THE OXFORD COMPANION TO THE BRONTËS

The Brontë sisters, oil painting by Branwell Brontë, *c.*1833–4.

THE OXFORD COMPANION TO THE

Brontës

Christine Alexander and
Margaret Smith

OXFORD
UNIVERSITY PRESS

OXFORD

UNIVERSITY PRESS

Great Clarendon Street, Oxford OX2 6DP

Oxford University Press is a department of the University of Oxford.
It furthers the University's objective of excellence in research, scholarship,
and education by publishing worldwide in

Oxford New York

Auckland Bangkok Buenos Aires Cape Town Chennai
Dar es Salaam Delhi Hong Kong Istanbul Karachi Kolkata
Kuala Lumpur Madrid Melbourne Mexico City Mumbai Nairobi
São Paulo Shanghai Taipei Tokyo Toronto

Oxford is a registered trade mark of Oxford University Press
in the UK and in certain other countries

Published in the United States
by Oxford University Press Inc., New York

© Oxford University Press 2003

Database right Oxford University Press (maker)

First published 2003

British Library Cataloguing in Publication Data
Data available

Library of Congress Cataloging in Publication Data
Data available

ISBN 0–19–866218–1

1 3 5 7 9 10 8 6 4 2

Typeset in Pondicherry, India
by Alliance Interactive Technology
Printed in Great Britain
on acid-free paper
by T.J. International Ltd
Padstow, Cornwall

In memory of
Rebecca Mary Alexander

ACKNOWLEDGEMENTS

This volume owes much to the many scholars who have worked in the field of Brontë studies over the years; without their dedication to research a reliable *Companion* would not be possible.

The Oxford Companion to the Brontës has been in production over a number of years and during this time many people have contributed assistance of various kinds. The authors would like to thank all those who have helped to make their task lighter and added to the accuracy of this volume. In particular we would like to thank the small band of contributors who gave so readily and so generously of their expertise: Carol Bock, Sue Lonoff, Victor Neufeldt, Herbert Rosengarten, Virginia Rushton, Patsy Stoneman, Beverly Taylor. Without their help the authors could not have completed the entries in time. The responsibility for the final form of the volume and for all errors and omissions, however, remains with the authors alone.

Christine Alexander would like to acknowledge with gratitude grants from the Australian Research Council and the Faculty of Arts at the University of New South Wales, that allowed her to check material in the UK and USA, and to consult with Margaret Smith in person.

We would like to express our thanks to Michael Cox, Pam Coote, Alison Jones, and Joanna Harris of Oxford University Press for their courtesy and patience, and to Rowena Anketell for her expert copyediting. Penny Boumelha, Kate Flint, John Maynard, Derek Roper, and Herbert Rosengarten also provided invaluable help in drawing up lists of topics. The assistance of the staff at the Brontë Parsonage Museum, especially that of Ann Dinsdale and Rachel Terry, and of Carole Heaton, Principal Librarian, Reference Library, Calderdale Council, Halifax, was invaluable. We are grateful for the help of Robert and Louise Barnard, Aimee Chan, Margaret and Robert Cochrane, Christopher Cooper, Bob Duckett, Professor Michel Fuchs, Robin Greenwood, Alan Shelston, and Stephen Whitehead; of Andrew Brammer and Rowland Hilder for their vital technical support; and thankful to Kathryn Nedeljkovic for her editorial assistance.

Christine's greatest debt goes to her family, to her husband Peter and her son Roland; together they survived personal tragedy. They also endured the stress of publishing deadlines over several years: she is grateful for their moral support and practical assistance. Finally, the authors would like to acknowledge the importance of collaborative research in literature; although contributors and authors were spread between three continents, we have benefited from each other's expertise and encouragement. The planning, organizing, editing, and research for most of the entries in the volume has been a stimulating and rewarding experience for the authors that has confirmed their commitment to Brontë studies.

CHRISTINE ALEXANDER and MARGARET SMITH

PREFACE

'They wanted learning. They came for learning. They would learn,' wrote Elizabeth Gaskell (Gaskell *Life*, 1. 246) of Charlotte and Emily Brontë's visit to Belgium, the only European country they visited and the furthest they travelled from their home at Haworth. Their aim was not so much to see as to understand the world. The books they read, the people they met and corresponded with, the landscapes they experienced, are integral components of their lives and works. *The Oxford Companion to the Brontës* aims to evoke the milieu in which the Brontës lived and wrote, to disseminate new reliable research, and to provide detailed information about their lives, works, and reputation. The Classified Contents List on pp. xv–xxv indicates that the *Companion* is designed to illuminate the active interrelation between the Brontës, their writings and activities, their own time and our time. Thus the volume is conceived as a whole, with interrelated entries that all contribute to our understanding of the rich imaginative life of this extraordinary family of writers.

In aiming for comprehensiveness *The Oxford Companion to the Brontës* provides detailed information about the life and work of the writers in the Brontë family: Charlotte, Branwell, Emily, and Anne Brontë, and their father Revd Patrick Brontë. There are long feature entries which survey their lives, their novels, poetry, juvenilia, letters, and artistic works; and there are feature entries relating to their education, to biographical research, and to the critical reception of their work from their own time to the present day. Other entries record their family, friends, and acquaintances; their pets, and their literary and political heroes; places they lived in and visited; individual stories, devoirs, poems, fictional characters and places; aspects of their careers as writers, governesses, and artists; historical events they engaged with, such as Chartism, the Peterloo Massacre, and the Ashantee Wars, and contemporary debates which they followed keenly, on exploration, slavery, and religion; contemporary attitudes to alcoholism, phrenology, and gendered accomplishments; manuscript collections, collectors, critics, and the varied critical reception of their works in both the academy and the market place. Selected entries on the Brontë juvenilia—a vast repository of biographical and literary material whose sheer volume is greater than the sum of all the published Brontë novels—provide a glimpse into their early imaginative worlds; and entries on film, ballet, and musical adaptations indicate the extent to which their works have inspired others.

Despite their short lives and relatively slender individual published output, the Brontës have received more critical attention than most other 19th-century writers. There are long entries in the *Companion* to guide readers through the variety of critical assessments that range from biographical responses to psychoanalytic and post-colonial readings. These entries are designed to reflect both historical and contemporary directions in literary study and to provide readers with a guide to current approaches to scholarship, criticism, and theory, as they apply to the Brontës. Thus the *Companion* also provides a guide to current Brontë studies.

What the *Companion* does not do is annotate the Brontës' works. There are entries on authors they drew upon, including explanation of allusions, but there are no specific entries on quotations or attempts to gloss the Brontës' vocabulary—information which is readily available in excellent editions recommended throughout the *Companion*. There is, however, a detailed survey of the Brontës' use of dialect in Dialect and Obsolete Words, pp. 573–82.

The Oxford Companion to the Brontës aspires to be an up-to-date, informative, and wide-ranging reference work that will serve the interests of specialists and general readers alike. It enables the reader to see the Brontës in their intellectual and social milieu, and to trace their enduring influence on other writers and readers. It is a book not only to consult but to browse in, and one which the editors hope will inspire further reading.

CHRISTINE ALEXANDER and MARGARET SMITH

CONTENTS

LIST OF MAPS

EDITORS AND CONTRIBUTORS

Authors and General Editors

CHRISTINE ALEXANDER, Professor of English at the University of New South Wales, Fellow of the Australian Academy of the Humanities, and former Australian Research Council Senior Research Fellow. Her critical study on *The Early Writings of Charlotte Brontë* (1983) won the British Academy Rose Mary Crawshay Prize; and she has edited a multi-volume *Edition of the Early Writings of Charlotte Brontë* (1987, 1991; vol. 3 forthcoming 2004). Other publications include the entry on Charlotte Brontë for the new *DNB*; a *Bibliography of the Manuscripts of Charlotte Brontë* (1982); an edition of *High Life In Verdopolis: A Tale from the Glass Town Saga* (1995); and *The Art of the Brontës* (1995), co-authored with Jane Sellars. Much of her Brontë work has been translated into Italian, German, and Japanese.

MARGARET SMITH, Honorary Fellow of the Institute for Advanced Research in Arts and Social Science, University of Birmingham; and a Vice-President of the Brontë Society. She was the textual editor of the Clarendon and World's Classics editions of Charlotte Brontë's novels, being awarded the British Academy Rose Mary Crawshay Prize for work on *The Professor* (1989); and editor of *The Letters of Charlotte Brontë* (3 vols.: 1995, 2000; vol. 3 forthcoming 2004). She was the textual editor of vols. 1 and 2 of the Oxford English Texts edition of *The Poetical Works of Robert Browning*, ed. Ian Jack (1983, 1984); and (with Rowena Fowler) textual editor of vol. 4 of the same edition (1991). She has also written the entry on Anne Brontë for the new *DNB*.

Contributors

CB CAROL A. BOCK, Associate Professor of English at the University of Minnesota Duluth. She is the author of *Charlotte Brontë and the Storyteller's Audience* (1992), and has published articles on the Brontës in journals such as *Victorian Literature and Culture*, *Journal of Narrative Technique*, and *Tulsa Studies in Women's Literature*. Her essay on the Brontë juvenilia appears in the *Cambridge Companion to the Brontës* (2002).

SL SUE LONOFF, Senior Associate of the Derek Bok Center at Harvard University and a member of the Harvard Extension School faculty. Her publications include a critical bilingual edition of Charlotte and Emily Brontë's *Belgian Essays* (1997), *Wilkie Collins and His Victorian Readers* (1982), and an anthology, *The College Reader* (1992). She is currently co-editing *Approaches to Teaching Emily Brontë's Wuthering Heights*. She has also published numerous essays on Victorian fiction and on pedagogy.

VN VICTOR NEUFELDT, Professor Emeritus of the Department of English at the University of Victoria, British Columbia, and Life Member of Clare Hall, Cambridge. He has published editions of the poems of Charlotte Brontë (1985) and Branwell Brontë (1990),

a bibliography of Branwell's manuscripts (1993), *The Works of Patrick Branwell Brontë* (1997, 1998, 1999), and has prepared the entry for Branwell Brontë in the new *DNB*. He is co-editor of *George Eliot's Middlemarch Notebooks* (1979), and has published articles on Branwell and Emily Brontë, Robert Browning, and George Eliot.

HR HERBERT ROSENGARTEN, Professor of English and former Head of the English Department at the University of British Columbia, where since 1997 he has been Executive Director of the President's Office. He has edited *The Tenant of Wildfell Hall*, *Shirley*, *Villette*, and *The Professor* (the last three with Margaret Smith) for the Clarendon Edition of the novels of the Brontës. Other publications include *The Broadview Anthology of Poetry* (with Amanda Goldrick-Jones).

VR VIRGINIA RUSHTON, professional singer and voice teacher whose initial undergraduate and postgraduate studies were in French and English literature. A commission from the National Trust to present a programme of words and music about the Brontë sisters led to a continuing research project into the influence of music in their lives and works, which has resulted in a number of papers for literary and voice-related conferences. During the 1990s she served on the Council of the Brontë Society, including a year as Chairman.

PS   PATSY STONEMAN, Reader in English at the University of Hull (UK), where she has taught since 1966. She has written a monograph on Elizabeth Gaskell (1987), the Introduction and Notes to the Wordsworth Classics edition of *North and South* (2002) and the Introduction to the Oxford World's Classics edition of *Wuthering Heights* (1995). She has edited the Macmillan New Casebook on *Wuthering Heights* (1993) and *Wuthering Heights: A Reader's Guide to Essential Criticism* (Icon Books, 2000). Her most recent publications are an essay on the Brontë Myth in the *Cambridge Companion to the Brontës* (2002) and a monograph, *Brontë Transformations: The Cultural Dissemination of Jane Eyre and Wuthering Heights* (1996). She is currently

preparing an edition of eight Victorian stage plays based on *Jane Eyre* for the Ashgate Press.

BT   BEVERLY TAYLOR, Professor of English and Director of Graduate Studies at the University of North Carolina at Chapel Hill, author of *Francis Thompson*, co-author of *The Return of King Arthur: British and American Arthurian Literature since 1800* and *Arthurian Bibliography: The Middle Ages*, and co-editor of two essay collections: *The Cast of Consciousness: Concepts of the Mind in British and American Romanticism* and *Gender and Discourse in Victorian Literature and Art*. She has published articles on 19th-century authors including Byron, Shelley, Carlyle, Elizabeth Barrett Browning, Robert Browning, Tennyson, Arnold, and Elizabeth Siddal. She is currently writing a study of Elizabeth Barrett Browning's works and co-editing an edition of her complete poetry.

CLASSIFIED CONTENTS LIST

Entries are arranged alphabetically by headword beneath the topic headings, except in the case of *Early writings* which are arranged chronologically.

Lives of the Brontës

Brontë Family
Brontë, Anne [Acton Bell]
Brontë, (Patrick) Branwell [Northangerland]
Brontë, Charlotte [Currer Bell]
Brontë, Elizabeth
Brontë, Emily Jane [Ellis Bell]
Brontë family
Brontë, Maria
Brontë, Mrs Maria, née Branwell
Brontë, Revd Patrick

Relatives of the Brontës
Branwell, Elizabeth
Branwell family
Kingston, Eliza Jane

Charlotte Brontë's Husband and his Relatives
Bell family
Nicholls, Revd Arthur Bell

Homes of the Brontës
Drumballyroney
Hartshead
Haworth
Haworth Parsonage
Ireland
Penzance
Thornton

Life in Haworth Parsonage
accomplishments
Aykroyd, Tabitha
books owned by the Brontës
books read by the Brontës
Brown, Martha
finances of the Brontës
geography, knowledge of and books
health of the Brontës
music
portraits of the Brontës
Ratcliffe, Tabitha
servants of the Brontës

The Natural World
Adelaide
animals and birds in the works of the Brontës
dogs in the Glass Town and Angrian saga
Flossy
Grasper
Gytrash, the
Keeper
landscapes associated with the Brontës
Natural History and the Brontës
Nero
pets owned by the Brontës
Plato
Tiger
Tom
Victoria (goose)
Yorkshire

Education and Teachers of the Brontës
Andrews, Anna
Bradley, John
education of the Brontës
Evans, Ann
Heger, M. Constantin Georges Romain
Plummer, Thomas
Robinson, William
Sunderland, Abraham Stansfield
Wooler, Katherine Harriet (Catherine)
Wooler, Margaret

Places of Education or Employment of the Brontës
Blake Hall
Broughton-in-Furness
Brussels
Cambridge
Cowan Bridge
Dewsbury
Heald's House
Heger, Pensionnat
Law Hill, Halifax
Lothersdale
Luddenden Foot
Mirfield
Roe Head
Sowerby Bridge
Stonegappe
Swarcliffe Hall
Thorp Green Hall
Upperwood House
Wellington, Shropshire
Wethersfield

Travel by the Brontës and Places Visited
Ambleside
Athénée Royal
Banagher
Birstall
Black Bull
Bolton Priory
Bradford
Bridlington (or Burlington)
Brookroyd
Chapter Coffee House
Crystal Palace

Classified Contents List

Writings by the Brontës

Poems

Anne Brontë

Novels

Classified Contents List

Classified Contents List

Classified Contents List

Other Writings by the Brontës

Classified Contents List

LIST OF ABBREVIATIONS

Chapter references to Brontë novels are to editions with continuously numbered chapters.

Page references to novels by the Brontës are to the Clarendon editions published by Oxford University Press under the general editorship of Ian Jack. Novels by the Brontës are referred to by their full titles, except for Anne Brontë's *The Tenant of Wildfell Hall*, which is abbreviated to *Tenant*.

Alexander *EEW*	*An Edition of the Early Writings of Charlotte Brontë*, ed. Christine Alexander, vol. 1 (1987); vol. 2 (1–2) (1991)
Alexander *EW*	Christine Alexander, *The Early Writings of Charlotte Brontë* (1983)
Alexander & Sellars	Christine Alexander and Jane Sellars, *The Art of the Brontës* (1995)
Allott	Miriam Allott, *The Brontës: The Critical Heritage* (1974)
Barker	Juliet R. V. Barker, *The Brontës* (1994)
'Biographical Notice'	*Wuthering Heights and Agnes Grey* . . . A New Edition Revised, with a Biographical Notice of the Authors . . . by Currer Bell (1850)
Brontëana	*Brontëana: The Rev. Patrick Brontë, A. B., His Collected Works and Life*, ed. J. Horsfall Turner (1898)
BST and *BS*	*Brontë Society Transactions* (1895–2001); retitled *Brontë Studies* (Mar. 2002–); references are to vol., pt., and pp.; e.g. 17. 90. 339–40
Chadwick	Mrs Ellis H. (Esther Alice) Chadwick, *In the Footsteps of the Brontës* (1914)
Chapple & Pollard *Gaskell Letters*	*The Letters of Mrs Gaskell*, ed. J. A. V. Chapple and Arthur Pollard (1966)
Chitham *ABP*	Edward Chitham, *The Poems of Anne Brontë* (1979)
Chitham *Birth of WH*	*The Birth of 'Wuthering Heights'* (1998)
Chitham *EB*	*A Life of Emily Brontë* (1987)
DNB	*Dictionary of National Biography*
Duthie *Foreign Vision*	Enid Duthie, *The Foreign Vision of Charlotte Brontë* (1975)
ELH	*English Literary History*
Gaskell *Life*	E. C. Gaskell, *The Life of Charlotte Brontë* (2 vols., 1857) (1st edn. unless otherwise stated)
Gérin *BB*	Winifred Gérin, *Branwell Brontë* (1961)
Gérin *CB*	Winifred Gérin, *Charlotte Brontë: The Evolution of Genius* (1967)
Gérin *EB*	Winifred Gérin, *Emily Brontë* (Oxford, 1971)
Gérin *Five Novelettes*	Winifred Gérin, *Five Novelettes* (Folio Press, 1971)
Gezari *EBP*	*Emily Brontë: The Complete Poems*, ed. Janet Gezari (1992)
Hatfield *EBP*	*The Complete Poems of Emily Jane Brontë*, ed. C. W. Hatfield (1941)
Leyland	Francis A. Leyland, *The Brontë Family, with Special Reference to Patrick Branwell Brontë*, 2 vols. (1886)
Lock & Dixon	John Lock and W. T. Dixon, *A Man of Sorrow: The Life, Letters and Times of the Rev. Patrick Brontë* (1965)
Lonoff	*The Belgian Essays: Charlotte Brontë and Emily Brontë*, ed. and trans. Sue Lonoff (1996)
McNees	McNees, Eleanor, (ed.), *The Brontë Sisters: Critical Assessments*, 4 vols. (1996)

List of Abbreviations

Miscellaneous Writings	*The Miscellaneous and Unpublished Writings of Charlotte and Patrick Branwell Brontë* (2 vols., 1936, 1938) (Shakespeare Head Brontë edn.)
Neufeldt *BBP*	*The Poems of Patrick Branwell Brontë*, ed. Victor A. Neufeldt (1990)
Neufeldt *BB Works*	*The Works of Branwell Brontë*, ed. Victor A. Neufeldt, 3 vols. (1997, 1998, 1999)
Neufeldt *CBP*	*The Poems of Charlotte Brontë*, ed. Victor A. Neufeldt (1985)
OED	*Oxford English Dictionary*
PMLA	*PMLA: Publications of the Modern Language Association of America*
Poems 1846	*Poems by Currer, Ellis, and Acton Bell* [Charlotte, Emily, and Anne Brontë] (Aylott and Jones, May 1846)
Roper *EBP*	*The Poems of Emily Brontë*, ed. Derek Roper with Edward Chitham (1995)
SEL	*Studies in English Literature, 1500–1900*
Shorter *Circle*	Clement K. Shorter, *Charlotte Brontë and her Circle* (1896)
Smith *Letters*	*The Letters of Charlotte Brontë*, ed. Margaret Smith, 3 vols. (1995, 2000, 2004 forthcoming)
Stevens, Joan	*Mary Taylor, Friend of Charlotte Brontë: Letters from New Zealand and Elsewhere* (1972)
Wise & Symington	*The Brontës: Their Lives, Friendships and Correspondence*, ed. T. J. Wise and J. A. Symington, 4 vols. (Shakespeare Head Brontë edn., 1932).
Wroot	Herbert E. Wroot, *Sources of Charlotte Brontë's Novels: Persons and Places* (Publications of the Brontë Society, suppl. to vol. 8(4); 1935)

Manuscript Collections

Beinecke, Yale	The Beinecke Rare Book and Manuscript Library, Yale University Library
Berg, NYPL	Henry W. and Albert A. Berg Collection, New York Public Library, Astor, Lenox, and Tilden Foundations
BL	British Library
Bonnell, BPM	Bonnell Collection, Brontë Parsonage Museum, Haworth
Bonnell, Pierpont Morgan	Bonnell Collection, Pierpont Morgan Library, New York
BPM	Brontë Parsonage Museum, Haworth
Brotherton	Brotherton Collection, Brotherton Library, University of Leeds
Houghton, Harvard	Houghton Library, Harvard University
Huntington	Huntington Library, San Marino, California
Lowell, Harvard	Amy Lowell Collection, Harvard University Library
Montague, NYPL	Montague Collection, New York Public Library
NYPL	New York Public Library
Parrish, Princeton	Morris L. Parrish Collection, Princeton University Library
Pierpont Morgan	Pierpont Morgan Library, New York
Ransom HRC, Texas	The Harry Ransom Humanities Research Center, University of Texas at Austin
Rylands	The John Rylands University Library, University of Manchester
Taylor, Princeton	Robert H. Taylor Collection, Princeton University Library
Widener, Harvard	Harry Elkins Widener Collection, Harvard University Library

CHRONOLOGY

Year	The Lives of the Brontës	Literary and Artistic Events	Historical Events
1777	Patrick Brontë (Brunty) born (17 Mar.) at Emdale in the Parish of Drumballyroney, County Down, first of ten children, to Hugh Brunty and Eleanor (Alice) McClory.	Sheridan, *The School for Scandal* published.	American War continues (began 1775).
1778		Burney, *Evelina* published.	French-American alliance. Britain declares war on France.
1779		Johnson, *The Lives of the Poets* (1779–81) published.	Crompton invents spinning mule. Spain declares war on England and seizes Gibraltar.
1780			Yorkshire petition for parliamentary reform. Gordon Riots develop from a procession to petition parliament against the Catholic Relief Act.
1781		Schiller, *Die Räuber*; Sheridan, *The Critic*; Rousseau, *Confessions* published.	
1782		Gilpin, *Observations on the Wye and South Wales* published.	
1783	Maria Branwell born (15 Apr.) at Penzance, Cornwall seven years after the birth of her sister Elizabeth (Aunt Branwell) (2 Dec. 1776).		Shelburne ministry; Fox-North coalition; William Pitt the Younger's first ministry. Peace of Versailles at which Britain recognizes the independence of the American colonies.
1784			Pitt's India Act. James Watt develops an improved steam engine (1st patented 1769).
1785		Cowper, *The Task* published.	Pitt's motion for parliamentary reform defeated. Cartwright invents the power loom.
1786		Beckford, *Vathek*; Burns, *Poems, Chiefly in the Scottish Dialect*; Gilpin, *Observations on Cumberland and Westmorland* published.	Eden commercial treaty with France. Coal gas first used for lighting.
1787	Patrick Brontë hears John Wesley preach.	Bernardin de Saint Pierre, *Paul et Virginie* published.	Association for the Abolition of the Slave Trade formed. US Constitution signed.
1788		Gibbon, *Decline and Fall of the Roman Empire* (1776–88), vols. 4–6.	Trial of Warren Hastings begins. First Fleet under Captain Arthur Phillip lands in Botany Bay.
1789	John Wesley stays with William Tighe at 'Rosanna', County Wicklow (25 June), on his last	Blake, *Songs of Innocence*; White, *Natural History of Selborne* published.	French Revolution begins.

Chronology

Year	The Lives of the Brontës	Literary and Artistic Events	Historical Events
1789	visit to Ireland. Patrick commences work as a part-time assistant to the local blacksmith (autumn).		
1790		Bewick, *General History of Quadrupeds*; Blake, *The Marriage of Heaven and Hell*; Burke, *Reflections on the Revolution in France*; Radcliffe, *A Sicilian Romance*; Charlotte Smith, *Ethelinde* published.	
1791		Burns, *Tam o'Shanter*; Boswell, *The Life of Samuel Johnson*; Gilpin, *Forest Scenery*; Paine, *The Rights of Man*, pt. 1; Radcliffe, *Romance of the Forest* published.	Birmingham Riots. Flight to Varennes and capture of the French royal family. Death of Mirabeau. Canada Act.
1792		Gilpin, *Essays on Picturesque Beauty*; Wollstonecraft, *Vindication of the Rights of Woman*; Young, *Travels in France* published.	French royal family imprisoned. September massacres.
1793	Patrick obtains a position as a teacher at Glascar Hill Presbyterian School under Revd Alexander Moore.	Blake, *Visions of the Daughters of Albion*; *America*; Burns, *Songs and Poems*; Godwin, *Political Justice*; Smith, *The Old Manor House* published.	Voluntary Board of Agriculture set up. Commercial depression. Execution of Louis XVI and Marie Antoinette; Reign of Terror under Robespierre; murder of Marat. Britain joins war against France.
1794	The Brunty family move to Ballynaskeagh.	Blake, *The Book of Urizen* and *Songs of Innocence and Experience*; Godwin, *Caleb Williams*; Paine, *Age of Reason*; Radcliffe, *The Mysteries of Udolpho* published.	Habeas Corpus Act suspended. Danton and Robespierre executed.
1795		Boswell dies.	Wet cold summer contributes to high food prices, scarcity. Speenhamland System Food Riots. Methodist secession from Church of England. French Directory established.
1796		Burney, *Camilla*; Lewis, *The Monk*; Southey, *Joan of Arc* published.	Failure of attempted French invasion of Ireland. Buonaparte's Italian campaign successful. Vaccination against smallpox introduced.
1797		Bewick, *History of British Birds*; Southey, *Poems*; Wilberforce, *Practical Christianity* published.	Naval mutinies. Defeat of Dutch fleet at Camperdown.
1798	Patrick goes to teach at a school at Drumballyroney and becomes tutor to the children of Revd Thomas Tighe, half-brother of William Tighe.	Malthus, *Essay on Population*; and Wordsworth and Coleridge, *Lyrical Ballads* published.	Tax of 10% on incomes over £200 introduced. Revolt in Ireland (May). French land in Ireland (Aug.). French in Syria and Egypt. Nelson victorious in the Battle of the Nile.
1799		Campbell, *The Pleasures of Hope*; More, *Strictures on the Modern System of Female Education* published.	Commercial boom (1799–1801). Religious Tract Society formed. Corresponding Society and other radical groups suppressed.

Year	The Lives of the Brontës	Literary and Artistic Events	Historical Events
1799			Combination Acts against the formation of unions. Buonaparte appointed first consul in France.
1800		Edgeworth, *Castle Rackrent*; and Burns, *Works* published.	Widespread food riots. Owen founds model factory at New Lanark. Highland clearances. Union of Ireland with Britain.
1801		Edgeworth, *Belinda*; Opie, *Father and Daughter*; Southey, *Thalaba* published.	Economic distress and higher food prices. Pitt resigns on refusal of George III to assent to Catholic Emancipation; Addington becomes prime minister. First British census. Danish fleet seized at Copenhagen.
1802	Patrick enters St John's College, Cambridge and registers as 'Patrick Branty' (1 Oct.), changing his entry two days later to 'Patrick Brontë'.	Scott (ed.), *The Minstrelsy of the Scottish Border* published. *Edinburgh Review* begins.	Peel introduces First Factory Act. Peace of Amiens between Britain and France. Buonaparte made first consul for life; takes name of Napoleon.
1803			General Enclosure Act simplifies process of enclosure of common land. War with France renewed.
1804		Blake, *Jerusalem* and *Milton*; and Schiller, *Wilhelm Tell* published.	Addington resigns. Pitt becomes prime minister. British and Foreign Bible Society formed. Napoleon becomes emperor and prepares to invade England.
1805		Campbell, *Collected Poems*; and Scott, *The Lay of the Last Minstrel* published.	Pitt dies; Ministry of All the Talents, with Grenville as prime minister. Battle of Trafalgar: Nelson defeats the French and Spanish fleets.
1806	Patrick receives his BA (23 Apr.). He applies to the Bishop of London as a candidate for Holy Orders (4 July). He goes to London and stays for the first time at the Chapter Coffee House, Paternoster Row (Aug.); ordained Deacon at Fulham Chapel (Sunday, 10 Aug.). He moves to a curacy at Wethersfield, Essex (Oct.), at a stipend of £60 p.a., lodging at the home of a Miss Mildred Davy where he forms an association with her niece, Mary Burder.	Byron, *Fugitive Pieces* published.	Napoleon closes Continental ports to British ships. French defeat Prussians at Jena.
1807	Patrick ordained priest at the Chapel Royal of St James, Westminster, by the Bishop of Salisbury (21 Dec.).	Byron, *Hours of Idleness*; Charles and Mary Lamb, *Tales from Shakespeare*; Thomas Moore, *Irish Melodies*, (1807–35); Wordsworth, *Poems* published.	Resignation of Grenville over Catholic question; Portland becomes prime minister. Abolition of the slave trade in the British Empire. French invade Spain and Portugal.
1808		Goethe, *Faust*; Hemans, *Poems*; Scott, *Marmion* published. Leigh Hunt founds the *Examiner*.	Beginning of repeal of laws requiring death penalty for minor crimes. Peninsular War begins.

Chronology

Year	The Lives of the Brontës	Literary and Artistic Events	Historical Events
1809	Patrick leaves Wethersfield to be assistant curate at All Saints church, Wellington, Shropshire (7 Jan.), leaving there to become curate at All Saints church, Dewsbury, Yorkshire, under Revd John Buckworth (4 Dec.).	Byron, *English Bards and Scotch Reviewers*; Goethe, *Wahlverwandtschaften* (*Elective Affinities*); Hannah More, *Coelebs in Search of a Wife* published. *Quarterly Review* (Tory) founded (William Gifford first editor).	Perceval becomes prime minister. Sir John Moore killed at Corunna. Wellesley in command in Portugal. Commercial boom (1809–10).
1810	Publication of Patrick Brontë's first work, 'Winter-Evening Thoughts. A Miscellaneous Poem'.	Crabbe, *The Borough*; Scott, *The Lady of the Lake*; Southey, *The Curse of Kehama* published.	
1811	Publication of Patrick Brontë's book, *Cottage Poems*. He begins duties as a curate at Hartshead, near Dewsbury (3 Mar.).	Austen, *Sense and Sensibility*; and Scott, *Vision of Don Roderick* published.	Depression because of Orders in Council. Luddite riots in Nottinghamshire and Yorkshire (1811–12). Prince of Wales becomes regent because of madness of George III.
1812	Wesleyan Academy at Woodhouse Grove opens (8 Jan.), originally for eight pupils (70 by 1813); John Fennell, an associate of Patrick appointed First Master and Patrick appointed an examiner. Luddites attack William Cartwright's Rawfolds Mill at Liversedge and receive their first defeat (11–12 Apr.) (later used in *Shirley*). Patrick meets Maria Branwell, who is staying with her cousin John Fennell (June); Patrick proposes to and is accepted by her whilst on a visit to the ruins of Kirkstall Abbey (end Aug.–Sept.). Maria Branwell hears of the shipwreck resulting in the loss of most of her personal belongings being sent from Penzance (14 Nov.). Marriage of Patrick Brontë and Maria Branwell, at Guiseley church, near Leeds, conducted by William Morgan, and of William Morgan to Jane Fennell, conducted by Patrick Brontë (29 Dec.), both brides given away by John Fennell.	Byron, *Childe Harold's Pilgrimage*, cantos I and II; and Hemans, *The Domestic Affections and Other Poems* published.	Perceval murdered; Liverpool becomes prime minister. War between UK and USA. French retreat from Russia.
1813	Publication of Patrick Brontë's *The Rural Minstrel*. Patrick and Maria Brontë set up home at Clough House, Hightown, Liversedge (Jan.).	Austen, *Pride and Prejudice*; Byron, *Giaour* and *Bride of Abydos*; Scott, *Rokeby*; Shelley, *Queen Mab* published. Southey made Poet Laureate.	East India Company's monopoly abolished. Wellington celebrates victory at Vittoria. Battle of Leipzig between the Allies and Napoleon's forces.
1814	Maria Brontë, their first child (born 1813 or early Jan.), christened by William Morgan with himself and his wife Jane and Mrs Fennell as godparents (23 Apr.).	Austen, *Mansfield Park*; Byron, *The Corsair* and *Lara*; Scott, *Waverley*; Wordsworth, *The Excursion* published.	Allies capture Paris; Napoleon abdicates and retreats to Elba. Treaty of Ghent ends war with USA. Stephenson develops the steam locomotive.

Year	The Lives of the Brontës	Literary and Artistic Events	Historical Events
1815	Elizabeth Brontë born (8 Feb.). Patrick moves to St James's church, Thornton (19 May). Mrs Brontë's sister Elizabeth Branwell of Penzance, comes to stay with the Brontës (early June). First visit by Elizabeth Firth to the Brontës (7 June). Elizabeth Brontë christened (26 Aug.). Publication of Patrick's *The Cottage in the Wood* (Dec.).	Byron, *Hebrew Melodies*; Cowper, *Poems* (ed. J. Johnson); Scott, *Guy Mannering*; Wordsworth, *The White Doe of Rylstone* and *Poems* published.	Corn law passed forbidding import of corn until home price of wheat reached 80s. per quarter. Commercial boom (1815–17). Battle of Waterloo: Napoleon defeated; Congress of Vienna: peace in Europe. Restoration of Louis XVIII; Napoleon exiled to St Helena.
1816	Charlotte Brontë born at Thornton (21 Apr.). Nancy Garrs becomes house servant to the Brontës (July).	Austen, *Emma*; Byron, *Childe Harold's Pilgrimage*, canto III and *Parisina*; Coleridge, *Christabel* and *Kubla Khan*; Lady Caroline Lamb, *Glenarvon*; Moore, *Sacred Songs*; Peacock, *Headlong Hall*; Scott, *The Antiquary*, *The Black Dwarf*, and *Old Mortality*; Shelley, *Alastor* published. The Royal Institution founds *Quarterly Journal of Science, Literature, and Art*. Byron leaves England for the last time.	Income Tax abolished. Riots in East Anglia and manufacturing districts. Elgin marbles bought by the British Museum.
1817	Births of Mary Taylor (26 Feb.) and Ellen Nussey (20 Apr.). (Patrick) Branwell Brontë born (26 June).	Byron, *Manfred*; Coleridge, *Biographia Literaria*; Godwin, *Mandeville*; Hazlitt, *The Characters of Shakespeare's Plays*; Hemans, *Modern Greece*; Hogg, *Dramatic Tales*; Keats, *Poems*; Moore, *Lalla Rookh*; Owen, *Report to the Committee on the Poor Law*; Scott, *Rob Roy* published. *Blackwood's Edinburgh Magazine* begins. Martin exhibits *The Bard* at the Royal Academy. Jane Austen and Mme de Staël die.	Seditious Meetings Bill drives democratic societies underground. Commercial slump. Death of Princess Charlotte, daughter of the Prince Regent. Monroe becomes president of the USA.
1818	Publication of Patrick Brontë's *The Maid of Killarney*. Birth of Arthur Bell Nicholls at Killead, County Antrim (6 Jan.). Emily Jane Brontë born (30 July). Sarah Garrs employed as children's nurse to the Brontës and Nancy Garrs promoted to cook and assistant housekeeper (Aug.). Second edition of Patrick Brontë's *The Cottage In The Wood* published.	Austen, *Northanger Abbey* and *Persuasion*; Byron, *Beppo* and *Childe Harold's Pilgrimage*, canto IV; Egan, *Boxiana* (1818–24); Susan Ferrier, *Marriage*; Hazlitt, *Lectures on the English Poets*; Keats, *Endymion*; Charles Lamb, *Collected Works*; Peacock, *Nightmare Abbey*; Scott, *Heart of Midlothian*; Mary Shelley, *Frankenstein* published.	Congress of European Alliance at Aix-la-Chapelle, attended by Castlereagh.
1819	Vicar of Bradford appoints Patrick as curate of Haworth but does not seek Trustees' approval (2 June); trustees of Haworth suggest to the Vicar of Bradford that Patrick preaches in Haworth church so that they can judge him (c.17 July). Patrick refuses	Byron, *Don Juan*, cantos I and II and *Mazeppa*; Hemans, *Tales and Historical Scenes*; Macaulay, *Pompeii*; Polidori, *The Vampire*; Scott, *The Bride of Lammermoor*, *Legend of Montrose*, and *Ivanhoe* published.	Peterloo Massacre: troops intervene at mass reform meeting. 'Six Acts' restrict right to hold meetings and freedom of press. Poor Relief Act. Queen Victoria born.

Chronology

Year	The Lives of the Brontës	Literary and Artistic Events	Historical Events
1819	and says that the Trustees must come to Thornton to hear him (21 July). He preaches at Haworth church for the first time (10 Oct.), but formally resigns the curacy of Haworth to the Vicar of Bradford (21 Oct.). The Vicar of Bradford appoints Revd Samuel Redhead to Haworth, again without seeking Trustees' approval (25 Oct.); Samuel Redhead officiates at Haworth church and the whole congregation walks out (31 Oct.). Patrick Brontë signs the register at Haworth for the first time (17 Nov.), at a funeral, and looks after both Haworth and Thornton until a decision is made about the curacy.		
1820	Anne Brontë born (17 Jan.). Patrick Brontë licensed to the Perpetual Curacy of Haworth after a compromise between the Vicar of Bradford and the Trustees (25 Feb.). The Brontë family move to the Parsonage, Haworth (Apr.).	Barrett [Browning], *Battle of Marathon*; Bulwer-Lytton, *Ismael*; Clare, *Poems Descriptive of Rural Life and Scenery*; Keats, *Hyperion* and *Lamia, Isabella, The Eve of St Agnes and Other Poems*, and *La Belle Dame Sans Merci*; Lamartine, *Méditations poétiques*; Malthus, *Principles of Political Economy*; Maturin, *Melmoth the Wanderer*; Scott, *The Monastery* and *The Abbot*. Shelley, *Prometheus Unbound*; Southey, *The Life of Wesley and the Rise and Progress of Methodism* published. *London Magazine* and *John Bull* begin.	Death of George III, accession of George IV. Trial of Queen Caroline. Revolution in Portugal and Spain. First iron steamship.
1821	Mrs Maria Brontë taken ill and found collapsed (29 Jan.). Patrick Brontë's *The Maid of Killarney* appears in the *Cottage Magazine*. Elizabeth Branwell ('Aunt Branwell') arrives in Haworth from Penzance because of her sister's illness (early May). Mrs Maria Brontë dies, aged 38, from cancer (15 Sept.).	Byron, *Sardanapalus, Cain*, and *Don Juan*, cantos iii–v; Clare, *The Village Minstrel*; De Quincey, *Confessions of an English Opium Eater*; Egan, *Life in London*; Hazlitt, *Table Talk*; James Mill, *Elements of Political Economy*; W. E. Parry, *Journal of a Voyage for the Discovery of a North-West Passage* (1821–4); Scott, *Kenilworth*; Shelley, *Epipsychidion* and *Adonais*; Southey, *A Vision of Judgement* published. Keats dies. John Martin exhibits *Belshazzar's Feast* at the British Institution.	Famine in Ireland (1821–3). Measures for Catholic Relief. Death of Napoleon. Greek War of Independence begins.
1822		Byron, *The Vision of Judgement* and *Werner*; Hemans, *Welsh Melodies*; Hogg, *Three Perils of Man*; Lockhart, *Adam Blair*; Scott, *Fortunes of Nigel, The Pirate*, and *Peveril of the Peak*; Wilson ('Christopher North'),	Suicide of Castlereagh; Canning Foreign Secretary; Peel Home Secretary.

Year	The Lives of the Brontës	Literary and Artistic Events	Historical Events
1822		*Lights and Shadows of Scottish Life*; Wordsworth, *Ecclesiastical Sketches* and *Description of the Scenery of the Lakes* (1st separate edn.) published. *Blackwood's Edinburgh Magazine* begins publishing the 'Noctes Ambrosianae' (1822–35). Leigh Hunt founds the *Liberal* (with Byron and Shelley). Shelley drowns. E. T. A. Hoffmann dies.	
1823		Byron, *The Island*, and *Don Juan*, cantos VI–XIV; Lamb, *Essays of Elia*; Lockhart, *Reginald Dalton*; Scott, *Quentin Durward*; Mary Shelley, *Valperga*; Southey, *History of the Peninsular War* (1823–32) published.	Agricultural discontent. Building of British Museum begins. War between France and Spain. Mechanics' Institute founded in London.
1824	Maria and Elizabeth go to Clergy Daughters' School, Cowan Bridge, near Kirkby Lonsdale (21 July), joined by Charlotte (10 Aug.) and Emily (25 Nov.). Tabitha Aykroyd ('Tabby') engaged as servant.	Byron, *Don Juan*, cantos XV–XVI; Carlyle's translation of Goethe's *Wilhelm Meister's Apprenticeship*; Susan Ferrier, *The Inheritance*; Hogg, *Private Memoirs and Confessions of a Justified Sinner*; Landon, *The Improvisatrice*; Parry, *Journal of a Second Voyage, 1821–1823*; Scott, *Redgauntlet* published. *Westminster Review* begins. Death of Byron. National Gallery opened.	Commercial boom. Repeal of the Combination Acts.
1825	Mechanics' Institute, Keighley, founded. Maria dies of pulmonary tuberculosis (6 May), having been fetched from school by her father (14 Feb.). Elizabeth sent home from school 'in decline' (31 May); Patrick Brontë brings Charlotte and Emily home (1 June); Elizabeth dies of pulmonary tuberculosis (15 June). Brontë children remain at home under the supervision of their aunt Elizabeth Branwell.	Hazlitt, *The Spirit of the Age*; Scott, *The Betrothed* and *The Talisman*; Wolfe, *The Burial of Sir John Moore*; Pepys's Diary published.	Industrial and financial crisis. Trade Unions legalized. Stockton to Darlington railway opened; Stephenson's steam engine *Action* (later renamed *Locomotion*) conveys first railway passengers. George IV opposes further measures for Catholic Emancipation. John Quincy Adams becomes president of the USA.
1826	Patrick Brontë returns from a clerical conference in Leeds with a box of toy soldiers for Branwell (5 June). The Young Men's Play begins, leading to the Brontë children's imaginary sagas of Glass Town, Gondal, and Angria.	Chateaubriand, *Les Aventures du dernier Abencérage*; J. Fenimore Cooper, *Last of the Mohicans*; Disraeli, *Vivian Grey*; Hone, *Every-Day Book* (1826–7); Scott, *Woodstock* published. Mendelssohn, Overture to *A Midsummer Night's Dream* performed. John Martin publishes a mezzotint of *Belshazzar's Feast*.	Destruction of powerlooms by unemployed weavers. End of Liverpool's ministry. England sends troops to Portugal. Royal Zoological Society founded.
1827	Branwell's earliest extant manuscript, 'Battell Book', illustrated with pencil and watercolour (12 Mar.). Our Fellows Play (July) and the Islanders' Play begin (Dec.).	Carlyle, *German Romance: Specimens of its Chief Authors*; Clare, *The Shepherd's Calendar*; Heber, *Hymns*; Keble, *The Christian Year*; Landon (L.E.L.), *Poetical*	Death of Canning. Battle of Navarino: Turkish fleet destroyed by British, French, and Russian fleets. University College, London, founded.

Chronology

Year	The Lives of the Brontës	Literary and Artistic Events	Historical Events
1832	Birstall (Sept.).	*Illustrations of Political Economy* (1832–4); Robert Montgomery, *The Messiah*; Scott, *Count Robert of Paris*, and *Castle Dangerous*; Tennyson, *Poems* (dated 1833); Frances Trollope, *Domestic Manners of the Americans* published. Constable paints *The Grove, Hampstead*. Scott and Goethe die.	
1833	Patrick Brontë joins Keighley Mechanics' Institute, with access to the library, reading room, and lectures. Ellen Nussey's first visit to Haworth (19 July). The Brontës visit Bolton Abbey with the Nusseys (Sept.).	Bulwer-Lytton, *England and the English*; Carlyle, *Sartor Resartus*; Hartley Coleridge, *Poems*; Keble et al., *Tracts for the Times* (1841); Lamb, *Last Essays of Elia*; George Sand, *Lélia* published.	Factory Act limits child labour. Oxford Movement in Anglican Church begins. First steamship crossing of the Atlantic.
1834	Installation service of the new organ at Haworth parish church (Mar.). The Brontës visit the summer exhibition of the Royal Northern Society for the Encouragement of the Fine Arts, in Leeds; Charlotte exhibits two pencil drawings, 'Bolton Abbey' and 'Kirkstall Abbey' (June); William Robinson also exhibits and is later engaged as art teacher for Branwell. Emily and Anne write their first extant Diary Paper, including earliest mention of Gondal (24 Nov.).	Ainsworth, *Rookwood*; Balzac, *Le Père Goriot*; Blessington, *Conversations with Lord Byron*; Bulwer-Lytton, *Last Days of Pompeii* published. Coleridge and Lamb die.	Melbourne (Whig) is briefly prime minister, followed by Robert Peel (Cons.) (1834–5). New Poor Law: parish workhouses instituted. Robert Owen founds the Grand National Consolidated Trade Union. Action by government against 'illegal oaths' in unionism results in failure of GNCTU and transportation of six 'Tolpuddle Martyrs'. Houses of Parliament burnt down. Slavery abolished in the British colonies.
1835	Branwell visits Liverpool, purchases Byron's *Childe Harold's Pilgrimage* (30 May). He drafts a letter to the Royal Academy of Arts asking where and when to present his drawings (June–July). Charlotte tells her friend Ellen Nussey of plans for Branwell to go to the Royal Academy, Charlotte to go to Roe Head as a teacher, and Emily to accompany her as a pupil (2 July). Charlotte and Emily leave Haworth for Roe Head (29 July). Branwell's course of art lessons with William Robinson, in Leeds, completed (11 Sept.). Anne replaces Emily at Roe Head (late Oct.). Branwell writes to Robinson to arrange a further course of lessons for 'the ensuing Winter' in preparation for entry to the Royal Academy schools (16 Nov.). He asks the editor of *Blackwood's Magazine* to take him on in place of James Hogg (Dec.), but receives no reply to this or later letters.	Browning, *Paracelsus*; Clare, *The Rural Muse*; Hartley Coleridge, *Lives of Illustrious Worthies*; Wordsworth, *Yarrow Revisited, and Other Poems* published. Turner paints *Burning of the Houses of Lords and Commons*.	Melbourne (Whig) becomes prime minister. Municipal Reform Act extends local government franchise to all ratepayers.

Chronology

Year	The Lives of the Brontës	Literary and Artistic Events	Historical Events
1838	teaching post at Miss Patchett's school at Law Hill, near Halifax (end Sept.). Charlotte leaves Margaret Wooler's school for the last time (Dec.).		
1839	Emily returns to Haworth from Law Hill (Mar.). Charlotte rejects a proposal of marriage from Ellen Nussey's brother Revd Henry Nussey (5 Mar.). Anne goes as governess to the Inghams, Blake Hall, Mirfield (8 Apr.). Branwell gives up his unsuccessful studio in Bradford, returning to Haworth; begins translation of Horace's *Odes* (mid-May). Charlotte goes as governess to the Sidgwicks at Stonegappe, near Skipton (May), returning to Haworth on 19 July. Branwell visits Liverpool (July). Charlotte refuses a proposal of marriage from Revd David Pryce (late July). She writes her last novelette, *Caroline Vernon* (July–Dec.). William Weightman comes as curate to Haworth (Aug.). Charlotte goes with Ellen Nussey to stay three weeks at Easton, and one week at the sea nearby, at Bridlington (then called Burlington) (Sept.). She writes her *Farewell to Angria* (late Sept.). Anne leaves her position with the Inghams (Dec.).	Carlyle, *Chartism*; Longfellow, *Voices of the Night*; Harriet Martineau, *Deerbrook*; Thackeray, *Catherine* published. Turner paints *The Fighting Téméraire*.	Custody of Infants Act gives women separated from their husbands the right to petition Chancery for access to infant children and custody of children under age of 7. Chartist riots. First Opium War between Britain and China (1839–42). Fox Talbot and Daguerre announce rival photographic processes.
1840	Branwell installed as tutor to the Postlethwaites at Broughton-in-Furness (1 Jan.). Branwell writes to Hartley Coleridge, asking him for his opinion of his poem, 'At dead of midnight' and his translations of two of Horace's *Odes* (20 Apr.); he visits Hartley Coleridge at Rydal Water, near Ambleside, and is encouraged by him (1 May). Anne goes as governess to the family of Revd Edmund Robinson at Thorp Green Hall, Little Ouseburn, near York (?8 May). Branwell sends translation of Book I of Horace's *Odes* to Hartley Coleridge (27 June). Branwell dismissed by the Postlethwaites and returns to Haworth (June). He is engaged as Assistant Clerk in Charge at Sowerby Bridge Railway Station (31 Aug.).	Browning, *Sordello*; Dickens, *Old Curiosity Shop* (1840–1); Poe, *Tales of the Grotesque and Arabesque*; Thackeray, *Paris Sketchbook* published.	New Houses of Parliament begun by Barry and Pugin (completed 1852). First presentation of the People's Charter to Parliament. Victoria marries Prince Albert. Nelson's column erected in Trafalgar Square. Introduction of Penny Post.

Chronology

Year	The Lives of the Brontës	Literary and Artistic Events	Historical Events
1842	English and Emily music in return for board and tuition (Sept.). William Weightman dies of cholera, aged 28 (6 Sept.). Branwell's article 'Thomas Bewick' published in *Halifax Guardian* (1 Oct.). Martha Taylor dies of cholera, aged 23, in Brussels (12 Oct.). Elizabeth Branwell dies, leaving a legacy of £350 for each of her nieces (29 Oct.); Anne returns to Haworth for the funeral (3 Nov.). Charlotte and Emily return to Haworth (8 Nov.). Anne returns to Thorp Green Hall (29 Nov.).		
1843	Branwell joins Anne at Thorp Green, where he is to be tutor to Edmund Robinson, jun. (?21 Jan.). Charlotte leaves Haworth (27 Jan.) to return to Brussels as both teacher and pupil; she gives English lessons to M. Heger and his brother-in-law. She enjoys the company of Mary Dixon, a cousin of the Taylors (Mar.). Charlotte's feeling of depression and isolation at the pensionnat increases (1 May); she is lonely and homesick in Brussels during the long vacation and goes to confession at Ste Gudule (Aug.–Sept.). She distrusts Mme Heger and gives in her notice, but M. Heger countermands it (Oct.); by 17 Dec. she has decided to come home.	Borrow, *The Bible in Spain*; Carlyle, *Past and Present*; Dickens, *A Christmas Carol*, and *Martin Chuzzlewit* (1843–4); Hood, 'Song of the Shirt' (*Punch*); Horne, *Orion*; Macaulay, *Essays*; Ruskin, *Modern Painters* (1843–60), vol. 1; Thackeray, *Irish Sketchbook* published. Wordsworth becomes Poet Laureate.	Theatre Regulations Bill (monopoly removed from Covent Garden and Drury Lane theatres).
1844	Charlotte leaves Brussels (1 Jan.) to return to Haworth. Upon her return she finds her father's eyesight is rapidly deteriorating. She wishes to start a school but cannot leave her father (end Jan.). Emily begins to transcribe her poems into two notebooks, one titled 'Gondal Poems', the other untitled (Feb.). Reunion of Charlotte and Ellen Nussey with Mary Taylor, returned from teaching in Germany (May). Charlotte tries to get pupils for a school at the Parsonage (July). She writes to M. Heger: if her sight permitted, she would write a book and dedicate it to him; she longs for an answer from him (24 July). Joe Taylor takes another letter from Charlotte to M. Heger: she is grieved by his six months' silence, and counts on	Barrett [Browning], *Poems*; Dickens, *The Chimes*; Disraeli, *Coningsby*; Thackeray, *Barry Lyndon* published. Turner paints *Rain, Steam and Speed*.	Royal Commission on Health in Towns. Bank Charter Act. Rochdale Co-Operative Society founded. Railway mania: massive speculation and investment leads to building of 5,000 miles of track (1844–5). Marx meets Engels in Paris.

Chronology

Year	The Lives of the Brontës	Literary and Artistic Events	Historical Events
1846	Charlotte asks publishers Aylott and Jones if they would publish a collection of poems (28 Jan.); she sends them the manuscript as the work of three relatives, the Bell brothers (6 Feb.); and pays them £31. 10s. for printing the poems (3 Mar.). Charlotte asks whether Aylott and Jones would publish three tales: *The Professor, Wuthering Heights,* and *Agnes Grey* (6 Apr.); Aylott and Jones refuse but offer advice. Branwell goes to Halifax for three days 'on business' (Apr.). *Poems* by Currer, Ellis and Acton Bell published (*c.*22 May). Revd E. Robinson dies (26 May); Branwell believes that Mrs Robinson is prevented from seeing him; he is distraught. Date at the end of Charlotte's manuscript of *The Professor* is 27 June. *Poems* well received in *Athenaeum* and *Critic* but only two copies are sold; Charlotte requests permission (4 July) to send '3 tales' to the publisher H. Colburn, who eventually rejects them (during the next year they are sent to and rejected by about four more publishers). Mr Brontë is now blind. Charlotte goes with her father to Manchester for an eye operation (19 Aug.); they remain there until 25 Sept. Patrick Brontë operated on for cataract in the left eye (25 Aug.). *The Professor* rejected. Charlotte begins writing *Jane Eyre.*	Balzac, *La Cousine Bette*; Dickens, *Dombey and Son* (1846–8); George Eliot, trans. of Strauss, *Life of Jesus*; Lear, *Book of Nonsense*; Thackeray, 'Snobs of England' (1846–7, in *Punch*) published.	Famine in Ireland. Repeal of the Corn Laws. Russell (Whig) becomes prime minister. First Christmas card designed.
1847	Aire Valley railway from Leeds extended to Keighley (16 Mar.). Charlotte feels her 'youth is gone like a dream' (24 Mar.). Fictional date at end of *Tenant* is 10 June; also presumed to be the final composition date. *Poems* remain unsold; Charlotte and her sisters send complimentary copies to Wordsworth, Tennyson, De Quincey, Hartley Coleridge, John Lockhart, and Ebenezer Elliott (16 June). Emily's *Wuthering Heights* and Anne's *Agnes Grey* accepted for publication by Thomas Cautley Newby, but not Charlotte's *The Professor* (July). Charlotte sends *The Professor* to Smith, Elder and Co. (15 July); she acknowledges their reasons	G. H. Lewes, *Ranthorpe*; Tennyson, *The Princess*; Thackeray, *Vanity Fair* (1847–8) published.	Factory Act restricts hours worked by women and children to ten hours. First Californian gold rush.

Chronology

1847   for rejecting it, but mentions that a work of 'more vivid interest' is nearly completed (7 Aug.). She sends MS of *Jane Eyre* to Smith, Elder by rail (24 Aug.), accepting their terms for its publication but refusing to revise it 'a third time' (12 Sept.). Charlotte stays with Ellen Nussey at Brookroyd, correcting proofs of *Jane Eyre* while there but not admitting authorship (9–23 Sept.). *Jane Eyre: An Autobiography*, edited by Currer Bell, published in three volumes by Smith, Elder and Co. (19 Oct.). Charlotte receives the first of many favourable reviews by 26 Oct. She continues to correspond with Ellen Nussey about Amelia Ringrose, not mentioning *Jane Eyre* (29 Oct.) and writes her first letter to G. H. Lewes (6 Nov.), in reply to one from him. Emily and Anne receive the last proof-sheets of *Wuthering Heights* and *Agnes Grey* (17 Nov.). Charlotte writes three beginnings to her next novel but discards them; she wishes to recast *The Professor*. Emily and Anne receive six copies of *Wuthering Heights. A Novel*, by Ellis Bell, and *Agnes Grey. A Novel*, by Acton Bell, published together in three volumes (14 Dec.). Charlotte sends a revised preface (21 Dec.) for the second edition of *Jane Eyre*, which will appear on 22 Jan. 1848, with a dedication to Thackeray. She disclaims authorship of *Wuthering Heights* and *Agnes Grey* (31 Dec.).

1848   Newby offers to make arrangements for 'Ellis Bell's' 'next novel' and offers advice on 'her new work' (15 Feb.). *The Tenant of Wildfell Hall* by Acton Bell, published in three volumes by Thomas Newby (*c.*27 June). Charlotte and Anne travel to London to prove there is more than one author named 'Bell'; they go to the opera with George Smith and his sisters, visit the Royal Academy Exhibition and the National Gallery (7–11 July). Second edition of *Tenant*; Branwell receives threat of court

    Gaskell, *Mary Barton*; Leigh Hunt, *A Jar of Honey from Mount Hybla*; Kingsley, *Yeast* (in *Fraser's Magazine*); G. H. Lewes, *Rose, Blanche and Violet*; Marx, *Communist Manifesto*; Thackeray, *Pendennis* (1848–50) published. Founding of Pre-Raphaelite brotherhood.

    Outbreak of cholera in London. Public Health Act. End of the Chartist movement. The 'Year of Revolutions' (in Paris, Berlin, Vienna, Rome, Prague, and other cities). Second Republic in France: Louis Napoleon becomes president. Roman Republic declared. Queen's College for Women founded in London.

Year	The Lives of the Brontës	Literary and Artistic Events	Historical Events
1848	summons for non-payment of debts (22 July). Branwell dies of chronic bronchitis and marasmus (wasting of the body), aged 31 (24 Sept.). Emily very ill, refuses to see a doctor; scarcely allows her condition to be referred to (Nov.). Anne receives visit from her former pupils, the Misses Robinson (Dec.). Emily dies of pulmonary tuberculosis, aged 30 (19 Dec.).		
1849	The doctor reports that Anne is unlikely to live (Jan.). Anne decides to use the £200 legacy left her by her godmother, Miss Outhwaite, to go to Scarborough (8 May). Charlotte, Anne, and Ellen Nussey leave for Scarborough, via York (24 May). Anne dies of pulmonary tuberculosis (28 May), aged 29, and is buried in St Mary's Churchyard, Scarborough. Charlotte and Ellen Nussey go down the east coast to Filey and Bridlington (7 June), before returning to Haworth. *Shirley* finished (29 Aug.); sent to publishers (8 Sept.). *Shirley. A Tale* by Currer Bell, published in three volumes by Smith, Elder and Co. (26 Oct.). Charlotte goes to London (29 Nov.), staying with the Smiths (until 15 Dec.); meets Thackeray, visits a Turner exhibition at the National Gallery, sees Macready in *Othello* and *Macbeth*.	Arnold, *The Strayed Reveller and Other Poems*; Dickens, *David Copperfield* (1849–50); Froude, *Nemesis of Faith*; Kingsley, *The Saint's Tragedy*; Macaulay, *History of England* (1849–61), vols. 1 and 2; Mayhew, *London Labour and the London Poor* (1849–50); Ruskin, *The Seven Lamps of Architecture* published. Dante Gabriel Rossetti paints *Girlhood of Mary Virgin*. Poe dies. Dostoevsky sentenced to penal servitude in Siberia.	Disraeli becomes Conservative leader. F. D. Maurice, Charles Kingsley, and Thomas Hughes preach Christian Socialism. Bedford College for Women founded in London.
1850	Charlotte visits London (30 May), again staying with the Smiths (until 25 June); visits the Royal Academy, sees the Duke of Wellington, and has her portrait drawn by George Richmond. She goes to Edinburgh (3–6 July), meeting George Smith there. She goes to stay with Sir James Kay-Shuttleworth at Briery Close, near Windermere, where she meets Elizabeth Gaskell (19 Aug.). Charlotte's 'edited' edition of *Wuthering Heights* and *Agnes Grey*, with 'Notice' about her sisters, published (10 Dec.). She stays with Harriet Martineau at The Knoll, Ambleside (16–23 Dec.).	Barrett Browning, *Sonnets from the Portuguese*; Sydney Dobell, *The Roman*; Gaskell, *The Moorland Cottage*; Hawthorne, *The Scarlet Letter*; Kingsley, *Alton Locke*; Tennyson, *In Memoriam AHH*; Thackeray, *Rebecca and Rowena*; Turgenev, *A Month in the Country*; Wordsworth, *The Prelude*; *Household Words* (ed. Dickens) published (1850–9). Millais paints *Christ in the House of his Parents*. Dante Gabriel Rossetti exhibits *Ecce Ancilla Domini*. Wordsworth dies; Tennyson succeeds him as Poet Laureate.	Wiseman made cardinal; Roman Catholic hierarchy restored in England. Miss Buss starts North London Collegiate School for Girls.

Chronology

Year	The Lives of the Brontës	Literary and Artistic Events	Historical Events
1851	Charlotte dubious about possible marriage to James Taylor (5 Apr.). She goes to London (28 May–27 June); attends Thackeray's lecture, sees the Great Exhibition five times, sees Rachel act twice, and visits Dr Brown, a phrenologist, where she and George Smith (as Mr and Miss Fraser) have their characters read.	Beecher Stowe, *Uncle Tom's Cabin*; Borrow, *Lavengro*; Gaskell, *Cranford* (1851–3); Melville, *Moby Dick*; Ruskin, *The Stones of Venice* (1851–3), pt. 1 published. Millais paints *Mariana*. Verdi, *Rigoletto* performed. Turner dies.	Great Exhibition in London. Louis Napoleon's *coup d'état*.
1852	Charlotte revises *Shirley* (Mar.). She sends final volume of *Villette* manuscript to Smith, Elder (20 Nov.). Arthur Bell Nicholls proposes marriage, but Mr Brontë's apoplectic reaction causes Charlotte to refuse (13 Dec.).	Arnold, *Empedocles on Etna and Other Poems*; Dickens, *Bleak House* (1852–3); Newman, *University Education* (later *Idea of a University*); Tennyson, *Ode on the Death of Wellington*; Thackeray, *Henry Esmond* published. Millais paints *Ophelia*. Holman Hunt paints *The Light of the World*.	Derby (Cons.) becomes prime minister, followed by Aberdeen (Coalition) (1852–5). Death of Duke of Wellington. Louis Napoleon proclaimed emperor with title Napoleon III.
1853	Charlotte makes her last visit to London (Jan.). *Villette* by Currer Bell, published in three volumes by Smith, Elder and Co. (28 Jan.). Charlotte goes to stay with Elizabeth Gaskell at Manchester (21–8 Apr.); Elizabeth Gaskell visits Charlotte at Haworth (19 Sept.). Charlotte visits Ellen Nussey, then goes to stay with Margaret Wooler at Hornsea (?16–13 Sept.). She writes *Emma*, the opening chapters of a new novel (Nov.).	Arnold, *Poems*; Gaskell, *Ruth*; Maurice, *Theological Essays*; Surtees, *Mr Sponge's Sporting Tour*; Thackeray, *The Newcomes* and *English Humourists of the Eighteenth Century* published.	Gladstone's first budget. Crimean War begins, defending European interests in the Middle East against Russia (ends 1856).
1854	Charlotte marries her father's curate Revd Arthur Bell Nicholls, and leaves for a honeymoon in Ireland (29 June), where she meets Nicholls's aunt who brought him up. Charlotte and Nicholls return to Haworth, to live at the Parsonage and look after Patrick Brontë (1 Aug.).	Dickens, *Hard Times*; Sydney Dobell, *Balder*; Patmore, *Angel in the House* (1854–63); Tennyson, *Charge of the Light Brigade*; Thoreau, *Walden* published. Holman Hunt paints *The Scapegoat*. Frith paints *Ramsgate Sands*.	Preston cotton spinners' strike. F. D. Maurice founds Working Men's College, London. Battles of Alma, Inkerman, and Balaclava in the Crimean War.
1855	Charlotte dies (31 Mar.), aged 38, of phthisis according to the death certificate, but possibly of hyperemesis gravidarum, excessive sickness during pregnancy. Patrick Brontë asks Elizabeth Gaskell to write an account of Charlotte's life with 'some remarks on her works' (16 June); she agrees, and begins to gather material.	Browning, *Men and Women*; Dickens *Little Dorrit* (1855–7); Gaskell, *North and South* (1854–5); Kingsley, *Westward Ho!*; Longfellow, *Hiawatha*; Martineau completes 2 vols. of unpublished *Autobiography*; Tennyson, *Maud*; Thackeray, *The Rose and the Ring*; Trollope, *The Warden*; Whitman, *Leaves of Grass* published. Millais paints *Blind Girl*.	Palmerston (Lib.) becomes prime minister. Metropolitan Board of Works. Repeal of Stamp Duty on newspapers. Fall of Sebastopol. Livingstone discovers Victoria Falls.
1856		Flaubert, *Madame Bovary*; Froude, *History of England*, (1856–70), vols. 1 and 2 published.	Second Opium War (1856–60) opens China to European trade.

Year	The Lives of the Brontës	Literary and Artistic Events	Historical Events
1857	Elizabeth Gaskell's *Life of Charlotte Brontë* published in two volumes (27 Mar.). *The Professor, A Tale* by Currer Bell, published in two volumes by Smith, Elder and Co., with a preface by Nicholls (6 June).	Barrett Browning, *Aurora Leigh*; Baudelaire, *Les Fleurs du Mal*; Eliot, *Scenes of Clerical Life*; Hughes, *Tom Brown's School-days*; Thackeray, *The Virginians*; Trollope, *Barchester Towers*; published.	Matrimonial Causes Act makes divorce available without special act of Parliament. Indian Mutiny: siege and relief of Lucknow (1857–8).
1858		Ballantyne, *The Coral Island*; Carlyle, *Frederick the Great.* Frith paints *Derby Day.*	Derby (Cons.) becomes prime minister; Brunel's *Great Eastern* launched. Suppression of Indian Mutiny, abolition of East India Company, and establishment of viceroyalty.
1859		Beeton, *Book of Household Management*; Collins, *The Woman in White* (1859–60); Darwin, *Origin of Species*; Dickens, *Tale of Two Cities*; Eliot, *Adam Bede*; Fitzgerald, *Rubáiyát of Omar Khayyám*; Meredith, *Ordeal of Richard Feverel*; John Stuart Mill, *On Liberty*; Smiles, *Self Help*; Tennyson, *Idylls of the King*; *All the Year Round* (ed. Dickens) published.	Palmerston (Whig–Lib.) becomes prime minister; Gladstone Chancellor of Exchequer. Franco-Austrian War.
1860		Dickens, *Great Expectations* (1860–1); Eliot, *The Mill on the Floss*; Ruskin, *Unto This Last* published. *Cornhill Magazine* founded with Thackeray as editor.	Italian unification.
1861	Patrick Brontë dies (7 June), aged 85; Nicholls returns to Ireland, later marrying his cousin, Mary Anna Bell (25 Aug. 1864).	Eliot, *Silas Marner* published.	Prince Albert dies. American Civil War (1861–5).

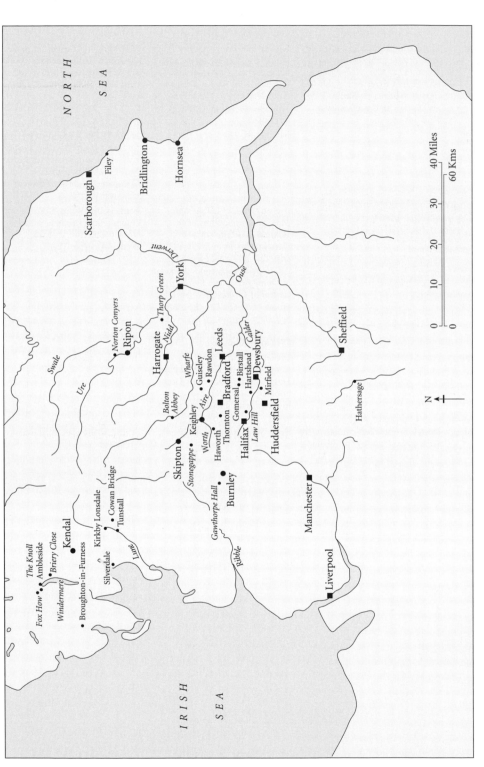

The north of England: places associated with the Brontës.

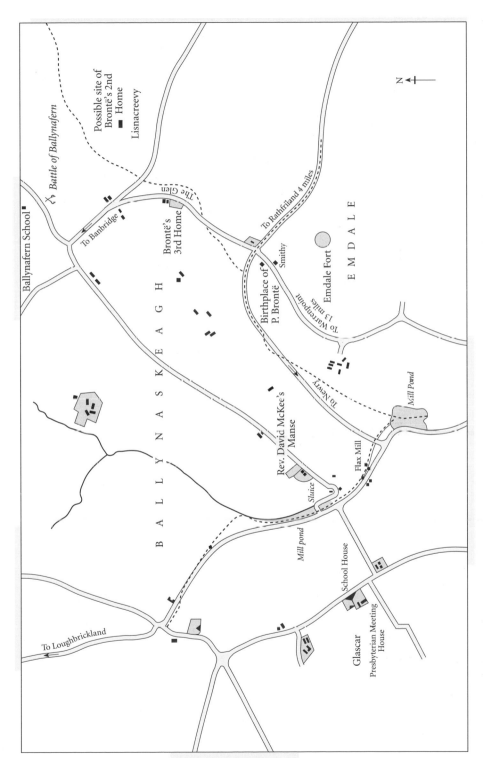

Ireland: places associated with Revd Patrick Brontë and his family.

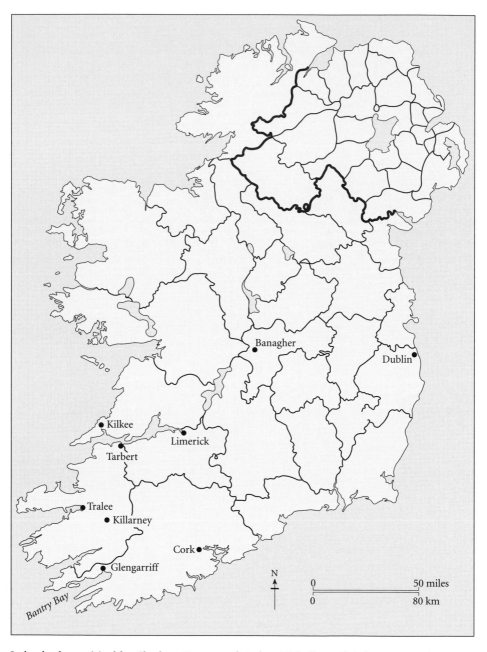

Ireland: places visited by Charlotte Brontë and Arthur Nicholls on their honeymoon journey.

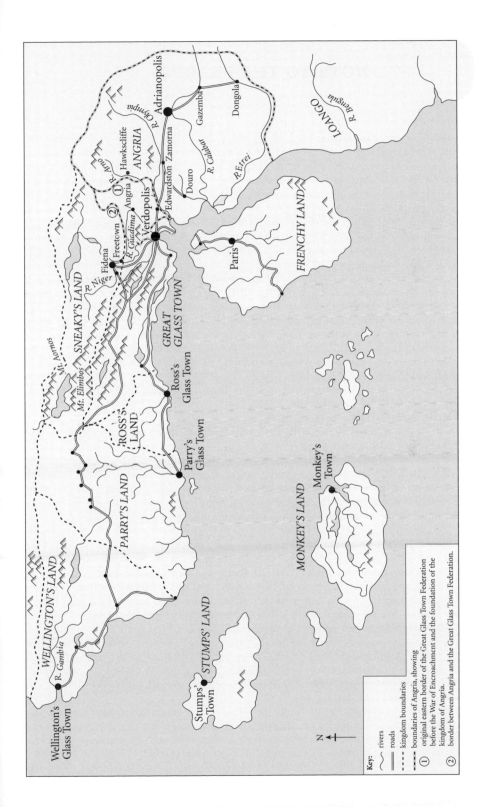

The Glass Town Federation and the kingdom of Angria (based on Branwell Brontë's frontispiece to 'The History of the Young Men' (1831), with Angria added). (Christine Alexander)

Key:
- rivers
- roads
- kingdom boundaries
- boundaries of Angria, showing
- ① original eastern border of the Great Glass Town Federation before the War of Encroachment and the foundation of the kingdom of Angria.
- ② border between Angria and the Great Glass Town Federation.

WELLINGTON'S LAND

R. Gambia

Mt. Aornos

SNEAKY'S LAND

Mt. Elimbos

'ROSS'S LAND'

PARRY'S LAND

Ross's Glass Town

Parry's Glass Town

GREAT GLASS TOWN

STUMPS' LAND

Stumps' Town

MONKEY'S LAND

Monkey's Town

Paris

FRENCHY LAND

LANGO

R. Bengula

Adrianopolis

R. Olympia

Gazemba

Dongola

Edwardston

Zamorna

Douro

R. Calabar

R. Etrei

ANGRIA

Hawkscliffe

R. Arno

Angria

Verdopolis

Freetown

R. Gradima

Fidena

R. Niger

N

NOTE TO THE READER

Entries in this *Companion* are arranged in letter-by-letter alphabetical order by their **headwords**, which appear in bold type, except for 'St', which is treated as if it were spelled 'Saint'. The headwords of works by the Brontës in French and German are in English with the foreign language title in brackets, as in '"Butterfly, The" ("Le Papillon")'. Married women are listed under the names by which they are best known by readers interested in the Brontës: for example, 'Beck, Mme; Brontë, Mrs Maria, née Branwell; Franks, Mrs Elizabeth; Gaskell, Elizabeth; Huntingdon, Helen'. A number of characters and place names in the Brontë juvenilia metamorphosed over time. In such cases, the original name is used as the headword and subsequent names are recorded in brackets (thus, 'Sneaky (Sneakie, Sneachi, Sneachie), Lady Maria'; 'Parry's Land (Parrysland, Parrisland)'). This practice is followed consistently, except in the few cases where major Glass Town and Angrian characters are more commonly known by their later titles: namely, 'Zamorna, Duke of (Arthur Augustus Adrian Wellesley, Marquis of Douro, King of Angria)'; 'Northangerland, Duke of (Alexander Augustus Percy, Rogue (Rougue), Lord Ellrington (Elrington))'; and 'Fidena, Prince John Augustus Sneaky (Sneachi, Sneachie), Duke of'. A further complication arises where Charlotte and Branwell spell the names of their characters differently. The headwords use Charlotte's spelling, with Branwell's spelling recorded in brackets: thus, 'Ellrington (Elrington) family'; and Charlotte's spelling is used consistently throughout the entries. Further alternative spellings that commonly occur in the juvenilia are also given in brackets in the headword: thus, 'Guadima (Guardina) River' or 'Almeida (Almeda), Augusta Geraldine (A.G.A.)'. There are also a number of signpost entries: these are headwords which act as cross-references, directing the reader to the entry under which the subject is covered, e.g. 'Bell, Currer, Ellis, and Acton. See PSEUDONYMS USED BY THE BRONTËS.'

Readers wishing to read about the lives of the Brontës should turn to the entries on each member of the family. There are in-depth entries on Charlotte, Emily, and Anne Brontë, and on their brother Branwell and their father Patrick. A survey of the many interpretations of their lives can be found in 'biographies to 1940' and 'biographies from 1940'. The critical response to the sisters' work is divided between a number of entries: 'critical reception to 1860'; 'criticism 1860–1940'; and 'criticism from 1940', with additional entries on a range of current critical approaches, such as 'post-colonial theory'. General contextual and historical entries, such as natural history, visual arts, contemporary writers, publishing, education, emigration, refer to thinkers or artists whose individual entries may be consulted for more detailed information. Entries on the sisters' novels follow a similar format, with sections on composition, plot, early editions of the novels and reception. Surviving original manuscripts and related manuscripts are described, as are the novels' sources and context or their antecedents. These and other substantial entries are followed by short lists of **further reading**. These are designed to point the reader towards further sources of information, and are not necessarily lists of references used in writing the entries. There is also a **general bibliography** on pp. 583–6.

Entries in the *Companion* are extensively cross-referenced. **Cross-references** are indicated either by an asterisk in front of a word, indicating that it has its own entry (e.g. 'The sisters were taught art as one of the female *accomplishments'), or by the use of 'see' or 'see also', followed by the headword in small capitals, e.g. '(see ART OF THE BRONTËS)'. Cross-references are designed to facilitate navigation between entries, leading the reader to other related entries, perhaps to entries that provide historical context, or more detailed information.

There is a **Classified Contents List** on pp. xv–xxv. This is a list of entries arranged under major subject headings, such as lives of the Brontës, the Brontës' early writings, the literary context, politics and government. It offers another means of accessing the information in the *Companion*, providing the reader with lists of all the entries relating to a particular subject.

Note to the Reader

References to chapters in the Brontë novels are to editions with continuously numbered chapters. Page references to novels by the Brontës are to the Clarendon editions, for which see the entry on 'Editing history of the mature novels'. References to multi-volume works such as *The Letters of Charlotte Brontë*, ed. Margaret Smith, vol. 1. *1829–1847* (1995), and vol. 2. *1848–1851* (2000), are by volume and page number, preceded by the abbreviation: e.g. 'Smith *Letters*, 2. 16–22'. References to *Brontë Society Transactions* (1895–2001) (retitled from March 2002 *Brontë Studies*) are to date, volume, part, and page[s]: e.g. *BST* (1999) 24. 1. 50–4. For quotations from critical or biographical works references are to page numbers: 'Lonoff, p. 434' indicates *The Belgian Essays: Charlotte Brontë and Emily Brontë*, ed. and trans. Sue Lonoff (1996), p. 434. For a list of abbreviations, used for the most frequently cited works, see pp. xxvii–xxviii.

A **chronology** covering the lives of the Brontës, as well as literary and artistic, and historical events, can be found on pp. xxix–xlvii.

Most of the entries in the *Companion* were written by the authors, Christine Alexander and Margaret Smith, and these entries are unsigned, but significant contributions were also made by other Brontë scholars. You can find a list of contributors to the *Companion* on pp. xiii–xiv, together with short biographies. Entries not written by the authors are signed using a system of initials, set ranged right, beneath the main text of the entry. A key to these initials can also be found on pp. xiii–xiv.

Readers' comments: every effort has been made to ensure that the information in the *Companion* is accurate. But minor errors and inconsistencies are inevitable, and readers are invited to call attention to any they discover, or to comment on the entries, by writing to:

The Oxford Companion to the Brontës, Trade and Reference Department, Academic Division, Oxford University Press, Great Clarendon Street, Oxford, OX2 6DP, UK. Readers' comments will be passed on to the authors.

A—— is a 'fashionable watering place' in *Agnes Grey*. See SCARBOROUGH.

Abbot, Martha, in *Jane Eyre*, the spiteful, sycophantic lady's maid to Jane Eyre's Aunt Sarah *Reed. She respects her employer for her money and despises Jane for her lack of it: Jane, as a dependant, and less than a servant because she does not work for her keep, should be subservient to her benefactress and to her young 'Master', John Reed. Unsympathetic to Jane's terror in the redroom, Abbot regards her screams as underhand tricks, threatens that God may strike her dead, and has no pity for such a plain 'little toad'. Unlike *Bessie, Abbot presumably neglects Mrs Reed on her deathbed.

Abercorn, Lord. An extravagant young nobleman in the *Glass Town and Angrian saga, who is compelled to sell his estate, Brushwood Hall, to pay his gaming debts. In *High Life in Verdopolis*, he and his cronies Eagleton, Molyneux, Lascelles, and Fitzroy (whose names all echo those of British and Irish aristocracy) are the unsuccessful suitors of Ellen *Grenville. Later, he becomes a general in the Angrian army yet remains 'a fop and a coxcomb under all' (*Julia*).

accomplishments, including 'fancy' needlework, were important for the social and professional mobility of middle-class women in the 19th century. Defined by the *OED* as 'an ornamental attainment that completely equips or perfects a person for society', ladylike accomplishments increased a young woman's chances of marriage, relieved the boredom of long leisure hours for the 'gentlewoman', and, in the case of the Brontës, added to their professional skills as teachers and governesses. Accomplishments usually denoted 'extras' in a school curriculum, subjects not considered part of a basic education but likely to be decorative additions to one's skills, such as French and German, music, drawing, and embroidery (see FOREIGN LANGUAGES). Needlework, French, German, Latin, music, and drawing were to be offered at the proposed 'Misses Brontës' Establishment' (Barker, pp. 439–40). Skill in such accomplishments might be acquired through hard labour and diligence, yet be viewed by society as ornamental assets rather than involving serious professionalism. Emily's attitude to *music, and Charlotte's and Anne's attitudes to drawing were exceptions to this general attitude to accomplishments (see ART OF THE BRONTËS). Schoolfellows were astonished by the sisters' diligence in acquiring accomplishments, which they intended to help them find employment. Both Emily and Anne had piano lessons (Charlotte was too short-sighted);

and all three sisters received lessons in drawing and sewing, the latter directed by their aunt Elizabeth Branwell.

The report on Charlotte's entry at Cowan Bridge School notes that at the age of 8 she 'works neatly' but knows nothing of 'Accomplishments' (Barker, p. 129). 'Working' usually denotes plain sewing and the Brontës are known to have made items such as shirts for Branwell (Smith *Letters*, 1. 207). As governesses they were required to assist with the household sewing, a task Charlotte clearly resented. She complains of Mrs Sarah *Sidgwick overwhelming her 'with oceans of needlework, yards of cambric to hem, muslin nightcaps to make, and, above all things, dolls to dress' (Smith *Letters*, 1. 191). Aunt Branwell, too, insisted on competence in plain sewing and, according to Mary *Taylor, 'used to keep the girls sewing charity clothing'.

For most women of the Brontës' class, however, needlework consisted of 'fancy work', classified as an accomplishment. Charlotte underlines the distinction in a letter describing her activities on her return from *Roe Head (Smith *Letters*, 1. 114). She describes her afternoons spent sewing ('plain' domestic sewing) and 'after tea' her evenings are spent either reading, writing, drawing, or doing 'a little fancy-work'. As children, the sisters made at least two samplers each to demonstrate their sewing skills. A group of three embroidered samplers with biblical passages from Proverbs are all dated January 1830, Emily's being the neatest (Anne's is illustrated in *Sixty Treasures*, ed. J. R. V. Barker (1988), pl. 27). The only surviving relics of the two eldest Brontë children, Maria and Elizabeth, are two faded samplers stitched by Maria at 8 years and Elizabeth at 7 (BPM). The BPM also owns a multicoloured patchwork quilt believed to have been worked by the Brontë sisters. However, the embroidered 'rustic scenes' listed under 'Art Needlework' in the *Binns sale catalogue (Saltaire, 1886) and said to be by the Brontës are unlikely to be by them (W. W. Yates, 'Some Relics of the Brontës', *New Review*, 59 (Apr. 1894), 485–6).

In *Shirley* (ch. 23), Charlotte attacks the genteel skill of needlework and fancy decoration, which she saw as 'naturally in a state of warfare with intellectual development'. The 12-year-old Rose Yorke (see YORKE FAMILY) (modelled on Mary Taylor) complains that such domestic tasks are a waste of a woman's talents if there are no more stimulating activities to supplement them. When Lucy Snowe disparages her paintings as mere copies she does so in terms of the fashionable simplified embroidery of the time that used brightly coloured Berlin wools and provided squared patterns for the needlewoman to follow (*Villette*, ch. 35). Yet although she did not particularly enjoy sewing, the surviving contents of Charlotte's rosewood workbox show that she did use the requisite lace, silk ribbon, and braid to trim bonnets and dresses (illustrated in *Sixty Treasures*, pl. 50). The existence of patterns for elaborately embroidered cuffs and collars, found in Charlotte's portable writing desk, also suggests that she practised this accomplishment (Alexander & Sellars, pp. 265–7).

Many 19th-century women, from private servants to titled ladies, practised not only 'fancywork' but also the making of ornamental articles for 'Fancy Fairs'. They were taught to apply their amateur drawing and painting skills to a range of papier mâché objects: letter boxes, card-holders, fans, and fire screens. Several fan-shaped drawings by the Brontës indicate that the Brontës and their friends were not exempt from making needlecases and similar fancy items as gifts or to be sold at a church fair (Alexander & Sellars, pp. 50–1, 189, 213). There is a faded needlecase made by Charlotte, lined and bound with pink silk and decorated with two tiny pencil drawings of a bird's nest and spaniel; a circular animal painting sewn into a silk binding; a pattern for a coin-purse; and a miniature painting by Charlotte with two needleholes at the top where it has been sewn into a small leather case (Alexander & Sellars, pp. 199–200, 267). The skilful decoration of objects was a requisite sign of the accomplished Victorian lady. Even more typical was the popular pursuit of painting on velvet, a fashion Charlotte never indulged in, possibly because of the cost involved; but while she was staying with her other close friend, Mary Taylor, she did try her hand at the accomplishment of painting on silk (p. 198).

Hesketh, Sally, 'Needlework in the Lives and Novels of the Brontë Sisters', *BST* (1997), 22. 72–85.

Acrofcroomb, a city and province of Ashantee, which features only in the early stages of the *Glass Town and Angrian saga. It is home to a tribe of cannibals ruled by ten brothers, who attack the Glass Town and eat Cheeky, Crackey, and Gravey.

In revenge, the *Twelves (under King Frederic and Arthur Wellesley) destroy Acrofcroomb.

Adelaide, one of the Brontës' two tame geese (see PETS OWNED BY THE BRONTËS), named after Queen *Victoria's aunt, the widowed Queen Adelaide.

Adrian, King. See ZAMORNA, DUKE OF (ARTHUR AUGUSTUS ADRIAN WELLESLEY, MARQUIS OF DOURO, KING OF ANGRIA).

Adrianopolis, capital city of the Kingdom of Angria in the *Glass Town and Angrian saga, named after its founder and ruler Arthur Augustus Adrian Wellesley, Marquis of Douro, Duke of *Zamorna, King of Angria. The *Spell describes the building of the new capital and *'My Angria and the Angrians' mocks the exodus of fortune-hunters from *Verdopolis seeking a new life in the brash new capital, 'the marble toy-shop of Adrianopolis, the mushroom of the Calabar'. Presided over by Zamorna's élite circle who own marble mansions, in 'light, lofty, open Grecian or Italian style', along the Calabar River, the inhabitants are chiefly the nouveaux riches and entrepreneurs from the 'old world' of Verdopolis, 150 miles away. To an even greater extent than Verdopolis, the architecture of Adrianopolis resembles that of John *Martin's recreations of the cities of the ancient world, and it gradually takes over Verdopolis's epithet as the 'Babylon' of the Glass Town and Angrian saga. The decadence of the new city is constantly compared to the restraint and classical purity of Verdopolis, despite the latter's previous reputation for corruption. During the Angrian wars, Adrianopolis suffers siege and occupation by Quashia *Quamina's Ashantee tribes; A *Leaf from an Unopened Volume hints at the doom awaiting the now imperial city.

'Advantages of Poverty in Religious Concerns, The', by Mrs Maria Brontë. This short undated essay of some 1,500 words, now in the Brotherton Collection, is endorsed by Revd Patrick Brontë: 'The above was written by my dear wife, and is for insertion in one of the periodical publications. Keep it as a memorial of her.' The essay is a well-meant pious effort to persuade 'poor but honest and industrious' Christians that religious faith is sufficient to comfort them, even when they lack food for their children and hear their 'heart-rending cries', for they can look forward to the 'everlasting bliss' of heaven. Naïvely, Mrs Brontë adds that honest Christians are 'scarcely ever suffered to languish in extreme want', and that any temptation to believe that God has forgotten them comes from the devil, 'the enemy of [their] immortal interests'. Poverty, she assures them, has many positive advantages: they are neither tempted to amass earthly treasure, corrupted by luxury, nor afraid of robbery, and they sleep peacefully after honest labour. If they both profess and practise religion they will be respected. No worldly learning or philosophy will cloud their understanding of biblical truth; indeed, though without leisure to read, they can 'nurture the life of God in the soul' by meditation and prayer. Only the irreligious whose bad conduct has made them poor need fear endless misery. The essay, implicitly accepting the class structure and the inevitability of poverty, might have suited the *Cottage Magazine* or *Pastoral Visitor*. It was first published in Shorter *Circle*, but was probably seen by Charlotte in February 1850 when her father put into her hands 'a little packet of letters and papers' written by her mother. Deeply touched, Charlotte found the papers a record of a mind 'of a truly fine, pure, and elevated order': 'I wish she had lived, and that I had known her'.

'Adventure in Ireland, An'. See 'TWO ROMANTIC TALES'.

'Adventures of Ernest Alembert, The' (25 May 1830), a tale by Charlotte Brontë, written in cursive script rather than her typical minuscule hand (MS in Carl H. Pforzheimer Library, NYPL). Inspired by stories of spirits who visit men shortly before their deaths, the tale is not obviously related to the Glass Town and Angrian saga, although it is similar to stories told in the *'Young Men's Magazine'.* The hero Ernest longs to visit the land of Faery, so Rufus Warner, a fairy, appears to him one autumn evening and takes him to witness the wonders of the supernatural world: splendid palaces of lapis lazuli and liquid diamond, paradisal gardens, a city with streets of precious stones. After many years, Ernest wishes to return home and a magic potion transports him to a green valley (perhaps the Valley of Verdopolis) where he meets an old man who had also been captured by fairies but who experienced the horrors of the bottom of the ocean. Ernest decides to spend the rest of his days in this valley which appears to have an eternal summer.

Alexander *EEW*, 1. 154–69.

'Adventures of Mon Edouard de Crack, The'. See DE CRACK, MON[SIEUR] EDOUARD.

Aesop's Fables, one of the formative *books read by the Brontës. The Fables are a collection of brief moral tales attributed to a Greek slave said to have lived about 600 BC, but probably 'Aesop' is simply a name invented to provide an author for fables centring on beasts. Most of the characters are animals that talk and act like human beings, illustrating the foibles and virtues of humans in a humorous way, as in 'The Fox and the Grapes', 'The

City Mouse and the Country Mouse', and 'The Ant and the Grasshopper'. Aesop's fables have survived through the centuries because of their widespread appeal. They have been retold and expanded by later writers, such as the 17th-century French poet and fabulist Jean de *La Fontaine. It is difficult to establish which edition the Brontë children read but Charlotte clearly states that the characters of *Our Fellows' Play were taken from Aesop's fables (Alexander *EEW*, 1. 6). Winifred Gérin states that the Brontës owned an 1825 edition translated from the French by Samuel Croxall (Gérin *CB*, p. 25), but two of the Brontë characters are not found in this edition.

Afghan War, a subject in Branwell Brontë's poetry. In November 1837 Mohammed Shah of Persia, with Russia's approval, besieged Herat in western Afghanistan. Perceiving a threat to British supremacy in India, the governor-general, Lord Auckland, ordered an invasion of Afghanistan, in order to restore Shah Shuja, its former ruler, instead of the supposedly pro-Russian Dost Mohammed. In April 1839 the British army entered Kandahar, crowned the Shah, went on to capture Ghazni in July 1840, and installed Shah Shuja in Kabul. The Afghans resented British occupation and the restoration of a detested ruler. The deposed Dost Mohammed won a battle at Parwandarah on 2 November 1840, but surrendered the next day to the British in Kabul. Though the British forces remained for two years, inadequate food, medical, and military supplies made their position untenable. During negotiations for withdrawal their political agent, Sir William Macnaghten, was shot by Akbar Khan, and his body was slashed by the knives of Ghazi tribesmen. The Afghans captured the British military store, and on 6 January 1842 about 4,500 British and Indian troops, with 12,000 camp-followers, offered a safe-conduct by Dost Mohammed, left Kabul to make their way in the intense cold of winter down the Khyber Pass, and so to India. Thousands died of cold and hunger, others were attacked and mutilated by Afghans; only one man, the army surgeon William Brydon, reached Jalalabad on 13 January 1842. In summer 1842 the new governor-general, Lord Ellenborough, decided that British troops should leave Afghanistan. Branwell Brontë imagined a family thinking of a 'well-loved wanderer' dying 'on foreign shores' (25 Apr. 1842; Neufeldt *BBP*, p. 221), resurrected a poem of 1837, 'On the callousness produced by cares', where the dying soldier's eyes are 'blind | To comrades dying' (*Bradford Herald* and *Halifax Guardian* (5 and 7 May 1842); Neufeldt *BBP*, p. 222), and wrote 'The Affghan [*sic*] War' urging England to avenge the slaughter of her 'children'

Africa

by Moslem sabres (*Leeds Intelligencer* (7 May 1842); Neufeldt *BBP*, p. 223). See also POETRY BY BRANWELL BRONTË.

Africa. The 'dark' continent of Africa held an exotic fascination for Romantic writers and painters, and it was seen as a site of opportunity by explorers, missionaries, politicians, and commercial interests in the 19th century. The choice of Africa by the Brontë children as the location for their imaginary kingdoms of *Glass Town and *Angria reflects how far the colonial experience had penetrated the psyche of the British public at that time. Articles in *Blackwood's Edinburgh Magazine* convey the image of an empty continent, apart from scattered barbaric tribes and sporadic Muslim invaders, with great rivers waiting to be navigated and a lucrative trade in natural resources waiting to be tapped. This mysterious vacuum (as they perceived it) enabled the young Brontës to create a new (imaginary) society, where they as children could wield unprecedented power and indulge in physical and moral anarchy (see JUVENILIA OF THE BRONTËS).

The Brontës' earliest encounter with Africa was probably in the pages of their geography book, Revd J. Goldsmith's *Grammar of General Geography* (1823), where the maps of Africa are crude (and inaccurate) and where the corresponding text represents the prevailing attitudes of the time. For example, 'The most civilized and intelligent quarter of the world is Europe; the most barbarous is Africa' (p. 79). *Blackwood's* was a particularly fertile source for information about Africa: it carried articles on the wealth and trade of Muslim merchants in Timbuctoo and Hausa, European exploration and the death of Mungo Park, the course of the Niger River, British emigration to the Cape of Good Hope, and the activities of the numerous Church Missionary Societies which were also regularly reported in publications like the *Cottage Magazine*. Revd Patrick Brontë was a founding member of the Bradford Church Missionary Society which, like the African Association mentioned so often in *Blackwood's*, sponsored not only missionaries to Africa but also sent Bibles. The Brontës read in *Blackwood's* about the 'Mission from Cape Coast Castle to Ashantee' (1819) and accepted the need to re-educate the 'savage', adopting in their stories the prevailing paternalism of the magazine (*Blackwood's*, 5 (1819), 175–83). The *Ashantee (Ashanti) kings described in this article, Sai Quamina and Sai Too Too, also became part of the Brontë saga together with the imaginary Quashia *Quamina who becomes a central character.

Branwell's early map of the Glass Town Federation (illustrated in Alexander *EEW* 2(2),

frontispiece) corresponds to those in their early geographies and particularly to a map in *Blackwood's* based on recent explorations in northern and central Africa (see GLASS TOWN AND ANGRIAN SAGA). The Brontës establish their imaginary colony at the mouth of the *Niger River in the Gulf of Guinea, the site recommended in the accompanying article in *Blackwood's* (June 1826; updated 1831). The resistance their *Young Men encounter from the native Ashantees and the presence of French territory near Glass Town (see PARIS (IN FRENCHYLAND)), reflect the political situation at the time when European powers such as Portugal, France, and Britain were seeking to establish commercial bases along the west coast of Africa, commonly known as the Gold Coast. Their battles were inspired by reports of the *Ashantee Wars of the 1820s in newspapers and journals; and numerous geographical names from these sources are absorbed into the saga, such as *Jibbel Kumri, *'Coomassie' (now 'Kumasi'), *Dahomey, Benin, *Guadima, *Calabar, *Etrei, *Dongola, and *Loango. Apart from names, however, and sporadic attempts to describe a desert scene, the landscape of the Brontës' early stories is basically a re-creation of that of Britain rather than Africa.

Branwell was still displaying his knowledge of Africa in 1845 when, in his unfinished novel *And the Weary are at Rest, he referred to Fort Elmina and Cape Coast Castle, within 6 miles of each other on the Gold Coast. Elmina was the earliest European settlement on the Gold Coast, built by the Portuguese in the 15th century, captured by the Dutch in 1637, and transferred to Britain in 1867, when conflict with the Ashantee (now 'Ashanti') flared again. Cape Coast Castle, also known as Carbo Corso (Branwell uses both names), was a British fort from 1664 and capital of British territory until 1876 (Neufeldt *BB Works*, 3. 458). See also ANNUALS; GEOGRAPHY, KNOWLEDGE OF, AND BOOKS; POSTCOLONIAL THEORY.

Alexander, Christine, 'Imagining Africa: The Brontës' Creations of Glass Town and Angria', in P. Alexander, R. Hutchinson, and D. Schreuder (eds.), *Africa Today: A Multi-Disciplinary Snapshot of the Continent* (1996), 201–19.
Meyer, Susan, *Imperialism at Home: Race and Victorian Women's Fiction* (1996), 29–59.

'African Queen's Lament, The'. See QUAMINA, QUASHIA.

Alexander *EEW* 2(1), 3–6.

A.G.A. See ALMEIDA (ALMEDA), AUGUSTA GERALDINE; GONDAL SAGA.

Agars, the. Henry, Richard, and William Agar are members of the powerful Angrian *Warner family, including Howards and Agars, whose head is Warner Howard Warner. They feature chiefly in 'A Day Abroad', a story in Charlotte Brontë's *'Corner Dishes' (Alexander *EEW*, 2(2). 97–137).

Agnes Grey. *See page 6*

Ainley, Miss Mary Ann, one of two old maids (the other is Miss *Mann) in *Shirley* befriended by Caroline *Helstone. Fifty years old, she lives alone. Her ugliness and poverty make her an object of mockery to some, but Caroline discovers that she is saintly by nature, and possessed of a 'practical excellence' that outweighs any lack of sophistication or intellect. She is summoned to *Fieldhead to help administer charitable relief to the destitute poor of *Briarfield, drawing from a fund of £300 given by Shirley *Keeldar. The narrator claims that Miss Ainley is not 'a figment of imagination— no—we seek the originals of such portraits in real life only' (p. 204). In a letter of 8 January 1850 commenting on his own portrayal in *Shirley* as Revd Mr Hall, Revd William Margetson Heald, Vicar of Birstall, told Ellen Nussey that his sister Mary 'thinks she descries Cecilia Crowther & Miss Johnson (afterwards Mrs Westerman) in 2 old maids' (Smith *Letters*, 2. 325). In her 'Reminiscences of Charlotte Brontë', Ellen speaks of Charlotte's having been impressed, while a pupil at *Roe Head school, 'with the goodliness and saintliness of one of Miss W[ooler]'s guests,—the Miss Ainley of *Shirley*, long since gone to her rest' (*Scribner's Monthly*, May 1871). HR

'Albion and Marina: A Tale', by Lord Charles Wellesley (12 Oct. 1830) (MS in Wellesley College Library). Written by Charlotte Brontë when she was 14 years old, 'Albion and Marina' is her first love story in which she explores the triangular relationship between the young Duke of *Zamorna, his childhood sweetheart Marian *Hume, and her sophisticated 'Frenchified rival' Lady Zenobia *Ellrington. The story is based on a secret romance of the historical Duke of *Wellington's eldest son, and is significant for its dual setting in England and *Glass Town (representing a final merging of the *Islanders' Play and *Young Men's Play) and for its use of the supernatural which parallels similar events in *Jane Eyre. The tale is also an excellent example of Charlotte's early observation of her own creative process: she carefully records 'I wrote this in four hours', and undercuts her romantic story through the ironic observation of the mischievous narrator Lord Charles *Wellesley, who delights in confusing fact and fiction. Lord Charles claims that he wrote the story 'out of malignity' towards his brother Arthur (Marquis Douro, later Zamorna); and that although the conclusion is a falsehood, the essence of the story is

founded on 'fact'. The deliberate obfuscation by the narrator is part of the increasingly complex relationship between creator and created in the *Glass Town and Angrian saga and Charlotte's growing sense of relationship to an audience.

The narrator disguises the Glass Town characters under the 'thin veil' of altered names. The heroine Marina Angus (Marian Hume) resides in a secluded forest with her father, Sir Alured Angus (see BADEY, DR HUME (LATER SIR ALEXANDER HUME, DUKE OF)), the Scots physician to the Duke of Strathelleraye (*Strathfieldsay). Despite her humble origins, Albion (Arthur Wellesley, Marquis of Douro) falls in love with her, but they are young and must wait. The Duke removes his family from England to the African Glass Town, promising his son may marry Marina when they return. Arthur then meets the accomplished Lady Zelzia (Zenobia) Ellrington but before she can seduce him, Marina's apparition warns him not to forsake her. He returns to England to find that Marina had died at the exact moment of his vision of her. A number of critics have pointed to this incident as a precursor to similar visions and voices surrounding the separation and reunion of Rochester and Jane Eyre, in particular the mysterious voice Jane hears when tempted by St John Rivers (*Jane Eyre*, ch. 35), and such visions as the 'illustration' of a young man who 'thought his love slept sweetly' but 'finds she is stone-dead' (ch. 36).

Alexander *EEW*, 1. 285–97.
McMaster, Juliet, et al. (ed.), *Albion and Marina by Charlotte Brontë* (1999).

alcohol. See HEALTH OF THE BRONTËS; BRONTË, (PATRICK) BRANWELL.

Alcona, Rosina, an ambitious, haughty member of the Gondal aristocracy, seen by Fannie Ratchford to be the same person as A.G.A. (see ALMEIDA (ALMEDA), AUGUSTA GERALDINE). She causes Julius Brenzaida's imprisonment but later appears to have married him. She supports his campaigns for power in Gaaldine and mourns his death and burial in Angora in Gondal (*'Remembrance').

Alderwood, formerly Badey Hall, the secluded home of Marian *Hume and her widower father, Sir Alexander Hume, Duke of *Badey (later Duke of Alderwood), near Grassmere Manor in Wellington's Land, *Glass Town and Angrian saga. It was inherited by her son Ernest Edward Gordon Wellesley, who lived there for the first three years of his life, neglected by his father, the Duke of Zamorna.

Alembert, Ernest. See 'ADVENTURES OF ERNEST ALEMBERT, THE'.

A NNE Brontë's first published novel, *Agnes Grey* (1847), concerned as it was with a socially anomalous governess protagonist, was not untypical of fiction by women writers in the early 19th century. An anonymous novel entitled *The Governess* was published by Smith, Elder in 1836; the Countess of Blessington was the author of a two-volume novel with the same title in 1839; and, also in 1839, Harriet Martineau's *Deerbrook* portrayed a highly intelligent governess who plays a part in the unfolding of the plot. Charlotte Brontë's *Jane Eyre*, the governess-novel par excellence, though published before Anne's novel, was actually written after it.

Composition
The first undoubted reference to *Agnes Grey* occurs in Charlotte Brontë's letter to the publishers *Aylott and Jones on 6 April 1846, when she asked their advice on behalf of 'C. E & A Bell' about publishing 'three distinct and unconnected tales which may be published either together as a work of 3 vols. of the ordinary novel-size, or separately as single vols' (Smith *Letters*, 1. 461). By that date the three works (Charlotte's The *Professor*, Emily's *Wuthering Heights*, and Anne's *Agnes Grey*) were being prepared for the press, and Anne ('Acton') must have estimated that her manuscript (which does not survive) would fill rather more than 300 printed pages—the usual size of one volume in a 'three-decker' novel. We do not know exactly when Anne completed her fair copy, but her estimate of its size was accurate enough: the novel takes up 363 pages in the first edition. The first five chapters of *Agnes Grey* may have been written during, or more probably after, her governess-ship in the *Ingham family, which lasted from 8 April until ?December 1839. Her experience of 'life-wearing exertion' to keep unruly, violent children in order provided plenty of material, though (one hopes) no exact models, for Agnes's weary, persevering, ill-rewarded efforts to corral the obnoxious Tom and Mary Ann *Bloomfield and persuade them to learn their lessons. Yet she was afterwards accused of 'extravagant over-colouring in those very parts that were carefully copied from the life, with a most scrupulous avoidance of all exaggeration' (preface to 2nd edn. of *Tenant*). Chapters 7–23 of *Agnes Grey* draw on some of Anne's experiences as governess in the *Robinson family. Though we do not know how closely the *Murray family resemble Anne's employers and pupils, there is a general similarity in the description of *Horton Lodge and its park of fine old trees amid flat, fertile countryside to *Thorp Green Hall in the vale of York, and in the family's attitude to marriage. Rosalie Murray's mother encourages her to marry the rich Sir Thomas Ashby, regardless of his manners and morals, as Mrs Lydia *Robinson (according to her daughters) urged them to contract loveless marriages, regardless of their happiness. Rosalie's eventual respect and affection for her governess is matched by the fondness of the two younger Robinson girls for Anne. Anne certainly aimed to combine moral teaching with entertainment in her novel, and she succeeds in making virtue attractive by giving Edward *Weston the generous spirit and sincere faith she had admired in Revd William *Weightman, and in setting his proposal in the seaside resort she loved so much—for '*A——' is transparently *Scarborough, which Anne had so often visited with the Robinsons.

It is possible that in Anne's Diary Paper of 31 July 1845, written seven weeks after she had left Thorp Green, she refers to the progress of *Agnes Grey* or of an early version of it. She writes: 'I have begun the third volume of passages in the life of an Individual. I wish I had finished it.' The title suits the straightforward linear structure and auto-biographical form of *Agnes Grey*; but the mention of a 'third' volume, preceded and followed by references to the *Gondal chronicles, may indicate a quite different work.

Early editions

Once completed, *Agnes Grey* was offered, along with *Wuthering Heights*, and at first with *The Professor* also, to a series of publishers from July 1846 until July 1847, when Thomas Cautley *Newby accepted the first two for publication. But though the first proof-sheets were in the press at the beginning of August 1847, exhausting delay and procrastination followed until Newby, encouraged by the outstanding success of 'Currer Bell's' *Jane Eyre* in October 1847, managed to send the last of the proof-sheets of 'Ellis and Acton's' novels for correction by 17 November. On 14 December Charlotte reported to W. S. *Williams that the two novels were at last published, and the authors had received their six copies. The format of the first edition, published at the usual three-decker price of 31*s.* 6*d.*, meant that *Agnes Grey* seemed little more than a tail-piece, for it appeared as the third of the three volumes, following the two taken up by *Wuthering Heights*. Its separate authorship is not made clear in the title-pages of volumes 1 and 2, which begin: 'WUTHERING HEIGHTS | A NOVEL, | BY ELLIS BELL, | IN THREE VOLUMES.' However, notices in the *Publishers' Circular* (15 December 1847), pp. 37 and 418, assigned the novels correctly. The printing, which was also by Newby, bears out Charlotte's claim that the spelling and punctuation of the books were 'mortifying', for Newby had not incorporated most of the authors' proof-corrections (Smith *Letters*, 1. 580). *Agnes Grey* was very shabbily treated: even its title appears as 'ANGES GREY' on six pages in volume 3. The Clarendon editors quote examples of carelessness such as 'she had swear like a trooper', and note misplaced letters, literal errors, omitted words, and erratic, often misleading punctuation. They adopt most of the 121 corrections Anne herself inserted in the Morris L. Parrish first edition, now at Princeton, and provide textual notes. Newby's financial dealings were equally de-plorable. Emily and Anne had paid him £50 towards the publication of their novels, on condition that it should be repaid to them when enough copies had been sold to cover expenses; but no money was returned to them. Newby had at first undertaken to print 350 copies, but he later declared that he had printed only 250. He told the authors that the sale of 250 copies would leave a surplus of £100 to be divided— presumably between himself and the 'Bells'. Under pressure from George *Smith and Charlotte, Newby eventually, long after the authors' death, sent Charlotte a cheque for £30, acknowledged by her on 18 March 1854.

By 18 September 1850 the first English edition was out of print. *Smith, Elder and Company, having failed to contact the elusive Newby, evidently decided he had no claim to copyright in the two novels. Accordingly, Charlotte agreed to correct a copy of the first edition, and completed her task despite the distressing memories it aroused. A revised second edition of the two novels in a single volume was there-fore published by Smith, Elder in December 1850, the price being 6*s.* Charlotte had not used the copy of *Agnes Grey* which Anne had annotated, and though she cor-rected many of Newby's misprints, her text was not authoritative. She altered the paragraphing and the style of punctuation, sometimes 'improved' the grammar, omitted (or failed to notice the omission of) some words, and made minor adjustments in the dialect speeches. In accordance with her own principle of 'truth to life', she arranged for expletives to be printed in full. It is not certain that Anne would have approved. For a detailed discussion, see the Clarendon edition (1988), pp. xv–xxii. Fifteen thousand copies of a new cheap edition based on the 1850 publication were printed on 22 March 1858 and published by Smith, Elder that month.

In America *Wuthering Heights* was first published by Harper & Brothers on 21 April 1848. *Agnes Grey* first appeared from 22 December 1849 to 19 January 1850 in the *Saturday Gazette*, published by Cummings and Peterson in Philadelphia. T. B. Peterson of 98 Chestnut Street, Philadelphia, then published it in volume form as '*Agnes Grey, An Autobiography*. By the Authors of "Jane Eyre," "Shirley," "The Tenant of Wildfell Hall," etc etc, etc.' It was puffed in *Godey's Magazine and Lady's Book* (a Philadelphia publication) for March 1850 as 'thought by many' to be superior to 'any of the former productions' by the same author, and *Godey's* editor commended 'the enterprise of Mr. Peterson, who received it in proof impressions from the London-press, in advance of its publication in that city'. This was either a lie by Peterson or Newby, or a sign of Peterson's tardiness rather than his enterprise in publishing the work.

Plot

Agnes and Mary Grey are the daughters of a curate in a North-of-England moorland parish. His upper-class wife has been disinherited because of her marriage to him, and he loses his patrimony through an unwise speculation. The 18-year-old Agnes, believing that she can help her family, becomes a governess in the household of a wealthy retired tradesman, Mr Bloomfield of *Wellwood. Treated at first with cold courtesy by his wife, Agnes realizes she will not be able to complain to her about her disobedient, rude, and destructive pupils: the bullying and sadistic 7-year-old Tom, and his mischievous and deceitful younger sisters Mary and Fanny. Both parents blame Agnes, in the children's presence, for their deteriorating behaviour, but do nothing to support her authority. Mr Bloomfield's mother, after apparently favouring Agnes, becomes her enemy, and persuades Mr Bloomfield to spy on and blame her. His brother-in-law, 'Uncle Robson', encourages Tom's cruelty. Agnes is dismissed, despite her modest progress in teaching the children, after less than a year. She then becomes a governess in the household of the upper-class Murrays of Horton Lodge. She sees little of Mr Murray, and is treated with condescension by his wife, who expects her to improve her daughters' prospects in the marriage market by teaching them showy accomplishments, and to cram her two unteachable sons with Latin grammar. The pretty, talented 16-year-old daughter Rosalie cares only to attract men, while the younger daughter Matilda is a careless, swearing hoyden. At 18 Rosalie boasts of her many 'conquests', but accepts the proposal of the vicious, wealthy roué Sir Thomas Ashby. Meanwhile Agnes appreciates the evangelical preaching of the new curate, Edward Weston, and the Christian charity he shows to Nancy Brown, in whose cottage Agnes first meets him personally. Rosalie, in jealous pique, boasts to Agnes of her long meetings with Weston, and prevents the anxious and bitter Agnes from seeing him. Just before her marriage to Ashby, Rosalie relents, and kisses Agnes affectionately. When Agnes meets Weston again, he pleases her by his quiet sarcastic comment on Matilda's cruel gloating over a leveret's death. Agnes is called home by her father's illness and death, and agrees to help her mother run a school. During a last visit to Horton, Agnes admits to Weston that she would be very glad to see him again. Agnes and her mother establish their school at A——. In June Agnes accepts an invitation from Rosalie, now Lady Ashby, to visit her at Ashby Park, and is warmly welcomed; but she is shocked by Rosalie's detestation of her husband, indifference to her baby daughter, and revelation that her encouragement of a previous lover has caused Ashby to withdraw the household from London to the country. Back at A——, Agnes walks along the sands one fine summer morning, and is suddenly greeted with excited yelps from her own former pet, the small terrier Snap. To Agnes's wondering delight, the dog is followed by Edward Weston, its rescuer and now its owner. A warm greeting follows, and Weston asks if he may call on Agnes and her mother, for he now has a living about 2 miles from A——. He proposes to Agnes on the castle hill, and a happy marriage follows.

Reception

The critical reception of *Agnes Grey* was influenced by its third-volume position as an appendage to *Wuthering Heights*, by the fact that both these novels were published after the best-selling *Jane Eyre*, and by Newby's exploitation of these circumstances and of the veil provided by the common 'Bell' pseudonym. In *Douglas Jerrold's Shilling Magazine* (5 Feb. 1848) *Agnes Grey* and *Wuthering Heights* were advertised as 'By the successful New Novelist'—implying 'Currer Bell's' authorship. Here and elsewhere, for example in the *Examiner* and the *Athenaeum* (29 Jan. 1848), Newby advertised the works by quotations from reviews, designed and adapted to suggest association with the successful *Jane Eyre*. Only the quotation from the *Athenaeum* mentioned 'two tales': the others failed to mention *Agnes Grey*, referring only to 'A work', 'this story', or specifically, *Wuthering Heights*. In his own catalogue of 'New Works by Popular authors' (Mar. 1848), Newby imitated the subtitle of *Jane Eyre* when he advertised *Wuthering Heights* and *Agnes Grey*, absurdly, as 'An Autobiography by Ellis and Acton Bell'. Inevitably, therefore, both novels were assessed by comparison with *Jane Eyre*, not as independent works. Unlike the uniquely powerful, indeed 'savage', *Wuthering Heights*, *Agnes Grey* seemed diminished in *Jane Eyre*'s shadow. If it was welcomed as less extreme than its companions, it was found lacking in imaginative qualities and power, a mere makeweight to complete the conventional three-decker. According to the *Spectator* (18 Dec. 1847) it was 'not of so varied or in its persons and incidents of so extreme a kind' as *Wuthering Heights*; 'but what it gains in measure is possibly lost in power'. In *Agnes Grey*, as in the Bells' other works, there was a 'choice of subjects that are peculiar without being either probable or pleasing; and considerable executive ability, but insufficient to overcome the injudicious selection of the theme and matter'. Henry Fothergill Chorley in the *Athenaeum* showed an equal distaste for the Bells' choice of 'painful and exceptional subjects:—the misdeeds and oppressions of tyranny . . . [and] physical acts of cruelty'. While *Agnes Grey* was more acceptable than the gloomy *Wuthering Heights*, it was less powerful: admittedly, Agnes 'undergoes much that is the real bond of a governess's endurance' but her trials are more ignoble than those in *Jane Eyre*. Chorley warned the authors against spoiling tales with 'so much feeling for character, and nice marking of scenery' by emphasizing eccentric and unpleasant elements. On the whole, reviewers unsurprisingly concentrated on *Wuthering Heights*, and concluded that little needed to be said about *Agnes*

Grey. The reviewer in the *Atlas* (22 Jan. 1848) found that *Agnes Grey* left 'no painful impression on the mind—some may think it leaves no impression at all'; it seemed to be 'a somewhat coarse imitation of one of Miss Austin's [*sic*] charming stories'. Anne Brontë had to take what comfort she could from comments on her true-to-life presentation of the torments and tediums of governess life, and from general remarks that her novel was worth reading, and had the negative virtue of being less extreme than *Wuthering Heights*. The most favourable review was probably that in the *New Monthly Magazine* (Jan. 1848): the simple tale 'fills the mind with a lasting picture of love and happiness succeeding to scorn and affliction, and teaches us to put every trust in a supreme wisdom and goodness'.

Later editions

The Clarendon edition (1988), edited by Hilda Marsden and Robert Inglesfield, has an introduction covering composition, publication, and textual history; a descriptive list of the early English and Continental editions; a text based on the first edition; explanatory notes; and an appendix listing selected textual variants in the 1850 edition of the novel. The explanatory notes include a useful list of articles on *governesses on p. 210. The World's Classics edition (1988) reprints the Clarendon text and explanatory notes, and has a helpful critical introduction and brief note on the text by Robert Inglesfield.

Allott.

Ewbank, Inga-Stina, *Their Proper Sphere: A Study of the Brontë Sisters as Early Victorian Female Novelists* (1966).

Frawley, Maria, *Anne Brontë* (1996).

Nash, Julie, and Suess, Barbara A. (eds.), *New Approaches to the Literary Art of Anne Brontë* (2001).

Peterson, M. Jeanne, 'The Victorian Governess: Status Incongruence in Family and Society', in Martha Vicinus (ed.), *Suffer and Be Still: Women in the Victorian Age* (1972).

Alexander, Lord of Elbë, the second love of A.G.A. in the *Gondal saga. It is unclear whether he is her husband or lover. He dies in her arms on the shores of Lake Elmor, while recalling Elbë Hall in his distant sunny home in the south.

The name 'Alexander' appears a number of times in the Gondal saga but seems to refer to different people. Thus Emily Brontë writes of a boy of 14 called Alexander who arranges to meet a young girl Zenobia in Araby in two years' time by a little spring in Exina's woods ('Fair was the evening and brightly the sun'). In April 1826, an Alexander is in a dungeon in the Southern Palace of Instruction. Anne Brontë writes of another Alexander whose surname is Hybernia.

Alford, Dr, physician to the royal household of Wellington's Land in the *Glass Town and Angrian saga. He attends the dying Marian Hume and her son Lord Julius, and is a witness to Marian's will. He is present at all the Duke of Zamorna's illnesses and at the birth of his and Mary Percy's twin sons.

He is derived from Henry Halford, a Palace School surgeon and one of Anne Brontë's 'chief men' in the *Islanders' Play, who is based on Sir Henry Halford, physician to Mrs Charles Arbuthnot, a close friend of the historical Duke of *Wellington.

Alfred, Lord. See SIDONIA, LORD ALFRED.

Allbutt family. Revd Thomas Allbutt (1800–67) married Mary Anne (Marianne) Wooler (1801–43) on 9 July 1835, the year he became the vicar of *Dewsbury. They had two children: Marianne Maria (1840–1906) and the distinguished physician Sir Thomas Clifford Allbutt (1836–1925), Regius Professor of Physic at Cambridge 1892–1925, whose bequest to the Fitzwilliam Museum, Cambridge, included 33 manuscript letters from Charlotte Brontë to his aunt Margaret *Wooler. The Allbutt family came from Shelton, Hanley, in Staffordshire, where Thomas Allbutt sen. is listed as druggist, printer, bookseller, stationer, book binder in the 1818 *Directory*. His son Thomas is said to have once been the editor of a newspaper at the

Staffordshire potteries (Smith *Letters*, 1. 139 n.), before he graduated MA at Cambridge in 1838, where he was first at St John's (Revd Patrick Brontë's old college) and then at St Catharine's College. He then became curate to Mr Buckworth (Mr Brontë's friend and former vicar) at All Saints church, Dewsbury, in 1832 and succeeded him after his death in 1835. He also took over the editorship of the evangelical *Cottage Magazine*, to which Mr Brontë had contributed. After the death of his first wife, Allbutt married Sarah Isabella Chadwick, née Skelton, in 1849, and moved to Suffolk in 1862.

At Cambridge Thomas Allbutt had known Henry *Nussey, who was his curate at Dewsbury from September 1835 until July 1837, during the time Charlotte was a teacher at *Roe Head. Charlotte and her friend Ellen *Nussey saw much of the Allbutts through this connection and through Margaret Wooler. Marianne had taught at Roe Head when Charlotte was a pupil and she and Ellen Nussey had followed the romance with Thomas Allbutt with interest (see Smith *Letters*, 1. 138). Charlotte's appointment as a teacher was to fill Marianne's place when she left to marry Thomas Allbutt. Charlotte thought Marianne a 'most tender and thoughtful' mother (Wise & Symington, 4. 83) but disagreed with Thomas Allbutt's Calvinist views on 'the Sin of Dancing' (Smith *Letters*, 1. 133).

Thomas Allbutt's sister Sidney Maria (1806–32) was the first wife of Dr William Moore Wooler (see WOOLER FAMILY), elder brother of Marianne. In 1832, Sidney Maria died of cholera in York, where her husband may have been working at the time (Smith *Letters*, 1. 116 n). Thomas Allbutt's brother, Dr George Allbutt (b. 1812) of Batley, Yorks., married Anna Maria Brooke (b. 1818) (see BROOKE FAMILY OF DEWSBURY) in August 1842, from another family known to the Brontës. It is through this branch of the Allbutt family that the *Roe Head Album was handed down (now in BPM).

Allen, Louisa. See VERNON, LOUISA (MARCHIONESS OF WELLESLEY).

Allison, William, coachman at *Thorp Green from 1843 until February 1847, when he accompanied the widowed Mrs *Robinson to the home of Sir Francis Edward Dolman *Scott. He returned to take his family to Great Barr in April 1847. According to Branwell Brontë, Mrs Robinson sent Allison to see him in June 1846, when he gave Branwell a heart-rending account of the agony caused her by her husband's will, which allegedly prohibited her from seeing Branwell on pain of forfeiting property left in trust for the family. Mrs Robinson's account book shows that she paid £3 to 'Wm for journey' on 11 June.

Almedore, a kingdom in *Gaaldine in the *Gondal saga and the name given to Emperor Julius *Brenzaida.

Almeida (Almeda), Augusta Geraldine, Queen of Gondal, 'author' as 'A.G.A.' and subject of many of Emily Brontë's poems. Born in Gondal, to whose natural landscape of snowy mountains, heather, and bluebells she is deeply attached. She is a passionate dark beauty, ruthless in both political and personal relationships; a female alternative to the Byronic heroes of the *Glass Town and Angrian saga. When she tires of *Amedeus, the lover of her childhood friend *Angelica, she sends both into exile. After an affair and marriage with Alfred *Sidonia of Aspin Castle, she abandons him to die of a broken heart. Her relationship with *Alexander, Lord of Elbë, also ends in his violent death by Lake Elmor. Fernando de *Samara too she loves, imprisons, then drives into exile and suicide. And when her 'passionate youth was nearly past', she is murdered by the outlaw *Douglas at the instigation of Angelica, while alone on Elmor Hill. The faithful Lord Eldred contemplates her tempestuous life that inspired both hate and devotion but never fulfilled its promise.

Fannie Ratchford reads the 'G' in 'A.G.A.' as 'Geraldine' and argues that 'Geraldine S. and Rosina *Alcona are the same person as A.G.A.' (*Gondal's Queen* (1955), 26–7). Edward Chitham points out that Emily did find it hard to let go of her powerful female heroine. After writing about A.G.A.'s death in May 1844, she restored her again in December, and then 'reincarnated' her as A. G. Rochelle in 'The prisoner' (Chitham *Birth of WH*, p. 71).

Her Christian name recalls Byron's half-sister 'Augusta' and Augusta di Segovia, Branwell's wicked femme fatale in the Glass Town and Angrian saga. Her surname, like Arthur Julius, Lord Almeida, from the same saga, derives from Almeida in Portugal, captured by Wellington in the *Peninsular Wars (Alexander *EW*, p. 24).

Almeida, Lord Julius, Marquis of. See WELLESLEY, ARTHUR JULIUS (LORD ALMEIDA).

Alnwick, a large town in the far north-west of the *Glass Town Federation, which becomes the temporary seat of government after Verdopolis is evacuated during the final stages of the *War of Encroachment in the *Glass Town and Angrian saga. The town and *Alnwick Hall, the Duke of Northangerland's ancestral home, are based on the historic Alnwick Castle and town in Northumberland, England.

Alnwick Hall, the 'Noble second country residence' of the Duke of *Northangerland in *Sneaky's Land, in the *Glass Town and Angrian saga. Based on Alnwick Castle, the ancestral home of the Percys in Northumberland, England, the Alnwick of the Glass Town and Angrian saga is also the Percy ancestral home, where Northangerland's mother Lady Helen *Percy lives. It is used by the Council of Six during their evacuation from Verdopolis in the *War of Encroachment; and Mary *Percy is sent into exile at Alnwick Hall by the Duke of Zamorna and nearly dies there during the Angrian Wars.

Ambleside. By the 1840s this small market town in Westmorland on the northern shore of Lake Windermere had long been attractive to tourists eager to enjoy the sublimities of the Lake District. In December 1840 Charlotte Brontë wrote to Hartley *Coleridge, who lived at 'The Knabbe', near Ambleside, which Branwell had visited earlier in the year. In December 1850, after repeated invitations, Charlotte visited Harriet *Martineau in her home, The *Knoll. Martineau delivered lectures to Ambleside artisans, and established a successful building society which enabled a number of working men to live in healthy dwellings instead of crowded, rented cottages.

Amedeus, lover of A.G.A. and, with his old sweetheart *Angelica, possibly the murderer of Julius *Brenzaida, in the *Gondal saga.

Andrews, Anna, head-teacher and temporary superintendent at *Cowan Bridge early in 1824; mistakenly identified as the cruel Miss *Scatcherd (*Jane Eyre*) in the *Leeds Mercury* and *Halifax Guardian* correspondence following the publication of Gaskell's *Life* in 1857. She was the mother of Hamilton Andrews Hill, who wrote angrily to Elizabeth Gaskell in August 1857, objecting to this identification. (Chapple and Pollard, *Gaskell Letters*, p. 465). She married a Mr Hamilton Hill in 1826 and emigrated to Oberlin, Ohio, where her husband became the secretary and treasurer of Oberlin College. Both the Hills worked for the abolition of slavery, and showed much practical kindness.

BST (1975), 16. 85. 364.
BST (2000), 25. 2. 136–46.

And the Weary are at Rest is Branwell Brontë's unfinished novel (in Berg, NYPL; Taylor, Princeton), begun in the summer of 1845. Alexander Percy is a guest of the Thurstons in Yorkshire for some grouse shooting. He becomes reacquainted with Maria Thurston, now trapped in a loveless, lonely and brutal marriage, with whom he had been in love ten years earlier. He woos her again, and she responds, agonizing over the terrible choice facing her: to remain confined in her loveless marriage or betray her sacred marriage vows and become an outcast in the sight of God and society, the same dilemma Anne was to take up in *Tenant*. The piece is a reworking of a fragment of prose narrative Branwell composed at the end of 1837, the first located outside Africa. In the fragment Maria Thurston is a contented lady of the manor, happily supervising preparations for her husband's return with Percy, whom she had last met when she was 14. It is the strange union in Percy of 'debauched profligacy', 'impassioned feeling', 'restless ambition', and 'embittered melancholy' that excites and attracts Maria, but the fragment does not include Percy's reappearance in the guise of a Methodist preacher—Brother *Ashworth—and it breaks off as Percy is about to begin seducing her. See also THURSTONS OF DARKWALL MANOR. VN

Neufeldt *BB Works*, 3. 420–66.
Shorter, C. K. (ed.), *And the Weary are at Rest* (1924).

Angelica, raised as a child in the same house as A.G.A. in the *Gondal saga. She falls in love with a dark boy called *Amedeus, who is lured away by the treacherous A.G.A. After A.G.A. tires of Amedeus, she sends both him and Angelica into exile where they live a life of crime, waiting to avenge themselves on Gondal's Queen. Angelica later persuades *Douglas, who has always loved her, to murder A.G.A.

Angora, a kingdom in the north of Gondal, homeland of Julius *Brenzaida, also referred to as 'Angora'. Another character in the *Gondal saga is the Royalist Henry Angora.

Angria, city of. Capital of the province of *Angria, it is known as the 'holy city of Angria', an ancient site endowed with a minster that towers over the surrounding moors and the *Warner Hills seen from Richmond Bridge. Landmarks include the Howard Road, which leads into the city from Verdopolis 120 miles away, and *Warner Hall (House), home of Warner Howard *Warner.

Angria, kingdom of, on the eastern borders of the Verdopolitan or *Glass Town Federation. (See map p. 48.) The name is traceable to a pirate kingdom on the Malabar Coast of India, named after its founder Kanhoji Angria and famous in the late 17th and early 18th centuries for its successful repulsion of European powers, until its defeat by Clive in 1756. The Brontës' Angria has some of the same legendary wealth and dubious notoriety as this Indian kingdom.

Angria consists of seven provinces created for the Duke of *Zamorna in 1834 from the area he heroically defended for the Federation during the *Wars of Encroachment against the French and Ashantees: *Zamorna, *Angria, *Douro, *Calabar, *Northangerland, *Arundel, and *Etrei. See GLASS TOWN AND ANGRIAN SAGA; MY ANGRIA AND THE ANGRIANS.

*Adrianopolis is built as a new capital for the new nation, which has the rising sun as its symbol, a war cry 'Arise!', and the national anthems 'Sound the loud Trumpet' and 'Welcome Heroes'. Angrians are characterized by a 'love of ostentatious pomp and flashy display'; they are straightforward and unsophisticated compared to the inhabitants of the 'old world' of Verdopolis.

Angria, province of. Eighty miles long and 180 miles broad, the province of Angria is the Yorkshire of the kingdom of Angria, in the *Glass Town and Angrian saga. Its 1,492,000 inhabitants, including its lord lieutenant, Warner Howard *Warner, speak in dialect, and its capital city of *Angria is surrounded by moorland, the Warner and Howard Hills, and distinctive mountains like Pendlebrow and Boulshill. See PENDLETON.

Angria and the Angrians. Between May 1834 and April 1839, Branwell Brontë chronicled the history of the new kingdom of *Angria in five volumes, now badly fragmented, scattered, and with many portions lost, but with 284 pages extant (MSS in Brotherton; BPM; Ransom HRC, Texas; Symington, Rutgers University Library; Berg, NYPL; Bonnell, Pierpont Morgan; Taylor, Princeton; BL; Bonnell, BPM; Roger W. Barrett, Chicago). The title-page is missing, but the title is referred to in the text.

Beginning with the coronation of the Duke of *Zamorna as King Adrian I, and the installation of his father-in-law, the Duke of *Northangerland, as prime minister, Branwell traces Northangerland's various attempts to undermine the king and his ministers and to replace the monarchy with a republic. All this is further complicated by the machinations of a government faction in Verdopolis, led by the Marquis of *Ardrah, heir to the throne of Parrysland and opposed to the independence of Angria, and by a war with the Ashantees under Quashia *Quamina, who have been encroaching upon Angrian territory, secretly aided by France and Northangerland. After the war with the Ashantees, Branwell chronicles the highly acrimonious parliamentary debates in *Verdopolis regarding Angria's independence and the reform of the corrupt Verdopolitan Navy (Ardrah is First Lord of the Admiralty), and an election campaign. Eventually Angria is forced into a ruinous civil war with Ardrah's forces (aided by a dismissed and exiled Northangerland, the French, and the Ashantees) who occupy *Adrianopolis and much of Angria, forcing Zamorna's forces to flee into the hills. Northangerland then turns on and defeats Ardrah's forces and proclaims the kingdom a re-

public with himself as lord president. Zamorna is captured and exiled to Ascension Island, his eldest son is murdered, and his wife Mary—Northangerland's daughter—dies of a broken heart. The Angrian troops under Warner Howard *Warner, the Duke of *Fidena, and the Duke of *Wellington rally and defeat Northangerland's forces. Zamorna is restored and begins to rebuild Angria, Northangerland and his supporters become fugitives, and Northangerland returns to his wife a broken man waiting to die.   VN

Alexander & Sellars, pp. 313, 324–5 (illustrations). Neufeldt *BB Works*, 2. 199–443, 454–86, 496–9, 518–60, 564–79, 597–668; 3. 1–13, 17–20, 59–60, 108–13, 117–18, 132–77, 185–93, 208–18, 246–72.

Angria House, large stone residence of Warner Howard *Warner in the city of *Angria; used as the Duke of Zamorna's headquarters during the Angrian Wars.

Angrian saga. See GLASS TOWN AND ANGRIAN SAGA.

Angrian wars. See GLASS TOWN AND ANGRIAN SAGA.

Angus, Sir Alured. See 'ALBION AND MARINA: A TALE'.

Angus, Marina. See 'ALBION AND MARINA: A TALE'.

animals and birds in the works of the Brontës. Evidence of the Brontës' love and knowledge of animals can be found throughout their writing and in their many drawings and paintings of birds and beasts (see ART OF THE BRONTËS). Dogs are particular favourites with all four Brontës. Their *pets *Grasper, *Keeper, *Flossy, and the hawk *Nero become the subjects of paintings and sketches (illustrated in Alexander & Sellars, pp. 376, 380, 384, 388, 390, 392, 408–10), and both Keeper and Nero also feature as 'characters' in their writing (see DOGS IN THE GLASS TOWN AND ANGRIAN SAGA). Cats are defended by Emily in the first of her *devoirs: 'The Cat' ('Le Chat', 15 May 1842), in language that excuses their faults in human terms such as 'hypocrisy, cruelty, and ingratitude'; she believes they are 'extremely like us in disposition' (Lonoff, p. 56). The Brontës' interest in physiognomy also manifests itself in this relationship between human and animal characters in both the juvenilia and the novels (Graeme Tytler, *Physiognomy in the European Novel: Faces and Fortunes* (1982), 249–52). Perhaps the most obvious example in Charlotte's writing is Jane Eyre's symbolic relationship with domestic birds and Rochester's association with the eagle. Nowhere, however, do we find in the Brontës' novels the sentimentality that so often accompanies Victorian verbal and pictorial references to animals (as for example in Edwin *Landseer's dog portraits, one of which Charlotte attempted to copy: Alexander & Sellars, p. 334). Surprisingly, it was Branwell who responded more conventionally to Landseer's anthropomorphic images by writing a sonnet 'On Landseer's painting—"The Shepherd's Chief Mourner" A dog keeping watch at twilight over its master's grave' (28 Apr. 1842; Neufeldt BBP, p. 456).

In the novels of Charlotte and Anne, however, there is the typical Victorian equation between concern for animal welfare and the moral well-being of a character. Ellen Nussey observed that 'The Brontës' love of dumb creatures made them very sensitive of the treatment bestowed upon them, for any one to offend in this respect was with them an infallible bad sign, and blot in their disposition' (Smith Letters, 1. 606). In Anne's Agnes Grey, for example, characters are judged according to their response to pet animals. The old widow Nancy Brown distinguishes between the good and bad clergyman in conventional (almost parodic) terms: when the cat jumps on Edward *Weston's knee 'he only stroked her, and gave a bit of a smile: so I thought that was a good sign; for once, when she did so to th'Rector, he knocked her off, like as might be in scorn and anger, poor thing' (ch. 11). Furthermore, the ability to feel another creature's pain takes on a moral status. Those, like Tom *Bloomfield and his uncle, who are unable to value animals as part of God's creation, are condemned. The scene in which Tom prepares to torture a nest full of young birds (ch. 5) is based on Anne's own similar experience of such 'sport' while a governess. Her authorial use of the event, however, carries an educational and moral lesson that is entirely different from Emily's casual reporting of Hareton's hanging of a litter of puppies (Wuthering Heights, ch. 17).

Animal imagery in Wuthering Heights is particularly disturbing and is associated with Emily Brontë's view of the animal world as unregenerate (see NATURAL HISTORY AND THE BRONTËS; IMAGERY IN THE BRONTËS' WORKS). But she also challenges (particularly in 'Le Chat') the assumption of earlier naturalists like Buffon that animals are inferior to humans. Her anthropomorphism is at odds with the more conventional attitudes of her teacher M. Constantin Heger (Lonoff, pp. 66–7, 383 n. 90). For her, animals hold a similar, if not superior, status to humans. The dogs at Wuthering Heights, for example, wield as much power and hospitality as the inmates, and their genealogy is as precise as that of their 'masters'. The brutality of these working dogs superficially contrasts with the 'civilized' lapdogs at Thrushcross Grange, yet it is there that Catherine is savagely attacked by bulldogs. Lisa Surridge argues that the cultural collision manifested in conflicting patterns of inheritance, labour, and architecture in Wuthering Heights also reveals itself in the different status of animals and underscores class, property, and power differentials ('Animals and Violence in WH', BST (1999), 24. 2. 161–73). She argues that one of the reasons for the novel's poor reception was 'that its view of animal-human relationships was so far removed from the Victorian middle-class norm' and the popular practice of pet-keeping. See BEWICK, THOMAS.

Davies, Stevie, Emily Brontë: Heretic (1994), ch. 3.

Newman, Hilary, 'Animals in Agnes Grey', BST (1996), 21. 6. 237–42.

Tytler, Graeme, 'Animals in Wuthering Heights', BS (2002), 27. 2. 121–30.

'Anne Askew'. *Devoir by Charlotte Brontë (2 June 1842), (MS in Huntington). Subtitled 'Imitation [of Eudorus]', it is modelled on a passage from the vicomté de *Chateaubriand's The Martyrs (Les Martyrs), which she transcribed in her notebook of *dictations. In both texts, the martyrs resist the temptation to renounce their faith. But instead of portraying a 4th-century Christian who is publicly tempted in the Roman arena, Charlotte portrays a 16th-century Protestant tortured by Catholics. She converts the historical Anne Askew, a woman who openly defied her opponents, into a terrified maiden confined in a dungeon out of Gothic romance.   SL

annuals, prized by the young Brontës particularly for their engravings, were generously illustrated little books of tales and verse, essays, and sketches, designed chiefly for women as Christmas, New Year, or birthday gifts. They began in 1822 as a publishing venture by Rudolph Ackermann, who combined the popular pocket diary and almanac, similar to the German Taschenbuch, an annual contributed to by Goethe, Schiller, and their contemporaries. The English productions were more expensive and more elegant than their Continental rivals; yet, like them, they were a direct result of the revolution in engraving, which allowed for reasonably priced books with steel engravings to reach a large middle-class market. As such they represented and reinforced the manners and morals of the times. Their very titles reflect their intended appeal to a female audience: *Forget Me Not, *Friendship's Offering, the Graces, the Keepsake, the *Literary Souvenir, the Gem, and Book of Beauty, to name a selection (the first five in order of appearance); and their use as copybooks for countless young women learning to draw, reinforced the gendered ideal of women as decorative and accomplished—not overtaxed by weighty articles but entertained with romantic tales and light verse (so light that respectable authors like Sir Walter

Scott, Wordsworth, Byron, and Shelley refused to sign the poetry they published in these elegant little volumes). Ironically, because they were unsigned, many fine lyrical poems like Samuel Taylor Coleridge's 'Youth and Age', Wordsworth's lyric on 'Scott's Departure for Italy', and some of the best poems of Felicia Hemans and Elizabeth Barrett Browning went unappreciated on their first appearance in the annuals. The young Tennyson contributed poetry for some five years to various annuals, Leigh Hunt contributed essays to the *Keepsake*, Macaulay published his poem 'Armada' in *Friendship's Offering* (1833), and even the scornful Charles Lamb who termed the annuals 'ostentatious trumpery' was persuaded by his editor friends to contribute to the *Bijou* (1827) and the *Gem* (1829). Despite the snobbery of writers like *Lockhart (who tried unsuccessfully to establish an annual himself) and *Thackeray (who deplored the degenerate artistic taste of annuals yet was not above contributing to them himself), the annuals included plates 'by the first artists and engravers' like Wilkie, Stothard, Leslie, Turner, Westall, *Finden, and *Martin. Such 'modern' painters appreciated the wide circulation of their works in highly finished engravings, making their names familiar as never before. One such engraving by Edward Finden, based on a drawing by Turner, and printed in the *Literary Souvenir* of 1829, was the model for Charlotte Brontë's copy of 'Bolton Abbey', one of the two works she exhibited in the summer exhibition of the *Royal Northern Society for the Encouragement of the Fine Arts in Leeds in 1834.

The Brontës' artwork clearly testifies to the popularity of the annuals as copybooks, a function not previously ascribed to them. Charlotte, Branwell, and Emily copied eleven engravings from the annuals they owned: *Friendship's Offering* (1829), the *Literary Souvenir* (1830), and the *Forget Me Not* (1831). The 12-year-old Branwell made a bold attempt to imitate John Martin's grandiose style, translating Edward Finden's engraving of Martin's 'Queen Esther' back into colours like the original (Alexander & Sellars, pl. XII). A portrait of Byron from a drawing by Richard Westall in the *Literary Souvenir* (1830) was appropriated by Charlotte for her own picture of the Glass Town poet Young *Soult the Rhymer (Alexander & Sellars, p. 19). Names and opinions from the annuals also provided inspiration for the Brontës' early writings. De Lisle, for example, appears in a sentimental poem by 'L.E.L.' (Letitia Elizabeth Landon) that accompanies an engraving copied by both Charlotte and Emily from the *Forget Me Not* (1831) (Alexander & Sellars, pp. 15, 177–8). The frequent picturesque and *Gothic description in the Brontë juvenilia was clearly influenced by the text

and plates, such as 'Bessy Bell and Mary Gray' (Alexander & Sellars, pp. 176–7). But the Brontës' borrowing was not undiscriminating. Charlotte reviewed three engravings from *Friendship's Offering* (1829), criticizing the mismatch between engraving and text, caused by the usual practice in the annuals of the poetry or prose being commissioned to accompany an already completed engraving (Alexander *EEW*, 1. 283). Many contributions to the annuals were lightweight, what Lockhart called 'toy-shop literature', pandering to social snobbery and materialistic values; yet it is worth noting that not only the Brontës but also John Ruskin first gained a love of art from annuals like the *Forget Me Not*. Charlotte was as interested as other young women in the society beauties that graced the pages of annuals like the *Drawing Room Scrap Book* (dated 1832 though it appeared for Christmas 1831) and Charles Heath's the *Book of Beauty*, edited by 'L.E.L.' in 1833 and then from 1834 to 1849 by Lady *Blessington. The elegant bindings too were of interest to Charlotte and Branwell whose juvenilia show that they appreciated every aspect of the book trade, referring as they do in early manuscripts to moroccos, velvets, watered silks, embossed papers, and gilded bindings. The annuals encouraged not only the fine arts of painting and engraving (Heath was himself a prominent engraver), but also the industrial arts of ornamental binding and embossing, and quality printing.

The heyday of the English annual lasted until about 1845. Some 200 were founded with the average issue of each volume at least 2,000. Some had a print run of over 10,000 for the first edition; others survived only one issue. At first the books were produced in a small pocketbook size but gradually increased to octavo and then full quarto drawing-room books, such as *Fisher's Drawing Room Scrap Book* which survived 20 years. Artists profited from the 'craze' for illustrative engravings; the average volume had between twelve and twenty plates. Publishers prospered less well as they sought to compete with splendid volumes like the *Picturesque Annual* with engravings after Clarkson Stanfield or the *Continental Annual* with engravings of paintings by Samuel Prout. The Brontës may have owned and certainly had access to the large *Sacred Annual* (1834) containing Robert Montgomery's 'The Messiah: A Poem'; Charlotte copied one of the hand-coloured lithographs and found inspiration for Glass Town in the frontispiece by John Martin (Alexander & Sellars, pp. 14, 21, 27, 243, and pl. XIII). In the earlier years important literary names were sought to attract sales (Charles Heath offered Scott and Southey large sums for trifles) and in the 1830s the snobbery associated with aristocratic editors, like Lady Blessington, Lady Emmeline Stuart Wortley, and the Hon. Caroline Norton, was used to attract sales. Curiously, the same publishers issued rival productions, and editors of some annuals were also contributors to others, such as Thomas Hood, Thomas Pringle, and Alaric A. Watts. Juvenile annuals were also popular, one of the best being Ackerman's *Juvenile Forget Me Not*.

Alexander & Sellars, pp. 14–21.
Alexander, Christine, 'Art and Artists in Charlotte Brontë's Juvenilia', *BST* (1991), 20. 4. 186–9.
——— ' "That Kingdom of Gloom": Charlotte Brontë, the Annuals, and the Gothic', *Nineteenth-Century Literature*, 47/4 (Mar. 1993), 409–36.
Miller, Lucasta, *The Brontë Myth* (2001).
Renier, Anne, *Friendship's Offering* (1964).

Aornos, Mount. A high mountain north of *Verdopolis, this is the 'Mt Olympus' of the *Glass Town and Angrian saga and reputed home of the god-like Chief *Genii. It features only in the early stories of the saga and is presumably part of the *Jibbel Kumri. The Aornos is a huge rock near the Ganges River in India, a natural fortress with a flat summit of arable land and water. The Brontës would have read of its capture in the campaigns of Alexander the Great.

Ape of the Hills, the common name for Donald of the Standard, the ancient and gigantic standard bearer of *St Clair and 'the lads of the mist' from the Highlands of the *Glass Town Federation, in the *Glass Town and Angrian saga.

Arabian Nights, or *Arabian Nights' Entertainment*, also called *The Thousand and One Nights*, is a collection of about 200 folk tales from Arabia, Egypt, India, Persia, and other countries, written in Arabic in the 1500s. Jean Antoine Galland translated it into French in the early 1700s, and this was immediately translated into English. Numerous subsequent translations, both from the Arabic and French, were made throughout the 19th century. Winifred Gérin suggests that the young Brontës read a translation of Galland's text, made in 1706 and reprinted in 1787 (Gérin *CB*, p. 26 n.), but this is difficult to verify and they could have read one of a number of 'family versions' or even extracts published in the *Lady's Magazine*. The tale-within-a-tale structure of the *Arabian Nights* provided Charlotte with a narrative model for her earliest stories. The *Nights* is one of the sources for the Brontës' conception of genii that play a major role in the early Brontë juvenilia (see GENII, CHIEF (LITTLE KING AND QUEENS)). Many of Charlotte's early tales of magic and the supernatural are reworkings of stories from the *Nights*. The adventures of Mirza Abduliemah in volume 4 of *'Tales of the Islanders', for example,

reflect Charlotte's reading of both 'Sinbad the Sailor' from the *Nights*, Swift's *Gulliver's Travels*, and possibly Addison's *Visions of Mirza* (Alexander *EEW*, 1. 208). 'Silence' in the 'Young Men's Magazine' (28 Aug. 1830) is the story of Houssain, an old man from Isfahan in Persia, who chooses an heir by judging various young men's reactions to a revelation of Paradise seen through a magic silver tube given to him by a genius (Alexander *EEW*, 1. 242–7). In 'Arthuriana', Charlotte's Glass Town characters use the magic carpet of Prince Houssain from 'The Story of Prince Ahmed' in the *Nights* (Alexander *EEW*, 2(1). 259). Episodes in *The Foundling* echo several tales from the *Nights* (Alexander *EEW*, 1(2). 120). Characters from the *Nights*, such as the fairy Maimoune and the evil *Danhasch, are transposed into the Glass Town saga (Alexander *EEW*, 1. 8 and 347; 2(1). 120). Early descriptions of the Glass Town landscape with its deserts and oases of palms, olives, myrtles, and vines, are derived more from the *Nights* and similar tales than from contemporary descriptions of the African landscape itself (see, for example, Alexander *EEW*, 1. 131). Allusions to the *Nights* also appear in the Brontë novels, particularly in *Wuthering Heights*, *Jane Eyre*, and *Villette*. See also RIDLEY, JAMES, TALES OF THE GENII.

Brontë, Charlotte, *The Professor* (Clarendon edn.), 330.
Caracciolo, Peter L., *The 'Arabian Nights' in English Literature* (1988), 25–8.

Ardrah, Marquis of, Arthur Parry, heir to Parry's Land (Parrisland), a contemporary and rival of the Duke of Zamorna in the *Glass Town and Angrian saga. As 'the scoundrelly Scot', commander of the Verdopolitan Navy and leader of the Reform Party in Verdopolis, he opposes the creation of Angria as an independent state. He uses his position as editor of 'The Northern Review' to attack the Duke of Zamorna (see 'SCRAP BOOK, THE'). With MacTerrorglen leading the Verdopolitan Reform Army, Ardrah takes the navy up the *Calabar River to besiege *Adrianopolis and overthrow Zamorna, but is subsequently defeated by his former ally the Duke of Northangerland.

Ardsley House, in the Olympian Hills, Angria; 1 mile from the town of Ardsley, site of the Battle of Ardsley, turning point in the Angrian wars for the Duke of Zamorna and his forces. Owned by George Turner *Grey, it was used by grouse shooters, but sacked during the Angrian wars by Scottish troops under Captain Wilson (later murdered by Grey).

Armitage family. In *Shirley*, Mr Armitage is a cloth manufacturer in the West Riding of Yorkshire, one of a small group of merchants associated with Robert Gérard *Moore in the defence of *Hollow's Mill against *Luddite rioters. Like Mr *Pearson, another cloth merchant, Armitage is the target of an attempted assassination. He has five daughters, the eldest of whom ('the red-haired Miss Armitage', p. 29) is at one time rumoured to be a possible wife for Robert Moore. The name is common in Yorkshire; the family of Sir George Armytage lived at Kirklees Hall (*Nunnely Priory) near Margaret *Wooler's school at *Roe Head.

HR

Arno River. This runs through the Duke of Zamorna's Angrian estate, *Hawkscliffe Forest. Zamorna's son Victor Frederick Percy *Wellesley is given the title Marquis of Arno.

Arnold, Matthew (1822–88), poet and influential social critic. Before he established a literary reputation, Charlotte Brontë met Arnold (21 Dec. 1850) and discerned 'genuine intellectual aspirations' beneath 'seeming foppery' (to James Taylor, 15 Jan. 1851). He described her as 'plain, with expressive gray eyes' and reported that they talked about French novels, curates, and her Brussels education (to Frances Lucy Wightman, 21 Dec. 1850). Arnold judged *Villette* 'hideous' and 'constricted', because Charlotte's mind contained 'nothing but hunger, rebellion, and rage' (to A. H. Clough, 21 Mar. 1853; to Mrs Forster, 14 Apr. 1853). His obituary poem 'Haworth Churchyard' (*Fraser's Magazine*, May 1855) commends Charlotte as 'Puissant' genius; Anne as 'Sweet and graceful'; celebrates Emily's 'Passion, . . . grief, | Daring'; and laments Branwell's troubled talent. The elegy's conclusion alludes to the end of *Wuthering Heights*, describing the Brontës as 'Unquiet souls' who will 'find' themselves 'In the dark fermentation of earth'. He was disconcerted to learn from Elizabeth *Gaskell (1 June 1855) that all the Brontës, except Anne, were buried not in the churchyard but in the church itself, which he considered 'the wrong, uncongenial spot' (Allott, p. 306).

BT

Collini, Stefan, *Arnold* (1988).
Honan, Park, *Matthew Arnold: A Life* (1981).

Arnold family. In August 1850 Charlotte Brontë visited Fox How, the Arnolds' home, in an 'exquisitely lovely' situation below Lough Rigg, near *Ambleside. Dr Thomas Arnold (1795–1842), headmaster of Rugby, bought the estate in 1832 and built a summer home there. When Charlotte read Arthur Penrhyn Stanley's *The Life and Correspondence of Thomas Arnold, D.D.* (2 vols., 1844) she considered Arnold 'not quite saintly . . . , almost a little hard', but the 'greatest of Working Men', of high intellect, stainless rectitude, and true-hearted affection: his happy life seemed almost without

experience of mortal illness among his family. Arnold married Mary Penrose of Fledborough, Notts., in August 1820. Six of their nine surviving children were born at Laleham, Middlesex, the three youngest at Rugby. Jane Martha (1821–99) married William Edward *Forster (1818–86) in August 1850; Matthew (1822–88) married Frances Lucy Wightman in June 1851. The others were Thomas (1823–1900), Mary (1825–88), Edward Penrose (1826–78), William Delafield (1828–59), Susanna Elizabeth Lydia (1830–1911), Frances Bunsen Trevenen Whately (1833–1923), and Walter Thomas (1835–93). Dr Arnold was a tender and playful father, and the 'guide and life of the party' on the family's long walks over the Westmorland hills. Charlotte was at first disappointed by Mrs Arnold's conventional manner, but after her later visits in December 1850 appreciated the amiability and 'beautiful unity' of all the Arnolds. She underestimated their intellectual ability, and probably also the frankness, vivacity, and quickness of observation others praised in Mrs Arnold. During her visit to Ambleside in December 1850 Charlotte was taken by Harriet *Martineau to meet Matthew *Arnold. When Jane Arnold Forster and her husband visited Haworth, probably early in 1851, she was saddened by the desolate-seeming parsonage, but reflected that Charlotte, though 'entombed' there, enclosed within herself 'a force of strong fiery life' (Gaskell *Life*, 2. 188, 190). Despite her promise to visit the Forsters in the ensuing spring, Charlotte never did so.

art collections. See ART OF THE BRONTËS.

art of the Brontës *See page 18*

Arundel. Province in the kingdom of *Angria, 165 miles long by 90 miles wide, known for its fertile green pastures and woods. Governed by the Earl of Arundel, it has a population of 971,000, and its capital is Seaton.

Arundel, Lord Frederic Lofty, Earl of, a close friend of the Duke of Zamorna, who creates him grand chamberlain in the *Glass Town and Angrian saga. Arundel is an accomplished horseman (nicknamed 'The Chevalier') and popular field-marshal in the Angrian army. He was thought to have died on the battlefield at Velino, during the *War of Encroachment in which Zamorna won the kingdom of Angria. His younger brother, Macara *Lofty, a Verdopolitan scoundrel, encouraged the rumour so that he would inherit his title. Arundel is married to Edith, eldest daughter of the King of Sneaky's Land. Arundel is an ancient English peerage, with lands in Sussex including Arundel Castle. The name also appears in *Shakespeare's history plays, such as *Henry IV* and *Henry VI*.

T HE Brontës had a profound and continuing interest in the visual arts. Their habit of reading pictures and their own practice of drawing and painting were crucial to their development as writers. Charlotte was an exhibited artist in her own lifetime, her earliest aim was to be a visual artist, and Branwell practised as a professional portrait painter from May 1838 to May 1839. Elizabeth Gaskell notes the strong yearning the Brontës had for the art of drawing and their habit of analysing 'any print or drawing which came their way' (*Life*, 1. 96). The sisters were taught art as one of the female *accomplishments and in preparation for their careers as teachers; Branwell progressed from watercolours to oils and had lessons with the professional portrait painter William *Robinson. Their earliest drawings date from about 1828 when Charlotte was 12, Branwell 11, Emily 10, and Anne 8; the sisters continued to draw until about 1845 when the publication of *Poems* by Currer, Ellis, and Acton Bell occupied their attention, and Branwell drew self-deprecatory sketches and illustrated his *letters until his death in 1848. There are approximately 180 extant drawings by Charlotte, just over 130 by Branwell, 29 by Emily, and 37 by Anne, with new paintings still coming to light after years in private hands. During the Brontës' lifetime many were given away as gifts, some discarded and others used as barter for frames (see WOOD, WILLIAM). A number of drawings survived through the collections of Revd A. B. *Nicholls and Martha *Brown in particular. The majority of Brontë art works are meticulously copied pencil drawings and delicate water-coloured portraits. A number of manuscripts and *books owned by the Brontës are annotated with sketches. At least ten large professional oil portraits by Branwell are extant, plus his two famous early portraits of his sisters.

There is no evidence that the Brontës had formal art lessons before Charlotte went to Roe Head in 1832. John *Bradley, a local Keighley painter, seems to have given them some lessons at Haworth Parsonage, and Thomas *Plummer, son of a schoolmaster friend of Revd Patrick Brontë, gave Branwell a few lessons in Keighley. They all began by copying woodcuts of birds and vignettes from *A History of British Birds*, by Thomas *Bewick (1816), and seem to have examined and imitated whatever illustration came their way, from plates in annuals to drawing manuals of picturesque scenes and trees. At *Roe Head school the sisters were exposed to the conventional art education of every middle-class Victorian young woman. They were taught to paint flowers, trees, picturesque views, and the hands and facial features important in 'taking a likeness'. Charlotte and Anne copied many of the same exercises of eyes, ears, noses, lips, profiles, and classical heads; and on her return from school Charlotte taught her younger sisters from the copies she had made (Alexander & Sellars, pp. 180–7, 400, 404–5, 331). In Brussels, Charlotte and Emily continued sketching from prints: in July 1842 Charlotte reported Emily's rapid progress in French, German, music, and drawing (Smith *Letters*, 1. 289). Emily's large pencil 'Study of a Fir Tree' is amongst her most discerning works, made 'en plein air' during the holidays. She and Charlotte actually sketched the same ruined tree and although both girls are imitating a picturesque vocabulary, Charlotte's resulting 'Landscape with Fallen Trees' is considerably less dramatic (Alexander & Sellars, pp. 118–21).

From the beginning Branwell's art education was distinguished from that of his sisters. At the age of 11, while they were copying prints, he was already drawing 'from nature'. At 12 he made a skilful watercolour copy of Martin's *Queen Esther*, carefully scaling up the perspective of the grandiose buildings from the tiny engraving in the *Forget Me Not* annual. He shared with his sisters a love of Bewick: his copy of the *Gos Hawk* (1833) is particularly noteworthy, and his article on the 'quiet poetry' of Bewick in the *Halifax Guardian* (1 Oct. 1842) also reveals his own taste in poetry and art (Alexander & Sellars, pl. II; *BST* 24 (1999), 1. 11–15). The same 'quiet truths to nature' that Branwell finds in Bewick's vignettes can also be found in Branwell's own meticulous sketches of moorland stone buildings or his lodgings at 'The Old Hall, Thorpe Green' (Alexander & Sellars, pp. 304–5, 346, and pl. LX). Eleven large oil portraits, mostly commissions from Branwell's professional days in *Bradford, survive, as well as a number of pencil sketches of friends and associates (see, for example, his fine portraits of John *Brown, Margaret *Hartley, and the *Kirbys: Alexander & Sellars, pls. XXIX–XXXII). Some of his most powerful work can be seen in his robust pen-and-ink sketches: his portraits of his heroes Alexander Percy (Duke of *Northangerland) and the Duke of *Zamorna have the same imaginative flare that one associates with his descriptions of these characters (Alexander & Sellars, pls. LXI–II). The equally vigorous pen-and-ink sketches on his many letters to Joseph Bentley *Leyland and in Mary *Pearson's commonplace book are a sad reminder of his alcohol and drug addiction and a talent lost. He had, after all, at only 17, painted two of the best-known and best-loved literary portraits in the world: the group 'The *Brontë Sisters' and the fragment portrait *'Emily Jane Brontë', both now in the NPG in London.

For Charlotte, art was particularly important as a means of refining her mind. Mary Taylor noted that she 'picked up every scrap of information concerning painting, sculpture, poetry, music, etc., as if it were gold' (Wise & Symington, 1. 92). At 13, Charlotte compiled a 'List of painters whose works I wish to see', listing chiefly Italian renaissance painters (Gaskell *Life*, 1. 91). In her early writings she refers frequently to galleries like the Louvre, to 'dark Salvators and Carracis and Corregios', to Corinthian pillars, and the symmetry and proportion of particular styles of architecture that reflect certain ethical values. Her Angrian heroes are patrons of the arts, since like their author they rate the artist's vocation as one of the highest in life. Charlotte believed that the artist is not only the most conscious of beings but is also capable of awakening his fellows to consciousness of a new beauty and truth. Thus she worked hard to emulate her models, believing 'that the art-faculty consisted of little more than mechanical dexterity, and could be obtained by long study and practice in manipulation' (Leyland, 1. 124, 139). She was encouraged by the acceptance of two pencil drawings, 'Bolton Abbey' and 'Kirkstall Abbey' (Alexander & Sellars, pp. 52, 228–9), for the summer exhibition of the *Royal Northern Society for the Encouragement of the Fine Arts in Leeds, 1834. The majority of her highly finished copies of engravings were made between 1834 and 1835 when she was 18 or 19, before she concluded, like Lucy Snowe in *Villette*, that her precious drawings were 'about as valuable as so many achievements in worsted-work' (ch. 35). Several of her later portraits, both fictional ('Woman in a Leopard Fur', Oct. 1839) and realistic ('William Weightman', Feb. 1840), show considerable skill and some flair. But the majority of her works may be classed as extremely competent, detailed, but conventional illustrations, with little sign of the vigour and originality of the pictures she saw with her 'spiritual eye' but, like Jane Eyre, was 'quite powerless to realize' (*Jane Eyre*, ch. 13). Her *Roe Head Album indicates that her art works are not to be distinguished from similar amateur female productions of the period. When *Smith, Elder asked her to illustrate the second edition of *Jane Eyre* herself, in 1848, she replied: 'It is not enough to have the artist's eye; one must also have the artist's hand to turn the first gift to practical account', and she felt 'much inclined to consign the whole collection of drawings to the fire' (Smith *Letters*, 2. 40–1).

Anne's detailed copies of engravings were as skilfully executed as those of Charlotte and several of them, such as 'Woman Gazing at a Sunrise' (13 Nov. 1839) and 'What you please' (25 July 1840), suggest imaginative deviations from the print she was copying (Alexander & Sellars, pp. 406–8). She occasionally made a practice of sketching from life during her periods from home as a governess. Thus we have records of the landscape around Thorp Green and possible portraits of her charges (Alexander & Sellars, pp. 410–17). Anne was particularly fond of sketching trees and her unfinished sketches of *Flossy again show that she was more venturesome than Charlotte in drawing 'from nature' (Alexander & Sellars, pp. 398–403, 416–17, and 408–10).

It is, however, Emily's love of nature that is manifested as much in her painting as in her writing. Like her sisters, she copied prints as exercises but it was not long before she was sketching all the *pets owned by the Brontës. Her endearing studies of 'Grasper—from life', 'Keeper—from life', 'Nero', and 'Flossy' (Alexander & Sellars, pls. III–VI) show a skilful use of the brush and an empathy with the animals that make these illustrations not only evidence of Emily's superior skill in watercolour but also highly prized Brontë relics. Of her 29 extant drawings, only nine are not connected with the natural environment. There are several hasty but vigorous pen-and-ink sketches illustrating *Diary Papers, and four of her copies of engravings survive, although we know of a possible 10 that she made. Only in three rough sketches do we find hints of her intensely private world: a sadistic scene, 'Images of Cruelty', that accompanies a fragment of drama; and 'doodles' in the margins of poetry manuscripts suggestive of a mind receptive to a life force in nature (Alexander & Sellars, pp. 102–3, 380–2). There are no caricatures like the one Lockwood finds in *Wuthering Heights* made by the first Catherine of Joseph, 'rudely yet powerfully sketched' (ch. 3); yet one suspects some may have been made. Two of Emily's copies of engravings may have *Gondal associations: the strong-featured 'Woman's Head with Tiara' (6 Oct. 1841) and 'The North Wind' (1842), the latter from William *Finden's engraving of Richard Westall's 'Ianthe', published as the frontispiece to Thomas *Moore's 1830 *Letters and Journals of Lord Byron, with notices of his Life* (pp. 384–7), but possibly copied from a foreign edition. The expression of Emily's Ianthe is more challenging than the original, her eyes piercing and void of the wide-eyed innocence of Westall's version.

Drawing and writing about Glass Town, Angria, and Gondal were practised in close association. The earliest record of the Brontës' art practice is the copying of lakeland views from Westmorland when the children were staying with their aunt and uncle *Fennell in September 1829 (Smith *Letters*, 1. 105). At the same time they were busy writing about the *Young Men's Play and the *Islanders' Play, creating fictitious art reviews (modelled on those in *Blackwood's Edinburgh Magazine* and *Fraser's*

Anne Brontë, pencil drawing of a woman gazing at a sunrise, 13 November 1839.

Magazine), and fictitious Glass Town sculptors and painters modelled on historical counterparts (Sir John Martin *Dundee, Frederick *De Lisle, Sir Henry *Chantrey, William *Etty). The *juvenilia of Charlotte and Branwell abound in references to artists and their works, to the techniques of painting, and to the role of the artist in society. Despite its ostensibly African setting, the landscape and architecture of Glass Town and Angria were in large part inspired by the liquid landforms and Palladian structures of Martin's dramatic paintings (four of his prints hung on the Parsonage walls), and the picturesque prints like those from Westmorland or from the pages of the *annuals or illustrated works of Lord *Byron. The physique and facial features of Angrian heroes and heroines are modelled on images of the statues of Apollo and Diana by Chantrey, on plates of heroes like Wellington and Napoleon, on contemporary literary figures or beauties like the Countess of *Blessington, or on fictitious heroines again in the works of Byron. The engraving by William Finden of *The Maid of Saragoza* in Thomas Moore's *Letters and Journals of Lord Byron*, for example, was copied in watercolour by Charlotte and then transformed into the Angrian heroine Mina Laury in descriptions in novelettes like *High Life in Verdopolis* (Alexander *EEW*, 2(2). 53). The juvenilia of both Charlotte and Branwell display a precocious understanding of artistic debate, preferring the sublime and picturesque to the mere beauty evinced in the 'mechanical skill' of portrait painting (Alexander *EEW*, 1. 92). They are aware of the importance of contrast and the use of chiaroscuro in engraving techniques. The studios of their fictitious artists are crowded with professional apparatus, like lay figures and camera lucidas (Alexander *EEW*, 2(1). 329). At 13, from reviews and prints, Charlotte was familiar with 'the vigorous sternness of Michael Angelo, the grace and beauty of Raphael and the glorious colouring of Titian, together with the exquisite finish of Leonardo da Vinci, the living portraits of Vandyke [*sic*] and the sacred sublimity of Fra Bartolommeo' (Alexander *EEW*, 1. 116). She even wrote her own reviews of three engravings in the annual *Friendship's Offering* (1829).

The training and habit of drawing and painting had a profound effect on the writing style and content of the Brontë novels. The many descriptive passages of landscapes and interiors, particularly in Charlotte's work, are structured as if the narrator is reading a painting, framing the scene and constructing its elements with conscious regard to foreground, middle-distance, and background (for example, *Shirley*, ch. 12). Much of Nelly Dean's story in *Wuthering Heights* is told as a series of vignettes, in which even the climactic scene between Catherine and Heathcliff 'made a strange and fearful picture' (ch. 15). The narrator of *The Professor* also organizes his experience pictorially: 'Three—nay four pictures line the four-walled cell where are stored for me the Records of the Past' and he then proceeds to describe them (ch. 7). For Jane Eyre, a new face is 'like a new picture introduced to the gallery of memory' (*Jane Eyre*, ch. 12). Heroines in all the novels practise *physiognomy and *phrenology as they scrutinize the countenance of other characters, just as their authors did for so many years. Charlotte's schooling in Brussels afforded her the opportunity to see many of the great paintings she had read about or seen only in black and white engravings. Mary Taylor records that in London, on the way to the Continent, Charlotte seemed to think 'our business was and ought to be, to see all the pictures and statues we could' (*Life*, 1. 146). Her experience is put to good use in *Villette* when Lucy Snowe visits various picture galleries and pronounces judgement on a Rubenesque painting of Cleopatra as 'an enormous piece of claptrap' because it is 'not a whit like nature' (ch. 19).

Charlotte's early intense response to Bewick's images is reflected in the young Jane's imaginative response in *Jane Eyre* (ch. 1), and the sublime pictures Charlotte would have liked to have painted herself are suggested in the surreal images Rochester finds amongst the conventional illustrations of Jane's portfolio (ch. 13). Characters in *Wuthering Heights* draw pictures in books, on window panes and in words; and books with 'costly pictures' help in the reconciliation between Catherine Linton and her cousin Hareton and aid in the latter's reclamation from brutality (ch. 32).

Most significant of all is Anne's *Tenant*, which is unique in Victorian literature in having a woman artist as heroine. Helen *Huntingdon's work as a painter exemplifies women's disadvantages in the art field in her lack of professional training and need for a male representative to market her work (see WOMEN, POSITION OF). Nevertheless through her art Helen is able to assert the value of work for middle-class women: the respectability, comfort, financial security, and especially the independence it guarantees. Her affinity with nature and her belief in universal salvation also find expression through her art and reflect the artistic values and experience of her author. Helen works directly from nature and reads it with the eye of a professional artist, recording the effect of light on leaves (chs. 6 and 9). She is conscious that such artistic preoccupation might deprive her of the full enjoyment of nature; yet, in her conversation with Gilbert *Markham, she also expresses the kind of satisfaction and pleasure that all the Brontës must have gained from their practice of art:

'I am always troubling my head about how I could produce the same effect on canvass [sic]; and as that can never be done, it is mere vanity and vexation of spirit.'
'Perhaps you cannot do it to satisfy yourself, but you may and do succeed in delighting others with the result of your endeavours.'
'Well, after all I should not complain: perhaps few people gain their livelihood with so much pleasure in their toil as I do.' (ch. 9)

Alexander, Christine, 'Art and Artists in Charlotte Brontë's Juvenilia', *BST* (1991), 20. 4. 177–204.
—— *Charlotte Brontë's Paintings: Victorian Women and the Visual Arts* (1993).
Alexander & Sellars (*catalogue raisonné*).

Ascension Isle, off the east African coast, where the Twelves fought the Dutch in the early *Glass Town and Angrian saga and where the Duke of Zamorna is exiled during the Angrian wars.

Ashantee (now spelt 'Ashanti'), the area of west *Africa colonized by the *Twelves in the *Glass Town and Angrian saga and identified as the *Glass Town Federation. The area is based on the Ashantee empire of the 18th and 19th centuries, a state wealthy in gold and active in the slave trade until it finally fell under British domination in the 1860s and 1870s. The southern provinces of Ashantee became the Gold Coast Colony in 1874, now southern Ghana.

The area of Ashantee encountered by the Twelves in the Brontës' imaginary saga is roughly equivalent to the 19th-century Gold Coast including the Kingdom of Guinea. Its boundaries (1,700 miles wide by 500 miles long) comprise the desert to the east, the Atlantic to the west, the Gulf of Guinea to the south, and the *Jibbel Kumri (Mountains of the Moon) to the north. The Ashantee tribes, enemies of Glass Town and Angria (originally represented as ninepins in the Brontë children's childhood play), are the displaced indigenous people of this land. The destruction of their capital, *Coomassie (based on Kumasi, the historical capital of the Kingdom of Ashanti), by the Twelves, was inspired by reports of the *Ashantee Wars of the 1820s in newspapers and journals. Quashia *Quamina, sole survivor of Ashantee royalty and son of the slain Sai-Too-Too *Quamina, plays a major role in the Glass Town and Angrian saga. In her poem 'O Hyle thy waves are like Babylon's streams', Charlotte compares the Ashantees to the Jews in captivity (Neufeldt *CBP*). See also KING BOY AND KING JACK; AFRICA.

Ashantee Wars, 1820s, between Britain and the Ashanti (formerly spelt *'Ashantee') empire, a west African state that occupied what is now southern Ghana. From the 18th century Ashanti had supplied slaves to Portuguese, Dutch, and British traders on the coast and even earlier to their Arab allies in Ethiopia and Abyssinia. By the 19th century, after a period of territorial expansion, Ashanti had established a strong centralized state with an efficient system of communications. Ashanti occupied southern Fanti territory around British headquarters at Cape Coast in 1807, the same year that Britain outlawed the slave trade. Trade relations declined and disputes arose over the Fanti region that led to warfare in the 1820s. The Brontës read in the pages of their local newspapers of the defeat of a British force in 1824 by the Ashanti, and throughout the 1820s newspapers and *Blackwood's Edinburgh Magazine* carried reports on the 'Ashantee Wars'. The skirmishes and battles inspired the Brontës' own imaginary penetration into 'Ashantee' land in their saga and the transposition of details from current articles into their juvenilia. For example, *Blackwood's* raised the problem of 'Arab jealousy' and 'Moorish rivalry' as an impediment to British interests in Africa (19 (June 1826), 698, 708); and the Brontës responded by creating 'Moorish' allies for their 'Ashantee' warriors, who (Charlotte tells us) are 'detested by the British'. In 1831 the Ashanti made peace and avoided conflict for 30 years, when they again challenged the British by sending forces to occupy the coastal provinces. Not until 1874 did a British force actually occupy Kumasi (the Ashanti capital, formerly spelt 'Coomassie') and then only for one day (although the Brontës' *Twelves and their forces had defeated *Coomassie in the early days of their *Glass Town and Angrian saga).

Ashworth ('Long disuse of a pen that was once frequently handled . . .'), Charlotte Brontë's first attempt at a realistic novel: an incomplete, untitled story, written between December 1840 and March 1841 (see Alexander *EW*, p. 289 n. 4, for dating). A three-volume novel was planned but only three manuscript chapters and an early draft of chapter 4 exist (in Widener, Harvard). The narrator tells us that the hero is to be Arthur Ripley *West (a reincarnated Duke of *Zamorna) yet the surviving chapters replay much of Branwell's early

material on the life of his hero the Duke of Northangerland—a possible reason for Charlotte's abandonment of the story. *Ashworth* is probably typical of what Charlotte referred to in her preface to *The Professor* as 'many a crude effort destroyed almost as soon as composed' during which she 'got over any such taste as I might once have had for the ornamented and redundant in composition'. Despite its reference to Angrian material, however, much of *Ashworth* looks forward to her later novels, especially to *The Professor* and *Shirley* in the rivalry between two brothers and the social unrest amongst the 'smutty' mechanics of Manchester and the West Riding (Alexander *EW*, pp. 206–9, 220–1). The later Jane *Eyre is prefigured in the characters of Ellen Hall and Marian Fairburne, and Mary Ashworth, the Yorkshire heiress who is 'As proud as Lucifer!', suggests the heroine Shirley *Keeldar.

The central character of the beginning of this draft novel is Mr Alexander *Ashworth, a landowner in West Yorkshire, based (almost without change) on Alexander Percy (Duke of *Northangerland) from the Brontë juvenilia. Chapter 1 describes his birth, wedding, bankruptcy, and wild early life (including the episode with the *Thurstons of Darkwall Manor, which suggests that Charlotte may have recently read several of Branwell's manuscripts). Chapter 2 tells of the fate of his two disowned sons and his daughter's experience at a private boarding school in London, where she meets Ellen Hall who is destined to become a nursery governess. Chapter 3 records the attitude of his neighbours General West (a revamped Duke of Wellington) and Mr De Capell (who recalls both General *Thornton and his father Alexander *Sneaky) to his entrance into Yorkshire society; the frank dialogues between West and De Capell prefigure those between Mr Helstone and Hiram Yorke in *Shirley*. In chapter 4, the interest centres on Ashworth's daughter Mary and her relations with the younger generation of Wests and De Capells (including the quiet but astute Marian Fairburne).

Four fragmentary manuscripts relating to an early version of *Ashworth* can be found in the Pierpont Morgan Library, New York (see Alexander *EW*, p. 288 n. 2, for details); extracts are printed in *BST* (1940) 10. 50. 15–24. At the end of chapter 3 is a cryptic plan for the novel: 'School-Scene/ Introduction to Yorkshire/ Gillwood, Ripley Towers—De Capell-Hall/ Miss Thornton & Miss Percy were'. The fragments relate to a Percy/West story that Charlotte sent to Hartley Coleridge in the late summer of 1840. His reply has not survived but Charlotte's subsequent letter to him suggests that he intimated that 'Messrs Percy and West' were 'not gentlemen likely to make an impression upon the heart of any Editor in Christendom' (fair copy letter to H. Coleridge, 10 Dec 1840; *TLS* (14 May 1970), 544; Smith *Letters*, 1. 239).

> Alexander *EW*, pp. 203–11, 220–4.
> Monahan, Melodie (ed.), 'Ashworth: An Unfinished Novel by Charlotte Brontë', *Studies in Philology*, 80/4 (1983).

Ashworth, Alexander, central character in the opening chapters of Charlotte Brontë's first abortive attempt at a realistic novel, known as *Ashworth.* Born in Hampshire (Ashworth Hall), he moves with his daughter Mary to the West Riding of Yorkshire, where he is a landowner and master of Gillwood Hall. The detailed description of his former life is a thinly disguised version of that of Alexander Percy, Duke of *Northangerland, from the *Glass Town and Angrian saga.

> Alexander *EW*, pp. 205–7.

Ashworth, Brother, an alias of Alexander Percy (Duke of *Northangerland), used chiefly when he preaches at Slugg St Methodist Chapel in *Verdopolis, in the *Glass Town and Angrian saga. The 'disguise' is employed to disseminate republicanism amongst the masses. Branwell, in particular, uses Brother Ashworth to parody Methodist revival meetings and Primitive Methodist hymns (see, for example, Neufeldt *BBP*, pp. 506–8, and Neufeldt *BB Works*, 3. 439).

Ashworth, Edward, eldest son of Alexander *Ashworth in Charlotte Brontë's story *Ashworth.* Disowned by his father, he and his brother William are rescued from obscurity by their grandmother and sent to school at Harrow where Edward 'pushed his way through the rough life of a school boy', while his less athletic brother endured by cynicism and daydreaming. When at the age of 18, Edward's grandmother dies, the brothers are plunged into poverty but there are suggestions that they will rise through their industry in the wool trade, as their prototypes did in Branwell's *The *Wool Is Rising.* The disparate characters and the antagonism of the two brothers are well-established motifs from the juvenilia and they appear again in *The Professor* (in Edward *Crimsworth and William *Crimsworth) and, more subtly, in *Shirley* and in *'Willie Ellin'. For a possible source, see HEATON FAMILY.

> Alexander *EW*, pp. 206, 219–24.

Ashworth, Mary, daughter of Alexander *Ashworth and sister of Edward and William in Charlotte Brontë's story *Ashworth.* Mary is a beautiful and intelligent heiress, educated at a private boarding school in London and then introduced into Yorkshire society at the age of 17. Like her prototype Mary Henrietta *Percy, she is considered proud and aloof, but the narrator hints that this may be a self-protective mask. In the story, we see her compassion for poor Ellen Hall and her sensitivity towards the retiring Marian Fairburne.

Ashworth, William, the younger disowned son of Alexander *Ashworth in Charlotte Brontë's story *Ashworth.* Like his prototype in the juvenilia (Captain Sir William *Percy), he is constantly victimized and physically maltreated by his elder brother Edward. He harbours his resentment within a well-controlled exterior and develops taciturnity and cynicism. Unlike his brother, he is scholarly—a forerunner of William Crimsworth in *The Professor* and Louis Moore in *Shirley.* For his early life and rivalry with his brother, see ASHWORTH, EDWARD.

Aspin Castle. See SIDONIA, LORD ALFRED.

Athénée Royal, Brussels. The upper school or college for boys in which M. Constantin *Heger held a position as professor. One of the first institutions of its kind in the recently established (1830) nation of Belgium, it prepared students for the university as well as for special schools. Heger chose to teach the youngest boys, who would have been about 12. Charlotte Brontë's contact with the school was limited, but she certainly attended the prize-day ceremony of 15 August 1843 to hear Heger deliver an address on emulation. She returned to Haworth with copies of that speech and his earlier speech of 1834. She alludes to a school for boys in *The Professor* and *Villette,* the latter clearly based on the Athénée.   SL

'Athènes sauvée par la poësie'. See 'ATHENS SAVED BY POETRY'.

'Athens Saved by Poetry' ('Athènes sauvée par la poësie'). *Devoir by Charlotte Brontë (6 Oct. 1843, MS in BPM; second version 22 Dec. 1843, MS in Berg, NYPL), probably based on an episode in Plutarch's *Lives.* At a victory banquet the Spartan general Lysander threatens to annihilate Athens, but first he summons a captive Athenian poet to entertain his soldiers. Initially reluctant, the poet decides to try taming the Spartans through his music. Adopting the voice of Electra he recalls the death of Agamemnon. When he pauses he discovers that his drunken audience has fallen asleep. Nonetheless Lysander spares the city. M. Constantin *Heger corrected the devoir lightly and chided Charlotte for its mocking conclusion, but there are grounds for thinking he admired it. Since this is her only classical essay, as well as her most ambitious effort, it may be the source of the scene in *Villette* where

Paul Emanuel brags of Lucy Snowe's knowledge (ch. 35). SL

Lonoff, pp. 334–57.
Duthie *Foreign Vision*, pp. 49–54.

Atkinson family. Revd Thomas Atkinson (1780–1870), a nephew of Hammond *Roberson, was a graduate of Magdalene College, Cambridge, and perpetual curate at *Thornton until May 1815, when he exchanged livings with Revd Patrick Brontë (then at *Hartshead) in order to be nearer Frances *Walker of Lascelles Hall, whom he married in December 1817. After their marriage, the Atkinsons moved to the Green House, *Mirfield, but Mr Atkinson continued at Hartshead until 1866. Frances Atkinson was related to the *Firth family, kind friends of the Brontës at Thornton. Through this connection friendship with the Brontës developed and the Atkinsons became Charlotte Brontë's godparents. It was probably Frances Atkinson who recommended Margaret Wooler's school at *Roe Head to Mr Brontë since they lived less than a mile from it and her niece Amelia Walker was there at the time. There is no evidence that the Atkinsons paid Charlotte's school fees, as suggested by W. W. Yates in *The Father of the Brontës* (1897), p. 100, but Patrick would have asked them to keep an eye on his daughter's welfare and she paid a number of visits to Green House while at Roe Head. As a teacher there, Charlotte taught Caroline Atkinson (b. 1822), daughter of Revd Christopher Atkinson, incumbent of St Paul's church, Leeds, and brother of Revd Thomas Atkinson.

Augusta Almeda. See ALMEIDA (ALMEDA), AUGUSTA GERALDINE.

Austen, Jane (1775–1817), novelist. In his review of *Jane Eyre* in *Fraser's Magazine* (Dec. 1847) George Henry *Lewes claimed that Jane Austen's 'correct representation of life' made her one of the greatest of English novelists. Having briefly contemplated following Austen's uncongenial example, 'to finish more, and be more subdued', Charlotte Brontë was provoked into formulating her own artistic creed: the belief that an author should not resist overmastering creative power. She wrote to Lewes on 12 January 1848 that Austen's *Pride and Prejudice* seemed to her 'An accurate daguerreotyped portrait of a common-place face; a carefully fenced, highly cultivated garden' without 'open country' or 'bonny beck'; her characters lived in 'elegant but confined houses'. Austen was only shrewd and observant, not 'sagacious and profound' (Smith *Letters*, 2. 10). Austen had what Lewes admired, 'the nicest sense of means to an end', but she was not great: 'Can there be a great Artist without poetry?', Charlotte demanded. Aus-

ten was 'sensible, real (more *real* than true)', she wrote to Lewes on 18 January, but without poetry she could never be great (Smith *Letters*, 2. 14). Reading Austen's *Emma* merely confirmed Charlotte's opinion: on 12 April 1850 she wrote to Lewes that Austen delineates 'the surface of the lives of genteel English people curiously well' but 'the Passions are perfectly unknown to her . . . what throbs fast and full, though hidden, what the blood rushes through, what is the unseen seat of Life and the sentient target of Death—*this* Miss Austen ignores; . . . if this is heresy—I cannot help it' (Smith *Letters*, 2. 383).

Aykroyd, Tabitha, (?1771–1855; 'Ackroyd' is a variant spelling of the surname). Revd Patrick Brontë engaged 'Tabby' as a servant at the Parsonage in 1824, when she was 53 years old, and a class-leader at the West Lane Methodist chapel. Her tombstone includes the names of George Aykroyd of Haworth Hall, d. 6 January 1839 aged 76, and Susannah Wood, d. 23 April 1847 aged 90. Elizabeth Gaskell, who met her in September 1853, described her as a 'thorough specimen of a Yorkshire woman of her class, in dialect, in appearance, and in character'. Shrewd, practical, and plain-spoken, she ruled the 'bairns', or 'childer' as she called them, pretty sharply, but was devoted to them, taking pride in their cleverness. She liked to be taken into the family's confidence as a friend, so that when she became very deaf, Charlotte had to tell her private news out on the moors where it could not be overheard. Tabby recalled the days when packhorses came through Haworth once a week, taking hand-spun wool over to Lancashire before the great mills had been built, driving away the fairies, or 'fairishes' from the streams or 'becks': 'It wur the factories as had driven 'em away' (Gaskell *Life*, 1. 81–2). Martha, the housekeeper in *Shirley*, has similar memories. Tabby's dialect speech was broader than that of Martha *Brown, and Emily Brontë recorded her telling Anne to 'pillopatate', i.e 'peel a potato'. Her great-nephew William Wood remembered her taking refuge in his house, for she was sure 'yon childer's all gooin mad, and aw darn't stop 'ith hause ony longer wi' 'em' (Barker, p. 151). *Hannah in *Jane Eyre* is closely modelled on Tabby. Ellen Nussey recalled her as quaint-looking, retaining her duties as long as she could, accompanying the girls if Branwell was not available as escort on long walks, and seizing letters from the postman, to carry them 'with hobbling step and shaking head and hand' to Charlotte (Smith *Letters*, 1. 597–8). All the Brontë sisters were loyally affectionate to Tabby, tolerating her foibles and tending or visiting her when she was ill. When Tabby slipped on ice just before Christmas 1836, she was taken to the Parsonage dangerously ill, with a shattered and dislocated leg. The sisters had to do almost all the housework as well as nurse Tabby, and three years later visited her at her sister's home when an ulcerated leg made her lame. In 1849 the presence of Tabby and Martha comforted Charlotte after Anne's death, and when Tabby fell off her chair with 'her head under the kitchen grate', Charlotte cared tenderly for her: as Tabby told Elizabeth Gaskell, 'her own mother could not have had more thought for her nor Miss Brontë had' (Gaskell *Life*, 2. 122). In August 1852 Tabby was ill with cholera, but she recovered. In January 1855, when Charlotte herself felt sick and faint, she had to send for the local surgeon Mr Ingham to attend Tabby, whose health had totally given way, and who died on 17 February at the home of her great niece Mary Ratcliffe (née Wood) in Stubbing Lane (now Sun Street), Haworth. Revd A. B. *Nicholls took her funeral service on 21 February. See also WOOD, WILLIAM.

Aylott and Jones, stationers, booksellers, and publishers, who published *Poems 1846. Aylott (d. 1872) founded the firm in 1828 in Chancery Lane, according to his daughter Mrs Martyn. From there he moved to 8 Paternoster Row, his address in 1846 during Charlotte Brontë's correspondence with the firm. A Mr Jones was his partner 'for a few years', but he was apparently a 'hard man', who did not pull together well with the amiable and genial Mr Aylott, and that partnership was dissolved. When a new partnership was formed the firm became 'Aylott and Co', the name used in Hodson's *Booksellers, Publishers and Stationers Directory*, where they are listed as booksellers and publishers. When Mrs Martyn's brother was taken into partnership, the firm traded as 'Aylott and Son', until Mr Aylott sen. retired in 1866. Mrs Martyn described him as 'ra-

ther old-fashioned', with 'very narrow views regarding light literature'. Though he had agreed to publish the 'Bells'' *Poems* (at their own expense), he was not interested in undertaking the 'three distinct and unconnected tales' about which Charlotte asked his advice on 6 April 1846, though he was willing to name other firms who might accept the manuscripts, and to advise on the best way to approach them. Mrs Martyn's comment that he preferred 'publishing classical and theological books' is borne out by the predominance of such works in the firm's lists: the 1845 list included Dr G. B. Cheever's life of Bunyan, and Clara Coulthard's *Prayers and Hymns; to which is added, the Millennium, a Poem*, and on their 1846 list was J. Aldis's *Six Lectures on . . . Christian Union*. They also exported books for the *Church Missionary Society's work in West Africa, and acted as a centre for the Church of England Book Hawking Union. They did, however, publish other poems, and in January 1850 brought out the first number of *The Germ: Thoughts towards Nature in Poetry, Literature, and Art* for D. G. Rossetti and his Pre-Raphaelite colleagues.

Mr Aylott lent Elizabeth Gaskell Charlotte's letters to him and allowed her to quote from them in the *Life*, where she commented on the 'thorough probity' of the firm. They had dealt fairly with the 'Bells', had advertised and sent copies for review as Charlotte requested, naming also additional journals and thus securing a 'not discouraging review' in the *Athenaeum* (4 July 1846) and a most encouraging article in the *Critic* on the same day. The suggestion that the edition—with 961 copies out of the original 1,000 still unsold—might be transferred to Smith, Elder and Co. seems to have come from Aylott and Jones. It was a sensible move, and on 7 December 1848 Charlotte acknowledged the receipt of £24 0s. 6d. paid by Smith to Aylott, and duly sent on to her.

B

Badey (Bady, Badry, Badhi, Badhri), Dr Hume (later Sir Alexander Hume, Duke of Badey). Originally simply 'Bady', the notorious surgeon of the early *Glass Town and Angrian saga, who dissects stolen bodies and resurrects people in his 'macerating tub'. Dr Hume Badey derives from both the *Young Men's Play, where he is a drinking crony of the fictional Duke of *Wellington, and the *Islanders' Play, where he is one of the *Palace School doctors. Although he is not one of the Twelves, he soon achieves the status of a Twelve (possibly replacing the original surgeon Cheeky) and becomes a respected elderly physician from Wellington's Land. He is the father of Marian *Hume, second wife of the Duke of Zamorna, who lived with her widower father at *Alderwood (originally Badey Hall). On Badey's death, Zamorna inherits his estate and changes the title from Duke of Badhi to Duke of Alderwood. The name 'Hume' and medical character derive from Sir John Robert Hume, who was the historical Duke of *Wellington's surgeon during the *Peninsular War, but Badey's practice is more akin to that of Dr Robert Knox, the doctor involved in the notorious *bodysnatching case of the *Burke and Hare trials.

Badey Hall. See ALDERWOOD.

Baines, Edward (1774–1848), proprietor and editor of the Whig newspaper the *Leeds Mercury* from 1801, when he bought the copyright, goodwill, and materials of the printing business from his former employers Binns and Brown, booksellers and publishers of Leeds (having completed his apprenticeship with them in 1797). He had three sons—Matthew Talbot, Edward, and Thomas—all of whom worked at the newspaper at various times, Edward (1800–90) becoming editor in 1818 and knighted in 1880. The 13-year-old Charlotte Brontë satirizes Edward Baines and his sons in volume 1 of *'Tales of the Islanders', 30 June 1829 (Alexander *EEW*, 1. 25–8), characterizing them as rats for the newspaper's articles against the Duke of *Wellington, the Brontë family hero who was now prime minister. The Baines were strong advocates of Roman *Catholic emancipation, which the Duke opposed at this time. They were also staunch Methodists, supporting the cause of the Dissenters, and they promoted parliamentary reform, advocating representation for industrial towns and cities like Leeds. In 1834, following the first *Reform Bill (1832), Edward Baines sen. became MP for Leeds. Despite the difference in politics, the Brontës respected Baines and subscribed to the *Mercury*, which reflected a Whig (later, a Whig-Liberal) position. Baines's vigorous views supporting the commercial interest (especially at the time of the *Luddite riots) are represented in *Shirley* by Robert Gérard *Moore and Hiram *Yorke. *Baines's Directory* is an important source of local information for the 1820s. The *Peterloo Massacre was witnessed by Edward Baines jun.

Rosengarten, H., 'Charlotte Brontë's *Shirley* and the *Leeds Mercury*', *Studies in Literature* 16 (1976), 593–600.

ballet adaptations. Martha Graham was the first of a series of choreographers to be inspired by the lives of the Brontës rather than by their works. Her ballet *Deaths and Entrances* was first performed by the Graham Dance Company in New York in 1943, having been previewed at Bennington College Theatre, Vermont. The music was by Hunter Johnson. In Britain, the Royal Ballet premièred Ronald Hynd's *Charlotte Brontë* at the Alhambra Theatre, Bradford, in 1974, with Margaret Barbieri in the role of Charlotte, Vyvyan Lorrayne as Emily, and Jeanetta Laurence as Anne. Reviewer Brian Horsfall described the ballet as a 'gripping hour-long work to a stark, strident score from Douglas Young'. Donna Armistead produced a more modest ballet under the title *The World Within*, in 1984, at the Nichols School Dance Department, Nottingham. In 1995, the Northern Ballet Theatre gave the first performance of *The Brontës*, a ballet choreographed by Christopher Gable and Gillian Lynne, at the Grand Theatre, Leeds, with a score by Dominic Muldowney. The première cast included Jayne Regan as Charlotte, Shannon Lilly as Anne, Charlotte Broom as Emily, William Walker as Branwell, and Peter Parker as Revd Patrick Brontë. During March, April, and May, the ballet toured England and Wales, appearing in Darlington, Halifax, Nottingham, Plymouth, Cardiff, Sheffield, Woking, and Newcastle. The scenario, which was devised in consultation with Brontë scholar Brian Wilks, was structured through the recollections of the aged Mr Brontë, and offered a remarkably detailed representation of the Brontë lives, from the courtship of Mr Brontë and Maria to Mr Brontë's lonely old age. In an interview with Richard Wilcocks, the

Northern Dance Theatre's spokesperson Anna Izza said, 'It will flow like a film, so we will not follow the pattern of *pas de deux*—applause—blackout—and so on.' Another unusual feature was that 'Christopher Gable decided to weave in text, where what we wanted to say could not be said in any other way: there's a backing tape throughout, with extracts from letters and novels, and poems' (*Yorkshire and Humberside What's On*, Mar. 1995). Sir Derek Jacobi and Dame Judi Dench provided the voices of Mr Brontë and Charlotte.

In France, Roland Petit choreographed a ballet based on *Wuthering Heights*, entitled *Les Hauts de Hurlevant: histoire d'une passion*. It was first performed by the Ballet National de Marseille in Paris in 1982, with Dominique Khalfouni and Jean Charles Gil as Catherine and Heathcliff. David Dougill, reviewing the first performance, reports that 'Petit and the author of his scenario, Édmonde Charles-Roux, have simplified the plot to concentrate on the four principal characters—Catherine, her lover Heathcliff, her brother Hindley, and her husband Edgar Linton. But brooding over their tortured relationships—manipulating them, in fact—is "la lande", the wild moor itself . . . Petit has collaborated again with Marcel Landowski (the composer of his *Phantom of the Opera*, 1980). The score—partly orchestral, partly electronic, but all on tape—is aptly menacing' (*Dance and Dancers* (Apr. 1983), p. 19). **PS**

> Stoneman, Patsy, *Brontë Transformations: The Cultural Dissemination of 'Jane Eyre' and 'Wuthering Heights'* (1996).

Banagher, Ireland, *c*.80 miles west of Dublin, in King's County (now Offaly), home town of Revd A. B. *Nicholls. From the age of 7 when he was adopted by his uncle and aunt, Dr Bell and his wife Harriet, Nicholls lived with them at Cuba House, Banagher, where Dr Bell was headmaster of the Royal Free School. Banagher is a small town clustered around the main street which rises uphill from the bridge over the Shannon River to the church. Winifred Gérin notes that its close-packed 18th-century stone houses resemble those of Haworth (Gérin *CB*, p. 544). From the church it was a quarter of a mile to Cuba House.

Nicholls took his wife Charlotte Brontë to visit his former home during their honeymoon in Ireland. Charlotte was impressed by the elegant Georgian Cuba House with its extensive grounds, 'externally like a gentleman's country-seat' and 'handsomely and commodiously furnished' (Wise & Symington, 4. 134). After Revd Patrick Brontë's death, Nicholls returned to Banagher to live with his aunt and her daughter Mary Anna who had moved from Cuba House to the smaller Hill House, at the top of a rise overlooking the town and Shannon River (*BST* (1950), 11. 60. 374). In 1864 he married Mary Anna and continued to live at Hill House, Banagher (still in existence), until his death.

Bany, Chief Genius. See GENII, CHIEF (LITTLE KING AND QUEENS).

Barbier, Auguste (1805–82). French poet whose most famous poem, 'The Idol' ('L'Idole'), attacks the revival of *Napoleon worship by representing France as a proud young racehorse whom the Corsican rides to her death. Charlotte Brontë translated it in March 1843 as a student at the Pensionnat *Heger (MS in Pierpont Morgan). In the manuscript of *Shirley* she praised Barbier's 'rude vigour' and quoted the first two verses in French (see *Shirley* (Clarendon edn.), 559); however, she removed the reference later. **SL**

> Duthie *Foreign Vision*, pp. 39–40.
> Neufeldt *CBP*, pp. 355–6 and 488–9.

Barraclough, Moses, a tailor and Nonconformist preacher who denounces Robert Gérard *Moore as Satan, and leads a group of disaffected working men to ambush wagons bringing new machinery to Moore's cloth mill in *Briarfield, in *Shirley*. He is 'a broad-shouldered fellow' with a 'demure face and cat-like, trustless eyes . . . a wooden leg and stout crutch . . . a kind of leer about his lips' (p. 149). A few days following the frame-smashing, Barraclough leads a group of working men to Moore's mill with the demand that he get rid of his 'infernal machinery' and hire more 'hands'. However, warned by Fred *Murgatroyd of Barraclough's intentions, Moore is ready for him and has him arrested by *Sugden, the constable from *Whinbury, and carried off to prison in *Stilbro'. Wroot states that Charlotte Brontë took the name 'Barraclough' from a well-known Nonconformist family living in Haworth (Wroot, p. 112); this may have been the family of John Barraclough, a clockmaker whose shop was situated close to Haworth Parsonage, and who owned the cottage rented by a John *Greenwood, possibly the Haworth stationer of that name (?1807–63) who was acquainted with the Brontë family. John Barraclough's eldest son was called Zerubbabel, the name given to an ancestor of the *Yorke family (*Shirley*, ch. 34). **HR**

'Battell Book'. Branwell Brontë's earliest extant manuscript (in BPM), dated 12 March 1827, this is a hand-sewn booklet of eight pages. Five pages contain sketches: soldiers in red and blue uniforms with cannon and standard-bearers, entitled 'Battell of Wshington [*sic*]'; a map of North and South America; soldiers with a large blue flag; a castle entitled 'Bandy castle'; a moated castle with a blue flag; and a one-sentence entry referring to the Battle of Washington fought in August 1814 during the American War against Britain of 1812–14.

VN

Alexander & Sellars, pp. 174–8 (illustrations).
Barker, J. R. V. (ed.), *Sixty Treasures* (1988), item 35.
Neufeldt *BB Works*, 1. 1.

Beck, Mme, directress of a pensionnat in *Villette, in Charlotte Brontë's novel of the same name; in essence an acid portrayal of Mme Zoë *Heger. A trim, fresh-complexioned, blue-eyed little widow, she engages Lucy *Snowe as a 'gouvernante' despite her lack of references, but counteracts her apparent rashness by scrutinizing Lucy's possessions and making wax impressions of her keys. With ruthless coolness she evicts Lucy's drunken predecessor, Mme Sweeny. Mme Beck's judgement is untempered by sympathy for individuals, despite her general charity to the poor. Habitually serene, motherly, and benevolent in appearance, she can be effusively courteous when it is in her interest to be so, and is not without admirable qualities. An excellent administrator, she rules with outward mildness, providing for the physical well-being of her pupils in a liberal, salutary, and rational manner. But her stern features, narrow forehead, and hard mouth match her unscrupulous pursuit of her own interest. She likes honesty, and respects it in Lucy, but uses underhand means and corrupt tools to maintain order and retain power. Ultimately she breeds moral corruption in those she purports to educate or control. Coolly unresponsive to her youngest child's affection, she tacitly condones the vices of the eldest, Désirée, by failing to correct her, and by using deceit to outwit her. Her skill in 'seeming' has become a fine art: she counterfeits concern for the malingering Désirée, in order to encourage Dr John *Bretton's visits to the school, then feigns absence in order to discover secrets by eavesdropping. She pretends concern for his health, in order to attract him, replaces in perfect order the letters she secretly 'borrows' from Lucy, and erects a façade of modest unconsciousness of the preparations for her fête. 'La Convenance' and 'La Décence' (Propriety and Decorum) are her two deities. From chapter 28 onwards the undercurrent of her malevolent jealousy runs nearer to the surface, as she becomes aware of M. Paul *Emanuel's love for Lucy. Exercising her manipulative talents, but lacking feeling and imagination, she does not foresee that the means she devises for Lucy to learn of Paul's former love for Justine Marie will make Lucy see him as her 'Christian Hero'. The desperate expedient of sending him to the West Indies proves equally self-defeating, for she increases Paul's determination to declare his love for her rival. Yet ultimately she is the victor: Fate decrees that Paul is separated from Lucy by death, and Mme Beck 'prospers all the days of her life'. See also REUTER, MLLE ZORAÏDE.

bed plays. Secret plays begun by Emily and Charlotte Brontë on 1 December 1827, probably the result of conversations between the two before going to sleep at night. They shared the same bed and same small bedroom, a common practice in cramped conditions at the time; but Charlotte's comment, 'Bed plays mean secret plays; they are very nice ones' ('The *History of the Year'), has given rise to speculation that they involved a sexual element. Their secrecy, however, is more likely to relate to the exclusion of Branwell and Anne from these plays. See ISLANDERS' PLAY.

Alexander *EW*, p. 26.

'Believe not those who say', poem by Anne Brontë (24 Apr. 1848); entitled 'The Narrow Way' by Charlotte in her 1850 edition. Though the Christian's journey is not smooth, it is the only road to heaven, and will be brightened by hope. Arm yourself for the fight, act justly, give up earthly treasure, and disregard scorn, for God promises heavenly rest. Anne's depiction of the Christian as a heroic pilgrim uses metaphors from *Bunyan, traditional lyric verse (the thorn and the rose), and the *Bible. 'Earnest of his rest' echoes Ephesians 1: 14. The poem's short-metre quatrains, evangelical message, and style, have led to its use as a hymn by Methodist and other denominations.

Chitham *ABP*, p. 16.

Bell, Currer, Ellis, and Acton. See PSEUDONYMS USED BY THE BRONTËS.

Bell family. Revd A. B. *Nicholls's uncle and guardian, Revd Alan Bell LLD (1789–1839) of *Banagher, King's County, married Harriette Lucinda Adamson (1801–1902). In July 1854 the newly married Charlotte Brontë found her 'quiet, kind and well-bred', and observed that she had been brought up in London. She nursed Charlotte, whose cough had been made worse by fatigue and excitement, with 'kindness and skill', and pleased her by speaking of Mr Nicholls with 'affection and respect'. She had cared for her two nephews as well as her own five sons and four daughters. Capable, sociable, and hospitable, she was active well into old age. During her honeymoon visit, Charlotte wrote to Catherine Wooler on 18 July that she 'was greatly surprised to find so much of English order and repose in the family habits and arrangements' (Wise & Symington, 4. 136). She was impressed by Mr Nicholls's brother Alan, a 'sagacious well-informed and courteous man', who was the manager of the Grand Canal from Dublin to Banagher, and by his cousin Joseph Samuel Bell, later LLD (1835–91), a brilliant student who had gained three prizes at Trinity College Dublin, and who eventually became rector of Kells and canon of St Patrick's, Dublin. She also met Arthur's cousin Mary Anna Bell, 'a pretty lady-like girl with gentle English manners', whom he was to marry as his second wife. Mary's brother Revd James Adamson Bell, like all the Bells a Trinity graduate and 'thoroughly educated' gentleman, was headmaster of the Banagher Royal School for about 20 years from 1848. His visit to Charlotte and Mr Nicholls at Haworth in January 1855 gave them great pleasure, for Charlotte had written to Ellen Nussey on 19 January 1855 that he was a 'true gentleman by nature and cultivation' (Wise & Symington, 4. 171).

Bellingham, James Everard, a rich English banker who visits Verdopolis in the early *Glass Town and Angrian saga, and writes a series of letters to his friend in London, 'published' as *'Letters from an Englishman' by Captain Sir John *Flower (Branwell Brontë). Bellingham becomes embroiled in the revolutionary unrest of the time, especially while on a trip through the Glass Town Federation with the Marquis of Douro (Duke of Zamorna), Lord Charles Wellesley, and Young Soult. He helps finance the counter-revolutionary effort (for which he is temporarily imprisoned by Rogue (Duke of Northangerland) and threatened with death. He later becomes vital to Zamorna's Angrian wars, supporting him in the way that Nathan and James Rothschild supported the historical Wellington's *Peninsular War.

Alexander *EEW*, 1(1). 213.
Neufeldt *BB Works*. 1. 118–24, 180–221, 230–8.

Belmontet, Louis (1798–1879), French poet, now largely forgotten. Charlotte Brontë translated his poem 'Les Orphelins' in February 1843. Her version, 'The Orphans', with the first stanza missing, was published in the *Manchester Athenaeum Album* (1850). SL

Duthie *Foreign Vision*, p. 39.
Neufeldt *CBP*, pp. 353–5 and 485–7.

Bennoch, Francis (1812–90), head of a wholesale silk business in Wood Street, London, friend of Nathaniel Hawthorne and Mary Russell Mitford, and self-proclaimed patron of authors and literature. He called briefly at Haworth on 20 September 1853. Elizabeth Gaskell encountered him on the Parsonage steps—a 'ruddy kind-looking man of no great refinement'—and agreed with Charlotte Brontë on the impertinence of such visits. But Revd Patrick Brontë was captivated, and Charlotte wrote courteously to Bennoch afterwards. He

thought her a 'little, quiet, gentle person' whose conversation had power and charm. In 1854 Charlotte's imminent marriage prevented her visiting him and his wife.

Beresford, Thomas, also Thomas Beresford Bobadill (Bobbadil), military companion of Arthur Wellesley, Duke of Wellington, in *'Tales of the Islanders' and in the early *Glass Town and Angrian saga. After 'An *Interesting Passage' (17 June 1830), he becomes General Bobadill of the army of Wellington's Land, maintaining order during the heated Glass Town elections and serving in the *War of Encroachment. He is modelled on General William Carr Beresford, friend of the historical Duke of *Wellington and marshal of the Portuguese army which assisted Wellington's victories in the *Peninsular War; but the character Bobadill is based on the boasting, cowardly soldier Bobadilla in Ben Jonson's play *Every Man in his Humour* (1598).

Bernardin de Saint-Pierre, Jacques-Henri (1737–1814), French writer best known for his *Nature Studies* (*Études de la Nature*) and his novel *Paul and Virginia* (*Paul et Virginie*). M. Constantin *Heger gave Bernardin's complete works to Charlotte Brontë on 15 August 1843, and the traces of that gift can be seen in her novels. Louis Gérard *Moore advises Shirley Keeldar to read from Bernardin's 'Fragments de l'Amazone' (*Shirley*, ch. 27), and Paul *Emanuel sails for Guadaloupe on a ship named the *Paul et Virginie* (*Villette*, ch. 39). Charlotte's techniques of describing skies and clouds have also been linked to Bernardin's. SL

Duthie *Foreign Vision*, pp. 190–2.
Ware, John N., 'Bernardin de Saint-Pierre and Charlotte Brontë', *Modern Language Notes*, 40 (1925), 381–2.

Bertha. See ROCHESTER, BERTHA.

Bessie. As a young nurse at *Gateshead Hall in *Jane Eyre*, capable, brisk, slim, and pretty, with dark hair and eyes, Bessie Lee enthrals Jane with her nursery tales and songs. She is superstitious, believing in the *Gytrash, an ominous black dog. Despite her capricious temper and frequent scolding, she sees Jane's real terror in the *red-room, and tends her kindly afterwards. Later, married to the coachman Robert Leaven, she brings news to Jane at *Lowood of the *Reed family, and of her uncle John Eyre's enquiries about her. Finally she arranges for Jane to travel from *Thornfield Hall to hear Mrs Sarah *Reed's deathbed confession.

Bewick, Thomas (1753–1828), a Newcastle wood engraver, credited with having revived the art of wood-engraving by his superior technique of using the end grain of hard wood and by his realistic illustrations. Revd Patrick Brontë—following the enthusiastic lead of *Blackwood's Edinburgh Magazine*—had a particular reverence for this north-country artist, with his keen observation of nature and human life. The Brontë children pored over both engravings and text in Bewick's most famous publications, copying his illustrations and transposing their suggestive ideas into their writing.

Bewick's most original and characteristic work is found in the lovingly executed wildlife images and vignettes of country life in *A General History of Quadrupeds* (1790) and *A History of British Birds*, 2 vols. (1797, 1804), both known to the Brontës. The Brontës owned the 1816 edition of *British Birds* that was basically the same as the first edition. The text of volume 1 was written chiefly by Bewick's partner Thomas Beilby, to whom he had formerly been apprenticed, and Bewick himself was responsible for the text of volume 2. The writers' arrangement of birds into various classes and their observations are confirmed throughout the text by reference to the scientific authorities of the day—the 'celebrated Count de *Buffon' and his British popularizer *Goldsmith, Gilbert White of Selborne who is quoted extensively, Thomas Pennant, John Latham, Baron *Cuvier, Linnaeus, Werner, and others—but the popularity of the book was undoubtedly due to the realistic lively engravings and to a text that expressed real empathy for its subject. Bewick said that when he first undertook his labours in natural history his 'strongest motive' was to lead young minds to 'the Great Truths of Creation' and contemporary reviews indicate that the educational value of his work was immediate and immense (S. Roscoe, *Thomas Bewick: A Bibliography Raisonné* (1953), 62). Like Gilbert White, whose work Charlotte had recommended, together with Bewick's, to her schoolfriend Ellen Nussey in July 1834 (Smith *Letters*, 1. 131), Bewick could infuse deep feeling into what he described and communicate it both visually and verbally. This is the 'quiet poetry' that Branwell Brontë so admired in his article *'Thomas Bewick' published in the *Halifax Guardian* (1 Oct. 1842).

In *'Lines on the Celebrated Bewick' (27 Nov. 1832), Charlotte speaks of 'the enchanted page | Where pictured thoughts that breathe and speak and burn | Still please alike our youth and riper age' (Neufeldt *CBP*, p. 25). The young Arthur Huntingdon's book in *Tenant*, that 'natural history with all kinds of birds and beasts in it, and the reading as nice as the pictures', is probably *British Birds* (Winifred Gérin, *Anne Brontë* (1959), p. 55). In *Villette* (ch. 25), Lucy Snowe studies the deep impression 'an old Bretton book—some illustrated work of natural history' had made on Paulina Home; and the young Jane Eyre, in particular, reflects the formative influence Bewick had on the young Brontës. In *Jane Eyre* (ch. 1), the unloved orphan retreats to a window seat and momentarily escapes into the world of *A History of British Birds*, a world of arctic wastes and the habitats of water birds that becomes a powerful analogue for Jane's own desolate position. The child is immediately attracted to the illustrations (from *British Birds*, vol. 2), as the young Brontës were themselves.

Bewick had a considerable influence on the Brontës as visual artists. Both his large ornithological plates showing each bird in its habitat and the tiny rural scenes or 'tail-pieces' provided excellent copy for their first drawing lessons in outline. Between 1828 and 1833, Charlotte, Branwell, Emily, and Anne made six copies of Bewick's miniature wood engravings from volume 1. *Containing the History and Description of Land Birds*; and five more copies from volume 2. *Of Water Birds*, the volume that so impressed the young Jane Eyre. Other drawings exist, of ruins, castles, and animals, that also indicate the influence of Bewick in these formative years, and no doubt further copies once existed, owned by local Haworth residents like William *Wood. It is also likely that the Brontës owned and copied other books embellished by Bewick (such as *Aesop's Fables* referred to in Charlotte's earliest juvenilia).

Charlotte made a watercolour version of Bewick's 'Mountain Sparrow' (Alexander & Sellars, p. 169) but omitted the image of the gibbet seen in the background of Bewick's original, one of those 'terrifying objects' passed over by Jane Eyre. Branwell's watercolour copy of Bewick's black-and-white plate of a goshawk shows that he translated meticulously every detail of its markings described in the text (Alexander & Sellars, pp. 303–4). Emily made two detailed pencil copies of local moorland birds: 'The Whinchat' and the 'Ring Ouzel' both from the first volume of Bewick's *Birds* (Alexander & Sellars, pp. 370–2). An article in *Blackwood's* (July 1825), notes that Bewick's birds and animals are personified: 'This is far beyond the mere pencilling of fur or feathers. It is the seizure and transference of countenance.' Jane Stedman observes how often in *Jane Eyre* characters are likened to varieties of birds: Jane to a linnet, dove, and skylark; Rochester to a 'fierce falcon' or 'caged eagle'; and Bertha Mason to 'a carrion-seeking bird of prey' ('Charlotte Brontë and Bewick's *British Birds*', *BST* (1966), 15. 76. 38–9). Stedman notes too that both Charlotte and Anne assimilated Bewick's technical term 'irides', as in Eliza Millward's eyes in *Tenant* having 'the irids, black or very dark brown', or

Frances Henri in *The Professor* having 'irids of bright hazel—irids large and full, screened with long lashes' (ch. 18).

The grim Hogarth-like humour and small size of Bewick's vignettes would have appealed to the creators of the miniature magazines of Glass Town. Emily copied 'The farmer's wife' (Alexander & Sellars, p. 371; titles from Alexander & Sellars not from Bewick's untitled sketches); Branwell copied 'Farmyard scene with dog and chickens' and 'Rural scene with two figures, cottage and castle' (Alexander & Sellars, pp. 286–7, 291); and Charlotte copied 'Fisherman sheltering against a tree' (Alexander & Sellars, p. 167). As a schoolgirl Jane Eyre, like Charlotte, copied vignettes of 'picturesque ruins and rocks', 'wrens' nests enclosing pearl-like eggs, wreathed about with young ivy sprays' (Alexander & Sellars, pp. 199 200, shows a similar illustration by Charlotte who even copied a sketch by one of Bewick's pupils (p. 199)). Anne drew 'Cottage with trees' and 'Magpie standing on a rock' after Bewick, and several other of her early sketches are also probably from this source, such as 'Church surrounded by trees' and 'Three juvenile sketches' (Alexander & Sellars, pp. 396 7). It was Bewick's recurring images of mortality, however, that caught hold of the imagination of the tormented young Branwell. Bewick's gibbets, tombstones, and fiends with pitchforks haunted him throughout his life and Bewick's headstones reappear as Branwell sounds his own deathknell in his letters to his artist friend Joseph Bentley *Leyland (see Alexander & Sellars, pp. 295, 359–62).

For all the Brontës, as for Jane Eyre, 'Each picture told a story' (*Jane Eyre*, ch. 1). In *The Professor* William Crimsworth pictures himself as 'a lean cormorant, standing mateless and shelterless on poverty's bleak cliff' (ch. 21), an image suggested by Charlotte's own copy of Bewick's vignette of a cormorant (Alexander & Sellars, p. 160). Again this same image is transmuted—via Milton who (in Bewick's words) made 'Satan personate the Cormorant' (in *Paradise Lost*)—into Jane Eyre's macabre watercolour of 'a drowned corse [*sic*]', glancing through the green water and sinking below the mast and the bird (*Jane Eyre*, ch. 13). Further, Bewick's images are reflected in Jane's surreal images of 'a half-submerged mast' on the 'swollen sea' (recalling the earlier 'wreck just sinking' of ch. 1) or the 'pinnacle of an iceberg piercing a polar winter sky'. Later at Gateshead Jane again sketches 'a glimpse of sea between two rocks; the rising moon, and a ship crossing its disk' (ch. 21), suggested by Bewick's tailpieces. Bewick's 'quiet solitary churchyard, with its inscribed headstone' (ch. 1) reappears at the death of Helen Burns (ch. 9), and also informs the grave scene of Rosamund

*Wellesley in the juvenilia and Branwell's 1842 sketch 'Resurgam' (Alexander & Sellars, p. 345).

Stevens, Joan, 'A Sermon in Every Vignette', *Turnbull Library Record* (Mar. 1968), 1. 3. 12–28.

Bible, the. In chapter 11 of her *Life* of Charlotte Brontë, Elizabeth Gaskell observed that Charlotte often took characters and scenes from the Old Testament for her Brussels essays, and that the 'picturesqueness and colour . . . the grandeur and breadth of its narrations, impressed her deeply. To use M. *Héger's expression, "Elle était nourrie de la Bible" [she was brought up on the Bible]' (*Life*, 1. 264). For all the Brontës, familiarity with the Bible was inevitable, brought up as they were in the home of a Protestant minister whose own writings, and of course his preaching, were permeated by biblical language. The use his children made of it reflected their personalities, reading, and experience. For Charlotte, the Bible was part of her patriotic Englishness; she believed it was a closed book to Catholics, especially those living abroad. She responded emotionally and imaginatively to its poetry and profundity, but, like Emily, she knew that its words and doctrines could be travestied by narrow-minded Sabbatarians, tub-thumping preachers, and self-seeking hypocrites. Branwell, reacting against his upbringing, had little respect for the Bible, though he responded ecstatically to the music of Handel's *Messiah*, and to other sacred motets and oratorios based on Scripture. Anne studied her Bible closely, seeking enlightenment on the difficult questions of love and forgiveness, sin and punishment, and the nature of eternity. Bible-based didacticism is integral to her novels, as spiritual searching is to many of her poems.

Other books read by the Brontës reinforced the impact of the Bible. *Bunyan, *Milton, and *Cowper all used biblical images and provoked thought about its theology. On the other hand, the notorious 'Chaldee Manuscript' in *Blackwood's Edinburgh Magazine* irreverently applied pseudo-biblical language to a secular conflict, as the Brontës were to do in the parodic preaching of the Duke of *Northangerland. The vast biblical landscapes painted by John *Martin also excited the Brontës' imagination. His *Destruction of Sodom and Gomorrah* is echoed in *The Professor*. Hunsden Yorke *Hunsden, with the 'profanity in quoting scripture disagreeably' that Elizabeth Gaskell had deplored before the novel's publication, greets William Crimsworth with 'Just so must Lot have left Sodom, when he expected fire to pour down upon it, out of burning brass clouds' (ch. 4). Hunsden also mockingly refers to 'Rebecca on a camel's hump' (ch. 18), an episode Charlotte uses with dramatic effect in the *Jane Eyre* charades.

Elsewhere she refers to the Bible's picturesque scenes and tragic or heroic Old Testament figures, her allusions giving her modern stories some of the grandeur or pathos of their deeds: Rochester is like the blinded Samson, or Nebuchadnezzar with his 'thick and long-uncut locks'. St John Rivers and Agnes Pryor both 'wrestle with God' in earnest prayer, like Jacob at Peniel.

Recognition of biblical allusions, readily picked up by most 19th-century readers, is essential to a full appreciation of the Brontës' writings. Without it, the resonance and nuances deriving from the biblical context cannot be savoured, ironies may be missed, emotional depth reduced, and the nature of characters like St John *Rivers not fully understood. As Ian Jack points out (*Essays in Criticism*, 32 (Oct. 1982), 331), *Lowood pupils in *Jane Eyre* spend Sunday evening repeating the catechism and Matthew 5–7, and listening to a long sermon, during which some 'enact the part of Eutychus', falling down 'if not out of the third loft, yet off the fourth form'. 'To be ignorant of the fate of Eutychus [Acts 20: 9] is to miss an amusing parallel, but to be unaware that [the chapters of Matthew's gospel] contain the Sermon on the Mount would be to lose a powerful effect of irony.'

It is no accident that quotations from St Matthew's gospel outnumber those to other books of the Bible in Charlotte's writings; but they also predominate in Anne's work, especially in *Tenant*. Anne's moral lessons are underlined by references to the gospel parables—the sower and the seed, the house built on sand, pearls cast before swine, and the unfruitful fig tree—all appropriate in a novel where Mr Arthur Huntingdon and his cronies disastrously waste their talents. Anne is also preoccupied with the New Testament, especially the first epistle of John and 1 Corinthians 13, in *Agnes Grey*. In chapter 11, Nancy recounts Edward *Weston's clear, kindly exposition of the great commandments, to love God, and to love one's neighbour. He has explained to her the message of 1 John 4, 'Beloved, if God so loved us, we ought also to love one another'. But Anne knows too that Scripture can be misapplied, or distorted by selective quotation. In *Tenant* Huntingdon maliciously counters Helen's Bible-based exhortations with texts which support his self-indulgence or his pernicious encouragement of Lowborough's drinking—'Use a little wine for thy stomach's sake' (ch. 22; 1 Timothy 5: 23). On his deathbed he scornfully recalls the story of Dives and Lazarus, accusing Helen of considering herself an 'immaculate angel' who would not dip a finger to cool his tongue as he burns in hell (ch. 49; Luke 16: 19–31). Helen, like Anne Brontë, is also selective in her use of Scripture, for she has searched the Bible thoroughly to find 'nearly thirty passages, all tending' to support her belief in the doctrine of *universal salvation (ch. 20).

Charlotte quotes from at least 47 books of the Bible, most often from Genesis, Samuel, Job, the Psalms, Isaiah, Matthew, and Revelation. The most poetic of these are eloquently used in her novels and letters. In *Shirley* Caroline Helstone goes through the Valley of the Shadow of Death (Psalm 23). *Jane Eyre* ends with the penultimate verse of the Revelation of St John the Divine, 'Surely I come quickly', and St John Rivers's response, 'Amen; even so come, Lord Jesus!' In Charlotte's letter to W. S. Williams of 2 October 1848 there is a heartbreaking reference to Mr Brontë's grief after Branwell's death, when he 'cried out for his loss like David for that of Absalom—My Son! My Son! And refused at first to be comforted' (2 Samuel 18: 33 and Psalm 77; Smith *Letters*, 2. 122).

In *Wuthering Heights* Emily Brontë uses the Bible principally as a means of characterizing the repulsive servant Joseph, showing his ineffective tyranny over the rebellious Cathy and Hindley. He insists on their reading 'good books' on Sundays, but Cathy uses the margins of her Testament to caricature and express her resentment against him. The tracts which the children tear up have biblical titles, *The Helmet of Salvation* (Ephesians 6: 17) and *The Broad Way to Destruction* (cf. Matthew 7: 13). But Joseph, despite his preaching, is quite devoid of Christian virtues. Most of the few biblical quotations in *Wuthering Heights* are to be found in his speeches, and in the surreal context of Lockwood's nightmare. Emily's 'almighty ever-present Deity' is God within her breast, not the orthodox God of the New Testament. Yet in her poem of faith, 'No coward soul is mine', some of the central images echo the Bible. 'Faith shines equal arming me from fear' recalls St Paul's exhortation to faith in Ephesians 6: 13–17, 'Take unto you the whole armour of God'. 'Anchored on | The steadfast rock of Immortality' recalls the parable of the house built on the rock in Matthew 7: 24, and Christ's declaration to St Peter, 'Upon this rock I will build my church' (Matthew 16: 18).

See also RELIGION; BOOK OF COMMON PRAYER, THE.

Brontë, Charlotte, *The Professor* (Clarendon edn.), app. 7A.

Thormählen, Marianne, *The Brontës and Religion* (1999).

Binns family, tailors in Haworth at the time of the Brontës. Their name figures largely in the provenance of Brontë items, which were still being purchased for the BPM from Binns descendants well into the 20th century (for example, Branwell's oil painting of John *Brown: Alexander & Sellars, p. 323). When Martha *Brown (the Brontës' surviving servant) died in 1880, she left her substantial collection of Brontë items (including a portfolio of pencil drawings and watercolour sketches) to her five sisters, all of whom soon sold their 'relics' to collectors. The eldest sister Ann had married Benjamin Binns in 1845 and, after living with John Brown for a time, Binns had set up his tailor business in Saltaire. Martha Brown lived with them on her return from Ireland until her death, leaving Ann the bulk of her collection. When Ann became a widow, she sold 30 drawings and other Brontë items in an auction of contents of her home at Saltaire on 26 and 27 January 1886. Interest generated by this sale led to increased collecting of Brontë 'relics' among local Yorkshire magnates and to various small exhibitions of Brontëana, such as that at the Bradford Free Library Art Gallery in April 1886 (Alexander & Sellars, pp. 437–8). There is a curious inscription on the back of Charlotte Brontë's early sketch 'Lady Jephia Bud' that suggests that one of the Binns family may have featured in the *Glass Town and Angrian saga (Alexander & Sellars, p. 168). In 1896, Joseph Binns, a retired tailor of Manningham, Bradford, who had lived in Haworth as a young man, lent several items to the Brontë Society. The Binns family were also connected with Binns and Brown, booksellers and publishers of Leeds, who owned the *Leeds Mercury newspaper from October 1794 to March 1801, when it was acquired by Edward *Baines.

'Biographical Notice of Ellis and Acton Bell' (19 Sept. 1850) was written by Charlotte Brontë to introduce her 1850 edition of her sisters' *Wuthering Heights*, *Agnes Grey*, and selected poems; to explain the origin and authorship of the 'Bells'' works; and to correct the assumption that they were by one person. Recalling that when the sisters were reunited in about 1845 they did not know what progress each had made in their writings, Charlotte described her excitement on finding a manuscript volume of Emily's verse, and the subsequent publication of *Poems 1846. Misleadingly, she claimed that the 'ill-success' of the volume inspired the sisters to write *Wuthering Heights*, *Agnes Grey*, and *The Professor*; in fact all were begun before *Poems appeared. Charlotte then described the publication of the first two and of *Jane Eyre*, the assumption by many reviewers that there was only one 'Bell', and the alleged failure of all critics but one (Sydney *Dobell) to appreciate Emily's work. She also unfairly implied that the reception of *Tenant* was entirely unfavourable, and attributed this to Anne's mistaken choice of subject, designed to warn against misuse of talents. She then briefly but movingly described her sisters'

illnesses and deaths, touched on their differing but 'genuinely good and truly great' characters, and added valuable, partly biographical, prefaces to *Wuthering Heights* and the poems.

biographies from 1940. *See page 36*

biographies to 1940. *See page 42*

Birrell, Augustine (1850–1933), barrister, man of letters, Liberal MP 1889–90, 1906–18. As Chief Secretary for Ireland 1907 to May 1916, he prepared the third Home Rule Bill, introduced by Asquith in April 1912; but, relying on the Irish leader John Redmond's assurances about the state of Ireland, Birrell was taken unawares by the Easter Rising of 1916, accepted responsibility, and resigned office in May. He was successful as an urbane, fluent writer, praised for his *Obiter Dicta* (1884), *Life of Charlotte Brontë* (1887), and the biographies, sketches, recollections, and edition of Disraeli's letters (1928) which followed. His amiable *Life* of Charlotte provided new information about Revd Patrick Brontë's first love, Mary *Burder, derived from her daughter, Mrs Lowe, who described their early meetings and walks together, and alleged that Mary's uncle Robert Burder, unhappy about Mr Brontë's Irish origins and lack of prospects, had secluded Mary in his house at Great Yeldham, intercepted and destroyed Patrick's letters, and caused the engagement to be broken off. Juliet Barker points out that letters of 1808–10 had survived until 1823, since Mary Burder wrote to Mr Brontë on 8 August of recently 'perusing' them (Wise & Symington, 1. 64). When Ellen *Nussey sought Birrell's advice in 1889 on publishing Charlotte's letters to her, he advised her to publish '*at once* & in America' (Smith *Letters* 1. 49), where Revd A. B. *Nicholls could not prevent her doing so by claiming copyright. Birrell offered to negotiate good terms for her, but by 7 November 1889 had found Scribner's 'nervous' about the legal aspect of the publication. He explained to Ellen that she did not own the copyright, and that even if the letters were published in America, copies could not be introduced into Britain if Mr Nicholls objected. After December 1889 Ellen turned to new advisers, ultimately falling into the hands of T. J. *Wise.

Birstall, an extensive parish forming part of *Gomersal township in the Yorks. woollen district, 6 miles south-east of *Bradford. Charlotte Brontë quite often visited the *Nussey family there. She admired their early home, *Rydings, and was welcomed later at *Brookroyd, in Batley parish. Ellen Nussey's father, brothers, and other Nussey and Walker relatives were involved in the woollen trade. Ellen was born at Birstall Smithies near one of the
(*cont. on page 41*)

INTEREST in Brontë biography remained strong throughout the 1900s in spite of the chilling effect which the New Criticism had on historical approaches generally at mid-century (see CRITICISM FROM 1940). The publication of Fannie Ratchford's *The Brontës' Web of Childhood* in 1941 provided new impetus for research into the Brontës' early lives in particular. An evaluation of the *juvenilia rather than a biography as such, Ratchford's work assesses the significance of the early writing in relation to each of the four Brontës' developing personalities. In her view, Branwell became a 'complete slave' (p. 5) to the imaginary world the children had created in their writing, whereas Charlotte eventually freed herself from its stunting influence; Anne, supposedly the least imaginative of the four, gradually grew weary of the fiction, while Emily remained fiercely and self-destructively loyal to it. Ratchford's book was important for later biographical studies, including Laura Hinkley's *The Brontës: Charlotte and Emily* (1945) and Charlotte Maurat's *The Brontës' Secret* (1969), because it provided evidence about the inner experience of the young Brontës and contributed to the understanding of their developments as writers. The conclusions Ratchford draws about the influence of the juvenile writing experience on each of the Brontës respectively are, of course, open to debate; and the record of the Brontës' collaborative writing was considerably enlarged and re-examined in the more authoritative *The Early Writings of Charlotte Brontë* (1983) by Christine Alexander. Such works pointed to a rich source of primary material to be examined by future biographers intrepid enough to undertake such a project.

Impelled in part by such studies of the Brontë children's early writing, biographical studies published after 1941 have often focused on the family unit, or on the four siblings or the three sisters. The most important of these family biographies is Juliet Barker's massive book *The Brontës*, published in 1994. Formerly the curator of the BPM, Barker conducted extensive research in preparing to write this biography, which also draws on new findings by a number of Brontë scholars. She provides a much fuller record of Revd Patrick Brontë's activities than previous scholars, and as a result, he emerges as an interesting, and often admirable figure in his own right. Barker also presents much new information about *Haworth and its environs during the time of the Brontës, contributing substantially to our understanding of the cultural, religious, social, and political contexts in which they grew to maturity. Apart from Daphne du Maurier (*The Infernal World of Branwell Brontë*, 1960), she is the first biographer to challenge the generally dismissive attitude toward Branwell taken by most writers since the publication of Elizabeth *Gaskell's *Life of Charlotte Brontë*. Thoroughly documented, Barker's book is an essential reference work for any student of the Brontës, despite her tendency to denigrate Charlotte. Earlier important biographical studies of the Brontë family include Rebecca Fraser's *Charlotte Brontë* (1988) (simultaneously released in the United States as *The Brontës*), Tom Winnifrith's *The Brontës and their Background* (1973), Phyllis Bentley's *The Brontës* (1948), and *The Four Brontës* (1949) by Lawrence and E. M. Hanson.

Of the many biographies devoted to individual members of the Brontë family since 1940, most have been on Charlotte and Emily. Charlotte's life has been an especially fertile area of research for a variety of reasons: she lived longer than her siblings, she interacted more with important figures beyond Haworth, and she left more primary evidence in the way of *letters and other written documents. The aim of Margaret Lane's *The Brontë Story* (1953) is to show 'the general reader' (p. ix) how evidence discovered since the publication of Gaskell's biography requires a revised view of Charlotte, particularly with respect to her relationship with M. Constantin *Heger. Two years later, Margaret Crompton's *Passionate Search* (1955) offered a view of Charlotte similar to Gaskell's, but depicted both Mr Brontë and the children's aunt, Elizabeth *Branwell, more sympathetically than many previous biographies. Considerably more influential than Lane and Crompton's books is Winifred Gérin's *Charlotte Brontë: The Evolution of Genius* (1967), which set a high standard for subsequent biographers with respect to specificity and comprehensiveness. For good reasons, Gérin's was long considered the definitive account of Charlotte's life, and she is still known as one of the most important Brontë biographers, having published separate lives for Anne (1959), Branwell (1961), Emily (1971), and Elizabeth Gaskell (1976) as well. Like Irene Willis before her (see BIOGRAPHIES TO 1940), Gérin actually lived in Haworth and was able to write with apparent authority about people and places in *Yorkshire. She also had unrestricted access to the increasingly good collection of Brontë artefacts housed locally in the BPM (for example, samplers stitched by the Brontë girls under their aunt's direction). Gérin makes use of correspondence and other manuscript materials, such as the juvenilia, that were gradually becoming more accessible to scholars, and she approaches her study of the eldest Brontë already well informed about other members of the family. In spite of some errors and a tendency toward reductive biographical interpretation of the novels, Gérin's book on Charlotte remains one of the pre-eminent Brontë biographies.

Other influential accounts of Charlotte's life followed Gérin's at a steady pace during the seventies and eighties, stimulated in part by the influence of feminism during this time. In *Unquiet Soul* (1975), Margot Peters begins with the claim that Charlotte's 'life and art were . . . an eloquent protest against the cruel and frustrating limitations imposed upon women' and, taking for granted the findings of previous biographers, Peters shows how the known 'facts of [Charlotte's] life fall into a new pattern' when viewed from this perspective. Conceding that Charlotte was 'not officially a feminist', Peters contends that she was 'feministic in the deepest sense' because she defied convention in order to fulfil her creative potential (p. xv). Helene Moglen's *Charlotte Brontë: The Self Conceived* (1976) presents Charlotte's life as a struggle to free herself from a masochistic need to be dominated by male figures. Predictably, earlier depictions of Mr Brontë as a household ogre are resurrected by Moglen, who also accepts Ratchford's assertion that Branwell was the controlling author of the juvenile stories he and Charlotte wrote together. According to Moglen, Charlotte eventually (but temporarily) achieved artistic and personal independence from male dominance when she rejected her brother for acting out her own fantasies of self-annihilating romantic enthralment in his relations with Mrs Lydia *Robinson. Pauline Nestor's *Charlotte Brontë* (1987) is brief, readable, and mildly feminist in its presentation of Charlotte's life. Tom Winnifrith's *A New Life of Charlotte Brontë* (1988) presents new evidence—for example, he cites a few previously unpublished letters and a 'scrappy and unsatisfactory' diary kept by Ellen *Nussey in 1844 (p. 62)—and offers a judicious account of Charlotte's life. Winnifrith's attention to the evidence leads him to important insights, including his observation that Emily was probably more actively involved in the effort to publish her poems than has generally been thought. In *Charlotte Brontë: A Passionate Life* (1994), Lyndall Gordon writes persuasively about Charlotte's connections with Heger and George *Smith, explaining her relations with them as ones experienced, first and foremost, through writing (in school exercises for Heger, novel manuscripts for Smith, and letters to both). In this way, Gordon convincingly interprets the endlessly rehearsed facts of Charlotte's romantic attraction to Heger and Smith within the context of the 'passionate life' she lived as a writer. Biographical work on two of Charlotte's closest friends—Joan Stevens's edition of Mary *Taylor's letters (*Mary Taylor*, 1972) and Barbara Whitehead's study of Ellen Nussey's relationship with Charlotte (*Charlotte Brontë and her 'dearest Nell'*, 1993)— have further enriched our understanding of Charlotte's experience and personality.

Although many books have been written on Emily Brontë since 1940, few can be called biographies in the usual sense of the word. For example, Muriel Spark's extended essay in *Emily Brontë: Her Life and Work* (1953), co-authored with Derek Stanford, is a meditation on Emily's personality rather than a history of her life. Like Simpson before her, Spark concludes from the little evidence available that Emily was a relatively normal and happy girl: unusual only in her strong commitment to her writing, Emily was the least neurotic of the three sisters, in Spark's view. Less motivated by 'a desire to get on in the world' than Charlotte, Branwell, or Anne, Emily wilfully chose a reclusive life at Haworth because it allowed her to dedicate herself fully to her work (pp. 45–6). Spark sees the Belgian sojourn as a crucial experience in Emily's life because Heger forced her to think through the implications of her developing philosophy of life, a romantically self-destructive ideal which she explored brilliantly in her one novel and performed tragically in the final days of her life. Most biographers after Spark have agreed that Emily was initially a fairly normal child, and they point out that her reputation as a 'sphinx' developed after her death out of an abundance of speculation and a dearth of hard evidence. That Emily was at least peculiar by the time of her death is conceded by all biographers, though when, why, and to what degree she became so is debated. In an attempt to demystify Emily's life and death, John Hewish's *Emily Brontë: A Critical and Biographical Study* (1969) offers intelligent readings of her poetry in relation to her experience. Hewish also provides more information about Emily's professional activities and draws attention to the way in which her Belgian school exercises demonstrate the toughness of a mind that was no less intellectual and ethical for being mystical and poetical (see DEVOIRS). Gérin's biography (1971) takes a quite different view of Emily's decline, which she attributes to the combined effect of Branwell's self-destructive behaviour, beginning in 1845, and Emily's revulsion at the publication of her own writing in 1846 and 1847, a claim that Robert Barnard's recent biography (2000) dismisses as 'nonsense' (*Emily Brontë*, p. 73). Richard Benvenuto's succinct account of Emily's life (1982) also claims that she ceased writing after completing *Wuthering Heights*, though he sees this withdrawal as consistent with her 'strength and self-acceptance' (p. 14) rather than as a symptom of emotional weakness or mental instability. Without taking an explicitly Freudian approach, Stevie Davies and Edward Chitham both locate the origin of Emily's emotional troubles much earlier, in traumatic childhood experience. Davies's *Emily Brontë: The Artist as a Free-Woman* (1983) echoes Virginia Moore's thesis that Emily felt more orphaned than any of the other Brontë children after their mother's death, which she identifies as the crucial experience of Emily's life.

Chitham's book *A Life of Emily Brontë* (1987) makes responsible use of the limited evidence to trace a series of traumatic events that happened to Emily when she was 6 years old: first, she was nearly killed in a freak bog explosion on the moor; then, within a month's time, she was sent to school at *Cowan Bridge, where she was pampered as the youngest child at the same time that she was forced to witness the abusive treatment of her two eldest sisters, who died shortly thereafter, just as her mother had died three years previously. Out of these early encounters with death and near-death, according to Chitham, Emily developed a sense of guilt and an obsession with dying that are evident in her writing and in her response to her final illness. Katherine Frank's 1990 biography, *A Chainless Soul*, presents Emily as 'a woman who lived bravely, consistently and purely, with unassailable integrity' (p. 2) while suffering from anorexia nervosa. A subsequent writer, Steve Vine, has enlarged Frank's thesis to argue that Emily's life was a series of willed 'retreats' and 'withdrawals' in which she used hunger, solitude, and silence as 'a gesture of resistance' and self-empowerment (*Emily Brontë* (1998), 2). Vine recounts a darker, more tragic life for Emily than many previous biographers, though his emphasis on her rebellion against convention echoes Peters's more triumphant story of Charlotte's life.

While relatively few 20th-century biographers have chosen to study Anne, recent work on her suggests that she may be emerging as the most interesting and positively portrayed of the four Brontës. Earlier biographies tended to echo Charlotte's somewhat maudlin description of Anne's character as well as her patronizing attitude toward the youngest Brontë's literary achievement. Estelle Trust's *Anne Brontë* (1954), published by The Story Book Press, is a readable narrative apparently designed for younger readers, but it is inaccurate, badly out of date, and cannot be taken as serious scholarship. The first important biography of Anne, by Winifred Gérin (1959), singles out Elizabeth Branwell as the most influential person in Anne's early experience and blames her for instilling in the child an overpowering sense of guilt that plagued her for the rest of her life. Gérin correctly observes that the Methodist controversy over redemption was a troubling issue for Anne, but, as Elizabeth Langland later pointed out, placing responsibility for Anne's religious anxiety solely on Aunt Branwell doesn't accord with the older woman's affiliation with the branch of *Methodism that took the more hopeful view of salvation, rather than the gloomy Calvinistic position that Anne found so disturbing. Like all Gérin's biographies of the Brontës, her account of Anne's life is enriched by its specificity and local colour but weakened by an assumption that the author's work should be interpreted as quite directly autobiographical. In a book published the same year, Ada Harrison makes judicious use of Anne's writing and draws intelligently on Charlotte's memoir of Anne, whom she interprets in relation to her two older sisters. Not surprisingly, Anne is presented as less powerful than Emily or Charlotte, but she also appears to be the most likeable of the four siblings in Harrison's account. Harrison argues that Anne was not, in fact, harmed by her aunt's religious teachings in childhood and attributes her melancholy to events that occurred later. First, like Gérin, Harrison accepts the theory that Anne was in love with Revd William *Weightman, one of Mr Brontë's curates, and presents his early death as one of the great griefs of Anne's short life. Second, she emphasizes Anne's difficulties as a governess, particularly in the Robinsons' home at *Thorp Green Hall, where Branwell's misconduct added greatly to his sister's anxiety and unhappiness. But in addition to these trying experiences,

Harrison also draws attention to Anne's success as a publishing writer and argues that all of the Brontë sisters, Anne not the least among them, were hopefully ambitious authors. Thirty years after Harrison's study, Elizabeth Langland further developed this more inspiring view of Anne in her brief biography, *Anne Brontë: The Other One* (1989). Langland argues that the death of Mrs Brontë when Anne was a toddler not only produced enduring feelings of guilt in the child but also gave her a sense of responsibility and a capacity for independence that set her apart from, and arguably above, the rest of her siblings. Langland notes that Anne's experiences were different from those of her sisters, both in childhood (she did not go to school at Cowan Bridge, for example, but remained safely at home with Branwell in the care of her aunt and father) and in maturity (she remained employed as a governess and lived away from home longer than either Emily or Charlotte). The view of Anne that emerges in Langland's book is that of a determined if reserved young woman, physically delicate but psychologically strong, sceptical of the romantic posturing exhibited by her older siblings and free of the emotional dependencies that hobbled Branwell in particular. Edward Chitham's *A Life of Anne Brontë* (1991) acknowledges its debt to Langland in a brief but useful overview of Brontë biographies and related developments in Brontë scholarship from Gaskell on. As in his other biographies of the Brontës, Chitham dutifully considers conflicting evidence about Anne's experiences. Maria Frawley's 1996 Twayne English Authors volume begins with a biographical chapter that offers interesting discussions of Anne's interests in art, music, and reading. Like other books in this series, Frawley's presents a reading of Anne's experience and personality that sets the stage for later chapters in which the works are interpreted according to an identified preoccupation; in this case, the idea of isolation. Arguing that Anne 'embraced and nurtured privacy' (p. 21), Frawley's biography is more tragically romantic than either Langland's or Chitham's.

Although there has been notable scholarly work published on Branwell's writing in recent years, his life has been largely neglected. Daphne du Maurier's *The Infernal World of Branwell Brontë* (1960) assesses Branwell's development much as Ratchford had done in 1941, saying that the cause of his great unhappiness was his inability to distinguish between reality and fantasy. The end result of her announced aim—to reinstate Branwell within his proper place in the Brontë family—is that he is fixed all the more firmly in the position of black sheep. Far less talented than his sisters, according to du Maurier, Branwell had exhausted his literary invention by the time he was 21. Gérin (1961) accepts Gaskell's claim that Branwell was seduced by Lydia Robinson, whereas du Maurier asserts that the supposed liaison between Branwell and his employer's wife was his own fabrication from start to finish. Joan Rees's 1986 publication, *Profligate Son: Branwell Brontë and his Sisters*, is more speculative than scholarly. Recent work on Branwell's life includes reliable sources not obviously biographical in nature, such as the introductions in Victor Neufeldt's editions of Branwell's writings and Jane Sellars's essay in Alexander & Sellars (pp. 65–99). These essays, combined with Neufeldt's article on 'The Writings of Patrick Branwell Brontë' (*BST* (1999), 24. 2. 146–60) and Barker's biography, offer a new and more inspiring view of Branwell as a moderately successful young regional author with ambition and considerable talent.

Of the many illustrated books on the Brontës, three of the best biographical introductions are *The Brontës at Haworth* (1992) by Juliet Gardiner, *The Brontës:*

An Illustrated Biography (1975) by Brian Wilks, and *The Brontës and their World* (1969) by Phyllis Bentley, though Wilks and Bentley both reproduce a portrait of Johanna Sang as that of 'Aunt Branwell' (see *BST* (1987), 19. 3. 126–7), together with Emily's painting of Flossy misattributed to Charlotte and a John Martin lithograph thought for many years to be Charlotte's painting of the Bay of Glass Town (Alexander & Sellars, pp. 388 and 21). A comprehensive biography of Mr Brontë is given in *A Man of Sorrow* (1965) by John Lock and Canon W. T. Dixon. The Brontës' Irish ancestry is discussed in John Cannon's *The Road to Haworth* (1980) and Edward Chitham's *The Brontës' Irish Background* (1986).   CB

Barker.

Barnard, Robert, *Emily Brontë* (2000).

Gordon, Lyndall, *Charlotte Brontë: A Passionate Life* (1995).

Langland, Elizabeth, *Anne Brontë: The Other One* (1989).

Neufeldt, Victor A., 'The Writing of Patrick Branwell Brontë', *BST* (1999), 24. 2. 146–60.

family mills, the other being at Brookroyd. Turnpike roads, constructed in the 1820s, formed important lines of communication, especially with *Leeds, *Huddersfield, and their cloth halls, but most of the area was pleasantly rural, with clear streams and light woodland. *Oakwell Hall, standing in its own spacious grounds in the northern part of the parish, was Charlotte's model for Fieldhead in *Shirley*. Batley, to the south, was more crowded and industrialized. In 1840 Ellen's sister Ann owned nine cottages and a more substantial house in Birstall, and her brother John owned Rydings and thirteen other properties. John lived in London, but allowed his mother-in-law, Mrs Mary Walker, and her unmarried daughters to live in Rydings. Through Ellen Charlotte came to know many 'Birstallians', notably the gentle and scholarly Revd William Margetson *Heald Jun. and his wife and sister. Like the 'Gomersalians', the people of Birstall were quick to recognize the originals of characters in *Shirley*, and in January 1850 Mr Heald, in a letter to Ellen, claimed that since he was generally supposed to be the 'black, bilious', dismal, and sometimes dialect-speaking Cyril Hall, he should be '*let into the secret of the company*' he had got into. He and his family had already recognized the *Yorke family, Robert Gérard *Moore, and Revd Matthewson *Helstone, and his wife suspected that 'Cecilia Crowther & Miss Johnson' were the two old maids in chapter 10 (Smith *Letters*, 2. 325).

birthday papers. See DIARY PAPERS.

Black Bull, inn near the top of Haworth Main Street, next to the church. In 1857 Thomas Akroyd heard that William Grimshaw, incumbent of Haworth 1742–63, 'would sometimes set his choir to sing the 119th Psalm, and then dash into the "Bull"' to whip 'unfortunate boosers' into the church.

A sturdy, dark gritstone building, with a barn, stables, and brewhouse in the early 19th century, it accommodated the meetings of the Three Graces Masonic Lodge until 1833. Branwell Brontë, who frequented it, was popular with customers and the innkeepers Abraham Wilkinson (1822–41) and Enoch Thomas (1841–8). By 1851 the landlord was William Sugden.

Blackwood's Edinburgh Magazine. Established by William Blackwood in 1817 as a rival to the Liberal *Edinburgh Review*, *Blackwood's Magazine* also offered readers an alternative to the Conservative *Quarterly Review*. Like the *Quarterly*, *Blackwood's* political leanings were Tory, but as a monthly miscellany it offered more variety in its materials, a livelier tone, and reading entertainment at more frequent intervals. Having produced six rather dull issues, the first editors were dismissed by Blackwood, who assumed editorial control and recruited John Gibson *Lockhart, John *Wilson, and James *Hogg as primary contributors. Together these three writers gave 'Maga', as it was known, its distinctive character, which the Brontë family and many other readers found so appealing. One of the magazine's first productions, 'The Chaldee Manuscript' (supposedly a translation of a recently discovered ancient text) was a hilarious spoof which satirized many contemporary public figures, some to the point of libel. Blackwood was forced to pay damages, but as a result of his writers' wicked wit, circulation figures rose and overnight his magazine became a force to be reckoned with in the literary world. In the same year Lockhart began his attack 'On the Cockney School of Poetry', now infamous for its harsh reviews of Keats in particular; scurrilous but brilliantly satirical, this series added to

(*cont. on page 47*)

INTEREST in lives of the Brontës began early, as reviewers speculated about the true identities of the three pseudonymous authors 'Currer, Ellis, and Acton Bell'. By 1850, after the deaths of Emily and Anne, rumours about 'the Bells' were so plentiful that Charlotte felt obliged to set the record straight in a *'Biographical Notice' attached to a new edition of *Wuthering Heights* and *Agnes Grey*. Charlotte's notice, along with short prefaces to her sisters' works, presented an enduring though hardly objective view of the two youngest Brontës. Eager to defend her sisters against the charge of 'coarseness' and to preserve a positive image of them in the public memory, Charlotte depicted Emily as an unsophisticated 'nursling of the moors' whose writings were romantically inspired by the rugged landscape and rustic inhabitants of her native *Yorkshire. Anne was described as a pallid, 'blameless' figure: sensitive, timid, and 'slightly morbid', she was guided by a principled adherence to duty which, according to Charlotte, darkened her life and sometimes marred her writing. Though Charlotte says little about herself in this note, biographers have frequently made use of her comments about Emily and Anne to reconstruct her own personality and to explain the dynamics of the three sisters' relationships. This first biographical commentary on the Brontës, written by the last remaining sibling, has consequently had considerable influence on our understanding of their lives and characters.

When Charlotte died in February 1855, a number of gossipy, inaccurate obituary pieces appeared in the periodical press. Goaded into action by Ellen *Nussey, Revd Patrick Brontë asked Charlotte's friend and fellow novelist Elizabeth *Gaskell to write a reliable account of his daughter's life. In a number of respects, his choice of biographer could not have been better. More than anyone else outside the Brontës' narrow circle of family and friends, Gaskell had managed to thaw Charlotte's habitual reserve with strangers, and the two women had enjoyed a warm if not intimate relationship. Equally important, Gaskell was an established author whose popularity ensured that the biography would be widely read. She was eager to undertake the commission, and her publisher, George *Smith, enthusiastically supported the project, as he had been the publisher of Charlotte's novels too. With the promise of assistance from Mr Brontë and Charlotte's widower, Revd A. B. *Nicholls, Gaskell soon began collecting materials for what would become one of the most famous biographies of the 19th century. She visited *Haworth, interviewed and corresponded with people who had known Charlotte, examined hundreds of letters that Ellen Nussey made available (in expurgated form), and looked through Charlotte's voluminous juvenile manuscripts. She travelled to *Brussels to visit the Pensionnat *Heger, where Charlotte and Emily attended school in the early 1840s, though in writing her book she suppressed the most interesting information gained there: knowledge of Charlotte's warm regard for her teacher, M. Constantin *Heger, a married man and father of five children.

Gaskell's *The Life of Charlotte Brontë* was published in March 1857, a second, slightly revised, edition being published in April, but the threat of legal proceedings forced Smith to withdraw the book from the market almost immediately. First, Mrs Lydia *Robinson, wife of Branwell's employer when he was a tutor in the Robinsons' home, objected to Gaskell's depiction of her as a seducer who contributed to the young man's ruin. Then the family of Revd W. Carus *Wilson protested against Gaskell's depiction of *Cowan Bridge, the charitable institution run by Wilson and on which Charlotte had modelled *Lowood School in *Jane Eyre*. Faced with two potential libel suits, Gaskell was compelled to print a retraction and revise her work for republication. In preparing the third edition of the *Life*, she not only reworked the two objectionable parts of her book, but also excised some mistakes that Mr Brontë had pointed out and added new material she had recently received from Mary *Taylor, Harriet *Martineau, and others. While some have thought the revised version published in August 1857 less interesting for its deletions, the additions provide a different kind of interest that arguably strengthens the work.

Considered a masterpiece of biography, Gaskell's *Life* continues to be an important source of information for the student of the Brontës' lives and writings, though it should be read along with more recent accounts that include material she suppressed or of which she was unaware. Her characterization of Mr Brontë is overdrawn, and her information regarding his early life and later activities in Haworth is minimal. Her account of Branwell's decline is inadequate and misleading; and, most obviously, her refusal to include the Heger material results in a serious omission. To understand why Gaskell concealed what she had learned in Brussels—and, more generally, to understand the strengths and limitations of the *Life*—one must know that, even before Mr Brontë had contacted her, Gaskell had been determined to save Charlotte from her detractors. Stung by the public perception of 'Jane Eyre' as a coarse and fiery malcontent, she wanted to 'make the world . . . honour the woman as much as they have admired the writer' (Chapple & Pollard *Gaskell Letters*, p. 345). For that reason, Gaskell deliberately emphasized the tragedies in Charlotte's family life in order to present her friend as a figure of selfless feminine fortitude and noble suffering. In doing so, however, she neglected those aspects of Charlotte's experience which called out her capacities for ambition, humour, and liveliness—most notably, her experience as an aspiring author and a successful literary professional. Gaskell's desire to emphasize 'the woman' over 'the writer' was reinforced by the officious over-involvement of Ellen Nussey, who knew virtually nothing about Charlotte's literary and professional interests and was primarily interested in defending her friend's reputation against charges of immorality and coarseness. Gaskell's portraits of Emily and Anne closely follow Charlotte's own account of them in the 'Biographical Notice', and her view of Branwell is merely that of an unfortunate youth led astray. The result is a vividly evoked and moving narrative which contains much information but is excessively dark, as more than one of Gaskell's contemporaries recognized.

Ellen Nussey's 'Reminiscences of Charlotte Brontë', published in *Scribner's Magazine* (May 1871), fills out the picture of Charlotte's schooldays and adds some detail to Gaskell's depiction of family life at *Haworth Parsonage. Ellen's aim in publishing the memoir was to defend her friend against the charge of irreligion, and the image she paints of Charlotte is consequently quite similar to that depicted in Gaskell's *Life*. George Smith, apparently disappointed that Ellen had given her 'Reminiscences' to another publisher, wrote his own essay on 'The Brontës' for *Cornhill Magazine* (July 1873). Smith relies almost exclusively on Gaskell's biography and reinforces her view of the Brontës' lives. T. W. *Reid was the first biographer to offer a corrective to Gaskell's *Life*. Critical of Gaskell's depiction of the Brontës' childhood as unrelievedly gloomy, he contends that Charlotte was, in fact, a 'happy and high spirited girl' (Reid, *Charlotte Brontë: A Monograph* (1877), 3) at least up until her departure for Brussels in

1842. Because he was able to draw on Charlotte's letters to Ellen Nussey from as early as 1832, Reid sensed some of the cheerful energy that enlivened the Parsonage in the 1830s, when the children were often happily absorbed in their early writing. Originally published in *Macmillan's Magazine* (1876), Reid's study was republished as a monograph in 1877 and was immediately followed by Swinburne's fulsome *A Note on Charlotte Brontë* (1877) and then by a sharply critical response from Leslie Stephen in the *Cornhill Magazine* (Dec. 1877). Bio-critical rather than biographical, the pieces by Smith, Swinburne, and Stephen depend on the research and commentary of previous biographers and are typical of the kind of writing that began to dominate Brontë studies by the 1870s: from that point on biography and criticism on the Brontës seem almost inseparable (see CRITICISM 1860–1940).

The articles by Smith and Stephen also anticipate another trend in Brontë biography: a tendency to focus on Charlotte's life (since evidence in the form of letters and other documents was scarce for the other three siblings) but to depict Emily as the true genius in the family. Peter Bayne's *Two Great Englishwomen* (1881) asserts that Emily was a better writer than her older sister, whom he nevertheless calls 'the head of this unique and most interesting Yorkshire school of literature' (p. 332). Bayne's somewhat confusing assessment of Emily and Charlotte's respective merits results in large part from his view of Charlotte as the more competent sister: neither of the younger sisters, he suggests, would have been capable of sustained literary careers, Anne being limited by her excessive reserve and Emily by the fact that, in *Wuthering Heights*, her genius had miraculously already expressed itself in its full maturity. More powerful than Anne and less imaginative than Emily, only Charlotte showed potential for professional development as a novelist, according to Bayne.

The overwhelming majority of biographical studies published on the Brontës over the next 60 years, from the 1880s to 1940, are either about Charlotte or focus on her as the dominant figure in the family. Augustine *Birrell's 1887 biography of Charlotte paints a somewhat more appreciative portrait of their father, whom he credits for positively influencing their education, and provides new information about Mr Brontë's life prior to meeting his future wife, Maria Branwell. Birrell also contends, like Bayne and Reid before him, that the Brontës' lives could not have been as uniformly grim as Gaskell had claimed. For Charlotte, he says, authorship was a source of hope and happiness. The 1890s saw the founding of the *Brontë Society, which continues to foster public as well as scholarly interest in the Brontës' lives today, and the publication of the seven-volume Haworth edition of Charlotte, Emily, and Anne's works (1899–1900), with introductions by Mrs Humphry *Ward and additional documents such as Charlotte's letters to George Smith. Having overseen the publication of the Haworth edition, Smith published an article on 'Charlotte Brontë' in *Cornhill Magazine* (Dec. 1900), drawing on his own correspondence with Charlotte, on Gaskell's biography, and on letters regarding Charlotte from various contemporary authors such as William Makepeace *Thackeray and his daughter Anne *Thackeray.

Important biographical material published on the Brontës between 1890 and 1941 is to be found in C. K. *Shorter's two books—*Charlotte Brontë and her Circle* (1896) and *The Brontës: The Life and Letters* (1908)—in Mrs Ellis H. (Esther Alice) *Chadwick's *In the Footsteps of the Brontës* (1895), and in the Shakespeare Head edition of the letters, ed. T. J. *Wise and J. A. *Symington (1932). Though Shorter's work is not without its errors, viewed amid the welter of opinion, gossip, anecdotal evidence, and partial truths that had characterized much work on the Brontës since the publication of Gaskell's *Life*, his first volume is a remarkable achievement. Given access to 370 of Charlotte's letters to Ellen Nussey, Shorter travelled to Ireland, where Mr Nicholls gave him all manner of papers: Charlotte's letters to Haworth from Brussels, Maria Branwell's love letters to Mr Brontë, all Charlotte's juvenile manuscripts and some of Branwell's, Emily and Anne's *Diary Papers, and more. Shorter was also able to obtain the use of Charlotte's letters to Mary Taylor, W. S. *Williams, James *Taylor, Laetitia Wheelwright (see WHEELWRIGHT FAMILY), and others. He consulted parish records and transcribed baptismal accounts for the Brontë children; he studied Pigot's *Directory* of Yorkshire to learn more about Haworth; and he queried Constantin Heger's son, who assured him (mistakenly, as it turned out) that no letters from Charlotte to his father were extant. Simply put, Shorter did his research thoroughly and offered an informed, reasonably objective account of the Brontës' lives. In 1905, he supplemented the information from the 1896 book, which he rightly described as 'a bundle of correspondence' rather than a real biography (Shorter *Circle*, p. 500), and recast it in narrative form as *Charlotte Brontë and her Sisters* for Scribner's Literary Lives series; subsequently he reprinted *Charlotte Brontë and her Circle*, combined with new material, in a two-volume edition of the *Life and Letters*. Mrs Ellis H. (Esther Alice) Chadwick, one of Elizabeth Gaskell's early biographers, presented a comprehensive account of the Brontës' lives and offered new material on Emily's experience as a teacher at *Law Hill, Halifax, in her book *In the Footsteps of the Brontës* (1914). After Shorter's death, Wise and Symington gained permission to incorporate the bulk of Shorter's two-volume work into their own four-volume edition of *The Brontës: Their Lives, Friendships, and Correspondence* (1932), which also reprints material from numerous other published sources, including several previous biographies. Wise and Symington's volumes have been an extremely important biographical resource for Brontë studies, but because of their cut-and-paste method of compilation and editing, they contain many omissions and inaccuracies.

E. F. Benson's *Charlotte Brontë* (1932) was the first biography to offer a frankly negative interpretation of the eldest Brontë. Benson was related to the *Sidgwick family, for whom Charlotte had worked as a governess in 1839, and he was anxious to redress the injury done to his family in Gaskell's *Life*, where they are depicted as insensitive, obtuse, and supercilious. Charlotte emerges in Benson's book as abnormally shy, irritable and unreasonable. Countering the long-standing romantic view of Charlotte, Benson suggests that she was not only excessively sensitive but also self-righteous, impossible to please and quick to take offence. Though controversial, Benson's critical portrait of Charlotte gained some currency, in part because there is a bit of truth in it and in part because trends in literary criticism at the time were causing a devaluation of Charlotte's literary reputation in relation to Emily's. Nearly always inseparable, critical and biographical reassessments of the Brontës worked hand in hand in the 1930s to accelerate the decline in Charlotte's status begun in the late 1800s.

Publication of Charlotte's letters to Heger in *The Times* in 1913 also undercut the idealized view of Charlotte that had been typical of Brontë biographies since the appearance of Gaskell's *Life*. While the discovery of the letters did not significantly change some biographers' understanding of Charlotte's personality, in the minds of many readers they provided clear evidence of a rather pathetic susceptibility to romantic enthralment. Frederika Macdonald, who had seen the letters when she visited Brussels and vaguely hinted at what she knew in 1894, felt free to tell the full *Secret of Charlotte Brontë* in 1914, and the history of the letters themselves was recounted by M. H. Spielmann in 1919 (*The Inner History of the Brontë–Heger Letters*).

As critical estimates of Emily's writing rose, several biographers turned their attention to the Brontë whom Shorter called 'the sphinx of our modern literature' (Shorter *Circle*, p. 144). Because she left so little in the way of direct evidence (three letters, a few Diary Papers, an account book, some school exercises), Emily's biographers have been forced to rely on the memoirs of people who knew her and on the indirect evidence of her writing. As a result, biographical studies of Emily tend to interpret her character more than they recount the few known facts of her rather uneventful life. The first biography of Emily, written in 1883 by A. M. F. *Robinson, added virtually no new information, but her passionately dark rendering of life at Haworth Parsonage left its mark on popular perceptions of the entire family. Robinson exaggerates Gaskell's already overdrawn depiction of Mr Brontë as a domestic tyrant and presents Branwell as vile and pathetic. Emily herself emerges as a kind of romantic genius-saint, loyal to her undeserving brother and elevated above all others by virtue of her spiritual strength and imaginative insight. Biographies by Romer Wilson (*All Alone: The Life and Private History of Emily Jane Brontë*, 1928) and Virginia Moore (*The Life and Eager Death of Emily Brontë: A Biography*, 1936) treat her poems and novel as autobiographical; arguing that Emily felt herself to be a lonely outcast like *Heathcliff. Moore contends that Emily's death was 'a virtual suicide' (p. 355). In contrast, Charles Simpson (1929) contends that the actual hard evidence, though scant, shows that Emily was a happy child who did not become the tragical being we know her as until the last three years of her life.

The dearth of direct evidence similarly hampered biographical research on Anne, who, moreover, had attracted less attention because her writing was less valued and because she herself was seen as a less intriguing figure than the mysterious Emily. The only study of Anne published before 1954 is William T. Hale's monograph, 'Anne Brontë: Her Life and Writings' (*Indiana University Studies*, 16 (1929), 3–44), which relies heavily on Gaskell's *Life* and Shorter's *Circle*. Although he offers no new evidence, Hale paints Anne in a more positive light than previous biographers, admiring the strength of her will in matters of duty and pointing out that her gentle pliability in other respects made her the most amiable of the four siblings. However, few readers today will be able to appreciate Hale's conclusion that Anne wrote only because she could not fulfil her 'true' vocation, that of wife and mother.

Robinson's casting of Emily as a romantic heroine is matched by her presentation of Branwell as the villain of the family, an interpretation made possible by the scarcity of facts about Branwell and prompted by two publications that attempted to defend him: a piece by George Searle Phillips in the *Mirror* (1872) and a chapter from F. H. *Grundy's *Pictures from the Past* (1879). The fact that Phillips and Grundy knew Branwell—as other biographers, from Gaskell on, had not—gave their memoirs some currency, though the wilder claims, such as Grundy's insistence that Branwell was the true author of *Wuthering Heights*, have always been difficult to take seriously. A longer and more level-headed account of Branwell was presented in Francis A. *Leyland's *The Brontë Family* (1886). Because Leyland's brother, Joseph Bentley, was Branwell's friend and a professional sculptor, the biography contains more information about contemporary artistic and literary influences on Branwell and provides a more informed analysis of Branwell's attraction to *pugilism, opium, and alcohol. Alice Law's book *Patrick Branwell Brontë* (1923) unfortunately revives Grundy's theory that Branwell wrote *Wuthering Heights* and relies entirely on Leyland and Gaskell in recounting his life.

Other works of biographical interest that appeared prior to 1940 include William Wright's unreliable *The Brontës in Ireland* (1893), Angus Mackay's *The Brontës: Fact and Fiction* (1897), May Sinclair's *The Three Brontës* (1927), Ernest Dimnet's *The Brontë Sisters* (1927), Irene Willis's *The Brontës* (1933), and E. M. Delafield's *The Brontës: Their Lives as Recorded by their Contemporaries* (1935).   CB

Blackwood's reputation as an entertaining and provocative periodical. In 1819, William Maginn began contributing as *Blackwood's* 'Irish correspondent' and officially joined the writing staff in 1821. He contributed heavily to one of the magazine's most popular series, the 'Noctes Ambrosianae', before leaving for London in 1830, where he helped establish *Fraser's Magazine*, also read by the Brontës. Collaboratively written in its early years, the 'Noctes' was a series of fictitious conversations between literary figures, some imaginary and some real, who supposedly met for bibulous dinners at Ambrose's tavern, an actual inn located near Blackwood's office in *Edinburgh. Some characters in these conversations are pseudonymous figures ('Ensign Morgan O'Doherty' is really Maginn; John Wilson appears as the crusty *Blackwood's* editor 'Christopher North' (see WILSON, JOHN); and James Hogg keeps his well-known public persona 'the Ettrick Shepherd'). But actual authors such as Lord *Byron and Thomas *De Quincey, in addition to wholly fictitious ones, are also made to participate. Over food and abundant drink, these tippling literati discuss the news of the day, with particular attention to books and politics, thus providing *Blackwood's* readers with an opportunity to enter imaginatively into that literary life which so attracted the Brontë children and made *Blackwood's* such an important influence on their early writing.

The Brontës never subscribed to *Blackwood's Magazine*, as they did to *Fraser's*, but they borrowed copies from a 'Mr. Driver', as 12-year-old Charlotte recorded in her *'History of the Year' (1829), where she calls the magazine 'the most able periodical there is' (Alexander *EEW*, 1. 4). The children evidently had access to copies dating back as far as 1818, so they had full exposure to the magazine's early, most recklessly written issues. In the April 1818 issue, they would have seen an advertisement for their father's novella *The *Maid of Killarney* (published anonymously when Char-

lotte was barely 2); and in the 1822 issues they delightedly read and reread the first instalments of the 'Noctes Ambrosianae'. Like *Fraser's* and the provincial newspapers to which the Brontës subscribed, *Blackwood's* provided both material and a model for the children's early writing. Such periodicals were largely responsible for the lively if crude satirizing of each other that the siblings engaged in through pseudonymous personae, such as Charlotte's Charles Townshend (see WELLESLEY, LORD CHARLES ALBERT FLORIAN) and Branwell's Duke of *Northangerland; and they help to account for the juvenilia's pervasive representation of authorship as a career of high-spirited rivalry and aggressive competition. From *Blackwood's* pages the children also drew many of their characters, including the Tory Duke of *Wellington, whom 'Maga' revered, and the Arctic explorers Sir William Edward *Parry, Sir John *Ross, and Sir James Clark *Ross, whose expeditions had been recounted in issues from 1818, 1820, and 1821. Similarly, the landscapes for the juvenile stories were drawn largely from *Blackwood's*: the children set their imaginary kingdom of *Glass Town on the west coast of *Africa in the *Ashantee kingdom, as it was described in an 1819 *Blackwood's* review of the recently published book *Mission from Cape Coast Castle to Ashantee*.

The most obvious evidence of *Blackwood's* early influence on the Brontës is the series of miniature magazines Charlotte and Branwell collaboratively produced beginning in 1830. Modelled on its real-life counterpart, this periodical was first named *'Branwell's Blackwood's Magazine', and then became 'Blackwood's *Young Men's Magazine' when Charlotte took editorial control. Under both young editors, their magazine resembled the adult periodical and contained many of the same features and departments, including serialized fiction, short narratives, poetry, reviews, advertisements, personal notices, and a section called 'Conversations', based on the 'Noctes Ambrosianae'. The influence of both *Blackwood's* and *Fraser's* also helps to explain why Charlotte's and Branwell's early writings reveal a fascination with inebriated characters, particularly literary figures, since the trope of brilliantly drunk literati was one of Maginn's prominently featured contributions to both magazines.

Branwell felt the spell of *Blackwood's* more powerfully and for a longer period of time than his sisters. As a boy, he was perhaps more responsive to the magazine's impressive treatment of classical writers, and his early works show that he was inspired by *Blackwood's* articles on literary criticism and theory. Like his sisters and countless other English readers, Branwell was also indebted to *Blackwood's* for his early appreciation of German Romantic literature. It is not surprising, then, that he turned first to *Blackwood's* in an effort to become a professional author. As a young man, he wrote repeatedly to Alexander Blackwood, who had succeeded his father as editor, requesting that he be considered for a position on the magazine's writing staff. Branwell's numerous applications to become a *Blackwood's* writer lay unanswered in the publisher's files until Margaret Oliphant discovered them in 1897 and included them in her *Annals of a Publishing House*. See also CONTEMPORARY WRITERS, BRONTËS' CONTACTS WITH, AND ATTITUDES TO.   CB

> Alexander, Christine, 'Readers and Writers: Blackwood's and the Brontës', *Gaskell Society Journal*, 8 (1994), 54–69.
> Bock, Carol, *Charlotte Brontë and the Storyteller's Audience* (1992).

'Blackwood's Young Men's Magazine'. See 'YOUNG MEN'S MAGAZINE'.

Blake Hall, near Mirfield church, Yorks., the scene of Anne Brontë's first experience as a governess, 8 April–?December 1839. An ancient hall on the same site had been rebuilt from c.1748 in a plain Georgian style. The wealthy Joshua Ingham (see INGHAM FAMILY) had moved there in 1824. Round the hall were 32 acres of parkland and a 12-acre home-farm, screened by trees from the surrounding lanes, but with a more open view towards Hopton woods and the River Calder. The hall was extended in 1845, sold in 1924, and eventually demolished in 1954, by which time the grounds had been sold for housebuilding. See WELLWOOD.

Blessington, Countess of (1789–1849), London society hostess, writer of 'silver-fork' novels dealing with the lives of the wealthy and fashionable, editor of *annuals, and friend of Lord *Byron. Her name was constantly before the public during the 1830s and 1840s, and her lifestyle and association with Byron appealed to the young Brontës as a model for their heroines in the *Glass Town and Angrian saga, in particular Lady Zenobia *Ellrington. Her irregular private life with her husband and the Count d'Orsay, and her friendship with Byron in Italy were well documented in the press. Even her portrait may have been copied by Charlotte from an engraving in one of the popular annuals (Alexander & Sellars, p. 217). In 1832 she published her 'Journal of Conversations with Lord Byron'. In 1834, she took over the editorship of *Heath's Book of Beauty* (until 1849), and from 1841 until her death she edited the *Keepsake*, both annuals familiar to the Brontës. Her literary contacts, maintained through lavish dinners to which she invited potential contributors, made the literary quality of her annuals superior to their rivals. Lady Blessington also regularly contributed verse and prose to other annuals of the time, living in later years (unknown to her friends and audience) a life of writing drudgery in order to support her social position.

> Sadleir, Michael, *Blessington-D'Orsay: A Masquerade* (1933).

Bloomfield family. Mr Bloomfield, a retired newly-rich tradesman, employs Agnes Grey as a governess, in *Agnes Grey*. He is between 30 and 40 years old, pale, unprepossessing, and peevish. He rudely accuses Agnes in his children's presence of not keeping 'Miss' and 'Master' Bloomfield in order. He is quarrelsome, threatens his children with violent punishments, and believes the accusations of his capricious and treacherous mother that Agnes neglects them. His wife is tall, thin, and black-haired, with cold grey eyes and a sallow complexion. Frigidly formal towards Agnes, she indulges her children, praising the 'noble' spirit of the eldest, Tom, and expecting Agnes to share her room with and act as nursery-maid to the 5-year-old Mary Ann. Agnes is not allowed to punish them herself; yet Mrs Bloomfield rebukes them mildly, believes their lies, blames Agnes for their deterioration, and condones Tom's cruelty. Despite her best efforts, Agnes is dismissed after half a year, allegedly for lack of firmness and care.

The 7-year-old Tom is a selfish, possessive bully who, encouraged by his parents and uncle, traps and tortures birds and other small creatures. He defies Agnes, and kicks her and his sisters. Though he has some ability, he sometimes has to be held down until he completes his tasks.

Mary Ann is tall and strong for her age, careless, indifferent to affection, slow to learn, disobedient, rude, and destructive; she craves notice, exploits her mother's indulgence, and is encouraged in her conceit by her uncle Robson. Her younger sister Fanny is mischievous, intractable, untruthful, and deceitful, given to spitting or bellowing when thwarted.

The Bloomfields collectively disabuse Agnes of her naïve belief that it must be charming to educate children, making 'Virtue practicable, Instruction desirable, and Religion lovely and comprehensible' (*Agnes Grey*, ch. 1). Anne's portrait of the Bloomfield family was probably influenced by her experiences as governess to the *Ingham family.

Blücher, General (1742–1819), Prussian general, field marshal, Prince of Wahlstadt in Silesia. He was instrumental in the defeat of *Napoleon Buonaparte and the overthrow of the First Empire in France. With the return of Napoleon, he took command of the Army of the Lower Rhine and, after a severe defeat and injury at Ligny (June 1815), he came to the assistance of the Duke of *Wellington and led the Pussian Army with decisive effect in the Battle of Waterloo, enabling the allies to re-enter Paris on 7 July. He features with Wellington during this occupation period in Charlotte Brontë's 'Journal of a Frenchman' (Alexander *EEW*, 1. 223).

Boarham, Mr, in *Tenant*. As his name suggests, he is a dreadfully dull interminable talker, who despite being over 40 is encouraged as a suitor of the 18-year-old Helen Lawrence by her aunt, Mrs *Maxwell. Helen prefers to spell his name 'Bore'em', and is grateful to Mr Arthur *Huntingdon for her rescue from his conversation and company. Unfortunately Mr Boarham throws Huntingdon's qualities into favourable relief.

Boaster, a military character '10 miles high', is Branwell Brontë's chief man in *Our Fellows' Play, taken from *Aesop's Fables* (1825 edn., trans. Samuel Croxall, DD). Boaster, the ruler of Lorraine, is a character in *'History of the Rebellion in My Fellows', where he defeats Charlotte's character Goodman.

Bobadill, General, (also Thomas *Beresford) one of the fictional Duke of Wellington's officers in the *Glass Town and Angrian saga. He is a dark, tall, ugly man with a particularly long chin; and is present at the officers' gatherings at *Bravey's Inn. Bobadill is based on the boasting, cowardly soldier Bobadilla, in Ben Jonson's play *Every Man in his Humour* (1598).

bodysnatching. The ghoulish activity of bodysnatchers or 'resurrectionists' is a prominent feature of the early Brontë juvenilia. It involves trade in newly buried corpses and their sale to surgeons for dissection. The practice was widely reported in journals like *Blackwood's Edinburgh Magazine*, where the Brontës read about the notorious *Burke and Hare, whose victims were smothered so that their bodies could be sold to the Edinburgh surgeon Dr Robert Knox. Branwell's devilish Glass Town character *Sdeath delights in bodysnatching, as do all the *'Rare Lads' of the *Glass Town and Angrian saga and Dr Hume *Badey. The plot of 'An *Interesting Passage' is based on bodysnatching, and the Earl of *Arundel is saved at the Battle of Velino through Sdeath's ghoulish activity (in *High Life in Verdopolis*). The activity is also carried on in the taverns of *Paris (in Frenchyland) (see DE CRACK, MON[SIEUR] EDOUARD).

Bolton Priory. The picturesque ruins of an Augustinian priory in Wharfedale, Yorks, founded in 1121, and dissolved in 1540. Part of the Gothic nave is used as the parish church for Bolton Abbey village. The younger Brontës visited it in *c*.August 1833. Ellen Nussey recalled that the shy Emily and Anne hardly spoke except to each other, but (no doubt like Charlotte) were 'drinking in pleasure', while Branwell was in 'ecstacies [*sic*]' (Smith *Letters*, 1. 124–5, 602–3). Charlotte made a drawing of 'Bolton Abbey, Wharfedale' (BPM; Alexander & Sellars, pp. 26, 52, 228–9).

Bonnell, Henry Houston (1859–1926), an important collector of Brontëana who bequeathed the greater part of his extensive collection to the trustees of the BPM. Bonnell graduated BA and MA from the University of Pennsylvania, and entered the New York publishing business of Dodd, Mead & Company. He was secretary of the Christian Literature Society of New York, a private man with a wide range of philanthropic and educational interests. He was the author of *Charlotte Brontë, George Eliot, Jane Austen: Studies in their Works* (1902), *Gloria: Twenty-Five Hymns* (with music by Sydney Thomson, 1903), and the words and hymns for *Via Crucis, The Way of the Cross, Cantata for Solo Voices, Chorus, and Organ* (1913). He visited England many times and his interest in collecting works of the Brontës began in the 1890s, and led to his purchase of material from the Nicholls sales of 1907 and 1914, from public auctions, London dealers, and private collectors such as T. J. *Wise. His chief interest was the Brontë sisters: 'The one aggravating feature of Brontë collecting is the mass of worthless dross one is obliged to accumulate for the sake of association, under Branwell's name' (25 Apr. 1922; BPM). He planned that 'Eventually the whole collection will go to the Brontë Museum, at Haworth' (interview with the Philadelphia *Public Ledger*, 1916), but after his death in 1926, at his home in Philadelphia, a substantial portion of his Brontë collection was bequeathed to his widow who later donated it to the Pierpont Morgan Library in New York. The larger

Charlotte Brontë, pencil drawing of Bolton Priory, c.May 1834, after Edward Finden's engraving of J. M. W. Turner's 'Bolton Abbey, Warfedale', that appeared in *The Literary Souvenir*, 1826. Exhibited by Charlotte Brontë at the Exhibition of the Royal Northern Society for the Encouragement of the Fine Arts, 1834.

portion of his collection came to Haworth in 1929, where it was housed (according to Bonnell's instructions) in the fireproofed dining room of the newly opened BPM. The importance of this gift added substantially to the international reputation of the museum as a centre for Brontë research. The Bonnell Collection in Haworth, housed since 1960 in the specially constructed Bonnell Room, contains books formerly owned by the Brontës, manuscripts of works and letters, 32 paintings and drawings, samplers, and other items such as Emily's writing desk and its contents. The Bonnell Collection at the Pierpont Morgan Library comprises an important range of manuscripts, which formed the nucleus of their 1995 *Exhibition of the Art of the Brontës*.

Book of Common Prayer, The. The version used by Anglican churches in the 19th century was that of 1662, reached after many revisions following Cranmer's first Prayer Book of 1549. At its heart are the Orders for Morning and Evening Prayer and the Sacraments, and the metrical psalter. Its solemn, archaic, beautifully cadenced language, familiar to the Brontës from their childhood, is echoed especially in the work of Anne and Charlotte. Their quotations from the Psalms are usually from the Prayer Book version. In *The Professor* and *Villette* Charlotte uses the striking metaphor 'the iron entered into his soul' (Psalm 105), not the *Bible*'s 'he was laid in iron'; and she prefers the Prayer Book's 'ungodly. . . flourishing like a green bay-tree' to the Bible's wicked man 'spreading himself' (Psalm 37; *The Professor* and *Shirley*). Prayers, too, are recalled in 'the changes and chances of this mortal life', 'as it was in the beginning', 'in heaven above or in the earth beneath'. Elizabeth Gaskell and orthodox Anglican reviewers complained of Charlotte's 'profanity in quoting texts of Scripture disagreeably'; but few would cavil at the great *coup de théâtre* in *Jane Eyre* where the Prayer Book's solemn warning in the Service of Matrimony, 'I require and charge you both (as ye will answer at the dreadful day of judgment . . .' is followed by the stranger's words, 'The marriage cannot go on' (ch. 26).

books owned by the Brontës. *See page 52*

books read by the Brontës. *See page 54*

Boue-Marine ('Sea-Mud') in *Villette* is Charlotte's contemptuous name for the port at which Lucy *Snowe disembarks—no doubt the equivalent of Ostend. Compare *Villette* ('little town'), *Labassecour* ('poultry-yard'), and 'Bouquin-Moisi' (mouldy old book) for Louvain.

Boulshill, village and mountain in the Warner Hills, province of Angria; based on Boulsworth

Hill in the Pennines, west of Haworth. In the *Glass Town and Angrian saga, the village of Boulshill (near *Pendleton) is the home of Miss West, and Charles Townshend's friend Tom Ingham has a farm at the foot of Boulshill.

Boultby, Revd Dr Thomas, the Rector of *Whinbury in *Shirley*. He is 'a stubborn old Welshman, hot, opinionated, and obstinate, but withal a man who did a great deal of good, though not without making some noise about it' (p. 303). A somewhat pompous figure, he is seen on Whit Tuesday at the head of his parish Sunday school, dressed 'in full canonicals, walking, as became a beneficed priest, under the canopy of a shovel-hat, with the dignity of an ample corporation, the embellishment of the squarest and vastest of black coats, and the support of the stoutest of gold-headed canes' (p. 331). Dr Boultby is based on an old friend of Revd Patrick Brontë's, Revd William *Morgan (1782–1858), a Welshman and vicar of Christ Church, Bradford, who had officiated at the marriage of Revd Patrick Brontë to Maria Branwell in 1812, and baptized four of the Brontë children. Describing a visit to Haworth by Mr Morgan in a letter of 17 March 1840, Charlotte Brontë complained to Ellen Nussey about 'that fat Welchman's prosing' (Smith *Letters*, 1. 211).   HR

boxing, Brontë interest in. See PUGILISM, BRONTË INTEREST IN.

Bradford, the West Yorks. wool town *c*.12 miles south-east of Haworth, was comparatively small in 1800. The installation of its first steam-powered mill in 1798 attracted more manufacturers, so that it had 67 textile mills by 1841, and a population growth rate of at least 50 per cent in each decade between 1811 and 1851, by which time it was the 'Worstedopolis' of England. Its dark gritstone houses lined narrow streets, its high mill chimneys belched smoke, and its canal was known as the River Stink, so obnoxious were its waters from human and factory effluent. Rich employers built opulent mansions at a distance, while their mill hands remained in the town, the victims of diseases exacerbated by poverty, filth, occupational hazards, and the dire effects of trade depressions. The stoppage of Rouse and Sons in 1846 threw 3,000 out of work and 888 families lacked the means of subsistence. Distress led to riots in 1837, 1839, 1842, and 1844; in May 1848 the military had to be called in yet again to quell violent pro-Chartist riots.

In *The Professor* Charlotte Brontë recreates, in *X——, the atmosphere of towns like Bradford or *Huddersfield: the home of 'Steam, Trade, Machinery', it is held in a 'cup' between low hills, its
(*cont. on page 56*)

A NUMBER of inscribed and annotated books owned by the Brontës still exist, chiefly in BPM but also in other libraries (Bonnell, Pierpont Morgan; Parrish, Princeton; NYPL), and several in private hands. Maria Branwell, the Brontës' mother, possessed Thomas à Kempis's *A Treatise on the Imitation of Christ*, James Thomson's *The Seasons* (1803) (dates of publication refer to editions owned by Brontës), and the *Union Dictionary* (1806), books that had come from Penzance to Yorkshire and possibly survived the same shipwreck as her numbers of the *Lady's Magazine* that Charlotte later read with so much interest (Smith *Letters*, 1. 240). Elizabeth *Branwell kept a set of 'mad Methodist Magazines' at Haworth Parsonage, and probably *Friendship in Death: In Twenty Letters from the Dead to the Living* (1728) by Elizabeth Rowe (*Shirley*, pp. 440, 773 n.). The Brontës inherited two books from their mother's aunt, Jane Fennell (see BRANWELL FAMILY): John Wesley's *A Christian Library* (1752) and Edward Young's *Night Thoughts* (1790); and from her daughter Jane Morgan (see FENNELL, REVD JOHN) who died in 1827, a *Greek Prayer Book* and Johnson's *Lives of the English Poets* (1797).

All the Brontës quote the *Book of Common Prayer and various hymns, especially those of Charles Wesley and Isaac Watts. They each owned their own copies of such books, including their own Bibles which were also used for translation exercises. Charlotte's '1st Book' was her mother's copy of Thomas à Kempis's *Imitation of Christ* (1803), given to her in July 1826. The BPM has a New Testament in French given to Charlotte by Margaret Wooler as a prize in 1831, a German New Testament given to her by 'Herr Heger' in 1843; and a Gospel according to St Matthew owned and decorated with sketches by Branwell. Anne's Bible was given to her by her godmother Elizabeth Firth, who instructed her father to give it to her at '10 years of age' (Pierpont Morgan); and she also acquired a book of religious poetry in 1845, in which she marked certain poems: *Sacred Harmony* (1841).

The majority of surviving books and those that betray signs of the most use are those owned by Revd Patrick Brontë, several of which he gained as prizes at Cambridge, such as his editions of Homer and Horace. A pupil at Cambridge also gave him Lempriere's *Bibliotheca Classica; or A Classical Dictionary* (1797). These he used in the classics lessons he gave his children and they would also have been familiar with his own publications. He also used a *Concordance to the Bible* 'containing a note . . . of his intention to read with his son Branwell certain classics, and a memorandum of what was accomplished' (*Bonnell Catalogue* (1932), 19). Mr Brontë's copy of Thomas John Graham's *Modern Domestic Medicine* (1826) is probably the most heavily annotated, with comments by him on contemporary treatments and his own observations on diseases. This he supplemented with *A System of Anatomy* (1847). Patrick Brontë owned Humphry Davy's *Elements of Chemical Philosophy* (1812), Hannah More's *Moral Sketches* (1819), Burke's *A Philosophical Enquiry into the Origins of our ideas of the Sublime and Beautiful* (1827), and the first volume of *The Gardens and Menagerie of the Zoological Society Delineated* (1830), which was used by his children and contains sketches by Anne. The young Brontës used their father's copy of Dryden's translation of *The Works of *Virgil* (1824), annotating especially the *Aeneid* and decorating the inside covers with faces and the names of characters from the

*Glass Town and Angrian saga; and the Brontë copy of Milton's *Paradise Lost* (1797) that still exists is likewise heavily marked.

Branwell also made numerous marginal notes and sketches in his own books. For his tenth birthday in June 1829, Charlotte gave him James Macpherson's *Poems of Ossian*, the pseudo-scholarship of which he imitated in his own early writing; and in the same year, probably also for his birthday, he was given the *Description of London* (1824), a volume illustrated with *prints of various public buildings which he further embellished with his own sketches. He annotated his copy of *Rambles by Rivers* (1844), by James Thorne, with observations made on his walks while at *Broughton-in-Furness; and also covered the pages of De la Motte's *Characters of Trees* (1822), a drawing manual used by Anne in particular, with a variety of architectural and figure sketches, mainly of soldiers.

Books by Lord *Byron and Sir Walter *Scott were favourites of the family. Branwell's pocket copy of *Childe Harold's Pilgrimage* (1827) which he bought in Liverpool in May 1835 is well used with numerous pencil jottings. Mr Brontë owned Byron's complete works, and most likely Thomas Moore's *Life of Byron*. He also had a number of volumes by Scott, probably his collected poetry and several of his novels. Scott's *Lay of the Last Minstrel* (1806) and George Allan's *Life of Sir Walter Scott* (1834) were on his shelves, and in 1828 Elizabeth Branwell gave her nephew and nieces Scott's *Tales of a Grandfather*. In 1838, Charlotte was given *The Vision of Don Roderick* (1811 and 1813) for her services as a teacher at Miss Wooler's school.

Various English and French grammars, spelling books, and dictionaries used by the Brontë children at school at *Roe Head and in *Brussels still survive. *The Doctrine of the Passions* (1791) by Isaac Watts (signed 'C Brontë') contains children's scribbles; and Richmal Mangnall's *Historical and Miscellaneous Questions* (1813) has the names of some of Charlotte's Roe Head schoolfellows inside the front cover. Charlotte owned Schiller's *Sämmtliche Werke* which she used in 1843 in Brussels for her translations into English and French (see NOTEBOOKS (CAHIERS)) of works by Schiller (Neufeldt *CBP*, pp. 357–64).

The 'Catalogue of Sale of Brontë effects held at Haworth Parsonage' (1 Oct. 1861) lists numerous other books owned by the Brontës: among them histories of Ireland, England, Rome (in Latin) and the Church; Rollin's *History*; various dictionaries including *Johnson's Dictionary*, a biblical dictionary, a German grammar and New Testament; music books; and an 'Encyclopedia'. Thackeray gave Charlotte a copy of *Fables de la Fontaine* (1839), and her friend Susan Carter (née Wooler) (see CARTER FAMILY) gave her Jeremy Taylor's *The Golden Grove* (1849) as a wedding gift but there is no evidence that she read it. See also ANNUALS; GEOGRAPHY, KNOWLEDGE OF AND BOOKS; FOREIGN LANGUAGES; BOOKS READ BY THE BRONTËS; NATURAL HISTORY AND THE BRONTËS.

Alexander & Sellars, app. A: 'List of Books Owned by the Brontës, with sketches and scribbles'.

THE writing of the Brontës is characterized by a particular richness of literary allusion that reflects their extensive reading and eclectic interests. The Brontës knew intimately the *Bible (they each owned their own copy) and their father's collection of Sir Walter *Scott and Lord *Byron, that inspired not only characters but also landscape descriptions in their juvenilia, poetry, and novels. Charlotte and Branwell were well acquainted with the poetry of *Milton, especially *Paradise Lost*, and the Romantic and pre-Romantic poets generally formed a staple part of their reading: in particular Robert *Burns, Thomas *Campbell, Samuel Taylor *Coleridge, Oliver *Goldsmith, James Macpherson, Thomas *Moore, Robert *Southey, James *Thomson, Edward *Young, and William *Wordsworth. The last was a favourite of Revd Patrick Brontë, who was inspired by Wordsworth's educational philosophy. He also appears to have encouraged a thorough knowledge of *Shakespeare, since from the time of their earliest manuscripts his children were familiar with his plays.

For Charlotte, *Bunyan's *Pilgrim's Progress* had a formative influence that is strongly reflected in the imagery and narrative structure of her writing. At Cowan Bridge she was introduced to Revd W. Carus *Wilson's monthly issues of the *Children's Friend* and possibly to *Johnson's *Rasselas*, which inspired her own *'Search after Happiness'. She had also read *Swift's *Gulliver's Travels* at an early age and Ben Jonson's plays *The Poetaster* and *Every Man in His Humour*. Both she and Branwell were well versed in Elizabethan and Jacobean revenge drama; and Branwell is said to have known *Peregrine Pickle* and other novels by Smollett (Robert G. Collins (ed.), *The Hand of the Arch-Sinner* (1993) p. xxv). William *Cowper was a great favourite with Anne, but all the Brontës knew his work well and felt keenly his tragic personal situation. Mary Taylor told Elizabeth Gaskell that they all, including Branwell, 'at times appreciated, or almost appropriated' Cowper's poem 'The Castaway' (Gaskell *Life* (3rd edn.), ch. 8). Again, *Shelley is said to have been a favourite of Emily, since his transcendentalism is most clearly reflected in her poetry, but all the Brontë writing indicates some familiarity with his work. In most cases, what one Brontë read the others are likely to have read also, except on the occasions when they were away from Haworth and subject to different influences.

Like the young Jane Eyre, the Brontë children delighted in the pages of Thomas *Bewick's *History of British Birds* and the exotic fantasy of the *Arabian Nights*. Together with *Aesop's Fables*, James *Ridley's *Tales of the Genii*, and *Blackwood's Edinburgh Magazine*, these five sources provided the chief literary entertainment that inspired the Brontës' early plays and led to their voluminous *juvenilia. *Blackwood's* introduced the children not only to an array of political and cultural interests but also to the main Scottish writers of the day, including John *Wilson, John Gibson *Lockhart, and James *Hogg. Hogg's tales of terror featured among *Blackwood's* Gothic offerings and as adolescents the Brontës were familiar with his *Private Memoirs and Confessions of a Justified Sinner*. The family took local newspapers like the *Leeds Intelligencer* and the *Leeds Mercury*; and Aunt Elizabeth Branwell subscribed to *Fraser's Magazine* and owned a set of the *Methodist Magazine*. Charlotte read her mother's copies of the *Lady's Magazine*, devouring its Gothic romances with enthusiasm (Smith *Letters*, 1. 236–42), and all four children absorbed the pages of various *annuals such as *Friendship's Offering, *Forget Me Not, and the Keepsake, several of which they owned, and copied the engravings. From the annuals, the Brontës became familiar with the poetry of Felicia Hemans and it is interesting to note that in 1842 Charlotte gave her friend Ellen *Nussey a copy of Hemans's Songs of the Affections and Other Poems (1841).

In July 1834, Charlotte recommended a list of authors she had read to Ellen Nussey, including (apart from those mentioned above) Pope ('I don't admire him'); the history writers Hume and Rollin; the *natural history authors Bewick, *Audubon, *Goldsmith, and White of Selborne; and 'For Biography, read Johnson's lives of the Poets, Boswell's life of Johnson, Southey's life of Nelson, Lockhart's life of Burns, Moore's life of Sheridan, Moore's life of Byron, Wolfe's remains' (Smith Letters, 1. 130–1). She enthusiastically states 'read Scott alone all novels after his are worthless'; but her later letter to Hartley *Coleridge (10 Dec. 1840) shows that by the age of 24 she was familiar with a range of novels from authors as various as Samuel *Richardson, Jean-Jacques Rousseau, Charlotte Smith, Revd George Moore, Charles *Dickens, James Fenimore Cooper, Edward *Bulwer-Lytton and Samuel Warren (Smith Letters, 1. 241). She read Frances Burney's Evelina and Ann Radcliffe's The Italian (see GOTHIC NOVELS). From the *Taylor family of Gomersal Charlotte had borrowed French newspapers and books, including the novels of George *Sand. Later she read William Makepeace *Thackeray's works and, at the suggestion of George Henry *Lewes, Jane *Austen's Pride and Prejudice, and subsequently Sense and Sensibility and Emma, all of which she received from her publishers (Smith Letters, 2. 361–2).

Scott's Life of Napoleon (1827) was read by all but was probably a particular favourite of Branwell, who had an early enthusiasm for France and its heroes. He loved the Greek myths and legends, frequently alluding to classical texts in his writing and transposing Greek battles into a Glass Town setting. He read Homer, Horace, and *Virgil in the original with his father, and also used Dryden's translation of Virgil's Aeneid. There is evidence that Emily Brontë also translated parts of the Aeneid and Horace's Ars Poetica as exercises in Latin (see FOREIGN LANGUAGES). At the age of 14 Charlotte made 'A *Translation into English Verse of the First Book of M. *Voltaire's Henriade'. In Brussels, M. Constantin *Heger introduced Emily and Charlotte to the French Romantics, including *Bernardin de Saint-Pierre, *Chateaubriand, Nodier, *Lamartine, *Hugo, *Millevoye, Alfred de Musset; and also earlier writers like *Buffon. At the age of 12, Branwell had already shared a knowledge of Chateaubriand with his sisters when, as *'Young Soult the Rhymer' (spelt 'Ryhmer' by Branwell), he wrote a miniature volume of Glass Town poems with notes and commentary by 'Monseiur de La Chateaubriand Author of Travles in Greece the Holy land &c.'. In Brussels, Emily also got a grounding in German that reinforced her taste for the German literature that she had encountered in translation in Blackwood's. It seems likely, for example, that she knew E. T. A. *Hoffmann's Das Majorat (The Entail), if only through Scott's essay on Hoffmann (Wuthering Heights (Clarendon edn.), 418 n.), and that she read Blackwood's series of translations of *Schiller (1842–3). It would be unusual, too, if the Brontës were not familiar with Goethe's Faust and The Sorrows of Young Werther, if only in translation.

Much has been written and contested about the sources of the Brontës' reading. It is likely they had access to the valuable library of their father's parishioners at *Ponden House, and that they borrowed some books from the *Keighley Mechanics' Institute

Library. There were no libraries in *Haworth when the Brontës were young; by 1847 John *Greenwood (stationer) may have lent books on subscription. Margaret Smith notes that the Haworth Subscription Library which closed on Easter Monday 1844 was probably short-lived (Smith *Letters*, 1. 114 n.). Benjamin *Binns recalled seeing the Brontës trudging 4 miles to *Keighley to procure books 'at a lending library kept by Mr Hudson, a bookseller and druggist in the High Street' (*Bradford Observer* (17 Feb. 1894), p. 6), but he provides no date for this occurrence. In 1848, Charlotte protested to Lewes that she had 'no access to a circulating library' (Smith *Letters*, 2. 14). After she became one of their authors, Smith, Elder sent Charlotte regular packages of new publications.

See also BOOKS OWNED BY THE BRONTËS; GEOGRAPHY, KNOWLEDGE OF AND BOOKS; ART OF THE BRONTËS; MUSIC; NATURAL HISTORY AND THE BRONTËS; PENINSULAR WAR; NAPOLEON BUONAPARTE.

Brontë, Charlotte, *The Professor* (Clarendon edn.), app. 7 (index of quotations and literary allusions in Charlotte's novels).

tall, cylindrical chimneys vomit soot, producing a 'dense, permanent' brooding vapour; and a mill quivers 'through its thick brick walls with the commotion of its iron bowels' (ch. 2). William Crimsworth's task of translating German business letters was common in Bradford, where in 1847 there were 34 foreign worsted merchants, and a warehouse district known as 'Little Germany'. X—— has radical agitators on the one hand, and on the other, employers who go bankrupt, compound with their creditors, and within six weeks flourish again. Branwell depicts a similar milltown, with 'great smoking chimneys' and yellow choking sky, tremulous factory-walls and sudden eruptions of noise, in *The *Wool is Rising* (1834).

There was a strong Dissenting presence in Bradford, but the Church of England reached few workers there until, in the early 19th century, evangelicals encouraged ministers to regard it as a mission field. Revd Patrick Brontë, influenced by them, accepted posts in *Dewsbury, *Hartshead, and then *Thornton, all of them near Bradford. He took an active part in its religious life, and his *The *Cottage in the Wood*, *The *Maid of Killarney*, and writings on the Haworth bog-burst (1824) were printed and sold by T. Inkersley of Bradford; the *Bradford Observer published letters from him on 13 May 1841, 15 February 1844, and 25 April 1844, and later, an appreciative review of *Jane Eyre* on 2 December 1847. The paper's would-be rival, the Tory *Bradford Herald*, established 6 January 1842, published eight of Branwell Brontë's poems between 28 April 1842 and 25 August 1842.

Branwell already knew Bradford well. He met some of the writers and artists—Hartley *Coleridge, Joseph Bentley *Leyland, William Dearden, John Hunter *Thompson, and others—who gath-

ered at the George Hotel, a respectable inn opened in 1829 in Market Street.

There were many improvements in the amenities of Bradford during the Brontës' lifetime. It already had a richly endowed grammar school. In the early 19th century the churches built Sunday and day schools. A mechanics' institute was established in 1832, and an appropriate building for it erected in 1839. The Bradford and Leeds railway was completed on 31 May 1846; conditions in the factories were improved after the Ten Hours' Act of 1847; a number of streets were widened and insanitary buildings demolished from 1850 onwards. For Charlotte it remained, on the whole, a town she travelled through to visit Ellen Nussey in Birstall, but it must have contributed to her understanding of the 'condition of England' question which concerns her in *The Professor* and *Shirley*.

Bradford Herald. A short-lived (Jan.–Oct. 1842) Tory counterpart of the liberal *Bradford Observer, this local weekly newspaper published eight of Branwell Brontë's poems between April and August 1842, four years before the appearance of his sisters' book of *Poems in 1846. Several of the poems Branwell sent to the *Bradford Herald* were printed simultaneously in the more established and reputable *Halifax Guardian, also a politically Conservative provincial paper. Branwell's poem 'Noah's Warning over Methuselah's Grave' appeared in the *Bradford Herald* on 25 August 1842. See also POETRY BY BRANWELL BRONTË.   CB

Bradford Observer. A local weekly newspaper, Liberal in politics and paying particular attention to literature, the *Bradford Observer* was much longer-lived than its Tory counterpart, the *Bradford Herald*. The *Bradford Observer* reported regularly on the Revd Patrick Brontë's activities in the 1830s, positively reviewed *Jane Eyre* in 1847, and publicized the true identity of 'Currer Bell' in February 1850, making it impossible for Charlotte to retain her local anonymity after that date. After Elizabeth *Gaskell's *Life* of Charlotte appeared in 1857, the *Observer* published exaggerated reports of Mr Brontë's harshness to his children. It also ran several letters defending Mr Brontë and reprinted a querulous rejoinder from Harriet *Martineau, originally published in the *Daily News*.   CB

Bradley, Revd James Chesterton (1818–1913), the model for Revd David *Sweeting in *Shirley*. He graduated BA from the Queen's College, Oxford, 1841, was ordained deacon and licensed to a curacy at Keighley in July 1842, ordained priest June 1843, and licensed to a curacy at Oakworth, about 2 miles from Haworth, October 1844. He worked assiduously to organize the parish and build a church, but overwork led to illness, resignation, and a long rest. He became curate of All Saints' Paddington, 1847–55, and married Caroline Rumsey in January 1856, curate at Corfe Castle, Dorset, 1856–62, and rector of Sutton-under-Brailes, Glos., 1863–1903. He took the funeral of Elizabeth *Branwell at Haworth on 3 November 1842.

Bradley, John (1787–1844), founder-member of the *Keighley Mechanics' Institute and art teacher to the young Brontës during 1829–30. His self-portrait (illustrated in Alexander & Sellars, p. 23) hangs in the Keighley Public Library. *Baines's Directory* of 1823 lists him as a house and sign painter of Wellington Street, Keighley, but he preferred to call himself an artist. Much of his surviving work belongs to his early career, such as his scenes of Keighley in pencil and ink wash executed in August 1820. He was not a professional teacher but had exhibited in the gallery of the Royal Northern Society in the 1820s (Alexander & Sellars, p. 33 n.). Tradition has it that he gave art lessons to the Brontës as a favour to Revd Patrick Brontë, a fellow member of the Keighley Mechanics' Institute Library, and that the children visited his house 'many times' in New Bridge Street, Keighley (William *Dearden in the *Bradford Observer*, 27 June 1861). John Bradley is said to be the painter of one of the few surviving *portraits of Mr Brontë and may well have encouraged Branwell in his enthusiasm for oil painting and architecture (Alexander & Sellars, pp. 33 n. and 23). In July 1831, Bradley and his family emigrated to the United States where he hoped to make a living as a portrait painter in Philadelphia, but he returned disillusioned in 1833. He resumed his position in the Mechanics' Institute and was 'architect' of its new building in 1834.

Dewhirst, Ian, 'Drawing Master to the Brontës', *Yorkshire Ridings Magazine* (June 1968), 26–7.

Branderham, Revd Jabes. Branderham's 'pious discourse', divided under 490 heads and delivered in the chapel of *Gimmerton Sough, forms the substance of *Lockwood's first nightmare in *Wuthering Heights*. He is said to be based on Revd Jabez *Bunting, a fanatical Methodist leader in the Halifax area. There was also a Scotsman with Presbyterian leanings whom Emily Brontë would often have heard preach: a Mr John Hope, who officiated at St Anne's church, near *Law Hill, Halifax, and who married Elizabeth *Patchett.

Branii Hills (variously spelt Brani, Branii, Brannii). The vast, wild mountain range in the north of *Sneaky's Land; the 'Highlands' of the *Glass Town Federation.

Branwell, Elizabeth (1776–1842), elder sister of Mrs Maria *Brontë and one of the eleven children of Thomas Branwell (1746–1808) (see BRANWELL FAMILY) in whose comfortable home she was brought up. He left £50 to each of his daughters, and she was able to save some of her income. The attractive young woman of 23 shown in an early portrait was never to marry. At 56 she seemed to Ellen Nussey a 'very small antiquated little lady' who 'wore caps large enough for half a dozen of the present fashion, and a front of light auburn curls over her forehead'; she recalled the social pleasures of her life in *Penzance with regret, but though precise in manner, she remained 'very lively and intelligent in her talk, and tilted argument without fear against Mr. Brontë' (Smith *Letters*, 1. 597). In 1815 Elizabeth stayed with the Brontës in *Thornton, and in 1821 was at Haworth, helping to look after the family during her sister's mortal illness. After Maria's death she moved permanently to Haworth. Disliking the cold northern weather, she kept her own room upstairs warm, and when downstairs wore pattens to keep her feet from the cold stone floors of the Parsonage. But she kept the household in good order, helped to educate Charlotte, Emily, and Anne, allowed them to read romantic tales in her ancient copies of the *Lady's Magazine*, and gave them Sir Walter Scott's *Tales of a Grandfather* in 1828. She would also read aloud to Revd Patrick Brontë, who was grateful to her for sharing his 'labours and sorrows'. His daughters respected her, though they occasionally resented her discipline, and her insistence that their love of animals be kept in subjection. It was perhaps Miss Branwell who gave away Nero the hawk and two pet geese while Charlotte and Emily were away in Brussels. But Charlotte at least was grateful to her for habits of order, neatness, and punctuality, and for her training in household work—though Mary *Taylor observed sourly that she insisted on her nieces sewing 'charity clothing' for the good of the sewers, not the recipients. Mary's view that Miss Branwell discouraged any other culture than sewing is questionable, for she responded generously to Charlotte and Emily's wish to study foreign languages. She had offered a loan of £100 towards setting up a school in the Parsonage, but agreed instead to finance their stay abroad. She regularly paid for her board at the Parsonage, and by her will left the residue of her estate (under £1,500) to be divided equally among her Haworth nieces and their cousin Eliza Jane *Kingston—thus indirectly financing the publication of *Poems* 1846. According to Mary Taylor, she made a great favourite of Branwell Brontë, who wrote with real grief of her illness and death, which deprived him of the 'guide and director' of his happy childhood days (Smith *Letters*, 1. 295). She had been afflicted with obstruction of the bowel, and for two nights Branwell witnessed her agonizing suffering. She left him no money, probably assuming that he could earn his own living. There is no evidence that Miss Branwell exercised a 'tyranny of the spirit' over Anne Brontë or her siblings. In *Anne Brontë* (1959), p.36, Winifred Gérin attributes to her a harsh Calvinistic belief in the eternal punishment of those not 'elected' to salvation; but since she had been brought up as a Wesleyan Methodist, she would have been more likely to emphasize God's grace. Evidence that a portrait formerly said to be hers is that of Johanna Margarethe Sang, née Weppler, appears in ' "Aunt Branwell" Portrait Re-Identified', *BST* (1987), 19. 3. 126–70. *See* BOOKS OWNED BY THE BRONTËS.

Oram, Eanne, 'Brief for Miss Branwell', *BST* (1964), 14. 74. 28–38.

Branwell family. Mrs Maria *Brontë, née Branwell, came of a Cornish family. Her paternal grandparents were Richard Branwell (b. 1711) of Penzance and Margaret, née John, the daughter of a blacksmith. Maria's father Thomas Branwell (1746–1808) married in 1768 Anne Carne (1744–1809), the daughter of a silversmith. Thomas was a prominent citizen in the busy seaport, importing luxury goods such as tea, which he sold wholesale or through his Market Square grocery shop. He also owned or leased a brewery, the Golden Lion Inn, Tremenheere House, and other property. Local tin mines were the main source of wealth for Bolitho's bank, in which the Branwells had substantial funds. Thus Thomas was able to bequeath to each of his daughters, Jane, Elizabeth, Maria, and Charlotte, life annuities of £50.

Jane (1773–1824) married a Wesleyan Methodist preacher, John Kingston, and went with him to America after he was dismissed from his ministry in disgrace in 1807. He was an unsatisfactory husband, and in 1809 soon after the birth of her fifth child, Elizabeth ('Eliza') Jane (1808–78), Jane Kingston left him and the older children to return with her baby daughter to the family home in Penzance. After her mother's death Eliza Jane *Kingston's small investments in railways and Cornish tin mines proved to be precarious sources of income. Unproductive mines often gave no income at all for several years, gradually draining her resources until her death in extreme poverty.

The Penzance Branwells were staunch Wesleyan Methodists. Maria Brontë's Aunt Jane Branwell (1753–1829) married Revd John *Fennell in 1790, when he was a Methodist class leader, regularly holding meetings for prayer and Bible study with the group of Methodists over whom he had pastoral care. He was also the headmaster of the Wesleyan school in Penzance. It was through Fennell's appointment to *Woodhouse Grove school that Maria, his niece by marriage, met Revd Patrick Brontë in 1812. In Penzance the Branwells contributed substantially to the building of the town's first Methodist chapel in 1814. It was very near to their home, 25 Chapel Street, a sturdy granite house faced with brick, fronting directly on to the street, but with a walled garden to the rear.

According to Ellen Nussey, Elizabeth *Branwell, Maria's elder sister, 'talked a great deal of her younger days, the gaities [*sic*] of her native town . . . the soft warm climate &c. She very probably had been a belle among her acquaintance' (Smith *Letters*, 1. 597.) Penzance had a ladies' book club founded in 1770, a scientific and literary society, concert rooms, and assembly rooms built in 1791 by Elizabeth's uncle Richard Branwell, 'where balls were held throughout the winter months' (Barker, p. 49).

This Richard Branwell, the tenant of the Golden Lion, was the owner of 25 Chapel Street, but he allowed his sister-in-law Anne and her daughters to live there after his brother Thomas's death. Richard's son Thomas (b. 1778), a lieutenant in the Royal Navy, was drowned in December 1811, when the *St George* sank in a violent storm off the coast of Denmark. Richard Branwell died a few months later. Three of Richard's grandchildren, the sons of his son Joseph (1789–1857), also went to sea. One of them, Joseph, died at sea early in 1846, and another, Charles Henry (b. 1830) said to have been a midshipman in the Royal Navy, died in 1851. A third son, William (d. 1876), was at sea at the time of his brother Joseph's death, and Charlotte Brontë sympathized with the distress of his parents, especially her 'poor Aunt Charlotte', who had 'received no tidings' of William for some time. In May 1846 Charlotte Brontë shared their relief

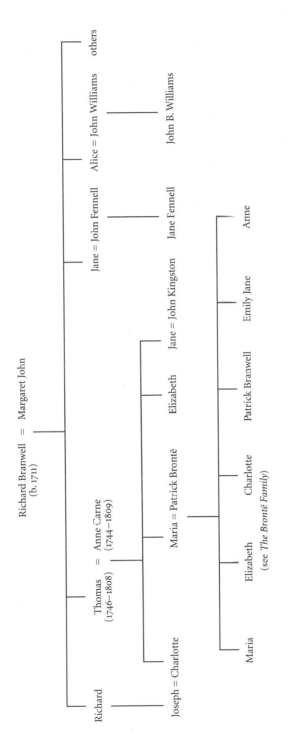

THE BRANWELL FAMILY

that William, safely returned, had abandoned a sailor's career (Smith *Letters*, 1. 456–7, 472–3). For Charlotte storms at sea and their tragic consequences were part of her family's experience, and were realized with imaginative intensity in the fate of M. Paul *Emanuel in *Villette*.

Joseph Branwell sen. (1789–1857) had married his cousin Charlotte (1791–1848), the youngest sister of Maria Branwell. Their wedding at Madron church, the parish church of Penzance, was arranged for 29 December 1812—the day of the double wedding of Maria and Patrick Brontë, and Maria's cousin Jane Fennell and Revd William *Morgan at *Guiseley church, Yorks. In 1830 Joseph Branwell is named in Pigot's *Directory* as the master of a day school in Queen Street, Penzance, but he later joined the staff of Bolitho's bank. One of Charlotte Branwell's six sons was named Thomas Brontë Branwell (1817–97), and Joseph Branwell of Thamar Terrace, Launceston, was included in Charlotte Brontë's wedding-card list in June 1854.

It was apparently Thomas Brontë Branwell who visited the Brontës in Haworth, staying for several days in September 1851, though Wise and Symington's authority (Wise & Symington, 3. 280 n.) for identifying him as the unnamed visitor is not given. Possibly Thomas took the opportunity of visiting his famous cousin and her father, who was probably his godfather, for the first time. He married Sarah Hannah Jones in 1852, and was, or later became, a clerk in the War Office. His daughter Charlotte died in December 1896. Descendants of some of his sons keep in touch with the Brontë Society.

Other Branwell cousins had connections with Redruth, Cornwall. In early August 1840, the Brontës received a visit from John Branwell Williams, cousin of Mrs Maria Brontë, the son of her aunt Alice Branwell and John Williams 'gentleman' of Redruth. John Williams had been staying with his wife and daughter at the home of his uncle by marriage, John Fennell, at Cross-Stone, near Todmorden, on the Lancs.–Yorks. border. In 1840 the Branwell Williamses' home was in London. Charlotte Brontë found the tall vigorous Mr Williams frank and sagacious, but thought his wife and daughter Eliza assumed the grand airs of Southerners. She was amused by Eliza, a 'bouncing good-looking girl' spoilt by a 'Mistaken Education' into a 'languishing affected piece of goods'.

Ratchford, F. E., 'The Loneliness of a Brontë Cousin [Eliza Jane Kingston]', *BST* (1957), 13. 67. 100–10.

'Branwell's Blackwood's Magazine'. In January 1829 Branwell Brontë began publication of a tiny Glass Town magazine (5.2 × 3.3 cm) in minute print writing, modelled on *Blackwood's*

Edinburgh Magazine, avidly read by the Brontë children, especially Branwell. Only the issues for January, June, and July are extant (in Lowell, Harvard), but it is clear from internal references that there was a May issue and possibly others (Alexander *EW*, 36). In August 1829 Charlotte, who had been contributing, took over the editorship, changing the name to 'Blackwood's Young Men's Magazine'. Branwell continued to contribute until December 1829, when he ended his involvement, citing the frivolity and foolish romances that had replaced soberness and gravity (see Neufeldt *BB Works*, 1. 73–5). In keeping with the original model Branwell's issues contained poems, natural history, articles on travel, letters to the editor, prose fiction, literary notices and commentary, advertisements, and a dramatized dialogue entitled 'The Nights', modelled on the 'Noctes Ambrosianae' in *Blackwood's*, of which Branwell was particularly fond. A significant feature is the knowledge of current events the magazines reflect: arctic exploration, American politics and trade policies, the Roman *Catholic Emancipation Bill, events of the Napoleonic era, the children's interest in Macpherson's *Ossian*. VN

Alexander, Christine, *Branwell's Blackwood's Magazine* (1995).
Alexander & Sellars, p. 289 (illustrations).
Neufeldt *BB Works*, 1. 7–31.

Bravey (Bravi), Sir William, one of the original 'glorious Twelves', his role in the *Glass Town and Angrian saga degenerates into that of the corpulent landlord of *Bravey's Inn. A tall and imposing old-fashioned figure, he presides over the African Olympic Games, and is the uncle of Lady Emily Charlesworth, heroine of The *Green Dwarf.

Bravey's Inn (Hotel), an impressive edifice in the centre of the Great Glass Town (*Verdopolis), in the *Glass Town and Angrian saga. Named after its corpulent landlord William *Bravey, the Inn is the meeting place for the Young Men and literati of the city. Its distinctive architecture, with 'its peerless dome and portico', is a Verdopolitan landmark.

Brenzaida, Emperor Julius, sometimes called Julius Angora, in the *Gondal saga. Educated with Gondal's other nobles, but imprisoned in 1825 (Gondal chronology) for his involvement with the ambitious Rosina Alcona whom he probably married. Other lovers include Geraldine S., whom he left grieving over their child in Zedora. He conquers Almedore in Gaaldine and, as king, breaks his promise of union with Gerald Exina, warring against him for the throne of Gondal. Eventually he is made emperor, but soon assassinated (possibly by *Amedeus) in his palace, where Rosina lies ill (Roper *EBP*, pp. 12–13). Fifteen years later, Rosina laments his loss over his grave 'on Angora's shore', probably on his estate (see 'REMEMBRANCE').

Bretton. In *Villette*, Lucy *Snowe's godmother, Mrs Louisa *Bretton, lives at first in a large, handsome house on St Ann's Street, a fine, quiet, thoroughfare leading towards the towers of the minster in the 'clean and ancient' English town of Bretton. Charlotte Brontë perhaps recalled *York or *Bridlington priory.

Bretton, Dr John Graham. In *Villette*, Bretton is first seen as a handsome, auburn-haired 16-year-old schoolboy, somewhat spoilt and whimsical, teasing the child Paulina *Home, but eventually becoming her adored playmate. Though he sometimes distresses her, he can be patient, friendly, and kind. He reappears, unrecognized, as the distinguished-looking young gentleman who helps Lucy *Snowe on her arrival in Villette, and is later recognized by her as the doctor attending patients at the pensionnat. As George *Smith acknowledged, he was Bretton's 'original', recognizable in his tall figure, expressive profile, shrewdly sparkling blue eyes, and vigorous energy. Regarded as the master of the household by Mrs Louisa *Bretton, he is teasingly affectionate to her. She has supported his persevering struggle through financial entanglements not of his own making, as Mrs Elizabeth *Smith had supported her son. He helps the unconscious Lucy when she faints outside the Villette Béguinage, takes her to *La Terrasse, superintends her recovery, and, when she is eventually recognized as his mother's goddaughter, becomes a genial friend, writing her cheering letters, and accompanying her (as George Smith had accompanied Charlotte Brontë) on visits to art galleries and theatres. Though he never fully understands her, regarding her as 'a being inoffensive as a shadow', Lucy respects his goodness, philanthropy, and compassion to his poor patients as well as to her. He can forget that he has not spoken to her for three months, yet she believes he keeps 'one little closet' in his heart for her. Using traits not derived from George Smith, Charlotte shows his development from immature infatuation with Ginevra *Fanshawe to a more shrewd assessment of her character. He is also a kindly, efficient doctor for the child Fifine Beck, but, less worthily, plays a part in the farce of her sister Désirée's pretended illness. His masculine vanity is tickled by Mme *Beck's wish to encourage his visits, and his suspicion that she is enamoured of him. Finally his courtship of Paulina proceeds rapidly. Having helped to rescue her from the theatre panic, he is attracted by her beauty, modesty, and intelligence, enhanced for him by her wealth and social rank, and by memories of her childhood adoration of him. References to his descent from a Highland chief, and portrayal of him as a handsome rider greeting his graceful lady, or driving with her in a carriage drawn by spirited horses, recall the romantic figure of the Duke of *Zamorna.

Bretton, Mrs Louisa Lucy, Lucy *Snowe's godmother in *Villette*, a doctor's widow. Tall, handsome, cheerful, alert, sensible, vivacious brunette, she is modelled on George *Smith's mother Elizabeth *Smith. Sweet and kind when young, she is sometimes peremptory in middle age, but shows much practical kindness to Lucy and Paulina *Home. She is devoted to her son, Dr John Graham *Bretton, proud of his success and professional skill, and persistent in her efforts to retrieve the inheritance that should be his. Indulgent to him in minor matters, she insists that he should marry neither a fool nor a usurping 'goddess'; both enjoy the resulting argument, a half-serious 'skirmish'. Usually serene and equable, she can be impetuous, retaining some of the freshness of youth. Her nature is unlike Lucy's, and she would be unable to comprehend Lucy's inner tensions and emotional turmoil. But she is warmly hospitable to Lucy both in *Bretton and in *La Terrasse, and it is through her that Lucy meets Paulina. Mrs Bretton's integrity contrasts with the duplicity of Mme *Beck, whose 'catherine-wheel' sparkle of compliments during her visit to the Brettons' house gives way to a gravity 'sterner than a judge' when she leaves them.

Brewster, Sir David (1781–1868; knighted 1831), distinguished Scottish physicist and Royal Medallist. He made important discoveries in optics, invented the kaleidoscope in 1816, improved the technique used in stereoscopes, and published many important books and scientific papers. Elizabeth Gaskell's father contributed to his *Edinburgh Encyclopaedia* (1808–29). He was an acquaintance of the *Kay-Shuttleworths and of Janet Kay-Shuttleworth's cousin Caroline Davenport, who probably arranged for him to accompany Charlotte Brontë on the last of her five visits to the *Crystal Palace, on 23 June 1851. She appreciated his explanations of exhibits there, given with reassuring simplicity and good nature.

Briar-chapel, in *Shirley,* 'a large, new, raw, Wesleyan place of worship' (p. 161), 100 yards from the *Yorke family residence at *Briarmains. This is probably where Moses *Barraclough and his followers are in the midst of a noisy 'revival' complained of by Revd Matthewson Helstone (ch. 1). A new Wesleyan Methodist church was erected in

1827 in Gomersal, not far from the home of the *Taylor family at the Red House; Joshua Taylor, Mary *Taylor's father, was one of its first trustees. Charlotte Brontë may also have had in mind a small brick chapel built in Gomersal in the early years of the 19th century by Mary Taylor's grandfather John Taylor, who let it be used by members of the Methodist New Connexion. Nonconformity was very strong in West Yorkshire, and the 19th century saw the erection there of many places of worship by Dissenters. HR

Peel, Frank, *Nonconformity in Spen Valley* (1891).

Briarfield, a manufacturing village in the West Riding of Yorkshire, in *Shirley*, home of Revd Matthewson *Helstone and his niece Caroline *Helstone, and the location of Robert Gérard *Moore's wool-making enterprise at *Hollow's Mill. Charlotte Brontë based it on the village of *Birstall where her friend Ellen *Nussey lived, first at Rydings (which is thought to have suggested *Thornfield Hall), then (after 1836) at Brookroyd. Birstall is contiguous to Gomersal, where the *Taylor family lived (the *Yorke family of *Shirley*). HR

Briarmains, the home of the *Yorke family in *Shirley*. It stands near the *Stilbro' highway, 1 mile from *Briarfield and close to *Briar-chapel, a new Wesleyan chapel. The interior, with its paintings, books, and vases, reflects 'the taste of a travelled man, a scholar, and a gentleman' (p. 50). It is to Briarmains that Robert Gérard *Moore is taken after the attempt on his life, and there he is cared for by Mrs Yorke. For the location and interior of Briarmains, Charlotte Brontë drew on the *Red House in Gomersal, the home of her friend Mary *Taylor and the *Taylor family; the house, a solid brick structure erected by William Taylor in 1660, has been turned into a museum. The name 'Redhouse' is given in the novel to a local inn lying between Briarfield church and *Fieldhead. HR

Bridewell. A house of correction referred to in *Jane Eyre*, mainly for vagrants and prostitutes, named after St Bride's Well in Bridge Street, Blackfriars, London; originally a training centre for apprentices, given by Edward VI to the City. The greater part of the building was demolished by 1864. The name was used generically for a prison or house of correction, as it is in the third scene of the charades in *Jane Eyre* (ch. 18), and in the Surrey Bridewell, St George's Fields, London, and Tothillfields Bridewell, Westminster.

Bridlington (or Burlington). In September 1839 Charlotte Brontë and Ellen Nussey stayed at *Easton, near the east Yorks. market town of Bridlington, before moving to lodgings at Bridlington Quay for a week. Inland, a pleasant street of Georgian houses led to the fine Norman church. Bridlington Quay was an attractive resort and 'bathing-place', where Charlotte was moved to tears by her first sight of the sea. She later recalled the waves 'roaring roughly' in the 'great brewing tub of Bridlington Bay' (Smith *Letters*, 1. 202). In 1841 she briefly contemplated establishing a school there, and in June 1849, after Anne's death, stayed there for a week.

British and Foreign Bible Society. For Protestants, access to the *Bible in language they can understand is essential. The Society, founded in March 1804, was strongly supported by members of the evangelical Clapham Sect, including Revd Patrick Brontë's benefactors Henry Thornton (treasurer of the new society) and William *Wilberforce, and by Thomas Gisborne (father of Lydia *Robinson) who was made an honorary governor for life. The aim was to provide copies of the Scriptures, translated into an appropriate language 'without note or comment' for all who needed them, free or at an affordable price. Six 'distinguished foreigners', and 30 representatives equally divided between the Church of England and Nonconformists, formed the committee, and the issue of Bibles and Testaments began in December 1805. The Society developed rapidly, with auxiliary groups both at home and abroad. The Roman Catholic Church did not participate, because, believing itself the custodian and interpreter of Holy Writ, it could not countenance scriptures without note or comment. Mr Brontë wholeheartedly approved of such spreading of the gospel, and in 1812 addressed the first anniversary meeting of the Bradford Auxiliary Society which he had helped to found. He established a Haworth auxiliary in 1823. In The *Maid of Killarney he compared the parent society to 'a noble and spacious edifice . . . affording . . . separate apartments for Christians of all denominations . . . and constituting an impregnable bulwark against the common enemy', and to 'the mighty Nile . . . spreading flowery verdure, and golden harvests, over the surrounding country!' (ch. 5). In 1848 Mr Brontë and Charlotte read George Borrow's *The Bible in Spain* (1843) with 'great interest'. Borrow had worked for the Society in Russia, Portugal, and Spain, and his work included the distribution of his translation of St Luke's gospel into the Spanish gypsy tongue.

Howse, Ernest Marshall, *Saints in Politics: The 'Clapham Sect' and the Growth of Freedom* (1953).

Brocklehurst, Revd Robert, in *Jane Eyre*. To the child Jane he seems like a black pillar, with a grim, mask-like face for its capital. As treasurer and manager of *Lowood, he insists on the rules:

the pupils should endure temporary deprivation of food with fortitude, for extra provisions would feed their 'vile bodies' but starve their immortal souls. Ignoring his own family's costly dress and curled hair, he requires pupils to be soberly clothed, and have their curls cut off, conforming to Christian grace and humility befitting their position. An extreme Calvinist, he believes wicked children are doomed to hellfire, and, publicly accusing Jane of deceit, he warns pupils to shun her and teachers to watch her. Charlotte's passionately indignant presentation of Brocklehurst, based on recollections of Revd W. Carus *Wilson, is barbed with irony, as in his 'sublime' exhortation that the waters of healing should not 'stagnate' round ungrateful Jane, whose 'benefactress' separated her from her own 'pure' offspring lest she contaminate them. Jane sums him up as a harsh, pompous, meddling man, who for economy's sake bought bad sewing equipment and starved the pupils, bored them with long lectures, and frightened them with readings from his own books about sudden deaths and judgements.

Bromley, Mr, minister of the Wesleyan Methodist Chapel, Slugg St, Verdopolis, and Methodist class leader in the *Glass Town and Angrian saga. Bromley, a short, broad, athletic man characterized as 'That great apostle of methodism', is an associate of Brother *Ashworth and a figure of satire with his exaggerated ejaculations on behalf of his hypocritical congregation. Branwell Brontë later gives the name Slugg (Revd Simon Slugg) to the preacher in his novel *And the Weary are at Rest, a character modelled on Bromley. See also PASSING EVENTS.

Brontë, Anne. *See page 66*

Brontë, (Patrick) Branwell. *See page 73*

Brontë, Charlotte. *See page 80*

Brontë, Elizabeth (1815–25), second daughter of Revd Patrick Brontë and Mrs Maria Brontë, born at *Hartshead, baptized 26 August 1815 at *Thornton. In 1823 the 'patient, sensible' Elizabeth and her sister Maria briefly attended Crofton Hall school, Wakefield. On entry at *Cowan Bridge on 21 July 1824 she could read little, write pretty well, but do no arithmetic. Her sewing was very poor, and she knew no grammar, geography, history, or 'accomplishments'. A servant, Mrs Hardacre, accompanied her to Haworth on 31 May 1825, when she was already seriously ill with pulmonary TB. She died on 15 June 1825.

Brontë, Emily Jane. *See page 88*

Brontë, Maria (?1813–25), Charlotte's eldest sister, and her model for Helen *Burns in *Jane Eyre*; born at *Hartshead, baptized there 23 April 1814.

In 1823 she briefly attended Crofton Hall school, Wakefield. On entry at *Cowan Bridge on 21 July 1824 she read tolerably, wrote pretty well, knew some arithmetic, grammar, and French, but sewed very badly and knew little geography or history. As a future governess, she took two 'extras', French and drawing. Though seriously ill with pulmonary TB by December 1824, she patiently endured an under-teacher's harsh treatment (see ANDREWS, ANNA). Charlotte recalled her remarkable intellect, mildness, wisdom, and fortitude. On 14 February 1825 Revd Patrick Brontë took her home, where she died on 6 May.

Brontë, Mrs Maria, née Branwell (1783–1821), wife of Revd Patrick Brontë; 8th child of Thomas and Anne Branwell (see BRANWELL FAMILY), and brought up in their comfortable Penzance home. Early in 1812 she travelled to Yorkshire to help her aunt Jane, née Branwell, wife of Revd John *Fennell, governor of *Woodhouse Grove school, where she met Mr Brontë some time before he examined the pupils in classics in July 1812. Nine charming, warm, frank letters from Maria to him, written between 26 August and 5 December that year, show their mutual attraction, Maria's gentle piety, and a lively sense of humour which enabled her to tease 'dear saucy Pat'. They were married at *Guiseley church on 29 December 1812, and began their married life at *Hartshead, where Patrick was curate. Maria's essay on 'The *Advantages of Poverty in Religious Concerns' (MS in Brotherton, with Maria's letter to Mr Brontë, 18 Nov. 1812), perhaps written after her marriage, is a well-intentioned piece, where the narrow limits of her piety and experience of life are revealed in her conviction that poverty cannot be an evil to those who are spiritually enlightened (see Wise & Symington, 1. 8–27).

Maria bore six children in quick succession between 1813 and 1820. At Thornton she had the help of a nursemaid and the thoughtful friendship of Elizabeth Firth (see FIRTH FAMILY). In 1815 her sister Elizabeth also came to help; but Maria was physically weak when the family removed to Haworth in April 1820. She fell dangerously ill on 29 January 1821, and endured agonizing pain from what was probably uterine cancer. Mr Brontë called in doctors and engaged a nurse, but they could do no more than give palliatives. Though her mind was 'often disturbed' in the last conflict, she died calmly and in faith on 15 September (Wise & Symington, 1. 58–60).

Brontë, Revd Patrick. *See page 98*

Brontë family. The surname is spelled 'Brunty' or (on one occasion) 'Bruntee' in Drumgooland

(cont. on page 72)

Maria Branwell, Mrs Brontë as a young woman: anonymous portrait.

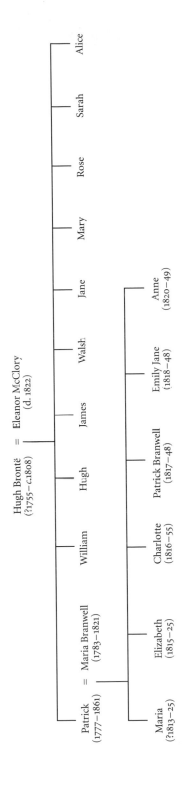

THE BRONTË FAMILY

ANNE BRONTË

ANNE Brontë ('Acton Bell', 1820–49) was born on 17 January 1820 at the parsonage in Market Street, *Thornton, the sixth and youngest child of Revd Patrick *Brontë and his wife Mrs Maria *Brontë. She was baptized at Thornton on 25 March 1820 by her father's friend Revd William *Morgan, with Elizabeth Firth (later Mrs Elizabeth *Franks) and Frances *Outhwaite as her godmothers. By 20 April 1820 the family had moved to *Haworth, where Mr Brontë had been appointed perpetual curate. After their mother's death, the Brontë children were cared for by their aunt, Elizabeth *Branwell. The early deaths of Anne's elder sisters Maria and Elizabeth in 1825 probably increased the family's protective care for the delicate, and later asthmatic, Anne. She was not sent to Cowan Bridge school, but was educated at home by her aunt and her father until mid-1832, when Charlotte Brontë helped to teach Anne and her inseparable companion Emily. These two were like twins, as Ellen Nussey said, and 'in the very closest sympathy which never had any interruption'. Ellen thought 'dear gentle Anne' quite different in appearance from her sisters. Her pretty light brown hair 'fell on her neck in graceful curls', she had 'lovely violet blue eyes' beneath fine pencilled eyebrows, and a 'clear, almost transparent complexion' (Smith Letters, 1. 598). Charlotte's pencil drawing of her in profile, dated 17 April 1833, was identified as an excellent likeness by two of Martha *Brown's sisters. Both this graceful drawing and Charlotte's less attractive watercolour of the same year show Anne's curls, tiny mouth, slightly receding chin, and slender neck (Alexander & Sellars, nos. 91 and 92 on pp. 210–11, and pl. VIII). Her pretty colouring is evident in Charlotte's watercolour of 17 June 1834 and Branwell Brontë's oil painting of his sisters (Alexander & Sellars, nos. 119 and 225 on pp. 230 and 310 and pl. XXIV). Anne was her aunt Branwell's favourite niece, and still had lessons from her, especially in sewing, after Charlotte returned from Roe Head. She and Emily also had piano lessons, as their *music books show. Anne preferred 'soft harmonies', and had a very sweet, though weak, singing voice.

Like Emily, Anne was fond of animals, and helped to look after the family pets. The silky-haired King Charles spaniel *Flossy, said to have been a gift from her *Thorp Green Hall pupils in 1843, was devoted to her. A drawing and two watercolours, probably made at Thorp Green, show a black, tan, and white spaniel, his head and ears finished in loving detail, which may have been Flossy (Alexander & Sellars, nos. 355–6, on pp. 409–10). Anne abhorred cruelty to animals, and it is likely that Agnes *Grey's intense distress at the *Bloomfield family's brutal treatment of them reflects Anne's own feelings. She delighted in the natural world: studies of trees, gracefully outlined and shaded, figure prominently among her drawings, poems such as 'The Bluebell' reveal her belief that 'A fine and subtle spirit dwells | In every little flower', and excellently observed landscapes and seascapes are evoked in her novels. Pure exhilaration, unexpected in the quiet Anne, inspires the theme and rhythm of her lines 'Composed in the Long-Plantation on a wild bright windy day', written on 30 December 1842, probably in a wood near Kirby Hall, Thorp Green Hall's neighbouring mansion. Her love for nature was enhanced, but also transcended, by her belief that God's wisdom and power was displayed in his works. In her poem 'In Memory of a Happy Day in February', finished on 10 November 1842,

Water colour of Anne Brontë, by her sister Charlotte, 17 June 1834.

the 'smile of early spring' is sweet, 'But most throughout the moral world I I saw his glory shine' (Chitham *ABP*, pp. 82–3, 88).

From an early age, Anne and Emily created and wrote about the exotic, imaginary land of *Gondal. No prose stories of Gondal survive, but some 23 of Anne's poems tell of the loves and griefs of its romantic heroes and heroines. They reflect the sisters' delight in oriental tales and in the works of Sir Walter *Scott and Thomas *Moore; for example, 'Verses by Lady Geralda' (Dec. 1836) and 'Alexander and Zenobia' (1 July 1837; Chitham *ABP*, pp. 49–59). Both poems also show Anne's erratic spelling, a trait still evident in her letters of the 1840s. She continued to write about the Gondals, mainly during her holidays at home, until at least September 1846, though in her *Diary Paper for 31 July 1845 she recorded that the Gondal chronicles of Republicans and Royalists begun three and a half years before were unfinished, and the Gondals were not 'in first rate playing condition' (Smith *Letters*, 1. 410).

In July 1835 Charlotte became a teacher at *Roe Head school. Mr Brontë wished to keep 'dear little Anne' at home for another year under her aunt's tuition and his own, but Emily, who accompanied Charlotte as a pupil, longed for freedom and rapidly declined in health. The 15-year-old Anne replaced her at Roe Head from October 1835. Five minutely detailed landscapes, two drawings of trees probably copied from engravings, and other pencil drawings, including one of Roe Head, testify to Anne's conscientious progress there under the instruction of her teachers. She was a quiet, diligent pupil, concerned to improve her skill in languages and other branches of learning so that she could eventually earn her own living. In 1836 she received a copy of Isaac Watts's *The Improvement of the Mind, with a Discourse on the Education of Youth* (1741) in J. F. Dove's English Classics edition of 1826. It was inscribed: 'Prize for good conduct. Presented to Miss A Brontë with Miss Wooler's kind love. Roe Head, December 14 1836' (Gaskell *Life* (Haworth edn., 1900), 147 n. 1). Though Charlotte recorded in her *Roe Head Journal* that she saw Anne's 'quiet image, sitting at her lessons on the opposite side of the table' (*c*.March 1837) we know little more of her activities there, but her affectionate nature and her ability to inspire affection in others are shown in her warm friendship with her young, beautiful fellow pupil Ann Cook (1825–40), the daughter of a Dewsbury banker. Both Charlotte and Anne were to grieve over her early death. Margaret *Wooler later showed a special concern for Anne during her mortal illness in 1849, but in December 1837 it was only Charlotte who became desperately worried about her. Anne had become 'wretchedly ill', suffering from pain and difficult breathing, and perhaps also from gastric fever. She was visited more than once at this time by the Moravian Bishop, Revd James *La Trobe, who recalled her gratitude: 'The words of love, from Jesus, opened her ear to my words . . . her heart opened to the sweet views of salvation, pardon, and peace in the blood of Christ' (William *Scruton, 'Reminiscences of the late Miss Ellen Nussey', *BST* (1898), 1. 8. 27). Possibly a spiritual crisis had accompanied, or been caused by, Anne's illness; and she would be comforted by the Moravian belief in the doctrine of *universal salvation—a belief Anne was to make her own, and to express through Helen Huntingdon in *Tenant*. Yet Miss Wooler not only seemed unconcerned about Anne's state, but thought Charlotte a fool for her anxiety. A quarrel ensued which made Miss Wooler cry. She complained to Mr Brontë, who sent for his daughters the day after he received her letter. At Haworth Anne soon became much better, and it is possible that she, as well as

Charlotte, returned to Roe Head for another year, as Mr Brontë claimed she did in a letter to Elizabeth Gaskell, quoted in Gaskell *Life* (3rd edn., i. 190–1).

Anne's work as a governess began on 8 April 1839, when she insisted on going alone to *Blake Hall, Mirfield, where she was to teach the eldest children in the *Ingham family, Joshua Cunliffe (1832–77) and Mary (1834–1922). Anne had thought she could summon more courage if nobody accompanied her. Her courage was needed, for though Mrs Ingham was kind, Anne's pupils were spoilt little dunces whom she was not allowed to punish when they misbehaved, as they constantly did. Informing their mother was therefore out of the question, so like Agnes Grey she had to scold, coax, and threaten, stick to her first word, and get on as well as she could. Charlotte was surprised by Anne's 'sensible, clever' letter from Blake Hall, but feared Mrs Ingham might conclude that the shy and silent Anne had a 'natural impediment of speech'. Anne endured the 'life-wearing exertion' of her task until the end of the year, when her employment ceased, probably by the Inghams' decision.

January and February 1840 were enlivened by the cheerful presence of Revd William *Weightman at the Parsonage, and by a visit from Ellen Nussey. On 14 February each of the girls received a Valentine card from Weightman—the first they had ever had. Two years later, on 20 January 1842, when Anne was at home on holiday, Charlotte told Ellen that he sat opposite to Anne at church 'sighing softly—& looking out of the corners of his eyes to win her attention—& Anne is so quiet, her look so downcast—they are a picture' (Smith *Letters*, 1. 279). Though the handsome, flirtatious Weightman differed in many ways from the plain, serious Edward *Weston in *Agnes Grey*, both were sincere evangelical preachers and pastors, generous, gentle, and understanding in their care for poor parishioners. Anne's poem 'I will not mourn thee, lovely one', written in December 1842 after Weightman's death, shows her trying to control her grief for the loss of one whose 'angel smile . . . Could my fond heart rejoice'.

Anne became a governess in the family of Revd Edmund *Robinson at Thorp Green Hall near York on or about 8 May 1840, and remained until June 1845. For a salary of £40 per annum she taught Lydia Mary, Elizabeth Lydia ('Bessy'), and Mary, and she may have taught Latin to the only son, Edmund. Agnes Grey's time at *Horton Lodge is partly based on Anne's experiences at Thorp Green, while her descriptions of the 'broad, bright bay' of A—— recall Anne's delight in *Scarborough where she accompanied the family on their summer holidays, and was (if her poem 'The Blue Bell', written on 22 August 1840, is autobiographical) 'Less harassed than at other times'. It is tempting to conclude that the 'weary' and 'lonely' life she describes in a poem written on 28 August 1840 at Thorp Green is a personal experience, but we have no reliable information about her life there until early April 1841, when she had reported that she was well. Anne returned to Haworth for three weeks, from 2 to 24 June 1841, but then had to join the Robinsons at Scarborough in their spacious lodgings at Number 2, Cliff, or rather, as Charlotte said, to return to 'the land of Egypt and the House of Bondage' (Smith *Letters*, 1. 258). In her *Diary Paper of 30 July 1841, written in Scarborough, Anne recorded that she disliked her situation and wished to change it for another, and Emily, in her own Diary Paper, sent 'an exhortation of courage courage! to exiled and harassed Anne'. Charlotte grieved at the thought of the lonely, susceptible Anne suffering as a patient, persecuted stranger among grossly insolent, proud, and tyrannical people. Anne meanwhile ruefully assessed her own faults, and made the most of her hard-earned wisdom, experience, and 'a little more self-posses-sion'. Like Emily, and like Agnes Grey, she hoped that she could eventually help to establish a successful school.

Anne returned home for the Christmas holidays in December 1841 in a despondent mood about her spiritual lethargy. She had also decided to leave Thorp Green, partly in order to help Miss Branwell and Martha Brown when Charlotte and Emily went to Brussels. But she had rendered herself so valuable in her difficult situation that the Robinsons begged her to return. She consented, experienced a resurgence of joy in February 1842, and eventually won the affection of the two younger Robinson girls. She accompanied the family to Scarborough again in July–August 1842. Soon after-wards she must have heard of Weightman's death on 6 September 1842. The painful death of Elizabeth Branwell followed on 29 October, and Anne had leave to go home for the funeral, returning to Thorp Green on 29 November 1842. Her composition of a poem 'in the Long-Plantation', near Thorp Green, on 30 December 1842 may indicate that she did not spend Christmas at Haworth. Materially Anne benefited by her aunt's bequest of a quarter-share of effects valued at under £1,500, and in due course had the pleasure of buying books, music, and drawing materials, perhaps more readily than in previous years. She also continued to study Latin and German, for as the Brontës' optimistic prospectus for their school shows, they intended to offer these languages, along with French, as 'extras' (Smith *Letters*, 1. 365). Meanwhile, on or about 21 January 1843 Branwell Brontë arrived at Thorp Green to become tutor to the young Edmund Robinson. By 1 May Charlotte, still in Brussels, had heard that he had been in poor health and spirits, but was doing well generally, and that Anne was 'pretty well'. Probably both Branwell and Anne accompanied the Robinsons to Scar-borough in July. According to Branwell, Mrs Lydia *Robinson had already become 'damnably too fond' of him, was always making him presents, and talking to his sister about him. Charlotte reported to Ellen Nussey on 23 January 1844 that both he and Anne (who had returned home for Christmas) were 'wonderously valued in their situation'—an impression more likely to be gained from Branwell's account than from the modest Anne. There is no firm evidence that Anne suspected Mrs Robinson of anything other than normal behaviour towards her brother in 1843, or in 1844, either at Thorp Green or in Scarborough. Her poems written between 28 May 1843 and 16 December 1844 include prayers for faith and praise for faith attained, a poem of longing for home ('How brightly glistening'), and one perhaps recalling William Weightman ('Yes thou art gone'). Others appear to be Gondal poems, with no ob-vious relevance to Branwell's or Mrs Robinson's behaviour. But before Anne resigned her post and returned to Haworth on or about 12 June 1845, she had 'very unpleasant and undreamt of experience of human nature' (Diary Paper of 31 July 1845). Anne kept her own counsel about this experience; whatever it was, it did not give her a per-manent dislike of two places associated with the Robinsons: *York and Scarborough. She and Emily enjoyed themselves very much during their trip to York from 30 June to 2 July 1845, and Anne especially desired to visit both places again on the last journey she ever took, just before her death. On the other hand, when Branwell led his family to believe he was dismissed from his tutorship because Mr Robinson had discovered an attachment between Branwell and his wife, and threatened to shoot him if he re-turned, Anne apparently did not contradict this version of events, and it was Anne who informed Charlotte of the 'immediate cause' of Branwell's illness after his dismissal.

From July 1845 onwards Anne witnessed with pain and revulsion Branwell's descent into increasingly heavy drinking and drug-taking, grieving over his wasted talent and his moral and spiritual degeneration. In her preface to the second edition of *Tenant* she defended her realistic presentation of 'vice and vicious characters' as the best method of warning inexperienced youth to avoid the 'snares and pitfalls of life'. Branwell's behaviour led his sisters finally to abandon their plan for a school at the Parsonage. But when in the autumn of 1845 Charlotte discovered Emily's poems in manuscript, Anne quietly produced some of her own poems, and by about 22 May 1846 *Aylott and Jones had published *Poems* by Currer, Ellis, and Acton Bell, including 21 poems by 'Acton' (Anne). The volume was reissued by Smith, Elder and Co. in 1848. In the same year, *Fraser's Magazine* published Anne's poem 'The *Three Guides' in August, and her hymn *'Believe not those who say' in December.

It is likely that Anne wrote *Agnes Grey* in 1845–6, and that she was making a fair copy of it by April 1846, when Charlotte asked Aylott and Jones for advice on the publication of 'three distinct and unconnected tales' (Smith *Letters*, 1. 461). Soon after 27 June 1846 it was sent with *Wuthering Heights* and *The Professor* to an unknown number of publishers before its acceptance by T. C. *Newby in July 1847. From 21 August 1846 until late September Anne and Emily, with the help of the servants, had to cope with Branwell while Charlotte was away in Manchester caring for her father after his cataract operation. Anne was forced to contemplate at close quarters the instability and, often, self-inflicted illness of an undisciplined character, and the resulting pain for those near to him; the distress was to continue for all the family, with little remission. In February 1847 Bessy and Mary Robinson, Anne's former pupils, who had corresponded with her until their father's death on 26 May 1846, and had then stopped writing, suddenly wrote to her almost every day for a fortnight, warmly asserting their 'endless esteem and gratitude' to her, and speaking affectionately of their mother, showing no knowledge of her alleged errors. The contrast between the Robinsons' way of life and Branwell's state of mind and body must have impressed itself on Anne as she began, or continued to write, her next novel, *The *Tenant of Wildfell Hall*. Despite her fragile health she persevered with what she regarded as a moral duty, courageously depicting a wife who leaves her debauched and adulterous husband in order to protect her young son, and returns to nurse him in his mortal illness in the hope that he will seek and receive God's mercy. There was little comfort for Anne from the progress of *Agnes Grey*, for its publication was postponed by Newby until December 1847. Then, though critics greeted it with faint praise for its 'minute observation', it was accused of an emphasis on the eccentric and unpleasant, and of exaggeration in 'parts carefully copied from the life', as Anne recalled in the preface to the second edition of *Tenant*. Nevertheless the combined three-volume edition of *Wuthering Heights* and *Agnes Grey* sold well enough for the authors to wish to stay with Newby as publisher, instead of transferring to Smith, Elder—the publishers of *Jane Eyre*.

Before Newby published *Tenant* on or about 27 June 1848, he informed the American publishers Harper & Brothers that it was the latest work of 'Currer Bell'. Since Smith, Elder had arranged that Harper's should publish the first American edition of Currer Bell's next work, George *Smith demanded an explanation. Charlotte and Anne made their hasty 'pop visit' to London from 8 to 11 July, astonishing

Smith by identifying themselves as two of the famous 'Bells', and confronting Newby with his chicanery. On the day they travelled to London, the *Spectator* admitted the power of Acton Bell's novel, but condemned the writer's morbid love for 'the coarse, not to say the brutal' (21 (1848), 662–3). Anne, distressed by the incomprehension of such reviews, wrote a forceful preface to the second edition, defending her moral purpose in describing the 'coarse' as it really was.

For her, the need to follow the difficult upward path of Christian faith, and to guide others into it, was paramount. Her religious poems, eloquent in their self-analysis and exhortation, include the hymn 'My God! O let me call Thee mine!'. Her last and most moving poem, 'A *dreadful darkness closes in', was written in January 1849, after Dr *Teale's diagnosis had confirmed that her symptoms were those of an advanced stage of TB. It moves from that torturing darkness to a prayer for patience, fortitude, and hope. As courageous as Emily, but more amenable, she accepted medical help and wished strongly for recovery. Her journey to Scarborough in May 1849 in the company of her sister Charlotte and Ellen Nussey was undertaken in the hope of improvement; but on 28 May she died—with almost her last breath saying that she was happy, and thanking God that 'death was come, and come so gently'. Her funeral service was taken by Revd J. W. Whiteside at Christ Church, Scarborough, on 30 May, and she was buried in St Mary's churchyard on Castle Hill.

Chitham *ABP*.
—— *A Life of Anne Brontë* (1991).
Gérin, Winifred, *Anne Brontë* (1959).
Nash, Julie, and Suess, Barbara A. (eds.), *New Approaches to the Literary Art of Anne Brontë* (2001).

Parish Registers. 'Prunty' is a variant of the name, and like the entry 'Branty' for Mr Brontë under the date 1 October 1802 in the register of St John's College, Cambridge, probably indicates a variant pronunciation. 'Branty' was corrected to 'Bronte' in the Residence Register for 3 October, perhaps because Patrick recalled that Horatio Nelson had been made Duke of Bronte in Sicily in 1799. Revd Patrick *Brontë was the son of Hugh Brontë (*c*.1755–*c*.1808) and his wife Eleanor McClory (d. *c*.1822). Their children were:

Patrick (17 March 1777–7 June 1861), married Maria Branwell (15 April 1783–15 September 1821); six children: Maria, Elizabeth, Charlotte, Branwell, Emily Jane, Anne.

William, born Ballyroney, baptized March 1779, d. 1862 or 1864; married and had issue.

Hugh, born Lisnacreevy, baptized May 1781, d. March 1863, unmarried.

James, born Lisnacreevy, baptized November 1783, d. 1870, unmarried.

Walsh, sometimes called Welsh, born Lisnacreevy, baptized February 1786, d. November 1868; married and had issue.

Jane, born Lisnacreevy, baptized February 1789, d. 1819, unmarried.

Mary, born Lisnacreevy, baptized May 1791, d. 1866, unmarried.

Rose, born *c*.1793, place unknown; date of death unknown.

Sarah, twin sister of Rose, born *c*.1793, place unknown; d. 1875; married and had issue.

Alice, born *c*.1795/6 Ballynaskeagh, d. January 1891, unmarried.

On 20 June 1855 Patrick Brontë described to Elizabeth Gaskell his parentage and upbringing. His father Hugh Brontë 'was a native of the South of Ireland, and was left an orphan at an early age . . . He came to the North of Ireland, and made an early, but suitable marriage. His pecuniary means were small—but renting a few acres of land, He, and my mother, by dint of application, and industry, managed to bring up a Family of ten Children, in a respectable manner' (Rylands MS, in Lock & Dixon, 494). Welsh Brontë's granddaughter Miss Shannon said that Hugh Bronte sen. and his sister lived with their mother's brother in Drogheda before Hugh moved north. Hugh is said by Dr William *Wright to have married Alice McClory 'in 1776 in the Protestant Church of Magherally', County Down.

(*cont.* on page 79)

B RANWELL Brontë (1817–48) used the pseudonym 'Northangerland' for his published writings. With the exception of Francis Leyland's 1886 *The Brontë Family*, biographies before Juliet Barker's 1994 *The Brontës* treat Branwell rather unfairly because of their over-reliance on Elizabeth Gaskell's very negative portrayal in the *Life* and on the unreliable anecdotal evidence of acquaintances like Francis Grundy. These biographers (including Leyland) also had little knowledge of how much and what Branwell had written or of his publications. Only with the completion of the three-volume edition of Branwell's writings by Neufeldt in 1999 were biographers finally able to assess accurately Branwell's life and achievement.

Branwell was born on 26 June 1817 at *Thornton, West Yorkshire, the fourth child of Revd Patrick *Brontë (1776–1861) and Mrs Maria *Brontë, née Branwell (1783–1821). In April 1820 Mr Brontë, having accepted the position of perpetual curate, moved his family to *Haworth, where his wife died in September 1821.

Branwell was mainly educated at home by his father, who every morning after prayers and breakfast instructed his children in the classics, history, geography, the Bible, and other basic skills (see EDUCATION OF THE BRONTËS). Branwell soon developed a fondness for classical languages, translating passages from the New Testament and the works of Homer, *Virgil, Horace, and Ovid. Like his sisters he read widely from an early age, including such authors as James Macpherson, *Shakespeare, *Milton, Defoe, Ben Jonson, *Bunyan, John *Dryden, Gray, Addison, *Goldsmith, Pope, *Burns, Sir Walter *Scott, Lord *Byron, Isaac Watts. He was particularly fond of *Blackwood's Edinburgh Magazine*. With his sisters he received art and music lessons by the time he was 12.

From the outset, Branwell was blessed with a lively imagination and intellectual curiosity. Though 'a little below the middle height' according to Francis Leyland, he was slim and agile, and at the age of 22 'good looking, with a shock of red hair brushed forward over his high forehead, long side-burns and a straight prominent nose. Vivacious and witty, he excelled at conversation and was impressively erudite.' His voice, Leyland recalled, 'had a ringing sweetness, and the utterance and use of his English were perfect' (Barker, pp. 334, 348). His self-portrait appears in Alexander & Sellars (p. 336).

After the death of their mother in 1821 and the two eldest sisters in 1825, Branwell and his remaining sisters, stimulated by their reading, and using such toys as wooden soldiers, ninepins, and musicians, began to make up and act out plays. Under the leadership of Charlotte and Branwell these 'Young Men' plays evolved into the complex saga of the imaginary *Glass Town Federation, situated in the Ashantee country of West Africa, which Charlotte and Branwell in turn developed into a story of the kingdom of Angria, and finally abandoned in 1839, while Emily and Anne, rebelling against the dominance of their older siblings at the end of 1831, developed the Gondal saga. See JUVENILIA; GLASS TOWN AND ANGRIAN SAGA.

Branwell's earliest known piece of writing dates from March 1827, but with the production of his 'Magazine' in January 1829, which quickly became *'Branwell's Blackwood's Magazine', he fully revealed his ambition to become the poet and man of letters he saw exemplified by Christopher *North and James *Hogg in *Blackwood's*.

In December 1835, at the age of 18, on hearing of Hogg's death, Branwell wrote to offer himself as Hogg's replacement. In all, between 1835 and 1843 he wrote to *Blackwood's* six times offering his services and samples of his prose, and sending samples of his poetry.

From 1829 to 1837 Branwell maintained a prodigious output of poems, verse drama, and prose, some of it in collaboration with Charlotte. His literary activities in 1829, his first full year of writing, at the age of 11–12, can best be described as a kind of volcanic eruption with all the sense of undisciplined exuberance that image suggests. From January 1829, he produced over the next twelve months, in addition to at least four and possibly seven issues of the magazine, a two-volume travel book, at least 34 poems or verse fragments (including an attempt at Latin verse), and a *verse drama. Several of his poems were written in collaboration with Charlotte (see UT AND WT); twenty were his own. A number of his poems were included in the magazine he and Charlotte produced in 1829, which became 'Blackwood's Young Men's Magazine' when Charlotte assumed the editorship in August. Eleven poems appeared in two volumes of poems 'published' (i.e. in Glass Town) by 'Young *Soult the Rhymer' (spelt 'Ryhmer' by Branwell), and the verse drama was also a separately 'published' volume. Branwell was more venturesome in experimenting with verse form, rhyme patterns, and metrics than Charlotte at this time. His experimentation was part of the image of himself as poet and man of letters he was consciously propagating at the time, an image with some contradictory features. On the one hand there is the sober and scholarly Sergeant *Bud, who after receiving a copy of Macpherson's *Ossian* from *Chief Genius Taly (Charlotte), writes to the editor of their magazine: 'upon an attentive perusal of the above said works I found they were most sublime and exelent I am engaged in publishing an edition of them in Quarto—3 vols—with notes and commentarys &c I am fully convinced that it is the work of Ossian who lived a 1000 years ago—and—of no other there is a most intense anxiety prevailing amongst literary men to know its contents in a short time they shall be gratified for it will be published on the first of July, 1829.' The same scholarly persona reappears in the guise of Moses *Chateaubriand, who not only provides elaborate learned commentaries on Young Soult's poems, but also censures the poet's excesses and irregularities. On the other hand there is the rebellious and undisciplined Young Soult the Rhymer, whose romantic posturing is the subject of a number of satirical comments and sketches by Charlotte (see Neufeldt *CBP*, p. 397; Alexander *EW*, 64–6; Alexander *EEW*, 1. 127, 180 ff., 309). Branwell was himself quite capable of laughing at his poetic posturings (see Neufeldt *BB Works*, 1. 175). Soult's rebelliousness is evident in his experimentation, in his bohemian appearance and behaviour, in his derivation—he is the son of one of Wellington's major adversaries in the Napoleonic campaigns—and in his praise of and sympathy for *Napoleon and France.

Up to the end of 1831 Branwell mainly thought of himself as Young Soult, the poet of Glass Town, published in Glass Town. After 1831, however, Young Soult rapidly disappears and a new dual self-conception begins to emerge. On the one hand Branwell continues as chronicler of the Glass Town and Angrian saga in the persons of Captain Sir John *Flower (Viscount Richton), Captain John *Bud, Henry *Hastings (the poet of Angria), and Charles *Wentworth. On the other hand Branwell is also P. B. Brontë, producing poems in his own right. Between 1832 and 1836, the year in which he first submitted a poem for publication, Branwell composed 51 poems, totalling almost

40,000 lines, in addition to a massive amount of prose related to Glass Town and Angria. Ten of these poems are fair copies, and seven of the ten are in ordinary cursive handwriting as opposed to the usual print writing; three others, while in the print writing, are part of a manuscript volume of very legible fair copies. All are dated and either signed by Branwell or have his initials at the beginning with the date. While the separation from Glass Town and Angria is obviously not complete, many of the poems are of a classical and philosophical bent; even Percy (Branwell's protagonist) is retrospective and reflective in most of his poems during this time, discussing the nature of human existence and the transitoriness of human happiness. All this suggests that from May 1832 on, at the age of 14, Branwell was beginning to think of publication in the real world. Four years later, in April 1836, he sent *Blackwood's* the manuscript of his poem 'Misery', offering to provide both poetry and prose in the future. He signed the poem 'Northangerland', his first use of the pseudonym that he was to adopt for the rest of his life.

Branwell's division of interest between chronicling the history of Angria and being a poet in his own right worried Charlotte. In her famous caricature of him in 1834 as 'Patrick Benjamin *Wiggins' (Alexander *EEW*, 2(2). 245–53), it is precisely his inability to act with undivided purpose that she sees as potentially dangerous. Not only was Branwell's perception of himself as writer divided; that role also had to compete with his interests in music and painting. His poetic ambitions notwithstanding, he had decided as early as 1833 that he wanted to become a professional portrait painter and possibly as early as 1834 began to take lessons from William *Robinson, the society portrait painter in Leeds. The two family portraits—the 'Pillar Portrait' or 'The *Brontë Sisters' portrait and the 'Gun Group'—date from this period (see Alexander & Sellars, pp. 73–6; 307–12). About the time that Charlotte wrote her description of Wiggins, Branwell began to plan to enrol in the *Royal Academy of Arts in 1835, a plan that seems never to have materialized (Barker, pp. 227 ff.). As a result of his music lessons, he had become proficient on the flute, had learned to play the piano, and with the installation of an organ in his father's church in 1834, learned to play it under the tuition of the Keighley parish organist Abraham *Sunderland. In addition he taught in the Haworth Sunday School, established in 1832, and was a secretary of the *Temperance Society, established in Haworth in 1834.

His response to his failure to enrol in the Royal Academy was not only an immediate return to writing, but also a feverish attempt to gain literary employment and to get himself published. In December 1835, he sent the now famous letter to *Blackwood's* offering himself as a replacement for James *Hogg. In April 1836 he sent *Blackwood's* his poem 'Misery', and in January 1837 he again wrote to the magazine's editor, requesting an interview to present a sample of his prose. His bombastic tone ensured that his letters went unanswered (see Christine Alexander, 'Readers and Writers: *Blackwood's* and the Brontës', *Gaskell Society Journal*, 8 (1994)). This last appeal was contemporaneous with Charlotte's letter to Robert *Southey, the Poet Laureate, to ask his advice on whether she could earn a living from her writing. Not to be outdone, Branwell wrote to *Wordsworth, sending him the manuscript of 'The Struggles of flesh with Spirit Scene I—Infancy', a revised version of 'Still and bright in twilight shining' (Neufeldt *BB Works*, 2. 588), asking the poet to pass judgement on the poem because at the age of 19 Branwell wished 'to push into the open world' with his writing. At the same time he continued to prepare himself to become a portrait painter. He was also very interested and involved in local politics; in January 1837 he helped establish the Haworth Operative Conservative Society, serving first as secretary, then as chairman.

Unfortunately neither *Blackwood's* nor Wordsworth replied to his letters, so Branwell continued to compose and revise poems for publication, unchecked and unguided, while also continuing with his Angrian chronicles, though it was becoming increasingly clear during 1837 that the imaginative impetus for the latter was failing. During 1837 and early 1838—until he left for Bradford—he added five poems to the notebook he had begun in late 1835 with the first draft of 'Misery', all fair copies signed or initialled, although some are incomplete. More significant, however, is a new notebook into which he entered between March 1837 and May 1838 revisions of 26 earlier poems, eight new poems, and translations of six odes of Horace.

These notebooks, especially the second one, reveal Branwell's gradual resolution of his dual conception of his role as writer. While Richton, Hastings, and Wentworth continue to produce some pages of narrative concerning Angria, from 1837 on it is P. B. Brontë who reaffirms his dedication to poetry in his poem 'The Spirit of Poetry', one of the two poems in the notebook not originally composed by an Angrian persona. The poems related to Angria are divorced from their original context and are all 'corrected', 'altered', 'enlarged', and 'transcribed' by 'P. B. Brontë'. Closely related to this change is a move toward long narrative poems, with a strongly reflective cast. Also, at the very end of 1837 he began work on a prose narrative which, although still featuring Alexander Percy, is set not in Africa but in Yorkshire, and in which he rebukes Charlotte as a 'writer who loved more to dwell upon Indian Palm Groves or Genii palaces than on the wooded manors and cloudy skies of England' (Neufeldt *BB Works*, 3. 186). Although he did produce a few more prose fragments in 1838–9, Branwell essentially abandoned Angria at the end of 1837 and turned more and more to writing long poems not based on an Angrian source and complete in themselves: public pieces meant for publication.

Early in 1838 Branwell decided to try to set up as a professional portrait painter in *Bradford, but the precise date of his move to Bradford is not known. Although he received some commissions, the venture was not a success (see Alexander & Sellars, pp. 82–4, 315, 323, 327–34) and he returned to Haworth in February 1839. Except for the first draft of *'Sir Henry Tunstall', he seems not to have composed any new poems while he was at Bradford, nor immediately after his return, when he began a regulated programme of study with his father, presumably, since painting was not to be his profession, to prepare him to take up teaching.

However, while at Bradford he had become actively involved with an artistic and literary circle which included Joseph Bentley *Leyland and his brother Francis. His literary aspirations were stimulated by the friendship he developed with Joseph, and he began the practice of passing manuscripts on to Leyland for criticism. Those aspirations seem to have been further stimulated by his programme of study with his father, for while he worked as tutor for the *Postlethwaite family at *Broughton-in-Furness, January to June 1840, he attempted once more to establish a literary career, this time as poet and translator. On 15 April 1840 he sent Thomas *De Quincey a revised draft of 'Sir Henry Tunstall' and translations of five *'Odes of Horace'. Five days later he sent Hartley *Coleridge a revised draft of the poem 'At dead of midnight—drearily' and translations of two odes by Horace. He wrote to Coleridge that he was 'about to enter active life' and needed to ascertain whether he could earn a living by 'periodical or other writing' and by translations of classic authors. While De Quincey did not reply, Coleridge obviously responded positively, for Branwell spent 1 May with him at Nab Cottage, near Rydal Water, and encouraged by the visit, continued work on the translations, sending Coleridge Book 1 of the Odes on 27 June, just after he had been dismissed from his post as tutor. The reasons for Branwell's dismissal appear various; neglect of his pupils, alcohol, and an illegitimate child have been suggested as possibilities. Although Coleridge began to draft a very positive and encouraging reply, he unfortunately never completed and sent the letter.

Meanwhile Branwell's literary activity was once more curtailed by his appointment as assistant clerk at the *Sowerby Bridge railway station on the newly opened Leeds and Manchester *railway on 31 August 1840, and not until he became clerk in charge of the station at *Luddenden Foot, 1 April 1841, did he once more find time and energy for literary composition.

Contrary to the traditional view that Branwell's days at Luddenden Foot consisted of little more than lack of attention to duty, idleness, and drunken debauchery, the move from Sowerby Bridge provided new impetus to his literary aspirations. Just over a month after the move, on 5 June 1841, he achieved his lifelong ambition when his poem 'Heaven and Earth' appeared in the *Halifax Guardian* under the pseudonym 'Northangerland', the first of eighteen to appear in various Yorkshire newspapers, all but one under the same pseudonym. That traditional view of Branwell's time at Luddenden Foot is based to a large extent on his own comments to his friend Francis *Grundy on 22 May 1842, in which he speaks of his 'grovelling carelessness, the malignant yet cold debauchery . . . which too often marked my conduct when there' (Wise & Symington, 1. 264), and underscores the difficulty of taking Branwell's descriptions of his own behaviour at face value. The delightful and witty conversationalist was also guilty, at times, of unpleasantly boastful and exaggerated accounts of his drinking exploits, mixed with crass sexual innuendo (see, for example, Barker, pp. 320–3; Alexander & Sellars, p. 347).

In August he not only published a second poem in the *Guardian*, this time a political satire over his own initials, but he also began to enter drafts of poems into a small notebook. Some of the poems are autobiographical, indicating an awareness that he was not making the most of his talents because of his overabsorption in the pleasures of the present. Most of the poems, however, are full of ambition, energy and optimism, and both the quality and quantity of the poems belie the usual description of Branwell's existence at Luddenden Foot. Some of the credit for all this activity must be given to his circle of artistic friends in *Halifax: the Leyland brothers, the artist John Wilson Anderson, the poets William *Dearden, John Nicholson, William Heaton, and possibly Thomas Crossley. The writers in this group met at various hotels and inns to read their manuscripts aloud to one another for criticism. See also THOMPSON, JOHN HUNTER.

Branwell's dismissal from his post in March 1842 because of a discrepancy in the accounts (he was never suspected of theft or fraud) did not dampen his literary activity. Instead it seems to have spurred him on to even greater efforts to establish himself as a poet to compensate for his failure. Between April 1842 and January 1843, when he left to become tutor at *Thorp Green Hall, he published nine poems—three of which were new; six were revisions of the new poems in the 1837–8 notebook—and one prose article; these appeared in three newspapers: the *Bradford Herald*, and the *Leeds Intelligencer* as well as the *Guardian*. In addition, he wrote one other new poem and revised six others, all intended for publication. He also made an effort to draw attention to his poems, sending samples of his work to James Montgomery, *Blackwood's*, Caroline Bowles, James and Harriet *Martineau, and Leigh *Hunt.

However, Branwell still had to earn a living, and so from January 1843 to July 1845 he was employed as tutor by the Robinsons at Thorp Green, where his sister Anne was already employed as a governess. During this time he produced only six new poems, but his desire to publish had not waned—he published two of the new poems and two written earlier in the *Yorkshire Gazette* within ten weeks of his dismissal from Thorp Green because of 'proceedings . . . bad beyond expression'—possibly an affair with Mrs Lydia *Robinson. What the actual details of the alleged affair were is not clear, but Branwell apparently believed that Mrs Robinson's affection for him was sincere and that she would marry him when her invalid husband died (see Barker, pp. 458–69; Neufeldt *BB Works*, 3. 403, 470, 473, 481, 482). However, Branwell's claim that Mr Robinson prevented any such marriage by changing his will so as to disinherit Mrs Robinson should she do so is false. The reasons for the claim are unclear; it may have been a face-saving story; it may have been a story created by Mrs Robinson to forestall any advances by Branwell (Barker, pp. 493–6).

Despite his distraught state after his dismissal, Branwell embarked on several ambitious projects during 1845–6. Immediately after his dismissal he began revisions of three earlier poems, the second of which was to be the first canto of a long poem. However, the first two remained unfinished; the third became part of his unfinished novel *And the Weary are at Rest*, begun in the summer of 1845. He set out to write the novel, he wrote to Joseph Leyland, because 'in the present state of the publishing and reading world a Novel is the most saleable article, so that where ten pounds would be offered for a work the production of which would require the utmost stretch of a man's intellect—two hundred pounds would be a refused offer for three volumes whose composition would require the smoking of a cigar and the humming of a tune' (Wise & Symington, 2. 61). Branwell's contempt for novels was consistent. Ten years earlier, in 'The *Life of Alexander Percy', volume 2, the narrator had written 'but Here I wish Reader that I had words to express the Heavenly beauty both in person and in mind of Mary Henrietta Wharton She was not one of those unnatural (for I will not call them supernatural) beings which disfigure the already worthless pages of sentimental Novels with their amazing ignorance and inanity beings who if they lived with their "purities" and perfections ought to be left withering like a sapless leaf in winter' (Neufeldt *BB Works*, 2. 182). Before the end of 1845 he completed four new poems, two of which were published in the *Halifax Guardian*. In July 1845 he left with John *Brown for *Liverpool, hoping to restore his bodily and mental health.

He began 1846 with another poem in the *Guardian*, composed seven others, including a topical poem on the heroism of Sir Robert Sale and Sir Henry Hardinge intended for publication, and began an epic in several cantos about Morley Hall which was connected with the Leyland family. Although the death of Mr Robinson on 26 May and Mrs Robinson's rejection of him greatly upset and distracted Branwell, by October he was back at work on 'Morley Hall' and two other poems concerned with historical figures facing defeat and despair, begun in late 1846 or early 1847 (Neufeldt *BB Works*, 3. 492, 494). He wrote to Joseph Leyland about the 'hopelessness of bursting through the barriers of literary circles, and getting a hearing among publishers . . . . Otherwise I have the materials for a respectably sized volume, and if I were in London personally I might try Henry Moxon [i.e. the publisher Edward Moxon],—a patronizer of rhyme' (Wise & Symington, 2. 92). In all, he produced ten poems in 1846, and did not go into total collapse even after the death of Mr Robinson and the failure of his plan to marry Mrs Robinson, boarding for a time at Ovenden Cross (see PEARSON, MARY).

In 1847 it became apparent, however, that whatever his intentions might be, Branwell's will and ability to write were fading rapidly. After Lydia Robinson's rejection Branwell lapsed into chronic alcoholism, dependence on opiates and debt, and caused the family much distress, embarrassment, and on the part of Charlotte, bitterness over talent wasted. He seems to have been unaware of his sisters' 1846 volume of poetry and of the novels published in 1847, and there is no evidence that any of his family were aware of his publications. Yet he published one poem in the *Halifax Guardian*, fittingly entitled 'The End of All' just four months before the publication of *Jane Eyre*, and sent another to Leyland asking if 'it would be worth sending to some respectable periodical like Blackwood's Magazine' (Symington & Hatfield, p. 42). Even now the *Blackwood's* dream had not died, but his health had deteriorated seriously and he died at the Parsonage on 24 September 1848, probably of tuberculosis aggravated by delirium tremens, although the death certificate states the cause as 'chronic bronchitis—Marasmus'. He was buried in the family vault in his father's church on 28 September.   VN

See also FREEMASONRY; ART OF THE BRONTËS; VERSE DRAMA BY BRANWELL BRONTË.

Alexander *EEW*.

Alexander *EW*.

Alexander & Sellars.

Barker.

Grundy, Francis Henry, *Pictures of the Past* (1879).

Leyland.

Neufeldt *BBP*.

Neufeldt *BB Works*.

Neufeldt *CBP*.

Symington, J. Alexander, and Hatfield, C. W. (eds.), *Patrick Branwell Brontë: A Complete Transcript of the Leyland Manuscripts* (1925).

Hugh's granddaughter Rose Heslip and great-granddaughters the Misses Shannon referred to his wife as Alice, but Drumgooland baptismal registers named her 'Elinor Brunty' and 'Eleanor McClory'. She remained 'a specially fine woman' in old age (*Brontëana*, 290–2).

William joined the United Irishmen, founded in 1791 mainly to secure the political emancipation of Catholics and Dissenters, and fought in the serious affray at Ballynahinch. Later in life 'Billy Brunty' kept a public house. By his wife, née Jane Shaw (1803–66), William had six sons, Hugh, Patrick, James, Matthew, William, and John. All but James married and had issue. Matthew emigrated to the USA and John to New Zealand. The great-great-grandchildren of Matthew's son William Emmett Brontë (1841–1900) have been traced. Patrick Brontë's niece Esther Jane, daughter of William, had a son William (b. 1835) whose great-great-grandsons have been traced.

Hugh was a tall man, a road-maker by trade, who, with his brother Welsh, had a reputation for good substantial work. His niece Rose Heslip rejected Wright's stories of his trying to coax a ghost out of his sister's house by playing the fiddle, and visiting Haworth before travelling to London to 'castigate' the writer of the *Quarterly*'s review of *Jane Eyre*. Mrs Heslip said that his only visit to England was in his boyhood, when he 'got employment in corn-thrashing and also in a sugar-factory. He then became ill', visited Haworth, and was given 10 guineas by Mr Brontë, who 'also took him to see Robin Hood's grave' at Kirklees. On 20 November 1843 Patrick wrote to him asking (*cont. on page 87*)

C HARLOTTE Brontë ('Currer Bell', 1816–55) was born at Thornton, near Brad-ford, Yorks., on 21 April 1816, the third child of Revd Patrick and Mrs Maria Brontë. Named after her mother's sister Charlotte Branwell, she was baptized on 29 June 1816 by Revd William *Morgan in the Old Bell Chapel in Thornton. Her younger siblings, Branwell, Emily, and Anne, were born in quick succession in 1817, 1818, and 1820. Charlotte's early memories of Haworth Parsonage, to which the family moved on 20 April 1820, were of sadness and loss, for her mother died on 15 September 1821.

The unhealed wound of motherlessness made its mark on her life and writings. When her father let her read the letters Maria had written to him during their court-ship, Charlotte was 'curiously touched . . . I wished she had lived and that I had known her' (to Ellen Nussey, ?16 Feb. 1850; Smith *Letters*, 2. 347.) In the *juvenilia loving mothers die young, and in *Shirley*, Caroline *Helstone's yearning is uncon-vincingly satisfied by the revelation that 'Mrs Pryor' is her long-lost mother.

In the Brontë household, the children's aunt Elizabeth *Branwell took on the mother's duty of caring for the children, earning Charlotte's respect rather than affection. Fortunately all the Brontë servants except Mrs Brontë's nurse were devoted to the family. The Garrs sisters (see SERVANTS OF THE BRONTËS) accompanied the children on their walks, and sometimes joined in their high-spirited games. Tabitha *Aykroyd's fierce protectiveness of the 'childer', like that of *Hannah in *Jane Eyre*, was rewarded by their lifelong loyalty.

On 10 August 1824, Charlotte was taken to join her sisters Maria and Elizabeth at *Cowan Bridge school. Emily followed on 25 November 1824. The school register records that the new pupil 'Reads tolerably—Writes indifferently—Ciphers [under-stands arithmetic] a little and works neatly [does plain sewing]. Knows nothing of Grammar, Geography, History or Accomplishments [French, music, and draw-ing]. . . . Altogether clever of her age but knows nothing systematically' (Barker, p. 128). She was to take the higher level of education in preparation for becoming a governess. At Cowan Bridge, unforgettably depicted as *Lowood in *Jane Eyre*, Charlotte suffered from the harsh discipline, dirty or inadequate food, enforced exercise, and walks in icy winds. She hated the insensitivity and appalling doctrines preached by Revd W. Carus *Wilson, and she fiercely resented what she saw as the cruel treatment of her sister Maria, whom she depicted as Helen *Burns. Maria was taken home seriously ill, and died at the Parsonage on 6 May 1825, while Charlotte and Emily were still at school. Helen Burns's death at 'Lowood' did not match the real circumstances; but Elizabeth Brontë, brought home on 31 May, the day before Mr Brontë brought back Charlotte and Emily, died at the Parsonage a fortnight later.

For the next five years Charlotte was educated at home by Elizabeth Branwell, perhaps with some instruction also from her father. One of Mr Brontë's great gifts to his children was the privilege of apparently unrestricted access to his books, and to the magazines and newspapers he bought or borrowed (see EDUCATION OF THE BRONTËS; BOOKS READ BY THE BRONTËS). Charlotte knew too the *Lady's Magazines* which had belonged to her mother or her aunt, and which she read by stealth with exquisite pleasure. Charlotte, imaginative and highly intelligent, had a

Carte-de-visite photograph of Charlotte Brontë, 1854.

natural gift for language, a retentive memory, and an inventive mind. With Branwell she enthusiastically developed the *Young Men's Play he had initiated in June 1826 into the exciting *Glass Town and Angrian saga. She began to chronicle the 'Young Men's' adventures in March 1829. Charlotte's satirical pieces, such as her mockery of her brother in the person of 'Patrick Benjamin *Wiggins', show her lively sense of humour and exuberant fluency. Until late 1839, when she bade *'Farewell to Angria', her tales of picturesque heroes and heroines allowed her to escape into an imaginary world. The skills evident in her mature novels were honed in these years of private creation.

On 17 January 1831 Charlotte became a pupil at Margaret *Wooler's school, *Roe Head, where she met Ellen *Nussey and Mary *Taylor. When she first arrived, she was shy, and Ellen thought her 'anything but pretty; even her good points were lost. Her naturally beautiful hair of soft silky brown being then dry and frizzy-looking, screwed up in tight little curls, showing features that were all the plainer from her exceeding thinness and want of complexion, she looked "dried in"' ('Reminiscences of Charlotte Brontë', in Smith *Letters*, 1. 590). She was to remain short in stature, and her hands and feet were tiny. During her visits to London in the 1850s she did not help matters by wearing an obvious brown silk 'hair-piece'. Elizabeth Gaskell attributed her 'nervous dread of encountering strangers' to her fixed idea that her personal ugliness made them reluctant to look at her: 'A more untrue idea never entered into anyone's head'; her 'pleasant countenance, sweet voice, and gentle timid manners' attracted many people to her (Gaskell *Life*, 2. 290).

Charlotte was fairly soon at ease at Roe Head, for Margaret Wooler was a kindly woman, who 'had a remarkable knack of making' her pupils 'feel interested in whatever they had to learn' (Gaskell *Life*, 1. 113). Charlotte responded well to her lessons, and the work helped her to become systematic in her approach to new tasks. She gained the French prize, a New Testament in French, presented with 'the Miss Woolers' kind love' on 14 December 1831.

Her private writing ceased during the school terms; but Mary Taylor told Elizabeth Gaskell that Charlotte would 'sit or stand still, often with a book' in the playground rather than play games with the other girls (Gaskell *Life*, 1. 108). At night, in the dormitory, she was 'an invaluable story-teller', frightening the other pupils 'almost out of their wits' (*Life*, 1. 112). Once she told of a somnambulist, walking on shaking turrets: 'She brought together all the horrors her imagination could create . . . surging seas . . . high precipices, invisible chasms and dangers', terrifying an invalid pupil, to her own distress and remorse (Ellen Nussey, 'Reminiscences'; in Smith *Letters*, 1. 592). Her ability to create haunting scenes was to be deployed in climactic episodes in her mature work, such as Jane Eyre's first sight of the ruined *Thornfield Hall, and the phantasmagoric Park sequence in *Villette* (ch. 38). Her strong visual imagination was ultimately more effectively embodied in writing than in art; but she already drew pictures much more quickly and skilfully than the other girls, and at Roe Head she was given a more formal training in drawing by Margaret Wooler's sister Susan, later Mrs E. N. Carter.

In September 1832, after she had left the school, Charlotte paid her first visit to Ellen Nussey at *Rydings, a turret-roofed house in *Birstall. The rookery and storm-riven but still-living old chestnut tree on the lawn were perhaps recalled by Charlotte in her evocation of Thornfield in *Jane Eyre*. Apart from this visit, Charlotte was at home in

Haworth from c.20 June 1832 until 29 July 1835. Though Ellen became her closest friend, Charlotte did not share with her the secret of her private writing or her uncensored reading. On 4 July 1834 she solemnly advised Ellen not to read *Shakespeare's comedies or *Byron's *Don Juan*; yet in the same month Charlotte wrote *The *Spell, An Extravaganza*—a lurid, amoral, and entertaining tale in which Charlotte's quotations from *Don Juan* show her complete familiarity with the poem. Ellen could not have suspected this from Charlotte's account of her daily occupations in a letter of 21 July 1832: 'In the morning . . . I instruct my Sisters and draw, then we walk till dinner after dinner I sew till tea-time, and after tea I either read, write, do a little fancy-work or draw, as I please' (Smith *Letters* 1. 114). In fact Charlotte, intent on self-improvement, was reading widely and producing an extraordinary number of paintings and drawings, for she seriously thought of making her living as an artist. Her pencil drawings of Bolton Abbey (see BOLTON PRIORY) and *Kirkstall Abbey, copied from engravings, were exhibited in Leeds in summer 1834. In 1833–4 she also wrote 26 prose works in the Glass Town and Angrian saga. A perfect spate of *poetry came from her eager pen, ranging from the ornate 'The Bridal' of 14 July 1832 to the deliberately doggerel 'Jeffry my turtle' of November–December 1834.

On 29 July 1835 Charlotte returned to Roe Head as a teacher, accompanied by Emily as a pupil. By mid-October Emily seemed literally ill with homesickness; Charlotte was intensely anxious about her, and Emily returned home, Anne taking her place. Charlotte's mundane life of lessons with recalcitrant or stupid pupils was sharply at odds with her inner life. After one such day, alone for the first time, she recalled that 'this moment of divine leisure—had acted on me like opium & was coiling about me a disturbed but fascinating spell such as I never felt before. . . . I quite seemed to see with my bodily eyes, a lady standing in the hall of a Gentleman's house as if waiting for some one' (*Roe Head Journal* fragment, Bonnell BPM MS 98(8)).

On 29 December 1836 Charlotte sent specimens of her poetry to Robert *Southey, telling him of her ambition to be for ever known as a poetess. Though he warned her that literature could not be the business of a woman's life, he did not discourage her from using her gift: poetry written for its own sake would be more likely to bring deserved fame. Charlotte took note, and continued writing poems in abundance. The year 1837 was especially prolific.

At the same period Charlotte's fondness for Ellen Nussey became extreme; she hated to be separated from her, and longed for her return when she went away to visit relatives. Because Ellen had a docile, unquestioning piety, she seemed unattainable and admirable, whereas Charlotte was afflicted with feverish doubts and fears, longing for holiness and terrified by the shadow of spiritual death. Her self-torments culminated in a nervous crisis in May 1838, when she had moved with the school to *Heald's House, Dewsbury Moor. The 'dreadful doom' of hypochondria made Charlotte's life a waking nightmare. Fortunately she recuperated at home, and the lively company of Mary and Martha Taylor, during their visit to Haworth in June 1838, helped to restore her to a healthier frame of mind. Back at the school, however, her moods fluctuated erratically; often she hated herself for her miserable touchiness and morbidity. Though she could not control her moods, she could analyse them, and her observation of her own experience was to contribute to her novels. Charlotte left Miss Wooler's school in December 1838.

For the first five months of 1839 Charlotte was at home. In March she received and refused a proposal of marriage from Ellen's brother, Revd Henry *Nussey, on the grounds that he should marry a mild, pious lady, not a romantic, eccentric-seeming, satirical person like herself. In May she took a temporary post as a governess in the *Sidgwick family. Her letters to her sister Emily described her detestation of her humiliating position as an 'inferior' who was not 'considered as a living and rational being except as connected with the wearisome duties she has to fulfil' (6 June 1839, in Smith Letters 1. 191). Sometime after her return home in July, she was astonished to receive another proposal of marriage from Revd David *Pryce, whom she had met only once, and again sent a refusal. In September she saw the sea for the first time, when she went with Ellen to *Easton and *Bridlington on the Yorkshire coast. The Parsonage was enlivened in 1840 by the frequent company of the handsome young curate Revd William *Weightman. Charlotte's exuberant high spirits at this period give the lie to the idea that she was always subdued and repressed. She was also busy writing, for in November 1840 she sent the opening chapters of a novel (probably *Ashworth) to Hartley *Coleridge, and was not (or so she said to him on 10 December 1840) unduly cast down by his opinion that her novel would not 'make an impression upon the heart of any Editor in Christendom' (Smith Letters, 1. 239). From the end of February until December 1841 she was employed as a governess by the *White family of Rawdon. She endured the last few weeks the more willingly because she had decided to go abroad: Mary Taylor had stimulated her 'wish for wings'. 'A fire was kindled in my very heart which I could not quench—I so longed to increase my attainments to become something better than I am', she wrote to Ellen Nussey on 2 November 1841 (Smith Letters, 1. 271). She and Emily planned to acquire the extra skills in French, German, and music which would enable them to set up a school of their own.

Thus on 8 February 1842 they travelled with their father and Joseph and Mary Taylor to Brussels, where they became pupils in Mme Zoë *Heger's pensionnat. After five months of tuition they were invited to stay on, Charlotte to teach English and Emily music in return for their board and tuition. The end of the year was overshadowed by the deaths of Martha *Taylor in Brussels and of William Weightman and Elizabeth Branwell in Haworth. Charlotte and Emily hurried back to Haworth, but were too late for their aunt's funeral. On 29 January 1843 Charlotte returned alone to the Pensionnat *Heger, where she continued to teach English, to learn German, and to improve her knowledge of French. During the first half-year she gave lessons in English to M. Constantin *Heger and his brother-in-law, and became increasingly devoted to M. Heger. By midsummer Mme Heger's former kindness had changed to a cool reserve. Miserably isolated and homesick, Charlotte returned to Haworth in January 1844.

Charlotte's two years in Brussels were of crucial importance in her life and writing. M. Heger's inspired teaching, his generous gifts of French books, his lessons in composition and literary analysis, all widened Charlotte's insular horizons, developed her conscious appreciation of different styles of writing, and encouraged her to control and shape the material suggested for *devoirs. She delighted in being the pupil of a cultured, intelligent master, and his autocratic, volatile temperament combined with his real kindness added to the piquancy of the situation. His characteristics are brilliantly displayed in Lucy Snowe's 'Master', M. Paul *Emanuel in Villette, where

Mme Heger is pilloried as the treacherous Mme *Beck. Some of their traits are also detectable in *The Professor*, in William *Crimsworth's 'mastery' as a teacher, and in Mlle *Reuter's devious arts.

In 1844 and 1845 Charlotte wrote letters to Heger, at first frequently in the confident expectation that he would respond as her friend and teacher, but later with indiscreet assurances of her never-ending affection, and a burning impatience for his rare replies. Four of her letters were seen by Elizabeth Gaskell, who concealed their full significance. M. Heger had torn up and thrown away all but one letter, but his wife had saved them and pieced them together with cotton or gum. It was not until 1913 that the Heger family gave permission for the four letters to be published.

From July to November 1844 Charlotte did her best to find pupils for the school she and her sisters hoped to set up in the Parsonage, but none were to be had. Her depression increased when Mary Taylor left England to sail to New Zealand on 12 March 1845. A visit to Hathersage from 3 to 26 July gave Charlotte a welcome change. Ellen Nussey was supervising improvements to *Hathersage vicarage in preparation for her brother Henry's homecoming with his bride, Emily Prescott.

Charlotte was greatly shocked when she returned to Haworth to find that Branwell Brontë had been dismissed from his tutorship at *Thorp Green Hall for conduct 'bad beyond expression'. He let it be known that Lydia *Robinson, his employer's wife, had shown him more than ordinary feeling, and implied that he had been intimate with her. Charlotte's reaction was complicated by her apparent refusal to admit to herself that her own feelings for M. Heger might be comparable to Branwell's infatuation with Mrs Robinson. For the rest of Branwell's life his drinking, bouts of lethargy, irritability, and his self-abandonment when Lydia failed to marry him after her husband's death, were a hardly tolerable burden on his family. Charlotte tried to conquer her depression by writing poems and grafting on to a fragmentary story about two brothers chapters of what became *The Professor*.

In the autumn of 1845 she made her famous discovery of a manuscript volume of verse in Emily's handwriting, which led to the sisters' first publication, *Poems* by Currer, Ellis, and Acton Bell, 1846. Charlotte took the initiative in arranging for its production by *Aylott and Jones. Though only two copies were sold, the three reviews it received were appreciative, and the sisters were encouraged to believe that they might also publish the 'work of fiction—consisting of three distinct and unconnected tales' (*The Professor*, *Agnes Grey*, and *Wuthering Heights*) which the 'Bells' were preparing for the press. Aylott and Jones had advised them to try other firms for this venture, but none of the three novels was accepted in 1846. On 25 August that year, when Charlotte was in Manchester while her father was being operated on for cataract, *Jane Eyre* was begun when *The Professor* received yet another curt rejection.

On 15 July 1847, after her sisters' novels had been accepted by T. C. *Newby, Charlotte sent *The Professor* to *Smith, Elder and Company. Their courteous refusal, accompanied by an offer to consider a three-volume novel, encouraged Charlotte to complete *Jane Eyre*. On 24 August she sent it off. Accepted immediately by George *Smith, it was published on 19 October, and rapidly became the most widely read novel in the country. Whether it was praised by reviewers as the best novel of the season, or vilified as a stab in the dark for religion and morality, it sold so well that a second edition was published on 22 January 1848 and a third in April 1848.

Anne Brontë's second novel, *The Tenant of Wildfell Hall*, was published by Newby in June 1848. He had implied in his advertisements and in his letters to American publishers that the three 'Bells' were one. An indignant letter from Smith, Elder, to whom Charlotte had promised her next novel, led to Anne and Charlotte's sudden visit by the night-train to London, which they reached on the morning of 8 July. They proved their separate identity to the astonished publishers, who were to become Charlotte's personal friends. By September Charlotte had completed the first volume of *Shirley*; but in the same month came the first of a series of tragic events which brought the progress of the novel to a standstill.

On 24 September Branwell Brontë died of 'chronic bronchitis and marasmus' (wasting), a state which had been exacerbated by drink and opium. Charlotte became ill, the shock and trouble having brought on a bilious fever. Her closest ally in childhood had died, with the promise of his early years unfulfilled. By 9 October it was obvious that Emily too was seriously ill. Her terrifyingly rapid decline began, when she wrung her sisters' hearts by refusing all help. After Emily's death from tuberculosis on 19 December Charlotte recurred again and again in her letters to Emily's being 'torn out of life'.

In early January 1849 Dr *Teale of Leeds pronounced that Anne was in an advanced stage of pulmonary tuberculosis. Anne longed for improvement and wished for a change of air. Charlotte, racked by fear that a move would hasten Anne's death, postponed the journey that Anne desired. Then in May, as a last resort, Charlotte and Ellen Nussey took her to *Scarborough, where she died on 28 May. After the funeral Charlotte and Ellen stayed in *Filey for a week, and then in *Easton. At home in the desolate Parsonage Charlotte completed *Shirley*. It was fair-copied by 29 August, collected by James *Taylor, Smith, Elder's managing clerk, on 8 September, and published on 26 October. Reviews were on the whole appreciative, though less enthusiastic than for *Jane Eyre*. Charlotte was relieved and cheered, until a savage attack by the 'thundering *Times*' on 7 December reduced her to tears. By that time she had accepted the invitation of George Smith and his mother to stay with them in London. Through them she met her much admired literary hero, William Makepeace *Thackeray, and she introduced herself to Harriet *Martineau.

In 1850 her friendship with George Smith flourished. She once again stayed at his home in London, where she roundly scolded Thackeray for his faults. There were also portrait sittings to the artist George Richmond (see PORTRAITS OF THE BRONTËS), and a meeting with George Henry *Lewes. The visit was followed by a three-day stay in *Edinburgh in the company of Smith, his brother, and a sister, when she had the delight of seeing places associated with Sir Walter *Scott. Charlotte's acquaintance with Sir James *Kay-Shuttleworth and his wife, initiated by him in March 1850, continued with her stay at their summer home, Briery Close in the Lake District, in August. Her fellow guest was Elizabeth *Gaskell, with whom there was an immediate rapport. In September Charlotte accepted W. S. *Williams's suggestion that she should produce an edition of her sisters' works. The one-volume edition of *Wuthering Heights* and *Agnes Grey* which appeared on 7 December contained Charlotte's emotional, invaluable *'Biographical Notice' of Emily and Anne.

Charlotte published nothing in 1851, but by 28 November she was making slow progress with *Villette*. In early April James Taylor called at the Parsonage before leaving the country for Bombay. Strange, inconclusive conversations with him showed he was attracted to Charlotte, but he departed without any definite proposal of marriage. Charlotte's most interesting stay in London followed, from 28 May until 26 June. The Smiths, and later Sir James Kay-Shuttleworth, arranged for her visits to the *Great Exhibition, Thackeray's lectures on 18th-century humorists, fine picture galleries, and a demonic performance by the actress *Rachel. George Smith accompanied her to a phrenologist, Dr J. P. *Browne. The year ended with a depressive illness made worse by Dr Ruddock's attempted cure: mercury pills which caused acute poisoning well into 1852.

Villette, completed after many delays by 20 November 1852, and generally well reviewed after its publication on 28 January 1853, had gained a less than enthusiastic reception from George Smith, who recognized himself and his mother in John *Bretton and Mrs *Bretton. On 13 December 1852, before she went to their home in London to complete the proof-correcting, Charlotte received an emotional proposal of marriage from Revd A. B. *Nicholls. Mr Brontë's extreme, almost apoplectic, reaction left her no choice but to refuse him. She let him know, however, that though he should not hope for acceptance, she did not wish to give him pain. In 1853 they corresponded during his absence at Kirk Smeaton, and met secretly when he visited friends near Haworth. Despite her reservations about his unintellectual tastes and narrow Puseyism, she came to appreciate his goodness and deep love for her, and to contemplate marriage with him. She told Ellen Nussey of this change of heart in late June or early July 1853. Ellen, jealous of Nicholls as the usurper of her place in Charlotte's affection, was estranged from her until February 1854, when Margaret Wooler assisted their reconciliation.

George Smith's letters, formerly frequent, had become rare and less confidential in 1853. In December that year, hearing that he had become engaged to Elizabeth Blakeway, Charlotte congratulated him coolly. By January 1854 she had persuaded her father to look more favourably on a marriage with Nicholls, and they became engaged in April. Their quiet wedding on 29 June 1854 was followed by a honeymoon in *Ireland and by an increasingly happy married life. She came to love her 'dear boy' wholeheartedly. He was her 'tenderest nurse' during the distressing illness, probably caused by excessive sickness during pregnancy, which began early in 1855 and ended three months later with her tragic death on 31 March.

Alexander *EEW*.
Barker.
Gaskell *Life*.
Gérin *CB*.
Smith *Letters*.

for news of the family, and advising him that in view of the imminent danger of civil war in Ireland, Protestants should arm and organize themselves, though they should not break the law (Barker, p. 429). On 20 January 1853 he sent Hugh a cheap edition of *Jane Eyre*, now in the BPM, and on 20 June 1855 made his will, bequeathing £40 to Hugh 'to be equally divided amongst all my Brothers and Sisters to whom I gave considerable sums in times past' (Wise & Symington, 4. 246).

James, like Hugh, was a favourite with children, and 'very smart and active with his tongue'. He was a shoemaker, but 'took a hand at everything'. It may have been on an early visit by James to Haworth that Mr Brontë sent a silver pencil-case for each of his brothers and a silver thimble for each sister. James afterwards described Charlotte as 'tarrible sharp and inquisitive'. Mrs Heslip remembered hearing of the visit, and of James's report that Charlotte 'had a very wee foot and small arms, (*cont. on page 97*)

T HE life of Emily Brontë ('Ellis Bell', 1818–48) remains the most enigmatic of the Brontë family, despite a number of fascinating early and more recent biographical studies. As John Hewish noted, 'This author's life and personality are monolithic and tend to be biographer-proof' (Hewish, *Emily Brontë* (1969), 9). The only evidence we have of the mind that created *Wuthering Heights*—itself an extraordinary *tour de force* that remains something of a conundrum—consists of four fragmentary *Diary Papers she wrote with her sister Anne, a few terse comments recorded by friends and family, some 200 *poems and fragments, and three perfunctory letters. Further contradictory evidence exists, refracted through the recollections of family and acquaintances, such as Charlotte's friend Ellen *Nussey, the Brussels schoolmaster M. Constantin *Heger, the Haworth stationer John *Greenwood, and in particular Charlotte herself who sought to interpret both Emily and her novel to a hostile Victorian audience. In her 1850 *'Biographical Notice' and Editor's Preface to the second edition of *Wuthering Heights*, Charlotte began the characterization of her sister (adopted with some scepticism by Elizabeth *Gaskell) as both Romantic genius writing 'from the impulse of nature, the dictates of intuition' and 'unobtrusive' woman with 'retiring manners and habits', living in contented seclusion and domesticity: 'I have never seen her parallel in anything. Stronger than a man, simpler than a child, her nature stood alone.' Since then, biographers have sought to account for the dichotomy between the 'simpler' feminine outside and the strong internal will— the 'secret power and fire that might have informed the brain and kindled the veins of a hero' (*Wuthering Heights* (Clarendon edn.), app.).

Emily Jane Brontë was born on 30 July 1818, in the village of *Thornton, near *Bradford, the fifth of six children. She was christened soon after on 20 August by Revd William *Morgan in the Old Bell Chapel where her father Revd Patrick *Brontë officiated as perpetual curate of Thornton. Jane Morgan and her parents, the *Fennells, are said to have been godparents (Gérin *EB*, p. 1) although there are no records in the baptismal register. A white china christening mug with her name in gilt lettering (now in the BPM) is all that remains to record the event. In April 1820, after the birth of Anne and when Emily was just under 2 years old, the family moved to *Haworth, where Emily was to spend all but two years of her short life.

There are few events of great moment in Emily Brontë's life. When she was 3, her mother Mrs Maria *Brontë died at the age of 38, and her mother's sister Elizabeth *Branwell took up residence in the Parsonage to care for her sister's six little children. Despite the death of their mother, evidence exists of a normal boisterous childhood for the young Brontës, with lessons in the morning and romps on the moors in the afternoon. On one such occasion in 1824, when Branwell, Emily, and Anne were out walking with the servant Sarah Garrs (see SERVANTS OF THE BRONTËS), they experienced a dramatic storm and eruption of bog on the moor behind the Parsonage at Crow Hill. Fortunately they were warned in time to reach safety and witness the spectacular natural event: a 7-foot-high torrent of mud, peat, and water that swept down the valley towards Ponden where they sheltered. The event no doubt provided the young Emily with an early experience of the power of nature.

Emily Jane Brontë, oil portrait by Branwell Brontë, *c*.1833–4.

On 25 November 1824 Emily joined her three elder sisters at the Clergy Daughters' School at *Cowan Bridge. The school register records 'Emily Brontë 5¾ [she was actually 6¼] 1824 Novbr 25th H Cough Reads very prettily & Works a little Left School June 1st 1825 Governess' (Chitham *EB*, pp. 36–7). She spent just over five months at the school, her departure hastened by a typhoid epidemic and the rapid decline of her eldest sisters Maria and Elizabeth, both of whom were sent home to die of consumption. Elizabeth returned home soon after Maria's death in May, and Charlotte and Emily were hastily withdrawn from the school in time to witness Elizabeth's death on 15 June. Emily's favoured position as the 'pet nursling of the school' (she was referred to by Miss Ann *Evans, the superintendent, as 'little petted Em') seems to have protected her from Charlotte's horrific experiences recorded in the account of *Lowood school in *Jane Eyre*. Nevertheless, she would still have experienced Revd W. Carus *Wilson's obsession with the deaths of young children, and the commonplace occurrence of death both at school and at home must have helped form early impressions about the place of human life in the natural world.

Emily played a lively part in the children's games of history and romance that led eventually to their written sagas. The early biographer Esther Alice *Chadwick tells of Emily playing Prince Charles escaping from the Parliamentary forces after the Battle of Worcester in the English Civil War and hiding by perching on the branch of her father's favourite cherry tree (rather than the oak tree of legend). The branch apparently broke and despite attempts to conceal the break with soot, Mr Brontë discovered the damage but not the culprit. (There are several versions of this story; Barker (p. 110) gives a different account derived from Marian Harland, *Charlotte Brontë at Home* (1899), 32, in which Sarah Garrs is responsible for the broken branch.) Emily showed the same interest in politics, current events, and literary debate, gleaned from local newspapers and the pages of *Blackwood's Edinburgh Magazine*, as her siblings. With Charlotte, she created the *bed plays in December 1827, 'making out' before going to sleep at night imaginary adventures based on the historical and political events they had read or heard about that day. Charlotte's *'Tales of the Islanders' gives us some indication of their early closeness and also the gradual dominance of Charlotte, which came to be resented by Emily (Alexander *EW*, p. 47). From about 1829, Charlotte and Branwell were clearly the leaders of the main family games, centred on the *Glass Town and Angrian saga. Emily and Anne had distinct roles as presiding *Chief Genii, directing the action of their characters Sir William Edward *Parry and Captain John *Ross respectively, both foremost Arctic explorers of their time. Gradually the interests of the younger sisters deviated from those of Charlotte and Branwell, showing an early preference for realism over romanticism that is clearly articulated in the mundane lives, meals, and architecture of *Parry's Land (see Alexander *EEW*, 1. 229–33).

Branwell appears to have had little time for his youngest sisters. His contempt for Emily is reflected in *Wiggins's comment: 'Emily's sixteen, lean and scant, with a face about the size of a penny' (Alexander *EEW*, 2(2). 250). Thus when Charlotte went to school at *Roe Head in January 1831, the younger sisters broke from the Glass Town and Angrian saga and formed their own kingdom of *Gondal, a partnership in which Emily could dominate. Unfortunately there is little surviving evidence of Gondal (only a few comments in Diary Papers and lists, no surviving prose manuscripts) and the events in the saga are a matter of considerable speculation (see GONDAL SAGA). It is clear from the poetry, however, that Gondal was a world of windswept nature, wild passion, broken alliances, vengeance, imprisonment, and death, a world from which Emily could draw sustenance and creative energy. It provided, as J. Hillis Miller noted, a 'myth kitty . . . always there to be returned to and recreated in poetry' (Miller, *The Disappearance of God* (1963), 160). Throughout her life, Emily was to sustain an uneasy mix between this imaginary world and her confined Parsonage existence of family, servants, animals, and domestic chores.

In November 1834, Emily and Anne began their joint Diary Papers, brief yearly records of family affairs written chiefly on their birthdays until about 1845. Here we see the two sisters peeling potatoes and apples; slacking in their 'bed work', lessons, and music practice; and preferring 'to go out to play'. The relationship between the sisters at this time was 'like twins, inseparable companions, and in the very closest sympathy which never had any interruption', according to Ellen Nussey who stayed at the Parsonage in July 1833 (Smith *Letters*, 1. 598). It is from Ellen Nussey that we have the best picture of the young Emily, with her dark grey-blue 'kind, kindling, liquid eyes' that seldom looked at you, and her poor complexion, odd hairstyle, and 'lithesome, graceful figure'. She was thought of as 'the prettiest of the children' (Gaskell *Life*, 1. 49), though the servant Nancy Garrs (see SERVANTS OF THE BRONTËS) recalled Emily as a child with 'the eyes of a half-tamed creature' who cared little for anybody's opinion and was happier with her pets. The only surviving paintings of her are those made by Branwell when she was 16: the famous group portrait of 'The *Brontë Sisters' and the portrait fragment from the so-called 'Gun Group', both now in the National Portrait Gallery in London (Alexander & Sellars, pp. 74–6, 307–12). The latter was preserved by Nicholls because of its likeness. Its muted tones and Emily's intense, far-off, almost haunting gaze in both the portraits have done much to foster her mysterious image.

In the Diary Papers Emily is at her most relaxed, drawing hasty sketches of herself, Anne, and her pets, writing in a rough minuscule scribble with frequent dashes, lack of punctuation, and dreadful spelling for a teenager. Her humorous imitation of the servant Tabitha *Aykroyd's Yorkshire dialect suggests her keen ear for local nuances (so successfully registered in Joseph in *Wuthering Heights*), and it is significant that animals feature equally with humans in her Diary Papers, especially her favourite *Keeper (the model for *Tartar in *Shirley*). Her delicate watercolours of family *pets—the dogs *Grasper, Keeper, and *Flossy, the hawk *Nero, and the cat Tiger—were all executed at this time. She shows little interest in the outside world. Written at the height of election fever in Haworth, when the King had just died and Mr Brontë and Branwell played a considerable role on the hustings, her Diary Paper of 26 June 1837 mentions only the accession of the young Queen *Victoria, one of the few public personalities to attract the attention of Emily Brontë. Her interests are clear: what the family is reading and writing, the welfare of her pets, her household duties, and her plans for the future.

The need for a career and prospective income weighed heavily on the Brontë sisters in the 1830s and early 1840s. In the limited Victorian context, some form of teaching was the inevitable choice for such middle-class women. Education, then, was not simply a passion for Emily but also a necessity. Recognizing this, she accompanied Charlotte to Margaret Wooler's school at *Roe Head on 29 July 1835, her education to be paid for by Charlotte's position as a teacher. Before this Emily had flourished on lessons from Mr Brontë and Charlotte, on her free access to her father's bookshelves, on journals such as *Blackwood's* and **Fraser's*, and on volumes from local lending libraries and such possible sources as the library at **Ponden House. But formal education, especially the rote learning of the time, was a different matter. It seems to have had little appeal for the independent and enquiring mind of Emily and she withdrew into herself. This reaction is usually attributed to shyness. Apart from the brief early stay at Cowan Bridge, this was her first encounter with society outside her close family circle. Ellen Nussey recalled the young Emily's reserve with strangers and Charlotte characterized Emily's ailment at Roe Head as acute homesickness for 'home and the moors' (*Wuthering Heights* (Clarendon edn.), 446). Robert Barnard, however, suggests that this ailment may have been more deliberate than Charlotte cared to acknowledge (*Emily Brontë*, p. 27). Certainly Emily appears to have always gained what she wanted in life and, given the restraints imposed by her position as a relatively poor Victorian woman, she preferred to live at home. Within three months, Emily had returned to Haworth and Anne had replaced her at Roe Head.

It seems that Emily was determined to earn her own keep on her own grounds. At the end of September 1838, at the age of 20, she took up a teaching post at Miss Patchett's school at **Law Hill, **Halifax, despite Charlotte's scepticism: 'Hard labour from six in the morning until near eleven at night with only one half hour of exercise between—this is slavery I fear she will never stand it' (Smith *Letters*, 1. 182). Nevertheless, despite some 40 pupils (including 20 boarders) and the formal learning she disliked, Emily was able to write some of her best-known poems at this time, such as 'Loud without the wind was roaring', 'A little while, a little while', and 'The bluebell is the sweetest flower' which express her yearning for the moors and her Parsonage home. Even Gondal continued to flourish at Law Hill, as witnessed by such poems as 'Light up thy halls!'. Since 12 July 1836 (her first extant poem), Emily had begun preserving her poems which from 1837 she kept in three notebooks (see POETRY BY EMILY BRONTË). The Law Hill area, with its panoramic views, thriving cultural town nearby, and stories of dispossession, is thought to have played a significant part in Emily's creative life. And it seems she was 'not unpopular' with her pupils, although she told them that the house-dog 'was dearer to her than they were'. Emily's second term at Law Hill, however, was less happy; she seems to have been unable to write and again her health broke down. Furthermore, 'she could not easily associate with others, and her work was hard because she had not the faculty of doing it quickly' (Chadwick, p. 124). By March 1839 she was at home again.

In her Diary Paper of 30 July 1841, her 23rd birthday, Emily records with some enthusiasm a scheme for the sisters to set up their own school with the prospect of becoming financially independent. In such an arrangement Emily would have control over her own time for writing and her single-minded pursuit of knowledge. By 1838 she had begun learning Latin with her father; several manuscript fragments of her translation of Virgil's *Aeneid* and Horace's *Ars Poetica* survive, and she also read *The Four Gospels*. Emily's degree of linguistic perception shown here is judged by Edward Chitham to be considerable and to have influenced the drama and economy of her later writing (Chitham *Birth of WH*, p. 18). Like her siblings, she continued to practise her drawing by copying manuals and popular prints from **annuals or books like Thomas **Bewick's *History of British Birds* or Thomas **Moore's *Life of Byron* (Alexander & Sellars, pp. 110–14). Although her later animal paintings and 'Study of a Fir

Tree' are executed 'from life', she was well aware of the accepted method of imitation of models in art education. Her skill in foreign languages, however, needed honing and with this in mind Emily agreed to accompany Charlotte to the Pensionnat *Heger in *Brussels in 1842.

Her year in Brussels was one of the most intellectually formative of her life. She and Charlotte left Haworth on 8 February, accompanied by Joseph and Mary *Taylor and escorted by Mr Brontë. They stayed three days in *London en route visiting historic buildings and galleries. They were to study French and German, expenses for board and education in the second half of the year being defrayed by Charlotte's teaching of English and Emily music. All available time was spent on study, although Emily did find time to write some Gondal poetry (Barker, p. 394). Charlotte reported that Emily 'works like a horse' to improve her French (Smith *Letters*, 1. 285). Unfortunately she and the master M. Constantin *Heger 'don't draw well together at all', yet her nine surviving *devoirs or essay exercises attest to her remarkable progress. Devoirs such as 'The *Butterfly' or 'The *Palace of Death' illustrate not only the dramatic quality of her argument but themes later encountered in *Wuthering Heights*: her distrust for civilization and her view of nature as a principle of destruction. Emily objected strongly—and vocally—to composing under order in the style of various models, fearing that she might lose her originality; but Heger's experimental methods paid dividends, as Lonoff explains, and he chose to preserve some of Emily's devoirs 'because I saw the genius in them' (Lonoff, p. 48). Heger admired Emily's 'head for logic' and her ability to argue, but he believed this was impaired by her 'stubborn tenacity of will, which rendered her obtuse to all reasoning where her own wishes, or her own sense of right, was concerned' (Gaskell *Life*, 1. 253).

It is no surprise that her social relationships in Brussels were less successful. At ease with the Taylors who were close friends of Charlotte, Emily had no time for the remainder of the small English society there. She resented the time spent on petty social ritual instead of study, refusing to speak even at an evening where only the Taylors and their cousins were present. As she explained in 'Le Chat', she considered politeness in humans to be little more than a form of hypocrisy. When Charlotte made concessions to the current style in dress, Emily defiantly refused to alter her old-fashioned clothes, which accentuated her height and thinness. She responded angrily and somewhat illogically to teasing: 'I wish to be as God made me' (Chadwick, p. 226). Pupils resented her practice of giving piano lessons outside her precious school time, although one pupil, Louise de Bassompierre, formed a rare friendship with Emily and was given her 'Study of a Fir Tree'. Charlotte reported Emily's rapid progress in *music and Ellen Nussey recalled the 'precision and brilliancy' of her playing (Smith *Letters*, 1. 289, 599). Beethoven was a particular favourite, as her surviving music books in the BPM attest. Emily was prevented from taking lessons from one of the foremost teachers in Brussels only by her abrupt departure for home on 8 November 1842, after the news of the sudden death of Aunt Branwell. A bequest from Elizabeth Branwell of just under £300 to each of the Brontë sisters relieved Emily of the immediate urgency of a teaching career.

There was no necessity now to leave Haworth and Emily quickly re-established the routine under which she thrived for the remainder of her short life. She assumed responsibility for the housekeeping, at times alternating pistol practice with baking according to the Haworth stationer John Greenwood (Chitham *EB*, p. 159). As Charles

Morgan suggested (*Reflections in a Mirror* (1944), p. 131) that the strict domestic routine functioned like that of a monastery, preserving her contemplative and creative energy for release elsewhere. Her poetry suggests she viewed life as a type of confinement, joyless and solitary. In poems like *'To Imagination' and *'Julian M. and A. G. Rochelle' we sense that the most important and most satisfying experience in life for Emily was some mystical union with 'the Invisible', the exploration of a spiritual world she could conjure up and retreat to after the busy practical routine of the day.

In 1844 she began copying her poems into two notebooks, possibly with thoughts of publication. The Diary Papers confirm continued preoccupation with Gondal and a cheerful routine of writing and household concerns. In 1845, after Anne's resignation from her governess position at *Thorp Green Hall, she and Emily took a brief trip to *York by train, impersonating Gondal characters like two young schoolgirls. There is the suggestion in Anne's 1845 diary, however, that Anne was less charmed by Gondal now and the intimacy between the sisters less intense. Juliet Barker points out the gaps in the Diary Papers, indicating Emily's imperviousness to the sufferings of her siblings (Barker, pp. 455–6). Anne would have been aware of the injustice of Emily's impatience with the despondency of those around her who must go elsewhere to earn a living (Diary Paper, 30 July 1845) while she remained in her home sanctuary. Certainly Anne's poetry suggests 'jarring discords' caused by Emily's scorn of Anne's conventional Christian faith (see 'SELF-COMMUNION'). Emily's religious beliefs were not atheistic, as is often thought, and her pantheism was in tune with other Romantic poets of the time; yet her cynicism about 'the thousand creeds | That move men's hearts' and her dogmatic certainty in her personal creed would have been both confronting and controversial to family and public alike (see 'NO COWARD SOUL IS MINE'). Nor would she deign to proselytize: as in all debatable matters she maintained silence. When Mary Taylor once commented that religion was a matter between God and herself, Emily famously replied 'that's right'.

When Charlotte discovered one of Emily's poetry notebooks in September 1845 and suggested it should be published, Emily's silence was used as a weapon of punishment for her sister's intrusion. Charlotte put the best possible gloss on the event in her 'Biographical Notice of Ellis and Acton Bell' (*Wuthering Heights* (Clarendon edn.), p. 436), explaining that Emily was not one 'on the recesses of whose mind and feelings, even those nearest and dearest to her could, with impunity, intrude unlicensed; it took hours to reconcile her to the discovery I had made, and days to persuade her that such poems merited publication'. Eventually Emily agreed to a joint publication with her sisters after punctuating and polishing her selection. Gender-neutral pseudonyms were chosen and about £36 paid by the authors for the publication by Aylott and Jones of *Poems* by Currer, Ellis, and Acton Bell, in May 1846. Only two copies sold, but the impetus to publish had been set in train.

The sisters were already well advanced in writing their first novels and in the summer of 1846 the manuscripts began the rounds of possible publishers. No manuscript survives to date the composition of *Wuthering Heights*. Planning such a complex narrative structure, chronology, and legal detail would have required time, and the possible sources for characters, buildings, and themes suggest a gestation period reaching back as far as Emily's period at Law Hill. The actual writing, however, is thought to have started about October 1845 (*Wuthering Heights* (Clarendon edn.), p. 16). In July 1847, the publisher Thomas Cautley Newby agreed to publish *Wuthering*

Heights together with Anne's *Agnes Grey* making up the third of a three-volume work, but not until after the successful publication of *Jane Eyre* by Smith, Elder in October 1847 did Newby move with any haste, hoping to profit from a confusion of the names of the three authors. (See WUTHERING HEIGHTS. A NOVEL.)

Newby's chicanery continued, yet Emily, as intransigent as ever and probably because Charlotte advised otherwise, stuck by the dishonest publisher, later even assuring him that he might publish her next novel (Smith *Letters*, 2. 26). Charlotte and Anne were obliged to travel to London to explain to Smith, Elder that the three Bells were three sisters. Emily, however, was incensed by the betrayal of her identity and caused Charlotte to bitterly regret her mention of Emily's name (Smith *Letters*, 2. 94). There is no record of Emily's reaction to the unfavourable reviews that labelled *Wuthering Heights* as 'coarse and disagreeable'. If anything, the reviews would have hardened her habitual scorn for public opinion but they would also have confirmed her sense of her own genius. The *Britannia*, for example, termed her novel 'strangely original'; and *Douglas Jerrold's Weekly Newspaper* felt confident that the writer 'wants but the practised skill to make a great artist; perhaps, a great dramatic artist' (Allott, pp. 223, 228).

Before she was 30, Emily Brontë had produced a novel that is seen as Shakespearian in its dramatic scope and power. It is a tremendous feat, achieved by that single-minded purpose and intensity of concentration she fought so hard to preserve. Muriel Spark observed that 'All her "peculiarities" and prejudices and domestic considerations are explicable only if her work is placed in the centre of her existence' (Spark and Stanford, *Emily Brontë: Her Life and Work* (1953), 92). This helps us to understand a personality that might otherwise be thought of in terms of 'stern selfishness' (Gaskell's phrase from a deleted passage in the *Life*). Even as a child, Emily valued discipline and self-control. In the famous mask incident, related by Mr Brontë to Elizabeth Gaskell, the young Emily (under cover of a mask) was asked by her father what she might do with her brother Branwell when he was naughty. She confidently answered: 'reason with him, and when he won't listen to reason, whip him' (Gaskell *Life*, 1. 59). An early interest in the sadistic side of human nature, later to surface in *Wuthering Heights*, is found in the crude sketches of flagellation that accompany Emily's translation of Horace's *Ars Poetica* (Alexander & Sellars, p. 381).

M. Heger was clear about her strength of character: 'She should have been a man—a great navigator. Her powerful reason would have deduced new spheres of discovery from the knowledge of the old; and her strong, imperious will would never have been daunted by opposition or difficulty; never have given way but with life.' There is a heroic quality here that manifested itself in several dramatic incidents told and retold by biographers, such as Emily's brave self-cauterizing of a dogbite without word to her family until the danger had passed, or her feisty separation of fighting dogs while the local lads looked on cowed (Gaskell *Life*, 1. 308–9; Gérin *EB*, p. 146). Both dog incidents were transposed into *Shirley*, the heroine being Charlotte's representation of Emily 'had she been placed in health and prosperity' (Gaskell *Life*, 2. 116). Shirley *Keeldar's reference to herself as 'Captain Keeldar' echoes 'The Major', a nickname given to Emily by Revd William *Weightman, an attribution that further confirms the perception of her as strong-willed, 'male' and unconventional. Charlotte admired and stood in awe of Emily. She acknowledged 'a certain harshness in her powerful, and peculiar character' (Smith *Letters*, 2. 133), and allowed Emily (Heger considered) 'to exercise a kind of unconscious tyranny over her'. As Robert Barnard suggests, Emily manoeuvred Charlotte into the position of subordinate and apologist (Barnard, *Emily Brontë*, p. 55). Charlotte is much blamed nowadays for her earnest role as interpreter of her sister, yet such a position was one that Emily herself sanctioned if not encouraged. It is unlikely Charlotte would have destroyed the literary remains of one she so revered, unless directed to do so. A letter from Newby survived in Emily's writing desk that indicates a second novel was well advanced (Chitham *EB*, pp. 226–8). It seems that the uncompromising Emily was reluctant to allow anything unfinished to be seen; it is likely that she either destroyed the draft herself or asked her sister to do so, together with any remaining Gondal prose that might indicate the tenor of her novel.

She was equally uncompromising in human relations. What has been seen as shyness in Emily, can also be interpreted as an innate aversion to conventional social intercourse. She seldom answered the Parsonage door and was the only Brontë not to teach Sunday school. Contemporaries reported that they preferred not to be seated next to her at a church function or afternoon tea. Mary Taylor commented to Ellen Nussey (Feb. 1843): 'Imagine Emily turning over prints or "taking wine" with any stupid fop & preserving her temper & politeness!' (Smith *Letters*, 1. 309). Hartley Merrall Jun., an early friend of Branwell, annotated his copy of Leyland's *The Brontë Family*: 'E. was not timid in her way she was the reverse' (Leyland, 1. 87–9). Her intransigence and silence gave her power. She had written with satisfaction and pride, 'I have persevered to shun | The common paths that others run' ('To Imagination', in Roper *EBP*, p. 155).

In *Wuthering Heights*, Lockwood's assumed misanthropy is ridiculous beside Heathcliff's genuine antipathy to all except those nearest to him in nature. All else would be hypocrisy. Emily believed that people should act according to the natures they are endowed with and, like animals, carry no blame on earth for their faults (a view also expressed in her poem beginning 'Well, some may hate, and some may scorn', in Gezari *EBP*, p. 26) (see also NATURAL HISTORY AND THE BRONTËS). This notion underscores her attitude to Branwell and his disastrous career. As an adolescent she had written on one of his manuscripts in French: 'Heavens! you're a bad boy, and you'll be a very unpleasant man' (Neufeldt *BB Works*, 1. 170). When it was suggested that the Haworth Sunday school pupils be taught manners and respect for betters, Emily reportedly said, 'Vain attempt!' She had no more illusions about Branwell or the ability of a person to change his or her nature than Catherine had about Heathcliff.

Her resignation towards this 'hopeless being', her brother, echoes the determinism that permeates all her writing. In 'The Butterfly', she argues that the world exists on 'a principle of destruction' and man is part of a great natural cycle, where the strong simply survive a little longer than the weak. The delightful story of the 15-year-old Emily philosophizing about the tadpoles at the 'Meeting of the Waters' on the moor near Haworth, is seen by most biographers as formative of this later belief. Ellen Nussey tells how she 'played like a young child with the tad-poles in the water, making them swim about, and then fell to moralising on the big and the little, the brave and the cowardly, as she chased them about with her hand' (Smith *Letters*, 2. 599). Throughout her life, Emily fought tenaciously to preserve the liberty to be herself, a condition she saw as essential for survival.

Emily Brontë's death was consistent with her actions in life. Following Branwell's death and funeral in September 1848, the family all suffered from winter colds and coughs. But Charlotte noticed that Emily looked particularly thin and pale. 'I fear she has pain in the chest—and I sometimes catch a shortness in her breathing when she has moved at all quickly . . . Her reserved nature occasions one great uneasiness of mind—it is useless to question her—you get no answers—it is still more useless to recommend remedies—they are never adopted' (Smith *Letters*, 2. 130). She would have no truck with doctors or medicines and, resigned as she was to her inevitable part in the natural cycle, she refused to make concessions to her condition until illness left her no choice. She insisted on dressing each day, reading downstairs, and even feeding the dogs. 'The spirit was inexorable to the flesh', Charlotte reported (Biographical Notice, in *Wuthering Heights* (Clarendon edn.), p. 439). As a concession to her family and only when it was too late, she agreed to see a doctor on 19 December 1848. A few hours later she died of pulmonary tuberculosis, aged 30.

Barnard, Robert, *Emily Brontë* (2000).

Chitham *EB*.

Davies, Stevie, *Emily Brontë: Heretic* (1994).

Hewish, John, *Emily Brontë* (1969).

Lonoff.

Pykett, Lyn, *Emily Brontë* (1989).

Spark, Muriel, and Stanford, Derek, *Emily Brontë: Her Life and Work* (1953).

and was sighted' (dim of sight), but her eyes were 'as clear as diamonds' (*Sketch*, 10 Jan. 1897).

Welsh, a man of some culture, 'an amateur fiddler, and prosperous road-maker', had 'a great fight with Sam Clark at Ballynafern', and for some time kept a public house. There is no firm foundation for Wright's story that he was named after a Heathcliff-like foundling in the previous generation. He married Elizabeth Campbell. One son, Walsh, was drowned while fording the Bann, the other, Cornelius, 'occasionally drank to excess', but according to relatives alive in 1898, was, like the rest of the family, an 'ordinary upright' person and a regular church-goer. Welsh's daughter Margaret married Samuel Shannon. Maggie Shannon, one of their daughters, wrote 'trenchant replies to false statements and foolish gossip respecting her maternal ancestors', and provided Joseph Horsfall *Turner with family notes and a portrait of her great-aunt, Alice Brontë.

Jane, Mary, and Rose, like their sister Sarah, were 'tall, red-cheeked, fair-haired, handsome women, with dark eye-lashes'. Rose Heslip remarked that 'You would not have seen nicer, cleaner women anywhere' (*Sketch*, 10 Feb. 1897).

Sarah made a runaway marriage with Simon Collins and had ten children. In extreme old age she was a widow, 'nearly blind', and had 'only the wages of her grandson, 5s. weekly, to sustain her'. Her daughter Rose Ann married David Heslip,

and had a daughter Emily Jane, who married Hugh Bingham and had children, but died before 1897. On 10 February 1897 an interview with Mrs Heslip was published in the *Sketch*, along with a photograph of her. She was then a 'hale old lady', housekeeping for her son-in-law in a village near Bradford. The interviewer was impressed by her good memory and indignant denial of most of Wright's stories about the Brontës. She had previously been interviewed by a Bradford journal and in the *Globe*, and was a prime source of information about her Brontë relatives.

Alice was living in comfortable circumstances with her brothers and sisters in their 21-acre farm in 1861, and died in Aghaderg parish. In March 1882 she was granted an annuity of £20 by Pargeter's Old Maids Charity Trustees, Birmingham. A well-built woman of robust health, she spoke like 'the last minstrel' in language with a 'decided Scottish flavour', and gave reliable accounts of her parents to Revd J. B. Lusk of Ballynaskeagh.

Brontëana, pp. 267–304.

Brontës, self-portraits by the. See PORTRAITS BY THE BRONTËS.

'Brontë Sisters, The' (portrait), portrait by Branwell Brontë (*c*.1834); famous for its primitive haunting beauty and rare subject, the three Brontë sisters themselves. They are depicted against a (*cont. on page 104*)

R EVD Patrick Brontë (1777–1861) was said by Dr William *Wright to have been born in a thatched peasant cabin in Emdale in the parish of *Drumballyroney, County Down, Ireland. He was the eldest of the ten children of a farmer, Hugh Prunty or Brunty, and his wife Eleanor, sometimes called Alice, McClory. By 1781 the family had moved to a larger house in the district of Lisnacreevy, about 1 mile from Emdale, and by 1796, when the family was complete, they were living in a large stone farmhouse in Ballynaskeagh. Patrick may have stayed on at a local school near Glascar as a pupil-teacher before establishing his own school at the age of 16. By 1798 or 1799 he had become a tutor in the family of an influential Protestant evangelical minister, Revd Thomas Tighe JP, a graduate of St John's College, *Cambridge, a friend of John Wesley, and now vicar of Drumballyroney and rector of Drumgooland. Mr Tighe may have given Patrick instruction in the classics, a prerequisite for his admission to St John's College, Cambridge, as a sizar on 1 October 1802. Patrick worked hard, gaining first class in all except his final examinations, winning prizes each year, and supplementing the exhibitions he was awarded in 1803 and 1805 by teaching pupils. Having decided to take orders in the Church of England, he also obtained, through the future missionary Henry *Martyn, promises of a total of £20 a year from Henry Thornton—a prominent member of the evangelical Clapham Sect—and from William *Wilberforce. Patrick was impressed by the preaching and teaching of Charles Simeon at Holy Trinity church, Cambridge. In 1804 his patriotic ardour was gratified when he and his friend John Nunn drilled as members of the university volunteer corps, of which Lord Palmerston was in charge.

On 23 April 1806 Patrick graduated BA, and on 28 June was appointed curate to Joseph Jowett at *Wethersfield, Essex, but did not take office until two months after his ordination as deacon by the Bishop of London at Fulham chapel on 10 August 1806. His duties were comparatively light, though they included a large number of burials during an outbreak of typhus fever. Having secured the necessary testimonials from the incumbents of two parishes near Wethersfield and from the Vicar of St Peter's, Colchester, Patrick was ordained priest on 21 December 1807 in the Chapel Royal of St James's, Westminster.

In Wethersfield he fell in love with his landlady's niece, the pretty 18-year-old Mary Mildred Davy *Burder. Her family lived on a large farm, The Broad, about 1 mile from the village. Mary's father had died, but his brother, and the rest of her family, disapproved of what seems to have been their tacit engagement in 1808. Mary was removed to her uncle's farmhouse at Great Yeldham, about 6 miles away, and Patrick contemplated accepting a curacy at Glenfield, near Leicester, which he visited for a time in September–October 1808. He refused the curacy, but by January 1809, when he finally left Wethersfield, he had apparently given up his intention of marrying Mary Burder—possibly because she was a Nonconformist—but had not told her clearly that the engagement was broken off: when he tried to renew his proposal to her in 1823, she angrily recalled duplicity on his part. He in turn claimed that she had not replied to the letters he wrote to her in 1810.

In January 1809 he moved to *Wellington, Shropshire, to become curate to the Vicar of All Saints' church, the Simeonite evangelical Revd John Eyton, notable for his

The Revd Patrick Brontë in old age.

pastoral concern and zeal for improving the education of the poor. In Wellington Patrick met his fellow curate Revd William *Morgan, and the Methodist schoolmaster Revd John *Fennell, both of whom were to become his relatives by marriage. He also found spiritual encouragement at the house of Mary Fletcher, widow of the Wesleys' friend John Fletcher of Madeley, and was confirmed in his adherence to Arminian rather than Calvinistic theology.

A curacy at the Yorkshire woollen town of *Dewsbury followed from December 1809 until early 1811. Though it was surrounded by pleasant fields and woods, conditions within the town were poor. Inadequate drainage, along with the poverty of the millworkers and handloom weavers in a time of industrial depression, contributed to the appalling number of deaths during Patrick's curacy. He became devoted to the evangelical Vicar at All Saints, Revd John *Buckworth, in whose house he lived for several months. He assisted in his Vicar's arduous parish duties, and taught in the Sunday school. On 20 July 1810 Patrick was licensed to the perpetual curacy of *Hartshead, but did not begin his duties there until March 1811. In August 1811 he was relicensed to the Hartshead curacy, since he had not formally 'read himself in'. Before he moved there, he had taken a leading part in helping to acquit William Nowell, falsely accused on 25 September 1810 of being an army deserter (see Barker, pp. 37–8). Patrick's duties were lighter in the hilltop villages of Hartshead and Clifton, and he was able to continue the writing of verse, moral tales, and articles on faith and doctrine he had begun in 1810. As he explained in his introduction to his first publication, *Winter Evening Thoughts: A Miscellaneous Poem* (1810), he intended to mix the '*Profitable* and *Agreeable*', and declared that if he succeeded in 'adding to the comforts of any individual, or . . . reclaiming but *one*, from the error of his ways, he [would] esteem himself amply recompensed for his labours'.

In 1811–12 working-class discontent, exacerbated by the use of new machines in the textile industry, and the resulting unemployment or impossibly low wages, erupted in the *Luddite riots. Cropping machines were smashed on Hartshead Moor in February 1812, and on 11 April men from Mr Brontë's parish joined others to attack Rawfolds Mill—the *Hollow's Mill of *Shirley*, in which Charlotte Brontë probably used some of her father's recollections. He condemned the violence of all 'insurrectionary movements', but may have had some sympathy with the Luddites' grievances.

Early in 1812 Patrick was invited by John Fennell to examine the pupils in classics at *Woodhouse Grove school. On a visit there in June, in preparation for the examination in August, he was immediately attracted to Fennell's niece by marriage, Maria Branwell (see BRONTË, MRS MARIA). Their courtship proceeded apace. The lovers enjoyed pleasant walks in the neighbourhood, and further afield among the towering ruins of Kirkstall Abbey—celebrated in one of Patrick's more successful poems, the picturesque 'Kirkstall Abbey, A Fragment of a Romantic Tale' in the *Rural Minstrel* (1813). Maria's answers to Patrick's letters show that most of his were warmly affectionate and admiring, if sometimes 'saucy', for she addresses him playfully on 18 November 1812 as 'My dear saucy Pat'. By 26 August 1812 he had proposed marriage, and the wedding took place in *Guiseley church on 29 December 1812. His charming 'Lines, Addressed to a Lady, on her Birthday' invoke 'hope, and joy, celestial pair' on the sweet 'April morn' of Maria's 30th birthday, 15 April 1813, and they also were published in *The Rural Minstrel*. Their first two daughters, Maria and Elizabeth, were probably born at Clough House, Hightown, about 1 mile from Hartshead. From 1813 onwards Patrick was actively associated with work in Bradford in support of the Church Missionary Association there, the Bradford and Dewsbury Bible Societies, and the Society for Promoting Christianity among the Jews. He was therefore willing to exchange livings with Revd Thomas Atkinson (see ATKINSON FAMILY), perpetual curate of *Thornton near Bradford, a large parish where the living was worth £140 per year—considerably more than his Hartshead curacy. On 19 May 1815 he and his family moved to Thornton, where his three younger daughters and his son Branwell would be born. They were warmly befriended by Dr John Scholefield Firth (see FIRTH FAMILY) and his daughter Elizabeth, later Mrs Elizabeth *Franks. At Thornton Patrick contributed three homiletic articles on conversion, in dramatized first-person form, to William Morgan's magazine the *Pastoral Visitor for 1815. The last article, on the convert's acceptance of Christ, echoes John Wesley in its fervid joy: 'Blessed be my God and Saviour, who plucked me as a brand out of the burning!' (see BST (1988), 19. 6. 271–5). He also published in 1815 The *Cottage in the Wood, inculcating the value of education, and sought to strengthen the Sunday school at Thornton by inviting Miss Firth and other competently educated ladies to teach there. In April 1818 his The *Maid of Killarney was advertised in *Blackwood's Edinburgh Magazine—a significant conjunction, for both his works and his children's reading of the magazine encouraged their precocious authorship. Towards the end of 1818 Patrick initiated and supervised the renovation of his decrepit church, the now ruined Old Bell Chapel.

When he was nominated to the perpetual curacy of Haworth in May–June 1819 by the Vicar of Bradford, Revd Henry *Heap, he was at first rejected by the Haworth church trustees as an assertion of their right to choose their own minister; but he was finally accepted by them in February 1820, and the family moved to Haworth in April. He had pastoral responsibility for the scattered moorland villages of Stanbury, Oxenhope, Cullingworth, Oakworth, and even Trawden, 8 miles away, as well as Haworth itself. In addition to the Sunday services he had to officiate at an exceptionally high number of baptisms. Since the mortality rate was also high, funeral services included those for many babies and small children. He continued his conscientious duties even during the illness of his wife from January 1821 until her tragically early death from what was probably uterine cancer on 15 September. Though he engaged a day nurse, he tended Maria at night, distressed by her pain, and by the additional anxiety of their children's being taken ill with scarlet fever—often, in those days, a fatal disease. As he later told John Buckworth (27 Nov. 1821), 'There were seasons when an affectionate, agonizing *something* sickened my whole frame' (Wise & Symington, 1. 59). The arrival of Maria's sister Elizabeth *Branwell provided help and comfort, but Maria's death left her husband prostrated and unable to perform his clerical duties for two weeks. He was also in financial straits caused by medical and nursing expenses, but was relieved by gifts and loans from friends in Bradford and elsewhere, and in summer 1823 was to earn a fee for again examining Woodhouse Grove pupils in classics. He may have proposed, unsuccessfully, to Elizabeth Firth in 1821, and to Isabella, sister of his friend Theodore Dury (see DURY FAMILY), in 1822 or 1823. His proposal of marriage to Mary Burder in 1823 met with a sharp refusal. One of his motives had undoubtedly been to find a kindly helpmeet who would care for his children and share his concern for them. There was no truth in most of the gossip passed on to Elizabeth Gaskell by Janet *Kay-Shuttleworth about his denying the children meat, burning their coloured boots, and slashing his wife's silk dress to ribbons, for they were the inventions or exaggerations of the nurse he had dismissed after her attendance on Maria. The accusations were denied by Patrick himself—though he admitted to some eccentricities—and by his cook Nancy Garrs, a more reliable witness than the nurse. The schoolmaster William *Dearden also testified to Patrick's kind companionship with his children. He bought toy soldiers for them, knew about their 'little plays', was interested in their development, and enjoyed discussing the topics of the day with his precocious daughter Maria. He transmitted to them his interest in the Napoleonic Wars and enthusiastic admiration for the Duke of Wellington, so helping to inspire the *Glass Town and Angrian saga. He also allowed them free access to books they delighted in: Sir Walter *Scott's novels and poems, the *Arabian Nights, James *Ridley's Tales of the Genii, Macpherson's Poems of Ossian, *Bunyan's The Pilgrim's Progress, Thomas *Bewick's Book of British Birds, among others—thus permanently enriching their imagination and art. They also inherited from him, and were encouraged in, their love of animals and birds. See BOOKS OWNED BY THE BRONTËS; EDUCATION OF THE BRONTËS.

In 1824 Patrick took his four older daughters to *Cowan Bridge school. All the children were brought home in 1825. Maria and Elizabeth died soon after their return, and their father, too distressed to take their funerals himself, asked William Morgan to do so. He decided that the other children should be educated at home for the time being, and shared the duty of teaching them with Elizabeth Branwell. He later engaged art and music teachers for them.

His letters to newspapers during the 1820s show a comparatively enlightened if limited liberalism. In three letters on Catholic Emancipation, published in the Leeds Intelligencer on 15 and 19 January and 5 February 1829, he advocated the granting of civil rights to Roman *Catholics as both just and expedient, since it would avert extremist action, though he opposed Catholic participation in national government. He was later to inveigh fiercely against the Pope's appointment of *Wiseman as cardinal-archbishop of Westminster, and the concomitant signs of 'Papal Aggression' in the late 1850s. Then, as in 1829, he condemned anything that might undermine Catholic allegiance to British authority. As might be expected from his comments on capital punishment in The Maid of Killarney, he also supported the Leeds Mercury's campaign to liberalize the harsh laws which sentenced to death by hanging both the petty thief and the multiple murderer. His letter published on 10 January 1829 found guilty all those who tolerated, enacted, and executed such laws; and in April and May 1830 he helped to organize petitions for the restriction of capital punishment and for the abolition of slavery. Such efforts, and the heavy burden of his parish work, especially during a smallpox epidemic in early 1830, led to exhaustion and acute illness in June and July of that year. In January 1831 he arranged for Charlotte to go as a pupil to *Roe Head school. In summer 1831 he obtained a grant from the National Sunday School Society towards the building of a Sunday school in Haworth, opened in 1832. He supported the Parliamentary Reform Act passed in that year. Before the Parliamentary elections of 1835 his support for Peel antagonized the powerful Whigs in Haworth, and his opposition to the Whig candidate Lord Morpeth was intensified by the Whig espousal of church disestablishment, a policy Patrick opposed in his pamphlet, Signs of the Times (see SERMONS AND TRACTS BY REVD PATRICK BRONTË). Strong objections by Dissenters to the payment of Church rates meant that he and his curate Revd William *Hodgson were embroiled in much local dissension in the late

1830s, though he had been well supported by Methodists and Baptists in his successful campaign to set up a Haworth Temperance Society in November 1834.

In 1838 Mr Brontë applied unsuccessfully to John Driver of Liverpool for help in securing clerical work in a bank for his son Branwell, and in 1839 helped to prepare Branwell for a tutorial post at *Broughton-in-Furness by reading with him works by Virgil, Homer, and Horace, and the four gospels in Greek. After Branwell's return from Broughton, Mr Brontë supported his application for a railway clerkship in August–September 1840. In February 1842 Mr Brontë accompanied Charlotte and Emily on their journey to *Brussels, and took the opportunity to visit the field of Waterloo. He was deeply grieved by the death of his young curate Revd William *Weightman on 6 September 1842, and in his funeral sermon said that they had been 'always like father and son'. After the death of Miss Branwell on 29 October 1842 Emily and the servants took care of the housekeeping at the Parsonage.

Rumours that Mr Brontë had been drinking to excess at this period may have been caused, as he alleged, by the smell of a lotion for his eyes, which were very weak. Cataracts developed, and he had to depend increasingly on the assistance of the Revd A. B. *Nicholls, his curate from May 1845. His troubles were increased by the dismissal of Branwell in disgrace from his tutorial post to Revd Edmund *Robinson in July 1845. By mid-1846 Mr Brontë was almost completely blind; in August Charlotte took him to Manchester, where a successful operation for cataract was performed by Dr William James *Wilson. At home he suffered the constant burden of Branwell's drinking bouts, unstable temper, and deteriorating health. When Branwell died on 24 September 1848 his father 'cried out for his loss like David for that of Absalom—My Son! My Son! And refused at first to be comforted' (Smith *Letters*, 2. 122). The death of Emily on 19 December 1848 and of Anne on 28 May 1849 meant that Mr Brontë became increasingly protective of and dependent on his only remaining daughter. He was proud of Charlotte's success as a novelist, and took pleasure in her friendship with her publishers and with Elizabeth Gaskell.

He continued to work for local causes, and in 1849–50 took the lead in organizing a petition to the Board of Health to procure a much-needed supply of clean water for Haworth. Though a government inspection by Benjamin Herschel Babbage revealed the appallingly insanitary conditions in the village, vested interests delayed progress until 1856. In 1851 Mr Brontë welcomed a visit to the Parsonage by James *Taylor, a member of the *Smith, Elder publishing firm, and would have permitted Charlotte to marry him providing the marriage was deferred for five years. She was not attracted to Taylor and did not become engaged; but when she told her father of Mr Nicholls's proposal on 13 December 1852, he was so violently opposed to the match that he was in danger of apoplexy. He was gradually brought round to a more favourable view during Nicholls's absence from Haworth from May 1853 until April 1854, when he consented to their engagement. After her marriage on 29 June 1854 Patrick remained on amicable terms with Mr Nicholls, who continued to respect and care for him after Charlotte's death.

Between 1855 and 1857 Mr Brontë co-operated with Elizabeth Gaskell in her writing of Charlotte's *Life*. The finished work gave him both pleasure and pain, but he thought it well done, and asked only for the correction of 'a few trifling mistakes', despite her misrepresentation of him as a violent man and harsh husband. In August–September 1856 Mr Nicholls read to him Charlotte's unpublished novel *The Professor*, and together they decided what deletions should be made before its publication by Smith, Elder in June 1857.

Mr Brontë was bedridden for a few months before his death on 7 June 1861. He bequeathed the residue of his estate to his 'beloved and esteemed son-in-law' Arthur Nicholls. Though he had become somewhat prejudiced, self-absorbed, and reclusive with age, he was a man of integrity, with a staunch evangelical Christian faith, a lively social conscience, and a deep attachment to his family. He had a profound influence on the character, development, and writing of Charlotte and Anne in particular, and though his upbringing of Branwell perhaps had its shortcomings, he can hardly be blamed for his son's tragic failure to fulfil his early promise.

Barker.
Brontëana.
Lock & Dixon.
Smith *Letters.*

very dark background, with a yellowish-brown pillar separating the figures of Anne and Emily from that of Charlotte. The painting has often been referred to as the 'Pillar Portrait', but underneath the 'pillar' the painted-out figure of Branwell can now be discerned. He was clearly unhappy with the composition and with his own self-portrait. It is a work of Branwell's immaturity, perhaps one of his first attempts at working in oils, and is poor in technique. Certainly Elizabeth *Gaskell thought little of the craftsmanship when Charlotte showed it to her in Haworth in 1853, but she noted its likeness to Charlotte and the moving expressions on the faces: 'One day, Miss Brontë brought down a rough, common-looking oil-painting, done by her brother, of herself,—a little, rather prim-looking girl of eighteen,—and the two other sisters, girls of 16 and 14, with cropped hair, and sad, dreamy-looking eyes' (Chapple & Pollard, *Gaskell Letters*, p. 249). In her *Life*, Gaskell referred to it as 'not much better than sign-painting', but noted that 'Emily's countenance struck me as full of power; Charlotte's of solicitude; Anne's of tenderness' (1. 155). Charlotte herself must have disliked it since she told her publishers (29 Sept. 1850): 'I grieve to say that I possess no portrait of either of my sisters' (Smith *Letters*, 1. 479); and her husband Revd A. B. Nicholls, who inherited it, simply folded it up and stored it on the top of a wardrobe at his home in Banagher, Ireland, where it was found together with the *'Emily Jane Brontë' portrait after his death in 1914. He had concealed its presence from C. K. *Shorter who visited him in 1895 in search of Brontë relics and even his second wife Mary Anna Nicholls was unaware of its existence until after 50 years her nurse found it when dusting. Now the prized possession of the National Portrait Gallery, London, the picture's extraordinary story of survival and poor physical condition (fold marks are discernible and paint is flaking) add to its enigmatic quality.

Brontë Society, the. In 1893, the Bradford librarian Butler Wood, J. Horsfall *Turner, William Walsh Yates, and Mr (afterwards Sir) John Brigg invited admirers of the Brontës to meet in Bradford Town Hall on 16 December to consider forming a Brontë Society and Museum. They decided to establish a museum to contain Brontë drawings, manuscripts, paintings, relics, editions of their works, writings about them, and photographs of places with Brontë associations. A committee was appointed, and met on 13 January 1894. The first president was Lord Houghton (1858–1945), son of Robert Monckton *Milnes. Vice-presidents included T. Wemyss *Reid, A. *Birrell, A. M. F. *Robinson, George *Smith, and Dr William *Wright. After the first annual meeting, held in Dewsbury in December 1894, the terms of membership were defined, and a committee meeting on 8 March 1894 decided the museum should be in Haworth. A room above the Yorkshire Penny Bank premises was rented at £12 per annum, and officially opened with celebratory speeches on 18 May 1895, in the presence of visitors from far and wide. During the following summer nearly 10,000 people visited the museum. A curator was appointed to officiate during the summer months of 1896, with a retaining fee during the winter closure.

The reopening in April 1897 was performed by C. K. *Shorter. The 1898 *Transactions* described both Shorter and T. J. *Wise as 'disinterested' devotees of the Brontë genius. After the Society's excursion to *Cowan Bridge, *Tunstall church, and Casterton in 1899, such outings became annual events. The Society was granted a Charter of Incorporation in 1902, and from 1902 to 1906 published Herbert Wroot's *Sources of Charlotte Brontë's Novels: Persons and Places* (revised reprint 1935). Annual reports, printed along with papers read at meetings, were entitled *Brontë Society Publications*, with a subtitle, *Transactions*, until 1950, when they became simply *Brontë Society Transactions (BST)*. Membership increased steadily, and in 1905 the 50th anniversary of Charlotte's death was marked by a well-attended memorial service in Haworth church. After Revd A. B. *Nicholls's death on 3 December 1906 the Society bought several Brontë items, some from his widow, others at Sotheby's *sales in 1907 and 1914. The centenary of Charlotte's birth, 21 April 1916, was marked by services in Haworth on 16 April and 17 June 1916, and by publication of *Charlotte Brontë 1816–1916: A Centenary Memorial* (1917) ed. Butler Wood.

About 5,000 people visited the museum in 1925, and by 1926 there were 87 life members and 255 annual members. The rented museum premises were inadequate for such large numbers and for the safe storage and display of its collections. Through the generosity of Sir James Roberts, a native of Haworth, the Society acquired the Parsonage, officially opened as a Brontë Museum on 4 August 1928 (see MUSEUMS; EXHIBITIONS OF BRONTËANA). The honorary curator, J. A. *Symington, who had compiled a *Catalogue of the Museum & Library* (1927), suddenly resigned in 1930 after the Society failed to find items which should have been in the Museum. The Museum remained open during the war, with its ceilings strengthened, windows blocked, and the room devoted to the *Bonnell collection closed. Annual excursions were temporarily abandoned, but there were Jubilee celebrations and a Commemoration issue of *Transactions* in 1943. Special services in Haworth church on 25 October 1947 and 19 December 1948 marked the centenaries of the publication of *Jane Eyre* and the death of Emily Brontë.

At the 1952 annual meeting Helen Greene Arnold, honorary American representative 1952–72, made her first report. In 1953 the Society celebrated its Diamond Jubilee and the museum's Silver Jubilee of the opening of the Parsonage Museum (BPM). It was in a flourishing state, with 687 members, over 40,000 visitors, and £3,600 cash in hand, and two special funds. In 1955 services in Westminster Abbey and at Haworth marked the centenary of Charlotte's death, and the annual meeting discussed plans for extending the museum to provide a Bonnell Collection room, strongroom, and improved housing for the Custodian. In 1956 a plaque was unveiled on Mr Brontë's alleged birthplace in Emdale, County Down. Irish membership increased, and an Irish section of the Society was eventually formed in June 1963.

1959 saw the completion of the Parsonage extension, which unfortunately gained much bad publicity. A letter in the *TLS* (Aug. 1962) describing it as the Society's 'disastrous binge' initiated a heated correspondence, and in 1963 six members of the Society's council resigned over the appointment of a young actress, Joanna Hutton, as curator. More bad publicity followed, but the new curator's offer to resign was not accepted, and she remained to serve the Society loyally for over five years.

Membership of the Society increased, reaching 1,152 in 1964, when it was registered as an educational charity. In 1967 the Society's archivist, Amy Foster, completed an analytical index of *BST*, updated in 1978. In June 1974 Dr Donald Hopewell retired after a distinguished presidency of 42 years. 1974 was also marked by the gift to the Society of a great collection of Brontë documents by George Smith's granddaughter, Mrs Elizabeth Seton Gordon. The bicentenary of Mr Brontë's birth was celebrated in a service at Haworth on 28 May 1977, and commemorated by the publication of Jocelyn Kellett's *Haworth Parsonage: The Home of the Brontës*. In 1982 the Society, with Meckler Publishing, published Christine Alexander's *A Bibliography of the Manuscripts of Charlotte Brontë*. Dr Juliet Barker, curator 1983–9, wrote and compiled the attractive *Sixty Treasures* (1988), commemorating the Diamond Jubilee of the acquisition of the Parsonage. Her successor, Jane Sellars, ensured that the BPM deserved the registration with the Government's Museum Registration Scheme which it achieved in 1990; but in the same year dissension arose in the Council over new plans for a Parsonage extension. At the annual meeting in 1991 members elected the leading dissentient, Miss Chris Sumner, and six other critics of the Council's proposed development. Four Council members who had been in favour of it resigned at the next Council meeting, and at the annual meeting in 1992 eight vacancies were filled by nominees opposed to the original Council plans. In September 1993 a Brontë Society office was opened at 74 Main Street, Haworth, with meeting and study rooms, used especially for educational work. Efficient and devoted work in the museum, library, shop, and offices continues, and the society has arranged successful conferences, study days, and lectures.

Membership continues to expand worldwide, with Brontë Society representatives in Canada, Germany, and the United States. A Brontë Society of Japan was established in 1987 by reforming the Japan Brontë Centre, a small group led by Professor H. Nakaoka (formed 1986). Its headquarters are located in Komazawa University, Tokyo, with a branch office in Tezukayama-Gakuin University, Osaka. The first president was a famous

Brooke family of Dewsbury

Japanese woman novelist Taeko Kono, and in 1997, the Brontë Society of Japan completed a twelve-volume Japanese edition of the Brontës' works, under the general editorship of Professor Nakaoka. In 1998 the Australian Brontë Association was established, with headquarters in Sydney and (like the Japanese Society) with affiliations to the Brontë Society.

Lemon, Charles, *A Centenary History of the Brontë Society 1893–1993* (1993).

Brooke family of Dewsbury, known to Revd Patrick Brontë and to Charlotte, who went to school with Leah and Maria Brooke. Mr John Brooke of Aldams House, later of Fall House, was a partner in the firm of Halliley, Brooke, and Hallileys, important woollen manufacturers specializing in blankets and carpets, with substantial banking interests in Dewsbury and elsewhere. As a young attorney's clerk, he had shown commercial ability and was offered a place at Aldams Mills by Mr Halliley, where he subsequently became a partner (together with John Halliley jun.) and married Halliley's daughter Sarah (d. 1828) on 30 May 1808 (W. W. Yates, *The Father of the Brontës* (Leeds, 1897), pp. xv–xvi). Another daughter Rachel Halliley (b. 1781) married Revd John *Buckworth in 1806; Patrick Brontë lodged with this couple in December 1809 at the beginning of his curacy at Dewsbury and remained on friendly terms with them. The Hallileys and Brookes were all members of the congregation at St Stephen's, Dewsbury, and among the manufacturing élite of the district, despite the financial crisis caused by their London house of Halliley and Carter (1834) and subsequent bankruptcy. By 1848 they had recovered enough for Charlotte Brontë to write of them as typical of 'all their class—respectable, well-meaning people enough—but with all that petty assumption of dignity, that small jealousy of senseless formalities which to such people seems to form a second religion' (Smith *Letters*, 2. 68).

John and Sarah Brooke had three daughters: Leah Sophia Brooke (b. 1815); Anna Maria, also called Mary (b. 1818); and Elizabeth (christened 1817). Leah and Mary were both at Roe Head with Charlotte. Mary was a particular friend of Mary Taylor and Leah is known to have corresponded occasionally with Charlotte (Smith *Letters*, 1. 114 and 254).

Anna Maria (Mary) married Dr George Allbutt (b. 1812) of Batley, in August 1842, brother of Revd Thomas Allbutt (see ALLBUTT FAMILY), who succeeded Revd John Buckworth as vicar of Dewsbury. She appears not to be the same person as Mary Brooke, the governess who later married a Halifax solicitor, Mr Michael Stocks (Smith *Letters*, 1. 210–11), and of whom Yates writes:

Mary 'alone or with a sister . . . conducted a school of high repute near Fall Lane, Dewsbury. She was a devoted churchwoman, and highly respected in the town and neighbourhood' (p. xvi).

It is possible that Emily Brontë first heard of her situation as teacher at Elizabeth Patchett's school at Law Hill through the Brookes, since Maria Patchett had married Titus Senior Brooke of Dewsbury (Barker, p. 294). In March 1839, Charlotte Brontë also heard that the family of Thomas Brooke of Northgate House, near Huddersfield, prosperous manufacturers, required a governess, but nothing came of this, possibly because music and singing were essential, as in the case of other unsuccessful applications by Charlotte (see, for example, Smith *Letters*, 1. 232 n.).

Brookroyd House, Birstall, Yorks., was Ellen Nussey's home from September 1836, when her widowed mother and family moved from *Rydings after the death in 1835 of Ellen's uncle Richard Nussey, builder of the comfortable, spacious, plain Georgian house. The Nusseys welcomed Charlotte Brontë's visits, and she corrected some of the proofs of *Jane Eyre* there, without revealing her authorship. After Ann *Nussey's marriage to Robert Clapham in September 1849 the house was rearranged to provide separate living quarters for them. After Mrs Nussey's death in 1857 Ellen and her sisters moved into part of the old *Gomersal Cloth Hall.

Brotherton, Lord (formerly Sir Edward) (1856–1930), important collector of Brontë books and manuscripts; member of the Brontë Society from 1924, president 1927–9. From humble beginnings Brotherton built up the largest private chemical manufacturing firm in Britain. He married in 1882 but tragically his wife died in childbirth a year later and from then on books and public office filled the vacuum in his personal life. He was twice MP for Wakefield (1902–10, 1918–22), mayor of Wakefield (1902–3), lord mayor of Leeds (1913–14), a Freeman of both cities, deputy lieutenant of the West Riding, Justice of the Peace, and honorary colonel of the 15th Battalion, the West Yorkshire Regiment he raised and equipped at the beginning of World War I. He was created a baronet in 1918 and made a peer of the realm in 1929.

Lord Brotherton built up a distinguished personal library at his home, Roundhay Hall, in the last eight years of his life. His assembly of some 35,000 printed books and pamphlets, 400 manuscripts, 4,000 deeds, and 30,000 letters constituted the nucleus of the Brotherton Collection housed in the Brotherton Library, the building he paid for and endowed at the University of Leeds, intending it to be a national library for the north-east of England. Letters and early manuscripts of the

Brontë family with their West Yorkshire origins were a particular favourite, as were the works of Sir Walter Scott. The Brotherton library still holds the richest collection of the writings of Patrick Branwell Brontë, together with some of Charlotte's letters and many of C. K. *Shorter's papers and correspondence.

His collecting was influenced by a number of librarians, dealers and bibliophiles, including Dr Henry Guppy of the John Rylands Library and, in Brotherton's last few years, the later-infamous Thomas James Wise, who found a ready outlet for his trade in books and manuscripts at Roundhay Hall. Those who worked particularly closely with Brotherton in building his collection were his niece-in-law and heir, Dorothy Una Ratcliffe (later Mrs McGrigor Phillips), and John Alexander *Symington, his part-time librarian. Symington has left an endearing glimpse of his patron, a great Yorkshire book collector and benefactor: 'The late Lord Brotherton had a particularly charming way of asking, when books were placed before him, "And what is the excuse for this publication?" The explanation needless to say, had to be a detailed account of the author's intentions, the scope and utility of the work, together with an estimate of its worth and right to occupy an allotted space in his Lordship's library' (*Some Unpublished Letters of Sir Walter Scott* (1932), p. v).

Alexander, Christine, 'Roundhay Hall: The Library of Col. Sir Edward Allen Brotherton, Bart., LL.D. (1926)', *Dictionary of Literary Biography, 184. Nineteenth Century British Book-Collectors and Bibliographers* (1997), 37–45.
Cox, D., 'The Brotherton Collection: its Beginning and Development', *University of Leeds Review*, 28 (1985/6), 41–59.
Symington, John Alexander, *The Brotherton Library: A Catalogue of Ancient Manuscripts and Early Printed Books Collected by Edward Allen Baron Brotherton of Wakefield*, 2 vols. (1931).

Broughton-in-Furness is an attractive small market town on the southern edge of the *Lake District. It stands on rising ground in the estuary of the Duddon—the river celebrated in Wordsworth's sonnet sequence of 1820, as Branwell Brontë knew when he became tutor to John and William Postlethwaite (see POSTLETHWAITE FAMILY) at Broughton House in January 1840. The substantial Georgian house is in Griffin Street, opposite the 17th-century Old King's Head Inn, and just below the spacious, tree-shaded Market Square with its central stone obelisk, where the weekly market and the annual fair for locally spun and woven woollen cloth were held. Branwell lived away from the centre, at High Syke farmhouse, the home of the surgeon Edward Fish. From high ground west of Duddon Bridge Branwell could see 'far off, and half revealed' on the horizon the peak of Black Combe, 'invincible in tempests', and the inspiration for his sonnet on the mountain (Neufeldt *BBP*, p. 209). He found the scenery of the Duddon valley delightful, and visited the small town of Ulpha as well as Seathwaite-in-Dunnerdale, where the devout 'Gospel Teacher', Revd Robert Walker (d. 1802), had ministered. Mr Walker had been praised in Wordsworth's Sonnet 18, 'Seathwaite Chapel', with its accompanying Memoir.

Brown, John (1804–55), Haworth sexton and stonemason who was Branwell Brontë's friend and confidant despite the disparity in their ages and social standing. He was 16 when the Brontës arrived in Haworth, almost fourteen years older than Branwell. John Brown succeeded his father, William Brown, as sexton in 1835 and named the cottage he had built in Parsonage Lane, next to the Haworth National School (also used as a Sunday school), 'Sexton House'. He and his wife Mary (née Ackroyd) had one son who died in infancy and six daughters: Ann (1826–94, married Benjamin Binns (see BINNS FAMILY)); Martha *Brown (1828–80); Eliza (1831–1901, married Henry Popplewell); Tabitha (1836–1910, married Robert Ratcliffe (see RATCLIFFE FAMILY) 1861); Mary (b. 1839, married John Jopling 1863); and Hannah (b. 1841, married James Hartley). Sexton House must have been crowded: not only did Ann's husband and new baby join the household, but Revd A. B. *Nicholls also lodged with the Browns during his curacy, from May 1845 until not long before his marriage to Charlotte Brontë in June 1854. John Brown was one of the few witnesses at their wedding (Barker, p. 757); and not quite a year later, Nicholls himself officiated at John Brown's funeral in August 1855.

As an experienced stonemason, John Brown worked closely on a number of memorials and other local commissions with the sculptor Joseph Bentley *Leyland. Both were confidants of Branwell and both appear to have heard the story of his relations with Mrs Lydia *Robinson of Thorp Green as they occurred. John Brown even received a letter asking advice on whether to risk such a sexual relationship, Brown being experienced in such extramarital matters (Barker, pp. 459–60). Branwell's letters to the older and more worldly John Brown (occasionally addressed as 'Old Knave of Trumps'), however, are not always reliable. They are usually written in a swaggering style (not unlike characters in his juvenilia) and reveal the crude, boasting, and unpleasant side of Branwell (Barker, p. 323, quotes a letter with 'a stream of schoolboy obscenities'). The insecure Branwell was always anxious to adopt a macho image with the older John Brown, a trait that did little to steady his behaviour.

It is difficult to assess the influence of John Brown on the younger Branwell. Branwell's large half-length portrait of him in 'the grand manner', against a stormy sky, indicates a strong-featured man with a resolute personality (see Alexander & Sellars, p. 323, and pl. xxix). He was hardworking and reliable in his job, loyal to Mr Brontë and trusted by him to take care of Branwell. In July 1845, Branwell was sent under Brown's care to *Liverpool, popular with holidaymakers at the time, to give the Parsonage family relief from Branwell's binge drinking (following the 'affair' with Mrs Robinson) and to allow him to recover from his 'frantic folly' (Smith *Letters*, 1. 412). They took a steamer trip along the Welsh coast, where Branwell sketched Penmaenmawr mountain from the sea and later wrote a poem inspired by it (Neufeldt *BBP*, pp. 276–8). Brown was also instrumental in encouraging Branwell to join the Three Graces Lodge of Freemasons in April 1836, which would have provided Branwell with a wider social context and the male company he lacked in the Parsonage. Brown had been initiated into the lodge in 1830 and by June 1831 had risen through the ranks to the position of Master of the Lodge (see FREEMASONRY). He is said to have possessed a number of books and been quite well read, yet he also shared in much of Branwell's dissipated behaviour, aiding and abetting his worst habits. Branwell's last extant letter, *c*.late August 1848, is indicative of a role Brown often played: it is a pathetic appeal to Brown to 'contrive to get me Five pence worth of Gin' while the rest of the Brontë family were at church (Smith *Letters*, 2. 110–11). John Brown was with the declining Branwell just before he died on 24 September 1848 (Barker, p. 567).

Brown, Martha (1828–80), servant at Haworth Parsonage from July 1841, aged 13, until the death of Revd Patrick *Brontë in 1861, when she accompanied Revd A. B. *Nicholls back to his home in Ireland and remained with him for about a year before returning to Haworth by Christmas 1862. Martha was the second eldest daughter of Mary and John *Brown of Sexton House, Parsonage Lane, Haworth. Although her family were close to the Parsonage, she lived with the Brontës from the time she was 'officially' employed. Previous to that she had probably run errands for them when their servant Tabitha *Aykroyd broke her leg in December 1836. 'Tabby' became increasingly lame and Anne Brontë noted in her *Diary Paper of 30 July 1841: 'Tabby has left us, Martha Brown has come in her place.' Although Tabby returned in May 1843, Martha continued in service,

taking the heavier share of the housework. She would return home only briefly when she was ill, such as in March 1846 when she was 'ill with a swelling in her knee and obliged to go home' (Smith *Letters*, 1. 459). She served the Brontës loyally over many years. When Mr Brontë died he left £30 to Martha 'as a token of regard for long and faithful services to me and my children'.

Following Mr Brontë's lead, Martha took a dislike to Mr Nicholls at first but was soon won over by his devotion to Charlotte. She made a number of visits to him in Ireland and continued to correspond with him until her death. He sent her gifts of money and urged her to make her home with him and his second wife. She chose to remain in Haworth, living first with her widowed mother at Sexton House until she died in August 1866, and then with her sister Ann and husband Benjamin Binns (see BINNS FAMILY) until 1877. In 1865, she spent a brief period working for Dr Amos *Ingham who had attended Charlotte in her last illness, but otherwise divided her time in helping her sisters with their large families. Her final home was a rented cottage in Stubbing Lane (now Sun Street), Haworth, where she entertained Brontë admirers and was herself something of a celebrity since Gaskell's *Life*. When Elizabeth *Gaskell had stayed with Charlotte in September 1853, Martha had apparently been rather garrulous and supplied her with some picturesque details about the Brontë sisters and their habits (Barker, p. 740). Martha died in January 1880, aged 51, and was buried in Haworth churchyard. Her large collection of Brontëana passed to her sisters and was dispersed.

Dinsdale, Ann, 'Martha Brown: life after the Brontës', *BST* (1999), 24. 1. 96–101.

Brown, William. See BROWN FAMILY.

Brown family, probably among the first to greet the Brontës on their arrival in Haworth on 20 April 1820, and witnesses to the many tragedies in the Brontës' personal lives. William Brown (1781–1835), son of John Brown of Haworth, was sexton of St Michael's for 27 years, from March 1807 during the ministry of Revd James Charnock and then under Revd Patrick Brontë. He died aged 55 years and was succeeded first by his eldest son John *Brown (1835) and then by his third son William (1855). As sextons their relationship with the incumbent clergyman was important to the success of the parish. They lived near the Parsonage and took care of the church and churchyard, including the graves, and also performed the role of the modern verger in church services. Like many sextons, the Browns were all trained stonemasons and could supplement their small stipend by supplying tombstones and inscriptions. John's second daughter Martha *Brown became a servant at the Parsonage from the age of 13 and other members of the Brown household, particularly Eliza who occasionally assisted Martha, were hired to perform various tasks for the Brontës over the years.

William Brown sen. married Mary Bowcock in November 1803. They had three sons: John (1804–55), Robert (1806–61), and William (1808–75). The family lived in the Ginnel (now Changegate) near the church and the house passed to William jun. on the death of his father. John Brown built his own house nearby in Parsonage Lane. Robert Brown became a grocer in Haworth, was married twice and had a large family. William jun. married Ann from Westmorland and had three sons and six daughters, most of whom worked as power-loom weavers in factories. Branwell Brontë's large portrait of William Brown is illustrated in Alexander & Sellars (p. 328). With the death of William in 1875, the office of sexton of Haworth came to an end, and was replaced by that of verger. The Brown family had connections with the Three Graces Lodge in Haworth (see FREEMASONRY).

Emsley, Kenneth, 'The Browns, Sextons of Haworth, and their Families, 1807–1876', BST (1992), 20. 5. 296–303.

Browne, Dr J. P., a *phrenologist; possibly James P. Browne, MD Edinburgh 1829, listed at 32 Cadogan St, Chelsea, in London Medical Directory 1851. After Charlotte Brontë and George *Smith visited Browne at 367 Strand, London, as 'Miss and Mr Fraser', copies of his phrenological 'estimates' of their characters were sent to them, dated 29 June 1851. Impressed by the 'imaginative power' of the unknown lady, he detected with surprising aptness 'organs' indicating 'strong and enduring attachments', sensitivity, anxiety to succeed, poetical enthusiasm, intellectual and linguistic capacity. Though less successful with Smith, he observed accurately enough an 'active and practical' nature.

Brunswick, Frederick. See YORK, FREDERICK GUELPH, DUKE OF.

Brunty. See BRONTË FAMILY.

Brushwood Hall, an old manor house purchased by the Englishman Samuel Smith from Lord Abercorn, in the *Glass Town and Angrian saga. Rich in game, the small estate is in a deep glen which runs into the main Verdopolitan Valley, 2 miles from Verdopolis.

Brussels was Charlotte Brontë's 'promised land' when in 1841 she and Emily planned to go abroad to improve their knowledge of French and other languages. Attracted to the city by reports of Mme Zoë *Heger's pensionnat there, they reached it from Ostend on 14 February 1842. Approaching through the porte de Flandre in the north-west, they would cross over the Canal de Charleroi, completed in 1832, catch a glimpse of the tree-lined boulevards which formed a promenade round the shield-shaped city, and pass by the quays, markets, and tall huddled houses of the old town or 'Basse Ville' on their way to the fine broad streets, squares, and park of the 'palatial and royal Haute-Ville', as Charlotte calls it.

Brussels had first grown up as a market centre where an east–west trading route crossed the river Seine. By the 11th century it was protected by encircling ramparts with seven fortified gateways. In The Professor William *Crimsworth strolls beyond the Porte de Louvain at the north-east angle of the city, and reaches, beyond the wide fields, drear, 'treeless and trackless', the cemetery on land given to the Protestants by Napoleon—where Charlotte and Emily walked with Mary *Taylor to mourn her sister Martha, and where in the novel Crimsworth found Frances *Henri weeping for her aunt.

Within the original ramparts, from the 12th to 14th centuries, wealthy Brabantine merchants controlled trade; after 1421 they had to share power with the craft guilds. In 1357 the liberation of the city from the invading troops of the Count of Flanders was followed by the construction of huge fortified walls, most of them eventually demolished to give place to boulevards between 1818 and 1840. From about 1430 to 1477 the duchy of Brabant merged in the territories of the Duke of Burgundy. Fine, ornate buildings such as the Hôtel de Ville date from this period, as does the church of St Michel and St Gudule ('St Jean Baptiste' in Villette) near the rue d'Isabelle, named after the Spanish Infanta Isabella, who reigned over Brabant with the Archduke Albert 1598–1621, and as governor for her nephew Philip IV of Spain until her death in 1633. Charlotte imagined Lucy *Snowe confessing in a church of the Spanish period, the baroque St Jean Baptiste.

French invasions in the late 17th century resulted in the replacement of some old wooden buildings by those of the superb Grande Place. From 1713 to 1795 the southern Netherlands were ruled by Austria. The rococo Chapel Royal in the Place du Musée, formerly a private royal chapel, now became part of the grand sequence of neo-classical buildings in the vicinity of the Place Royale, the rue Royale, and the great Parc—the scene of the hallucinatory 'festal night' in Villette.

From 1795 the southern Netherlands were under French republican rule, but after the battle of Waterloo (1815) they became part of the Kingdom of the Netherlands. From 23 to 27 September 1830 Belgian nationalists, including M. Constantin *Heger, fought at the barricades for independence. Charlotte saw, and described in *Villette* (ch. 20), the first king of the independent nation, Leopold I.

Bryce. See PRYCE, REVD DAVID.

Buckworth, Revd John (1779–1835), evangelical vicar of *Dewsbury during Revd Patrick Brontë's curacy there; matriculated at St Edmund Hall, Oxford, 1801, graduated BA 1805, MA 1810; curate to Revd Matthew Powley at Dewsbury from 1804, vicar from 1807; a fine preacher and hymnwriter. In January 1806 he married Rachel Halliley, one of the influential Hallileys of Aldams mills in Dewsbury. Mr Brontë lodged temporarily in the Vicarage from December 1809, helped in the Sunday school Buckworth founded in 1810, and liked and respected him. Buckworth trained young men for *Church Missionary Society work, and with other local clergymen founded the *Cottage Magazine*.

Bud, Captain John, pseudonym of Branwell Brontë. Bud is a contemporary of the Duke of Wellington and an eminent Glass Town political writer. He is father of Sergeant *Bud and author of (among other works) 'The *History of the Young Men' and 'The *Life of Alexander Percy'. Despite his unpleasant, irregular appearance, he is the friend and mentor of young Lord Charles *Wellesley. He lives in Quaxmina Sq. with other aged antiquarians, including his great friend John *Gifford. Bud's botanical name was a feature of the *'Young Men's Play'.

Alexander *EEW*, 1. 126–7.

Bud, Sergeant, son of Captain *Bud and a survivor of the *'Young Men's Play', in the *Glass Town and Angrian saga. Sergeant Bud, 'a clever lawyer and a great liar', is a member of the Inner Temple and of Gray's Inn, London; and also a publisher, bookseller, and scrivener to Chief Genius Talli (Charlotte Brontë). His character is likened to parchment and his writing is a 'long dry thing' much like Bud himself.

Alexander *EEW*, 1. 128.

Buffon, Georges-Louis Leclerc, comte de (1707–88). French Enlightenment scientist, author of a 36-volume *Natural History* and originator of the phrase 'The style is the man himself'. M. Constantin *Heger dictated an extract from his essay 'The Horse' ('Le Cheval') to Charlotte Brontë and mentioned him to stress the importance of technique in correcting her devoir, 'The *Fall of the Leaves'. Emily's *devoir 'The Cat' ('Le Chat') may refute Buffon's article of the same title,

though the evidence for this remains conjectural.
SL

Lonoff, pp. 66–7 and 246–7.

Bulwer-Lytton, Edward (1803–73) (Bulwer before 1843; Bulwer-Lytton after 1843; first Baron Lytton, 1866), reforming politician, prolific novelist and poet, extremely popular in his time despite an often inflated, artificial style. Emily Brontë's *Diary Paper of 26 June 1837 reports Branwell's reading Bulwer's *Eugene Aram* aloud to Charlotte. Charlotte was familiar with a number of his novels, which she judged effeminate, vapid, and unoriginal: she observed to Hartley Coleridge on 10 December 1840 that Bulwer-Lytton and *Dickens often write 'like boarding-school misses' (Smith *Letters*, 1. 241). Bulwer-Lytton provided a standard against which she asserted the artistry of *Shirley*: 'Truth is better than Art. *Burns' Songs are better than Bulwer's Epics', she wrote to W. S. Williams on ?1 March 1849 (Smith *Letters*, 2. 185). Reviewers often preferred *Jane Eyre* to Bulwer-Lytton's work.
BT

Christensen, Allan Conrad, *Edward Bulwer-Lytton: The Fiction of New Regions* (1976).

Bunting, Revd Jabez (1779–1858), *Methodist leader of the Halifax Circuit during the *Luddite riots. He was known to Revd Patrick *Brontë, who disliked his arrogance, and is said to be the chief original of Revd Jabes *Branderham in *Wuthering Heights*. He is a man of some stature in ecclesiastical history; he helped to organize a corporate Methodist church after its separation from the Church of England in 1795, and was a trustee and member of the management committee of the Wesleyan Academy at *Woodhouse Grove. In 1813, before Maria Branwell Brontë's uncle John Fennell left his position as 'acting governor' of Woodhouse Grove in September that year, Bunting secured the appointment of his brother-in-law, Revd Thomas Fletcher, as a tutor, with a seat on the management committee, to replace the classical master, William Burgess, who had left in August 1812. After Mr Fennell's departure, Mr Fletcher became 'acting headmaster' for a time under the new governor, Revd James Wood. When Bunting delivered one of the sermons marking the dedication of the new school chapel in 1833, 'so many people tried to get into the chapel . . . that unruly scenes occurred, provoking the considerable wrath of the dignitary in the pulpit!' (F. C. Pritchard, *The Story of Woodhouse Grove School* (1978), 101). The pandemonium was widely reported, and Mr Brontë would certainly have heard about it and told Emily (Lock & Dixon, pp. 147–8).

Bunyan, John (1628–88), author of *The Pilgrim's Progress* (1678, 1684), a book well known to the

Brontës, who possessed an edition of 1743. In Charlotte's early writings the 'Slough of Despond' is recalled in a 'slough of criminality . . . deceit, meanness', and Lord Charles frees himself from the 'Castle of Giant Despair' (Alexander *EEW*, 1. 170. 2(2). 244). Bunyan's monstrous Apollyon, King of Hell, confers the glamour of wickedness on the Duke of *Northangerland's grandson, Prince Alexander, a 'young Apollyon', and the Duke of *Zamorna exults as his savage dogs Moloch and Apollyon attack the trembling Lord Lofty—an episode recalled later when the terrified Revd Joseph *Donne begs Shirley *Keeldar to hang the ferocious dog Tartar, as Christiana's sons beg for the Gatekeeper's 'filthy cur' to be hanged.

In Charlotte's mature works 'Apollyon' is no longer a concept used half in jest. St John *Rivers has the 'sternness of the warrior Greatheart, who guards his pilgrim-convoy from the onslaught of Apollyon' (ch. 38). In *Villette* M. Paul *Emanuel is also pitted against Apollyon; 'Emanuel' means 'God with us', and in *The Pilgrim's Progress* the 'Delectable Mountains' are 'Immanuel's Land' from which one may 'see to the gate of the Celestial City'. When Lucy *Snowe's enemies seek to put an impassable chasm between her and M. Emanuel, it seems to her that Apollyon straddles across the chasm 'breathing flames', and she asks 'Could my Greatheart overcome?' (ch. 38). Bunyan's Greatheart, the guardian of Christiana and Mercy, overcomes giant fiends, Grim, Maul, Slaygood, and Despair, and guides the women through the Valley of Humiliation, where Christian battled with Apollyon, but where one may meet with angels. So in *Villette* M. Emanuel walks with Lucy 'by moonlight—such moonlight as fell on Eden . . . haply gilding a path glorious, for a step divine—a Presence nameless' (ch. 41).

The protagonists of *The Professor* and *Jane Eyre* envisage a land of bliss like Christian's Celestial City, afar off, but seemingly attainable. In *Jane Eyre*, after the rescue of Rochester from his burning bed, Jane imagines beyond wild waters 'a shore, sweet as the hills of Beulah', which, says Bunyan, is where the 'contract between the bride and bridegroom was renewed'. But at the heart of *Shirley* is the dark Valley of the Shadow of Death.

Anne Brontë's perception as life as a difficult path, akin to Bunyan's vision, is evident in her poems of spiritual self-examination. The last two stanzas of 'When sinks my heart' evoke the 'awful river . . . Perchance of all the pilgrim's woes Most dreadful', but the poet sees beyond it the 'blessed shore'. In 'The *Three Guides' she presses forward on the narrow upward path, guided by the Spirit of Faith, while the soul struggles on the hard path in *'Self-Communion'; and in her best-known hymn she warns, *'Believe not those who say the upward path is smooth', adjuring the pilgrim to 'Arm, arm thee for the fight'.

Wheeler, Michael D., 'Literary and Biblical Allusion in *The Professor*', *BST* (1976), 17. 86. 46–57.

Buonaparte, Napoleon. See NAPOLEON BUONAPARTE.

Burder, Mary Mildred Davy (?1789–1866), niece of Revd Patrick Brontë's *Wethersfield landlady. She lived at a farmhouse, The Broad, met him at her aunt's house, fell in love, and accepted his proposal in 1808. Her uncle Robert Burder allegedly secluded her at Great Yeldham on discovering his Irish origins; but Mr Brontë recalled difficulties caused chiefly by her. His letter to John Campbell of Glenfield of 12 November 1808 shows that he gave up the affair as an 'unequal yoke', perhaps because she was a Congregationalist. She replied tartly to his renewed proposal of 28 July 1823, implied he had broken his former promise, and refused to see him again. She married Revd Peter Sibree, Dissenting minister at Wethersfield, in 1824, and had four children.

Burke and Hare, notorious for *bodysnatching, used as models for low life in the *Glass Town and Angrian saga. Their story intrigued the young Brontës and became part of the plot of *'Letters from an Englishman' and other early tales. William Burke (1792–1829) was an Irish criminal who went to Scotland in about 1817 where he boarded in a lodging house kept by another Irishman William Hare. Bodysnatching was rife at the time and when one of Hare's lodgers died late in 1817, the two men realized they could make good money by the sale of corpses to Dr Robert Knox, a leading Edinburgh anatomist. They then began a 'business', inveigling obscure travellers and others to Hare's lodging house, making them drunk and then smothering them so that the bodies would have no marks of violence. Dr Knox paid from £8 to £14 per body and not until fifteen bodies had been disposed of were suspicions aroused and Burke and Hare arrested. The latter turned king's evidence and Burke was hanged in Edinburgh in January 1829.

Burns, Helen. Charlotte Brontë insisted that Helen Burns in *Jane Eyre*, based on her sister Maria, was 'real'. Elizabeth Gaskell recorded Charlotte's 'unavailing indignation at the worrying and the cruelty to which her gentle, patient, dying sister Maria had been subjected' at *Cowan Bridge. At *Lowood the motherless Helen dreams about her home at Deepden in Northumberland, and finds companionship in reading books such as Samuel *Johnson's *Rasselas*. She is often publicly disgraced or flogged by Miss *Scatcherd for petty misdemeanours or slatternliness; but Jane marvels at her wide knowledge, skill in languages, and eloquence in the congenial company of Miss *Temple. Helen's pallor, thinness, and sunken grey eyes show that she is far advanced in consumption; yet, spiritually strong, she befriends Jane, imparting courage by her inner radiance, preaching patience, Christian love which overcomes hate, and calm faith in Eternity as a home, not an abyss. Like Charlotte and Anne, she believes in the doctrine of *universal salvation, trusting that the 'pure spark' of spirit will return to the Creator and even perhaps 'brighten to the seraph'. Thus she resigns herself to death; and Miss Temple finds Jane at dawn, asleep in the arms of Helen, who has died during the night.

Burns, Robert (1759–96), Scottish poet. Burns's poems and songs remained very popular, especially in the first half of the 19th century. Some of his phrases passed into the common currency of speech, and editions were readily available. Henry Garrs, brother of the Brontës' servants Sarah and Nancy, and himself an aspiring poet, owned a cheap copy of the *Poetical Works*, with a memoir, engravings, and glossary, printed and published in Halifax in 1843. We do not know which edition the Brontës possessed, but they knew his works well. Charlotte in particular cherished them as the voice of nature and feeling rather than art: 'Truth is better than Art. Burns' Songs are better than Bulwer's Epics,' she wrote to W. S. Williams in March 1849 (Smith *Letters*, 2. 185). Again, on 3 April 1850, contrasting the thoughtful working man John *Greenwood (stationer) of Haworth who appreciated *Jane Eyre* with the clever George Henry *Lewes who denigrated *Shirley*, she defended her preference for the heart's kindly feeling by quoting from Burns's warm, outspoken, and indecorous 'First Epistle to John Lapraik': 'No man ever yet—"by aid of Greek climbed Parnassus" '. She perhaps expected Mr Williams to recall that the poet continues: 'Gie me ae spark o' Nature's fire, that's all the learning I desire . . . My Muse, tho' hamely in attire, | May touch the heart' (Smith *Letters*, 2. 185, 375).

Significantly, while she advised the ladylike Ellen Nussey to read J. G. *Lockhart's *The Life of Robert Burns* (1828), she did not recommend his poems. But Charlotte and Branwell, who liked all things Scottish, read and quoted from them freely. Lines and phrases from Burns's 'To Dr Blacklock', 'Address to the Deil', 'My Heart's in the Highlands', and 'O my Luve's like a red, red Rose' can be found in Charlotte's early writings. Branwell's song by Percy, 'Should old acquaintance be forgot', is a variation on Burns's 'Auld Lang Syne'—less picturesque, fresh, and moving, but capturing

something of the rhythmic, songlike quality (Neufeldt *BBP*, p. 193). In *Penmaenmawr* Branwell laments his lost love, Mrs Lydia *Robinson, in lines inspired by Burns's 'Ye banks and braes', an air Branwell heard played by the band on board the steamer 'while sailing under the Welsh mountain' (Neufeldt *BBP*, p. 276). In *Shirley*, Charlotte leads affectingly to Agnes *Pryor's revelation of her motherhood when she breaks down in singing 'Ye banks and braes,' and Caroline, unaware of the truth, thinks she is 'weeping at the pathos of the air' (ch. 24) (see MUSIC). The idea of 'Auld acquaintance' recurs in *Shirley* and in *Villette*, where it also forms the title of a chapter. Charlotte quotes too from Burns's more lively, bold, and satirical verses: 'Tam O'Shanter', 'The Twa Dogs', 'To a Louse', and 'Last May a braw Wooer'. Anne and Emily Brontë make few references to Burns; but Anne's quotation from his 'Country Lassie' in *Tenant* (ch. 31) aptly underlines Helen's bitterness: 'Sine as ye brew, my maiden fair, | Keep mind that ye maun drink the yill'.

'Butterfly, The' ('Papillon, Le'). Devoir by Emily Brontë (11 Aug. 1842; MS in Berg, NYPL). The speaker, walking in the forest in a bitter mood, observes that Nature 'exists on a principle of destruction'. She picks a flower, only to notice a caterpillar's blighting effects. This observation prompts the claim that an evil world should have been annihilated. Suddenly, a gold and purple butterfly appears, a sign from the Creator that rebukes her judgement as well as a symbol of transformation in 'the world to come'. 'The Butterfly' has drawn more critical attention than any of Emily's other essays, largely as a statement of her religious views and essentially misanthropic temperament. However, the fact that Charlotte wrote a matching devoir, 'The Caterpillar' ('La Chenille') (11 Aug. 1842, MS in Heger family), suggests that it is also a response to an unidentified assignment. Charlotte's essay is overtly moralistic, drawing an analogy between the stages of the caterpillar's life and man's. Just as the gross, offensive worm undergoes a transformation in its coffin-like cocoon, so corrupt mortals will be resurrected and arise in glory after the last trumpet. The essay attests to her religious orthodoxy and increasing ability to handle French syntax, but it lacks the power of Emily's. SL

Benvenuto, Richard, *Emily Brontë* (1982), 78–80.
Lonoff, pp. 176–92.
Miller, J. Hillis, *The Disappearance of God* (1975), ch. 4.

Byron, George Gordon, Lord (1788–1824), the most popular and influential of English poets during the Romantic period; seen initially by contemporaries as the successor to Sir Walter

*Scott. Apart from Scott, Byron—his life and works—had perhaps the single greatest influence on the writing of the Brontës. His aristocratic background, liberal views, and unconventional life captured the imaginations of the adolescent Brontës and engendered not only a sexual and psychological complexity in the heroes of their early writings, but helped to inspire the complex characters of two of the Brontës' most famous fictional heroes: *Heathcliff and *Rochester. As John Maynard argues in the case of Charlotte, the impact of Byron's life and work 'definitively negated her milieu's tendency to deny awareness of a sexual life to a young woman' (*Charlotte Brontë and Sexuality* (1984), p. 12).

At the age of 10, after spending his childhood in Scotland, Byron inherited the title and the estate of Newstead Abbey in Nottinghamshire from his great-uncle, the 'wicked' Lord Byron. He went to Harrow and then Trinity College, Cambridge, where he wrote his first volumes of poetry that were scathingly attacked in the *Edinburgh Review*. He hit back by publishing the anonymous satire *English Bards and Scotch Reviewers* (1809), and then set off for the tour of Spain and Greece that provided the material for the first two cantos of *Childe Harold's Pilgrimage* (1812), the poem that made him famous overnight among the most elite sections of the reading public (a quarto bound copy of the poem cost 50s.) and that provided readers like the young Brontës with a travelogue of picturesque scenes, exotic characters, and a hero whom people readily identified with Byron himself. He became known as a poet of love and constancy, and this reputation was sustained by the development of the Byronic Hero in his popular *Oriental Tales—The Corsair, The Giaour, The Bride of Abydos*, and *Lara* (1812–14)—together with cheaper poems like *Ode to Napoleon Bonaparte, Siege of Corinth, Hebrew Melodies*, and *The Prisoner of Chillon*, all devoured by and subsequently quoted by the Brontës.

After 1816, however, Byron's reputation and sales fell with the scandal of his separation from his wife and child, the rumours of an incestuous affair with his half-sister, and his subsequent exile from England to a Europe that appreciated his radical politics and satire. In England he was no longer a safe poet, politically or morally, as his *Childe Harold*, cantos 3 and 4, the personal verse drama *Manfred*, the political Italian dramas, and the anticlerical and political satire of *Cain* and *Don Juan* demonstrate. Cheap editions of *Don Juan* restored Byron's popularity and gained him a wider middle and lower-middle class readership, but, unlike the Brontës, these readers were not much interested in the early works of Byron. By the time the Brontës entered the market in the early 1830s, there was a thriving trade in pirate and cheap Continental editions, like the pocket copy of *Childe Harold's Pilgrimage* (Paris 1827) that Branwell Brontë owned. There was also a prosperous second-hand market for the earlier expensive volumes, plus remaindered unsold new stocks. It is possible that Revd Patrick Brontë's edition of Byron's works came from such a source, given his low income, or it might equally have been one of the many volumes of Byron's collected works advertised by Parisian publishers 'at a third to an eighth of London prices' (William St Clair, 'The Impact of Byron's Writings', in Andrew Rutherford (ed.), *Byron: Augustan and Romantic*, 1990). The sale catalogue of Mr Brontë's effects (BPM) simply cites 'Books Byrons' and there is no evidence for Winifred Gérin's statement that he owned the *Complete Works* (1833) ed. Thomas *Moore ('Byron's Influence on the Brontës', *Keats-Shelley Memorial Bulletin*, 17 (1966)). Furthermore, no single edition of Byron before 1839 contained all six of the plates copied by the Brontës; nor were they all to be found in Thomas Moore's *Letters and Journals of Lord Byron: With Notices of his Life* (commonly known as his *Life of Byron*). The Brontës' edition is unlikely to have been illustrated and, like other eager young artists or Byron enthusiasts, they probably bought or had access (at school or elsewhere) to a series of engravings in one of the many 'Byron Galleries' bound separately from the editions themselves (Alexander & Sellars, pp. 16–17).

It is remarkable that the Brontë children were free to read Byron's complete texts with enthusiasm, rather than the bowdlerized versions of 'Beauties of Byron' produced for ladies lucky enough to be allowed a taste of the poet who had been pronounced the author of 'moral vomit' and 'ordure' (Rutherford (ed.), *Byron: The Critical Heritage* (1970), 2–3). Southey, admired and consulted by Charlotte, had described *Don Juan* as 'a high crime . . . against society', a poem of 'mockery . . . mingled with horrors, filth with impiety, profligacy with sedition and slander' (to editor of the *Courier*, 8 Dec. 1824). It is clear that Charlotte was aware of contemporary opinion of the material she and her siblings read, since she advised her schoolfriend Ellen Nussey to omit 'the Don Juan, perhaps the Cain of Byron though the latter is a magnificent Poem' (Smith *Letters*, 1. 130). She herself read all of Byron 'fearlessly'.

The young Brontës may have first encountered Byron's name in the pages of *Blackwood's*. The issue for February 1825 carried a long, impassioned defence and eulogy of the recently deceased poet. This was followed in August by a discussion of Parry's *Last Days of Lord Byron*, and in December with a letter from Byron to John Galt. In 1828,

Blackwood's reviewed Leigh Hunt's *Lord Byron and Some of his Contemporaries*, and Moore's *Life of Byron* was reviewed soon after it appeared early in 1830. By 1834 Charlotte had read the latter, that included the first publication of Finden's engraving of Lady Jersey, copied by Charlotte (Alexander *EW*, p. 82). She quotes freely from *Childe Harold*, *Manfred*, *Cain*, and *Don Juan* in particular throughout her juvenilia. Her early poem 'The trumpet hath sounded' (Neufeldt *CBP*, pp. 91–3) is based on Byron's 'The Destruction of Sennacherib', and her 'African Queen's Lament' (Alexander *EEW*, 2(1). 3–6) is reminiscent of Byron's *Hebrew Melodies*. In *Caroline Vernon* Charlotte describes how the reading of Lord Byron can 'half-turn' the head of a romantic young girl; yet she also mocks Zamorna's Byronic pretensions in this last of her novelettes. Both Charlotte and Branwell describe the young Mary Percy's infatuation for Byron and his Verdopolitan equivalent the Marquis of Douro (Duke of *Zamorna).

By the age of 18, Charlotte herself had become infatuated by Byron. Her novelettes at this time— *High Life in Verdopolis* and The *Spell* in particular—focus on her increasingly Byronic hero Zamorna, with his changing, vengeful moods, his cynicism, pride, and defiance of conventional morality. He is 'passion and fire unquenchable. Impetuous sin, stormy pride' (Alexander *EEW*, 2(2). 93). Heroines become enslaved by his 'basilisk's fascination' and he adopts the pose of the oriental despot or pirate king of Byron's Oriental romances (Alexander *EW*, pp. 117–20). Byron's Scottish heritage is woven into the background of Zamorna by the addition of a boyhood marriage to Lady Helen Victorine, Baroness *Gordon, thus allying him with 'the dark—malignant, scowling Gordons', like Byron himself (his mother Catherine Gordon was a Scottish heiress descended from James I of Scotland). Gradually Zamorna adopts the darker side of the Byronic hero, demonstrating a restless fascination for evil that draws him closer to his political rival in the Glass Town and Angrian saga, namely Alexander Percy, Lord Northangerland, Branwell Brontë's particular hero and alter ego. But whereas Zamorna's satanic qualities manifest themselves chiefly in sexual misdemeanour and political insurrection, Percy combines these features with a religious angst and search for personal happiness that haunted both Byron and his heroes. Numerous manuscripts such as Charlotte's long narrative poem known as 'Zamorna's Exile'—a poem in two cantos reminiscent of *Childe Harold* in its outburst of anguish and despair but using the stanza pattern of *Don Juan* (Neufeldt *CBP*, pp. 194 and 209)—analyse the relationship between Zamorna and Northangerland. The struggle between these characters throughout the Brontë saga dramatizes the ambiguities within the Byronic Hero evident in the dual nature of the proud, defiant womanizer of *Childe Harold* and the unredeemed Faustian figure of *Cain*.

Branwell identified closely with the dark side of the Byronic Hero, displaying near the end of his life the same sense of Calvinistic guilt that plagued Byron. He identified with Manfred's struggle to reconcile the existence of good and evil in the world, and seems to have adopted the persona of the doomed outcast. Between a Byronic image of Alexander Percy and a corpse on a bier, both drawn by Branwell in 1846 (Alexander & Sellars, p. 357), he has quoted Byron: 'No more—no more—Oh never more on me | The freshness of the heart shall fall like dew, | Which, out of all the lovely things we see | Extracts emotions beautiful and new!' (*Don Juan* 1. 214), a reference not only to the past and present self of his alter ego Northangerland (alias Percy) but to himself. In his letters to Joseph Bentley *Leyland, his language is as extravagant as Byron's: he is 'in torment', 'a martyr bound at the stake', and 'roasting at a slow fire night and day', all typical phrases in his correspondence (Leyland). Branwell's writing is as replete with Byronic reference as that of Charlotte, but unlike her he never seems to have relinquished his obsession with Byron. At the age of 12 he was writing poetic dramas in imitation of Byron (see VERSE DRAMA BY BRANWELL BRONTË). His story 'The *Pirate' and drawing of the same name (Alexander & Sellars, p. 322) are in imitation of Byron's *Lara* and *The Corsair*. The magician on Philosopher's Island is none other than Byron's *Manfred, who features in both Charlotte's and Branwell's early Glass Town stories.

Byron also had a major influence on the Gondal saga of Emily and Anne: his moods, themes, characters, even phrases are readily recognizable. The numerous outlaws, bandits, exiles, and prisoners derive in part from his poetry. The names of Emily's heroine Augusta and her lover Lord of Elbë have Byronic associations (Augusta was Byron's half-sister and 'Albë' was *Shelley's name for Byron). Emily was deeply impressed by the superhuman struggle of the individual will against the forces of nature and against the rule of God and man that she encountered in *Childe Harold* (especially canto 3), *Manfred*, and *Cain*. The full measure of this Byronic impact can be seen in *Wuthering Heights* and particularly in the character of Heathcliff. Contemporary reviewers were the first to notice the connection: 'Like the Corsair, and other such melodramatic heroes, [Heathcliff] is "Linked to one virtue and a thousand crimes"' (*Examiner*, in Allott, p. 220). Charlotte's later hero Rochester also reflects the long influence of Byron.

Like Conrad in *The Corsair,* he blames fate for his early disastrous marriage, he scorns society's codes and, like Manfred, is prepared to flout God's laws; but in his relationship with Jane he attains a remorse and repentance unknown to the Byronic Hero. Anne was less obsessed by Byron's romanticism, although there are scenes in *The Tenant* not unlike episodes in *Don Juan.*

Engravings illustrating the poetry and life of Byron were the greatest single influence on the subject and style of the Brontës' drawings (Alexander & Sellars, p. 17). Emily made a copy of William Finden's engraving of Westall's 'Ianthe', the 11-year-old Lady Charlotte Mary Harley to whom Byron dedicated *Childe Harold* (Alexander & Sellars, pp. 385–7). Westall's illustrations to Byron were first published in 1819, but later appeared in Moore's *Life of Byron,* in *Finden's Illustrations of the Life and Works of Lord Byron* (1833–4) and in *The Poetical Works of Lord Byron* (1839). Emily's illustration, however, was probably copied from one of the many foreign editions, since it was made in 1842 while she was in Brussels and given to the *Heger family. It was from Edward and William *Finden's engravings which dominated Byron publications of the 1830s that Charlotte produced her many copies of Byronic scenes and heroines. Other plates, such as 'Guicciola' and 'Clare' are typical of her Byronic beauties and heroes. In 1833, she copied a portrait of Byron himself from the *Literary Souvenir (Alexander & Sellars, p. 19) and renamed him 'Alexander *Soult', a Glass Town poet; and at the same time also copied Byron's friend the Countess of *Blessington, whom she renamed for the Glass Town bluestocking Zenobia Ellrington (Alexander & Sellars, pp. 216–17). Byron's characters, scenes, and friends provided models for Glass Town and Angrian equivalents, such as Mina *Laury (Byron's 'Maid of Saragoza') and Marian Hume (Byron's friend the Countess of Jersey) (Alexander & Sellars, pp. 236–7). Charlotte may also have copied an engraving of Byron's friend Leigh Hunt and Branwell's friend Francis *Grundy tells how Branwell sent a poem to Hunt for critical judgement (Alexander & Sellars, p. 275).

It is thought that the *Diary Papers, written by Emily and Anne, were modelled on Byron's early journals scribbled in a schoolbook at Harrow and described in Moore's *Life* (Gérin *EB,* p. 38). Branwell followed with enthusiasm Byron's favourite sport of *pugilism. Nor did Byron's fetish for pet animals go unnoticed by the Brontës: they had their own menagerie of *pets and Byron's penchant for enormous dogs is replicated by the Angrian hero Zamorna and by Rochester in *Jane Eyre* (see DOGS IN THE GLASS TOWN AND ANGRIAN SAGA). Direct and indirect verbal echoes of Byron abound in the Brontës' writings (see *Professor* (Clarendon edn.), p. 331). Bertha Rochester in *Jane Eyre,* for example, is referred to as Rochester's 'mad, bad, and embruted partner' (320), echoing Caroline Lamb's famous description of Byron as 'mad, bad, and dangerous to know'. Zamorna adopts Byron's motto and Caroline *Vernon (possibly named after Caroline Lamb, whose pursuit of Byron echoes throughout the juvenilia) follows Byron's model of female infatuation for the hero—an example deliberately abandoned by Charlotte in Elizabeth *Hastings and Jane *Eyre (Alexander *EW,* pp. 196–7). It was probably from Byron that the Brontës gleaned a knowledge of Zoroastrianism, encountered especially in *Manfred* and reinforced by Byron's friend Moore's poem 'The Fire-Worshippers' in *Lalla Rookh* (Alexander *EW,* p. 240). The myriad allusions to Byron's life and work in the writings of the Brontës have never been fully documented; his unconventional lifestyle, his insistence on political and sexual liberty, his writings on the nature of love and his scorn for hypocrisy, his apostrophes to nature, his atheism and cynical attitude to society had a profound and pervasive effect on the minds of the adolescent Brontës.

See also GOTHIC NOVELS; BOOKS OWNED BY THE BRONTËS.

Brown, Helen, 'The Influence of Byron on Emily Brontë', *Modern Language Review,* 34 (1939), 374–81.

Gérin, Winifred, 'Byron's Influence on the Brontës', *Keats–Shelley Memorial Bulletin,* 17 (1966), 1–19.

C

Calabar, province of, in Angria in the *Glass Town and Angrian saga; 190 miles long and 130 miles broad. Governed by the Lord-Lieutenant Thornton Wilkin *Thornton, its capital is Gazemba and its population numbers 59,000. The 'Campaign of the Calabar' during the Angrian Wars is the subject of Henry *Hastings's first prose work (Alexander *EW*, p. 277; Neufeldt *BB Works*, 2. 278–379).

Calabar River flows through Angria to the Gulf of Guinea in the *Glass Town and Angrian saga. The Duke of Zamorna establishes *Adrianopolis on the banks of the Calabar which are then lined by the white domes and pillars of the capital's classical architecture. The Angrian river is named after a river of the same name to the west of the Niger Delta in Africa. Calabar is also the name of a town similarly situated in southern Nigeria.

Calvinism entails controversial beliefs which affected the faith and writings of the Brontës. John Calvin (1509–64), born in Picardy, was intended for a career in the Catholic Church, but, convinced of his mission to reform it, resigned his benefices in 1534. In 1535–6, after moving to Berne to escape persecution, he published his seminal work, *Christianiae Religionis Institutio*, defining and vindicating *Protestantism. In Geneva in 1556–8 he helped to establish the reformed faith. His preaching, incessant doctrinal disputes, and laborious concentration on his exegetical works affected his health and led to his early death. Calvinism's distinctive dogma, that of predestination, was developed in its harshest, deterministic form by Calvin's friend and successor Theodore Beza (1519–1605): souls are chosen by God to be either saved or damned; God is omnipotent and his decrees are unalterable; nevertheless, his gifts of sufficient grace and perseverance are given to those 'elected' to salvation.

Revd Patrick Brontë was an orthodox Anglican in his belief in hell as a real place of punishment for impenitent sinners, but he was not a Calvinist. He condemned the extreme Calvinist belief that God destined individuals, irrevocably, to be either 'elect' (saved by grace to eternal life) or 'reprobate' (eternally damned). He told J. C. Franks in January 1839 that such appalling doctrines were 'decidedly derogatory to the Attributes of God' (Lock & Dixon, p. 292). In late 1836 Charlotte was 'smitten at times to the heart with the conviction that' ghastly Calvinistic doctrines were true; if they were she was already an outcast, for she could neither profess herself a true Christian, nor take her rebellious thoughts to their logical, atheistic, conclusion. She perhaps knew that Revd Henry *Nussey had been troubled by Calvinist-inspired fears. Perhaps too she had not fully escaped from the nightmarish childhood experience of Revd W. Carus *Wilson's Calvinistic insistence that even a small child might be doomed to everlasting torment. By March 1845, she had put such fears behind her, for Mary *Taylor had heard her 'condemn Socinianism, Calvinism, and many other "isms" inconsistent with Church of Englandism' (Gaskell *Life* (1900), p. 142). Branwell at times believed that that he was already the '*dead alive*', doomed to hell; but he could also sardonically mock the belief, or, writing as the Byronic Percy, delight in posing as a damned soul. His Satanic Azrael defies the Calvinistic God who 'though he loves our race so well . . . hurls our spirits into Hell!' (Neufeldt *BBP*, p. 231). Though Anne sympathized with William *Cowper's fear that he was a castaway, her poem 'A Word to the Calvinists' conveys strong belief in a loving God who saves her from such fears. Emily agreed with Mary Taylor that her religion was 'between God and' herself (Gaskell *Life* (1900), p. 142), but she invoked God as 'Undying Life' in *'No coward soul is mine'.

Cambridge. When Revd Patrick Brontë entered St John's College on 2 October 1802 it was the largest of Cambridge's twelve colleges. Before her death in 1509 Lady Margaret Beaufort, Countess of Richmond, approved the foundation of a new college, replacing the Hospital of St John, and it was established in 1511. In 1802 it consisted of three courts, entered by great gateways, to the east of the Cam, with a library on the north side of the third court. Mr Brontë entered as a sizar, one of the least privileged students, and probably shared a room with his fellow sizar John Nunn, in the third storey of the front quadrangle (Barker, p. 7). At the other side of the college the Old Bridge across the river dated from 1696. The 'Bridge of Sighs' leading to 19th-century Neo-Gothic buildings on the west bank was not built until 1827–31. Further south, beyond Trinity, Caius, and Clare, is King's College, Henry VI's foundation (1441) with its magnificent 15th–16th-century chapel and James Gibbs's Fellows' Building of 1724. Over the central archway of this building lived Revd Charles *Simeon, Fellow of King's and incumbent of Holy Trinity church 1783–1836, responsible for the spiritual fostering of many evangelical clergy and laymen. To matriculate, Mr Brontë required an adequate knowledge of Latin and Greek. He had been a tutor in the family of Revd Thomas Tighe, Rector of *Drumballyroney, an evangelical St John's man himself, who helped and recommended him. Examinations in subjects other than mathematics took the form of exercises performed in disputation, and Mr Brontë achieved a first class in each of his classics examinations. Cambridge men whom he knew then or later included Charles Simeon; Henry *Martyn (St John's); J. C. Franks, Evan Jenkins (Trinity); Revd Henry *Nussey, Thomas Atkinson (Magdalene) (see ATKINSON FAMILY); and Theodore Dury (Pembroke) (see DURY FAMILY).

Campbell, Thomas (1777–1844). On 4 July 1834 Charlotte Brontë recommended this popular Scottish Romantic poet to Ellen Nussey as 'first rate'. In *High Life in Verdopolis, Jane Eyre,* and *Villette* she quotes from Campbell's *The Pleasures of Hope,* 'The Soldier's Dream', 'The Turkish Lady', and 'The Battle of the Baltic', and she enhances the 'silence deep as death' when the Duke of Zamorna appears in 'The *Scrap Book' by quoting from Campbell's 'The Beech-Tree's Petition'. Revd Patrick Brontë knew and probably admired Campbell's work too, for in a letter to her father of 4 June 1850 Charlotte enthusiastically describes 'a grand, wonderful picture of [John] Martin's' from Campbell's 'The Last Man' (Smith *Letters,* 1. 130).

'Caractacus'. See VERSE DRAMA BY BRANWELL BRONTË.

Carey (Cary), Captain Lucius, degenerate follower of Rogue (Duke of *Northangerland), sometime pirate and member of the *Elysium in the early *Glass Town and Angrian saga. His name is often associated with a similar minion of Rogue, Captain C. Dorn, and he also appears as a bookseller for the August 1829 issue of 'Blackwood's *Young Men's Magazine'.

Carlisle, 7th Earl of, George William Frederick Howard (1802–64), Viscount Morpeth from 1825, Earl of Carlisle from 1848. As a Liberal MP for Yorks. from August 1830, he spoke at a Haworth political meeting in 1832 of the state's duty to provide more churches in large towns, offending Revd Patrick Brontë by calling most rural churches 'dark lanterns'. Morpeth's liberal supporters tried to shout Mr Brontë down at an electioneering meeting on 20 July 1837; but Morpeth himself was gentle, generous, cultured, a supporter of *Mechanics' Institutes. He introduced himself to Charlotte

Brontë on 29 May 1851 before William Makepeace *Thackeray's second London lecture.

Carlyle, Thomas (1795–1881), essayist, historian, biographer, and prominent Victorian sage. In *Fraser's Magazine* the young Brontës would have read Carlyle's *Sartor Resartus,* and his early essays and translations from the German, writings which affirmed the organic, spiritual nature of the universe, asserted transcendent moral absolutes accessible through intuition, and celebrated charismatic 'heroes'. By the 1840s Carlyle's vision of paternalistic captains of industry caring for workers influenced the 'condition-of-England' novels (see NOVEL IN THE MID-19TH CENTURY, THE). Though Charlotte criticized his idiosyncratic style—his 'Germanisms'—to W. S. Williams, on 15 June 1848 (Smith *Letters,* 2. 74), reading his *Critical and Miscellaneous Essays* while she worked on *Shirley* confirmed her appreciation of his passion for truth and celebration of individuals' intrinsic worth (to W. S. Williams, 16 Apr. 1849, Smith *Letters,* 2. 202). BT

Kaplan, Fred, *Thomas Carlyle: A Biography* (1983).
Rosenberg, John D., *Carlyle and the Burden of History* (1985).

Caroline Vernon ('When I concluded my last book'). This is the last of Charlotte Brontë's Byronic novellas of the *Glass Town and Angrian saga. The plot traces the beginning of a teenage infatuation for the now middle-aged but still rapacious Duke of *Zamorna. The narrator is the cynical Charles Townshend, an older version of the young Lord Charles *Wellesley, who has disguised his regal identity in order to gain access to a greater variety of situations and to pursue his favourite hobby, eavesdropping. The adolescent heroine is Caroline *Vernon, by whose name the story has become known. (The title 'Caroline Vernon' was first used by Fannie Ratchford in *The Brontës' Web of Childhood* (1941).)

The untitled manuscript is divided into two parts, both located in Widener, Harvard (67 pages). Neither part is signed or dated, but from internal dating (Charlotte habitually set her stories at the time of composition) and from biographical evidence, it is possible to suggest that the two parts were written late July–early August and late November–early December 1839 (see Alexander *EW,* p. 198; Barker, p. 337, arbitrarily extends the date to spring 1840 with no evidence). The manuscript is carelessly written: there are no title-pages or prefaces, and the text includes several versions of some episodes. The surviving text of *Caroline Vernon* is, strictly speaking, a draft.

Despite its ostensibly repetitive material (Barker dismisses the story as 'the usual tiresome tale'),

Carter family

Caroline Vernon demonstrates a shift in Charlotte's narrative stance and greater realism in her writing. Zamorna has been domesticated, reduced to 'a clod-hopper' farmer whose property and interests are based on Charlotte's recent experience of North Yorkshire. Palaces are reduced to country houses and relationships to domestic comedy (Alexander *EW*, pp. 193–5). The Duke of *Northangerland and Zamorna clash like two old 'bulls', and even Zamorna's gradual seduction of Caroline, Northangerland's illegitimate daughter, is viewed ironically, as the final fling of a superannuated roué who can think of nothing better to do with his guardianship than revert automatically to old habits. Real insight is shown in the sensitive portrait of the impressionable and wilful adolescent Caroline, suggested perhaps by Caroline Lamb, one of *Byron's more wilful mistresses. Not for nothing did Ratchford call this story Charlotte's 'last Byronic fling': it abounds in Byronic allusions. It also reflects Charlotte's latest passion for French novels (see Alexander *EW*, p. 198).

Having fed imaginatively on the exploits of Byron, Bonaparte, and Wellington during her neglected childhood, Caroline (like her author) hungers for excitement and romance. Zamorna appears to embody her ideal hero. She creates her own romance and the now enervated Zamorna simply obliges. Psychologically a prisoner of her own dreams, Caroline is morally her own worst enemy (a situation Charlotte Brontë herself was now keenly aware of and feared). When the 15-year-old Caroline arrives on Zamorna's doorstep, he makes no attempt to restrain himself: 'Her Guardian was gone—Something terrible sat in his place'. A powerful scene follows in which we see the young girl, struggling against the hypnotic sexual power of a practised seducer, aware for the first time of her own impulses and desires, titillated yet terrified by the experience. The fate Jane Eyre later escapes is a foregone conclusion for Caroline. She is too young to win the battle between passion and conscience ('passion tempted, conscience warned'). As the narrator suggests, she is clay in the potter's hand; yet, ironically, her fervid imagination had already determined the outcome.

Zamorna takes Caroline to Scar House, Ingleside, the isolated location where Rosamund *Wellesley, one of his former mistresses who died of heartbreak, lies buried in the churchyard—a move which presumably foreshadows the fate Charlotte had planned for Caroline. The outcome of the story is also significant in the long-standing rivalry between Northangerland and Zamorna: Zamorna ultimately triumphs, flaunting his power over Northangerland's two daughters (he is already married to the eldest, Mary Percy) and depriving his rival of his 'last & only comfort'.

Alexander *EW*, 192–9.
Gérin *Five Novelettes*, pp. 271–367.

Carter family. Revd Edward Nicholl Carter (1800–72) was the curate at Mirfield parish church, not far from *Roe Head, when Charlotte Brontë was a pupil there. He probably prepared her for confirmation at Liversedge on 24 September 1831. On 30 November 1838 he was licensed to the newly built Christ Church, Lothersdale, where J. B. *Sidgwick was patron of the living. He and his family lived at Lower Leys Farm until a new house was ready for them in the village. In 1842 he became perpetual curate at Heckmondwike, near Leeds, and remained there, respected and loved, until his death. St Saviour's church, Heckmondwike, was built in his memory. In December 1830 he married Susanna[h] (Susan) Wooler (1800–72), who taught drawing at Roe Head until the birth of her first son in 1832. Her pencil drawing of the school is reproduced in Alexander & Sellars, p. 42. She trained her pupils to make copies of the same view, and of the school's collection of engravings. The Carters' first son, Edward, probably died in infancy, but a second son born in 1835 was given the same name. His three sisters were Ellen (b. 1834), Susan Margaret (1837–94) and Catherine (Kate, b. ?1840). While Charlotte was a governess at *Stonegappe, Lothersdale, she came to have a friendly regard for the Carters, and was grateful when Mr Carter brought her news of Anne Brontë's good health at *Blake Hall. On 28 August 1848 Charlotte advised Mrs Carter, who was considering sending Ellen to the Clergy Daughters' School, that it had improved since its removal from *Cowan Bridge. Catherine and Susan Margaret Carter had become schoolmistresses at *Oakwell Hall by c.1871, when they had two assistants, eighteen girl pupils, and domestic staff. Catherine was still there in 1894.

Carus Wilson, Revd William. See WILSON, REVD W. CARUS.

Castlereagh, Frederick Stuart, Viscount, a dandified early friend of the Duke of *Zamorna, who becomes Earl of Stuartville and an Angrian minister. He features in the *Islanders' Play as a member of the Duke of Wellington's cabinet, and one of Charlotte Brontë's *Twelves includes Francis Stewart, the family name of Castlereagh. In the *Glass Town and Angrian saga he is Zamorna's contemporary. Originally from Ireland, he joins the *Elysium and loses his estate in gambling debts. When he rescues Lady Harriet Montmorency (see CASTLEREAGH, HARRIET) from an unwelcome marriage to Thornton Wilkin *Sneaky, Zamorna gives him the post of secretary of the Foreign Office and Castlereagh marries Harriet himself.

He distinguishes himself in the *War of Encroachment, becomes a member of the Council of Six and lord lieutenant of the province of Zamorna in Angria, where he has the estate of Stuartville Park. Even as an Angrian statesman, Castlereagh maintains 'the habits of the coxcomb', with curled hair, perfumed silk handkerchief, fancy waistcoats, snuffbox, and gold repeater. He is based on Robert Stewart, Lord Castlereagh, Marquis of Londonderry, a distinguished British statesman, who was born in Ireland in the same year as the Duke of Wellington and constantly promoted his friend Arthur Wellesley's career, until he tragically committed suicide in 1822.

Castlereagh, Lady Harriet, daughter of Hector *Montmorency and sister of Julia Montmorency in the *Glass Town and Angrian saga. A pale, graceful beauty with dark curls, she marries Viscount Frederick Stuart *Castlereagh when he rescues her from an unwelcome marriage to Thornton Wilkin *Sneaky. She is given away by the Duke of Zamorna, to whose coterie she and her husband belong.

Castle Tavern, Holborn, London. See PUGILISM, BRONTË INTEREST IN.

'Caterpillar, The' ('Chenille, La'). See 'BUTTERFLY, THE' ('PAPILLON, LE').

Catholicism, Roman. Revd Patrick Brontë's home parish of *Drumballyroney had a sizeable minority of Roman Catholics, and he must have been aware of the discriminatory laws which denied them access to government and the professions. In 1797 Pitt ordered the disarming of Ulster to undermine the United Irishmen's efforts to secure Catholic emancipation and parliamentary reform. The result was the unsuccessful United Irish rebellion of 1798, after which the Act of Union of 1800 abolished the Irish parliament, but did not fulfil implicit promises of emancipation. In early 1829, when Irish constituencies with overwhelming Catholic majorities were still represented at Westminster by Protestant landowners, Mr Brontë's overriding concern that a violent 'convulsion' of rebellion should be avoided led him to support the bills for emancipation and relief. Writing to the Tory *Leeds Intelligencer on 15 and 29 January and 5 February 1829, he supported civil rights for Catholics, provided that 'the Protestant monarch or legislature' was empowered to remove Catholics from 'places of trust or influence' if danger threatened. Their father's keen interest aroused the young Brontës to 'breathless anxiety' as they listened to his reading of the 'terms on which the Catholics were to be let in' when the main bill was passed on 29 April. Charlotte's eloquent, dramatic account in *'Tales

of the Islanders', volume 2, shows how intensely she and her siblings could sympathize with a just cause, even though they knew of Catholics only by repute. During their adolescence, Catholics may still have seemed to them distant, alien, associated with popish priests who held sway over peasants ignorant of the Bible, subject to the confessional, and imposed on by rituals performed in an arcane language. The Brontës' view of such 'mummery' and 'idolatry' would be coloured by *Gothic novels. Such associations are prominent in *Villette*, along with the idea of entrapment: Lucy *Snowe's visit to the confessional entangles her in a sinister, priest-led plot, though the mutual love of Lucy and M. Paul Emanuel eventually overrides religious prejudice. The initial impact of the real *Brussels on Charlotte in 1842 had been to intensify her fierce Protestantism: papistry was humbug, priests had an 'idiotic, mercenary, aspect'. This attitude predominates in *The Professor*. Yet Charlotte admitted that some Catholics were 'as good as any christians can be to whom the Bible is a sealed book and much better than scores of Protestants' (Smith *Letters* 1. 290). Her own 'real confession' in September 1843, love for M. Constantin Heger, and perception of the beauty of some Catholic prayers even while she disparaged them ('Rose céleste, reine des Anges . . . Tour d'ivoire, maison d'or') modified and complicated her attitude to Catholics. The Pope's elevation of *Wiseman to the status of cardinal in 1850 led to hysterical, jingoistic anti-Catholic rantings in the British press (except in a few papers like the tolerant *Leader*) and to the public burning of effigies of Wiseman and the Pope. Mr Brontë feared that the Church of England would be perceived as a Romish nursery because of its Anglo-Catholic adherents. Charlotte satirically pictured the staff of Smith, Elder installing an oratory, and the *Leader* walking 'bodily back into the True Fold'. Yet though she saw Wiseman as an 'oily, sleek hypocrite' in June 1851, she went to hear him speak, just as she had voluntarily attended some of Newman's lectures on Anglican difficulties 'in Submitting to the Catholic Church' in June 1850.

Cave, Mary, in *Shirley*, a woman from *Briarfield, 'the beauty of the district' (p. 247) who was wooed by both Hiram *Yorke and Revd Matthewson *Helstone in their younger days, and who has died some years before the action of the novel commences. Mary chose Helstone, then a curate, above the young wool staplers who were her other suitors because he held an office that invested him 'with some of the illusion necessary to allure to the commission of matrimony' (p. 61). Once they were married, Helstone largely ignored her. However, being 'a remarkably still, silent person' (p. 247), Mary did not make her feelings known to her husband; within five years, she fell into a decline, and died. At the time of her death Mr Helstone's 'dry-eyed and sober mourning' gave rise to false stories that he had treated Mary harshly; the rumours have intensified Hiram Yorke's lasting and bitter animosity towards him. Mary's portrait hangs in the dining room at the Rectory, and elicits from Agnes *Pryor the observation that she was unlikely to have been a woman of spirit. The story of Mary Cave underlines Mr Helstone's rather cool, unsympathetic nature, his tendency to treat women with contempt, and his failure to recognize in Caroline *Helstone, his niece, the same symptoms of loneliness and emotional need that appear to have carried off his wife.   HR

Caversham, Captain George Frederick, Baron of. An excellent jockey, gambler, and card shuffler, Caversham is a handsome Glass Town villain and associate of Alexander Percy (Duke of *Northangerland), who murdered Caversham's wealthy father in a duel at Percy Hall. Percy's own father had been a friend of Caversham sen., who lent Percy money and helped Augusta di *Segovia to murder Percy's father for payment. Caversham is a colonel in the Dragoons during the *War of Encroachment, and he becomes an enemy of the Marquis of Douro (later Duke of *Zamorna) when he dupes him in a horse race (see SOMETHING ABOUT ARTHUR).

Celia Amelia. See WEIGHTMAN, REVD WILLIAM.

Cervantes' *Don Quixote* may be recalled in the two graceful dark-eyed Zoraydas in Charlotte Brontë's *The *Foundling* and *A *Leaf from an Unopened Volume*, perhaps named after the Algerian maid Zoraida who elopes with her lover in *Don Quixote* (pt. 1, bk. 4, ch. 13). Mlle Zoraïde *Reuter in *The Professor* recalls both the Zoraidas and Mme Zoë *Heger, her prototype. Charlotte uses a picturesque, Cervantean image in *Villette* (ch. 39) for the power of imagination, which can transform a 'way-side, hedge-munching animal' into a phantom, much as the Don imagines his decrepit nag Rosinante is a gallant charger.

Chadwick, Esther Alice (Mrs Ellis H. Chadwick), author of *In the Footsteps of the Brontës* (1914), and editor of *Kitty Bell, the Orphan* (1914). Mrs Chadwick lived at various times in Haworth, the *Shirley* country, and near *Woodhouse Grove. She met people who had known the Brontës, including Dr Amos *Ingham, Tabitha *Ratcliffe, and Tabitha *Aykroyd's great-nephew, William Wood, who made coffins for all the Brontë family except Anne. She made 'repeated pilgrimages' to every 'Brontë shrine' in England and Belgium, where she

was welcomed in houses now demolished, and met Frances Wheelwright (see WHEELWRIGHT FAMILY) and Mlle Louise de Bassompierre (former pupils at the Pensionnat *Heger), M. Constantin Heger's son Dr Paul Heger (see HEGER FAMILY), and M. l'Abbé Richardson, whom M. Heger had advised on the art of teaching. Writing soon after the publication of Charlotte Brontë's letters to M. Heger, she had more insight into that relationship than most of her predecessors, and was free to comment on it. She was sensibly cautious about accepting Dr Wright's stories of the Brontës' Irish background, and herself endeavoured to see and transcribe documentary material such as the entries in St John's College registers. She recorded Tabitha Ratcliffe's moving recollections of Charlotte on her deathbed, so worn and thin that light showed through her hands. She did make errors of fact and judgement, alleging, for example, that Revd Henry *Nussey proposed to the daughter (not the sister) of his former vicar; that Emily Brontë was at Law Hill in 1836; and that 'Kitty Bell the Orphan' was written by Charlotte as an early version of *Jane Eyre* (see K.T.). More recent biographers and editors have corrected most of her errors, and her work remains of value for its records of the Brontës by those who knew them, or the places they lived in.

Chantrey, Sir Henry, a Glass Town sculptor, one of the group of talented artists that surrounds the young Marquis of Douro (Duke of *Zamorna) in the *Glass Town and Angrian saga. His various busts and statues, such as his Apollo and Diana in the likeness of Douro and Zenobia, adorn the palaces of *Verdopolis. When Zamorna becomes king of Angria, Chantrey is knighted and becomes a member of the Angrian court circle. He is based on the historical Sir Francis Legatt Chantrey (1781–1841), an English sculptor from Derbyshire, famous for his portrait statues and busts, and church monuments.

Chapter Coffee House, 50 Paternoster Row, London, an old building with low-beamed ceilings, wainscotted walls, a shallow, broad, dark staircase, and high narrow windows overlooking the booksellers' shops in the Row. An 18th-century meeting place for booksellers, publishers, writers, and country clergymen, it was familiar to *Goldsmith, *Johnson, and Chatterton. Revd Patrick Brontë occasionally stayed there in 1802–7, and again in February 1842 when he accompanied Charlotte and Emily to Brussels. Charlotte and Anne used it during their London visit, 8–11 July 1848. It was closed in 1854, reopened as a tavern *c.*1856, rebuilt after 1885, and eventually demolished.

Charlesworth, Lady Emily, Countess of St Clair, the niece of Bravey and of the stern Marquis of Charlesworth, who is also her guardian, in the *Glass Town and Angrian saga. Tutored by *Gifford, she is more interested in her role as 'Rewarder of the victors' at the African Olympic Games. Lady Emily is the romantic heroine of The *Green Dwarf which tells the story of her courtship by the artist Mr Leslie (actually Earl *St Clair in disguise), her abduction by Alexander Percy (Duke of Northangerland) to whom she is engaged, and her rescue and marriage to St Clair.

Chartism. The Reform Bill of 1832 left five out of six working men without votes. Attempts to gain more bargaining power through amalgamating trade unions failed, and in 1837 William Lovett and Francis Place, realizing that workers needed votes before they could effect social change, formulated demands which were embodied in the People's Charter published in May 1838. Its six points were annual parliaments, universal male suffrage, equal electoral districts, removal of the property qualification for MPs, secret ballot, and payment of MPs. The more radical wing was led by James Bronterre O'Brien and Feargus O'Connor, an unreliable demagogue, who established the inflammatory Northern Star. For a time O'Connor encouraged the idea of violent revolution, which gained ground in 1837 and 1838, especially among half-starved northern workmen, and there were mass meetings by torchlight. The powerful conflicting emotions stirred by such events inform Charlotte Brontë's recreation of the earlier *Luddite riots in Shirley. The Birmingham Political Union suggested a National Petition, which was ready for presentation to Parliament on 6 May 1839; on 7 May the government resigned on an unrelated issue, and there was a long postponement. The Chartists' convention moved on 13 May to Birmingham, where riots took place and Lovett was briefly imprisoned. After 12 July, when the Commons refused to consider the petition, the Convention dissolved. In November O'Connor failed to support a rising in Monmouth which was quelled by troops. Fourteen Chartists were killed, ten died of wounds, and three leaders were sentenced to death, but the sentence was commuted to transportation. O'Connor agitated for a second petition, which received over 3,000,000 signatures, and emphasized the demand for universal suffrage. On 2 May 1842 the Commons rejected a motion that the petitioners should be heard. In the 1840s the Chartist movement was weakened by dissension over the movement to repeal the Corn Laws, but gathered momentum in 1848, at a time of distress and unemployment at home and violent revolutions abroad. Chartists celebrated in London after hearing of the establishment of a French Republic on 25 February, and began to plan a non-violent campaign. Charlotte's patriotic loyalty cannot have approved of their mass meeting in Leeds on 10 March, when the French republican flag was hoisted. Later that month several thousand Chartists met near Haworth, in early April the Haworth Chartist Abraham Lighton addressed a meeting of 8,000 near Kildwick, and elsewhere Chartists drilled, bought guns, and sharpened pikes. Serious plans for an insurrection were made in London. Wellington was put in charge of defences against the great Chartist gathering expected on Kennington Common before the presentation of another monster petition. Both events were humiliating fiascos for the Chartists: they were not allowed to process to Parliament, and the petition proved to contain many bogus signatures such as 'Victoria Rex, April 1', fictitious names, and obscenities. Charlotte Brontë's comments were temperate and comparatively liberal, for she agreed with W. S. Williams on 20 April 1848 that Chartist grievances should not be neglected 'nor the existence of their sufferings ignored. It would now be the right time, when an ill-advised movement has been judiciously repressed to examine carefully into their causes of complaint and make such concessions as justice and humanity dictate' (Smith Letters, 2. 51). Sporadic Chartist activities continued, and there were serious riots in Bradford at the end of May. Though Charlotte avoided writing about this contemporary issue in Shirley, she applied to the *Luddite riots the views she had developed in considering the Chartist cause.

Chateaubriand, François-René, vicomte de (historical) (1768–1848). A founder of French Romanticism and one of its leading authors, he was also admired in England. Twelve-year-old Branwell, writing as Young *Soult, alludes to his Travels in Greece, Palestine, Egypt, and Barbary (1812). This translation of Itinéraire de Paris à Jérusalem (1811) was in the *Ponden House library; it is also cited in a *Blackwood's Edinburgh Magazine article on Chateaubriand's work (1821). Charlotte read Chateaubriand in French as a student at the Pensionnat *Heger. Her notebook of *dictations includes brief passages from The Genius of Christianity (Le Génie du Christianisme, 1802) and The Martyrs (Les Martyrs, 1809). These became the basis for two of her *devoirs, 'Evening Prayer in a Camp' and *'Anne Askew'. She also transcribed a passage from his Atala (1801), which Heger titled 'Niagara Falls'.   SL

Chateaubriand, Moses (fictional). Napoleon's valet in the *Young Men's Play, Chateaubriand enters the *Glass Town and Angrian saga as a pedantic literary critic of Young *Soult's poetry. He appears only in Branwell's early manuscripts and is modelled on François-René, vicomte de *Chateaubriand.

Chénier, André (1762–94). Poet of French and Greek ancestry, born in Constantinople and brought up in Paris. An early partisan of the French Revolution, he was later imprisoned and executed. Most of his work remained unpublished until 1819; then he was recognized as a leading 18th-century poet. As M. Constantin *Heger's student, Charlotte read his poem 'The Young Captive' ('La Jeune Captive'). In her *devoir 'The Sick Young Girl' she paraphrases two of its lines: 'And though the present hour has griefs and cares | I would not die so soon.' In *Shirley*, Caroline *Helstone recites it to Hortense and then to Robert Gérard Moore. Caroline finds it deeply moving, though the narrator regards it more sceptically (chs. 5 and 6). SL

Lonoff, pp. 21–2.

'Chenille, La' ('Caterpillar, The'). See 'BUT-TERFLY, THE' ('PAPILLON, LE').

childhood and childhood reading of the Brontës. See BOOKS READ BY THE BRONTËS; JUVENILIA OF THE BRONTËS.

Children's Friend, The, an evangelical children's magazine edited by Revd W. Carus *Wilson, founder of the School for Clergymen's Daughters at *Cowan Bridge, model for *Lowood School in *Jane Eyre*. 'The Child's Guide' given to Jane by Mr *Brocklehurst in chapter 4 is probably based on the *Children's Friend* (1824–1930), though Wilson's magazine was similar to many other juvenile periodicals published by religious groups in the first half of the 19th century. Featuring cautionary accounts of naughty children who die unexpectedly, such magazines must have been anathema to the young Brontës, who thrived on lively adult periodicals such as *Blackwood's Edinburgh Magazine* and *Fraser's Magazine*.

CB

Althoz, Josef L., *The Religious Press in Britain, 1760–1900* (1989).
Drotner, Kirsten, *English Children and their Magazines, 1751–1945* (1988).

Church Missionary Society (CMS), originally 'The Society for Missions in Africa and the East'. The evangelical founders of this independent voluntary society in April 1799 included Revd Charles *Simeon and Revd John Venn (1759–1813). Inspired by Christ's words in Mark 16: 15, 'Go ye into all the world, and preach the gospel to every creature', they sent the first two CMS missionaries to Sierra Leone in 1804. Access to India was at first blocked by the East India Company's refusal to permit English missionaries to sail in their ships. Henry *Martyn had to go out in 1805 as a salaried chaplain to the Company. In 1813 *Wilberforce and other members of the Clapham Sect petitioned Parliament to allow 'the natives of India, our fellow-subjects' to share the blessings of Christian light and to free them from the evils of human sacrifice 'at the temple of Jaggernaut [*sic*]', the burning of widows, infanticide, and the shackles of caste. Reports of Wilberforce's great speech of 22 June 1813 would have been known to Revd Patrick Brontë, who had probably helped Revd John *Buckworth of Dewsbury to prepare young men for ordination and mission. 'Missionary intelligence' in magazines and newspapers kindled Charlotte's imagination, for she refers to suttee in the *Glass Town and Angrian saga (Alexander EEW, 2(2). 193), and describes the 'Sacrifice d'une veuve indienne' as a 'spectacle déchirant' in her devoir of 17 April 1842 (Lonoff, pp. 2–7). Her poem 'The Missionary' appeared in *Poems* 1846, published by *Aylott and Jones, who 'did a very great deal in export with the Church Missionary Society in West Africa' (C. K. Shorter, *The Brontës*, (1908), 1. 320 n.). In the poem she imagines the missionary's agonizing parting from his love, Helen, and his resolve to 'plant the gospel vine, | . . . Where thickest shades of mental night | Screen the false god and fiendish rite'. In *Jane Eyre* Mr *Brocklehurst accuses Jane of being worse than 'a little heathen who . . . kneels before Juggernaut', Jane teasingly assures Rochester she will not be 'hurried off in a suttee', and finally pays tribute to St John *Rivers, hewing down 'the prejudices of creed and caste' in India. In *Villette* Lucy Snowe feels beforehand the Juggernaut's 'annihilating craunch'. CMS work expanded during Mr Brontë's lifetime to the wider world, from New Zealand in 1809 to Mauritius in 1856. Women worked in the mission field from the early years, usually alongside their husbands. Thus St John Rivers's demand that Jane Eyre should accompany him as his wife is reinforced by the custom and authority of the Church. CMS missionaries spread the gospel through preaching, education, training in industry, crafts, and household skills, medical care and training for work in hospitals and dispensaries. The missions were funded by subscriptions to auxiliary societies, collections at special services, and such devices as the 'Missionary basket' to which women contributed ornamental articles for sale to the men of the household. Probably Charlotte, like Caroline *Helstone, lacked enthusiasm for this method of funding 'the regeneration of the interesting coloured population of the globe' (*Shirley*, ch. 7). Her satirical tone here resembles William Makepeace Thackeray's constant sniping at dismal evangelical sermons, typically 'on behalf of the mission for the Chickasaw Indians'. Perhaps she also recalled Branwell's parodic missionary meeting in *And the Weary are at Rest*.

Howse, Ernest Marshall, *Saints in Politics* (1953; repr. 1976).

Church of England, the Church to which Revd Patrick Brontë and his family belonged. The immediate reason for establishing a Church separate from Rome in 1533–4 was Pope Clement VII's refusal to grant Henry VIII's request for annulment of his marriage to Catherine of Aragon, so that he could marry Anne Boleyn. But many English people, already critical of the Catholic church's wealth, and its spiritual and legal dominance, welcomed Convocation's recognition of Henry as Supreme Head on earth of the Church of England in 1534. Though public worship was still celebrated in Latin, except for the English Litany, Henry's decree that the *Bible should be placed in all churches was in line with *Protestant emphasis on the Word of God revealed through the Scriptures. In 1571 the Thirty-Nine Articles, the central statements of doctrine still endorsed by Anglican clergy, were ratified. After the dissensions of the 16th and 17th centuries, the Church was re established in 1660, and use of a revised *Book of Common Prayer* was enforced by the Act of Uniformity of 1662.

In the early 19th century the Church needed reform. In 1813 more than 10 per cent of churches had no resident clergyman; some rectors had wealthy livings, but resided elsewhere, paying *curates a pittance to do the work of their church; others had several poor livings. Many midland and northern parishes were much too large. The ecclesiastical commission of 1835 worked to create extra parishes: 877 new churches were built between 1835 and 1845. An Act of 1843 initiated a more equitable distribution of wealth, and improved conditions for clergy working in squalid urban parishes. In February 1846 Mr Brontë's curate Revd J. W. *Smith became perpetual curate of Eastwood, a new district carved out of expanding industrial *Keighley. The unpromising Revd J. B. *Grant became a hard-working perpetual curate of the new district of Oxenhope, formerly part of *Haworth parish. Mr Brontë was also a perpetual curate—the equivalent of a vicar, nominated by a lay rector (purchaser of the right to receive tithes) or by trustees, or appointed to a new district. His Irish birth was no obstacle to his ministry in England. The established (episcopal) Church of Ireland and the Church of England were linked by the Act of Union of 1800 as the United Church of England and Ireland. Thus he could enter Cambridge, graduate, and receive ordination. The ordinand's

oath of allegiance to the sovereign was entirely congenial to his patriotism. The Bible and the Book of Common Prayer influenced the aims, content, and style of almost all his writings, giving them at their best cogency and a touching solemnity. His funeral sermon for Revd William *Weightman recognized the minister's duty to speak so as to be understood by his hearers, but still to expound God's word 'in the pure and dignified language of Scripture'. In his support for Church of England day and Sunday schools and for *temperance, *Church Missionary, and Bible societies Mr Brontë proved himself a worthy member of the evangelical wing of the Church.

From about 1780 Anglican evangelicals had brought into it a reforming zeal akin to that of the *Methodists, though their adherents tended to be middle, not working, class. Evangelicals emphasized the need for personal commitment to Christ, belief in his saving grace, as revealed in the Scriptures, and the Christian's duty to spread the gospel. Distinguished secular members of the evangelical Clapham Sect included *Wilberforce and Henry Thornton, both of whom helped Mr Brontë at Cambridge, and the clergymen Henry *Martyn, Revd Charles *Simeon, and John Venn (1759–1813), a founder of the Church Missionary Society, and the son of Henry Venn, Vicar of Huddersfield, 1759–71. The evangelical network in the West Riding of Yorkshire included several of Mr Brontë's friends, notably Revd William *Morgan, Revd John *Buckworth, and Theodore Dury (see DURY FAMILY). Evangelicals were often caricatured in the 18th century, as they were in the works of Dickens and Thackeray; but Mr Brontë earnestly exhorted a young clergyman, in the evangelical manner, to 'Shew Jesus in a saving light' and 'Remember still to fear the Lord, | To live, as well as preach, his word' (J. Horsfall Turner (ed.), *Brontëana*, (1898), p. 60). Anne's portrayal of a sincere evangelical clergyman, Edward *Weston, in *Agnes Grey* is effective because his kindness, pastoral care for the poor, and clear exposition of Christ's message to 'love one's neighbour' are contrasted with the harsh formalism of the vain, mercenary, toadying 'High Church' Revd Mr *Hatfield.

Charlotte was loyal to, but not uncritical of, the Church of England. In her works she presented a variety of Anglican clergymen: the harsh *Calvinist Revd *Brocklehurst, the militant Tory rector Revd Matthewson *Helstone, the gentle scholar Revd Cyril *Hall, the idealistic but tyrannical, self-immolating missionary St John *Rivers, and the brash young curates who gabble about theology but never talk of piety. Her more severe critics believed that in *Jane Eyre* religion was 'stabbed in the dark', and that in *Shirley* her curates were like 'a bevy of goblins', and her scriptural allusions unseemly and offensive. But it was precisely because Charlotte honoured the essential religious principles of the Church of England that she criticized its less than ideal representatives. A favourable notice of *Jane Eyre* in the *Church of England Journal* (16 Dec. 1847) gratified her because, she told W. S. Williams, 'I love the Church of England. Her Ministers, indeed I do not regard as infallible personages, I have seen too much of them for that—but to the Establishment, with all her faults—the profane Athanasian Creed *ex*cluded—I am sincerely attached' (Smith *Letters*, 1. 581). The Brontës had no love for the High Church tendencies of the *Oxford Movement, but like Anne, Charlotte admired some unorthodox liberal Anglicans. Of all the preachers she heard in London, she preferred F. D. Maurice (1805–72), a Christian Socialist sympathetic to Unitarianism and the doctrine of *universal salvation. She was shocked by his dismissal from his professorship at King's College London in October 1853 after his denial in his *Theological Essays* that sinners were doomed to an eternity of torment. A. M. F. *Robinson in 1883, followed by Eanne Oram (*BST* (1957), 13. 67. 131–40), thought that Emily was a disciple of Maurice. See RELIGION.

Thormählen, Marianne, *The Brontës and Religion* (1999).

'Chute des feuilles, La'. See 'FALL OF THE LEAVES, THE' ('LA CHUTE DES FEUILLES').

Cirhala River, and plain, in the *Glass Town and Angrian saga, on which the town of *Evesham, in the province of *Edwardston (formerly Edward Parry's Land), in the Verdopolitan Federation, is situated.

Clapham, Mrs Henry. See ROBINSON FAMILY OF THORP GREEN.

Clapham, Mrs Robert. See NUSSEY, ANN.

class. See TWO NATIONS, THE.

Cliffbridge, a 'fashionable watering-place' in *Shirley* where Shirley *Keeldar first meets Sir Philip *Nunnely. The few details provided by the narrator (there are gardens, cliffs, and a bridge) suggest the spa town of *Scarborough, where Anne Brontë died in May 1849 in a house quite close to the Cliff Bridge (constructed 1827).

HR

'cloud of recent death is past away, The'. See 'LINES ON THE CELEBRATED BEWICK'.

Cockney, Old Man. See 'TALES OF THE ISLANDERS'.

Cockney School, The, a term of abuse for a group of London poets including Leigh *Hunt, Keats, Hazlitt, and their friends, and first used by *Blackwood's Edinburgh Magazine* (Oct. 1817), in a disparaging article signed by Z (the editors J. G. *Lockhart and John *Wilson, Brontë heroes). This was the first of a series of vicious attacks in the Tory magazine against what it saw as a group of literary upstarts whose humble origins were unsuited to a poetic calling (Charlotte's 'The *Poetaster' gives a similar view). The famous review of autumn 1818, in which Keats's 'Cockney' rhymes and 'immature verses' were savagely derided, was said to have contributed to his premature death. The term 'Cockney' was well-known slang for a Londoner, but the young Brontës picked up the connotations suggested by *Blackwood's* and used the word in their juvenilia. In *'Tales of the Islanders', for example, Charlotte refers to 'wicked cockneys' who must be punished in the dungeons of the Palace School (Alexander *EEW*, 1. 24). There is also an 'Old Man Cockney' in the *Islanders' Play, who appears to be a servant of the Duke of Wellington.

Colburn, Henry (d. 1855), publisher. On 4 July 1846 Charlotte Brontë sent the manuscripts of *The Professor*, *Wuthering Heights*, and *Agnes Grey* to Colburn, who asked what kind of stories they were and what the authors had already published. If he did see the novels, he must have rejected them. Of obscure origins, he worked in William Earle's bookseller's shop in Albemarle Street, London, then moved to Morgan's Conduit Street Circulating Library, which he owned before 1810. He founded the *New Monthly Magazine* in 1814, and the *Literary Gazette* in 1817, the latter acquired by its editor William Jerdan in 1842. Both journals reviewed the Brontës' novels. The *Gazette* notoriously 'puffed' works published by Colburn, who moved to New Burlington Street in 1824. As a publisher he dominated the circulating-library market for three-volume novels, publishing for example works by Edward *Bulwer-Lytton, Disraeli, Theodore Hook, and Lady Morgan. Richard Bentley, Colburn's junior partner from June 1829, later became his rival, vying with him in exploiting popular trends. On 8 September 1851 Charlotte asked George *Smith to scotch a rumour that she was about to publish with either of the rivals. Colburn died, a wealthy man, at the house to which he had retired in Bryanston Square.

'Cold in the earth'. See 'REMEMBRANCE'.

Coleridge, Hartley (1796–1849), essayist and poet. Eldest son of the poet Samuel Taylor *Coleridge, Hartley (named after philosopher David Hartley) was admired as a precocious child of nature by his father (in 'Frost at Midnight') and William *Wordsworth (in 'To H.C., Six Years Old' and 'Ode: Intimations of Immortality'). In boyhood Hartley wrote about an imaginary world called Ejuxria, which (anticipating the Brontës' practice) he shared with his younger brother Derwent (see JUVENILIA OF THE BRONTËS). At Oxford (his tuition paid by his father's friends), Hartley's disappointment in failing three times to win the Newdigate Prize for English poetry contributed to intemperance which cost him a fellowship at Oriel College. In London he wrote briefly for the *London Magazine* (from 1820), relapsed into alcoholism, and in 1823 returned to Ambleside to teach school. He established a literary reputation beginning in 1833, when he published both a collection of biographies of *Worthies of Yorkshire and Lancashire* and a volume of well-received verse. He published verse and literary criticism in *Blackwood's Edinburgh Magazine* and compiled biographies for a collection of Elizabethan playwrights (*Dramatic Works of Massinger and Ford*, 1840). Increasingly reclusive and eccentric after his father's death in 1834, Hartley Coleridge contracted fatal bronchitis while carousing in inclement weather.

In April 1840 Branwell sought Hartley Coleridge's opinion on his prospects for a literary career, submitting his poem 'At dead of midnight—drearily' and translations of two of Horace's Odes (see 'ODES OF HORACE, THE'). Receiving encouragement, Branwell visited Coleridge's home near Rydal Water (1 May) and corresponded further about his translations of Horace, which Coleridge praised effusively in an incomplete draft of a letter that was never sent. In November 1840 Charlotte, writing as 'CT', sought Coleridge's evaluation of a manuscript, probably *Ashworth*. Her 10 December reply to his letter expresses pleasure that her prose left her sex indeterminate but implies that his assessment was discouraging. On 16 June 1847 'Currer Bell' sent Coleridge a copy of the Brontë sisters' *Poems* 1846 'in acknowledgement of the pleasure and profit we have often derived from your writings' (Smith *Letters*, 1. 531).   BT

Hartman, Herbert, *Hartley Coleridge: Poet's Son and Poet* (1931).

Coleridge, Samuel Taylor (1772–1834), Romantic poet and literary critic, much admired by the young Brontës, who embraced his exaltation of spontaneous, untutored imagination over rationalism. Though Branwell particularly admired 'Kubla Khan' (1797), Coleridge more evidently influenced Emily's poetry—a connection observed by her first biographer (A. M. F. *Robinson, 1883), who described their poetry in terms of 'surplus of imagination', 'instinctive music and irregular rightness of form, . . . effects of landscape', and 'scant allusions to dogma' (ch. 12). Traces of Coleridge appear in Emily's imagery, her use of nature to emblemize the human condition, and her delineation of creativity's disruptive aspects; in Charlotte's imagery there are specific echoes of Coleridge, notably 'the silent sea' of Sir John *Rivers's soul, and pervasive use of nature imagery to portray characters' psychology.   BT

Ashton, Rosemary, *The Life of Samuel Taylor Coleridge* (1996).
Bate, Walter Jackson, *Coleridge* (1968).

Collins, Revd John, possible model for Mr Arthur Huntingdon in *Tenant*; BA 1828, MA 1832, Trinity College Dublin. He assisted Revd Theodore Dury (see DURY FAMILY) from c.March 1839; was ordained priest in January 1840, and was curate at *Keighley, 1840–5/6. At Haworth in March 1840 he preached a clever, bold sermon attacking Dissenters. But in November Revd Patrick Brontë advised Mrs Collins to leave him: he was drunken, extravagant, deeply indebted, profligate, and treated her and her child savagely. By April 1847, after an infamous career of vice in England and France, he had abandoned her and her two children in Manchester, where she eventually recovered from the 'hideous' disease inflicted on her.

Colne-moss Tarn, home of the *Hastings family near *Pendleton in the province of *Angria in the *Glass Town and Angrian saga. The name recalls the moorland scenery of west Yorkshire, Colne being the name of a town across the Pennine range from Haworth.

communications. After 1784 letters could be conveyed by mailcoach along a network of post roads, and from 1794 provincial penny posts could be operated around large towns. Thus on a letter of 28 April 1831 from Revd Patrick Brontë were stamped the words 'Bradford Yor[ks] | P[enn]y Post'; following normal practice, he had written the address on the outside of the folded and sealed letter. Addressees might receive local post the following day, but letters sent for longer distances were expensive, and might take two, three, or more days, especially in winter. Before 10 January 1840 the cost of postage was usually paid by the recipient. The lowest rate for a single-sheet letter by the general post was 4d. up to 15 miles, rising to 1s. for a distance up to 300 miles, a double letter of two sheets paid twice these rates, 'heavy' letters were charged by the quarter ounce. On 21 July 1832 Charlotte Brontë assured her 'dearest Ellen' that she would not 'grudge double postage' to obtain a lock of her hair (Smith *Letters*, 1. 115). The higher cost of sending more than one sheet, or, after 1840, of 'heavy' letters, led correspondents, including Charlotte and Anne, to cross-write some single-sheet letters. Letters might be carried by *railway from the early 1830s. In January 1840 a uniform, prepaid penny rate of postage came into operation throughout Britain. The printed formula 'PAID ONE PENNY' could be hand-stamped on letters sent before 6 May 1840, when ready-stamped envelopes and adhesive stamps were introduced. Charlotte exchanged letters with her London publishers at an enviably rapid rate, her corrected proofs being normally received on the day after posting. Letters to Europe, carried by packet-boats, were costly, and temporary residents abroad, like Charlotte and Emily in Brussels in 1842/3, sent home packets of letters by travelling friends for distribution in England. So also did Mary *Taylor, writing from New Zealand. From the late 1840s European reports might be transmitted to newspapers by electric telegraph.

Daunton, M. J., *The Royal Mail* (1985).

'Confidence' ('Oppressed with sin'), poem by Anne Brontë (1 June 1845), written at Thorp Green, soon after two poems expressing rebellion and despair. Anne acknowledges her depression and weakness, but affirms that God will give her strength. She commits herself wholly to him, in her Redeemer's name. The poem is a hymn, in the musically effective Short Metre (66. 8. 6) skilfully used in familiar evangelical hymns such as James Montgomery's 'Stand up, and bless the Lord', and Isaac Watts's 'Come we that love the Lord'. The most important of many biblical allusions is to Psalm 27, 'The Lord is my light'.

Chitham *ABP*, p. 114.

contemporary writers, Brontës' contact with and attitudes to. Except for Charlotte, the Brontës had little direct contact with the well-known authors of their day. In varying degrees, all three sisters preferred privacy to the public exposure that would make them known personally to other contemporary writers. Moreover, Emily and Anne died not long after the release of their pseudonymously published novels, and the true identities of 'Ellis and Acton Bell' remained unknown during their short lifetimes. As a young man, Branwell lived away from home in a number of different places and had more opportunity to make acquaintances among the provincial authors and artists he met in *Yorkshire; but he, too, published under a pseudonym and died early, without achieving the kind of recognition that would bring him into contact with the more important literary figures of his day. Living seven years longer than her siblings, Charlotte was the only one to form significant connections with the literary world beyond Yorkshire.

Charlotte's and Branwell's letters and early writings reveal their enthusiasm for the literary figures of their youth: Sir Walter *Scott, Lord *Byron, J. G. *Lockhart, Thomas *Campbell, John *Wilson, James *Hogg, Robert *Southey, Thomas *Moore, William Maginn, and others. It comes as no surprise, then, that the two oldest Brontës tried to gain support from established writers when they began to contemplate authorship seriously themselves. In addition to offering his services repeatedly to the editor of *Blackwood's Edinburgh Magazine* between 1835 and 1842, Branwell wrote to several well-known authors, asking their opinions of his writing and seeking counsel about how best to launch his anticipated career as an author. Five months before his twentieth birthday, Branwell sent a sample of his verse to William *Wordsworth, but, according to Robert Southey, Wordsworth found his letter (printed in Smith *Letters*, 1. 160–1) so fulsome in its flattery and so flippant in its treatment of other poets that Wordsworth was too disgusted to reply. Three years later, Branwell tried again, this time sending an original poem and several verse translations to Thomas *De Quincey, a regular contributor to *Blackwood's*, and to Hartley *Coleridge, son of Samuel Taylor *Coleridge and a respectable poet in his own right. De Quincey apparently did not reply, but Hartley Coleridge sent an encouraging response and invited Branwell to visit him in the *Lake District. Soon after, the two spent a pleasurable day together at Coleridge's home on Rydal Water, conversing about poetry and reading their work out loud to each other. This experience seems to have boosted Branwell's confidence and strengthened his determination to pursue a career in writing (see 'ODES OF HORACE, THE'). However, when in the following month he sent his new-found mentor a revised draft of the poem he had enclosed with his original letter, Branwell waited in vain for a reply. We now know that Coleridge finally began to draft a response to Branwell a full five months later, but the letter was never sent. Like Branwell's letters to Wordsworth, De Quincey, and Alexander Blackwood, his hopeful correspondence with Hartley Coleridge led the aspiring young author nowhere.

Coleridge's half-hearted effort to write back to Branwell in November 1840 must have been prompted by his recent receipt of a similar request for advice from another inhabitant of *Haworth Parsonage, a mysterious 'CT'. This, of course, was Charlotte, writing under one of her juvenile *pseudonyms. She, too, sent a sample of her work—in this case the opening chapters of a novel—and while Coleridge did write back to 'CT', his response was not encouraging (see ASHWORTH). Charlotte had had a similar experience three years earlier, when she had written to Southey for his opinion of her poetry. Sending him a sample of her verse shortly before Branwell wrote to Wordsworth for the same purpose, Charlotte waited two and half months for Southey's now infamous warning: 'Literature cannot be the business of a woman's life' (Smith *Letters*, 1. 165–6). Her response was to thank Southey demurely for his advice; in return he sent a courteous, kindly-meant if rather patronizing reply which concluded their correspondence. Charlotte's later correspondence with Hartley Coleridge—initiated by her under a gender-neutral pseudonym and concluded by her in a light-hearted, satirical vein—shows that Charlotte gradually became more politic in her handling of the famous authors to whom she applied. Perhaps shrewder than Branwell in this respect, she was at any rate more successful at getting them to respond.

Branwell did get to know a number of provincial writers, however, and, to a degree never possible for his sisters, he benefited from the company and collegial advice of these peers. While working as a portrait painter in *Bradford, he was introduced to the local antiquarian John James and to Robert Storey, a poet widely published in the local press. Later, at *Luddenden Foot, where he was employed by the Leeds and Manchester railway, he was part of a circle of local poets who met regularly to combine conviviality with the reading and discussing of each other's work. Included in this group of literary friends were William *Dearden, known as the 'Bard of Caldene'; 'The Airedale Poet' John Nicholson; and Thomas Crossley, the 'Bard of Ovenden'. After being dismissed from his position with the railway in March 1842, Branwell made yet another effort to forge useful literary connections, sending samples of his writing to Leigh *Hunt; Caroline Bowles, wife of Robert Southey and herself a respected poet; James Montgomery, a well-known Sheffield poet; and James and Harriet *Martineau. Unlike his Yorkshire acquaintances, however, Branwell never became a locally famous poet, and, like Emily and Anne, he had no direct personal contact with any of the leading writers of the day.

The case was different for his older sister. When Charlotte, Emily, and Anne's book of poems had sold only two copies a year after its release, she resourcefully sent presentation copies to six established authors—Thomas De Quincey, Alfred Lord *Tennyson, Ebenezer *Elliott, William Wordsworth, Hartley Coleridge, and J. G. Lockhart—in an unsuccessful attempt to gain influential 'friends' in the literary world. Later, after having made her reputation as the author of *Jane Eyre*, she had copies of *Shirley* sent to Elizabeth *Gaskell and Harriet Martineau, so initiating her friendship with them, and was personally introduced to contemporary literary society by her well-connected publisher

George *Smith and his reader, W. S. *Williams. During Charlotte's four visits to *London, she was hosted by Smith and Williams, through whom she met numerous authors including Julia *Kavanagh, George Henry *Lewes, Richard Monckton *Milnes, and William Makepeace *Thackeray. In addition to her future biographer Elizabeth Gaskell, the most important contemporary literary figures in Charlotte Brontë's life were Lewes, Martineau, and Thackeray.

Charlotte had long admired Thackeray, whom she set above all other writers as 'the first of Modern Masters' (Smith *Letters*, 2. 98). It is likely that she knew his pseudonymous work published in *Fraser's Magazine* and *Punch*, and she had a high opinion of *Vanity Fair*, which was published in monthly instalments from January 1847, the same year in which *Jane Eyre* appeared, until July 1848. Thackeray, in turn, responded enthusiastically to Charlotte's first novel, which she dedicated to him in its second edition. The two novelists met four times, with mixed results. It seems that Charlotte expected Thackeray to live up to the ideal notion she had conceived of him from his writings, while he, for his part, refused to play that role. Their first personal contact, at a dinner party arranged by George Smith in December 1849, was disappointing for Charlotte, who 'spoke stupidly' because she was so nervous, as she later recalled (Smith *Letters*, 2. 312). The following summer, when she was again staying with the Smiths in London, Thackeray paid a two-hour morning call during which she lectured him on his literary faults, surely a discomfiting experience for him. Shortly after, she attended a dinner in her honour at Thackeray's home, a disastrous social event that his daughter, Anne *Thackeray, later recounted in painful detail. Things did not improve the following year when Thackeray ostentatiously referred to Charlotte as 'Jane Eyre' in her presence at one of his well-attended lectures in London; averse to such 'lionizing,' she was furious and made him feel the full force of her anger when he called the following day. Smith, always diplomatic, managed to soothe Charlotte's ire, and the two novelists parted amicably, never to meet again. In her letters, Charlotte continued to be critical of Thackeray for his failure, as she saw it, to live up to his potential as a novelist, but she also consistently praised his masterly writing. In 1853, George Smith sent her an engraving of Samuel Laurence's portrait of Thackeray, which she hung next to that of her other hero, the Duke of *Wellington.

Unlike Thackeray, G. H. Lewes was not known to Charlotte when he first wrote to her in November 1847. Learning from his letter that he intended to review *Jane Eyre* favourably in the next issue of *Fraser's Magazine*, she applied to Williams for information about Lewes's standing in the literary community. His review of *Jane Eyre* was glowing, and he had much praise to offer in his letter as well, but he also warned Brontë against her inclination to melodrama. He recommended that she study the novels of Jane *Austen (which she had not read) as models of realistic fiction. Charlotte politely thanked him for his rather patronizing counsel, which she acknowledged was good advice, but she also defended her own romantic writing in contrast to Austen's elegantly satirical style. Brontë made a point of reading Lewes's novels, which she praised to him but evaluated less generously in letters to Williams. The rift in their relationship, as far as Charlotte was concerned, came when Lewes reviewed her second novel, *Shirley*, for the *Edinburgh Review* (Jan. 1850). Once again, he wrote to Charlotte before the review appeared, telling her that he disliked the opening chapter and was intending to say so in print; he also mentioned his growing certainty that 'Currer Bell' was a woman. Charlotte wrote back promptly, urging him not to think of her as a woman because the novel would be reviewed more fairly if critics believed Currer Bell to be a man (Smith *Letters*, 2. 275). In the event, however, Lewes's review not only harshly criticized *Shirley* but also revealed Charlotte's identity as the unmarried 'daughter of a clergyman' from Yorkshire. Understandably, Charlotte was very angry, and she fired off a hot reply: 'I can be on my guard against my enemies, but God deliver me from my friends!' (Smith *Letters*, 2. 330). Lewes apparently failed to understand the pain he had inflicted and forced her to explain herself in yet another letter: 'I will tell you why I was so hurt by that review . . . not because its criticism was keen or its blame sometimes severe; . . . but because, after I had said earnestly that I wished critics would judge me as an *author* not as a woman, you so roughly—I even thought—so cruelly handled the question of sex,' she complained, alluding to the review's insinuation that she had failed to write credibly about motherhood because she herself was childless and single (Smith *Letters*, 2. 332–3). When Charlotte and Lewes finally met over luncheon at the Smiths' the following summer, he once again offended her by tactlessly quipping that they had both written 'naughty books'. She responded indignantly but parted from him in friendship, though her respect for him was always tempered by a dislike for his apparently reckless insensitivity towards other people's feelings, especially her own.

Harriet Martineau, like Thackeray, had long been an admired figure at Haworth Parsonage. On Charlotte's second visit to London in 1849, she asked Smith to introduce her to the older writer, who was then visiting relatives nearby. She had already sent Martineau a copy of *Shirley* with a note expressing warm admiration for her first novel, *Deerbrook* (1839). In spite of their many differences, Brontë and Martineau got along well for some time, corresponding and spending time together at Martineau's home at *Ambleside in the Lake District, where Charlotte met the young Matthew *Arnold, who displeased her until she saw that his foppishness was a cover for genuine modesty and high intellectual attainments. Martineau once tried unsuccessfully to mesmerize Charlotte at her friend's request; and Charlotte tried, with no more success, to broker a book contract for Harriet with the firm of *Smith, Elder and Company. She was appalled by Martineau's atheism but defended her new friend in the face of objections from other, more conventional acquaintances. Charlotte had genuine respect and admiration for this hardworking, independent-minded, unmarried woman writer, but, as with Lewes, a breach in their relationship eventually occurred. Famous for her strong opinions and forthright expression of them, Martineau frankly criticized *Villette*, both in her review for the *Daily News* (3 Feb. 1853) and in a personal letter she sent to Charlotte. She found the book 'intolerably painful' and objected to what she considered its monomaniacal view of love and its bigoted representation of Roman *Catholicism. Stung to the quick by these criticisms, Charlotte quickly sent Martineau a very angry reply, and, having fumed for several weeks over her friend's seeming betrayal, finally wrote a letter that ended all communication between them. After Charlotte's death, Martineau prepared an appreciative obituary which appeared in the *Daily News*; later, as fractious as ever, she engaged in an extended quarrel over Elizabeth Gaskell's representation of her in the *Life*.

In contrast to these troubled literary friendships, Charlotte's attachment to her biographer remained sincerely warm, though not intimate, from their first meeting to their final correspondence. As with Martineau, Charlotte initiated the relationship by sending Gaskell a copy of *Shirley* 'with the author's compliments' in 1849. Moved by the novel's scenes of sickbed suffering, Gaskell sent a sympathetic reply, which Charlotte answered in a letter revealing her identity as a woman, something she had never done before. Getting to know each other through letter writing (a genre at which both excelled), the two authors eventually met at the Lake District home of Sir James *Kay-Shuttleworth, who had invited them both for a visit in August 1850. Normally shy with strangers, Charlotte greeted Elizabeth with uncharacteristic warmth, and their friendship developed rapidly as they spent much time alone together during their week-long visit. Subsequently, Charlotte stayed with the Gaskells in *Manchester on three occasions, and Elizabeth was one of the very few house guests at Haworth Parsonage. Charlotte's and Elizabeth's minds were not made from the same mould, however, and those differences prevented them from ever becoming intimate friends. Elizabeth was as curious as she was sympathetic about what she saw as Charlotte's tragically lonely life, and Charlotte was not quite sure that Elizabeth could truly be her '*own woman*' as an author while responding to the constant demands of her lively household, busy social life, and wifely duties as a minister's spouse (Wise & Symington, 4. 76). But they were each eager in their respective ways to be kind to the other. Charlotte graciously agreed to delay the publication of *Villette* to avoid competition with Elizabeth's *Ruth*, which was scheduled to be released at the same time; and Elizabeth tried to clear Charlotte's father's objection to her engagement with Revd A. B. *Nicholls by secretly attempting to arrange a pension or a more lucrative clerical appointment for Nicholls. She was invited to visit Haworth when the couple had returned from their honeymoon, in spite of Mr Nicholls's reservations about his wife's friendship with the wife of a well-known Unitarian minister. Unfortunately, Elizabeth did not visit Haworth again while Charlotte was living. When Revd Patrick Brontë requested that she write his daughter's biography, she eagerly complied and in less than two years finished what would become one of the finest 19th-century literary biographies.

Though Charlotte's personal acquaintances among contemporary writers were relatively few, her letters often refer to the authors whose work she was reading at the time. George Smith and W. S. Williams regularly sent box loads of recently published books and periodicals to the Parsonage, which gave her additional exposure to contemporary literature. With Williams in particular she established a steady correspondence in which she aired her opinions about the volumes he had sent. From these letters we know that she greatly admired the works of John *Ruskin, preferred George *Sand to Jane *Austen and Honoré de Balzac, had reservations about Ralph Waldo Emerson and Thomas *Carlyle, disliked *In Memoriam* (though Emily seems to have liked Tennyson's earlier poems), was intrigued by George Borrow, and could speak quite contemptuously of generally admired writers such as fellow novelists Charles *Dickens and Edward *Bulwer-Lytton and poets Robert and Elizabeth Barrett Browning. Charlotte also corresponded with several lesser-known authors including Catherine *Gore, R. H. Horne, John Stores *Smith, Julia Kavanagh, and Sydney *Dobell. Toward the latter three, who were younger and less professionally secure than

she, Charlotte adopted a kindly meant if not-altogether flattering attitude of support and patronage. CB

Coomassie (now spelt 'Kumasi'), capital of the west African empire of Ashanti and used by the Brontës in their *Glass Town and Angrian saga. Their imaginary *Ashantee capital of Coomassie has 500,000 inhabitants and is located on the deep Red River near Rosedale Hill, site of the Duke of *York's death. Destroyed in an attack by the *Twelves, it is described in *'Letters from an Englishman' (by Branwell) as a majestic ruin. It was after the Battle of Coomassie and the death of King Sai Too-Too Quamina that the Duke of Wellington found the young Quashia *Quamina. See also AFRICA; ASHANTEE WARS.

'Corner Dishes', 'Being A small Collection of Mixed and Unsubstantial Trifles In Prose and Verse By Lord Charles Albert Florian Wellesley' (16 June 1834). This is a collection of three items by the 18-year-old Charlotte Brontë, written in a hand-sewn booklet of nineteen pages (Huntington): 'A Peep into a Picture Book', 'A Day Abroad' in four chapters, and 'Stanzas on the Fate of Henry Percy'.

'A Peep into a Picture Book', as its title suggests, is a series of portraits of Charlotte's favourite characters analysed by Lord Charles as he looks through the pages of *Tree's Portrait Gallery of the Aristocracy of Africa,* modelled on such popular English *annuals as Heath's *Book of Beauty*.

'A Day Abroad' records Lord Charles's visits to *Warner Hotel, *Wellesley House, and *Ellrington Hall. Chapter 1 is a highly successful comic scene that might well be acted on the stage. The *Warner family breakfast, a sedate affair presided over by the taciturn and exacting head of the family of Howards, Warners, and Agars, is intruded upon by the swaggering drunk Arthur *O'Connor, a crony of Warner's wayward clerical brother Dr Henry Warner. At Wellesley House Lord Charles observes petitioners to Mary Percy, including the pugilist Maurice *Flannagan, Henry Bramham *Lindsay, and Patrick Benjamin *Wiggins, whose obsession with noses causes him to desecrate the sacred Percy nose! The episode satirizes Branwell's current enthusiasms for pugilism and music. At Ellrington Hall, Lord Charles is no more than a diminutive spy, reporting the reminiscences of the Duke of Northangerland and his plan to destroy the friendship between the Dukes of *Zamorna and *Fidena.

'Stanzas on the Fate of Henry Percy' describes the final days and murder of Lieutenant Henry *Percy while on a voyage to the South Sea Islands. The youngest son of Northangerland, he is murdered at the instigation of his father, by Captain Steighton (see STEATON, TIMOTHY).

Alexander *EEW*, 2(2). 83–147.

Cornhill. See SMITH, ELDER AND COMPANY.

Cornhill Magazine. Established in 1860 by Charlotte Brontë's publisher, George *Smith, the *Cornhill Magazine* was an innovative periodical that enjoyed great success in its early years. Priced at only 1s., it deliberately eschewed political and social controversy in an effort to reach a younger, more general audience than those addressed by the earlier literary reviews. In an effort to provide polite entertainment, intelligent non-partisan reviewing, and high-quality writing, every monthly issue included instalments of two serialized novels (instead of the usual one) by well-known authors, plus essays, short fiction, and reviews by other exceptionally talented writers. Smith persuaded William Makepeace *Thackeray to be the first editor as well as a major contributor and recruited many other prominent writers by offering much higher payments than most magazines. Notable contributors include Matthew *Arnold, Wilkie Collins, George Eliot, Elizabeth *Gaskell, Thomas Hardy, and Anthony Trollope. Under Thackeray's editorship and with the assistance of Revd A. B. *Nicholls, *Cornhill* posthumously published Charlotte's last, unfinished narrative, *Emma*, with an introduction by Thackeray, in April 1860. Two previously unpublished poems by Charlotte and one by Emily also appeared in the *Cornhill Magazine* over the next year and a half. When ill health forced Thackeray to give up his editorial duties in 1862, the magazine was edited by a committee that included Smith and George Henry *Lewes, a great admirer of Charlotte's first and last novels. In 1868, Ellen *Nussey suggested that Smith publish her letters from Charlotte in *Cornhill*, an offer he eagerly took up until he realized that frosty relations between Ellen and Mr Nicholls would make securing permission to print the letters unlikely. Smith himself wrote two articles on the Brontës for inclusion in his magazine (July 1873; Dec. 1900). Leslie Stephen, who served as editor from 1871 to 1882, provided a more negative assessment of Charlotte's work in the issue for December 1877.
CB

Cottage in the Wood, The, or *The Art of Becoming Rich and Happy* by Revd Patrick Brontë (Bradford, 1815); prose section reprinted in the *Cottage Magazine* (June 1817; 2nd edn. 1818). In his introduction Mr Brontë deplores the 'sensual novelist's' unreal equation of palaces with misery and cottages with ideal happiness. Quoting Milton's 'The mind is its own place', he preaches that only goodness and wisdom can bring happiness.

His story is unpretentiously told: the cottagers' daughter Mary, taught to read the Bible at Sunday school, earns a small salary there as a teacher, and brings happiness to her parents by converting them. When William Bower, a wealthy, drunken rake and atheist, asks her to be his mistress, she refuses. After a patiently endured time of poverty, she is bequeathed £4,000 by a pious lady. Bower, impoverished by riotous living, but converted after miraculously escaping death, gives poor children free tuition in Sunday school, and meets Mary there. Their eventual marriage is both happy and pious. Though the reversal of fortunes is too neat, the little story moves forward rapidly, and the characters and speeches have some touches of realism: Mary's perfection includes common sense. As always, Mr Brontë's language is permeated with biblical allusions. See POETRY BY REVD PATRICK BRONTË.

Cottage Magazine (1812–47), the first of several magazines designed by evangelical Anglicans for rural working-class readers. Its editor, Revd John *Buckworth, was vicar at *Dewsbury, where Revd Patrick Brontë served as curate during the time of *Luddite riots in that area. Similar to Revd William *Morgan's *Pastoral Visitor* and Revd W. Carus *Wilson's *Friendly Visitor*, the *Cottage Magazine* reprinted Mr Brontë's didactic narrative The *Cottage in the Wood* in June 1817. Buckworth's wife, Jane, also contributed to the magazine and may have inspired Maria Branwell Brontë to write her essay 'The *Advantages of Poverty in Religious Concerns' for inclusion in its pages.
CB

Althoz, Josef L., *The Religious Press in Britain, 1760–1900* (1989).

Cottage Poems (Halifax, 1811), by Revd Patrick Brontë, who aimed to write simply, plainly, and perspicuously so that the 'lower classes' might understand; and to show that to be truly happy, one must be religious. He signally failed to write simply, except in 'The Cottager's Hymn'. The poems range from the amiably pious 'Epistle' to Revd John *Buckworth—fluent enough but marred by a jogging rhythm and pouncing rhymes—to the ambitious 'Winter-Night Meditations', a variation on the storm descriptions interspersed with meditations in, for example, Thomson's *The Seasons* (1726–46). It begins with verve, but becomes inchoate, with a clodhopping use of *L'Allegro*-type octosyllabics, and some woefully bathetic lines on the Highlander's blade which 'with horrid whistle' 'lops off heads, like tops of thistle'. More attractive poems are 'The Rainbow', a fairly lively verse-sermon; the epistle to Revd Joshua Gilpin with its brisk satire on the

'Bond-street beau' preacher that 'smooths its chin, and licks its lip, I and mounts the pulpit with a skip'; and 'The Spider and the Fly', which combines nice observation with a brief moral. The 'Epistle to a Young Clergyman' borrows a version of William *Cowper's phrase, to 'dazzle me with tropes' (*The Task*, bk. 2). The worst poem is 'The Cottage Maid', with its virtuous 'sweet maiden', ludicrous metre, appalling occasional feminine rhymes ('Jesus' paired with 'frees us', 'ease us', and 'appease us'), and flat, hobbling rhymeless lines concluding each stanza, worthy of McGonagall on a bad day. Happily, *The *Rural Minstrel* is an all-round improvement on this volume.

Coventry, J. Roy (d. 1942), Brontë collector during the early 1900s, whose bequest to the Brontë Society in 1955 enriched its collection. He was a frequent visitor to Haworth from his home in Guernsey and corresponded regularly with Martha *Brown's sister Tabitha *Ratcliffe and her niece Mary Popplewell. Most of his collection came from this source and since the owners were reluctant to sell off large batches of relics, he bought items individually over a period of time.

Alexander & Sellars, pp. 375, 378–9, 384, 396, 438.

Cowan Bridge. The Clergy Daughters' school in the hamlet of Cowan Bridge, Lancashire, founded by Revd W. Carus *Wilson, was opened in January 1824. Wilson's aim was the intellectual and religious improvement of the pupils, through an education enabling them 'to return with Respectability and Advantage to their own Homes, or to maintain themselves in the different Stations of Life to which Providence may call them'. Girls requiring a more liberal education to fit them for teaching were charged more than the basic £14 per year, plus £1 towards the cost of books. Donors and subscribers recommended pupils, especially daughters of needy and exemplary clergy. Patrons included Hannah More, Revd Charles *Simeon, William Wilberforce, and Frances Currer of Eshton Hall. Wilson had purchased a row of stone cottages at right angles to the Settle to Kendal turnpike road, and added a long schoolroom with dormitory above, as at *Lowood. This wing faced a veranda used for winter exercise, at the other side of a square plot divided into small gardens for the pupils to cultivate. The school lay in a lush green valley, below the wooded slopes of Leck Fell, and near the brawling Leck Beck. The school had enrolled 20 girls by the end of July 1824, including Maria Brontë aged 10 and Elizabeth Brontë aged 9 on 21 July. Charlotte, aged 8, arrived on 10 August 1824, the thirtieth to be enrolled, and Emily, aged 6¼, the forty-fourth, on 25 November. Summer uniform consisted of buff nankeen frocks, brown pinafores, and black stockings, with white clothes for Sundays; purple woollen frocks and cloaks were worn in winter. Long hours were spent in prayers and other religious exercises, and Sunday attendance at Wilson's church in Tunstall, over 2 miles away, was obligatory, until he enlarged the nearer Leck chapel. Strict discipline included public beating and the wearing of 'untidy badges'—a punishment perhaps overused by an under-teacher rather than by Miss *Andrews (formerly identified, unfairly, with Miss *Scatcherd), temporary superintendent of the school until the appointment of Ann *Evans, c.July 1824. According to Elizabeth Gaskell, who visited the school at Casterton in March 1856, the original diet had not been bad or unwholesome, but the food was often contaminated, burnt, or rancid owing to the carelessness of a dirty, wasteful cook. After the outbreak of 'low fever'—probably typhus—early in 1825, Wilson sought out an efficient nurse, ordered liberal supplies of food and medicine, and eventually discharged the cook. But of twenty pupils who left by September 1825, eleven left in ill health, of whom three, including Maria and Elizabeth Brontë, died of consumption soon after leaving; two others died of typhus. Four girls had died at the school by 1831; and of fifteen who left in ill health between 1826 and 1831, eight died soon afterwards.

When the school moved in 1832 to new buildings at Casterton, about 3 miles away, it left behind its 'sad ricketty infancy' and provided an excellent education.

Fermi, Sarah, 'The Brontës at the Clergy Daughters' School: When Did They Leave?', *BST* (1996), 21. 6. 219–31.
——and Smith, Judith, 'The Real Miss Andrews: Teacher, Mother, Abolitionist', *BST* (2000), 25. 2. 136–46.

Cowper, William (1731–1800). All the Brontës knew Cowper's poems. Revd Patrick Brontë quoted from them, and Elizabeth Gaskell remarked how deeply they impressed Charlotte (Gaskell *Life*, 1. 154). In *Life* (3rd edn.) she added a comment by Mary Taylor: 'Cowper's poem, "The Castaway," was known to them all, and they all at times appreciated or almost appropriated it. Charlotte told me once that Branwell had done so.' In *Jane Eyre* St John Rivers prays that in going to seek Mr Rochester Jane 'may not indeed become a castaway' (ch. 35), doomed to the eternal damnation Calvinists threatened and Cowper feared. Jane's persistence in seeking Rochester rejects Calvinistic dogma, and affirms redemptive power. In *Shirley* Caroline recites the whole poem, 'realizing' Cowper's anguish vividly, but hoping that he is 'safe and calm in heaven now' (ch. 12). Anne Brontë, too, traced the language of her 'inmost heart in every line' of Cowper's poems: her hard-won faith in universal salvation coexisted with an empathic awareness of the terrors of the soul fearing damnation (see 'TO COWPER'; 'SELF-COMMUNION'; 'CONFIDENCE'). In *Tenant* Lowborough's conviction that he is 'not a cast-away' is a tragic irony; for Arabella loves him for his money, not himself. 'The Castaway' was a posthumous publication, and though it was adumbrated in some of Cowper's letters to Newton describing his 'gloomy chamber' of despair, it was unlike much of Cowper's work. *The Task* (1783) is often relaxed and amiable, and poems such as 'John Gilpin' show his lively sense of humour; but Charlotte, like Anne, had been more impressed by his sombre aspects: her reference to the 'stricken deer' in *Shirley* (ch. 14) is from Cowper's *The Task* (3. 108–11) and in chapter 24 she uses the phrase 'strong to strew the sea with wrecks' from Cowper's grim, intense poem, 'The Negro's Complaint'.

Crack(e)y. See DE CRACK, MON[SIEUR] EDOUARD.

Craik, Dinah Mulock. See SEQUELS AND 'INCREMENTAL LITERATURE'.

Crashey (Crashie), Captain Butter, one of the *Twelves in the *Glass Town and Angrian saga. Captain of the *Invincible* which brought the founders of Glass Town to Africa, he is 140 years old and becomes the venerable patriarch of Glass Town, revered for his wisdom and semi-divine powers, like his brother the magician *Manfred. He lives in the *Tower of All Nations, where he arbitrates from a golden throne, dispensing peace when necessary.

Crimean War (1853–6). Tsar Nicholas I of Russia, seeking to extend his empire in south-east Europe, claimed to protect Orthodox Christians in the Turkish dominions, and in July 1853 occupied Wallachia and Moldavia. After Turkey declared war on 4 October, Russia sank a Turkish fleet at Sinope. Revd Patrick Brontë's and Charlotte's sympathies were 'all with Justice and Europe against Tyranny and Russia' (Wise & Symington, 4. 109). Since Britain distrusted Russia's potential threat to India, and France resented Orthodox privileges in the Palestinian Holy Places, they sent a combined fleet into the Black Sea on 3 January 1854 and declared war on Russia on 28 March. In September they landed troops in the Crimea, where they besieged Sevastopol. After the Battle of Balaclava on 25 October, in which the Light Brigade rode to its death, Russians gained command of the road to the British base, but were repulsed on 5 November 1854 after the desperate Battle of Inkerman. During the Crimean winter conditions were terrible: food and clothing were scanty, transport animals perished, and camp hospitals lacked basic equipment. The troops suffered cholera, scurvy, dysentery, and fever: 420 out of every 1,000 men died in Scutari hospital before Florence Nightingale began her reforms. Dispatches in *The Times* bringing news of these conditions led to the foundation of a National Patriotic Fund. Bradford citizens raised £3,000 at the end of October. Mr Brontë, using Charlotte and Revd A. B. Nicholls as his amanuenses, convened a meeting 'in the Haworth National School on Saturday' 16 December to consider 'raising a General Subscription in aid of the Patriotic Fund' (MSS Woodhouse Grove School near Leeds and West Yorkshire Archive Service Bradford). Charlotte's youthful patriotism had given way to a belief, as she wrote to Margaret Wooler on 6 December 1854, that war was 'one of the greatest curses that can fall upon mankind. I trust it may not last long . . . no glory . . . can compensate for the sufferings which must be endured' (Wise & Symington, 4. 164). The war ended with the Treaty of Paris in March 1856.

Crimsworth, Edward, tyrannical mill owner and elder brother of William *Crimsworth in *The Professor*, one of a series of such characters deriving from stories in the *Glass Town and Angrian saga. Antagonistic pairs of brothers, most of them named Edward and William, recur in Charlotte's writings from the 1830s until their final manifestation as Edward and *Willie Ellin in three fragments written in 1853. The wealthy Edward Crimsworth has a mill and warehouse in *X——, and a grand mansion, *Crimsworth Hall, outside the town. His ruthless mastery of a vicious horse is an Angrian motif. Powerfully built, light-complexioned, handsome, but with cold, avaricious eyes, he is alert and abrupt, speaking in a guttural northern accent, but treating his wife with 'playful contention'. He grudgingly employs his brother William at a shabby wage to deal with foreign correspondence, under threat of instant dismissal for any faults. But neither his blasphemous sarcasms nor his cold neglect enable him to penetrate William's reserve and self-control. His malignity exacerbated by William's southern accent, education, impeccable morals, and punctual industry, he treats him like a dog or a slave. Provoked by Hunsden Yorke *Hunsden's public attack on him as a family despot, Edward threatens William with a heavy gig-whip; William defies him, breaks the whip, and threatens to charge him with assault. In sullen amazement, Edward dismisses him. Later, in Brussels, William learns that Edward's business had failed, and his ill-treated wife had left him but returned after he compounded with his creditors at tenpence in the pound. He was flourishing again, though he had sold Crimsworth Hall. Finally this somewhat crudely sketched Angrian villain is brought up to date, some ten years later, when William hears that he is, appropriately enough, making a fortune through dubious *railway speculations.

Crimsworth, William, protagonist of *The Professor* and successor of a number of younger brothers in the juvenilia, such as William *Percy and William *Ashworth. Charlotte was determined that her hero should work his way through life like a real living man, and that he should not marry a beautiful, rich, or high-ranking lady. So the orphaned Crimsworth rejects aristocratic patronage, and becomes clerk to his manufacturer brother, Edward *Crimsworth. William endures his slavery until Edward, angered by Hunsden Yorke *Hunsden's exposure of his tyranny, threatens William with a gig-whip for his alleged tale-bearing. William breaks the whip, declares he is leaving a prison, and, feeling light and liberated, quits the mill for ever. On Hunsden's advice he travels to Belgium, where Hunsden's recommendation to a Mr Brown helps him to secure a teaching post at M. François *Pelet's school. At first appalled by his blundering pupils, he masters them by demonstrating his own superiority, adapting lessons to their dull capacity, and despotically quelling insubordination. William is less shrewd in his approach to the devious Mlle Zoraïde *Reuter, for he temporarily succumbs to the illusion that she is charming and lovable; but, once disillusioned, he treats both her and her silly or sullen pupils with cold indifference. Like Lucy *Snowe, he tries to master feeling by reason. But he recognizes that Mlle Reuter's assistant teacher, Frances *Henri, who becomes his pupil, is his ideal. An exacting master because he wishes to challenge Frances's withdrawn personality, recognizes her ability, and realizes that his formality sets her at ease, he becomes (though he does not tell her so) her willing slave. Their eventual marriage is one of great happiness; yet he is ultimately the master, for he insists, despite Frances's reluctance, that their son should go to Eton. William embodies many of Charlotte's own characteristics: her strong passions, her love of freedom and independence, her integrity, her disconcerting reserve in uncongenial company—'looking frigidly shy at the commencement of a party; confusingly vigilant about the middle and insultingly weary towards the end' (ch. 22). William's curious, wary, love-hate relationship with Hunsden, epitomized in their boyish tussle in chapter 24, is probably a hangover from the mutual fascination and antagonism of the two brothers, Charles and Arthur Augustus Wellesley (Duke of *Zamorna), in the

*Glass Town and Angrian saga. Psychologically interesting but not fully integrated with William's other qualities, it is one consequence of the novel's piecemeal construction.

Crimsworth Hall in *The Professor.* Edward *Crimsworth's large house and grounds lie amid fields and woods 4 miles from *X——. A portrait of the Crimsworths' gentle, sensitive mother hangs in the oak-panelled dining room, and a long room is used for a grand birthday party. Edward sells the hall during his temporary bankruptcy.

critical reception to 1860. *See page 134*

criticism 1860–1940. *See page 142*

criticism from 1940. *See page 147*

Crosby, Dr John (1797–1859, MRCS 1818), medical practitioner in Great Ouseburn, Yorks., where memorials describe him as esteemed, urbane, skilled, and sympathetic to the poor. As the physician to the *Robinson family of Thorp Green, he was presumably au fait with events there. He kept in touch with the dismissed Branwell Brontë, who alleged that Crosby reported Mrs Lydia *Robinson's 'inextinguishable love' for him. This and similar messages may be fabrications; but it is perhaps credible that a Robinson trustee ordered Crosby to return, unopened, a letter from Branwell to Lydia. Branwell also claimed to have received money through Crosby's hands.

Cross of Rivaulx, a pretty lodge on the edge of *Hawkscliffe estate in Angria, where Mina *Laury stays and where Louisa *Vernon is kept prisoner for a time, in the *Glass Town and Angrian saga. It is named after an old obelisk with a crucifix sculpted in its side that lies nearby, halfway between the city of Angria and the foot of the Sydenham Hills. Rievaulx is the name of an abbey and village in north Yorkshire, but the scene of the lodge and obelisk was inspired by an engraving copied by Charlotte Brontë on 23 June 1836 (Alexander & Sellars, p. 244).

Alexander *EW*, pp. 234–5.

Crystal Palace, Hyde Park, London, site of the *Great Exhibition (1851). From July 1849 Prince Albert, Sir Henry Cole, and others actively promoted an international industrial exhibition. Royal commissioners, appointed in July 1850, eventually accepted Joseph Paxton's design, based on his innovative iron and glass Lily House at Chatsworth. The prefabricated building rose swiftly, and after its grand opening by Queen Victoria on 1 May 1851 was visited by six million people before its closure on 15 October. Charlotte Brontë, who visited it five times, regarded it as a

(*cont. on page 141*)

ALTHOUGH all four Brontës had published work prior to 1847, *Jane Eyre* was the first of their writings to receive significant critical attention. The sisters' book of *Poems* 1846 had received mildly approving comment from the few critics who had read it, and it is worth noting that most of these reviews singled out Emily's verse as superior to that of Charlotte and Anne. But the book had sold no more than two copies by 1847, so their poems can hardly be said to have been 'received' by contemporary critics. *Jane Eyre*, on the other hand, was an immediate success when it was published in October 1847, and the sensation caused by 'Currer Bell' only intensified when 'Ellis and Acton Bell' (see PSEUDONYMS USED BY THE BRONTËS) released their own novels less than two months later. The publication of Anne's second novel, *The Tenant of Wildfell Hall*, the following summer fuelled the fire of controversy over the Bells' writing and further piqued public curiosity about the authors' identities. By the time *Shirley* was released late in 1849, Charlotte's true identity and the sad story of her siblings' deaths were starting to be publicly known. With the publication of her *'Biographical Notice' and preface to the 1850 edition of *Wuthering Heights* and *Agnes Grey*, early critical response to the Brontës moved into a second phase, one largely characterized by an attitude of admiration and pity for this remarkable trio of women writers. The publication of *Villette* in 1853 for the most part reinforced that attitude, as did the flurry of respectful obituary pieces that followed Charlotte's death in 1855. These publications, along with Elizabeth *Gaskell's enormously influential *Life*, in 1857, are the milestones which mark the history of the critical reception of the Brontës' work from 1846 to 1860.

Before 1850, reviews of Charlotte's, Emily's, and Anne's novels tended to confuse and conflate the identities of the three authors, sometimes asserting that Currer, Ellis, and Acton Bell were one person. Certainly the Brontës' silence about their actual identities allowed for such confusion, which Anne's publisher, T. C. *Newby, exploited when he advertised *The Tenant of Wildfell Hall* as a new work by Currer Bell. But reviewers were also inclined to think of the Bells as a single writer because the features which made their works similar to each other were the same ones that set them apart, in the critics' opinions, from the run of ordinary novels. The qualities in the Brontës' writings that were most often discussed by reviewers were 'originality', 'vigour', and 'coarseness', the last a broad term that meant something slightly different for each reviewer. There was also considerable debate over two issues in particular: first, whether the novels were 'true', or credible, as their supporters claimed, or wildly improbable as their detractors insisted; and second, whether the Bells were moral writers or the reverse.

Many early reviews of *Jane Eyre* observed that it was 'different' from conventional novels and praised it for being 'new', 'fresh', and 'original'. They also acknowledged the powerful and distinctive voice of the author, who wrote with uncommon 'vigour' and 'boldness', offering the reading public a narrative full of 'refreshing unconventionalities'. But it was these very qualities, in combination with the novel's supposed coarseness, which made *Jane Eyre* objectionable to some of the early critics, particularly those who thought that Currer Bell might be a woman. For some, *Jane Eyre*'s coarseness lay in its indecorous presentation of romantic and sexual content.

The unidentified reviewer for the *Spectator* (6 Nov. 1847), for example, not only thought it unlikely that a man like Edward *Rochester would confess the history of his intimate relationships to a young governess in his employ; the critic also felt positively offended by the 'low tone' of such improbable conduct (McNees, 3. 4). While British reviewers tended to criticize such passages as 'vulgar' and 'improper', their American counterparts were inclined to see them as assaults on the virtue of susceptible young readers. In this view, *Jane Eyre* contained morally unacceptable 'ribaldry' and 'blasphemy', the latter an allusion to the frank—or 'coarse'—manner in which Charlotte deals with religion in her novel.

But for every critic who took offence at what was considered the novel's immorality or indecorousness, and for every reviewer who objected that the story was not credible, there were just as many who thought that *Jane Eyre* was both moral and 'true'. *Era*'s anonymous reviewer, for example, declared that 'there is nothing but nature and truth about' the novel, which presents a moral 'victory of mind over matter. . . reason over feeling' (Allott, pp. 78–9). One explanation for these divergent opinions, of course, lies in the differing political, religious, and class allegiances of the various periodicals which printed reviews of *Jane Eyre*. As a staunchly middle-class journal, the *Spectator* could not approve any of the Brontës' unorthodox novels except for the last, *Villette*, which is notable for its sombre if ambivalent acceptance of suffering and silence. The *Examiner*, a politically radical review, on the other hand, typically ran favourable assessments of the Brontës' novels because it approved of the bold individualism and contempt for mere propriety they expressed. 'High Church' periodicals, such as the *Christian Remembrancer*, condemned the Brontës for the same reasons that the *Examiner* praised them.

Almost all reviewers agreed on the literary merit of *Jane Eyre*, however. Critics were struck by the compelling particularity that made Charlotte's writing so absorbing. One review noted that the author 'fixes you at the commencement, and there is no flagging on his part—no getting away on your's—till the end' (Allott, p. 79). William Makepeace *Thackeray complained to W. S. *Williams, who had sent him a copy, that '*Jane Eyre* . . . interested me so much that I have lost (or won if you like) a whole day in reading it at the busiest period' when he should have been working on his own novel, *Vanity Fair* (Allott, p. 70). An anonymous reviewer for **Fraser's Magazine* recalled a similar experience: 'We took up *Jane Eyre* one winter's evening, somewhat piqued at the extravagant commendations we had heard, and sternly resolved to be as critical as Croker. But as we read on we forgot both commendations and criticism, identified ourselves with Jane in all her troubles, and finally married Mr. Rochester about four in the morning' (Allott, p. 152).

In one of the best early reviews of *Jane Eyre*, George Henry *Lewes discusses this quality of Charlotte's writing with perceptiveness and clarity. Like other reviewers, Lewes praised the novel's unusual capacity for holding the reader's attention and attributed its success in this regard to its strong evocation of 'reality': 'The story . . . fastens itself upon your attention, and will not leave you. The book is closed, the enchantment continues. . . . your interest does not cease . . . Reality—deep, significant reality—is the great characteristic of the book' (Allott, p. 84). Quoting a passage from the first chapter, Lewes rhetorically asks, 'Is not that vivid, real, picturesque?' and then explains how Charlotte's powerful 'faculty for objective representation' is the same faculty that allows her to represent inner experience in such a compelling manner. He identifies a feature that many critics have thought distinctive of all the Brontë novels when he says that Charlotte has 'the power . . . of connecting external appearances with internal effects—of representing the psychological interpretation of material phenomena' (Allott, p. 86). The 'reality' which is evoked in their novels is, according to Lewes, felt by the reader to be both objective and subjective, material and psychological; hence it is unusually comprehensive and compelling—one might say more 'true' than the verisimilitude of most novels.

The problem with this remarkable faculty of description for some early reviewers, however, was that the Bells applied it to what was often considered objectionable material: to characters that were indiscreet, uncouth, and immoral; to places that were outlandish or improbable; and to action that was unrefined or indecent. Readers who found such 'coarseness' distasteful or alien resented being compelled by the power of the author's writing to feel the vivid reality of what they could not condone or wish to believe. If the pen that compelled such a response was in a woman's hand, the author was especially vulnerable to charges of effrontery and coarseness. Inferring from details in *Jane Eyre* that Currer Bell was a woman, the *Christian Remembrancer* (Apr. 1848) asserted that 'a book more unfeminine . . . would be hard to find in the annals of female authorship'. The anonymous reviewer objected to 'the authoress' whose novel made use of slang, quoted scripture for the sake of humour, depicted passionate love scenes, and provided trenchant analysis of 'the worst parts of human nature'— features of the novel that 'commend our admiration, but are almost startling in one of the softer sex'. Such 'masculine hardness, coarseness, and freedom of expression' (Allott, p. 89) from a woman writer was seen as a form of sedition: 'Every page [of *Jane Eyre*]', the reviewer complained, 'burns with moral Jacobinism' (Allott, p. 90).

An anonymous review, written by Elizabeth *Rigby, in the *Quarterly Review* (Dec. 1848), raised similar objections but expressed them in an exceptionally offensive tone of class arrogance. Conceding that *Jane Eyre* 'is a very remarkable book' by which 'it is impossible not to be spellbound', Rigby also declared that it was 'pre-eminently an anti-Christian composition' with 'a decidedly vulgar-minded woman' as its heroine. To Rigby, the romantic individualism of Charlotte's novel was both blasphemous and seditious:

There is throughout [the novel] . . . a proud and perpetual assertion of the rights of man, for which we find no authority either in God's word or in God's providence—there is that pervading tone of ungodly discontent which is at once the most prominent and the most subtle evil which . . . civilized society . . . has at the present day to contend with. We do not hesitate to say that the tone of the mind and thought which has overthrown authority and violated every code human and divine abroad, and fostered Chartism and rebellion at home, is the same which has also written *Jane Eyre*. (Allott, pp. 109–10)

Rigby also declared that, if one accepted the unlikely proposition that *Jane Eyre* was written by a woman, then the author must be 'one who has . . . long forfeited the society of her own sex' (Allott, p. 111), a comment that especially wounded and angered Charlotte.

In the meantime, *Wuthering Heights* had been both praised and criticized for many of the same features that drew critical attention to *Jane Eyre*. Emily's novel was described as 'powerful' and 'original' and praised for its 'vigour', 'genuineness', and ability to hold the reader's interest. It repelled some critics by its coarseness and

bemused many by its 'strangeness'. The brutality of the characters, their violent behaviour and crude language; the atmosphere of gloom that pervades the entire first
half of the novel; the wildness of its setting; and, most of all, the story's moral
ambiguity—all these disturbing features were seen as more prominent in this novel
than in those written by Charlotte and Anne. Some reviewers claimed to be unconcerned about the potential of *Wuthering Heights* to corrupt its readers because the
novel was simply too chaotic and strange to engage readers' attention in the way *Jane
Eyre* did. The novel's oddly objective juxtaposition of violence with love, beauty with
horror, and the narrative's refusal to authorize a conventional response to those
opposing forces, often left critics confused and suspicious of writing they were nevertheless forced to admire.

Anne's first novel received little attention compared to that given *Jane Eyre* and
Wuthering Heights. Critics were quick to find a family likeness between *Agnes Grey*
and the other stories by the Bells, so it received some criticism for being 'unpleasant',
'improbable', and 'peculiar'. But most reviewers found it more 'acceptable', more
'agreeable', more 'measured' and 'sunnier' than *Wuthering Heights*, to which it was
usually compared. On the other hand, it was also considered less powerful and less
interesting. One critic remarked that though 'it leaves no painful impression on the
mind—some may think it leaves no impression at all' (Allott, p. 233). Such was not the
case with Anne's next novel, *The Tenant of Wildfell Hall*. While noting that Acton
Bell's second work was more 'powerful and interesting' than her first, the critics
condemned its subject matter as 'disgusting' and accused the author of having 'a
morbid love for the coarse' (Allott, p. 250). Her characters were thought 'disagreeable'
and their actions either improbable or overdrawn. A reader for *Sharpe's London
Magazine* reported that the book was 'so revolting' that it ought not be reviewed,
a recommendation that was ignored for fear that 'the powerful interest of the story
[and] the talent with which it is written' would attract readers to a 'work unfit for
perusal' (Allott, p. 263). As this quotation suggests, the literary skill shown in *Tenant*
was almost universally admitted in spite of the critics' distaste for Anne's subject. Like
Jane Eyre and *Wuthering Heights*, *Tenant* was said to demonstrate 'considerable abilities ill applied' (Allott, p. 250). The American journal *Literary World* thought the
mind of the author 'coarse almost to brutality' and noted that such coarseness was not
at all 'natural': 'it is the writer's genius which makes [the novel's] incongruities appear
natural. . . . No matter how untrue to life her scene or character may be, the vividness
and fervor of her imagination is such that she instantly *realizes* it' (Allott, pp. 258–9).
One of the great virtues of Anne's novel, then, was the remarkable reality of description that characterized her sisters' writing as well. Like *Wuthering Heights*, which is
also double-plotted and features two sets of characters, *Tenant* was said to be poorly
constructed, a judgement that recent criticism has sought to overturn (see CRITICISM
FROM 1940).

When *Shirley* appeared in October 1849, it received considerable attention, most
of it polite if not enthusiastic. Some reviewers approvingly noted that it was less
sensational than its predecessor, but many also recognized that what was gained
through restraint did not make up for a loss of interest and power. *Shirley* was
criticized, usually mildly, for some improbabilities and for its awkward construction,
but praised for its faithful presentation of *Yorkshire scenes and characters. Charlotte
was especially pleased by an intelligent critique by Eugène Forçade in the *Revue*

des deux mondes (Allott, pp. 142–6) and must have been gratified by a largely favourable review in *Fraser's Magazine* (Allott, pp. 152–5), to which the Brontës had subscribed. She was shocked and angered, however, by an attack from another quarter where she had not expected to find an antagonist. In an article for the *Edinburgh Review*, Lewes—who had written so positively about *Jane Eyre* and with whom Charlotte had been corresponding—pronounced that '*Shirley* cannot be received as a work of art.' He complained that it was uninteresting, coarse, inartistic, and saturated with 'such vulgarities as would be inexcusable—even in a man' (Allott, p. 165). Lewes had recently discovered Charlotte's true identity, and his review alludes repeatedly to Currer Bell's gender—in spite of the fact that Charlotte had specifically asked him to 'not think of Currer Bell as a woman' (Smith *Letters*, 2. 330). Ignoring her request, Lewes identified the author of *Shirley* as an unmarried daughter of a clergyman from Yorkshire and made a point of chastising her for provincial coarseness.

No longer able to maintain her anonymity, Charlotte prepared a biographical memoir of her sisters, including commentary on their writing, for the 1850 edition of *Wuthering Heights* and *Agnes Grey*. There she set out distinctions between the works of Emily and Anne that have influenced critical response to their novels ever since. Emily is described as an unconscious genius who wrote from inspiration, capturing the reality of her rustic environment without being tainted by its coarseness. As 'a nursling of the moors' (Smith *Letters*, 2. 748), Emily remained, like the moors themselves, unviolated by the dark forces that played over her work. Anne, on the other hand, is described as 'blameless', morbid, pure, and well-intentioned but incapable of the heroic genius that Emily brought to bear on similarly dark subject matter (Smith *Letters*, 2. 745). *Tenant*, in Charlotte's view, was 'an entire mistake', and the negative reviews it received fully justified (as in her commentary on *Wuthering Heights*, she says nothing about the favourable judgements that critics had made about Anne's novel) (see 'BIOGRAPHICAL NOTICE').

Charlotte's rating of her sisters' respective merits in the 'Biographical Notice' helps to account for the diminishing interest in Anne's writing in the 1850s and beyond. Emily, on the other hand, found at least two favourable critics in the decade following her death: Sydney *Dobell, writing for the *Palladium* in 1850, even before Charlotte's 'Biographical Notice' had appeared, praised Emily's 'instinctive art' and pointed out the 'unconscious felicities' and 'native power' of *Wuthering Heights* (Allott, pp. 279–80). (He also thought that Ellis and Currer Bell were one and the same person.) Seven years later, Peter Bayne compared Emily to 'a Titan host' overthrowing the canons of literary decorum to produce a work that is 'monstrous' but true in the way that dreams are true (Allott, pp. 322–3), though he also lamented the brutalizing effect the novel had on the reader. The responses of both critics accord with Charlotte's view of her sister as an unconscious genius and anticipate the many Freudian and psycho-social readings of *Wuthering Heights* that appeared in the following century (see PSYCHOANALYTIC APPROACHES). Other critics were not as taken with Emily's work as Dobell and Bayne, however; as Nicola Diane Thompson has shown, most reviews of *Wuthering Heights* written in 1850 were both less severe and more condescending than those published before Emily's identity—and gender—were known (*Reviewing Sex: Gender and the Reception of Victorian Novels*, 1996).

Villette, the last of Charlotte's novels to be published in her lifetime, received generally favourable reviews when it appeared in 1853. Charlotte's identity and tragic losses were now widely known, and such knowledge often influenced critical remark on her book. Many thought the book excessively morbid but would only 'touch upon' this flaw 'with respect, because [they found] it difficult to disconnect from it a feeling of the bitterness of experience actually undergone' by the author (Allott, p. 175). Always a perceptive critic of Charlotte's work (though capable of great insensitivity to her feelings), Lewes noted that 'as a novel, in the ordinary sense of the word, *Villette* has few claims'; but, he continued, as 'the utterance of an original mind' with extraordinary 'capacity for all passionate emotions', it is 'a work of astonishing power' (Allott, pp. 210–11). The novel was faulted for its bigoted attitude toward Roman *Catholicism by two reviewers, Anne Mozley of the *Christian Remembrancer* and Harriet *Martineau of the *Daily News*. Martineau and Mozley also criticized *Villette* for its treatment of the theme of romantic desire, though from opposite perspectives. In Mozley's mind, both the author and her heroine were deemed 'unfit' for the love and domestic happiness they seemingly desired because they were repellently 'self-reliant' and too 'contemptuous of prescriptive decorum . . . [to] inspire . . . man's true love' (Allott, p. 207). Martineau, as a feminist, complained on the other hand that 'in real life' few women are as preoccupied with 'the need of being loved' as Charlotte imagined. Martineau's review begins and ends with abundant praise for *Villette*, but she found the book 'almost intolerably painful' in its sustained expression of 'subjective misery' (Allott, pp. 172–3)—a reaction diametrically opposed to Lewes's passionate response to the 'strong, struggling soul' whose 'cry of pain' both critics heard (Allott, p. 211).

When *The Professor* was published posthumously in 1857, it was respectfully noticed but given little serious critical attention. It was seen as an inferior version of *Villette* and in its general tenor a mere draft of all Charlotte's later work. Its opening was pronounced 'clumsy', its characters uninteresting, and its overall structure ill-designed. But, since it was considered an apprentice piece which had not been published during the author's lifetime, most critics felt 'disposed rather to err on the side of gentleness than rigour' in assessing the early effort of an admired, and tragically deceased, author (Allott, p. 344). As Catherine Malone has pointed out, the release of *The Professor* immediately after the publication of Gaskell's popular biography ensured that the novel would attract interest and helps to account for the largely sympathetic response from reviewers, who spent less time criticizing the weaknesses they recognized and more time relating the story to Charlotte's life and other works (' "We have All Learned to Love Her More Than Her Books": The Critical Reception of Brontë's *The Professor*,' *Review of English Studies*, NS 47 (1996), 175–87).

Throughout the 1850s, the Brontës remained a topic of critical interest, one that elicited sympathizing wonder at the authors' tragic experiences and remarkable achievements. Charlotte's death in 1855 added to this interest, and the appearance of Gaskell's *Life* in 1857 was greeted with an overwhelming response from readers and critics alike. Commentary on the Brontës that appeared after the *Life*, emphasized the influence of their 'wild' and rustic environment, which Gaskell had described in evocative detail, and further developed the idea that their 'genius' was distinctive and innate.

Branwell's work received no notice in the press until Gaskell briefly discussed his poetry in her biography of Charlotte. Her assessment of his literary ability was favourable, but the role he played in her account of his sister's life precluded much interest in his work at that time. During his lifetime, Branwell had received private review of his work, some of it favourable, from correspondents including Hartley *Coleridge, Joseph Bentley *Leyland, and, possibly, James and Harriet Martineau, and the poet James Montgomery.

Important reviews, 1846–60

Poems 1846

Anon., *Critic* (4 July 1846).

[Sydney Dobell], *Athenaeum* (4 July 1846).

[William Archer Butler], *Dublin University Magazine* (Oct. 1846).

Anon., *Spectator* (11 Nov. 1848).

Jane Eyre (1847)

[A. W. Fonblanque], *Examiner* (27 Nov. 1847).

Anon., *Era* (14 Nov. 1847).

[G. H. Lewes], *Fraser's Magazine* (Dec. 1847).

Anon., *Christian Remembrancer* (Apr. 1848).

Eugène Forçade, *Revue des deux mondes* (31 Oct. 1848).

E. P. Whipple, *North American Review* (Oct. 1848) (also reviews *Wuthering Heights* and *Agnes Grey*).

[Elizabeth Rigby], *Quarterly Review* (Dec. 1848).

Shirley (1849)

[A. W. Fonblanque], *Examiner* (3 Nov. 1849).

Anon., *Britannia* (10 Nov. 1849).

Anon., *Spectator* (3 Nov. 1849).

Eugène Forçade, *Revue des deux mondes* (15 Nov. 1849).

Anon., *Fraser's Magazine* (Dec. 1849).

G. H. Lewes, *Edinburgh Review* (Jan. 1850).

Villette (1853)

[Harriet Martineau], *Daily News* (3 Feb. 1853).

Eugène Forçade, *Revue des deux mondes* (15 Mar. 1853).

G. H. Lewes, *Westminster Review* (Apr. 1853).

[Anne Mozley], *Christian Remembrancer* (Apr. 1853).

The Professor (1857)

Anon., *Examiner* (20 June 1857).

Anon., *Athenaeum* (13 June 1857).

Wuthering Heights (1847)

Anon., *Examiner* (8 Jan. 1848).

Anon., *Atlas*, 22 Jan. 1848 (also reviews *Agnes Grey*).

[G. W. Peck], *American Review* (June 1848).

Sydney Dobell, *Palladium* (Sept. 1850).

Charlotte Brontë, 'Editor's Preface to the New Edition of *Wuthering Heights* and *Agnes Grey*' (1850) (also discusses *Agnes Grey* and *The Tenant of Wildfell Hall*).

Peter Bayne, *Essays in Biography and Criticism* (1857).

Agnes Grey (1847)

H. F. Chorley, *Athenaeum* (25 Dec. 1847) (also reviews *Wuthering Heights*).

The Tenant of Wildfell Hall (1848)
  [H. F. Chorley], *Athenaeum* (8 July 1848).
  Anon., *Literary World* (12 Aug. 1848).
  Anon., *Sharpe's London Magazine* (Aug. 1848).
  [Charles Kingsley], *Fraser's Magazine* (Apr. 1849).   CB

Alexander, Christine, and Rosengarten, Herbert, 'The Brontës', in Joanne Shattock (ed.), *The Cambridge Bibliography of English Literature*, vol. 4 (3rd edn., 1999).
Allott.
McNees.

great Vanity Fair such as 'eastern Genii might have created' (Smith *Letters*, 2. 631).

cultural criticism. In literary studies, the term cultural criticism is sometimes used very broadly to refer to any consideration of literature in relation to the culture within which it was produced and/or received. In this broad sense, it has greatly enhanced studies of the Brontës' novels. In a more restricted sense, it denotes a large body of fairly recent criticism that draws on a number of overlapping fields: Marxism; discourse theory; new historicism, especially the writings of Michel Foucault (1929–84); and psychoanalytic theories about the formation of identity, particularly as developed by Jacques Lacan (1901–81). Defined most narrowly, cultural criticism is a Marxist-oriented form of critical practice which emerged in the mid-sixties and which studies the relationship of literature to ideology. Noting that the categorical distinctions between 'high' and 'low' culture are themselves ideological constructs subject to critical investigation, cultural critics have challenged the privileging of 'high culture' and 'great books', over mass culture and 'popular' writing; they have insisted on the importance of analysing texts that previous critics had dismissed as 'sub-literary' (for instance, popular magazines and cartoons) and cultural formations that had been traditionally excluded from the purview of literary criticism (legal documents and medical treatises, for example). The value of understanding literary texts as part of larger fields of discourse has now generally been accepted within the discipline of literary studies, and critics today rarely feel compelled to defend their decision to write about non-canonical literature, non-literary texts, or non-verbal cultural artefacts.

Although cultural criticism has sometimes been defined in opposition to new historicism (because the latter is less politically orientated than the former), in practice it is often difficult to separate these two approaches. New historicists reject several of the premises upon which traditional historical studies have relied, and, in turning their attention to discourse, they transform the historical study of literature as well. Challenging the assumption that history is an objective, linear narrative of causally connected events, new historicists contend that history, like literature, is fundamentally interpretation rather than factual account; history is the representation of events that have been subjectively selected, ordered, interpreted, and even invented by particular historians situated within particular cultures in particular places and points in time—a 'situatedness' that influences the historical narratives they write. History, like all forms of discourse including literature, is simply one of the many ways in which culture represents itself to itself. The goal of new historical study, then, is to understand the various ways in which culture has represented itself to itself over time. Indebted to the work of Foucault, new historicists also conceive of power not in terms of class dominance and oppression (as classical Marxists do), but rather as a productive force that circulates through the exchange of material goods, people, and discourse within a particular society. Culture to the new historicist is this activity of exchange: an economy of power in which social formations (the mechanisms by which such exchanges occur, for example, the institutions of marriage, adoption, and slavery, or the systems of literary trade and patronage) and social subjects (people in their individual and group identities as participants within this economy) are mutually constituted. That is, individuals are constituted as social subjects by cultural influences and social formations which these social subjects help to produce. Discourse is a social language that develops out of, and simultaneously helps to create, culture; it is the means by which ideology is disseminated to, and transformed by, people through language. Because literature is only one of the means by which discourse circulates within culture, cultural critics necessarily study literary texts in their relation to other forms of discourse, including, for example, those produced in the fields of medicine, law, and sociology. In the study of the Brontës,

(*cont. on page 146*)

A FTER the flood of reviews that followed the publication of Elizabeth *Gaskell's *Life* and the posthumous release of *The Professor* in 1857, there was a period of about twenty years in which relatively few critical assessments of the Brontës' works were published. Two of the more interesting, both on *Villette*, address the important question of authorial subjectivity. In an 1866 article for *Harper's Monthly Magazine*, Susan M. Waring praised *Villette* as Charlotte's finest work because, of all of her protagonists, Lucy *Snowe is the 'most minutely informed with [the author's] own experience' ('Charlotte Brontë's Lucy Snowe', in McNees, 3. 623). Waring rejects as naive the idea that Lucy and her creator are 'coincident' but asserts that Charlotte's heroine is a perfect 'medium for expressing her own experience and temperament' (McNees, 3. 631). In contrast, William Wirt Kingsley argued that Charlotte was not a subjective writer like Lord *Byron, as was often claimed, but attained the kind of imaginative objectivity seen in *Shakespeare's work; 'her imagination', he comments, 'got the better of her self-consciousness' and gave her the self-forgetfulness characteristic of great authors (McNees, 3. 617). The question of the Brontës' relationship to their narratives—is it one of instinctive and emotional self-expression, or one of controlled aesthetic detachment, or something different from either of these polar alternatives?—arises repeatedly in criticism of their work, so it is not surprising that it made itself felt even during a decade when relatively little attention was given to their writings. Its emergence as a controversial topic in the 1860s also points to a tension in Brontë criticism that developed out of the two main approaches taken to their work from about this time: biographical interpretation and varieties of textual study that can be loosely called formalist.

Fascination with the Brontës' lives and surroundings was so strong during this period that it often overshadowed interest in their works, a fact lamented in the mid-20th century by textual critics who eschewed the biographical approach to literary analysis (see CRITICISM FROM 1940). But identifying the 'real-life' sources of characters, settings, and plots in the novels has been a productive and enduring form of research in Brontë studies, one given considerable impetus in the 1890s by the founding of the *Haworth-based *Brontë Society. Works published between 1860 and 1940 that make use of this kind of criticism include A. M. F. *Robinson's 1883 biography of Emily, which compares passages from Branwell's letters with lines from *Wuthering Heights* to argue that Hindley *Earnshaw's drunken ravings were modelled on Branwell's behaviour during his decline; Robert Smith Keating's 1902 *Tatler* essay, which identifies Revd J. W. *Smith as the real-life counterpart of Revd Peter Augustus *Malone, a minor figure in *Shirley* ('A Well-known Character in Fiction', in McNees, 3. 479–82); E. A. *Chadwick's *In the Footsteps of the Brontës* (1914); and H. E. Wroot's *Sources of Charlotte Brontë's Novels: Persons and Places* (1935), an influential book that is still widely available today. With the rise of historically oriented *cultural criticism in the 1980s and 1990s, the potential usefulness of these exercises in sleuthing out sources is now more evident than it has sometimes been. For example, Wroot's 1906 essay 'The Politics of 1812' identified the *Leeds Mercury* as Charlotte's source of information about the *Luddite riots depicted in *Shirley* (McNees, 3. 483–7), thus laying the groundwork for later analyses of the process by which she appropriated actual history for use in fictional narrative. Such analyses include Herbert Rosengarten's 'Charlotte Brontë's *Shirley* and the *Leeds Mercury*' (*Studies in English Literature*, 16 (1976), 591–600) and Patrick Collier's 'The lawless by force . . . the peaceable by kindness': Strategies of Social Control in Charlotte Brontë's *Shirley* and the *Leeds Mercury*' (*Victorian Periodicals Review*, 32 (1999), 279–98). Mrs Humphry *Ward's recognition that 'the monstrous' in the Brontës' writing derived from the 'Germanism' of the 1830s and 1840s as it was presented through *Blackwood's Edinburgh Magazine* and *Fraser's Magazine* also paved the way for better understanding of their work within the context of early 19th-century discourse ('Introduction' to *Wuthering Heights*, in McNees, 2. 45). Other critics writing before 1940 who have tried to understand the Brontës' writings by studying their relationship to the history of literary forms such as the novel, the Gothic romance, and the contemporary periodical include George Saintsbury, who claimed in 1899 that Charlotte's novels mark 'the intersection of . . . the romance proper and the novel proper' ('The Position of the Brontës as Origins in the History of the English Novel', in McNees, 1. 287); Edith M. Fenton, who in 1920 identified *Wuthering Heights* as a 'subjective' romance qualitatively different from the 'superficial' Gothic mode from which it evolved ('The Spirit of Emily Brontë's *Wuthering Heights* as Distinguished from that of Gothic Romance', in McNees, 2. 57–70); Romer Wilson (*All Alone: The Life and Private History of Emily Jane Brontë*, 1928); and Leicester Bradner ('The Growth of *Wuthering Heights*', *PMLA* 48 (1933), 129–46), who each identified different sources for Emily's novels within issues of *Blackwood's* published in the 1840s. Contemporary critics analysing the Brontës' work from *post-colonial and cultural studies perspectives are indebted to these earlier critics for their research on the social and cultural contexts in which their books were produced and received, though it may also be necessary to consult more recent sources to verify facts.

Along with a continued interest in biographical background, a second trend in Brontë criticism between 1860 and 1940 was a decline of Charlotte's reputation and a concomitant rise in Emily's. This reversal was partly due to a loosening of moral codes that occurred near the end of the century: having been quite rigid in the late 1840s and 1850s when the Brontë novels were first released, such prescriptive codes of decorum gradually gave way to the more relaxed attitudes of the late Victorian era and then to the decidedly bohemian mores of the *fin de siècle*. What had struck early reviewers as especially 'coarse' and 'immoral' in *Wuthering Heights* no longer shocked critics in the 1890s. Charlotte's novels, on the other hand, began to look more and more staid as time went by. Additionally, as the aesthetic movement took hold in the 1880s, Emily's artistry gained increasing attention and respect. In the 20th century, recognition of the impressive formal properties of her writing secured her reputation as the pre-eminent literary artist in the Brontë family.

But before these developments could occur, the Brontës had to be recognized as enduring figures in the history of English literature, and there were many critics in the last third of the 19th century who did not expect that to happen. While interest in the Brontës' lives remained strong, it was not unusual for their works to be dismissed as *passé* after the 1860s. More than one critic observed that *Wuthering Heights* was 'practically unread' by the late 1870s, and even those who thought highly of the novels noted that they had fallen out of favour. In *Blackwood's* (June 1883), Margaret Oliphant claimed that *Jane Eyre* was no longer read; indeed, she scoffed, the book could hardly be found outside 'the old-fashioned circulating libraries' and was fit only for taking to the spa or seaside as a reminder of the past 'happy days of the Victorian era' (pp. 757–8). One astute critic pointed out, however, that the decline in the popularity of the Brontë novels was probably a necessary precursor to a development of serious critical interest in them, and, in fact, such interest did begin to develop slowly in the last twenty years of the 19th century.

In 1877, *Wuthering Heights* was still relatively neglected by the critics. Like their predecessors from the 1850s and 1860s, many late 19th-century readers remained perplexed by what Sir Thomas Wemyss *Reid called 'the weirdest story in the English language' (Reid, *Charlotte Brontë: A Monograph* (1877), p. 209). Reid is one of the many reviewers who were both repelled and awed by *Wuthering Heights*: 'repulsive and almost ghastly', it nevertheless displays 'vast . . . intellectual greatness' and skilled craftsmanship (pp. 202, 204). He noted that Emily was the best poet in the family, but reserved his highest praise for Charlotte, and particularly for *Villette*, which he considered a 'great masterpiece' that 'hold[s] its own among the ripest and finest fruits of English genius' (p. 128) and 'remains . . . without a rival in the school of English fiction to which it belongs' (p. 145). Reid's assessment of Emily's and Charlotte's respective merits was not universally accepted, however. In the same year Leslie Stephen, editor of the *Cornhill Magazine, published an influential essay that identified what he considered the serious limitations of Charlotte's work—'her view of life is [not] satisfactory or even intelligible' (*Hours in a Library*, no. 17. 'Charlotte Brontë', in McNees, 1. 242)—and it is interesting to note that, during the time in which the Brontës were becoming canonical literary figures, there was a lack of critical consensus about which of these two sisters truly deserved the honour. Anne was never seriously considered—except by George Moore, whose extravagant praise of *Agnes Grey* in *Conversations in Ebury Street* (1924) as 'the most perfect prose narrative in English literature' (McNees, 2. 4) must strike even Anne's most admiring fans as an eccentric literary judgement—and Branwell's work remained virtually unknown. But an increasing number of critics, including A. C. Swinburne ('Emily Brontë', *Miscellanies* (1886), 260–70) and Peter Bayne (*Two Great Englishwomen*, 1881) began to publish admiring appraisals of Emily's poetic genius—which they saw displayed in her fiction as well as in her verse—in the last 25 years of the 19th century. A. M. F. Robinson's 1883 biography enhanced Emily's reputation as the most mysterious and interesting member of the family, and Mrs Humphry Ward's introduction to the Haworth edition of *Wuthering Heights* (1900) confidently asserted that 'Emily's genius was . . . greater' than Charlotte's (McNees, 2. 42).

The decline of Charlotte's reputation and the rise of Emily's during this period was directly related to the gradual ascendancy of formalist literary methods, a trend that began with the aesthetic movement of the 1880s and culminated in the influential work of the Russian formalists and the American New Critics in the mid-20th century. Virginia Woolf's essay '*Jane Eyre* and *Wuthering Heights*', written in 1916, anticipates the claims of later critics in asserting that Charlotte's narratives lack the aesthetic control that makes Emily's novel superior. According to Woolf, both the Brontës (characteristically, only Charlotte and Emily are considered) are 'poetic': that is, their 'meaning [is] inseparable from [their] language, and [is] itself rather a mood than a particular observation' (McNees, 3. 71), a judgement that aligns the novels of both sisters with the formalist programme for celebrating the coincidence of form and content. But Woolf's essay also echoes Mrs Ward's 1900 remark that the only attraction of Charlotte's novels is the 'contact which they give us with her own . . . personality' when she calls Charlotte a 'self-centred and self-limited' author whose 'overpowering personality' leaves its impress on everything she writes; 'all her force', according to Woolf, 'goes into the assertion, "I love", "I hate", "I suffer"' (McNees, 3. 69). 'Emily was [not only] a greater poet than Charlotte', in Woolf's view; she was also a superior novelist because she was able to objectify her feelings in dialogue, action, and setting, so that readers reach 'summits of emotion not by rant or rhapsody' but through the power of dramatic presentation. 'There is no "I" in *Wuthering Heights*', Woolf notes, and in this respect she finds it a far better novel than *Jane Eyre* (McNees, 3. 71).

Woolf's argument regarding Emily's artistic control was immeasurably bolstered ten years later, when C. P Sanger published his now famous essay 'The Structure of *Wuthering Heights*'. Sanger definitively disproved the claims of 19th-century critics who insisted that the novel was poorly constructed and 'chaotic'. He shows that Emily was knowledgeable about contemporary laws of property ownership and inheritance and that she applied that knowledge accurately in working out the plot of her story; he presents a detailed chronology to demonstrate that the dating of events and identification of characters' ages are scrupulously correct; he illustrates the 'symmetry of the pedigree' of the two families in the novel; and he proves that this complex and emotionally tumultuous 'tale [is] kept together' by the author's extraordinarily skilful deployment of her materials (McNees, 2. 73).

In 1934, the gradual reversal of Charlotte and Emily's literary reputations was made complete by Lord David Cecil's *Early Victorian Novelists: Essays in Revaluation*, which dismisses Charlotte as a 'subjective novelist' who was 'hardly a craftsman at all'. According to Cecil, she wrote books that are 'badly constructed' and 'incoherent' because she used fiction as a mere 'vehicle for self-revelation'. 'Once fully launched on her surging flood of self-revelation, Charlotte Brontë is far above pausing to attend to so paltry a consideration as artistic unity' ('Charlotte Brontë', in McNees, 1. 393), Cecil acidly comments. With *The New Criticism* about to be published in 1941, no more damaging assessment could have been made. Cecil's essay on Emily, on the other hand, secured a place in the canon for *Wuthering Heights* and provided a reading of the book which has become a kind of orthodoxy in critical interpretation today (see STRUCTURALIST APPROACHES). Far from being incoherent, the 'general outline' of Emily's novel is, in Cecil's words, 'as logical as that of a fugue' ('Emily Brontë and *Wuthering Heights*', in McNees, 2. 113). He sees the story as structured by two 'principles', that of 'storm' and that of 'calm', by which the cosmos is ordered (in Emily's view) and along which all of the elements of her novel are aligned: the violent *Earnshaw family, the windswept moors, and *Wuthering Heights itself are expressions of the principle of storm, whereas the refined *Lintons and *Thrushcross Grange, which is partitioned off from the uncultivated moors, are associated with the principle of calm. Cecil repeatedly compares Emily to William Blake, arguing that, unlike other Victorian novelists, she was a mystic and metaphysician who evolved a perfect form for her writing from the power of her 'lonely genius', which owed nothing to the influence of past authors or contemporary literary conventions. Cecil's claim that Emily did not have 'ready-made [literary] conventions to help her' (McNees, 2. 125) cannot really be borne out, but his reading of *Wuthering Heights* as organized according to two opposing principles has achieved wide and probably permanent currency in Brontë criticism, which continues to refine and modify his reading of the novel to this day.

A smattering of critical pieces on the Brontë sisters' poems was published between 1860 and 1940; all agree that Emily was the best poet, and at least two attempt to study her *Gondal poems in order to show their relationship to 'The Growth of *Wuthering Heights*' (Leicester Bradner, *PMLA* 48 (1933), 129–46) and to the 'The Gondal Saga' itself (Helen Brown and Joan Mott, *BST* (1938), 9. 48. 155–72). The first efforts to analyse the juvenilia occurred during this time as well; most notable is Fannie Ratchford's 1931 article 'The Brontës' Web of Dreams', in the *Yale Review*, followed by her important book *The Brontës' Web of Childhood*, completed in 1940. Though there was some awareness that Branwell's poetry had not received the recognition it deserved, efforts to publish his poems during this period were not very successful. His work does receive some brief critical attention in the biographical studies (see BIOGRAPHIES TO 1940). Except for George Moore, whose comments on Anne are mentioned above, and a few rather dismissive passages in Brontë biographies, Anne's work was virtually neglected between 1860 and 1940. See also REPUTATION.   CB

Allott.
McNees.

this has meant a return to studying the historical and cultural contexts in which their works were written, but it has been a return with a difference.

In addition to essays on *Wuthering Heights* ('Emily Brontë in and out of her Time', *Genre*, 15 (1982), 243–64, and 'Imperialist Nostalgia and *Wuthering Heights*' in Linda H. Peterson (ed.), *Wuthering Heights* (1992), 428–49), cultural critic Nancy Armstrong has written substantially on the Brontës in her important book *Desire and Domestic Fiction: A Political History of the Novel* (1987), where she argues that *Jane Eyre* and *Wuthering Heights* are hegemonic rather than ideologically subversive texts. Armstrong contends that in creating the impression that social convention opposes individual desire (especially female desire), these popular books helped to obscure social oppression in the Victorian era by reconstructing it as sexual repression; *Jane Eyre* and *Wuthering Heights* helped to produce the modern female sexual subject and in the process contributed to the suppression of the female social self. In spite of the power of these novels to constitute the female subject within the parameters of sex, romance, and private life, however, the Brontë sisters themselves were professionally, if not socially, empowered by this form of subjective identification, according to Armstrong. Because they had from an early age 'prepared themselves to be novelists the way that other women supposedly prepare themselves to be wives and mothers', Charlotte and Emily did not experience writing as 'ontologically different and

ideologically opposed' to desire; rather, authorship was for them a means of producing (and continually re-producing) both self-identity and desire (p. 189). Sally Shuttleworth's *Charlotte Brontë and Victorian Psychology* (1996) contends that in the 19th century new notions of subjectivity emerged in conjunction with the consolidation of authority by medical science, thus paving the way for the development of modern psychoanalytic theory and the psychiatric profession. Shuttleworth studies Victorian psychological discourse in a variety of fields to show how writing in social theory, medicine, economics, and literature (especially the novel) made use of a 'shared vocabulary and metaphoric base' which helped to form the ideology of the modern psychological subject (p. 16): a construct in which interiority (later identified by Freud as the unconscious) is privileged as the site of the 'true self' whereas the 'surface' manifestations of behaviour and conscious thinking are seen as the distorted expressions of an inner truth that must be interpreted by psychological science. One of the most compelling aspects of Shuttleworth's book is her focus on texts to which the Brontës actually had access and by which their lives were certainly influenced; most notable, perhaps, is their father's heavily marked copy of Thomas John Graham's *Modern Domestic Medicine* (1826). Alan Bewell shares Shuttleworth's interest in medical discourse, and in 'Jane Eyre and Victorian Medical Geography' (*English Literary History* 63 (1996), 773–808) he shows that

(*cont. on page 151*)

T HE number of publications on the Brontës has doubled nearly every decade since 1940, the vast majority being interpretations of *Jane Eyre* and *Wuthering Heights*; *Villette* and *Shirley* have also received significant critical attention during this time. Under the influence of feminism, interest in Charlotte's novels rose dramatically in the 1960s, while Anne's work—especially *The Tenant of Wildfell Hall*—has attracted increasingly sophisticated and appreciative treatment since the early 1980s. Emily's reputation remains undiminished. That Branwell's writing has received relatively little attention is understandable: his work is qualitatively different from his sisters'; moreover, most of it was not published until the last decade of the 20th century.

Criticism on the Brontës since 1940 has, for the most part, followed trends in critical practice and literary theory as they have developed over the last 60 years. From the 1940s until about 1970, literary criticism was dominated by so-called intrinsic approaches such as American New Criticism, Russian formalism, and structuralism, all of which encouraged close analysis of the formal properties of literary texts and warned against the 'intentional fallacy' committed by biographical critics who supposedly assume that interpretation is merely a matter of figuring out what the author intended to say. In this critical climate, many academicians veered sharply away from biographical approaches to the Brontës' writing and devoted their energies to analysing the novels as self-contained works of art. Fascination with the Brontës' lives remained strong among non-professional readers at this time, however, and biographical interpretation regained currency in the 1970s as the women's movement gave rise to *feminist approaches to literary criticism. Such new 'women-centred' perspectives, in combination with the powerful tools of literary analysis provided by formalism, led in the early seventies to an extraordinary outpouring of criticism on works by Charlotte, Emily, and, to a lesser extent, Anne. Then, in response to de-velopments in post-structuralist theory, critics (including feminists) began to lose confidence in the practice of identifying the formal properties and 'deep structures' by which literary texts are organized and through which they convey supposedly deter-minate meaning. Such scepticism about the stability of texts produced, in the 1980s, a number of deconstructionist readings which stressed the indeterminacy of the Brontës' novels, *Wuthering Heights* and *Villette* in particular. As more and more critics began to agree that the internal structures of texts are actually inseparable from the external contexts in which such texts are written and read, less text-centred analyses of the Brontë novels became increasingly common. Over the last twenty years, criticism on the Brontës, like literary criticism in general, has been heavily informed by post-structuralist versions of older, so-called extrinsic approaches (Marxism in its more recent permutations as a variety of *cultural criticism, for example), and by new schools of criticism, such as new historicism and *post-colonial theory, that have developed since the early eighties.

In the 1940s and 1950s, many critics applied formalist and *structuralist approaches to the study of the Brontë novels, *Wuthering Heights* in particular. In 'Fiction and the Matrix of Analogy' (*Kenyon Review*, 11 (1949), 544–50), Mark Schorer shows how *Wuthering Heights* uses an intricate 'matrix' of natural and elemental images ('fire, wind, water') to express Catherine *Earnshaw's and *Heathcliff's powerful personalities (McNees, 2. 184), though he denies that Emily was in control of this remarkable deployment of metaphors. Without adopting Schorer's patronizing attitude, Dorothy Van Ghent ('The Window Figure and the Two Children Figure in *Wuthering Heights*', *Nineteenth-Century Fiction*, 7 (1952), 189–97) also emphasizes the coherence of *Wuthering Heights* by showing how the two plots are bound together by the unifying presence of Heathcliff, by the frame of Ellen *Dean's and *Lockwood's narratives, and by the pervasive 'two children figures'. Through these formal devices, Van Ghent argues, the 'passionate immoderacy' of the characters' actions is held within an aesthetic structure 'of intense compositional rigour' (McNees, 2. 204). Numerous similar readings of *Wuthering Heights* were published in the 1950s and 1960s, the most comprehensive being Elisabeth Van de Laar's analysis of the novel's 'inner structure' of related images and symbols (*The Inner Structure of 'Wuthering Heights*', 1969). The 1950s also produced many essays on the narrators of Emily's novel, a development that reflects a structuralist concern with narrative poetics and the New Criticism's interest in devices such as the 'unreliable' narrator.

Although Lord David Cecil had dismissed Charlotte as a mere 'subjective' writer in 1934, formalist readings of her work eventually returned her to critical favour by the 1960s, and she has shared this position with Emily ever since. An essay by Richard Chase ('The Brontës: A Centennial Observance', *Kenyon Review*, 9 (1947), 487–506) was one of the first to draw attention to the formal patterns in *Jane Eyre*, as well as in *Wuthering Heights*, and to argue that Charlotte and Emily transformed Victorian domestic plots and 'social customs . . . into the forms of mythical art' (McNees, 4. 74). Numerous articles on the structural and symbolic functions of image patterns in *Jane Eyre* subsequently appeared during the sixties, along with a handful of formalist analyses of *Shirley* and *Villette* and no fewer than three book-length studies of Charlotte's literary 'art': Robert Martin's *The Accents of Persuasion: Charlotte Brontë's Novels* (1966), Wendy Craik's *The Brontë Novels* (1968), and Earl A. Knies's *The Art of Charlotte Brontë* (1969). In addition, psychoanalytic readings of both Charlotte's and Emily's novels began to appear during the fifties and sixties. One of the more influential of these was Robert Heilman's 'Charlotte Brontë's "New" Gothic', which shows how Charlotte modified the conventions of the Gothic mode in *Villette* to create a new kind of novel that explores psychological 'depths and intensities' that had previously been beyond the purview of narrative fiction (McNees, 4. 160). The first Marxist readings of *Wuthering Heights* also appeared during this time, though it would be another twenty years before other Marxists turned their attention to the Brontës.

Many feminist studies of the Brontës were published in the 1960s, two of the most notable being Inga-Stina Ewbanks's *Their Proper Sphere: A Study of the Brontë Sisters as Early-Victorian Female Novelists* (1966) and Kate Millett's *Sexual Politics* (1969), which famously described *Villette* as 'one long meditation on a prison break' (p. 40). The milestones of feminist criticism in Brontë studies in the seventies are Adrienne Rich's article '*Jane Eyre*: The Temptations of a Motherless Woman', published in the popular magazine *Ms* (Oct. 1973), pp. 89–106; Elaine Showalter's discussion of Charlotte's novels in *A Literature of their Own* (1977); and, most famously, chapters on Emily's and Charlotte's writing in Sandra M. Gilbert and Susan Gubar's *The Madwoman in the Attic* (1979). The inclusion of *Jane Eyre* in Gilbert and Gubar's widely used *Norton Anthology of Literature by Women* (1985, 1996), which features interpretative commentary by the editors, further disseminated their particular take on what Gayatri Spivak later called this 'cult text of feminism' ('Three Women's Texts and a Critique of Imperialism', *Critical Inquiry*, 12 (1985), 243). Belonging to a phase of feminism which has since come under scrutiny by more recent critics (including feminists), such 'high feminist' interpretations approach the Brontë novels as stories about women who struggle to define themselves authentically within an oppressive system of patriarchy. Following the publication of Terry Eagleton's influential *Myths of Power: A Marxist Study of the Brontës* in 1975, some Marxist-feminists took issue with his assessments (for example, the Marxist-Feminist Literature Collective, 'Women's Writing: *Jane Eyre, Shirley, Villette*, and *Aurora Leigh*', *Ideology and Consciousness*, 3 (1978), 30–5) while others, like Nancy Pell ('Resistance, Rebellion, and Marriage: The Economics of *Jane Eyre*', *Nineteenth-Century Fiction*, 31 (1977) 397–420), and Jina Politi ('*Jane Eyre* Class-ified', *Literature and History*, 8 (1982), 56–66) built more constructively on his work. In either case, these feminist responses to Eagleton's analysis demonstrate how productive the intersection of feminist and socio-economic perspectives within the field of Brontë studies can be.

In general, the tendency of feminist criticism since about 1980 has been toward a greater engagement with other critical perspectives, so that after the seventies it is difficult to isolate feminist readings of the Brontës' work in a separate category; rather, one finds the influence of feminism throughout the various critical approaches that have together dominated Brontë studies in the last 25 years. One can divide those approaches roughly into two categories if one allows for considerable overlap and innumerable mutual influences across the groupings: (1) text- and language-centred forms of deconstruction and contemporary psychoanalytic criticism, and (2) interpretations that are less obviously text-oriented because they examine the Brontës' writing within the larger field of cultural discourse. Early *deconstructionist approaches to *Wuthering Heights* are perhaps best exemplified in articles by Carol Jacobs ('*Wuthering Heights*: At the Threshold of Interpretation', *boundary 2: a journal of postmodern literature and culture*, 7 (1979), 49–71) and J. Hillis Miller (*Fiction and Repetition in Seven English Novels*, 1982), who argue that any reading of the novel will inevitably be undone by some detail that contradicts the totalizing interpretation; all our efforts to penetrate the narrative layers of *Wuthering Heights* lead not to its hidden significance, according to Jacobs, but only to more interpretation. Of Charlotte's novels, *Villette* has lent itself to deconstructionist interpretation exceptionally well, particularly when combined with feminist psychoanalytic theories about subjective identity. One of the first and best of such readings is Christina Crosby's 1984 interpretation of *Villette* as a novel that subverts the very oppositions upon which identity itself is based, according to modern psychoanalytic theory: the conscious mind and its hidden counterpart, the unconscious ('Charlotte Brontë's Haunted Text', *Studies in English Literature*, 24 (1984), 701–15).

Less obviously influenced by deconstruction, Margaret Homans's analyses of Charlotte's and Emily's work in two books (*Women Writers and Poetic Identity: Dorothy Wordsworth, Emily Brontë, and Emily Dickinson* (1980) and *Bearing the Word: Language and Female Experience in Nineteenth-Century Women's Writing* (1986)) and several articles published over a period of about twenty years beginning in 1978 have kept pace with the emergence of Lacanian theory by focusing on women writers' problematic relationship to language. Similarly, in *Monsters of Affection*

(1982) Diane Sadoff considers the ways in which Charlotte's female protagonists attempt to gain 'mastery' through language; in addition, Sadoff reinterprets the nature of the father-daughter bond in Charlotte's writing by drawing on feminists' adaptations of Lacan's theory of 'the gaze', the means by which identity is supposedly constituted during 'the mirror stage' of psychic development.

The second category of recent critical perspectives on the Brontës can be thought of as contextual approaches that have been transformed by post-structuralist thought. Cultural criticism and the overlapping school of new historicism have drawn attention to various kinds of discourse that contributed to the Brontës' writing and, indeed, to which their novels may be said to belong. Most notable, perhaps, is Sally Shuttleworth's *Charlotte Brontë and Victorian Psychology* (1996), which examines contemporary psychological discourse in a variety of fields to show how writing in social theory, medicine, economics, and literature (including Charlotte's novels) paved the way for the development of modern psychoanalysis and its construction of the modern psychological subject. In an earlier book, *Desire and Domestic Fiction* (1987), Nancy Armstrong made the related argument that the popularity of *Jane Eyre* and *Wuthering Heights* helped to produce the modern female sexual subject and, in the process, contributed to the suppression of the female social self within 'the political unconscious', a term previously coined by Frederic Jameson. One other important example of recent cultural criticism on the Brontës (though of a very different kind from Shuttleworth's and Armstrong's) is Patsy Stoneman's *Brontë Transformations* (1996), which traces the cultural dissemination of *Jane Eyre* and *Wuthering Heights* through the adaptations and derivatives made in the 150 years since the novels were first published.

Closely allied with cultural criticism and new historical approaches, post-colonial theory has also found fertile soil in the Brontës' writing. Gayatri Spivak's 1985 article, 'Three Women's Texts and a Critique of Imperialism' (*Critical Inquiry*, 12 (1985), 243–61), is the original text in this rich vein of contemporary criticism, which examines the tropes by which imperialist discourse operated in 19th-century British writing, especially in novels. Other work that has contributed to the study of the Brontës' writings from a post-colonial perspective includes Christopher Heywood's research on Yorkshire slavery ('Yorkshire Slavery in *Wuthering Heights*', *Review of English Studies*, 38 (1987), 184–98, and 'Africa and Slavery in the Brontë Children's Novels', *Hitotsuhashi Journal of Arts and Sciences*, 30 (1989), 75–87); Firdous Azim's 1993 book, *The Colonial Rise of the Novel*, on the influence of imperialism in the development of the novel form; Terry Eagleton's discussion of *Wuthering Heights* within the context of Irish immigration during the 1840s in *Myths of Power* (1975) and his article 'Heathcliff and the Great Hunger' in his book of the same title (1995), pp. 1–26; Christine Alexander's article 'Imagining Africa: The Brontës' Creations of Glass Town and Angria' (in P. Alexander, R. Hutchinson, and D. Schreuder (eds.), *Africa Today: A Multi-Disciplinary Snapshot of the Continent* (1996), 201–19); and Susan Meyer's book *Imperialism at Home* (1996), which includes important chapters on the writing of Charlotte and Emily Brontë in relation to race. See also MARXIST APPROACHES; PSYCHOANALYTIC APPROACHES. CB

McNees.

topographical metaphors of disease in literary and non-literary discourse contributed to the formation of class and national identities in Victorian England, an approach that makes his work compatible with *post-colonial theory. Nicholas Dames's essay 'The Clinical Novel: Phrenology and *Villette*' (*Novel*, 29 (1996), 348–59) draws on Foucault's idea of the 'clinical gaze' to explain how Charlotte's characters produce both desire and subjective identity through a process of 'reading' each other as a clinician would read a psychiatric patient. In all these works, the cultural critics are concerned with the relationship between cultural discourse and the construction of individual and group identity.

A different approach to study of the Brontës within a cultural context is Patsy Stoneman's *Brontë Transformations: The Cultural Dissemination of 'Jane Eyre' and 'Wuthering Heights'* (1996), the only extensive study of the cultural dissemination of the Brontës' writings published so far. Stoneman discusses in chronological order the many ways in which *Jane Eyre* and *Wuthering Heights* have been adapted by a culture that has both transformed and been transformed by these powerful texts. In the introductory chapter, she situates her study within the field of discourse theory, but the strength of her work lies in its recovery of the numerous derivations and adaptations that have been made from these two novels. Stoneman's book concludes with an impressive list, more than 60 pages long, of 'derivatives' made from *Wuthering Heights* and *Jane Eyre*. CB

Shuttleworth, Sally, *Charlotte Brontë and Victorian Psychology* (1996).

Stoneman, Patsy, *Brontë Transformations: The Cultural Dissemination of 'Jane Eyre' and 'Wuthering Heights'* (1996).

curates played a significant part in the lives and writings of the Brontës. Their social position on the lowest rung of the ecclesiastical ladder was in some ways anomalous. Most Anglican curates were graduates of Oxford, Cambridge, Durham, or Trinity College Dublin; some were non-graduates trained at theological colleges like St Bees in Cumberland (founded in 1816 and no longer extant), or Chichester (founded 1839). Literate ministers of the Church of England, they had theoretically become 'gentry' whatever their parentage; but most of them had miserably small stipends, so that they could hardly contemplate marrying until they secured a reasonable living, or married for money. Yet single women like Ellen *Nussey, reasonably well educated but not wealthy, often hoped to marry a curate. Two of Ellen's admirers were John Gorham, who became a schoolmaster, and Revd O. P. *Vincent, who had many curacies before ob-

taining a rectorship at the age of 60. In some cases the system of patronage helped. Many livings were 'in the gift' of wealthy aristocrats or Oxbridge colleges, so that having the right social contacts could be useful. Sir James *Kay-Shuttleworth and Richard Monckton *Milnes both suggested suitable livings for Revd A. B. *Nicholls, which to his credit he refused out of loyalty to Charlotte and Revd Patrick Brontë. Revd Charles *Simeon bought up livings so that he could help to place evangelical ministers in areas where they were specially needed. In this case patronage worked for good; but not all curates entered the Church with a true sense of religious vocation. Apart from the still-lingering tradition that in titled families, eldest sons inherited the title and estate, second sons entered the armed services, and third sons went into the Church, some young men used the Church to fulfil more worldly ambitions. Charlotte had the misfortune to know the appalling Revd John *Collins, sometime curate in Keighley, who exploited his natural gift of oratory in the pulpit, but totally lacked moral standards. Revd Peter Augustus *Malone of *Shirley* is Charlotte's merciless *reductio ad absurdum* of the coarse-grained and ultimately dishonest curate Revd J. W. *Smith, whose education served only to elevate his self-esteem and increase his determination to marry a rich wife. In real life, Mr Brontë's opposition to Charlotte's marrying Mr Nicholls was based partly on his lowly position and small salary. For a meagre reward of £90 per annum or less, depending on whether help had been provided by the Church Pastoral Aid Society (founded 1836) or the High Church 'Society for Promoting the Employment of additional Curates', curates had to perform the routine tasks of innumerable baptisms and burials, and to assist in pastoral work. They might have to do most of the work of the parish if their vicar or rector was elderly or a frequent absentee, and they often eked out their income by taking private pupils. Yet they could not automatically command the respect normally accorded to the incumbent. If they had imbibed reformist or extreme ideas at their college or university, they might have an uphill struggle to introduce them in a traditionally run parish. Anne Brontë depicts with vivid sympathy the efforts of the evangelical Edward *Weston to counteract the unchristian doctrinaire harshness of the rector, Revd Mr *Hatfield, who calls Nancy Brown a 'canting old fool', insists that she must come to sacrament, and that if she does her best to get to heaven and 'can't manage it', she must be one of those unable to 'enter in at the strait gate'. Weston resembles in some ways the thoroughly good curate Revd William *Weightman, whose death was caused by his visiting the sick. George Eliot was later to depict with profound sympathetic insight the hardships of the evangelical curate Amos Barton, and the brutal opposition of those who resented, without understanding, his willingness to help and preach to the poorest and most ignorant of the townspeople. In contrast, Charlotte unsympathetically presented the curates in *Shirley* as being fashionably preoccupied with superficial theories, but ignoring the fundamentals of Christianity—not even arguing on 'theology, practical or doctrinal; but on minute points of ecclesiastical discipline' (ch. 1). Visiting the sick they found 'dull work', and preferred to visit each other, eat and drink to excess, and argue uproariously. Charlotte excepts from her strongest criticism the amiable Revd David *Sweeting and the generally 'rational, diligent and charitable' Mr *Macarthey; and she admits that Revd Joseph *Donne 'did some good with his cash: he was useful in his day and generation' (ch. 37). Critics who perceived her satire of the curates as a damaging betrayal of religion missed the point: she criticized them precisely because their follies brought into disrepute the *Church of England, which she loved.

Cuvier, Baron Georges de (1769–1832), famous French zoologist who established the sciences of comparative anatomy and palaeontology. His work was known to the young Brontës chiefly through their copy of *The Gardens and Menagerie of the Zoological Society Delineated* (in BPM) and through their interest in *phrenology. Like Lavater, Cuvier composed tables to indicate the facial angles of men and different animals as a means of measuring intellectual faculties. In May 1829 Charlotte labelled a tiny sketch of a figure 'Baron de Cuvier', and in September of the same year a reference to him in Branwell's juvenilia suggests that he had become a character from 'Frenchy Land' in the *Glass Town and Angrian saga (Alexander & Sellars, pp. 28, 292; Neufeldt *BB Works*, 1. 62).

Dahomey, Plains of. The fertile plains beyond the delta of Fernando Po, chosen by the *Twelves as the site of the *Glass Town. To the far north, the *Jibbel Kumri or Mountains of the Moon encircle the plains of Dahomey. See also AFRICA.

Dance, Louisa. See VERNON, LOUISA (MAR-CHIONESS OF WELLESLEY).

Danhasch (Danash, Danasch), son of Schemhourasch, a genie rebellious to God in the *Arabian Nights, who appears as an evil genie in the early *Glass Town and Angrian saga. He tries to kill Frederick Guelph, Duke of *York, when he rescues Zorayda but is prevented by Maimoune, daughter of Damriel, king of a legion of genii in the *Arabian Nights*. Again, Danhasch tries to destroy the Duke of York's son, Edward Sydney, but is prevented by Crashie and Manfred, the 'two wondrous brothers' (*The *Foundling*).

Darkwall Manor. See THURSTONS OF DARKWALL MANOR.

'Day at Parry's Palace, A'. See 'YOUNG MEN'S MAGAZINE'.

Dean, Ellen (Nelly), unmarried housekeeper at *Thrushcross Grange and narrator of most of the story of *Wuthering Heights to the tenant Mr *Lockwood. Her story includes both eyewitness accounts and interpolated narratives, such as a letter from Isabella *Linton and reports from *Zillah. Her mother had nursed Hindley *Earnshaw and Nelly spent her childhood with Hindley and Catherine at Wuthering Heights, becoming a servant first to the Earnshaws and then to *Heathcliff. When Catherine marries Edgar Linton she is forced to leave her 'nursling' Hareton *Earnshaw and accompany her mistress to Thrushcross Grange. Her happiest years are as nurse to the Linton's daughter, the young Cathy, to whom she is deeply attached. Her often gratuitous interference in events and her moralizing and common-sense narration provide a realistic barrier between the reader and the passionate lives of her story.

Dearden, William (1803–89), a Keighley schoolmaster and friend of Revd Patrick and Branwell Brontë. After Elizabeth Gaskell's biography of Charlotte, Dearden sprang to the defence of 'this venerable clergyman' and corrected a number of stories about Mr Brontë, at the same time recording his own memories of the family in letters to the *Bradford Observer (20 Aug. 1857, p. 8, and 27 June 1861, p. 7). He interviewed the servant Nancy Garrs (see SERVANTS OF THE BRONTËS) and reported that Patrick did not dine alone during her time at the Parsonage, that he taught his children 'at stated times during the day', and that 'His children were the frequent companions of his walks.' Dearden him-

self remembered seeing the young Brontes with their father in the Keighley studio of John *Bradley.

Dearden had originally come from Hebden Bridge and after his period as schoolmaster in Keighley, he moved to Huddersfield, where he was principal of the King Street Academy. He had always written poetry, published in the local papers, and was known as the 'Bard of Caldene'. He was part of the *Halifax circle of writers and artists and encouraged Branwell Brontë in his poetry when Branwell was introduced to the group by Joseph Bentley *Leyland. Branwell thought Dearden's Death of the African Bloodhound and The Star-Seer (1837) were 'surely models of excellence'. In 1842 Dearden and Branwell agreed to write 'a drama or a poem, the principal character in which was to have a real or imaginary existence before the Deluge' (quoted in Barker, p. 399, from Halifax Guardian, 15 June 1867). They were to meet in a month at the Cross Roads Inn and produce their results. Dearden wrote 'Demon Queen' and Branwell produced 'Azrael, or the Eve of Destruction', a long poem dramatizing the confrontation between Noah and Azrael over Methuselah's grave (Neufeldt suggests this poem was actually begun much earlier, in BB Works, 3. 196). Dearden believed that if 'Azrael' had been published it would 'prove to the world that Branwell was not inferior in genius and power to the gifted Currer Bell' (Bradford Observer, 27 June 1861; part of the poem was published on 25 August 1842, Neufeldt BB Works, 3. 375). In the actual event at the inn, however, Branwell brought the wrong manuscript and read instead a story that Dearden later thought resembled Wuthering Heights, so giving rise to claims that Branwell rather than Emily had written the novel.

'Death of Moses, The' ('Mort de Moïse, La'). *Devoir by Charlotte Brontë (17 July 1843?; MS in Heger family) that demonstrates her thorough knowledge of the Bible and her religious ardour. In describing her subject's last hours, she initially follows Deuteronomy: Moses blesses the tribes of Israel and starts to climb Mount Nebo. Then she pauses to ask whether such biblical stories should be taken literally. Rejecting scepticism she affirms that faith should prevail over reason; this interruption was criticized by M. Constantin *Heger. When Charlotte resumes her account, she develops her own version of Moses's dying vision. She imagines him seeing not only the promised land but also centuries of biblical history. The devoir concludes with a revelation of angels heralding the birth of a Messiah who, though unnamed, is evidently Jesus. Rough notes that accompany the devoir (in Bonnell, BPM) further explore this revelation. SL

Gaskell *Life*, 1. 264.
Lonoff, pp. 310–33.

'Death of Napoléon, The' ('Mort de Napoléon, La'). Devoir by Charlotte Brontë (31 May 1843; MS in BPM). Ostensibly an examination of *Napoleon Buonaparte's life and exile on St Helena, it becomes a panegyric on the Duke of *Wellington, Charlotte's childhood hero and Napoleon's conqueror, as well as a comparison between two men of genius. Several passages obliquely refer to her unhappiness. She denounces a cold, cruel 'mediocrity' who seems suspiciously like Mme Zoë *Heger and alludes to the charity of a male 'stranger' who feels only pity for the exile. M. Constantin *Heger massively corrected the devoir, striking out its introduction and confessional remarks. He made further emendations in the version he prepared for Elizabeth *Gaskell (in Rylands), which she published in her *Life* (1. 290–5). SL

Lonoff, pp. 270–309.

De Capell family, neighbours of Alexander Ashworth in West Yorkshire, in Charlotte Brontë's fragmentary story *Ashworth. The family consists of Mr De Capell, his two sons and daughter, who all live at De Capell Hall. Mr De Capell is a colourful Yorkshire personality with a heavy dialect, forthright manner, and keen association with the manufacturers of Leeds and Bradford. He recalls General Thornton and particularly his father Alexander Sneaky in the *Glass Town and Angrian saga; and prefigures Hiram Yorke in *Shirley*. The daughter Amelia is spoilt and unthinking: she may be based on Amelia *Walker whom Charlotte considered 'utterly spoilt by the most hideous affectation' (Alexander *EW*, p. 208). At boarding school in London, she bullies the humble Ellen Hall into repacking her trunk, and is equally condescending towards her poorer cousin Marian Fairburne. John and Thornton De Capell are based on John Augustus Sneaky (Duke of *Fidena) and his brother General *Thornton in the Angrian saga. Like their

prototypes, the eldest, John, is a proud, self-controlled young man who studies law in London, whereas Thornton (as his name suggests) is 'a thorn in his father's side' (Alexander *EW*, p. 220).

deconstructionist approaches. The term deconstruction refers to a philosophy of language pioneered by Jacques Derrida (b. 1930) and to a school of literary criticism derived from that philosophy. The multi-layered text of the major Brontë novels, especially *Wuthering Heights* and *Jane Eyre*, has led critics to use deconstruction in interpreting them. Sometimes called post-structuralism (though the term post-structuralism also refers more broadly to criticism in general as it developed after structuralism), deconstruction evolved logically out of basic contradictions in structuralist thought. On the one hand, the founder of structuralist linguistics, Ferdinand de Saussure (1857–1913), invalidated long-standing assumptions about the referential nature of language by showing that, in fact, there is no innate or necessary connection between particular words (signifiers) and what they represent (signifieds); that 'cat' stands for our idea of a cat is merely a matter of convention, an arbitrary connection that developed out of language use itself. Words are thus not inherently meaningful; rather, Saussure argues, meaning arises out of our use of linguistic elements in relation to each other—out of differences that allow us to distinguish one element from another and to put them together in particular ways when we speak or write. Saussure's work therefore rejects the common-sense idea that words express pre-existent truths (signifieds) and instead leads to the conclusion that there is no truth beyond language, no meaning before, or outside, discourse. On the other hand, in his effort to establish a science of signs (semiology), Saussure posited the existence of an underlying structure, or grammar, which determines how linguistic elements are put together to make meaning, just as his colleague, the anthropologist Claude Levi-Strauss, theorized an innate structuring activity of the mind which accounts for universally recurring patterns in human culture, such as those found in all primitive myths (see MYTH AND SYMBOL). Both Saussure and Levi-Strauss, the two founding figures of structuralism, thus fall back on the very notion that structuralism supposedly invalidates: the belief in the presence of some truth that is ontologically anterior to, and more fundamental than, the world as it is structured by human use, particularly the use of language.

In exposing this fundamental contradiction, Derrida pushed structuralism into its next permutation as deconstruction. In *De la grammatologie* (1967), he shows how works by Saussure, Levi-

Strauss, and others undo themselves at key points which he calls *aporia*: points where a text says both 'A' and 'not A', asserting an opposition that it simultaneously contradicts, thereby producing textural instability or indeterminacy. All texts dismantle, or deconstruct, themselves in this way, Derrida argues, because it is the very nature of language to do so. Efforts at textual interpretation result, therefore, not in the discovery of determinate meaning, but in the production of more interpretation—in other words, more text. The kind of writing we call literary is valued by deconstructionists because, rather than gloss over its indeterminacy as most writing tries to do, literature deliberately draws attention to its instability by using language that is more obviously ambiguous and overfilled with multiple potential meanings. Deconstructionists focus on the high degree of self-reference in literary language (since all language, in fact, refers to itself more than to the things it represents) and often show how literary texts are, fundamentally, about themselves: about the endlessly challenging processes of interpretation, reading, communicating, understanding, and becoming ourselves through language.

That *Wuthering Heights* has attracted numerous deconstructionist readings over the last 30 years is not surprising given the persistence with which critics have tried to explain how the formal features of Emily's novel function in relation to each other and make up a unified underlying structure for the text (see STRUCTURALIST APPROACHES). As early as 1959, Allen Brick noticed that by eliciting the reader's identification with one narrator after another (not just with Lockwood and Nelly, but also with other characters, like Isabella and Heathcliff, who recount their own embedded stories), *Wuthering Heights* engages us in a series of efforts, none entirely successful, to understand the core message of the novel ('*Wuthering Heights*: Narrators, Audience, and Message', *College English*, 21 (1959), 80–6). Later exemplary deconstructionist readings by Carol Jacobs ('*Wuthering Heights*: At the Threshold of Interpretation', *boundary 2: a journal of postmodern literature and culture*, 7 (1979), 49–71) and J. Hillis Miller (*Fiction and Repetition in Seven English Novels*, 1982) each focus on slightly different features of the text but offer essentially the same argument: *Wuthering Heights* creates the impression that there is a centre, or core of meaning, or hidden secret, that we can find if only we read properly, but its felt promise of determinate meaning is never fulfilled. There is always some remaining detail in the text that undoes whatever totalizing interpretation a reader may propose, and our efforts to penetrate the narrative layers lead, not to the novel's hidden significance, but only to more interpretation.

One of the earliest deconstructionist discussions of *Wuthering Heights*, in Frank Kermode's *The Classic* (1975), nicely illustrates how the application of a structuralist approach can lead, by way of interest in the reader, to deconstructionist interpretation. Though Derrida has been credited with turning structuralism into deconstruction nearly overnight (he published three books on the subject in 1967), in fact, post-structuralist literary theory developed more slowly and circuitously than that. Kermode's observation that the meaning found in a novel changes over time as reading audiences change, and his references to theorists like Wolfgang Iser, point to the fact that structuralist theory first led to questions about the reader's role in the processes of signification before it arrived at deconstruction's conclusions regarding the indeterminacy of the text (indeed, not every structuralist made that final step into deconstructionist practice). For some, Bakhtin's theories of narrative polyphony provided a more compelling response to the unsettling of structuralist assumptions that occurred in the late sixties. Feminists like Suzanne Rosenthal Shumway ('The Chronotype of the Asylum: *Jane Eyre*, Feminism, and Bakhtinian Theory', in Karen Hohne and Helen Wussow (eds.), *A Dialogue of Voices: Feminist Literary Theory and Bakhtin* (1994), 152–74), for example, have made use of both Bakhtin and French feminism (which adapts Derrida's theories to its own perspective) in order to explain the relationship between language, gender identity, and the formal features of a dialogic text like *Jane Eyre*. Others have adopted reader-response approaches to the Brontës, interpreting them as stories which are not only about reading, storytelling, and interpretation but which also enact the hermeneutic challenges that constitute that theme. Criticism of this type includes a rash of articles on readers and reading published in the 1980s (Mark M. Hennelly, Jun., 'Jane Eyre's reading Lesson', *ELH* 51 (1984), 693–717; Joseph Dupras, 'Charlotte Brontë's *Shirley* and Interpretive Engendering', *Papers on Language and Literature*, 24 (1988), 301–16; Gregory S. O'Dea, 'Narrator and Reader in Charlotte Brontë's *Villette*', *South Atlantic Review*, 53 (1988), 41–57; Brenda Silver, 'The Reflecting Reader in *Villette*', in Elizabeth Abel, Marianne Hirsch, and Elizabeth Langland (eds.), *The Voyage In: Fictions of Female Development* (1983), 90–111; John P. Farrell, 'Reading the Text of Community in *Wuthering Heights*', *ELH* 56 (1989), 173–208), and one book, Carol Bock's *Charlotte Brontë and the Storyteller's Audience* (1992), which is the most comprehensive treatment of the subject, covering Charlotte's writing from the juvenilia through *Villette*.

In addition to this preoccupation with reading, post-structuralist interpretations of Charlotte's and Emily's novels have also emphasized the problem of self-identity. Pointing to the recurring pairs of opposites that structure Charlotte's novels—for example, fire–ice, Rochester–St John, Helen–Bertha in *Jane Eyre*—these readings show how each pair reverses and undoes itself, thus dismantling the very foundation on which the text is built, and in the process pointing to the problematic nature of self-identity. For example, Richard Benvenuto ('The Child of Nature, the Child of Grace, and the Unresolved Conflict of *Jane Eyre*', ELH 39 (1972), 620–38) shows that Jane Eyre is depicted as both a 'child of nature' and its opposite, a 'child of grace': on the one hand, she is a strong individual guided by a sense of her own worth and rights; on the other, she also firmly identifies herself within the prescriptive framework of divine and social authority. The contradiction, though unintended, is no flaw, Benvenuto argues, because Charlotte herself was (unconsciously) so dually identified. Similar interpretations of *Villette* are made by Susan Watkins ('Versions of the Feminine Subject in Charlotte Brontë's *Villette*', *Critical Studies*, 8 (1997), 218–25), who contends that the novel exposes the instability and inadequacy of the feminine split subject (itself a binary opposite), and by Christina Crosby ('Charlotte Brontë's Haunted Text', *Studies in English Literature*, 24 (1984), 701–15), who reads the ghostly nun as 'an agent of indeterminacy' in a novel that subverts the oppositions upon which identity itself is based, according to modern psychology: the deep truth of interiority (the unconscious) and the supposed distortions of surface representation.

Like Crosby's and Watkins's articles on *Villette*, deconstructionist readings of *Wuthering Heights* frequently engage with modern psychoanalytic theory in order to explore the issue of identity (for two quite different examples, see Jay Clayton's *Romantic Vision and the Novel* (1987) and Leo Bersani's *A Future for Astyanax* (1976)) but other approaches have also been greatly enriched by deconstruction (see FEMINIST APPROACHES; POSTCOLONIAL THEORY; MARXIST APPROACHES; CULTURAL CRITICISM). For example, in *Literary Fat Ladies: Rhetoric, Gender, and Property* (1987), Patricia Parker draws on feminist theory, the ideas of Derrida, and the work of cultural historian Michel Foucault (1929–84) to explain the relationship between the novel's form, its materialist concerns with 'place' and 'property', and the issue of identity (both human and textual). Other critics who deal more narrowly with the novel's linking of identity to text or language include John T. Matthews ('Framing in *Wuthering Heights*', *Texas Studies in Literature and Language*, 27 (1985), 25–61), John Allen Stevenson ('Heathcliff Is Me: *Wuthering Heights* and the Question of Likeness', *Nineteenth-*

Century Literature, 43 (1988), 60–81), and Michael S. Macovski ('*Wuthering Heights* and the Rhetoric of Interpretation', *ELH* 54 (1987), 363–84). Macovski's essay is perhaps the most optimistic deconstructionist reading of a Brontë novel. While critics like Jacobs and Miller dwell on the ways in which *Wuthering Heights* demonstrates the futility or impossibility of interpretation, Macovski shows that the novel 'continually keeps the possibility of interpretation open by sustaining a rhetorical process of understanding' which, though never entirely successful, nevertheless demonstrates how the self is fashioned in moments of 'rhetorical exposure before another' (p. 368). 'The listener's function' in relation to the speaker is thus both 'interpretive and ontological', a claim one might also make about the reader in relation to the literary work: the work is what comes into being when the language of the text is read. In this way, Macovski's essay takes important deconstructionist arguments about *Wuthering Heights* into account and yet arrives at a more hopeful conclusion that tallies with the Brontës' strong sense of themselves as self-defined through language and discourse.   CB

Farrell, John P., 'Reading the Text of Community in *Wuthering Heights*', *ELH* 56 (1989), 173–208.
Jacobs, Carol, '*Wuthering Heights*: At the Threshold of Interpretation', *boundary 2: a journal of postmodern literature and culture*, 7 (1979), 49–71.
Miller, J. Hillis, *Fiction and Repetition in Seven English Novels* (1982).

De Crack, Mon[sieur] Edouard, the hero of Lord Charles Wellesley's (Charlotte Brontë's) tale 'The Adventures of Mon Edouard de Crack' (Alexander *EEW*, 1. 133–40); possibly a descendant of Cracky, one of the original *Twelves in the *Glass Town and Angrian saga. On the death of his parents in the countryside of Frenchyland, de Crack journeys to *Paris where he encounters the squalid underworld of the city and its motley assemblage of characters. His money is stolen and he is forced to work in a tavern of dubious notoriety, where corpses are traded (possibly owned by *Pigtail). After five years, he is swept up by a black giant and swoons on seeing a vision of genieland with its 'four beings of immeasureable height' (the young Brontës). When he wakes, a man in green, Eugene Beauchamp, directs him to Glass Town. Rescued by the Marquis of Douro (Duke of Zamorna) from assault by Richard (Young Man) *Naughty, he is given employment as head overseer in the factory of Captain Mourout, and presumably lives happily ever after.

De Hamal, Colonel Alfred, a curly-haired dandy in *Villette*, who drops adoring letters to Ginevra *Fanshawe from his nephew's *Athénée window. Disguised as a nun, he climbs into the pensionnat for secret meetings with her, and they make a runaway marriage. His pseudo-*Gothic 'haunting' adds to Lucy *Snowe's nervous terrors.

Delancy (De Lancy), Alexander, also called 'Monsieur Like-to-live-in-lonely-places' in 'The *Search after Happiness', a Frenchman who accompanies Henry *O'Donell on his search for happiness, only to return home again and become a rich merchant in the city of *Paris, where he is highly favoured by the Emperor *Napoleon. Delancy's name was probably suggested by that of Sir William de Lancey, a Peninsular colleague of the Duke of *Wellington, who was mortally wounded fighting near the Duke at the Battle of Waterloo, 1815.

De Lisle, Frederick (or Sir Edward), an eminent Verdopolitan portrait painter, patronized by the Duke of Zamorna and the Earl St Clair, and later by Edward Percy, in the *Glass Town and Angrian saga. Having taught Marian *Hume painting, he is a beneficiary in her will. Characterized as 'great in the beautiful' (Alexander EEW, 1. 129–30), he appears to be modelled on Sir Joshua Reynolds (see ROYAL ACADEMY OF ARTS).

Delph, Victoria, a famous heiress in the *Glass Town and Angrian saga whose fortune has 'turned more than one Peer's coronet, & a great Earl's bald-head, & magnificent Monarch's crowned one into the bargain'. Her name is bandied about when anyone wants a rich wife, it is used to name steamboats ('Little Vic') and hairstyles ('à la Victoria Delph'), but the woman herself seldom features.

De Quincey, Thomas (1785–1859), author admired by Branwell Brontë and his sisters. His *Confessions of an English Opium Eater* (London Magazine, 1821; vol. form 1822), *Suspiria de Profundis* (Blackwood's Edinburgh Magazine, 1845), and 'The English Mail-Coach' (Blackwood's, 1849) have phantasmagoric dream evocations akin to some of the visionary sequences in the Brontës' early writings, and in Charlotte's transformation of the park in Villette (ch. 38) into a 'land of enchantment'. Branwell may have been encouraged to take opium by the Confessions, for though De Quincey intends to warn his readers against the drug, his descriptions of its pleasures, of the strangely enhanced 'phantoms of the eye' and music 'heard in dreams', would appeal to the escapist and the musician in Branwell, despite their attendant 'state of gloom'; for he was promised, paradoxically, an 'abyss of divine enjoyment', and (supposedly) protection against consumption. De Quincey also wrote with personal knowledge of other writers in the Brontës' Pantheon: his 'Lake

Reminiscences', first published in journals 1834–40, later revised for his *Collected Works* in 1853, describe vividly, and critically, S. T. Coleridge, Wordsworth, Southey, and their circle. In spring 1840 Branwell sent to De Quincey translations of five *'Odes of Horace', and his long poem 'Sir Henry Tunstall', a version of a poem originally written in Bradford in 1838. This was carefully revised at Broughton-in-Furness before 15 April 1840, and evidently highly regarded by Branwell himself, for he offered it in newly revised form to *Blackwood's* on 6 September 1842 (see Neufeldt BBP, pp. 474–86, 526–30). Unfortunately De Quincey, ill, harassed by creditors, and surrounded by a chaos of papers in his Edinburgh lodgings, did not reply. On 16 June 1847 Charlotte Brontë sent a copy of *Poems 1846 to De Quincey in acknowledgement 'of the pleasure and profit' the 'Bells' had 'often and long derived from' De Quincey's works.

devoirs. *See page 158*

Dewsbury, a town about 7 miles south of *Bradford, in the Calder valley. During Revd Patrick Brontë's curacy there from December 1809 to early 1811 many inhabitants were hand-loom weavers, though there were already large textile mills near the river. Rapid expansion, facilitated by steam-driven machinery, abundant coal supplies, good turnpike roads, and navigable waterways, soon made it a principal centre for the manufacture of blankets, carpets, druggets, and worsted yarns. In the timber-framed vicarage, dating from the 14th century, Mr Brontë lived for several months and became a friend of the vicar, Revd John *Buckworth. All Saints church, with its Norman nave, retained some Anglo-Saxon carvings. Through his wife Rachel, née Halliley, Buckworth was connected with Dewsbury's most influential family, the Hallileys of Aldams Mills. Leah Sophia and Anna Maria Brooke (see BROOKE FAMILY OF DEWSBURY), the daughters of John Brooke and his wife Sarah, née Halliley, were later Charlotte's schoolfellows at *Roe Head. Mr Brontë visited cottages, helped in the Sunday school, and officiated at hundreds of baptisms and burials. He perseveringly championed William Nowell, wrongly charged with desertion from the army, from September 1810 until he was cleared of guilt in August 1811. Mr Brontë's bold defiance of a drunkard who obstructed a Whit Tuesday procession is recalled in *Shirley*. Charlotte knew many people in or near Dewsbury, mainly through the Woolers. Revd Thomas *Allbutt (see ALLBUTT FAMILY) (to whom Revd Henry *Nussey was curate from 1835 to July 1837) was Buckworth's curate from 1832 to 1835, then vicar of Dewsbury 1835–62. His first wife was Marianne Wooler, and his *(cont. on page 162)*

THE plural of the French word for 'duty', 'devoir' is also the common term for 'homework'. Often it refers to student compositions, the exercises that remain a basic feature of the French and Belgian educational systems. When Charlotte and Emily Brontë studied at the Pensionnat *Heger (Charlotte in 1842–3, Emily in 1842), they wrote devoirs under the guidance of their professor, M. Constantin *Heger. Nineteen by Charlotte and nine by Emily have survived, and two others are known but untraceable.

The earliest account of these Belgian essays appears in Elizabeth *Gaskell's *Life of Charlotte Brontë*. She says that after observing both sisters Heger proposed to teach them French by adopting a system he had used with his more advanced students. Instead of giving them conventional drills he would read them extracts by major French authors, analyse the structure and leading features with them, and ask them to respond by expressing their own views in a corresponding manner. Emily balked at the idea of writing to imitate, but Charlotte agreed to try. In fact, despite Emily's initial reluctance, both sisters wrote essays that followed his instructions, although he also encouraged them to choose subjects that engaged their hearts and minds. Thus even when his assignments were confining, the devoirs express the contrasting dispositions and interests of their authors. As the sisters became more advanced he introduced them to what he called 'synthetical teaching'. He read excerpts by several writers on the same subject, directing them to observe similarities and differences, and indicating how each writer's position might affect his account. The sisters were then to 'sift and collect the elements of truth' (*Life*, 1. 254–5, 258–9).

Gaskell interviewed Heger in 1856, thirteen years after Charlotte left the pensionnat and a year after her death. What he told her does not always accord with the evidence in Charlotte's copybooks and devoirs. Charlotte kept a notebook of *dictations (*dictées*), which she may have transcribed as she sat in Heger's classes, rather than in private lessons. Furthermore, while several of the devoirs imitate a passage in content or style, others fill in an outline that he set or have no apparent links to famous authors. Then too, as her French improved she took more licence. The devoirs of 1843, the second year of her stay in Brussels, differ in length and complexity from those that she composed in 1842. Nonetheless Gaskell's account is invaluable both for explaining Heger's system of instruction and for providing his view of the sisters' capacities and characters. She also reproduced two of Charlotte's devoirs, 'Imitation: Portrait of Peter the Hermit' ('Portrait de Pierre l'Hermite [*sic*]', 31 July 1842) and 'On the *Death of Napoleon' ('Sur la nom [*sic* for 'La Mort'] de Napoleon', 31 May 1843, both in Rylands).

A later English student, Frederika MacDonald (*The Secret of Charlotte Brontë* (1914)), has described the process of composition that students were expected to follow. They were first to write a draft in their notebooks, leaving space in the margins for corrections. They then prepared a copy for Heger, which was also to include a wide margin. When he returned it, they were to take note of his corrections and make a new copy with changes. Whether Charlotte and Emily always followed these steps cannot be ascertained from the evidence. The surviving manuscripts show, however, that they carefully prepared what they submitted. Both wrote neatly on hand-ruled pages, sometimes sewing the left edges together to make a booklet. Charlotte lettered several titles in ornamental script and occasionally set off proper names. Heger's markings, though far less tidy, attest to his conscientious efforts to improve grammar, clarity, and style. Corrections that range from light to massive appear on seventeen of the surviving manuscripts, including one, Charlotte's *'Human Justice' ('La Justice humaine') (6 Oct., in Bonnell, BPM) with his and her revisions in three layers. He was also liberal in expressing his approval; 'Bon' and 'Très bon' or their initials recur next to passages he liked. This process represents a radical departure from Charlotte's earlier methods of composing. The devoirs were not spontaneous compositions; they had to be thought out and were subject to inspection by a teacher whom Charlotte, at least, respected.

The sisters differed widely in their attitudes toward these exercises. Emily appears to have written with reluctance and to have resisted Heger's intervention, whereas Charlotte strove to perfect her French and please the 'master' she increasingly admired. Heger gave Gaskell the impression that Emily had the greater genius, but he paid more attention to Charlotte's devoirs, showing her how to choose words effectively and adding observations on technique and style. This disparity may reflect the sisters' different levels of proficiency. Whereas Charlotte had won the French prize at Margaret Wooler's school (see FOREIGN LANGUAGES), Emily knew little French when they arrived and, in Charlotte's words, 'work[ed] like a horse' (Smith *Letters*, 1. 285). Yet despite her limited fluency Emily's devoirs have impressed most critics as more powerfully written than her sister's. Whatever their linguistic limitations, their originality is evident.

In the sisters' first weeks at the pensionnat (they arrived on 15 February 1842), their writing assignments probably focused on grammar exercises and dictations, the standard drills for language acquisition. Charlotte may have done translations as well, but since all but one *notebook from this period are undated, the sequence cannot be traced with certainty. She wrote her first devoir of record, 'L'Ingratitude', on 16 March; it has since disappeared. Her earliest surviving essay is 'Sacrifice of an Indian Widow' ('Sacrifice d'une veuve indienne', 17 April, in BPM). Its narrator, an outraged European, describes the procession that precedes the sacrifice, the widow's refusal to resist the act of suttee, and her death on the lighted pyre.

Charlotte's next two devoirs suggest that Heger was putting his method into practice, in that both correspond to passages in her notebook of dictations (in Bonnell, BPM). 'The Sick Young Girl' ('La Jeune Fille malade', 18 April, in Parrish, Princeton) is similar in subject to the first notebook entry, Alexandre Soumet's sentimental poem 'The Poor Girl' ('La Pauvre Fille'). She probably also drew on André *Chénier's poem 'The Young Captive' ('La Jeune Captive'). In all three texts, the speaker expresses her fear of dying, but only Charlotte's ends optimistically: God restores the girl to health. The fourth dictation in the same notebook is an excerpt from the vicomte de *Chateaubriand that Heger titled 'Evening Prayer on Board a Ship'. Charlotte imitates its title and its description of a radiant sunset in her devoir 'Evening Prayer in a Camp' ('La Prière du soir dans un camp', 26 April). But she sets her scene in an Egyptian desert, and the men who pray are Protestant, not Catholic.

The Protestantism of both sisters became more pronounced in a school and country where the vast majority were Catholics. The pensionnat's promotional circular refers to 'the course of instruction, based on Religion' (Chadwick, p. 190), and the excerpts Heger chose confirm this statement. Charlotte responded with professions of faith that not infrequently defied Catholic tenets, but Heger never commented on her convictions; he focused instead on their expression. In 'The Nest' ('Le Nid', 30 April, in Berg, NYPL), she makes the observation of a bird's eggs an occasion for marvelling at God's handiwork. Heger revised her French extensively, adding a comment on the function of details, and proposed that they analyse *Lamartine's poem 'The Infinite' ('L'Infini'), for its use of detail. Subsequently Charlotte wrote 'The Immensity of God' ('L'Immensité de Dieu'), a devoir whose speaker begins by contemplating the night sky and ends by reflecting on the infinitude of creation. She also refers to the telescope and light rays, evidence of an interest in astronomy that may have developed at the pensionnat.

As Gaskell says, the sisters expressed their nationalism whenever they could. In response to a letter on St Ignatius that Heger read and asked her to imitate, Charlotte wrote a devoir about English missionaries sent by the Church to Africa ('Lettre d'un missionaire, Sierra-Leone, Afrique', now lost). Emily also chose subjects that enabled her to write from her English experience. In her first extant devoir, 'The Cat' ('Le Chat', 15 May, in Berg, NYPL), a fox-hunting landowner becomes an example of human cruelty. Despite errors in French the essay trenchantly defends cats against their detractors. Their 'hypocrisy, cruelty, and ingratitude', she points out, only underscore their likeness to people. National and religious feeling combine in her devoir *'Portrait: King Harold before the Battle of Hastings' (June, in Rylands), as they do in Charlotte's devoir *'Anne Askew' (2 June, in Huntington). The instructions for the latter composition are unknown, but Heger told Gaskell that 'Harold' imitates Victor *Hugo's essay 'On Mirabeau', as does Charlotte's matching devoir, 'Portrait Peter the Hermit' ('Pierre l'Ermite', 23 June, in BL). In fact, Charlotte's essay has a more direct source: a dictation in her notebook from Joseph-François Michaud's account of Peter's role in the Crusaders' capture of Jerusalem.

Several other devoirs exemplify matching responses to a common assignment. In essays titled 'The Siege of Oudenarde' ('Le Siège d'Oudenarde', n.d., in Friends Historical Society, Swarthmore College), each sister recounts an episode from 15th-century Burgundian history in which a general must choose between surrendering to the enemy or letting his captured sons die. The facts in the two accounts are nearly identical and probably follow an outline Heger dictated, but Charlotte accentuates the father's anguish, whereas Emily stresses the patriotism that stems from his belief in liberty. She also observes that the women, 'that class condemned by the laws of society to be a heavy burden in any situation of action and danger, on that occasion cast aside their degrading privileges' to share in the defence of their city. In Charlotte's version the general's wife shows herself worthy of being his mate. Another matching pair consists of party invitations that the invited guest declines to accept. Despite the rigid format they again express the sisters' personalities. Emily, who was taking piano lessons, addressed her 'Letter' (16 July, in BPM) to a music teacher whose reply points out the student's lack of talent. Charlotte addressed hers (21 July, in Rylands) to a clergyman who replies that Duty must conquer Inclination. Two further sets of paired essays are extant: Emily's 'The *Butterfly' ('Le Papillon') (11 August, in Berg, NYPL) and Charlotte's 'The Caterpillar' ('La Chenille', in Heger family), and the pair titled 'The *Palace of Death' ('Le Palais de la Mort') (Charlotte's 16 October, Emily's 18 October, both in BPM).

Emily submitted her remaining three devoirs within a ten-day period. In 'Letter (My dear Mama)' ('Lettre. [Ma chère Maman])', 26 July, in Heger family), a young invalid complains of loneliness and urges her mother to visit. The plea has been read as an expression of Emily's longing for home and maternal affection, but the essay could as plausibly respond to an assignment like the one that produced Charlotte's 'The Sick Young Girl'. Analogously, 'Filial Love' ('L'Amour filial', 5 August, in Bonnell, BPM) could be linked to Charlotte's missing devoir 'Ingratitude'. Emily claims that the biblical commandment 'Honour thy father and thy mother' contains an implicit reproach: the love that children should naturally feel for their parents must be compelled. She attacks those who live in 'moral chaos', violating their parents' devotion, and warns of divine retribution. The last line, 'Let angels and men weep for his fate— he was their brother', connects it to a devoir also dated 5 August, 'Letter from one brother to another' ('Lettre d'un frère à un frère', in Ransom HRC, Texas). In this confession an unnamed correspondent acknowledges the anger that estranged him from 'Edward' and sent him into bitter exile. He admits to having secretly entered his brother's house, observed only by the dog whose recognition he rebuffed. Now repentant, he pleads to be reconciled. Although all three of these devoirs might be read biographically (Branwell had lost his job after charges of negligent supervision), this is the only one with clear connections to the Brontës' early writings and to *Wuthering Heights*. Charlotte and Branwell had both written tales of brothers named Edward and William who fall out (see PERCY, EDWARD and WILLIAM; ASHWORTH, EDWARD and WILLIAM) and when Heathcliff breaks into the Grange to see Catherine, the dog knows that he is not a stranger.

Several of Charlotte's devoirs seem to express veiled personal feeling. In 'The Aim of Life' ('Le But de la vie', 24 August 1842?, in Berg, NYPL), a student 'now past twenty' accuses himself of deception: his teachers applaud his industry, but he knows that he lives in studious retirement because he lacks the qualities to shine in society. Berating himself for yielding to selfishness, he resolves to find the energy to grapple with the world, to use his knowledge for the benefit of others or at least bear up under adversity. The date of this devoir places it within the long vacation, a time when other students and teachers were on holiday, except for a newly arrived English family, the *Wheelwrights, whom the sisters were to teach and look after. The conflict between inclination and duty, expressed here by a narrator with traits like his author's, recurs with far more impact in *Jane Eyre*. A similar conflict, together with a longing to escape the 'flat country' and flee to the mountains, arises in the unfinished draft *'My Dear Jane' ('Ma chère Jane') (undated, in Bonnell, BPM). 'The Death of Napoleon' (31 May, in BPM) also has digressions that appear to bear on life at the pensionnat.

Charlotte wrote the latter two devoirs during her second year in Belgium, a period marked by growing depression. The death of Aunt Elizabeth *Branwell at the end of October had brought a sudden end to the sisters' studies, and though Emily refused to leave Haworth again, Charlotte had accepted the Hegers' invitation to work as a teacher and continue learning French and German. The half-dozen essays from 1843 differ in quality and length from their precursors. Only one, 'The *Fall of the Leaves' ('La Chute des feuilles') (30 March, in Heger family), is written in response to a dictation. Others may have followed Heger's instructions but are far more ambitious in scope and style than anything she wrote the year before. 'The *Death of Moses' ('La Mort de Moïse') (27 July, in Heger family) displays her knowledge of the

Old Testament. *'Athens Saved by Poetry' ('Athènes sauvée par la poësie') (6 Oct., Bonnell, BPM; second version December, Pierpont Morgan) weaves Greek history, myth, and geography into a twenty-page narrative. 'Letter from a Poor Painter to a Great Lord' ('Lettre d'un pauvre peintre à un grand seigneur') (17 October, in Berg, NYPL) features another man in his twenties who has suffered because of his difference from his fellows, this time a painter who believes in his own genius and seeks a patron to launch his career. He recounts his past, emphasizing the transition from a life of inaction to one of struggle, and adds that he has learned his craft successfully. While the devoir is highly romantic in tone, it also endorses the neoclassic principles that Heger believed in: emulation as a means of learning, the necessity of studying technique, and directing art to moral purposes.

No other Belgian essays have survived. Charlotte sent four letters to Heger after her return to Haworth, but when that one-sided correspondence ended she also stopped composing in French. Still, she preserved her memories of devoirs together with tangible proofs of her experience: copybooks, manuscripts, gift books from Heger, and a certificate attesting to her competence. Most significantly, three of her four novels create classroom contexts and episodes in which a student submits devoirs to a mentor. Frances Evans *Henri of *The Professor* writes an essay on King Alfred (ch. 16). Shirley *Keeldar writes 'The First Blue-Stocking', her version of the myth of divine inspiration (*Shirley*, ch. 27). Lucy *Snowe writes 'Human Justice' and an unnamed classical essay (*Villette*, ch. 35). In all cases the devoirs reveal a woman's abilities to a man who values them and loves her.

In sum, as a series of French language compositions the devoirs hold a special place within the Brontë canon, and not just because of their foreignness. Apart from *Wuthering Heights* and her Diary Papers, they are Emily's most significant prose writings. As such they offer fresh perspectives on her convictions and capacities. Charlotte's devoirs provided an incentive to break away from the *Glass Town and Angrian saga and write for an audience beyond her family. They increased her interest in style and technique, serving too as important agents of transition between her earlier and later work. The manuscripts themselves reveal this process of development and document her relations with the teacher whose influence would permeate her fiction.   SL

Barker, pp. 382–92, 413–19.
Chitham *Birth of WH*, ch. 4.
Duthie *Foreign Vision*, ch. 2.
Gaskell *Life*, vol. 1, chs. 11–12.
Lonoff (from which quotations of the devoirs here are taken).

brother-in-law was Dr William Moore Wooler (see WOOLER FAMILY). Margaret *Wooler moved her school to *Heald's House, Dewsbury Moor (west of Dewsbury) in 1838, when Charlotte was a teacher there. In January 1850 Charlotte commented that *Shirley*'s 'notoriety' in Dewsbury was 'almost as good as an emetic' to her (Smith *Letters*, 2. 334).

Dewsbury Moor. See HEALD'S HOUSE.

Diary Papers. *See opposite page*

Dickens, Charles (1812–70), magazine editor, social reformer, and phenomenally popular novelist—the standard against which reviewers measured his contemporaries. His realistic, sympathetic depictions of outcasts and social evils charted a new direction in Victorian fiction and may have influenced Charlotte's transition from her juvenile writing: on the back of *'Farewell to Angria' she noted the oppressive school and child abuse in *Nicholas Nickleby* (1838–9). Intolerant of (*cont. on page 166*)

A LSO known as Birthday Notes, written by Emily and Anne Brontë. These are brief four-yearly records of events in the family, descriptions of everyday parsonage life, progress in the imaginative worlds of *Gondal and Angria (see GLASS TOWN AND ANGRIAN SAGA), and concern about the future. They include the following manuscripts:

24 November 1834, Diary Paper signed by Emily and Anne

MS in BPM, with a tiny sketch in the left margin labelled 'A bit of Lady Julet's hair done by Anne'. The handwriting is Emily's although both girls composed the paper. The informal style and dialogue paint a vivid picture of Charlotte boasting about her apple puddings, Tabitha *Aykroyd (Tabby) urging Anne to 'pilloputate' (peel a potato), Aunt Elizabeth *Branwell asking Anne where her feet are, and Sally Mosley washing. Dinner is to be boiled beef, turnips, potatoes and apple pudding. Abraham *Sunderland is due to come for piano lessons but the girls have not yet practised their B major scale. Emily's imitation of Tabby's dialect is amusing, but the scrawled handwriting and poor spelling makes it hard to credit that this is written by an intelligent 16 year old. The paper contains the sisters' first reference to Gondal and ends by wondering about what they will be doing in 1874 (some 25 years after their deaths). As Revd A. B. *Nicholls noted of the papers, 'They are sad reading, poor girls!' (*The Brontës: Life and Letters* (1908), 1. 215).

26 June 1837, Diary Paper signed by Emily and Anne

MS in BPM (Bonnell). Despite the joint signature, the note was written by Emily on the evening of Branwell's twentieth birthday and includes a sketch by her of the two sisters sitting at the table composing their Diary Paper. Books, papers, and 'The Tin Box' in which the papers are kept are labelled in the sketch. While the younger sisters are writing in the drawing room, Branwell is reading *Bulwer-Lytton's novel *Eugene Aram* to Charlotte, who is sewing. A coronation is in preparation in Gondal (see GONDAL SAGA), coinciding with Queen *Victoria's accession to the throne. Charlotte and Branwell's characters the Dukes of *Northangerland and *Zamorna are mentioned, confirming that the four children still share information about their 'plays'.

30 July 1841, Diary Paper signed by Emily

MS unavailable; formerly in the *Law Collection; facsimile in Shorter *Circle*. The paper has two thumbnail sketches on either side of the heading, illustrating Emily alone in the dining room, writing at her 'desk-box' on the table and standing contemplating the 'bleak look-out' at the window. She notes that her aunt has just been reading *Blackwood's Edinburgh Magazine* to Mr Brontë and describes where everyone, including the *pets, is situated. Charlotte, Branwell, and Anne are away from home, yet it is clear that there has been correspondence about the scheme for 'a school of our own', a preferable alternative to 'dragging on in our present condition'. Emily notes the importance of 'cash in hand' that such a venture will provide. She refers only briefly to Gondal, noting that the princes and princesses are at the *Palace of

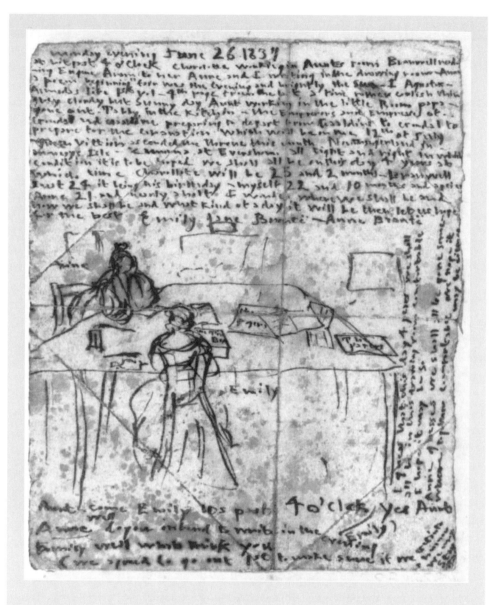

Emily Brontë's Diary Paper, 1837.

Instruction and that she has made little progress with her 'many books on hand'. She has 'just made a new regularity paper!' and means 'to do great things'.

30 July 1841, Diary Paper signed by Anne

MS unavailable; formerly in the Law Collection. This paper was written at *Scarborough, where Anne is 'engaged in writing the fourth volume of Solala Vernon's Life'. She notes that she dislikes and wishes to change her situation as governess with the *Robinson family of Thorp Green. She too places hope in 'setting up a school of our own' but notes how few of the events she records were foreseen by the sisters in their previous paper of July 1837. Providence and the passing of time occupy her thoughts.

30 July 1845, Diary Paper signed by Emily

MS owned by William Self; facsimile of part in Shorter *Circle*. This paper was actually written on 31 July, the day after Emily's birthday, as the following paper by Anne makes clear. It includes a sketch of Emily writing with her 'desk-box' on her lap in her bedroom, with the animals Keeper, Flossy, and the cat. She notes the abandonment of the 'school-scheme' and her return from *Brussels because of her aunt's death but records nothing about this seminal event in her life. Her trip with Anne to York and their impersonation of Gondal characters is clearly more significant at this time. Again, it is Emily who notes the financial situation and, since her aunt's small legacy to the sisters, the fact that they have 'cash enough for our present wants with a prospect of accumolation [sic]' (Emily took charge of investing the money in railway shares). Mr Brontë's deteriorating eyesight, a hope for Branwell's improvement, and the situation with the pets are noted. In particular, Emily notes her own self-discipline and resignation: 'not as idle as formerly . . . having learnt to make the most of the present and hope for the future with less fidgetness that I cannot do all I wish'. She wishes that the rest of her family could be as content and comfortable as she is. Her reference to Tabby asking her 'as formerly to—"pilloputate"', suggests that she has just reread the first Diary Paper of 1834.

31 July 1845, Diary Paper signed by Anne

MS owned by William Self. Anne has just 'escaped' from *Thorp Green Hall, after what she describes as 'some very unpleasant and undreamt of experience of human nature', presumably owing to the behaviour of Branwell and Mrs Lydia *Robinson. Anne's phrase hoping that Branwell 'will be better and do better' echoes Emily's allusion to him above, suggesting either that this was a phrase often used in reference to Branwell or that they had just discussed his situation. Despite the dismal wet evening, Anne gives a vivid picture of domestic life, with Charlotte sewing in the dining room, Emily ironing upstairs, Mr Brontë in the parlour, Tabby and Martha the servants in the kitchen, and she herself in the rocking chair in front of the dining-room fire with her feet on the fender. By the end of the Diary Paper, Emily has joined Anne downstairs in the dining room and is writing her own paper of the same date. Anne also refers to the aborted school scheme, to Charlotte's wish to go to *Paris, and to a grey silk frock she is making. Anne seems no longer so enthusiastic about the Gondal 'play' and notes that the 'Gondal chronicles' begun three and a half years ago have not been finished. Her mood is unusually despondent in this paper and she believes she could not be 'flatter or older in mind' than she is now.

Although the earliest surviving Diary Paper is dated 24 November 1834, the practice of reviewing yearly events and wondering about the future may have begun earlier. Emily and Anne were 16 and 14 respectively when this first extant paper was written and they continued the practice until 1845, when they were in their twenties. The agreement was that they should open the papers every four years, usually on Emily's birthday, take stock of their situation in relation to the earlier paper, and write another to be locked away in the tin box for another four years, rather like a time capsule though in the 1845 papers they plan to open them in 1848. The two girls were clearly concerned about the future yet equally aware of their inability to divine it. Anne underscores this in her echo from Byron: 'How little know we what we are | How less what we may be!' (Smith *Letters*, 1. 265 n.). What is remarkable is their general buoyancy and good faith in 'Providence'.

The papers and their accompanying illustrations are valuable for their biographical evidence, in particular for the way the imaginative world of Gondal formed an integral part of their everyday experience. A much-quoted passage demonstrates this point: 'papa opened the parlour Door and gave Branwell a Letter saying here Branwell read this and show it to your Aunt and Charlotte—The Gondals are discovering the interior of Gaaldine Sally mosley is washing in the back-Kitchin' (24 Nov. 1834). It is through the Diary Papers that we learn for the first time about Gondal and hear that Gondal prose manuscripts definitely existed. The papers reveal, too, the nature of the Gondal relationship between the sisters. The two girls act out the imaginary events and read each other their prose manuscripts, but although Anne knows that Emily is writing poetry she is kept ignorant of its content (31 July 1845 Diary Paper).

Family activities, trips away from home, and what everyone is reading are carefully documented. The only public events recorded are Robert Peel's invitation to stand as MP for Leeds (1843) and the accession of 'Queen Vittiora' to the throne (June 1837), an event of particular significance to Emily. The chief preoccupation is with the organization of their own lives, with self-discipline, and with writing. Both are concerned about their pets. For Emily, the coming and going of Brontë pets are as important to her as the movements of servants. The departure and return of Tabby and Martha are mentioned in the same breath as those of Flossy, Tiger, Nero, and the geese (Diary Paper of 30 July 1845).

When Clement King *Shorter acquired the Diary Papers of 1841 and 1845 from Mr Nicholls, he described the tin box in which they were kept as 'about two inches long' and noted that the papers were 'neatly folded to the size of a sixpence' (Shorter *Circle*, p. 146).

Alexander & Sellars, pp. 378, 383, 392, 398 (illustrations).
Ratchford, *Gondal's Queen* (1955), app. 2 (complete text of all Diary Papers).
Smith *Letters*, 1. 262–5, 407–11 (last four Diary Papers).

rebellious heroines, Dickens never read *Jane Eyre*; Charlotte criticized Esther Summerson as a caricature (to George Smith, 11 Mar. 1852, in Wise & Symington, 3. 322). It remains uncertain whether the two met in London (see Smith *Letters*, 2. 642 n. 2). Soon after Charlotte died, Dickens wrote to Frank Smedley on 5 May 1855, refusing to publish a biographical essay on her in *Household Words* (Smith *Letters*, 1. 27 n. 1), regarding it as an invasion of her privacy.   BT

Kaplan, Fred, *Charles Dickens: A Biography* (1988).

dictations (*dictées*). Exercises done by Charlotte Brontë and probably by Emily at the Pensionnat *Heger in Brussels. In this still common form of language instruction, the teacher reads a passage aloud to students who transcribe it as accurately as they can. Charlotte preserved a *notebook of her dictations that includes six poems and fourteen prose selections, one of the latter in two versions (in Bonnell, BPM). Two other notebooks also include dictations (in Brotherton, and Ransom HRC, Texas). These exercises served several purposes: they trained the students to write French correctly, provided a basis for M. Constantin Heger's lectures, and sometimes became models that the students imitated or analysed in essays of their own. At least five of Charlotte's *devoirs are linked to passages that she transcribed, and according to Elizabeth *Gaskell, Emily's *'Portrait: King Harold before the Battle of Hastings' also stems from the one on Mirabeau.

Heger took occasional liberties in preparing dictations for his students, increasing their dramatic effects or censoring what he judged improper. Many of his choices bear out the school's claim that its course of instruction was 'based on religion'. But he also gave extracts from classic authors, for example Bossuet and Buffon, as well as from current Romantic writers: vicomte de *Chateaubriand, Nodier, *Lamartine, and *Hugo. These excerpts and accompanying lectures expanded Charlotte's knowledge of French literature and became a source for Caroline Helstone's and Shirley Keeldar's lessons in *Shirley*.　　　SL

Alexander, Christine, *A Bibliography of the Manuscripts of Charlotte Brontë* (1982), pp. 181–2, 185.

Duthie *Foreign Vision*, pp. 231–2.

Lonoff, pp. vii–ix, lvi–lvii.

Dimdims throne, a chain of mountains near the Lake of the Genii, presumably part of the *Jibbel Kumri, in the early *Glass Town and Angrian saga.

Disraeli, Benjamin (1804–81), novelist and politician (prime minister 1868 and 1874–80). *Sybil: or, the Two Nations* (1845) shares concerns with *Shirley* and other 'condition-of-England' novels (see NOVEL IN THE MID-19TH CENTURY), and reviewers compared Charlotte Brontë's works with Disraeli's. His trilogy of *Coningsby* (1844), *Sybil*, and *Tancred* (1847), articulated a paternalistic ideal of a noble, naturally appointed aristocracy leading the working classes, and ideas in *Sybil* are evoked in *The Professor* (ch. 24). Whereas Charlotte sympathized with Haworth's opposition to the Corn Laws (the community in 1840 petitioned Parliament for repeal, and in 1846–7 agitated anew), Disraeli savagely opposed 1845 efforts to repeal the tariff. In a letter to Ellen Nussey of 23 March 1852 (Wise & Symington, 3. 325), Charlotte invoked Disraeli to express her cynicism about 'all ministries and all oppositions. . . . Confound them all.'　　　BT

Blake, Robert, *Disraeli* (1998).

Vincent, John Russell, *Disraeli* (1990).

Dissent is a general term for Christian denominations separate from the *Church of England and its sister churches abroad. Most repudiate any link between church and state, and regard the Bible as the supreme authority. Baptists insist on adult believers' baptism. General Baptists, founded in the 17th century, repudiate *Calvinism. Particular Baptists, founded *c*.1633 as an offshoot of Independent churches, are Calvinist. Both sects emphasize educational and mission work, and consider that individual churches should be self-governing. In this they differ from Wesleyan *Methodists, whose system of circuits (groups of churches in the same area) forms part of a network organized and controlled by the Methodist Conference. In Haworth the first West Lane General Baptist chapel was erected in 1752 by voluntary contributions, the principal subscribers including the mill owning Greenwoods of Bridge House; the enlargement in 1775 was assisted by their relative, William Greenwood of Oxenhope, and the Baptist tradition continued in the Greenwood family. James (1793–1857) and William (1770–1858) were also Anglican Church trustees, and therefore could resist or approve the nomination of Revd Patrick Brontë as the incumbent. In later years he was friendly with William, but less so with James, who helped to found the Hall Green Particular Baptist chapel (completed 1825), and whose daughter married its first minister, Revd Moses Saunders. The West Lane pastor from 1785 to *c*.1830 was Revd Miles Oddy, with whom Mr Brontë had a good relationship; but his successor, Revd John Winterbotham (ordained September 1831), vociferously opposed Anglican privileges. In December 1833 Independents and Baptists held meetings in Bradford, supporting a proposal 'to remove the bishops from the House of Lords, abolish tithes and other Church dues and open the universities to non-Anglicans (Barker, p. 217). Mr Brontë's subsequent letters to the *Leeds Intelligencer* provoked sarcastic replies from Mr Winterbotham, to which Mr Brontë responded scornfully that access to university would be useless to Winterbotham, who lacked Greek and Latin. Thereafter, in Haworth, with its large Dissenting population, there were 'annual battles' over church rates leading to a crisis in 1836, when powerful opposition to the rates, led by James Greenwood, made Mr Brontë fear there was a real danger of disestablishment of the Church of England. He tried to prevent the appointment of a Whig (and therefore pro-Dissent) magistrate, and succeeded in having the Anglican (and Tory) Joseph Greenwood appointed. The political alignment roughly reflects a class distinction: prosperous Dissenters, aspiring to be considered gentry, not seldom became Anglicans. When in *Shirley*

Mr Helstone sees the 'Dissenting and Methodist schools, the Baptists, Independents, and Wesleyans, joined in unholy alliance' to obstruct the Church school procession, Shirley significantly comments 'Bad manners!', and the well-organized ranks of the Establishment press forward to alarm the 'enemy', led by a 'large greasy' tradesman.

Independents and Presbyterians, sometimes regarded as 'Old Dissent', since they were long-established Puritan-inspired groups, were not very familiar to the younger Brontës, though Mr Brontë must have known many Presbyterians in his youth. All his family would, however, know of their sturdy faith, endurance, and dogmatism through reading Sir Walter *Scott's novels, especially *Old Mortality* and *The Heart of Midlothian*. Like the *Moravians, Presbyterians were not prime targets of the Brontës' ridicule.

divorce laws in the early 19th century.

Before 1857 divorce was extremely rare. Ecclesiastical courts granted divorce for adultery, extreme cruelty, and desertion, but prohibited remarriage for either spouse. Secular divorce, which allowed remarriage, required a bill in the House of Lords and, costing the petitioner £600–700, was limited to the wealthy. Because wives' property became their husbands' upon marriage, men had greater access to divorce, and divorce statutes institutionalized a sexual double standard: men could divorce wives for adultery, but even after the 1857 Matrimonial Causes Act, a wife had to prove additional charges against her husband such as bigamy, extreme cruelty, or incest. Between 1800 and 1857, Parliament granted about ten divorces annually; only three were ever obtained by women.

Until 1857 a divorced or separated woman had virtually no economic rights. She could not inherit or bequeath property, and her husband (even a deserter) could claim her earnings. A husband's property rights extended to his wife's body (enforceable by writ of habeas corpus) and to his children. A father could take his children from their mother and dispose of them as he wished. Though married women continued to have no legal control over their children, from 1839 divorced or separated women—who had not been named adulterous—could request custody of children under the age of 7 (the court might still rule otherwise). Previously, regardless of his character or circumstances, a father automatically took custody of children.

The Brontës' novels foreground divorce laws' inequities. Because insanity did not constitute grounds for divorce, *Jane Eyre*'s Edward *Rochester is permanently shackled to Bertha *Rochester. In *Tenant* Helen *Huntingdon violates the law by locking her bedroom door against her husband, then fleeing his estate with her son. Without legal claim to the child or to any property, personal effects, or earnings, she can support herself and retain her son only by concealing her identity. In *Wuthering Heights* neither Isabella *Linton nor Catherine *Linton can divorce their husbands despite *Heathcliff's physical and psychological abuse, and through a husband's rights to his wife's property Heathcliff eventually secures ownership of *Thrushcross Grange.　　　　BT

Bodichon, Barbara Leigh Smith, *A Brief Summary, in Plain Language, of the Most Important Laws Concerning Women* (1854).

Horstman, Allen, *Victorian Divorce* (1985).

Norton, Caroline, *Caroline Norton's Defence: English Laws for Women in the Nineteenth Century* (1854).

Dixon, Mary (1809–97), Mary *Taylor's cousin, whom Charlotte Brontë met at the *Dixon family home in Brussels after Martha Taylor's death in October 1842. In early 1843 Charlotte enjoyed Mary Dixon's company, finding her elegant, ladylike, accomplished, and kind, and submitting resignedly to Mary's offer to draw a portrait of her 'unfortunate head'. Mary's health was delicate, and Charlotte missed her when she left Brussels in summer 1843 to take hydropathic treatment in Germany and in Ilkley, Yorks. Mary later kept house for her brothers in Birmingham until they married, and probably lived with them or other relatives thereafter.

Dixon family. Charlotte Brontë met several members of this family, including Mary *Dixon, whose father, Abraham Dixon sen. (1779–1850), was a foreign commission agent in Leeds, following the collapse of the family bank in Birmingham in 1825, until c.1842. He then became an 'inventor' at 11 rue de la Régence, Brussels, endeavouring to sell patent processes and gadgets to wool merchants and others. He had married in 1808 Laetitia (1780–1842), sister of Joshua *Taylor of Gomersal. His eldest son, Joshua (?1810–85), attended Leeds Grammar School, worked in the USA for several years, and, dying unmarried at Winslade, Exeter, bequeathed pictures, marble statues, and other artefacts to Bethnal Green Museum, London. His surviving early letters to his brothers give the impression that the Dixons were a united and affectionate family. Abraham or Abram Dixon jun. (1815–1907) worked for Rabone's, precision tool manufacturers and export merchants, in Birmingham from c.1838, and married Margaret, daughter of Richard Rathbone of Liverpool, in June 1847. They lived until after 1851 at Hay Hall, Yardley, Birmingham—a timbered 15th-century hall, partly rebuilt in brick in 1538. Charlotte declined their invitation to stay there for Christmas 1849. They later moved to Cherkeley Court, Leatherhead, Surrey. William Taylor Dixon (1818–84) graduated BA from St Catharine's College, Cambridge, 1846, MA 1850, and was ordained priest in 1847. He was headmaster and chaplain of the Training School, Leeds, 1848–50, and vicar of Buslingthorpe, Yorks., 1850–60, before moving to Somerset. Charlotte probably met him in Brussels, as she did George Dixon (1820–98) who frequently travelled to the Continent for Rabone's. He and his brother Thomas (1821–65) carried letters to England for her. Thomas learnt German in Brussels, became an engineer, and, with Joseph *Taylor, visited Charlotte in Haworth.

Dobell, Sydney Thompson (1824–74), poet and critic, famous for his dramatic poem *The Roman* (Apr. 1850), inspired by sympathy with oppressed nationalities, but less successful with *Balder* (1854), written in the frenetic style pilloried by W. E. Aytoun as 'Spasmodic'. He and his wife Emily, née Fordham, lived at Coxhorne House near Cheltenham, in idyllic surroundings in the Cotswolds. Charlotte Brontë was grateful for his perceptive critique of *Wuthering Heights* (*Palladium*, Sept. 1850), and sent him her 1850 edition of her sisters' works, but in May 1851 she refused his invitation to accompany him and his wife to Switzerland.

dogs in the Glass Town and Angrian saga: Roland, Roswal, Angria, Calabar, Condor, Sirius, Moloch, and Apollyon. Roland is Mary *Percy's Newfoundland guard dog, owned by her before her marriage and first described by Branwell Brontë in *The *Politics of Verdopolis*; he is named after the most famous of Charlemagne's paladins, the flower of French chivalry and subject of romance. The other dogs belong to the Duke of *Zamorna and appear to represent his association with Sir Walter *Scott and with Lord *Byron, both of whom had large dogs. Their names illustrate the eclectic nature of the Brontës' knowledge: Roswal is Zamorna's favourite stag-hound; Angria and Calabar are named after Angrian provinces (see ANGRIA, PROVINCE OF; CALABAR, PROVINCE OF); Condor suggests the huge South American vulture of that name; Sirius, the Dog-Star; Moloch, an Ammonite deity worshipped with human sacrifice and fire (from the *Bible and *Milton's *Paradise Lost*); and Apollyon is the Greek name of the king of hell (in Revelation, used especially by *Bunyan in *The Pilgrim's Progress*). Rochester's dog, Pilot, in *Jane Eyre*, was also a Newfoundland dog, another link with Byron's similar dogs, Boatswain and Lyon. In Italy, according to Shelley, Byron had 'eight enormous dogs' (Elizabeth Longford, *Byron* (1976), 138). Sir Walter Scott had a favourite deerhound, which Charlotte says is a breed used for

hunting in Cape Province, South Africa (Alexander *EEW*, 2(2). 45), a statement not yet verified, since she cannot be referring to the Cape Hunting Dog, a wild hyena-like animal that hunts in packs. See PETS OWNED BY THE BRONTËS; ANIMALS AND BIRDS IN THE WORKS OF THE BRONTËS.

Dongola, capital city of the Angrian province of *Etrei on the east bank of the River Etrei. Its garrison protects the southern border of Angria but the town suffers a ferocious massacre by the *Ashantees. The Brontës' copy of Goldsmith's *Grammar of General Geography* cites Dongola as 'a province of Nubia'; the name is still preserved there as the town of Dongola in southern Sudan. See also AFRICA.

Donne, Revd Joseph, curate to Revd Dr Thomas *Boultby, Rector of *Whinbury, in *Shirley*. 'All about him was pragmatical and self-complacent, from his turned-up nose and elevated chin to his clerical black gaiters, his somewhat short, strapless trousers, and his square-toed shoes' (p. 331). One of the three 'youthful Levites' mocked by the narrator in the novel's opening chapter, Donne is a snob, a 'lisping cockney' (p. 324) who looks down on the natives of Yorkshire and complains of 'the want of high society' (p. 129), despite his own vulgarity. He is put to flight by Shirley *Keeldar's dog *Tartar, then expelled from her house when he insults Yorkshire people in her presence. The narrator gives him credit at the end of the novel for becoming 'an exemplary domestic character, and a truly active parish-priest, . . . His little school, his little church, his little parsonage, all owed their erection to him' (p. 723). Donne's original was Joseph Brett Grant (d. 1879), who served as Revd Patrick Brontë's curate in Haworth in 1844–5 before becoming the incumbent of the neighbouring parish of Oxenhope, where he remained until the end of his life. He was appointed headmaster of the Free Grammar School near Oxenhope in 1844, and thanks to his persistence as a fund-raiser, helped to secure enough money to build a church (St Mary the Virgin, consecrated in 1849). Speaking of the favourable reception given *Shirley* in Yorkshire, Charlotte Brontë wrote to W. S. Williams on 3 April 1850 that even the curates 'shew no resentment. . . . Mr. Donne was—at first, a little disturbed; for a week or two he fidgetted about the neighbourhood in some disquietude—but he is now soothed down, only yesterday I had the pleasure of making him a comfortable cup of tea and seeing him sip it with revived complacency' (Smith *Letters*, 2. 376). HR

Dooley, Lucile, author of 'Psychoanalysis of Charlotte Brontë, as a Type of the Woman of

Dorn, Captain C.

Genius', *American Journal of Psychology*, 31 (July 1920), 221–72. Dooley ascribed Charlotte's death to neurosis over marriage and motherhood; but Charlotte's letters written from the time of her engagement to Revd A. B. *Nicholls until her death show at first a level-headed awareness of his limitations, and eventually a spontaneous happiness in and gratitude for his affection, with no sign of neurosis. Dooley also regarded the occasional sexual metaphors in Charlotte's early writing as the ignorant and compulsive expression of a neurotic unconsciousness. See PSYCHOANALYTIC APPROACHES.

Dorn, Captain C. See CAREY, CAPTAIN LUCIUS.

Douglas, M, lover of E. R. *Gleneden and possibly the same man 'Douglas' who became a traitor and then, at the instigation of another lover *Angelica, murderer of A.G.A., in the *Gondal saga.

Douro, Marquis of. See ZAMORNA, DUKE OF.

Douro, River, and province, in the *Glass Town and Angrian saga. Named after the Duke of *Zamorna's early title of Marquis of Douro, the river flows through the Angrian province (130 by 100 miles) of the same name, governed by Lord *Jordan. The capital city, with a population of 71,000, is also called Douro.

Douro Villa, the small Grecian palace of the Marquis of Douro (Duke of Zamorna) and Marian *Hume in the early *Glass Town and Angrian saga, set in a picturesque landscape in the Vale of Verdopolis; Marian's retreat and final home.

'dreadful darkness closes in, A', Anne Brontë's last poem (7 and 28 Jan. 1849). Written after Dr Teale had diagnosed an advanced stage of pulmonary tuberculosis, the poem moves from her shocking and bewildering realization that she is mortally ill to a review of what she had hoped for in life, and a prayer that God will make her suffering a means of serving him more wisely. Anne's torturing mental pain makes a powerful impact, and the poem is moving in its honesty, humility, and, ultimately, spiritual fortitude, when the self is subsumed in Christian devotion. The urgent pressure of Anne's appeal is more evident in the very lightly punctuated manuscript than in the printed text. Metrically, inversions of the usual iambic foot coincide with intense words conveying Anne's agony ('Crushed with sorrow, worn with pain'). The many biblical allusions, especially Revelation 2: 10 ('be thou faithful unto death, and I will give thee a crown of life'), add to the poem's solemn resonance.

Chitham *ABP*, p. 163.

Drinkwater, John (1882–1937), playwright, poet, and critic, one of the first to give (qualified) acknowledgement of Branwell Brontë's talents. He was manager of the Birmingham Repertory Company (from 1909) and is chiefly known for his historical plays, such as *Abraham Lincoln* (1918). At one time he owned the manuscript of Branwell's translation of 'The Odes of Horace' (27 June 1840; now in the Brotherton), which he had privately printed in 1923, at the Pelican Press, with an influential introduction in which he makes a careful study of Branwell's work and judges his translations of Horace to be Branwell's best achievement as a poet: 'they also have a great many passages of clear lyrical beauty, and they have something of the style that comes from a spiritual understanding, as apart from merely formal knowledge, of great models'. Drinkwater also owned the manuscript of Branwell's dramatic poem 'Caractacus' (26 June 1830; Brotherton) (see Neufeldt *BBP*, pp. 48–62; Alexander & Sellars, pp. 296–7).

> Drinkwater, J. (ed.), *The Odes of Quintus Horatius Flaccus, book 1*, trans. Branwell Brontë (1923); repr. in *The Miscellaneous and Unpublished Writings of Charlotte and Patrick Branwell Brontë*, vol. 2 (1938); Shakespeare Head Brontë).
> Neufeldt *BBP*, app. A.

drugs in the early 19th century. See HEALTH OF THE BRONTËS.

Drumballyroney, the parish in County Down, Northern Ireland, in which Revd Patrick Brontë was born. It was mainly arable land, with the 'frontier declivities' of the Mourne mountains to the south-east, and was a vicarage, with a Protestant church. The parish formed part of the benefice of Drumgooland. In the two parishes there were in 1834 1,787 churchmen (Anglicans); 9,369 Presbyterians; and 8,191 Catholics. Dr William *Wright alleged that Mr Brontë's birthplace was a small thatched farm cottage in Emdale (or Emdel), north-west of Rathfriland. The Drumballyroney registers for 1779–91 show that his brother William was born in Ballyroney, and the next three brothers and two sisters in nearby Lisnacreevy.

Dryden, John (1631–1700), poet and dramatist. The Brontës' copy of Dryden's translation of *The Works of Virgil* (1824; BPM bb 64) includes pencilled lists of Angrian names, Charlotte's signature after book 10, and drawings by Branwell, whose later translations from Horace show his absorption of Virgilian vocabulary. Charlotte's knowledge of the *Aeneid* may derive from this volume, and in *Wuthering Heights* the fir-branch transformed into a bleeding limb may recall the 'bleeding branch' in *Aeneid* 3. 34–44. Rochester refers obliquely to Dryden's play *All for Love, or The*

World Well Lost in *Jane Eyre* (ch. 24), and in *Tenant* (ch. 21) Mr Arthur Huntingdon declares the 'world well lost' for love.

Dubois, Victoire, one of Charlotte Brontë's pupils at the Pensionnat *Heger. Charlotte wrote to her on 18 May 1844 (Smith *Letters*, 1. 346–7) after receiving letters from pupils of the first class there. In response to Victoire's loyal and affectionate letter, Charlotte promised to think of and love her former pupils, and to visit Victoire and 'Clémence' if she ever returned to Brussels.

Dugdale, Crawshaw (b. *c*.1838), medical assistant to Dr Amos *Ingham. He was not a doctor, and did not sign Charlotte's death certificate (as suggested in Gerin *CB*, p. 562, and Lock & Dixon, p. 474), but he may sometimes have attended her during her last illness in February–March 1855.

Dundee, Sir John (George) Martin, in the *Glass Town and Angrian saga. Dundee is Glass Town's best landscape painter, especially in the sublime, hence the later addition to his name reflecting his association with John *Martin. Dundee's paintings, including the 'Spirit of Cawdor', are reviewed in the *'Young Men's Magazine', and he has published a volume of the scenery of the Glass Town countries in five quartos. Together with Frederick *De Lisle, the portrait painter, he is one of the Duke of Zamorna's artistic coterie.

Dury family. Revd Theodore Dury (1788–1850), evangelical rector of *Keighley 1814–40, friend of Wilberforce and also of Revd Patrick Brontë, was born in Hadley, Middlesex, 2nd son of Lieutenant-Colonel Alexander Dury. After Harrow he matriculated at Pembroke College Cambridge 1807, and graduated BA 1811, MA 1830. Ordained deacon in 1812, he became a curate at Totteridge, Middlesex, until in 1814 his friend and schoolfellow the sixth Duke of Devonshire presented him to the rectory of Keighley. His first wife, Caroline Bourchier, whom he married in 1815, died in 1820, leaving him with a son and a daughter Caroline, who was briefly Revd William *Weightman's 'object of Devotion' in June 1840, and the recipient of 'most passionate' verses (Smith *Letters*, 1. 222). In February 1823 rumour reported that Dury's sister Isabella had quarrelled with him about 'poor Mr Bronte'—a rumour she dismissed as ridiculous and unfounded: 'I never should be so very silly as to have the most distant idea of marrying anybody who had not some fortune, and six children into the bargain' (Barker, p. 113). In 1822 Dury married Anne Greenwood (1795–1881, sister of Mrs Sarah *Sidgwick née Greenwood), by whom he had five sons and two daughters. Anne Dury perhaps recommended Charlotte Brontë to apply for the governess post at *Stonegappe. A generous man with strong educational ideals, Dury was a 'guiding spirit' of the *Keighley Mechanics' Institute, gave liberal treats to Keighley Sunday school children, and preached at Haworth on behalf of the Sunday school there. He was a friend of Revd W. Carus *Wilson, and by 1827 he and his wife, sister, and father were all either donors or subscribers to *Cowan Bridge school, of which he was a trustee. In 1833 he was appointed an executor of Elizabeth *Branwell's will, though he renounced the executorship on leaving Keighley for West Mill, Herts.

Keighley Past and Present (1858; rev. 1879).

Earnshaw, Catherine, daughter of Mr *Earnshaw of *Wuthering Heights. Her name and childhood diary entry of an escapade on the moors with *Heathcliff precipitate Lockwood's second nightmare in which she appears as a ghostly 'waif'. She and the 'gipsy-brat' Heathcliff form an inseparable bond in childhood that survives even her marriage to the more civilized Edgar Linton. She believes it would degrade her to marry the uneducated Heathcliff, yet realizes she is violating her own nature by marrying Linton. The violence she does to her own soul weakens her otherwise hardy and wilful nature and she suffers mental delirium. She is nursed tenderly by her husband but their peaceful happiness is destroyed by the surprise return of Heathcliff. His intrusion during the final stages of Catherine's pregnancy involves a meeting of intense ecstasy and recrimination, which precipitates her death in childbirth. Her daughter Catherine Linton survives and the mother is buried in Gimmerton churchyard, with her husband and Heathcliff later being buried on either side of her. True to her threat never to rest till Heathcliff joins her, she haunts him until his death 25 years later, and country-people believe both their ghosts frequent the moors on wild nights.

Earnshaw, Frances. Secretly married to Hindley *Earnshaw, she arrives with him to live at *Wuthering Heights after his father's death. She is thin, bright-eyed, and excitable. They both deny her consumptive symptoms but she dies soon after the birth of her son Hareton, leaving her devoted husband devastated.

Earnshaw, Hareton, son of Hindley and Frances Earnshaw; heir to *Wuthering Heights, whose inheritance is usurped by *Heathcliff. The name of his forebear, 'Hareton Earnshaw', is carved over the door of Wuthering Heights. Despite his father's love, Hareton is in constant danger from Hindley's intemperate behaviour, fuelled by Heathcliff as part of his plans for revenge. Heathcliff also encourages the degradation of Hareton (a similar situation occurred at *Law Hill, Halifax), developing his brutality and love of cruelty, reducing him as low as Heathcliff himself once was. Ironically, Heathcliff cannot stamp out Hareton's innate good nature: Hareton feels affection for his oppressor and is the only character to mourn Heathcliff's death. Both Hareton and his cousin Catherine resemble Catherine Earnshaw, especially in their eyes, so that in the end Heathcliff cannot bear to look at them. His cousin's contempt for his ignorance inspires Hareton's efforts to improve himself, though they are initially checked by her further scorn. Their reconciliation through Catherine's encouragement of Hareton's reading and their creation of a flower garden at the Heights prepare the way for their expected marriage and move to Thrushcross Grange on New Year's Day.

Earnshaw, Hindley, brother of Catherine *Earnshaw and son of Mr *Earnshaw of *Wuthering Heights. He is like a foster-brother to Ellen *Dean, having been nursed by her mother, and regards *Heathcliff as an interloper and usurper of his father's affection, bullying him mercilessly as a child and degrading him after Mr Earnshaw's death. Mr Earnshaw had sent Hindley to college and he returns for his father's funeral with a young wife Frances *Earnshaw, who dies of consumption after giving birth to a son Hareton *Earnshaw. His grief for his wife's death is as violent and destructive as the passions of Heathcliff and Catherine: 'For himself, he grew desperate; his sorrow was of that kind that will not lament; he neither wept nor prayed—he cursed and defied—execrated God and man, and gave himself up to reckless dissipation' (*Wuthering Heights*, ch. 8). After three years' absence, Heathcliff exacts his revenge on Hindley, encouraging his drinking and gaining his property through gambling debts. Joseph suspects Heathcliff of hastening Hindley's early death at the age of 27.

Earnshaw, Mr, the owner of *Wuthering Heights and kind but severe father of Hindley and Catherine. His return from business in Liverpool with the orphan waif he calls Heathcliff and his partiality for the boy begin the decline in his family's fortunes.

Easton, a tiny hamlet 2 miles inland from *Bridlington, situated where the valley of the Gypsey Race levels out towards the coastal plain. Charlotte recalled her stay there with Ellen Nussey in September 1839 in the hospitable home of John and Sophia *Hudson, and their walks to nearby Harlequin or Hallow Kiln Wood and picturesque Boynton as a 'green spot' in her life, looked back on with real pleasure. She and Ellen stayed there again for a week, less happily, in June 1849 after Anne's death in Scarborough. Charlotte's watercolour of Easton farmhouse is reproduced in Gérin *CB*, opposite p. 156.

Ebenezer Chapel, in Verdopolis, under the care of Mr *Bromley, in the *Glass Town and Angrian saga. The chapel is attended by Louisa Dance (see VERNON, LOUISA) and the Duke of *Northangerland, in his Methodist guise as Brother Ashworth. Scenes at the chapel are Charlotte Brontë's earliest satires on *Methodism.

Eden-Cottage, in the *Glass Town and Angrian saga, 4 miles from *Fidena in the north of the Verdopolitan Federation, where Louisa *Vernon first held court and entertained Mr Percy the Drover who had given her the cottage. Their daughter Caroline *Vernon is raised there and sees it not as 'Eden' but as 'Siberia', a place of exile 300 miles from Verdopolis.

Edinburgh. George *Smith persuaded Charlotte Brontë to meet him, his sister Eliza, and brother Alick in Edinburgh for a brief stay from 3 to 6 July 1850. The visit gave her intense pleasure, heightened by her enthusiasm for the works of Sir Walter *Scott, *Burns, *Campbell, and the *Blackwood's Magazine writers, and by the expert knowledge of a guide. She was exhilarated by her ascent of Arthur's Seat, and the view from the summit. Scott's 'romantic town' seemed to her bright, clear, and vital—a lyric compared with the prose of London—and she was moved by the Scott monument, completed in 1844.

editing history of the juvenilia. See JUVENILIA OF THE BRONTËS: EDITING HISTORY.

editing history of mature novels (late reprints of minor textual significance are excluded).

Anne Brontë: (1) *Agnes Grey. A Novel*

1847 (Dec.) *Agnes Grey. A Novel*, by Acton Bell; 1st English edn., published and printed by T. C. *Newby as vol. 3 of three, following *Wuthering Heights* in vols. 1 and 2. Notorious for its careless spelling and punctuation, and garbled phrases. The Parrish collection in Princeton University library has a list of corrections in Anne's hand.

1850 (Jan.) *Agnes Grey. An Autobiography.* By the authors of 'Jane Eyre', 'Shirley', 'The Tenant of Wildfell Hall', etc. [*sic*]. 1st American edn., 1 vol., published by T. B. Peterson, Philadelphia. Based on 1st English edn.
(Dec.) *Agnes Grey* by . . . Acton Bell; with *Wuthering Heights* in 'A New Edition revised, with a biographical notice of the authors, a selection from their literary

remains, and a preface by Currer Bell'; 1 vol., published by *Smith, Elder, and Company, printed by Stewart and Murray. Obvious misprints corrected, punctuation improved, but Charlotte broke up long sentences, changed dialect words, and altered paragraphing.

1851 *Agnes Grey* by . . . Acton Bell; Continental edn., repr. of 1850, published by Bernhard Tauchnitz, Leipzig; pp. 57–268 in vol. 2 of two.

1931 *Agnes Grey. A Novel* by Acton Bell; 1 vol., Shakespeare Head edn., Blackwell, Oxford; based on 1st edn. collated with 2nd; some misleading punctuation altered.

1988 *Agnes Grey*, ed. Hilda Marsden and Robert Inglesfield; Clarendon Press, Oxford; limited emendation taking into account Anne's correction list. Each Clarendon edn. has an introduction covering composition and textual history; a descriptive list of early editions; explanatory and textual notes and appendices.

(2) *The Tenant of Wildfell Hall*

1848 (June) *The Tenant of Wildfell Hall* by Acton Bell; 1st English edn., 3 vols., published by Newby, printed by J. Billing.
(28 July) *The Tenant . . .* by 'Acton Bell, author of "Wuthering Heights"' [*sic*]; 1st American edn., published by *Harper & Brothers, New York.
(Aug.) *The Tenant . . .*; 2nd English edn., with corrections: a reissue of unexpended 1st edn. sheets with a revised title-page and author's preface dated 22 July 1848; 3 vols., published by Newby, printed by J. Billing.

1854 *The Tenant . . . .* English Parlour Library edn.; 1 vol., published by Thomas Hodgson, who bought the copyright from Newby. A corrupt text, omitting the first four pages of Markham's letter to Halford, many expletives, about 25 complete paragraphs, and most of ch. 28. (See G. D. Hargreaves on incomplete texts in *Tenant* in *BST* (1972), 16. 82. 113–17 and (1977), 17. 87. 115–21.)

1859 *The Tenant . . .* by Acton Bell (Miss Anne Brontë); a new impression of the Parlour Library edn., published by Smith, Elder, who bought the copyright from Messrs Darton.

1931 *The Tenant . . .* by Acton Bell; 2 vols., Shakespeare Head edn.; based on 2nd edn., with many corrections of misprints.

1992 *The Tenant . . .*, ed. Herbert Rosengarten; Clarendon Press, Oxford; based on 1st issue, augmented by preface to 2nd edn.; most emendations based on 2nd edn. and/or 'author's own copy' in Princeton University Library.

Charlotte Brontë (1) *Jane Eyre. An Autobiography*

1847 (Oct.) *Jane Eyre. An Autobiography*, ed. Currer Bell; 1st English edn., 3 vols., published by Smith, Elder, printed by Stewart and Murray.

1848 (Jan.) *Jane . . . by* Currer Bell; 2nd edn., published by Smith, Elder, printed by Stewart and Murray. Includes dedication to Thackeray and preface by 'Currer Bell' dated 21 Dec. 1847. Some minor textual revisions and corrections of misprints; but more misprints are introduced.
(Jan.) *Jane. . .,* by Currer Bell; 1st American edn., 1 vol., published by Harper & Brothers, New York.
(Apr.) *Jane . . .,* by Currer Bell; 3rd English edn., 3 vols., published by Smith, Elder, printed by Stewart and Murray. Reprints dedication and preface, and adds note by Currer Bell dated 13 Apr. 1848, explaining that her 'claim to the title of novelist rests on this one work alone'. Some revisions and corrections, but new errors are introduced.
Jane . . ., by Currer Bell; 1st Continental edn., ?2 vols, published by Bernhard Tauchnitz, Leipzig.

1850 (Apr.) *Jane . . .,* by Currer Bell, author of "Shirley"; 4th English edn., 1 vol., published by Smith, Elder, printed by Spottiswoodes and Shaw. Reprints introductory material, corrects a few misprints.

1931 *Jane. . .,* by Currer Bell; 2 vols., Shakespeare Head edn., based on 3rd edn., collated with 1st, 'variations of wording' checked with second. Obvious misprints corrected.

1969 *Jane Eyre,* ed. Jane Jack and Margaret Smith; Clarendon Press, Oxford; based on 1st edn. with emendations mainly from holograph manuscript and 2nd and 3rd edns.

1975 Reprint of above, with corrections and additional notes.

(2) *Shirley. A Tale*

1849 (Oct.) *Shirley. A Tale,* by Currer Bell, author of 'Jane Eyre'; 1st English edn., 3 vols., published by Smith, Elder, printed by Stewart and Murray.
(22 Nov., postdated 1850 on title-page) *Shirley. A Tale,* by Currer Bell, Author of "Jane Eyre"; 1st American edn., 1 vol., published by Harper & Brothers, New York.
Shirley. A Tale by Currer Bell, author of 'Jane Eyre'. Copyright Edition. 1st Continental edn., 2 vols., published by Bernhard Tauchnitz, Leipzig.

1852 (Nov.; postdated 1853 on title-page) *Shirley. A Tale,* by Currer Bell, author of 'Jane Eyre'; a New Edition, 2nd English edn., 1 vol., published by Smith, Elder and Co., London, and Smith, Taylor, and Co., Bombay; printed by Oliver and Boyd, Edinburgh. Some authorial corrections and revisions; some footnotes omitted.

1931 *Shirley: A Tale* by Currer Bell, author of 'Jane Eyre'; 2 vols., Shakespeare Head edn., set from 1st edn. and collated with 2nd.

1979 *Shirley,* ed. Herbert Rosengarten and Margaret Smith. Clarendon Press. Based on 1st edn. with emendations mainly from holograph manuscript and 2nd edn.

(3) *Villette*

1853 (Jan.) *Villette,* by Currer Bell, author of 'Jane Eyre', 'Shirley', etc.; 1st English edn., 3 vols., published by Smith, Elder & Co., London, and Smith, Taylor & Co., Bombay, printed by Stewart and Murray. Title-page includes the words 'The Author of this work reserves the right of translating it.'
(4 Mar.) *Villette,* by Currer Bell, author of 'Jane Eyre', 'Shirley', &c; 1st American edn., 1 vol., published by Harper & Brothers, New York.
Villette, by Currer Bell, author of 'Jane Eyre'; Copyright Edition; 1st Continental edn., 2 vols., published by Bernhard Tauchnitz, Leipzig.

1855 *Villette,* by Currer Bell, author of 'Jane Eyre', 'Shirley', etc., a new edn.; 2nd English edn., 1 vol., published by Smith, Elder and Co., London, and Smith, Taylor and Co., Bombay; printed by Smith, Elder & Co. Numerous minor textual variants from 1st edn., but no firm evidence that they are authorial.

1931 *Villette* by Currer Bell, author of 'Jane Eyre', 'Shirley', etc. Shakespeare Head edn., 2 vols., based on 1st edn.

1984 *Villette,* ed. Herbert Rosengarten and Margaret Smith. Clarendon Press. Based on 1st edn., with emendations taking into account holograph manuscript, proof-sheets in Sterling Library, University of London, and authorial revisions in BPM copy formerly belonging to Revd A. B. Nicholls.

(4) *The Professor. A Tale*

1857 (6 June) *The Professor, A Tale,* by Currer Bell, author of 'Jane Eyre', 'Shirley', 'Villette', &c.; 1st English edn., 2 vols., with preface by 'Currer Bell', and note by the editor, A. B. Nicholls. Published and printed by Smith, Elder & Co., London.

(27 June) *The Professor, A Tale*, by Currer Bell, author of . . . &c.; 1st American edn., 1 vol., published by Harper & Brothers, New York.
The Professor. A Tale, by Currer Bell, author of . . . &c. Copyright edition. . . . *[The right of Translation is reserved.]*; 1st Continental edn., 1 vol., published by Bernhard Tauchnitz, Leipzig.

1931 *The Professor*, by Currer Bell, author of . . . etc.; Shakespeare Head edn., 1 vol., based on 1st edn.

1987 *The Professor*, ed. Margaret Smith and Herbert Rosengarten, Clarendon Press, Oxford; based on holograph manuscripts of preface and text; includes list of additions and corrections to the Clarendon editions of Charlotte's and Emily's novels.

Emily Brontë: *Wuthering Heights. A Novel*

1847 (Dec.) *Wuthering Heights A Novel,* by Ellis Bell, 'in three volumes' (actually in vols. 1 and 2 of three), vol. 3 containing *Agnes Grey*; 1st English edn., published and printed by Thomas Cautley Newby. Notorious for its careless spelling and punctuation, and garbled phrases.

1848 (21 Apr.) *Wuthering Heights. A Novel. By the author of 'Jane Eyre.'* [*sic*]; 1st American edn., 1 vol., published by Harper & Brothers, New York.

1850 (Dec.) *Wuthering Heights and Agnes Grey*, by Ellis and Acton Bell, a new edn. revised (see 1850 *Agnes Grey* above).

1851 Title as for 1850 edn., with '*Copyright Edition*' added; 1st Continental edn., 2 vols., published by Bernhard Tauchnitz, Leipzig.

1931 *Wuthering Heights A Novel,* by Ellis Bell; Shakespeare Head edn., 1 vol., based on 1st edn., collated with 2nd; punctuation sometimes emended; includes 'Biographical Notice' and 'Editor's Preface' from 2nd edn.

1976 *Wuthering Heights*, ed. Hilda Marsden and Ian Jack; Clarendon Press, Oxford; based on 1st edn., with emendation of faulty accidentals. Appendices include 'Biographical Notice' and 'Editor's Preface' from 2nd edn.

A selection of collected editions

1889–95 *The Life and Works of Charlotte Brontë and her Sisters.* 7 vols., Smith, Elder. Illustrated by Edmund Morison Wimperis with sketches of places identified by Ellen Nussey as the originals of some fictional settings.

1899–1900 *The Life and Works of Charlotte Brontë and her Sisters.* Haworth edition. 7 vols., Smith, Elder. Introductions to each novel by Mrs Humphry Ward. Introduction and notes to Gaskell *Life* by C. K. *Shorter. Illustrated with photographs of places and people associated with the works.

1905 *The Novels of the Brontë Sisters.* 10 vols., Dent. Illustrated by Edmund Dulac. 60 colour plates.

Alexander, Christine, and Rosengarten, Herbert J., 'The Brontës', in Joanne Shattock (ed.), *The Cambridge Bibliography of English Literature* 4 (3rd edn., 1999)

education. Primary education became available to more children during Revd Patrick Brontë's lifetime, but it was not until after his death that W. E. *Forster's Education Act of 1870 and a subsequent Act of 1880 provided for the compulsory education of all children up to the age of 13. The lot of child workers in textile mills (such as those in Haworth) improved somewhat after 1833, when the first Factory Act prohibited the employment of children under 9, and stipulated that children under 13 should attend school for at least two hours per day. In Haworth before 1844, free education was limited to the Haworth Grammar School, which taught the three Rs to small children—though it had not enough room for the 200 pupils allegedly enrolled there—and the Stanbury Baptist Free School, which had about 60 scholars in 1833. Private schools, such as the one Mr Brontë established in County Down at the age of 16, had always existed for those who could afford them. In 1844, the Brontë sisters proposed to set up a school at *Haworth Parsonage, charging £35 per annum 'for the board and education of a limited number of young ladies', with French, German, Latin, music, and drawing as 'extras' at a guinea each per quarter. Charlotte claimed that the retired situation of Haworth meant 'moderate' terms could be offered; but no pupils applied, and the project was abandoned. In 1844 the *Haworth National School was set up with a grant from the Church of England National Society (founded 1811). Some north Yorkshire schools had notoriously taken advantage of 'retired' situations to exploit the unwanted orphans and other unfortunates delivered into their hands. In 1823 William Shaw of Bowes Academy had been prosecuted for negligence when two pupils went blind: *Dickens's nightmarish 'Dotheboys Hall' had a foundation in reality. On 31 October 1847 the *Observer* commented that *Lowood in *Jane Eyre* was a ' "Do-the-Girls Hall" . . . How many similar establishments are there at this moment in merry England.' Revd W. Carus *Wilson, the 'Mr Brocklehurst' of Lowood, was well intentioned, unlike Squeers, but the regimen he imposed at

*Cowan Bridge in the early years had dire results. Harsh discipline, spartan conditions, and dreary memorized lessons were fairly typical of charitable foundations where subscribers and patrons expected docility from those they helped, as at *Woodhouse Grove and the Bradford School of Industry set up to train 'girls of poor parents' (see Barker, p. 72). Regular 'repetitions' were used even at the comparatively enlightened *Roe Head. Until the mid-century, when training colleges for teachers began to be set up on the model of Sir James *Kay-Shuttleworth's pioneering Battersea College of 1840, schools for the poor might use Joseph Lancaster's monitorial or Andrew Bell's 'Madras' system of teaching some of the older boys and setting them to teach younger pupils. Similar systems were in use at some grammar schools, where the foundation statutes might provide some free places. The statutes might also stipulate that Latin and Greek should be taught, and that the master should be a graduate. Haworth Grammar School, founded in 1638, and inadequately endowed, could not attract such graduates, and was not untypical.

Private education was a lottery both for teacher and taught, employer and employed, as the Brontës knew to their cost. Charlotte and Anne dramatized the frustrations and humiliations of the *governess's life in their novels, and Charlotte satirically quoted Elizabeth *Rigby's defence of such social inequity in the speeches of 'Miss Hardman' in Shirley. But Jane Eyre's nurturing of Adèle and Louis Moore's 'taming' of Shirley are intended to demonstrate the benefits of wise educational principles. In Wuthering Heights the younger Cathy's teaching of Hareton counteracts Heathcliff's deliberate neglect.

University education was not open to women, and education abroad was exceptional. Charlotte's decision that she and Emily should improve their knowledge of languages had far-reaching consequences. They were fortunate in having their aunt's financial help and the *Hegers' generosity, for their Brussels experience was educational in the widest sense, influencing the sisters' intellectual, moral, and emotional development as well as their linguistic skills, and contributing dynamically and creatively to their writing. Education is a central theme in all Charlotte's novels. Anne's work, like her father's, has a strong didactic element, enforcing the primacy of moral education.

education of the Brontës. *See opposite page*

Edwardston, chief manufacturing town in the province of *Zamorna, Angria, just east of Verdopolis; founded on the Olympia River by the woollen manufacturer and entrepreneur Edward *Percy. The Duke of Zamorna and his army are defeated here by Reformist forces during the Angrian Wars.

Edwardston Hall, country house of Edward *Percy on the edge of Edwardston village and contiguous to Girningham Park, in part of the Valley of Verdopolis that is subsumed into the province of *Zamorna, Angria.

Elbë, Alexander, Lord of. See ALEXANDER, LORD OF ELBË.

Elbë Hall, Hill, and Lake. See ALEXANDER, LORD OF ELBË.

Elimbos (Elymbos), Mount and Palace of. A high mountain in the barren north of *Sneaky's Land, home of the *Ape of the Hills and his strange Highland tribe in the *Glass Town and Angrian saga. Elimbos Palace is the residence of King Alexander *Sneaky in Sneaky's Land on the northern reaches of the River Niger.

Ellen, George Frederick, the unredeemed Squire of Hallows Hall, Aynsham, and Ellenshill, Alnwick, two properties in Sneaky's Land, in the *Glass Town and Angrian saga. Captain Henry *Hastings falls under the spell of this 'son of Nicholas', whose single object in life is to corrupt all his acquaintances. In his later manuscripts, Branwell Brontë describes with delight the violent bacchanalian scenes caused by Ellen in the 'beer shops' of the secluded *Coomassie mountains.

Neufeldt BB Works, 3. 141–56.

Elliott, Ebenezer (1781–1849), Sheffield ironmaster and former Chartist, whose Corn Law Rhymes (1831) supported abolition of Protectionist corn laws. Charlotte Brontë sent him Poems 1846, probably with an appreciative letter like others of 16 June 1847. His copy (Bonnell, BPM MS 294) is inscribed in an unknown hand 'Presented to Ebenezer Elliott by the Misses Brontë'.

Ellrington (Elrington), Lady Zenobia, Countess Northangerland, the Verdopolitan Mme de Staël, 'a masculine soul in a feminine casket', in the *Glass Town and Angrian saga. Zenobia is a learned woman who reads Herodotus and Aeschylus in the original. She is often referred to as the 'Empress of Women' for her great mental and physical abilities; and is named after the historical Zenobia, Queen of Palmyra and the East, described in Peacock's poem 'Palmyra' and Edward Gibbon's The History of the Decline and Fall of the Roman Empire, read by Charlotte Brontë.

Disappointed in her early love for the Duke of Zamorna, she becomes the Duke of Northangerland's third wife, stepmother to his daughter

(cont. on page 179)

T HE Brontës experienced little formal schooling, instead deriving most of their education from literary, social, political, and religious influences within and around their parsonage home. As a sole parent Revd Patrick Brontë's approach to education was to allow his children to pursue their own interests apparently without rigid supervision or interference, a method which was unusual for the time. He gave his children basic lessons in literacy, geography, history, maths, and a little French; and was assisted by the children's aunt, Elizabeth Branwell, who also endeavoured to train the girls in the female accomplishment of sewing. Samplers survive in the BPM as witness to the standard of their skill by 1830, and various extant workboxes and their contents indicate the lifelong chore of 'working', i.e. needlework including plain hemming and shirtmaking. *Music and *art were also part of their home education, with the children taking lessons from teachers both at home and in Keighley. Branwell never went to school. Mr Brontë tutored him at home, particularly in Latin and Greek, and there is evidence to suggest that he also gave his daughters some lessons in Latin and *natural history. Above all, the wide random reading of the Brontë children encouraged their own exploration of learning and provided the rich imaginative experience that led to their *juvenilia. See BOOKS READ BY THE BRONTËS; BOOKS OWNED BY THE BRONTËS; GEOGRAPHY, KNOWLEDGE OF AND BOOKS.

Mr Brontë was an excellent role model for independent learning. Largely self-taught and an avid reader, he soon gained experience as a teacher. After his basic schooling at Glascar, Ireland, he is thought to have trained as a pupil-teacher before establishing his own school at the age of 16, an extraordinary feat for a young man from a humble Irish family at the time. He then became a tutor to the children of Revd Thomas Tighe (in c.1798–9), before entering St John's College, *Cambridge, as a sizar in 1802, where he helped pay his way by teaching other students. He maintained his interest in education throughout his life, in a range of activities from being an examiner at the Wesleyan Academy at *Woodhouse Grove to being instrumental in establishing the *Haworth National School and (with Revd A. B. Nicholls) a school in Stanbury.

The Brontë sisters did experience some formal schooling. Maria and Elizabeth attended boarding school at Crofton Hall, Wakefield, for a short time in 1823. In 1824 Maria, Elizabeth, Charlotte, and Emily were sent to the Clergy Daughters' School, *Cowan Bridge, but were brought home in 1825, the two eldest girls dying soon after as a result of pulmonary TB exacerbated by the poor conditions at the school, immortalized in Lowood School in *Jane Eyre*. The school offered 'plain and useful Education', unless the pupil was to be educated as a teacher and governess, as in the case of Maria Brontë who was taught French and drawing for an extra fee of £3 a year. The list of Charlotte's 'Acquirements on Entering' gives some indication of the kind of systematic education valued at the school: 'Reads tolerably—Writes indifferently—Ciphers a little [i.e. arithmetic] and works neatly. Knows nothing of Grammar, Geography, History or Accomplishments'. From January 1831 to mid-June 1832, Charlotte attended Margaret Wooler's school at *Roe Head, Mirfield, where the curriculum offered the same basic subjects and the 'extras' French, music, and drawing. On her return home she immediately took over the supervision of her sisters' studies, passing on all she had learned in the previous year and a half. She was also appointed the first superintendent at the new Sunday school in Haworth (1832). At the end of July 1835 Emily attended school at Roe Head for three months and was then replaced by Anne in December 1837. Anne remained there as a pupil for about a year or possibly more (see Smith *Letters*, 1. 175), her fees paid by Charlotte's work as teacher there.

The Brontë sisters' experience of elementary education was typical of that provided by religious societies before the days of government regulation. Fees were paid by parents or charitable subscribers, and 'intellectual and religious Improvement' according to the pupils' 'different Stations of Life' was the aim (Clergy Daughters' School prospectus, *Leeds Intelligencer*, 4 Dec. 1823). Religious instruction was paramount, and the philosophy of self-help and self-improvement particularly strong in small middle-class schools like that at Roe Head. Charlotte's immediate response to this ideal, already encouraged at home, is evident in her letters of 1832–4 in which she is concerned for her own and her friends' improvement (see, for example, Smith *Letters*, 1. 111, 121, 128, 130). It is fortunate, however, that the systematized rote learning, the question and answer method displayed in Richmal Mangnall's *Historical and Miscellaneous Questions* (1813) that was used at both Crofton Hall and Miss Wooler's school, failed to dampen the innate intellectual curiosity of the Brontës. They were keen to excel in formal schooling since it meant vocational training and might equip them eventually to establish their own school.

With this view in mind, Charlotte and Emily sought a Continental education and encountered a quite different method of teaching that was to have a major effect on their later career as writers. On 15 February 1842, they enrolled in the Brussels pensionnat run by Mme Zoë *Heger, where they received French and German lessons from her husband, and where Emily was encouraged in her music. M. Constantin *Heger was an inspiring teacher whose 'system' involved the imitation of celebrated literary and historical examples in order to develop understanding and personal style (see DEVOIRS). His commitment to students as individuals meant that he adapted his teaching to suit the older Brontës (Charlotte was 26, Emily 24) and also gave them some individual tutoring. Sue Lonoff demonstrates the importance of Heger's role as a critical reader of their devoirs and confirms Dessner's view that for Charlotte, especially, this was 'a time of crucial intellectual and artistic growth' (Lonoff, p. xxiv). Heger's legacy was not only to introduce her to new sources but to develop her critical faculty and make her a more reflective writer. Emily left Brussels in November 1842 and Charlotte remained a further year, leaving on New Year's Day 1844. Charlotte, Emily, and Anne each had personal experience as teachers when they became *governesses. See also ACCOMPLISHMENTS.

Alexander & Sellars.
Baumber, Michael, 'Patrick Brontë and the Development of Primary Education in Haworth', *BST* (1999), 24. 1. 66–81.
Barker.
Lonoff.
Morris, Lord, 'The Brontës and Education, Education, Education', *BST* (1997), 22. 1–18.

Mary and therefore, ironically, Zamorna's mother-in-law. Northangerland (then Percy) assumes Zenobia's name and title on marriage to her, becoming Lord Ellrington. Her father, old Earl of Ellrington, and mother Lady Paulina Louisada, a Latin beauty of dubious morals, die early in the saga. Their deaths leave her as guardian to her young brothers. See ELLRINGTON (ELRINGTON) FAMILY.

The 'swarthy', raven-haired Zenobia is renowned for her pride, choler, and statuesque figure, inherited from her mother, and her rages are particularly violent after Zamorna (then Marquis of Douro) refuses to marry her. In 'Visits in Verreopolis' and 'The Bridal', Lord Charles Wellesley, whose curiosity makes him a frequent recipient of her rage, presents her as having been driven mad by her jealous love. Her usual dress of rich crimson velvet robes, with dark plumes in her turban, and gold jewellery, indicates her decadent background and contrasts with the purity of her rival Marian *Hume. After her abduction by Rogue (Northangerland) in 'The *Pirate' and marriage to him, she becomes a matronly figure, maintaining a prestigious salon in Verdopolis but often neglected by her husband. She remains loyal to Zamorna and Angria, where she spends the summer months. Zenobia and Northangerland are separated during his revolutionary activities and the Angrian wars, but reconciled after his final defeat by Zamorna.

Ellrington (Elrington), Lord. See NORTH-ANGERLAND, DUKE OF; ELLRINGTON (ELRINGTON) FAMILY.

Ellrington (Elrington) family. Henry, Earl of Ellrington (spelt 'Elrington' by Branwell), contemporary of Wellington in the *Glass Town and Angrian saga, married Lady Paulina Louisada, a Latin beauty of dubious morals, who died after producing a daughter Zenobia and three sons: Alsand, Myrtillus, and Surena (a friend of Lord Charles Wellesley, who later boards with him). Old Lord Ellrington brings his family to Verdopolis but they are captured en route by Rogue (Duke of *Northangerland) in his pirate ship (see 'PIRATE, THE'). After several years, Lord Ellrington dies and his name and title are taken by Rogue who marries Zenobia and purchases Ellrington Hall.

Ellrington (Elrington) Hall in the *Glass Town and Angrian saga, often referred to as Ellrington House, home of Zenobia *Ellrington and Alexander Percy (Duke of *Northangerland) in Verdopolis, where only French is spoken. It is a vast building purchased by Percy from old Lord Ellrington (Zenobia's father) and then extended.

(The alternative spelling reflects Branwell's preference for a single 'l'.)

Elm Grove Villa. A small elegant villa built among a grove of tall elm trees on the Olympian River, 2 miles from *Zamorna in Angria, this is the home of the Duke of *Fidena (as Mr Seymour) and Lily *Hart for the four years that their marriage remains a secret. It is the birthplace of their son John Augustus Sneaky, and is later purchased by Captain Sir William *Percy.

Elysium, a secret male society in *Verdopolis, also known as Pandemonium, 'that splendid temple of Hell' in the *Glass Town and Angrian saga. Its activities consist of initiation rites, drinking, gambling, and fighting; and there are suggestions of scandal, orgies, and secret alliances. Members (chiefly the young aristocrats of Verdopolis) must be over 15, have slain a man, and have an income over £5,000 a year. The Dukes of *Northangerland and *Zamorna (still Lord Ellrington and Marquis of Douro when the Elysium features in the saga) preside as president and vice-president respectively, explaining in part their otherwise mysterious early alliance. The leaders put an end to the Elysium when war disrupts their 'evil' pursuits. The name and unregenerate behaviour of this male club was suggested by the rumbustious conversations at Ambrose's Tavern, Elysium, in the 'Noctes Ambrosianae' of *Blackwood's Magazine. The idea of a secret society also reflects the Brontës' early awareness of *Freemasonry.

Emanuel, Paul, a professor at the lycée next door to his cousin Mme *Beck's pensionnat, where he also teaches, in *Villette. A small, dark, spare, bespectacled man of great talent and integrity, his character is closely modelled on that of M. Constantin *Heger, to whom Charlotte became passionately devoted, as Lucy *Snowe does to M. Paul, though the course of the novel's action is imaginary. Ultimately Paul returns Lucy's love, but the novel ends, it is implied, with his death by drowning, before their love can be consummated in marriage. It is M. Paul who advises Mme Beck to accept Lucy as a *gouvernante*. Harsh in appearance, irritable, impatient, fiery, vehement, passionate, and temperamental, he can storm furiously at stupid or slow pupils with a fluency of rebuke which makes even the most recalcitrant quail; yet he is at heart pure, devout, loyal, and self-sacrificing in providing for needy dependants, and tender-hearted to real suffering. He is perceptive of real talent (though he jealously guards his own prerogative as a professor and examiner) and is a talented teacher of literature. His touchy suspicion that Lucy lacks respect for him, and his jealousy of her newly found friends, particularly Dr John

*Bretton, accompany an increasing realization that he and Lucy have an 'affinity'. Aware that his unjust harshness has hurt her, he becomes gentle and comforting; yet he still springs on her an impromptu examination to test her supposed classical and scientific learning. Despite the tempestuous vagaries of their relationship, Lucy comes to esteem him as her 'Christian Hero' and to love him as her 'Master'. The jealous Mme Beck seeks to separate him from Lucy and prevent him from seeing her before he leaves for the West Indies. In obedience to his spiritual director, Père *Silas, and in a spirit of Christian charity, he is to nurse Mme *Walravens's estate back to prosperity, despite her previous injustice and harshness to him. During a crucial last-minute conflict between Paul and Mme Beck in chapter 41 he becomes Lucy's 'preux chevalier', roused to love and pity for her distress. He takes her to the house where he has prepared a schoolroom in which she can teach during his absence. Her lingering fear that Paul loves his ward, Justine Marie, impels her to an outburst of jealous anger, which delights Paul as proof of her ardent love for him. An Eden-like peace ensues after his proposal of marriage and her acceptance. During his absence abroad, he writes loving letters to her by every vessel. Constant, honourable, and noble, and still adhering to his Catholic faith, he is willing for Lucy to remain a Protestant, for he loves that faith in her. The last pages of the novel imply that he perished at sea in the wreck of the ship in which he was returning to Europe. Thus Charlotte at one level symbolically represents the impossibility of a union between herself and M. Heger. At another level the wrecking tempest is the ultimate destructive embodiment of the storms, real and metaphorical, which recur in *Villette*.

emigration from the British Isles increased dramatically during the 19th century. Between 1837 and 1867 more than three million people from Great Britain and some two million from Ireland emigrated, most of the Irish emigrants leaving in the desperate years following the potato famine of 1847. Some of Revd Patrick Brontë's relatives joined the exodus: his brother William's son John emigrated to New Zealand, John's brother Matthew became a carriage-maker in Tennessee, and Matthew's son William Emmett (1841–1900) settled in Arkansas. Mr Brontë's great-great-nephew William Stewart was an apothecary in South Africa. Eliza Jane *Kingston, a Branwell relative with whom Charlotte Brontë kept in touch, was born in Baltimore, Maryland, where her father had emigrated.

Emigration to Britain's overseas colonies had been promoted since 1815 as a remedy for distress and unemployment. A failed expedition to New Zealand followed the setting up of a commercial company in 1825, of which the banker John Dixon of Birmingham (a relative of Mary *Dixon) was a director. In 1829 Edward Gibbon Wakefield (1796–1862) proposed centrally controlled state-aided emigration to the colonies. The proceeds of land sales to selected emigrants would assist further settlement, and colonies would become self-governing as soon as possible. The ideas of Wakefield and the Radical 'Colonial Reformers', embodied in an Act of 1834, formed the basis of later settlement, especially in Australia and New Zealand. Wakefield was among the directors of a commercial New Zealand Company set up in August 1838, which actively sought investors and invited prospective settlers, sent a survey ship to New Zealand in July 1839, and negotiated the sale of large areas at Port Nicholson, Nelson, Wanganui, and Taranaki. Early arrivals in Wellington on the west shore of Port Nicholson included Mary *Taylor's brother Waring in April 1842, and three Greenwoods from the Gomersal area, related to the *Greenwood family of Haworth and Keighley. Mary Taylor left London on 12 March 1845, and arrived in Wellington on 24 July. Branwell's two poems on emigration (Neufeldt *BBP*, p. 263; May 1845) were topical. But all the Brontës were fascinated by the romantic idea of storm-tossed voyages into exile. Charlotte imagined Mary's voyage—'Sickness—Hardship—Danger are her fellow-travellers' (Smith *Letters*, 1. 388)—and admired her strength and courage. Mary's letters from New Zealand to Charlotte and Ellen Nussey reveal much about the characters of all three. They influenced Charlotte's feelings and writings about exile, gave a special point to her references to 'Rose Yorke' (see YORKE FAMILY) as 'a lonely emigrant' in 'some virgin solitude' in *Shirley*, to Shirley's threat to 'emigrate to the western woods', and Louis Gérard *Moore's preference for freedom in exile rather than tutor-slavery. There are perhaps echoes too in M. Paul *Emanuel's voyage to the West Indies in *Villette*. Mary's emigration, and that of her cousins Ellen and William Henry Taylor, probably increased Charlotte's interest in the work of Alexander Harris (1805–74), an emigrant to Australia, and author of *Testimony to the Truth* (1848) and *The Emigrant Family* (1849), which she discussed in her letters to W. S. Williams. In 'Anne Brontë, *Agnes Grey* and New Zealand', *BST* (1990), 20. 2. 97–9, Jane Stafford discusses Anne's 'arresting image' of the emigrant to 'Port Nelson, New Zealand, with a world of waters between himself and all that knew him' (*Agnes Grey*, ch. 7).

'Emily Jane Brontë' (portrait) by Branwell Brontë, c.1833–4; the enigmatic image of Emily

Brontë that, despite its physical fragility and poor technical execution, has caught the imagination of generations of viewers. The painting was originally part of the larger 'Gun Group' portrait inherited by Revd A. B. *Nicholls after the deaths of all the Brontës. He considered it such a poor likeness of all but Emily that he preserved only her image, cutting it from the larger canvas which he destroyed and taking the fragment with him to Ireland. During the Brontës' lifetime, however, John *Greenwood (stationer) of Haworth made pencil tracings of the figures of the three sisters that, together with an 1879 photo of a daguerreotype or ambrotype of 1858–61 of the intact portrait (BPM), give us some idea of the content and composition of the 'Gun Group'. The horizontal format comprised Anne, Charlotte, Branwell, and Emily sitting behind a table on which lies a collection of objects including game, books, and papers, representative of the preoccupations and status of the subjects. A surprisingly tall Branwell holds a gun in the crook of his arm, hence the popular title 'Gun Group'. A contemporary who saw the painting called it 'a shocking daub, not up to the rudest sign board style. The artist himself stands in the middle with bright red hair divided from the centre, and a straight line along the nose to mark its highest point' (John Elliot Cairnes, in BST (1984), 18. 94. 293). During the late 1870s Nicholls lent the 'Emily Jane Brontë' fragment to Martha Brown. After his death it was found lying on the top of a wardrobe in his home in Banagher, Ireland; it is now in the National Portrait Gallery, London.

Alexander & Sellars, pp. 307–10, pl. XXIII.
Barker, Juliet, 'The Brontë Portraits: A Mystery Solved', BST (1990), 20. 1. 3–11.

Emma ('We all seek an ideal in life . . .') (MS dated 27 Nov. 1853, in Taylor, Princeton), Charlotte Brontë's fragmentary commencement of a novel, left incomplete by her death in March 1855. The two chapters of Emma were written later than the 'Willie Ellin' fragments but they feature an urbane Mr Ellin who is probably associated with the earlier plot. This 'last sketch' focuses on Miss Matilda Fitzgibbon, a motherless young pupil who attends an English boarding school where she is bullied by Miss Wilcox when the latter discovers Mr Fitzgibbon has given a non-existent address and does not intend to pay his daughter's fees. The child and her circumstances are not dissimilar to material found in an early fragment relating to *Ashworth, which describes 'Miss Percy . . . a pupil in Mrs Turner's Seminary at Kensington' (Ashworth, ed. Monahan, Studies in Philology (1983), 80. 4. 97). This material is recast in Ashworth (ch. 2) and revived again in Emma

after Villette. Susan Meyer points out that towards the end of chapter 2 of Emma, Matilda is revealed to be 'of a race, or at least a physical appearance, that renders her susceptible to [racist] insult', suggesting that race was to play an important figurative role in this novel (Imperialism at Home: Race and Victorian Women's Fiction (1996), 62–3).

Charlotte's bereaved husband, Revd A. B. *Nicholls, had allowed Elizabeth *Gaskell to see Emma when she was gathering material for Charlotte's biography, published in 1857. When Gaskell later wished to add it to a proposed new edition of the Life 'to make the book more attractive, & likely to sell', she told George *Smith about 'the fragment of a tale she [Charlotte] left' (1/ Mar. 1858). She was sceptical about obtaining Nicholls's permission, so Smith wrote and obtained a surprisingly warm consent and offer by Nicholls to transcribe the 20-page, much revised, manuscript draft in pencil. The fragment was published in April 1860 in Smith's new *Cornhill Magazine, under the title 'The Last Sketch' and with an introduction by its editor William Makepeace *Thackeray. Both Mr Nicholls and Revd Patrick Brontë were deeply moved by Thackeray's generous personal tribute to Charlotte. In a letter to George Smith, Mr Nicholls said how much he prized Emma as being 'the last thing of the kind written by the Author' (The Professor (Clarendon edn.), 304). He also gave Smith a graphic description of how Charlotte had read him the manuscript in the winter of 1854, a description repeated by Thackeray in his introduction. On the suggestion of Nicholls, the Cornhill text retained the deleted last page of the manuscript, where Mr Ellin protects the distressed child Matilda Fitzgibbon, but included several misreadings.

Brontë, Charlotte, Emma (new transcription from the manuscript), in The Professor (Clarendon edn.), app. 6.

Enara, Henry (Henri) Fernando di, an Italian known as 'The Tiger' in the *Glass Town and Angrian saga. He is commander in chief of the Duke of *Zamorna's Angrian forces and a friend of General Lord Edward *Hartford. His foreign features with black hair, stern brow, and penetrating eyes, make him an object of suspicion to Angrians but he is well supported by Zamorna, who creates him baron of Etrei and governor of the Angrian province of *Etrei. His raven-haired daughters Maria, Gabriella, Giulietta, and Francesca are contemporaries of Caroline *Vernon.

Enoch, Frederick (b. ?1827), song-writer, author of the once-famous song 'My sweetheart when a boy', the four-part 'Sweet Vesper Hymn' to music by Henry Smart, and other works. The son of

John Enoch of Warwick, Boot and Shoemaker, Auctioneer and Appraiser, Frederick Enoch was working for his father as a 'Printer, Stationer, and Shop Assistant' in 1851. One of the two purchasers of *Poems 1846, he wrote to the authors through their publishers, *Aylott and Jones, in admiration of their work, requesting their autographs. The signatures they sent him, as the 'Bells', are in the BPM, BS Picture 256.

Etrei River and province that form the southern desert frontier between Angria and the ousted *Ashantees in the *Glass Town and Angrian saga. The province (named after a district in Ethiopia), governed by the Lord Lieutenant Henry (Henri) Fernando di *Enara, has a population of 4,000 and its capital city is *Dongola (after a province in Egypt). The Etreian campaign is the last of the Angrian Wars.

Etty, William, RA (historical) (1787–1849), Yorkshire painter who was born and died in York. The most celebrated painter of the nude in British art, he was a lifelong attender of the *Royal Academy of Art life classes and aimed to produce grand style history paintings as advocated by Reyolds. He features as a model for the Angrian artist of the same name in the Brontë juvenilia (see ETTY, WILLIAM (FICTIONAL)). The Brontës may even have seen originals of his voluptuous nudes that were strongly influenced by those of Rubens and the Venetians. Thus, Lucy Snowe's reaction to 'the indolent gypsy-giantess, the Cleopatra' in *Villette* (ch. 19) may owe something to Charlotte's early knowledge of Etty, as well as her later experience of Rubens.

Etty, William (fictional), Angrian artist, named after William *Etty, RA. The historical Etty illustrated many of Sir Walter *Scott's novels, including *The Pirate* which includes his portrait of the heroine Minna (see LAURY, MINA). The fictional Etty lives in *Adrianopolis in one of the marble mansions built for the Duke of Zamorna's artistic coterie. His dark hair and swarthy complexion betray his origins as the unacknowledged son of Northangerland and his first wife Augusta (or Maria) di *Segovia. He married Julia Montmorency but she and their infant daughter, Zorayda, mysteriously disappeared while he was on a painting expedition in the *Jibbel Kumri. Zorayda returns when she is 18, having been raised by Quashia Quamina (A *Leaf from an Unopened Volume).

Evangelical Alliance. This international association of Protestant churches and individuals was founded in London early in 1846 at a meeting of more than 800 clergymen and laymen representing 50 denominations. United in their protest against Roman *Catholicism and *Puseyism, they adopted nine articles: the primacy of the divinely inspired Scriptures, interpreted by the believer's private judgement; humanity's depravity; the incarnation of the Son of God, and His atonement for the sins of all; justification by faith alone; 'the work of the Holy Spirit as sanctifier; the immortality of the soul; the resurrection of the body; the final judgment by Jesus Christ; and the divine institution of the Christian ministry' (*Encyclopaedia Britannica* (1982), 3. 1009). Both Revd Patrick Brontë and Charlotte approved of these tenets, and of the ideal of cooperation, but their local experience meant that they could also see difficulties in an alliance including *Dissenters. The Baptists of Haworth resented and opposed the rights and privileges of the established Church, and neither side was willing to give way. Charlotte commented on D'Aubigné's letter advocating the Alliance in the Anglican journal, the *Record* (12 Mar. 1846): 'The evangelical alliance part is not very practicable yet certainly it is more in accordance with the spirit of the Gospel to preach unity amongst Christians than to inculcate mutual intolerance & hatred' (Smith *Letters*, 1. 459–60). In 1851 both Charlotte and her father appreciated the ideals expressed in Ruskin's pamphlet, *Notes on the Construction of Sheepfolds*, but Mr Brontë commented that the proposal that all Protestant sects could unite 'by keeping simply to Scripture' was 'impracticable' (Smith *Letters*, 2. 584). Yet Charlotte retained something of a vision which transcended petty distinctions, for in *Villette* she enabled Lucy Snowe to wonder at 'the minute and unimportant character of the differences between' the Presbyterian, Lutheran, and Episcopalian denominations and 'at the unity and identity of their vital doctrines: I saw nothing to hinder them from being one day fused into one grand Holy Alliance' (ch. 36).

evangelicalism. See RELIGION.

Evans, Ann (1792–1857), model for Miss *Temple; daughter of William and Winifred Evans of Gosport, Hants. In July 1824 she became the superintendent at *Cowan Bridge, taking over from the temporary superintendent Miss *Andrews. A former pupil, 'CMR', described her to Nicholls on 26 May 1857 as a kind person who had her energies 'severely tasked' and did not always know how the pupils were treated. Her sympathetic letter of condolence to Revd Patrick Brontë of 23 September 1825 shows her fondness for 'dear Charlotte' and 'little petted Em' (MSS private). She left the school after her marriage at Tunstall church in July 1826 to Revd James Connor (1792–1854), rector of Knossington, Leics., from 1845.

Evesham, on the Cirhala River in the north of the Glass Town (Verdopolitan) Federation. During the Angrian Wars it is occupied by the Duke of *Northangerland's revolutionary forces (under Macterrorglen), and the Battle of Evesham (won by the Duke of *Zamorna's troops under General Thornton) becomes the last major battle of the *Glass Town and Angrian saga, returning Zamorna to power. During the battle Zamorna's head-quarters are at Clarence Wood. Charlotte Brontë's poem 'The Town besieged' describes Evesham before the battle (Neufeldt *CBP*, p. 261; see also Alexander *EW*, pp. 158–9, 170–1).

exhibitions of Brontëana began with individual Haworth villagers, as Charles Lemon reports in his book *Early Visitors to Haworth* (1996), and in 1889 a 'Museum of Brontë relics' was opened at 123 Main Street' (*Brontëana*). When the *Brontë Society was formed in 1893, one of its major objects was 'to acquire literary, artistic and family memorials of the Brontës' and 'to place the same at Haworth . . . for public examination' (quoted in Charles Lemon, *A Centenary History of the Brontë Society* (1993), 4). From 1895, these acquisitions were displayed in the former Yorkshire Penny Bank (now the Haworth Tourist Office) and from 1928 in Haworth Parsonage, which, as the BPM, became the major depository of objects, manuscripts, and printed sources relating to the Brontë family. Branwell's portraits of his sisters are, however, in the National Portrait Gallery. Bronteana early acquired considerable market value, and many objects passed into private ownership, helped by dealers such as T. J. *Wise, a Brontë Society member described in *Brontëana* as 'a notorious forger and literary vandal'. In complete contrast was the American Henry H. *Bonnell, who donated his extensive collection of manuscripts to the Parsonage Museum in 1929. In 1959 extensions to the Parsonage included a dedicated 'Bonnell Room' to allow these acquisitions to be displayed. From about this time, the Society has aimed to restore the Parsonage itself to the appearance of the Brontës' home by gradually removing museum-type display cases from the living rooms. In 1982 the first of a number of changing exhibitions were mounted in the bookshop foyer, and since 1984 a semi-permanent exhibition entitled 'The Brontës: A Family History' has been housed in the upper rooms of the 1878 'Wade extension'. In 1999 the Bonnell Room was restructured to accommodate a more extensive changing exhibition, beginning with 'The Brontës: A Passionate Response', an account of how writers and film-makers have reproduced and extended the Brontë texts and lives.

One notable exhibition held outside the BPM was 'The Breath of the Wilderness of Haworth: the Brontë Sisters and *Wuthering Heights*' held in Tokyo and Osaka, Japan, in 1987. The Brontë Society loaned first editions and personal possessions of the Brontës for the exhibition, which also included a screening of the film *Osimaru*, a Samurai version of *Wuthering Heights* directed by Yoshige Yoshida (1988), and other items showing the influence of the Brontës in Japan. In 1989 the Yorkshire Museum at York included Brontë items in its exhibition 'Treasures of Yorkshire and Humberside'. 'Branwell Brontë and his Circle' was the title of an exhibition organized by the City of Bradford at Cartwright Hall from October 1994 to January 1995.

Throughout 1995, the BPM offered an exhibition entitled 'The Art of the Brontës: New Discoveries', based on research by Christine Alexander and Jane Sellars, and in February and March a more extensive exhibition entitled 'The Art of the Brontës: Paintings and Drawings by Charlotte, Branwell, Emily and Anne Brontë' appeared at Sotheby's, London, to launch their book *The Art of the Brontës* (1995). A travelling 'Art of the Brontës' exhibition, modified to incorporate local holdings, appeared at Bodelwyddan Castle, North Wales (Apr.–July 1995) and the Pierpont Morgan Library, New York (Jan.–Apr. 1996). The exhibition and the related book provided for the first time a scholarly catalogue and analysis of the Brontës' activity in the visual arts.   PS

J. Horsfall Turner (ed.), *Brontëana* (1898).
Stoneman, Patsy, *Brontë Transformations: The Cultural Dissemination of 'Jane Eyre' and 'Wuthering Heights'* (1996).

Exina, a province in the south of *Gondal, which has a sea-green standard. 'Exina' is the surname for several Gondal characters, including Arthur Exina, a noble who is imprisoned, and Gerald Exina, probably ruler of Exina province (Julius *Brenzaida reneges on his pact with Gerald and causes his captivity and death). Anne Brontë's characters Eustace and Henry Sophona also come from Exina.

'extraordinary dream, An'. See 'YOUNG MEN'S MAGAZINE'.

Eyre, Jane, heroine of Charlotte Brontë's novel of the same name. Small, plain, poor, and an orphan, Jane is discordant and unloved at *Gateshead Hall, where her Aunt Sarah *Reed ignores her efforts to do her duty, and punishes her cruelly by isolation in the terrifying *red-room. Jane's suffering impels her to retaliate with threats to reveal her aunt's tyranny; but when her resentment subsides, she is desolate, longing above all for love, and grateful for *Bessie's capricious affection. At *Lowood Jane is furiously indignant at Miss *Scatcherd's treatment of Helen *Burns. She hates her as an oppressor like Mrs Reed, at whose instigation Revd Robert *Brocklehurst accuses Jane of deceit. But the benevolent Miss *Temple, who exonerates her, restores Jane's self-respect and increases her self-control and ability to moderate her vengeful feelings, though, tenacious of all impressions, she cannot forget her ordeals. By her patient magnanimity, Helen Burns also has a lasting influence on Jane—evident later when Jane seeks reconciliation with her dying aunt. Jane's perseverance in study brings her calm though limited satisfaction at Lowood, and later in teaching Adèle *Varens and her *Morton pupils, and in studying with Diana and Mary *Rivers. After Miss Temple leaves Lowood Jane's longing for change leads her to welcome a 'new servitude' at *Thornfield Hall; her equal longing for the liberty and action women lack but men take for granted is at first unsatisfied. Edward *Rochester's arrival opens new mental horizons, and brings her the excitement of helping him during the crises caused by Bertha *Rochester's attacks. After she rescues him from his burning bed, he ardently claims an affinity with her, but then chooses to dissimulate by his pretended wooing of Blanche *Ingram—rousing Jane to realize her love for him despite his faults. When he tells her she must leave Thornfield before his marriage, Jane's 'vehemence of emotion, stirred by grief and love', masters her: departure from him would be like death—yet she could not stay to become 'nothing' to him, for she claims equality with him in heart and spirit. As an equal, Rochester begs her to marry him and is accepted; and as an equal, she resists his attempts to shower gifts upon her as a sultan might upon a slave. Secretly, however, he is her idol. After Bertha is revealed as Rochester's wife, Jane, in anguish, leaves him, fearing to be the instrument of evil to one she wholly loves. At *Moor House Jane recognizes in St John *Rivers a noble austerity which elevates Christian mission above human love but which would destroy half her self if she agreed to be his wife. Saved by the supernatural call which leads to her reunion with the maimed and blinded Rochester, she finds in her marriage liberty and fulfilment. In Jane, aspects of *Richardson's Pamela and the archetypal Cinderella fuse with Charlotte's own sufferings and ardours, especially her passion for M. Constantin *Heger. See also GOVERNESSES; HASTINGS, ELIZABETH.

Faction du Mange (Manège), a secret society led by Jean, Prince of Ponte Corre, in Frenchyland (see PARIS), dedicated to the overthrow of the Emperor *Napoleon in the *Glass Town and Angrian saga. The society is given financial support by a branch in Verdopolis, funded by the Duke of *Northangerland's coterie. Based on the similar historical society reported in *Blackwood's Edinburgh Magazine*, the name (also a French surname used in the juvenilia: see NAUGHTY, RICHARD (YOUNG MAN NAUGHTY)) is probably a playful Glass Town construction referring to eating (the French verb *manger*, 'to eat'). References to the cruelty of the Faction Du Mange and its connection with *Pigtail and his Prussian Butter and bread (a virulent poison), support a reading based on *Manger*. Wise & Symington (2. 482) suggest that the alternative spelling 'Manège' (used by Branwell, Neufeldt *BB Works*, 1. 16), indicates a reference to this French faction as a riding school where intricate manoeuvres and stylish horsemanship are practised. ('Manège' can also mean 'wile, stratagem, trick'.) Alexander (*EEW*, 1. 119) makes the further suggestion that Charlotte may refer to '*le parti du manche,* based on the expression *être du côté du manche*, literally "to be on the right side of the broomstick" (presumably those in power)'.

Fairburne, Marian, the humble cousin of the proud Amelia De Capell in Charlotte Brontë's fragmentary story *Ashworth*. Despite her retiring nature, she has a discernment that recalls that of Elizabeth Hastings in the juvenilia and is a favourite of Arthur Ripley West, who refers to her as his snowdrop (a name the Duke of Zamorna used for his early wife Marian Hume). A scene in which Arthur examines Marian's portfolio of drawings prefigures Rochester's examination of the reticent Jane Eyre's art portfolio in *Jane Eyre* (ch. 13).

Fairfax, Mrs Alice, the mild, kindly, slightly deaf housekeeper at *Thornfield Hall, in *Jane Eyre*, widow of the second cousin of *Rochester's mother. Though ignorant of the details of his past, she thinks him unlikely to marry the comparatively poor and much younger Blanche *Ingram. Deeply shocked to see him kissing Jane, and sceptical about his intentions, she warns Jane to be on her guard. After Jane leaves Thornfield, Rochester settles an annuity on Mrs Fairfax and sends her to live with distant friends. She replies to the lawyer's enquiries about Jane, but not Jane's enquiries about Rochester.

fairy tales. The Brontë children, inspired by the *Arabian Nights*, James *Ridley's *Tales of the Genii*, and traditional tales like those told by *Bessie in *Jane Eyre*, invented their own fairy tales, in which wicked enchantresses, handsome princes,

ill-treated virtuous ladies, dwarves, and child-eating ogres lived in castles or imprisoning towers. Charlotte recalled Charles Perrault's 'La Barbe-Bleue' in all three major novels—most effectively in *Jane Eyre*, where the third storey at *Thornfield Hall resembles 'some Bluebeard's castle'. *Jane Eyre* also groups characters in threes, uses the motif of the lost wanderer or seeker, and has the satisfying contours of the Cinderella story, and perhaps of 'Beauty and the Beast'. In *Villette* Mme *Walravens, like 'Malevola, the evil fairy', descends a 'mystic winding stair'. See FOLKLORE.

'Fall of the Leaves, The' ('Chute des feuilles, La'). *Devoir by Charlotte Brontë (30 March 1843, MS in Heger family; photocopy in BPM). Subtitled 'An Essay on Style' ('Devoir de style'), it begins as an analysis of *Millevoye's poem of the same name, which she transcribed in a notebook of *dictations. However, it soon shifts to a defence of genius and passion as the source of 'all true poetry'. Though she concedes that writing poetry requires thought and method, she argues that inspiration sparked by powerful feeling matters more. M. Constantin *Heger challenges her romantic ideas in marginal comments and a long 'observation', and insists that she herself 'study form'. A prime example of the dialogue between teacher and student, this devoir has been reprinted more than any other. SL

Duthie *Foreign Vision*, pp. 38–9.
Lonoff, pp. 240–59.

Fanny and Eliza, maids at the Rectory in *Briarfield, in *Shirley*. Fanny shows compassion to her downcast and lonely young mistress Caroline *Helstone, whom she encourages to visit the old maids Miss *Ainley and Miss *Mann (ch. 10). HR

Fanshawe, Ginevra, a pretty, blonde coquette in *Villette*, whom Lucy *Snowe first meets during her crossing to 'Boue-Marine'; said to be modelled on Maria Miller, whom Charlotte had known at the Pensionnat *Heger. The daughter of a half-pay captain with aristocratic connections, she is a frank, selfish hedonist, a 'butterfly' who does little serious work at Mme *Beck's school, concentrating on accomplishments which will enable her to shine in society and eventually secure a wealthy husband. She prefers the brainless gamester Count de Hamal to the skilled Dr John *Bretton, but enjoys her conquest of the latter. Knowing that Lucy takes her at her lowest as 'ignorant, and flirting, and fickle, and silly, and selfish', she feels at ease with her, and despite their wrangling, she and Lucy are never totally alienated. But her discourteous 'quizzing' of Mrs Louisa *Bretton disillusions 'Dr John', and her empty chatter disgusts her uncle, Mr *Home, Count de Bassompierre, who has paid her school bills. Piqued by her cousin Paulina's marriage, she elopes with De Hamal, and calls out lustily for aid with his gambling debts. Pretty sure to get what she wants in the end, she suffers 'as little as any human being' Lucy has ever known.

Farewell to Angria ('I have now written a great many books') (*c*.late 1839), Charlotte Brontë's brief fragmentary farewell to her *Glass Town and Angrian saga (BPM). Like an addict who bids farewell to an old habitual 'friend', Charlotte acknowledges the repetitive hold her Angrian fantasy has on her imagination and its resulting 'ornamented and redundant composition' (a phrase relating to her juvenilia in her preface to *The Professor*). The extended image she uses is that of an artist who has exhausted her model and is ready to paint 'from the life'. She longs to 'quit . . . that burning clime where we have sojourned too long—its skies flame—the glow of sunset is always upon it—the mind would cease from excitement and turn now to a cooler region' (Alexander *EW*, p. 199). Following this statement, Charlotte wrote the commencements of several novels, few of which survive (see ASHWORTH); not until *The Professor* was she satisfied with her 'subdued' composition.

Brontë, Charlotte, *Jane Eyre*, ed. Richard Dunn (Norton 2nd edn.), 426; (3rd edn.), 424.

Farren, William, in *Shirley*, an unemployed millworker laid off by Robert Gérard *Moore, put out of work like many others in the West Riding of Yorkshire by the advent of new machinery in the early years of the 19th century. He is a member of a delegation led by Moses *Barraclough and *Noah o' Tims that demands Moore leave the country, or part with his machinery and employ more mill-hands. However, Farren bears no ill will towards Moore; his wish is only 'to mak' a effort to get things straightened, for they're sorely acrooked' (p. 153). Moved by his extreme poverty, Revd Cyril *Hall lends Farren a little money, and Moore persuades Hiram *Yorke to give Farren work in

the fruit gardens at Yorke Mills. Through her portrait of Farren, Charlotte Brontë seeks to give a sympathetic and balanced account of the plight of the working class; while schemers like Moses Barraclough try to advance their cause through violence and social disruption, William Farren struggles to maintain a sense of dignity for himself and his family through honest toil, and rejects the 'scoundrels that reckons to be the "people's friends," and knows naught about the people, and is as insincere as Lucifer' (p. 367). Charlotte's portrait of the decent and honourable working man trapped by circumstances anticipates Dickens's similar treatment of Stephen Blackpool in *Hard Times* (1854). HR

feminist approaches. Although important assessments of the Brontës were made by early feminists, including their contemporary Harriet *Martineau (1802–76) and in the 1920s Virginia Woolf (1882–1941), feminist criticism of their work was not really plentiful until the 1970s, when the women's movement began radically to change the study of women's writing. By the mid-seventies, most Western universities had established women's studies programmes (often heavily staffed by literature faculty members) and were offering a variety of courses on women writers, women in literature, and issues in women's writing. The canon of traditionally taught works was expanded and reshaped by the inclusion of women's texts that feminist scholars had 're-covered' from various depths of obscurity (Anne's *The Tenant of Wildfell Hall* is one example); and works by women already in the canon (*Jane Eyre* and *Wuthering Heights*, for instance) were being reinterpreted from new, feminist perspectives. The flood of feminist literary criticism published at that time was a result of popular interest in, and strong institutional support for, the study of women's lives and literature.

The significant impact of feminism on literary studies since the early 1970s is partly due to the versatility and heterogeneity of feminism itself, and to the extraordinary range of critics who engage in feminist analysis and scholarship. Often referred to as a perspective rather than an interpretative method, feminism has been able to accommodate many other approaches and appropriate their methodologies to produce theoretically engaged and technically sophisticated interpretations of literary texts. Moreover, like Marxism, feminism has often questioned its own underlying assumptions just as vigorously as it has critiqued those it opposes. This eagerness to debate the contested issues within feminism itself has made it an enormously fertile area of study, one which reaches out to the theories and scholarship of other fields and continually evolves under their influence. The very richness, diversity, and fluidity of feminist literary criticism makes it impossible to describe with any kind of precision the large body of feminist work on the Brontës that has been published over the last 40 years. The reader is therefore advised to consult entries on other critical approaches for additional examples of the ways in which feminists have interpreted the Brontës' writing. What follows is a broad summary of feminist criticism on the Brontës as it has evolved in three overlapping stages from the late sixties to the present.

The first phase of this criticism began with the publication of works which reflected a new and distinctly feminist awareness of Charlotte, Emily, and Anne as *women* writers. (The fact of their gender had always been an issue in Brontë criticism, but the feminist perspective on this issue was new in the 1960s.) Inga-Stina Ewbank's *Their Proper Sphere* (1966) discusses 'the state of female authorship in the 1840s' (p. 3), providing a description of the market for women's writing when the Brontës began to publish which is still a useful introduction to the topic today. Hazel Martin's mildly feminist *Petticoat Rebels* (1969) examines Charlotte's works as 'novels of protest against the social prescriptions that limited women's behavior and opportunities' (p. 90) in the Victorian era. More radical than either Martin's or Ewbank's works is the chapter on *Villette* in Kate Millett's controversial book, *Sexual Politics* (1969). Millett argues that in Lucy Snowe we see the devastating 'effects [that] . . . a male-supremacist society has upon the psyche of a young woman' (p. 140) whose narrative is 'one long meditation on a prison break' (p. 146). Two years later, Carol Ohmann's equally provocative essay on the 'sexual prejudice' of male critics of *Wuthering Heights* ('Emily Brontë in the Hands of Male Critics', *College English*, 32 (1971), 906–13) demonstrated not only the bias of Victorian reviewers but also the sexist attitudes of contemporary male critics who admired the book but patronized the author, calling her in one case 'the intense, inhibited spinster of Haworth' (quoted in Ohmann, p. 911) and denying that she had artistic control of her work.

Well launched by such publications, feminist criticism on the Brontës flourished in the seventies with the aid of formalist analytic techniques, producing innumerable textual readings that focus on women's experience in patriarchy, particularly the inner, psychological experience of the embattled feminine self. This kind of criticism, which Gayatri Spivak later called 'high feminism' and correctly identified with American critics of the seventies in particular, has been enormously influential, in part because much of it was printed in widely disseminated and eagerly received publications. Appearing in the popular magazine *MS* in 1973, Adrienne Rich's essay '*Jane Eyre*: The Temptations of a Motherless Woman' explains Charlotte's novel as a tale about a young woman who, at each stage of her development, is able to resist 'traditional female temptations' (such as masochism and 'victimization') because 'the image of a nurturing or principled or spirited woman on whom she can model herself, or to whom she can look for support' (McNees 3. 226–7) appears to her, either in the form of an actual woman, like Miss Temple, or in dream figures such as the lunar 'matriarchal spirit' (McNees, 3. 236) that communicates with Jane on the night she leaves Thornfield. Like Rich, Ellen Moers approaches the Brontës from a perspective that is both formalist and psychological in her well-known book *Literary Women* (1976). Tracing patterns of Freudian images in their writing, she analyses the literary means by which anger and erotic impulses are displaced and sublimated in women's narratives. In this respect, Moers' book is similar to the work of Sandra M. Gilbert and Susan Gubar, whose *The Madwoman in the Attic: The Woman Writer and the Nineteenth-Century Literary Imagination* (1979) achieved nearly monumental status in the early eighties, as did their widely used anthology of women's writing in English (*Norton Critical Anthology*: *Literature by Women*, 1985, 2nd edn. 1996). In Charlotte's and Emily's novels Gilbert and Gubar discover patterns, imagery, and modes of literary expression that they contend are peculiar to the women, for example, the 'spectral' image of the feminine self that appears in all four of Charlotte's works (Bertha Mason, Lucia in *The Professor*, the Titan-woman in *Shirley*, and Lucy Snowe's ghostly nun) and that Emily brilliantly embodies in Catherine Earnshaw's alter ego, Heathcliff.

Gilbert and Gubar's book belongs to the second phase of feminist criticism on the Brontës, which sought to situate them within a specifically feminist version of literary history and within a newly identified 'tradition' of women's writing. Drawing on Harold Bloom's ideas about the productive 'anxiety of influence' which literary 'fathers' such as Milton induce in their male heirs, Gilbert and Gubar contend that such anxiety was especially acute for female authors in the 19th century and that it was largely responsible for the distinctively feminine patterns of images, archetypes, and symbols one sees in women's writing. Arguing that 19th-century women's writing in general is covertly subversive, Gilbert and Gubar read *Wuthering Heights* as 'a rebelliously topsy-turvy retelling' of Milton's *Paradise Lost* which recounts the fall of woman (Catherine Earnshaw) and her Satanic 'shadow self' (Heathcliff) (*Madwoman*, p. 255). Nine years later, Stevie Davies built on and refuted Gilbert and Gubar's assertions about Emily's anxiety-driven relationship to Milton, celebrating her 'strong' affiliation with her literary forefather and calling her 'Milton's legitimate daughter' (*Emily Brontë* (1988), 18). The effort to place the Brontës within feminist literary history also received considerable support from Gilbert and Gubar's inclusion of Emily's poetry and the entirety of *Jane Eyre* in their *Norton Anthology of Literature by Women*, as well as by the earlier appearance of Elaine Showalter's book, *A Literature of their Own: British Women Novelists from Brontë to Lessing* (1977). Dividing the history of British women's novel writing into three stages—'feminine, feminist, and female'—Showalter describes *Jane Eyre* as a 'classic feminine novel' which combines realistic narrative techniques with symbolic devices that Showalter sees as peculiar to women's literature; for example, the use of spatial metaphors of rooms and houses to represent female sexual and psychosexual experience (the red-room thus signifies menarche, whereas Lowood suggests the repression of female sexual drives and Thornfield allows for the reassertion of the 'animal' aspects of womanhood). Margaret Homans, whose first critical essay on the Brontës was published in 1978 ('Repression and Sublimation of Nature in *Wuthering Heights*', *PMLA* 93. 9–19), is also interested in women's psychology and has attempted to situate the Brontës within the history of 19th-century women's writing. Her work, however, is more strictly Freudian and Lacanian than the feminist criticism discussed so far. Well versed in Romantic poetry, Homans is interested in the process of 'figuration' by which nature (associated by both psychoanalysis and Romanticism with the material, the literal, the maternal, and, more generally, the feminine) is repressed and sublimated into words: signs that stand for, or figure forth, that which they replace. Homans thus finds Lacanian theories about gender and language acquisition useful. Drawing on the work of feminist psychoanalytic theorists such as Helene Deutsch and Nancy Chodorow, she develops a feminist-Lacanian study of 19th-century women authors' relationship to their writing in her book *Bearing the Word: Language and Female Experience in Nineteenth-Century Women's Writing* (1986), which develops many of the ideas that she had begun to explore in earlier works on the Brontës (*Women Writers and Poetic Identity: Dorothy Wordsworth, Emily Brontë, Emily Dickinson* (1980), and 'Dreaming of Children: Literalization in *Jane Eyre* and *Wuthering Heights*', in Juliann E. Fleenor (ed.), *The Female Gothic* (1983), 257–79) (see PSYCHOANALYTIC APPROACHES).

Homans's work is compatible with the high feminism which flourished in the seventies, especially in the USA, in that it focuses on the individual female self and her inner, psychological experience. But Homans's engagement with Continental theory (Derrida and deconstruction as well as Lacan) also affiliates her with other developments in feminist literary criticism which have at times produced rather sharp objections to the work of the first wave of feminists. Dissatisfaction with the narrowness of the high feminist approach began as early as the late seventies, when Marxist-oriented critics such as Nancy Pell ('Resistance, Rebellion, and Marriage: The Economics of *Jane Eyre*', *Nineteenth-Century Fiction*, 31 (1977), 397–420) and the members of the Marxist-Feminist Literature Collective ('Women's Writing: *Jane Eyre, Shirley, Villette, Aurora Leigh*', *Ideology and Consciousness*, 3 (1978), 30–5) began to draw attention to the importance of economic realities and social relationships in the Brontë novels. Countering the overwhelming prevalence of non-social interpretations of *Jane Eyre*, Pell argues that the difficulties of young Jane's situation are from the outset shown emphatically to be of socio-economic origin and that the celebrated 'romantic individualism and rebellion of feeling' in the novel are 'controlled and structured by an underlying social and economic critique of bourgeois patriarchal authority' (p. 399), especially the system of inheritance and primogeniture. Pell also notes that the gaining of fortunes in *Jane Eyre* depends on the exploitation of colonial peoples (Jane's legacy and Bertha's dowry both come from Jamaican slave plantations), a point considerably elaborated upon by later, post-colonial feminists. Jina Politi's Marxist-feminist interpretation similarly observes that the novel depends on references to the foreign other (in this case France) in its construction of a new female stereotype—the English governess—which 'perfectly suited the imperialistic, militaristic temper of the period' in which Brontë was writing ('*Jane Eyre* Class-ified', *Literature and History*, 8 (1982), 89). Addressing Gayatri Spivak's 1985 critique of feminist readings of *Jane Eyre* which are based on an 'isolationist admiration for the literature of the female subject in Europe and Anglo-America' ('Three Women's Texts and a Critique of Imperialism', *Critical Inquiry*, 12 (1985), 511), critics in the late eighties and nineties offered interpretations of the Brontës' work that combine feminist and *post-colonial perspectives in order to illuminate the connections between the construction of femininity and the social formation of subjects with the context of imperialism and nationalism.

Along with these post-colonial readings, some of the most interesting and enlightening feminist interpretations of the Brontës' works published since the mid-eighties have been ones that contextualize the writings within social and/or cultural history and the evolution of literary forms, particularly the novel. Theories regarding the formation of the social subject and the construction of the self, derived from the work of cultural historian Michel Foucault and Marxist theorists such as Pierre Macherey and Louis Althusser, are joined in such analyses with accounts of the novel's rise as a literary form in the 19th century and with feminists' long standing interest in the construction of feminine identity to show how novels by the Brontës both reflect and contribute to this particular ideological task within culture. For example, Nancy Armstrong's *Desire and Domestic Fiction* (1987) and several pieces by Anita Levy ('The History of Desire in *Wuthering Heights*', *Genre*, 19 (1986), 409–30; *Other Women: The Writing of Class, Race, and Gender, 1832–1898* (1991); '*Jane Eyre*, the Woman Writer, and the History of Experience', *Modern Language Quarterly*, 56 (1995), 77–95) demonstrate the ways in which Charlotte's and Emily's novels helped to produce a reconfigured modern female self associated with the private, asocial life of desire and family relationships. In a similar fashion, Beth Newman ('The Situation of the Looker-On: Gender, Narration, and Gaze in *Wuthering Heights*', *PMLA* 105 (1990), 1029–41) provides an impressively rich interpretation of *Wuthering Heights* using Freudian and Lacanian psychoanalytic theory in order to demonstrate how the modern gendered subject and literary techniques which we today call 'point of view' developed in conjunction with the emergence of the bourgeois family and the evolution of the novelistic genre in the 19th century. Like Armstrong, Bette London relies on Foucault in her reading of *Jane Eyre*, not as a tale of a young woman's struggle toward freedom and psychic wholeness, but as a 'textbook of self-discipline' which produces, in both Jane and the reader, willing participants in a system that constructs 'the rebellious [female] self' and 'conventional femininity' by the same mechanism. In writing her autobiography, London argues, Jane 'composes' her naturally undisciplined self, constructing in the process a 'no longer willful Jane' and a 'willing reader' who approves of her self-constructed feminine docility ('The Pleasures of Submission: *Jane Eyre* and the Production of the Text', *ELH* 58 (1991), 209, 202). Other important works by feminist critics include Marci M. Gordon's article on *Wuthering Heights* ('Kristeva's Abject and Sublime in Brontë's *Wuthering Heights*', *Literature and Psychology*, 34 (1988), 217–24); Patricia Yaeger's *Honey-Mad*

Women: Emancipatory Strategies in Women's Writing (1988); and a series of short pieces on *Wuthering Heights* in *Feminists Reading: Feminist Readings* (1989), edited by Sara Mills et al.

CB

Newman, Beth, 'The Situation of the Looker-On: Gender, Narration, and Gaze in *Wuthering Heights*', *PMLA* 105 (1990), 1029–41.

Spivak, Gayatri Chakravorty, 'Three Women's Texts and a Critique of Imperialism', *Critical Inquiry*, 12 (1985), 243–61.

Stoneman, Patsy, 'Feminist Criticism of *Wuthering Heights*', *Critical Survey*, 4 (1992), 147–53.

Fennell, Revd John (1762–1841), born Madeley, Shropshire; as a young man he was a Methodist local preacher and class-leader in *Penzance. In December 1790 he married at Madron church, Cornwall, Jane Branwell (1753–1829) (see BRANWELL FAMILY). In 1809 he was the headmaster of a day school in *Wellington, Shropshire, where he met Revd Patrick *Brontë and William *Morgan. Appointed first governor of *Woodhouse Grove school on 25 September 1811, with his wife as governess, he invited Mr Brontë to examine in classics. Thus Patrick met Maria Branwell *Brontë. At the school the Fennells proved to be pious and humane, but poor organizers. Their daughter Jane (1791–1827) married William Morgan, on 29 December 1812. In September 1813, intending to seek ordination in the Church of England, Fennell became curate to Revd John Crosse, Vicar of *Bradford. Mrs Fennell was godmother to Mr Brontë's daughter Maria, Mr Fennell baptized Elizabeth Brontë on 26 August 1815 and Branwell on 23 July 1817; they and their daughter were Emily's godparents. In September 1829, after Mrs Fennell's death in May, the Brontë children and Elizabeth *Branwell stayed with Mr Fennell at Cross-Stone, Todmorden, where he was incumbent April 1819–13 October 1841. Either he or another local John Fennell married Elizabeth Lister of Leeds in 1830 and had five children by her.

Ferndean Manor is an old house with dank, green walls, deep within a gloomy wood, about 30 miles from *Thornfield Hall, in *Jane Eyre*. Its unhealthy situation had deterred Rochester from hiding his mad wife there, but after he was maimed in the fire at Thornfield, he himself lived in it. Jane saw him straining to see the sky above the amphitheatre of trees. In the fields beyond the wood Jane agreed to marry him. Ruined *Wycoller Hall, in a deep wooded valley about 9 miles from Haworth, resembles Ferndean in its situation and antiquity, not in its architecture.

Fidena, the elegant capital of *Sneaky's Land, the 'Scotland' of the Glass Town or Verdopolitan

Fidena, Prince John Augustus Sneaky (Sneachi, Sneachie), Duke of

Federation and important for its strategic position: north of the Verdopolitan Valley, the crossroads to *Wellington's Land to the west and northern Angria to the east. The city is burnt by Rogue (Duke of *Northangerland) in his republican rebellion in the early *Glass Town and Angrian saga, but recaptured by Wellington at the Battle of Fidena (March 1832) and miraculously rebuilt. See also FIDENA, PRINCE JOHN AUGUSTUS SNEAKY, DUKE OF.

Fidena, Prince John Augustus Sneaky (Sneachi, Sneachie), Duke of, eldest son and heir of Alexander Sneaky, King of Sneaky's-Land, in the *Glass Town and Angrian saga. As a young man, he and his friend the Duke of Zamorna (Douro) fight bravely in the Great Insurrection and the rebellion in Sneaky's Land. He is wounded but, disguised as 'Mr Seymour', he woos and marries Lily *Hart, a humble seamstress. The marriage remains a secret for several years, during which a son is born, John Augustus Sneaky Jun., Marquis of Rossendale. Thanks to his sisters, Edith and Maria, Fidena and his wife are reconciled to his tyrannical father, who has already disinherited one son (*Thornton). Fidena's grave and fair character make him a sought-after leader. He becomes foreign secretary and then leader of the Constitutionalist Government in Verdopolis and later commander-in-chief during the *War of Encroachment. He is the only son of the four kings whom they all trust, so he is made prime minister of the Verdopolitan Federation.

Fidena is not a member of Zamorna's Angrian coterie; yet despite this and his antipathy to Zamorna's character, Fidena is Zamorna's most respected and trusted friend. He is hailed as a Christian philosopher, who has 'calm cool wisdom, noble integrity, stern resignation to the decrees of duty' that prefigure the character of St John *Rivers. Fidena watches over and comforts the dying Marian *Hume as she is neglected by Zamorna, and constantly tries to dissuade Zamorna from his relationship with Northangerland. Amongst the various leaders of the Glass Town Factions 'Fidena alone holds up the standard of justice and Religion' (Neufeldt *BB Works*, 2. 528).

Fidena Palace, in *Verdopolis; federal residence of the king of *Sneaky's Land and his family in the *Glass Town and Angrian saga.

Fieldhead, the home of Shirley *Keeldar in *Shirley*. A 'gothic old barrack' that has been tenantless for ten years, it lies between *Hollow's Mill and Briarfield Rectory. It brings its owner 'a property of a thousand a year', as well as precedence in the district. It is large enough to accommodate the whole *Sympson family—father, mother, and three children, together with their tutor Louis Gérard *Moore—when they pay Shirley a visit, and its dairy supplies the cottagers on the estate with milk and butter. Charlotte Brontë based Fieldhead on *Oakwell Hall, a manor house in *Birstall built in 1583 and substantially remodelled in the 17th century. The Hall is still extant, and with its latticed windows and its interior marked by a high gallery and oak-panelled walls, it appears much as Charlotte would have seen it on her visits to the *Nussey family, who lived at the *Red House in nearby Gomersal. From 1838 to 1852 Oakwell Hall was in use as a girls' boarding school run by Hannah Cockill (1810–93) and her sisters Sarah and Elizabeth, who were relatives of the Nussey family; Elizabeth had been at *Roe Head school with Charlotte. The name 'Fieldhead' was doubtless suggested by the neighbouring hamlet of that name lying close to Oakwell Hall and Birstall, and celebrated as the birthplace of the scientist and theologian Joseph Priestley (1733–1804).   HR

Filey, a small East Yorks. fishing town and resort. Charlotte Brontë and Ellen Nussey stayed there from 7 to 14 June 1849 after Anne's death, seeking the seclusion which *Scarborough could not provide. From Cliff House lodgings, kept by a Mrs Smith in North Street (now Belle Vue Street), Charlotte wrote to her father of the 'black desolate reef of rocks' (Filey Brigg, recalled in *Shirley*, ch. 32). In late May 1852 she returned to Filey alone to recuperate after a period of ill health and depression.

Berry, Kevin, *Charlotte Brontë: The Novelist's Visits to Bridlington, Scarborough, Filey and Hornsea* (1990).

film adaptations and biographies. *Jane Eyre* attracted some of the earliest film makers: there was a silent Italian film in 1909, and Theodore Marston adapted and directed a one-reel film for Thanhauser Pictures in 1910, with Irma Taylor and Frank Crane as Jane and Rochester. More is known, however, about the four-reel film adapted by John William Kellette and directed by Martin J. Faust for Blinkhorn Photoplays, New York, in 1914. The Brontë Parsonage Museum has stills (showing that the film was acted in modern dress), and a plot summary which is fairly close to the novel except that Adèle is the daughter of Rochester and Bertha, and melodramatic tension is produced at the end when Jane saves the blind Rochester from plunging over a precipice. Also in 1914, Frank H. Crane directed a two-reel film for Imperial-Universal Pictures, with Ethel Grandin and Irving Cummings. The year 1915 saw at least five film versions: a three-reel adaptation by Travers Vale for the Biograph Company, with

Louise Vale and Franklin Ritchie; three others, with Alan Hale, Richard Tucker, and Conway Teale as Rochester; and an Italian version entitled *The Castle of Thornfield*. Paul West's adaptation of 1918 appeared under the title *Woman and Wife*; directed by Edward Jose for Select Pictures, it was five reels long and featured Alice Brady as Jane, Eliott Dexter as Rochester, and Leonora Morgan as the insane wife. In this version, Rochester believes his mad wife to be dead until she is brought to the house for purposes of blackmail. Having interrupted the wedding, she is finally drowned. In 1921, Hugo Ballin adapted, produced, and directed a seven-reel film for the W. W. Hodkinson Corporation, with Mabel Ballin and Norman Trevor. Stills survive from this production. In 1920 a film was produced in Hungary under the title *The Orphan of Lowood*, and thus presumably derived from the German version of Charlotte Birch-Pfeiffer's 1870 play, *Die Waise Von Lowood*. *Die Waise Von Lowood* was also the title of Curtis Bernhardt's German adaptation, filmed in 1926. The Brontë Society also have photographs of the filming of *Shirley* at Wycoller Dene, near Haworth, in 1922, in which heavy wagons are shown negotiating difficult terrain for the frame-breaking scenes. Carlotta Breeze, Clive Brook, and Harvey Braban were the principal actors.

The first sound movie was adapted by Adèle Comandini, directed by Christy Cabanne, and produced by Ben Verschleiser for Monogram Pictures in 1934. Virginia Bruce was Jane and Colin Clive was Rochester. Stills show Jane as buxom and very blonde, in gingham and pantaloons. A curiosity is Jacques Tourneur's 1943 film, *I Walked with a Zombie*. Produced by Val Lewton from a screenplay by Curt Siodmak and Ardel Wray, it is described as 'based on an Original Story by Inez Wallace', but despite the Caribbean voodoo setting, it seems loosely based on the 'triangle' plot of *Jane Eyre*. 'Jane' is employed to nurse the 'possessed' wife of a Caribbean planter, a supercilious blonde who sleepwalks in diaphanous robes.

Still the best-known of all *Jane Eyre* films is the 1944 version with Orson Welles as Rochester, Joan Fontaine as Jane, and the young Elizabeth Taylor as Helen Burns. The film was adapted by Robert Stevenson, Aldous Huxley, and John Houseman, directed by Robert Stevenson and produced by William Goetz for Twentieth Century-Fox. The film has many Gothic trappings and the musical score by Bernard Herrmann contributes a great deal to its eerie weather-bound atmosphere. Like the contemporary Eichenberg lithographs (see ILLUSTRATIONS OF THE BRONTËS' WORKS), the film exaggerates gender-polarization; Joan Fontaine, who played the girl who becomes the second Mrs de Winter in *Rebecca* (1940), is a subdued and subservient Jane who fills Rochester's footbath at their first meeting, while Orson Welles is an overwhelming Rochester. Jane's rebellious speeches are toned down, and the plot severely truncated, omitting Jane's flight and the Rivers family, thus suggesting that all Jane needs is her man. This is a memorable film which owes only its bare elements to Charlotte Brontë.

By contrast, Delbert Mann's 1970 film tries hard to place *Jane Eyre* in the context of the burgeoning women's movement. Produced by Frederick Brogger for British Lion Pictures from a screenplay by Jack Pulman, the film features Susannah York as Jane and George C. Scott as Rochester, and its tone is quiet enough to allow considerable focus on their dialogue rather than Gothic architecture or dramatic surprises. Appearing only shortly after Jean Rhys's novel, *Wide Sargasso Sea* (1966) (a sympathetic account of the first Mrs Rochester: see SEQUELS AND 'INCREMENTAL LITERATURE'), this film presents a new kind of Bertha, young, pretty, and vacant. Rochester is given a scene alone with her in which the poignancy of their situation appears without 'shock-horror' tactics, while Jane is given new speeches to explain why, in modern terms, it is impossible for her to stay with Rochester without violating another woman's rights. The trials of Jane's journey over the moors, and her quiet triumph as a village schoolmistress, are given due weight. This is a well-intentioned film; if it fails to convince, it may be because Susannah York is too tall, too pretty, and too modern in her gestures.

Franco Zeffirelli's 1996 film, produced by Dyson Lovell for Miramax, restores the filmic grandiloquence of the Orson Welles version, augmented by colour and all the devices of modern photography. Its landscapes are large and its Thornfield Hall is Haddon Hall, the ancient and massive Derbyshire castle, despite Jane's description of Thornfield as 'a gentleman's manor-house, not a nobleman's seat'. Rochester is strongly played by William Hurt, and Jane by Charlotte Gainsbourg, a suitably 'plain and little' heroine. The screenplay by Hugh Whitemore presents Jane as an outspoken and rebellious child; she insists, for instance, on sharing Helen's sentence of hair-cutting, so that they wear their cropped hair like a symbol of female victimhood. The later scenes, however, subtly commute this independent spirit. When Jane runs away from Thornfield, instead of battling through the storm to her independent life, she is allowed to swoon into waiting arms; and the image of Jane and Rochester reunited at the end freezes into a simulacrum of a Victorian end plate to any romantic story.

The film history of *Wuthering Heights* begins with a distinguished six-reel silent version directed

'Oh, my heart's darling, hear me *this* time': Laurence Olivier as Heathcliff begs Catherine to return in William Wyler's 1939 film of *Wuthering Heights*.

by A. V. Bramble for The Ideal Film Renting Company in 1920. The screenplay was by Eliot Stannard, and the film was shot largely on location in Haworth, with the co-operation of the Brontë Society. No copy of the film survives, but the Society has an extensive collection of stills not only from the film but also of the processes of filming—carrying the heavy cameras onto the moor, for instance. Haworth Old Hall was used for the exterior of Wuthering Heights, and authenticity of detail was carefully attended to. Three actors were used for Heathcliff, and two for Hindley and Edgar, to make sure that they 'grew up' convincingly. Even more surprising, given that the film lasted no more than an hour and a half, was the fact that all the second-generation characters were included, and that Hareton and the second Catherine also had child and adult versions. The adult Heathcliff and Catherine were played by Milton Rosmer and Anne Trevor. The gestures of the actors resemble those of the Victorian stage melodrama, but the dramatic still of Catherine's death scene combines heightened gestures with realistic indications of her illness. Interestingly, the film was billed as 'Emily Brontë's tremendous Story of Hate', though according to Brontë Society member Jonas Bradley, 'the more gruesome elements of the story have been minimised' to suit the 'A' certificate (quoted in Patsy Stoneman, Brontë Transformations (1996), 115).

By far the most influential of all the Brontë films was the 1939 Samuel Goldwyn production of Wuthering Heights, directed by William Wyler to a screenplay by Ben Hecht and Charles MacArthur, with Laurence Olivier and Merle Oberon as Heathcliff and Catherine, David Niven as Edgar, and Flora Robson as Nelly. Comparisons were made between this film and the exactly contemporary film of Gone With the Wind; Olivier had wanted Vivien Leigh (who played Scarlett O'Hara) to play Catherine, and Alfred Newman's music for Wuthering Heights was felt to be in the same style as the other film. Unlike the 1920 Wuthering Heights, the Hollywood film takes considerable liberties with the plot and characterization. The character of Heathcliff is softened (Goldwyn originally wanted to call the film He Died for Her) and Catherine's is sharpened so that she appears as a coquettish social climber who loses interest in Heathcliff because of his inability to fulfil her ambitions. The plot is severely truncated to end with the death of the elder Catherine, which is elevated to tragic status by gestures toward the 'other-worldly' aspects of the novel. In particular, Penistone Crag serves throughout the film as a lovers' tryst, where Catherine declares that she wants 'everything to stop' so that they can be frozen in their youthful togetherness. Developed into a filmic motif, a snowbound Penistone Crag becomes the site of Heathcliff's death and of his ghostly reunion with Catherine. The strength of the film lies in such emotive scenes, especially the scene in which Heathcliff leans from the window to beg Cathy's ghost to return; but by recasting the story into what Wagner calls 'the story of the stable-boy and the lady' (Geoffrey Wagner, The Novel and the Cinema (1975), 234) and removing the second-generation characters, Wyler's version domesticates the novel, locating the tragedy safely in a costume-drama past whose social structures need not trouble the modern world. The film had, however, a tremendous impact on the reputation of Emily Brontë's novel, and more copies of the novel were sold in the three weeks after the first showing of the film than in the previous five years (C. M. Edgerley, 'Wuthering Heights as a film', BST (1939), 9. 49. 239–41).

A curiosity of Brontë film history is Luis Buñuel's 1953 version, shot in Mexico under the ironic title Abismos de Pasion (Depths of Passion). Buñuel himself had a hand in the screenplay, which was produced by Oscar Dancigers with Jorge Mistral and Irasema Dilian as the Heathcliff and Catherine characters. This version, which transposes the story to a Latin, Catholic society, is focused on the economic and ideological constraints within which sexual relationships must function. Lacking any transcendent quality, the film has no childhood scenes and no second generation. The story opens with Heathcliff and Edgar in open competition for the heavily pregnant Catherine, and ends with Heathcliff being shot by Hindley, leaving Catherine's son to carry on the patriarchal lineage. A final scene in an underground tomb, invoking Romeo and Juliet, with music from Wagner's Tristan and Isolde, shows the dead lovers in what Philip Strick describes as 'an ironically futile romantic achievement the surrealists found glorious to contemplate' (Programme note for first UK screening at the National Film Theatre (14 Feb. 1984)). In contrast, A. R. Kardar's Indian version Dil Diya Dard Liya (Give Your Heart and Receive Anguish), filmed for Kary Productions, Bombay, in 1966, reverts to the romanticism of the early 19th century, including shipwrecks, wanderings, songs, and dance. The Heathcliff character, played by Dilip Kumar, is eventually discovered to be the heir to a dead maharajah and he and 'Catherine' (Waheeda Rehman) are married. In 1988 the Japanese director Yoshige Yoshida made a Samurai version of Wuthering Heights entitled Onimaru, with Yuko Tanaka in the Catherine role; Yusaka Matsada plays the Heathcliff character as an inarticulate warrior. The film was inspired by Georges Bataille's essay on the novel in his book La Littérature et le mal

(*Literature and Evil*, 1957), which focuses on the dramatization of sexuality and death.

The first colour film of *Wuthering Heights* was directed by Robert Fuest and produced by John Pellatt for American International Pictures in 1970 from a screenplay by Patrick Tilley, with Timothy Dalton as Heathcliff and Anna Calder-Marshall as Catherine. The film clearly derives from the 'permissive' 1970s, but drastically curtails and limits the potentialities of the novel. It begins with Catherine's burial and goes on, like Buñuel's version, to show Heathcliff being shot by Hindley. The rest of the story is in flashback and there is no second generation. Fuest, who later became known as a director of horror films, has combined some ghoulish aspects of the novel with an overtly sexual atmosphere in which Nelly, with an expanse of white bosom, is infatuated with Hindley, and Heathcliff, who is very probably Mr Earnshaw's illegitimate son, invites the young Catherine to 'a tumble'. In a *BST* review (1971), David Drew is unconvinced by 'the juxtaposition of earthy sex and blanched ghosts' (16. 81. 59).

The most elaborate film of *Wuthering Heights* so far is the 1992 Paramount version entitled *Emily Brontë's Wuthering Heights* (because Samuel Goldwyn holds the copyright of the simple title). Directed by Peter Kosminsky to a screenplay by Anne Devlin, the film is both highly coloured and very detailed, including all the second-generation plot. Ralph Fiennes makes an intense Heathcliff with a good Yorkshire accent, but controversy was raised by the casting of Juliette Binoche, who never quite sounds English, in the roles of both Catherines. The set shows Gothic heightening, with Wuthering Heights represented as a turreted castle; the photography, however, is brilliant, with changeable exterior and gloomily convincing interior scenes. There is little new about the interpretation; indeed, by introducing Emily Brontë herself (played by the popular singer Sinead O'Connor) into the opening sequence, the film subscribes to the Romantic theory of literary inspiration ('something whispered to my mind and I began to write') which allows us to read the film as a fantasy of a single mind.

Given the huge number of biographies and semi-fictional books based on the lives of the Brontës, it is surprising that their lives have not attracted many film makers. There seems to have been a 1943 film called *Three Sisters of the Moors*, with Molly Lamont and Lynne Roberts, but little is known of this. The most notorious example appeared three years later: the Warner Brothers' film *Devotion*, directed by Curtis Bernhardt to a screenplay by Keith Winter, produced by Robert Buckner and released in 1946, with Olivia de Havilland as Charlotte, Ida Lupino as Emily, and Nancy Coleman as Anne. Arthur Kennedy played Branwell, Montagu Love played Mr Brontë, and the Austrian actor Paul Henreid played Arthur Bell Nicholls. The music is by Erich Korngold. There is little attempt at visual authenticity and stills of the three sisters, dressed in rich fabrics and adorned with lace and flowers, are interchangeable with those of Meg, Jo, and Amy from MGM's *Little Women* (1949). The title, *Devotion*, derives from a plethora of biographical books and plays which appeared during the 1920s and 1930s speculating on the precise relationships between the Brontë siblings. *Devotion* shows all three sisters willing to sacrifice themselves to further Branwell's career, while he uses the proceeds from a successful picture to send them to Brussels. There is, however, a further twist to their mutual devotion improbably based on the assumption that Emily is in love with Revd A. B. Nicholls, who is in love with Charlotte. Emily, who is visited from time to time by premonitions of death represented by a dark horseman, proves her devotion to Charlotte by dying, finally carried off by the horseman, and as she dies, she tells Charlotte that 'loving is the only thing that matters'. Thackeray (in person) comments that they 'appear to have indulged in quite an orgy of self-denial'. The film was described by a Brontë enthusiast as a 'vulgar distortion of the life story of the Haworth immortals' (*BST* (1946), 11. 56. 38).

In complete contrast is the four-part drama *The Brontës of Haworth*, written by Christopher Fry for Yorkshire Television, directed and produced by Marc Miller, and broadcast in 1973. Emily was played by Rosemary McHale, Charlotte by Vickery Turner, Anne by Ann Penfold, Branwell by Michael Kitchen, and Mr Brontë by Alfred Burke, and even the most searching of observers found an 'uncanny' resemblance between the distinguished television cast and their originals. Much of the action was shot on location in Haworth, including the interior of the Parsonage, and the camera filters were manipulated to produce a muted light. As might be expected from a dramatist of Christopher Fry's stature, the writing is poetic, and the sensitive, responsive acting drew viewers into a fascinated engagement with a family at once extraordinary and believable.

The same could not be said for André Téchiné's *Les Sœurs Brontë*, produced for Action Films, Paris, in 1979 to a screenplay written by Téchiné with Pascal Bonitzer. Selected for the Cannes Film Festival, this 'lavishly-costumed bio-pic' (Jacques Siclier, *Weekly Guardian* (26 May 1979)) was described by Philip French as 'a copper-bottomed disaster' and a 'risible romantic farrago' (*Observer* (20 May 1979)). Isabelle Adjani (Emily), Marie-France Pisier (Charlotte), and Isabelle Huppert

(Anne) all appear extremely pretty in the Brigitte Bardot style.

Delbert Mann, who had directed a film of *Jane Eyre* in 1970, went on in 1983 to direct *Brontë*, a film about Charlotte Brontë which began life as a one-woman play by William Luce for Irish Radio, with music by Arthur Harris. The play was filmed as a Sonny Fox Production with Irish landscape settings realistically standing in for Yorkshire. *Variety*'s reviewer describes the film as 'a miniature treasure' (15 Dec. 1983). Two video-films dealing with Brontë biography have also been prepared in association with the Brontë Society. *In the Shadows of the Brontës* (1990) is a rather pedestrian compilation of still photographs with a commentary written by Peter Harker and narrated by Martin Plenderleith for Classic Productions, Bridlington. *A Wild Workshop: Yorkshire and the Brontës* (1992), is more imaginative, with wonderful landscape photography including costumed performers as members of the Brontë family (Ann Dinsdale, the current Museum Librarian, can be seen as Charlotte). Voices-over read a selection from Brontë letters, novels, and poetry. The film was written and directed by Richard Spanswick, who also wrote the music, and produced by Heather Saycell for Videolink, Cheshire. See also THEATRE ADAPTATIONS AND BIOGRAPHIES; TELEVISION AND RADIO ADAPTATIONS. PS

Klein, Michael, and Parker, Gillian (eds.), *The English Novel and the Movies* (1981).

Nudd, Donna Marie, 'Bibliography of Film, Television and Stage Adaptations of *Jane Eyre*', *BST* (1991), 20. 3. 169–72.

——'Rediscovering *Jane Eyre* through its Adaptations', in Diane Hoeveler and Beth Lau (eds.), *Approaches to Teaching Jane Eyre* (1992).

Stoneman, Patsy, *Brontë Transformations: The Cultural Dissemination of 'Jane Eyre' and 'Wuthering Heights'* (1996).

finances of the Brontës. As a sizar at *Cambridge Revd Patrick Brontë would pay £10 on admission, 6s. 4d. quarterly tuition fees, and matriculation and graduation fees. To meet these expenses he taught pupils, and obtained three exhibitions, one of £5 per annum, a half-share of another (£1 13s. p.a.), and 14s. from a Goodman exhibition. In addition William *Wilberforce and Henry Thornton agreed to pay £10 each per annum. He must have welcomed the £60 p.a. of his *Wethersfield curacy. The value of his *Wellington, Shropshire, and *Dewsbury curacies is not known; his *Hartshead living was worth £62 p.a. plus a small lodging allowance. His living at *Thornton was nominally £140 p.a., but in practice only £127, and he applied for help from Queen Anne's Bounty on 27 January 1820. The *Haworth living was £170 p.a., with the parsonage rent-free;

but medical expenses for his wife in 1821 left him heavily in debt. Friends subscribed £200 for him, a charity provided £50, and Elizabeth *Branwell helped by paying for her keep and sharing in the teaching of the children. In 1825 Mr Brontë paid £80 2s. 2d. in fees to *Cowan Bridge school. Mrs Thomas Atkinson (see ATKINSON FAMILY) may have contributed to Charlotte's fees at *Roe Head, and from 1838 the Church Pastoral Aid Society paid for Mr Brontë to have a curate. After the deaths of Emily and Anne, their assets of under £450 and under £600 respectively, with unspecified amounts in funds, would go to their father. In his will Mr Brontë bequeathed £40 to be distributed to his brothers and sisters, £30 to Martha *Brown, and the residue to Revd A. B. *Nicholls. At his death in 1861 he left estate of under £1,500.

Much of Charlotte's salary as a teacher at Roe Head and *Heald's House was absorbed in buying necessities for herself and Anne. The amounts she earned there, and in the *Sidgwick household, are unknown. At *Upperwood House her nominal salary of £20 per annum was reduced to £16 because she was charged for the cost of laundry. In 1843 Charlotte earned £16 as a teacher at the Pensionnat *Heger. Elizabeth Branwell's bequest of under £1,500 to be divided among four nieces meant that by early 1843 the Brontë sisters had each received a quarter-share which they invested in York and North Midland railway shares. For some years they received dividends of 10 per cent, and they were able to pay £31 10s. plus advertising expenses to publish *Poems* 1846. Charlotte invested £500 received for *Jane Eyre* in railway shares. In January 1853 George *Smith reinvested the proceeds of their sale (£521 17s. 6d.) in 3¼ per cent reduced bank annuities. He had already invested for her £500 for the copyright of *Shirley*, £100 for the cheap edition of *Jane Eyre*, and £480, part of the £500 paid for *Villette*. In April 1853 he invested £82 10s. for the foreign copyright of *Villette*. Before her marriage Charlotte tied up her capital (£1,678 9s. 9d.) in a trust for herself and any children she might have. It would have gone to her father on her death, had she not bequeathed it in her will (17 February 1855) to Mr Nicholls.

Anne's salary at *Blake Hall is unknown. At *Thorp Green Hall she earned £40 p.a., a total of £203 10s. for the time she stayed there. Other sources of her assets at her death would include her quarter-share of Elizabeth Branwell's estate, £50 from T. C. *Newby for *Tenant*, and Frances *Outhwaite's legacy of £200. Emily's estate of under £450 reflected the short time she had worked as a teacher, and her lack of earnings from *Wuthering Heights*, for she and Anne paid Newby £50 towards the cost of publishing it but received nothing back. Branwell's early attempts to become

Charlotte Brontë, 'English Lady', pencil copy of William Finden's engraving of Lady Jersey, after the painting by E. T. Parris, in *The Poetical Works of Lord Byron* (1839).

a professional artist cannot have been very profitable. His salary as tutor at *Broughton-in-Furness is unknown. As clerk at *Sowerby Bridge station his salary was £75 p.a., and as clerk-in-charge at *Luddenden Foot £130, from which £11 1s. 7d. was deducted on his dismissal. At Thorp Green he earned £80 p.a. from January 1843 until his dismissal in July 1845. Since he was frequently in debt or appealing for money thereafter, his assets at the time of his death were probably negligible.

Finden, Edward and William, 19th-century English line engravers. William (1787–1852) and his younger brother Edward (1791–1857), worked in conjunction first on engraving illustrations for books and then on large-scale plates such as Sir Thomas Lawrence's portrait of King George IV, and the Highlander's Return and Village Festival by Wilkie. In Charlotte Brontë's 'A Peep into a Picture Book' (in *'Corner Dishes') her young narrator Lord Charles Wellesley browses through the pages of 'Tree's Portrait Gallery of the Aristocracy of Africa', engraved by Edward Finden from paintings by Frederick De Lisle, the Joshua Reynolds of Glass Town (Alexander EEW, 2(2). 84–96). The detailed description of the engravings, binding, and paper suggests that she has at least seen one of the sumptuous editions of Finden's Royal Gallery of British Art, Finden's Portraits of the Female Aristocracy, or Finden's Byron Beauties, possibly at the home of Mary Taylor or at Roe Head where the volumes may have been used in art lessons. (The single 'Finden' in the titles here refers to William, who owned the studio.) It is clear too that Branwell was aware of the quality of the Findens' engravings, since he and his sisters chose to copy several of their plates from the popular *annuals. Branwell reproduced Edward Finden's engraving of John *Martin's Queen Esther in watercolour (Dec. 1830), and at the same time Charlotte copied his Bessy Bell and Mary Gray, after a painting by J. R. West, both in the *Forget Me Not (1831). In May 1834, Charlotte copied Edward Finden's crisp view of Bolton Abbey, Wharfedale, based on Turner's well-known drawing of 1809, which appeared in the Literary Souvenir (1826), a drawing she exhibited at The *Royal Northern Society for the Encouragement of the Fine Arts.

A series of landscape and portrait illustrations to the life and works of Byron executed by the Findens proved particularly popular. A number of these are reproduced by Charlotte and Emily in pencil and paint. Charlotte copied Edward Finden's Santa Maura (23 Sept. 1833) and Geneva (23 Aug. 1834); and William Finden's Bridge of Egripo (c.1834), Countess of Jersey (renamed 'English Lady' by Charlotte, 15 Oct. 1834), and The

Maid of Saragoza (c.1834). Emily copied William Finden's engraving of Westall's Ianthe, which she retitled 'The North Wind' (1842). These Finden engravings appeared in numerous editions of Byron published by John Murray, such as The Works of Lord Byron: With His Letters and Journals and His Life, ed. Thomas Moore, 14 vols. (1832); Letters and Journals of Lord Byron: With Notices of His Life, ed. Thomas Moore, 3 vols. (3rd edn., 1833); and The Poetical Works of Lord Byron, 8 vols. (1839). The engravings also appeared in separate volumes without Byron's poems, such as Finden's Illustrations of the Life and Works of Lord Byron, 3 vols. (1833–4) and Finden's Landscape and Portrait Illustrations to the Life and Works of Lord Byron (1834).

Alexander & Sellars, pp. 298, 176–7, 213–14, 228–9, 233–7, 385–6.

Finic(k), the mute dwarf servant of the Marquis of Douro (Duke of *Zamorna) in the *Glass Town and Angrian saga. He is the offspring of an early affair between Douro and Sofala, a Negress whom the 18-year-old Douro forsook and who, before she died, prayed that her son might shame his false father (reported in A *Leaf from an Unopened Volume). His appearance is particularly repugnant to Douro, with whom he communicates in sign language. He stands three feet high, has a huge head covered by a shock of coal-black hair, and has small bead-like eyes which gleam with an expression of fiendish malignity.

Firth family. Dr John Scholefield Firth (1757–1820), physician and wealthy landowner, of Kipping House, *Thornton, befriended the Brontës at Thornton with his daughter Elizabeth, later Mrs *Franks. Revd Patrick Brontë had exchanged livings with Revd Thomas Atkinson (see ATKINSON FAMILY), husband of Frances, née Walker, daughter of Dr Firth's sister Esther. Dr Firth married in December 1793 Elizabeth Holt (1758–1814), who was killed instantly when a horse bolted and she was thrown violently out of a gig in July 1814, in Kipping lane, opposite the kitchen window of her home. He married secondly in September 1815 Ann Greame (?1761–1846), Mr Brontë's friend Revd William *Morgan performing the ceremony in Bradford. She was the twin sister of Frances *Outhwaite of Bradford. On 26 August 1815 John and Elizabeth Firth, with Elizabeth *Branwell, were godparents at the baptism of Elizabeth Brontë; and the second Mrs Firth shared the family's interest in and kindness towards the Brontës. They were invited to Kipping House, took walks together, and met at other houses. Dr and Mrs Firth were Branwell Brontë's godparents at his baptism on 23 July 1817. The Firths' thoughtful

Fitzarthur

benevolence towards the Brontës continued after they moved to Haworth. Mr Brontë stayed several times at Kipping House on his way to Bradford, and on 8 September 1820 Elizabeth Firth and her father visited Haworth Parsonage. Mr Brontë recalled his time at Thornton as the happiest in his life, though its associations were saddened for him by the illness and death, in December 1820, of Dr Firth, with whom he used to take 'sweet counsel' (Smith *Letters*, 1. 142). Mr Brontë visited him on 13 and 21 December 1820, and took his funeral on 2 January 1821. On 26 May 1821, during Mrs Brontë's last illness, Elizabeth Firth and Frances Outhwaite took Maria and Elizabeth Brontë back to Kipping for a month.

Fitzarthur. See WELLESLEY, ERNEST EDWARD GORDON; 'FITZARTHUR'.

Flannagan (Flanigan), Maurice, a famous boxer in the *Glass Town and Angrian saga, a favourite of the Duke of *Zamorna (who gives him a secretarial job so he can spar regularly with him) and particularly admired by Patrick Benjamin *Wiggins (Branwell). He has 'a most pugnacious aspect', fiery red hair, 'shoulders like Atlas', and is nicknamed 'Pratee' after a champion of the ring at the time of the Brontës. See 'CORNER DISHES'; PUGILISM, BRONTË INTEREST IN.

Flossy, a King Charles spaniel given to Anne Brontë by her pupils, the Robinson girls at Thorp Green, and brought to Haworth about 1843. Flossy wore a brass collar (still extant in the BPM), as he does in Emily's famous painting 'Flossy' (misattributed to Charlotte in J. R. V. Barker (ed.), *Sixty Treasures*, (1988), p. 17; see Alexander & Sellars, pp. 388–9). The dog features in a number of Brontë sketches by both Emily and Anne (Alexander & Sellars, pp. 389–92, 408–10). Apparently Flossy sired another 'Flossy' that was given to Ellen Nussey (Smith *Letters*, 1. 362 n.). Flossy features regularly in correspondence and diary papers over a period of eleven years. On 26 January 1848, Anne wrote to Ellen that 'Flossy is fatter than ever, but still active enough to relish a sheep hunt' and Ellen refers affectionately to the dog as 'long silky haired black and white Flossy' (Smith *Letters*, 1. 600). He outlived his mistress by many years, eventually dying in December 1854.

Flower, Captain Sir John, later Viscount Richton, from Wellington's Land, contemporary of the Duke of Wellington and associated with the *Young Men's Play. In the *Glass Town and Angrian saga he initially plays a political and military role, becoming secretary of the War Office for the Constitutional Party, then a military leader under *Fidena in the *War of Encroachment, and subsequently Lord Richton, Verdopolitan

ambassador to the kingdom of *Angria. Married, with several daughters and a son, his residence in Verdopolis, Flower House, is the scene of numerous parties for young and old. As Branwell Brontë's pseudonym from 1831 to 1834, Flower chronicles the rise of the new kingdom of Angria in (among others) The *Politics of Verdopolis and *Real Life in Verdopolis. He is an eminent scholar and the official Glass Town historian.

folklore. Tabitha *Aykroyd remembered when 'fairies frequented the margin' of the Haworth beck (Gaskell *Life*, 1. 82). The Brontës learned much folklore from her and from their reading. Charlotte refers playfully to 'fairishes', elves, brownies, and sprites, but, like Branwell, she also knows about the ominous *Gytrash or black dog, vampires, deceptive marsh-spirits, and Banshees. *Wuthering Heights* is haunted by the presence of the other world: the unquiet spirits of the dead, Cathy's belief that she is unable to die, Heathcliff's agonized pleas to her to haunt him, and his final 'walking' with her, terrifying the little boy who dares not pass their spirits.

foreign languages. Five of the Brontë children studied languages other than English. All of them had access to translations of Greek, Roman, French, and German literature through books on Revd Patrick Brontë's shelves, the family's magazine subscriptions, and access to local libraries.

As the only male child and therefore the one entitled to an education in the classics, Branwell learned Latin and Greek. Mr Brontë had studied those languages at St John's College, *Cambridge, and, since he did not want to send his son away to school, undertook to teach the boy himself. In tutoring Branwell he drew on the New Testament in Latin and the Prayer Book in Greek, as well as texts by classical authors. Branwell proved an eager and precocious learner, reading Homer and *Virgil by the age of 10. He also incorporated Latin and Greek phrases into his early writings. In 1838 he began to translate Horace's *Odes* (see 'ODES OF HORACE, THE'; DRINKWATER, JOHN). Two years later he sent some of his translations to Hartley *Coleridge and Thomas *De Quincey. In 1839 he embarked on a further course of study with his father, probably to gain a position as tutor to Robert Postlethwaite's two sons (see POSTLETHWAITE FAMILY).

Since girls were not traditionally instructed in the classics his sisters did not study them as he did. Nonetheless evidence exists that they knew some Latin, whether directly through their father's agency, by indirectly sharing in Branwell's lessons, or by teaching themselves. Charlotte's work includes classical references, and in Brussels she wrote a *devoir, *'Athens Saved by Poetry', that is based

198

on an episode in Plutarch's *Lives*. Emily read at least part of three books in Latin: Virgil's *Aeneid*, Horace's *Ars Poetica*, and *The Four Gospels*. She undertook translations from the first two, which, as Edward Chitham has shown, are of considerable sophistication and subtlety (Chitham *Birth of WH*, pp. 17–32). Additionally, she made notes on tragedies by Aeschylus and Euripides. The extent of Anne's knowledge of the classics is not known, but while she was a governess she bought and inscribed a Latin textbook, possibly to tutor her pupil Edmund Robinson (see ROBINSON FAMILY).

While it was atypical to teach girls Greek and Latin, they were encouraged to learn French and German if they wished to be considered 'accomplished'. Charlotte persuaded her Aunt Elizabeth *Branwell to pay for a year of study abroad by claiming that she and Emily had to learn those languages if they were to open their own school. Her fascination with French literature and culture was apparent by the time she was 13. Among her writings from that period are five instalments of 'A Frenchman's Journal' (1830; see 'YOUNG MEN'S MAGAZINE'). In the same year she made a *'Translation into English Verse of the First Book of M. Voltaire's Henriade'. She entered Margaret *Wooler's school in 1831 with her own copy of Tocquot's *A New and Easy Guide to the Pronunciation and Spelling of the French Language*; at the end of her second term, she won the French Prize, a copy of the New Testament in French. Her French, however, was far from perfect, as a letter to Ellen Nussey demonstrates (Smith *Letters*, 1. 118–19). Mary *Taylor's father later lent her French books, which she considered 'the best substitute for French Conversation' (Smith *Letters*, 1. 226). But she only acquired a firm grasp of the language during her two terms at the Pensionnat *Heger, as attested by the progress she made in writing devoirs, the certificate of competence that M. Constantin *Heger gave her, and the letters she subsequently sent him. She introduced French phrases into all four novels—*Villette* contains extensive passages in French—and conveyed the ambience of a Belgian boarding school there and in *The Professor*. More broadly the French Romantics she had studied influenced the style of her writing. After her return from Brussels she maintained her reading knowledge of the language. But aside from later references to George *Sand and Balzac (to whose work G. H. Lewes first alerted her), she seems to have lost the fascination for things French that she had shown before her Belgian experience.

Emily also studied French in Brussels. Whether she knew much of the language before that trip remains a matter of conjecture. In her three months as a student at Miss Wooler's school she probably had lessons in French, which would have been included in any curriculum designed for the improvement of young ladies. When Anne replaced Emily at the school she would have had a similar grounding, and Aunt Branwell, who read French, may also have tried to impart what she knew to her charges. But clearly, Emily came to the Pensionnat Heger with less basic knowledge of the language than Charlotte and remained for only nine months. Nonetheless as her eight surviving devoirs demonstrate she made remarkable progress. Unlike Charlotte, however, she did not continue to bring French into her writings.

Several critics have argued that German was Emily's language of preference. As early as 1848 a review refers to parallels between *Wuthering Heights* and tales by E. T. A. Hoffmann, most notably *Das Majorat* (*The Entail*). *Schiller and Novalis have also been suggested as influences on her novel and poetry. As Mary Ward first observed, however, Emily would not have needed to know German to read them since *Blackwood's* and *Fraser's* regularly published German authors in translation. Charlotte's portrayal of Diana and Mary *Rivers in *Jane Eyre* (ch. 28) struggling through Schiller with a dictionary may be obliquely biographical, hinting at her own sisters' efforts. However, as Chitham accurately comments, 'real evidence is hard to come by' (Chitham *EB*, p. 149).

What is certain is that Charlotte studied German at the pensionnat, especially in her second year (1843). She composed an imaginary letter to a friend ('Meine liebe Freundinn') and translated poems by Schiller, and other pieces, into French and English. Later she portrayed young women in her novels engaged in the study of German. Like the Rivers sisters, Jane Eyre labours to learn it; Lucy Snowe and Paulina de Bassompierre take lessons with Fräulein Anna Braun (*Villette*, ch. 26). In contrast, William Crimsworth enters *The Professor* with a working knowledge of German (ch. 2).

While Charlotte did not study any other language, she sprinkled Italian words into her writings and continued to dispatch her characters to Rome, Florence, Venice, and Naples. In these and other ways, she and her siblings manifested a lifelong interest in cultures other than their own. See also BOOKS OWNED BY THE BRONTËS; BOOKS READ BY THE BRONTËS; ACCOMPLISHMENTS.   SL

Alexander *EW*, pp. 66–7.
Barker, pp. 147, 166, 867.
Chitham *Birth of WH*, pp. 17–32, 57–66.
Chitham *EB*, pp. 141–9.
Duthie *Foreign Vision*, pp. 179–98.
Neufeldt *CBP*, pp. 343–70, 484–90.

Forget Me Not (1823–48), the first of the *annuals, established by the publisher Rudolph Ackermann as 'a Christmas, New Year's and birthday present' and edited during its 26 years by Frederic Shoberl. (The first issue only appeared under the editorship of William Combe, the well-known author of the *Tour of Dr Syntax*.) It was a particularly popular annual, surviving 180 of its almost 200 competitors. Early copies of the *Forget Me Not*, including that of 1831 owned by the Brontës, cost 12s. each, were bound in engraved green paper wrappers, and issued in a cardboard case with the same green paper designs. Its contributors (often anonymous) included names familiar to the Brontës, such as Thomas Campbell, Thomas Hood, Thomas *Moore, James Montgomery, James *Hogg, and Mrs Hemans. The *Forget Me Not* also included the first publication of *Byron's earliest verses and some unpublished lines by James Thomson.

Although the date of the Brontës' copy is 1831, they received their annual by November of the previous year, since it was common practice for the volumes to be issued in time for Christmas. Thus their copies of the engravings are all dated November and December 1830. Charlotte made watercolour copies of the engraving on the title-page of a woman with a lyre from a drawing by F. Burney; *Bessy Bell and Mary Gray*, an engraving by W. *Finden after J. R. West that accompanied a tale by 'Delta' (David *Moir); *The Italian Scene* engraved by Freebairn after a painting by Barrett; and *The Disconsolate*, an engraving by C. Rolls after H. Corbould, that accompanied a poem of the same name by 'L.E.L.' (Letitia Elizabeth Landon). Emily also copied *The Disconsolate* and Branwell copied *Queen Esther* from a painting by John *Martin.

> Alexander & Sellars, pp. 15, 112–13, 175–9, 298, 372–3 (illustrations).
> Tallent-Bateman, Chas. T., 'The Forget Me Not', *Manchester Quarterly: A Journal of Literature and Art*, 21 (1902), 78–98.

Forster, William Edward (1818–86), statesman. Forster married Jane Martha Arnold (1821–99) in August 1850, shortly before Charlotte Brontë's first visit to the *Arnold family. Forster entered the Bradford woollen trade in 1842. A strong Liberal, honest, unselfish, and practical, he urged the Bradford *Chartists to espouse moral, not physical, force in 1848. Jane Forster was quiet, pious, and kind-hearted. After visiting Haworth with Forster, in ?late January 1851, she wrote a memorable account of Charlotte moving about like a spirit in the joyless parsonage. They called again in October 1852, but Charlotte refused their invitations to stay with them at Rawdon, near Leeds.

> Gaskell *Life*, 2. 187–90.

Fort Adrian, the castle-like mansion of the Duke of *Zamorna, on the east bank of the *Calabar River, in *Adrianopolis, Angria. Lying 5 miles across the water from the city batteries, it houses a garrison and can be seen from Zamorna Palace. It is here that Zamorna's son Ernest is housed for a time and where Louisa *Vernon is imprisoned.

Fossette, rue. Like the rue d'Isabelle in *Brussels, the rue Fossette, formerly the 'Fossé aux Chiens' (the site of the kennels for the ducal hounds in the 13th century), is a quiet street to which one descends by an 'old and worn flight of steps'. In it stands Mme *Beck's pensionnat, in Charlotte Brontë's *Villette*.

Foundling. A Tale of Our Own Times, The, 'By Captain Tree' (31 May–27 June 1833), a booklet of eighteen pages with an elaborately decorated title-page (illustrated in Alexander *EEW*, 2(1). 42; MS in BL Ashley); once attributed to Branwell, the novelette is definitely the work of Charlotte, narrated by her character Tree (Alexander *EW*, pp. 95–6) in the *Glass Town and Angrian saga. The story traces the fortunes of Edward *Sydney from his foundling status in England to his patronage by the Marquis of Douro (Duke of *Zamorna) in the 'Utopian Colony' in Africa, and subsequent discovery of his true identity as Prince Edward of York, son of Frederick Guelph, Duke of *York and King of the *Twelves. His arrival in the Glass Town provides Charlotte with an opportunity to complicate her narrative with descriptions of the Great Glass Town, now *Verdopolis, its architecture and society, and its college for nobles on *Philosopher's Island. The early Glass Town is also recalled, many of 'the glorious Twelves' are reintroduced, and the Chief *Genii make their final appearance in Charlotte's juvenilia. A secondary plot involves the relationship between Zamorna's cousin Lady Julia *Wellesley and Sydney, which Charlotte analyses as the infatuation of a suitor and the whim of 'a foolish petted little girl'. Their unsuitable marriage provides material for future comic marital strife in the juvenilia. Lord Charles Wellesley later refers to this tale by Tree as 'one wild farrago of bombast, fustian and lies' (Alexander *EEW*, 2(2). 94). Tree's narrative is one of Charlotte's series of alternative visions of the Glass Town world and part of the continuing rivalry between its narrators.

> Alexander *EEW*, 2(1). 43–125.

Franks, Mrs Elizabeth, née Firth (1797–1837), daughter of Dr Firth (see FIRTH FAMILY) of *Thornton, and friend of the Brontë family. Her diary records the pleasant social life of her girlhood, her attendance at Richmal Mangnall's Crofton Hall school (1812–13), her friendship with Frances *Outhwaite, her acquaintance with Revd Thomas Atkinson (see ATKINSON FAMILY), and the tragic death of her much-loved mother. Elizabeth was godmother to Elizabeth and Anne Brontë, and perhaps stood proxy for Charlotte *Branwell at Charlotte Brontë's baptism. She became fond of Elizabeth *Branwell, who was 'much affected' on parting from her in July 1816. After Mrs Brontë's death she contributed two guineas to a subscription fund for Revd Patrick Brontë. From 8 to 10 December 1821 he visited the Firths at *Kipping House, and it is likely that he proposed marriage to her in a letter she received on 12 December. In what she describes in her diary as her 'last letter' to him on 14 December she must have refused him; but on her wedding tour after her marriage in September 1824 to Revd James Clarke Franks (1793–1867), Vicar of *Huddersfield, she visited and gave presents to the three elder Brontë girls at *Cowan Bridge school. Her kindness to Charlotte, Anne, and probably Emily Brontë was shown during their stay at *Roe Head school in gifts of clothes, and an invitation to Charlotte and Anne to visit her for a week in June 1836. The Franks had five children: John Firth (1826–1917), James Coulthurst (1828–?1928), Henry James (1830–54), Elizabeth (1831–97), and William Walker (1833–64). Mrs Franks's health declined after a serious attack of influenza, and she died in September 1837. In 1853 her widower married Jane Coates of Huddersfield (d. 1884).

Fraser's Magazine. Founded in 1830 as a rival to *Blackwood's Edinburgh Magazine*, *Fraser's Magazine* was a lively and highly diverse periodical edited by William Maginn, previously an important contributor to *Blackwood's*. The Brontës began receiving *Fraser's* in 1832 when *Blackwood's* was no longer available to them, and its influence, like that of its predecessor, is evident in their juvenile writings. Maginn adopted a fictitious editorial persona, 'Oliver Yorke', whose pervading presence—like that of the fictitious *Blackwood's* editor 'Christopher *North' (John *Wilson)—unified a magazine otherwise notable for its variety of styles, viewpoints, and types of writing. Like the Brontës, Maginn and his staff were politically conservative, and much of the magazine's emphasis was on politics, social issues, and religion. However, it also published serialized fiction, short stories, poetry, extensive book reviews with lengthy extracts from the novels and poems of the day, and advice to aspiring contributors. Independent of any publishing house (unlike many other contemporary magazines, including *Blackwood's*), *Fraser's* boasted that its book reviews were based strictly

on merit. In the 1830s, *Fraser's* published its 'Gallery of Illustrious Literary Characters', a series of engravings of contemporary authors by Daniel Maclise, with satiric commentary provided by Maginn. *Fraser's* tried, often successfully, to outdo *Blackwood's* in its own speciality: parody of public figures, brilliant invective, and topical satire that bordered on (and sometimes amounted to) libel. Contributors during the Brontës' time included John Gibson *Lockhart, James *Hogg (both from *Blackwood's*), Robert *Southey, William Makepeace *Thackeray, and George Henry *Lewes. Lewes's long and laudatory assessment of *Jane Eyre* for *Fraser's* (Dec. 1847) is one of the most perceptive early reviews of that novel. In the last year of her life, Anne published two poems in *Fraser's*, one under her well-known pseudonym, Acton Bell. Matthew *Arnold's poetic tribute to the Brontës, 'Haworth Churchyard', appeared in *Fraser's* two months after Charlotte's death.   CB

Bock, Carol, 'Authorship, the Brontës, and Fraser's Magazine: Coming Forward as an Author in Early Victorian England', *Victorian Literature and Culture*, 29 (2001), 241–66.

Freemasonry was thought to have originated in Scotland among stonemasons in the early 17th century, growing out of the secrecy of skilled trade associations. Meetings used a system of secret initiation and ritual centred on the symbolism of King Solomon's Temple. Members committed themselves to moral and political regeneration and many 'lodges' (as the separate groups were called) adopted mystical metaphysical traditions derived from Renaissance Neoplatonism. Non-professional members interested in the mystical nature of mathematics and proportion soon joined the various lodges and the movement spread throughout Europe by the end of the 18th century, absorbing as it did so various eclectic beliefs. During the Enlightenment Freemasonry became closely associated with deism and universalism, and especially with pre-revolutionary radical politics, although in Britain the movement was less subversive than in Europe. By the time of the Brontës, British Freemasonry was better known for its middle-class sociability than for its occult or scientific speculation. The Brontës may first have encountered Masonic secret societies as a source of terror in the *Gothic novel and they may also have been aware of Percy Bysshe *Shelley's interest in the idea of a mystical-scientific intelligentsia—a conspiracy of revolutionaries, freethinkers, and Masonic illuminati—ruling Britain (a vision presented in *Queen Mab*, a poem probably read by the Brontës: Alexander & Sellars, p. 387). Although Branwell was familiar with Mozart's church music, there is no evidence that he knew *The Magic Flute*, Mozart's popular opera that is so heavily based on Masonic ideals and symbolism.

Throughout their childhood, however, the Brontës encountered Freemasons from the local Three Graces Lodge, that met first at the Black Bull Inn at Haworth (from 7 July 1806), then moved to the King's Arms in 1821, and finally—under the energetic leadership of John *Brown—moved to premises in Newell Hill (Lodge Street), in February 1833. Brown, Haworth sexton and stonemason, had been initiated into the lodge in 1830 and by June 1831 he had already risen through the ranks to become Master of the Lodge. Through his enthusiasm and organizational skills Haworth Freemasonry thrived, drawing on a cross-section of society from cabinetmakers and masons to schoolmasters, organists, clockmakers, textile manufacturers, and shopkeepers. (The Brown leadership continued in 1855 when William Brown succeeded his elder brother as Master, and William's son Edmund, a coal agent, also became Worshipful Master in 1892.) On 2 September, 1833, the Three Graces Lodge conducted a procession and service at St Michael's church, at which Revd Patrick Brontë preached the sermon. The fascination with male camaraderie and secret alliances in the Brontë juvenilia may owe something to this early knowledge of Freemasonry. The *Elysium, in particular, that secret male society in Verdopolis, with its social drinking, songs and toasts, and initiation rites, reflects the few facts that were public knowledge about masonic activities in Haworth at the time.

It was John Brown who introduced Branwell to the Lodge of the Three Graces, where he was initiated as a Brother on 29 February 1836, at the age of 19. Brown as Worshipful Master and Joseph Redman as Secretary of the Lodge (and also Mr Brontë's parish clerk) had applied to the Provincial Lodge at Wakefield for a special dispensation for Branwell to be admitted before the usual age of 21, arguing that his father 'is Minister of the Chapelry of Haworth, and always appears to be very favourable to Masonry' (MS in BPM). They were at first refused, but after a second letter stating that 'this young Gentleman is a Pourtrait Painter and for the purpose of acquiring information or instruction intends going on to the Continent this Summer', special permission was granted. Like Brown, Branwell proceeded rapidly through the ranks (probably because of his planned trip): he attended a meeting on 28 March and then, on 20 April, at an extraordinary meeting, he was promoted to the degree of Fellowcraft, and at the next regular meeting, only five days later, he was raised to the degree of Master Mason (Feather, p. 44). It appears, however, that Branwell's plans (like his earlier plans to enter the *Royal Academy of Arts) did not eventuate. Records show that he attended almost every Masonic meeting in Haworth throughout 1836 and 1837 (Masonic records in private hands). He acted as lodge secretary for about a year (1837) and as organist on Christmas Day 1838, but after his initial enthusiasm his participation waned to only erratic visits about once or twice a year until 1847. Branwell's association with the Lodge may have helped him obtain portrait commissions, since at least three of his substantial oil portraits are of local masons: John and William Brown, and William Thomas, whose father held high office in the Three Graces Lodge when Branwell was secretary (Alexander & Sellars, pp. 323, 328, and 333). W. Thomas sen. and his brother R. Thomas, wine and spirit merchants of Haworth, also owned a Masonic apron painted by Branwell and displayed at an exhibition of 'Masonic Treasures' at the Masonic Hall, Duncombe Place, York, 1979 (Alexander & Sellars, pp. 325–6). Other members of the Three Graces Lodge at the time Branwell was secretary include a number of well-known Haworth names: Jas Brown, John Bland, Jas. Akroyd, John Feather, John Greenwood, W. C. Greenwood, William Hartley, W. Mosley, and John Roper.

Feather, W., *A Centenary History of the Three Graces Lodge, 408, Haworth, 1792–1931*, Keighley, [1931].

Freetown, on the River Niger, in *Sneaky's Land, in the *Glass Town and Angrian saga. It commands the road north of Verdopolis and is of strategic importance during the *War of Encroachment. Named after Freetown, the British settlement in Sierra Leone.

French essays. See DEVOIRS.

French revolutions, 1830 and 1848. The Bourbon king Charles X of France who succeeded to the throne in 1824 after the death of his brother, the constitutional monarch Louis XVIII, had led the Ultras, the party of extreme reaction, during Louis's reign. Once in power, he dissolved the Chamber of Deputies on 25 July 1830, restricted voting rights to payers of land tax, and banned all newspapers not authorized by government. The suppressed journalists banded together with Parisian workmen and students under republican leaders, and successfully opposed government troops in two days of desperate fighting behind barricades. By the evening of 29 July, they had occupied the Louvre and the Tuileries, and set up a provisional republican government. The king, too late, offered to submit, but members of the dissolved parliament offered the crown to Louis Philippe, son of Philippe 'Egalité' of Orléans. The 'July Revolution' was to spark off rebellions elsewhere in Europe, notably in *Brussels, where

M. Constantin *Heger fought at the barricades for Belgian liberty. Revd Patrick Brontë wrote to Mrs Franks on 28 April 1831 that the French revolution was a warning of what would happen in England unless moderate reform was effected (Smith *Letters*, 1. 106).

Louis Philippe had supported the 1789 revolution until he deserted to the Austrians after his father was guillotined in 1793, despite his republican principles. But in 1815 Louis joined the liberal opposition to the restored Bourbon monarchs, and when he accepted the crown he relied on the support of the moderates. Later, alarmed by rebellions and attempts on his life, he became increasingly repressive, and refused to extend the franchise. When his government banned a demonstration in the form of a patriotic banquet on 22 February 1848 there were violent clashes in the streets of Paris. Louis's dismissal of the hated minister Guizot and his abdication in favour of his grandson were of no avail, and Louis and his queen escaped in disguise to England, where he died on 26 August 1850. A provisional government, led by Lamartine, was proclaimed and confirmed on 24 February 1848. In the same year there were revolutionary movements in Italy, Austria, Hungary, and Germany. Charlotte Brontë's correspondent William Smith *Williams, a keen republican, rejoiced in the French revolution, but Charlotte had reservations: she wrote to him on 25 February 1848, saying that she considered Louis Philippe an 'unhappy and sordid old man', who like Guizot deserved his 'sharp lesson'. Both were men of dishonest hearts, and 'every struggle any nation makes in the cause of Freedom and Truth has something noble in it; something that makes us wish it success; but I cannot believe that France—or at least Paris—will ever be the battle-ground of true Liberty' (Smith *Letters*, 2. 29–30). As in *Shirley*, she maintained that real strength which would not bend 'but in magnanimous meekness' was needed for thorough reform.

Frenchyland. See PARIS (IN FRENCHYLAND).

Friendship's Offering, or Annual Remembrancer (1824–44), an *annual bound in red silk, was begun by Lupton Relfe, then taken over by *Smith, Elder and Company (Charlotte Brontë's publishers). The editorship also changed hands from T. K. Hervey to Thomas Pringle in the 1830s and then to Leitch Ritchie. Poetry by Thomas Hood, Mackworth Praed, Mrs Hemans, L.E.L. (Letitia Elizabeth Landon), Robert *Southey, and James Macaulay graced the pages of this annual, although its engravings were at first not considered to be the equal of the *Literary Souvenir*. The Brontës owned the sixth (1829) volume of *Friendship's Offering*. On 15 July 1830, Charlotte made a watercolour copy of one of its 'embellishments': an engraving by J. A. White of a painting of a child and dog by E. Landseer, entitled *Hours of Innocence* (the dog is replaced in Charlotte's painting with a flowering bush). In September of the same year, she wrote a critique of three other engravings in her copy of *Friendship's Offering*, based on the art reviews in *Blackwood's* (Alexander *EEW*, 1. 281–3). The engravings accompany the following texts: a poem 'Campbell Castle' by Delta (David *Moir); a play 'The Will' by Leitch Ritchie; and a poem 'The Minstrel Boy' by the Ettrick Shepherd (James *Hogg).

Alexander, Christine, 'Art and Artists in Charlotte Brontë's Juvenilia', *BST* (1991), 20. 4. 186–9 (includes illustrations of engravings).

Gaaldine, a large island in the south Pacific, discovered by the Gondals. It is divided into a large province, Zedora, governed by a viceroy, and five kingdoms: Alexandria, Almedore, Elseraden, Zelona, and Ula. Conceived as a contrast to Gondal, its landscape and climate are tropical, with palms, cedars, bright blue skies, and heat. Constant warfare and revolution govern the destinies of the rulers of Gaaldine. In 1837, Emily Brontë refers to the siege and capture of Tyndarum and the victory of Almedore, which flies a crimson ensign. In her *Diary Paper of 26 June 1837, she records the departure of various emperors and empresses for a coronation in Gondal. See GONDAL SAGA.

Gale, Mrs, in *Shirley*, one of the three landladies (the others are Mrs Hogg and Mrs Whipp) who must put up with noisy and unwelcome visits by the curates Revd Joseph *Donne, Revd Peter Augustus *Malone, and Revd David *Sweeting to each other's lodgings, visits described by the narrator as a 'system of mutual invasion' (p. 10). Mrs Gale's husband John is a small clothier and former churchwarden in *Whinbury. Donne lodges with the Gales, and it is at their house that the curates are dining (and arguing) when the novel's action begins. Through Mrs Gale's dour reactions to their behaviour, Charlotte Brontë conveys her own impatience with the curates' real-life counterparts and their sense of superiority (her letter of 18 June 1845 to Ellen Nussey describes the curates' unexpected arrival for tea at the Parsonage, and their ensuing abuse of Dissenters: Smith *Letters*, 1. 399). Revd James Chesterton Bradley (the model for Mr Sweeting) disputed her view of their behaviour, maintaining that the three curates met weekly at each other's lodgings to take tea and discuss the Greek Fathers (see P. F. Lee, cited by Wroot, p. 133).
HR

Gambia River, on which the Duke of Wellington's Glass Town (Glasstown) is situated in the *Glass Town and Angrian saga. *Wellington's Land is later called Senegambia, after the country of that name similarly located in west *Africa and through which flows the Gambia River.

Garrs family. See SERVANTS OF THE BRONTËS.

Gaskell, Elizabeth, née Stevenson (1810–65), novelist and biographer of Charlotte Brontë; born in London, daughter of a former Unitarian minister, William Stevenson. Her mother, née Elizabeth Holland, died in October 1811, and her daughter was cared for in Knutsford, Cheshire (the fictional 'Cranford' or 'Hollingford'), by her mother's sister Hannah Lumb. The child's visits to her father and his second wife, the unsympathetic Catherine Thomson, are reflected in some of Molly Gibson's experiences in *Wives and Daughters*, written 1864–5. From about 1821 to 1825 Elizabeth attended the Miss Byerleys' excellent school at Barford, near Warwick, which they moved to Stratford-upon-Avon in 1824, and was happy there. Afterwards her home life in Knutsford was varied by visits to her mother's relatives, and to the family of the Unitarian Revd William Turner of Newcastle. With Mr Turner's daughter Ann she apparently spent a sociable season in Edinburgh in 1830. In March 1832 Elizabeth became engaged to Revd William Gaskell (1805–84), a graduate of Glasgow University, junior minister at Cross Street Unitarian chapel, Manchester. After their marriage on 30 August 1832 they lived first in Dover Street, then Rumford Street, and finally from 1850 at 84 Plymouth Grove, a large house in a pleasant garden. Elizabeth had a stillborn baby girl in July 1833, and four more daughters (see GASKELL FAMILY). The Gaskells' first son died in infancy, and the birth of a second son, William, in October 1844, brought great joy to both his parents. When William died of scarlet fever in August 1845 Elizabeth collapsed. To distract her from her grief her husband suggested she should write. She had already written with him the first of a proposed series of 'Sketches among the Poor' in 1837, and had sent to William Howitt a sketch of Clopton House. Three of her early stories appeared in *Howitt's Journal* (1847–8). Acting on her husband's suggestion, Elizabeth wrote her powerful anonymous novel *Mary Barton* (1848), set against the grim background of Manchester, where workmen suffered from the fluctuations of the cotton trade. A plea for social justice and understanding between master and man, it was a great success, though it brought the author, whose identity was soon recognized, the angry resentment of some influential Manchester employers. Charlotte Brontë read it after she had begun to write *Shirley*, and found it a 'clever though painful tale'. It may have influenced her decision not to develop in detail her own story of the working man, William Farren. In less serious vein, and at Mary Howitt's suggestion,

Elizabeth Gaskell wrote 'The Last Generation in England', for the American *Sartain's Union Magazine* (July 1849)—a precursor of her semi-autobiographical *Cranford* (in *Household Words*, 1851–3). In February 1849 Charlotte 'negatived' Mary Howitt's proposal that she too should write for 'an American periodical', probably *Sartain's*. In November 1849 Charlotte sent a copy of *Shirley* to the 'author of *Mary Barton*'. The friendly relationship thus begun was confirmed by the first meeting of the two authoresses at the *Kay-Shuttleworths' holiday retreat, Briery Close, in August 1850. They found each other congenial, shared many literary tastes, and began a correspondence. Charlotte wrote warmly about Elizabeth's Christmas story for 1850, *The Moorland Cottage*, and her short visit to the Gaskells' home in June 1851 brought renewed appreciation of the charm of Elizabeth's presence and the happy activity of her family. In 1852 Charlotte deferred the publication of *Villette* until Elizabeth's controversial *Ruth* had come out, in early January 1853. The story of a 'fallen' woman, based in part on Elizabeth's knowledge of the fate of seduced girls who rapidly descended into prostitution and disease, it was a plea for Christian charity towards them, expressed in practical help towards building a new life, as Elizabeth herself helped to arrange the emigration and future employment of such girls.

Before Elizabeth published the first instalment of her next full-length novel, *North and South*, in September 1854, Charlotte had married Revd A. B. *Nicholls. Elizabeth Gaskell had secretly furthered the match by enlisting the aid of Richard Monckton *Milnes in augmenting Mr Nicholls's income, perhaps by a pension. Milnes had instead offered him the choice of two posts, which he declined; but Milnes may still have helped financially in some way, for Elizabeth Gaskell thanked him 'most truly about Mr Nicholls' in a letter written at about the time of the marriage.

Soon after Charlotte's death on 31 March 1855 Revd Patrick Brontë asked Elizabeth Gaskell to write a biography of his daughter. She had already expressed a wish to write down her personal recollections of Charlotte so that 'people would honour her as a woman'; for this full-scale biography she wished to show the development of Charlotte's character, and to let Charlotte tell her life story in her own words wherever possible. Elizabeth therefore wrote to or visited as many of Charlotte's correspondents as she could, and requested the loan of Charlotte's letters. She saw and used letters to, among others, Mr Brontë and Emily, Margaret *Wooler and the *Wheelwright family, W. S. *Williams, James *Taylor, George Henry *Lewes, and George *Smith. She also used some 330 letters which Ellen *Nussey selected from

about 500 written to her between May 1831 and February 1855. Remarkably, M. Constantin *Heger either read to Elizabeth Gaskell or allowed her to read Charlotte's letters to him, and sent her carefully chosen extracts from them, with an illuminating account of the way he taught his two most gifted pupils. Ellen censored passages in the letters to her, and Elizabeth Gaskell selected and shaped the material she was sent in order to remove any trace of impurity in a writer whose novels had been criticized for coarseness and irreligion. Thus she explained the 'silent estrangement' between Mme Zoë *Heger and Charlotte during 1843 by reminding the reader of Charlotte's staunch Protestantism and her 'gnawing, private cares' about Branwell's behaviour and her father's eyesight. Neither Elizabeth Gaskell nor her amanuenses were totally reliable copyists of the letters, and she accepted as true the malicious gossip of a dismissed servant about Mr Brontë's eccentricities. Yet Gaskell's personal friendship with Charlotte, fellow-feeling for her as a writer, conversations with her about her method of composition, and the sheer quantity of original material she used, make the biography irreplaceable. The first edition appeared on 27 March 1857, the second in April or May 1857, and the third, extensively revised, in August 1857.

Chapple & Pollard, *Gaskell Letters*.

Gaskell, Elizabeth, *The Life of Charlotte Brontë*, ed. Angus Easson (1996).

Uglow, Jenny, *Elizabeth Gaskell: A Habit of Stories* (1993).

Gaskell family. Charlotte Brontë met Elizabeth *Gaskell's husband and family in *Manchester, where Revd William Gaskell, MA (1805–84), was junior minister at Cross Street Unitarian chapel from 1828, senior minister from 1854. An accomplished scholar with a strong social conscience, he actively promoted working men's education. He proof-read the *Life* of Charlotte, but after its publication had to direct his solicitor to retract all statements imputing guilt to the former Mrs Lydia *Robinson. The Gaskells' daughters were Marianne (1834–1920), Margaret Emily ('Meta', 1837–1913), Florence Elizabeth ('Flossy', 1842–81), and Julia Bradford (1846–1908) who enchanted Charlotte and is perhaps recalled in Paulina *Home.

Gateshead Hall is the home of Jane Eyre's Aunt Sarah *Reed, in *Jane Eyre*. A fine mansion about 100 miles from *Thornfield Hall, it is approached by a carriage road, and has extensive grounds with hothouses, a kitchen garden, and a fir plantation. Crucial scenes take place in the ghostly *red-room, the breakfast room, and Mrs Reed's bedroom. Charlotte Brontë drew on her knowledge of various houses of the 'gentry', such as *Stonegappe, where she was a governess in the Sidgwick family. There is also a manuscript fragment about a house called Gateshead, Bonnell, BPM MS 118(8), May 1843 (printed in *The Professor* (Clarendon edn.), p. 338).

Gawthorpe Hall, near Burnley, Lancs., the ancestral hall of the Shuttleworths, and the home of Sir James *Kay-Shuttleworth and his wife Janet. Built in 1600–5, it was renovated, enlarged, and ornamented in 1849–52. The architect Charles Barry added an extra storey to the tower, with a carved stone parapet. Charlotte Brontë visited it reluctantly from 12 to 15 or 16 March 1850, but found the picturesque, grey, stately house very much to her taste. She stayed there again for three days in January 1855 with her husband, but became seriously ill soon after her return home.

Gazemba, Fort, at the town of Gazemba, 60 miles south-east of *Adrianopolis in Angria on the banks of the Calabar, in the *Glass Town and Angrian saga; under the command of Henry (Henri) Fernando di *Enara.

Genii, Chief (Little King and Queens), the four Brontë children in their roles as Chief Genii in the early *Glass Town and Angrian saga; Brannii (Branwell), Tallii (Charlotte), Emmii (Emily), and Annii (Anne). Their names are spelt with a variety of double and single letters, reflecting the word 'genii' (Brani, Branii, Brannii, etc.). The concept of four protectors derived from the *Young Men's Play, but other plays had similar presiding beings. Little King and Queens were the equivalent of the Chief Genii in the *Islanders' Play. Here they play a direct role in events, corresponding with characters, disciplining and rescuing them, and having a great deal of fun in their disguise as old washerwomen for the Duke of Wellington (much to the disgust of Branwell who refuses to co-operate). See 'TALES OF THE ISLANDERS'.

The invention of Chief Genii allowed the young Brontës to account for their own participation in the initial physical play with the toy soldiers, as they moved them around and protected their own favourite characters. When as authors Charlotte and Branwell invented a prehistory for the Glass Town and Angrian saga, they established the presence of a supernatural power in Ashantee that assists the *Twelves. These are the legendary genii, who dwell in the *Jibbel Kumri or Mountains of the Moon (like the Greek gods on Mount Olympus, an idea reflecting Branwell's current lessons in the Classics). Some genii, like *Danhasch, are evil; and Branii himself has to be restrained from unjust acts against the Young Men, who eventually rebel against the tyranny he initiates (Alexander *EEW*, 1. 39).

Initially inspired by the Brontës' reading of the *Arabian Nights* and James *Ridley's *Tales of the Genii*, the Glass Town genii also take on biblical features, especially from the Book of Revelation. Glass Town mortals are often blinded and fall 'as dead' before the genii and their splendid palaces and thrones of precious stones. The Chief Genii speak with a trumpet-like voice, and appear on clouds in the midst of lightning and thunder (see Branwell's illustration of a Chief Genius 'Mentor' on the title page of 'The *History of the Young Men' (in Alexander & Sellars, p. 299). His figures of justice also suggest a godlike presiding presence over his 'publications' (Alexander & Sellars, pp. 300–3).

Written as the saga is from the point of view of Glass Town characters, the narrators see the dimly focused huge creatures who read their minds and intervene in their events, transporting them to safety and resurrecting them when necessary, as guardians of the land, protectors, and often arbitrary judges. Charlotte's 'Strange Events' recounts Lord Charles Wellesley's experience of the symbiotic relationship between the creator genii and himself (and his relationship with his historical counterpart) (see Alexander *EEW*, 1. 257–8).

Branwell appears to have disliked the role of protector, preferring to go on the rampage now and then, uttering 'the horrible howl of [his] war-cry' (Alexander *EEW*, 1. 39). After the rebellion of the Young Men, the four Chief Genii are formally expelled from the saga in Charlotte's poem 'The trumpet hath sounded' (11 Dec. 1831), modelled on *Byron's 'The Destruction of Sennacherib' (Neufeldt *CBP*, pp. 91–2; Alexander *EW*, pp. 75–6). In subsequent juvenile manuscripts, they are evoked only occasionally when the early Glass Town is referred to (in The *Foundling or The *Green Dwarf) or when Branwell chooses to admonish Emily and Anne for abandoning the Glass Town and Angrian saga, in an editorial tirade in his *'Monthly Intelligencer' (Neufeldt *BB Works*, 1. 250).

geography, knowledge of and books. The Register at the Clergy Daughters' School, *Cowan Bridge, 1824, records that Charlotte Brontë 'Knows nothing of Grammar, Geography, History or Accomplishments'. Geographical education in girls' schools at the time, however, was at best a rudimentary study of 'Globes', and it is more likely that the Brontë children's early geographical knowledge was acquired from old text books at home and from *Blackwood's Edinburgh Magazine. They had inherited, for example, *Geography for Youth* (Dublin, 1795; BPM), by Abbé Lenglet Du Fresnoy, originally owned by Hugh Brontë in 1803 (see BRONTË FAMILY). In 'The *History of the Year'

(1829), Charlotte mentions 'an old geography' given to her sister Maria (Alexander *EEW*, 1. 4). The heavily annotated *A Grammar of General Geography* (1823; BPM), by Revd J. Goldsmith, bears witness to frequent use by the four surviving Brontës, and is a particularly valuable biographical source with its sketches and *Gondal place names. Its pages contain maps of the continents, and crude woodcuts of people and buildings illustrate the corresponding text, which identifies each region from an Anglocentric perspective (see AF-RICA). At Margaret Wooler's school at Roe Head, Charlotte used the earlier *Geographical and Historical Grammar* (by Salmon, 1771; BPM), with its even cruder maps of Africa. There was a dramatic instability of knowledge about Africa and other non-European countries in the early 19th century (see JIBBEL KUMRI) and news reports of Arctic and African exploration would have caused great excitement generally. There is no doubt that articles on such subjects, often reporting missionary-related endeavours to 'unknown' areas of the world, helped inspire the young Brontës' acquisition of imaginary islands and the eventual settlement of their fictional explorers on the central west coast of Africa. *Blackwood's* carried numerous geographical and travel articles, particularly on current exploration in the Arctic and in Africa, with accompanying maps. A fourth extant geography used by Charlotte was probably bought for Roe Head and then taken to Brussels: Russell's *General Atlas of Modern Geography* (*c*.1831; Pierpont Morgan). Inside the back cover Charlotte records her homesickness, alone in Brussels 'amongst foreigners' (14 Oct. 1843). The book may also have been used later by Branwell since pencil lines on a map of England indicate various routes in West Yorkshire and particularly the way from Haworth to *Liverpool and on round the Welsh coast to Anglesey. All her life Charlotte Brontë yearned to travel, possibly to emigrate to new lands like her friend Mary Taylor, but as an adult she was realist enough to know that emigration to distant lands did not always bring female colonists the desires and freedoms she had experienced in her early representation of 'Africa'. Brussels was the furthest she and Emily travelled, stopping in London en route; Emily and Anne had made their first long journey together to *York in June 1845; Anne accompanied Charlotte to *London in July 1848; and Branwell made trips to Liverpool and the *Lake District, where he was a tutor at *Broughton-in-Furness. See also COMMUNICATIONS; RAILWAYS; TRAVEL BY THE BRONTËS; CHURCH MISSIONARY SOCIETY.

Geraldine, lover of Emperor Julius *Brenzaida whose child she bears, in the *Gondal saga. Persuaded by others, she no longer supports him politically, so he leaves her and returns to those who love him unreservedly.

German essays. See DEVOIRS.

Gifford, John, elderly Glass Town lawyer and antiquarian and, later, chief judge in the *Glass Town and Angrian saga. Gifford assists his great friend Captain John *Bud in the research for 'The *History of the Young Men'. He is based on William Gifford, first editor of the *Quarterly Review*, famous for his conservative criticism. Like his model, John Gifford disapproves of all 'modern' poetical excesses including those of the Marquis of Douro (Duke of Zamorna) who therefore satirizes him in 'The Red Cross Knight' (Alexander *EEW*, 2(1). 232–4).

Gill, Mrs, in *Shirley*, the cook and housekeeper at *Fieldhead, whom Shirley *Keeldar detects in some minor irregularities in the handling of household accounts, but who is not taken to task because her mistress is loth to see her 'brought to shame and confusion of face' (p. 299). Thanks to Shirley's forbearance, Mrs Gill becomes attached to her, and is the only person besides Louis Gérard *Moore whom Shirley will permit near her in case of illness after her dogbite (ch. 28).   HR

Gimmerton, the nearest village to *Wuthering Heights and *Thrushcross Grange, in *Wuthering Heights*. The doctor, lawyer, and *Zillah, the servant at the Heights, all come from Gimmerton, which also has a band that visits houses of the gentry at Christmas. Edgar *Linton, Catherine *Earnshaw, and *Heathcliff are buried in Gimmerton churchyard. Gimmerton Sough chapel, where Revd Jabes *Branderham preaches his 'Pious Discourse', is thought to be based on Chapel-le-Breer near Sough Pastures, near *Law Hill, Halifax. A 'sough', or water-channel, runs into Shibden Beck just above the chapel. Gimmerton first appears in *Wuthering Heights* as 'Gimmerden' ('ewe valley'), and has the same etymological meaning as Shibden ('sheep valley'), north of Law Hill, suggesting that this area was transferred to the moors above Haworth for the locality of *Wuthering Heights* (Charles Simpson, *Emily Brontë* (1929), 58–60).

Girnington Hall, General *Thornton's country estate in the province of *Angria; a rambling Gothic mansion, fine wooded property and thriving farmland. In early Brontë manuscripts, Girnington Hall is near Douro Villa in the Vale of Verdopolis, but it soon becomes a very Angrian estate when part of the Vale is subsumed into the new kingdom of Angria.

Glass Town (Glasstown). See VERDOPOLIS; GLASS TOWN FEDERATION; GLASS TOWN AND ANGRIAN SAGA.

Glass Town, Valley of. See VERDOPOLIS, VALLEY OF.

Glass Town and Angrian saga. *See opposite page*

Glass Town Federation (Verdopolitan Federation), formed by the *Young Men from the union of four kingdoms—*Wellington's Land, *Sneaky's Land, *Parry's Land, *Ross's Land— with the addition of *Monkey's Island and *Stumps' Island. The federal capital is the Great Glass Town (see VERDOPOLIS), and each of the four kingdoms has its own capital Glass Town (or 'Glasstown' as it is later spelt). The area is roughly synonymous with the Gold Coast of *Africa, including the kingdom of *Ashantee and extending north to what is now Senegal (see Map). The early Brontë stories relating to this geographical area are known as 'the *Glass Town and Angrian saga'. Later juvenilia by Charlotte and Branwell relate almost exclusively to the Valley of *Verdopolis and especially to the kingdom of *Angria, an extension of the Glass Town or Verdopolitan Federation.

Gledhill, Alfred, a Keighley dealer who bought a number of Brontë drawings and other items in January 1886, when Ann Binns sold at auction the contents of her home, including items inherited from her sister Martha *Brown. In January 1889 he exhibited many of these, including Charlotte's 'Laughing Child' and 'Crying Child' and Emily's charming drawing of Flossy (attributed to Charlotte) at a 'conversazione' in the *Keighley Mechanics' Institute. He sold his collection to Martha's cousins Francis and Robinson Brown, but most of it was later bought by the Brontë Society in 1898 and 1950.

Alexander & Sellars.

Gleneden, family name for a number of patriotic *Gondal characters who helped restore peace in Gondal after a period of tyranny. References to them are cryptic. E. R. Gleneden is a woman loved by M. Douglas ('Honour's Martyr', Gezari, *EBP*, p. 26). Her brother Arthur Gleneden was killed or imprisoned ('Gleneden's Dream', Gezari, *EBP*, p. 69; 'From our evening fireside now', Gezari, *EBP*, p. 94). E. Gleneden elopes with a Mary R. ('Thy Guardians are asleep', Gezari, *EBP*, p. 147). See also UNIQUE SOCIETY, THE.

Goldsmith, Oliver (?1730–74). On 4 July 1834 Charlotte advised Ellen Nussey to read Goldsmith's poems and *History of Earth and Animated Nature,* and all the Brontës would have known The

Vicar of Wakefield. Charlotte quotes *The Traveller* in describing the Marquis of Douro (later Duke of *Zamorna) and his rascally companions in 'The *Secret', who anticipate Rochester in *Jane Eyre* (ch. 13), with so much 'unconscious pride in his port'. Revd Patrick Brontë's copy of Goldsmith's *Roman History* is the source for Jane's comparison of John Reed to 'Nero, Caligula, &c'. Charlotte enjoyed *She Stoops to Conquer,* for she refers in *Shirley* and elsewhere to Tony Lumpkin and to his companions' 'concatenation accordingly'.

Gomersal, Great and Little, a wooded and pleasant township on rising ground above the River Spen, 5 miles south-east of *Bradford in the Yorks. woollen district. The population grew fairly rapidly in the mid-19th century, more than doubling in size from 6,189 in 1831 to 12,880 in 1871. The staple trade, the manufacturing and merchandizing of army cloth, was followed by Joshua Taylor of the *Red House; the *Taylor family of Gomersal was well known to the *Nusseys and Brontës. Joshua's father, John (1736–1805), had been an admirer and friend of John Wesley, and had built a small redbrick chapel for the 'New Connexion' Methodists on the Oxford Road in Gomersal. Charlotte came to know personally or by repute other Nussey acquaintances, such as the Swaines, flannel and cloth merchants, and the Burnleys of ancient Pollard Hall, worsted spinners for four generations. James Burnley had been the prime mover in building Grove Congregational Chapel, opened in 1826. Both Ann and Mercy Nussey were for a time associated with the Gomersal *Moravian community and chapel, whose minister, Revd Richard Grimes, vouched for Mercy's sincerity in applying to join the Fulneck Moravians. The Nusseys were related by marriage to the Carrs— solicitors and surgeons—of Gomersal, and both families are mentioned in Charlotte's letters. Rumours of her authorship of *Jane Eyre* circulated in the area, and she had to warn Ellen Nussey (who suspected but had not yet been told the truth) as early as 3 May 1848 that if 'any Birstalian or Gomersalian' bored her on the subject, she was to assure them that Miss Brontë disowned such accusations (Smith *Letters,* 2. 62). 'Currer Bell's' identity became known beyond a doubt after the publication of *Shirley,* with its easily recognizable portrayal of the Taylors as the *Yorke family.

Gondal, a large island in the north Pacific, with Regina as its capital, in the *Gondal saga. Divided into four provinces: Gondal, Alcona, Angora in the north, and Exina in the south. The landscape and climate reflect that of Yorkshire and Scotland, with their moorlands of heather, fern, and bluebells, snowy mountains, and cold winter winds.

(*cont. on page 215*)

T
HE Glass Town and Angrian saga originated in three plays associated with the Brontë children's toy soldiers (*Young Men's Play, *Our Fellows' Play, and *Islanders' Play), that were initially acted out and then documented in a series of magazines, poems, articles, dramas, speeches, short stories, and novelettes. This fictitious world, established in *Africa, centred first on the *Glass Town Federation and its principal city *Verdopolis (initially called the Great Glass Town), and then moved to Angria, a new kingdom created in 1834 to the west of the Federation (see Map). (The saga is most commonly referred to as the 'Glass Town Saga'; 'Angrian Saga' is often used by writers to refer to later stories centred on the kingdom of *Angria, but no separate saga is involved.)

By the end of 1830, the Young Men's and Islanders' Plays had fused and the central characters and features of the Glass Town and Angrian saga were clearly established. Inspired by a set of twelve wooden toy soldiers, all four of the Brontës had created favourite characters and woven a fictitious world around their central players. Charlotte's early hero was the Duke of *Wellington, soon replaced by his two sons, Arthur, Marquis of Douro, Duke of *Zamorna, and Lord Charles *Wellesley (based on the historical duke and his sons). Branwell initially 'played' *Napoleon, then Alexander *Sneaky, before settling with Alexander Percy ('Rogue', later Lord Ellrington and Duke of *Northangerland), a name derived from the historical Percys of Northumberland. Emily and Anne chose the Arctic explorers Captain Sir William Edward *Parry and Sir James Clark *Ross.

The young authors were both writers and players in their fiction, assuming the identities of Glass Town literati, acting as protectors for their particular heroes and presiding over the saga as Chief *Genii. Supernatural events are common in the early stories, where the genii play an active role resuscitating characters who have been 'killed' in a previous story. The mixture of fact and fiction, and the way real events impinge on those of the saga, is a central feature of this imaginative world. No Glass Town manuscripts by Emily and Anne survive, but those of Charlotte and Branwell are voluminous. Branwell assumed responsibility for documenting the historical, military, and political events; Charlotte recorded the social scene and edited the *'Young Men's Magazine'. A large selection of individual Glass Town and Angrian writings can be found in this Companion.

In 1831, when Charlotte departed for *Roe Head, Emily and Anne broke away from the Glass Town and Angrian saga and formed their own play of *Gondal. Despite an ongoing rivalry, Charlotte and Branwell continued in close literary partnership until about 1837, when they appear to have agreed to take the saga their own separate ways. In late 1839, the 23-year-old Charlotte formally took leave of the Glass Town and Angrian saga (see 'FAREWELL TO ANGRIA'), although she recurred indirectly to it in such fragments as *Ashworth* and many of its features can be traced in her later novels. Branwell continued to write under the influence of his imaginary world until his death at the age of 31 (see JUVENILIA OF THE BRONTËS).

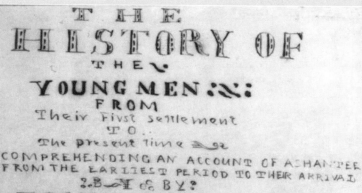

THE
HISTORY OF
THE
YOUNG MEN
FROM
Their First settlement
TO
The present Time or
COMPREHENDING AN ACCOUNT OF ASHANTEE
FROM THE EARLIEST PERIOD TO THEIR ARRIVAL
&B &c BY

JOHN BUD ESQ'R

CAPTAIN IN THE
&10 REGT OF HUSSARS
VICE PRESIDENT OF THE ANTIQUARIAN society
FELLOW OF THE LITERARY SOCIETY
FELLOW OF THE ASSOCIATION FOR
THE REWARD OF LEARNING
CHEIF LIBRARIAN TO
THE ROYAL GLASS
TOWN LIBRARY
&c &c &c &c

IN   VOLUMNS

VOL I.

"IT IS my TASK
"To Explore The Dark recesses of the past
"And Bring to light the deeds of Former ages"
Marquis Douro's
School of Learning v139

1831

Great Glass town Printed and sold by Seargent Tree

Branwell Brontë's title page to 'History of the Young Men', by the narrator Captain John Bud, who describes the establishment of the Glass Town Federation in West Africa.

History

The history of the Young Men became the history of the Glass Town and Angrian saga. The *Twelves were a brave band of adventurers who sailed from England, fought against the Dutch on Ascension Island, and then established a colony in the kingdom of *Ashantee on the west coast of Africa. They encounter resistance from the Ashantees and after a brief peace, war ensues. The king of the Twelves (see YORK, FREDERICK GUELPH, DUKE OF) is slain at the Battle of Rosendale Hill, and replaced by the Duke of Wellington, who later defeats the Ashantees and kills Sai-Too-Too *Quamina at the Battle of *Coomassie. Wellington adopts Sai-Too-Too's son Quashia *Quamina, sowing the seeds of future antagonism against Glass Town and Angria.

Meanwhile the Twelves establish their capital city, with the aid of supernatural help (from the Chief Genii), in the Gulf of Guinea, at the mouth of the Niger and opposite the island of Fernando Po. This is the Great Glass Town, centre of a federation of four kingdoms ruled by the original four heroes of the young Brontës: *Wellington's Land, *Sneaky's Land, *Parry's Land, and *Ross's Land, each of which has its own provincial 'Glass Town' capital (such as 'Wellington's Glass Town'). As the Great Glass Town becomes a centre of commerce and civilization, its name changes first to 'Verreopolis' and then to *'Verdopolis' to reflect its growing sophistication. The spelling of 'Glass Town' and other place names also fluctuates inconsistently: for example, 'Glass Town' becomes 'Glasstown', 'Wellington's Land' becomes 'Wellingtonsland', 'Sneaky's Land' becomes 'Sneakysland/Sneachisland/Sneachiesland', and so on. Branwell also spells certain character names slightly differently to Charlotte (for example, 'Rougue' for her 'Rogue', Elrington' for her 'Ellrington', 'Wellesly' for her 'Wellesley'); Charlotte's version is the most often used by scholars and has been adopted in this Companion, with Branwell's version recorded in brackets.

Wars and political upheavals dominate the events of the saga throughout its history, transposed from relatively recent real events such as republican uprisings, the *Ashantee Wars, or the *Peninsular War (see also WELLINGTON, DUKE OF (FICTIONAL); NAPOLEON (FICTIONAL)). They are chronicled in obsessive detail by Branwell (see ANGRIA AND THE ANGRIANS) and form the background to many of Charlotte's stories (see PASSING EVENTS). In March 1831 there is insurrection in Verdopolis, the Great Rebellion, in which Rogue sets up a provisional government on the French model of 1789. Order is restored miraculously by Captain Butter *Crashey, but a year later Rogue again leads a rebellion in the north (Battle of *Fidena) which is eventually defeated by Alexander *Sneaky, King of Sneaky's Land, and his son Prince John, Duke of *Fidena—assisted by forces from the other kingdoms. The Ashantees are a constant threat to the east of the Federation. In 1833 they are joined by the Arabs and the French in the *War of Encroachment against the united Verdopolitan forces. This proves to be a watershed for the Federation in which the new kingdom of Angria is created from the spoils of war. Zamorna and Percy (formerly Rogue), who defeated the Ashantees in the east, demand the territory from the Verdopolitan Parliament and are also given the new titles of king of Angria and duke of Northangerland respectively. Constant parliamentary battles ensue to win equal representation for Angria in the old Federation.

From now on, Glass Town political alliances are cemented into distinct factions and leaders: the Constitutionalists (formerly Wellington's and Sneaky's party, now led by

Glass Town and Angrian saga

John Duke of Fidena), the Angrians (Zamorna), the Reformers (Arthur, Marquis of *Ardrah, who controls the navy), the Republicans (Lord Macara *Lofty, and Hector *Montmorency), and the Destructives or Revolutionists (Alexander Percy, Duke of Northangerland). The Reformers are the greatest threat to peace and to Angria, since they have powerful allies: the French (Napoleon), the Ashantees (Quashia Quamina), the Negroes (King Jack), and the Bedouin Arabs (John, Earl of Jordan). Northangerland also plays fast and loose with these 'allies' and secretly rules another party with French connections, the *Faction Du Mange (derived from the Young Men's Play).

Zamorna, as king of Angria, appoints Northangerland (now his father-in-law) as prime minister, but Northangerland remains in league with his old republican associates and leads a rebellion against Zamorna. The ensuing Angrian wars ravage the country, and Zamorna is driven into exile before returning triumphant. Angria is again invaded by the Reformers under Ardrah and Zamorna is again exiled; but Ardrah is deposed by Northangerland who sets up a republic before being defeated by Zamorna and the loyal native Angrians under Warner Howard *Warner, with the help of the Verdopolitan Constitutional forces under Fidena.

Glass Town and Angrian Society

Glass Town's social history is equally developed and becomes extraordinarily complex. The royal families of each of the kingdoms have an entourage of friends, associates, servants, and retainers who follow them between their palaces in the Great Glass Town and their country houses. In the capital itself there are lower-class groups of *'rare lads', bodysnatchers, vagabond Frenchmen (see PIGTAIL), servants, and *pugilists who interact with the 'High Life' in various ways. The professionals and the military mix freely with the aristocracy, united by political alliances and by a common enthusiasm for literature in which many of them take an active part. The Twelves are venerated as the elders of society, but considered too authoritative and serious by the younger generation of gallants. Stumps and Monkey (original Twelves) are retired to islands off the Glass Town coast (see STUMPS' ISLAND; MONKEY'S ISLAND), whose inhabitants are mocked by Verdopolitans for their bizarre dialect and old-fashioned manners and dress. Branwell's original Frenchyland (see PARIS) from the Young Men's Play, an island adjacent to Verdopolis, continues to exercise a political presence through the machinations of Northangerland and Montmorency. Several Glass Town institutions, such as *Bravey's Inn, the *Elysium, and the university on *Philosopher's Island, have a significant impact in the lives of the inhabitants.

Social life focuses on a group of characters: the Duke of Wellington and his two sons, their friends and admirers, and their enemies. As Wellington becomes an elder statesman (like his friend Lord *St Clair), Zamorna moves into centre stage, accompanied by his sometime friend and enemy Northangerland. Lord Charles Wellesley records Zamorna's marriages (to Lady Helen *Gordon, Marian *Hume, and Mary *Percy), his mistresses (chiefly Mina *Laury, *Sofala, Rosamond *Wellesley, and Caroline *Vernon), children (see WELLESLEY, ARTHUR JULIUS; WELLESLEY, ERNEST 'FITZARTHUR'; WELLESLEY, JULIUS WARNER DI ENARA; WELLESLEY, VICTOR FREDERICK), friends and political associates (such as Fidena, *Thornton, Warner, Viscount *Castlereagh, Lord *Arundel, Lady Zenobia *Ellrington, and Lady Julia *Wellesley).

Zamorna also surrounds himself with artists and writers, all of whom record their own versions of his life and character. Prominent members of Glass Town's literary society include Captain 'Andrew' *Tree (prose writer), Sergeant *Tree (publisher and bookseller), Captain John *Bud (political writer and historian), Sergeant *Bud (a lawyer), Alexander *Soult (poet), Henry *Hastings (poet), and Viscount Richton (historian and politician) (see FLOWER, CAPTAIN SIR JOHN).

Northangerland has an equally colourful coterie, ranging from former pirates, cattle thieves, and revolutionaries (for example Richard *Naughty, Baron of *Caversham, Jeremiah *Simpson and Arthur *O'Connor) to French noblemen (like Hector *Montmorency) and the Ashantee leader Quashia. As with Zamorna, Glass Town's authors constantly analyse Northangerland's character as it develops from the early pirate and republican revolutionary 'Rogue' (spelt 'Rougue' by Branwell) into a sinister and embittered aristocrat on his marriage to Zenobia Ellrington (spelt 'Elrington' by Branwell), and finally evolves into the Luciferian villain-hero of Romantic literature. His marriages (to Augusta (or Maria) di *Segovia, Maria *Wharton, and Zenobia Ellrington) and mistresses (especially Harriet *O'Connor and Louisa *Vernon) are as confusing and difficult to reconstruct from individual stories as those of Zamorna. His pathological hatred for his sons, however, contrasts with Zamorna's love for his children. Despite their abandonment as babies, Edward *Percy and Captain Sir William *Percy work their way back into aristocratic society and continue the theme of rivalry between two brothers, begun by Wellington's two sons (see Alexander EW, pp. 219–33).

The driving force of the Glass Town and Angrian saga is the complex love-hate relationship of Northangerland and Zamorna. Zamorna's early conflicting attitudes to the 'vile demagogue' are complicated by his marriage to Northangerland's beloved daughter Mary. She becomes a pawn in their political rivalry during the Angrian wars, for which Northangerland is basically responsible. The wars originate in the republican Northangerland's inability to work for long with any constitutional leader, even his own son-in-law and sometime friend Zamorna. Their struggle is that of two gigantic personalities fascinated by each other but both lusting for the same power. Resolution of their relationship is impossible and only old age finally subdues their fiery antagonism. Branwell traces Northangerland's career relentlessly to the doors of Pandemonium, in a series of unstructured chronicles. Charlotte at first moves her ideal hero (the early Arthur Wellesley) closer to Northangerland's ruthlessness, indulging in the Byronic personality she now creates for Zamorna (Arthur's new name not only reflects his new title but also his modified personality); but she maintains a realistic attitude towards her egotistical hero through her cynical narrator Lord Charles. In her final Angrian stories, Zamorna is viewed as a comic figure, a spent womanizer and despotic ruler; and Charlotte's conventional heroines are superseded by the independent Elizabeth *Hastings.

Geography

The young Brontës were well acquainted with the topography of west Africa, from travel books, school geographies, Blackwood's and other magazines and newspapers. The site of the Great Glass Town can be linked directly to Blackwood's, 19 (June 1826), 705, which contained an article by James McQueen (also a character in the saga) and an accompanying map based on Denham and Clapperton's explorations in northern and central Africa from 1822 to 1824 (see Alexander *EEW*, 2(2), frontispiece). Not only did Branwell copy this map for his own illustration of Glass Town locations in his *'History of the Young Men' (1830), but he and his sisters followed the author's advice on the most favourable site for a new colony: one that 'would COMMAND the trade, the improvement, and the civilization of all North Central Africa'. The establishment of Glass Town and Angria, then, can be seen as an imaginary exercise in colonization.

Although ostensibly African, the geographical features of the four kingdoms of the Glass Town (or Verdopolitan) Federation are modelled on parts of the British Isles: *Parry's Land and *Ross's Land are roughly equivalent to Yorkshire and lowland Scotland; *Sneaky's Land represents northern England and also Scotland; and *Wellington's Land in the far west is equivalent to Ireland, birthplace of the historical Arthur Wellesley, Duke of Wellington. The federal area itself, comprising the Valley of *Verdopolis and Verdopolis as federal capital, is roughly equivalent to southern England. Rivers, such as the *Niger, distinguish particular locations; and familiar landmarks distinguish the cities (for example, the *Tower of All Nations and *St Michael's cathedral).

To a large extent Angria repeats the geography of the Federation itself. The major rivers (*Olympia, *Guadima, *Calabar, *Etrei, and *Douro) flow west from the mountains in the north-east and east to the Gulf of Guinea. Major towns lie along the rivers: *Zamorna, *Edwardston, *Angria, Seaton, *Pequene, Douro, *Gazemba, and *Dongola. Deserts lie to the south. Geographical names and phrases echo throughout the saga providing a solid reality to the imaginary world: 'the forests of *Hawkscliffe', 'the savannah of *Arundel', 'the banks of the *Cirhala', the *Sydenham Hills, *Warner Hills, and Warner and Howard Moors. See also ARDSLEY HOUSE; BOULSHILL; PENDLETON; EVESHAM; CROSS OF RIVAULX; LOANGO, BATTLE OF.

There are also mythic associations with the landscape of the early Glass Town Federation that reflect Branwell's classical studies. He not only introduced the Great African Games (modelled on the Olympic Games), but also created a Mt *Aornos which (like Mt Olympus) is the home of the 'gods', the Genii, who also inhabit the *Jibbel Kumri (or Mountains of the Moon) to the north-east of the Federation, the great Sahara Desert to the north-west, and Hylle, the vast stormy Lake of the Genii, which has religious significance.

The writing of the saga

The nature of the Brontës' early writing is further described under *juvenilia of the Brontës. Not only is there a large number of manuscripts comprising the Glass Town and Angrian saga, but they are also written in a variety of genres, ranging from short stories, speeches, fragmentary tales, and poems, to plays, novelettes, magazines, and newspaper articles. Charlotte often groups miscellaneous stories and poems on similar topics into a single volume under such titles as 'Arthuriana Or Odds & Ends' (Alexander *EEW*, 2(1). 207–62), 'The *Scrap Book', or 'Corner *Dishes'. Several items are untitled, but have been given names over the years by various Brontë scholars as indicated in individual entries. The titles of substantial novelettes are printed in italics in this Companion; the titles of early works and collections of short works are in inverted commas.

The Glass Town and Angrian stories are richly intertextual, with place names, titles of characters, their personalities, and myriad other references derived from sources as various as the *Bible, the *Arabian Nights*, school *geography books, classical history, *Shakespeare, *Bunyan, *Milton, *Wordsworth, Sir Walter *Scott, *Byron, Thomas *Moore, *Southey, James *Hogg, local newspapers, magazines (like *Blackwood's*) and fashionable *annuals (see CHILDHOOD AND CHILDHOOD READING OF THE BRONTËS). Paintings too form the intertext of the saga, with verbal references to visual works by contemporary artists like *Martin and *Finden (see ART OF THE BRONTËS).

Much of the saga was formulated only in discussion amongst the creators; knowledge was assumed between the four collaborators, who had no need to explain circumstances or background in individual stories. A self-referential world emerged, with fictitious writers and editors jockeying for authorial power over an increasingly complex Glass Town and Angrian society. Individual stories from the saga can be bewildering, since the Brontës were continually rewriting events and reinventing the personalities of their characters. The multiplicity of names given to one person and the frequent changes of title can cause further confusion. This summary, together with numerous individual entries on people, places and stories, can only be an introduction to what is a vast hinterland of romance and adventure. See also POETRY BY CHARLOTTE BRONTË; POETRY BY BRANWELL BRONTË; VERSE DRAMA BY BRANWELL BRONTË; AFRICA; and selected individual stories. See Classified Contents (pp. xv–xxv) for lists of Glass Town and Angrian works that have entries in the Companion.

Alexander *EW*.

Alexander *EEW*.

Alexander, Christine, 'Victorian Juvenilia', in William Baker and Kenneth Womack (eds.), *A Companion to the Victorian Novel* (2001).

Barker, Juliet (ed.), *Charlotte Brontë: Juvenilia 1829–1835* (1996).

Collins, Robert G. (ed.), *The Hand of the Arch-Sinner* (1983).

Conover, Robin St John, 'Creating Angria: Charlotte and Branwell Brontë's Collaboration', *BST* (1999), 24, 1, 16–32.

Gérin *Five Novelettes*.

Miscellaneous Writings.

Neufeldt *CBP*.

Neufeldt *BB Works*.

Ratchford, Fannie E., *The Brontës' Web of Childhood* (1941).

Gondal saga. *See page 216*

Gooch, George, railway engineer known to Branwell Brontë and to Francis Henry *Grundy; probably related to the railway pioneers Sir Daniel Gooch and Thomas Longridge Gooch. He was company engineer for the Manchester and Leeds railway *c*.1837–41, and worked with Grundy near Haworth on the Bradford and Keighley line, 1847. Branwell saw him at about the time of Revd Edmund *Robinson's death in 1846 (see Smith *Letters*, 1. 490–1).

Goodman (Goody). See OUR FELLOWS' PLAY; 'HISTORY OF THE REBELLION IN MY FELLOWS, THE'.

Gordon, Edward Ernest 'FitzArthur'. See WELLESLEY, ERNEST EDWARD GORDON 'FITZARTHUR'.

Gordon, George. See BYRON, LORD; GORDON, CAPTAIN JULIAN.

Gordon, Lady Helen Victorine, Baroness, first wife of the Duke of *Zamorna and sister of the villainous Captain Julian *Gordon in the *Glass Town and Angrian saga. She is 'the young and beautiful lily of Loch Sunart', wooed and married by a youthful Zamorna who was sent to 'Scotland' to become a man. He leaves her for *Philosopher's Island, 600 miles away, to complete his education at the University for Glass Town

(cont. on page 221)

G ONDAL is the imaginative world created by Emily and Anne Brontë. Unlike the *Glass Town and Angrian saga devised chiefly by Charlotte and Branwell, the Gondal epic cannot be easily reconstructed. Poetry manuscripts (often with only cryptic references) and several Diary Papers and fragments are the only evidence we have of the secret life that nurtured the writing of the two youngest Brontës. Gondal appears to have functioned as an imaginative storehouse for Emily, one to which she resorted throughout her life to experiment with intense emotional states and relationships. Anne was less passionate about and less reliant on Gondal, her interest waning as she grew older.

Origins

The origins of Gondal lie in the childhood play that grew up around the Glass Town and Angrian saga. All four children helped to chronicle the original adventures of the *Young Men's Play and the *Islanders' Play in miniature magazines and books, but the written contributions of Emily and Anne to this literature (if indeed there were any) have been lost.

We know from the surviving manuscripts of Charlotte and Branwell, however, that Emily and Anne were not always happy with their role in the Glass Town and Angrian saga. As the youngest players, they always had second choice: Emily's toy soldier had been 'a grave-looking fellow: we called him Gravey'; whereas Anne's was 'a queer little thing very much like herself': he was called 'Waiting Boy'. Their characters could not help but pale in stature beside Charlotte's and Branwell's choice of the Duke of *Wellington and *Napoleon, the two greatest antagonists of the age.

There are allusions throughout the early Glass Town manuscripts to the differing tastes of the younger siblings: when they changed the names of their chief characters they chose the Arctic explorers Sir William Edward *Parry and Sir James Clark *Ross, a choice removed from the African exploration that caught the imagination of Charlotte and Branwell. 'A Day at Parry's Palace' (see 'YOUNG MEN'S MAGAZINE') reveals Lord Charles *Wellesley's (and therefore Charlotte's) disgust at the blunt, unpolished northern manners of Parry and Ross, whose territories reflect a mundane Yorkshire landscape with its stone walls and factories 'breathing thick columns of almost tangible smoke'. Parry's palace is the antithesis of the imperial Verdopolitan structures: a square stone building with a blue slate roof. Lord Charles understands little of 'their majesties'' (Parry and Ross's) heavy northern dialect, he finds their table manners uncouth and their diet of roast beef, Yorkshire pudding, mashed potatoes, apple pie, and preserved cucumbers 'intolerably dull'. This was the world of realism to which Emily and Anne were becoming increasingly committed as a setting for their own epic, while Charlotte and Branwell were moving steadily in the opposite direction.

As Emily and Anne grew older they resented the authority of their siblings: they had their own ideas, preferring the cold-climate northern hemisphere they knew so well to the balmy African landscape and the high life of the Verdopolitan nobility. The Brontës had 'always liked Scotland as an idea', as Charlotte told her publisher after she eventually visited *Edinburgh in 1850 (Smith Letters, 2. 427), and for Emily, in particular, the northern landscape of lakes and mountains—filtered through the pages of Sir Walter *Scott's historical romances and James *Hogg's writings on Scottish folklore in *Blackwood's Edinburgh Magazine*—had a special appeal. The Yorkshire beginnings of Parry's and Ross's Lands were gradually transformed first into the Scottish northern provinces of Glass Town and then into the setting so often evoked in the Gondal poems, which appears to be a cross between Yorkshire and Scotland. Even the names of Gondal heroes, like those from Parry's Land, were predominantly Scots (Alexander, Douglas, Gleneden, Lesley, and Stewart for example).

Before the literary partnership between Charlotte and Branwell became solidly established, Emily had collaborated with Charlotte in what were called 'bed plays' or 'secret plays'. These may have been the origin of the Islanders' Play in which Emily appears to have played a major role, again in league with Charlotte. In *'Tales of the Islanders', the young authors enter their own dramas, interacting with the characters and experiencing their adventures. One of these escapades involves Charlotte and Emily alone, amid Emily's preferred landscape, where 'the wind sweeps with more fearful blast over this wild bleak moor', where mountain sheep graze on the heath and find shelter among the rocks, where the lark springs from his mossy bed as the authors approach. Further, when Charlotte had grown tired of the Islanders' Play (recorded by her in vol. 2, October 1829), it was Emily who took the lead, initiating the School Rebellion which looks forward to a central theme of Gondal. There is mutiny at the Palace of Instruction and the ringleaders are her characters, 'little Johnny Lockhart' and Princess Victoria (see VICTORIA, QUEEN). Eventually, Charlotte's hero, the Duke of Wellington, quells the rebellion with a single autocratic threat.

The concept of a female authority figure seems to have been peculiar to Emily. Her early fascination with Princess Victoria, only ten months younger than herself, informs the Gondal saga, setting it apart from the male-dominated power structures of Glass Town. Suddenly thrust into the limelight in 1830 as heir to the British throne, Princess Victoria was adopted as a central player by Emily, with her character and fortune melded to that of another Brontë heroine *Mary Queen of Scots. Seven years later her interest had not abated: she recorded Victoria's imminent accession to the throne in her *Diary Paper of 26 June 1837, and (according to Fannie Ratchford) she transposes the event into a coronation in her Gondal setting (Hatfield *EBP*, pp. 18 and 67).

When Charlotte left home to go to *Roe Head school in 1831, Emily and Anne saw this as an opportunity to break away from Charlotte's control, leaving Branwell to pursue his own extravagant military and political schemes. They took with them much of the Glass Town formula: the concept of islands, the wild moorland scenery, a powerful princess, the struggles of a predominantly royalist world, and even some names. The name *'Almeida', for example, reappears in Gondal as 'Almeda'. The names Adrian and Julius also derive from Glass Town; and the young lovers Alexander and Zenobia suggest Charlotte's and Branwell's Alexander Percy and his third wife Zenobia. Much of the Duke of *Zamorna's early 'Scottish' past, including his marriage and desertion of Lady Helen Victorine Gordon, is replayed in Gondal. The Gondalian *'Unique Society', wrecked on a desert island, recalls the secret society of Glass Town nobles on Philosopher's Island. As in the Islanders' Play, the 'Princes & Princesses' of Gondal are besieged within the *Palace of Instruction, some kept as prisoners in vaulted dungeons. In the earlier play, it was Emily who kept the key to the cells for 'naughty school children': 'These cells are dark, vaulted, arched and so far down in the earth that the loudest shriek could not be heard by any inhabitant of the upper world, and in these, as well as the dungeons, the most unjust torturing might go on without any fear of detection' (Alexander *EEW*, 1. 24). Dungeons proliferate in Gondal. Savage passion, imprisonment, and rebellion were to be the hallmarks of the new saga.

Surviving manuscripts and the reconstruction of Gondal

The earliest evidence we have of Gondal is the *Diary Paper written by Emily on 24 November 1834. Here we find the enigmatic sentence that so fascinated the early Brontë scholar Fannie Ratchford: 'The Gondals are discovering the interior of Gaaldine'. This led to her 'reconstruction' of the plot, first as an introduction to C. W. Hatfield's *Complete Poems of Emily Brontë* (1941) and then in her *Gondal's Queen* (1955), a hazardous operation given that the evidence consists largely of short lyrics and fragments with few narrative references. Ratchford's arrangement of all Emily's poetry as an epic—'the life story of A.G.A., from dramatic birth, through tempestuous life, to tragic death' (*Gondal's Queen*, p. 27)—with her own narrative prose links and her grouping of characters to reflect a prefiguring of relationships in *Wuthering Heights* is to a large extent speculative, designed to show that Gondal represents '*Wuthering Heights* in the making' (p. 37). The main problems with this reconstruction are the identification of three characters as the single heroine Augusta Geraldine *Almeida (A.G.A.) and the grouping of poems to fit this pattern. Yet many of Ratchford's hunches have proved correct and her conviction that all of Emily's verse 'falls within the Gondal context' has the merit of seeing Emily's work whole. Other critics followed suit, in particular Mary Visick in *The Genesis of Wuthering Heights* (1958), who saw Gondal as an early draft of the novel, focusing on the imaginative transformation of Gondal characters into Catherine, Heathcliff, and Edgar. In *An Investigation of Gondal* (1958), W. D. Paden argued for a less unified narrative that was 'only mildly suggestive' of patterns in the later novel. Summaries of Gondal reconstructions by Laura Hinkley, Fannie Ratchford, and W. D. Paden can be found in Roper *EBP*, app. 7.

Subsequent critics maintained a rigid separation between Gondal and non-Gondal poetry, reducing the importance of Gondal and arguing its 'regressive' (Chitham *ABP*, p. 118) influence on the quality of both Emily's and Anne's work (see POETRY BY EMILY BRONTË). More recent critics, while acknowledging an ostensible Gondal and non-Gondal division, prefer to see Emily's work as a whole. Lyn Pykett's analysis of Emily's Gondal verse (*Emily Brontë* (1989), 69), for example, reveals the same preoccupations as those of her non-Gondal poems, an exploration of the constraint and limitation of human existence:

The heroic exiles and outcasts of Gondal rise above the limitations of their situations by rebelling against their society and taking political and military power into their own hands. In the non-Gondal poems the restrictions on the active life provide an impetus for an intense focus on the inner life, and in particular for an exploration of those inner resources of vision and imagination which might be a means of rising above the external limitations of the female condition.

Whether or not we accept that Emily Brontë's lyrics all grew out of a Gondal context, it is clear that even after the publication of *Wuthering Heights* she still found in her epic world a source of inspiration for her personal concerns. As late as May 1848, seven months before her death, she was working on a Gondal civil war poem: she never totally abandoned her imaginary world. As she stated in her *Diary Paper of 30 July 1845: 'We intend sticking firm by the rascals as long as they delight us'.

Anne, too, continued to exploit the Gondal context but her involvement with the saga was never as intense or as committed as that of Emily. Comparatively few poems by Anne exist, approximately 53 compared to some 200 by Emily, and of these just under half were composed within an obvious Gondal context. Anne's Gondal poems can be divided into two groups, based on periods when she was at home: her earliest extant poems written between 1836 and 1838, when she was 16 to 18, and those written between late 1845 (after she left Thorp Green) and 1846. This does not appear to have been accidental. From the beginning she seems to have followed Emily's lead, writing about Gondal at home almost entirely under her influence (see DIARY PAPERS: 30 JULY 1841, for the sole exception).

As Anne matured and gained a greater experience of the outside world than Emily, she seems to have deliberately distinguished, in a way that Emily never did, between the fantasy she wished to retain for Emily's sake and her own increasingly personal concerns about her role in life and her relationship with God. Comparisons between her few letters and her personal poetry reveal that Anne Brontë's own practice was that of Agnes Grey, who considered her poems as 'relics of past sufferings and experience, like pillars of witness set up in travelling through the vale of life, to mark particular occurrences' (*Agnes Grey*, ch. 17). The heroine of Anne's earliest poem ('Verses by Lady Geralda', 1836) reflects keenly her author's endurance and determination: despite a profound sense of loss and sadness, this Gondal heroine leaves home, as Anne herself did two months before, happy in the prospect of activity. Even in her 'purely' Gondal poetry, Anne was already articulating the personal concerns that were to become the hallmark of her philosophical and religious poems.

Apart from the poetry and the six Diary Papers with brief references to Gondal, the only remaining evidence of Emily and Anne's saga is five lists of Gondal names. These include: (1) a list of place names written by Anne into the 'Vocabulary of Names and Places' at the back of *Goldsmith's Grammar of General Geography* (BPM); (2) a list of 26 names recorded by Anne on a scrap of paper (Ransom HRC, Texas); (3) a list of sixteen names recorded by Anne on a poetry manuscript ('A prisoner in a dungeon deep', BPM); (4) a list of the personal features of five characters made by Emily on a poetry manuscript known as D8 (Bonnell, BPM), containing a fragment dated 28 July 1842 (Roper *EBP*, pp. 130 and 255 n. 91; David R. Isenberg, 'A Gondal Fragment', *BST* (1962), 14. 72. 24–6); and (5) several more names listed by Emily on a fragmentary poetry manuscript known as F2 ('But the hearts that once adored me', Ransom HRC, Texas). These contain only the most cryptic references to the Gondal saga, yet, together with six poems containing 'Gondal dates' (Roper *EBP*, p. 303), they suggest that the Gondal saga was composed using memoranda and chronologies. Having agreed verbally on the basic course of events, Emily and Anne could use a specific narrative context as the springboard for their individual poems and stories, writing them at different times and about different episodes in the Gondal narrative. As Derek Roper points out, the actual composition dates Emily attached to her poems are no guide to Gondal chronology (Roper *EBP*, p. 10). Though usually written in physical proximity (see Emily's sketch in Alexander & Sellars, p. 378), their compositions appear to have been independently conceived: only a few character names were used by both sisters and, though they read prose passages to each other, Anne records her ignorance of the content of Emily's poetry (Diary Paper, 31 July 1845).

It is possible that much of Gondal was acted out rather than recorded in writing, as with the early Glass Town and Angrian saga. Even when she was 27, Emily was keen to continue this role-playing: on 30 July 1845, she and Anne, then 25, went on a rare excursion together to York, during which 'we were, Ronald Macelgin, Henry Angora, Juliet Augusteena, Rosobelle ?Esualdar, Ella and Julian Egramon[t] Catherine Navarre and Cordelia Fitzaphnold escaping from the palaces of Instruction to join the Royalists who are hard driven at present by the victorious Republicans' (Smith *Letters*, 1. 408).

The rate of Gondal prose composition was definitely slower than that of Glass Town. In the 1845 Diary Paper, Anne admitted 'We have not yet finished our "Gondal chronicles" that we began three years and a half ago'. Emily confessed that although she had 'a good many books on hand', she usually made 'small progress with any' (Diary Paper, 30 July 1841). The Diary Papers confirm the existence of four prose manuscripts: 'Augustus-Almedas life 1st v.' composed by Emily during June 1837 ('Augustus' is thought to be a mistake for 'Augusta'); 'the fourth volume of *Solala Vernon's Life*' by Anne (30 July 1841); and two works recorded in July 1845: 'a book by Henry Sophona' by Anne and 'a work on the First Wars' by Emily (also referred to by Anne as 'the Emperor Julius's life'). These and any other prose manuscripts have disappeared without trace. Whether Charlotte was responsible for their loss or whether Emily and Anne themselves destroyed the bulk of the evidence of their secret world, we shall probably never know.

The Kingdom of Gondal and its significance

Without the prose manuscripts, however, we can only glimpse and guess the nature of the kingdoms they created, chronicled, and possibly painted (Alexander & Sellars, pp. 106, 384, 386). Despite the character lists, names remain confused and uncertain: the same Gondal character may be referred to in different ways, by initials, titles, Christian or full name, or the same initials may stand for more than one person. There are few narrative clues since the poems represent moments in the Gondal epic, points of intensity or crisis that lend themselves to expression in poetry rather than prose. Only the barest framework can be safely pieced together from available evidence.

The centre of focus is Gondal, an island in the North Pacific, divided into four kingdoms ruled by rival families, suggesting a latter-day Romeo and Juliet saga. In a landscape of wild moorland, harsh winter winds and snows, a drama of rebellion and betrayal in love and war is played out, as the rivalries between the central characters are explored. The poems focus especially on the violent passions of the strong-willed heroine Augusta Geraldine Almeida and on the power struggle of Julius Brenzaida, who at one time was either her husband or lover. The action moves between Gondal, whose capital is Regina, and the recently discovered *Gaaldine, an island in the South Pacific, also divided into kingdoms but with a contrasting tropical climate and verdant landscape. After friction between the Royalists, civil war breaks out and the Republicans gain the upper hand.

The background plot might be brief and hazy but we cannot miss the regularity with which certain themes and images repeat themselves in a way that smacks of obsession. Time and again the sisters return to situations of isolation, exile, and death. Life in Gondal is dominated by a pervading sense of confinement: sometimes physical and sometimes spiritual, where the actor is chained by powerful emotions, memories, and the consequences of action. In such a world, death becomes a liberating alternative. Unlike the Glass Town and Angrian saga, where relationships can be redeemed and lives remade, events in Gondal are final and players in 'Earth's dungeon tomb' must reconcile themselves to a life of 'change and suffering' (*'Cold in the earth').

Gondal is of particular importance in relation to Emily Brontë's only novel, *Wuthering Heights.* The relationship between the two is inescapable: not only do we find similar themes, associations, and images which strongly suggest that the novel grew out of the epic, but Emily clearly returned to Gondal after *Wuthering Heights* was completed. In September 1846, she began copying into her 'Gondal Poems' notebook a civil war poem which she later revised in May 1848, the year of her death. Mary Visick's *The Genesis of Wuthering Heights* (1958; repr. 1965) provides a useful list of 'possible parallels' between Gondal and the novel. In his recent *Birth of 'Wuthering Heights'*, Edward Chitham extrapolates from Gondal poems Emily's working techniques in *Wuthering Heights* and supports his detailed chronology for the composition of the novel by showing how Gondal was transposed into *Wuthering Heights.*

The mood of Gondal is predominantly elegiac. Characters lament their exile and imprisonment, or their separation from a loved one, often as a result of death. Like the relationship between Heathcliff and Catherine, their loyalties are strong and their emotions violent. The beauties of nature, especially the wind and the moors, console and bring spiritual release to Gondal's prisoners. Their cry for liberty echoes that of their creator. For Emily herself, the Gondal saga provided a similar imaginative freedom. It was habitual and sustaining, a visionary world she hailed as 'My Slave, my Comrade and my King!' (Roper *EBP*, p. 156).

Brontë, Emily, *Wuthering Heights* (Clarendon edn.), app. 4.
Chitham *Birth of WH.*
Evans, Barbara, and Lloyd, Gareth, *Everyman's Companion to the Brontës* (1982).
Ratchford, Fannie E., *The Brontës' Web of Childhood* (1941).
—— *Gondal's Queen: A Novel in Verse by Emily Jane Brontë* (1955).

nobles, and she dies in childbirth believing she has been forsaken. Her son is Ernest Edward *Gordon 'Fitzarthur', because her marriage was never officially recognized ('Fitz' being the form of name used for a child of a morganatic marriage).

Gordon, Captain Julian, an early associate of the Duke of *Northangerland and villainous brother of Lady Helen Victorine, Baroness Gordon, first wife of the Duke of Zamorna, in the *Glass Town and Angrian saga. He supports Northangerland against the Verdopolitan Federation and Angria in the Angrian Wars. One of the 'dark—

malignant, scowling Gordons' (Alexander *EW*, p. 196), he is based on the Scottish Gordon relatives of George Gordon, Lord *Byron. He reappears in Charlotte's *Ashworth* as Charles Gordon and a similar character, George Gordon, appears in Branwell's *And the Weary are at Rest.*

Gordon, province and Mountains. A northern province associated with the four kingdoms of the *Glass Town Federation; like Angria, Calabar, and Northangerland, it is part of the area defended by the Duke of Zamorna during the *War of Encroachment and demanded by him for his new kingdom of *Angria. The Gordon Mountains, located 100 miles from Verdopolis, are home to Ashantee tribes who threaten the Federation.

Gore, Catherine Grace Frances, née Moody (1799–1861), prolific novelist, successful dramatist, and an acquaintance of *Bulwer-Lytton, *Dickens, *Disraeli, and William Makepeace *Thackeray. In August 1850 and June 1851 she tried in vain to meet the elusive Charlotte Brontë in London, and wrote friendly notes to her. Her most famous novel was *Cecil: The Adventures of a Coxcomb* (1841). Her *Peers and Parvenus* (1846), contemporary with Charlotte's *The Professor*, contrasts nouveau-riche characters with the poor but honest tutor Philip Fairfax. Mrs Gore gave a copy of her novel *The Hamiltons* to Charlotte, who admired it as 'original'.

Gorfin, Herbert E., T. J. *Wise's agent from 1898, selling for him from an address in New Cross, London, both forged pamphlets and legitimate rare books and manuscripts. In 1899 the *Brontë Society bought, through him, many drawings listed in Alexander & Sellars. He had joined Wise's firm as office-boy in 1892, and with a short interval remained in their employ until 1912, when he bought from Wise legitimate stock and (apparently ignorant of the forgery) the remainder of the pamphlets, and set up as an antiquarian bookseller in Charing Cross Road, later moving to Lewisham. He was exonerated from complicity by Carter and Pollard in 1934.

Gothic novels, fiction characterized by an atmosphere of terror generated by ominous setting, threatening mysteries, and supernatural phenomena. The genre, familiar to and enjoyed by the Brontës from an early age, stems from Horace Walpole's *Castle of Otranto: A Gothic Story* (1764), set in an apparently haunted medieval castle with labyrinthine subterranean passages, a gigantic supernaturally menacing suit of armour, a family curse, and threats of sexual ravishment. Novelists who subsequently contributed to the tradition included William Beckford (his *Vathek, an Arabian Tale* (1786) added Oriental opulence to Gothic ingredients), the immensely popular Ann Radcliffe (especially known for *The Mysteries of Udolpho*, 1794), and Matthew Gregory Lewis (whose *The Monk* (1796) contributed more transgressive sexuality and Faustian themes).

Besides supernatural elements (for which Radcliffe often eventually offered rational explanations) and an atmosphere of brooding terror, the genre developed other conventions which rapidly became formulaic. Gothic novelists set their stories in a remote past thought to be superstitious and emotional, and in physical settings ominously associated with oppression, such as castles, prisons, dungeons, monasteries, and nunneries. They evoked a brooding atmosphere with burial vaults, ruins, shadows, and stormy nights. They employed melodramatic action including violence and threatened sexual violations, and subordinated characterization to alarming plot twists. Generally lacking psychological depth, heroines were damsels in distress who passively resisted physical and emotional victimization. The male protagonist often became a composite Hero–Villain in the Romantic mode of *Byron's Lara or Manfred—moody, haughty, demonic, violent, self-destructive, yet rendered sympathetic by his guilt, persecution, suffering, and isolation. Mary Shelley wedded such complexity of characterization to complexity of theme in *Frankenstein* (1818), one of the more sophisticated works in the genre.

Critics of Gothic literature link its aesthetics, devised to excite readers' passions and evoke fear and awe, to the aesthetics of the Sublime articulated by Longinus in the 1st century and revived in the mid-18th century by Edmund Burke's *A Philosophical Enquiry into the Origins of our Ideas of the Sublime and Beautiful* (1757). Cultural trends which contributed to the rise and popularity of Gothic fiction in the late 18th and early 19th centuries include the medievalism of English antiquarianism and feudal nostalgia, the passionate excesses of German *Sturm und Drang* and Romantic diabolism, the disruptive impulses of the French Revolution, and English nationalism and anti-Catholicism (Victor Sage, in Marie Mulvey-Roberts (ed.), *The Handbook to Gothic Literature* (1998), 82–3).

By the time *Frankenstein* appeared, the stereotyped and exaggerated conventions of the Gothic novel were parodied in Thomas Love Peacock's *Nightmare Abbey* and Jane *Austen's *Northanger Abbey* (both 1818). Austen satirizes not only formulaic Gothic setting, mood, villain, and heroine, but also the naive female readership of such fiction. Despite such ridicule of Gothic excesses, the tradition continued to flourish in 19th-century periodicals familiar to the young Brontës, for the pages of the *annuals and of the *Lady's Magazine, *Blackwood's Edinburgh Magazine, *Fraser's Magazine, and the *New Monthly Magazine* featured lively Gothic thrillers, poems, and tales of hauntings and mysterious happenings. The appeal of Gothic conventions to the Brontës is evident in the *juvenilia, with their melodramatic plot twists, exotic settings, violence, victimized women, and diabolical villain/heroes. During the same period Edward *Bulwer-Lytton's novels increasingly transported the Gothic elements conspicuous in his early *Falkland* (1827) and *Pelham* (1828) into the modern era, providing a model for later sensation mysteries set in contemporary England such as Wilkie Collins's *The Woman in White* (1860).

Anticipating this grafting of the Gothic on to contemporary realism, the Brontë sisters masterfully employed Gothic trappings in their novels not merely to generate narrative excitement, but also to delineate complex psychologies and subjective apprehension of the horrors of the everyday. Schooled by melodramatic tales in periodicals and annuals, Charlotte furnished her early writings with settings and actions vividly Gothic, effects which she turned to sophisticated uses in her mature fiction. As Robert Heilman has argued in 'Charlotte Brontë's "New" Gothic' (1958), Charlotte's frequent invocations of mysteries and apparently supernatural phenomena, while often quickly defused with irony, humour, and rational explanation, function seriously to depict her heroines' passionate intensity, sexual energy, and emotional repression. *Jane Eyre*'s madwoman in the attic and *Villette*'s apparition of the nun, for example, convey the heroines' resistance to the prevailing feminine ideal, and anger at their constraining social and economic circumstances. In Charlotte's hands evocations of oppressive convents and Catholic confessionals, the frisson of ghostly glimmerings, abrupt vanishings, and lightning storms become tools for psychic exploration and social protest.

In *Wuthering Heights* Emily radically transforms the heroine of Gothic story by making Catherine Earnshaw as complex as Charlotte's more realistic protagonists, and also overtly aggressive and aware of her own demonic nature. Like *Jane Eyre*'s Rochester, Heathcliff owes his diabolic energy and emotional power to Gothic lineage, as does the brooding atmosphere of *Wuthering Heights*. Emily was more willing than Charlotte to conjure ghosts, macabre dreams and hallucinations, and a generally Gothic aura, without offering rational explanation. Her spirits and other supernatural elements succeed partly through her strategy of employing limited, mundane narrators who are themselves affected by moods and phenomena which they cannot comprehend.

Without the more overtly Gothic trappings of inexplicable apparitions or dreams through which the supernatural penetrates the ordinary, Anne in *Tenant* evokes the Gothic with such elements as the partly derelict mansion, the heroine's mysterious past, and her monstrously oppressive husband. Such vestiges of Gothic machinery invest the novel's consideration of contemporary issues (such as *divorce and child custody laws) with the intensity of the exotic to expose the genuine horror of the commonplace experience of many women.

BT

Alexander, Christine, '"That Kingdom of Gloom": Charlotte Brontë, the Annuals, and the Gothic', *Nineteenth-Century Literature* (1993), pp. 409–36.

Heilman, Robert B., 'Charlotte Brontë's "New" Gothic' (1958); repr. in Ian Watt (ed.), *The Victorian Novel: Modern Essays in Criticism* (1971), 165–80.

Homans, Margaret, 'Dreaming of Children: Literalization in *Jane Eyre* and *Wuthering Heights*', in Juliann E. Fleenor (ed.), *The Female Gothic* (1983), 257–79.

Mulvey-Roberts, Marie (ed.), *The Handbook to Gothic Literature* (1998).

governesses. If the social position of the private governess in the 19th century was difficult to define, so also was her name, for the word 'governess' has had various meanings. In England the salaried governess is first heard of in Tudor times. In the 17th and 18th centuries the honourable position of royal governess was usually held by a learned and noble lady. But a 'governess' also meant any woman who had charge of a person: Moll Flanders' 'governess', her son's nurse, is the pawnbroker with whom she shares her stolen goods. As J. W. Beattie points out in *The Story of the Governesses' Benevolent Institution* (1962), 'during the latter part of the eighteenth century, the status of the governess underwent a change, and it was then that the word "schoolroom" first came into use'. Wealthy parents preferred to keep a resident governess rather than send their child to school. 'It was considered bad manners to be rude to the governess, nor was she slighted in public by her pupils.' (p. 5.) 'Governess' might also mean the female supervisor of a school, or an assistant schoolteacher. The number of private governesses increased in the early 19th century. Young women like the Brontës had few other opportunities to earn money, for shopkeeping was not genteel, clerical posts for women were almost non-existent, and becoming a seamstress was a last resort. Though women might be driven by necessity to teach, their learning and skills might be minimal. They might have little natural capacity for or experience of teaching, and certainly no training or formal qualifications. Dorothea Beale, recalling the benefits of examinations for intending governesses at Queen's College, London, described the difficulty of choosing a governess in about 1840: 'My mother advertised and hundreds of answers were sent. She began by eliminating those in which bad spelling occurred . . . next the wording and composition were criticised, and lastly, a few of the writers were interviewed, and a selection made. But alas! an inspection of our exercise books revealed so many uncorrected faults, that a dismissal followed, and another search resulted in the same way' (*The First College Open to Women: Queen's College London*, ed. Mrs Alec Tweedie, 1898). After her painful experience as a governess with the *Sidgwick family, and her more bearable but still harassing time at *Upperwood House, Charlotte advised W. S. *Williams in May 1848 that the 'great qualification' for a governess was the 'faculty, not merely of *acquiring* but of *imparting* knowledge; the power of influencing young minds; that natural fondness for—that innate sympathy with children'. Though she considered the Governesses' Benevolent Institution excellent in some ways, it was 'absurd and cruel to attempt to raise still higher the standard of acquirements. Already Governesses are not half nor a quarter paid for what they teach—nor in most instances is half or a quarter of their attainments required by their pupils . . . It is true the world demands a brilliant list of accomplishments; for £20. per ann. . . . the demand is insensate' (Smith *Letters*, 2. 63–5). Advertisements for and by governesses implied that they were or should be paragons of learning: in *The Times* (26 Feb. 1848) a governess claimed that she was 'fully competent to instruct without masters, in English, geography, history ancient and modern, French (acquired by a long residence in Paris), Italian, music, writing, and arithmetic'. An advertisement in the *Leeds Intelligencer* (21 Dec. 1839) was for 'a young Lady, as GOVERNESS, of an amiable disposition, and some experience, willing to make herself generally useful, and competent to teach Music, French, and Drawing, with the usual Branches of a good Education'. As Charlotte found at *Stonegappe, being 'generally useful' might involve a 'tremendous burden of sewing' and being expected 'constantly to amuse as well as instruct' 'a set of pampered, spoilt & turbulent children'. Charlotte's position was humiliating, for Mrs Sidgwick made it clear that her children were not supposed to 'love the governess'. Most governesses were paid very small salaries. Charlotte's salary at Upperwood House was 'nominally £20., but the expense of washing' was deducted. At *Thorp Green Hall Anne earned £40 per annum—half her brother's salary. Elizabeth *Rigby snobbishly deplored the overstocking of the governesses' profession by 'underbred' daughters of ambitious farmers and tradespeople who had 'brought down the value of salaries and interfered with the rights of those whose birth and misfortune leave them no other refuge'. But she emphatically pointed out the injustice of the governess's position: 'A mother satisfies her conscience when she gives the patient drudge who not only retails to her children every accomplishment and science of the day, but also performs the part of maternal factotum in every other department, the notable sum of 40l. or 50l a-year; and then, when she has lived in the family for perhaps fifteen years . . . dismisses her . . . without a fragment of help in the shape of a pension or

provision to ease her further labours or approaching incapacity' (*Quarterly Review*, 83 (Dec. 1848), 180). In 1829 a Governesses' Mutual Assurance Society was formed to alleviate such hardships, but it ended in about 1838. Little progress was made with a new 'Governesses' Benevolent Institution' formed in 1841 until Revd David Laing became honorary secretary in 1843. He reported that there were 600 subscribers by January 1844, and arranged the first annuity in May 1844. By May 1847 the Institution had established a teachers' registry, an employment agency, elective and provident annuities, a savings bank, and a home for governesses between their engagements. Donations were invited towards setting up an asylum for aged governesses, a college for governesses, and a diploma. In 1848 Laing and several professors from King's College, London, founded the 'Queen's College for Female Education, and for granting Certificates of Qualification to Governesses'. The college was opened in Harley Street (where it remains, as an independent school) in May 1848, with Frederick Denison Maurice as chairman of its Committee of Education and Professor of Theology. Charlotte was pleased when Louisa Williams obtained a place there. Though the college encountered difficulties of organization, it was a pioneer in improving the qualifications and status of governesses.

Graham, Mrs Helen. See HUNTINGDON, HELEN 'MRS GRAHAM'.

Grant, Revd Joseph Brett (?1820–1879), model for Revd Joseph *Donne. He graduated BA 1843, MA 1868 from Emmanuel College Cambridge, was ordained deacon 1843, and appointed headmaster of Haworth Free Grammar School 1844, when he became Revd Patrick Brontë's curate. Ordained priest in 1845, he became curate-in-charge, and (by March 1846) perpetual curate of the new district of *Oxenhope, where he worked energetically for the establishment of a National School and church. He married Sarah Ann Turner at Woodford, Essex, in January 1846. Grant assisted Revd A. B. *Nicholls at Branwell's funeral service. Nicholls stayed with the Grants before his marriage to Charlotte, and they were asked to the wedding breakfast.

Grasper, an Irish terrier belonging to Revd Patrick *Brontë, the first of many *pets owned by the Brontës. Emily's sensitive pencil sketch shows Grasper wearing his leather collar, required by the dog tax of the time (Alexander & Sellars, p. 376). Grasper lived at Haworth Parsonage from about 1834 until about early 1838 when his successor *Keeper is first mentioned.

Grassdale Manor, the residence of Mr Arthur *Huntingdon and Helen *Huntingdon after their marriage in *Tenant*. Described by Gilbert *Markham as a 'stately mansion in the midst of its expansive grounds' (ch. 52), it is the setting for many of the painful events which force Helen to flee her husband. After his death, Helen does not return to Grassdale, except when necessary. It later becomes the residence of her son, Arthur *Huntingdon.

Grassmere Manor House, a handsome old castellated manor house in Grassmere, a secluded part of *Wellington's Land, near Badey Hall, in the *Glass Town and Angrian saga. Home of the faithful Mina *Laury, when she becomes the Duke of *Zamorna's mistress and guardian of his two eldest sons.

Gravey, Edward (later spelt Gravii), the Metropolitan Archbishop of Verdopolis in the early *Glass Town and Angrian saga; initially chosen by Emily Brontë as her soldier in the *Young Men's Play. A clergyman of 'remarkably grave and venerable aspect', he is the only prelate who can marry members of the royal family. Thus, he performs the clandestine marriage between Lily *Hart and Seymour (Duke of Fidena). His revered position derives from his status as one of the *Twelves.

Great Exhibition, the (1851), held in the *Crystal Palace from 1 May to 15 October. An 1836 Parliamentary committee had shown that Britain's lead in manufacturing was threatened by Continental rivals, and the exhibition's chief promoters, Prince Albert and Henry Cole, hoped to inspire manufacturers to use designers to make artefacts more desirable. More grandiosely, they proclaimed it as a 'tournament of peace', tending towards the unity of mankind by displaying exhibits from foreign countries as well as Britain and her colonies. An invitation from George *Smith's mother to Charlotte Brontë to visit London at the time caused Charlotte to forget her prejudices about 'a series of bazaars under a magnified hot-house', and to pay five visits there, the first on 30 May, the last with Sir David *Brewster on 22 June. Though it was 'not much in her line', she evoked its 'strange and elegant but somewhat unsubstantial effect' in a letter to her father of 31 May 1851: 'The brightest colours blaze on all sides—and ware of all kinds—from diamonds to spinning jennies and Printing Presses are there to be seen—It was very fine—gorgeous—animated—bewildering— but I liked Thackeray's lecture better' (Smith *Letters*, 2. 625). She would see for example the Koh-i-noor diamond, and the immense, complex Applegath's Patent Vertical Printing Machine.

She confessed to Amelia *Taylor on 7 June 1851 that it was wonderful but tiring: 'you come out very sufficiently bleached and broken in bits' (Smith *Letters*, 2. 633). On 13 June the sight of the 'ex-royal family of France' at the Exhibition must have reminded her of the dramatic events during the *French Revolution of 1848. She was amused by one of the more eccentric exhibits, a bed which silently ejected its occupant at a given hour, and she suggested its use by the dilatory Thackeray as a spur to completing *Henry Esmond* (Smith *Letters*, 2. 655–6).

Great Glass Town (Glasstown). See VERDOPOLIS.

Green, Henry S., founder member of the *Brontë Society and collector of drawings. In 1896 he lent to the Brontë Museum exhibition Charlotte's 'River Scene with Trees' (4 Aug. 1842), Branwell's ink sketch of his lodgings at *Thorp Green Hall (25 Aug. 1844), and a piece of paper with pencil sketches by Branwell on the verso showing figures engaged in indecent behaviour. Green later moved from Dewsbury to Moss Side, Manchester. His son and daughter A. H. and Emily Green gave the pictures to the BPM in 1947. He perhaps owned for a time Emily's watercolour of her merlin, *Nero.

Alexander & Sellars, pp. 258, 346, 347, 384.

Green Dwarf. A Tale of the Perfect Tense, The ('By Lord Charles Albert Florian Wellesley'; 2 Sept. 1833), a novella of the *Glass Town and Angrian saga. This is Charlotte Brontë's most obvious attempt to imitate the historical romances of Sir Walter *Scott, in particular *The Black Dwarf*, *Ivanhoe*, and *Kenilworth* (see Alexander *EEW*, 2(1). 127, 143, 146, 163). The manuscript of this classic story within a story is 26 pages of minuscule script, originally a hand-sewn booklet (Ransom HRC, Texas). The young Lord Charles records Captain John Bud's narrative of twenty years ago, recalling the early Glass Town scene and the first African Olympic Games (celebrated in Branwell's 'Ode on the Celebration of the Great African Games'; Neufeldt *BBP*, pp. 79–83), which under Charlotte's pen became a medieval tournament. The 'rewarder of victors', Lady Emily *Charlesworth is engaged to Alexander Percy but secretly loves Earl *St Clair with whom she plans to elope. The lovers are outwitted by the crafty Percy, who abducts Lady Emily and imprisons her in a ruined tower in a dark forest. Meanwhile St Clair and Percy join the Duke of Wellington's forces in battle against the Ashantee tribes under Quashia *Quamina. Percy contrives with the assistance of Quashia and St Clair's servant lad, 'the green dwarf', to discredit St Clair as a traitor. The Duke of Wellington secretly intervenes, St Clair's innocence is proved, and the lovers are married. Percy is exiled (see NORTHANGERLAND, DUKE OF) and Lord Charles delights in telling us that the scoundrelly green dwarf, who is sentenced to ten years labour in the galleys, is none other than his literary rival, Captain 'Andrew' *Tree, in his youthful days.

In *The Green Dwarf*, Charlotte gives Branwell's character Percy a past and a more interesting psychology, to use as a foil to her still-embryonic hero Douro (Duke of *Zamorna). She examines the duplicity suggested by Percy's sinister eyes and deceitful smile, modelling his villainy on that of Varney in Scott's *Kenilworth*, which she had recently read and admired (Smith *Letters*, 1. 121). This 'Tale of the Perfect Tense' also includes an interpolated anecdote about *Napoleon, that was published separately by Clement Shorter as *Napoleon and the Spectre: A Ghost Story* (1918).

Alexander *EEW*, 2(1). 127–206.

Greenwood, Mr John (fictional), music master to the Duke of Zamorna's wife Mary and chief organist at *St Michael's cathedral, Verdopolis, in the *Glass Town and Angrian saga. He is worshipped by Patrick Benjamin *Wiggins who first meets Greenwood in the city of Zamorna, Angria, where he is staying with his friend Mr Sudbury Figgs (organist at *Howard). Greenwood plays at the opening of the new organ at Howard (a reference to the installation of an organ at St Michael's church, Haworth, in March 1834). In a brilliant comic scene Wiggins debases himself before Greenwood and offers to be his 'toadie' (Alexander *EEW*, 2(2). 251–3). Greenwood is based on the famous *Leeds organist of the same name (see GREENWOOD, JOHN (ORGANIST)) and Figgs on Abraham Stansfield *Sunderland, the *Keighley organist who gave lessons to the young Brontës.

Alexander *EEW*, 2(2). 109–15.

Greenwood, John (organist) (1795–1837), the famous *Leeds musician who made a career for himself in *London; caricatured in the Brontë juvenilia (see GREENWOOD, MR JOHN). Greenwood showed precocious musical ability on almost all instruments at an early age and was organist at Keighley parish church at 13, where he remained until 1821 when he moved to Leeds. A hasty marriage to one of his pupils compelled him to leave for France but he returned to London where he taught and published two volumes of Psalmody. He travelled widely in America and returned to the position of organist at South-Parade Chapel, Halifax, in 1834. Branwell Brontë was an enthusiastic admirer of Greenwood (see WIGGINS, PATRICK BENJAMIN), who played at the Haworth Music Festival of January 1834, performing 'an astonishing

extempore fugue' at the Wesleyan Methodist Chapel, and again at the opening of the organ in Haworth church (March 1834), an event satirized by Charlotte (Alexander *EEW*, 2(2). 251–2).

Greenwood, John (stationer) of Haworth, (1807–63). Originally a woolcomber, John Greenwood became the stationer and bookseller from whom the Brontës obtained their writing paper. In March 1850 he wrote an appreciation of *Jane Eyre* which came into Charlotte's hands. She described him as 'a modest, thoughtful, feeling, reading being', and arranged for him to sell *Jane Eyre* (1850 edition) and other *Smith, Elder and Company publications. His daughter Jane Helen ('Ellen'), later Widdop, inherited ten drawings by Anne and one by Charlotte from him. His tracings of a painting facilitated identification of the NPG portrait of Emily, and he wrote an account of the Brontës reproduced in *BST* (1951), 12. 61. 35–8.

Greenwood family of Haworth and Keighley. The Brontës knew several branches of this manufacturing family, descendants of John Greenwood of Bridge House, Haworth (1659–1737). His great-great-grandson Joseph Greenwood, JP, of Spring Head (1786–1856) about half a mile from Haworth Parsonage, was about a Tory member of the Church of England, a trustee of Haworth church lands, and friend of Revd Patrick Brontë. From about 1810 he lived in a house near his worsted mill, which he leased to other manufacturers from about 1822, when he retired from trade. Joseph and his sons were bankrupted in 1853. The Brontë sisters were friendly with Joseph's daughters, Ann (b. 1820), who died of TB in 1838, and Martha Clapham (1818–76), who went mad, probably in the 1840s, and was cared for in an upper room at Spring Head.

Joseph's brother James (1795–1857), a woollen merchant and manufacturer, moved from Bridge House to Woodlands, a mansion which he built in 1832 in secluded grounds to the south of Haworth. Charlotte mentions the unemployment and distress of many millworkers following James's bankruptcy in 1848. James's sister Mary Ann (1786–1834) married the wealthy manufacturer William Sugden (1786–1834) of Eastwood House, Keighley. Sugden had an illegitimate son, Edward, by his wife's sister Elizabeth (1789–1849), who was married off to the alcoholic local doctor William Cannan (1790–1842). James's uncle John Greenwood of The Knowle, Keighley, was the father of Charlotte's employer Mrs Sarah *Sidgwick. Her brother Frederick Greenwood, JP (1797–1862), lived from 1848 at *Norton Conyers. Mr Brontë's friend Revd Theodore Dury (see DURY FAMILY), Rector of Keighley, married as his second wife Mrs Sidgwick's sister Anne Greenwood (1795–1849).

The Brontës also knew and visited William Greenwood (1800–93) of Old Oxenhope Hall and Mill, and his relatives, scions of the same family.

Fermi, Sarah, 'A "Religious" Family Disgraced: New Information on a Passage Deleted from Mrs Gaskell's *Life of Charlotte Brontë*', BST (1992), 20. 5. 289–95.
—— and Greenwood, Robin, '*Jane Eyre* and the Greenwood Family', BST (1997), 22. 44. 53.
Greenwood, Robin, 'Haworth's Landowners', typescript (3rd edn., June 1999).

Grenville, Ellen, daughter of the wealthy Glass Town mill owner General Thomas *Grenville in the *Glass Town and Angrian saga. She is initially the protégée of Lady Zenobia *Ellrington, whose lessons in the classics and astronomy earn Ellen the reputation of a 'youthful blue'. Her conversation is recondite yet she still retains her unpretentious, girlish simplicity. The Duke of Zamorna refers to her as his 'little bluebell' and encourages his friend Warner Howard *Warner's courtship of her in *High Life in Verdopolis*. After her marriage to Warner, the Angrian prime minister, she retains her blue eyes but loses her coquettishness and her intelligence, dwindling into 'a quiet, nice little woman'.

Grenville, Colonel John Bramham. See GRENVILLE, GENERAL THOMAS.

Grenville, General Thomas (also Colonel John Bramham Grenville), wealthy Verdopolitan mill owner, member of Earl *St Clair's cabinet and speaker in the House of Commons; based on Lord William Grenville, prime minister of the coalition 'Ministry of all the Talents' (1806), who gave Wellington his first seat in the British Parliament. During the Great Rebellion of the Verdopolitan Federation, Grenville is shot when he refuses the demands of workers for more wages (an incident that prefigures Robert Gérard Moore's experience in *Shirley*). He later takes part in the *War of Encroachment. His wife is a portly, cheerful woman and they have two sons and a daughter, Ellen *Grenville, who marries Warner Howard Warner, the Duke of Zamorna's Angrian prime minister.

Grey, Agnes. Anne Brontë endowed her eponymous heroine with some of her own courage, determination, and sensitivity. While, unlike Helen *Huntingdon and Jane *Eyre, Agnes remains, on the whole, within the bounds of acceptable feminine behaviour, she is capable of asserting her own will, speaking out against cruelty, and retaining an inner resilience and self-respect despite the condescension, coarseness, or unfairness of her employers. She has, too, Anne's clarity of vision, insight into character, capacity to learn from experience, firm moral code, and strong religious faith. Yet Anne does not make the mistake of depicting a paragon. Though Agnes analyses her father's character with acute psychological insight as an 'ingenious self-tormentor', she presents her own younger self as amusingly naïve: 'How charming to be intrusted with the care and education of children! . . . I felt I was fully competent to the task' (ch. 1). The novel will show her learning otherwise in the hard school of experience, at the hands of the *Bloomfield family, the *Murray family, and their acquaintances. Anne convincingly demonstrates Agnes's capacity for love, at first for her mother and sisters, later for Edward *Weston, and her responsiveness to affection: thus we sympathize with her vulnerability as an unloved, tormented *governess employed by those who see her as a useful tool to be discarded when she is no longer of service. Agnes's instinctive fondness for animals and birds—a trait she shares with her creator—accompanies a strong sense of the duty to protect them from harm; and as the novel progresses, her maturing judgement of human beings is powerfully influenced by their attitude towards the animal creation. At the risk of making herself sick and incurring the wrath of her employers Agnes drops a 'large flat stone' on the nestlings Tom Bloomfield intends to torture. All the Bloomfields, Matilda Murray, and Revd Mr *Hatfield are judged and condemned for their cruelty; Edward Weston's goodness is symbolized in his rescue of Agnes's dog from the brutal rat-catcher. Yet Agnes is no sentimentalist: Rosalie Murray's heartless pursuit of Weston is bitterly likened to the dog 'gorged to the throat', who begrudges the 'smallest morsel' to a starving brother (ch. 18); and when Rosalie wishes to defer her mercenary marriage so that she can continue her mischievous coquetry, Agnes has 'no more pity for her'. While Agnes's own love for Weston is hardly a grand passion, it is delicately and gradually presented so that the reader sympathizes with her fluctuations of hope, happiness, anxiety, and depression; and her sense of fulfilment after the proposal is brilliantly imaged in the height of the 'steep rugged hill' where the two lovers watch 'the splendid sun-set mirrored on the restless world of waters at our feet' (ch. 25).

Grey, George Turner, the owner of Ardsley Hall, a liberal and noble Angrian gentleman in the *Glass Town and Angrian saga, whose hospitality to grouse shooters during the hunting season is legendary. When he returns from the Battle of *Edwardston to find his house invaded and his daughter Catherine murdered, his own throat is cut by the intruders. A faithful follower of the Duke of Zamorna, Grey's name becomes a watchword, inspiring the troops and providing the subject of song.

Grimsby, Mr. The worst of Mr Arthur *Huntingdon's depraved friends, Mr Grimsby achieves almost demonic proportions in the eyes of Helen *Huntingdon in *Tenant*. He embodies every vice from which Helen tries to shield her young son. Not content with his own wicked behaviour, Grimsby tries to entice his friends into the same corruption, especially delighting in tormenting Lord *Lowborough. The most forcefully malignant character in the novel, Grimsby meets his end when he is killed in a drunken brawl by a gambler he has cheated.

Grimshaw, Revd William (1708–63), BA Christ's College, Cambridge, incumbent of Haworth 1742–63. A close friend of John Wesley, he 'thought it his duty to countenance, and to labour with' Haworth *Methodists, for whom he built a chapel in 1758. The resultant flourishing state of Haworth Methodism was a cause of anxiety and resentment to Revd Patrick Brontë and to Charlotte. Self-denying, and a tireless pastor, Grimshaw enlarged Haworth church, and was also an effective preacher, using everyday incidents to teach spiritual lessons. Leaving the church during the psalm before the sermon, he would seek out idlers and drive them into the church, where he inveighed against sin so 'as to make even the profane and profligate tremble'. Elizabeth Gaskell used John Newton's *Life of William Grimshaw* (1799) to portray the local brutality and vice which Grimshaw reduced, but, using other sources and her own observations, gave evidence of the falling back into 'wild rough heathen ways' after his death (Gaskell *Life*, 1. 23–7).

Grundy, Francis Henry (b. ?1822), son of the Unitarian Revd John Grundy (1782–1843). The energetic and flamboyant Francis was an engineer and surveyor on the Manchester and Leeds Railroad 1841–2, when he met Branwell Brontë in *Halifax and *Luddenden Foot. After working elsewhere, Grundy returned in *c*.1845 to work on the Skipton extension line from Bradford, and again met Branwell. In *Pictures of the Past* (1879) Grundy gives a lively, inaccurate account of Branwell, quoting misdated and garbled extracts from his letters. In the 1850s he emigrated to Australia, dug for gold, and worked as a land surveyor.

Guadima (Guardina) River flows majestically over the Plains of *Dahomey, through the Valley of Verdopolis, and surrounds the Great Glass Town (*Verdopolis). Its upper reaches flow through the city of *Angria, in the north of the kingdom of Angria. The occasional spelling 'Guadiana' suggests its name was derived from the River Guadiana in southern Spain, scene of action during the *Peninsular Wars and mentioned in *Wellington's dispatches.

Guelph, Frederic. See YORK, FREDERICK GUELPH, DUKE OF.

Guiseley, Yorks., a township 6 miles north of *Bradford. St Oswald's church dates back to Norman times, and has a fine 13th-century transept and beautiful chancel arch. Since it was the parish church for *Woodhouse Grove, it was there that Revd Patrick Brontë married Maria Branwell *Brontë and Revd William *Morgan married Maria's cousin Jane Fennell on 29 December 1812, the double wedding taking place by special licence. Revd John *Fennell gave away his daughter and niece, the two young clergymen acted alternately as bridegroom and officiating minister, and the two cousins as bride and bridesmaid (Barker, p. 56).

Gytrash, the, northern dialect for an apparition, spectre, ghost, that usually takes the form of an animal. The *OED* cites Charlotte Brontë's use of it in *Jane Eyre* (ch. 12), when Rochester on his horse comes suddenly upon Jane one evening in a country lane, as the earliest literary use of the word (1847). She describes it as a spirit that, 'in the form of horse, mule, or large dog, haunted solitary ways, and sometimes came upon belated travellers'. Branwell tells us that the Gytrash most commonly appears as 'a Black Dog dragging a chain a dusky calf nay even a rolling stone or a self impelled cart wheel' (Neufeldt *BB Works*, 3. 187). He may have heard of the Horton gytrash, a huge black dog with rattling chains, 'seen' in Horton village near *Thornton. See THURSTONS OF DARKWALL MANOR for a gytrash based on local Haworth tradition.

Halford, Henry. See ALFORD, DR.

Halford, J., the addressee and primary auditor of *Tenant*, although the majority of British editions (until recently) omitted the opening pages that begin 'To J. Halford, Esq' (see TENANT OF WILDFELL HALL, THE: COMPOSITION, MANUSCRIPT, AND EARLY EDITIONS). Halford's relation of past events in his life is the motivation for Gilbert Markham's own epistolary revelations. Halford himself has no voice in the narrative, but is known to have married Gilbert's sister, Rose, and latterly become Gilbert's intimate friend.

Halifax, one of the principal wool towns in the Calder valley, Yorks. Merchants traded their 'pieces' (lengths of cloth) in the classical Piece Hall, completed in 1779, with its great inner quadrangle surrounded by colonnaded tiers of 315 apartments 'for the reception of goods'. St John's parish church dated from 1470, and there were other fine buildings, but population growth from 12,000 in 1801 to 34,000 in 1851 led to overcrowded, insanitary dwellings for the millworkers. When Branwell Brontë was at *Sowerby Bridge and *Luddenden Foot he often visited Halifax, and met his friends Francis *Grundy and Joseph Bentley *Leyland. Local poets and musicians met at the Talbot and the early 17th-century Old Cock, frequented by Branwell along with the Commercial Inn. He took an interest in the musical life of the town, which was famous for its choral society, and was visited by such famous composers as Liszt and Mendelssohn. In March 1846 Branwell wrote to John Frobisher, organist of the parish church, enclosing verses set to an air by Gluck which he loved for its 'mingled majesty and tenderness'. Branwell probably had access to the Leylands' circulating library, and there was also a subscription library at the Old Cock. Several of his poems were published in the *Halifax Guardian between June 1841 and June 1847. Unfortunately Halifax was, as he remarked in a letter to Leyland of c.January 1847, an 'ensnaring' town to him (Wise & Symington, 2. 121). In April 1846 he stayed there three days instead of three hours, tempted to 'get *out* of' himself. In January 1848 he mentioned a 'fainting-fit' at the Talbot, and depicted a drinking scene there. On 17 June 1848 he reported, in desperation, that Thomas Nicholson, landlord of the Old Cock, had threatened a court summons if he did not pay his bill.

Halifax Guardian, a reputable provincial newspaper established in 1832, which regularly devoted space to literature. The *Halifax Guardian* published twelve of Branwell Brontë's poems, all but two under the pseudonym *'Northangerland', and an article on Thomas *Bewick (Oct. 1842; printed in *BST* (1999), 24. 1. 11–15) over a period of six years, beginning in June 1841. The paper had high standards for accepting pieces to include in its poetry columns, which featured many of the well-known poets of the day as well as original work by promising writers such as Branwell. From 1832 to 1837, the *Halifax Guardian* was published by a relative of Joseph Bentley *Leyland, Branwell's friend, but there is no evidence that Leyland influenced the decision to print Branwell's poems in the 1840s. Three of these poems appeared simultaneously in the *Bradford Herald*. Those appearing only in the *Halifax Guardian* are 'Heaven and Earth' (5 June 1841), 'On Melbourne's Ministry' (14 Aug. 1841), 'Real Rest' (8 Nov. 1845), 'Penmaenmawr' (20 Dec. 1845), 'Letter from a Father on Earth to his Child in her Grave' (18 Apr. 1846), 'Speak Kindly to Thy Fellow Man' (19 Sept. 1846), and 'The End of All' (5 June 1847). Conservative in its political orientation, the *Halifax Guardian* also printed Revd Patrick *Brontë's letter 'on the ominous and dangerous vagaries of the times' (quoted in Barker, p. 428) on 29 July 1843. Emily's 'Death Scene' was reprinted in the *Halifax Guardian* five months after Charlotte, Emily, and Anne's *Poems* appeared in May 1846. In 1857, the paper printed a series of letters in which the son of William Carus *Wilson conducted an acrimonious debate with Revd A. B. *Nicholls over the representation of Wilson's school at *Cowan Bridge as *'Lowood Institution' in *Jane Eyre*. By this time, the *Halifax Guardian* had the fourth highest circulation among newspapers circulating in the West Riding of *Yorkshire.   CB

Hall, Revd Cyril, the charitable vicar of Nunnely in *Shirley*. He is first described as perhaps 40 years old, 'plain-looking, dark-complexioned, and already rather gray-haired' (p. 156). Later he is said to be 'forty-five years old, slightly bald, and slightly gray' (p. 304). Frank and unaffected, he speaks with a strong northern accent. He is attentive to Caroline, but as a friend only; living with his sister

Hall, Ellen

Margaret, 'he was wedded to his books and his parish' (p. 304). When the laid-off worker William *Farren and his family face starvation, Mr Hall steps in to lend him money. His role is to provide a contrast to the other clergymen in the novel by offering a model of good clerical conduct. 'The original of Mr. Hall I have seen,' Charlotte Brontë wrote to William Smith Williams on 21 September 1849; 'he knows me slightly, but he would as soon think I had closely observed him or taken him for a character—he would as soon, indeed, suspect me of writing a book—a novel—as he would his dog—Prince' (Smith *Letters*, 2. 260). Charlotte was referring to Revd William Margetson *Heald (1803–75), Vicar of *Birstall 1836–75, who was evidently quite amused by his fictional portrayal: to Ellen Nussey on 8 January 1850 he wrote: 'In that Mr Hall is represented as black, bilious, & of dismal aspect, stooping a trifle & indulging a little now & then in the indigenous dialect,—this seems to sit very well on your humble servant—other traits do better for my good father than myself' (Smith *Letters*, 2. 325). The elder Heald (1767–1837) preceded his son as vicar of Birstall 1801–36.   HR

Hall, Ellen, the 'drudge-like' half-boarder at the girls' boarding school in London in Charlotte Brontë's fragmentary story *Ashworth*. She reveals her lonely background to the sympathetic Mary *Ashworth, and Mary's scorn for Ellen's future fate as a nursery governess reflects Charlotte's own loathing for her recent similar role with the *Sidgwick family. A mysterious Miss Hall 'from Lincolnshire' is mentioned by both Charlotte and Mary Taylor in their letters (Smith *Letters*, 1. 116).

Halliley family. See BROOKE FAMILY OF DEWSBURY.

Hamilton, Edwin, an eminent architect in the *Glass Town and Angrian saga, patronized by the Marquis of Douro (Duke of *Zamorna), who later gives him a knighthood and marble palace in *Adrianopolis. Wellesley House with its 'chaste magnificence' and marble staircase is one of Hamilton's Palladian masterpieces, and he also tries his hand at writing tragedies (see 'The Tragedy and the Essay', in 'Arthuriana'; Alexander *EEW*, 2(1). 234–43). The Brontës had probably heard of several artists named Hamilton, including Gavin Hamilton (1723–98), a painter and excavator at Rome, known for his classical taste; William Hamilton (1751–1801), a painter of historical and Shakespearian subjects who studied in Italy and whose portraits included John Wesley and Mrs Siddons (also mentioned in 'The Tragedy and the Essay'); and David Hamilton (1768–1843), a Scottish architect.

handwriting and Brontë signatures. Branwell Brontë and his sisters used a minute print-style script, usually in ink, in their juvenilia, private writings such as *Diary Papers, and some poem drafts. Anne forms most of her letters unambiguously, spacing them out clearly; 'n' is usually distinguishable from 'u', and 'e' from 'c'; 't' is distinctly crossed, and in her Diary Paper of 31 July 1845 becomes an obolus; 'g' has a rudimentary descender, 'y' a straight descender with no hook or loop. The letters are upright or slope slightly backwards. Branwell's 'Monthly Intelligencer' of 27 March 1833 has clearly formed, rather angular letters; the cross-stroke of 't' is confined to the left side of the upright, 'y' has a hooked or curved descender, and the descender of 'g' has no loop. In his 'History of Angria IV' the letters look flattened; 'e' resembles 'c', 'r' may look like 'v'. The distinctive 't' is retained, and in chapter 2 the figure 4 is made backwards. Charlotte's writing in 'A Fragment' (11 July 1831) is unambiguous; the letters are set close together, and may be joined. 'g' is formed with two loops, without lifting the pen. The descender of 'y' is straight, or slightly angled. In her 'Verdopolitan Intelligencer' (16 Mar. 1835) most letters are well defined, though 'm' may be loosely made; 'g' remains as in 1831, but 'y' often has a curled descender. In Emily's joint Diary Paper with Anne of 24 November 1834 the letters are rudimentary and angular; 'a' sometimes looks like 'c' made backwards, while 'c' may be confused with 'e', 'r' with 'v'. The descender of 'g' has no loop. Letters are even more minimal in her poem manuscript 'That wind I used to hear' (28 Nov. 1834): 'g' is merely an irregular downstroke, 'n' and 'u' look much alike. The letters 'th' may be linked together. Emily's fair copy of 'There shines the moon' (Feb. 1844) is slightly clearer: 'g' has a looped descender, 'e' is more distinct; 't' and 'h' may be joined, but legible.

When the Brontës in adulthood use a cursive hand in their letters, devoirs, fair copy manuscripts, or other documents, their different styles are more readily identifiable. In her letters Anne's writing is a very clear, careful, rather spiky version of copperplate, with generously spaced letters and lines, and large capitals, ascenders, and descenders; 't', 'd', and 'h' have long upstrokes making an acute angle with the downstrokes, so that there is a space between the two at the lower end. Sometimes Anne lifts her pen after the first letter of a word.

Branwell could write with either hand. He used his right hand in, for example, his letter of 4 January 1837 to the editor of *Blackwood's Edinburgh Magazine*. The writing is quite large, clear, rather spiky, with a strong slope to the right. Large elaborate forms of capital 'I' are prominent, with stems descending below the baseline. 't' has a long, bold cross-stroke, and the double-looped 'f' is made without lifting the pen. He more often wrote with his left hand, using upright, or slightly backward-sloping, irregularly formed letters. In some words ascenders and descenders slope haphazardly. 't' normally has a long cross-stroke, except as a final letter. Capital initials are used rather at random, and emphasis may be given by heavily underlined printed capitals. The prominent capital 'I' recurs.

Emily's cursive hand, a clearly legible, angular variant of copperplate, is usually written with a fine nib, and slants steeply and evenly to the right. 'f', 'g', and 'y' have long narrow-looped descenders, and the 't' cross-strokes are long. The minuscule letters are small in proportion to the average height of a line of writing.

Charlotte's cursive script changed over the years. From c.1829 to 1837 she used a fairly well-spaced copperplate style, sloping to the right, with elongated ascenders and descenders. 'y' might have a narrow downward loop or long backward curve. In 1838–40 she often used a bolder, less regular hand with long ascenders and descenders. Final 'y' might have a straight descender, smooth backward curve, or angled hook. The ascender of final 'd' might be straight or looped backward. From 1841 to 1843 there was a change from a small but slightly disjointed hand with occasional blotted loops to a neat, regularly sloped, very small, clear style. Final 'y' might be sharply angled, or have a narrow loop. Medial and final 'd' were often neatly curved backward. By 1844–5 her writing was usually small, fluent, even, slightly and regularly sloped to the right. A final 'd' might curve or loop back smoothly towards the beginning of a word.

When Revd Patrick Brontë's sight was good, he produced a rapid, inelegant script with a steep slant to the right, normally using dark ink and a fairly thick nib. Final 'd' and the word 'of' might be almost encircled by a loop, and 'g' might be either straight-stemmed or a figure-of-eight. Long cross-strokes on 't' sometimes extended to the following word. Capital initials, idiosyncratically used, were large, and some words began with an enlarged minuscule. He often inserted superfluous commas. His writing became larger and more irregular with age, but remained clearly legible. See the examples of handwriting and signatures on p. 408.

Hannah, an elderly, rustic, dialect-speaking servant in *Jane Eyre*, who has been with the Rivers family for 30 years. She is honest, outspoken, and stubborn, like Tabitha *Aykroyd. Concerned to protect her 'childer' at *Moor House, she shuts out the destitute Jane, suspecting her of being in league with housebreakers, but later admits she was unchristian to consider poverty a crime, and becomes Jane's friend. When Diana and Mary *Rivers leave to go to B——, Hannah accompanies St John *Rivers to *Morton, but returns to help Jane clean Moor House and prepare a Christmas welcome for her cousins.

Hardman family, in *Shirley*, 'a family of considerable pretensions to good birth and mental superiority' (pp. 422–3) by which Agnes Grey (later Mrs Agnes *Pryor) is employed as a governess. Mrs Pryor recounts her sufferings at the hands of the Hardmans to dissuade Caroline *Helstone from pursuing the idea of becoming a governess (ch. 21). Through Mrs Pryor's history Charlotte Brontë was doubtless recalling her own unhappiness as a governess in the *Sidgwick household, but the Hardmans' cold and snobbish observations about governesses are adapted from Elizabeth *Rigby's unkind review of *Jane Eyre* in the *Quarterly Review* (Dec. 1848): see SHIRLEY: 'A WORD TO THE "QUARTERLY"'. HR

Hareton. See EARNSHAW, HARETON.

Hargrave, Esther, the younger sister of Millicent and Walter Hargrave and a friend of Helen Huntingdon, in *Tenant*. Like Helen, Esther is strong-minded. She learns from Helen's advice and experience in marriage, and defies the wishes of her mother and brother, who wish her to marry the rich Mr Oldfield. Esther is entrusted with the care of Helen's son Arthur when Mr Huntingdon lies dying, and she makes a good match in Helen's brother, Frederick *Lawrence. It is thought that Esther Hargrave may be based on one of the younger girls of the *Robinson family of Thorp Green, to whom Anne Brontë acted as governess and friend.

Hargrave, Millicent, in *Tenant*, Helen *Huntingdon's good friend, despite being Annabella Wilmot's cousin. Unlike Helen and unlike her own young sister Esther, Millicent is gentle and submissive. She obeys her mother's wishes and marries Ralph *Hattersley, the son of a rich banker and a friend of Mr Arthur *Huntingdon. She patiently endures Hattersley's dissolute behaviour, until Helen intervenes and Millicent herself gains courage enough to reveal her suffering to her husband who reforms. With their two children, Ralph and Helen (who eventually marries Helen Huntingdon's son Arthur), Millicent and her husband settle into a respectable and happy country existence. Millicent's situation, being forced by her mother to make a mercenary marriage, is similar to that of one of the younger girls of the *Robinson family of Thorp Green, to whom Anne Brontë was governess (Smith *Letters*, 2. 21).

Hargrave, Walter, friend of Mr Arthur *Huntingdon and brother of Millicent and Esther, in *Tenant*. His home is with his mother and sisters at The Grove, but he spends most of his time away from it, living a life of fashion and self-indulgence in London and Paris. Millicent hoped he would marry her friend Helen and when instead she marries Huntingdon, Hargrave tries to gain Helen's affection by supporting her against her husband. As the Huntingdons' marriage deteriorates, Hargrave declares his love for Helen and is decidedly rejected. When he returns from Paris, he resumes the pursuit, skilfully presenting his seduction as morally justified, since he will rescue her and her child from Huntingdon's abuse. His genuine feeling for Helen and his cultivated taste and manner place her in real danger of being 'inextricably entangled in [his] snare' (ch. 33). Spoilt and wilful from boyhood, his main concern in marriage is to secure a fortune, but he eventually marries a plain, 40-year-old spinster with a moderate fortune. The handsome, crafty Hargrave may owe part of his conception to the unpleasant Sir Hargrave Pollexfen in *Richardson's *Sir Charles Grandison* and to the aristocratic rake Lovelace in *Clarissa* (*Tenant*, p. 503).

Harlaw (Harlow), Marquis of. See ROSS, EDWARD TUT.

Harper & Brothers, principal American publishers of the Brontë novels in the 19th century. In 1817 James Harper (1795–1869) and his brother John (1797–1875) established a printing business in New York, as 'J & J Harper, Printers', which soon became a publishing firm, and was joined by two other brothers. From 1833, as 'Harper & Brothers', they rapidly gained a reputation for shrewd business enterprise. The house merged in 1962 with Row, Peterson & Co., with the imprint 'Harper & Row, Publishers'. Harpers asked two questions about manuscripts they were offered: 'Is this book moral as well as interesting and instructive?' and 'Is this a plagiarism?' (Exman, p. xiv). On the matter of international copyright they were theoretically in favour of authors receiving just compensation: in 1844 Wesley Harper signed a petition to Congress favouring a change in copyright status, but the brothers were reluctant to be more aggressive. Thus they made the most of the profitable market in British books, on which no copyright had to be paid, publishing works by, for example, Dickens and Thackeray in volume form and in their magazines, *Harper's Weekly* (1857–1916) and *Harper's New Monthly Magazine* (founded 1850), and they were keen to publish the Brontës' works. Eugene Exman states that when *Jane Eyre* was acclaimed by British reviewers, 'Sampson Low quickly dispatched an early copy' to Harpers, who published it in their 'Library of Select Novels' on 4 January 1848 at 25 cents. It was followed by a 'subedition' in cloth on 22 November 1849, and Harpers also subleased sets of plates to other publishers, such as Derby and Jackson of New York and Cincinnati. Harpers published the first American edition of *Wuthering Heights* 'By the Author of "Jane Eyre"' on 21 April 1848 in paper covers, simultaneously with clothbound copies. Good sales of *Jane Eyre* in America meant that they bid high for the first sheets of 'Currer Bell's' next work, which *Smith, Elder and Company promised to let them have. Smith, Elder were therefore alarmed when they heard from Harpers in early July 1848, that a 'rival publisher' (T. C. *Newby) had informed them that 'he was about to publish the next book by the author of "Jane Eyre"', under her other *nom de plume* of Acton Bell—Currer, Ellis, and Acton being, according to him, one person. Charlotte and Anne hastened to London, arriving on 8 July, to explain that the new work offered to Newby was Anne's *Tenant*. Harper & Brothers, still confused, published the first American edition of *Tenant* 'by the Author of Wuthering Heights' (1 volume, purple cloth) on 28 July 1848, followed by a 2-volume edition in paper wrappers the same year. Smith, Elder had negotiated with Harper's to sell them advance sheets of Charlotte's next book to give them an advantage over other American publishers. Harper's duly paid £50 to Smith, Elder for advance sheets of each of Charlotte's three other novels, publishing *Shirley* on 22 November 1849 ('1850' on title-page), *Villette* on 4 March 1853, and *The Professor* on 27 June 1851, only a few weeks after the first English publications. Apparently Harper's did not publish an early edition of *Agnes Grey*.

Exman, Eugene, *The Brothers Harper* (1965) (inaccurate on the Brontës).
Smith, W. E., *The Brontë Sisters* (1991).

Harrogate. By c.1840 two villages, High and Low Harrowgate, about 16 miles north of *Leeds, were rapidly becoming one town, the principal 'watering-place' in the north of England. It had five wells or spas drawing from sulphurous or chalybeate springs, used in treating 'scorbutic, cutaneous and chronic [rheumatic] disorders' (Thomas Dugdale, *Curiosities of Great Britain: England and Wales Delineated* (c.1837–41), 934). On 6 June 1820 Revd Patrick Brontë signed a petition to a charity so that a poor Haworth woolcomber might go there to relieve his scorbutic complaint (Barker, p. 101). Charlotte was a governess at *Swarcliffe Hall near Harrogate in July 1839. In August 1844 she refused Ellen Nussey's invitation to join the Nusseys there.

Hart, Lily, Duchess of Fidena, wife of Prince John and mother of John Augustus Sneaky, Jun., Marquis of Rossendale, in the *Glass Town and Angrian saga. She is the heroine of 'Lily Hart' (see SECRET AND LILY HART, THE), Charlotte Brontë's fairy-tale love story of the Duke of *Fidena's clandestine courtship of the seamstress Lily. Her name and story were probably inspired by that of 'Emily Hart', the early assumed name of Emma Lyon, later Lady Hamilton, mistress of Lord Nelson, Duke of Bronté.

Hartford, General Lord Edward, nobleman and feudal landowner in the province of Zamorna, in the *Glass Town and Angrian saga. He lives at Hartford Hall, the scene of numerous parties, horse races, and shooting matches. He is an old schoolfriend of Captain Sir John *Flower (Richton), a strong supporter of the Duke of Zamorna and a commander of his troops at the Battles of Westwood and Leyden. Hartford is a dark, moustachioed, arrogant aristocrat, but honourable and handsome (except for a scar on his forehead), 'a sort of Angrian Great-heart in the field & in the council'. He is unsuccessful in his attempt to win the affections of the Duke of Zamorna's mistress Mina *Laury, and after being wounded by Zamorna in a duel over her, he recovers to court Jane *Moore, daughter of Hartford's lawyer and tenant. No longer endorsed by Zamorna, he is rejected as an ambassador although he represents one of the oldest families in Angria. He is jealous of the success of Captain Henry *Hastings, his tenant's son; when Hastings is disgraced, Hartford pursues him like a bloodhound and presides as judge at his court martial.

Hartford Hall (House), a decayed Elizabethan mansion, Angrian country seat of General Lord Edward *Hartford in Hartford Dale, Zamorna, in the *Glass Town and Angrian saga. The Olympian River flows through the property, which includes tenanted farms. Massinger Hall and *Kirkham-Lodge are on Hartford's land, and *Girnington Hall is nearby.

Hartley, Margaret. See KIRBY, MR AND MRS ISAAC.

Hartley, Michael, in *Shirley*, 'a frantic Antinomian in religion, and a mad leveller in politics' (p. 726). Declaiming verses from Proverbs and the Book of Job, he shoots Robert Gérard *Moore as the latter is riding back to *Briarfield from *Stilbro' in the company of Hiram *Yorke. Though Hartley is known to be the perpetrator, Moore does not pursue him, and he dies 'of delirium tremens' a year after the attempt. Charlotte Brontë adapted the episode of the attempted assassination from the real-life attacks in April 1812 on West Riding

mill owners William Cartwright and William Horsfall. The former escaped injury, but Horsfall died of his wounds. During the attack on Cartwright's mill at *Rawfolds, one of the two rioters killed was Samuel Hartley, a cropper formerly employed by Cartwright. See LUDDITE RIOTS.   HR

Hartley family. Hartley is a well-known family name that existed in Haworth and the local area before the arrival of the Brontës. A James Hartley became the first minister of West Lane Baptist church, Haworth, erected in 1752. He had been a convert of William *Grimshaw, Revd Patrick Brontë's famous predecessor, and one of his former lay preachers who had lived with him at Sowdens. A descendant of his, Joseph Hartley at Church Gates, objected to paying for new water supplies in 1851 (a move instigated by Mr Brontë for the health of *Haworth residents) since his house Sowdens already had water. Joseph owned a number of buildings, including a butcher's shop and house, stable, and privy close to the old Haworth church which was 'an intolerable nuisance' (demolished 1886; Barker, p. 97) and a cottage at 'Ducking Stool in Stubbing Lane' (Lock & Dixon, pp. 435, 438). Another member of the Hartley family was postmaster of Haworth during the Brontës' time. Charlotte Brontë used the name Hartley for the crazed Antinomian weaver who shoots Robert Gérard Moore in her novel *Shirley* (see HARTLEY, MICHAEL). She was probably thinking of Samuel Hartley, the 24-year-old cropper of Halifax, who was killed at the attack on *Rawfolds Mill, owned by William Cartwright, during the Luddite riots of 1812.

Hartshead. Revd Patrick Brontë moved westwards from *Dewsbury in early 1811 to his curacy at the tiny hilltop village of Hartshead and the more populous Clifton. He lodged at Lousy Thorn farm opposite Hartshead's small Norman church of St Peter until his marriage, when he and Maria moved to Clough House, Hightown. Many parishioners worked in the woollen industry, and in February 1812 angry *Luddites smashed William Cartwright's new cropping frames on Hartshead Moor. On the night of 11 April 1812 Luddites gathered at the Dumb Steeple, south of the moor, before attacking *Rawfolds Mill. Both incidents are recalled in *Shirley*.

Hastings, Elizabeth, loyal Angrian and 19-year-old sister of Captain Henry *Hastings in the *Glass Town and Angrian saga. Her home is Colne-Moss Tarn in *Pendleton. Her father, a gentleman farmer and tenant of Warner Howard *Warner, is—like his children—an obstinate passionate man, who disowns his son Henry when he is disgraced. Elizabeth leaves home when her father strikes her for supporting her brother, yet she still respects both him and Mr Warner. Much of Charlotte Brontë's attitude to Branwell and his early failures is embodied in Elizabeth's outlook towards her wayward brother.

Elizabeth Hastings's character and experience prefigure that of Jane *Eyre. Her features are irregular though expressive, with handsome brown eyes, and her hair is plaited on her forehead in smooth braids. She is little and thin and dresses like a Quaker, yet she is a keen observer, a 'person of quick perceptions & dexterous address'. She lacks openness, and conceals intense emotions beneath her skilful address. She is intensely proud of her hard-won independence as a teacher. Her first job is as companion to the Angrian beauty Jane *Moore, to whom she teaches French and Italian. While looking after Massinger Hall in the Moores' absence, she harbours her fugitive brother and is interrogated by Captain Sir William *Percy. She then successfully establishes a school with pupils from among the wealthy manufacturers and aristocrats of the province of Zamorna. She is respected and depends on nobody, yet she still longs for 'a warmer, closer attachment'. She is tempted by William Percy's declaration of love but refuses to become his mistress, the first of Charlotte Brontë's heroines to rank self-respect above romantic love. See HENRY HASTINGS.

Hastings, Captain Henry, popular young Angrian soldier of the 19th Infantry regiment and author, who degenerates into a drunken murderer, in the *Glass Town and Angrian saga. A later pseudonym of Branwell Brontë, he composes songs and national anthems which bring him sudden fame. But he is selfish and vain, and naïvely confident of his ability to charm. He insults Richton and Hartford in the presence of Warner Howard *Warner, his patron, who never again helps him. When he is cashiered for shooting his superior officer Adams, he becomes a fugitive, pursued especially by General Lord Edward *Hartford and Captain Sir William *Percy. He assumes the name of Wilson, joins the Revolutionary forces (opposed to Angria), and becomes involved in a plot to kill the Duke of Zamorna. After eighteen months on the run, Hastings is captured and court-martialled, but prevents his execution by turning King's evidence.

Hastings comes from Colne-Moss Tarn in *Pendleton, Angria, where his respected elderly father is a farmer tenant of Warner. His sister Elizabeth *Hastings is intensely loyal to her brother, leaving home because of him, sheltering him from police at Massinger Hall, pleading for him with Warner and Mary Percy, and, despite his public infamy, still thinking well of him. Hastings

gradually comes to embody Branwell's own social failure despite his early promise, his increasing addiction to drink, and his instability of character. Charlotte's often sensitive and penetrating presentations of Hastings (as, for example, in *Julia) contrast with Branwell's seemingly unconscious bravado and justification of drinking and debauchery in the voice of Henry Hastings in his own Angrian manuscripts. Charlotte's novelette *Henry Hastings includes a sensitive portrayal of this brother–sister relationship.

Hatfield, C. W. (d. 1942), collector and editor. A Customs and Excise officer whose hobby was the collection of Brontëana, he was a vice-president of the *Brontë Society for fourteen years, contributed many articles and transcriptions to BST, supplied corrections for John Alexander *Symington's 1927 catalogue of the Brontë museum items, and prepared a catalogue of the *Bonnell Collection at Haworth in 1932. His edition of Emily Brontë's poems in 1941, with its lucid introduction, carefully established texts, and manuscript collations, was the most scholarly work on the Brontës produced by that date. His familiarity with the Brontës' handwriting enabled him to confirm his surmise that C. K. *Shorter's 1910 edition, supposedly of Emily's poems, contained 25 that were not by her. In 1926 Davidson Cook sent him copies of manuscripts in the Law Collection which proved that Shorter's 1923 edition was neither complete nor entirely accurate. Derek Roper, editor of the Clarendon edition of Emily's poems (1995), pays tribute to Hatfield's work, noting that the canon is essentially that which he established in the 1941 edition. Hatfield also did the editorial work for Shorter's limited editions of Brontë letters. By 1926, the year of Shorter's death, he had gathered together unpublished poems by Charlotte, unpublished letters, and hundreds of corrections and additions to those already printed, and hoped to have them included in a Library edition of the Brontë works and letters. A modest and retiring person, indifferent to his personal gain or prestige, he was happy to assist Symington in the preparation of the Shakespeare Head Brontë letters, a task he began in 1931. His name did not appear in the half-title, but Symington acknowledged his help with 'particular gratitude and thanks', and ensured that Hatfield shared with him the honours of The Miscellaneous and Unpublished Writings in 1936.

Hatfield, Revd Mr, Rector of *Horton in Agnes Grey. A conceited, worldly toady and snob, he aspires to marry the upper-class Rosalie Murray (see MURRAY FAMILY). After she scornfully refuses him, he marries a wealthy spinster. A High Church ritualist, he is concerned with outward form, not with the teaching of Christ, and is a total contrast to the sincere, truly Christian Edward *Weston. In chapter 10, the staunchly evangelical Anne Brontë writes in scathing condemnation of such clergymen, who 'bind heavy burdens, and grievous to be borne, and lay them upon men's shoulders . . . and that make the word of God of none effect by their traditions, teaching for doctrines the commandments of men'. See also OXFORD MOVEMENT.

Hathersage, a Derbyshire village, like *Morton, on the eastern edge of the Peak District; in the 19th century inhabited mainly by farmers and workers in local needle factories. Charlotte Brontë stayed with Ellen *Nussey from c.3 to 26 July 1845 in the vicarage, which was being renovated and enlarged before the return of the vicar, Ellen's brother Revd Henry *Nussey, and his bride. St Michael's church has memorials to the Eyre family dating back to the 15th century, and a charity board naming 'Joan Morton'. Charlotte and Ellen visited the widowed Mary Eyre's home at *North Lees Hall, and borrowed her pony to visit Castleton and Cavedale.

Hattersley, Ralph, son of a rich banker, and a dissolute friend of Mr Arthur *Huntingdon in *Tenant*. He wishes for a quiet wife who will let him do as he pleases 'without a word of reproach or complaint' (ch. 25). He finds exactly this in Millicent *Hargrave. He loves his children and his wife, despite the fact that her dutiful submissiveness irritates him and exacerbates his habits of drunken revelry and gambling. However, he tires of his friends and decides to reform, his decision confirmed by Helen Huntingdon's advice on his treatment of the unhappy Millicent and by his witnessing the death of his friend Arthur Huntingdon. In later life he settles in the country as a respectable gentleman farmer with his wife and children, and becomes famous for the horses he breeds.

Haussé, Mlle, a teacher at Mme Zoë *Heger's pensionnat. She is probably the 'Mademoiselle Marie' whom Charlotte Brontë describes as 'talented and original—but of repulsive and arbitrary manners'. She and 'Mlle Blanche' hate each other like two cats, and are 'on a system of war without quarter' (Smith *Letters*, 1. 284, 319). Charlotte seems to have used traits from both teachers for the characters of Zélie de *St Pierre in *Villette* and Mlle Zéphyrine in *The Professor*.

Hawkscliffe, the Duke of Zamorna's country estate in the province of *Angria, including Hawkscliffe Forest and Hawkscliffe Castle on the River Arno. The lodge of the *Cross of Rivaulx lies on the edge of Hawkscliffe Forest. In her last Angrian stories, Charlotte Brontë reduces Hawkscliffe House to 'a handsome pile—but by no means so large nor so grand as the extent of the grounds seemed to warrant' (*Caroline Vernon*); and the estate is now a working farm where even the Duke of Zamorna helps with haymaking.

Haworth, home of the Brontë family from 1820, is a village built on the steep sides of the Worth valley and its tributary on the eastern edge of the Pennines. Before the Brontës' day packhorses used to bring wool and cotton over the Pennine hills and moors to the West Riding mills. The approach to 'the dreary black-looking' village of Haworth via Bridge House in the valley was 'one of the steepest hills' Jane Forster (see FORSTER, WILLIAM EDWARD) had ever seen, and Elizabeth Gaskell recorded that the street was paved with flagstones placed end-ways, that the horses' feet 'may have something to cling to, and not slip down backwards' (Gaskell *Life*, 2. 297). In Main Street the dark stone houses stand in an irregular line, most of them shoulder to shoulder, some with alleys in between. There may be three or more storeys at the back of a two-storey fronted house, with upper windows looking out over the valley.

In the early 19th century Haworth was a vast parish: White's Yorkshire *Directory* (1853) noted 'many scattered houses' in a township that contained '6848 souls, and 10,540 acres of land . . . nearly half of it uncultivated heaths and commons'. Well-known family names that have existed in Haworth and its vicinity since Saxon times include Appleyard, Aykroyd, Binns, Brown, Feather, Greenwood, Heaton, Hartley, Holmes, Horsfall, Hoyle, Murgatroyd, Pickles, Pighills, Ratcliffe, Rushworth, Shuttleworth, Sugden, Sutcliffe, Taylor, Toothill, Whittaker, Wood. Revd Patrick Brontë walked many miles visiting parishioners on remote farms with rough pasture fields or high stony arable land where oats, but few other crops, were grown. For his daughters, in their childhood and young womanhood, the moorlands were a place of freedom and delight, and the source of inspiration. Emily had a particular love for them, so that when Charlotte was the sole surviving sister the moors seemed a 'wilderness, featureless, solitary, saddening . . . not a branch of fern, not a young bilberry leaf nor a fluttering lark or linnet but reminds me of her. The distant prospects were Anne's delight . . . she is in the blue tints, the pale mists, the waves and shadows of the horizon' (Smith *Letters*, 2. 403).

But Haworth itself was a busy manufacturing village. There were already eighteen small textile mills in the township by 1820, three within the village proper at Bridge House, Ebor Mill, and Mytholmes, the rest in Oxenhope and Stanbury. In addition woolcombers worked at home, in the steamy heat needed for the task. The unusually wide upper windows of some cottages bear witness to the other home industry of handloom weaving, for which all the daylight hours were precious. Some of the mills were already lit by gas, which meant that even in winter the workers' day might start at or before 6 a.m. Women and children might be employed either in the mills or at home, and there were several related trades. The parish registers record wool-sorters, heald-thread makers, shuttlemakers, and various other craftsmen: stonemason, wheelwright, clockmaker, blacksmith, joiner, and so on. Several villagers combined farming with other occupations, so that horses, cows, and pigs contributed to the 'insalubrious' state of Haworth's roads and backyards. Innkeeping and shopkeeping were other employments. Visitors often put up at the *Black Bull, but there was no lack of other inns: the White Lion, King's Arms, Fleece, and Sun, with four beerhouses recorded in the 1837 *Directory*, and a temperance hotel in 1853. The landlord of the White Lion, and later briefly of the Bull, was Enoch Thomas, whose relatives, the wine and spirit merchants, owned the squalid workers' cottages known as 'Brandy Row' behind the Main Street. Haworth was not a healthy village. Polluted water, to which the overcrowded churchyard with its flat-topped tombstones contributed, inadequate privies, open drains, and heaped up middens near dwelling-houses, meant that Haworth's mortality rate was 25.4 per thousand, with a mortality rate for infants under 6 years of 41.6 per cent, and an average life expectancy of just under 26. Mr Brontë and his curates officiated at an appalling number of burials. On 29 August 1849 Mr Brontë, Revd A. B. *Nicholls, and two local surgeons 'headed a petition to the General Board of Health for assistance in procuring a better water supply' (Barker, p. 635). Benjamin Herschel Babbage's damning report after his inspection on 4 April 1850 recommended among other things the closure of the churchyard. But progress was slow owing to the self-interest of too many of the Haworth landowners and tradesmen, measures of reform were half-hearted, and the churchyard was not finally closed until 1856.

Most of the buildings in Haworth are of dark, sturdy millstone grit, and the older ones are roofed with heavy stone slabs. A few larger houses date from the 17th century: the attractive Town End farmhouse, the Old Hall at the lower end of Main Street, and no. 8 Fern Street. Their stone-mullioned windows are like those imagined by Emily in *Wuthering Heights*. Other houses of some dignity are the 18th-century *Haworth Parsonage, the Manor House at Cook Gate, and Bridge House, all built to a similar design with a central pedimented front door and symmetrically placed

windows. A wide-fronted building in Main Street now used as the 'Villette' coffee house was formerly the Haworth *Mechanics' Institute. In the steep, rough-surfaced Lodge Street, once Newell Hill, is a room formerly used for meetings of the Three Graces Freemasons' Lodge to which Branwell belonged. Almost a mile outside Haworth to the south is an isolated, spacious, stone-built house in extensive grounds, known as Woodlands, built in 1832 by the mill owner James Greenwood (1798–1857) (see GREENWOOD FAMILY OF HAWORTH AND KEIGHLEY). His bankruptcy in 1848 threw many of the poor of Haworth out of employment and occasioned great distress in the village.

James Greenwood had owned and operated Bridge House mill, the oldest in Haworth, now extant as a much enlarged building erected mainly by the Butterfields after 1850, and still in industrial use. In the Brontës' day the local worsted mills were worked by steam power. Charlotte describes such mills dramatically. Hurrying in the frosty dawn towards his brother's mill, William Crimsworth found that the factory workpeople had preceded him by nearly an hour and the mill was all lighted up and in full operation (*The Professor*, ch. 5). It was 'vomiting soot from its long chimney and quivering through its thick brick walls with the commotion of its iron bowels' (ch. 2). In *Shirley* the child workers come 'running in' to the mill during the raw morning, and are reprimanded by Robert Gérard *Moore and Joe Scott, if they are late; but 'neither Mr. Moore nor his overlooker ever struck a child in the mill'; and the narrator hopes 'they have enough to eat' when, 'released for half an hour from toil' at eight o'clock, they betake themselves to their breakfast. In William Greenwood's Old Oxenhope worsted spinning mill, within Haworth township, one boy and three girls under 10, and six boys and five girls under 14 were employed in 1833; only one shift of children was needed 'during one adult shift' as they 'only work 12 hours'; and though work stopped earlier on Saturdays, the 'deficiency' was 'made up usually on previous Thursday or Friday'. The Factory Act of 1833 secured the exclusion of all children under 9 from textile factories (except in the silk industry), limited the work of children under 13 to 48 hours a week, or nine hours in any one day. Children under 13 were to attend school for not less than two hours per day.

Until 1833 such child workers in Haworth might obtain little if any education, except at Sunday schools provided by the churches. In 1802 the *Methodists had revived an earlier school, and the West Lane Baptists had established one before 1832, when Mr Brontë organized the building of a church Sunday school, still extant, on the other side of the lane from the Parsonage. The schools aimed to provide a basic education, inculcate discipline, and enable their scholars to read the Bible. Branwell, Charlotte, and Anne were all Sunday school teachers. A typical Whitsuntide Sunday school feast and procession, described in *Shirley* (chs. 16 and 17), recalls one of the more cheerful sides of contemporary village life as well as the sectarian hostility which might erupt there. The Church of England *Haworth National School was not founded until 1844. The endowed Free Grammar School in Haworth, founded in 1636, was in decline. An inspection in 1827 found that 200 pupils were on the roll, but the schoolroom would scarcely hold 100, no classics were taught, and the master was not a graduate. In 1844 Revd William *Scoresby arranged for the replacement of the master in charge, the Wesleyan Mr Ramsbottom, by the Cambridge graduate Revd J. B. *Grant. He was said to be a good classical scholar, and was in charge until 1849. But the 1868 report called the school the worst in the district, with eighteen pupils ill-taught and ill-supplied with books. Yet some intelligent and determined artisans succeeded in furthering their education: John Farish, a founder-member of the *Keighley Mechanics' Institute, had attended a night school while apprenticed to a silk-reed maker in Macclesfield, and when he later became a woolcomber and then a reed-maker in Haworth he pursued his studies in mathematics and applied sciences by reading far into the night. The establishment of the Haworth Mechanics' Institute in 1849 showed that there was an interest in such further education; and the eagerness of the members to acquire copies of Charlotte's novels in 1850 is evidence of both literacy and local pride. There was also justifiable local pride in a strong tradition of vocal music, and concerts were held both in the church and a room over the Black Bull. See also FREEMASONRY.

Haworth suffered periods of political and social unrest. In the mid-twenties poor trade and the collapse of banks caused distress and unemployment in and around Haworth. Again, in 1840, trade depression, harsh weather, and unemployment meant that the poor lacked both food and fuel: Mr Brontë and his then curate, William Weightman, successfully organized appeals for subscriptions and gifts, and arranged the distribution of cotton shirting, blankets, oatmeal, and potatoes (Barker, p. 328). In 1842 local *Chartist risings were joined by some workers from Haworth; and in 1846, when the local mill owners were holding out against strikes of woolcombers and powerloom workers against low wages, a Wool-Combers' Protective Society was formed. But by 1850 Charlotte's assistance in enabling the woolcomber and stationer John *Greenwood to sell the cheap edition of *Jane Eyre*,

and other books, indicated that Haworth had at least some readers not too impoverished to spend money on non-essentials.

It is true that the Bible might be the only book in most houses in Haworth. Methodist class-leaders, for example, expected their members to meet for Bible-reading, study, and prayer. The first Methodist church in Haworth had been founded in West Lane by Revd William *Grimshaw in 1758, enlarged by the addition of a gallery in about 1805 to accommodate increasing numbers, and again enlarged in 1822; the West Lane Baptist chapel was built in 1752, enlarged in 1775, and rebuilt in 1844, again because of growing attendance. Both chapels are unpretentious stone buildings set near the road, backing on to fields. The Hall Green Chapel of the Particular Baptists, erected in 1824, is large, rather austere, and set in its own small graveyard. Mr Brontë had on the whole a good relationship with Haworth Methodists, but was harassed by opposition from the West Lane Baptist minister, Revd John Winterbotham, especially over the question of church tithes from 1834 onwards.

All the Brontë family except Anne, who died in Scarborough, were buried in the family vault beneath the floor of the old *Haworth church of which Mr Brontë was the incumbent, and Mr Brontë's name was the last to be added to the family memorial tablet. Other old memorials, such as that bearing a touching tribute to William Weightman, were re-erected in the new church built by Mr Brontë's successor, Revd John Wade, in 1879. Here the Brontë memorial chapel is to be found and the Brontë Society holds an annual service of thanksgiving for the lives and works of the Brontës.

Haworth church. The old church of St Michael was a small, undistinguished 18th-century stone building, with tall arched windows, a high three-tier pulpit (now in Stanbury church), narrow wooden box pews, a larger square pew used by the Brontës next to the east wall and near the altar, and heavy wooden galleries. The tower, which survives, is of more ancient date. John Wesley preached in Haworth when his friend Revd William *Grimshaw was the incumbent. So great was the congregation that wooden platforms outside the church were erected to accommodate the people. The greenish glass windows and the galleries built in front of them made the church dim, and a visitor in the 1850s thought it a 'queer, ugly, half old, half modern looking place'. Ellen Nussey described the 'stolid look of apathy' of the people who 'sat or leaned in their pews' during the services. 'The sexton with a long staff continually walked round in the aisles "knobbing" sleepers when he dare, shaking his head at and threatening unruly children, but when the sermon began' a 'rustic untaught intelligence' or a 'daring doubting questioning look' appeared in the faces of those listening to Revd Patrick Brontë's extempore preaching, expressed 'in the simplest manner . . . so as to be perfectly intelligible' (Smith Letters, 1. 600). In this old church Charlotte was married on 29 June 1854, in a simple white muslin dress with 'delicate green embroidery, a lace mantle and a white bonnet, trimmed with lace and a pale band of small flowers and leaves' (Barker, p. 757). But it was also here, in a vault beneath the floor, that all the Brontës except Anne were buried. In 1858 Mr Brontë had a new family memorial tablet installed, for the old one was too small. Revd A. B. Nicholls ensured that the old tablet should not be sold to souvenir-hunters by ordering the sexton, William Brown, to smash it and bury the pieces deep in the Parsonage garden. Special authority from the Secretary of State had to be obtained for Mr Brontë's burial on 12 June 1861, for the churchyard had been closed in 1856. In the Brontës' time the graveyard, where '44,000 burials are said to have taken place', was bleak and treeless. Trees were planted there in 1864 'to help disperse the corpses' (Barker, p. 98). By 7 August 1866 some of the newly planted trees had been 'again and again maliciously broken down', and other and more revolting nuisances took place there. The vicar, John Wade, asked the Ecclesiastical Commission whether the entrances might be closed up (BST (1998), 23. 1. 72). In the church itself, despite improvements and repairs, the floors beneath the box pews were rotten, the church was dank owing to the large number of coffins beneath it, and the entire Grimshaw aisle was decrepit. The usual subscribers to church improvements declined to shore up the old building any longer. Mr Wade eventually accepted £5,000 from the Haworth manufacturer Michael Merrall towards the construction of a new building, finally opened in 1879 (see BST (1997), 22. 96–112). See SUNDERLAND, ABRAHAM STANSFIELD.

Haworth National School. In the first half of the 19th century most elementary *education in England was provided by the 'National Society for promoting the education of the poor in the principles of the established church', founded in 1811, whose schools taught the liturgy and catechism of the Church of England, and by the Nonconformist 'British and Foreign School Society', founded in 1814, which enforced Bible-reading, but excluded denominational teaching. Both kinds of school taught the rudiments of education to children who might otherwise have remained illiterate, but both depended on the generosity of subscribers for their survival. In 1833 Parliament voted £20,000 for

education to be shared between the two societies, who used it to build new schools. The grant was available only when voluntary contributions met half the cost. By July 1843 a move towards state-controlled education had been defeated by Nonconformists as an infringement of religious liberty. Revd Patrick Brontë deplored this Nonconformist 'sophistry' and, aware of the ignorance of most of his parishioners and the 'skismatical' ideas of those with a little learning, wrote urgently to the National Society, 'seeking a grant towards a new school in Haworth' (Barker, p. 430). This was obtained, and the school was established with the encouragement of Revd William *Scoresby, in the Sunday school premises (founded 1832). On 28 January 1843 the *Bradford Observer reported that it was to be opened on 2 January 1844 and 'conducted by Mr *Rand from the National Society's Central School London. The children will be taught spelling, reading, English grammar, ancient and modern history, geography with the use of globes, writing, common and mental arithmetic, the Scriptures and singing on Hullah's system . . . books, slates, pencils etc. are to be provided gratis but the charge will be 2d. a week for each child.' Special evening classes were held for factory children. Mr Rand's wife was appointed schoolmistress, and the school was an immediate success, though Mr Brontë had to ask the 'principal inhabitants of Haworth' for extra money to supplement the £20 provided by the Society for the teachers' salaries. By 27 July there were 160 scholars, and the children had made 'considerable progress in learning and good manners' (Smith Letters, 1. 351). Charlotte invited Mrs and Miss *Taylor of Stanbury to meet the Rands and Mrs Rand's mother for a celebratory tea at the Parsonage on 19 July following the inspector's examination. As she observed in a letter to Mrs Rand of 26 May 1845, numbers did not increase much under the Rands' successor, Mr Purnell, partly owing to Nonconformist opposition. Sutcliffe Sowden probably underestimated the numbers at c.60 scholars when Revd A. B. *Nicholls first came to Haworth in May 1845, but was perhaps on firmer ground when he implied that Nicholls's hard work helped to raise the numbers to 'between two & three hundred' pupils by January 1853 (Lock & Dixon, p. 457). The building of the Haworth Board Schools in 1896 brought about 'the demise of the Church and Methodist day schools in Haworth' (BST (1991), 20. 3. 161).

Haworth Parsonage in Church Street dates from 1778–9. Beyond the house rough pasture land and then high moorland stretch westward towards the Lancashire border. In the Brontës' day a perimeter wall surrounded the house, front garden, and backyard, and small trees and bushes

Haworth Parsonage, ambrotype photograph taken before 1861.

bordered the garden, but there were no tall trees: the present stone-pines were planted in 1854, and the churchyard trees beyond in 1864. Nor was the house surrounded by graves, for the churchyard lay only to the east of the house. The front windows, facing east, had the benefit of morning light and a clear view towards Brow Moor. In design the Parsonage closely resembles the Manor House and Bridge House in Haworth. Before Revd John Wade added a gable wing to the north in 1872, the front was pleasingly symmetrical, with its central door beneath a handsome classical portico, flanked by two windows on each side, with five windows on the first floor below the stone-flagged roof. The walls are of local millstone grit, weathered to a dark grey, with some Elland stone. During Revd Patrick Brontë's incumbency, a back kitchen used for washing jutted out into the backyard. Charlotte, self-exiled in Brussels, nostalgically recalled it and Tabitha *Aykroyd's domain, the large inner kitchen, where she would like to 'be cutting up the hash', while Emily ensured that Tiger and Keeper had the best pieces of mutton, and Tabby blew the fire (Smith Letters, 1. 331). At the north-west corner of the backyard was a building probably used as a peatstore; at the south-west corner, a two-seater privy; and nearer the house a well, fed from the hillside above, and thus, unlike many houses lower down, uncontaminated by drainage from the churchyard. Within the house, the square dining room to the left of the front door was the Brontë sisters' usual sitting room, and their sanctum for discussing together the plots of their novels. Behind it was a storeroom, altered to become Revd A. B. *Nicholls's study in 1854. Like the servants' room above, it was originally entered from outside the house. Mr Brontë usually took all his meals except tea by himself in his study, to the right of the front door. Behind the study is the kitchen, and above it Mr Brontë's bedroom. The main bedroom, over the dining room, was shared by Mr and Mrs Brontë until her death in 1821, then used by Elizabeth Branwell, and later no doubt by her nieces. In 1850 it was Charlotte's bedroom, and, like the dining room below, was enlarged then or in 1851 at the expense of the adjacent room. Thus the so-called 'children's study' over the hall became the narrow slip of a room we see today. Behind Mr Brontë's bedroom is another room which Branwell Brontë may have used as a studio. In 1928 the house was bought by Sir James Roberts and presented to the Brontë Society for use as a museum and library. It has been restored as far as possible to its appearance in the Brontës' day.

Kellett, Jocelyn, Haworth Parsonage (1977).

Hay is a hillside hamlet, half-lost in trees, 2 miles from *Thornfield Hall, in Jane Eyre. Beyond it becks thread the passes of the hills, and on the lonely lane leading to it Jane Eyre first sees and helps Rochester. Their interrupted wedding begins in Hay church, just beyond Thornfield gates.

Heald, Revd William Margetson, jun. (1803–75), son of the 'surgeon and divine' of the same name (1767–1837), whom he succeeded as vicar of *Birstall in 1837; Hon. Canon of Ripon 1855–75. A graduate of Trinity College, Cambridge (BA 1826, MA 1829), and friend of Revd Henry *Nussey, he was 'spiritual, scholarly, gentle, liberal-minded and generous' (J. A. Venn, 'Heald', in Alumni Cantabrigenses 1752–1900, pt. 2 (1922–54)). With his father, he was the prototype for Revd Cyril *Hall. His sister Harriet ('Margaret Hall') called Jane Eyre a 'wicked book' on the authority of the *Quarterly Review. He married in April 1844 Mary Carr (1811–?1854), daughter of Charles Carr, solicitor, of Gomersal (?1777–1832).

Heald's House, Dewsbury Moor. Bought by Revd Hammond Roberson in 1795 as a home and school, it was the birthplace of Revd William Heald jun. Early in 1838 Margaret *Wooler moved her school from Roe Head to this house near *Dewsbury, probably in order to be nearer to her elderly parents at Rouse Mill, Batley. Charlotte Brontë had been teaching at Roe Head, and moved with the school. Heald's House is a long, low 18th-century house on a hill about a mile west of the town centre—an 'unlovely' place by 1948, according to Ernest Raymond, but in more attractive surroundings in 1838. The building survives, overshadowed by Dewsbury Hospital. Charlotte's 'hypochondria' while she was there—a state of acute depression and physical illness—made her recall it as a 'poisoned' place, where she must have been no better company than a 'stalking ghost'. It is possible that Anne was with her there for part of the time, but for a fortnight and two days in April–May 1838 Charlotte was there 'quite alone' after being asked to return early from her Easter holiday owing to Mr Robert Wooler's illness and his death on 20 April. Ellen Nussey, usually near at hand in Birstall, was with relatives in the south of England, and Miss Wooler was 'detained in the interim at Rouse-Mill' (Smith Letters, 1. 177). By mid-May Charlotte's 'health and spirits had utterly failed' her, and on medical advice she returned to Haworth, probably on 23 May, to recover. She returned to endure her governess-slavery from July or August until 22 December 1838. At Christmas 1838 Margaret Wooler handed over the management to her sister Eliza, who failed to make it prosper. Charlotte tried in vain to find pupils for it, and Eliza relinquished the school early in 1841. Charlotte accepted Margaret Wooler's invitation to 'work it up to its former prosperity', but by 29 September 1841, having heard nothing more of the plan, had decided to go abroad instead.

health and medicine. By 1800 the structure of the body was almost fully known, thanks to improved methods of microscopy and of injections. Knowledge of physiology increased later in the century owing to the discoveries of Johannes Peter Müller (1801–58) whose *Handbuch der Physiologie des Menschen* (1833–40) was translated into English as *Elements of Physiology* (1838–42). In 1800 the surgeon's professional status was recognized when the Company of Surgeons became the Royal College of Surgeons of London, reconstituted (1843) as the Royal College of Surgeons of England. The work of the Royal College of Physicians of London (founded 1518) was coordinated by the General Medical Council, established in 1858. Edinburgh University's medical faculty (founded 1726) provided a prestigious medical training. James Kay, later *Kay-Shuttleworth, an Edinburgh graduate, carried out well-conceived research into the pathology of disease, especially that of the lungs. The Society of Apothecaries (founded 1617) was given powers of examination and granting of licences to practise medicine in 1815. The Pharmaceutical Society was founded in 1841. In London medical students were trained at several hospitals, including Guy's and St Thomas's, and Charlotte Brontë received advice from the eminent London practitioner Dr John Forbes during Anne's mortal illness. Leeds had a good reputation for medical care, and Manchester benefited from the work of Dr William James *Wilson as did Revd Patrick Brontë. Medical research was disseminated through the London and provincial medical journals, and medical directories included the qualifications of practitioners.

The advance of scientific medicine in the 19th century was helped by important discoveries. Inoculation against smallpox by cowpox matter was already practised, thanks to its discovery in 1796 by Edward Jenner (1749–1823). Nevertheless, high mortality followed the smallpox epidemics of 1825 and 1839–40, and led to the first statute directed against the disease in 1840, designed to enable the poor to get their children vaccinated at the cost of the ratepayer, and to prohibit under penalties the old inoculation by amateurs. Smallpox continued at a steady rate until the serious epidemic of 1871–2, after which its incidence declined.

In other areas the principal medical advances were the invention of the stethoscope by R. T. H. Laënnec (1781–1826) in 1816, and its pioneering use in England by such doctors as John Forbes, John Elliotson, and Thomas Pridgin *Teale. By 1847 ether was in use as an anaesthetic. General anaesthesia by chloroform was used by Sir James Simp-son in November 1847, and came to supersede ether for long operations. It gained general acceptance after Dr John Snow gave it to Queen Victoria during the birth of Prince Leopold in 1853.

'Alternative medicine' was widely practised. Homœopathy was a system founded in *c.*1796 by Samuel Hahnemann (1755–1843) according to which diseases are treated by administering very small doses of drugs which would produce in a healthy person symptoms like those of the disease being treated. In London Dr Paul Francis Curie established a Homœopathic Dispensary in Holborn, and there was a homœopathic hospital in Hanover Square, where Dr John Epps (1805–69) lectured on the materia medica from 1851. Charlotte sent a statement about Emily's symptoms to Dr Epps in December 1848. Emily called homœopathy 'Quackery', and it was useless in her case, but it served as a harmless alternative to extreme measures such as bloodletting, purging, and dosing with toxic drugs such as the mercury pills which caused acute poisoning when Dr Ruddock prescribed them for Charlotte in December 1851. Other alternative systems included hydropathy, the 'water-cure' originally developed by Vincenz Priessnitz (1801–51) in Silesia, widely used at Continental spas, and introduced into England in the early 1840s. Ilkley and Harrogate in Yorkshire flourished as spa towns. Mesmerism, named after Franz Anton Mesmer (1734–1815), was enthusiastically adopted by Harriet *Martineau, and was used by some respected physicians; but the exaggerated claims made by some practitioners for cures of almost any complaint from rheumatism to epilepsy brought it into discredit.

Tuberculosis (like cancer) remained intractable. It affected the poor more than the rich, because their living conditions—close proximity in ill-ventilated houses, poor diet, infected milk—were conducive to its rapid development. Because it was not recognized as infectious, precautions were taken too late in households of all classes. The sharing of beds in the Brontë household undoubtedly increased the risk. Death might be delayed, as perhaps it was for Anne, by prescriptions of cod liver oil and carbonate of iron, and by advice to remain at an even temperature. Those who could afford it went abroad, to the sanatoria of Switzerland in the later years of the century, or to a warmer part of Britain, like Penzance—a place recommended by Dr T. J. Graham in Mr Brontë's copy of *Modern Domestic Medicine* (1826).

Measures designed to improve public health were spurred on by devastating epidemics. An epidemic of 'relapsing' and enteric fevers in 1817–19 coincided with distress caused by unemployment and low wages after the Napoleonic Wars. It was especially prevalent in 'poor-houses', in filthy overcrowded London lodging houses, and in the slums of northern manufacturing towns such as Rochdale and Leeds. It occasioned a revival of bloodletting, which some doctors found to 'answer well'. Even more serious was the 1830–1 outbreak of typhus gravior, characterized by 'a mottled, measly, or rubeoloid rash', which did not respond to bloodletting. A recurrence of virulent typhus gravior in 1837–8 resulted in 9,047 deaths in the last six months of 1837, and 18,775 deaths in 1838. Liverpool, Manchester, and Salford were badly affected; Leeds and Bradford also suffered, but less seriously. In *Mary Barton* (1848), which Charlotte read, Elizabeth *Gaskell described the appalling tenement and cellar dwellings of Manchester which were ravaged by fever in 1839–41. The 'Irish fever' which followed the potato famine of 1845–6 spread through Irish immigration into England, typhus causing 30,320 deaths in 1847. The worst affected places were Liverpool and Manchester. In *Ireland itself general dropsy, scurvy, malignant dysentery, and relapsing fever decimated the southern and western areas. County Down in the north, Mr Brontë's home county, was less affected.

Influenza epidemics, such as those in 1803 and 1831, caused more deaths among people living in better housing than among the typhus-afflicted poor, but the consumptive, asthmatic, and the aged of all classes were most at risk. The very severe influenza of 1833 affected both town and country dwellers. Leeds, York, and Birmingham were hard hit. The 'great influenza' of 1847–8 began in London in November 1847, lingered there until January, then spread to the rest of the country. Charlotte and her sisters had either influenza or colds in January 1848. In England as a whole, this epidemic caused more than 5,000 deaths. Other outbreaks followed in 1855 and 1889–94. There were also dangerous epidemics of measles: in 1839 measles caused 773 deaths in Manchester and 383 in Leeds, compared with smallpox deaths of 237 and 171 and scarlatina deaths of 264 and 35 respectively.

The malignant Asiatic cholera which reached Sunderland in late October or early November 1831, and spread from there throughout Britain, had been reported in Lower Bengal in 1817, in European Russia in August 1829, and was transmitted to Britain via sailors or passengers in vessels using the north German Baltic ports. The highest mortality was among impoverished dwellers in filthy, especially low-lying areas where ordure accumulated and scavenging was rare or inefficient. Ships arriving in London from the north-east were quarantined, but cases began in London riverside parishes in mid-February 1832. In London, from 15 June to 31 October 1832 there were 4,266 deaths from cholera, the total for the year being 5,275. In the rest of the country Lancashire was again hard

hit, and there were 702 deaths in Leeds. Dr John Parkin suspected that the disease was not, as many people believed, 'atmospherically' transmitted, but might derive from noxious matter in water (*London Medical and Surgical Journal*, 1 Sept. 1832). Charlotte would have been even more concerned about the 'Cholera . . . slowly advancing' in January 1832 had she realized that the water supply for most parts of Haworth was abominably polluted. Different treatments for Asiatic cholera were tried in vain: opiates sometimes mixed with acetate of lead, bloodletting, or saline drugs given orally or intravenously. The greatest lesson taught was the need for sanitary reform. The Public Health Act of 1848 was adopted in some 200 places, including several growing industrial towns such as Bolton, Bradford, and Sunderland. It was to the Board of Health that Mr Brontë and his fellow-petitioners addressed their request for an inspection of Haworth's water supply and drainage system, or lack of it. Despite the horrifying findings of the inspector, Benjamin Herschel Babbage, in April 1850, and his recommendations—the installation of sewers, a piped-water supply, at least one watercloset for every three houses, the closure of the churchyard—vested interests delayed most of these reforms until 1856 or later. The Board itself proved to be inefficient, and it was abolished in 1858. In 1865–6 a further outbreak of cholera led to the legal adoption of compulsory powers. Local authorities were required to appoint sanitary inspectors and to undertake the provision of sewers, water supply, and refuse disposal.

The 19th century also witnessed reforms in the treatment of the insane. At the end of the 18th century reformers uncovered neglect and brutality at 'madhouses' such as the London 'Bedlam' and the York Asylum, where sufferers were routinely shackled. A pioneer of humane treatment was William Tuke, who founded the York Retreat, opened in 1796. Dr John Conolly (1794–1866) introduced humane treatment into Hanwell asylum from 1839. An Act of 1808 made publicly funded psychiatric asylums possible, and an Act of 1845 made their provision compulsory. Other establishments were founded with the help of subscribers, or run by doctors such as Henry S. Belcombe of York, at whose Clifton House asylum Ellen *Nussey's brother George was cared for. Enlightened private homes might provide varied interest through music or gardening. Some private asylums catered for paupers paid for by the local Poor Law Guardians, and several pauper asylums accepted paying patients. The rich, like 'Mr Rochester', might keep their afflicted relatives at home. The vast, secluded asylums generally associated with the Victorian age were built in the later years of the century.

See also HEALTH OF THE BRONTËS.

Shuttleworth, Sally, *Charlotte Brontë and Victorian Psychology* (1996).

health of the Brontës. Revd Patrick Brontë's longevity, despite his serious inflammation of the lungs in June–July 1830, recurrent attacks of bronchitis, and serious strokes in July 1852 and June 1853, shows a remarkably sound constitution. He may have been mildly infected with the tubercle bacillus as a boy, recovered, and become immune to the disease. He also survived a painful operation for cataract in August 1846. From October 1860 he was confined to bed, but was 'pretty well' until January 1861, when he gradually lost strength after a severe relapse, but retained unimpaired mental faculties. He was seized with convulsions early in the morning of 7 June 1861, and died that afternoon.

Maria Branwell Brontë shows little sign of physical weakness in her courtship letters, though she wished she had Patrick's arm to assist her as she toiled uphill on one of her many walks (Wise & Symington, 1. 11). But her marriage was followed by six pregnancies in rapid succession, and she must have been exhausted when she suddenly became dangerously ill on 29 January 1821. She may have had either uterine cancer or 'chronic pelvic sepsis together with increasing anaemia' (*BST* (1972), 16. 82. 102). On 15 September 1821 she died, terribly emaciated, after seven months of agonizing pain.

Her daughters Maria and Elizabeth both died of pulmonary tuberculosis. Like Emily and Charlotte, before going to *Cowan Bridge they had measles and whooping cough—viral infections which Dr Mollie Davidson suggests might have reactivated previous undiagnosed mild tubercular infection (private communication).

Charlotte's references to Branwell having 'two or three times fallen down in fits' may mean that he was epileptic, possibly from boyhood—a condition not made public because it was regarded as a stigma. If so his epilepsy would be exacerbated by his drinking, which grew worse after his dismissal from *Thorp Green Hall in 1845. He also took opium, readily available as laudanum (alcoholic tincture of opium) or as a solid. The first recorded instance of his drug-taking occurred in August 1839, when he resorted to opium to alleviate tic douloureux during a visit to Liverpool. He deteriorated sharply both physically and mentally in the last year of his life. Before 9 January 1848 he had 'five months of . . . utter sleeplessness violent cough and frightful agony of mind'. In addition, Charlotte said, he was 'always sick'; and Elizabeth *Gaskell mentions frightful 'attacks of delirium tremens' (Gaskell *Life*, 1. 332). These could be triggered by sudden deprivation of alcohol. Two or three days before he died, he was so frail that

he had to 'catch hold to the door side'. Dr John *Wheelhouse, called in on Saturday 23 September 1848, said that death was imminent, and Branwell died the following day. The death certificate stated the cause as 'Chronic bronchitis—Marasmus' (wasting with no apparent cause). Dr Davidson points out that 'Branwell must have had liver damage and chronic gastritis and been unable to absorb food, therefore marasmic; but in such an infected household tuberculosis could not be ruled out.' This was Charlotte's belief, for she told W. S. *Williams that 'consumption has taken the whole five' (Smith *Letters*, 2. 93, 121, 216).

Charlotte described Emily as 'highly nervous', and unable to endure the disciplined routine of school. After only three months at *Roe Head, Emily's health was 'quickly broken: her white face, attenuated form, and failing strength threatened rapid decline'. Only a return to her unrestricted life at Haworth restored her to 'pretty good health'. In late 1847 or early 1848 influenza probably reactivated a latent tubercular infection; and after Branwell's death in September her health began to fail. By early December 1848 she was in a state of extreme emaciation, suffering paroxysms of coughing, expectoration, and shortness of breath 'aggravated by the slightest exertion'—a stage of miliary tuberculosis when infection had invaded the whole system. Refusing all medical intervention until it was too late, she died on 19 December after 'agonies, proudly endured to the end' (Smith *Letters*, 2. 155).

Emily had probably already infected Anne, who had also had influenza earlier in the year. Anne, who suffered from asthma, had always been delicate, and her spiritual crisis at Roe Head in December 1836 was accompanied by severe physical pain and difficulty in breathing. When Dr Thomas *Teale diagnosed pulmonary tuberculosis in January 1849, she accepted medical help. Her gradual decline was marked by remittent fever, and she became even more emaciated than Emily had been. She died peacefully on 28 May 1849, thanking God that death had come.

Charlotte, like her sisters, suffered periods of acute tension. In early 1838 she had 'weeks of mental and bodily anguish' and had to return home from school. In *Brussels in late 1843 she felt oppressed 'to an excess', though she was 'well in health'. Her desperate letters to M. Constantin *Heger, especially those of 1845, reveal mental torment in which she found 'neither rest nor peace'. She had bouts of ill health in 1846–50, some of them associated with toothache. The most serious was her total collapse into 'bilious fever' after Branwell's death. In late 1851 an autumn of depression culminated in treatment by Dr Ruddock which gave her acute mercury poisoning. The resulting weakness lasted until well into 1852. After a period of anxiety and distress caused by Mr Brontë's reaction to Revd A. B. *Nicholls's proposal on 13 December 1852, Charlotte's health improved when he eventually agreed to their marriage. During her honeymoon a cold was made worse by 'fatigue and excitement'; but after it, until the end of November 1854, when she again caught cold, her health was very good. In January 1855 her cold may have been aggravated by her walk in thin shoes on damp ground at *Gawthorpe Hall. By 19 January 1855 she was suffering from 'indigestion and continual faint sickness', and she continued to be oppressed with nausea, sickness, irritation, a slow feverish feeling, and consequent lack of appetite and digestion. She died on 31 March 1855 after 'nights indescribable—sickness with scarce a reprieve—I strain until what I vomit is mixed with blood' (letter to Amelia *Taylor, Feb. 1855; Wise & Symington, 4. 176). Dr Ingham certified the cause of death as 'Phthisis'—a term associated with TB—but the Haworth servants, and probably Charlotte herself, believed she was pregnant. If she was, the likeliest cause of death was hyperemesis gravidarum, severe vomiting in pregnancy. See also HEALTH AND MEDICINE.

Barker.

Gallagher, H. W., 'Charlotte Brontë: A Surgeon's Assessment', BST (1985), 18. 95. 363–70.

Maynard, John, Charlotte Brontë and Sexuality (1984).

Rhodes, Philip, 'A Medical Appraisal of the Brontës', BST (1972), 16. 82. 101–9.

Shuttleworth, Sally, Charlotte Brontë and Victorian Psychology (1996).

Smith Letters.

Heap, Revd Henry (1789–1839), Vicar of Bradford 1816–39. Admitted sizar at St John's College Cambridge in 1814, he gained a Lambeth BD as a '10 year man' (external mature student) in 1834. He antagonized Bradford Dissenters, but helped to alleviate distress in 1825 and to establish the Bradford Dispensary. In 1819 he defied the Haworth church trustees' refusal to accept his nomination of Revd Patrick Brontë as perpetual curate, and after the latter's withdrawal, nominated Samuel Redhead, who was riotously rejected. After meeting the trustees, Heap permitted them to join him in nominating Mr Brontë, an agreement ratified on 8 February 1820.

Heathcliff, a boy found starving in the streets of *Liverpool by Mr *Earnshaw, named after a dead son of the Earnshaws, and raised as one of the family at *Wuthering Heights. He is a dirty, ragged, gipsy-looking child, 'as dark almost as if it came from the devil' (Wuthering Heights, ch. 4), yet Mr Earnshaw favours him over his own son, Hindley, and his daughter Catherine and Heathcliff roam the moors as inseparable companions. Hindley bullies Heathcliff, who remains sullen and apparently insensible even when degraded to a farmhand after Mr Earnshaw's death. But Heathcliff nurses his pride and resentment, particularly when Catherine is courted by Edgar *Linton. When he hears Catherine admit that it would degrade her to marry him, he suddenly disappears for three years. His origin and his activities during these three years remain a mystery, yet he returns a dignified man of means with a foreign accent. However, he is as ruthless and violent as ever. His systematic revenge on Hindley *Earnshaw and the Lintons is chilling. First Heathcliff encourages Hindley's drinking and gaming habits until he becomes mortgagee of Wuthering Heights at Hindley's death; then he deliberately degrades and brutalizes Hindley's son Hareton *Earnshaw; he elopes with Linton's sister Isabella though he hates her and tires of tormenting her simply 'from pure lack of invention' (ch. 14); and after Isabella's death, he tyrannizes over and manipulates his sickly son Linton *Heathcliff into marriage with the young Catherine *Linton to secure *Thrushcross Grange. His quarrel with Edgar Linton and the mental anguish caused by his violent passion for Catherine also precipitate her death. Eighteen years later when Edgar dies, Heathcliff digs up Catherine's coffin and embraces the decaying corpse, at the same time loosening the boards on the side of her coffin where he intends to be buried. He believes in ghosts and is continually tormented by Catherine's spirit. It is only his growing obsession with her vision that weakens his thirst for final revenge on the two young survivors of the families, Catherine Linton and Hareton Earnshaw. His visions eventually distract him from eating and he dies in the haunted bedroom, with a sneer on his lips and his eyes fixed in a 'frightful, life-like gaze of exultation' (ch. 34).

It is little wonder that at the end Ellen *Dean asks 'Is he a ghoul, or a vampire? . . . where did he come from, the little dark thing, harboured by a good man to his bane?' (ch. 34). When Isabella writes to Ellen she asks 'Is he a devil?' and even Catherine compares him to Satan. Yet Catherine understands his character: 'Heathcliff is—an unreclaimed creature, without refinement, without cultivation; an arid wilderness of furze and whinstone. . . . he's a fierce, pitiless, wolfish man' (ch. 10). Although she loves him, she is not deluded like Isabella by his handsome, powerful *Byronic exterior. Like Emily Brontë herself, Catherine is aware of the realism behind the Romantic hero, the savage brutality and egotism. Heathcliff's unorthodox devotion to one consuming passion, his love for Catherine who dominates him while alive and dead, partly redeems him in the eyes of many readers. Although Ellen Dean moralizes about him, there is no authorial judgement of his diabolic actions and his distorted nature is seen as the result of perverse treatment. There is something elemental about him, as his name and his association with the harsh aspects of nature (the north wind, cliffs, wilderness, whinstone, and wolves) suggest. He is an integral part of the natural rather than the civilized world. When he is buried in the earth next to Catherine, 'dissolving with her' (ch. 29), he will have attained his 'heaven' and 'that of others is altogether unvalued and uncoveted' (ch. 34) by him. His mysterious origins, speculated on by Ellen Dean and Lockwood who suggest he may have been kidnapped, or 'an American or Spanish castaway' (ch. 6), or a descendant of the Emperor of China or an Indian queen (ch. 7), have been explored by a number of critics (see CRITICISM FROM 1940).

Heathcliff, Linton, son of *Heathcliff and Isabella *Linton, born a few months after she escapes from her husband and Wuthering Heights to the south of England. His mother dies when he is 13 and although his uncle at Thrushcross Grange wishes to be his guardian, his father immediately claims him. The dark, powerful Heathcliff despises the fussiness and apathy of his fair, blue-eyed son who resembles Edgar Linton. However, Heathcliff's plans for revenge involve making his sickly son Linton master of Hindley Earnshaw's son and lands. Lack of sympathy makes the boy malicious and selfish, and he is terrorized into luring his cousin Catherine Linton across the threshold of Wuthering Heights where she is imprisoned until they are married. Through their marriage he (and hence, his father Heathcliff) gains her fortune and lands on the death of her father. Having served his purpose, Linton Heathcliff is allowed to die without medical help, and with only Catherine to nurse him.

Heaton family, of *Ponden House, Stanbury, where they had lived since 1513; an old yeoman family who, by the Brontës' time, were regarded as the local equivalent of gentry. They were on relatively friendly terms with the Brontës, although the only surviving letters between the two families are brusque and business-like (Lock & Dixon, pp. 337–8). The Heatons had been farmers for generations, and also ran quarries, a small coal mine, a cotton mill, and a corn mill in the time of the Brontës (Flintoff, *In the Steps of the Brontës* (1993), 89). Robert Heaton the 6th (m. Elizabeth Murgatroyd) and his half-brother William Heaton were partners in the Ponden Cotton Mill from 1798

to 1815. Their personal and business relationship is said to parallel that of Edward and William Crimsworth in *The Professor*, and that of their predecessors in Charlotte and Branwell's juvenilia (Edward *Percy and Edward *Ashworth, for example). Robert Heaton (the 7th of the line; 1787–1846) married Alice Midgley of the Manor House, Haworth, in May 1821, the year after the Brontës arrived in Haworth. Both he and later his son Robert (8th; 1822–98, unmarried) were, like their predecessors, trustees of Haworth Church Lands; yet they were also involved in the Scar Top Methodist Chapel (built 1818), about a mile west of Stanbury. Heaton family members occupied various substantial farmhouses in the district. Robert Heaton (7th) had a brother who lived nearby, Michael Heaton of Royd House, also a church trustee and onetime chairman, who died a few months before Revd Patrick Brontë and whose heirs obtained special leave from the Secretary of State (after a refusal from Revd A. B. *Nicholls) to have Mr Brontë buried beside his wife in part of Haworth church graveyard that had been closed (Lock & Dixon, p. 529). Robert and Michael Heaton were both middle-aged when the Brontës were children, and the eldest of Robert's five sons was several years younger than the youngest Brontë, so it is unlikely they would have been particular friends although the Brontës may have gleaned some of the lurid family stories from the young Heatons.

The young Brontës are known to have occasionally called at Ponden House for shelter on their rambles across the moors to *Penistone Crags and possibly to borrow books from the Heatons' impressive private library, including a first folio edition of *Shakespeare. Branwell, who is known to have enjoyed shooting, may have joined some of the Heatons' shooting parties, as one of his pencil sketches suggests (Alexander & Sellars, pp. 316–17). Several shooting descriptions in Branwell's writings are set in Ponden Kirk, part of the Heatons' extensive sporting estate on Stanbury Moor, and one fragment actually mentions Ponden (Flintoff, p. 90) (see also SCOTT, SIR WALTER; AND THE WEARY ARE AT REST). Early local tradition also links Emily Brontë with the younger Robert Heaton (1822–46), the eldest of the five Heaton brothers, who is said to have planted a pear tree for her and possibly accompanied her on her walks to the 'Brontë waterfall' (which may have been at the head of the Ponden valley). John Heaton of Well Head, a woolcomber and one of the many Ponden House cousins, would have been known to Branwell as a fellow member of the Haworth Three Graces Lodge of *Freemasons (although he was ten years older than Branwell).

Legendary stories about the Heatons of Ponden House and their function as sources for the

Brontës' writings are a minefield of speculation. However, it does seem that gossip and rumours about their family history fuelled the minds of the young writers and were transformed in various guises into both their juvenilia and their later novels. William Shackleton's unpublished 'Four Hundred Years of a West Yorkshire Moorland Family' (1921; in BPM), tells of a bitter feud and tragic family saga involving a legendary ghost (or *Gytrash) and an inheritance dispute in the 17th century with circumstances not unlike those of the plot of *Wuthering Heights* and of Branwell's later Angrian fragments (see THURSTONS OF DARKWALL MANOR). All the Brontës appear to have used features of the Heaton legend in their writing and Brontë biographers have made much of this unsubstantiated but possible source (see, for example, Gérin *EB*, pp. 30–2; du Maurier, Daphne, *The Infernal World of Branwell Brontë* (1960), pp. 42, 85, 102). Ponden House also has architectural connections with *Wuthering Heights.

Edgerley, C. Mabel, 'Ponden Hall and the Heatons', *BST* (1945), 10. 55. 265–8.
Fermi, Sarah, 'A "Religious" Family Disgraced: New Information on a Passage Deleted from Mrs Gaskell's *Life of Charlotte Brontë*', *BST* (1992), 20. 5. 289–91.

Heger, M. Constantin Georges Romain

(1809–96), teacher of Charlotte and Emily Brontë in *Brussels. The family, of Viennese ancestry, had been established in Belgium for three generations when Heger was born in Brussels. His father, Joseph Antoine Heger, bankrupted in 1815 when his loan to a friend was not repaid, sent Constantin to Paris in 1825. There he worked as secretary to a solicitor, but could not afford to pursue a career in law. Visits to the Comédie-Française as a paid claqueur fostered the dramatic talent evident later in his readings and dynamic lessons: 'He made grammar cheerful; he brought syntax to life' (*L'Étoile belge*, 9 May 1896). In 1829 he became a teacher of French and mathematics at the *Athénée Royal, Brussels, and in 1830 married Marie-Josephine Noyer. From 23 to 27 September 1830 he fought at the barricades as a nationalist in the cause of Belgian liberty, when Belgians united in a successful struggle for independence from the Dutch, rulers of the Netherlands since 1815. His wife's young brother was killed at his side in the fighting, and in September 1833, she herself, with her child, died during a cholera epidemic.

After Heger met Mlle Zoë Claire Parent (see HEGER, MME), the directress of a girls' boarding-school (a 'pensionnat') in the rue d'Isabelle, he began taking the upper French classes there. They married in September 1836 and had six children (see HEGER FAMILY). Their son Paul recalled a happy, united household to which his generous,

ardent, lively, witty father and gentle, firm mother welcomed friends and made them feel at home. The family portrait of 1848 by Ange François shows a top-hatted, quite elegant man with dark hair, eyebrows, and beard: bespectacled but youthful-looking, alert, slightly quizzical. Joseph Gérard's portrait of him at 59 depicts a man of authority, with a high, broad forehead below receding hair, steady eyes, and firm mouth. Neither portrait matches Charlotte's portrayal of the temperamental 'professor of Rhetoric' as she first saw him in 1842, though she acknowledged his 'power as to mind': he seemed a choleric, irritable, little black ugly being who looked sometimes like an 'insane Tom-cat', sometimes 'a delirious Hyena', though on rare occasions 'not above a hundred degrees removed from . . . mild & gentleman-like' (Smith *Letters*, 1. 284). Paul Heger also recalled his father's fits of anger—'but they were so quickly over and followed by outpourings of kindness which revealed the magnanimity of his heart' (*BST* (1992), 20. 6. 344). M. Paul *Emanuel is recognizably based on M. Heger. All who knew Heger recognized his goodness. Elizabeth Gaskell, who met him in 1856, praised him in the *Life* as kindly, wise, good, and religious; one whose open, prepossessing ways made him especially beloved by children. A devout member of the Society of St Vincent de Paul, he helped the sick and needy, and gave instructive and entertaining evening lectures for poor people. He and his wife allowed special inclusive terms to Charlotte and Emily as the daughters of a minister of only moderate means, and invited Charlotte to return for a second year as a teacher, both to continue her studies and learn the art of teaching.

Heger was wise in his approach to teaching the two girls: having observed their characters and realized their exceptional talents he devised a specially adapted course, and gave them individual as well as class lessons. He 'loaded' Charlotte with well-chosen books: the works of Bernardin de St Pierre, Pascal's *Pensées*, an anthology, *Fleurs de la poésie française*, two German books, and his prize-giving addresses at the Athénée Royal for 1834 and 1843. In his letter to Revd Patrick Brontë of 5 November 1842 he praised their love of work, perseverance, and progress, and expressed his own and his wife's almost parental affection for them. Though Mme Heger's attitude to Charlotte cooled in mid-1843, Heger himself vehemently opposed Charlotte's decision to leave the school in October 1843. When she finally left, he provided a diploma certifying her ability as a teacher, and suggested she might take one of his daughters as a pupil—a suggestion she rejected, knowing it would not be 'agreeable' to Mme Heger. Heger's natural gift for teaching was supported by his intelligent analysis of aims and methods: he aimed to make his pupils dissatisfied with mediocrity, to revere and experience every kind and style of good literature, to use imagery to illuminate and interpret but not as a substitute for argument, to listen sensitively, alert to faults of style, to let a difficult sentence arrange itself while one walked or slept, instead of struggling with it, and to avoid reading work in a markedly different style from one's own before writing. He read masterpieces to Charlotte and Emily, impressing on them the effect of the whole, analysing the parts—arrangement, structure, style—and then asking them to choose and write on a similar subject. His corrections emphasized accuracy, clarity, relevance, focus, and appropriate style; his comments provided praise, and stimulated further thought by questioning and suggesting revisions. His belief that art could enhance inspiration, his insistence on 'le mot juste', and the models and practice he provided, were catalysts in Charlotte's move away from the comparatively undisciplined luxuriance of her Angrian tales towards the controlled shaping of her major novels. The impact of his strong personality, her increasing obsession with him, her resentment against Mme Heger as a 'rival', and her struggle to control her emotions, contributed to the informing passion of her work. No comparable influence on Emily is detectable; but the *devoirs she wrote for Heger show her independent judgement and idiosyncratic views of morality and the natural world. Heger's 'system' of education has been seen as anticipating that of the New Critics (Lonoff, p. xlvi; Dessner in *BST* (1973), 16. 83. 215–16) and others have found 're-markable parallels' between his teaching methods and those of F. R. Leavis (*BST* (1997), 22. 16).

M. Heger became principal of the Athénée in 1853, but resigned after two years because he could not accept the utilitarian methods advocated by the General Inspector of Schools. At his own request he resumed the teaching of the youngest class in the school. He continued to give lessons in his wife's pensionnat until he retired from teaching in about 1882. His obituary in *L'Indépendence belge* on 9 May 1896 praised his passionate belief in the importance of education, and the dynamism and authority of his teaching.

Gaskell *Life*, chs. 11 and 12.
Lonoff.
Macdonald, Frederika, *The Secret of Charlotte Brontë Followed by Some Reminiscences of the Real Monsieur and Madame Heger* (1914).
Smith *Letters*.

Heger, Pensionnat. The school in Brussels that Charlotte and Emily Brontë attended, Charlotte in 1842–3 and Emily in 1842. An 'Educational Establishment for Young Ladies' ('Maison d'éducation pour les jeunes demoiselles'), it was directed by Mme Zoë *Heger (née Parent), the niece of its founder. Her husband, M. Constantin *Heger, the school's professor of rhetoric and literature, also helped design the curriculum.

The pensionnat came to Charlotte's attention through the wife of the British chaplain in Brussels, Evan Jenkins; his brother, the Revd David Jenkins, was a longstanding friend of Revd Patrick Brontë's. Charlotte had been seeking a school in Brussels that would qualify her in French and other *foreign languages so that she could open her own school with her sisters. She had chosen Emily rather than Anne to go with her and persuaded Aunt Elizabeth *Branwell to pay their expenses. Mrs Jenkins first suggested a school in Lille, but she then heard such favourable accounts of the pensionnat that she recommended going there if the terms were right. Charlotte's subsequent letter to the Hegers so impressed them that they included what were normally extras in a single, reasonable fee. Thus the two sisters and their father left Haworth on 8 February 1842, visiting London en route to the Continent and arriving at 32 rue d'Isabelle on 15 February.

The site of the pensionnat has its own romantic history, as Elizabeth *Gaskell first observed. In the 13th century it had been occupied by kennels for the hounds of the reigning duke. Subsequently it had been a hospital or hospice, the garden of a religious order, and the field in which the guild of the cross bow men (les Arbalétriers du grand serment) held their annual matches. In the 17th century the Infanta Isabella gave the guild a mansion, but when Mme Heger bought the property in 1830 only the gate to its garden and part of the archery ground remained. The house that the school and her growing family occupied dated from about 1800. Additions were made in the Brontës' time and later, and the pensionnat continued to occupy the premises until 1894. The building was demolished together with the street in the early 20th century.

The best descriptions of the classrooms, garden, forbidden alley (*allée défendue*), and other features can be found in Charlotte's novels *The Professor* and *Villette*. Later interviews with Heger and his daughter Louise confirmed the precision of Charlotte's memory for physical details and instructional methods (see DEVOIRS; DICTATIONS (DICTÉES); NOTEBOOKS (CAHIERS)). At the time she and Emily entered, Charlotte estimated that 40 day students and a dozen boarding students attended. Gaskell, whose source was Constantin Heger, puts the number closer to 100. In any case the students were divided into classes on the basis of age and proficiency. Charlotte and Emily, who arrived at the ages of 25 and 23 respectively, were anomalous not only as older students but also as English Protestants. They were literally separated from the other boarders by having their own sleeping quarters in the large dormitory and set more profoundly apart by the resolve that drove them to excel at their studies. As Gaskell famously said, 'They wanted learning. They came for learning. They would learn' (*Life*, 1. 246).

The pensionnat's circular states that student health was 'the object of active surveillance', and whatever Charlotte later held against Zoë Heger she conceded that its regimen was sounder than that of any school in England. The food was ample and appetizing, time for recreation was allotted, and in fair weather there were expeditions to the neighbouring countryside. Three resident women taught the regular classes and seven masters visited to teach advanced subjects. Emily studied music with one of them in addition to French, German, and drawing. During her second year Charlotte joined the ranks of resident teachers. In exchange she continued to take lessons in German and French. However, her contacts with Heger diminished, probably because his wife suspected her of feelings more personal than scholarly. Active surveillance of another kind also drove her to increasing resentment: as was usual in Continental schools, Mme Heger kept watch over students and teachers, although she could scarcely have been as invasive as Charlotte's Mme *Beck and Mlle *Reuter.

Charlotte departed from the Pensionnat Heger on New Year's Day 1844, but she never left it fully behind her. *The Professor* and *Villette* portray daily life in a Brussels pensionnat for young women. *Shirley*'s Caroline Helstone and Shirley Keeldar study French with the Moores, who are half Belgian. The actual pensionnat continued enrolling local and foreign students; when the Hegers retired three of their daughters took over its management. By then, as a newspaper account of 1886 reported, they had 'educated hundreds of families, raised a whole society' (Chadwick, p. 219).

SL

Chadwick, pp. 205–12.
Gaskell *Life*, ch. 11.
Spielmann, Marion H., 'Charlotte Brontë in Brussels', *TLS* 113 (Apr. 1916), 177–9.

Heger, Mme Zoë Claire, née Parent (1804–90), one of the five children of an émigré who fled from the 1789 French Revolution to Brussels, where he married Charlotte, née Legrand. When his sister, a former nun, set up school in the rue du Bois Sauvage, her four nieces became her pupils. After her aunt's death Zoë established her own school at 32 rue d'Isabelle. Physically attractive, with blue eyes and auburn hair, she met the widower M. Constantin *Heger in 1834 and married him in September 1836. Though somewhat cool and formal in manner, she inspired affection in her family, and was said to be beloved by her pupils. Her son Paul remembered her as gentle but firm, with a single aim in life, to create happiness around her. Charlotte and Emily Brontë arrived at her highly recommended school in February 1842. At first Charlotte found her good, kind, and affable; and M. Heger's letter to Revd Patrick Brontë of 5 November 1842 speaks of the almost parental affection both he and his wife felt for the girls. Charlotte was aware of Mme Heger's talents as a directress, and paid tribute to them in *Villette* when she described Mme *Beck's 'easy, liberal, salutary, and rational' concern for the physical well-being of her pupils, and her arrangements for the distribution of lessons so that 'No minds were overtasked'. But in 1843 Charlotte found Mme Heger increasingly cool, distant, and reserved towards her, leaving her in solitude while others enjoyed a fête-day. By 13 October 1843 Charlotte had decided that Mme Heger was 'politic—plausible and interested'. Charlotte especially detested (and interpreted as spying) her practice of 'surveillance'. It is likely that she had realized Charlotte was becoming obsessively attracted to M. Heger. She would have accepted Charlotte's notice to leave in October had it not been countermanded by him. After her return to England Charlotte wrote so frequently to M. Heger—for a time she wrote twice a week—that his wife and he agreed she must write only once in six months. He 'let Madame write for him stiffly but not unkindly' (Frederika Macdonald to Robertson Nicoll, 26 Feb. 1894; MS in Brotherton) to that effect. Only four of Charlotte's letters survive—carefully preserved, indeed pieced together, by Mme Heger, probably as evidence that Charlotte, and not her husband, was at fault—but they are enough to reveal Charlotte's desperate longing for a warmer response from him. The publication of *Villette*, with its recognizable portrayal of the 'Directress' as devious, politic, jealous, and power-loving, understandably antagonized Mme Heger and her children, and she refused to see Elizabeth Gaskell when she travelled to Belgium in search of material for the *Life*. Mme Heger continued to run her pensionnat, assisted by her three elder daughters in the 1860s before she retired sometime before 1869. Charlotte's frustrated envy of Mme Heger's impregnable position as Constantin Heger's wife fuelled her biased presentations of the directress-figure in *The Professor* and *Villette* while it enhanced their dramatic tension.

Gérin *CB*.
Lonoff, Sue, 'An Unpublished Memoir by Paul Heger', *BST* (1992), 20. 6. 344–8.

Heger family. Constantin *Heger and his wife Zoë *Heger had three children before Charlotte and Emily Brontë arrived in *Brussels in February 1842: Marie Pauline (1837–86), Louise Florence (1839–1933), and Claire Zoë Marie (1840–1930). Their first son, Prospère Édouard Augustin (d. 1867) was born in March 1842, soon after the Brontës' arrival. Mme Heger was again pregnant during Charlotte's second year at the Pensionnat—a fact which perhaps intensified Charlotte's feeling of exclusion in the summer and autumn of that year, for Julie Marie Victorine (d. 1928) was born in November 1843. The sixth and last child was Paul François Xavier (1846–1925). M. Heger was devotedly fond of his children, as his son Paul testified, and as Charlotte recalled in her letter to M. Heger of 18 November 1845, when she wrote that he had never looked severe when Louise, Claire, and Prospère were near him. The elder daughters assisted Mme Heger at the Pensionnat in the 1860s until her retirement sometime before 1869, and continued to run the school after their mother's death until its transfer to the avenue Louise in 1894. Charlotte was fond of Louise Heger, portrayed her as Mme *Beck's second child, Fifine, 'an honest, gleeful little soul' in *Villette* (ch. 10), and singled her out as the daughter she specially remembered in her letter to Heger of 24 July 1844, because she had so much character, naïveté, and truthfulness (*vérité*) in her little face. Those who knew her in later life found her remarkable: she had a superb voice, was a masterly painter, and her conversation was shrewd and often mischievously witty. Prospère married a Mlle Jamar, but tragically died of typhoid on his honeymoon journey. Marie and Claire, like Louise, did not marry, but Victorine married Émile Picard, an ex-naval captain. Paul, professor of physiology at the University of Brussels, married Léonie van Mons. Of their three children, Marthe married Dr René Péchère, an honorary professor at the university, and Simone married M. Lucien Beckers; both these families eventually inherited and looked after some of the family papers. Before her mother's death Louise was shown by her the four surviving letters that Charlotte Brontë had written to M. Heger. His wife had kept them as evidence that might dispel any 'misapprehension'. After Mme Heger died in January 1890, Louise handed the letters 'in fear and trembling' to her father, who 'recognised them with astonishment, and, with a frown, flung them into' a basket of discarded papers, whence they were rescued and preserved by Louise (M. H. Spielmann, *The Inner History of the Brontë* [*sic*]–*Heger Letters*, 1919). In 1894 she showed them to Frederika Macdonald who advised her to keep them secret lest their nature might be misunder-

stood. But sometime after 1909 Louise told her brother Paul of their existence, and in 1911 the family sought the advice of the art-critic Marion Spielmann, who considered that they might safely be given to the British Museum, as they were in 1913, when Paul Heger also gave permission for them to be published in *The Times* (27 Sept. 1913). Their publication gave a startling insight into the nature of Charlotte's feeling for her *professeur*.

Helstone, Caroline, the niece of Revd Matthewson *Helstone in *Shirley*, who as a small child was abandoned by her mother and rescued from her drunken father. At the novel's commencement she is 'just eighteen years old' (p. 109; a little later she is 'eighteen years and six months', p. 222), and has lived with her uncle at the Briarfield Rectory for the past twelve years. Her father James Helstone (her uncle's brother) has been dead for ten years, and her mother's whereabouts are unknown. She is deeply in love with her cousin, Robert Gérard *Moore, who initially seems to reciprocate her interest; there is no mixture of blood, as Caroline's mother was the half-sister of Mr Moore's father. Caroline spends much time at *Hollow's Cottage with Robert's sister Hortense Gérard *Moore, who acts as her tutor; however, political differences lead to an estrangement between Mr Helstone and Robert Moore, and Caroline is forbidden to see her cousin. The situation is worsened by the arrival in their neighbourhood of Shirley *Keeldar, an heiress in whom Robert takes an increasingly obvious interest. Nonetheless, the young women become close friends and constant companions, and together witness the attack on *Hollow's Mill by machine-breakers. Later that summer Caroline, her constitution already weakened by low spirits, falls prey to a feverish illness, from which she is nursed to health by Shirley's companion Agnes *Pryor, who helps in Caroline's recovery by revealing that she is Caroline's mother, and who explains that she had given away her daughter from fear that Caroline would grow up dissolute and unfeeling like her father. Caroline's happiness is made complete by Robert's avowal of love, following his rejection as a suitor by Shirley and his close brush with death at the hands of a would-be assassin. They are married in August 1812, in a double ceremony shared with Louis Gérard *Moore and Shirley Keeldar.

Caroline Helstone is one of a number of Charlotte's heroines who were orphaned or abandoned as children and, to a greater or lesser degree, suffer neglect as adults. Frances Henri, Jane Eyre, Lucy Snowe: it is difficult not to see a strain of authorial identification with the frustration and yearning for affection felt by each of these young women.

According to T. Wemyss Reid (*Charlotte Brontë: A Monograph*, 1877), Charlotte's friend Ellen *Nussey 'is shadowed forth to the world in the person of Caroline Helston [*sic*]' (p. 101); against this unqualified assertion one must set the probability that Ellen herself was the source of Reid's attribution. Others have seen in Caroline's self-effacing nature and stoic conduct in illness a tribute to Charlotte's sister Anne, who contracted her fatal illness during the composition of *Shirley* and died before its completion. Some support for this reading is provided by the change in colour of Caroline's eyes from brown to blue (the colour of Anne's eyes) in the course of the narrative (see J. M. S. Tompkins, 'Caroline Helstone's Eyes', *BST* (1961), 14. 71. 18–28). Through Caroline Helstone, Charlotte explores the dilemma of many women of her own class: educated, sensitive, yearning to find some outlet for their feelings and yet forbidden by patriarchal convention from acting independently. Caroline's proposal that she become a governess, one of the few ways a respectable woman might earn her own living in the first half of the 19th century, provides Charlotte with an opportunity to comment on the miseries attendant on that profession while at the same time offering an ironic riposte to the unkind *Quarterly* review of *Jane Eyre* (see SHIRLEY: 'A WORD TO THE "QUARTERLY"'). On occasion the author's own views begin to obtrude upon Caroline's reflections about the plight of women, and stretch the fictional fabric beyond credibility (in the chapters 'Old Maids' and 'Two Lives'), but Caroline's desires and frustrations are otherwise convincingly portrayed.   HR

Helstone, James, in *Shirley*, the drunken and dissolute brother of Revd Matthewson *Helstone, husband to Agnes (later Mrs *Pryor) and father to Caroline *Helstone. Deceased some ten years before the novel's action begins, his influence is felt through Caroline's longings for familial love. The picture of him that hangs in the Briarfield Rectory (p. 247) shows him to have been handsome, and Caroline inherited his good looks to such an extent that her mother feared her child's nature and was led to abandon her. James kept Caroline with him for a few weeks until his drunken violence necessitated her rescue, after which she went to live with her uncle. Hiram *Yorke later describes James as 'handsome, dissolute, soft, treacherous, courteous, cruel' (p. 509).   HR

Helstone, Revd Matthewson, in *Shirley*, the fiercely patriotic 55-year-old Rector of Briarfield, uncle and guardian of Caroline *Helstone. A 'clerical Cossack' and staunch Tory, he is a friend and ally of the manufacturer Robert Gérard *Moore, helping the latter defend his mill against the depredations of machine-breakers, but political

differences drive them apart and Mr Helstone forbids his niece to continue her visits to *Hollow's Mill and her beloved cousins. In his youth he had successfully competed with Hiram *Yorke for the hand of Mary *Cave, but after their marriage his unfeeling treatment of Mary seems to have contributed to her early death. Helstone has a contemptuous view of women ('at heart, he neither respected nor liked the sex, and such of them as circumstances had brought into intimate relation with him had ever feared rather than loved him', p. 128), and 'the fixity of his feelings respecting the insufferable evils of conjugal existence' (p. 130) keep him from entering into a second marriage, and make him a less than perfect guardian for his lovesick niece. Nonetheless, he is capable of affection, as is demonstrated by his concern for Caroline during her illness. In his rugged, outspoken nature and his unwavering defence of the Church, he reflects the qualities of the man upon whom he was modelled, Revd Hammond *Roberson (1757–1841), incumbent of several West Riding livings including Dewsbury and Hartshead, and famous for his opposition to the *Luddites. Roberson was a friend of Revd Patrick Brontë's, from whom Charlotte may have heard stories about his warlike nature. She speaks of him as the model for Helstone in a letter of 21 September 1849 to W. S. Williams: 'I never saw him except once—at the consecration of a Church—when I was a child of ten years old. I was then struck with his appearance and stern, martial air. At a subsequent period I heard him talked about in the neighbourhood where he had resided—some mentioned him with enthusiasm—others with detestation—I listened to varied anecdotes, balanced evidence against evidence and drew an inference' (Smith *Letters*, 2. 260; see also Gaskell *Life*, 1. 118–21). Roberson gave strong support to William Cartwright, owner of *Rawfolds Mill, when the mill was attacked by a mob on 12 April 1812. Living at Heald's Hall, Liversedge, less than a mile from Rawfolds, he could hear the attack taking place, and immediately rode to the mill to assist Cartwright. Like Mr Helstone in *Shirley*, Roberson endowed a church (Christ Church, Liversedge, built 1812–16) and founded a school (established at Dewsbury, later moved to Heald's Hall). Some aspects of Mr Helstone's character and conduct are also derived from the personal history of Mr Brontë, such as his habit of keeping loaded pistols in his house, and his resolute handling of a band of Dissenters attempting to block a Whitsuntide procession. (For differing accounts of the latter incident, see Lock & Dixon, pp. 63–6; Wroot, pp. 78–9.)   HR

Henri, Frances Evans, heroine of *The Professor*. In her situation as a Protestant teacher and pupil in a foreign Catholic school, in her ardour for self-improvement, and in her growing love for a 'Master' who fosters her talents, Frances resembles Charlotte Brontë during her stay at the Pensionnat *Heger. But Charlotte endows her with grace and grants her a happy marriage to her teacher. Frances resembles the Angrian Marian *Hume who marries the Duke of *Zamorna despite the jealousy of her rival, in the *Glass Town and Angrian saga. Like so many of Charlotte's heroines, she is an orphan. She first appears as an 18-year-old teacher of lace-mending in Mlle Zoraïde *Reuter's school. Conventual-looking, like George Sand's heroine in *Consuelo* (1842–3), Frances suffers in her efforts to control her turbulent pupils. Her thin, intelligent face and large eyes are eventually animated by her happiness in William *Crimsworth's love. His interest is first aroused by her reading, in 'clear, correct English', and by the imagination and good principle shown in her essay on King Alfred. He discovers that her father was a Swiss Protestant pastor, married to an Englishwoman. Frances is determined to go to England, her 'promised land'. Mlle Reuter, jealous of William's interest in Frances, dismisses her, and he finds her after a long search, weeping at her aunt's grave in the Protestant cemetery. She greets him with glowing pleasure, and he delights in her kindred flame of feeling, controlled by reason, her integrity, and moral strength—ideal qualities to which heroines in Charlotte's other novels aspire. Frances energetically revolts against tyranny or injustice. After both Frances and William have secured good teaching posts, William visits her, and overhears her reciting verses by Sir Walter *Scott, and then her own poem, 'I gave, at first, Attention close', a version of Charlotte's wish-fulfilment poem (Neufeldt *CBP*, pp. 276, 333), written with M. Constantin *Heger in mind. Frances accepts William's proposal, but insists on continuing to teach. Later she enjoys verbal combats with Hunsden Yorke *Hunsden, captivating him by her charm and vigorous language. She and William eventually set up a school, where she proves to be a dignified, elegant directress, usually benignant, but severe in rebuke, and treating pupils of all ranks equally—resembling in this Ann *Evans, whose name she shares. The Crimsworths retire to England, where they enjoy the cosmopolitan company gathered at Hunsden's home. Frances submits reluctantly to William's decree that their son Victor needs school discipline, and must go to Eton.

Henry Hastings ('A young man of captivating exterior'), novella by Charlotte Brontë, recording later events in the *Glass Town and Angrian saga (in two parts dated 24 February and 26 March 1939 respectively; MS in Widener, Harvard). The story is remarkable for its psychological insight in the portrayal of Elizabeth *Hastings, prototype of Jane *Eyre and Lucy *Snowe. Through her cynical narrator Charles Townshend (see WELLESLEY, LORD CHARLES ALBERT FLORIAN), Charlotte, clearly and without illusions, presents her brother Branwell in the character of Captain Henry *Hastings, his degradation and his sister's involvement in his ruin. The first part includes Captain Sir William *Percy's diary and traces the capture of Hastings by Sir William and General Lord Edward *Hartford, despite his sister's efforts to shield him. Part 2 assumes an intervening manuscript, now lost (see Alexander *EW*, p. 184), and describes in six chapters Hastings's trial for the attempted murder of the Duke of *Zamorna and Sir William's unsuccessful attempt to seduce Elizabeth. The novella's wide range of situation and character focuses on the brother–sister relationship that reflects Charlotte's own loyalty to Branwell at this time, despite disillusionment with his character and prospects: 'It was very odd but his sister did not think a pin the worse of him for all his Dishonour. It is private meanness, not public infamy, that degrade a man in the opinion of his relatives.' Charlotte recognizes too that her old partnership with Branwell has gone (Elizabeth's brother 'was changed, she was changed, those times were departed for ever'), yet there is still some collaboration since his stories are useful as a butt for her satire and background for her character vignettes (see Alexander *EW*, pp. 161, 188).

Charlotte shows a surprising amount of self-analysis in her portrayal of Elizabeth Hastings. Her physical features, her demeanour, her irritable temper that made her unfit for teaching young children are reflected in her heroine (cf. Smith *Letters*, 1. 266), and even her habit of pacing up and down the dining room (Alexander *EW*, p. 187) is transferred to her heroine. Like Charlotte, Elizabeth prides herself on her ability to judge character, to conceal her own feelings and her scorn for her pupils and their families, including the Angrian beauty Jane *Moore to whom she acts as companion. Only Sir William divines Elizabeth's passionate nature and her intense longing for love. Like Rochester, Sir William has already had an affair in the Angrian equivalent of *Paris, and is now seeking a soulmate. Yet, like the later Jane Eyre, Elizabeth's conscience prevents her falling prey to him and to her own smouldering passion ('I am afraid of nothing but myself'). Her fortitude is strengthened by the example of the dead Rosamund *Wellesley who, like so many Angrian beauties, was wooed, won and then deserted by the Byronic Zamorna. Elizabeth is the first of Charlotte's heroines not to become the mistress of the man she loves:

self-respect is vital and she will wait for marriage or nothing.

Alexander *EW*, pp. 183–9.
Gérin *Five Novelettes*, pp. 171–270.

Hero. See NERO.

'He saw my heart's woe', poem by Charlotte Brontë (*c*.Dec. 1847), reflecting her anguish at M. Constantin *Heger's failure to respond to pleas for love or compassion. Intense opening stanzas, with extreme imagery of torture, mutilation, and unyielding stone, cumulative short clauses, and emphatic rhymes, culminate in stanza 4, where the poet's emotion meets the repeated negatives of lines 15–16. In the less forceful second half, the poet, self-condemned, withdraws to exile, looking only to God for comfort.

Neufeldt *CBP*, p. 340.

High Life in Verdopolis, 'or The difficulties of annexing a suitable title to a work practically illustrated in Six Chapters. By Lord C A F Wellesley' (Charlotte Brontë) (20 Mar. 1834). This Angrian novelette, a manuscript of 23 pages of minuscule script (in BL), is an exploration of relations between the sexes. The hero is Warner Howard *Warner, a newcomer to the Verdopolitan scene, and the plot centres on his search for a wife. His business-like attitude to courtship contrasts with the Duke of *Zamorna's complex liaisons and hypocritical flirtations, giving Charlotte the opportunity to document the infatuation of each of her heroines for her Byronic hero: the strongwilled Lady Zenobia *Ellrington, who has long struggled against Zamorna's attractions; the proud Lady Maria *Sneaky (Sneachie), who is subdued by the 'oriental despot'; the faithful Mina *Laury, who devotes her life to her 'master'; the otherwise feminist Ellen *Grenville, who marries Warner when his rival Lord Macara *Lofty is discredited; and, in particular, the relationship between Zamorna and his new bride, the brilliant Mary *Percy. This is the first appearance in Charlotte's manuscripts of Mary Percy, who is to become the saga's central heroine and was introduced by Branwell five months earlier in The *Politics of Verdopolis, which is specifically referred to in *High Life in Verdopolis*—indicating the close co-operation between Charlotte and Branwell at this time.

The relationship between Warner and Zamorna, founded on expediency rather than personal liking, is one of the most interesting in the *Glass Town and Angrian saga. Their characters are antipathetic, yet they respect and understand each other's strengths. The Duke of *Northangerland, too, is necessary to Zamorna's ambition: the combined power of these 'two great Drivers of

Verdopolis' is viewed as 'sublime'. Northangerland has little time for Zamorna's Angrian coterie in *High Life*. He is the sceptic, whose atheism is confirmed by quotations from Byron and who mocks Warner's gift of 'second-sight' as 'mummery'. In fact, Warner sees not a vision but Viscount Frederic Lofty, Earl of *Arundel, who was thought to have died at the Battle of Velino and who has been supplanted by his scoundrel brother. Arundel's appearance at the end of the story discredits his brother, releases Ellen to marry Warner, and leads to his own marriage to his fiancée Edith Sneaky. Zamorna is now the poet who surpassed *Byron, a womanizer with 'the basilisk's fascination'.

The text of *High Life* is rich with quotation especially from *Shakespeare and Byron. The story has been called 'an orgy of Byronism' (Fannie Ratchford, *The Brontës' Web of Childhood* (1941), 84), so replete is it with references to Lord *Byron, to his works, to his ancestry, and even to his breed of dogs (see DOGS IN THE GLASS TOWN AND ANGRIAN SAGA). Epigraphs to various chapters proclaim their allegiance to Byron's most famous poem, *Childe Harold's Pilgrimage*, and the characters of Zamorna and Northangerland now draw heavily on aspects of the Byronic Hero.

Charlotte Brontë treats her aristocratic gatherings (the grand parties, processions, masked balls, and picturesque country estates) as a theatrical performance, raising or lowering the curtain on a variety of set scenes organized for dramatic visual effect, as in a play or a painting. However, her handling of her narrator is particularly inconsistent in this story. She needs the urbane, cynical Lord Charles to puncture her high-blown portraits of the Verdopolitan aristocracy in which she so delights and to maintain control over her fascination for the immoral Zamorna; but she also needs the small, impish Lord Charles, the naughty boy who can wander into salons unobserved and overhear conversations, or sit on Mary Percy's lap and discover her intimate feelings about Zamorna. In this and other juvenilia, the reader can observe the young author experimenting with narrative control, reluctant to use her own unmediated voice and yet encountering problems of inconsistency.

Alexander *EEW*, 2(2). 3–81.
Alexander, Christine (ed.), *Charlotte Brontë's 'High Life In Verdopolis'* (1995).

High Sunderland Hall, demolished in 1950, was an ornate stone building at Northowram, in the Halifax area, within walking distance of Law Hill where Emily Brontë was a teacher. Built by the Sunderland family, the Elizabethan wooden edifice had been clad in stone early in the 17th century before the English Civil War. The family fortunes declined with those of the king, and the house then changed hands many times and slowly became a ruin over the centuries. The Priestleys, tenant farmers, lived in part of it during the time Emily was at Law Hill. The carvings above the door and over the gateway are similar to those on the façade of Wuthering Heights. They included two griffins on the inside of the gateway and two misshapen nude men, one on either side of the house door (early photos of these can be found in Ernest Raymond, *In the Steps of the Brontës* (1948)). A grotesque head formed the keystone to the arch of the gateway on the outside, while other heads with lewd faces peered from the cornices of the stonework (early photo in Charles Simpson, *Emily Brontë* (1929), opposite p. 68). The gateway façades and the house doors also contained armorial bearings and a number of Latin inscriptions (printed in full with translations in Simpson, pp. 72–3). Over the south door, for example, the Latin inscription reads: 'This place hates, loves, punishes, observes, honours. Wickedness, peace, crimes, laws, virtuous persons.' The exposed situation of the building, on the edge of a moor that rises to a summit and drops away to Halifax on one side and Shibden Valley on the other, again recalls the two houses in *Wuthering Heights* (Simpson, pp. 64–76).

Historical Narrative of the 'War of Encroachment', An, by Branwell Brontë, a narrative of 34 pages in two volumes, in two hand-sewn booklets (in Houghton, Harvard), written between November 1833 and January 1834. Volume 1 details the French invasion of the *Glass Town Federation, the rebellion of the Marquis of Douro (Duke of *Zamorna) and Lord *Ellrington (spelt Elrington by Branwell) against their military leadership, the involvement of Warner Howard *Warner in the war, the retreat of the Glass Towners to the hills of the province of Angria, and the refusal of the kings to provide the funds needed to counteract the French effectively and to defend *Verdopolis (Great Glass Town).

Volume 2, entitled 'An Historical Narrative of the War of Aggression', details the continued unwillingness of the kings and their ministers to prosecute the defence of the country effectively, the vote in the House of Commons to oust the ministers, the military occupation of the Commons by Ellrington and Douro, the execution of the prime minister, Earl *St Clair, the imprisonment of the kings, and the takeover of all government functions by a Council of Six. Verdopolis is evacuated, but the French are finally defeated with Douro and Ellrington emerging as great heroes.
VN

Neufeldt *BB Works*, 1. 365–446.

'History of the Rebellion in My Fellows, The', an eight-page, hand-sewn booklet by Branwell Brontë (dated 1 Sept.–1 Dec. 1827; MS in BPM), describing a battle between Goodman (a rascal inciting disaffected spirits to rebellion) and Branwell's forces, assisted by *Boaster, at the town of Lorraine. After an initial defeat Branwell's forces prevail and Goodman (Charlotte's character) has to agree to terms of peace that include paying homage to Branwell. Now at peace, Branwell begins to build numerous castles, churches, and other public buildings. 'My Fellows' refers to the *Our Fellows' Play established by the Brontë children in July 1827, based on *Aesop's Fables.   VN

Alexander *EW*, pp. 40 1.
Alexander & Sellars, pp. 287–8 (illustrations).
Neufeldt *BB Works*, 1. 2–6.

'History of the Year, The' (12 Mar. 1829; MS in BPM). An autobiographical fragment by Charlotte Brontë, describing a typical day in Haworth Parsonage with the servant Tabby (Tabitha *Aykroyd) washing the dishes, Emily sweeping the parlour, Anne watching some cakes cooking, and Branwell and Revd Patrick Brontë gone to Keighley to fetch the newspaper the *Leeds Intelligencer. Charlotte, writing in the kitchen, moves from a description of her surroundings to a discussion of the newspapers and journals read by the family, including *Blackwood's Edinburgh Magazine 'the most able periodical there is'; and then to a catalogue of the Brontë children's 'plays': *Young Men's Play, *Our Fellows' Play, *Islanders' Play ('our three great plays') and the secret bed plays about which nothing is known except that they are 'very nice'. The passage relating to the Young Men's Play is much quoted: it describes the children's dramatic response to the arrival of a box of toy soldiers and the naming of favourites, soon to be the heroes of their play.

Alexander *EEW*, 1. 4–6.
Alexander *EW*, pp. 25–8.

'History of the Young Men, The'. In a hand-sewn booklet of eighteen pages (dated 7 May 1831; MS in BL), Captain John *Bud (Branwell Brontë), in six chapters, details the establishment of the Glass Town Federation (see GLASS TOWN AND ANGRIAN SAGA) in the *Ashantee territory of West Africa, and includes a map of the Federation.

In the introduction Branwell describes how a set of toy soldiers became the Twelves who set sail for *Africa. Among the crew were Arthur Wellesley (spelt Wellesly by Branwell; see WELLINGTON, DUKE OF); Sir W. E. *Parry, Alexander *Sneaky, and Captain John *Ross, who represented Charlotte, Emily, Branwell, and Anne respectively and after whom were named the four kingdoms of the

Federation. En route they land at Ascension Island where they have a fierce battle with the Dutch garrison, but annihilate it. Having landed in Africa they elect Frederic Guelph, Duke of *York, as king, and send an exploratory party consisting of the four representatives into the interior, where they encounter the Chief *Genii who become their 'guardian demons'. After the completion of Twelves Town, a scouting party encounters a group of Ashantees, killing some and taking others prisoner. When the prisoners have been ransomed, the Twelves live and trade amicably with the Ashantee under their king, Kashna *Quamina. His son, Sai-Too-Too *Quamina, declares war on the British, who then march on the Ashantee Capital, *Coomassie, and defeat an Ashantee army of 13,000, but lose their king at the Battle of Rossendale Hill. After three years of peace the Ashantee once more attack Twelves Town, and are defeated after a desperate battle. In retaliation the Twelves destroy the Ashantee city of Acrofcroomb and massacre all its inhabitants. The British, having heard of the fighting prowess of the Twelves, send a deputation to find a leader for the British troops against *Napoleon. Arthur Wellesley is sent, defeats Napoleon, and returns with 30,000 veterans as Sir Arthur Wellesley, Duke of Wellington, and succeeds Frederic II as king. See also ASHANTEE WARS. VN

Miscellaneous Writings, 1. 61–95.
Neufeldt BB Works, 1. 137–69.

Hodgson, Revd William (?1809–74), Revd Patrick Brontë's curate, December 1835–May 1837. The Pastoral Aid Society granted £50 towards his annual salary in 1836. He supported Mr Brontë's speech against the new *Poor Law in February 1837. Though he antagonized local Dissenters by zealous preaching on divisive doctrines such as Apostolic Succession, he was popular with Anglicans in Haworth, where 236 people petitioned in April 1837 for his continuing to officiate. He became perpetual curate of Christ Church, Colne, Lancs., in May 1837. In August 1839 he visited the Brontës for a day, with his curate Revd David *Pryce.

Hoffmann, Ernst Theodor Wilhelm (Amadeus) (1776–1822), German romantic writer and music critic, celebrated for his supernatural tales with their motifs of the doppelgänger and evil-possession. A resemblance between Hoffmann's Gothic tales and Wuthering Heights was noted in the first reviews of Emily Brontë's novel, Das Majorat (The Entail) in particular being cited as a source (Allott, p. 32). The complex plot concerns the effects of fratricide and dispossession on the lives of three generations (John Hewish, Emily

Brontë (1969), p. 126). Emily may have read the original, although she could have known the story from an essay on Hoffmann by Scott, who refers to the 1826 English translation by F. Gillies (Allott, p. 376). Hoffmann's tales, such as The Devil's Elixir, appeared in translation in journals like *Blackwood's Edinburgh Magazine and *Fraser's Magazine. Another Hoffmann story, The Brigands, also has numerous parallels with Wuthering Heights (Augustin-Louis Wells, Les Sœurs Brontë et l'étranger (1937), 157–66).

Hogg, James (1770–1835), Scottish-born poet, novelist, writer of prose fiction, and major contributor to *Blackwood's Edinburgh Magazine in its early years. James Hogg was a self-taught shepherd in the Ettrick Forest, who began to publish poetry under the pseudonym 'the Ettrick Shepherd' in 1807. Joining Blackwood's writing staff in 1817, Hogg conceived the idea of the infamous 'Chaldee Manuscript', which secured the magazine's reputation, and contributed to the popular 'Noctes Ambrosianae', which Charlotte and Branwell imitated in the miniature versions of Blackwood's they wrote as children. A series of imaginary conversations between *Edinburgh literary figures, the 'Noctes' casts Hogg in his popular role of inspired shepherd-poet (much like his counterpart, the 'Heaven-taught ploughman' Robert *Burns) and is represented as speaking in Scots dialect. Charlotte's description of Hogg in 1829 as 'a man of most extraordinary genius' (Alexander EEW, 1. 5) shows how receptive the young Brontës were to this image of untutored literary genius. In the 1830s, Hogg was represented as the quintessentially successful author in *Fraser's Magazine, to which the Brontës subscribed.

Hogg's influence on the Brontës' writing can be seen in Wuthering Heights and in early stories by Charlotte and Branwell. Emily's presentation of *Joseph, who speaks in a nearly unintelligible Yorkshire accent, owes something to 'the Shepherd's' speech in the 'Noctes' and is most certainly indebted to the characterization of John Barnet in Hogg's novel The Private Memoirs and Confessions of a Justified Sinner (1824). In his writings, Branwell was repeatedly drawn to the issue of religious hypocrisy, a central theme of Hogg's Confessions as well. Branwell's juvenile tale 'The Pirate' (1833) and Charlotte's The Spell (1834) draw upon Hogg's novel in creating demonic doubles for their protagonists. After Hogg's death in 1835, Branwell offered to take his place on Blackwood's writing staff; understandably, Blackwood declined to respond to Branwell's tactless proposal. CB

Hollow's Cottage, in Shirley, the home of Robert Gérard *Moore and his sister Hortense Gérard *Moore. Close to *Hollow's Mill, it is 'a small, white-washed place, with a green porch over the door', 'a snug nest for content and contemplation, but one within which the wings of action and ambition could not long lie folded' (p. 72). Caroline *Helstone is a regular visitor to the Cottage, where Hortense tutors her in French, mathematics, and fine needlework. The cottage was perhaps suggested by a small house that stood next to Joshua Taylor's (see TAYLOR FAMILY OF GOMERSAL) mill at Hunsworth; John and Joseph *Taylor moved there after their father's death in 1840 (Smith *Letters*, 1. 242).   HR

Hollow's Mill, in *Shirley*, a cloth-mill near *Briarfield in the West Riding of Yorkshire, situated by a stream in a wooded hollow ('Hollow's Copse'). The mill is rented by Robert Gérard *Moore from the trustees of the *Fieldhead estate owned by Shirley *Keeldar. At the time of *Shirley*'s opening (February 1811), Moore has occupied the mill for two years, and is seeking to modernize the old structure by importing new machinery. His plans are delayed when his wagons, bringing new frames and shears from *Stilbro', are ambushed by a gang of machine-breakers led by Moses *Barraclough. In June 1811 Hollow's Mill comes under direct attack by a force of frustrated working men, but is successfully defended by Moore and his allies, including his overseer Joe Scott, a group of fellow merchants and manufacturers (see ARMITAGE FAMILY; RAMSDEN, TIMOTHY; SYKES FAMILY; WYNNE FAMILY), Revd Matthewson *Helstone and his curate Revd Peter Augustus *Malone, and half-a-dozen soldiers. For her description of the appearance and location of Hollow's Mill Charlotte Brontë may have drawn on the cloth-mill at *Hunsworth owned by Joshua Taylor (the original of Hiram *Yorke; see TAYLOR FAMILY OF GOMERSAL) and less than 2 miles from the *Red House at *Gomersal (*Briarmains). However, the details of the *Luddite attack on Moore's mill (given in *Shirley*, ch. 19) are adapted from the *Leeds Mercury* account of the assault on *Rawfolds Mill near Cleckheaton, leased by William Cartwright, on 11 April 1812 (see *Shirley*, (Clarendon edn.), app. A). Mrs Gaskell (*Life*, ch. 2. 114) tells us that Charlotte read back files of the *Leeds Mercury* as preparation for her venture into historical fiction, and the finished text indicates clearly that, while changing the timeline of the real events, she stayed close to this source in describing the attack on Hollow's Mill and the subsequent attempt on Robert Moore's life.   HR

Home, Mr, Count de Bassompierre, a distant relative of the late Dr Bretton in *Villette*, and uncle by marriage of Ginevra *Fanshawe. His Angrian antecedents were called *Hume in the *Glass Town and Angrian saga. Of mixed Scottish and French origin, he inherits family estates in France and the title 'Count de Bassompierre'. While he is abroad recovering after the death of his giddy, careless wife, Mrs Louisa *Bretton looks after his daughter Paulina *Home, on whom he dotes. Later, in Villette, he thinks of Paulina as still a child, and is deeply disturbed to find that she and Dr John Graham *Bretton are in love, but he finally consents to their marriage.

Home, Paulina Mary (Polly) in *Villette*. As a precocious 6-year-old child, who may have some of the traits of Elizabeth *Gaskell's daughter Julia, Paulina stays with Mrs Louisa *Bretton while her father, Mr *Home, Count de Bassompierre, is abroad. Doll-like, fastidious, and homesick, she mopes for him, praying intensely, for she has a 'one-idead' nature. Yet she is strong in her silent control of both grief and joy. At first she resents Dr John Graham *Bretton's teasing, but his real kindness makes her idolize him. Shocked, hurt, and angry when he shuts her out of his room during his schoolfriends' visit, she retreats into her wounded pride, but becomes friendly again. His preoccupied acknowledgement of the news that she is leaving causes her 'dedful' misery, soothed with difficulty when Lucy *Snowe takes her down to be reassured by a more affectionate farewell. Lucy meets her again in *Villette as a beautiful, delicately made 17-year-old heiress and countess. Dr Bretton helps to rescue her from a panic-stricken crowd escaping from a fire-threatened theatre, and attends her at her father's grand apartments in the rue Crécy. Though she can be haughty, she is refined, sensitive, thoughtful, alternating between childlike playfulness and shy dignity in conversation with Bretton, now recognized as the friend of her childhood. Like her precursors in the *Glass Town and Angrian saga, the Angrians Marian *Hume and Marina Angus, she most often dresses in pure white, with touches of vernal green. Her cousin Ginevra *Fanshawe's spiteful claims that Bretton is her devoted lover are disproved when he plainly prefers Paulina, recognizing her charm and the 'fine and penetrating sense' of her conversation with her father's learned friends. Lucy Snowe helps to bring Paulina's father round to the idea of her marriage with Bretton, and perceives that such natures as Paulina's are blessed with life's sunshine, in contrast to her own clouded fate.

Hook, Revd Walter Farquhar (1798–1875), clergyman and church historian, vicar of Leeds in 1837 and then dean of Chichester in 1859. He had been chaplain in ordinary to King William IV in 1827, and to Queen Victoria from 1839. His sympathies lay with the *Oxford Movement, prompting Charlotte Brontë to declare that her conscience 'will not let me be either a Puseyite or a Hookist'

(Smith *Letters*, 1. 214). Yet, like Revd Patrick Brontë, his practical Christianity helped to revive the Anglican Church and re-establish numbers in the industrial north of England lost to Methodism and Dissent (see RELIGION). Mainly through his energy and enthusiasm 21 churches were built in Leeds, along with 23 parsonages and 27 schools.

Horace. See 'ODES OF HORACE, THE'.

Horne, Richard Henry (later R. Hengist Horne) (1803–84), eccentric poet, journalist, and dramatist. He reported in 1841 for the Royal Commission on Employment of Children. From 1851, after separating from his wife, Catherine, née Foggo, he made a precarious living in Australia, having failed to find gold there, before returning to London in 1869. Charlotte Brontë praised his tragedy *The Death of Marlowe* (1837) and his epic poem *Orion* (1843), a copy of which he sent her in November 1847. She met him in London in 1850, probably at the home of George *Smith, who knew him well.

Hornsea, a small market town and resort, *c*.16 miles north-east of Hull, E. Yorks. With wide sands on the seaward side, and an attractive freshwater lake, Hornsea Mere, to the west, it had some fame as a spa. Charlotte Brontë stayed there for a happy week, walking on the sands or by the lake with Margaret *Wooler, from ?29 September 1853 to 5 October 1853. Miss Wooler had taken rooms at 4 Swiss Terrace, later 94 Newbegin (still extant). On the return journey in the coach between Hornsea and Hull, a small girl was sick in Charlotte's lap, but Charlotte made herself 'presentable' again at Hull station.

Horton is a small village near *Horton Lodge, in *Agnes Grey*, probably based on Little Ouseburn, near York. It has a single street, cottages with 'humble' inhabitants, and a shop where Berlin wool may be bought.

Horton Lodge is the house of the *Murray family, based on *Thorp Green Hall, in *Agnes Grey*. Spacious, with a stately portico and long windows, set in a wide deerpark amid fertile countryside, it is a day's journey from Agnes Grey's home. She is a governess there for more than two years.

Houghton, Lord. See MILNES, RICHARD MONCKTON.

Howard, a town in the *Warner Hills, province of *Angria, in the *Glass Town and Angrian saga. Scorned by Lord Charles Wellesley as 'a miserable little village, buried in dreary moors and moss-hags and marshes' (Alexander *EEW*, 2(2). 248), and home of Patrick Benjamin *Wiggins (Branwell) and his sisters, it is a thinly disguised version of *Haworth. The leader of the district,

Warner Howard *Warner, has his home here (*Warner Hall), and his residence in Adrianopolis is called Howard House.

Howard family. See WARNER FAMILY.

'How clear she shines'. See 'TO IMAGINATION'.

Huddersfield, Yorks., in the 1830s was a flourishing woollen-manufacturing and cotton-spinning town, not unlike X—— in *The Professor*. It had an immense oval brick cloth-hall, erected 1766–8, and large mills on the banks of the rivers Holme, Colne, and Calder. The vicar of St Peter's parish church was the scholarly James Clarke Franks (1793–1867), who had organized the rebuilding of his church in an ornate Gothic style by 1830. His wife, Elizabeth *Franks, was Elizabeth and Anne Brontë's godmother. Charlotte and Anne, who attended *Roe Head school just over 4 miles from Huddersfield, stayed with the Franks family for a week from 17 June 1836.

Hudson, George (1800–71), the 'railway king'. Originally a draper's apprentice in York, he gained wealth which he invested in North Midland and other *railway shares. In November 1837 he became chairman of the York and North Midland railway company, in which the Brontë sisters had shares—Charlotte's being reinvested for her in January 1853 in bank annuities. The 1845 and 1848–9 railway panics which ruined thousands were exacerbated by Hudson's fraudulent dealings, such as payment of dividends out of capital. From 1849 Hudson lived much abroad, but in 1868 friends raised £4,800 to purchase an annuity for his benefit.

Hudson, John (d. 1878) **and Sophia**, née Whipp (d. 1876), hosts of Charlotte Brontë and Ellen Nussey at *Easton, near *Bridlington, in September–October 1839. John Hudson, a gentleman-farmer, probably from a Burton Agnes family known to Revd Henry *Nussey, married Sophia in January 1831 at Yapham-cum-Meltonby. They kindly entertained Charlotte and Ellen at Easton House for a month before letting them move to lodgings in Bridlington. Charlotte recalled with pleasure this first visit and her 'romps with little Fanchon'—Mrs Hudson's niece Fanny Whipp (d. 1866)—but her second visit, 14–21 June 1849, was overshadowed by her sister Anne's death on 28 May 1849.

Hugo, Victor (1802–85). French novelist, poet, playwright, and essayist; a leader of the French Romantic movement. When Elizabeth *Gaskell interviewed M. Constantin *Heger in 1856, he told her of his lecture to Charlotte and Emily Brontë about Hugo's essay 'On Mirabeau' (see DICTATIONS (DICTÉES)). Subsequently the sisters wrote essays loosely based on it (see 'PORTRAIT: KING HAROLD BEFORE THE BATTLE OF HASTINGS'). Charlotte also transcribed two poems by Hugo in one of her notebooks: 'A night one heard the sea without seeing it' ('Une nuit qu'on entendait la mer sans la voir') and 'Poland' ('La Pologne'). She quotes the first verse of the former in *Shirley* (pp. 559, 779 n.). SL

Chitham *Birth of WH*, pp. 61–5.
Gaskell *Life*, 1. 258–9.

'Human Justice' ('La Justice humaine'). *Devoir by Charlotte Brontë (6 Oct. 1842?; MS in Bonnell, BPM). This essay, highly praised and corrected by M. Constantin *Heger, should not be confused with the one of the same name in *Villette* (ch. 35). It is an earnest student's composition that assails the manifold abuses of justice, offering as a case in point the story of a man who has been falsely accused. In contrast, when Lucy *Snowe's examiners force her to produce an essay, she satirically represents 'Human Justice' as a hag who cares only for her own comforts and leaves the wretched to their misery. SL

Lonoff, pp. 208–15.

Hume, Sir Alexander. See BADEY (BADY, BADRY, BADHI), DR HUME (LATER SIR ALEXANDER HUME, DUKE OF BADEY).

Hume, Lady Frances Millicent, the blind daughter of the Duke of Badey, who appears in the *Glass Town and Angrian saga only after her sister Marian *Hume's death. She has been neglected by her family but earns her living as governess to Euphemia (Effie) Lindsay, niece of Henry Bramham *Lindsay. After the death of her father she falls under the 'protection' of the Duke of Zamorna.

Hume, Marian, 'Marchioness of Douro, Duchess of Zamorna & Princess of the Blood of the Twelves', daughter of Alexander Hume *Badey, Alderwood Hall, and the Duke of *Zamorna's second wife, in the *Glass Town and Angrian saga. (She is referred to as Florence Hume in Charlotte Brontë's poem 'Stanzas on the Fate of Henry Percy'.) Marian's mother died when she was 14, having betrothed her child to Henry Percy, youngest son of her dearest friend Lady Maria *Percy (Mary Wharton) and the Duke of Northangerland. Henry Percy, however, dies at the hand of his father, releasing Marian to marry Zamorna (then Arthur, Marquis of Douro). Their marriage is recorded in 'The Bridal' (Alexander *EW*, pp. 80–3). Delicate, innocent and faithful, 'almost Quaker-like' (*'Albion and Marina') and dressed always in green and white, with a single pearl necklace, the auburn-haired Marian is the perfect

heroine and wife. As her husband increases in sophistication and duplicity she becomes boring both to him and to Branwell Brontë. Zamorna increasingly neglects her, and she and her son, Arthur Julius Wellesley, Lord Almeida, live alone at Douro Villa where she dies not only of consumption, but of a broken heart (see Alexander *EW*, p. 112).

Hunsden, Hunsden Yorke, in *The Professor*. He combines traits of Joseph *Taylor of Gomersal and his father Joshua, the model for Hiram *Yorke in *Shirley*. Original, cosmopolitan, radical in politics, scornful of cant, seasoning kind deeds with harsh words, mingling boldness with self-doubt and cynical jests with fitful gloom, Hunsden is a disturbing character, born of Charlotte Brontë's fascination with and bafflement by the complex real-life originals. He is young, tall, with a 'queer composite countenance', his small, even feminine, lineaments and long dark hair seeming at odds with his pugnacity. He detests aristocrats as a 'rotten order', and declares it is absurd that the 'aristocratic' William *Crimsworth should try to become a tradesman. Paradoxically, he takes pride in his ancient lineage. His books bear witness to his cultured tastes and knowledge of French and German, as well as to the radicalism which leads him, despotically enough, to spur William to rebel against his brother's despotism. By publicly denouncing Edward *Crimsworth's tyranny, he precipitates William's dismissal, and writes an effective letter of introduction to the influential Mr Brown in Brussels; yet he declares that he cares nothing for William personally; and he spoils William's heartfelt gratitude for a portrait of his mother, bought at the sale of *Crimsworth Hall, by accompanying the gift with a contemptuous note. Later, illogically shocked to learn that William intends to marry a lace-mender, he is captivated, to his own surprise, by her charm, and Frances *Henri scores some shrewd hits at his dogmatism. The friendly tussle with William that follows, and Hunsden's later admission of his former love for the glamorous Lucia, both derive from Angrian tales in the *Glass Town and Angrian saga, Lucia recalling Louisa *Vernon. Back in England, Hunsden enjoys the company of foreign politicians and savants, and of English freetraders; and he indoctrinates the Crimsworths' son, Victor, with his radical principles.

Hunsworth, Yorks. When Joshua Taylor (see TAYLOR FAMILY OF GOMERSAL) died in December 1840 his sons Joseph and John moved to a cottage near the family's Hunsworth Mill, in the Spen valley. It probably resembled *Hollow's Mill cottage in *Shirley*. In the cottage garden Mary *Taylor, Charlotte Brontë, and Ellen Nussey had a happy reunion in May 1844. Charlotte spent a week at Hunsworth in January 1845, before Mary's emigration to New Zealand, but suffered headaches and sickness caused, she suggested in a letter to Ellen Nussey of ?20 February 1845, by the 'malaria' of Hunsworth—'an abominable smell of gas' (Smith *Letters*, 1. 382). After October 1850 the cottage was the marital home of Amelia *Taylor and Joseph *Taylor.

Hunt, (James Henry) Leigh (1784–1859), radical essayist, editor, poet, and friend of W. S. *Williams. With his brother John he was sentenced in 1813 to a fine and two years' imprisonment for aspersions on the Prince Regent. George *Smith, who published his *Imagination and Fancy* (1844), *Wit and Humour* (1846), and other works, was at first amused by his impracticality, but later annoyed by his 'ingratitude and encroachment'. Charlotte Brontë praised his illustrated Christmas Book for 1847, *A Jar of Honey from Mount Hybla*, and the pleasant style and kindly spirit of *The Town* (2 vols., 1848).

Hunt, Thornton Leigh (1810–73), son of Leigh *Hunt; journalist who wrote for the *Spectator* 1840–60, and other papers. In 1849 he and George Henry *Lewes planned a new radical weekly, the *Leader* (Mar. 1850–Nov. 1860), advocating Chartism, republicanism, freedom of expression, and religious tolerance, with Lewes as literary and Hunt as political editors. They remained friends, even though Hunt fathered four children by Lewes's wife, Agnes. On 16 March 1850 Charlotte Brontë refused Hunt's invitation to write for the *Leader*, and on 23 November 1850, following its article on 'Justice for Catholics' sardonically congratulated both editors on their apparent conversion to Catholicism.

Huntingdon, Arthur Jun., named after his profligate father in *Tenant*, who tries to pervert his wife Helen's careful nurture of their son by encouraging the boy to drink and swear and 'to have his own way like a man, and send mamma to the devil' (ch. 35). When 'little Arthur' is about 5, his mother secretly escapes with him to *Wildfell Hall. Rescued from his father's corrupting influence, Arthur grows into a normal 'merry simple-hearted child'. His love of strong liquor is reversed by his mother by making him drink wine laced with small amounts of tartar emetic, which makes him sick. Arthur becomes friends with Gilbert *Markham and with his dog, Sancho, and Gilbert later gives Arthur a dog of his own. Arthur is instrumental in bringing his mother and Gilbert Markham together. He eventually inherits *Grassdale Manor and marries his childhood playmate Helen Hattersley, daughter of his mother's friend Millicent.

Huntingdon, Mr Arthur, the son of a rich old friend of Mr *Maxwell, uncle of Helen Lawrence in *Tenant*. Helen's aunt warns her that Huntingdon is 'destitute of principle, and prone to every vice that is common to youth' (ch. 16), for he has been brought up by a selfish uncaring father and an indulgent mother. Yet Helen finds him charming, especially beside Mr *Boarham, and she believes she might reform him. After their marriage, on the honeymoon in Europe and once settled at his estate, Grassdale Manor, Huntingdon's selfishness becomes apparent. He finds country life boring and is soon back in London leading a dissipated life again. Only in the shooting seasons does he join his wife, bringing with him his profligate friends Mr *Grimsby, Walter *Hargrave, Ralph *Hattersley, and Lord *Lowborough (with whose wife Annabella, Huntingdon has an affair). He recklessly squanders his own and Helen's money in gambling debts, drinks excessively, and delights in corrupting his own son by making him tipple and swear 'like a man' (ch. 35). His blatant affairs culminate in installing his mistress, Miss Myers, as little Arthur's 'governess'. Huntingdon's behaviour finally drives Helen to leave him for the sake of their son and her own moral sanity. His dissipated habits result in deteriorating health, and when he suffers a fall from a horse, he becomes seriously ill. Despite Helen's aid (she is the only one who will help him) he feels no repentance, only remorse and horror for the idea of his approaching death.

Huntingdon, Helen ('Mrs Graham'), whose journal forms the central narrative of *Tenant* (chs. 16–44). Born Helen Lawrence, she has lived since the death of her mother (when she was a small child) with her aunt and uncle, Mr and Mrs *Maxwell, at *Staningley Hall. Her own father showed little interest in her and eventually died of alcoholic poisoning. She has black hair and grey eyes, is a talented amateur painter, and at 18 is beautiful and strong-willed. She ignores the well-meaning but misguided advice of her aunt to marry the older Mr *Boarham and becomes infatuated by the rake Mr Arthur *Huntingdon. She sees his faults as a challenge and naively believes she might rescue him for salvation. She is soon disillusioned and finds him selfish and profligate with no redeeming features, unlike his friends Hattersley and Lord *Lowborough, the latter of whom she feels sorry for and admires when he tries to reform. Despite her efforts, the marriage proves a disaster. Huntingdon's prolonged absences, his drinking and gambling, his jealousy and deliberate perversion of their son Arthur, his affair with Lady

Lowborough, and finally his introduction of his mistress Miss Myers into their home as a 'governess', compel Helen to leave, for both her own sake and that of her son. Her strongly held, unorthodox views on education and the doctrine of *universal salvation are those of Anne Brontë herself (see RELIGION).

With the aid of her brother, Frederick *Lawrence, Helen escapes in secret and becomes 'the tenant of *Wildfell Hall', where she lives under her mother's maiden name of Graham, with only her son and faithful servant *Rachel. She supports herself by selling her paintings and living simply. However, her wish for anonymity is disturbed by her gossiping country neighbours (among them the *Wilson family, the *Millward family, and the *Markham family) who find the mystery surrounding her presence irresistible. She and Mr Lawrence (whom her son is thought to resemble) are suspected of a liaison by the gossip mongers of *Lindenhope.

Meanwhile Helen meets and falls in love with Gilbert *Markham, whose jealousy is mistakenly aroused by overhearing her and Mr Lawrence. To clear herself of false charges, she gives Gilbert her journal, containing the history of her marriage and the truth of her current circumstances. She and Gilbert agree not to meet for a year, and Helen returns to nurse her dying husband, still hoping for his salvation. After his death she inherits her uncle's handsome estate of Staningley Hall, where she goes to live with her aunt and son. When Gilbert Markham learns of her husband's death, he travels to Staningley Hall to propose, but without Helen's initiative in overcoming his sense of social inferiority they might never have been married. We are told that their marriage is a happy one and they are blessed with 'promising' children.

I

'I have now written a great many books'.
See FAREWELL TO ANGRIA.

illustrations of the Brontës' works begin
with the etchings provided by E. M. Wimperis
for the seven-volume *Life and Works of Charlotte
Brontë and her Sisters* (1872–3). The illustrations
are all of houses or landscapes with titles drawn
from the novels ('Valley of Gimmerton', 'The Park,
Brussels'). Other complete sets of illustrated works
include Smith, Elder's 'Haworth' edition of 1899,
which has photographs of people and places associated with the lives and writings of the Brontës;
those by Edmund Dulac (10 vols., Dent, 1905),
showing scenes from the novels in watercolour,
identified by quotations from the text ('"Come
in! come in!" he sobbed'); and the 'Shakespeare
Head Brontë' (11 vols., 1931–3), which has landscape illustrations following drawings or etchings
by Jack Hewer. The Folio Society produced illustrated editions in 1964–6 and 1991, each illustrated
by a different contemporary artist in a variety of
challenging styles. Almost the only individual illustrated editions, however, are of *Jane Eyre* and
Wuthering Heights.

A two-volume edition of *Jane Eyre* illustrated by
line drawings and etched plates was published by
Thomas Crowell (New York) in 1890. Two illustrated editions of *Jane Eyre*, by F. H. Townsend and
Edmund H. Garrett, appeared in London in 1897.
Townsend's illustration of '"That is *my wife*"' is
particularly telling. Ethel Gabain produced fine
lithographs for a large-format 'Édition du Souvenir
et de l'Amitié' (Paris, 1923). The scene where Jane
observes Bertha trying on the wedding veil is suggestive in that both women might appear in the
mirror. Barnett Freedman's coloured lithographs
for the 1942 Heritage Press edition (New York)
were closely followed by Fritz Eichenberg's black-
and-white lithographs for Random House (New
York, 1943), which include strong representations
of the young Jane at Lowood and of Jane and Rochester embracing under huge trees. The 1991 Folio
edition was illustrated by Simon Brett, who has

given visual representation to some of Charlotte
Brontë's metaphors: Jane stands thigh-deep in the
'surges of joy' described in chapter 15. The Brontë
Society also owns an oil painting by Thomas
Davidson depicting 'The first meeting of Jane
Eyre and Rochester' dating from about 1907; the
style is conventionally Victorian.

This Davidson painting is paired by another
showing Mr Lockwood's first meeting with
Heathcliff. Among book illustrations of *Wuthering
Heights*, notable are Clare Leighton's wood engravings for the 1931 Random House edition (New
York). Clean and flowing, these pictures focus on
the women characters and have a contemporary
feel. The frontispiece shows Catherine in short
skirt and wrinkled socks on a hilltop, extending
a helping hand to Heathcliff. In complete contrast
is a set of drawings intended (but not published) as
illustrations for *Wuthering Heights* by the French
artist Balthus (Balthasar Klossowski) in 1932–4;
there is also an oil painting, 'La Toilette de Cathy',
related to this series (now in the Georges Pompi-
dou Centre, Paris). All the Balthus illustrations
show jerkily articulated figures with a strong sexual charge. The 1939 William Wyler film had a huge
influence on popular illustrations after this date,
many of which show 'scenes'—such as Heathcliff
carrying Catherine to the window—which appear
in the film but not the novel (e.g. New York: Pocket
Book edition, 1939). Barnett Freedman's lithographs for the Heritage Press (New York, 1940)
verge on the grotesque. The Clare Leighton edition
was replaced in 1943 by the more famous Random
House edition illustrated by Fritz Eichenberg, and
these illustrations have been widely influential,
being reproduced, for instance, in Lucille
Fletcher's libretto to Bernard Herrmann's opera
(1965) and described in Jane Urquhart's novel,
Changing Heaven (1990) (see OPERATIC AND MU-
SICAL VERSIONS; SEQUELS AND 'INCREMENTAL LIT-
ERATURE'). Eichenberg's lithographs are darker
and more aggressive than Clare Leighton's. Of the
two Folio Society versions of *Wuthering Heights*,
that of 1964 is spikily illustrated by Charles Keeping, while the 1991 version by Peter Forster represents Heathcliff and, progressively, the other
characters, as having African features. In the late
1990s, the American artist Mary Haig produced an
extensive series of 'Images of *Wuthering Heights*'
in bright watercolours interspersed with quotations from the text, some of which were reproduced as large postcards.   PS

Stoneman, Patsy, *Brontë Transformations: The Cultural Dissemination of 'Jane Eyre' and 'Wuthering
Heights'* (1996).

imagery in the Brontës' works. Besides the
*landscape of the *Yorkshire moors and lowering

weather, inspiration for the Brontës' imagery came from their eclectic reading, ranging from *Milton's grandeur to *Gothic melodrama found in periodicals and *annuals, and from the sublime visual imagery of the painter John *Martin, with its eerie lighting and violent kinetic forms. In the *Glass Town and Angria saga, fantastic landscapes associated with passion, imagination, and individualism contrast with the familiar surroundings of England, its reason and control. Charlotte and Branwell's early writings rely primarily on concrete, detailed sensory descriptions of settings, scenery, and costume, and occasional metaphor. This rather literal imagery grounds the wild fantasy of the supernatural elements and the hyperbolic *Byronism of the characters and plots; it also focuses attention primarily on the surface narrative, while gesturing toward characterization and themes. Charlotte's poems and verse fragments (see POETRY BY CHARLOTTE BRONTË) exhibit often overwrought imagery which she later disparaged (using biblical allusion) in a letter to Elizabeth Gaskell of 26 September 1850: 'the sea too often "wrought and was tempestuous", and weed, sand, shingle—all turned up in the tumult' (Smith Letters, 2. 475). Whereas Charlotte's imagery in the *juvenilia evoked a sublime landscape, she felt that Emily's suggested a bleaker fantasy world (Alexander EW). Emily's poetry, including *Gondal material, depends heavily on nature imagery, biblical allusion, and evocations of nocturnal dream worlds and Gothic dungeons to create moods. Her imagery includes more symbolism than young Charlotte's, and her descriptions and metaphors consistently delineate characters' psychology. Anne's poetry, some associated with Gondal, is more austere, usually preferring concrete description and precise diction to figurative language.

Having formally bid adieu to Angria, Charlotte intended her mature novels to embrace commonplace realism, yet most readers remember her work for unusual events and emotional intensity, both heightened by acute, vivid imagery. As she announced regarding The Professor, she found no market for the 'plain and homely'; the book trade preferred 'the wild wonderful and thrilling—the strange, startling and harrowing' (preface). In The Professor she restrains her effusive imagery, using metaphors and leitmotifs rather sparingly, although there are notable exceptions such as Crimsworth's feeling 'barbarous and sensual as a pasha' when Mlle Reuter 'stole about me with the soft step of a slave' (ch. 20). Shirley initially promises to avoid 'passion, and stimulus, and melodrama', to be 'something unromantic as Monday morning'. The figurative language of this early passage indeed refers to homely subject matter, comparing the novel to Lenten fare suitable for Good

Friday ('cold lentils . . . unleavened bread with bitter herbs'). Having hinted that she will stray from Mondays to Good Fridays, her plentiful imagery ranges even further, sometimes offering sumptuous fare in intensely Romantic figurations (as when Shirley *Keeldar conceives of women as Titans or mermaids). In Jane Eyre and Villette, abundant and richly resonant imagery contributes substantially to making them 'wild wonderful and thrilling', and unlike the juvenilia's, the novels' imagery plays an important role in creating intricately nuanced, densely textured characters and themes.

Charlotte's imagery often sutures her romantic inventiveness in plot and description to the realism of her finely observed details and social criticism. She periodically personifies phenomena and abstractions such as Sleep, Death, Destiny, Hypochondria, Memory, Imagination, Feeling, Reason. These figures often appear in protagonists' dreams, visions, and writing—formats associated with imagination rather than reason. Her descriptions simultaneously domesticate the personified abstractions and make them vividly fanciful, as when Human Justice comes to life in Lucy *Snowe's essay as 'a red, random beldame with arms akimbo', ignoring 'a swarm' of sick, quarrelsome children at her feet while she enjoys her pipe and 'bottle of Mrs. Sweeny's soothing syrup' (ch. 35).

Charlotte's uses of Gothic imagery innovatively achieve an equilibrium between realism and romanticism. Beyond evoking readers' sensations of fear and wonder, her ruins, gloomy edifices, secret attics, stormy nights, apparitions, disturbing dreams, and unnatural phenomena portray characters' psychology, often intensifying their emotions to the brink of psychic disturbance, but ultimately achieving psychological realism, an aspect of her fiction that distinguishes it from the more common preoccupation among Victorian novelists with external realism. In her hands such Gothic elements do not demonstrate paranormal forces so much as they reveal characters' superstitions, transcendental beliefs, desires, and subconscious awareness. Ostensible Gothic mysteries express such psychological dimensions as rage normally deemed unsuitable for the period's heroines (see WOMEN, POSITION OF); they also suggest the horror of repression in women's everyday experience. Much of Charlotte's imagery conveys sexual themes not directly expressible within Victorian standards of decorum (see SEXUALITY). She not only identifies her female protagonists with unconventional passion, but also adumbrates the exhilarating as well as threatening aspects of phallic power, ranging from Rochester's piquant fancy of transporting Jane to the moon where she will warm herself among volcano tops and Paul Emanuel's puffing cigar smoke into the private interiority of Lucy's desk, to St John Rivers's identification as a white marble pillar suggestive of sexual repression. William *Crimsworth's subjection to a personified Hypochondria underscores the strain of repressed feeling, whereas the conflagration seemingly ignited by *Vashti's performance suggests the danger of expressing emotions. Charlotte at times invokes imagery of Eastern harems, sultans, and suttee to associate eroticism with the power dynamics of colonization and domination. In contrast, lush nature imagery suggestive of fertility and fruition often conveys positive sexual suggestions.

Nature imagery constitutes one of Charlotte's major resources, especially for establishing the haunting moods of her fiction. She also invests natural phenomena with transcendental significance and associates nature with human feelings. Nature imagery directly reveals psychology (as when a wild storm draws Lucy Snowe out onto the roof) and also functions symbolically in terms of plot and theme (as when Rochester and Jane confess their love to each other in an Edenic garden setting, beneath a tree which lightning soon splits). Reiterated references to natural phenomena often constitute a leitmotif linking various characters and scenes to develop thematic complexities, as when the moon, a multivalent emblem, associates Jane with both chastity and passion, with control and irrationality—and Bertha *Rochester's lunacy. Pervasive, multifaceted nature imagery has prompted critics to interpret the novels through numerous patterns, such as Jane's association with birds, or recurring oppositions between fire and ice.

Much of Charlotte's imagery forcefully protests against gender double standards and women's limited opportunities. Jane Eyre, Shirley, and Villette, for example, feature recurring imagery of starvation and feasting which manifests the heroines' hunger not only for love but for liberty to function outside the boundaries defined for their sex and socio-economic class. The novels similarly employ imagery of enclosure and imprisonment to explore the heroines' tendencies to self-effacement, on the one hand, and rebellion against oppressive conventions, on the other. In works narrated in the first person, imagery conveys subconscious feelings, desires, attitudes which the narrator would not understand or reveal about herself, as when Jane's dream that a burdensome child keeps her from catching Rochester suggests her unacknowledged unreadiness to marry him. Imagery sometimes replaces direct disclosure of facts, as exemplified when Lucy suppresses the traumas of her youth and of Paul's fate by invoking shipwreck metaphors. Clothing imagery is a frequent tool, and related imagery of cross dressing and cross-gender impersonation interrogates cultural practices, as in Rochester's gypsy disguise, Lucy's masculine garb and role in the school drama, and *De Hamal's amatory charade in nun's habit.

Charlotte's abundant literary allusions often function as imagery, formulated as similes, metaphors, and patterns which sketch the protagonist's milieu, define her nature, and convey her experiences through comparison to literary figures (as in relating Lucy Snowe's experiences to Christian's testing in Pilgrim's Progress). Biblical allusions provide an important fund of imagery (the Clarendon editions note references to 46 separate books of the *Bible—Matthew most often, some 50 times), as do her allusions to more than 200 other literary works, most frequently by *Shakespeare, Milton, Sir Walter *Scott, *Bunyan, and *Byron, and the *Arabian Nights. Jane's reading preferences, for example, develop characterization and themes by suggesting her longings for escape, rescue, and happiness. References to art provide equally salient indexes to the characters' inner lives, as in Jane's drawings and Lucy Snowe's evaluations of women's images in the art gallery.

The bold imagery of Emily's Wuthering Heights underscores its uniqueness and contributed to the shock registered by some Victorian critics. Evocative of Gothic fiction with its haunted *Wuthering Heights, its dreams and deliriums, and its physical setting amid brooding moors, blizzards, winds, and rains, the novel describes a deranged world in which inanimate objects become violently animated and nature expresses (perhaps produces) characters' psychic states, so much so that the characters have been categorized as children of calm and children of storm. The novel is Gothic, too, in its pervasive brutality described in vivid, often bloody, detail. From such prominent, indelibly delineated images as Mr *Lockwood's slicing the ghostly waif's wrist on the broken windowpane, to settings casually littered with mistreated *animals, the descriptions make even mundane domestic scenes seem aberrant. Much of the disturbing imagery is implicitly sexual, as when Catherine *Earnshaw's bloody wound from dogbite initiates her transition from girlhood to womanhood. Recurring animal imagery reinforces the pervasive violence and supports the dominant leitmotif, the story of Satan's rebellion and fall, filtered through a Miltonic lens and coupled with Byronic imagery simultaneously evoking mankind's angelic potential and bestial state.

Through imagery of wasting and starvation, Emily associates the recurring violence with self-destruction and also characterizes women's relative cultural impotence. Images of imprisonment underscore the socially transgressive nature of the characters and themes, delineating individual isolation which is partially countered by doublings and mirror imagery. Significantly, figurations of liminality (windows, doors, thresholds) sustain a tension with the imprisonment motif, and also suggest the permeability or interpenetration of natural and supernatural worlds. This quick inventory of a few of the novel's dominant image patterns merely begins to suggest the important functions imagery plays in this artfully crafted work. Fittingly, when Charlotte attempted to excuse what she viewed as the novel's transgressions, she employed resonant imagery to suggest its power and organic fitness, characterizing the work as 'moorish, and wild, and knotty as a root of heath', and as a statue rudely chiselled from 'a granite block on a solitary moor' (Editor's Preface to *Wuthering Heights* (1850 edn.)).

Like her poetry, Anne's novels use imagery more sparingly than her sisters' works, in both the amount and the fancifulness of her figurative language. *Agnes Grey*, with its severely unadorned plot, employs a plain style with flatly definitive similes; rather than stimulating multiple and complex imaginative associations in readers' minds, the similes fix a straightforward meaning, as in 'It came like a thunderbolt' or 'It was gall and wormwood to his soul'. Similarly, Anne's sensory imagery relies on concrete specificity rather than imaginative suggestiveness. Even so, she creates some forceful, memorable images, as in Agnes's smashing fledglings in their nest. *Tenant* employs Gothic imagery to generate interest and emotional force in its otherwise unflinchingly realistic tale. The brooding setting of *Wildfell Hall coupled with the heroine's initially mysterious background evokes an anxiety conventionally associated with Gothic antecedents, an emotional response the narrative eventually redirects against Mr Arthur *Huntingdon's domestic brutality. Juxtaposing moods and descriptions of the seemingly Gothic Wildfell Hall, its mundane agrarian neighbourhood, and *Grassdale Manor, transfers the terrors of Gothic fiction to the realities of everyday life involving alcoholism and spousal oppression. Among recurring motifs, Anne refers to Helen's paintings to reveal her psychology and to develop themes dealing with women's capacities, self-expression, and autonomy; and she employs Biblical allusions to explore ethical and spiritual issues.   BT

Alexander, Christine, ' "The Burning Clime": Charlotte Brontë and John Martin', *Nineteenth Century Literature*, 50 (Dec. 1995), 285–321.

Gilbert, Sandra M., and Gubar, Susan, *The Madwoman in the Attic: The Woman Writer and the Nineteeth-Century Literary Imagination* (1979).

Lashgari, Deirdre, 'What Some Women Can't Swallow: Hunger as Protest in Charlotte Brontë's *Shirley*', in *Disorderly Eaters: Texts in Self-Empowerment* (1992), 141–52.

Linder, Cynthia A., *Romantic Imagery in the Novels of Charlotte Brontë* (1978).

India. See CHURCH MISSIONARY SOCIETY; TAYLOR, JAMES.

industry and agriculture in Yorkshire.
In *c*.1839 Thomas Dugdale noted in his gazetteer, *England & Wales Delineated*, that of the 1,568,000 acres in the West Riding of Yorkshire, 700,000 provided pasturage, and 350,000 arable land. On the Pennine moorland beloved by the Brontës small cultivated areas could be found, though few crops would grow except oats, and even sheep-grazing was sparse. In the dales, which widen out from steep narrow Pennine gorges to flatter, lower, more fertile land, the population increased in the 19th century as the woollen industry developed, and local quarries were worked to provide millstone grit of the kind used in Haworth for houses, churches, and mills. Below the lower ground to the east and south lay the coal measures, extending southwards from just north of Leeds to Nottinghamshire and north Derbyshire, with *Halifax and *Huddersfield on their southern edge. Here there were more woods, meadows, and arable land. The *Nusseys and *Woolers owned farms in this kind of countryside, which forms the background to *Shirley. The southern part of the county did not impress William Cobbett in 1830: 'As to the land [between *Leeds and *Sheffield] viewed in the way of agriculture, it really does appear to be very little worth. I have not seen, except at Harewood and Ripley, a stack of wheat since I came into Yorkshire' (*Rural Rides*, ed. George Woodcock (Penguin, 1967), 495). Near Halifax and *Bradford, the only grain crops he saw were 'very miserable oats'; and on his way north to Durham from Leeds 'hardly any wheat at all, or any wheat stubble, no barley, the chief crops being oats and beans mixed with peas' (p. 505). Dugdale's gazetteer noted that the dales among the East Riding moors were well cultivated 'nearly a mile up the hills'. Further south the grassy wolds, which Charlotte Brontë would see on her way to *Bridlington, provided pastureland for sheep, and the flat land between Hull and the sea was 'of excellent quality, feeding very fine cattle, and producing the finest corn in great plenty' (Dugdale, p. 938). Hull was one of the most important ports in England, as the Brontës would realize through their contacts with the *Dixons, Nusseys, *Taylors of Gomersal, and *Ringroses. As long ago as the 1720s Defoe had observed that 'All the trade at Leeds, Wakefield and Halifax' was transacted in Hull, which was also the port for 'the lead trade of Derbyshire and Nottinghamshire'. 'The butter of the East and North Ridings' was 'brought down the Ouse to York', and thence to Hull, which traded with 'all

parts of the known world' (*A Tour through the Whole Island of Great Britain* (3 vols., 1724–6), vol. 3, letter 9).

Of the three Ridings of Yorkshire, the west was the most industrialized. All travellers remarked on the black southern towns, Rotherham, Barnsley, and Sheffield—the town of the 'knife-grinders and scissar merchants' disparaged by Rosamond *Oliver. In 1830 Cobbett observed, 'All the way along from Leeds to Sheffield it is coal and iron, and iron and coal. It was dark before we reached Sheffield, so that we saw the iron furnaces in all the horrible splendour of their everlasting blaze . . . from this one town and its environs go nine-tenths of the knives that are used in the whole world; . . . the trade of Sheffield has fallen off less in proportion than that of the other manufacturing districts', because North America needed its cutlery and tools, and because 'to make knives there must be the hand of man. Therefore, machinery cannot come to destroy the wages of the labourer' (*Rural Rides*, pp. 494, 495). The river Don provided navigable communication with the principal commercial towns. Industrial pollution of air and water, such as that described in *The Professor* and *Shirley*, was to persist into the 1950s. The need for iron and steel increased in the *railway age, and the industry was transformed and enlarged by the Bessemer and Siemens processes for manufacturing steel in bulk. Alum-shale deposits near the North Riding coast were worked to produce alum, used among other things as a mordant in dyeing, and there were chemical- and gas-works in industrial towns. By the 1820s most large industries used gas-lighting and steam-power, and so relied, indirectly, on coal. The mines, where children worked underground for up to sixteen hours each day as trappers or as hauliers of the coal-tubs, were notoriously dangerous, as Revd Patrick Brontë observed in 1824: 'In deep and extensive coal-pits . . . explosions take place, that scorch and force all things round them' (*Brontëana*, p. 214). Improvement was slow, despite the revelations of the Children's Employment Commission, and the resulting Mines Act of 1842.

The West Riding textile industry developed from small-scale hand-spinning and weaving in the workers' homes, or in small water-powered 'manufactories', to a mechanized industry based on steam. The cropping-frames, each doing work formerly done by five men, were the main source of the *Luddites' grievances in 1811–12, so forcefully described in *Shirley*. From the late 1820s more power-looms were installed in ever larger mills: in Halifax worsted power-looms multiplied from 'some hundreds' in 1830 to 4,000 in 1850. The countrywide financial crisis of 1825 exacerbated unemployment in the textile industry. In 1826

unemployed weavers destroyed power-looms, and in the later 1830s and 1840s supported the *Chartists. There was rioting in the 'Plug-plot' year, 1842, and in 1848 when Charlotte recorded widespread unemployment in *Haworth. Many woollen manufacturers known to the Brontës, such as the Greenwoods, Nusseys, Taylors of Gomersal, and Brookes of Dewsbury, experienced financial crises. The woollen industry as a whole expanded until the 1880s, and processed more foreign wool: 30,000,000 pounds of raw wool were imported from Australia in 1851 compared with none in 1815.

Cobbett, William, *Rural Rides* (Penguin edn., 1967), app.

influence on other writers. See SEQUELS AND 'INCREMENTAL LITERATURE'.

Ingham, Dr Amos (1827–89), the Haworth surgeon who attended Charlotte in February and March 1855 during her last illness and signed her death certificate. He had become a licentiate of the London Society of Apothecaries and member of the Royal College of Surgeons in 1852, and had married Mary Akeroyd, daughter of a wealthy worsted spinner, on 21 March 1854. He was ill in December 1854 when Charlotte asked him to send medicine for Tabitha *Aykroyd, the Parsonage servant, who was 'much troubled with diarrhea [*sic*]' and who died on 17 February 1855.

Ingham family. Joshua Ingham (1802–66), JP and deputy lieutenant of the West Riding of Yorks., and his wife Mary, née Cunliffe Lister (1812–99), employed Anne Brontë as a governess at *Blake Hall, *Mirfield, 8 April–?December 1839. Ingham's family were merchants, bankers, and coal-owners in the Calder valley. Originally Nonconformist, they turned to the Church of England when they prospered. Of Joshua and Mary Ingham's thirteen children, five had been born when Anne became governess: Joshua Cunliffe (1832–77), Mary (1834–1922), Martha (1836–1917), Emily (b. 1837), and Harriet (1838–9). In 1851 Joshua Ingham farmed 220 acres, employing 40 farm labourers, while as a mine-owner he employed 258 people, including 100 boys and 10 women. Charlotte Brontë told Ellen Nussey on 24 January 1840 that the Inghams had 'an unruly, violent family of Modern children . . . Anne is not to return—Mrs. Ingham is a placid mild woman— but as for the children it was one struggle of life-wearing exertion to keep them in anything like decent order' (Smith *Letters*, 1. 210). Agnes *Grey's trials in the *Bloomfield family almost certainly reflected Anne's with the Inghams, for Anne defended *Agnes Grey from charges of 'extravagant over-colouring in those parts . . . carefully copied from the life, with a most scrupulous avoidance of all exaggeration' (preface to *Tenant*, 2nd edn. (Aug. 1848)). Joshua Ingham's great-granddaughter Susan Brooke testified that he was irritable and on occasion tyrannical. His mother Martha, née Taylor, may have resembled the senior 'Mrs Bloomfield'.

> Brooke, S., 'Anne Brontë at Blake Hall', *BST* (1958), 13. 68. 239–50 (with portraits).
>
> Nussey, John, 'Blake Hall, Mirfield, and its Occupants', *Yorkshire Archaeological Journal*, 55 (1983), 134–41.

Ingram, Blanche, a fashionable beauty of 25, in *Jane Eyre*. She is a house-party guest at *Thornfield in the spring following Jane Eyre's arrival. Tall and dark, with noble features, like the Angrian Lady Zenobia *Ellrington, she is an accomplished pianist, and sings duets with *Rochester; but she is haughty and satirical, maliciously parades her knowledge of botany at the expense of Mrs Dent, discourteously uses her fluent French to make private remarks to her mother, and in Jane's hearing abuses governesses as detestable, ridiculous incubi. To make Jane jealous, Rochester insists on her being present while he apparently enjoys Blanche's company, and acts a charade of marriage with her. Blanche is confident that her accomplishments, affected regal manner, and proclaimed admiration of men 'with a spice of the devil in them' will ensure that Rochester proposes marriage. Jane is tortured to realize that he may, even though he perceives Blanche's barren heart, petty spitefulness to Adèle *Varens, and mercenary aims. After Rochester proposes to Jane, he assures her that Blanche will not suffer: he had circulated a rumour that his fortune was not a third of what was supposed, and the idea of his insolvency had 'extinguished' Blanche's flame in a moment.

'Interesting Passage in the Lives of Some Eminent Men of the Present time, An', by Lord Charles Wellesley (Charlotte Brontë) (18 June 1830; MS in Lowell, Harvard), a scandalous tale of a robbery at the Glass Town Public Library which tells us as much about the malicious narrator as about the participants in his 'fictitious' story. In order to malign his literary rival, Lord Charles *Wellesley publishes the gossip of Captain *Tree's servant who reports that prominent members of Glass Town's literary society (including the Chief Librarian Lieutenant Brock), secreted stolen books in a coffin in a large vault in the cemetery. While keeping watch, however, Tree is surprised by Dr Hume *Badey and the two Glass Town villains, Richard (Young Man) *Naughty and Ned *Laury, notorious bodysnatchers eager for fresh material for the doctor's medical research. Hume promises not to inform on Tree if he undertakes to provide him with a living subject each week (see BURKE

AND HARE), but when Tree threatens to tell of Hume's illegal activities, Hume kills him, but subsequently resuscitates him in his 'macerating tub'. Lord Charles is attacked for this story in 'The *Liar Detected' by Captain *Bud (Branwell) but reciprocates with yet another attack on Glass Town literati in 'The *Poetaster'.

> Alexander *EEW*, 1. 170–7.

Ireland. Both Revd Patrick *Brontë and Revd A. B. *Nicholls were born in the north of Ireland, Brontë in *Drumballyroney parish, County Down, Nicholls at Killead, County Antrim, though in 1825 he and his brother Alan moved to *Banagher. Emdale, Mr Brontë's alleged birthplace, is *c*.5 miles south-east of Loughbrickland, just off the road to Rathfriland. The family later lived in nearby Lisnacreevy, and Patrick's youngest sister Alice was born in Ballynaskeagh. In his day the undulating countryside of small pasture and arable fields was varied by the bleaching-greens of the local linen weavers. To the south-east rise the mountains of Mourne.

In 1777 Ireland was in a state of turbulence, when Volunteers raised during the time of the War of American Independence demanded political reform. In 1782–3 Ireland obtained legislative independence from Britain with the establishment of an Irish parliament. This gave more power to wealthy Protestant landowners, but greater misery to a mainly Catholic peasantry suffering from absentee landlordism, rackrenting, and eviction. In the 1790s agrarian discontent and the spread of French revolutionary ideas led to the formation of the United Irishmen, who aimed to secure Irish independence. Patrick's brother William joined the rebels, fought at the Battle of Ballynahinch in June 1798, and was fortunate to escape the ruthless suppression which followed. In later years both Charlotte and her father denounced violent rebellion, and supported the Act of Union of 1800 by which Pitt, after a campaign involving bribery and the suggestion of Catholic emancipation, suppressed the Irish Parliament. The Catholic Emancipation Bill was not passed until 1829.

The Irish famine, at its worst in 1846 and 1847, caused widespread distress and led to mass emigration and further weakening of the economy, exacerbated by American competition in the corn market. Political unrest increased, and there was a flicker of rebellion in the year of revolutions, 1848, when the Young Ireland movement tried but failed to win Irish liberty. Charlotte, unsympathetic to the Irish, prayed that England might be spared such 'frenzy-fits'. She associated Ireland with Roman *Catholicism, and with untrustworthy curates such as Revd James William *Smith and Revd John *Collins. Her happy marriage with

Mr Nicholls began with an Irish honeymoon which changed her ideas of the people and their country. After a calm passage from Holyhead to Kingstown and thence to Dublin on 4 July 1854, they admired Nicholls's alma mater, Trinity College, with its noble classical library, and ornate new museum. From Dublin they travelled by train to Birr, and thence by road to Banagher, where they were welcomed by Nicholls's relatives at Cuba House. Charlotte admired the lofty, spacious rooms of a house 'like a gentleman's country-seat', and liked the well-educated, well-bred family. By 18 July they had left Banagher to travel to Limerick and thence to Kilkee, County Clare, a 'wild and remote spot' (Wise & Symington, 4. 135) though it was already a favourite sea-bathing resort for Limerick citizens. They were exhilarated by the 'battling of waves with rocks' as the 'broad Atlantic' foamed and boiled against the cliffs (Wise & Symington, 4. 137, 148). Having crossed the Shannon by ferry to Tarbert, County Kerry, they went on via Tralee to *Killarney, where Charlotte narrowly escaped death after falling from her rearing horse in the Gap of Dunloe. They moved south across the Kenmare River and along the high, winding mountain road to picturesque Glengarriff at the head of Bantry Bay. Finally they journeyed to Cork, thence back to Dublin, and to England.

Islanders' Play, begun in December 1827, had the greatest influence on Charlotte Brontë's creative writing of all the early childhood plays. It concentrates chiefly on Charlotte's favourite characters, the Duke of *Wellington and his two sons, and involves politics and allegory rather than battles. Emily, too, appears to have been especially interested in this play, whose island setting and rebellion helped to inspire *Gondal. Charlotte gives two accounts of the origin of the Islanders' Play: an untitled fragment (Alexander EEW, 1. 6) and an account in chapter 1 of *'Tales of the Islanders', the only surviving manuscript relating exclusively to this play. Unlike the *Young Men's Play, the Islanders' was purely imaginary. One wet night in December the young Brontës were sitting round the fire, bored and silent, when Charlotte said 'Suppose we had each an Island of our own'. Imaginations ablaze, they each named islands and the chief men who would occupy them. The islands were all off the coast of Britain: the Isles of Man, Wight, Arran, Bute, and Jersey. (In the second account of events, Charlotte cites only the Isles of Man, Wight, Arran, and Guernsey (Alexander EEW, 1. 22).) For chief men, Branwell chose John Bull, Astley Cooper, and Leigh *Hunt; Emily chose Sir Walter *Scott, his son-in-law John Gibson *Lockhart, and grandson Johnny Lockhart; Anne chose Lord Bentinck, Michael Sadler, and Henry Halford; and Charlotte chose the Duke of Wellington, his sons, 'Christopher North', and his fictitious colleagues in *Blackwood's Edinburgh Magazine, Mr Abernethy and others.

As author-creators the Brontë children assumed a protective role over their respective islands and characters, intervening in events when necessary (as in their roles as Chief *Genii) and assuming the names of Little King and Queens. The adventures of the Islanders can be traced, from Charlotte's point of view, in 'The Tales of the Islanders' (Alexander EEW, 1. 21–33, 99–113, 140–54, 196–211). One of the adventures involving only Charlotte and Emily at night suggests its origins lay in the earlier *bed plays and its setting is similar to Emily's *Parry's Land in the Young Men's Play (Vol 1, ch. 4).

Judging from 'Tales of the Islanders', the only evidence we have, the Brontës developed the Islanders until October 1829 when their partnership lapsed, and Charlotte continued the play alone until June 1830 when the Islanders' British setting had almost completely merged with that of Glass Town. As early as August 1829, the Duke of Wellington was already beginning to fuse with his 'African' counterpart in the Young Men's Play and, given the similar guardianship roles of the Chief Genii and Little King and Queens, it was inevitable that the plays should combine into the single imaginary world of the *Glass Town and Angrian saga.

Alexander EW, pp. 42–52.

'I will not mourn thee, lovely one', by Anne Brontë (Dec. 1842). Written soon after William *Weightman's death. Anne does not mourn the dead man, for he knew little of sin or pain, and has attained the heaven he hoped for; but she laments her own loss of one whose smile and musical voice filled her with joy. The poem touchingly reveals the emotion Anne is trying to control: dazzling light, 'shining eye', and 'angel smile' contrast sharply with sombre clouds, and the silent, enclosing tomb.

Chitham ABP, p. 87.

Jane Eyre. See page 268

Jenkins, Revd Evan (?1797–1856), BA Trinity College, Cambridge 1823, MA 1829; British chaplain in *Brussels from 1826; chaplain to King Leopold. Through his relatives in Pudsey and Batley, Charlotte Brontë obtained his address at 304 chaussée d'Ixelles. His wife recommended the Pensionnat *Heger, gave Revd Patrick Brontë hospitality in February 1842, and issued a standing invitation to Charlotte and Emily to visit on Sundays and half-holidays, until she found it too difficult to entertain her taciturn guests frequently. But the Jenkinses would see the sisters at the Chapel Royal, and they invited Charlotte to dinner on Christmas Day 1843.

Jews, London Society for Promoting Christianity amongst the. An interdenominational society, still extant, founded in 1809 by the Christian Jew J. S. C. F. Frey (1771–1851). It initially distributed tracts and Bibles, began a Hebrew translation of the New Testament, opened schools for Jewish children, and established a printing-office and basket-making factory to provide work for converts cast off by their families. *Simeon and *Wilberforce spoke at the sixth annual meeting on 6 May 1814. Auxiliary societies like that in Leeds, supported by the *Nussey family, collected contributions, and circulated the fund-raising 'Jew-basket' dreaded by Caroline *Helstone in *Shirley*, where satirical fun is made of compulsory sales of unwanted fancy goods to the 'heathenish gentlemen' of the family. Charlotte Brontë, a slack contributor to 'silly Jew-basket work', failed to provide a drawing for it in March 1840.

Jibbel Kumri (Gibbel Kumri) or Mountains of the Moon form 'a misty girdle to the plain of Dahomey', in the *Glass Town and Angrian saga. Uninhabited, they are said to be 'Genii-haunted'. Shooting expeditions of Verdopolitan noblemen take place in the dark foothills of these northern mountains. When Quashia *Quamina initiates rebellion against the Glass Town, Ashantee tribes flock to his banner from the mountain glens and caverns of Jibbel Kumri where they have hidden since their defeat by the *Twelves. Early 19th-century maps site the Jibbel Kumri variously to the north and east of the Gulf of Guinea, confirming the young Brontës in their practice of disregarding geographical accuracy. See also AORNOS, MOUNT; TOWER OF ALL NATIONS.

John, Dr. See BRETTON, DR JOHN GRAHAM.

'John Henry'. See SHIRLEY: 'JOHN HENRY'.

Johnson, Samuel (1709–84), writer and lexicographer. Charlotte Brontë may have read Johnson's *Rasselas*, his moral fable on the 'choice of life', before writing 'The *Search after Happiness'; and Helen *Burns, who thinks 'on the choice of eternity', appropriately reads it. Johnson's *Lives of the English Poets*, which Charlotte recommended to Ellen Nussey on 4 July 1834, influenced her view of writers such as Richard Savage, whose miserable fate she recalled (Smith *Letters*, 2. 59). Sombre lines in *The Vanity of Human Wishes* about 'helpless man' who may 'Roll darkling down the torrent of his fate' are echoed in Jane Eyre's temptation to 'rush down the torrent of' St John *Rivers's will (ch. 35).

Jordan, John Julian, Lord, younger brother of Augusta di *Segovia, who squanders his fortune on her lover and later husband, Alexander Percy (Duke of Northangerland), in the *Glass Town and Angrian saga. As the 'Sheik Medina', he later affects Arabian dress and astonishes Verdopolis by his luxurious and profligate living. He and his troops ('a wild and motley host of mercenary Bedouins') are a constant threat to Angria, joining forces with Quashia *Quamina and Northangerland against the Duke of Zamorna. Jordan is killed at the Battle of Leyden.

Alexander *EW*, pp. 158–61.
Gérin *Five Novelettes*, pp. 83–121.

Joseph, the hypocritical old servant and farmhand at *Wuthering Heights, described by Ellen *Dean as 'the wearisomest, self-righteous pharisee that ever ransacked a Bible to rake the promises to himself and fling the curses on his neighbours' (ch. 5). He is a Calvinist, declaring 'all warks together for gooid tuh them as is chozzen, and piked aht froo' th' rubbidge'. He is loyal to the *Earnshaws but plagues everyone at Wuthering Heights with his sermonizing, believes the young Catherine practises witchcraft, and encourages the faults of his favourite Hareton, believing Heathcliff responsible and therefore damned. When Heathcliff dies he announces with great satisfaction: 'Th' divil's harried off his soul' (ch. 34). The Clarendon editors of *Wuthering Heights* (p. 415) attribute

(*cont. on page 275*)

A novel by Charlotte Brontë, published 1847. First published under the pseudonym 'Currer Bell', *Jane Eyre* attracted immediate attention by its powerful statement of woman's claim to independence.

Composition

From late June or early July 1846 Charlotte and her sisters repeatedly offered the manuscripts of *The Professor*, *Wuthering Heights*, and *Agnes Grey* to various publishers. None had been accepted when in August 1846 Charlotte took her father to Manchester for a cataract operation. The rejected *Professor* manuscript was returned to her there on the day of his operation, 25 August. She promptly sent it off again, and began to write a 'more imaginative and poetical' novel, *Jane Eyre*, in the hope that it would have more success. As she later told Elizabeth Gaskell, she could not write every day; long intervals might elapse before she was again possessed with her vision for the progress of a novel; but then she would search for the precise words to mirror her thoughts, before she wrote anything down. This she did in pencilled, tiny handwriting, on scraps of paper or in little square paper books held against a piece of board instead of a desk. Too few of these scraps survive for one to judge whether Elizabeth Gaskell was right in saying that there would occasionally be a sentence scored out, but seldom, if ever, a word or expression. In fragments such as that describing 'a large house called Gateshead' (BPM: Bonnell 118 (8); *The Professor* (Clarendon edn.), p. 338), 'John Henry' (see SHIRLEY: 'JOHN HENRY'), and **Emma*, single words and short phrases as well as sentences are revised. But Elizabeth Gaskell's observation might be true of the greater part of *Jane Eyre*, for though Charlotte had done little more than begin the novel by about 23 September, when she left Manchester, inspiration came rapidly on her return to Haworth. 'When she came to "Thornfield" she could not stop . . . On she went, writing incessantly for three weeks; by which time she had carried her heroine away from Thornfield, and was herself in a fever which compelled her to pause' (Gaskell *Life*, 2. 11–12). After her sisters' deaths Charlotte recalled how they used to read and discuss their work together in the evenings—though her own stories were so real to her that she rarely changed them at anyone else's suggestion. But she had once told her sisters that they were wrong to make all their heroines beautiful, and had declared she would show them 'a heroine as plain, and as small as myself, who shall be as interesting as any of yours'.

Manuscript and early editions

On 16 March 1847 Charlotte began to make a fair copy of *Jane Eyre*. Early in August 1847 *The Professor* received its seventh rejection, this time from *Smith, Elder and Company, who courteously suggested that a three-volume work would receive careful attention. Charlotte completed her fair copy of *Jane Eyre* on 19 August, and sent it off by rail to Smith, Elder on the 24th. They received the wonderfully clear and legible manuscripts which now form part of the George Smith bequest as BL Additional MSS 43474–6. This fair copy was used by the printers, Stewart and Murray, to set up the first edition, and has the compositors' names inscribed in the margins. On receipt of the manuscripts Smith, Elder's reader W. S. *Williams, probably seconded by James *Taylor, warmly recommended the novel to George *Smith, the head of the firm, for publication. Smith could not put the book down, finished reading it the same night, and immediately accepted it—though with a request that Charlotte should revise the first part since it might not suit the 'public taste'. Defending her work as 'true', Charlotte refused any revision, but accepted (with the comment that it was a small sum for a year's intellectual labour) Smith's offer of £100 for the copyright, and his stipulation that the firm should have the refusal of her next two works. In fact Smith, Elder eventually paid £500 for the three-volume editions of *Jane Eyre*. Printing and proof-reading went ahead without delay. By 24 September, when she thanked her publishers for punctuating the sheets in a more 'correct and rational' way than her own, Charlotte had already been correcting proofs during her stay at Ellen *Nussey's home, *Brookroyd, from 9 to 23 September—without revealing to Ellen the secret of what she had been writing. The proofs were completed at Haworth, and the novel was published in the customary three volumes at £1 11s. 6d. on 19 October. The title-page described it as 'An Autobiography. Edited by Currer Bell'. Its immediate popularity meant that a second three-volume edition, 'By Currer Bell', with some authorial corrections and revisions appeared on or before 22 January 1848. It was dedicated to W. M. Thackeray, and Charlotte's preface paid tribute to her publishers and to select 'generous critics', as well as to Thackeray as 'the first social regenerator of the day'. By 11 March 1848 a third edition had been called for. On 13 March Charlotte sent corrections for it, with a brief note (wrongly dated 'April 13th, 1848' in the printed edition) making clear that she was the author of *Jane Eyre* only, and not of *Wuthering Heights* and *Agnes Grey*, which had been attributed to her. The third edition, in three volumes, was published on or before 15 April 1848. A cheap 'fourth edition', in one volume, priced at 6s., with no obvious authorial corrections, followed in late April 1850. The first American edition had been published by *Harper & Brothers on 4 January 1848 at 25 cents. These and other early editions are described in *Jane Eyre* (Clarendon edn.), pp. xxi–xxvi, and Walter E. Smith, *The Brontë Sisters. A Bibliographical Catalogue . . .* (1991).

Text

The clarity of the *Jane Eyre* manuscript meant that the first edition reproduced the substantives of the text with a fair degree of accuracy; but Charlotte's punctuation was 'corrected' and toned down into a more conventional form. There are occasional clusters of authorial revisions in the manuscript, especially in passages of pictorial description where Charlotte is concerned to choose an apt word for the people or places she seemed to see 'with her bodily eye'. Thus 'crimson' furnishings at *Thornfield Hall become 'purple', or 'Tyrian-dyed', and Diana and Mary *Rivers have faces of 'distinction and intelligence' instead of the vaguer 'distinction and interest'. Longer deletions and additions seem intended to keep a fine balance between physical attraction and the more spiritual affinities of Jane and *Rochester: Charlotte cancelled a passage in which Rochester teasingly agreed with Jane that she could not compare with Blanche *Ingram in 'bulk and weight'—but he would 'graciously excuse deficiencies'. Charlotte made a few minor revisions in proof: Bertha *Rochester's 'dark' visage became 'wild' in the first edition (and was to become 'lurid' in the second); Rochester's 'sharp' sarcasm became 'pungent'. Some of the apparent revisions in the second edition may be misprints ('uttered' for 'muttered', 'western' for 'westering') but Charlotte did pick up a few errors in the first edition, and corrected 'sly' to 'shy' in chapter 25, 'use' to 'lose' in chapter 26, and so on. For the third edition she corrected 'testatrix' to 'legatee' in chapter 24, and the unseasonable May dahlias in chapter 9 became tulips. The textual notes and introductions in the Clarendon and World's Classics editions give further details.

Plot

Mrs *Reed of *Gateshead Hall dislikes her orphaned 10-year-old niece Jane *Eyre, encourages her children Eliza, Georgiana, and John to treat her as an inferior, and takes John's part when Jane retaliates against his cruel blows. By her aunt's orders Jane is locked in the *red-room, where the kindly Mr Reed had died. Terrified, she screams, imagining a gleam of light to be his spirit. When her aunt thrusts her back into the room she has a species of fit. Shortly afterwards Mrs Reed sends her to *Lowood charity school, warning its patron Revd *Brocklehurst of her 'tendency to deceit'. He publicly accuses Jane of lying, but Miss *Temple clears her name. Jane's friend Helen *Burns dies of consumption. After eight years at Lowood Jane's advertisement for a post as governess is answered by Mrs *Fairfax of Thornfield Hall. Before she leaves Lowood, the Gateshead servant *Bessie brings news that Jane's uncle John Eyre had called at Gateshead to enquire about her.

At Thornfield Mrs Fairfax welcomes Jane in the absence of its master, Mr Rochester, and Jane meets her pupil, Adèle *Varens. She hears laughter in the third storey and is told it is that of the servant, Grace Poole. One January afternoon Jane helps a rider whose horse has slipped on ice in *Hay Lane. He proves to be Mr Rochester, who is intrigued by Jane, admits he has been a 'hackneyed sinner', and describes his affair with the treacherous Céline Varens. During the night Jane hears a 'demoniac laugh', sees smoke coming from Rochester's room, finds his bed on fire, and quenches the flames. He clasps her hand as his 'cherished preserver'. During a house-party Jane has to endure the rudeness of Blanche Ingram, said to be Rochester's intended bride; but, disguised as a fortune-telling gipsy, Rochester disillusions Blanche about his supposed wealth. After he has told Jane's 'fortune', she recognizes him. He is 'convulsively' shocked when she mentions the arrival of a Mr Richard Mason. That night a savage cry from the third storey, followed by calls for help, alarms the guests. Rochester calms them, but asks Jane to tend the wounded Mason while he fetches a doctor. She hears canine snarls from the next room, but obeys him, and Mason leaves at dawn. Jane is then called back to Gateshead, where the dying Mrs Reed confesses that she had told Jane's uncle John that his niece, whom he wished to make his heir, had died. On her return to Thornfield Jane is welcomed by Rochester, who proposes marriage. After she has accepted, a storm rises, and lightning splits the chestnut tree under which they had been sitting. Ominous dreams precede the midnight visitation to Jane's bedroom of a vampire-like woman who tears the bridal veil in half. The wedding is interrupted by a stranger, accompanied by Mason, who declares that Rochester has a living wife. Rochester admits the truth, and invites all present to visit his wife—the madwoman of the third storey—who violently attacks him. Though Jane forgives Rochester, she refuses to be his mistress, and leaves Thornfield secretly. After many miles of travelling by coach and on foot, the starving Jane finds shelter in *Moor House, the home of the Rivers family. Concealing her identity, she accepts St John *Rivers's offer of work in *Morton school. Meanwhile a letter

'My strength is quite failing me': Edmund Garrett's illustration for the 1890 Crowell edition of *Jane Eyre*.

announces the death of the Rivers's uncle John, who has left all but 30 guineas to an unknown relative. Realizing that St John is suppressing his love for Rosamond *Oliver, Jane invites him to look at her portrait of Rosamond. He sees the name Jane Eyre on the covering paper, realizes she is his cousin, and tells her she is the heiress to £20,000. She shares the legacy equally with her three cousins, but still longs for news of Rochester. St John asks her to accompany him as his wife when he leaves for missionary work in India, and she is on the point of accepting when she hears Rochester crying out her name. She calls out in response, and returns post-haste to Thornfield, only to find it a fire-blackened ruin. She learns from an innkeeper that Rochester had tried in vain to save the life of the madwoman who set it alight, and had himself lost one hand and the sight of one eye. Jane hastens to him at *Ferndean Manor and reassures him of her continuing love. After their marriage Rochester recovers enough sight to see his first-born son.

Sources and Context

More than one reviewer believed Jane Eyre's resistance to Rochester recalled that of Richardson's Pamela to her 'Mr B': indeed *Douglas Jerrold's Weekly Newspaper* protested against 'Miss Eyre's Pamela-fashion of calling Mr. Rochester her master . . . before she loves him' (20 Nov. 1847). But Charlotte's attitude to Richardson was at best equivocal. In her 'Word to the "Quarterly"' (see SHIRLEY: 'A WORD TO THE "QUARTERLY"'), she referred to him satirically as 'the idiot (inspired or otherwise)', and in *Jane Eyre* itself Pamela is one of the sources of the tales told by Bessie, the servant, which please Jane's childish taste. Charlotte might well have insisted that the adult Jane was worlds apart from Pamela in character, motivation, and class. She certainly insisted that Rochester was a good man unfairly trapped by scheming relatives, not an ignoble and dissolute schemer. Nevertheless, Rochester inherited from the *Glass Town and Angrian saga the Byronic glamour of the Duke of *Zamorna, with his many mistresses, volatile moods of exultation and remorse, picturesque and melodramatic gestures, dark secrets, conflicting loyalties, and above all the masterful manner which fascinates and tantalizes those who serve or love him. But Jane, unlike Zamorna's mistress Mina Laury, for example, is not 'entangled in his spells past hope of rescue' (Alexander *EW*, p. 167). Her declaration that she is Rochester's equal is at the heart of the novel. Rochester inherits more directly from the Byron of *Childe Harold* his despairing wanderlust as he 'flew through Europe half mad; with disgust, hate, and rage', as his companions (ch. 24). In the dénouement, Byron is forgotten, as Rochester prays for strength to lead 'a purer life'. See also COWAN BRIDGE; FAIRY TALES; IMAGERY.

Reception

Jane Eyre astonished and delighted almost all of its first readers and reviewers. Even the captious *Spectator* (6 Nov. 1847) conceded that it showed skill, power, and vigour, and sustained a 'species of interest' throughout, despite its improbabilities, unnatural characters, and 'low' behaviour. Many newspaper reviews, especially the provincial weeklies, found nothing to criticize. Sated by a diet of 'fashionable' novels, they praised *Jane Eyre*'s novelty, vitality, unhackneyed freshness and individuality, its power to excite and move, to 'make the pulse gallop and fill the eye with tears', its sustained intensity, and the engrossing charm which made the book impossible to put down. They were impressed by its insight into the human heart, vigorous style, and above all its 'truth', enhanced by the author's choice of an unconventionally plain woman as heroine. Jane was presented with such insight that many believed the writer was a woman, despite the 'masculine firmness of touch'. The *Spectator* seems to have been the first to criticize Rochester's conduct as 'hardly "proper" . . . between a single man and a maiden in her teens', but the reviewer cavilled at the 'low tone of behaviour (rather than of morality)'. Until the end of November other critics either ignored or positively commended the novel's morality: the Roman Catholic *Tablet* found it 'healthful and profitable'; the *Critic* advised that circulating libraries might safely order it; while the *People's Journal* and the *Sun* discovered 'pure and healthy' or 'ennobling' moral sentiments; and the *Era*, the *Nottingham Mercury*, and the *Examiner*—journals widely differing in outlook and prestige—agreed in discerning an inherent moral excellence. At this date, fault-finding was directed at *Jane Eyre*'s melodramatic elements, improbabilities, or 'eccentricities' in the plot; and the *Atlas* complained of the unreality of Helen Burns. Yet other reviewers found nothing improbable at all: the *Newcastle Guardian* commended *Jane Eyre* as a simple narrative of events 'common in every-day life', very suitable for circulating libraries. Most criticisms were qualified by a modicum of praise. The *Spectator* considered real ability had been expended on poor, ill-chosen material, the *Britannia* carped at 'revolting' passages and a general want of construction, but considered that Currer Bell still deserved encouragement. G. H. Lewes's influential, perceptive review in *Fraser's Magazine* gave generous praise as well as criticism of *Jane Eyre*'s melodrama and improbable elements. Similarly appreciative but not uncritical estimates followed in, for example, the *Scotsman* (22 Dec. 1847), the *Courier* (1 Jan. 1848), the *Dublin University Magazine* (May 1848), and (most gratifying to Charlotte) *La Revue des deux mondes* (31 Oct. 1848). ('The censures are as well-founded as the commendations', Charlotte told W. S. Williams on 16 November (Smith *Letters*, 2. 140).) But alongside these generally fair reviews appeared, from December 1847 onwards, a series of hostile, sometimes hysterical attacks on *Jane Eyre*—perhaps in reaction against the general enthusiasm, perhaps symptomatic of the growing anxiety about perceived threats to established religion and society at this period. On 5 December 1847 *The Sunday Times* found in *Jane Eyre* innumerable faults, despite its cleverness: it was outré, unnatural, its savage hero had the repulsive manners of a boor, his interviews with his mad wife were too disgusting to quote, some scenes were so exaggerated as to be totally incredible, and there was a mass of improbable incidents; worst of all, perhaps, the writer actually boasted of overstepping conventional rules. The *Mirror of Literature, Amusement and Instruction* (Dec. 1847) was not amused: its reviewer ranted about insidious and debased tendencies, immorality, extravagant and disgusting scenes: religion was 'stabbed in the dark' by a novelist who attempted to level social distinctions and do away with morality. The strange violence of *Wuthering Heights*, which had appeared by mid-December, probably helped to fuel further attacks, for it was held to be typical of the 'Bell brothers'. Two religious journals, the *Tablet* (23 Oct. 1847) and the *Church of England Journal* (16 Dec. 1847), had praised *Jane Eyre* as 'healthful' or 'earnest', and a third, the High Anglican *Guardian* (1 Dec. 1847), had taken exception to Helen Burns's unorthodox creed as potentially mischievous, but had still praised the novel's 'rare reality' and admirably drawn characters. In contrast, several heavyweight religious quarterlies for 1848 condemned its morality outright. The *Christian Remembrancer* (Apr. 1848) believed that the book's power and even genius was overshadowed by its questionable morality: *Jane Eyre* was not positively anti-Christian, but it was preoccupied with the worst parts of human nature, and burning with 'moral Jacobinism', for it implied that all virtue was but well-masked vice. The *Church of England Quarterly Review* for the same month also admitted Charlotte's skill and power, but perceived in the book a mere morality which was not Christian. In September 1848 the *Rambler*, a liberal Catholic journal, condemned *Jane Eyre* as one of the coarsest books ever perused, tending perpetually towards the gross and animal aspects of human nature, seeking to palliate Rochester's detestable morality, and skilfully drawing an unattractive and unfeminine heroine. Secular periodicals took up the cry: the *North American Review* (Oct. 1848) acknowledged minor virtues, but condemned *Jane Eyre*'s offensive indelicacy, its moral paradoxes, flouting of convention, and the shocking profanity, brutality, and slang of Mr Rochester, who was involved in scenes showing mere animal appetite and courtship after the manner of kangaroos: Charlotte like the other Bells presented vice and degradation too literally, arousing disgust instead of teaching purity; sadly, the novel's dubious reputation meant that every American family soon had a copy of it. Most notoriously, in the **Quarterly Review* (Dec. 1848) Elizabeth **Rigby, later Lady Eastlake, concluded that *Jane Eyre* was pre-eminently anti-Christian, because it committed the highest moral offence of making an unworthy character interesting. That the novel was not devoid of tragic power, some brilliance, and 'wonderful scenes of suppressed feeling . . . stamped with truth' made it all the more dangerous. Not only was much of it in 'horrid taste', vulgar, unladylike, and coarse, but it subverted Christian ethics by showing an unregenerate, undisciplined heroine, with no more religion than a heathen, exerting moral strength. Jane also defied the divinely appointed social order of rich and poor and was thus akin to the insubordinate spirit that had overthrown authority abroad and fostered Chartism and rebellion at home. The *North British Review* (Aug. 1849) made similar accusations of indelicacy and of recklessness with regard to right and wrong; and as Miss Rigby had sneered that if *Jane Eyre* was by a woman, she must be one who had 'long forfeited the society of her own sex', so the *North British Review* considered that the author, if a woman, must be 'nearly unsexed'. Though Smith, Elder would not let Charlotte voice her indignation in her projected preface to *Shirley*, 'A Word to the "Quarterly"', she conveyed it clearly enough through Mrs Pryor's account of 'Miss Hardman' in *Shirley* (ch. 21).

Later editions

Whether *Jane Eyre* was regarded as moral or immoral, it continued to sell. The fourth edition was cheap enough for it to be sold by country booksellers such as John **Greenwood of Haworth. Following Elizabeth Gaskell's *Life* of Charlotte in 1857, an edition of 25,000 copies was sold, with two further printings of 1,000 copies in each of the next two years. It is probable that the novel was never out of print for long. Of special interest for *Jane Eyre* are the Haworth edition (1899) with a long and perceptive introduction by Mrs Humphry Ward; W. R. Nicoll's edition of 1902, which includes the fragment he entitled 'The Moores', now known as 'John Henry'; the Clarendon edition, edited by Jane Jack and Margaret Smith (1969, rev. 1975), annotated and based on the text of the first edition collated with and emended by reference to the manuscript, second and third editions; the Norton Critical Edition (New York,

1971; rev. 1987 and 2000), annotated, and including reviews of and critical essays on *Jane Eyre*. See also TRANSLATIONS OF BRONTË WORKS; CRITICAL RECEPTION TO 1860; EDITING HISTORY OF MATURE WORKS; CRITICISM 1860–1940; CRITICISM FROM 1940.

Allott.
Bock, Carol, *Charlotte Brontë and the Storyteller's Audience* (1992).
Ewbank, Inga-Stina, *Their Proper Sphere: A Study of the Brontë Sisters as Early-Victorian Female Novelists* (1966).
Gilbert, Sandra M., and Gubar, Susan, *The Madwoman in the Attic* (1979).
Glen, Heather (ed.), *New Casebooks: Jane Eyre* (1997).
—— *Charlotte Brontë: The Imagination in History* (2002).
Peters, Margot, *Charlotte Brontë: Style in the Novel* (1973).
Shuttleworth, Sally, *Charlotte Brontë and Victorian Psychology* (1996).
Stoneman, Patsy, *Brontë Transformations* (1996).
Tillotson, Kathleen, *Novels of the 1840s* (1954).
Winnifrith, Tom, *The Brontës and their Background* (1973).
Wroot, Herbert, *Sources of the Brontë Novels: Persons and Places* (suppl. to *BST* 1935).

Joseph's dialect and some other characteristics to Tabitha *Aykroyd, the Brontës' servant and a 'joined Methodist' of long standing. See LAW HILL, HALIFAX for another possible source.

Julia ('There is reader a sort of pleasure'), an Angrian novelette written by Charlotte Brontë in minuscule script on loose sheets of notepaper (19 June 1837; MS in Ransom HRC, Texas), during her summer holidays as a teacher at *Roe Head. *Julia* is an excellent example of Charlotte's habit of episodic writing developed during this period. Her narrator Charles Townshend (see WELLESLEY, LORD CHARLES ALBERT FLORIAN) allows himself to be 'rattled away' by his imagination: he records and analyses a medley of scenes and characters that he encounters on his travels. Meanwhile Branwell is organizing the Battle of *Evesham which forms the background to *Julia*, but Charles (and his author) have no interest in the war except as it affects the Angrian coterie: 'amid the daily deeds of strife passing round me, the recollection of domestic scenes is singularly soothing'. Two new characters are introduced to Charlotte's Angrian stories: Captain Henry *Hastings, already well established in Branwell's writing, and Caroline *Vernon as a child, a portrait that foreshadows the situation of Adèle *Varens in *Jane Eyre* and the delightful childhood prattle of Paulina *Home in *Villette*. There is a brilliant vignette of the naive young poet-officer Hastings 'in the blaze of his fame', being encouraged in his boastfulness by Lady Julia *Wellesley and Mary Percy. Julia makes only this brief appearance, the title reflecting a name of convenience that was attached by early Brontë collectors who had not read the manuscript (probably T. J. *Wise who sold the manuscript to John H. Wrenn: see

MANUSCRIPTS AND MANUSCRIPT COLLECTIONS). In another episode, Charlotte satirizes the Wesleyan Methodists when their Angrian class-leaders set on the local magistrate and his family in what they consider to be a conversion attempt: see METHODISM; RELIGION.

Julia. See WELLESLEY, LADY JULIA.

'Julian M. and A. G. Rochelle' (9 Oct. 1845); 152 lines in quatrains by Emily Brontë, from the Gondal Poems manuscript notebook. Lines 13–44 and 65–92, plus four extra lines, were published by Emily in *Poems* 1846 (with Gondal references removed) as 'The Prisoner (A Fragment)', one of her best-known poems. Lines 1–12 were published by Charlotte Brontë in 1850, with eight lines added by her, under the title 'The Visionary'. The whole original poem was first published in 1938 by the Shakespeare Head Press (*Gondal Poems*, ed. Helen Brown and Joan Mott).

'The Visionary' includes the opening narrative frame of the poem. The speaker (Julian M.) is alone in the silent house at night, awaiting the secret visit of 'the Wanderer' (A. G. *Rochelle, whom we learn from the original poem he has released some time ago). In the original poem, the speaker then launches straight into the dramatic story of their first meeting in prison (the content of 'The Prisoner (A Fragment)'), but Charlotte's interpolation suggests the speaker is the poet, waiting for her 'visitant of air', Imagination.

'The Prisoner (A Fragment)' omits the narrative frame of the larger poem and concentrates on the visit of the speaker who, with the gaoler, becomes the recipient of the prisoner's tale of visionary escape:

275

> A messenger of Hope comes every night to me
> And offers, for short life, eternal liberty.

Heralded by the west wind and in the silence of the evening, she experiences the 'Invisible': 'My outward sense is gone, my inward essence feels'. But the agony of returning sensation is unbearable:

> When the pulse begins to throb, the brain to think again,
> The soul to feel the flesh and the flesh to feel the chain.

The steady six-stress lines with their regular rhyme and strong central caesura suggest that the recurring vision is no different from other events in the narrative, it is a constant part of the prisoner's reality. The two witnesses are powerless to cause further woe to the captive: her visionary experience heralds death and her sentence given by man has been 'overruled by Heaven'. C. Day Lewis called the description of the vision 'the greatest passage of poetry Emily Brontë wrote' ('The Poetry of Emily Brontë', *BST* (1957), 13. 67. 92).

The lines following 'The Prisoner (A Fragment)' remove the focus on escape by death and restore the poem to the Gondal romance it was originally intended to be. Julian frees A. G. Rochelle from her chains and she chooses to remain in her dungeon, tended by Julian through thirteen weeks of illness. He eventually wins her love and she visits him secretly at night. Julian and Rochelle are from warring families, probably during the late Royalist-Republican wars in the *Gondal saga. They were childhood playmates but now Julian's family are fighting for 'freedom' and reproach him for not leading his forces like a true 'patriot'. Yet 'It needed braver nerve to face the world's disdain' and remain true to his love.

The poem is a powerful description of mystic experience, a 'divine vision' in which most commentators see Emily's own worship of Imagination. It abounds in conventional Romantic and Gothic images and themes: the gaoler with the rusty key, the dungeon, the childlike beauty as prisoner, the female captive like a bird in the cage, the imprisonment of the soul in the body, the spirit soaring free, visionary inspiration heralded by western winds, the wanderer and exile, and the individual defying the world's disdain.

Davies, Stevie, *Emily Brontë: Heretic* (1994), 226–30.
Gezari *EBP*, p. 177.
Hardy, Barbara, 'The Lyricism of Emily Brontë', in Anne Smith (ed.), *The Art of Emily Brontë* (1976), 98–100.
Hewish, John, *Emily Brontë* (1969), 83–6.
Roper *EBP*, p. 176.
Spurgeon, Caroline, *Mysticism in English Literature* (1913), 80–4.
Stanford, Derek, and Spark, Muriel, *Emily Brontë* (1953), 128–35.

'Justice Humaine, La'. See 'HUMAN JUSTICE'.

juvenilia of the Brontës. *See opposite page*

A PART from the juvenilia or early writings of Jane Austen, the Brontë juvenilia are the most famous in English literature. They are not only extraordinarily abundant, having occupied their authors from childhood, through adolescence and into maturity, but they are unique in their collaborative intensity and imaginative vision. It is not unusual for children to create imaginary worlds: both Hartley Coleridge and Anthony Trollope, for example, record doing this. Nor is it rare for children to collaborate in literary ventures, as the Stephen children did in their magazine, 'The Hyde Park Gate News'. Virginia Woolf records how she and her siblings produced 69 issues (still surviving in the British Museum) between February 1891 and April 1895. Such juvenilia, however, are usually written for an adult audience with all the necessary censorship of sexual fantasy and violence. For this reason, the secret world of the Brontë juvenilia reveals not only the children's apprenticeship as authors but their uninhibited development of the self. There is much of biographical interest in the juvenilia, and in their appropriation and transformation of material from the adult world, there is also a new take on the concerns, ideologies, and values of Victorian society. Where mature works, such as *Jane Eyre*, document the life of the child from an adult perspective, the juvenilia allow the unmediated voice of the child to be heard.

The term 'juvenilia' is something of a misnomer in relation to the Brontës. It generally refers to 'Literary or artistic works produced in the author's youth' (*OED*), and 'typically marked by immaturity of style, treatment or thought' (*Websters*). Branwell Brontë's massive body of writings, commonly referred to as juvenilia, include those he wrote when he was 31 and on the verge of death. Charlotte Brontë continued writing her novelettes until the age of 24 and they are frequently referred to as juvenilia: she herself considered them immature. Yet Keats died at 24, and we seldom refer to more than a handful of his poems as 'juvenilia'. Reference to Brontë juvenilia, then, should carry neither the exclusive implications of youth (works written under 20 years) nor the derogatory implications of immaturity.

The Brontë juvenilia are characterized by their miniature size and their minuscule script, written in imitation of newspaper print and fashioned into little hand-sewn booklets originally for use by the *Twelves, the original toy soldiers of the *Glass Town and Angrian saga. Paper was also expensive and scarce in the Brontë household; scraps of drawing paper, advertising brochures, sugar bags, and the like were often recycled to supply the children's 'scribblemania'. Except for the young Brontës who were short-sighted, the tiny hand-printed script is difficult to read without a magnifying glass, making the manuscripts illegible to adult eyes. Thus the preservation of the minuscule script throughout the extensive Brontë juvenilia helped to maintain a secret shared imaginative world.

Manuscripts of Brontë juvenilia are preserved in libraries, museums, and private collections in the UK and the USA (see MANUSCRIPTS AND MANUSCRIPT COLLECTIONS). In quantity they exceed the Brontës' combined published output. They include magazines, poems, plays, short stories, novelettes, and Diary Papers, written chiefly in the minuscule script of Charlotte and Branwell. These refer mainly to the Glass Town and Angrian saga, initially a collaborative enterprise among all four

Miniature magazines and volumes containing early writing by Charlotte Brontë.

siblings and later a literary partnership between Charlotte and Branwell. The relatively few manuscripts by Emily and Anne that survive tell the cryptic story of *Gondal, record brief autobiographical notes on scraps of paper (see DIARY PAPERS), or document in poetry the lyric voice of their authors (see POETRY BY ANNE BRONTË; POETRY BY EMILY BRONTË). All known Brontë juvenilia have now been published. Fannie Ratchford's pioneering work (*The Brontës' Web of Childhood*, 1941) still provides a valuable introduction to the Brontë juvenilia and its formative influence on their later writing; Christine Alexander's *The Early Writings of Charlotte Brontë* (1984) is a later comprehensive survey of all extant Brontë juvenilia, which concentrates on Charlotte's development, on her collaboration with Branwell, and on mapping the intricacies of the sagas; and Victor Neufeldt's introductions to his editions of Branwell's work shed new light on Branwell's early writings.

The earliest recorded juvenile manuscript is Branwell's *'Battell Book' (12 Mar. 1827), although Charlotte's undated manuscript *'There was once a little girl' is a close contender (c.1827–8). Both these manuscripts are typical of the children's early productions: little hand-sewn booklets as small as a large postage stamp, in rough paper covers, with occasional illustrations and minuscule script. Poor spelling and often non-existent punctuation are as much features of these teenage texts as are their complex intertextuality and rich allusiveness. Later novelettes of Charlotte and Branwell are written on larger, loose sheets of paper but still in the same minuscule script used by all four children. Most of Emily's poems are recorded either on small uneven scraps of paper or in one of three notebooks, whereas most of Anne's poems are preserved in fair-copy notebooks. The earliest extant Gondal reference by Emily is dated 24 November 1834, when she was 16, two years earlier than Anne's first surviving Gondal manuscript.

The juvenilia are a powerful record of the liberating effect of literary play. Like those of all normal children, their earliest games were physical: they encountered the adult world by re-enacting historical stories, probably derived from Sir Walter *Scott's *Tales of a Grandfather* which they read at an early age. Records survive of Emily Brontë breaking the branch of her father's favourite cherry tree while pretending to be Prince Charles escaping from the Roundheads. As their reading skills advanced, the literary dimension of the adult world became available to the young explorers. Their play likewise became literary rather than physical, and they began to document their various 'plays' as they called them, in particular the *Young Men's Play, the *Islanders' Play, and *Our Fellows' Play.

In the process, the young Brontës gained their apprenticeship as authors. Just as they appropriated material from the adult world, so they imitated the methodology of its literary scene. Local newspapers and the 19th-century quarterlies and reviews, especially *Blackwood's Edinburgh Magazine*, were their models. The children became editors, designers, illustrators, and publishers of their various productions, with all the freedom and authority this implies. Their imaginative recreation of their physical and social environment, their experimentation with different voices and styles, their rewriting of relationships in order to position and define the self, are all forms of play by which the Brontës grew towards maturity. Their shared imaginative vision provided 'a web of sunny air' (as Charlotte called it in her poem *'We wove a web in childhood') for the four motherless children, and led to mutual creative support, if not continued literary collaboration, that survived into their adult years. Within a close-knit sibling society they could achieve a security and power otherwise inaccessible to them.

Collaboration also brought rivalry between the child authors that is evident in their earliest articles and reviews. Under the guise of fictitious poets, historians, and politicians, they jockey for the Glass Town public's attention by writing scurrilous reviews of each other's work (like the *Blackwood's* review that so savaged the youthful Keats). In the process the young writers are not only playing with their material but with the process of narration itself. In one article Sergeant *Bud (Branwell's voice) scorns Charlotte's degenerate editorial policy; in the next, Lord Charles *Wellesley (Charlotte's voice) satirizes Emily's *Parry's Land with its Yorkshire puddings and dull landscapes (see 'YOUNG MEN'S MAGAZINE'). The young writers carry on a continual verbal battle in editorial notes, prefaces, afterwords, and the actual texts of their stories.

This playful assumption of a variety of masks allowed the young Brontës to practise writing in different genres and different styles, exercising vicariously the power of the author/editor they were denied as children or young women in real life. As in *Blackwood's*, the Brontës' fictitious contributors are all male. For Charlotte, the adoption of a male pseudonym and in particular of a male narrator for her first novel *The Professor* was not only to mask the woman writer, but was also a part of that assumption of literary authority practised since childhood.

The resulting game of storytelling, derived from authors like Scott and James *Hogg, is just one example of appropriation of the adult world that helps create the rich intertextuality of the juvenilia. 'The *Search after Happiness', for example, engages with *Johnson's *Rasselas* (1759), and the idea of the double associated with the personalities of the Dukes of *Zamorna and *Northangerland, heroes of the Glass Town and Angrian saga, echoes the Romantic personality of the Byronic Hero and the complex psychology in Hogg's *The Private Memoirs and Confessions of a Justified Sinner* (1824). The juvenilia record the Brontës' assumption and critique of Victorian religious, political and social ideology. In both narrative form and in content, for example, they engage with the question of the position of *women (Elizabeth *Hastings is a prototype for Jane *Eyre) and with the triumphs and evils of colonialization (see AFRICA; QUAMINA, QUASHIA).

The imaginative games recorded in the juvenilia absorbed their players over such a length of time and to such an intensity of commitment that all happiness for two at least of the players was inextricably bound up with playing the game. Branwell Brontë never escaped his fictitious Angrian world; and Emily continued to play the Gondal game until the year of her death. There is no evidence that Emily's imaginative world had anything but a constructive effect on her mature writing. It appears to have provided sustenance, security, and inspiration for her intensely secretive and self-contained personality. She moves freely in her poetry between Gondal and the real world; and although the Gothic power of Gondal may have combined with Scott and *Shakespeare to provide the inspiration for *Wuthering Heights*, the novel is solidly structured within the domestic world of a middle-class Victorian narrator. For Branwell, however, the game ran away with its player. His absorption in Angria and his devotion to his alter ego Northangerland blurred his ability to distinguish between reality and fiction. The freedom and power he wielded in Angria could not be replicated in the real world. His juvenilia, so various in form and narrative voice in his early years, continue unchanged in a never-ending chronicle of picaresque narratives centring on the life, fortunes, and increasingly complex and disturbed personality of Northangerland.

The power of literary collaboration in sustaining and fostering the Brontës' literary output cannot be underestimated; but it is also true that each of the Brontës had a unique imaginative life that became increasingly individual as they grew older. The development of Anne's moral sense led her increasingly away from Emily's often anarchic world and it is significant that Anne was not always party to innovations in Emily's Gondal plot (see DIARY PAPERS). Critics such as Barker have recently stressed the collaborative element of the juvenilia chiefly to privilege Branwell's literary contribution; yet, as Charlotte's assumption of various masks demonstrates, she was quite as capable of sparring with her own polyphonic voices as with those of Branwell. Even in an early tale like *'Albion and Marina', written at 14 years old, Charlotte's sharp observation of her own creative process is clearly evident. Unlike her brother, she was able to discipline her imagination and harness its creative energy in the cause of social justice. Her later juvenilia indicate an increasing engagement with reality and with her own position as a single woman in society.

Charlotte came to see her early writing as sinful fantasy (see ROE HEAD JOURNAL, THE); and characterized it as 'lurid' (*Farewell to Angria)—a hothouse of 'ornamented and redundant composition' (preface to The *Professor) from which she must withdraw for a time. Yet she also acknowledged the value of her 'practice of some years', the formative experiences without which her first novel could not have been written. Anne made the adjustment to Victorian domestic fiction without trauma, taking with her her early lessons in writing. Emily moved seamlessly from one personal imaginative world to another. Elements of the juvenilia can be traced in all three of the sisters' later novels and their early literary creations can be viewed as their apprenticeship as authors. It is important to stress, however, that the Brontë juvenilia are of interest in themselves, both for their own literary merit and for their biographical and historical value.

Alexander, Christine, *A Bibliography of the Manuscripts of Charlotte Brontë* (1982).
Alexander *EW*.
Alexander *EEW*.
Alexander, Christine, 'Editorial Creations and Editorial Compromise: The Art of the Possible in the Case of the Brontës', in M. Blackman, F. Muecke, and M. Sankey (eds.), *The Textual Condition: Rhetoric and Editing* (1995), 110–27.
—— 'Victorian Juvenilia', in William Baker and Kenneth Womack (eds.), *A Companion to the Victorian Novel* (2001).
—— and Rosengarten, Herbert J., 'The Brontës', in Joanne Shattock (ed.), *The Cambridge Bibliography of English Literature*, 4 (3rd edn., 1999), 12–24.
Barker, Juliet (ed.), *Charlotte Brontë: Juvenilia 1829–1835* (1996).
Collins, Robert G. (ed.), *The Hand of the Arch-Sinner* (1993).
Conover, Robin St John, 'Creating Angria: Charlotte and Branwell Brontë's Collaboration', *BST* (1999), 24. 1. 16–32.
Gérin *Five Novelettes*.
Miscellaneous Writings.
Neufeldt *BB Works*.
Neufeldt, Victor A. (ed.), *A Bibliography of the Manuscripts of Patrick Branwell Brontë* (1985).
Ratchford, Fannie E., *The Brontës' Web of Childhood* (1941).

K

Kashna (Cashna). See QUAMINA, KASHNA (CASHNA).

Kavanagh, Julia (1824–77), novelist and biographer, born in Ireland, daughter of the writer Morgan Peter Kavanagh (d. 1874). Many of her writings reflect a knowledge of France gained during her early life there. In June 1850 Charlotte Brontë pitied the poor little dwarfish woman, wasting 'her brain to gain a living' in London since her father's desertion of his family. Charlotte appreciated her *Madeleine* (1848), *Woman in France during the Eighteenth Century* (2 vols., 1850), and *Nathalie* (1850) with its *Rochester-like hero, but found her *Women of Christianity* (1852) too pro-Catholic, and *Daisy Burns* (1853) a 'tawdry deformity'. See also SEQUELS AND 'INCREMENTAL LITERATURE'.

Kay-Shuttleworth, Sir James (1804–77), doctor, educational reformer, writer, and acquaintance of Charlotte Brontë; born Rochdale, Lancs., MD Edinburgh 1827; practised as a doctor in *Manchester, 1828–35. His work and publications led to sanitary and educational reforms. After acting as assistant Poor Law commissioner in East Anglia 1835–9, he became first secretary to the Committee of the Privy Council on Education in London. Through his work as joint founder of the Battersea Training College (1839–40) he met his future wife, Janet Shuttleworth, whose surname he added to his own on their marriage in February 1842. A highly strung, obsessively hard-working man, he suffered a serious nervous breakdown after a prolonged epileptic fit in December 1848. He was eventually induced to resign from the Committee, and a baronetcy was conferred in December 1849. Rumours of 'Currer Bell's' identity reached the Kay-Shuttleworths at *Gawthorpe Hall by January 1850, when they invited her to visit them. She refused, but after they visited Haworth Parsonage on 8 March, reluctantly accepted, staying at Gawthorpe from 12 until 15 or 16 March. Sir James's invitation to stay in his London house that summer dismayed her: though genuinely kind, he had an insistent, too courtly manner which she found oppressive.

In the event his ill health meant that she stayed with the George *Smiths. In August she visited the Kay-Shuttleworths at Briery Close, Windermere, and saw Sir James again in December 1850. In summer 1851, they arranged for her to meet famous people and see splendid collections of paintings in London.

In November 1854, after Charlotte's marriage, Sir James offered her husband a curacy at Habergham, which he declined. A chill caught at Gawthorpe in January 1855 endangered her already precarious health. After her death Sir James visited the Parsonage with Elizabeth Gaskell, and coolly took away many manuscripts for her use in the *Life*.

Kay-Shuttleworth, Janet, Lady (1817–72), heiress of Robert Shuttleworth of *Gawthorpe Hall. In 1839 she asked James Kay's advice on improving Gawthorpe school. They married in 1842, and had five children: Janet Elizabeth (1843–1914), Ughtred James (1844–1939), Robert (1847–1934), Lionel Edward (1849–1900), and Stewart Marjoribanks (1851–87). Charlotte Brontë liked the children's governess, Rosa Poplawska, but Rosa encouraged Janet's religiosity and invalidism, and influenced her decision to separate from her husband from September 1854. Janet repeated to Elizabeth *Gaskell the slanderous gossip of Mrs Brontë's former nurse, attributing to Revd Patrick Brontë eccentricities afterwards proclaimed in the *Life*.

Keeldar, Shirley, the eponymous heroine of Charlotte Brontë's novel *Shirley*. At 21, she comes into a fortune of £20,000 and moves to *Fieldhead, the family mansion in the parish of *Briarfield in the West Riding of Yorkshire. She is accompanied there by her former governess and now companion, Mrs *Pryor. Strong-minded, articulate, and independent of spirit, Shirley holds her own with the local patriarchy headed by Revd Matthewson *Helstone. With the financial independence bestowed by an income of £1,000 a year, and holding a man's position in that she is 'lord of the manor', she acts and speaks with greater freedom and authority than might be expected of a young single woman in England at the beginning of the 19th century. She soon meets Robert Gérard *Moore, the manufacturer who leases *Hollow's Mill from her; they become close friends, and when he is in particularly desperate financial straits, she lends him £5,000. She attempts to help the poor of the neighbourhood through charity and 'good works', but her sympathies lie with Moore, and she has no time for the mob violence directed against his mill. Shirley also befriends Moore's cousin Caroline *Helstone; however, by encouraging Robert's friendship (which culminates in his unsuccessful proposal of marriage) she unwittingly separates Caroline from the man she loves. Shirley secretly loves Robert's brother Louis Gérard *Moore, who had been her tutor when she lived with the *Sympson family; that love blooms when Louis arrives with the Sympsons to stay at Field-head. Surviving a dogbite, the urgent attentions of Sir Philip *Nunnely, and the anger of her uncle and former guardian Mr Sympson, Shirley makes public her feelings for the impoverished tutor, and is eventually united with him in marriage.

Though there are similarities between Shirley and Charlotte's Angrian heroine Jane *Moore (see Ratchford, *The Brontës' Web of Childhood*, 1941), in a number of respects she embodies aspects of Emily Brontë's nature and experience: in her self-cauterizing after being bitten by a dog; in her stoical refusal to see a doctor despite illness; in her fierce insistence on liberty; and in her passionate love of wild nature. Mrs Gaskell maintains that Charlotte 'tried to depict [Emily's] character in Shirley Keeldar, as what Emily Brontë would have been, had she been placed in health and prosperity' (*Life*, 2. 116). Shirley may also resemble Emily in her almost mystical apprehension of nature, though the former's extrovert manner hardly reflects what we know of the desperately shy and private person that was Emily. Ivy Holgate ('The Structure of *Shirley*', *BST* (1962), 14. 72. 27–35) sees Shirley as an amalgam of Emily Brontë and Charlotte's outspoken and fiercely independent friend Mary *Taylor. Certainly Shirley acts with a vigour that Charlotte had identified in Mary years before, telling Ellen Nussey in 1841 that 'Mary alone has more energy and power in her nature than any ten men you can pick out in the united parishes of Birstal and Gomersal. It is vain to limit a character like hers within ordinary boundaries—she will overstep them—I am morally certain Mary will establish her own landmarks' (Smith *Letters*, 1. 242–3). A different approach is taken by Mrs Humphry Ward who proposes in her introduction to the Haworth edition of *Shirley* (1900) that 'Charlotte Brontë has expressed in the picture of Shirley that wilder and more romantic element of her own being, which found a little later far richer and stronger utterance in "Villette"' (p. xxvii). Most readers, however, are probably less preoccupied with the question of biographical or autobiographical elements than with the seeming change in Shirley's behaviour towards the end of the novel. Until Louis makes his appearance, Shirley embodies an individualism and a fierce independence that to modern critics mark her as protofeminist; but the brilliant heiress, the self-styled 'Captain Keeldar' who briskly gives orders and treats her subordinates with a self-assurance grounded in rank, must cede her strength and authority to the powerless and impoverished Louis Moore in order to make his conquest possible.

This somewhat improbable surrender is attributable in part to the writer's wish-fulfilment, a union bringing restoration of loved ones to secure and lasting happiness; it is also consistent with Charlotte's strong Tory belief in a class-based status quo, a view that sometimes struggles with her compassion for and identification with those, whether factory hands or women, who are marginalized in an industrialized and patriarchal society.   HR

Keeper, the 'tawny strong limbed' dog described by Ellen Nussey as 'Emily's favourite, he was so completely under her control she could quite easily make him spring and roar like a lion' (Smith *Letters*, 1. 600). She tells how Emily habitually read, kneeling on the hearth with her arm round Keeper, an image used by Charlotte in *Shirley* where Keeper is the model for *Tartar. The famous story of Emily's savage pummelling of the dog's head as punishment for his habit of lying on the beds upstairs was first told by Elizabeth Gaskell (*Life*, 1. 309–10). She also records how Keeper followed his mistress's coffin to the grave and moaned for nights outside her bedroom door. Keeper died three years later in December 1851 and is buried in the garden of Haworth Parsonage. To the local inhabitants of Haworth, Keeper seemed a ferocious dog. A contemporary, John Stores Smith, described him as a 'conglomerate, combining every species of English caninity from the turnspit to the sheepdog, with a strain of Haworth originality superadded' (quoted in Smith *Letters*, 1. 332).

Keighley, a populous manufacturing town with numerous mills, 4 miles from Haworth at the confluence of the rivers Aire and Worth, in the Yorks. woollen district. Its prosperity was increased by the nearby Leeds and Liverpool Canal, and the population expanded from 5,745 in 1801 to 18,258 in 1851. Some low-lying areas like Dalton Lane were notoriously overcrowded and filthy, and there was considerable unrest among the workers, unrest of the kind dramatized in the conflicts between hard masters and ill-treated workers in Charlotte Brontë's *The Professor* and *Shirley*. A woolcombers' strike began on 18 November 1846 and four to five thousand pro-Chartist workers gathered in Keighley market place in early 1848. Whole families depended on millwork for their livelihood: Henry Robinson, who wrote to Charlotte on 23 July 1851, belonged to a family of worsted spinners and manufacturers of Strong Close Mill, who then employed 63 men, 71 women, 12 boys, and 4 girls. Many of the mill owners' mansions stood in their own pleasant grounds: the Sugdens' classical Eastwood House, built in 1819 (still extant), stood in a spacious park. John Greenwood, Sarah *Sidgwick's father, lived at the Knowle, in

'Keeper—from life', watercolour by Emily Brontë, 24 April 1838.

a comparatively rural area; and the Greenwoods' relative, Henry Clapham, and his wife Mary, née *Robinson, lived in style at Aireworth House. After their marriage in 1848, the bride 'cut a dash' in her new carriage, infuriating the Keighley gentry.

Keighley's old parish church of St Peter was pulled down, rebuilt in 1805–6, and later replaced by a handsome Gothic church (for which Sarah Sidgwick's brother Frederick laid the foundation stone in 1846) consecrated 11 August 1848. Revd Patrick Brontë occasionally officiated at marriages for his friend Revd Theodore *Dury, and Dury's successor William Busfeild (1802–78). Possibly Charlotte heard how in March 1835 a mother of 'one of the parties' rose from her seat when banns were announced and said 'I forbid that'—to the amusement of the congregation (John Mayhall, *The Annals of Yorkshire from the Earliest Period to the Present Time* (1862), 1. 425). The wealthy Sugdens, like the Greenwoods, were benefactors of Keighley church, and were kind to the deserted wife of the curate John *Collins. Another Keighley curate, James William *Smith, absconded in 1848. The Roman Catholic St Anne's church by Pugin opened in North Street in 1840. The imposing Wesleyan Methodist chapel (1846) stands in Temple Street, where traditional stone 'setts' (small paving stones) and 19th-century cottages and shops survive. The Brontës walked or hired a gig to Keighley when they needed goods not available in Haworth, or attended meetings at the church or the *Keighley Mechanics' Institute. Possibly they borrowed books from a lending library kept by Thomas Duckett Hudson of 32 High Street, Bookseller, Stationer, Binder, and Chemist. Their longer journeys by coach, on the Leeds–Kendal turnpike road, or, from March 1847 by train on the Aire Valley *railway, involved a preliminary journey to Keighley; and the manuscript of *Jane Eyre* was despatched from Keighley's small 'station-house' on 24 August 1847, before the building of a more substantial station in c.1849. Visitors to Haworth could take a 'conveyance' from Keighley's coaching inn near the church, the Devonshire Arms, still extant under a different name.

Keighley Mechanics' Institute, founded in 1825 as 'a society for mutual instruction, and to establish a library for that purpose' by four *Keighley tradesmen: John *Bradley (house and sign painter and sometime artist), John Farish (reed-maker), William Dixon (tailor), and John Haigh (joiner) (*Yorkshire Ridings Magazine* (June 1968), 27). Bradley was the Institute's first secretary and was elected vice-president in 1831 and the architect of its new building, opened on 29 December 1834 (later the Yorkshire Bank, demolished in 1968).

Revd Theodore Dury, Rector of St Andrew's, Keighley, from 1814 to 1840, is also said to have been a guiding spirit (Lock & Dixon, p. 274). Revd Patrick Brontë joined in 1833, his membership number being 213 and admission fee 5s., plus a contribution of twopence per week. This entitled him to use the reading-room, the library and apparatus, and to attend lectures and classes. In 1833, the Mechanics' Institute had 93 members and 625 volumes in its library, chiefly on science, travel, and philosophy, although its catalogue includes many other books the Brontës are known to have read (Clifford Whone, 'Where the Brontës Borrowed Books', *BST* (1950), 11. 60. 344–58). Ian Dewhirst has pointed out that Mr Brontë's role in the Mechanics' Institute was not as great as has been assumed ('The Rev. Patrick Brontë and the Keighley Mechanics' Institute,' *BST* (1965), 14. 75. 35–7). His name is mentioned only occasionally in the Institute minutes and he is known to have taken part in the regular lecture programme sponsored by the Institute. The lectures were chiefly on scientific topics in the early days but later included other subjects, such as the popular course on 'Ancient British Poetry' in 1832, given by William *Dearden, former schoolmaster of Keighley and a friend of the Brontës. By 1835, free lectures were given fortnightly on such subjects as Napoleon, geography, and Poland. In April 1840, Charlotte Brontë noted that both her father and Revd William *Weightman had given several lectures (Smith *Letters*, 1. 214, 216 n.). The Brontë sisters and Ellen *Nussey attended Weightman's first lecture on 'The Advantages of Classical Studies' and were escorted to Keighley and back on foot by the very lively speaker. In early 1841, Mr Brontë gave a lecture on 'the Influence of Circumstances', but by 1846 his name was gone from the list of members (Dewhirst, p. 36). The Mechanics' Institute also sponsored concerts, the most memorable being in December 1834, to celebrate the opening of their new building for which they brought professional singers from *Leeds (Barker, p. 212). A Mechanics' Institute of which Charlotte Brontë was 'the most distinguished member and patroness' was established in nearby *Haworth (report in the *Leeds Mercury*, 14 Apr. 1855). See MECHANICS' INSTITUTES.

Kenneth, Mr, the doctor from Gimmerton who attends the inhabitants of Wuthering Heights and Thrushcross Grange in *Wuthering Heights*.

Killarney, County Kerry, Ireland, is near three beautiful lakes which lie between Macgillicuddy's Reeks and Mangerton. Charlotte Brontë and Revd A. B. *Nicholls stayed in Killarney during their honeymoon; but as she rode through the Gap of

Dunloe on the high, steep, narrow, rock-strewn track, she glimpsed the 'very grim Phantom' of imminent death, when her horse seemed suddenly to go mad, rearing and plunging so that she was thrown on the stones beneath it. Nicholls, holding it, was at first unaware of her fall. When he let go the horse sprang over her, miraculously leaving her untouched (letter of 27 July 1854 to Catherine *Winkworth, in Wise & Symington, letter 907).

King, Robert Patrick. See SDEATH, ROBERT PATRICK.

King Boy and King Jack. These two black military commanders lead Quashia *Quamina's *Ashantee forces during the Angrian Wars in the *Glass Town and Angrian saga. They become the subject of mockery in a poem in *Caroline Vernon*:

With King Boy & King Jack both genteely in black
Forming Holy Alliance & breathing defiance
Nor a Prince finding brandy every day coming handy
While he's conquering of lands with his bold nigger
      bands.

King Boy also appears in Branwell Brontë's *And the Weary are at Rest. The name derives from a reference in *Blackwood's* to 'King's Boys', liberated Africans in Sierra Leone who were taught trades, such as those of masons and carpenters. 'These men work when they please, and as they please' ('Sierra Leone: Civilization of Africa', *Blackwood's Edinburgh Magazine*, 21 (May 1827), 603).

Kingston, Eliza Jane (Elizabeth) (1808–78), cousin of the Brontë sisters; fifth child of Jane, née Branwell (1773–1855) (see BRANWELL FAMILY) and John Kingston (?1768–1824), a Methodist preacher and former missionary who was expelled from the Methodist Connexion in 1807. The family emigrated, and Eliza was born in Baltimore, Maryland. Jane Kingston left her husband in April 1809 and brought Eliza back to *Penzance. Charlotte Brontë's letters to her in 1846 are affectionate and sympathetic. She and the Brontë sisters had equal shares in Elizabeth *Branwell's legacy, but Eliza's Cornish mining investments proved unfortunate, and she declined into extreme poverty.

Kipping House, Kipping Lane, Thornton, home of Dr John Scholefield *Firth (1757–1820) and his daughter Elizabeth (later Mrs *Franks), good friends of the Brontës and godparents to several of the children. The Brontës regularly took tea at Kipping House during Revd Patrick Brontë's curacy at Thornton from 1815 to 1820, and when Anne Brontë was born (17 January 1820) the Brontë children spent the day there. When he moved to Haworth, Mr Brontë occasionally stayed at Kipping House en route to Bradford and after Mrs Brontë's death in 1821, Maria and Elizabeth Brontë spent a

month at Kipping House to relieve the burden of their distressed father. Kipping House, a Georgian structure made of stone, still survives.

Kirby, Mr and Mrs Isaac, of 2 Fountain Street, Bradford, where Branwell Brontë lodged for a year from May 1838, to pursue a career in portrait painting under the patronage of Revd William *Morgan who secured the accommodation for him. Kirby (d. 1844) was a wholesale 'dealer in London & Dublin, Double XX Stout, Porter etc' and 'Scotch Ales' (*Bradford Observer*, 4 May 1837), which he sold from his commercial premises opposite the Rawson Arms in Market Street. His wife Margaret ran a lodging house with a household of ten listed in the 1841 Census. Branwell rented two rooms, one of which he used as a studio. He appears to have lodged amicably with the family, growing fond of the Kirby's young nephew and niece, Thomas and Margaret Hartley, believed to be orphans and born in *Broughton-in-Furness, Cumberland, Mrs Kirby's home county. His portraits of Mr and Mrs Kirby and Margaret Hartley, probably painted in lieu of rent, are among the best of Branwell's oil paintings (Alexander & Sellars, pp. 329–32). The contrast between the swarthy, doleful Mr Kirby and his tight-lipped wife compared to their shy, sweet-faced niece suggests the different relationships between the artist and his sitters. Margaret Hartley had positive memories of Branwell: 'He was a very steady young gentleman, his conduct was exemplary, and we liked him very much' she later recalled (W. W. Yates, 'The Brontë Family: A Suggestion. Two Years in the Life of Branwell Brontë', *Dewsbury Reporter*, 25 Nov. 1893).

Kirkby Lonsdale, a handsome market town in the Lune valley, Westmorland (now Cumbria), on the road from Settle to Kendal, the model for *Lowton in *Jane Eyre*. The Leeds–Kendal coach used by Revd Patrick Brontë in taking his daughters to school passed through *Cowan Bridge, about 2 miles to the south-east. Kirkby had a free grammar school, shops, a coaching inn, carpet and blanket manufactories, and a churchyard from which an attractive view of the fells and of Casterton Hall, the home of Revd W. Carus *Wilson's parents, could be seen.

Kirkham-Lodge, near Kirkham Wood, in the province of *Angria, on the estate of Lord *Hartford, in the *Glass Town and Angrian saga; home of George *Moore and his daughter Jane, the 'lady of Kirkham Lodge'.

Kirklees Priory. The ruins of a 12th-century Cistercian priory, in the grounds of Kirklees Hall. They lie in a green valley west of *Hartshead. Elizabeth Gaskell describes its sunny glades, black shadows of yew-trees, 'grey pile of buildings', and 'mouldering stone in the depth of the wood, under which Robin Hood is said to lie'. The bow windows of *Roe Head overlooked pastureland ending in Kirklees woods, 'Sir George Armitage's park' (Gaskell *Life*, 1. 101). In *Shirley* (ch. 12) Caroline and Shirley plan to 'penetrate into Nunnwood', where the ruins of a nunnery lie in a deep hollow dell.

Kirkstall Abbey. The ruins of a Cistercian abbey founded by Henry de Lacy in 1147 in the Aire valley, north-west of *Leeds. Maria Branwell and Jane Fennell enjoyed the 5-mile riverside walk there from *Woodhouse Grove school in the company of Revd Patrick Brontë, who is said to have proposed marriage to Maria on one such visit (Wise & Symington, 1. 12, 18). He recalled its ruined tower and 'arches ivy-crowned' that 'enchant the heart' in 'Kirkstall Abbey, A Fragment of a Romantic Tale', in the *Rural Minstrel*. Charlotte made a watercolour and two drawings of Kirkstall Abbey (Alexander & Sellars, pp. 203–4, 229–30).

Kirkwall, Sir John, the quintessential Angrian; MP in the Verdopolitan Parliament, in the *Glass Town and Angrian saga. Like Warner's family in the province of Angria, the Kirkwalls are one of the oldest landed families in the province of Zamorna. John Kirkwall is the head and lives at Meadowbank. He and his wife always make an annual visit to the Moores, at Kirkham Wood, Arundel. Their son, Charles Kirkwall, was to marry Harriet Moore, Jane *Moore's eldest sister who died. Another son, Captain Frank Kirkwall, 'a scoundrelly young blade', is wounded (presumably in a duel) by Warner's youngest brother Sergeant Vincent James Warner. A brother, the Rt. Revd Dr Kirkwall, is primate of Zamorna. For the origins of the name Kirkwall, see ST CLAIR, LORD RONALD ROSLYN, EARL.

Knoll, The. A sturdy, compact, stone-built house on the outskirts of *Ambleside. In 1845 Harriet *Martineau enjoyed planning it and supervising its building before making it her home from April 1846, though she often travelled elsewhere in summer to escape the influx of Lake District tourists. Wordsworth planted two stone-pines in the garden, and helped to choose a sundial motto, 'Come, Light! Visit me!' During her stay there from 18 to ?24 December 1850 Charlotte Brontë found the house pleasant, neat, and comfortable, and spent the mornings in the drawing room while Harriet worked in her study; sociable afternoons and evenings followed.

Knox, Dr Robert. See BURKE AND HARE.

Kœkelberg, Château de. The so-called Château de Kœkelberg was a finishing school primarily for English pupils, kept by Mme Catherine Goussaert, née Phelps, at 123 Chaussée de Jette, west of *Brussels. Built after 1820, and demolished after 1888, it resembled *La Terrasse in *Villette*, with its garden, plantations, and avenue. It was situated where the Boulevard Leopold II now crosses the northbound railway line from the Gare de l'ouest (Joan Stevens, *Mary Taylor* (19/2) p. 172). Martha *Taylor attended the school from May 1841 until her death. Charlotte and Emily visited it after Mary *Taylor joined Martha there in February 1842, but it had many specialist teachers and was too expensive for them to attend.

K.T., a correspondent of Charlotte Brontë in November–December 1850, who introduced him (or her)self as an admirer of 'Currer Bell's' work, warning her that 'Kitty Bell, the Orphan', a plagiary of *Jane Eyre*, had begun to appear in G. W. M. Reynolds's *London Journal*, and offering to send opinions of *Shirley*. Charlotte replied courteously to the resultant verbose analysis of *Shirley's* inferiority to *Jane Eyre*. The unidentified K.T.'s letters indicate a 30-year-old Irish professional artist, possibly an engraver or scene-painter, using an accommodation address, 'Miss Kelly's, 153 Fleet St., London'; perhaps associated with the actress Frances Maria Kelly (*DNB*).

L

L——, a very large town in *Jane Eyre*, about half-way between *Gateshead Hall and *Lowood, where the coach taking Jane to school stops at an inn so that passengers may dine. Since *Cowan Bridge ('Lowood') was on the Leeds–Kendal coach route, Charlotte Brontë may be thinking of Leeds.

Labassecour (the 'poultry-yard' or 'farmyard') in *Villette* is Charlotte Brontë's condescending name for a country obviously based on Belgium, one of the 'Low Countries'. Its countryside, people, and history are all belittled. The fields are 'tilled like kitchen garden beds', the capital is Villette ('little town'), the prince is the Duc de Dindonneau, a young turkey. Mme *Beck's name recalls a bird's 'bec', the portress Rosine's surname is 'Matou' (tomcat), and Lucy's pupils are a 'swinish multitude'. The Park with its pasteboard splendours commemorates a little revolution, when brickbats 'and even a little shot' were interchanged. But Paul *Emanuel, we note, is neither Labassecourien nor French.

Lady's Magazine, The; Or Entertaining Companion for the Fair Sex (1770–1848), one of the most influential periodicals of the later 18th and early 19th century. Published monthly and sold for sixpence a copy, it promised to entertain and educate through poetry, short stories, and serialized fiction, chiefly Gothic romances intended to appeal to a female audience. In a letter dated 10 December 1840, Charlotte told Hartley *Coleridge that she had read the *Lady's Magazine* long ago 'before I knew how to criticize or object—they were old books belonging to my mother or my Aunt; they had crossed the Sea, had suffered shipwreck and were discoloured with brine—I read them as a treat on holiday afternoons or by stealth when I should have been minding my lessons—I shall never see anything which will interest me so much again—One black day my father burnt them because they contained foolish love-stories' (Smith *Letters*, 1. 240). She likens her own novel-ettes, in particular *Ashworth*, to stories in the

Lady's Magazine, such as A. Kendall's *Derwent Priory: A Novel. In a Series of Letters*, published anonymously in 22 parts from January 1796 to September 1797 (repr. in 2 vols, 1798). Coleridge had criticized the profusion of characters and the romantic tenor of the sample writing Charlotte had sent him (draft fragments of *Ashworth*), and she half-jokingly wished she had been 'born in time to contribute to the Lady's magazine' when 'my aspirations after literary fame would have met with due encouragement'. In *Shirley* (ch. 22) Caroline Helstone also cherishes 'some venerable Lady's Magazines, that had once performed a sea-voyage with their owner, and undergone a storm, and whose pages were stained with salt water'. Charlotte's mother had sent for her books from Penzance to Yorkshire after her marriage, but her trunk suffered shipwreck and very few articles were saved (see TRAVEL BY THE BRONTËS).

La Fontaine, Jean de (1621–95), French poet best known for his *Fables*. Since they first appeared, children have committed them to memory, a fact that two of Charlotte Brontë's novels dramatize. In *Jane Eyre* Adèle Varens declaims his fable 'The League of Rats' ('La Ligue des Rats') 'with an attention to punctuation and emphasis, a flexibility of voice and an appropriateness of gesture, very unusual indeed at her age' (ch. 11). In *Shirley* the protagonist warmly recalls reciting 'The Oak and the Reed' ('Le Chêne et le Roseau') under Louis Gérard *Moore's guidance (ch. 27). M. Constantin *Heger gave Charlotte an anthology that included this fable. He may also have paraphrased one of its lines in his revision of her devoir, 'The *Death of Napoleon'. SL

Lonoff, p. 434 n.

Lake District, in the former counties of Cumberland and Westmorland (now Cumbria), with the high peaks of Scafell, Scafell Pike, and Great Gable at its centre. Irregular mountain ridges stretch from the centre towards the lowlands bordering on the Solway Firth, Irish Sea, and Morecambe Bay. The Eden valley to the north-east forms a finger of lowland between Shap Fells and the Pennines. The lakes in the valleys between the ridges include the dark depths of Wastwater, between austere scree slopes, the milder beauties of Derwentwater and Windermere, and the sinuous long curves of Ullswater, on whose western shore *Wordsworth saw his daffodils and 'Aira force which thunders down the Ghyll'. Charlotte Brontë and her sisters were copying 'views of the lakes' when she wrote to her father on 23 September 1829. Paintings and drawings of the Lake District had proliferated since its 'discovery' as an English Arcadia in the mid-18th century. The Brontes associated it, too, with the Lake Poets and other writers whose work they loved: Charlotte and Branwell wrote to Wordsworth, Hartley *Coleridge, and *De Quincey, and Charlotte (famously) to *Southey. Branwell became familiar with the southern mountains, such as Black Combe, when he lived at *Broughton-in-Furness. In August 1850 Sir James *Kay-Shuttleworth acted as guide to Charlotte and Elizabeth Gaskell when they stayed at Briery Close, and only rain prevented them from meeting Tennyson, staying with his bride at Tent Lodge, Coniston; but Charlotte longed to drop unseen from the carriage and go away by herself 'amongst those grand hills and sweet dales' to drink in 'the full power of this glorious scenery' (Gaskell *Life*, 2. 173). She did, however, meet the *Arnold family in the 'exquisitely beautiful' surroundings of Fox How, both then and in December 1850, when she stayed with Harriet *Martineau in *Ambleside.

Lalande, Mme, *Northangerland's French mistress in the *Glass Town and Angrian saga, rival of Lady Georgina Greville and Louisa *Vernon. She owns the Château de Bois at Orleannois, and stays at Demry's Hotel when in Verdopolis.

Lamartine, Alphonse de (1790–1869), early French Romantic poet and politician. For classes with Emily and Charlotte Brontë, M. Constantin *Heger drew excerpts from two of his books, *Poetic and Religious Harmonies* (*Harmonies poétiques et religieuses*, 1830) and *Poetic Contemplations* (*Recueillements poétiques*, 1839). In his comment on Charlotte's *devoir 'The Nest', he proposes to analyse one of Lamartine's *Harmonies* with her 'from the point of view of the details'. Evidence that she read this poem, 'The Infinite' ('L'Infini'), can be found in her devoir 'The Immensity of God'. She also transcribed a *dictation of Lamartine's 'Epitaph for French Prisoners who Died in English Captivity' ('Épitaphe des prisonniers français morts pendant leur captivité en Angleterre'). Politically he was an idealist, a fact that Charlotte sceptically observed in writing to W. S. *Williams on 11 March 1848 about the French Revolution of that year: 'Lamartine, there is no doubt, would make an excellent legislator for a nation of Lamartines—but where is that nation?' (Smith *Letters*, 2. 41).   SL

Lonoff, pp. 42–3, 52–5, 188.

landscapes associated with the Brontës. Charlotte Brontë wrote in her preface to the second edition of *Wuthering Heights* that 'the wild moors of the north of England can for [strangers] have no interest' (*Wuthering Heights* (Clarendon edn.), app. 1); yet she and her sisters have been responsible for transforming what she saw as a 'mon-

otonous' but much-loved natural setting into one of the most famous literary landscapes in the English-speaking world. Elizabeth *Gaskell's dramatic opening to her *Life* of Charlotte also did much to evoke the atmosphere and scene which have become synonymous with the Brontë legend.

The landscape of the Yorkshire moors and villages with its windswept vegetation, its bird and animal life, its grey stone cottages and isolated farms plays a central role in the Brontë novels and also informs their childhood sagas, despite the ostensibly exotic settings (see GONDAL SAGA; GLASS TOWN AND ANGRIAN SAGA; YORKSHIRE; HAWORTH). The overwhelming effect of landscape on character in *Wuthering Heights*, in particular, accounts in large measure for the unique power of that novel. It reflects the moral and philosophical creed of its author and helps, in part, to explain Emily's intense attachment to her home locality (see NATURAL HISTORY AND THE BRONTËS). As Charlotte explained, 'where the love of wild nature is strong, the locality will perhaps be clung to with the more passionate constancy' (*Wuthering Heights*, app. 1). Thus Emily 'found in the bleak solitude many and dear delights; and not the least and best loved was—liberty'. The windswept Yorkshire moors have now become associated in popular culture, through books and films, with an image of freedom.

The more benign landscape of east Yorkshire and the coast near *Scarborough is associated with Anne Brontë and her novels. As with her sisters, her experience as a teacher provided her with a detailed knowledge of a number of fine old houses and estates (for example *Thorp Green Hall, *Oakwell Hall, and *Shibden Hall). The 'purple moors' and 'hollow vale' of the Peak District, where Charlotte visited, are said to be the models for the landscape surrounding *Moor House in *Jane Eyre* (ch. 30); and the former prosperous woollen-mill *Dewsbury district surrounding *Mirfield, where Charlotte was for so many years at *Roe Head school, has become known as 'Shirley Country'. Branwell's experience of the Lake District, where he was a tutor, can be seen in his later manuscripts, although the influence of Sir Walter *Scott also had a significant effect on his and Emily's landscape descriptions. Emily appears not to have been impressed by her sojourn in *Brussels, but the landscapes of both *The Professor* and *Villette* attest to the deep impression that city made on Charlotte's literary imagination.

DeCuir, Andre L., 'The Portrayal of Nature in Her Tribute to Emily: Charlotte Brontë's Shirley', *BST* (1999), 24. 1. 50–4.
Duthie, Enid L., *The Brontës and Nature* (1986).

Flintoff, Eddie, *In the Steps of the Brontës* (1993) (walking tours).

Heywood, Christopher, 'Pennine Landscapes in *Jane Eyre* and *Wuthering Heights*', BST (2001), 26. 2. 187–98.

Marsden, Hilda, 'The Moorlands: The Timeless Contemporary', BST (1990), 20. 1. 25–33.

Pollard, Arthur, *The Landscape of the Brontës* (1988).

Landseer, Sir Edwin Henry (1802–73), English painter, sculptor, and engraver of animal subjects, whose work was known to and copied by the Brontës. The bronze lions at the foot of Nelson's Monument in Trafalgar Square, London, were modelled by him (1859–66). His painting—widely disseminated through prints of engravings made by his brother—was immensely popular with the Victorian public and he was Queen Victoria's favourite painter. His historical and Highland subjects, such as the famous *Monarch of the Glen* (1850) and *Dignity and Impudence* (1839), despite their tendency to sentimentalize animals or moralise, were consonant with the Brontës' interest in Scotland and love of *animals. *The Old Shepherd's Chief Mourner* (1837) inspired Branwell's sonnet 'On Landseer's painting—"The Shepherd's Chief Mourner" A dog keeping watch at twilight over its master's grave', 28 April 1842 (Neufeldt *BBP*, pp. 456–7). In July 1830, Charlotte copied an engraving of Landseer's *Hours of Innocence* from the annual *Friendship's Offering*, but found the dog too difficult to draw, replacing it with a flowering shrub (Alexander & Sellars, p. 174).

Lascelles Hall, one of three halls at Lepton, east of *Huddersfield. The 17th-century New Hall incorporated Lowerside and Overside halls. The late 16th-century Old Hall was the home of Charlotte Brontë's fellow pupil at *Roe Head, Amelia *Walker. In 1809 Amelia's father, Joseph Walker, inherited it and began to 'gentrify' it by laying out extensive park-like grounds, but he neglected the rest of the estate buildings, some of which were used as commercial premises by Huddersfield firms. Charlotte visited it with Anne Brontë and Joseph Walker's cousin Mrs Elizabeth *Franks on 21 June 1836, and by herself in January 1839, when she wished 'the visit were well over' (Smith *Letters*, 1. 184).

La Terrasse is a secluded château beyond the Porte de Crécy in *Villette*. Lucy *Snowe is taken there by Père *Silas and Dr John *Bretton after her swoon near the Béguinage, and on waking she recognizes the furnishings of her godmother's English home. Charlotte was recalling the Château de *Kœkelberg.

La Trobe, Revd James (1802–97; elected bishop 1863). A pastor of Huguenot descent, La Trobe attended the *Moravian boarding school at Fulneck, Pudsey, Yorks., taught there 1821–7, and returned to the area as an ordained minister and director of the Mirfield Moravian boarding school 1836–41. His second wife Mary, née Grimes, had taught at the Gomersal Moravian Ladies' Academy, briefly attended by Ellen Nussey. Anne Brontë asked him to visit her during her serious illness at *Roe Head in late 1837. His emphasis on God's redeeming love brought her peace of mind, encouraging her to embrace the doctrine of *universal salvation.

Laury, Sergeant Edward (Ned), an early Glass Town soldier, *Rare Lad, and bodysnatcher in the *Glass Town and Angrian saga. He becomes a loyal retainer of the Duke of Wellington, retiring to Wellington's estates. *Something about Arthur* describes Laury's situation and his daughter Mina Laury's early infatuation for the Duke of Zamorna (Alexander *EEW*, 1. 7–40). A tall athletic man of 50, Edward Laury later serves Zamorna as chief ranger of his Angrian estates.

Laury, Mina, daughter of Sergeant Edward (Ned) *Laury, a loyal retainer of the Duke of Wellington, in the *Glass Town and Angrian saga, especially Charlotte Brontë's novelette of the same name, *Mina Laury*. A young peasant girl with dark curls, and large intense black eyes, she meets the youthful Duke of *Zamorna when she saves him from a tiger (Alexander *EEW* 2(1), 32–40). Their early love affair is nipped in the bud by Wellington, but she becomes maid first to Zamorna's mother and then to his second wife, Marian. After Marian's death she is entrusted with the care of Zamorna's children (see WELLESLEY, ERNEST) and becomes his devoted mistress. She loyally follows Zamorna wherever needed and goes into exile with him during the Angrian wars, but she lives chiefly as Zamorna's hostess at *Grassmere Manor and at the *Cross of Rivaulx. Courted by General Lord Edward *Hartford, she can think only of her idol, Zamorna. Charlotte Brontë's watercolour copy of William Finden's engraving of *The Maid of Saragoza* for *Byron's *Childe Harold*, inspired the description of Mina in *High Life in Verdopolis* and probably elsewhere. The name 'Mina' may be derived from Minna, lover of the pirate Cleveland in Sir Walter *Scott's *The Pirate*, illustrated by Sir William *Etty.

'Laussane A Trajedy'. See VERSE DRAMA BY BRANWELL BRONTË.

Law, Sir Alfred Joseph (1860–1939), owner and possibly contributor to the *Law Collection of manuscripts, letters, paintings, and rare books, which he inherited from his uncle William *Law. Alfred Joseph was the son of John Law, brother of William and Alfred Law who built up a successful flannel manufacturing firm in Lancashire. Alfred Joseph went into the family business, holding the position of governing director for many years and gaining a reputation as a 'model employer' (*Yorkshire Post*, 19 July 1939). He served as MP for Rochdale 1918–22, and for the High Peak Division of Derbyshire 1929 until his death. He was knighted for political services in 1927, prominent in Lancashire Freemasonry, a director of the Rochdale Canal Company, and he travelled overseas extensively.

Law, William (*c*.1836–1901), enthusiastic collector of paintings, manuscripts, and rare books, including a large number of Brontë manuscripts and relics. His important collection, now dispersed both by sale to subsequent collectors and inheritance, is known as the *Law Collection. A bachelor with a shy, retiring disposition, William Law led a very private life, quietly building up his valuable collection of literature and art, endowing his parish church where he was churchwarden and unobtrusively dispensing money to charity. His rare editions and manuscripts were housed in a fine library at his home 'Honresfeld', near Littleborough, in Rochdale. His collecting interests were supported by the highly successful flannel manufacturing firm of A. and W. Law, which he established with his brother Alfred, who inherited his collection and house. On the death of Alfred, also a bachelor, in 1839, William Law's fine collection passed to Sir Alfred Joseph *Law, the son of another brother John Law. William Law frequently visited Haworth in search of Brontë relics, purchasing a number of items from locals like William *Wood and Tabitha *Ratcliffe.

Law Collection, sometimes known as the Honresfeld Collection after the home of William *Law and his nephew Sir Alfred Joseph *Law in Littleborough, near Rochdale, Lancashire, where the collection was housed for many years and first inspected by the librarian Davidson Cook ('Literary Treasures of Honresfeld', *Bookman*, 68 (1925), 283–5). The collection was built up by William Law, a known collector of Brontëana in the 1890s, and when he died a bachelor in 1901 the collection and house passed first to his brother Alfred (d. 1913), and then to a nephew Alfred J. Law (son of John Law, another brother). It is unclear to what extent Alfred J. Law added to the collection, if at all, but he preserved the collection basically intact (some Brontë items were sold in 1933) in the magnificent Honresfeld Library (illustration in *Bookman*, 68 (1925), 283). The walls of Honresfeld were apparently adorned with paintings by Rembrandt, Turner, Holman Hunt, and others. Apart from business interests, William Law lived a retired life; and Sir Alfred's chief interest was politics. Thus the Law Collection was a well-kept secret from

its inception, just as the whereabouts of the remnants of the collection remain private today.

In its heyday the Law Collection contained a stunning array of items ranging from rare books such as 15th-century missals and medieval books of hours, a Shakespeare Quarto and First Folio, and the Kilmarnock Burns; to manuscript letters by Cowper, Jane Austen, Longfellow, and others; and original manuscripts of works by Burns, Scott (including that of 'Rob Roy'), Byron, and the Brontës. Many of these manuscripts have since been published, xeroxed, or transcribed; for example, the transcripts made by Davidson Cook in the BPM. William Law himself privately printed Burns's first Commonplace Book (1872) and in 1896 Clement K. Shorter published a facsimile of Emily Brontë's *Diary Paper of 30 July 1841, and several other items from the Law Collection, in *Charlotte Brontë and her Circle*. In 1895 William Law donated an oil painting by Branwell ('Jacob's Dream') to the Brontë Society, when the first Brontë Museum was opened, and lent a number of other items for exhibition including Emily Brontë's copy of *Poems* 1846. Davidson Cook describes a writing desk in the collection, belonging to Charlotte and 'crammed with relics' including 'several of the famous little MS. books' (*Bookman* (Nov. 1925), 101). William Law was particularly fond of Emily's work and one of his prize possessions was his leather-bound volume of her 'E.J.B. Notebook', transcribed in her hand and dated February 1844 (see POETRY OF EMILY BRONTË).

On 31 March 1933, a number of drawings and manuscripts from the Law Collection were offered for sale by Hodgson & Co. They were listed as 'The Property of a Collector' (obviously Sir J. Alfred Law). Approximately half of the items were sold, a number of them eventually reaching the BPM through the generosity of other collectors like J. Roy Coventry (see MANUSCRIPTS AND MANUSCRIPT COLLECTIONS). The BPM holds transcriptions (made by Davidson Cook and C. W. Hatfield) of most of the Brontë manuscripts in the Law Collection.

Alexander & Sellars.

Law Hill, Halifax, the site of Elizabeth *Patchett's school where Emily Brontë held a teaching post for almost six months, from the end of September 1838 until March 1839. The school was established in 1825 and listed as a 'Boarding Academy' in the *Halifax directories. Law Hill is a large square stone house with outbuildings, including a former wool-warehouse that was converted into a schoolroom for the 40 pupils, about half of whom were boarders who slept in the five large bedrooms on the first floor. There were also five attic rooms and spacious ground-floor reception rooms. The history and situation of the stone building, on a high hill exposed to the wind but with panoramic views, contributed to the story of *Wuthering Heights*. The building had originally been built by Jack Sharp whose behaviour was remarkably similar to that of Heathcliff. In the first half of the 18th century, Sharp, an orphan, had been adopted by his uncle John Walker of Walterclough Hall in Southowram. As he grew up, he 'developed an overbearing and unscrupulous character' and, 'abusing his uncle's kindness . . . gradually possessed himself of the main interests in the business' (Charles Simpson, *Emily Brontë* (1929), 54). On John Walker's death in 1771, his eldest son claimed his rights as heir and Sharp reluctantly left the Hall, promising revenge. He built Law Hill 1 mile away and enticed the easygoing son into gambling and ruin. He also managed to systematically degrade a young cousin of the heir (as Hareton Earnshaw was degraded), before becoming bankrupt himself and disappearing to London. Apparently Jack Sharp's manservant was called *Joseph and the surname of one of Miss Patchett's servants was *Earnshaw, a common name in the district.

Gérin *EB*, pp. 76–80.

Lawrence, Frederick, Helen *Huntingdon's brother, the squire of *Lindenhope and the owner of *Wildfell Hall, in *Tenant*. Though initially reluctant to endorse such a drastic step as leaving her husband, Frederick provides sanctuary for Helen and her son Arthur at the Hall. He himself lives at Woodford, in Lindenhope. His intimacy with Helen and resemblance to Arthur arouse suspicion amongst the residents of the village and eventually with the jealous Gilbert *Markham, who attacks him viciously with his whip, causing a head injury. However, Frederick forgives Gilbert when the truth is explained, and their friendship, strained as it is, is resumed. Gilbert gives Frederick good-natured advice about the dangers of marrying Jane Wilson (see WILSON FAMILY) and, in turn, he reluctantly accedes to Gilbert's requests for information about Helen after she has moved away. Gilbert believes Frederick disapproves of his desire to marry Helen, but it is really Gilbert's own reticence in enquiring about her and Frederick's natural reserve and passivity that are the cause of his silence about Helen. While staying with Helen after the death of her husband, Frederick meets and marries Esther *Hargrave.

Leaf from an Unopened Volume, A, 'Or The Manuscript of An Unfortunate Author. Edited by Lord Charles Albert Florian Wellesley' (Charlotte Brontë) (17 Jan. 1834). The manuscript of this Angrian novelette is a hand sewn booklet of nineteen pages (BPM), with title-page and preface by

the publisher Sergeant *Tree stating his determination 'to run all hazards in order to gratify public curiosity' despite the risk of offending those mentioned in the story. Lord Charles also addresses the reader, elaborately disowning responsibility for the contents of this 'volume' and explaining that he was forced to write 'mechanically as it were' at the dictation of a mysterious stranger. The narrative is a glimpse into the future of Angria, showing the Duke of *Zamorna at the height of his power but foretelling destruction and desolation for his family and friends. The drama centres on Zamorna's twin sons who re-enact the old rivalries between Zamorna and the Duke of Northangerland. Prince Alexander Ravenswood tries to thwart Prince Adrian Percy's plans to marry Zorayda, who believes she must avenge her supposed father Quashia *Quamina and kill Zamorna. She discovers that her mother was the daughter of Hector *Montmorency and her father was Sir William *Etty, the unrecognized son of Northangerland. Fannie Ratchford described this as 'The most melodramatic and unpleasant of all [Charlotte's] writing . . . a confused medley of intrigue, licentiousness, and fraternal hate, with illegitimate or disowned children, dwarfs, and Negroes playing leading parts' (*The Brontës' Web of Childhood* (1941), 83).

This is the first manuscript to describe the new kingdom of *Angria, which may suggest either that Charlotte had more to do with the establishment of Angria than previously thought or that the 'Unfortunate Author' is an alter ego of Branwell relating his plans (with Charlotte's obvious embellishments) for the future of the saga (Alexander *EEW*, 2(1). 324 n. 6; Alexander *EW*, p. 122). Whatever the case, the story indicates how far ahead the siblings planned their saga. The sense of internal corruption and the rise and fall of despotic empires conveyed here also suggests that the Brontës had some familiarity with Edward Gibbon's *The History of the Decline and Fall of the Roman Empire* (1776).

Alexander *EEW*, 2(1). 321–78.
Lemon, Charles (ed.), *A Leaf from an Unopened Volume* (1986).

Lee, Bessie. See BESSIE.

Leeds, Yorks., about 20 miles by road from Haworth. Now a city, Leeds was in the Brontës' lifetime a large and populous borough, the main centre of clothing manufacture in the north of England. Coaches plied on the turnpike roads radiating from its centre, and the Brontës reached *Cowan Bridge by coach on the route from Leeds to Kendal via *Keighley. Railways from Leeds were among the earliest to be built: the Leeds and Selby railway, begun in October 1830, and opened for passengers in September 1834, was used by Charlotte Brontë and Ellen Nussey on their way to *Bridlington in 1839. The Brontës' rail journeys to York and London were also made via Leeds.

The borough had several fine churches, many Dissenting chapels, a Roman Catholic chapel, and a free grammar school. Handsome houses lined the broad streets around Park Place and Park Square, but shoddy cottages were crowded in polluted courts and cul-de-sacs both in the centre and in the notoriously filthy suburbs of Hunslet and Holbeck. Asa Briggs notes that 75 cartloads of manure were removed from the Boot-and-Shoe Yard in Kirkgate during the 1831–2 cholera epidemic (*Victorian Cities* (1963), 145). The River Aire too was 'doubly-dyed' with waste from the mills. The terrifying spread of cholera from such areas is a recurring theme in Charlotte's letters.

Merchants, like the Brontës' friends the Taylors of Gomersal and the Nusseys, traded in the lofty 18th-century mixed Cloth Hall and the White Cloth Hall (1775). The borough had woollen and silk mills, several cotton mills worked by steam engines, metal foundries, chemical works, and other commercial enterprises. The principal streets were lit by gas, as were many of the factories. The General Infirmary, opened in 1771, and supported by benefactions and subscriptions, and the public dispensary, employed several distinguished doctors, notably the two Thomas Pridgin *Teales, father and son. Mr Teale sen. was called in to see Anne in January 1849, when he diagnosed pulmonary tuberculosis.

Mr Teale, like other well-educated Leeds citizens, was an active member of the Leeds Philosophical and Literary Society. A picture gallery belonging to the Northern Society for the Encouragement of the Fine Arts held regular exhibitions, in one of which (in 1834) drawings by Charlotte of Bolton Abbey and Kirkstall Abbey were displayed (Alexander & Sellars, pp. 228–9), as well as a colossal bust of Milton's 'Satan' by Branwell's friend Joseph Bentley *Leyland. Local printers and booksellers provided the two principal newspapers, the Whig *Leeds Mercury* and the Tory *Leeds Intelligencer*, both of them taken at Haworth Parsonage, and read by the whole family. Revd Patrick Brontë's best story, *The *Maid of Killarney*, published in London in 1818, was available from the booksellers Robinson & Co. in Leeds. More prosaically, Charlotte purchased special items of clothing, such as a white lace mantle, from shops in Leeds, and visited a dentist, Mr Atkinson, there. All in all, Leeds played a significant part in the lives of the Brontës.

Leeds Intelligencer. Established in 1754, the *Leeds Intelligencer* was one of the three local news-

papers read regularly in the Brontës' childhood home. Like *Blackwood's Edinburgh Magazine* and *Fraser's Magazine*, newspapers like the Tory *Intelligencer* and its Whig counterpart the *Leeds Mercury* gave the Brontë children access to a world of information and ideas they otherwise would not have known, and in this way contributed to their development as young writers. Stridently political, unabashedly personal, and sometimes libellous, such papers also provided Charlotte, Branwell, Emily, and Anne with models for their first writings, which often exhibit the lively, pugnacious style of early 19th-century provincial journalism. Alaric Watts's tenure as editor of the *Intelligencer* (1823–25) had already given the paper a touch of literary distinction when the young Brontës began to read it, and during the time of their most prolific juvenile writing, from 1829 through the 1830s, the warfare between the *Intelligencer* and the *Mercury* was conducted with unsurpassed virulence as well as verbal skill. Reinforcing this model of writing was the example set by their father, the Revd Patrick *Brontë, who submitted his own verse for publication in the *Intelligencer* and contributed a number of letters to its editor. For example, Mr Brontë's satirical poem on the Irish nationalist Daniel O'Connell, appearing in the *Leeds Intelligencer* on 21 January 1837 under his initials only, must have impressed his children, who were eagerly learning how to participate in the literary culture of their day. Not surprisingly, Charlotte and Branwell's juvenilia make frequent reference to newspapers and the periodical press. The characters of their imaginary city *Verdopolis avidly read, discuss, and reply to pieces published in local papers having names like 'The Verdopolitan Intelligencer', a title clearly derived from its real-life counterpart. Later in life, Branwell submitted poems to several provincial papers, including the *Leeds Intelligencer*, which published his topical verse 'The Affghan War [*sic*]' on 7 May 1842 (see AFGHAN WAR). The paper also reprinted Anne's poem, *'Believe not those who say', from *Fraser's Magazine* in December 1848. The *Intelligencer* ran a lengthy, favourable review of *Villette* (19 Feb. 1853), but also participated in the condemnation of Mr Brontë by the local press that followed the publication of Elizabeth *Gaskell's *Life*. It was in the *Leeds Intelligencer* that Mr Brontë found an advertisement for William Carus *Wilson's 'School for Clergymen's Daughters', to which he sent his four eldest girls, with tragic results, in 1824.   CB

Leeds Mercury. Established in its earliest form in 1717, the *Leeds Mercury* was one of three local newspapers taken at the Brontës' childhood

Lennox, Lord William

home, as Charlotte records in her *'History of the Year', dated 12 March 1829. Like its Tory counterpart, the *Leeds Intelligencer*, it widened the young Brontës' intellectual horizons, and inspired them to emulate its lively, belligerent style in their early writings. During the time of their most prolific juvenile writing, from 1829 through the 1830s, the conservative *Intelligencer* and the liberal *Mercury* conducted a viciously satirical war of words in their pages, which the children then imitated in their own miniature periodicals. Revd Patrick *Brontë contributed a number of pieces to the *Leeds Mercury*, primarily on controversial reform topics such as the softening of the criminal code, the repeal of the death penalty, the abolition of slavery, and the reduction of church rates. In the spring of 1812 when he was curate at *Dewsbury, he had read the *Mercury*'s reports on *Luddite riots in the area, in particular, the attack on Cartwright's mill in nearby *Rawfolds, which Charlotte later imaginatively recounted in *Shirley*. Charlotte herself consulted the *Mercury*'s archives when writing her novel, and she seems to have had a mixed reaction to the paper's liberal position. On the one hand, she was repelled by the free-trade cause as it was espoused in the pages of the *Mercury*, and she consequently has her narrator emphatically denounce the mill owners' attitude as reprehensibly selfish. On the other hand, her narrator's moral stance toward the rioting workers is reminiscent of the disapproving, paternalistic tone adopted in the *Mercury*'s accounts of the attack on Cartwright's mill. Recognizing the importance of this liberal paper, Mr Brontë sent a review copy of *Villette* to the editor, Edward *Baines, in 1853, but by that time the *Mercury* no longer reviewed books. Under the proprietorship of the Baines family, the *Leeds Mercury* developed a circulation of over 12,000 by the time of Charlotte's death; its readership extended well beyond *Yorkshire, and subscriptions were taken by major hotels, libraries, and newsrooms throughout England. One of Charlotte's earliest biographers, Sir Thomas Wemyss *Reid, was editor of the *Leeds Mercury* from 1871 to 1887. CB

Collier, Patrick, ' "The lawless by force . . . the peaceable by kindness": Strategies of Social Control in Charlotte Brontë's *Shirley* and the *Leeds Mercury*', *Victorian Periodicals Review*, 32 (1999), 280–98.

Rosengarten, Herbert J., 'Charlotte Brontë and the *Leeds Mercury*', *SEL*, 16 (1976), 591–600.

Lennox, Lord William, a young aristocratic coxcomb in the *Glass Town and Angrian saga; named after Lord William Lennox, one of the historical Duke of *Wellington's aides-de-camp.

letters by the Brontë family. *See opposite page*

'Letters from an Englishman'. Fourteen letters, in six hand-sewn booklets totalling 112 pages (in Brotherton), edited by 'John Flower' (Branwell Brontë). James *Bellingham, an English banker recently arrived in *Glass Town, relates to his relative, Adam Scott in London, his adventures as he travels about the Glass Town Federation with the Marquis of Douro (Arthur Wellesley, later Duke of *Zamorna), Charles *Wellesley, and Young *Soult the Rhymer. The first letter is dated 2 September 1830, the last 2 August 1832.

Bellingham marvels at the magnificence of Glass Town; relates his adventures at the home of Dr Hume *Badey who dissects bodies, living and dead (see BODYSNATCHING); and describes his travels across Twelveland, marvelling at the scenery, meeting the cattle rustler *Pigtail, mocking the bombastic poetry of Young Soult, and observing a boxing match. He makes an emergency return to Great Glass Town to witness an insurrection led by Alexander Rogue (Duke of *Northangerland), lends the government £13,000,000, for which Rogue sentences him to be executed after he captures the city, but is saved when the Twelves' forces recapture the city. Travelling again with Douro, he comes across Rogue in a remote area once more exhorting his followers to insurrection, is captured by them, witnesses the battle between the two forces and Rogue's ruthless execution of prisoners of war, the defeat of Rogue's forces by those of the Duke of *Wellington, and the execution of Rogue. By the end of the letters Branwell's focus has shifted from Wellington to Rogue and Douro. VN

Alexander & Sellars, pp. 298, 300–2 (illustrations).
Miscellaneous Writings, 1. 96–158.
Neufeldt *BB Works*, 1. 118–24, 170–202, 210–21, 230–8.

Lewes, George Henry (1817–78), writer, critic, and editor; correspondent of Charlotte Brontë and reviewer of her novels. As the partner of George Eliot from about September 1853 until his death, he supported her career as a novelist. An ugly, intelligent, versatile cosmopolitan, with a histrionic gift inherited from his grandfather, the comic actor Charles Lee Lewes (1740–1803), he acquired fluent French at schools in France and Jersey, and later wrote well-informed articles on French literature and philosophy. In London, in 1837, he became friendly with Thornton *Hunt and other free-thinking, unconventional minor writers, and was invited to meet Dickens, after reviewing his work in December 1837. In 1847–8 he acted in Dickens's amateur theatrical company. The early years of Lewes's marriage to the talented Agnes Jervis were happy, and they had four sons. W. S. *Williams knew them well, as did George *Smith,

(*cont. on page 302*)

B Y comparison with that of prolific writers like Dickens or the Brownings, the Brontës' correspondence is not vast. We know of about 950 letters from Charlotte, written between 1829 and February 1855, of which the manuscripts of about 860 have been located; over 240 from Mr Brontë, 1805–60 (about 220 manuscripts, 28 letters printed in newspapers, others printed without location in Lock & Dixon and elsewhere); more than 40 from Branwell, 1835–48, of which about 30 are extant in manuscript; and 9 from Maria Branwell to Mr Brontë before their marriage, only one of which has been located in manuscript. Emily declared that writing 'a proper letter' was a feat she had never performed. None of the letters she wrote to Charlotte seem to have survived, and all we have are three laconic notes (1843, 1845, 1846) to Ellen Nussey. There remain only five from Anne: to Ellen, 4 October 1847, 26 January 1848, and 5 April 1849—the last pathetically justifying her wish to improve her chances of survival by a change of air; to W. S. *Williams, 29 September 1848, written on Charlotte's behalf after Branwell's death; and to Revd David *Thom, 30 December 1849, concurring with his belief in the doctrine of *universal salvation. Many letters from the Brontës must have been destroyed or lost.

Charlotte Brontë

The lack of letters to Charlotte from her siblings makes one cherish her few letters to them: eight to Emily, two to Branwell, and a single brief message to Anne. Those to Emily witness to Charlotte's love for and trust in her; it is to Emily that she describes her 'real confession' in the *Brussels cathedral. Charlotte's letter to Branwell of 17 May 1832 is a formal school exercise; the other, written from Brussels on 1 May 1843, shows her elder-sisterly concern for his welfare, and frankly admits her alienation from all the 'stupid' inhabitants of the Pensionnat *Heger except M. Constantin *Heger and the cool Mme Zoë *Heger—'not quite an exception'. Her true companions are the 'old faces' of Angria (see GLASS TOWN AND ANGRIAN SAGA). We have fourteen of Charlotte's letters to her father, two of them fragmentary because he cut them up to send to autograph hunters after her death. The others are affectionate, concerned for his wellbeing, and careful in the choice of topics that will interest him. The six letters she wrote to him in 1851 include vivid descriptions of the *Great Exhibition and of W. M. *Thackeray's lectures. Regrettably, none of Charlotte's correspondence with Revd A. B. *Nicholls survives; indeed he told Elizabeth *Gaskell that he had burned all Charlotte's letters to himself. We do have Charlotte's four passionate letters to M. Heger, written in 1844 and 1845 after her return from Brussels, when she longed for more frequent replies from him. The complex emotions she reveals were to be a potent influence on her major novels.

Charlotte wrote more letters to Ellen Nussey than to any other correspondent and 394 are known, out of the 500 Ellen claimed to have received from her. Ellen destroyed many letters that she considered too sensitive for publication, before allowing Elizabeth Gaskell to see about 350 of them; but hitherto unknown letters surface occasionally. Some are known only because of the survival of postmarked envelopes, some only in garbled versions edited by Ellen for the suppressed edition produced by Joseph Horsfall *Turner. The letters to Ellen, written between May 1831 and February

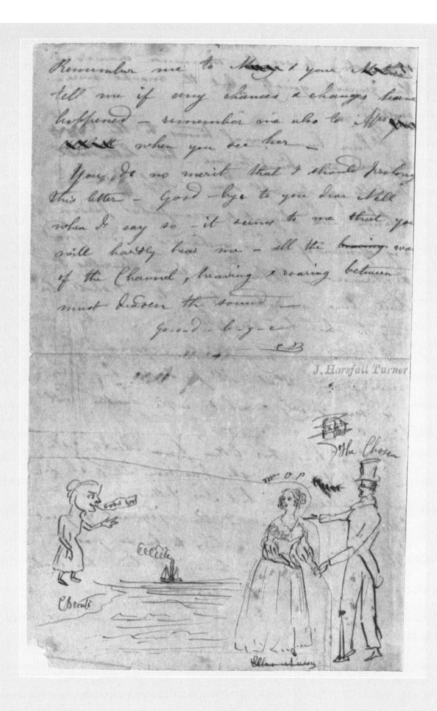

The last page of Charlotte Brontë's letter to Ellen Nussey of 6 March 1843, including a sketch of herself waving good-bye to Ellen across the sea from Belgium.

1855, provide much insight into Charlotte's life and personality. In many intimate, spontaneous letters she shares with Ellen the intense moods of adolescence, the joyous companionship of the sisters at the Parsonage before they separated to suffer the torments of governess life, the short-lived exhilaration of the early months in Brussels, the later 'dreary weight' of depression and isolation and of her belief that Mme Heger is 'a politic—plausible and interested person'; but the strength of Charlotte's attraction to Heger remains concealed. Yet Charlotte can be remarkably candid about her reactions to some of the men who found her attractive or proposed to her: the young curates—Revd Henry *Nussey in March 1839, Revd David *Pryce in August the same year; later, in 1851, James *Taylor. We learn too little of Mr Nicholls, of whom Ellen was jealous. No letters to Ellen survive from a period of alienation between the two women from summer 1853 to spring 1854. But we learn much from the correspondence as a whole about contemporary provincial life: about the difficulties of travel, the novelty of the railways, the friendly exchanges of long visits; the financial crises in households of women, the reluctant ventures into governess-ship or schoolteaching; the custom of 'bride-visits'; births, marriages, and deaths; the frightening prevalence of TB, the ineffectiveness of medicines, the periodic ravages of cholera, the tribulations caused by debauchery in the family, and by the painful necessity of confining and distress of visiting the insane. In Charlotte's letters to Ellen during the illnesses and deaths of her brother and sisters, we share her agony. We do not turn to Charlotte's correspondence with the unintellectual Ellen for detailed discussion of books, ideas, or politics, though all these are referred to, and Ellen's attempt to identify the originals of characters in *Shirley* elicits Charlotte's gnomic 'We only suffer Reality to *suggest*—never to *dictate*' (16 Nov. 1849, in Smith *Letters*, 2. 285).

An important series of eighteen letters written in 1846 to *Aylott and Jones, publishers of the Bells' *Poems*, survives almost intact. Brief, formal, and courteous, the letters reveal Charlotte's mixture of efficiency and naïveté in her approach to this exciting venture into publication. For more insight into Charlotte's methods of composition and for her response to the writing of others, we can turn to her correspondence with W. S. Williams. Some 125 letters to him written between 4 October 1847 and 6 December 1853 show a growing confidence in him as a discerning reader and sympathetic friend. These characteristics are most evident in the 70 or so letters of 1848–9. Their more sporadic correspondence during the slow gestation of *Villette* tails off to a sad, flat conclusion in Charlotte's laconic letter to Mr Williams of 6 December 1853, asking him not to 'select or send any more books. These courtesies must cease some day— and I would rather give them up than wear them out.' At their best, the letters to him are rich in personal insights and reflections of contemporary life. Charlotte writes about the French Revolution of 1848, Chartism, education, governesses, and the position of women; Emersonian philosophy, concepts of religion, Providence, and truth; reviews of her novels, her plans for those to come, and her opinions of her sisters' works; critics and criticism, novelists and novels. She extols Thackeray, and inveighs against Jane Austen's ignorance of the 'stormy Sisterhood of the Passions'. She deplores the iniquities of her sisters' publisher, Thomas Cautley *Newby, in comparison with the virtues of *Smith, Elder and Company. Of all the books sent to her by the firm, many of them chosen by Mr Williams, Ruskin's *Modern Painters* seems to her supremely illuminating.

From mid-1850 George *Smith became Charlotte's principal London correspondent. The brief business letters she had previously written to him—eight in 1848, ten in 1849—gave place to their friendly correspondence of late 1850, followed by 24 long, candid, warmly interested, often affectionately teasing letters in 1851. Their friendship continued, but there were fewer letters in 1852, and a rapid falling-off from the spring of 1853. This was partly due to the heavy burden of work which had oppressed Smith for the past year, and partly to his happier preoccupation with Elizabeth Blakeway, to whom he became engaged in November or December. The nadir of Charlotte's relationship with him was reached in her curt, contorted letter on his engagement: 'My dear Sir | In great happiness, as in great grief—words of sympathy should be few. Accept my meed of congratulation—and believe me | Sincerely yours | C Brontë.' The correspondence as a whole is of the first importance for understanding Charlotte's relationship with the young publisher whom she was to portray as Dr John Graham *Bretton in *Villette*. It is significant too in its references to her work, to books, writers, and contemporary society. We hear of the writing and reception of *Villette*; of Thackeray and his *Henry Esmond*, part of which Charlotte saw in manuscript; of Harriet *Martineau and her never-to-be-published novel *Oliver Weld*; of Charlotte's *portrait by George Richmond, commissioned by Smith; and of the current vogue for *phrenology, exemplified in Dr J. P. *Browne's 'estimates' of Charlotte and Smith in the guise of 'Miss and Mr Fraser'.

Charlotte's first impressions of Smith and Williams had been memorably conveyed in her only surviving letter to Mary *Taylor, that of 4 September 1848. The verve, dramatic impetus, and graphic portrayal of character in this letter intensify one's regret that Mary Taylor destroyed the rest of Charlotte's side of the correspondence. Fortunately Mary's letters to Charlotte and Ellen Nussey, and her two letters to Mrs Gaskell incorporated in the *Life*, tell us much about Charlotte's personality, and the interests she shared with this intelligent, original, enterprising friend (see Stevens, Joan, *Mary Taylor* (1972), esp. app. B).

Twelve, or possibly thirteen, letters from Charlotte to James Taylor survive. Most are carefully composed, earnestly offering opinions on the books he sent her, and on such subjects as Harriet Martineau's 'atheism', which they both deplored. Her last letter to him, addressed to Bombay, was written after she had taken the precaution of sounding Mr Williams on his enigmatic character. In it she writes eloquently of her horrified reaction to *Rachel's acting, and is carefully appreciative—but no more than that—in response to his two letters to her from India. Her letters to Ellen Nussey about him reveal her repulsion from his physical presence, and yet her sense of desolation after his departure for India.

An easier, more open relationship is evident in 39 letters from Charlotte to Elizabeth Gaskell. Charlotte freely exchanges views on people, places, and books with her congenial fellow writer, finds comfort in her sympathy, and amusement in her lively gossip. The correspondence, along with Elizabeth Gaskell's comments on it in letters to other friends, provides valuable insight into the friendship which forms the basis of the *Life*. It may be compared with Charlotte's letters to other women who showed a similar protective concern for her: 33 to Margaret *Wooler, her old schoolmistress, to whom Charlotte became more affectionate in her loneliness after her sisters' deaths; and thirteen somewhat formal but sincere notes to George Smith's mother. Nineteen letters to Amelia Ringrose (see TAYLOR, AMELIA) and nine to Laetitia *Wheelwright, less intimate than those to Ellen Nussey, nevertheless show an increase in warmth and sympathy over the years. It was to Ellen and these two friends that Charlotte wrote her last, infinitely touching letters on her deathbed.

Charlotte's letters to writers other than Elizabeth Gaskell are few but significant: letters to Robert *Southey on 16 March 1837 and his son Cuthbert on 26 August 1850 acknowledging the value of the poet's advice not to write verse for the sake of fame; to Hartley *Coleridge in December 1840, flippantly responding to his dismissal of her attempt at a novel, *Ashworth*; to George Henry *Lewes, disputing his taste for Jane Austen, and later resenting his unfair critique of *Shirley*, always revealing much about her own views of writing; and to Harriet Martineau, at first in admiration, but finally in pained rejection of Martineau's condemnation of the 'kind and degree' of love in *Villette*. Only one of Charlotte's letters to Martineau survives in manuscript. For the rest we have such scraps as Martineau chose to quote in her *Autobiography*, and those copied by other writers. Even more regrettable is the apparently total loss of Charlotte's correspondence with Thackeray, though there are some implausible and easily recognizable forgeries purporting to be her letters. There is a handful of notes to other authors: for example *De Quincey, Sydney *Dobell, Mrs Catherine *Gore, Richard H. *Horne, Julia *Kavanagh, Thornton *Hunt, R. M. *Milnes, and John Stores *Smith.

Charlotte's early letters are written with a fine nib in a copperplate hand which is not always easy to decipher, especially when the letters are cross-written. A somewhat smaller but more legible hand is used from about 1838—obscure only when Ellen Nussey deleted or scraped out words she considered too sensitive for publication, such as uncomplimentary references to her own family. A few draft letters written in pencil in a minute hand survive: in these, deletions, alterations, and loosely formed letters can present problems. Most of Charlotte's letters to Aylott and Jones, George Smith, and James Taylor, and many to W. S. Williams, are accurately dated, as are those to her family and friends written before 1840, which have integral addresses and postmarks. See COMMUNICATIONS. From 10 January 1840 onwards, when separate envelopes were commonly but not invariably used, dating can be difficult. Charlotte may give no date, the day of the week only, or an incorrect date, especially at the beginning of a month or year. In such cases approximate dates have to be derived from, for example, citations in biographies, editions, recollections, anecdotes, sale catalogues, autograph fragments or collections. The existence of other letters can be deduced from envelopes or from references in extant letters to, from, or about Charlotte. Few letters addressed to her survive. Most were presumably destroyed by Charlotte herself, by Mr Nicholls, or (less probably) Mr Brontë. But there are some: among others, an affectionate letter from a Belgian pupil, *Mathilde; six forthright letters from Mary Taylor; an invitation from C. A. Dana to contribute to the *New York Tribune*; a long letter from a missionary, Joseph Abbott, who had known her parents; and four verbose screeds from *'K.T.', who offers quite a shrewd critique of *Shirley*.

Revd Patrick Brontë

Manuscripts of more than 200 letters from Mr Brontë have been located. Twenty-eight letters to newspapers survive in printed form; and some letters are known only from transcriptions. Many, dealing with such matters as trustee appointments and meetings, witness to his conscientious daily work; others show concern to improve his church, build a Sunday school, provide testimonials or pastoral help for his parishioners. Numerous letters to the General Board of Health from 1850 onwards show his persistence in urging and achieving sanitary reform for Haworth. His social conscience and strong political and religious views give force to his letters to the *Leeds Mercury, Leeds Intelligencer, Halifax Guardian,* and *Bradford Observer,* while his more personal letters illumine his relationships with Mary *Burder, his clerical friends, his children, and the people he met or wrote to because of their interest in his daughters' work—notably to George Smith. Regrettably his 'kind, affectionate' letters to Maria Branwell have not been located. Two letters to Charlotte in January 1853 convey his animosity towards Mr Nicholls, yet in the same month Patrick writes a fine testimonial for him. Letters to Elizabeth Gaskell in 1855 provide information for the *Life* about himself and his children, and in 1857 he writes to her again with an astonishing degree of tolerance, even of sympathy for her, despite her allegations about him. Having secured some corrections for the 3rd edition he concludes in a letter of 30 July 1857, 'Let us both try to be wiser and better as Time recedes and Eternity advances.' Mr Brontë's large handwriting, often produced with a thick nib and dark ink, is generally legible. Though paragraphing, spelling, and punctuation become erratic in the letters of his old age, he remains for the most part clear and coherent, retaining the forms of courtesy to the end.

(Patrick) Branwell Brontë

Between 40 and 50 letters from Branwell are extant either in manuscript, in the form of notes entered in R. M. *Milnes's Commonplace Book, or as cited by F. H. *Grundy and others. There must have been many more—to his friends and family, and to the newspapers which published his *poetry. Two early letters—an apology to his art teacher, William *Robinson, 16 November 1835, and a draft letter to the Royal Academy—reflect his aspirations to be an artist. His insistent demands to the editor of *Blackwood's Edinburgh Magazine* in 1835, 1836, and 1837, express his conviction (not shared by the editor) that he would be a valuable new contributor. A more modest appeal to the editor on 6 September 1842 still produced no result. An admiring but tactless letter to Wordsworth on 19 January 1837 and a letter to De Quincey, both pleading for consideration of his poems, probably remained unanswered. Branwell was more deserving of the encouragement he received from Hartley Coleridge in 1840, especially for his translations from Horace. From the same brief period of tutorship at Broughton-in-Furness comes Branwell's bawdy letter of 13 March 1840 to John *Brown (see Barker, pp. 320–3). With less bravado Branwell writes to Grundy in 1842 in quest of work on the railways, and to J. B. *Leyland about a memorial to the Haworth surgeon Thomas Andrew. Letters to John Brown in 1843, written from Thorp Green, claim that Mrs Lydia *Robinson is 'damnably too fond' of him. In 1845, after his dismissal, he writes despairingly to Grundy and Leyland of his misery and illness; but he also tells Leyland about the novel he is writing 'to wile away his torment', and in March 1846 he writes very politely to J. Frobisher, the Halifax organist, about publishing one of his poems to music by Gluck. Letters to Grundy and Leyland written between 1846 and early 1848 tell of his continuing mental agony in the loss of Lydia, but also mention sporadic efforts to resume his writing. He illustrates several letters to Leyland by pen-and-ink drawings, typically showing himself chained to a stake, or hanged like a murderer (see Alexander & Sellars, pp. 347–62). Branwell's last surviving note is a request to John Brown to get him 'Five pence worth of Gin'. Branwell usually wrote with his left hand in a clear upright or slightly backward-slanting style, but he occasionally used his right hand to produce a right slant. Letters written at times of crisis, especially towards the end of his life, may be marked by minor slips and alterations.

Locations
The holograph manuscripts of the Brontës' letters are widely dispersed, largely owing to the activities of T. J. *Wise. The principal collections are in the *Brontë Parsonage Museum and the *Brotherton Library in Britain, and in the Huntington, Pierpont Morgan, and Princeton libraries, and New York Public Library in the USA. For these and other locations see MANUSCRIPTS AND MANUSCRIPT COLLECTIONS.

Publication
Apart from Mr Brontë's letters to newspapers, and his letter of 27 November 1821 to John Buckworth (published in the *Cottage Magazine* for 1822), the Brontës' letters were not published until after Charlotte's death in 1855. In her *Life* of Charlotte, published in 1857, Elizabeth Gaskell quoted extensively from her letters. Gaskell's selectiveness, expurgations, misreadings, misdatings, grouping together of extracts to different correspondents, and printing of letters in the wrong context, mean that her texts cannot be relied on. On the other hand, some of her transcriptions are accurate in all but punctuation, and she also quoted from some manuscripts which have vanished without trace. Thus, where manuscripts are lacking, her texts have to be taken into account. Significant later publications include the suppressed edition of Charlotte's letters produced at Ellen Nussey's request between 1885 and 1889 by J. Horsfall Turner. Ellen had arranged for the publication of expurgated versions of letters to her and to Margaret Wooler, but in 1889 she decided that more passages should have been omitted. Before 1892 the printed sheets of all but about a dozen copies had been burnt. Ellen annotated, and marked passages for omission, in several of the surviving copies; for example, those in the BPM and British Library. Unfortunately her unreliable texts are at present the sole authority for about 40 of Charlotte's letters.

C. K. *Shorter's *Charlotte Bronte and her Circle* (1896) has texts of variable accuracy, but one of his coups was the printing of Maria Branwell's letters to Mr Brontë. He also included transcripts and/or facsimiles of some of Emily and Anne's *Diary Papers. He printed many of Charlotte's letters to W. S. Williams, for some of which the manuscripts remain unlocated. His transcriptions of her letters to Laetitia Wheelwright are reasonably accurate, and he annotated her letter to Elizabeth *Branwell, '*Mrs. Gaskell's "Life." Corrected and completed from original letter in the possession of Mr. A. B. Nicholls*' (Shorter *Circle*, p. 97). Since Mr Nicholls probably destroyed this letter along with those to Emily, Shorter's text is important. Shorter's other texts, especially those of letters to Ellen Nussey and George Smith, are unreliable. He printed better versions of some of them in footnotes to *Life* (Haworth edn. 1900). In *The Brontës: Life and Letters* (2 vols., 1908) Shorter printed more letters, but again his editing was capricious, producing too many corrupt texts, passages from different manuscripts combined as one, incorrect personal names, misdated and wrongly addressed letters. But he printed seven appendices, including Mr Brontë's letters to Mrs Elizabeth

*Franks, J. Stores Smith's reminiscences of and letters from Charlotte, and extracts from the newspaper controversy about *Cowan Bridge as described in the *Life. The Brontës: Their Lives, Friendship and Correspondence* (4 vols., 1932), edited by J. A. *Symington, greatly assisted by C. W. *Hatfield, and (nominally) by T. J. Wise, contained more manuscript-based texts than previous editions, but relied on the 1st edition or 1900 Haworth edition of Gaskell's *Life* for most of Charlotte's letters to Elizabeth Gaskell, G. H. Lewes, and George Smith. Garbled texts of these were the result, with few indications of lacunae, and no indication of sources for individual letters. Annotation remained inadequate. Professor Mildred Christian produced a valuable census of Brontë manuscripts in the United States (*The Trollopian*, 1947–8), and generously bequeathed to the BPM her working papers and some photocopies for a projected edition of the letters. *The Letters of Charlotte Brontë*, ed. Margaret Smith (vol. 1, 1995; vol. 2, 2000) is as far as possible manuscript-based and fully annotated. A third and final volume is due for publication in spring 2004, covering letters from 1852 to 1855, with corrections and additions to the previous volumes. A comprehensive edition of Mr Brontë's letters, edited by Robert Barnard and Dudley Green, is projected, and it is to be hoped that an edition of Branwell Brontë's correspondence will be produced. Meanwhile readers have to use the 1932 Shakespeare Head edition, supplemented by letters printed in Barker *BST*, Smith *Letters*, Lock & Dixon, and other biographies and editions of the Brontë oeuvre.

Leyland.
Smith *Letters*, esp. 1. 27–76: 'The History of the Letters'.
Winnifrith *Background*.

who recalled Lewes as one of the best and most amusing raconteurs in the Museum Club. Though Charlotte was impressed by Lewes's display of learning in his novel *Ranthorpe* (1847) and by the realistic character of the Branwell Brontë-like Cecil Chamberlayne in his *Rose, Blanche, and Violet* (1848), she criticized the novels' structure and tone. She appreciated Lewes's generous reviews of *Jane Eyre* in *Fraser's Magazine* and the *Westminster Review*, but questioned his advocacy of a more subdued, Jane Austen-like style. His 'brutal and savage' review of *Shirley* in the *Edinburgh Review* (Jan. 1850) left her feeling cold, sick, and indignant, because he had perceived in it limitations characteristic of women and had judged it throughout on that basis—partly, perhaps, because he was preoccupied with his wife's current pregnancy with the first of four children she bore to Thornton Hunt. By registering the first two children as his own he made it impossible to divorce her. Before meeting Lewes at the home of George Smith in June 1850, Charlotte considered him 'clever, sharp and coarse', but she judged him more leniently thereafter, seeing in his face a moving resemblance to her sister Emily. In his review of *Villette* in the *Leader* (12 Feb. 1853), he admitted the novel's many faults, but proclaimed that 'In Passion and Power

. . . Currer Bell has no living rival, except George Sand'. Charlotte's correspondence with Lewes reveals some of her most passionately held beliefs about the art of writing and the nature of genius.

Leyden, battle of. The village of Leyden, in the *Glass Town and Angrian saga, is the scene of the Duke of *Zamorna's most famous victory over the Duke of *Northangerland's forces after his return from exile. General Lord Edward *Hartford and Captain Sir William *Percy both fight on Zamorna's side and Northangerland's ally Lord *Jordan (Sheik Medina) is killed. Northangerland is defeated again soon after Leyden at the Battle of Westwood.

Leyland, Francis A. (1813–94), an antiquarian who ran a bookshop and circulating library from his father's printing business, Roberts Leyland & Son, at 15 Cornmarket, *Halifax, publisher and printer of the *Halifax Guardian* until 1837. Leyland became a Roman Catholic and in 1845 married Ann Brierley (d. 1849). He had heard of Branwell Brontë from his brother Joseph Bentley *Leyland, and he first met Branwell after he was appointed assistant clerk in charge at Sowerby Bridge Railway Station, 4 miles outside Halifax, on 31 August 1840. It is through Francis Leyland that a more accurate description of Branwell and his talents at this time survives. He defended Branwell's reputation following Elizabeth *Gaskell's unfavourable portrayal of him in the *Life*, and Mary F. Robinson's repetition of this view in her *Emily Brontë* (1883). Swinburne's favourable review of the latter book in the *Athenaeum* prompted Francis Leyland to publish a reply in the same journal on 21 July 1883, announcing his intention to reveal the 'better side of [Branwell's] nature': 'I speak from personal knowledge of him, and I possess many of his writings in letters and poems, with which I hope at no distant day to demonstrate his power, and to dispose of many of the calumnies with which a hasty and ill-considered judgment has overshadowed his memory' (quoted in Charles Lemon, 'Branwell Brontë and the Leyland Brothers', *BST* (1999), 24. 1. 34). The result was Leyland's two-volume *The Brontë Family: With Special Reference to Patrick Branwell Brontë* (1886). On the death of his brother, Francis Leyland had inherited Branwell's correspondence, much of which he quoted in his book, before selling it to Edward Brotherton (later Lord *Brotherton) in the early 1920s. In 1925, Brotherton's librarian, J. A. *Symington, edited the correspondence with C. W. *Hatfield and it was privately printed in Leeds as *Patrick Branwell Brontë: A Complete Transcript of the Leyland Manuscripts*.

Leyland, Joseph Bentley (1811–51), sculptor friend of Branwell Brontë, with a studio in Swan Coppice, Halifax, where Branwell first met him, probably in 1839. Through Leyland and his family Branwell found an entrée into the local Halifax circle of writers and artists, which included William *Dearden, George Hogarth, John Nicholson, and John Wilson Anderson. Leyland had gained an early success in London, Manchester, and Leeds but, like Branwell, his promising talent was unfulfilled, he was constantly in debt and he died an alcoholic only three years after Branwell. He is best remembered for his statue of Dr Beckwith in York Minster, and for a sculpted group of African bloodhounds. The Brontës would have seen Leyland's group of English greyhounds and his huge sculpted head of Satan (before it achieved critical acclaim in London) at the 1834 Leeds exhibition of the Royal Northern Society for the Encouragement of the Fine Arts, at which the young Charlotte Brontë also exhibited two pencil drawings (see ART OF THE BRONTËS). His portrait medallion of Branwell can be seen at the BPM (a photograph of it is reproduced as a frontispiece in Gérin *BB*). Leyland often worked with John *Brown, the Haworth stonemason and confidant of Branwell, on commissions for local churches and memorials, such as the commission to design and execute

the memorial tablet to the Haworth curate, Revd William *Weightman (now in Haworth church), which Branwell was instrumental in securing for Leyland.

Leyland was probably Branwell's closest friend. He was not always a beneficial influence and seems to have encouraged not only Branwell's poetry but also his excessive drinking. A considerable correspondence from Branwell to Leyland survives and was first used by Leyland's brother, Francis A. *Leyland, in his book on the Brontë family (1886), and then privately printed in *Patrick Branwell Brontë: A Complete Transcript of the Leyland Manuscripts*, ed. J. Alex Symington and C. W. Hatfield (1925). The letters reveal much of Branwell's literary and artistic interest, and the 'sufferings' caused by his obsession with Mrs Robinson and his opium addiction, which are graphically illustrated in a number of the letters (see Alexander & Sellars, pp. 348–56, 360–2). Branwell was also in the habit of sending Leyland poems for comment, including his long poem 'Caroline', which was printed by Francis Leyland in *The Brontë Family: With Special Reference to Patrick Branwell Brontë* (1886). In 1846 Branwell began an epic poem on the Legend of Morley Hall, Leigh, Lancashire, the ancient seat of the Leyland family, in return for Leyland's medallion, but the poem was never finished (Neufeldt *BBP*, pp. 284–6). The introductory lines are a meditation on the past when the now ruined hall stood among pristine green fields unspoilt by noise, grime, and industrial buildings (Smith *Letters*, 1. 467, 476).

Leyland Manuscripts, a collection of 21 letters (in Brotherton), written by Branwell Brontë to his close friend and confidant, the sculptor Joseph Bentley *Leyland (except the last letter which is to John *Brown, sexton of Haworth and also a close friend), between 1842 and 1848. These letters, which include sixteen sketches and two new poems ('When all our cheerful hours seem gone forever' and 'Thy soul is flown'), reveal much about Branwell's state of mind and body after his dismissal by the Robinsons in 1845, his feelings for Mrs Lydia *Robinson, the disappointment of his hopes of marrying her after the death of her husband, and his continued efforts to write and publish poetry and to write a novel.   VN

Alexander & Sellars, pp. 92–5, 345–55, 359–63.
Symington, J. A., and Hatfield, C. W., *Patrick Branwell Brontë: A Complete Transcript of the Leyland Manuscripts* (1925).
Wise & Symington.

'Liar Detected, The', a prose tale of four chapters in a hand-sewn booklet of fourteen pages (in Bonnell, BPM), dated 19 June 1830, and subtitled 'The Liar Unmasked', by Captain John *Bud, one of Branwell Brontë's pseudonyms. In the first two chapters Bud attacks Lord Charles *Wellesley, one of Charlotte's personae, for his vicious attacks on fifteen individuals in 'An *Interesting Passage in the Lives of Some Eminent Men of the Present Time' by Charlotte, dated 18 June 1830 (see Alexander *EEW*, 1. 170–7), systematically refuting Wellesley's accusations against each individual. In the third chapter Wellesley is criticized for his behaviour and character, and his lack of literary talent as exemplified by his poem 'The Vision' (by Charlotte), dated 13 April 1830. The final chapter consists of a public admonition of Wellesley by Bud. Charlotte's response appears in 'The *Poetaster' and 'Conversations' (Alexander *EEW*, pp. 179–96; 224–7). VN

Alexander & Sellars, p. 287 (illustrations).
Neufeldt *BB Works*, 1. 92–7.

libraries, Brontës' access to. See BOOKS READ BY THE BRONTËS.

Life Of Feild Marshal the Right Honourable Alexander Percy, The [*sic*]. In a three-volume manuscript (in Brotherton) with 34 pages extant (most of vol. 3 has been lost), probably begun in the spring of 1834 and completed in 1836, Branwell Brontë once more revises the early history of Alexander Percy (Duke of *Northangerland) to provide him with a historical pedigree that will complement that of the Duke of *Zamorna (Arthur Wellesley). Percy's ancestors are now the Percies of Northumberland, with the family estate at *Alnwick. The narrator Captain John *Bud traces the arrival of Alexander's father in Africa, Alexander's birth and education with his early interest and proficiency in music and theological questions, his defiance of his father and his dissolute habits encouraged by his mentor *Sdeath, his secret marriage to Lady Augusta di *Segovia, his banishment to the college on the *Philosopher's Island, his association with a secret, atheistic, republican revolutionary group there, his payment of a £50,000 fine, and his final success as a Senior Wrangler. In the meantime his wife schemes to murder her father-in-law so that Alexander can inherit the estate, having heavily borrowed against his inheritance. Percy sen. is dispatched by Sdeath, but when Augusta counsels Alexander not to pay his debts to his fellow conspirators from whom he has borrowed heavily at extortionate rates, they have her killed. In the utter despair over his loss of Augusta are laid the foundations of Percy's later cruelty, coldness, atheism, and melancholy. However, in the midst of the dissipation that follows his wife's demise, Alexander meets Mary Henrietta Wharton (see PERCY, MARY HENRIETTA), whom he marries. The missing portion of volume 3 will

have covered the birth of his three sons, and his daughter Mary (later the wife of Zamorna). The youngest son is killed in the tropics (see Charlotte's poem, 'Stanzas on the Fate of Henry Percy', in Alexander *EEW*, 2(2). 139–47); the other two sons Percy orders to be destroyed but Sdeath fails to carry out his orders. The extant portion of volume 3 relates Mary's death and Percy's descent into dissipation, outlawry, and exile as a result. VN

Collins, Robert G. (ed.), *The Hand of the Arch-Sinner* (1993), pp. 1–118.
Neufeldt *BB Works*, 2. 92–190.

'Lily Hart'. See SECRET AND LILY HART, THE.

Linden-Car. Gilbert *Markham's family residence and the surrounding countryside that constitutes his farm in *Tenant* ('car' being a northern dialect word meaning 'pond' or 'low-lying boggy ground'; although it can also mean 'Grange'). Linden-Car was left to Gilbert to manage, somewhat reluctantly, after his father's death. It is left to Fergus *Markham to manage after Gilbert's marriage to Helen Huntingdon.

Lindenhope, a village in the neighbourhood of *Linden-Car and *Wildfell Hall in *Tenant*. It is the parish of Revd Michael Millward (see MILLWARD FAMILY) and home of the *Wilson family. In north-east dialect 'hope' means 'a small enclosed valley' (*OED*).

Lindsay, Henry (Harry) Bramham, the 'grim, gaunt, ghastly Scotchman' from Sneaky's Land, who becomes one of the Duke of *Zamorna's ministers in the *Glass Town and Angrian saga. He knew Zamorna when young, trained as a lawyer, and wrote for the 'Northern Review'. His father is the stern old Scots yeoman Jamie Lindsay, seneschal of the Duke of Wellington's court, who speaks in the broad northern tongue that characterizes his son. Lindsay's niece, Effie, seems to fall (with her governess Lady Frances Millicent *Hume) under Zamorna's protection.

'Lines on the Celebrated Bewick' ('The cloud of recent death is past away'), poem by Charlotte Brontë (27 Nov. 1832), first given this title on publication in the *TLS* (4 Jan. 1907). The Brontës delighted in Thomas *Bewick's vignettes. This poem praises his 'scenes to Nature true', where, on the 'enchanted page' both the birds and their surroundings seem 'pictured thoughts that breathe', and recall the love and light of childhood days. Eloquent and picturesque despite occasional clichés of poetic diction, the 20 alternate-rhymed quatrains move gracefully, and the intertwined description and emotion are satisfyingly framed by opening and closing elegiac stanzas.

Neufeldt *CBP*, p. 100.

Linton, Catherine (Cathy), daughter of Edgar *Linton and Catherine *Earnshaw, in *Wuthering Heights*, born two hours before her mother's death and brought up by her father and Ellen *Dean at *Thrushcross Grange. She has inherited traits from both her parents: 'She was the most winning thing that ever brought sunshine into a desolate house—a real beauty in face—with the Earnshaws' handsome dark eyes, but the Lintons' fair skin, and small features, and yellow curling hair' (p. 232). She is brave and high-spirited, rather a spoilt girl but not as wilful as her mother. A lover of nature, she is attracted by the view of *Penistone Crags and her secret excursion there on her pony Minny takes her for the first time to *Wuthering Heights where she meets her two cousins, Linton *Heathcliff and Hareton *Earnshaw. Her lively nature is summed up in her 'perfect idea of heaven's happiness', a description of the natural world that matches Emily Brontë's own idea of an earthly heaven: 'rocking in a rustling green tree, with a west wind blowing, and bright, white clouds flitting rapidly above; and not only larks, but throstles, and blackbirds, and linnets, and cuckoos pouring out music on every side, and the moors seen at a distance, broken into cool dusky dells; but close by, great swells of long grass undulating in waves to the breeze; and woods and sounding water, and the whole world awake and wild with joy' (ch. 24). Unlike Linton, who wants an 'ecstacy of peace', Catherine wants the world 'to sparkle, and dance in a glorious jubilee'. When her father is dying, she is tricked into marrying Linton Heathcliff so that he (and his father) can gain possession of Thrushcross Grange. Her happy good nature degenerates into sullenness when she is ill-treated by Heathcliff, who destroys her books, makes her work, and forces her to nurse her dying young husband alone without medical aid. Her initial snobbish contempt for Hareton gives way to friendship and then love. At the ages of 18 and 23 respectively, they are to marry and move to Thrushcross Grange.

Linton, Edgar, a fair, blue-eyed gentle boy from *Thrushcross Grange who becomes infatuated with the spirited Catherine *Earnshaw in *Wuthering Heights*. He is an obvious foil to *Heathcliff, whose jealousy he arouses when his social position, appearance, wealth, and amiability appeal to Catherine's snobbery and she agrees to marry him. His gentleness to his wife is seen partly as the yielding of a weaker, timid nature before her imperious tyranny. After six months their peaceful happiness is broken by Heathcliff's return and Edgar's jealousy is aroused by Heathcliff's constant visits to his wife. Their quarrel leads to Catherine's delirium from which she never recovers, despite Edgar's devoted nursing. A final visit by Heathcliff causes her death in childbirth and he does everything possible to avoid meeting Heathcliff again, becoming a recluse and resigning his magistracy. His consolations are his daughter and his books. He never forgives his sister Isabella for marrying Heathcliff, but is grieved when he is prevented from assuming the guardianship of her surviving son Linton Heathcliff, who is named after and resembles Edgar Linton. At first he opposes the friendship between his daughter and nephew, and although it is too late to change his will in her favour, Edgar dies hoping she will be provided for by her marriage to her cousin after all. Although Edgar appears feeble beside the 'elemental' Catherine and Heathcliff of the first half of *Wuthering Heights*, his quiet courage gains stature as Heathcliff's vindictiveness increases in the remainder of the novel. His devotion to his wife Catherine is as constant as Heathcliff's, though different in kind, and he too dies believing he will be reunited with her in death: 'I am going to her, and you, darling child, shall come to us' (ch. 28).

Linton, Isabella, sister of Edgar *Linton in *Wuthering Heights* and, like him, fair-haired, blue-eyed, and indulged as a child. At the age of 18 she becomes infatuated by *Heathcliff, whom she sees as a Romantic hero, and despite her sister-in-law Catherine's warning about his nature, Isabella elopes with him. There is something masochistic in her behaviour towards Heathcliff, who treats her with contempt and cruelty, and tells Ellen Dean that 'no brutality disgusted her—I suppose she has an innate admiration of it, if only her precious person were secure from injury!' (ch. 14). At first she is so wretched she desires 'to be killed by him' (ch. 17), but manages to escape and flee to the south of England, where she gives birth to her sickly and pampered son Linton *Heathcliff. She dies twelve years later, hoping her estranged brother will become her son's guardian and ignorant of the way he falls into Heathcliff's power instead.

Lister family. Mary Cunliffe Lister (1812–99) married Joshua Ingham of *Blake Hall, *Mirfield, where Anne Brontë was employed as governess from 8 April to ?December 1839. (See INGHAM FAMILY for similarities with the Bloomfields in *Agnes Grey*.) According to Ellen Nussey, Mary was 'an amiable conventional woman' and her younger sister, Harriet (b. ?1818), was the 'clever—but refractory' pupil Miss Lister, whom Charlotte found so annoying at Roe Head (Brotherton MS). Charlotte speaks of her loathing of Harriet Lister and her fellow pupils in the *Roe Head Journal* (in Richard J. Dunn (ed.), *Jane Eyre*, Norton Critical Edition (3rd edn. 2001), 403), at the same time mentioning an unrelated 'Ellen Lister' (p. 404). Harriet was to marry William Clement Drake Esdaile in 1846 (Smith *Letters*, 1. 158). Their father was Ellis Cuncliffe Lister, Liberal MP for Bradford after the Reform Bill.

Literary Souvenir (1825–34), known for the quality of its engravings, the fourth of the annuals to be established, by Longman, Rees, &c and edited by Alaric A. Watts, a minor poet. The Brontës owned the 1830 volume, which was used by both Charlotte and Branwell as inspiration for their own early tales and as a copybook for their art. In 1833, Charlotte copied *The Sisters of Scio* engraved by Henry Rolls after a painting by A. Phalopon and accompanying a poem of the same name by Felicia Hemans (Alexander & Sellars, pp. 223–4). In October she copied a portrait of *Byron engraved by E. Portbury from a drawing by Richard Westall, which she named 'Alexander *Soult' (15 Oct. 1833), a Glass Town poet and persona of Branwell Brontë (Alexander & Sellars, pp. 19, 218–19). The following year, *c*.May 1834, she made a copy of Edward Finden's view of *Bolton Abbey, Wharfedale*, one of the two works she exhibited in the summer exhibition of the *Royal Northern Society for the Encouragement of the Fine Arts in Leeds (Alexander & Sellars, pp. 228–9); and not long after (*c*.1834–8), as an exercise in oil painting, Branwell made a large copy of another engraving from the *Literary Souvenir*, *Jacob's Dream*, engraved by E. Goodall from a painting by W. Allston (Alexander & Sellars, pp. 81, 317–18).

Little King and Queens. See GENII, CHIEF (LITTLE KING AND QUEENS).

Liverpool, Lancs., in the early 19th century the principal British seaport for transatlantic and west-coast shipping. Maria Branwell *Brontë and Elizabeth *Branwell possibly reached Yorkshire from Penzance via Liverpool. In February 1838 Revd Patrick Brontë hoped John Driver, a Haworth man prospering as a wine-merchant in Liverpool, might find Branwell a post as a bank clerk. Driver probably identified 'Currer Bell' in a Liverpool paper in late 1849 (Gaskell *Life*, 2. 127–8). Branwell was sent to Liverpool with John *Brown to recover after his dismissal in July 1845. The city's association with the slave trade has led to the supposition that Emily intended Heathcliff, who was found there, to be of slave origins.

Liversedge, a township in the Yorks. heavy woollen district well known to the Brontës, 7 miles north-east of *Huddersfield, and about 1 mile north-east of *Hartshead. Revd Hammond *Roberson lived at Heald's Hall (built in 1766), the largest house in Liversedge, from 1795, when he also transferred his boys' school there.

Roberson erected at his own expense Christ Church, Liversedge, consecrated in August 1816, and was its first incumbent. *Rawfolds Mill, Liversedge, the original of Hollow's Mill in *Shirley*, was attacked by Luddites on 11 April 1812.

BST (1907), 4. 16. 32–3 (illustrations).

Loango, Battle of, fought during the last of the Angrian wars in the southern Loango area of *Etrei, in the *Glass Town and Angrian saga. According to the Brontës' 19th-century geography books, Loango was an area on the central west coast of Africa. Their copy of Goldsmith's *Grammar of General Geography* describes Loango as 'a country of western Africa, the inhabitants of which are the blackest in the world'. See also AFRICA; GEOGRAPHY, KNOWLEDGE OF AND BOOKS.

Lockhart, John Gibson (1794–1854), journalist, novelist, biographer; admired by the Brontës for his contributions to *Blackwood's Edinburgh Magazine*, and his biographies of his father-in-law Sir Walter *Scott (1837–8) and of *Burns (1828). Emily was especially intrigued by his young son Johnny Lockhart, for whom Scott wrote *Tales of a Grandfather*, owned by the Brontës. Scott, Lockhart, and Johnny Lockhart were her 'chief men' in the *Islanders' Play (see 'TALES OF THE ISLANDERS'). On 16 June 1847 Charlotte Brontë sent him *Poems* 1846, acknowledging the 'pleasure and profit' derived from his works. As editor of the *Quarterly Review* he asked Elizabeth *Rigby to review *Jane Eyre*, which he thought clever, and better than other contemporary novels, though Jane was 'rather a brazen Miss'; yet he accepted Rigby's unfair review. Smith, Elder and Company sent his 'Roman' novel *Valerius* (3 vols., 1821) to Charlotte on 18 March 1850.

Lockwood, Mr, tenant of Thrushcross Grange to whom Ellen *Dean tells the story of the Earnshaws and Lintons in *Wuthering Heights*. After a superficial love affair at a seaside resort in the south of England, he perversely withdraws from society and seeks the solitude of the northern moors. However, he is intrigued by his misanthropic landlord *Heathcliff and his beautiful widowed daughter-in-law Catherine *Linton. His visit to the Heights, enforced stay there during a snowstorm, his nightmare and subsequent illness, provide the excuse for Ellen's narrative during his convalescence over several weeks at the end of 1801 and the beginning of 1802. Nine months later, while on his way north during the shooting season in September he calls on Ellen and hears the story of Heathcliff's death and the impending marriage of Hareton *Earnshaw and Catherine Linton. Lockwood is an unreliable judge of character and his civilized, southern manners are out of place in the wild isolation and savage environment of *Wuthering Heights and its inhabitants.

Lofty, Viscount Frederic. See ARUNDEL, LORD FREDERIC (LOFTY), EARL OF.

Lofty, Lord Macara, the scoundrelly younger brother of Lord Frederick *Arundel, whose inheritance Macara tries to usurp in *High Life in Verdopolis, in the *Glass Town and Angrian saga. He is a contemporary of the Duke of Zamorna, duped by him in 'The Tragedy and the Essay' (Alexander EW, p. 105). Later he becomes the friend of Charles Townshend (Lord Charles *Wellesley) and sometime ally of the Duke of Northangerland and Ardrah in their coalition against Angria. He becomes Verdopolitan chancellor of the exchequer under Ardrah's Reformist government, and, later, chief secretary of Northangerland's Revolutionary Government in Angria. He eventually turns against both Ardrah and Northangerland, has a brief affair with Louisa *Vernon, and becomes a dissipated opium addict.

London. For the young Brontës, London seemed a 'great Babylon', a glamorous city of palaces inhabited by great men such as the Duke of *Wellington. It served as a model for their *Glass Town. Certainly magnificent buildings existed, the royal parks were green oases, the river and docks were thronged with ships; but much of London was noisy, dirty, and smelly. Its population was growing rapidly, approximately doubling between 1811 and 1851 to 2,263,341. Most of the poor lived in crowded, decrepit slums such as Seven Dials in St Giles's parish, or filthy back alleys in Westminster, Bermondsey, and the Borough. Industries included tanneries, chemical works, flour mills, and printing works, whose smoke, steam, and noise added to the pollution caused by horse-traffic and, from the 1830s, steam railway-engines.

The Brontë children gained their ideas of London from various sources. Their father knew the precincts of St Paul's and Paternoster Row, for he had stayed at the *Chapter Coffee House. The BPM has the Brontës' heavily annotated, illustrated volume, A Description of London (1824): Branwell could impress his friends with his knowledge of London though he had never been there. He and Charlotte read magazine reviews of London art exhibitions, so that when she visited London with Emily, her father, and Joe and Mary Taylor from 8 to 11 February 1842, en route to Brussels, she knew exactly where the pictures and statues were that she insisted on seeing. From the 1830s onwards the writings of, for example, *Dickens and *Bulwer-Lytton gave the Brontës a broader view of the city, though Charlotte did not become painfully aware of the reality of its dark under-

world until she read Henry Mayhew's London Labour and the London Poor in February 1851.

Emily's journeys through London made no obvious impact on her writing, but Charlotte vividly recalled the 'great bell of St Paul's' and its 'Dome, looming through a London Mist' in The Professor (ch. 7). Her solitary departure from London in January 1843 was hauntingly evoked in Villette (ch. 6). Her next visit, in Anne's company (7–11 July 1848), included meetings with George *Smith, W. S. *Williams, and T. C. *Newby, a visit to the National Gallery (opened 1838) and to Covent Garden for The Barber of Seville (transformed into the concert episode in Villette (ch. 20)). Anne's novels were written before she visited London, which figures in Tenant mainly as a corrupting influence on Huntingdon; but her contact with Newby perhaps induced him to correct the second edition.

From 29 November 1849 to 14 December 1849 Charlotte stayed at George Smith's family home in Westbourne Place, Paddington. Their move westwards from premises 'over the shop' was typical of the continuing exodus from the City. Charlotte met James *Taylor, John Forbes, Harriet *Martineau, William Makepeace *Thackeray, and some of the critics of her books, notably Samuel Phillips of The Times. She admired two superb collections of J. W. M. Turner's paintings, but did not admire Macready's performances in *Shakespeare's Macbeth and Othello.

During her happiest visit to London (30 May 1850–25 June 1850) a 'genial and friendly' George Smith escorted her to the Royal Academy Exhibition, probably leaving her there to enjoy the pictures, especially Landseer's Wellington at Waterloo and John *Martin's The Last Man, as Dr Bretton leaves Lucy in Villette (ch. 19). Smith and his mother accompanied her to an opera, perhaps Meyerbeer's The Huguenots; he escorted her to the Chapel Royal to see Wellington, to the House of Commons, and to the first of three sittings for her *portrait by George Richmond. She met George Henry *Lewes and Julia *Kavanagh, and she was an embarrassingly reticent guest at Thackeray's evening party. The heroines of her novels share her disconcerting habit of silent observation. She did not tell her father that she attended a lecture by Newman, but could safely describe to him the fascinating animals and birds at Regent's Park zoo, previously seen only in books.

Her longest London visit (30 May 1851–25 June 1851) was very much a West End experience. She visited the *Crystal Palace, and attended Thackeray's lectures in the luxurious Willis's Rooms. Paul *Emanuel's 'Qu'en dites-vous?' in Villette (ch. 27) recalls Thackeray's asking her for her opinion after a lecture. She perhaps met Dickens, or saw him act, and met other distinguished people at the 'patriarch-poet' Samuel Rogers's breakfast table. She was escorted to the magnificent art collections of the Marquess of Grosvenor and the Earl of Ellesmere, in marble halls reminiscent of the kingdom of *Angria. She appreciated sermons by three Protestant preachers, including F. D. Maurice, but thought the Catholic *Wiseman a 'sleek hypocrite'. George Smith took her to Richmond, and to visit the *phrenologist J. P. Browne.

During her last visit, in January 1853, she corrected the proofs of *Villette*, and determined to see the 'real' rather than the decorative side of London life. Accordingly she visited the Bank and the Royal Exchange. Possibly Mayhew's grim accounts of the 'real' led her to visit also grim old Newgate prison, and the so-called model prison, Pentonville (built 1840–2) with its harsh 'separate system' and treadmill régime. She saw the Foundling Hospital (1739), and the handsome buildings of Bethlem Hospital in Lambeth, currently replacing brutal by more humane treatment of the insane. Perhaps she intended to base her future writing on such realities. Her fragmentary *Emma* is concerned with a criminal parent and a distressed, abandoned child.

Lothersdale, a village in a green pastoral stretch of the Aire valley below *Stonegappe, c.4 miles south of Skipton. J. B. *Sidgwick was a prime mover in the building of Christ Church, Lothersdale, in 1838, and became its first churchwarden. Revd Edward N. *Carter, licensed as its first incumbent on 30 November 1838, was living at Lower Leys farm in 1839, but by 1841 had moved to Oakcliffe, the new parsonage house in the village. Charlotte Brontë probably recalled Lothersdale when she described the Duke of *Zamorna standing in a hayfield, 'varry good grazing land', in *Caroline Vernon* (ch. 2) (Gérin *Five Novelettes*, p. 285).

Lowborough, Lord. One of Mr Arthur *Huntingdon's dissipated friends in *Tenant*, Lord Lowborough is an interesting mixture of weakness and strength of character. In his youth his gambling losses drive away his fiancée, Caroline; after further losses, he decides to marry an heiress, Annabella *Wilmot, to whom he becomes devoted. She scorns him and mocks his desperate attempts to give up drinking and gambling. He becomes suicidal when he discovers she has been Huntingdon's mistress for two years, and when she elopes with another lover he divorces her. He retreats to his castle in the north of England with his children (a son and a nominal daughter), and later marries a very different wife—without beauty and wealth but with cheerfulness, integrity, and good sense.

Lowood is a charity institution in *Jane Eyre*, based on Charlotte's memories of the Clergy Daughters'

School at *Cowan Bridge. Fifty miles from *Gateshead Hall, and set in a picturesque forest dell, it is a many-windowed, irregular building, with a wide, long schoolroom where about 80 pupils study, and a long dormitory, where the water for washing is sometimes frozen hard. In winter the school day begins before dawn with prayers lasting an hour and a half. Meals are ill-prepared, scanty, or inedible, the girls' quaint uniforms are unbecoming, and discipline is harshly enforced, particularly by Miss *Scatcherd, who flogs Helen *Burns for slatternliness but ignores her intelligent answers during lessons. Miss Miller is an overworked underteacher, Miss Smith teaches sewing, and the 'strange foreign-looking elderly' Madame Pierrot teaches French. Only the superintendent, Miss Maria *Temple, is enlightened, refined, and sympathetic, mitigating the harsh régime imposed by Revd Robert *Brocklehurst, son of the founder Naomi Brocklehurst. In winter pupils become paralysed with cold during his services at Brocklebridge church, and their faces are almost flayed by the icy wind during their 2-mile walk there and back. All the pupils have lost one or both parents, and the £15 a year they or their friends pay is supplemented by benevolent subscribers: nevertheless semi-starvation, neglected colds, and inadequate clothing predispose the girls to infection by typhus, of which many die in the spring after Jane Eyre arrives. Since Mr Brocklehurst shuns the infected school, a new housekeeper is able to cater more liberally. Public enquiry leads to better regulations, more humane management, and new buildings on a new site, so that the school is transformed into 'a truly useful and noble institution'. There Jane is happy and studious, becoming a teacher during her last two years at Lowood.

Lowton (*Kirkby Lonsdale) is a 'little burgh' 2 miles from *Lowood, in *Jane Eyre*. Jane Eyre walks there to take her advertisement for a post as governess, and receives Mrs Alice *Fairfax's reply from the old dame at the post office. The coach for *Millcote leaves from the Brocklehurst Arms in Lowton.

Luddenden Foot, a hamlet situated where the wooded Luddenden valley opens into the ravine-like Calder valley c.4 miles west of *Halifax. It had two inns, a cornmill, and a railway station on the Leeds and Manchester railway, where Branwell was clerk-in-charge from 1 April 1841 to 31 March 1842. He lodged at Brearley Hall, near Luddenden village. The local people were mainly spinners, handloom weavers, woollen-mill workers, or watermen. Branwell drank with friends at the Lord Nelson (1654), and filled a notebook with jottings, sketches, and poems. He was dismissed because of a discrepancy of £11 1s. 7d. in the station accounts for which he was responsible.

Luddite riots, a major source for *Shirley* and other Brontë writings. In 1811–12 the west Yorkshire woollen trade, the Lancashire cotton trade, and the east midlands hosiery trade centred on Nottingham experienced widespread attacks on mills and the destruction of machinery. The general term 'Luddism' applied to the movement derives from the mythical leader of the Nottingham machine-breakers, General Ned Ludd, a pseudonym used in an anonymous threatening letter. Hardship caused by cyclical unemployment during the Napoleonic war years was exacerbated by the inability to trade with Europe or the United States. Manufacturers were hit first when Napoleon closed French ports to vessels from Britain or her colonies (November 1806) and then forbade neutrals to deal in British goods (December 1807). Britain responded with a number of 'orders in council' (edicts from the sovereign on advice from his ministers, allowing the government to act without parliamentary sanction) placing severe restrictions on trade with France by any neutral country. This particularly affected the United States which placed its own restrictions on both France and Britain to force them to lift their sanctions. Hard-hit manufacturers sought to reduce costs by dismissal of workers, lower wages, and especially the introduction of machinery and new techniques that made skilled workers redundant. This also affected cottage-based industries that were forced out of business because the efficient new machinery in the mills produced more cloth of better quality. Fuelled by political radicalism of the early 1800s and by economic hardship, artisans sought to extort concessions from employers by direct action. The machine-breakers targeted particular factories and workshops because of the use of new machinery, changes in production standards, or harsh employers. In 1811, Parliament, which had rejected recent campaigns for a minimum wage, passed a bill making frame-breaking a capital offence: the Brontës' hero *Byron was among those who spoke against the bill. In the summer of 1812, the government sent over 12,000 soldiers to areas under Luddite threat, more than the Duke of *Wellington had with him in the Peninsular War.

The cloth dressers of the West Riding of Yorkshire were at the centre of the Luddite troubles. The first attacks began in February 1812 in the *Huddersfield area, attacking a consignment of cropping machines as it crossed Hartshead Moor en route to *Rawfolds Mill, Cleckheaton. In 1806, the owner William Cartwright had introduced new shearing or cropping machines which gave the

cloth an attractive smooth finish. His and other mill owners' decisions to buy more, a move which would further displace cloth workers, sparked off a number of attacks on mills in the area. On 11 April, a large force of Luddites attacked Rawfolds Mill with pistols, hatchets, and bludgeons. Cartwright, who had publicly defied the Luddites, was well prepared for the 20-minute assault, which left two of the Luddites mortally wounded and the mill defenders (including a number of soldiers) unscathed. A week after the attack, Cartwright escaped an assassination attempt as he was returning from Huddersfield. On 28 April, William Horsfall, a woollen manufacturer from Marsden (near Huddersfield), was murdered. Vigorous searches and reprisals for those responsible for the attacks stamped out most Luddite activity, although groups of armed men continued to meet and drill in secret on the moors for some time after.

During this period Revd Patrick Brontë held curacies in areas affected by the risings: the Yorkshire woollen town of *Dewsbury and *Hartshead, 4 miles west of Dewsbury. Large numbers of those in the Rawfolds attack were among Mr Brontë's parishioners and although he supported the establishment in condemning the attack, he did not answer the alarm with a sword in hand as did his friend Revd Hammond *Roberson. However, it is thought that his lifelong habit of keeping a loaded pistol overnight in the house and discharging it each morning, stems from this troubled period. An apocryphal story tells how some of the bodies of the executed men responsible for the murder of Horsfall and the attack on Rawfolds were buried in secret at night in Hartshead churchyard and although Mr Brontë suspected the activity he said nothing.

The Brontë children were familiar from a young age with stories of the Luddites, gleaned chiefly from their father. Their early writings are full of insurrection, radical incitement of the workers and even mill attacks (see especially Alexander *EW*, pp. 83 and 177–8). The leader Sergeant Edward (Ned) *Laury (echoing 'Ned Ludd') and his *Rare Lads are based directly on the Luddite rioters (for example, *Something about Arthur). Charlotte also heard the Luddites spoken about when she was at Margaret Wooler's school, first at Roe Head, then at Dewsbury Moor, not far from Rawfolds Mill: 'Miss Wooler spoke of those times; of the mysterious nightly drillings . . . of the overt acts, in which the burning of Cartwright's mill took a prominent place; and these things sank deep into the mind of one, at least, among her hearers' (Gaskell *Life*, 1. 114–15). Gaskell notes that during Charlotte's research for *Shirley* she sent to Leeds for a file of the 'Mercuries' of 1812–14, possibly at the suggestion of her father who would have recalled reports of the

Luddite riots

Luddites in old issues of the *Leeds Mercury*, to which the Brontës still subscribed (Rosengarten *SEL* (1976), 16. 4. 593). Here Charlotte read articles on the riots and their causes, especially by the editor Edward *Baines, including arguments about the 'Orders in Council' (a phrase she uses in *Shirley*).

Kipling, Lesley, and Hall, Nick, *On the Trail of the Luddites* (n.d.).

Leeds Mercury (1812), excerpts in *Shirley* (Clarendon edn.), app. A.
Peel, Frank, *The Risings of the Luddites, Chartists and Plugdrawers* (2nd edn., 1888).
Rosengarten, Herbert, 'Charlotte Brontë's *Shirley* and the *Leeds Mercury*', *Studies in English Literature* (1976), 16. 4. 593–600.
Thompson, E. P., *The Making of the English Working Class* (1963, revd edn. 1968), ch. 14.

Macarthey, Mr, an Irishman in *Shirley* who succeeds Revd Peter Augustus *Malone as curate in *Briarfield. In a brief and humorous portrait he is said to be decorous, hard-working, and charitable, though too easily upset by Quakers and Dissenters. His original, Revd A. B. *Nicholls (1819–1906), became curate to Revd Patrick Brontë in May 1845 in succession to Revd J. B. *Grant; nine years later he and Charlotte Brontë were married. Following *Shirley*'s publication, Charlotte told Ellen Nussey that Mr Nicholls 'triumphed in his own character' (Smith *Letters*, 2. 337). HR

'Ma chère Jane'. See 'MY DEAR JANE'.

Macterrorglen, Sir Jehu. See SIMPSON, JEREMIAH (MACTERRORGLEN).

MacTurk, Dr William, MD, 1795–1872. On 29 January 1855 Revd A. B. *Nicholls, seeking better advice than Haworth could provide for the ailing Charlotte, sent for Dr MacTurk, reputedly the 'most able physician' in Bradford. On 30 January MacTurk predicted an illness 'of some duration', but perceived no immediate danger. Revd Patrick Brontë reported that both MacTurk and the local surgeon hoped her health would return 'after a few days'; but Charlotte declined rapidly before her death on 31 March. She had used the name 'Mac-Turk' for the skilled, autocratic surgeon, 'less of a humbug' than the local doctor, who attends Robert Gérard *Moore in *Shirley* (chs. 24, 32).

madwoman. See ROCHESTER, BERTHA.

Maid of Killarney, The (London, 1818) published anonymously, a 'modern tale' in which Revd Patrick Brontë aimed 'by a species of innocent guile' to 'allure to well-doing'. His slender thread of romance tells how the young, well-bred Englishman Albion falls in love with the pious Irish maiden Flora Loughlean, and, having been converted to devout Christianity, is allowed to marry her. The story is interwoven with 'cursory remarks on religion and politics' in the manner of Hannah More's *Coelebs in Search of a Wife* and other evangelical moral tales. But it is set, very attractively, in the picturesque surroundings of the Lakes of Killarney, and is told with occasional touches of humour: the young hero is teased for his 'inflated rhapsody' on the 'Queen of Lakes', and is miraculously cured of his jealous 'fever of body and mind' on hearing that his supposed rival is already married. Aiming to show real life, Mr Brontë describes, as well as poor mad Ellen's flower-decked retreat, an Irish mud cabin covered with 'thin green turf' or 'scraws'. He makes quite an exciting episode of the Whiteboys' attack on Loughlean Hall, and he describes vividly an Irish Wake, with its ritual laments: 'O! my dear honey,

why did you die? . . . Speak, ah! speak to your dear children.' His pictures of both pious poor and graceless grumblers are designed to show the benevolence of the virtuous gentry towards them; and his exemplary tale of the horrors of an impenitent deathbed is crudely overwritten. But on the whole his moderation shines through: 'Nanny' speaks gently of the 'dear sweet' priest who would call her a 'harrytic' for reading the Bible; the gentry object to Catholic emancipation, but praise the valiant Catholic soldiers who fought at Waterloo. In politics they advocate reform of inhumane laws which condemn both starving sheep-stealers and violent murderers to death.

Malone, Revd Peter Augustus, the most prominent of the three curates lampooned in *Shirley* (see also DONNE, REVD JOSEPH; SWEETING, REVD DAVID). He is curate to Revd Matthewson *Helstone, Rector of *Briarfield in the West Riding of Yorkshire. Malone's father, a member of the Irish gentry, was 'poor and in debt, and besottedly arrogant; and his son was like him' (p. 11). Loud and boisterous, Malone enjoys his glass of whisky and laughs often at his own jokes. He carries a loaded pistol and a shillelagh during his pastoral visits; this is a time of unpredictable violence by machine-breakers in Yorkshire, and Malone shows some courage in standing with Robert Gérard *Moore and Revd Helstone to defend *Hollow's Mill against attack by the rioting workers. His valour notwithstanding, he is drawn as a self-centred buffoon who believes he is attractive to women, and he imagines himself a suitor, first to Caroline *Helstone, then to the heiress Shirley *Keeldar. At the end of the novel the narrator speaks of 'the premature and sudden vanishing of Mr. Malone from the stage of Briarfield parish' (p. 724), but declines to provide any detail for fear of upsetting the reader. Through Malone and his fellow curates, Charlotte Brontë castigates the failure of the Church of England to rise above petty formalism and materialism to meet the spiritual needs of the people whom it was supposed to serve. Curates, she wrote to Ellen *Nussey on 18 June 1845, 'seem to me a self-seeking, vain, empty race. At this blessed moment we have no less than three of them in Haworth-Parish—and God knows there is not one to mend another' (Smith *Letters*, 1. 399). Malone's original was Revd James William *Smith (b. ?1815), graduate of Trinity College Dublin. He was curate to Revd Patrick Brontë 1843–4, then curate in the nearby parish of Keighley till his abrupt departure from England in 1847, leaving behind a mass of unpaid debts and suspicions that he had misappropriated money donated to charity (Smith *Letters*, 2. 33–4; Lock & Dixon, pp. 391–2). For a time he showed an unwelcome interest in Charlotte's friend Ellen Nussey, arousing Charlotte's contempt by his evident interest in Ellen's possible fortune. Mr Brontë was anxious that Ellen be dissuaded from thinking of Mr Smith, and Charlotte wrote to her on ?29 July 1844 to convey her father's view that 'Mr. Smith is a very fickle man—that if he marries he will soon get tired of his wife—and consider her as a burden—also that money will be a principal consideration with him in marrying' (Smith *Letters*, 1. 361). Wise & Symington (3. 3) print a letter by Revd James C. Bradley ('Mr Sweeting') of 3 May 1902, who insists that Mr Smith was 'a thorough gentleman in every sense of the word, and there was not the slightest ground for the insinuation [Charlotte Brontë] makes against him'. HR

Manchester. In 1841 Manchester and neighbouring Salford together had a population of 270,961, most of whom were crammed into a motley assemblage of old and new buildings in narrow streets or closes. The *Gaskells lived first in Dover Street, then in Rumford Street, and finally escaped from the city smoke to the garden-surrounded 84 Plymouth Grove, where Charlotte Brontë stayed, 27–30 June 1851, 22–8 April 1853, and 1–4 May 1854. But Elizabeth Gaskell's charitable work made her aware of the grim cellar-dwellings where a whole family might live in a single room, their livelihood subject to the uncertainties of Manchester's cotton trade. She described their plight graphically in *Mary Barton* (1848). Sir James *Kay-Shuttleworth, who practised as a doctor in Manchester 1828–35, also drew attention to the effects of poor housing, and to lung diseases caused by cotton dust.

On 19 August 1846 Charlotte took her father to Manchester for his cataract operation by William James *Wilson, in lodgings in unprepossessing Boundary Street. On the day of Revd Patrick Brontë's operation, 25 August, Charlotte received back the manuscript of *The Professor*, curtly refused by a sixth publisher, and soon afterwards began to write *Jane Eyre*.

Though in *Shirley* (ch. 37) Charlotte equated manufacturing Manchester with unpatriotic commercialism, she was aware of its active cultural life—an awareness later enhanced by her contacts with the Gaskells. In August 1848 she received, but refused, an invitation to the Manchester Athenaeum's annual soirée. This institution, opened in January 1836, had moved into a spacious new building designed by Charles Barry in October 1839, providing a library, newsroom, language classes, and a dining room. George Henry *Lewes lectured on speculative philosophy there in February 1849, Charlotte's 'The Orphans' appeared in the *Manchester Athenaeum Album* (1850) and William Makepeace *Thackeray lectured in October 1852.

Kay, Brian, and Knowles, James, 'Where "Jane Eyre" and "Mary Barton" were born', *BST* (1967), 15. 77. 145–8.

Welldon, J. E. C., 'The Brontë family in Relation to Manchester', *BST* (1910), 4. 20. 144–50.

Manfred, the magician in the early *Glass Town and Angrian saga, president of the university for Glass Town nobles on *Philosopher's Island. He is the brother of Captain Butter *Crashey, who also has supernatural powers. The Brontës had read *Byron's verse drama *Manfred*, whose solitary hero invokes spirits by sorcery.

Mann, Miss, a 'crabbed old maid' in *Shirley* who lives alone in *Briarfield, and is befriended by Caroline *Helstone. She is mocked and shunned for her plain looks, moroseness, and censoriousness, but Caroline discovers that beneath her unwelcoming exterior she is a caring and selfless person who 'had passed alone through protracted scenes of suffering, exercised rigid self-denial, made large sacrifices of time, money, health for those who had repaid her only by ingratitude' (p. 200). Robert Gérard *Moore sends his sister Hortense Gérard *Moore to stay with Miss Mann during the *Luddite troubles, and the two spinsters take a trip to Wormwood Wells, 'a noted watering-place' (p. 407). In Miss Mann and Miss Ainley, Caroline foresees her own likely fate as an unmarried woman of no fortune, and mentally exhorts the 'Men of England' to 'look at your poor girls . . . dropping off in consumption or decline; or, what is worse, degenerating to sour old maids' (p. 443), a fate that might be avoided were women given opportunities to engage in useful work. It is possible that both 'old maids' had real-life originals (see AINLEY, MISS). The need for women to have access to employment as a means of supporting themselves and giving their lives a purpose is an issue to which Charlotte Brontë returns frequently in her writing. Writing to W. S. *Williams on 3 July 1849 that her career as a writer has given her 'a hope and motive', she adds 'I wish all your daughters—I wish every woman in England had also a hope and motive. Alas! there are many old maids who have neither' (Smith *Letters*, 2. 227). HR

manuscripts and manuscript collections. *See page 314*

Marchmont, Miss, a rich, crippled old lady, morose, stern, and long confined to two rooms, in *Villette*. Lucy *Snowe agrees to become her companion, realizing Miss Marchmont's courage, originality, and truth of feeling, combined with powerful passions. One February night, after a violent storm, Miss Marchmont tells Lucy of the tragic fate of her fiancé, whom she had seen dragged behind his furiously galloping horse, and who had died in her arms. She determines to prepare for reunion with him by unselfishly making Lucy happy; but a stroke brings death the same night. This inset story prefigures the novel's tragic ending.

Markham, Gilbert, the hero (or anti-hero, since he is a rather unimpressive character) of *Tenant*. He is the narrator of the novel, through his letters to his friend Halford, but the vivid central story of Helen *Huntingdon's journal that he includes, means that he is sidelined for much of the novel. Despite his cultivated taste and penchant for reading, Gilbert's behaviour is often rude and brutal. He lacks charm and even perception at times, but his integrity forms a strong contrast to the dishonesty of the dissolute Mr Arthur *Huntingdon, and his natural, friendly relationship with the young Arthur *Huntingdon does much to redeem his character.

Gilbert, despite his ambitions, respects his father's dying wish that he remain a gentleman farmer and manage *Linden-Car. Initially the admirer of Eliza Millward (see MILLWARD FAMILY), Markham is intrigued by the mysterious Mrs Graham, and falls in love with her. His jealousy at witnessing affection between her and his friend Mr Frederick *Lawrence leads to his irrational and brutal assault on the latter. His coldness to Mrs Graham prompts her to give him her journal, whose contents he recounts to Halford and the reader. When he discovers Mrs Graham's true identity as Helen Huntingdon, and the reason she is in hiding from her dissolute husband, they are reconciled. When Helen leaves the district and Gilbert hears of her husband's death, he is surprisingly paralysed by a sense of social inferiority and his pride prevents him enquiring after her. A rumour that she is to be remarried galvanizes him into action, but even when he reaches her at *Staningley Hall he continues to be intimidated

until Helen reassures him of her disregard for their difference in wealth and position. They are married and live happily at Staningley Hall with Helen's aunt, the young Arthur, and their own 'promising young scions' (ch. 53).

Markham family, in *Tenant*. They live at *Linden-Car, a farm managed by Gilbert *Markham, the eldest son. Mrs Markham is a widow, a matronly housewife, proud of her three children and of her home-brewed ale that is particularly favoured by Revd Michael Millward. She is indulgent towards her sons, but disapproves of Gilbert's flirtation with Eliza Millward (see MILLWARD FAMILY) at the beginning of *Tenant*, and is further distressed by his interest in the mysterious Mrs Graham, about whom she and the village gossip. Her daughter Rose, a pretty, good-natured girl who later marries the recipient of Gilbert's letters, J. *Halford, is equally disposed to listen to the gossip about Mrs Graham. The adolescent Fergus prefers to bait his older, more serious brother about 'the tenant' of Wildfell Hall. Fergus is an unmannerly careless lad who loves shooting and hunting, but when he later falls in love with the Vicar of L——'s eldest daughter, he suddenly makes 'surprising exertions' (ch. 53) to improve himself. He inherits the farm when Gilbert moves to *Staningley Hall.

Marshall, Ann (?1809–47), nurse; later Lydia *Robinson's lady's maid. Branwell Brontë alleged that Ann saw him 'do enough to hang him' in his affair with Mrs Robinson, who had to swear, on her husband's deathbed, to 'complete severance' from Branwell. Like Winifred Gérin's suggestion that the £520 Ann deposited with Mr Robinson might be a reward for spying on her mistress (Gérin *BB*, p. 237), Branwell's statements remain unproven. Ann, like her fellow servants, probably entrusted her savings to her employer. Mrs Robinson paid the money into Ann's estate after her death, and also paid the Mr Atkinson who looked after Ann in her last illness.

Marsh End. See MOOR HOUSE.

Martin, John (1789–1854), painter, etcher, engraver, engineer and reformer. Like Thomas *Bewick, Martin was a Northumberland artist whose career and work was well known to the Brontës. Three of his large mezzotint prints hung on the Brontë Parsonage walls: *The Deluge, Belshazzar's Feast*, and *Joshua Commanding the Sun to Stand Still*; and a watercolour copy of his *Queen Esther* made by Branwell Brontë from *Finden's engraving in the *Forget Me Not* annual (1831) still survives in the BPM. Martin first exhibited at the *Royal Academy of Arts in 1811 and at the
(*cont. on page 317*)

T HE manuscripts of the Brontës' writings, many of them dispersed through the agency of T. J. *Wise, are scattered in many different locations in the UK and USA, and possibly elsewhere.

Novels and related manuscripts

The fair copy holograph manuscripts of Charlotte's major novels are extant. Those of *Jane Eyre*, *Shirley*, and *Villette* form part of the George *Smith memorial bequest in the British Library: BL Additional MSS 43474–6, 43477–9, and 43480–2. The manuscript of The *Professor, which passed into the hands of T. J. Wise, and was sold through Messrs J. Pearson & Co to J. Pierpont Morgan sen. in *c.*1900, is in the Pierpont Morgan Library, New York. All are written in a clear, cursive script in ink, and were used in the printing house to set up the first editions. Compositors' names are written at intervals in the margins or other spaces. *Jane Eyre* and *The Professor* have comparatively few revisions, though there are one or two heavily inked deletions of words or phrases in *The Professor*, probably made by Revd A. B. *Nicholls, who edited the novel for the press in 1857. The second and third volumes of *Shirley*, and the whole of *Villette* are considerably revised; there are numerous deletions, alterations, and insertions, and some passages or phrases have been literally cut out with scissors or a knife by Charlotte, who, in the traumatic period after the deaths of her sisters, often found it difficult to maintain the flow of composition or to be satisfied with her fair copies. For more information about these manuscripts, see the textual introductions and notes in the Clarendon and World's Classics editions. Some of the subsidiary manuscripts related to the four novels, most of them dispersed by T. J. Wise, are pencil drafts, written in a small, reasonably legible cursive hand, but roughly revised. Bonnell MS 118 (8) in BPM is an undeveloped fragment referring to a house called Gateshead, and a draft of part of the preface to the second edition of *Jane Eyre* can be found in Berg, NYPL. Bonnell MSS 124 and 125, in BPM, contain four fragmentary rejected beginnings or episodes relating to *Villette*. In the Pierpont Morgan Library are a draft preface and two fragments relating to *The Professor*, and Berg, NYPL, has another draft preface and a version of Frances *Henri's poem in chapter 23 of the novel, beginning 'At first I did attention give'. Charlotte's 'A Word to the "Quarterly"', intended as a preface to *Shirley* but not published with it (see SHIRLEY: 'A WORD TO THE "QUARTERLY"'), is a fair copy in ink, and now forms part of the Seton-Gordon collection at the BPM. Transcripts of all these manuscripts can be found in the Clarendon editions. See also EMMA; SHIRLEY: 'JOHN HENRY'; 'WILLIE ELLIN'. The manuscripts of *Wuthering Heights*, *Agnes Grey*, and *Tenant* have not been located. Possibly T. C. *Newby did not return them to their authors.

Other writings: UK locations

In the UK the largest collection is in the BPM, which has four main series of Brontë manuscripts.

1. The general collection purchased by or donated to the *Brontë Society since its inception in 1893; identified as BS, with a number.

2. Manuscripts from the collection of Henry H. *Bonnell, bequeathed by him to the Society, and received by the BPM in January 1929; identified as Bonnell or Bon, with a number, and listed in the Brontë Society *Catalogue of the Bonnell Collection in the Brontë Parsonage Museum* (1932). The Bonnell Collection also includes such relics as Emily's writing desk, and Brontë drawings, books, and administration papers.

3. The Seton-Gordon collection (SG MSS), containing almost all Charlotte's letters to George Smith and his mother. With other related documents, they were presented to the Brontë Society in 1974 by Mrs Elizabeth Seton-Gordon, Smith's only surviving granddaughter. After her death in December 1985 the Society received her bequest of the remainder of her large collection of Brontëana, including another letter from Charlotte to Mrs Smith, two pencil drawings by Charlotte, and a carte-de-visite photograph of her. This confirmed that an Emery Walker negative discovered in the National Portrait Gallery in 1984 was of Charlotte (*BST* (1982), 18. 92. 101–14, and (1986), 19. 1 & 2. 27–8, 41–3).

4. The Grolier collection (Gr MSS), 44 letters written by Charlotte and a devoir by Emily acquired from Christie's of New York at their sale on 25 March 1980 of manuscripts donated on behalf of the Grolier Club of New York.

The Brontë Society also owns some of Ellen *Nussey's correspondence and her transcriptions of some of Charlotte's letters, some of the correspondence of Brontë biographers and editors, many transcriptions by C. W. *Hatfield of manuscripts and other documents, copies of letters of administration, documents relating to Mr Brontë's parish duties, the Robinson papers, consisting of correspondence and other documents relating to the *Robinson family of Thorp Green, and many documents throwing light on the local history of the Haworth area. The Society has also benefited from the generous bequest by the American scholar Dr Mildred Christian (1901–89) of her working papers, transcripts of Brontë letters, photostats of letters in other libraries, including the now inaccessible *Law Collection, and photographs formerly owned by Joseph Horsfall *Turner.

Another major UK collection is T. J. Wise's Ashley Library of books and manuscripts of letters, poems, and juvenilia, now in the British Library, which also has separate collections and single items. These include Charlotte's letters to George Henry *Lewes, BL Add. MS 39763. The Brotherton Collection in the Brotherton Library, University of Leeds, has many letters, poems, and some juvenilia by Branwell Brontë, Charlotte's letters to Amelia Ringrose (see TAYLOR, AMELIA), and much supporting documentation, including some of the correspondence of C. K. *Shorter. The Fitzwilliam Museum, Cambridge, has Charlotte's letters to Margaret *Wooler, donated by her great-nephew, Dr Thomas Clifford Allbutt. The John Rylands University Library, University of Manchester, owns letters from Charlotte and Mr Brontë to Elizabeth *Gaskell, other Gaskell correspondence, and the manuscript of the *Life*. The John Murray archive owns Mr Brontë's letters to George Smith and some of the *Smith, Elder and Company ledgers, and there is other valuable material relating to the firm in the National Library of Scotland, which also has a typescript copy of Smith's 'Recollections'. Smaller collections of manuscripts written by or related to the Brontës can be found in the various depositories of West Yorkshire Archives; in Birmingham University Library; the Bodleian, Oxford; Trinity College, Cambridge; Trinity College Dublin; the Wordsworth Library, Dove Cottage, Grasmere;

Manchester Central Library; Sheffield University Library; the Penzance Library; and in other public and private collections.

Other writings: USA locations

In 1947–8 Professor Mildred Christian published *A Census of Brontë Manuscripts in the United States* in the *Trollopian*, later *Nineteenth-Century Fiction*. This included letters and other manuscripts in the Huntington Library, which owns the largest single collection of Charlotte's letters to Ellen Nussey in the USA. Other important manuscripts holdings are in Berg, NYPL, which has a rich and varied collection of Brontë letters, poems, drafts, devoirs, juvenilia, and some of the correspondence of Mary *Taylor and Ellen Nussey. NYPL also houses a small but significant group of letters in the Montague and Pforzheimer collections; although much of the Pforzheimer collection has recently moved to the Ransom HRC Texas, NYPL still retains Charlotte's six letters and her early story 'The Adventures of Ernest Alembert' (see ALEMBERT, ERNEST). Also to be found in New York are the great assembly of letters, poems, devoirs, and juvenilia in the Pierpont Morgan Library, and smaller collections or single manuscripts at Columbia University Library, New York University Library, and the University of Rochester Library. Ransom HRC Texas has Charlotte's letters to James *Taylor, a devoir by Emily, some of Mary Taylor's correspondence, and other related material, especially in the T. J. Wise collection. There are fine collections of Brontë manuscripts in the Houghton and Widener collections at Harvard, including some of the earliest miniature manuscripts and the important late fragments of 'Willie Ellin', Princeton University Library has exceptionally rich collections, notably the manuscripts collected by Morris L. Parrish and Robert H. Taylor. Single letters or good small collections can be found in the Beinecke Library, Yale University, Boston Public Library, Knox College Library, Maine Historical Society Library, the Denison Library at Scripps College, the Friends' Historical Library at Swarthmore College, Wellesley College, and in other academic, public, and private libraries.

Sources

Ancillary collections which throw light on the acquisition and dispersal of manuscripts are owned by the University of British Columbia Library and Rutgers University Library. Manuscript locations are given, wherever possible, in most recent scholarly editions of the Brontës' writings.

Alexander, Christine, *A Bibliography of the Manuscripts of Charlotte Brontë* (1982).
Alexander, Christine, and Rosengarten, Herbert J., 'The Brontës', in Joanne Shattock (ed.), *The Cambridge Bibliography of English Literature*, 4 (3rd edn., 1999).
Index of English Literary Manuscripts (1992), vol. 4.
Neufeldt, Victor, *A Bibliography of the Manuscripts of Patrick Branwell Brontë* (1993).

British Institution in 1813, but remained outside the academy because of his theatrical and flamboyant techniques. He became a popular rival to J. M. W. Turner when his career took off in the 1820s with his exhibition of *Belshazzar's Feast* (1826) and his 24 mezzotint illustrations to *Milton's Paradise Lost* (1827). His style combined the vast landscapes and architectural phantasmagorias of de Loutherbourg and Turner with tiny figures gesturing in the sublime mode like those of Henry Fuseli or Benjamin West, and his work was informed by recourse to a scientific knowledge of geography and perspective, giving him control over scale. *Blackwood's Edinburgh Magazine* referred to him as 'King of the Vast' (Nov. 1832). His choice of apocalyptic subjects, the use of a dominant colour, and strong contrasts of light and dark made his paintings particularly dramatic. His biblical and historical catastrophes had a reforming zeal that reflected his numerous engineering and town planning projects, including ventilating coal mines and sewage disposal systems for London that were ahead of their time. Branwell hoped to follow in the footsteps of men like Martin, an artist from the north of England who had made good in London (see ART OF THE BRONTËS). Branwell's good friend Joseph Bentley *Leyland had studied under Haydon, a friend of Martin who like him had been excluded from the Academy, and the Bradford artist W. O. Geller, whom Branwell also knew, had studied under Martin himself.

Between the years 1826 and 1839, while the Brontës were busy writing their juvenilia, Martin supplied over 27 designs for *annuals and journals from his now famous paintings. Most of these were available to the Brontës and we know that specific engravings had a profound effect on them. In 1828, for instance, they were able to see in *The Keepsake* a small line engraving by E. J. Roberts of Martin's *Sadak in Search of the Waters of Oblivion* (1812) that Winifred Gérin believes inspired a scene in one of Charlotte's earliest tales, 'An Adventure in Ireland' (Gérin CB, pp. 43–4). Numerous visionary landscapes in the Brontë juvenilia are recognizably 'Martinesque', such as a description in 'The Search After Happiness' that describes *The Deluge* which Charlotte saw every day on the Parsonage walls. Here her characters are perched 'on the top of a rock which was more than a thousand fathoms high', beneath them are 'liquid mountains tossed to and fro with horrible confusion', and above them is 'a mighty firmament, in one part covered with black clouds from which darted huge and terrible sheets of lightning' (Alexander *EEW*, 1. 46). The Great Glass Town, a city of marble pillars, solemn domes, splendid palaces and mighty towers, suggests the grandiose perspectives of Martin's lost cities of the ancient world: Babylon, Nineveh, Pompeii, and Herculaneum. His *Fall of Babylon* (1819), with its glass-like, translucent reflections of fairy-tale structures on the banks of the Euphrates, suggests perhaps an origin for the name of the Brontës' imaginary city itself; and the massive architecture of *The Fall of Nineveh* is mirrored in the new Angrian capital of *Adrianopolis (Alexander *EW*, p. 235). The Glass Town painter 'Dundee', later renamed 'Sir John Martin Dundee', is known for paintings of 'the most sublime majesty', such as 'The Spirit of Cawdor Ravine' that has all the hallmarks of Martin (Alexander *EEW*, 1. 64–5).

Apart from the three large Martin mezzotints mentioned above, two further framed engravings are recorded (with inadequate titles) in the newspaper Bill of Sale on the death of Revd Patrick Brontë: one is almost certainly Martin's print of *St Paul Preaching at Athens*, a separate small plate from Westall and Martin's *Illustrations of the New Testament* (1836), and the other was probably a pirated version of Martin's *Destruction of Pharaoh's Host*, retitled *Passage of the Red Sea* (although it could also be G. H. Phillips's engraving of Francis Danby's *The Passage of the Red Sea*, widely available at the same time (Thomas Balston, *John Martin 1789–1854: His Life and Works* (1947), 285–91)). The latter provides an analogue of Charlotte's actress Vashti in *Villette* (ch. 23), whose 'magian power' and 'prophet-virtue' could 'release and re-mingle a sea spell-parted'. In such works, Martin reinforced the language of *Byron for the Brontës: both were masters of the material sublime, both depended on the visual and spectacular for their effects.

Martin's many 'literary' works reproduced in mezzotint prints popularized his name and reinforced texts with which the Brontës were already familiar. Their subjects ranged from biblical scenes to those of Byron, Milton, Shelley, and Thomas Gray's poem *The Bard* (1817), to classical scenes like *Marcus Curtius* and *Clytie*. They would have known that Martin glossed his vision of Deluge by reference to 'that sublime poem' Byron's *Heaven and Earth* and that he relied on Byron's drama *Sardanapalus* for his image of self-destruction in the *Fall of Nineveh*. *Belshazzar's Feast*, too, has affinities with Byron's vision of *Belshazzar*. By the time Martin illustrated *Manfred* (1837), the young Brontës were well acquainted with Martin's visual analogues of their favourite poet. Charlotte could be sure, when she referred to *Belshazzar's Feast* in her 'Biographical Notice' to her edition of *Wuthering Heights* (1850), that her audience would be familiar with the image.

Charlotte ultimately denounced, in intellectual terms, Martin's artistic methods (as she did the passionate nature of her *juvenilia), but she always retained an emotional affinity for his visionary

Engraving of John Martin's *Belshazzar's Feast* (1821–3).

designs. We see this, for example, in Lucy Snowe's impression of the carnival in *Villette* with its exotic architecture and colour: 'a land of enchantment, a garden most gorgeous, a plain sprinkled with coloured meteors, a forest with sparks of purple and ruby and golden fire gemming the foliage; a region . . . of strangest architectural wealth—of altar and of temple, of pyramid, obelisk, and sphynx' (ch. 38). When Charlotte eventually saw an original Martin painting at the 1850 Summer Exhibition of the Royal Academy, it was an illustration of Thomas Campbell's poem 'The Last Man': 'a grand, wonderful picture . . . showing the red sun fading out of the sky, and all the soil of the foreground made up of bones and skulls' (Smith *Letters*, 2. 411). (The illustration said to be by Charlotte 'after' Martin and known as 'The Bay of Glass Town' in so many publications and displayed for so long in the BPM as such, is actually a hand-coloured lithograph by Martin, *The Temptation*, from the fourth edition of *The Sacred Annual: Being the Messiah, A Poem, In Six Books*, by Robert Montgomery (1834).)

Martineau, Harriet (1802–76), writer. Brought up in a Unitarian family in Norwich, she made her name with her *Illustrations of Political Economy* (1832–4), popularizing ideas of social reform through simple stories. In 'A Manchester Strike' she touched on themes later embodied in *Shirley*—a novel Charlotte Brontë presented to Martineau in November 1849, acknowledging the 'pleasure and profit' derived from her works, especially her novel *Deerbrook* (1839). Martineau's 'affectionate approbation' of the gift emboldened Charlotte to visit her in London on 9 December 1849, thus revealing 'Currer Bell's' identity. A friendly correspondence ensued, and Charlotte visited Martineau at The *Knoll, her *Ambleside home, from 16 to 23 December 1850. Charlotte relished her company, summing her up as 'both hard and warm-hearted, abrupt and affectionate—liberal and despotic'. Martineau's controversial *Letters on the Laws of Man's Nature and Development* (1851), written with Henry George Atkinson (?1815–84), was criticized as much for its credulity as its agnosticism. Charlotte was shocked by what she interpreted as atheism, considered the book a 'death-blow' to Martineau's future usefulness, but still wrote appreciatively. From July to December 1851 Charlotte acted for Martineau as an intermediary with George *Smith for the publication of her novel *Oliver Weld*, which Martineau wished to appear anonymously. Charlotte was not surprised by Smith's rejection of an unorthodox novel which advocated tolerance for Catholics, in this period of controversy over so-called 'Papal Aggression'. Martineau's critique of *Villette*

in the *Daily News* (3 Feb. 1853), mingling praise with objections to the 'atmosphere of pain' and the characters' obsession with love, caused the hurt and indignant Charlotte to break off the friendship. Despite this, Martineau paid tribute to Charlotte's 'force of integrity' in a fine obituary in the *Daily News* (6 Apr. 1855), expressing the 'deep grief of society that her genius will yield us nothing more'.

Martyn, Henry (1781–1812), missionary to India; a brilliant scholar at St John's College, Cambridge, and curate to Revd Charles *Simeon. An ardent evangelical, sympathetic to Revd Patrick Brontë, he helped to secure for him £10 per year from *Wilberforce and Henry Thornton, 1804–6. His austere commitment to missionary work inimical to his frail health, and his parting from Lydia Grenfell, may be echoed in St John *Rivers.

Marxist approaches. The debate about literature's relation to ideology and class—a debate which Karl Marx himself initiated when he revised his initial pronouncements on this subject in 1852—has developed within Brontë studies just as it has in other areas of investigation. Marx's economic theories have been elaborated, contested, and reformulated numerous times, so that it is no longer possible to speak of Marxism in the singular, if by that we mean one distinctive and internally coherent system of thought. Rather, we must refer to the varieties of Marxist theory as they have evolved over time and in relation to developments in other fields. A number of fundamental principles of Marxism have remained unchanged, however, and these can be recognized as the underpinnings of any form of Marxist literary criticism. First, Marxism holds that in modern societies, literature—like religion, politics, law, philosophy, and the non-literary arts—is part of a 'superstructure' which develops out of the 'economic base', or 'infrastructure', to which it is tied. As a result, literature cannot be properly understood without reference to the socio-economic conditions of its production, dissemination, and reception. Marxism thus insists on 'materialist' readings of the literary text, which it views both as the product of labour (made within a system of production and exchange, the effects of which can be seen in the text's form as well as in the uses to which the text is put within culture) and as the means by which the work of ideology is conducted by, and upon, the members of a particular society. Precisely how literature functions with respect to ideology has been a matter of considerable dispute among Marxists. Some have seen literature as a powerful cultural 'apparatus' which helps to reinforce the prevailing ideology and thus to reproduce the current class structure; others have

Marxist approaches

argued that literature has a greater degree of autonomy from the economic base than other components of the superstructure and that literary texts therefore have the capacity to expose the insufficiencies and inconsistencies of the dominant ideology, with a potentially liberating effect. Marxist readings of the Brontës' writing show how Marxist literary criticism has recently evolved into more broadly conceived forms of cultural criticism that effectively accommodate the insights and methods of other approaches to the study of literature.

Early Marxist assessments of the Brontës are now considered significant contributions to Brontë scholarship and criticism, but at the time of their initial publication they were met with notable indifference. The first of such pieces, an essay by David Wilson ('Emily Brontë: The First of the Moderns', *Modern Quarterly Miscellany*, 1 (1947), 94–115), fell on such barren ground that even a like-minded critic such as Raymond Williams wrote in apparent ignorance of this groundbreaking work. Such conspicuous oversight is explained partly by the inhibiting effect that formalism had on all contextual approaches to literary analysis from the early 1940s to the mid-1970s, even outside the United States, where Marxist political theory was long viewed with some suspicion. It must also be conceded, however, that Brontë studies in particular proved especially infertile soil for Marxist criticism in these early years. Because of a long-standing practice of viewing the Brontës as reclusive female authors—remarkable for their self-inspired genius rather than for their observations of the social world around them—claims about their novels' relevance to socioeconomic history were very slow to gain acceptance. Emily, the most esteemed of the Brontës at mid-century, was especially thought of as a writer whose work was 'above' the temporal and local conditions to which the Marxist critic attends. Wilson was well aware that his study of *Wuthering Heights* 'in light of West Riding social history' presented Emily 'in a new light' (p. 94). As later Marxist critics such as Terry Eagleton were to note, Wilson's article provides a very useful account of the history of class conflict in the Brontës' part of Yorkshire; it also presents convincing evidence that the Brontës must have seen the ravaging consequences of industrialization and class oppression in the streets of Haworth on an almost daily basis. Wilson looks at Emily's poems and novel for 'direct expression of [her] opinions upon the political and social conflicts' of the day, and he claims that she had 'a close understanding and sympathy with [working-class] people', who are represented in her novel through the figure of her embattled hero, Heathcliff. Emily is, in Wilson's

view, 'the first of the moderns' because she 'saw and wrote about the events of social history that mark the beginning of the modern era' (p. 104). *Wuthering Heights*, he concludes, is the forerunner of 'the proletarian novel' (p. 115).

Four years later, Arnold Kettle made the more modest (but at that time still largely unaccepted) claim that '*Wuthering Heights* is about England in 1847'; its central concerns are 'not with love in-the-abstract but with the passions of living people, with property-ownership, . . . the arrangement of marriages, . . . the relations of rich and poor' (*An Introduction to the English Novel* (1951), vol. 1, 139). Kettle sees Heathcliff in his youth as the novel's representative worker and, in his adulthood, as a capitalist. Initially 'degraded' within society, Heathcliff eventually adopts 'the classic methods of the ruling class, expropriation and property deals', in order to beat his oppressors at their own game. That Heathcliff loses his 'human values' in the process shows that Emily recognized the moral and spiritual price of survival within capitalist society (pp. 150–5). Unlike Wilson, Kettle is careful to insist on the formal sophistication of Emily's novel as well as its ideological importance. Emphasizing that 'there is nothing sloppy or uncontrolled' in the narrative presentation, he notes that her mode of writing is, like that of Dickens: 'intensely concrete' and yet fundamentally symbolic (pp. 139–40).

Twenty-two years later, Raymond Williams identified a materialist basis for the plot of *Wuthering Heights* in the conflict between the 'working Heights' and the 'renting Grange'; between, that is, an older, agrarian-based class of property-owners who worked their own land and a newer class of gentry whose economic relation to the land was mediated and indirect. When Catherine Earnshaw decides to marry Edgar rather than the propertyless Heathcliff, the lovers are so divided that the novel can offer no 'social solution' to their problem, according to Williams (*The Country and the City* (1973), 176). In an earlier essay, Williams compares Emily and Charlotte to Blake and other Romantic poets who wrote in a context of political and social turbulence which provoked 'an intensity of desire' along with a similarly 'intense [and] often desperate apprehension of isolation and loss' ('Charlotte and Emily Brontë', in *The English Novel from Dickens to Lawrence* (1970), 197–8). Like Kettle, Williams is attentive to the formal qualities of the Brontës' writing; specifically, he contrasts the 'multipersonal' narrative perspective of *Wuthering Heights* with the 'personal' relationship established between narrator and audience in *Jane Eyre* and *Villette*, though, like Kettle, he does little to show how these formal features are pertinent to his Marxist analysis.

Terry Eagleton's *Myths of Power* (1975) is a significant advance over earlier Marxist assessments of the Brontës in this respect. Drawing on structural and phenomenological models of interpretation, Eagleton identifies the 'categorical structures' of the Brontës' fiction—and their imaginative consciousnesses—as derived from the particular social history of the West Riding, Yorkshire. While previous critics had analysed the oppositions in the Brontës' narratives in other terms—for example, as the competing literary modes of realism and romance or as the expression of timeless impersonal forces such as David Cecil's 'force of storm' and 'force of calm' (see CRITICISM 1860–1940)—Eagleton was the first to argue that this two-part structure was ideologically based. In the works of all three Brontë sisters, Eagleton claims, one can see 'two ambiguous, internally divided sets of values' that are related to the 'tensions and alliances between the two social classes which dominated [their] world: the industrial bourgeoisie, and the landed gentry or aristocracy' (p. 4). Filled with conflict and interchange that stem from the convergences and antagonisms between the two classes, Charlotte's novels are energized by this tension; where she fails, in Eagleton's view, is in her attempt to fuse or balance these oppositions at the end of her narratives. The artistically problematic ending of *Jane Eyre*, for example, results from Charlotte's need to fall back on the middle-class fantasy of upward mobility, a myth that reinforces the very ideology that the novel earlier seeks to criticize. *Wuthering Heights*, on the other hand, is an aesthetically superior work in Eagleton's view because it is a formally coherent presentation of the ideological incoherence of the social world it describes. Eagleton finds Anne's novels the least successful because they have neither the dynamic ambivalence of Charlotte's novels nor the unified 'tragic vision' of *Wuthering Heights*.

Throughout the 1970s, Marxist interest in the Brontës focused largely on Emily's novel, though in 1978 members of the Marxist-Feminist Literature Collective countered Eagleton's critical judgement of Charlotte's writing with their own appreciative assessments of *Jane Eyre*, *Shirley*, and *Villette* ('Women's Writing: *Jane Eyre*, *Shirley*, *Villette*, *Aurora Leigh*', *Ideology and Consciousness*, 3 (1978), 30–5). Later Marxist-feminist readings of *Jane Eyre* tend to be more in line with Eagleton's, however. Jina Politi, for example, argues that 'the novel's movement is not towards liberation. It is towards a tidying, a consolidating of class positions' ('*Jane Eyre* Class-ified', *Literature and History*, 8 (1982), 90). Like Eagleton, she sees *Jane Eyre* as a 'conflicted' novel: beginning with rebellion, its narrative mode and its subject almost immediately split

into oppositions—realism versus fantasy, rebellious protagonist versus encultured bourgeois woman narrator—oppositions which are ultimately blended and reduced to the latter. Politi's observation that Charlotte's novel 'constructs a new female stereotype' (p. 89) by invoking the inferior otherness of foreign females (especially the French) enriches her Marxist reading by linking it with feminism, post-colonial theory, and Foucault's theories of subject formation. Unlike Eagleton, who passes a negative judgement on *Jane Eyre* ostensibly on aesthetic grounds, Politi underscores the cultural significance of the novel by showing how it contributed to the discursive formation of both national identity and the feminine subject in 19th-century England. In *The Politics of Story in Victorian Social Fiction* (1988), Rosemarie Bodenheimer also offers an appreciative reading of Charlotte's work (in this case *Shirley*) while conceding its aesthetic weakness and its ideological conservatism. The 'shapelessness' of *Shirley*'s plot derives, according to Bodenheimer, from its author's 'non-progressive view of history', or more precisely, from Charlotte's assumptions about the necessary role of paternalism within both the public (labour relations) and private (familial relations) spheres. It is these outdated assumptions, and Charlotte's admirable refusal to allow utopian solutions to the problems she depicts, that produces in *Shirley* 'an anatomy of paternalism more profound and disturbing than any other in the genre' (p. 555). Like the readings of Charlotte's novels by Politi, Bodenheimer, and other Marxist-influenced critics of the 1980s, Marxist criticism of *Wuthering Heights* during this decade increasingly drew upon developments in other areas of thought to make its literary analyses more subtle and informed. Frederic Jameson's *The Political Unconscious* (1981), for instance, is indebted not only to psychoanalysis but also to structuralist theories of narrative which allow him to argue that the novel is about 'impersonal forces' of history (rather than the ahistorical forces of the cosmos or metaphysics). Drawing on Vladimir Propp's *The Morphology of the Folk Tale* (1968), Jameson contends that Heathcliff should be analysed less as credible human 'character' than as a function of the text. As the 'actant' or 'donor figure' in a narrative about emerging capitalism, Heathcliff provides the fortune necessary for the working out of the plot and 'recodes the new economic energies [of the historical period] as sexual passion' (p. 128). *Wuthering Heights* is, in this reading, one of those significant literary texts that express 'our collective fantasies about history and reality' (p. 34). James Kavanagh's 1985 book *Emily Brontë* is even more synthetic in its use of concepts derived from other theorists and from other fields of study. Combining Freudian notions of family romance, Lacanian theories of 'the imaginary', feminist insights provided by critics such as Sandra Gilbert and Susan Gubar, Althusserian notions regarding the reproduction of social subjectivities, along with more traditional Marxist authorities, such as historian E. P. Thompson and Jameson himself, Kavanagh analyses the family unit in *Wuthering Heights* as a socio-economic institution undergoing historical change in its relation to labour. Originally 'the site of production of goods' (yeoman farming at Wuthering Heights), the family becomes 'instead the site where the social subjects necessary for a capitalist economy are formed'. In its new form, the family is 'an arena of psycho-sexual struggle': Heathcliff is the displaced father who seduces the daughter (Cathy), and Nelly is the 'phallic mother' who controls the narrative and speaks 'The Law of the Father'. Asserting that 'class and social questions . . . are intrinsic to the figuration of the Oedipal romance' in *Wuthering Heights*, Kavanagh shows how the family unit survives not only the disruption of desire (embodied in Heathcliff) but also the transforming effect of emergent capitalism (also represented through Heathcliff) (pp. 87–93). In 1989, John P. Farrell offered a different kind of Marxist reading of Emily's novel by showing how the 'heteroglossia' of the text (its multiplicity of voices) and the structures by which narrators and readers are related to each other are employed in the novel's search for 'community' and rejection of 'society', as those two concepts had been theorized by Victorian social critics including Thomas Carlyle, Émile Durkheim, and Marx himself ('Reading the Text of Community in *Wuthering Heights*', *ELH* 56 (1989), 173–208). Farrell thus blends Marxist theory and subject matter with the concerns and techniques of text-oriented reader-response criticism and narratology.

Marxist theory continued to be an important approach to the study of the Brontës' writing after the 1980s, but by this time it had combined with a number of other approaches to form more comprehensive and integrative fields of analysis. Often referred to as 'the sociology of literature' in the 1970s, Marxist-based literary criticism is today recognizable in the work of contemporary cultural criticism, which may be said have subsumed its more narrowly conceived forerunner. See also CULTURAL CRITICISM; FEMINIST APPROACHES; POST-COLONIAL THEORY; PSYCHOANALYTIC APPROACHES. CB

Eagleton, Terry, *Myths of Power: A Marxist Study of the Brontës* (1975).
Kavanagh, James, *Emily Brontë* (1985).
Wilson, David, 'Emily Brontë: The First of the Moderns', *Modern Quarterly Miscellany*, 1 (1947), 94–115.

Mary Queen of Scots (Mary Stuart) (1542–87) fascinated the young Brontës, especially Charlotte who modelled several of her heroines on this ill-fated historical character. She features in much of Sir Walter *Scott's work, such as his novel *The Abbot*, and especially his *Tales of a Grandfather*, read by the young Brontës. The daughter of James V of Scotland and Mary of Guise, she became a queen when she was a week old. At 6 she was affianced to the Dauphin, raised as a Roman Catholic in France and married first Francis II of France, then (following her return to Scotland) Lord Darnley and Bothwell, both of whom were murdered. As a Catholic and the focus of numerous plots, Mary Stuart was a threat to her Protestant cousin Elizabeth I who imprisoned her and finally had the young Queen of Scots beheaded. Both her tragic life and her physical features attracted Charlotte, who often described her resemblance as seen in portraits (see, for example, Alexander *EEW*, 2(2). 178 and 191). Mary Stuart's name and character probably suggested those of Mary Henrietta, Queen of Angria; and the Scottish wife of the Duke of Zamorna's double in *The *Spell* is clearly based on Mary Stuart. Charlotte is also thought to have written a poem, 'Lines on Mary Queen of Scots', that has since disappeared (note amongst Hatfield correspondence, BPM).

Mason, Bertha. See ROCHESTER, BERTHA.

Mason, Richard. A visitor to *Thornfield Hall, who claims to have been *Rochester's friend in the West Indies, in *Jane Eyre*. Feeble in character and physiognomy and probably doomed like the rest of his family to become insane, he retains some affection for the madwoman, his sister Bertha, married to Rochester fifteen years before, but she attacks him. Jane Eyre, ignorant of the truth, tends his wounds, and he is taken away secretly. But while he is staying with Jane's uncle John Eyre, the correspondent in Funchal, Madeira, of Mason's mercantile house, Jane's letter arrives announcing her forthcoming marriage to Rochester, and he intervenes dramatically to prevent it.

materials, writing, drawing, and painting. See ART OF THE BRONTËS; HANDWRITING AND BRONTË SIGNATURES.

Mathilde, a pupil at the Pensionnat *Heger, who replied affectionately to a letter from Charlotte Brontë in c.July 1844. Modest, and nervous about her imminent piano performance on Mme Heger's fête-day, 12 August, she was grateful for Charlotte's assurances of affection and esteem. The embossed monogram on Mathilde's letter may indicate high rank: in *The Professor* (ch. 25), Frances *Henri's pupil Mathilde is the 'heiress of a Belgian count'.

Maxwell, Mr and Mrs, the uncle and aunt of Helen *Huntingdon in *Tenant*. They provide a home for Helen at *Staningley Hall on the death of her mother, despite the fact that her neglectful father is still living. From the well-meaning but conventional Mrs Maxwell, Helen learns her religious and moral principles, but ignores her recommendations of Mr *Boarham as a suitor. Unfortunately the 18-year-old Helen also ignores her good advice against marrying Arthur Huntingdon, who is the son of an old friend of her uncle and becomes one of his shooting companions. On the death of her Uncle Maxwell, Helen inherits Staningley estate, but Aunt Maxwell remains there in her own apartments after her niece's second marriage.

mechanics' institutes. Dr George Birkbeck (1776–1841) established successful classes for mechanics in Glasgow after his appointment as professor of natural philosophy in 1799. They were continued by his successor after Birkbeck left for London in 1804. He founded the London Mechanics' Institute (now Birkbeck College) in 1823. The movement spread rapidly, and by the end of 1825 institutes were established in 21 towns in, or on the borders of, Lancashire and Yorkshire. The Manchester Mechanics' Institute (1824) provided classes in French and German, mathematics and drawing, so that warehouse employees as well as draughtsmen and managers became better qualified and could command higher wages. Many institutes arranged social outings, musical entertainments, educational visits, and exhibitions, and in all, the library was a vital facility: Revd Patrick Brontë borrowed books from the *Keighley Mechanics' Institute. In February 1850 Charlotte discovered that copies of *Jane Eyre* and *Shirley* were to be bought for the Haworth Mechanics' Institute, founded in spring 1849, and supported by Charlotte, her father, the mill-owning Merralls, and others. A. B. Nicholls became its President in December 1849. The history of the Leeds Institute (1824) is typical of the movement: once the largest in the country, its numbers had dwindled to 73 by 1850. Problems all institutes faced were the lack of elementary knowledge among some members, the difficulty of arranging suitable classes for different levels of knowledge and ability, and the high cost of engaging suitably qualified instructors. Many institutes had declined or closed by the 1870s, when their function was taken over by university extension courses and other forms of adult education. The movement spread overseas to the British colonies, and some mechanics' institutes (such as the Sydney Mechanics' School of Arts founded in 1833) still exist today.

Medina, Sheik. See JORDAN, JOHN JULIAN, LORD.

Merrall, Hartley (1819–95), boyhood friend of Branwell Brontë, younger brother of Michael (1811–81), and son of Hartley Merrall sen. (1777–1846), a local mill owner. Leyland records that when Merrall, 'an accomplished musician', accompanied Branwell on a visit to Liverpool in August 1839, he bought some sheet music for Branwell and in return Branwell painted his portrait (Alexander & Sellars, p. 333). Juliet Barker assumes that Michael Merrall was Branwell's friend (Barker, p. 195), but the identification of the younger Hartley is supported by Leyland's preface thanking him and William Woods, both early acquaintances of Branwell, and by the existence of a copy of Leyland's *Brontë family* which once belonged to Hartley and has his notes in the margins.

Leyland, 1. 87–9.

Methodism touched the lives of all the Brontës. It was founded by John *Wesley (1703–91), Fellow of Lincoln College Oxford, 1726–51. He led a group of students who were 'methodical' in attendance at Communion, Bible study, and prison visiting. When he and his brother Charles (1707–88) were unsuccessful as missionaries in Georgia in 1735–7, the *Moravian brethren helped to strengthen his faith. In Aldersgate chapel in London on 24 May 1738 he felt his heart 'strangely warmed' with the assurance of salvation. His lifelong itinerant preaching began in 1739 in Bristol, where he preached to the brutalized colliers of Kingswood. In 1740 his sermon on free grace marked his renunciation of *Calvinist doctrine, whereas George Whitefield (1714–70) left the Wesleyans to found Calvinistic Methodism. Charles Wesley also preached, and wrote more than 6,000 hymns, three of which are ridiculed, with their accompanying sighs and groans, in *Shirley* (ch. 9). John Wesley did not wish to secede from the Church of England, but separation eventually came in 1795. Revd Patrick Brontë's career was materially assisted by Wesley's friend, Thomas Tighe; in *Wellington, Shropshire, he was influenced by the Wesleyan Mary Fletcher, and at *Woodhouse Grove he met his Methodist wife Maria Branwell *Brontë. In Haworth Revd William *Grimshaw had built West Lane Methodist church. Nevertheless in 1837, when Haworth Dissenters were agitating for the abolition of church rates, Mr Brontë endorsed as 'just & Excellent' the virulent anti-Dissent opinions in *An Earnest Address to the Working Classes . . . by a Poor Man* (2nd edn., 1836), where 'noisy and uproarious' Wesleyan preachers are said to hold 'very little in common with Christians' (pp. 86–7). Mr Brontë apparently became more tolerant in his old age: Lock & Dixon assert that he attended some Methodist evening services (p. 346).

Anne Brontë was sympathetic to Methodism, echoing Charles Wesley in her poem, 'My God! O let me call thee mine', and copying his 'O for a heart to praise my God' in the music manuscript book she used between June 1843 and October 1844. But Charlotte, Branwell, and Emily regarded most Methodist preachers as oily, canting hypocrites (see BROMLEY, MR). For their mockery of excited Methodist meetings and publicity-seeking instant converts they had ample precedent in 18th-century caricatures: Tony Lumpkin's 'the rascals . . . always preach best with a skinful' in *Goldsmith's *She Stoops to Conquer* is echoed in *Julia* ('the preachers drank eight quarts of ale & now they're praying'). Branwell's Brother *Ashworth travesties Methodist sermons by preaching on the 'text', 'I came not to save but to destroy'. Timothy *Steaton of the juvenilia reappears in *The *Professor* as a 'joined Methodist' and 'engrained rascal'. In *Wuthering Heights*, Revd Jabes *Branderham perverts the biblical 'Seventy Times Seven' into an absurdity, and the servant *Joseph perverts the gospel into a repressive and retributive doctrine. There is an element of snobbery in the Brontës' satire, and for Charlotte at least, a concern lest what the church really stood for might be degraded. Much of Wesley's preaching had been directed at ignorant labourers uncared for by the established Church, and Primitive Methodism, one of a series of schisms, whose leaders from 1811–12 again held open-air revival meetings, was the special butt of Branwell Brontë's derision. See also RELIGION.

Methodist Magazine. Founded by Revd John *Wesley as the *Arminian Magazine* in 1778, the *Methodist Magazine* was designed to counter the narrow *Calvinism of other early Methodist magazines. In *Haworth, Elizabeth *Branwell kept a complete set which had belonged to the Brontë children's mother. Derisively described in *Shirley* as 'mad Methodist Magazines, full of miracles and apparitions, of preternatural warnings, ominous dreams, and frenzied fanaticism' (p. 440), the *Methodist Magazine* inspired some of the children's early supernatural tales. Joseph Benson, the editor from 1804 to 1821, when the issues owned by Mrs Brontë were published, was a learned and conservative man who increased the magazine's circulation to 20,000.   CB

Althoz, Josef L., *The Religious Press in Britain, 1760–1900* (1989).

Millcote, a large manufacturing town like Leeds (on the Aire) or Bradford, on the banks of the River A——, in *Jane Eyre*. It is 70 miles nearer London than *Lowood is. A smooth main road leads to *Thornfield Hall, 6 miles away. It has a coaching inn, and Rochester and Jane visit a silk warehouse there.

Millevoye,   Charles-Hubert   (1782–1816), minor French poet, noted in the early 19th century for his elegiac lyric 'The Fall of the Leaves' ('La Chute des feuilles'). M. Constantin Heger's *dictation of the poem appears in one of Charlotte Brontë's notebooks. She also wrote a devoir with the same title ('The *Fall of the Leaves') and referred to Millevoye in the manuscript of *Shirley*, although the poem she attributes to him there was actually written by André *Chénier.   SL

Lonoff, pp. 256–7.

Millward family. Revd Michael Millward, the widowed vicar of *Lindenhope in *Tenant*, is a tall, elderly but active man, with a preference for strong meats and malt liquors. His distinctive figure is characterized by a shovel hat, a stout walking stick, and knee breeches and gaiters that 'incased his still powerful limbs' (ch. 1). He is equally powerful 'in important dogmas and sententious jokes, pompous anecdotes and oracular discourses' (ch. 4). 'He was a man of fixed principles, strong prejudices, and regular habits,—intolerant of dissent in any shape, acting under a firm conviction that *his* opinions were always right, and whoever differed from them, must be, either most deplorably ignorant, or wilfully blind' (ch. 1). As Mr Millward ages and the duties of his parish become too much for him, he appoints Richard Wilson (see WILSON FAMILY) curate. Richard marries Millward's elder daughter Mary and succeeds him in the parish. Mary is plain, quiet, sensible, and scholarly, unappreciated by nearly everyone in the village, except her father, Mrs Graham, children, animals, the poor, and Richard Wilson. Her younger sister Eliza is the opposite: lively and bewitching. She is the object of Gilbert *Markham's affection before he encounters Helen Graham. Jealousy of the latter makes Eliza resentful, and she maliciously informs Gilbert of Helen's supposed wedding. She later marries a wealthy tradesman.

Milnes, Richard Monckton (1809–85, created Baron Houghton 1863), Conservative MP for Pontefract 1837, but later a Liberal. Philanthropic, cultivated, influential, hospitable, and a bibliophile (with a private collection of pornographic art), he introduced himself to Charlotte Brontë on 29 May 1851 after Thackeray's lecture, and afterwards privately described her 'insignificant' person, rustic speech, and odd constrained manner. She refused his invitations in 1851 and 1852. In 1854 he and Elizabeth Gaskell sought to improve Revd A. B. *Nicholls's income. In October 1859 he made notes on Branwell's letters to John *Brown about Mrs Lydia *Robinson and others.

Barker, pp. 333–4, 459–61.

Milton, John (1608–74), major poet and essayist. A favourite of Revd Patrick Brontë, Milton was familiar to the Brontë siblings from childhood, and his works echo in their juvenilia, novels, and Charlotte's letters. Though they allude most frequently to *Paradise Lost*, and Milton stands first among the poets Charlotte recommended to Ellen *Nussey (4 July 1834, in Smith *Letters*, 1. 130), by 1830 Charlotte was also familiar with at least some of Milton's prose (*Reason of Church Government*).

Milton's influence registers in Charlotte's visual images. She painted a watercolour (dated 4 March 1835) based on his pastoral elegy 'Lycidas', copying a shepherd from Henry Fuseli's *Solitude at Dawn* inspired by Milton (Alexander & Sellars, p. 238). The imagery of *Paradise Lost* resonates, too, in the visionary paintings in Jane Eyre's portfolio which arrest Rochester's attention: the 'Kingly Crown' and 'Shape which shape has none' recalling Death, the evening star, the colossal head, and the perching cormorant that evokes Milton's description of Satan when he first alights in Eden (*Paradise Lost*, 2. 666–73 and 4. 196). In her fiction Charlotte quotes from or directly alludes to *Samson Agonistes*, 'L'Allegro', 'Il Penseroso', and—in all four of her novels—*Paradise Lost*. Critics have suggested connections between Jane Eyre and the chaste woman in Milton's *Comus*, as well as between Rochester and Milton's Satan. In *The Professor* Milton's moral authority provides security when Frances is first alone with William Crimsworth in her home: reading *Paradise Lost* aloud as he corrects her intonation eases her embarrassment (ch. 19). A reference to Milton in *Shirley* captures a personal association for Charlotte: the *Yorke family's residence *Briarmains, an attractive site of both familial comfort and aesthetic culture, features stained glass windows depicting *Shakespeare and Milton, details derived from the home of her girlhood friend Mary *Taylor.

Emily's poetry and fiction echo Milton's diction in specific phrases and in the habitual use of intense, dynamic verbs. Her fascinating diabolic men suggest the influence of Milton's Satan as well as *Byron's characters. The thwarted power, tarnished beauty, and ultimate evil of Lucifer/ Satan resonate powerfully in the figure of Heathcliff, and *Wuthering Heights* has been interpreted through its evocations of *Paradise Lost* and inversions of the epic's themes and power relations: Stevie Davies reads the novel as a female myth of genesis, expulsion, and rebirth energized by Emily's admiration for Milton, whereas Sandra Gilbert and Susan Gubar interpret the work as a reversal of the patriarchal myth of the Fall expressing Emily's revolt against Milton's misogyny.

Charlotte captures Emily's rebellion against Milton's views in her character Shirley, who complains that Milton modelled his passive, domestic Eve on his cook (alluding to *Paradise Lost*, 5). Shirley describes her contrasting vision of the first woman as a Titan, an Amazon mother originally called 'Nature', with heart and strength to bear not only a Messiah, but to endure a thousand years of bondage (*Shirley*, ch. 18). BT

Cass, Jeffrey, 'Miltonic Orientalism: *Jane Eyre* and the two Dalilas', *The Dickens Studies Annual*, 32 (2003).
Davies, Stevie, *Emily Brontë* (1988).
Gilbert, Sandra M., and Gubar, Susan, *The Madwoman in the Attic: The Woman Writer and the Nineteenth-Century Literary Imagination* (1979).

Mina Laury ('The last scene in my last book'), 17 Jan. 1838, Angrian novelette written by Charlotte Brontë in minuscule script on loose pages (MS in Taylor, Princeton) in the Christmas holidays during her period as a teacher at *Roe Head. The cynicism of her usual narrator Charles Townshend (see WELLESLEY, LORD CHARLES ALBERT FLORIAN) is absent and although his voice is implied in comments to the reader, he is not named and not obviously the narrator. The novelette represents an advance in Charlotte's narrative technique, with clear emphasis on the presentation of character in action and a well-focused plot that concentrates on the love of Mina *Laury for the faithless Duke of *Zamorna. This involves Lord *Hartford's unsuccessful proposal to Mina, his duel with Zamorna, and the latter's subsequent treatment of Mina. A sub-plot, Zamorna's duplicity and neglect of his wife Mary, underscores his exploitation of Mina, whose selfless devotion to him is demonstrated especially in the description of her efforts to save Zamorna's eldest son, Ernest 'Fitzarthur' *Wellesley, from his hideous death. Mina is content to live in seclusion and neglect as housekeeper at the Angrian shooting lodge of Mr Pakenham (Zamorna).

Charlotte's treatment of love and her analysis of Mina's feelings foreshadow the honesty of her portrayal of women's passion in her later novels. Mina's attitude prefigures in part that of Jane *Eyre and even of Catherine *Earnshaw in *Wuthering Heights*: 'She had but one idea—Zamorna, Zamorna, Zamorna—! . . . she could no more feel alienation from him than she could from herself.' Mina's devotion, however, borders on masochism and is exploited by Charlotte for the last time; selfless adoration without moral conscience has its limitations for the ambitious writer. In this story Charlotte has kept the Northangerland–Zamorna relationship, which dominates so many of the Angrian manuscripts, in the background; but the fury of the Angrians at renewed relations between their king and the treacherous Duke of *Northangerland is represented in the heated dispute between Zamorna and his prime minister Warner Howard *Warner.

Alexander EW, pp. 165–8.
Gérin Five Novelettes, pp. 123–69.

Mirfield, a village and parish on the River Calder, 3 miles south-west of *Dewsbury, in the woollen district of Yorks. In the mid-19th century the chief manufactures were blankets, carpets, and cloth. Mirfield had its mill-chimneys, but the surrounding well-wooded countryside was beautiful, and Margaret *Wooler took her *Roe Head pupils on 'long scrambling walks' down its shady lanes (Gaskell Life, 1. 113). Anne's employers at *Blake Hall had a pew in Mirfield church, just outside their estate. Green House, the home of Thomas Atkinson (see ATKINSON FAMILY), and the *Moravian chapel at Wellhouse were also within the parish.

missionaries. See CHURCH MISSIONARY SOCIETY.

Moir, David (1798–1851), under the pseudonym 'Delta', regular contributor of poems and ballads to *Blackwood's Edinburgh Magazine between 1820 and 1844. The Brontës read his tale of 'Bessy Bell and Mary Gray: A Scottish Legend of 1666' in their *annual *Forget Me Not (1831), and Charlotte copied the accompanying engraving. Emily Brontë's Gondal poems echo Moir's ballads of Scottish history, especially the exploits of Douglas, a character adopted for Gondal. His descriptions of nature's beauty, his predilection for elegy, and his spare, simple style are also echoed in Emily's verse (Barker, p. 274). Moir's debt to Sir Walter *Scott and his celebration of Abbotsford, Scott's home, further reinforced the Brontës' love of Scotland and their early hero Scott.

Monkey's Island (Isle), 300 miles off the coast of Glass Town; a popular resort like nearby Stumps' Island in the *Glass Town and Angria saga. It was founded by Monkey, one of the original Twelve Young Men. The old-fashioned inhabitants of Stumps' and Monkey's Islands belong to an obsolete race of 'round rosy-faced, curly-pated, straight-legged, one-shoed beings', who speak in the old-fashioned Young Men's Tongue. These are the remnants of the original toy soldiers, referred to as antediluvians and mocked by the Verdopolitans for their fare of melons and rice, and for their prosy, old-fashioned

drawl. Branwell Brontë illustrated them at the end of his first magazine for 1829 (Alexander & Sellars, p. 187) and they are described in detail in Charlotte's The *Foundling (Alexander EEW, 2(1). 52).

'Monthly Intelligencer', a four-page newspaper in four columns by Branwell Brontë (in BPM), completed in April 1833 and probably modelled on the *Leeds Intelligencer, to which Revd Patrick Brontë contributed a number of letters to the editor. The contents include descriptions of a grand dinner hosted by Rogue (Duke of *Northangerland), a meeting of the General Senate of Glass Town, two sessions of the House of Commons in which Branwell skilfully imitates the verbatim reporting of parliamentary debates in the newspapers of his day; a leading article on 'Rogue [sic] in Public and Rogue in Private'; and a poem 'Song applicable to the present crisis' by Young *Soult the Rhymer. Both sessions of the Commons are dominated by Rogue demanding the abolition of the monarchy and the establishment of a republic.   VN

Alexander & Sellars, p. 303 (illustrations).
Miscellaneous Writings, 1. 183–201.
Neufeldt BB Works, 1. 250–65.

Montmorency, Hector Matthias Mirabeau, a Verdopolitan nobleman who maintains his original French connections in the *Glass Town and Angrian saga; contemporary of the Duke of Wellington, banker and 'familiar' of the young Alexander Percy (Duke of Northangerland). Montmorency is essentially a Gothic villain, sinister, dark, and constantly scheming. His country estate, Derrinane, is in *Wellington's Land. His marriage to Harriet *O'Connor, sister of Arthur O'Connor, is unsuccessful; she is seduced and then deserted by Percy, who leaves her to die in misery. Montmorency has two daughters: Harriet, who becomes Lady *Castlereagh, and Julia, who elopes with William *Etty. After the latter have been married two years, Julia and their child, Zorayda, are mysteriously abducted; Zorayda returns when she is 18, having been raised by Quashia *Quamina (see LEAF FROM AN UNOPENED VOLUME, A). Montmorency is recast as Thaddeus Daniels in Charlotte Brontë's fragmentary novelette *Ashworth.

Montmorency, Miss Julia. See MONTMORENCY, HECTOR MATTHIAS MIRABEAU.

Moore, George, lawyer and toady of General Lord Edward *Hartford, on whose land he has always lived, in the *Glass Town and Angrian saga. His fortune was made the night Angria was declared a nation, since he is also a merchant with a warehouse and ships at the port of Doverham, the chief port. His fortunes are on the rise and he has a new mansion, Kirkham Wood. A shrewd, unprincipled man of middle age, he becomes an Angrian magistrate. His eldest daughter Harriet is dead, but he has groomed his youngest, Jane *Moore, for an eminent position in society.

Moore, Hortense Gérard, the 35-year-old sister of Robert Gérard *Moore and Louis Gérard *Moore in *Shirley.* Hortense is tall and stout, with black hair and black eyes. A native of Antwerp, she is resolutely Belgian in the face of English custom in dress, speech, and housekeeping, though this puts her at odds with her English maid *Sarah. Hortense, who lives with Robert at *Hollow's Cottage in *Briarfield, holds a high opinion of herself, and a correspondingly low opinion of almost everyone else except her brothers. She acts as a kind of governess to her young cousin Caroline *Helstone, whom she tutors in several subjects, and in whom she attempts to inculcate 'the perfect control and guidance of her feelings' (p. 78). Her friends in Briarfield include the redoubtable Mrs *Yorke and the morose old maid Miss *Mann. Laetitia *Wheelwright and her sisters, who had attended the Pensionnat *Heger in Brussels from July 1842 to August 1843, maintained that they would have known 'that *Shirley* was by a Brussels pupil . . . from the absolute resemblance of Hortense Moore to one of their governesses—Mlle. Haussé' (Wise & Symington, 3. 52). Mlle *Haussé was one of the teachers at Mme Heger's school during the time in 1843 that Charlotte spent there as a teacher.   HR

Moore, Jane, an Angrian beauty known as 'The Rose of Zamorna' in the *Glass Town and Angrian saga. She has many admirers and is seen as quintessentially Angrian in her rounded form, plump neck, white shoulders, reddish-gold tresses, pride, flashiness, and lack of romance and sensitivity. William Percy calls her 'a superb animal' and is more interested in her 'shadow', her demure companion Elizabeth *Hastings. Jane is the youngest daughter of George Moore, lawyer and toady of General Lord Edward *Hartford whom Jane intends to marry.

Moore, Sir John (1761–1809), Scottish soldier who served in the American War of Independence, the Revolutionary Wars in France, the West Indies, Ireland, Holland, Egypt, Sicily, and Sweden. In 1808 he was sent to strengthen the English army in the *Peninsular War and assumed chief command; but Spanish apathy, French successes elsewhere, and English intrigues placed him in a critical position. With the fall of Madrid and *Napoleon Buonaparte advancing with 70,000 men, Moore was forced to retreat with only 25,000. The formidable march of nearly 250 miles through mountainous country in winter conditions, harassed by the enemy, and the desperate battle against French troops under Marshal Soult on 19 January 1809, is legendary. The French defeat, Moore's fatal wound in the moment of victory, and his burial early next morning are celebrated in Charles Wolfe's famous poem *The Burial of Sir John Moore* (1817), well known to the Brontë children (see, for example, Neufeldt *BB Works*, 1. 384).

Moore, Louis Gérard, in *Shirley,* the younger brother of Robert Gérard *Moore, tutor to young Henry *Sympson and formerly tutor to Shirley *Keeldar when she lived with the Sympsons. Though born in Belgium like Robert, he was educated in England, and has adopted teaching as his profession. By nature more reflective and deliberate than his brother, he carries out his duties uncomplainingly, despite the cool treatment he receives from the Sympson family. 'His pupil [Henry Sympson] loved him; he asked nothing more than civility from the rest of the world' (p. 514). Louis accompanies the Sympson family on its visit to *Fieldhead, and there his love for Shirley, first born when he was her tutor, is rekindled, but must remain unspoken because of the difference in their station. It is his calm strength that enables Shirley to overcome the fears aroused by the dogbite she has suffered. Her feelings for Louis are conveyed through her unexpected submissiveness to his quiet authority and her playful resumption of their former teacher-pupil relationship; his yearning finds clearest expression through internal monologues set down in a notebook (see chs. 29, 36). Brought closer together by trying circumstances (the attempted assassination of Robert, the hostility of Mr Sympson), they declare their love for one another, defy convention, and are married. While Louis superficially resembles William Crimsworth in his professorial role and sheltering strength, he is too much a compound of idealized traits to be wholly convincing as the man who wins Shirley's heart. Though he possesses a restrained passion and repressed desires that make him a potentially interesting contrast to his more forceful and unreflective brother, Louis remains incompletely realized, an uneasy hybrid of the qualities of *Rochester from *Jane Eyre* and William *Crimsworth from *The Professor.* Behind the fictional projection of all three of these figures lie Charlotte's yearnings for and memories of M. Constantin *Heger, her teacher in Brussels, the 'maître' whose influence upon her imagination would find fullest expression in her creation of the Belgian professor Paul *Emanuel in *Villette.*   HR

Moore, Robert Gérard, a cloth manufacturer in *Shirley* who leases *Hollow's Mill, near *Briarfield in Yorkshire, from Shirley *Keeldar. At the novel's commencement ('in eighteen-hundred-eleven-twelve') he has lived in the district for two years with his older sister Hortense Gérard *Moore. About 30 years of age, Moore is tall, thin, 'very foreign of aspect' (p. 33). His Belgian mother, Hortense Gérard, had married her father's English business associate Robert Moore, uniting two merchant families, but the fortunes and standing of the family business tumbled under the impact of the French Revolution. Now their Belgian-born son Robert seeks to discharge the debts that he has inherited, 'to rebuild the fallen house of Gérard and Moore on a scale at least equal to its former greatness' (pp. 34–5). In advancing his trade, he is determined to install the latest machinery in his mill, but his plans are frustrated both by the opposition of local workers and the depression of trade caused by the war with France and its impact on relations with America. In his dealings with workers he is harsh and unsympathetic, refusing to be intimidated by threats of violence against his mill and his person. When *Hollow's Mill is threatened by an organized force of machine-breakers, Moore is prepared, successfully repelling the attack with help from fellow manufacturers and a small group of soldiers. Subsequently he shows himself to be relentless in pursuit of the ringleaders. He is, however, capable of more humane feeling, as is apparent in his treatment of one deserving working man, William *Farren, whose suffering he attempts to alleviate. In his domestic relations he shows himself to be warm and considerate, especially to his 18-year-old cousin Caroline *Helstone, who spends much time with his sister at *Hollow's Cottage, and whose strong feelings for Robert are very apparent. Moore seems to reciprocate those feelings, but fears for his business cause him to draw back, and to look instead towards a possible connection with the young heiress Shirley Keeldar, newly arrived in the neighbourhood. For a time he courts Shirley, even proposing marriage, but she rejects him; only later does he learn of her strong feeling for his brother Louis Gérard *Moore. While away pursuing the rioters, and subsequently on a visit to London, he obtains new insights into the hardships of the working poor, and becomes more compassionate; ironically, at the very moment that he reveals his change of heart, he is shot by a crazed weaver, Michael *Hartley, and for several weeks lies seriously ill in the care of the *Yorke family at *Briarmains. He recovers, and guided by a new humility and self-understanding, turns to Caroline with strengthened love. With a change in Britain's military fortunes and revived commercial prosperity, Robert's prospects improve, and in August 1812 he and Caroline are married.

Robert is a descendant of the cruel older brother figure (Edward *Percy, Edward *Ashworth, Edward *Crimsworth, John Henry *Moore) that Charlotte Brontë repeatedly drew in her juvenilia (see Alexander *EW*, ch. 29), but much softened in outlook and conduct. His Belgian ancestry reminds us that *Shirley* grew out of an attempt to recast *The Professor*, which has a Belgian setting and which was the first of Charlotte's adult novels to adumbrate the pattern of a love between an experienced older man and an eager, deep-feeling young woman, a pattern derived in large part from Charlotte's memories and refashioning of her time at school in Brussels with M. Constantin *Heger. The detail concerning Moore's determination to rebuild his family's business was probably suggested by the story of Joshua *Taylor, father of Charlotte Brontë's close friend Mary *Taylor, whose banking business failed in 1825, and who is otherwise portrayed in *Shirley* as the manufacturer Hiram *Yorke. HR

Moore, Thomas (1779–1852), Irish poet, historian, and lawyer, famous in his lifetime for his *Irish Melodies* (1807–8 and 1834); his political satires and oriental poems, including *Lalla Rookh: An Oriental Romance* (1817); and his controversial *Letters and Journals of Lord Byron, with Notices of his Life* (1830). Moore's Irish heritage and songs would have appealed to the Brontës, and his close friendship with Byron would have confirmed their interest. In 1834 Charlotte recommended Moore's biographies of Byron and Sheridan (Smith *Letters*, 1. 131), and her novelette *Caroline Vernon* suggests she had also read Moore's biography of Lord Edward Fitzgerald (Alexander *EW*, p. 196). Charlotte also read *Lalla Rookh*, to which she alludes in all her novels (*The Professor* (Clarendon edn.), p. 186 n.).

Moor House, or Marsh End. The *Rivers' family home, in *Jane Eyre*, separated from *Morton by marsh and moor, where Jane finds shelter. Through a small latticed window in its low, mouldering wall, Jane sees a firelit kitchen like that at *Haworth Parsonage. She hears and answers Rochester's call in its moonlit parlour and garden. It resembles Moor Seats, near Hathersage, in the Peak District.

Moravians. A small Protestant denomination founded in 1457, and later strengthened by the leadership of Count Nikolaus von Zinzendorf (1700–60). Moravian missionaries eventually travelled widely, influencing other Protestant sects, notably Methodism. The *Nussey family had contacts with Moravian communities in Mirfield,

Gomersal, and Fairfield near Manchester, where Mercy *Nussey briefly became a sister. Through the Nusseys Charlotte Brontë perhaps heard of the Moravian Frances Jane Eyre of Fulneck near Leeds. Moravians live an orderly life, with daily prayers within communities under the spiritual authority of elected bishops, and believe in the doctrine of *universal salvation. Anne Brontë was visited and comforted by Revd James *La Trobe in 1837.

> Connor, Margaret, '*Jane Eyre*: The Moravian Connection', *BST* (1997), 22. 37–43.
> —— 'The Rescue: James La Trobe and Anne Brontë', *BST* (1999), 24. 1. 55–65.
> —— and Outram, Rosemary, ' "Miss Temple" and the Connors', *BST* (2001), 26. 1. 27–45.

Morgan, Revd William (1782–1858; BD 1823), a portly, loquacious Welshman, ordained priest 1805; 1806–12 assistant curate All Saints, *Wellington, Shropshire, where he became Revd Patrick Brontë's friend; incumbent of Bierley, Yorks., from 1812, curate to John Crosse of *Bradford, 1813–15; incumbent Christ Church, Bradford, 1815–51, rector of Hulcott, Bucks., 1851–8. He married Jane Branwell Fennell (1791–1827), Mrs Brontë's cousin, on 29 December 1812; baptized Maria, Elizabeth, Charlotte, and Anne Brontë; and buried Mrs Brontë, Maria, Elizabeth, and Branwell. A fervent, anti-Catholic evangelical, he founded and edited the *Pastoral Visitor*, to which Mr Brontë contributed. A possible model for Revd Dr Thomas *Boultby in *Shirley*, and an admirer of Charlotte's novels. He married Mary Alice Gibson (d. 1852) in 1836, married a third time soon after 1852, and died in Bath, 1858.

Morley, Babbicombe, pompous associate of the Angrian Party; later one of the Duke of Zamorna's Angrian ministers, in the *Glass Town and Angrian saga. He is characterized by his pretentious legal jargon (Alexander *EEW*, 2(2). 262).

Morley Hall. See POETRY BY BRANWELL BRONTË; LEYLAND, JOSEPH BENTLEY.

Mornington Court, residence of the fictitious Duke of *Wellington and his family in Wellington's Glass Town, in the *Glass Town and Angrian saga; a name derived from the title of the historical *Wellington's father and grandfather, Lord Mornington. The name is also used for one of the Duke of Zamorna's sons, Edward Mornington (*A* *Leaf from an Unopened Volume*).

Morpeth, Lord. See CARLISLE, 7TH EARL OF.

'Mort de Moïse, La'. See 'DEATH OF MOSES, THE'.

'Mort de Napoléon, La'. See 'DEATH OF NAPOLEON, THE'.

Morton, a village like *Hathersage, in a pastoral vale amid North-midland moors, in *Jane Eyre*. It is inhabited by farmers and workers in Mr Oliver's needle factory and iron foundry. The vicar, St John *Rivers, provides for Jane Eyre a cottage and schoolhouse facing quiet fields half a mile from the village and in sight of the Olivers' Vale Hall.

Murat, Joachim (fictional), 'the flower of French Chivalry', a survivor of the *Young Men's Play, in the *Glass Town and Angrian saga. He first fights with the Ashantees against the Duke of Zamorna in the *War of Encroachment, leading a regiment of French horsemen at the Battle of Little Warner, but then changes sides and becomes an Angrian minister. Murat is based on Napoleon's brother-in-law, Marshal Joachim Murat (1767–1815), the brilliant French cavalry officer who was made king of Naples in 1808 and who also changed allegiance several times during Napoleon's decline in power. Charlotte Brontë received a Napoleonic relic from M. Constantin *Heger given to him by Murat's son (see NAPOLEON BUONAPARTE).

Murgatroyd, Fred, in *Shirley*, a worker in the stables at *Hollow's Mill. He is one of the workers accompanying Joe Scott on the ill-fated expedition to procure new shears and frames for Hollow's Mill. He contends with the preaching tailor and agitator Moses *Barraclough for the attentions of *Sarah, the maid at *Hollow's Cottage. Their rivalry leads to a fight in which Fred is beaten; his revenge is to report to his employer, Robert Gérard *Moore, a conversation he overhears in which Barraclough reveals his role in the smashing of Moore's machinery and outlines his plans to lead a deputation of workers to meet with Moore. The report enables the mill owner to plan Barraclough's capture and arrest (ch. 8). HR

Murray family, in *Agnes Grey*. Agnes Grey's second post as governess is with the Murrays of *Horton Lodge. Mr Murray is a roistering foul-mouthed country squire, fox-hunter, and farmer. His handsome, dashing wife delights chiefly in parties and fashionable dress. She spoils her children, but expects Agnes to oblige, instruct, and refine her daughters, and to cram her reluctant sons with Latin grammar. She actively promotes her elder daughter Rosalie's marriage to the wealthy, vicious Sir Thomas Ashby.

Rosalie, a slender, fair beauty with some talent for music and languages, values showy accomplishments as assets in the marriage market. An unprincipled flirt, she leads the rector, Revd Mr *Hatfield, to propose, then scornfully refuses him. Though she comes to respect Agnes's good principles, she mischievously tries to spoil her relationship with Edward *Weston. Rosalie also encourages her admirer Harry Meltham even after her marriage to Ashby. Hating her husband, she seeks the friendship of Agnes, who advises her to try to improve him, or failing that, to find satisfaction in her own integrity and in cherishing her baby daughter.

The younger daughter, Matilda, is a more honest but self-willed hoyden with a careless disregard for lessons, happy only in riding, romping with her dogs, relishing the cruelty of hunting and the pleasure of shocking Agnes by her oaths, until her mother compels her to acquire more ladylike accomplishments. She supports her sister's attempt to separate Agnes and Weston. Both sisters amuse themselves by visiting poor cottagers, bestowing on them small gifts, but disregarding their feelings.

The Murrays' two sons, the unruly John and cowardly, capricious, selfish, malicious Charles, both prove unteachable despite Agnes's efforts, and are eventually sent to school. See also ROBINSON FAMILY OF THORP GREEN; GOVERNESSES.

museums. The *Brontë Society's first museum was opened on 18 May 1895 in a rented room over the Yorkshire Penny Bank at the top of Main Street, *Haworth. Brontëana on display that summer included the manuscripts of *Jane Eyre* and *Villette*, lent by *Smith, Elder and Company, and items lent by T. J. *Wise and C. K. *Shorter. In 1907 the Society purchased items from Revd A. B. *Nicholls's widow, including J. B. *Leyland's medallion head of Branwell, and more Brontëana from the Nicholls sale at Sotheby's in July. By 1926 gifts, loans, and purchases were straining the capacity of the little museum. New premises were needed, but the Society had cash assets of less than £50. Inquisitive tourists had made life difficult for Revd Patrick Brontë's successors at *Haworth Parsonage, and in 1927 the Ecclesiastical Commissioners offered it for sale, on condition that a new rectory be provided elsewhere. Sir James Roberts, a Haworth man who had made a fortune in wool and textiles, generously gave the purchase price of the Parsonage, with over £1,500 towards its conversion into a museum and library. The new wing added in 1878 by Revd John Wade was adapted as the library and council room, with accommodation for the custodian on the upper floor. On 4 August 1928 Sir James handed over the title-deeds to the Society's president, Lord *Brotherton. The Parsonage dining room was fireproofed to house the precious *Bonnell collection on its arrival in January 1929. In the 1930s many of the Brontës' original pieces of furniture, such as the sofa, kitchen table, and chairs, were returned to the house. During the Second World War years ceilings were strengthened, windows blocked up, and the dining room closed to the public, but the rest of the house remained open, and visitors actually increased between 1943 and 1949. In the 1950s it was realized that more space was needed for the rapidly growing collections, and for the more efficient movement of visitors. In 1957 it was decided to make the upper floor of the Wade extension part of the museum, restrict the library to researchers, rehouse the Bonnell collection in a secure exhibition room, reglaze the plate-glass windows with small Georgian-style panes, and build an extension to the rear of the house to accommodate the custodian. When the refurbished house was fully opened to the public in 1960, they could see the dining room rearranged with its original furniture, and the kitchen restored as far as possible to its appearance in the Brontës' day. When unsound roof beams had to be replaced in 1976, the Society also installed an air-conditioned, humidity-controlled strong-room for the storage of *manuscripts and rare books. In 1982 a single large exhibition area was created in the upper storey of the north wing to display chronologically, by means of photographs, portraits, facsimiles, artefacts, and explanatory captions, the history of the Brontë family. Other themed exhibitions are mounted each year, sometimes enriched by temporary loans. In 1989 all furniture which did not belong to the Brontë family was removed from display, except for a reproduction bed copied from a drawing by Branwell, and the main downstairs rooms were arranged to reflect their appearance in the 1850s, when visitors to the home of the famous 'Bells' began to record their impressions of the house. Thus the dining room (Charlotte's sitting room) displays the portraits of herself, the Duke of *Wellington, and *Thackeray, given to her and her father by George *Smith. Modern conservation techniques are used, security has been improved, and rare books and manuscripts may be consulted only in the presence of qualified staff. As a centre for Brontë research the museum is unsurpassed. See also EXHIBITIONS OF BRONTËANA.

*Oakwell Hall, *Birstall (*Fieldhead in *Shirley*) still retains something of its rural seclusion. Threatened with transportation to the USA, it was bought for public ownership in 1928 by Sir Norman Rae and Mr J. E. Sharman, and opened as a museum. It has been restored to recreate the atmosphere of 17th- and 18th-century life. Near the house an arboretum and formal gardens have been established. Within the hall one can see the oak-lined rooms, and the 'fine, dark' glossy-panelled great hall with its arched stone fireplace, gallery, oak staircase, and dog-gate, the setting for 'Mr *Donne's Exodus'.

The *Red House, *Gomersal (*Briarmains in *Shirley*), passed out of the *Taylor family's possession in 1920, and was bought by Spenborough civic authorities in 1969 for conversion into a Brontë and Local History Museum, opened on 19 April 1973. Owned by the Kirklees Metropolitan Council since 1974, it was closed for repairs in 1987, but reopened in 1990, well restored and displayed to look as it did in the 1830s, when Charlotte visited it. The painted windows she described have been restored, and the elegant parlour with its alcoves and early pianoforte is particularly attractive. In the barn an exhibition demonstrates the connection between the locality and *Shirley*.

Lemon, Charles, *A Centenary History of the Brontë Society* (1993).
Barker, Juliet R. V. (ed.), *Sixty Treasures* (1988).

music became a consuming passion of the newly leisured middle classes during the 19th century, spreading throughout the country to the increasingly wealthy industrial towns of Yorkshire. The local papers of the time report a rich musical culture of concerts, amateur and professional music societies, commercial enterprise in instrument manufacture, music publishing, and teaching.

Social position, education, and inclination meant the Brontës enjoyed a range of musical experiences. Evidence for their interest in music survives in their volumes of printed music, the music manuscript books of Branwell and Anne, and the cabinet piano with its small compass of six octaves played by Emily and Anne at the Parsonage.

The Brontës inherited their enthusiasm for music from their father. Relative to his income, Revd Patrick Brontë spent large sums of money on flute and organ lessons for Branwell, and piano lessons for Emily and Anne (see SUNDERLAND, ABRAHAM STANSFIELD). He spearheaded at least one concert in Haworth (1832) and organized the organ appeal for St Michael's church which culminated in an inauguration concert (23 March 1834); he was reputed to have been 'passionately fond of oratorio' (*Bradford Observer*, 17 Feb. 1894). The early history of this passion is unclear: Lock & Dixon's assertion (p. 8) that he 'assisted in conducting the music' at Glascar Presbyterian church is unsubstantiated. Two of his brothers played the (folk) fiddle; he may have been aware of a concert life in Belfast, and he may have heard music in the Cambridge college chapels.

Music plays a central role in Mr Brontë's romance *The *Maid of Killarney* (London, 1818): the heroine Flora so captivates the heart of Albion with her harp-playing and singing that he becomes 'absorbed and lost in the most agreeable and refined enjoyment' (pp. 57–8). The tale includes discussion of music, and the opinion that 'those performances have the most genuine music in them, which make us feel the most' (p. 59) possibly represents Mr Brontë's view.

Before 1834 all three sisters were playing the piano. Ellen Nussey and Mary Taylor recalled Charlotte's attempts at the piano and her interest in music. (She abandoned the piano because of poor eyesight.) Even before she attended *Roe Head, she was aware of and writing about music, enthusing in *'Tales of the Islanders' (1829) about 'that most sublime of all music, martial music, when the ringing trumpet and the rolling drum are sounding together' (Alexander *EEW*, 1. 107). She remained susceptible to military music throughout her life, describing the 'sweet music' of bugle, horn, and trumpet in *Villette* (ch. 36) as a 'sea breaking into song with all its waves'.

Emily and Anne made better progress with Keighley piano teacher Abraham Stansfield Sunderland, though they confess in the *Diary Paper of 24 November 1834 to not having practised. The earliest sheet music bearing their names is *Three Original Waltzes* by R. Andrews, dated 3 October 1832, for piano duet. They collected a number of duets, solos, and songs during the 1830s and early 1840s, most of the piano music vacuous and showy, written by obscure composers for the lucrative amateur market, but still requiring some technical competence. Works by better-known composers include arias and choruses from Handel's *Messiah*; waltzes by Beethoven, Mozart, and Weber; and the overture to *La Preciosa* by Weber— a composer referred to also by Branwell. The songs are unsophisticated ballads and traditional songs.

The *juvenilia of Charlotte and Branwell contain many musical scenes: set pieces of grandiose ceremonial, romantic serenades, heavenly visions, and solitary outpourings in which the music intensifies the dramatic and emotional moment. A significant experience for the teenage Brontës was the inauguration of the church organ. Charlotte's caricature of Branwell and his ecstatic reaction to the event in *'My Angria and the Angrians' provide useful clues to Branwell's impulsive personality and powerful attraction to music. In 1831 he was already copying hymn tunes and traditional songs arranged for flute into a small music manuscript book (*Branwell Brontë's Flute Book*). Having been a member of the organ appeal committee, on Christmas Day 1838 he acted as organist. He seems to have preferred sacred music, especially that of Handel. The portrayal of Alexander Percy (Duke of *Northangerland), for whom 'music formed the chief passion of his soul' ('Life of Northangerland'), is strong enough to suggest that Branwell was writing about himself.

Charlotte and Anne also understood the power that musicians wield over their audiences. In *Jane

musical settings of Brontë poems

Eyre, seeing and hearing Blanche *Ingram at the piano through Jane's eyes and ears, we sense Charlotte's own misery at her lack of accomplishment. Yet *Shirley* displays considerable versatility in the handling of musical scenes, including the comic flute-playing curate, soothing guitar music, and the affecting revelation of Mrs Agnes *Pryor's relationship to Caroline *Helstone through the song 'Ye Banks and Braes o' Bonny Doon'.

In *Tenant*, Anne uses music to emphasize social inequality, for emotional release, and even to foretell the story. During 1843, Anne filled a music notebook with 34 simple piano solos, hymns, and songs (*Anne Brontë's Song Book*). In November 1844 she acquired several printed copies of songs, some teaching material, and *The Musical Library* volumes of keyboard and vocal music.

Emily's early 'precision and brilliancy' as a pianist was recorded by Ellen Nussey, who noted that after her return from Brussels 'the expression was that of a professor absorbed heart and soul in his theme' (Gérin *EB*, p. 40). In Brussels, Emily had both studied and taught piano. In her pre-Brussels poetry, coinciding with the period of musical activity at Haworth, there are countless references to music, various instruments, singing, laments, and lullabies. The post-Brussels poetry, however, has less of these; the musical images come from nature rather than art, and carry spiritual significance. In 'A Day Dream' (5 Mar. 1844) the poet is transported through birdsong to an experience of heaven and spiritual enlightenment. Except for the Christmas Eve visit of the Gimmerton Band, there are no major musical scenes in *Wuthering Heights*: social refinement and social harmony as symbolized by music are among the victims of this novel. The closing passage, however, is accompanied by 'the soft wind breathing through the grass', the music Emily loved best.   VR

> Higuchi, Akiko (ed.), *Anne Brontë's Song Book and Branwell Brontë's Flute Book* (2002).
> —— 'Music in *Villette*', *BS* (2003), 28. 1. 25–36.

musical settings of Brontë poems. Relatively few Brontë poems have been set to music by remarkably few composers: 34 texts by Charlotte, Branwell, Anne, and Emily in settings by fourteen British and American composers are in the BPM collection. These settings date predominantly from the second half of the 20th century. As poets—and, therefore, as authors of potential song texts—the Brontës remained comparatively unknown during a period of prolific song-writing in England, from about 1840 to the First World War. Despite the publication of more editions of the poems, and Emily's recognition as a lyric poet, Brontë poetry remains neglected (or rejected) by composers.

The choice of two composers, Jack H. Rhodes and Alfred Jepson, of four of Anne's sacred verses as hymn texts is not surprising. The best known of Rhodes's three hymns is *The Narrow Way* ('Believe not those who say'), composed in 1948 and included in *Hymns Ancient and Modern* (revised); his other settings are 'I hoped that with the brave and strong', and 'Spirit of faith!'. Jepson's style is more successful with Anne's 'To greet with joy the glorious morn' (1962) than with Charlotte's 'Rochester's Song to Jane Eyre' in which the hymn-like music works against the passionate text. Arthur D. Walker's cycle of six poems by Emily, Anne, and Branwell, *Elegy* (1972–3), mixes regular and improvisatory styles in attempting contrasted voices at moments of heightened emotion in, for example, Emily's 'If grief for grief can touch thee'. In his *Six Poems of Emily Brontë*, Op. 63 (1989), John Joubert uses musical patterns and form to intensify verbal image and meaning. Joubert's effective sequence includes 'Harp of wild and dream-like strain', 'Tell me, tell me, smiling child', and 'High waving heather', culminating with 'No coward soul is mine' in an ecstatic conclusion.   VR

'My Angria and the Angrians', 'By Lord Charles Albert Florian Wellesley' (14 Oct. 1834), a medley of scenes describing Charlotte Brontë's favourite Verdopolitan characters who now form the new Angrian society. The Angrian capital of *Adrianopolis has just been completed, and the manuscript begins with the exodus from the old world to the new capital on the *Calabar River. In a clever parody of the biblical exodus of the Israelites from Egypt, Lord Charles ridicules the fortune-seekers on their way to Angria, pretending to align himself with the sober elements of the old Verdopolitan society who scorn 'Angrian ostentation and loftiness'. Still only 9 years old, despite his sophisticated narrative voice, Lord Charles refuses to accompany his new guardian General *Thornton and sets off alone 'to spy out the nakedness of the land'. After meeting Patrick Benjamin *Wiggins, he arrives at the city of *Zamorna where an election meeting is underway, providing further opportunity for Lord Charles to describe a variety of Angrian characters and to include several patriotic songs (namely Branwell's 'Welcome Heroes to the War' and the Angrian National Anthem 'Sound the loud trumpets o'er Afric's dark sea' by Captain Henry *Hastings).

The manuscript (in the *Law Collection) appears to have been written over a period of a week and is basically a series of composition exercises in a variety of styles, dense with literary allusion and exploring fragmentary episodes in the *Glass Town and Angrian saga. One fragment includes a drama relating to a promise the Duke of

*Zamorna and Lady Zenobia *Ellrington made to visit the Duke of *Northangerland's vault, should he die before them, and open his coffin. This is followed by Charlotte's poem 'The crypt, the nave, the chancel past'. The final fragments record the birth of twin sons to Zamorna and Mary Percy (including Hastings's song 'Hurrah for the Gemini!'), and their christening and ceremonial presentation to the people of Angria.

'My Angria' is especially noteworthy for its brilliant caricature of Branwell in the character of Patrick Benjamin *Wiggins, and for Charlotte's deprecatory sketch of herself and her sisters from Wiggins's point of view: 'Charlotte's eighteen years old, a broad dumpy thing, whose head does not come higher than my elbow. Emily's sixteen, lean and scant, with a face about the size of a penny, and Anne is nothing, absolutely nothing' (Alexander *EEW*, 2(2). 250).

Alexander *EEW*, 2(2). 239–93.
McMaster, Juliet, and Robertson, Leslie (eds.), *My Angria and the Angrians by Charlotte Brontë* (1997).

'My darling, thou wilt never know', poem by Charlotte Brontë (24 Dec. 1848, two days after Emily's funeral); first published in *The Woman at Home* (Dec. 1896) with the title 'On the Death of Emily Brontë'. The Huntington manuscript has many uncancelled variants, reflecting Charlotte's distress, conveyed also in agonizingly physical images—grinding, crushing, galled, pierced—for the pain of watching helplessly while Emily suffered. 'Wasting misery' combines Emily's own emaciation with the relentless eroding grief of the watchers. The last stanza is comparatively trite. See also 'THERE'S LITTLE JOY IN LIFE FOR ME'.

Neufeldt *CBP*, p. 341.
Winnifrith, Tom (ed.), *The Poems of Charlotte Brontë* (1984), p. 241.

'My Dear Jane' ('Ma chère Jane'). An incomplete draft that Charlotte Brontë wrote in French while studying at the Pensionnat *Heger (1843?; MS in Bonnell, BPM). The letter's imaginary writer is unnamed but closely corresponds to Elizabeth *Hastings, a character in *Henry Hastings*. Similarly, the Jane she addresses, who is not an early version of Jane *Eyre, corresponds to the Angrian Jane *Moore. The writer begins by berating her 'rich, young, and beautiful' friend for her indolence but then confesses to her own inertia, which stems from 'a heavy depression'. She envisions the demons that taunt her, expresses contempt for her current surroundings, and reveals her longing for the mountains. Still, she admits that there is one outstanding man who rises above the 'croaking frogs' of the low country. This increasingly autobiographical fragment breaks off with the words 'I continue'.   SL

Alexander *EW*, pp. 184–8.
Lonoff, pp. 260–9.

myth and symbol. Myth critics interpret literary texts by searching out recurring symbolic images, motifs, and narrative patterns that can be traced back to their origins in primordial myth. According to this view of literature, a text's power to move the reader is due to the presence of such primordial elements, which speak timelessly and universally to all human beings. The powerful impact made on their readers by the Brontës' novels, especially *Jane Eyre* and *Wuthering Heights*, has impelled critics to seek its source in myth and symbol. Myth criticism in literary studies developed in the mid-20th century out of work in the fields of anthropology and psychology. In the 1970s, feminists adapted the approach to their readings of women's texts. It has been difficult, however, for myth criticism to withstand the charges that more recent critics, many of them feminists, have directed against universalizing approaches to the study of cultural forms, and current interpretations that consider the relationship of literature and myth are likely to understand the latter as inextricably bound up with the work of ideology and culture.

In anthropology, the central figures in early myth studies are those affiliated with a group usually referred to as the Cambridge School: Jane Harrison (1850–1928), Gilbert Murray (1866–1957), F. M. Cornford (1886–1950), and, pre-eminently, Sir James Frazer (1854–1941), whose monumental, multi-volume study *The Golden Bough* (1890–1922) has had an inestimable influence on the study of literature. Frazer examined myths from numerous cultures widely separated in time and by geographical location, discovering in them fundamental similarities that he theorized must originate in some innate feature of the human mind. Among these recurring patterns are several associated with the rituals of sacrifice by which a people seeks to cleanse and rejuvenate itself (the killing and revival of the king-god, the figures of the scapegoat and the sacrificial virgin) and those more directly connected to rites of fertility and regeneration (for example, the mother-goddess). In the field of psychology, Carl Jung (1875–1961) contributed significantly to the development of myth studies by theorizing that particular structures in the human mind were the source of these primordial stories and the recurring elements they share. These psychic structures, or archetypal forms as Jung called them, predispose all humans to the activity of myth making and to corresponding interpretative behaviour which allows us to grasp intuitively the deep significance of the universal and timeless patterns found in myth. We all understand the meaning of mythic narratives (though we may not be able to articulate that meaning) because, in the words of Joseph Campbell, they 'touch some very deep chord' in what Jung called our 'collective unconscious' or 'racial memory', the storehouse of trans-cultural archetypes from which myths flow ('*The Masks of God*': *Primitive Mythology* (1959) 31). Jung also emphasizes the process by which individuals achieve psychic maturation over time (as opposed to Freud's contention that the psyche is shaped in infancy), and he conceptualizes various parts of the self which must be properly integrated in order for individuation to occur: the persona, which is the self that engages with the world outside the self; the anima (or, in a woman, the animus), which is the part of the self that mediates between the conscious and unconscious parts of the mind; and the shadow self, the part of our unconscious that bears unacceptable attributes that must be driven out of consciousness.

The most recent and fullest treatment of the Brontës from a Jungian perspective is Bettina L. Knapp's book *The Brontës: Branwell, Anne, Emily, and Charlotte* (1991). Knapp discusses both the lives and the writings (poetry as well as prose) of all four Brontës, presenting an assessment of their respective merits and weaknesses that generally conforms to earlier judgements. Branwell is shown to be psychically unstable, while Charlotte, Emily, and Anne are presented as far more successful in meeting the challenges that lead to maturity and individuation. As a Jungian critic, Knapp attributes the perennial appeal of the Brontë sisters' work to their ability to plumb the mysteries of human personality—'to make accessible what is hidden and buried in darkness' (p. 150)—but she also notes their remarkable ability to combine these mythic qualities with a genuine and intelligent interest in the social issues of their day, especially as they bore on the lives of women. In this latter respect, Knapp's book echoes an important essay by Richard Chase ('The Brontës: A Centennial Observance,' *Kenyon Review*, 9 (1947), 487–506). For Chase, Charlotte and Emily's great achievement is that they 'transmuted the Victorian social situation into mythical and symbolic forms' (McNees, 4. 86), thus pushing the novel beyond the normal limits of the genre and producing great 'mythical art' (McNees, 4. 74). The female protagonists in their novels, Chase says, are 'culture heroines', 19th-century feminine counterparts of mythic male 'culture heroes' such as Hercules or Prometheus; their function 'as mythical being[s] is to transform primeval society into a humane and noble order of civilization' (McNees, 4. 80). Jane Eyre and Cath-

erine Earnshaw do this, not by slaying monsters as the male figures do, but by putting into motion the warring God- and Satan-figures in each of these stories (both embodied in Rochester and Heathcliff) so that the 'principle of life' which the Brontës admired ('sexual and intellectual energy') can be cleansed of its impurities and revitalized (McNees, 4. 75). The novels thus take the mundane realities of women's social and economic condition in Victorian England and transform them into a narrative that, fundamentally, is a retelling of mythic tales about sacrificial death, sexual revitalization, and the regeneration of life.

Approaching the well-known oppositions in *Jane Eyre* from the perspective of myth criticism, Robert Heilman and R. E. Hughes emphasize the relationship of the novel's mythic elements to the heroine's effort to develop a mature and unified sense of self. In 'Charlotte Brontë's New Gothic' (in Robert C. Rathburn and Martin Steinmann (eds.), *From Austen to Conrad* (1958), 118–32), Heilman shows how Charlotte employs the recurring image of the moon in working out 'the conflict between reason-judgment-common sense and feeling-imagination-intuition' which constitutes the challenge Jane faces as she develops psychologically (McNees, 4. 166). These oppositions, expressed in characteristically Brontëan terms, are shown by Heilman to be identified with the archetypal images of the Apollonian sun god and the 'White Goddess' of the moon. Hughes's rather different reading, '*Jane Eyre*: The Unbaptized Dionysos' (*Nineteenth-Century Fiction*, 18 (1964), 347–64) defines these contraries similarly and argues that the novel demonstrates how the process of maturation and individuation requires Jane to make the difficult journey from the Dionysian Rochester to his Apollonian opposite, St John Rivers, in order to gain self-knowledge and return to a transformed and tamed Dionysus. Though their essays differ in many respects (for example, Heilman's is largely a formal analysis of image patterns, while Hughes's article is more psychologically oriented), these critics agree that Charlotte intuitively 'touched an archetypal chord' (McNees, 3. 128), as Hughes puts it, in writing *Jane Eyre*. Rebecca West, in an early essay, concurs with this view of the Brontë sisters ('The Role of Fantasy in the Work of the Brontës', *BST* (1954), 12. 64. 255–67), whom she calls 'sibyls, priestesses to whose care the sacred books had been confided' by their predecessors in 'the same hieratic system'. In the Brontë novels, West asserts, the personal obsessions of these 'Victorian gentlewomen' take the form of an 'inner vision [that] might have marked them as pre-Sumerian' (McNees, 4. 148).

In the 1970s, a number of feminist critics, including Adrienne Rich ('*Jane Eyre*: The Temptations of a Motherless Woman', *Ms.* (Oct. 1973), 89–106); Elaine Showalter (*A Literature of their Own: British Women Novelists from Brontë to Lessing*, 1973); Helene Moglen (*Charlotte Brontë: The Self Conceived*, 1976); Sandra Gilbert and Susan Gubar (*The Madwoman in the Attic: The Woman Writer and the Nineteenth-Century Literary Imagination*, 1979); and Stevie Davies (*Emily Brontë: The Artist as Freewoman*, 1983) adapted myth criticism to the needs of feminist literary analysis, producing some inspiring readings of Charlotte and Emily's novels. But as Rich's description of this appropriation suggests, a 'revisioning' of myth draws critical attention to the role that culture plays in the formation of such stories, thereby invalidating myth criticism's central premiss: that myths are made up of universal elements which derive from innate structures of the human mind and, in that sense, are fundamentally not subject to the influence of culture. In the wake of such challenges, myth criticism exists today in rather etiolated forms. See also FEMINIST APPROACHES; PSYCHOANALYTIC APPROACHES; IMAGERY. CB

mythology, classical. References to classical mythology in the works of Emily and Anne Brontë are rare, though in *Wuthering Heights* Emily refers, significantly, to the story of Milo, whose hands are held fast by the tree which he attempts to pull up by the roots. Catherine *Earnshaw will not be separated from *Heathcliff: ' "Who is to separate us, pray? They'll meet the fate of Milo!" ' (ch. 9). Branwell was 'steeped . . . in Virgilian' vocabulary by December 1829 (Neufeldt *BBP*, p. 369), and he gives the source of a quotation in 'The History of the Young Men' as 'Pope's Hom[er]. I.i'. Unsurprisingly, his Young *Soult the Rhymer converses with the 'planet Mars', identifying it with the fiery-haired Roman god of war: 'But *Mars* no more will brook this long delay' (Neufeldt *BBP*, p. 75). Elsewhere his deities, Brannii, and the rest, replace the Olympian gods Jove, golden Juno, and Phoebus with his 'beams divine'. His heroes outdo the

splendours of the Olympians: the conflict for the dead body of Patroclus on the shores of Troy must sink to nothing before the battle against the Ashantees, and the bravery of Captain Butter *Crashey and his companions is 'like that of Diomedes and Ulysses or Nisus and Euryalus. They penetrated into the very midst of the sleeping barbarians, killing hundreds' ('History of the Young Men'). In 'Letters from an Englishman' the giant who takes Bellingham prisoner has huge legs and feet 'enough to have dismayed Hercules himself'. On the other hand, some of Branwell's later poems recur to the idea of Lethe. The image is most developed in his sonnet contemplating death, when 'Charons boat prepares, oer Lethe's river I Our souls to waft, and all our thoughts to sever I From what was once life's light'—that is, from his beloved Mrs Lydia *Robinson (Neufeldt *BBP*, p. 283). Charlotte was familiar with classical works by November 1830, for, like Branwell, she had access to *Dryden's *The Works of Virgil, Translated into English Verse* (1824), and she probably knew also Pope's translations of the *Iliad* and the *Odyssey*. Her early writings display classical mythology used both as a stylistic ornament and a means of elevating heroic characters: the Duke of *Zamorna is likened to Apollo, graceful women resemble Hebe or Helen of Troy, characters lie locked in the chains of Somnus; the sun is Apollo's chariot, the sea the green 'realm of Neptune', and a barque, 'Neptune's noblest daughter', rides at anchor. Charlotte is fascinated, as always, by the gold-bearing garden, the Hesperides, by the creative Promethean fire, and Helicon the source of inspiration. Her use of myth is picturesque and romantic. In *Shirley* and *Villette* classical images may have a deeper resonance, like the 'dragon's teeth' already sown amongst Hiram *Yorke's children in *Shirley* (ch. 9). In *Villette* some mythological references are heavy with omen: in chapter 36, 'The Apple of Discord', Lucy solves the deadly 'Sphynx-riddle' of Père *Silas's connection with Paul *Emanuel. In *Jane Eyre* the omens are those of *folklore, the only mythical reference being Jane's allusion to Rosamond *Oliver as a Persian 'Peri'.

Napoleon Buonaparte (historical) (1769–
1821), soldier, politician, and emperor of France
(1804–15); admired by the Brontës as a 'great man'
and worthy adversary of their hero the Duke of
*Wellington. Although he had died as a prisoner
on St Helena, following his defeat six years earlier
at the Battle of Waterloo (1815), his fame in Britain
was still equal to that of Wellington and it haunted
Europe during the Brontës' childhood and well
into their adulthood. He was one of Thomas *Carlyle's examples of 'The Hero as King' in his series
of lectures published in 1841 (*On Heroes, Hero-
Worship, and the Heroic in History*). His extraordinary military and political career appealed
particularly to Branwell, who chose him as his
'chief man' in the Young Men's Play (Alexander
EEW, 1. 5). Branwell agreed with those who saw
Napoleon as the champion of republicanism, who
consolidated the French Revolution against the
tyranny of monarchy: his Glass Town character 'Rogue' (the early Duke of *Northangerland)
rouses rebellion amongst the masses and continues to hanker after republican ideals throughout the *Glass Town and Angrian saga despite his
alliances with monarchy. Except in her earliest
manuscripts, Charlotte sees Napoleon chiefly as
the enemy, as the cause of the *Peninsular War
and the symbol of all that is antipathetic to her
Tory hero Wellington. Whigs and radicals in Britain also saw Napoleon as a symbol of opposition to
Tory government and, even after his aggressive
imperialism and the establishment of his dynastic
empire, Whigs like *Byron and Hazlitt continued
to admire him. Byron especially saw Napoleon as
a model: in *Don Juan* he terms himself the 'grand
Napoleon of the realms of rhyme' (canto 11).
*Wordsworth had early admired Napoleon, com-
paring his own education and status as a poet with
such a man of action, but later saw his coronation
as a betrayal of revolutionary promise. For Samuel
Taylor *Coleridge, Napoleon was an example of
'Commanding Genius' (*Biographia Literaria*, 1817).
The Brontës would have been aware, too, of Napoleon's image in popular culture, where he was

portrayed in pamphlets and caricatures as either
'Little Bony' or an object of terror associated with
the devil. Texts representing Napoleon in terms of
*Milton's Satan would not have gone unnoticed by
Branwell, whose portrayal of Northangerland
owes much to Milton's rendering of God's fallen
angel (see, for example, Hazlitt's lecture 'On Shakespeare and Milton', 1818). Charlotte and Branwell
read Sir Walter *Scott's *Life of Napoleon Buonaparte* (1827) in early 1829 (Alexander *EEW*, 1. 28)
and referred to him in poems and stories in their
early juvenilia: he becomes the fictitious character
*Napoleon, ruler of Branwell's Frenchyland to
the south of Glass Town. In *Caroline Vernon*
the historical Napoleon is one of Caroline's heroes
(Alexander *EW*, p. 196). In March 1843, while in
Brussels, Charlotte made a translation of Auguste
*Barbier's 'L'Idole' (1831), which presents Napo-
leon as a tyrant (Neufeldt *CBP*, p. 355). Soon
after, she wrote an essay entitled 'The *Death of
Napoleon', as a *devoir for M. Constantin *Heger;
but the exercise becomes a panegyric on Napoleon's 'noble peer', the Duke of Wellington (Lonoff,
pp. 270–309). On 4 August that year, Heger gave
Charlotte a curious relic of Napoleon: a fragment
from his coffin that had come from Heger's friend
Lebel, secretary to Prince Achille Murat, Napoleon's nephew and son of Joachim *Murat (*BST*
(1978), 17. 88. 185–8). Charlotte's reaction to this
gift is not recorded but her attitude to Napoleon
appears to have been modified by her association
with Heger. In *Villette*, Lucy Snowe believes that
M. Paul *Emanuel (largely modelled on Heger)
has 'points of resemblance to Napoleon Bonaparte' (ch. 30); however, Mme *Beck is negatively
characterized as 'a little Bonaparte in a mouse-
coloured silk gown' (ch. 14).

Napoleon (fictional), ruler of Branwell's
Frenchyland in the *Glass Town and Angrian
saga. He and his son Young Napoleon are survivors
from the *Young Men's Play. Branwell originally
named his favourite toy soldier 'Bonaparte' in opposition to Charlotte's Wellington, but after the
historical *Napoleon Buonaparte's death in 1821,
he changed his soldier's name to *Sneaky, who
became one of the famous *Twelves. Napoleon,
however, survives throughout the saga as a background figurehead in *Paris. The character of
Branwell's Byronic hero, the Duke of *Northangerland, however, also retains much of the
original glamour, republican associations, and tyrannical behaviour of the original Napoleon, especially in his early manifestation as 'Rogue'.

Branwell's manuscripts feature Napoleon more
frequently and in more detail, usually in poems
by Young *Soult. 'Ode to Napoleon', for example,
refers to various episodes in Napoleon's career and

his superstitious nature (Neufeldt *BB Works*, 1. 58–60). In Charlotte's early stories the 'Emperor Napoleon' is basically a figurehead, who lives in Paris and arbitrates in such stories as 'The Enfant' (Alexander *EEW*, 1. 34–6). He is also the subject of earlier ghost stories, such as that retold in *The *Green Dwarf* (Alexander *EEW*, 2(1). 139–43), where 'Piche' (Charles Pichegru, the French general who led the conquest of the Netherlands but later conspired against Napoleon, was imprisoned in 1804, and found strangled in his cell) has returned to haunt his supposed murderer, Napoleon. The historical Napoleon's other commanders in the *Peninsular War and at Waterloo, such as Marshal André Masséna, Marshal Michel Ney, Marshal Jean Lannes, Marshal Joachim *Murat, Marshal Jourdan (*Jordan), and Marshal Soult (see SOULT, ALEXANDER), also become participants in the saga: for example, in Branwell's description of the Battle of Zamorna (1834; Neufeldt *BB Works*, 2. 22–3). Napoleon's fictitious son, 'Young Napoleon', features only in the early saga, as a haggard French rogue, a member of the infamous *Pigtail's gang.

natural history and the Brontës. *See page 338*

nature. See NATURAL HISTORY AND THE BRONTËS; LANDSCAPES ASSOCIATED WITH THE BRONTËS; ANIMALS IN THE WORKS OF THE BRONTËS; PETS OWNED BY THE BRONTËS.

Naughten, Richard. See NAUGHTY, RICHARD (YOUNG MAN NAUGHTY).

Naughty, Richard (Young Man Naughty), a Glass Town villain and bodysnatcher, 'champion of the poachers' and associate of Sergeant Edward *Laury in his 'Rare Lad' days. He is huge, cruel, and ruthless, delighting in torture and assassination (Alexander *EEW*, 1. 129). He is shot by the Marquis of Douro (Duke of *Zamorna) but 'made alive' again by Dr Hume *Badey. As Richard Naughten (or Mange) he rouses the lower classes in support of the Duke of *Northangerland in the Great Rebellion, and again during the Angrian wars against Zamorna, as leader of the People's Party. He is appointed commander of Northangerland's forces and lord lieutenant of Angria while there is a Revolutionary Government.

Needham, Alice Jane, a Blackburn resident who bought some Brontë relics at the Nussey sale of 1898. By courtesy of her daughter Sister Margaret Needham, T. J. Winnifrith described and analysed Ellen *Nussey's unreliable copies of some of Charlotte's letters (Winnifrith *Background*). Ellen originally copied them in 1868–9, hoping that George *Smith would publish them. Copyright difficulties led her to send them instead

to Scribner's magazine, *Hours at Home* (June–Sept. 1870). The 'Needham copies', now in the BPM, contain a few words found in no other text. See Smith *Letters*, 1. 37–8, 119, 128.

needlework and embroidery. See ACCOMPLISHMENTS.

Nelly. See DEAN, ELLEN (NELLY).

Nero, Emily Brontë's pet hawk rescued from an abandoned nest on the moors and kept in a cage until given away while she was in Brussels (see PETS OWNED BY THE BRONTËS). Emily's poem, known as 'The Caged Bird' ('And like myself lone wholly lone') and dated 27 February 1841, in which she identifies with a bird pining for liberty, may refer to Nero. Her detailed watercolour of a merlin is also likely to be of Nero, since it is clearly painted from close observation (Alexander & Sellars, pp. 384–5). The hawk was formerly referred to by Brontë biographers as 'Hero'—a misreading of Emily's *Diary Paper of 30 July 1845.

Newby, Thomas Cautley (?1798–1882), publisher from the late 1820s. In July 1847, when he accepted 'Acton Bell's' *Agnes Grey* and 'Ellis Bell's' *Wuthering Heights* for publication, his premises were at 72 Mortimer Street, Cavendish Square, London. He occupied a four-storeyed house at 30 Welbeck Street from 1850 until 1874, when he retired, selling his business to Messrs Morgan and Hebron. He died intestate in June 1882 at 12 Westbourne Gardens, Folkestone, the home of his son-in-law, Henry Bayly Garling, leaving a personal estate of only £38. Charlotte Brontë called him a shuffling scamp, but thought he might be a needy one too. He delayed publication of 'Acton and Ellis Bell's' novels until December 1847, after Currer Bell's *Jane Eyre* had proved to be a bestseller; he drove a hard bargain with his authors, demanding a £50 deposit which he failed to return despite selling at least the 250 copies which would have produced a profit of £100; the novels, which he printed as well as published, retained spelling and punctuation errors corrected by the authors in proof; and his advertisements implied that they were by the same author as *Jane Eyre*. Yet the good sales of her first novel encouraged Anne Brontë to give him *Tenant*, published in two editions in June and August 1848. He also wrote to 'Ellis Bell' on 15 February 1848, offering to take a second work, to be written in the author's own time, to ensure that it did not fall short of 'his' first achievement. But in June 1848 he caused great perturbation by informing *Harper & Brothers (apropos of *Tenant*) that he, not Smith, Elder, would be publishing 'Currer Bell's' next work. Both Charlotte and Anne confronted him with

(*cont. on page 340*)

REVD Patrick Brontë owned a considerable number of books on scientific subjects, including anatomy, pharmacology, chemistry, and zoology, and judging from the childish notes and scribbles in the margins all titles were available to the young Brontës without discrimination. His copy of *The Garden and Menagerie of the Zoological Society Delineated*, for example, has been embellished by a variety of pencil sketches by Anne Brontë, including a copy of the Pine Marten (Alexander & Sellars, p. 422). Only Mr Brontë's volume of Humphry Davy's *Elements of Chemical Philosophy* is unmarked, though reference is made to another of Davy's works, *Last Days of a Philosopher*, in Anne Brontë's novel *Tenant* (ch. 15). Naturalists like * Buffon were also included among the texts Heger excerpted for Charlotte and Emily's *devoirs in Brussels. It is clear from their writings and from the books and magazines they read and owned, that the Brontës had considerable knowledge of scientific subjects and were particularly interested in natural history.

The general interest in science and philosophy among the local Yorkshire population can be assessed by the chief interests of members of the *Keighley Mechanics' Institute Library, which Mr Brontë joined in 1833. The catalogue lists White's *History of Selborne*, Goldsmith's *History of the Earth*, Cuvier's *Theory of the Earth*, Loudon's *Natural History*, Lyell's *Geology*, Mantell's *Wonders of Geology*, Withering's *British Plants*—all seminal and popular works of the period available to the Brontës and in several cases cited by them. Even more significant is the availability of Paley's *Moral Philosophy*, Playfair's *Natural Philosophy*, and a number of Bridgewater treatises on animal and vegetable physiology, on astronomy, and probably Buckland's famous treatise of 1836 on the significance of fossil relics in confirming the biblical flood. These titles represent the spread of critical debate on natural history during the formative years of the Brontës. Contemporaries remember the Brontë sisters walking to Keighley to change books at a circulating library (Barker, pp. 148–9), which would probably have had the more popular, bowdlerized natural histories of the time. Here too they would have found botanical books to supplement flower-painting manuals for their art lessons (Alexander & Sellars, p. 49).

On 4 July 1834, the 18-year-old Charlotte advised: 'For Natural History read Bewick, and Audubon, and Goldsmith and White of Selborne' (Smith *Letters*, 1. 131). It is possible that the Brontës owned the works of all these writers at this time, except Audubon whose lavish *Birds of America* (1827–38) was too costly for a parsonage family (although Mr Brontë later acquired Audubon's *Ornithological Biography*, 1831–9). Charlotte's recommendation is probably based on the substantial review of Aububon and long extracts from his work over two issues of *Blackwood's Edinburgh Magazine* in 1831. Certainly they owned Thomas *Bewick's two-volume *History of British Birds*, the 'illustrated work of natural history' that so impressed the young Paulina Home in *Villette* (ch. 25) and that was a favourite of the young Jane Eyre (*Jane Eyre*, ch. 1). It was published first in 1797 following Bewick's highly successful *General History of Quadrupeds* (1790) and it articulated the traditional arguments of natural theology later re-enunciated in Paley's *Natural Theology* (1802). Bewick sees the hand of providence in every page of the 'great book of Nature', a phrase often repeated in the Brontë juvenilia. He views rapine in nature as Emily Brontë came to view it: as part of the 'law of Nature which devotes to destruction myriads of creatures to support and continue the existence of others'. Lonoff points out that although in Emily's essay 'The *Butterfly' a chain of being is implicit, 'she stresses antagonism rather than linkage, and the suffering that "seeds" the coming harvest' (Lonoff, p. 188). Yet the bitterness of the speaker gives way to a visionary faith: 'though the nature of nature is that "every being must be the tireless instrument of death to others," the butterfly heralds a God who is somehow going to validate this suffering and destruction.'

An intense interest in natural history accompanied the rise of Romanticism, and both—in the formative years of the Brontës—came under the sway of natural theology, which sanctioned the study of nature as a means of revering the earthly grandeurs and design of Creation. The church and science maintained a comfortable partnership in these pre-Darwinian days, before the implications of Lyell's *Principles of Geology* (1830–3) were worked out in *The Origin of Species* (1859). Natural history could be justified as morally useful, and the Evangelical movement (which Mr Brontë supported) gave religious sanction to such pursuits as birdwatching and geology. Mr Brontë was the typical naturalist clergyman of the period, observing and recording natural phenomena, such as the eruption of the bog on Haworth Moor in 1824. He believed it to be an earthquake and published a sermon on the subject, the same year as Buckland's *Reliquiae Diluvianae* appeared. The value of recording the natural flora and fauna was also learnt by Branwell Brontë. The annotations in his surviving copy of James Thorne's illustrated *Rambles by Rivers: the Duddon, the Mole, the Adur, Arun & Wey* (1844), demonstrate a keen interest in the places he had visited.

The Brontës, with their interest in *Blackwood's*, would have been aware that Cuvier had confirmed that a number of creatures occurring as fossils belonged to species now extinct. Their demise, however, was not yet accounted for by theories of the 'survival of the fittest' but put down to severe 'catastrophes', the most recent of which was the biblical Deluge, painted at the time by John *Martin (1826) after extensive research into this latest scientific theory. An engraving of this work hung on the Haworth Parsonage wall and, having read the eight-page descriptive brochure that accompanied Martin's plate, the Brontës would have been aware of the natural history behind it.

It is clear that the Brontës' lessons in natural history and art went hand in hand. Their copies of flowers were drawn not only from drawing manuals but also from botanical plates. The names of famous naturalists appear in their early writings and even on the backs of their art work (Alexander & Sellars, p. 163). Cuvier, the French anatomist and zoologist, for example, became part of the prolific world of Glass Town characters (Neufeldt *BB Works*, 1. 62). Cuvier's work is frequently discussed in *Blackwood's* and his name recurs throughout Bewick's *History of British Birds* with that of his earlier fellow countryman Buffon, as leading authorities of the day. Anne's close observation of the sea and her love of trees in particular is generally associated in *Tenant* with Helen *Huntingdon's practice of drawing and painting. Nature also takes on a symbolic role in the misshaped monstrous garden at *Wildfell Hall. Charlotte's pervasive references to natural phenomena in her novels reflect her close observation and symbolic use of nature (see IMAGERY).

It is in Emily Brontë's writing, however, that we find the greatest impact of natural history theory. Her passionate love for the natural world is expressed in such poems as 'The linnet in the rocky dells' and *'Shall Earth no more inspire thee', and *'No coward soul is mine' is often seen as a statement of pantheistic belief. Nature for Emily was a mysterious and powerful force, dominating life with unremitting will. There is none of the benignity that Wordsworth saw in the natural world. As Hillis Miller points out, her vision of a fallen world is close to that of Wesley, who believed that both man and animals were implicated in the fall from grace but that man surpasses the animals in cruelty since he acts 'of his free choice'. In the final analysis however, Wesley, like the Brontës, sees not a vision of destruction but a vision of a new heaven and a new earth in which the animal world will also be uncorrupted and free (Lonoff, pp. 189–90).

Wuthering Heights demonstrates a similar emphasis on earthly antagonism, yet there is a providence at work even among the most distorted creatures and in spite of a sense of the remorselessness of time. The novel has been characterized as 'a veritable bestiary of predators and victims' (Nancy Armstrong, 'Emily Brontë In and Out of her Time', *Genre* 15 (1982), *Desire and Domestic Fiction* (1987), p. 252). Even Ellen Dean enunciates a survival principle: 'Well, we *must* be for ourselves in the long run; the mild and generous are only more justly selfish than the domineering' (*Wuthering Heights*, p. 114). Yet Emily Brontë does not endorse Ellen's moral implications. Heathcliff might be 'a fierce pitiless wolfish man' and Edgar the leveret, but their behaviour, viewed in the natural scheme of things, carries no condemnation as is clear in her early poem beginning 'Well, some may hate, and some may scorn' (Gezari *EBP*, p. 26). The importance of nature in the novel, however, is not only to stress man's affinity with the instinctive world and an awareness of human corruptibility that is seen as consonant with natural history, but to convey a unity in creation. Every phase of the life of the characters is accompanied by nature: the gaunt thorn trees, the mist along *Gimmerton Valley, the moths under a benign sky. Emily is able to convey the rhythm of a larger natural life against which the inevitability of the individual evil represented by Heathcliff seems to dissolve.

his lies during their visit to London from 8 to 11 July 1848. Possibly the slightly revised 'second edition' of *Tenant* was a placatory gesture on his part. Since Newby had not acquired the copyright in *Agnes Grey* and *Wuthering Heights*, though he blustered about possessing it, he could not prevent Smith, Elder from publishing the novels in Charlotte's edition of 1850. She did not want them to reprint *Tenant*, which seemed to her a misdirected effort on Anne's part. It was only after her sisters' deaths that George Smith obtained for Charlotte from the 'Nubian desert', as he called the elusive publisher, some of the money Newby owed them. She acknowledged a cheque for £30 from him on 18 March 1854. It was probably part of the proceeds of his sale of copyright in the *Tenant* to Thomas Hodgson, who published a corrupt 'Parlour Library' edition in February 1854, the text of which was used in at least thirteen subsequent editions. Smith, Elder bought rights in the book from Darton & Co. in 1859.

Newby's shiftiness extended to his advertisements for the works of other authors, such as Mrs Mackenzie Daniel's *My Sister Minnie* (1848)

advertised in *The Times* with a quotation, allegedly from the well-known *Examiner*, but actually from the *Glasgow Examiner*: 'Its merits cannot fail to ensure success.' Trollope's first novel (*The Macdermots of Ballycloran*), published by Newby, did not involve the novelist in any expense but he experienced an even longer delay than the Brontës and comparable printing errors (Michael Sadleir, *Trollope: A Bibliography* (1928), 8–9). In Newby's favour it should be said that he advertised *Tenant* 21 times in the *Morning Herald* for July and August 1848, that a number of his authors continued to publish with him, and that he maintained a varied publishing list for nearly half a century.

Hargreaves, G. D., 'Incomplete Texts of "The Tenant of Wildfell Hall"', *BST* (1972), 16. 82. 113–17.

—— 'Further Omissions in "The Tenant of Wildfell Hall"', *BST* (1977), 17. 87. 115–21.

Nicholls, Revd Arthur Bell (6 January 1819– 2 December 1906), Mr Brontë's curate from May 1845 to 1861, and Charlotte's husband for a tragically short time, from 29 June 1854 until her death on 31 March 1855. He was born in Killead, County

The Revd Arthur Bell Nicholls about the time of his marriage to Charlotte Brontë.

Antrim, one of ten children of a Presbyterian farmer, William Nichols or Nicholl[s], and his wife Margaret, née Bell, an Anglican. In 1825 Arthur and his brother Alan were sent to the care of their uncle Alan Bell, headmaster of the Royal Free School at Banagher, King's County (now Offaly). They lived in Dr Bell's home, the impressive Georgian Cuba House, were brought up as Anglicans, and received a classical education. Dr Bell presumably paid Arthur's fees when he was admitted as a pensioner to Trinity College Dublin on 4 July 1836. He matriculated in January 1837, but, for some unknown reason, did not graduate until February 1844, when he obtained a second-class BA and a 'Testimonium' in Divinity. He eventually sought a 'Title for Orders' in England, possibly through advertisement in the *Ecclesiastical Gazette*. He was ordained deacon at Lichfield on 18 May 1845, and licensed to the curacy of Haworth on 5 June 1845, having already officiated there on 25, 28, and 29 May. Charlotte commented: 'He appears a respectable young man, reads well, and I hope will give satisfaction.' On 30 January 1854 Richard Monckton *Milnes described him in a letter to Elizabeth *Gaskell as 'a strong-built, somewhat hard-featured man, with a good deal of Celtic sentiment about his manner & voice—quite of the type of the Northern Irishmen'.

Mr Nicholls's religious views are probably reflected in the devotional works he acquired in 1848: sermons by Dr William Beveridge and selected works by Dr William Hall, reprinted and published by the Religious Tract Society; and *The Churchman's Companion* (Society for Promoting Christian Knowledge, 1845). Significantly, in or after 1848, that year of Brontë deaths, Mr Nicholls turned down the corner of a page in Dr Hall's 'Devout Meditations on Death'. Competence in the Classics is implied by William Cartman's gift of a 1671 Elzevir printing of *Valerii Maximi— Dictorum Factorumque Memorabilium Libri IX*. On the other hand Nicholls's copy of *Cranford* reminds one that his customary gravity could give way to mirth. His Haworth landlady, Martha Brown's mother, 'heard him giving vent to roars of laughter as he sat alone [reading *Shirley*]— clapping his hands and stamping on the floor. . . . he triumphed in his own character' (Charlotte to Ellen Nussey ?28 Jan. 1850, in Smith *Letters*, 2. 337). Fortunately Charlotte's portrayal of him as 'Mr Macarthey' ('Macarthur' in the *Shirley* manuscript) is benign. 'Decent, decorous, and conscientious', he 'laboured faithfully in the parish: the schools, both Sunday and day-schools, flourished under his sway' (ch. 37). The truth of this portrait is attested in the parish registers, where his name as officiating minister appears so frequently, and in the formal reference given by Revd Joseph

*Grant in January 1853: through Nicholls's work and influence, Haworth National School scholars had increased from 60 to between 200 and 300, church attendance was up sixfold, and the *Stanbury schoolroom and place of worship had been erected. Mr Nicholls also supported public-spirited efforts such as Mr Brontë's petition to the General Board of Health on 29 August 1849. In *Shirley* Charlotte qualifies her praise of 'Macarthey' by good-humoured mockery of his 'proper, steady-going, clerical faults . . . finding himself invited to tea with a Dissenter would unhinge him for a week . . . the thought of an unbaptized fellow-creature being interred with Christian rites . . . could make strange havoc in Mr. Macarthey's physical and mental economy; otherwise, he was sane and rational, diligent and charitable'. There is a hint here of the narrowness and *Puseyite tendencies which later troubled Charlotte, since she feared they might inhibit her friendship with the Unitarian Gaskells.

These tendencies, and his generally reserved, stiff manner, did not endear him to the parishioners, though there were stories of his kindness to individuals, and he visited poor parishioners almost every afternoon. After his successful campaign in 1847 against the Haworth women's custom of drying washing in the churchyard, Charlotte ruefully noted that many parishioners wished he would not return after his holiday in *Ireland. In July 1851, however, she observed a change in his customary behaviour; he was 'good—mild and uncontentious' when he took tea at the Parsonage. A year later, in a letter from Filey to her father of 2 June 1852, she sent the first of several friendly messages to Nicholls, with the comment that she was sure he would 'laugh out' at the 'ludicrous' behaviour of the singers in the mouldy, decayed church she had visited. But at home she began to observe with 'dim misgivings' his low spirits, 'threats of expatriation', 'constant looks' at her, and 'strange, feverish restraint'. They culminated in his proposal on 13 December 1852, when, 'shaking from head to foot, looking deadly pale' he made her feel 'what it costs a man to declare affection where he doubts response' (to Ellen Nussey, 15 December 1852, in Wise & Symington, 4. 29). Mr Brontë responded with apoplectic fury, Charlotte consequently refused Nicholls, and his misery culminated in his decision to leave Haworth.

In January 1853 he wrote to the Society for the Propagation of the Gospel, offering himself as a missionary to the Australian Colonies of Sydney, Melbourne, or Adelaide. Mr Brontë, one of six referees who praised his character and conduct, admitted that he had behaved 'wisely, soberly, and piously', and was 'sound and orthodox' in principles. Though invited for an interview, he changed his mind by 26 February, postponed his decision, then gave a return of his rheumatism as the reason for withdrawing his application. He remained miserable and touchy, and he broke down completely when he took the Whitsunday Communion service in the presence of Charlotte and a crowded congregation; but when questioned he told the churchwardens that his imminent departure was his own fault, not Mr Brontë's. On 25 May 1853 sympathetic parishioners presented him with a gold watch as a farewell gift. On 26 May Charlotte saw him lingering at the Parsonage gate after handing over the National School deeds to Mr Brontë: going out, she found him in a 'paroxysm of anguish' and let him know she was not 'cruelly blind and indifferent to his constancy and grief'. His duties were to be taken by the unsatisfactory George De Renzy, while he became curate to Revd Thomas Cator, MA (1790–1864) at Kirk Smeaton near Pontefract. His letters to Charlotte, at first unanswered, eventually led to their clandestine correspondence, meetings when he stayed with the Grants near Haworth, Mr Brontë's grudging permission for his daughter to become better acquainted with him, and finally to consent for their marriage. He had refused livings offered to him, through Monckton *Milnes's influence, because he knew he could never marry Charlotte unless he could return to Haworth, for she would not leave her father. He gained Mr Brontë's respect by proving himself 'disinterested and forbearing', and won from Charlotte 'more than mere cool respect', for 'with exquisitely keen feelings', he could still 'freely forgive'.

During the honeymoon in Wales and Ireland which followed their quiet wedding on 29 June 1854, he proved to be tenderly considerate to Charlotte, who learnt how highly valued he was by his relatives. Like her, he was exhilarated by the magnificence of the Atlantic waves; together they visited exquisite scenery at Kilkee, Glengariff, and *Killarney; and, by reacting swiftly when he realized she had fallen from her horse in the Gap of Dunloe, he helped to save her life. During their marriage their mutual love grew strong. By 26 December 1854 she could write, 'He is "my dear boy" certainly, dearer now than he was six months ago' (Wise & Symington, 4. 167). He did not discourage her from writing. C. K. *Shorter stated in his edition of Gaskell's Life (1900) that 'Mr. Nicholls repudiates . . . [the allegation] that he discouraged his wife's literary activities.' On the contrary, they had read her chapters of *Emma and 'chatted pleasantly over the possible development of the plot' (p. 634). She tolerated and was amused by his quirks of behaviour—as for example when he 'threatened to bolt' when the affected Amelia Tay-

lor visited the Parsonage, or when he demanded that Ellen Nussey should burn Charlotte's rash letters, which he thought as 'dangerous as lucifer matches'. During her last illness she wrote to Laetitia Wheelwright on 15 February 1855: 'No kinder better husband than mine . . . can there be in the world. I do not want now for kind companionship in health and the tenderest nursing in sickness' (Wise & Symington, 4. 174).

After Charlotte's death he cared faithfully for her father, and much against his own inclination, agreed to Mr Brontë's wish that Elizabeth *Gaskell should write a biography of her, even though he was horrified that she wanted to quote directly from Charlotte's letters, and that he was required to cede copyright for the quotations as used in the Life. He wrote indignantly to George *Smith that the matter had 'from beginning to end . . . been a source of pain and annoyance' to him. It continued to cause him distress after Elizabeth Gaskell's statements about *Cowan Bridge and Revd W. Carus *Wilson led to an acrimonious newspaper controversy from April to August 1857, in which Charlotte's motives in 'caricaturing' the school and making injurious 'misstatements' about it were questioned. Mr Nicholls wrote five indignant letters, his 'sole desire' being 'to defend the dead from the aspersions cast on her by interested individuals' (Wise & Symington, app. 1). His concern to protect her reputation led him to obliterate several phrases in the manuscript of The *Professor, which he edited for publication. He also supplied George Smith with the manuscript and a transcription of Emma, and three poems, one by Emily and two by Charlotte, for the *Cornhill Magazine (see BST (1987), 19. 3. 97–106 and (1994), 21. 4. 101–15).

Though many parishioners expected him to be the new incumbent after Mr Brontë's death on 7 June 1861, the church trustees voted against him by five to four. He immediately resigned. Before returning to Banagher, he gave away many items, especially to Martha *Brown and her sister Tabitha, retained private papers and other treasured Brontë possessions such as Charlotte's writing desk, workbox, and paintbox, and put up for the remaining contents of the Parsonage for auction on 1 October 1861 (see SALES OF BRONTËANA). In Banagher he lived at the Hill House (still extant), the home of his widowed aunt Mrs Harriette Bell and her daughter Mary Anna. Martha Brown visited frequently as a welcome guest and helper in the household. Nicholls corresponded with her when she returned to Haworth, taking a kindly interest in her life there, and occasionally sending gifts of money. On 26 August 1864 he married Mary Anna (1830–1914). Having known him from her childhood, she understood him well, recognizing the devotion to Charlotte which led him to place mementoes of her throughout the house. Shorter, who met both husband and wife at Banagher on 31 March 1895, described their marriage as one of 'unmixed blessedness'. He had found Nicholls 'in a home of supreme simplicity and charm, esteemed by all who knew him and idolised in his own household'.

Though he regularly attended church, Nicholls did not return to the ministry, possibly owing to throat trouble. He occupied himself with farming in a small way, and, unlike Ellen Nussey, did not attempt to edit Charlotte's letters or exploit his connection with her. Ellen had been hostile to him from shortly after Charlotte's death. She was jealous of him as the usurper of her position as Charlotte's closest friend, on the defensive about her failure to burn Charlotte's letters, and sceptical about his possession of copyright in them. The publication of Thomas Wemyss *Reid's articles on Charlotte in Macmillan's Magazine (Aug.–Oct. 1876), for which Ellen had provided much information, caused Mr Nicholls to break his long silence on Brontë matters, to protest against an ambiguous passage on Charlotte's 'sole failure of duty' and against the revelation of her feelings for 'Mr X' (James *Taylor). Nicholls blamed himself for not cautioning Ellen that his wife's letters were not 'hers for publication'. Shorter and T. J. *Wise were well aware of the laws of copyright. Shorter charmed his way into Mr Nicholls's good will, and on 23 November 1895 purchased the copyright in manuscripts which passed through his hands, paying Mr Nicholls £150. In fact most of Nicholls's manuscripts were passed on to Wise, and Nicholls was again distressed by the unscrupulous use of letters, when Charlotte's description of his breakdown at the Whitsuntide service was printed in Sotheby's catalogue for 28 February 1896 (and later printed in Shorter Circle). But he still apparently trusted Shorter in 1900, when his assistance was acknowledged in Shorter's edition of the Life (Haworth edn.).

During the last few years of his life, Nicholls's health declined. Mary Anna cared for him devotedly, helped by a professional nurse from the end of November 1906, when bronchitis was diagnosed. He died on 2 December 1906, and was buried in St Paul's churchyard, Banagher. Mary Anna, who died on 27 February 1915, lies in the same grave.

Cochrane, Margaret and Robert, My Dear Boy (1999).

Smith Letters.

Nicholls, Mary Anna. See BELL FAMILY.

Niger River, in the *Glass Town and Angrian saga, flows from *Sneaky's Land in the north through the Plain of Dahomey and the Vale of Verdopolis to the Gulf of Guinea, where *Verdopolis lies at its mouth and its confluence with the River Guadima. Wellesley House and other palaces are built on the Niger in Verdopolis. The river also forms the boundary between the Verdopolitan (or Glass Town) Federation and the new kingdom of *Angria.

During the early 19th century, newspapers and journals carried articles on numerous European explorations to find the course and termination of the Niger in *Africa. The travels of Mungo Park in particular caught the public imagination. The author of a *Blackwood's article for June 1826 recommended that the British move their unsuccessful settlements at Freetown and elsewhere on the Gold Coast to Fernando Po at the mouth of the Niger (still disputed at the time), so that they would command the trading routes of the river and its tributaries into central Africa (Alexander EW, p. 30). The young Brontës, not the British Government, agreed and established Verdopolis. The map associated with this article became the blueprint for the Glass Town Federation.

'Nightly Revel, The'. Appended to Revd Patrick Brontë's The *Cottage in the Wood, this retells in verse the story of William Bower's conversion. Based on real life, it recreates vividly in well-managed heroic couplets the 'idly fierce' quarrels of Bower and his drunken companions. Rapid, cumulative lines convey the crescendo of drunken folly and gambling, until 'three giant sots' gallop out through 'the tangling wood'. In a 'gusty storm', 'bright, and more bright, the quivering lightnings flash', but the riders escape death when their sheltering oak is struck. The two unrepentant sinners die at the hand of lurking murderers, and only Bower, standing apart in 'penitential prayer', survives.

Noah o' Tims, the somewhat shady and disreputable leader of the worker's delegation in Shirley that tries to force Robert Gérard *Moore to change his plans for the mechanization of Hollow's Mill. The formation of Noah's name follows the patronymic tradition that was still found in parts of the north of England at the end of the 19th century; another instance occurs in Shirley, p. 655 ('John-of-Mally's-of-Hannah's-of-Deb's') (Wroot, pp. 122–3). Noah is drawn as 'a little dapper strutting man, with a turned-up nose' (Shirley, p. 149), exhibiting 'an exceedingly self-confident and conceited air' (p. 150). Through his exaggerated formality and pretentious diction, Charlotte Brontë seeks to portray the hypocrisy of professional agitators who manipulate 'honest though misguided men' into committing acts of violence. Much like Dickens, who would caricature the union organizer through the character of Slackbridge in *Hard Times* (1854), Charlotte was sympathetic to the hardships of the working poor, but distrusted partisan movements that threatened the status quo. Referring to the French Revolution of 1848, she lamented to Margaret *Wooler in a letter of 31 March 1848 that 'convulsive revolutions put back the world in all that is good, check civilisation, bring the dregs of society to its surface' (Smith *Letters*, 2. 48). She expressed sympathy for the grievances of the Chartists, whose cause foundered after the failure of their petition in April 1848, but there is implicit relief in her letter to William Smith Williams of 20 April 1848 that 'an ill-advised movement has been judiciously repressed' (Smith *Letters*, 2. 51). HR

'No coward soul is mine' (2 Jan 1846), 28 lines by Emily Brontë, from the Honresfeld MS (see LAW COLLECTION); published by Charlotte Brontë in 1850, with the mistaken comment: 'The following are the last lines my sister Emily ever wrote.' The poem had been written during the process of selection and editing for *Poems* 1846, but it had not been included in that volume.

In contrast to such poems as 'The *Philosopher' that urge oblivion, this great poem by Emily is a jubilant affirmation of Faith in God. As with so many of her poems, the speaker may be a Gondal character, but the sentiments are consistent with what we know of Emily's own complex attitude to Christianity. Armed by Faith, the speaker defiantly rejects the 'Fear' of this 'world's storm-troubled sphere'. The spirit of God resides within her and this, in turn, gives her power in an eternal existence:

> O God within my breast
> Almighty ever-present Deity
> Life, that in me hast rest
> As I Undying Life, have power in thee

The speaker then damns all other creeds as 'un-utterably vain . . . To waken doubt in one | Holding so fast by thy infinity'. A number of critics have failed to read stanzas 3 and 4 as one sentence (there is little punctuation in this poem) and therefore erroneously interpret the speaker's obvious contempt for sectarian religion as a rejection of Christianity. The speaker is adamant, however, that belief in the eternity of God ('So surely anchored on | The steadfast rock of Immortality') will protect her from doubt and fear. God's spirit 'Pervades . . . Changes, sustains, dissolves, creates and rears'. Earth might cease to be and yet if 'thou wert left alone | Every Existence would exist in thee', an echo of Catherine's famous statement of affinity with Heathcliff (*Wuthering Heights*, ch. 9). Since God is everywhere there is no place for death to exist, and since God is everything, there is no atom of physical matter that death is capable of destroying.

Critics have also worried about the pride evinced in this boast of secure faith. Emily's Christianity was intensely personal and unorthodox but she was not atheistic. Stevie Davies points out that 'Serene self-confidence does not have to boast', and the contemptuous and retaliatory nature of the poem reflects a defence against both the religious fanaticism of the time (witness *Joseph in *Wuthering Heights*) and Emily's own 'strife within herself' (see, for example, 'The Philosopher') (*Emily Brontë: Heretic* (1994), 145). Margaret Maison identified a source for the phrase 'coward soul' in an ode by Hester Chapone that was printed in Elizabeth Carter's translation of *The Discourses of Epictetus* ('Emily Brontë and Epictetus', *N & Q*, NS 25 (June 1978), 230–1). Maison reads Emily's poem as a reply to Chapone's anti-Epictetus poem. For the influence of Epictetus on Emily see POETRY BY EMILY BRONTË. Derek Roper notes the affinity between Emily's pervading spirit and Coleridge's description of secondary imagination that 'dissolves, diffuses, dissipates, in order to recreate' (Roper *EBP*, p. 279).

Gezari *EBP*, p. 182.
Roper *EBP*, p. 183.

North, Christopher. See WILSON, JOHN (CHRISTOPHER NORTH).

Northangerland, province in Angria, in the *Glass Town and Angrian saga, 200 miles long and 270 miles broad, with a population of 376,000. Its capital city is Pequene and the Duke of *Northangerland is its governor.

Northangerland, Duke of (Alexander Augustus Percy, Rogue (Rougue), Lord Ellrington (Elrington)). Former pirate ('Rogue' or 'Rougue'), arch-demagogue, revolutionary, and politician, he is first friend and then foe of the Duke of *Zamorna, whose third wife is Northangerland's daughter Mary. Northangerland becomes Branwell Brontë's favourite persona and the central figure in his poetry and prose. So close did Branwell's identification with this character become that most of his later published *poetry (at least eighteen poems) appeared in local newspapers under the pseudonym 'Northangerland'.

His character is a complex amalgam of Branwell's enthusiasm for *Napoleon Buonaparte, *Milton's Satan and the dark side of the *Byronic Hero. His later psychology and various alter egos owe much to James *Hogg's portrayal of the doppelgänger motif in *The Private Memoirs and Confessions of a Justified Sinner*. There is an element too of Sir Walter *Scott's hero Rob Roy, who (like Northangerland) was a drover, a ruthless opponent of the government, and a powerful and dangerous outlaw.

Northangerland's biography emerges during the course of the *Glass Town and Angrian saga. He is first referred to by Charlotte as 'Old Rogue's youngest son, a promising youth' (Alexander *EEW*, 1. 176), and is a major player in the later volumes of Branwell's *'Letters from an Englishman'* (1830–2), where he is instrumental in the Great Rebellion of March 1831. He leads an insurrection in Verdopolis and sets up a provisional government on the French model of 1789. He again leads a rebellion in Sneaky's Land, where, after burning the city of Fidena, he is defeated and shot. Resurrected by Branwell, he appears as the hero of 'The *Pirate', outlawed captain of 'The Red Rover', who enters central Verdopolitan society as the new husband of Zenobia Ellrington, assuming the title Lord Ellrington (Elrington in Branwell's manuscripts).

As his name mutates from Rogue to Colonel Alexander Augustus Percy, Lord Ellrington, and Duke of Northangerland (sometimes Lord or Earl of Northangerland), his history and character become more complex. 'Rogue' is reserved as the 'professional' name of Percy, used chiefly in the early juvenilia in relation to the revolutionary activities of 'the vile demagogue Alexander Rogue'. Charlotte complicates his character in *The *Green Dwarf*, suggesting that beneath the handsome regular countenance of this accomplished soldier and gentleman lurks a villainy betrayed only by a sinister eye and deceitful mouth. It is this duplicity that fascinates the otherwise noble young Marquis of Douro (Zamorna), who cannot resist the lure of Percy's brilliant evil, in which he was trained early by the evil *Montmorency and the devilish *Sdeath. Percy develops into the Glass Town equivalent of Milton's Satan: 'bright with beauty, dark with crime'. As the young Brontës increasingly understand the possibilities of the Byronic Hero, they probe the recesses of Percy's (and, to a lesser extent, Zamorna's) duplicitous mind. His atheism and amorality, in particular, are explored repetitively. His restless energy knows no bounds. Aspiring to respectability and acceptance, he undermines stable personal and political relationships as soon as he creates them.

Percy is modelled on the Percys of Northumberland, England (hence, Northangerland), whose hot-headed and warring exploits feature in Shakespeare's history plays, probably the chief source for the Brontës since Alexander Percy is heir to the Duke of Beaufort, his uncle, who also appears in such plays as *Henry IV* and *Henry V*. Alexander Percy is tall and auburn-haired, like the historical Percys, and his Alnwick Hall is named after Alnwick Castle in Northumberland. Scott also tells of the legend of Alnwick and the Percys in *Tales of a Grandfather*, owned by the Brontës.

Percy is married three times and has numerous affairs. He appears incapable of loving anyone except his second wife and their daughter Mary. His father, Edward Percy, had disapproved his son's marriage to Augusta di *Segovia (in 1812) and sent him to Philosopher's Isle, where he formed the Society of Atheistic Republicans. On his return Percy and Augusta have a son but, like all Percy's sons, he disappears at birth, only to re-emerge as the artist William *Etty in later stories. Augusta and Percy arrange the murder of Edward Percy sen., in order to inherit his money, but Augusta herself is murdered when she tries to cross her accomplices. In 1814, he marries Lady Maria Henrietta Wharton with whom he is idyllically happy, living at Percy Hall in Wellington's Land. Three sons are born (Edward, William, and Henry) and a daughter (Mary) before Maria dies of consumption aggravated by the assumed death of her baby sons. (With an unnatural antipathy to sons, Northangerland ordered Sdeath to dispose of them but he disobeyed orders and left them in obscurity.) Heartbroken and further disillusioned, Percy lives a dissipated and anarchic life, gambling, cattle-dealing (he is a former drover), and participating in the 1831 and 1832 rebellions mentioned above. After an unsuccessful attempt to abduct and marry Lady Emily Charlesworth (engaged to Lord *St Clair), he elopes with Harriet *O'Connor, the wife of his evil 'familiar' Montmorency, and abandons her to die in misery. After sixteen years as a bandit and pirate, he marries Lady Zenobia *Ellrington with whom he maintains an uneasy relationship for the remainder of the saga, avoiding her rages and juggling a variety of mistresses including Lady Georgina Greville, Lady St James, Louisa (Dance) Vernon, Miss Pelfe, and Madame Lalande. His illegitimate daughter Caroline *Vernon is the pride of his latter years.

The central feature of the Glass Town and Angrian saga is the relationship between Lord Ellrington and the Marquis of Douro (later Northangerland and Zamorna). Together they preside over the scandalous activities of the *Elysium, and develop a love-hate relationship that affects the course of political events. Ellrington assists Douro (now Duke of Zamorna) in the *War of Encroachment against the Ashantees and the French. He becomes duke of Northangerland when Zamorna becomes king of Angria. Their relationship is further complicated when Northangerland becomes not only Zamorna's father-in-law but also his prime minister of Angria. Unable to maintain his support of monarchy, Northangerland turns on Zamorna and helps Ardrah defeat and occupy Angria. He then turns on Ardrah to try to establish a republican government in Verdopolis with himself as lord president of the Provisional Government (his constant 'Napoleonic' aim in life). He sends Zamorna into exile on Ascension Island, causing the near-death of his daughter Mary who is caught between the machinations of father and husband. When Zamorna regains power, Zamorna ignores the popular cry for Northangerland's death and preserves his life on condition that he lives quietly as a private citizen.

In later years, Northangerland occasionally assumes one of his early 'undercover' disguises as 'Brother *Ashworth', the Methodist preacher skilled in rousing the masses (chiefly against their leaders). Given Northangerland's atheistic beliefs, this bizarre practice is part of the Brontës' religious satire. The same name is used for the later character Alexander *Ashworth, who is a reincarnation of Northangerland.

Northangerland House, home of Lord Northangerland in the kingdom of *Angria, 'towering like some great theatre above the streets of Adrianopolis'; in the *Glass Town and Angrian saga.

Northern College. See PALACE OF INSTRUCTION.

North Lees Hall. In 1845 this ancient battlemented hall at Outseats near *Hathersage, owned by Miss Hannah Wright of Brookfield Hall, was inhabited by the widowed Mary Eyre, her son George, and three daughters. Nearby, a ruined Catholic chapel witnessed that the Eyres were an old Catholic family. During visits to the hall in July 1845 Charlotte saw the apostle cupboard (described in *Jane Eyre*, ch. 20) inherited in 1862 by Mrs Thomas Eyre's nephew, and acquired by the BPM in 1935. The first mistress of North Lees, Agnes Ashurst, reputedly went mad, was confined in a padded room, and died in a fire.

Norton Conyers. A house about 4 miles north of Ripon, originally 14th century, but now mainly Jacobean in style, with curved gables added in 1632. Traces of battlements are visible. The stable block, courtyard, walled garden, and orangery are 18th century. The rookery and sunk fence, oak hall, great staircase, and family portraits resemble those at *Thornfield Hall in *Jane Eyre*. Owned by the Graham family, with some intervals, since 1624, the house was often unoccupied during the lifetime of Sir Bellingham Graham (d. 1866). Charlotte Brontë might have visited it from *Swarcliffe Hall in 1839 with Mrs Sidgwick, whose brother Frederick Greenwood rented the house from 1848.

notebooks (*cahiers*). Charlotte Brontë returned from the Pensionnat *Heger with several notebooks filled with student exercises. The original number remains uncertain, since some were subsequently torn apart and rebound (on their mutilation, see WISE, THOMAS JAMES). The notebooks from 1842 (in BPM; BL; and Ransom HRC, Texas) contain grammar exercises and *dictations. During that year she also transcribed translations from English into French. In her second term of residence, in 1843, her agreement with the Hegers included German lessons. An undated notebook (in BPM) features six works by *Schiller translated into French: 'The Diver' ('Le Plongeur' in a prose version), 'The Maiden's Lament' ('La Plainte de la jeune fille'), 'The Alpen Hunter' ('Le Chasseur des Alpes'), 'The Knight of Toggenburg' ('Le Chevalier de Toggenburg') and 'Dirge for a Dead Indian' ('Chant funèbre [sic] pour l'Indien mort'). It also includes her translations of 'William Wallace', 'Un banquet égyptien', 'Roxburgh Castle', and 'Le Gladiateur', an excerpt from *Byron's *Childe Harold*. Another notebook (25 Apr. 1843, in BPM) includes six translations into English of German prose and poetry: 'The Diver' (in verse), 'The Count of Hapsburg', 'The Glove', 'Hector's Parting', 'The Ring of Polycrates', and 'The Pleasure of the Moment'. In addition, she translated part of Sir Walter *Scott's poem 'Coronach' into French and poems by *Belmontet and *Barbier into English. A further notebook from September 1843 contains exercises in arithmetic. SL

Alexander, Christine, *A Bibliography of the Manuscripts of Charlotte Brontë* (1982), pp. 181–5.
Neufeldt *CBP*, pp. 353–70, 485–90.

novel in the mid-19th century, the. In this period (often described as 'the age of the novel') the British novel achieved unprecedented artistic and popular stature. The Brontës' major novels, all published in mid-century, attained the prominence and wide readership previously accorded only to Sir Walter *Scott and Charles *Dickens. Charged with immorality and triviality in the preceding century, at the beginning of the 19th century the genre was represented largely by formulaic sentimentality and imitative Gothic sensationalism. Those now judged to be the major talents in fiction during the Romantic period—Jane *Austen and Scott—published their novels anonymously. Anonymity was common for women writers, but Scott's determination to conceal his authorship of novels suggests reluctance to sully his reputation as a leading poet. Beginning with his first novel *Waverley* (1814), however, his immensely popular historical fiction helped to reverse the fortunes of the novel by setting a trend toward greater realism. His antiquarian's attention to the

347

particulars of daily life, as well as to the sweeping social and political movements providing the backdrops for his human stories, satisfied a growing desire for authenticity in novels' depictions of life. Charlotte exhorted Ellen Nussey on 4 July 1834: 'For fiction—read Scott alone—all novels after his are worthless' (Smith *Letters*, 1. 130).

Novels that held an analytical mirror up to their world appealed strongly to mid-19th-century readers increasingly preoccupied with social problems. Victorians self-consciously regarded theirs as an age of transition, as the ideological uncertainties and unprecedented social ills associated with democracy, industrialization, urbanization, religious fragmentation, and growing scepticism challenged centuries-old social, political, and philosophical systems. Whereas the upper classes had previously constituted the principal audience for fiction, by mid-century increasing affluence, education, and leisure among the middle classes enlarged and transformed the audience for novels and elevated novel writing to more genteel professional status. The burgeoning middle classes, regarding themselves as cultural arbiters, welcomed novels that took up social questions, and utilitarian emphasis on the usefulness of literature made the novel rather than poetry the dominant literary form.

The principal mode of novel publication had long been the expensive three-decker, a work published in three separate volumes. Charlotte's three major novels and Anne's *Tenant* were all published in this format. Around 1840 two phenomena rapidly expanded novels' readership: the publication of novels in inexpensive monthly parts (slim paperbound booklets)—a development of the long-established weekly or monthly instalments in periodicals—and the growth of subscription libraries, especially the dominant Mudie's (begun in 1842), which allowed readers to borrow an unlimited number of three-deckers for a modest annual fee. Dickens revived the lapsed 18th-century practice of publishing novels in monthly parts with his first work of fiction, *The Pickwick Papers* (1836–7), producing profound results. Whereas an average edition of a three-decker novel numbered 750 copies (the phenomenally successful Scott reached 6,000), *Pickwick* eventually sold 40,000 copies per issue. At the same time that fiction was becoming more accessible financially, long-standing evangelical opposition to novels as morally objectionable began to weaken, while the dictates of Mudie's Library ensured that works in wide circulation would meet high standards of conventional taste and morals. As middle-class interests came to determine the success of individual novels, a number of fictional sub-genres popular in the first three decades of the

century lost appeal: the 'silver-fork novel' of fashionable life, melodramatic romances, and tales dealing with adventurers and highwaymen, fox-hunting and gentry life, and naval life.

Dickens's *Pickwick Papers* did more than explode circulation figures; with its lively attention to working-class life it also signalled changes in the content of the literary novel. Almost immediately hailed as the greatest novelist since Scott, young Dickens continued to cultivate readers' taste for immediacy and relevance in *Oliver Twist* (1837–9). Its workhouses and pickpockets addressed contemporary controversies over the Poor Laws and abandoned children, while readily accessible sentimentality, humour, and melodrama leavened its social consciousness. Lowood School in *Jane Eyre* reminded readers of Dickens's horrific Dotheboys Hall in *Nicholas Nickleby*. Dickens's spirited and sympathetic attention to the lower classes reflects some kinship with the large body of fiction consumed by labouring-class readers in the form of 'penny dreadfuls', unpolished narratives enlivened by sensationalism and comedy and marketed in instalments priced at just a penny. Popular authors of penny dreadfuls are unfamiliar today, such as Henry Cockton and George W. M. Reynolds, whose lurid tales such as *The Slaves of England (The Seamstress)* and *Wagner, the Wehr-Wolf* outsold even Dickens's works in the 1840s and 1850s. While the fiction in *Fraser's Magazine* and *Blackwood's Edinburgh Magazine*, like that of Dickens, portrayed the conditions of labourers' lives to middle-class readers, Dickens surpassed other novelists of the time in blending the comedy, melodrama, and vitality of the penny dreadfuls with serious social criticism and a high degree of artistry.

By the time Dickens published *Nicholas Nickleby* (1838), depicting the unhealthy conditions of cheap boarding schools and the struggles of a young woman to support herself, his principal fellow novelists included Frances Trollope, who satirized current social abuses such as child labour, and writers such as Charles Lever and Benjamin *Disraeli, who abandoned their earlier subject matter to concentrate on social problems. Charlotte considered that Frances Trollope had made a 'ridiculous mess' of her novel *Michael Armstrong: The Factory Boy*, and she determined that her own 'social problem' novel *Shirley* should be soundly based on historical facts. Lever turned from popular comedies of sporting life to treat the political problems arising from England and Ireland's unification. Disraeli forsook the worlds of fashionable society and exotic romance to publish a trilogy that focused first on the political and economic climate since the *Reform Bill, 1832 (*Coningsby*, 1844); then on the evils of industrialism and dangers of *Chartism (*Sybil, or the Two Nations*, 1845); and eventually on religion's role in ameliorating social problems (*Tancred*, 1847).

As Disraeli's trilogy exemplifies, a dominant category of fiction from the mid-1840s was the 'condition of England' novel, which focused on the social problems attending industrialization. Dickens approached such concerns in *Dombey and Son* (1846–8), which attacks the figure of the callous captain of industry and discredits the period's prevailing utilitarianism and materialism, and *David Copperfield* (1849–50), which exposes inequities in England's class structure. During the same period Elizabeth *Gaskell (who later became Charlotte Brontë's friend and first biographer) in *Mary Barton* (1848) and *North and South* (1854–5) examined the social chasms between rich and poor, the effects of Chartism, and problems wrought or exacerbated by industrialization and the sudden growth of industrial cities. Similar concerns dominate Charles Kingsley's 1848 *Yeast*, though it focuses on the plight of rural labourers, and his 1850 *Alton Locke*, which exposes the crass exploitation of sweatshops and squalid conditions of slums. These preoccupations in fiction reflect anxieties about the social unrest manifest in the domestic rise of Chartism during the 'Hungry Forties' and Europe's revolutionary movements of 1848. Similar topicality is evident in novels which address England's crisis of faith, such as James Anthony Froude's *Shadows of the Clouds* (1847) and *The Nemesis of Faith* (1849), and John Henry Newman's *Loss and Gain* (1848). Though not all fiction of the period addressed social problems, many novels that lacked topical resonance—by such writers as Frank E. Smedley, R. S. Surtees, and Edward Bulwer-Lytton—proved ephemeral.

William Makepeace *Thackeray, who became Dickens's chief rival for recognition as the greatest novelist at mid-century, though less aggressively concerned with specific social problems than Dickens or Gaskell, combined a journalist's commitment to authenticity and a satirist's delight in exposing foibles and folly. His first developed novel *Vanity Fair* (monthly parts began in January 1847), though set back in time some 30 years, focused on tensions wrought by social changes which remained compellingly contemporary: the aristocracy's decline and rise of a new business class, the blighting effects of unbridled materialism, the precariousness of women's status in the marriage market. Thackeray's tenets of realism prevented his idealizing any character, a practice suggested by *Vanity Fair*'s subtitle, 'A Novel without a Hero'. Like *Jane Eyre* and a number of Dickens's works, Thackeray's *Pendennis* (1848–50) contributed to the popularity of the *Bildungsroman*, or novel of personal development.

Mid-century fiction also included a large body of domestic novels, mostly written by women, notable for their limited concerns (usually courtship and marriage), romanticization of everyday experience, idealization of leading male and female characters, religious piety, formulaic plots, and sentimental tone. Though their authors—for example, Harriet Smythies, Anne Marsh, Mrs Stirling, Marmion Savage, Lady Georgina Fullerton—are almost entirely forgotten today, they established a standard for women's writing against which reviewers sometimes criticized the Brontës' works for lapses in taste or morality.

The Brontës' novels figure singularly in their mid-century context. While they pursue issues common to the fiction of the day, they remain remarkable for their originality. Even the Brontës' publishing format was unusual in terms of standard marketing practices. Of the major Victorian novelists, they alone never attempted serial publication (Charlotte flatly rejected this suggestion from her publisher), and their first manuscripts ignored the typical expectation for three-deckers (the publisher joined *Wuthering Heights* and *Agnes Grey* to constitute three volumes; *The Professor*'s brevity contributed to its rejection). Emily's *Wuthering Heights* dramatically eschews the mundane realism familiar to mid-Victorian readers, yet as Charlotte's 1850 preface to the novel maintains, its representation of Yorkshire dialect and rugged character types may more faithfully represent the life around her than her London readers imagined. Moreover the novel's conflicts arise from such phenomena scrutinized in other mid-Victorian fiction as the marriage market, class tensions, and changing economic structures. Attention to contemporary issues such as women's limited education and employment opportunities links Anne's and Charlotte's works to the dominant trends in fiction of the 1840s, a topicality which Charlotte pursued aggressively in the industrial themes of *Shirley*. Though their social concerns parallel those of their contemporaries, the Brontës' practice of examining these issues through the intense subjectivity of unusually passionate female characters set them apart from mainstream fiction of the day and drew adverse criticism from reviewers accustomed to more sentimental, genial novels by women writers. The rarity of the Brontës' success in combining contemporary realism and extreme emotional intensity is reflected in the bifurcation of these tendencies in novels of the 1850s and 1860s, a period when Anthony Trollope achieved fame with exquisitely rendered depictions of quiet everyday life and George Eliot established her reputation with meticulous realism, while such writers as Wilkie Collins and Mary Elizabeth Braddon earned immense popularity by arousing heightened feelings with sensation fiction and psychological thrillers. See also PUBLISHING 1800–1860. BT

Gilmour, Robin, *The Novel in the Victorian Age: A Modern Introduction* (1986).

Sutherland, J. A., *Victorian Novelists and Publishers* (1976).

Wheeler, Michael, *English Fiction of the Victorian Period* (2nd edn. 1994).

Nunnely, a West Riding town in *Shirley*, close to *Briarfield and *Whinbury. Nunnely is the oldest parish in the area with a 'low-roofed Temple and mossy Parsonage, buried both in coëval oaks, outstanding sentinels of Nunwood' (p. 328). Revd Cyril *Hall is vicar here, and Revd David *Sweeting his curate. Sir Philip *Nunnely and his family make their home in Nunnely Priory, 'an older, a larger, a more lordly abode than any Briarfield or Whinbury owned' (p. 535). Shirley *Keeldar and Caroline *Helstone walk over Nunnely Common and gaze upon Nunnwood, 'the sole remnant of antique British forest in a region whose lowlands were once all sylvan chase, as its highlands were breast-deep heather' (p. 237). At the centre of this forest, reputed to be one of the haunts of Robin Hood, lie the ruins of a nunnery. Nunnely is a fictitious rendering of Hartshead, the village where Revd Patrick Brontë was the incumbent 1811–15. Below Hartshead lies Kirklees Hall, in 1811–12 the home of Sir George Armytage (1761–1836), third Baronet of Kirklees; within the grounds of the Hall stand the ruins of Kirklees Priory, a former Benedictine nunnery. It was from this nunnery that the mortally wounded Robin Hood was said to have fired an arrow whose landing place would mark his grave, and in the woods about 600 yards away from the gatehouse of the nunnery a gravestone marks the famed outlaw's supposed burial site (see Gaskell *Life*, vol. 1, ch. 6; also Barker, pp. 39–40). HR

Nunnely, Sir Philip, a wealthy young baronet in *Shirley* who meets Shirley *Keeldar at 'the fashionable watering-place of *Cliffbridge' (p. 535). He is 'a good and amiable gentleman', unaffected and sensible, a lover of the arts (though he writes very bad poetry). Sir Philip is drawn by his interest in Shirley to visit Nunnely Priory, his ancestral home. There he proposes marriage to the heiress, but to the extreme chagrin of Shirley's uncle Mr *Sympson she declines. The figure of the 'boy-baronet' is one-dimensional, his role being to create another seeming obstacle to the fulfilment of Louis Gérard *Moore's yearnings, and to precipitate the angry scene between Shirley and her uncle that culminates in the latter's expulsion from *Fieldhead. HR

Nussey, Ann, later Clapham (1795–1878), eldest sister of Ellen *Nussey; a capable housekeeper for Revd Henry *Nussey, and later for the family at *Brookroyd. Charlotte Brontë appreciated her sympathy at times of bereavement. She married a land agent, Robert Clapham (?1788–1855) in September 1849, when separate quarters were arranged for them within Brookroyd.

Nussey, Ellen (1817–97), Charlotte Brontë's closest friend for almost 24 years. She was the twelfth child of John Nussey and his wife, née Ellen Wade (see NUSSEY FAMILY). Four of John Nussey's older children were born in his uncle Richard Walker's house, *Rydings. Ellen was born in a house in Smithies Moor Lane, but after John Nussey's death his wife and family moved back into Rydings. Ellen's brothers John and Joshua were then living in London, and she paid long visits to these relatives there or in their subsequent homes. In summer 1836 Ellen's mother, with her younger daughters and sons, moved to *Brookroyd. As a child Ellen first attended a small local school, then the *Gomersal *Moravian Ladies' Academy, and finally from January 1831 Margaret *Wooler's school at *Roe Head, where she first met Charlotte. Ellen comforted the homesick Charlotte, whose shy initial friendship for her became in adolescence an ardent obsession, transforming Ellen's mild kindness and conventional piety into an ideal Christian way of life which Charlotte longed to share. A more down-to-earth, easy relationship followed from September/October 1839, when Ellen and Charlotte holidayed together in *Easton and *Bridlington. During Ellen's visit to Haworth in January/February 1840 both girls enjoyed the lively company of Revd William *Weightman. Ellen readily made friends, and shared in her family's sociable activities. Though she was quite unlike the highly original Mary *Taylor, she kept up a correspondence with her. She wrote long gossiping letters to and about her friends Mary Gorham and Amelia Ringrose (see TAYLOR, AMELIA), and stayed with both of them for long periods. She was not intellectual or widely read, and she was not let into the secret of the Brontës' published work until after Emily's death on 19 December 1848. Then, during her stay at the Parsonage as a longed-for friend after the great strain of Emily's illness, she was told the truth, and given copies of the sisters' four novels. Ellen accompanied Charlotte and Anne on Anne's last journey to *Scarborough in May 1849; she tended the dying Anne, and helped to make her funeral arrangements. Her presence comforted Charlotte in the following weeks, when Charlotte resumed the writing of *Shirley*, transforming reality into the happy ending of the 'Valley of the Shadow of Death'. Ellen took a special

Portrait of Ellen Nussey a young girl.

interest in this novel, and came to see Caroline *Helstone as a portrait of herself.

In the 1850s Charlotte's life took on new dimensions when she was courted as a celebrity and introduced to the 'lions' of London society; but Ellen remained her confidante and solace. Charlotte wrote to W. S. *Williams on 3 January 1850:

Just now I am enjoying the treat of my friend Ellen's society and she makes me indolent and negligent—I am too busy talking to her all day to do anything else . . . When I first saw Ellen I did not care for her . . . we were contrasts—still we suited—affection was first a germ, then a sapling—then a strong tree: now—no new friend, however lofty or profound in intellect . . . could be to me what Ellen is, yet she is no more than a conscientious, observant, calm, well-bred Yorkshire girl. She is without romance—if she attempts to read poetry—or poetic prose aloud—I am irritated and deprive her of the book—if she talks of it I stop my ears—but she is good—she is true—she is faithful and I love her. (Smith *Letters*, 2. 323)

Charlotte's preoccupation with Revd A. B. *Nicholls during the year before her engagement caused 8 months of estrangement from Ellen, who was jealous of this new and absorbing attachment. The breach was healed by March 1854, but there was a slight constraint in their relationship after Charlotte's marriage, despite Charlotte's renewed affection. After her friend's death in March 1855 Ellen's loyalty to the memory of an idealized Charlotte became her leading principle for the rest of her life. She made a number of attempts to publish Charlotte's letters to her. In 1863 she asked M. Constantin *Heger to help her produce an edition. Unsurprisingly, he refused. In 1869 she sent expurgated copies of the letters to George *Smith, who pointed out that Mr Nicholls owned the copyright, and suggested that Ellen should instead incorporate some of the 'most characteristic' letters in a narrative of their friendship. He could offer her about £50 for two or three articles in the *Cornhill Magazine*. Ellen thereupon requested the return of her letters. Having learnt that copyright restrictions did not apply to American publications, Ellen arranged with Scribner's of New York to publish extracts from the letters in their magazine, *Hours at Home*. Textually corrupt and incomplete, they had been selected from her expurgated copies and published from June to September 1870. In 1871 she revealed to George Smith that she had also sent a narrative of her friendship to Scribner's, 'Reminiscences of Charlotte Brontë', published in *Scribner's Monthly* for May that year (see Smith *Letters*, app. to vol. 1). In 1876 and 1877 she helped T. W. *Reid with his articles and book on Charlotte, and between 1878 and 1882 briefly cooperated and then quarrelled with Alpheus Wilkes and Sidney Biddell on abortive projects involving

the letters. Between 1885 and the spring of 1889 J. Horsfall *Turner, at her request, arranged for the printing of such letters as she sent him. A thousand copies were put into type; but before they were completed by the addition of letters to Mary Taylor and Laetitia Wheelwright (see WHEELWRIGHT FAMILY), Ellen changed her mind, believing that more material should have been omitted. After an acrimonious dispute and legal intervention, the sheets were returned to Ellen. She still imagined they could be published without Mr Nicholls's permission, became even more paranoic about her manuscripts, and accused various people, including Turner, of stealing them. For their eventual fate, see SHORTER, CLEMENT KING; WISE, THOMAS JAMES. After her mother's death in 1857 Ellen and her sisters moved to a dwelling in the old Gomersal Cloth Hall, then from 1860 onwards to a succession of houses in Lane Side, Gomersal, Ingwell House in *Birstall, the hamlet of Fieldhead, and finally Moor Lane House, Gomersal, where she died.

Whitehead, Barbara, *Charlotte Brontë and her 'dearest Nell'* (1993).

Nussey, Revd Henry (1812–60), brother of Ellen *Nussey. An earnest, evangelical student, he graduated BA from Magdalene College, Cambridge, 1835, was curate to Thomas Allbutt (see ALLBUTT FAMILY) (Sept. 1835–July 1837), and to W. M. *Heald (Aug. 1837–Feb. 1838), when he became 'harassed in mind'. A head injury, the commission of an unspecified sin in March 1838, and his brother William's mental illness and suicide in June 1838 impaired his self-confidence and ability to speak in public. Despite his conscientious pastoral care as curate at Burton Agnes near *Bridlington in late 1838, his vicar, Charles Henry Lutwidge, asked him to leave owing to his inadequacy as a preacher. His health improved during his curacy at Donnington and Earnley with Almodington, Sussex (Dec. 1838–Apr. 1844). In February 1839 he proposed marriage to Margaret Anne Lutwidge, Charles's sister. Immediately after her refusal, he proposed to Charlotte Brontë, who, certain that she did not love him, refused, alleging that her disposition was not 'calculated to form' his happiness, and that she lacked the capital to succeed with the school he suggested near Donnington. Henry accepted her refusal with pious resignation to the 'Will of the Lord'. The episode is probably recalled in St John *Rivers's proposal. In April 1844 Henry became curate, and in August vicar, of *Hathersage and Derwent. In May 1845 he married the wealthy Emily Prescott at Everton, Lancs. Charlotte's three-week visit to Hathersage while Ellen Nussey helped to prepare the vicarage made her familiar with the name Eyre, and with scenery recalled in

Jane Eyre. Henry became mentally and physically ill at Hathersage. From July 1847 he and Emily travelled on the Continent, but he never recovered sufficiently to resume his clerical duties. The later years of his marriage were unhappy. He died in August 1860 at Wootton, Warwickshire.

Nussey, Mercy Mary (1801–86), sister of Ellen *Nussey. In early life associated with the *Gomersal *Moravian community, she was afterwards admitted to the Single Sisters' Moravian house, Fairfield, near Manchester. By 1831 she had returned to *Birstall, and later started a school for poor children at nearby Carlinghow. Charlotte Brontë often sends respects or love to Mercy in her letters to Ellen, but from 1848 onwards refers to her trying behaviour, poor judgement, and lack of self-government. Mercy lived with her sisters after their mother died, but in 1878 moved into lodgings near George Nussey's asylum in York.

Nussey family. Charlotte Brontë's friend Ellen *Nussey was one of a large family. Ellen's father John (1760–1826) was a woollen manufacturer and merchant in *Birstall, where the Nusseys had interests in the Smithies and Brookroyd mills. After his death his wife Ellen, née Wade (?1771–1857) returned to *Rydings with the children still living at home, sharing the house with its owner, her brother-in-law Richard Nussey (1763–1835). It was there that Charlotte first visited the family, whose fortunes gradually declined, partly owing to Mrs Nussey's poor management. The eldest son, John (1794–1862), left home at 14 to be apprenticed to his half-cousin, Richard Walker (1772–1825) of 17 St James Street, London. John became a master of the Society of Apothecaries in 1833, and was apothecary to George IV and his successors. He married his second cousin Mary Walker (1799–1868), and they lived in style at 4 Cleveland Row, St James's, where Ellen stayed with them for long periods, for example, in 1834–5 and 1837. John also had property in Birstall. Georgiana Nussey (1829–72), one of twelve children born to this family, was briefly Charlotte's 'sweet little correspondent', though later she apparently became spoilt. Nevertheless she and her brother Edward (1828–1911) and their mother behaved courteously to the famous 'Currer Bell' when they called on her in London in January 1853. Ellen's brothers Joseph (1797–1846), Richard (1803–72), and George (1814–85) carried on the family woollen business, while William (1807–38) joined John in London, and was a qualified apothecary when he suffered a nervous breakdown and committed suicide. Charlotte may not have known this, but she knew that Joseph was a dissolute character, and a burden on his mother and sisters who had to nurse him. Charlotte pitied his relatives, who also had to witness the gradual deterioration of George's mental health, which led to his becoming a permanent inmate of Dr Henry Stephen Belcombe's humanely run private asylums in York by August 1845. Charlotte had known and admired George as Ellen's handsome and beloved brother in the 1830s. Richard Nussey (1803–72) married a wealthy wife, Elizabeth Charnock, in 1846, and moved to Leeds, where he prospered as a mill owner and commission agent. Joshua Nussey (1798–1871) graduated BA from St Catharine's College, Cambridge, in 1822, MA 1825, and was ordained priest in 1824. He married Anne Elizabeth Alexander (1788–1875) in 1832. Ellen stayed with them in 1838 during his curacy at Batheaston, near Bath (1834–8), and in 1846 stayed at Oundle, Northants., where Joshua was Vicar from 1845 until his death. Charlotte made tart comments about his wife, and included him in her strictures on Ellen's cold-hearted brothers who (she believed) did not do enough to help their aged mother and poorly off sisters. Sarah Walker Nussey (1809/10–1843) was an invalid, possibly disabled in some way, whose death Charlotte regarded as a merciful release, though she sympathized with the family's loss and grief. See also NUSSEY, ANN; NUSSEY, REVD HENRY; NUSSEY, MERCY MARY.

Woledge, Geoffrey, *Oakwell Hall: A Short History* (1986).

O'Connor, Arthur, profligate associate of the youthful Duke of *Northangerland ('Rogue'), who seduces O'Connor's sister Harriet, in the *Glass Town and Angrian saga. He is a member of the *Elysium and a colonel in Northangerland's Revolutionary army. After disobeying orders when drunk and causing the deaths of 30,000 men, he attempts suicide, is caught and executed, but mysteriously reappears in later stories. A pugilist and gambler, O'Connor loses his inheritance to the Duke of Zamorna, who makes him head supervisor of the Angrian Excise. He again becomes one of Northangerland's henchmen, and ends as a dead maniac, buried in an asylum yard.

O'Connor, Harriet, sister of Arthur *O'Connor, O'Connor Hall, in the early *Glass Town and Angrian saga. A member of Augusta di *Segovia's court in Wellington's Land, her unhappy childhood under a severe stepmother ends in seduction by the youthful Duke of *Northangerland ('Rogue'). She marries Hector *Montmorency and they have two daughters, but his cruel treatment leads her to run away a second time with Northangerland, who leaves her to die at Fidena, delirious in an inn. Her sad story becomes the subject of song. Later, Charlotte Brontë weaves her story into the background of *Ashworth*.

Odes of Horace, The. Branwell Brontë translated odes 9, 11, 14, 15, 19, 31 from Book 1 in spring 1838, but only the last sixteen lines of ode 14 and the whole of ode 15 survive in the notebook of collected poems he began in 1837 (in the BPM). On 15 April 1840, while working as a tutor at *Broughton-in-Furness, Branwell sent Thomas *De Quincey a poem ('Sir Henry Tunstall') and translations of odes 9, 11, 15, 19, 31 (in Houghton, Harvard); five days later he sent a poem ('At dead of midnight—drearily') and translations of two odes to Hartley *Coleridge, asking if it would be 'possible to obtain remuneration for translations for such as these'. While De Quincey did not reply, Coleridge did, and Branwell spent 1 May at Nab Cottage, near Rydal Water (Coleridge's home). On 27 June 1840, encouraged by Coleridge, Branwell sent him translations of all of Book 1 (in Brotherton), except for ode 38 ('This ode I have no heart to attempt, after having heard Mr H Coleridges translation, on May day, at Ambleside'), asking Coleridge if he should 'pursue the work or let it rest in peace'. Coleridge began to draft a very encouraging reply: 'I think many of the odes might appear with very little alteration. Your versification is often masterly—and you have shown skill in a great variety of measures—There

---

Oakwell Hall, Birstall, 11 miles south-west of Leeds in Yorkshire; accepted as the model for Fieldhead in Charlotte Brontë's *Shirley*. Built in 1583 on the site of previous dwellings dating from the 12th century and altered in the 17th century to reflect the family's rising status, the house belonged to the Batt family, who prospered as stewards to the Saviles of Thornhill, Royalists during the Civil War. After 1789 it was let to a succession of tenants, including a Thomas Clapham whose family home was Fieldhead. Hannah G. Cockill (1810–93) and her sisters Sarah (1812–96) and Elizabeth (1813–54) kept a school at Oakwell Hall from about 1838 to 1852, during which time Charlotte must have visited although there is no record. Elizabeth Cockill was a fellow pupil of Charlotte at *Roe Head. Their mother Hannah (1810/11–92) was first cousin to Mrs Nussey (see NUSSEY FAMILY) (who had previously lived in part of the Hall) and friend of the *Taylor family of Gomersal (*BST* (1978), 17. 88. 210 and 3). After the Cockills, Oakwell continued as a girls' school run by the Misses Upton (1853–7) and then as a boys' school kept by Henry Millard (1861–6). By 1871 it was occupied by the Carter sisters, Ellen M. Carter and Catherine E. Carter, daughters of the Vicar of Heckmondwike and nieces of Miss Wooler who ran a 'ladies' boarding school'.

Charlotte's detailed descriptions of Fieldhead confirm Oakwell as the model. Apart from noise from the motorway on the brow of the hill behind, Charlotte would find little else changed. In *Shirley* (ch. 11) she termed it 'picturesque': 'Very sombre it was; long, vast, and dark: one latticed window lit it but dimly . . . The gallery on high, opposite the entrance, was seen but in outline, so shadowy became this hall towards its ceiling; . . . This was neither a grand nor a comfortable house: within as without it was antique, rambling, and incommodious.' Today Oakwell Hall is the property of Kirklees Metropolitan Council. See also MUSEUMS.

Pollard, Arthur, *The Landscape of the Brontës* (1988), 124–8 (illustrations).

is a racy english in your language which is rarely to be found even in the original . . . which considering how thoroughly Latin Horace is in his turns of phrase, and collocation of words—is proof of sound scholarship—and command of both languages.' Unfortunately Coleridge never completed the letter. In his letter to Coleridge, Branwell claims to have translated odes from Book 2 as well, but none of these has ever surfaced. In 1923 John *Drinkwater produced a privately printed limited edition of the translations to demonstrate Branwell's considerable abilities as a translator.   VN

Miscellaneous Writings, 2. 423–65.
Neufeldt *BB Works*, 3. 219–22, 286–90, 299–334.

O'Donnell, Henry. See 'SEARCH AFTER HAPPINESS, THE'.

'Often rebuked, yet always back returning', undated poem, of 20 lines by Emily Brontë, published by Charlotte in 1850. Since no manuscript has been found and since all of the other sixteen poems published by Charlotte came from one of Emily's manuscript notebooks, the authorship of this poem has been called into question. Hatfield (*EBP*, p. 255) believed it sounded more like Charlotte and others have suggested Anne (*BST* (1982), 18. 92. 143). More recently, Gezari has supported the claim for Charlotte's authorship since resemblances to Emily's poems are 'not striking', the iambic pentameter is more typical of Charlotte, and, in her deep conviction that it was her duty to act as Emily's 'interpreter', Charlotte composed a poem 'that her sister might have written' (Gezari *EBP*, p. 284). Roper supports this view (Roper *EBP*, p. 277), yet still includes the poem as part of Emily's oeuvre in his edition (p. 222). As Chitham points out, however (*BST* (1983), 18. 93. 222–6), much of the poem is characteristic of Emily and, although Charlotte as editor 'corrected' and even added verses to complete her sisters' poems, it is unlikely she would have represented one of her own poems as by Emily. Controversy is likely to remain.

Emily, like the speaker in the poem, continually retreated into her own 'shadowy region' and must often have felt 'rebuked' by her conscience; yet to reject that world of imagination, even for a day as the poem says, is unlike her. If by Emily, the poem certainly positions her on the side of realism and nature rather than romance. The speaker chooses to shun 'idle dreams' and to walk 'Where the grey flocks in ferny glens are feeding; | Where the wild wind blows on the mountain side'. Nature, like the visions rejected at least for 'Today', has power to awaken her emotions.

Gezari *EBP*, p. 222.
Roper *EBP*, p. 222.

'Old Stoic, The' ('Riches I hold in light esteem') (1 Mar. 1841), 12 lines by Emily Brontë, from the Honresfeld MS (see LAW COLLECTION); published by Emily in *Poems*, 1846, when it was given the title 'The Old Stoic'. The speaker, possibly a Gondal character, makes light of riches, love, and fame that, like dreams, vanish with the morn. Instead, as the lyric 'I' of the poem nears death, the speaker prays only for liberty: 'In life and death, a chainless soul, | With courage to endure'; an idea that recurs in such poems as *'To Imagination' and *'No coward soul is mine'. Margaret Maison points out that Emily may have known the Stoic writings of Epictetus as translated by Elizabeth Carter (1758) ('Emily Brontë and Epictetus', *N & Q* (1978), 223, 230–1). Certainly Emily was attracted to the notion that although the body is chained, a person with an unchained soul will be free. As Charlotte famously stated, 'Liberty was the breath of Emily's nostrils; without it, she perished' (*Wuthering Heights* (Clarendon edn.), app. 1, p. 446).

Gezari *EBP*, p. 30.
Roper *EBP*, p. 153.

Oliver, Rosamond, heiress of a rich *Morton factory owner, in *Jane Eyre*. Jane paints a portrait of this ideal, charming beauty with delicate features and long chestnut curls. Indulged but not spoilt, Rosamond generously provides the furniture and servant for Jane's school cottage. Aware that St John *Rivers loves her, she gently encourages him; but he represses his love, knowing she could not understand or cooperate with his missionary ideals. He fixes his departure date knowing that she will shortly marry a Mr Granby of S—— (*Sheffield) whom she has known for only two months.

Olympia River and Olympian Hills, in the Glass Town and Angrian saga. The cities of *Zamorna and *Edwardston are built on the Olympia River which flows from the Olympian Hills west to the sea, through the province of Zamorna in Angria. The country seats of many of Angria's aristocracy are situated along the Olympia (such as Hartford Hall, *Girnington Hall), and its waters are vital for Edward Percy's new mill at Edwardston.

'On the Death of Anne Brontë'. See 'THERE'S LITTLE JOY IN LIFE FOR ME'.

'On the Death of Emily Jane Brontë'. See 'MY DARLING, THOU WILT NEVER KNOW'.

operatic and musical versions. *Jane Eyre* and *Wuthering Heights* are the only Brontë novels to have been made into operas or musicals. 'The Little Orphan's Song' (which Bessie sings to Jane in chapter 3) was set to music by Joseph W. Turner as early as 1848, and in 1962 Alfred Jepson set

'Rochester's Song to Jane', but full-scale operas and musicals did not appear until the 1960s. A musical version of *Jane Eyre* with lyrics by Hal Shaper and music by Monty Stevens was performed in Windsor in 1961 with Dianne Todd as Jane, and revived in Hornsey, London, in 1966, in Canada during 1970–1 and again in Windsor in 1973. The adaptation removes most of what is distinctive about Charlotte Brontë's novel and converts the story into a conventional romance plot in which Jane falls in love with Rochester at first meeting and declares it to all and sundry. The musical numbers include 'If I'd never met you', 'Love came by', and 'Happily married'. Just as Mills and Boon romances follow the general plot outline of *Jane Eyre*, moreover (see SEQUELS AND 'INCREMENTAL LITERATURE'), so do several popular musicals of the 1960s, including *The Sound of Music* (1965).

Another musical version of *Jane Eyre* began as a play by Ted Davis with musical interludes by Chopin, produced in Monmouth, Maine, in 1984. Davis, who directed the American première of *Saigon Rose*, later asked David Clark to write a full score for *Jane Eyre*, and this musical version, with Davis's lyrics, was performed in Monmouth in 1988 and in New York State in 1990. The result is an odd mixture of syrupy Broadway melodies with an unmistakably feminist libretto. A recurrent lyric speaks of the 'Wild Birds' pictured in Jane's paintings, which for Rochester have 'a long way to fall', but for Jane, 'a long way to fly'.

There are three operatic versions of *Jane Eyre* to date. Nils Vigeland's *False Love/True Love*, commissioned for and performed by the Almeida Opera in 1992, is a chamber opera with only two performers—Jane and Rochester—and two scenes. In the first, Jane and Rochester have just returned from church after the interruption of their wedding; in the second, Jane returns to find him blind and crippled. The focus is psychological and emotional.

An opera entitled *Jane Eyre* by John Joubert is complete but still awaiting its first performance. The libretto by Kenneth Birkin was published by the St Nicholas Press (Richmond, N. Yorks) in 1995, and a performing score is in the hands of Maecenas Music. Joubert's opera is in three acts involving an orchestra of seventeen and a dozen solo singers, and lasts almost three hours. The action includes scenes at Lowood, Thornfield, and 'Whitecross' (Morton). Although the main interaction is between Jane and Rochester, the inclusion of singing roles for many of the male authority figures (Brocklehurst, Briggs, the Rector and his Clerk, St John Rivers) means that the unorthodox love story is acted out against a vocal representation of conventional attitudes. Many of the female roles—the Lowood girls,

Adèle, Blanche Ingram, and Bertha Mason—are non-singing parts, and the predominance of male voices emphasizes Jane's isolation.

Kenneth Birkin's libretto follows Charlotte's text to a certain extent, but has a tendency to translate it into slightly different terms. Jane's speech from chapter 12, including the words 'women are supposed to be very calm generally', develops in this version to a rhetorical exhortation which claims much more, more explicitly, than Charlotte's Jane: ' "Cast off your chains . . . essay great deeds and walk new ways, victorious and free!" ' (act 1, scene 1). If the libretto has more vehement class implications than Charlotte's text, however, it tones down Charlotte's claims in terms of gender. Jane's words in the garden, 'as if . . . we stood at God's feet, equal,—as we are!' (ch. 23) are given to Rochester, with the additional and crucial change to 'equal, as we now be', as if it is he who has conferred equality on Jane (act 2, scene 2). These words are used again to end the opera as Jane joins Rochester in the ruined Thornfield, and leave us with a sense of their equality which is subtly less challenging than Charlotte's version.

Michael Berkeley's *Jane Eyre*, performed at the Cheltenham, Buxton, and Huddersfield Festivals in 2000, is a major operatic work of considerable dramatic force and intelligence. The libretto by David Malouf has been independently published, and demonstrates very sharply the severe selection process demanded by operatic adaptation. Although this is a full-scale work lasting an hour and a half, its written text occupies only 27 pages. Gateshead, Lowood, and Ferndean are entirely excised, so that the opera, in two acts, focuses on the central relationship between Jane and Rochester. The handling of this relationship, however, suggests a rich context of events and relationships. The action arises from Jane's retrospective reverie in the silence and safety of her moorland schoolroom. The first word of the opera is 'Silence', emphasized by string glissandi reminiscent of the opening of Britten's *A Midsummer Night's Dream*. Against this quietness, however, arise the voices of the past. Berkeley was attracted by the subject because he sees the situation as 'essentially operatic even in the original story because it's predicated on the idea of voices—voices that are heard through a kind of telepathy, voices that come out of the ether' (*Independent*, 28 June 2000). In the opera, the voices are heralded by Jane's account of how she 'knocked' at the door of Thornfield, the word emphasized by being spoken, not sung, amid instrumental silence.

As well as Jane (soprano) and Rochester (baritone) there are three other female voices: Mrs Fairfax (mezzo-soprano), Adèle (girl soprano), and Mrs Rochester (contralto). The contrast between these voices—Jane repressed, Mrs Fairfax calm, Adèle youthful and romantic, and Mrs Rochester passionate and voluptuous—is emphasized by instrumental colour. Berkeley uses either a contrabassoon or a trombone to accompany Rochester's 'Jane, Jane'; Adèle is associated with the flute; and the more sombre Jane with oboe or cor anglais. Mrs Rochester's laughter is suggested by a bass clarinet. The opera also makes vivid use of musical quotation. As Jane remembers her introduction to Thornfield, Adèle introduces the lovers' duet from Donizetti's *Lucia di Lammermoor*, a lilting melody which, in context, gathers poignancy from the story's tragic outcome. Given the Brontës' known enthusiasm for Sir Walter Scott on whose story *Lucia* is based, this is a luminous invention, and Berkeley uses it in a variety of ways. Adèle demonstrates her love of Parisian gaiety by waltzing to the tune, just like her mother. Jane's uneasiness with Adèle's spontaneous enjoyment of bodily movement is suggested by a phrase recalling Britten's *The Turn of the Screw*, where another governess resists the possibility of her young pupils' sexuality, but as Adèle whirls Jane around and makes her laugh, it seems that Jane can learn from her; that she needs to unbend and 'thaw'. The tension between Romantic freedom and nervous repression is presented in terms of different musical styles: Donizetti versus Britten. Later, however, Adèle shows the sinister side to Romanticism by telling Jane the horrid story of Lucia, who went mad after killing the husband of a forced marriage. The relevance of this story to that of Jane Eyre is emphasized in the opera by the appearance of the first Mrs Rochester, first framed in an oriel window high up on the set and later on stage with flames intended to kill Rochester.

The abbreviation of the opera plot allows the identity of Mrs Rochester to be revealed much more quickly than in the novel, forcing the two women to confront the oddity of their relation to Mr Rochester. The stage set reinforces this sense of uncanny repetition by reflecting the action in an array of curved mirrors which draw connections between all the female characters. Although there is no doubt that Mrs Rochester is mad, she is treated sympathetically and allowed to question Rochester: 'Oh Edward, why, why have you sent me to a living grave?' Her version of the *Lucia* dance is at first one of innocent enjoyment rather like Adèle's; after the spoiled wedding, however, as Rochester tells the story of their marriage, her dancing becomes repugnantly abandoned. The mirrors reflect a bewildering kaleidoscope of fragments and images in which flames extinguish Mrs Rochester. As Jane's memories fade and the schoolroom re-establishes itself, Rochester's 'Jane! Jane!' forces itself on her consciousness and she

returns, never to leave him again; the opera ends on the words 'Never. Never.' Despite the severe pruning to Charlotte Brontë's plot, Berkeley and Malouf's opera is a rich investigation of its central themes and tensions: desire and discipline, longing and loss.

The various operatic versions of *Wuthering Heights* have certain things in common. They all derive more closely from the William Wyler film of 1939 than from Emily Brontë's novel, which means that the plot is severely truncated to focus on the potentially adulterous triangle, in which the simultaneous deaths of Catherine and Heathcliff end the story, acquiring tragic status from their association with wild nature. They all derive, moreover, from the Delius/Butterworth neo-romantic tradition of accessible music depending on familiar dramatic and emotional effects rather than musical innovation. Gerald Gover's opera was performed in Bradford in 1955, the Bradford *Telegraph and Argus* describing it as 'a major work, in three acts, with prologue and epilogue and employing full orchestra and a large chorus' (6 Oct. 1955).

The American composer Carlisle Floyd was commissioned to write an opera on *Wuthering Heights* for the Santa Fe Opera which was performed in New Mexico in 1958, by the University of North Carolina in 1982, and in Boston, Massachusetts, in 1993. A major feature of this work was its 'unforgettable portraits of Cathy and Heathcliff against the storm-tossed background of the wild countryside'. According to Robert Sabin, Floyd's 'bold, impassioned score' left 'both performers and audience shaken with the elemental power of the Brontë story' ('Carlisle Floyd's "Wuthering Heights"', *Tempo*, 59 (1961), 23–4).

The most notable work in this tradition is, however, the opera by Bernard Herrmann, who had composed the evocative wind-ridden music for Orson Welles's 1944 film version of *Jane Eyre*. His *Wuthering Heights* was conceived at the same time, but took many years to mature. A printed score was published in 1965 and the full opera was recorded in 1966, but was first performed, in a revised and shortened version, in Portland, Oregon, in 1982. The libretto, published at this time, was by Herrmann's wife, Lucille Fletcher, with illustrations by Fritz Eichenberg (see ILLUSTRATIONS OF THE BRONTËS' WORKS). Working entirely from 'the book of the film', Herrmann and Fletcher reproduce many of Wyler's revisions to the plot, so that an important dramatic moment occurs when Heathcliff carries the dying Catherine to the window (which does not occur in the novel) but like Floyd they transpose speeches from one character to another and also incorporate several of Emily Brontë's poems. Since Heathcliff (a baritone) is the representative of wild nature in this opera, this has the effect of making him an entirely articulate spokesman of a Romantic appreciation of nature, thus simplifying Catherine's choice to one of nature versus culture. Contemporary reviewers also disliked the 'hokey solution' (also used in the 1939 movie) of having the protagonists 'walk off into the sunset to find happiness in death' (Frank Kincaid, 'Portland, Ore.', *Opera News* (15 Jan. 1983), 43).

The opera itself makes fewer concessions to this popular sentimentality than the visual production, and some very dramatic moments are produced by the changes to the structure of the novel. Heathcliff's appeal to the child-ghost, for instance—'Oh, my heart's darling hear me this time'—is in the opera heard three times: once from Heathcliff in the prologue at the time of Lockwood's dream, once from Catherine when Heathcliff runs away, and finally from Heathcliff at the time of Catherine's death. At this point, her ghostly voice comes from outside the window, echoing his words, and the opera ends with the fading echoes of their mutual appeals. This is far from a 'happy ever after' conclusion. The 1966 recording was reissued on CD in 1992, with the Pro Arte Orchestra and Morag Beaton (soprano) and Donald Bell (baritone) as Catherine and Heathcliff.

Operatic versions of *Wuthering Heights* were not restricted to the English language. Philippe Hériat published a three-act opera entitled *Les Hauts de Hurle-Vent* in Paris in 1961, while Dino Milella's two-act *Una storia d'altri tempi* was published in Milan in 1972. Rather like Buñuel's film, Milella's opera places the story in the context of rigidly patriarchal kinship structures, in which both Catherine and her mother are victims of forced marriages. Unlike Emily Brontë's heroine, this Catherine is a 'saintly creature' who carries 'Heathcliff' off to a conventional eternity.

All the operatic versions of *Wuthering Heights* use musical style and allusion to claim their allegiance to high culture. Such pretensions were satirized by Bernard de Zogheb's *Le sorelle Brontë*, an 'opera in four acts' published in New York (Fibor de Nagy Editions, 1963). This Italian-language 'opera', according to its foreword, 'has never been performed for more than a handful of its Alexandrian-born poet's friends', and consists of a series of hilarious jingles set to tunes such as 'A Bicycle Made for Two', 'Tipperary', and 'This is the Army, Mr Jones'. Its dramatis personae include not only the Brontë sisters but also 'MacMillione, un editore avaro e ricco', and also Thackeray and Dickens, who notoriously bade one another 'Good Morning' in Robert Buckner's 1946 film, *Devotion*.

The novel has also inspired serious popular versions. In 1978 the singer Kate Bush scored a major triumph with her single, 'Wuthering Heights', whose extraordinary wailing tone creates a spellbindingly eery atmosphere. The song plays with Catherine's words: 'I've come home and I'm so cold, let me in', but the context is conventional, little more than 'I've lost my man'. In 1991 Silva Screen Records released cassette and CD recordings of a full-scale musical by Bernard J. Taylor with the Philharmonia Orchestra, Cantorum Choir, and major stars—Lesley Garrett, the opera singer, as Catherine, and Dave Willetts, who starred in 'Phantom of the Opera', as Heathcliff. The music is vigorous and dramatic, with a flavour of Andrew Lloyd Webber, but the lyrics do address the feeling shared by Catherine and Heathcliff of being 'outsiders' in numbers such as 'They say he's a gypsy' and 'I belong to the earth'. The plot, however, inevitably follows the Wyler pattern of 'star-cross'd lovers'.

In the early 1990s a number of fairly ephemeral musicals appeared including a 'popera' by Alek Keshishian (1992) and a 'romantic musical' by Paul Dick (Broadway, 1992). The version which has made the most impact, however, is *Heathcliff*, directed by Frank Dunlop with lyrics by Tim Rice (who wrote *Evita*) and music by John Farrar (who wrote the hit songs from *Grease*) as a vehicle for Sir Cliff Richard, with Helen Hobson as Catherine. The show appeared as a video for Balladeer in 1997. The immense publicity for this production makes it plain that 'Mr Good Guy', Cliff Richard, has been 'obsessed' with the figure of Heathcliff since adolescence, associating the story with that of Romeo and Juliet. The musical makes the familiar changes to the plot, so that the lovers die together on the snow-covered moors. Sir Cliff's particular purpose in reproducing the story, however, is to ask whether Heathcliff is 'a devil incarnate' or 'misunderstood man', and the answer is very clear: misunderstood. The blame for their tragedy is uncompromisingly heaped on Catherine, and Heathcliff's response to her death is less lament than exhortation: 'learn what your sin has done . . . nothing justifies I Reckless inhuman lies'. There is a good deal of passion in the delivery of the songs, but the clear-cut morality of the lyrics and the easy sentimentality of the musical style is at odds with the harsh conflicts of Emily Brontë's novel.

See also FILM ADAPTATIONS AND BIOGRAPHIES.

PS

Stoneman, Patsy, *Brontë Transformations: The Cultural Dissemination of 'Jane Eyre' and 'Wuthering Heights'* (1996).

Our Fellows' Play, begun by the Brontë children in July 1827 and replaced by the Islanders' Play in December of the same year. The children each had an island inhabited by people 6 miles high, with names from *Aesop's Fables*: Hay Man (Charlotte), Boaster (Branwell), Hunter (Emily), and Clown (Anne). Only Boaster is found in the one story clearly relating to Our Fellows: Branwell's **'History of the Rebellion in My Fellows'* (1828). Charlotte's description of 'the origin of the O'Dears' (variously transcribed O'Deans and O'Deays), refers to Our Fellows, suggesting that the young Brontës humorously called the characters in this play 'O Dears' as they were always in some kind of trouble. (For a similar Brontë humour see PARIS (IN FRENCHYLAND).) An article on 'Natural History' in Branwell's first magazine is written by 'O Dear' (Neufeldt *BB Works*, 1. 7)

Based on toy soldiers and consisting chiefly of battles organized by Branwell between Boaster and Goodman (Charlotte), Our Fellows' Play seems to have had little interest for the Brontë sisters. Branwell's penchant for France (French place names are used) and Frenchmen (see PIGTAIL) also dominates this play. A relic of Our Fellows survives in a letter referring to the 'young men', written in the 'old' Young Men's tongue from Goody or Goodman to the editor of 'Branwell's Blackwood's Magazine' for January 1829, demonstrating that elements from the various plays coalesced in the imaginations of the children (see YOUNG MEN'S PLAY). It is also clear that the children acted the parts of their characters before documenting events, and that they entered their fiction sometimes in their own character. Branwell's 'History of the Rebellion in My Fellows', for example, includes a letter from Goodman to 'Little Branwell' declaring war on him.

Alexander *EEW*, 1. 6.
Alexander *EW*, pp. 35, 40–1.
Alexander, Christine (ed.), *Branwell's Blackwood's Magazine* (1995), pp. 2, 36.
Neufeldt *BB Works*, 1. 2–6.

Outhwaite, Frances (1796–1849), sister of Dr John *Outhwaite; a schoolfellow and friend of Elizabeth *Franks, and niece of the second Mrs J. S. Firth (see FIRTH FAMILY). She showed much practical kindness to the Brontës at *Thornton and afterwards, and was one of Anne Brontë's godmothers. Since she and her mother were patrons of the Bradford School of Industry, she may have recommended Nancy Garrs, who was trained there, as a *servant of the Brontës. She bequeathed £200 to Anne Brontë, enabling her to take comfortable and airy lodgings at No. 2, Cliff, *Scarborough, in May 1849.

Outhwaite, Dr John (1792–1868), MD Edinburgh 1818. A respected Bradford physician, he was a friend of Revd Patrick Brontë for many years, though a more rigid Tory than he. In Oc-

tober 1843 Outhwaite recommended an 'excellent collyrium' for Mr Brontë's eyes, but by September 1844 had become a former friend who had 'afflicted' him. After graduating, Dr Outhwaite had spent time in Manchester with the oculist William James *Wilson. In Bradford, having inherited wealth from his father and grandfather, both surgeons, he often gave medical help gratis to the poor. For more than twenty years he was virtually managing director of the Bradford Infirmary, Exchange, and Library.

Oxenhope, a steep hillside village south of Haworth, part of Revd Patrick Brontë's parish until 1845, when it became a new ecclesiastical district. Revd J. B. *Grant raised funds to build its first Anglican church, St Mary's, consecrated on 11 October 1849. A Wesleyan Methodist chapel dated from 1805. By the mid-19th century Near Oxenhope had four textile mills, and Far Oxenhope twelve, plus a weaving shed. The mill owner William Greenwood (1759–1823) of Old Oxenhope Mill was senior church trustee of Haworth in 1820–1, and his nephew William (1800–93) and niece Sarah (1811–93) were friendly with the Brontës.

Oxford Movement. This movement provoked an intensely emotional and generally hostile response in the Brontë family. It began in 1833 after John Keble (1792–1866) preached the Assize Sermon at Oxford on 14 July 1833. Published as *National Apostasy*, it alerted the *Church of England to the danger posed by the government's abolition of ten Irish bishoprics via the Irish Church Temporalities Bill, which became law on 14 August 1833. Other laws seemed to open the way to Church disestablishment. Keble exhorted the Church to do everything possible to advance its cause. John Newman proposed the formation of a society at Oxford to rouse the clergy, emphasize Apostolical Succession (uninterrupted transmission of spiritual authority from the Apostles), defend the Prayer Book, and circulate books and tracts. Keble contributed 7, and Newman 24, of the 90 'Tracts for the Times' published 1833–41. They asserted the absolute doctrinal authority of a church which was 'catholic' in its adherence to the teaching of the early and undivided church, and sought to arouse it to awareness of its divine mission. Edward Bouverie *Pusey joined the 'Tractarians' soon after their inception. Unlike Newman, Pusey remained within the Church of England; but the practices he advocated were distrusted, especially by Anglican Evangelicals such as Revd Patrick Brontë. Pusey deprecated 'any innovations in the way of conducting the Service, anything of Ritualism, or especially any revival of disused

Vestments', and Newman was indifferent to such revivals. But Tractarian insistence on the high dignity of the Church and its services led to an increasing use of ritual from the late 1840s. Charlotte viewed 'Puseyites' with a mixture of amusement, contempt, and alarm, and Mr Brontë was angrily hostile; yet both of them liked William Weightman, who in April 1840 gave a 'noble, eloquent high Church, Apostolical succession discourse—in which he banged the Dissenters most fearlessly and unflinchingly'. Branwell, who for much of his life had little respect for the Church, was desolated by Weightman's death. The so-called 'Papal Aggression' of 1850–1 intensified Mr Brontë's detestation of Puseyite 'poison', and Charlotte praised Lord John Russell for putting the blame for the 'Pope's insult to the Church and State' (his elevation of *Wiseman to the rank of cardinal) on 'Anglo-Catholic enemies within the gates, indulging in their mummeries of superstition' (Smith *Letters*, 2. 501–2 n.). In *Jane Eyre* the self-righteous, spiteful Eliza *Reed regularly studies a Common Prayer Book, concentrating on the 'Rubric' (directions for the conduct of services) and stitching an enormous gold and crimson altar cloth for a new church. Clearly Eliza, preoccupied with the 'outside of the cup and platter', is already a High Churchwoman, halfway to the Catholic nunnery she eventually joins. In *Shirley* Charlotte ridicules the Puseyite curates, and in *Villette* criticizes Catholic practices she associated with Puseyism. She was unrepentant and unsurprised when High Church journals such as the *Guardian*, *English Churchman*, and *Christian Remembrancer* were offended by her anti-Romanism. But Charlotte's personal emotions and moral judgement ultimately outweighed her sectarian prejudices, for she came to realize that the Puseyite Revd A. B. Nicholls had a 'most sincere love of goodness' wherever he saw it, and might even change his feelings about the Unitarian Mr Gaskell if he knew him.

'Palace of Death, The' ('Le Palais de la Mort'). Allegorical *devoirs by Charlotte Brontë (16 Oct. 1842) and Emily (18 Oct. 1842, both in BPM), probably based on a fable by Jean-Pierre Florian. According to the outline that precedes each essay, presumably dictated by M. Constantin *Heger, Death has become so busy that she needs a viceroy. She summons the candidates to her palace, where they must justify their claims to the position. She has difficulty making a choice until Intemperance arrives and wins. Both devoirs fill in this outline, but Charlotte concentrates on elaborate descriptions of the palace and the claimants, whereas Emily develops encounters between candidates, succinctly dissects folly and vice, and introduces Civilization as a new agent of evil. Heger corrected Charlotte's version extensively and seems to have preferred it to Emily's, unlike all subsequent critics.   SL

> Lonoff, pp. 216–37.
> Maxwell, J. M., 'Emily Brontë's "The Palace of Death"', *BST* (1967), 15. 77. 139–40.

Palace of Instruction, where the princes and princesses of *Gondal are educated. Beneath the North and South Colleges lie dungeons where the young nobility are often imprisoned and write poems on their prison walls. Even A.G.A., Gondal's Queen, suffers this fate at one time. The isolated Palace of Instruction recalls the education of young nobles on *Philosopher's Island in the Glass Town and Angrian saga and the *Palace School with subterranean dungeons in the Islanders' Play.

Palace School, where 'Little King and Queens' and Governors supervise the education of the young nobility in the *Islanders' Play. The school is in a magnificent Corinthian palace that towers over the silent grandeur of Vision Island. It has a subterranean dungeon where rebellious children and 'wicked cockneys' are tortured and kept in cells. To control the unjust discipline of Colonel Naughty and his gang (including Branwell Brontë with his large black club), the Little Queens Charlotte and Emily keep the keys. The Palace School is abandoned after the school rebellion. It is probably similar to the 'Palaces of Instruction', referred to in the Young Men's Play, and performs the same role as the university on Philosopher's Island in the *Glass Town and Angrian saga. The idea of a prison for nobles is preserved throughout the *Gondal saga of Emily and Anne, in the *Palace of Instruction. See 'TALES OF THE ISLANDERS'.

'Palais de la Mort, Le'. See 'PALACE OF DEATH, THE' ('LE PALAIS DE LA MORT').

Pamela. See RICHARDSON, SAMUEL.

'Papillon, Le'. See 'BUTTERFLY, THE' ('LE PAPILLON').

Paris (in Frenchyland), capital of Frenchyland, a large island off the coast of Glass Town. This is exclusively Branwell Brontë's interest, where his hero the Duke of *Northangerland, a latter-day *Napoleon Buonaparte, is seen as a type of king, ruler of various 'dark Revolutionary Coteries', the Republican factions of the Dupins, the Barras, and the Bernadottes (based on French equivalents during Napoleon's reign). Bernadotte, for example, is an early associate of Northangerland and later military leader of Frenchyland, who sides with Quashia *Quamina, the Marquis of *Ardrah, and Northangerland against Angria.

Paris of the *Glass Town and Angrian saga is a remnant of the earlier Young Men's Play and of Branwell's early obsession with Republican France and *Napoleon, who rules Frenchyland. It is a replica of its namesake, with a reputation in Verdopolis for 'wickedness, rioting, idleness and grandeur'. Few Frenchmen in the juvenilia have any redeeming features. The noblemen are usually sinister and plotting intrigue either against Napoleon or the Glass Town; to the Verdopolitans, all Frenchmen are revolutionaries at heart. *Pigtail is typical of the 'low villains' in Paris, who are known for their cruelty to children. Theatre, intrigue, and mistresses loom large on the Parisian scene (see VERNON, LOUISA), where Northangerland brings his daughter Caroline to learn about fashion and life.

A particular feature of Frenchyland is the curiously whimsical names of its inhabitants, often referred to simply by their initials. For example, MH refers to Moses Hanghimself, 'Moses' being a humorous rendering by the young Brontës of 'Monsieur' (see CHATEAUBRIAND, MOSES; DELANCY, ALEXANDER). Other examples of fanciful names used particularly by Branwell include 'Moses ride-on-the-back-of-an ass', 'M. De la Qack', and 'M. walk-20-miles-a-hour'. The inhabitants of

Verdopolis constantly scorn 'the ridiculousness of French names' (Neufeldt *BB Works*, 1. 173).

See also FACTION DU MANGE; DE CRACK, MON EDOUARD.

Parker, Thomas (1787–1866), a local Haworth celebrity who later won considerable fame as a tenor when he sang before Queen Victoria. The Brontës heard him sing as early as 20 July 1829, at a major concert of sacred music in Haworth church. He often sang at the annual vocal and instrumental concert of the Haworth Philharmonic Society (founded *c.*1780), held in the Black Bull Inn. He and his musical family, all named after famous musicians, were professionals who helped foster community music (Barker, p. 210). On 22 December 1838, Branwell completed an oil portrait of Parker, represented with a viola or cello as symbol of his profession (Alexander & Sellars, p. 327).

Parry, Sir William Edward (fictional), King of Parry's Land (Parrisland), formerly Captain Parry, the friend and ally of Captain John *Ross, and father of Arthur, Marquis of *Ardrah, who is friendly with Ross's son. Parry is Emily Brontë's chief man in the Young Men's Play, replacing the original 'Gravey' soldier. He continues as her responsibility in the *Glass Town and Angrian saga, where the friendship between the two kings Parry and Ross, and between their sons, reflects the close association between Emily and Anne in the early part of the saga. Parry is realistic and down-to-earth. The lack of romance in his person, palace, and country is a disappointment to Lord Charles Wellesley (Charlotte), when he spends 'A Day at Parry's Palace' (see Alexander *EEW*, 1. 229–33) and meets Lady Emily Parry and their child 'Little Eater'. Like the fictional Ross, Parry is based on the historical Captain Sir William Edward *Parry, a famous Arctic explorer whose exploits in the Polar Sea were reported in *Blackwood's Edinburgh Magazine* during the 1820s.

Parry, Sir William Edward (historical) (1790–1855), Arctic navigator adopted by Emily Brontë as her 'chief man' in the Young Men's Play and the Glass Town and Angrian sagas (see PARRY, SIR WILLIAM EDWARD (FICTIONAL)). He served against the Danes in 1808 and was sent to the Arctic to protect whale fisheries in 1810. He commanded five expeditions to Arctic regions: in 1818 (under Sir John *Ross), 1819, 1821–3, 1824–5, and 1827, all documented in *Blackwood's Edinburgh Magazine* and newspapers accessible to the young Brontës. *Blackwood's*, for example, reported on the 'North-West Passage: Expedition under Captain Ross and Lieutenant Parry' (4 (1818), 339–44); 'Remarks on Captain Parry's Expedition' (8 (1820), 219–23); and 'Captain Parry's

Voyage' (9 (1821), 289–99). Parry also published his own accounts of his travels, such as his *Journal of a Second Voyage for the Discovery of a North-West Passage* (1821). Parry's close collaboration with both Sir John Ross and Sir James Clark *Ross is reflected in the Brontë juvenilia. A portrait of Sir William Edward Parry is reproduced in Robert Barnard, *Emily Brontë* (2000), p. 17.

Parry's Land (Parrysland, Parrisland), kingdom of the fictional Sir William Edward *Parry, formerly Captain Parry, one of the Twelves and Emily Brontë's hero in the *Glass Town and Angrian saga. The capital is Parry's Glass Town. It borders Wellington's Land in the west, the Gulf of Guinea in the south, Ross's Land in the east, and Sneaky's Land in the north-east; but few roads traverse it except the main road from Sneaky's Land to Wellington's Land. Like its ruler, the country is rough and unexciting to the Verdopolitan élite, much too similar to Yorkshire with its stone walls and factories. Charlotte's author Lord Charles Wellesley mocks the rustic nature of Parry's Land and its ruler in 'A Day at Parry's Palace' (Alexander *EEW*, 1. 229–33). See also 'YOUNG MEN'S MAGAZINE'.

Parry's Palace, official residence of the fictional Sir William Edward *Parry, King of Parry's Land, in the *Glass Town and Angrian saga. With its Yorkshire stone and slate roof, it is basically a replica of Haworth parsonage and the antithesis of *Waterloo Palace (see Charlotte Brontë's 'A Day at Parry's Palace', in Alexander *EEW*, 1. 229–33).

Passing Events (21–9 Apr. 1836), untitled Angrian novelette in the *Glass Town and Angrian saga begun by Charlotte Brontë on her 20th birthday at Haworth during her Easter holiday break from teaching at *Roe Head. The manuscript comprises about 15,000 words in minuscule script, written on loose sheets of notepaper (Bonnell, Pierpont Morgan). Suddenly confronted with an imaginative freedom she has denied herself for so long, Charlotte finds it difficult to settle to a subject: 'my mind is like a prism full of colours but not of forms'. Her narrator Charles Townshend, the successor to Lord Charles Albert Florian *Wellesley, describes a series of episodes in the lives of favourite Angrian characters and the effects that Branwell's recent wars have had on them while Charlotte has been at Roe Head. We witness a crisis in the relationship between the Duke of *Northangerland and his wife (formerly Lady Zenobia *Ellrington), and Mary *Percy's desperate efforts to escape becoming a pawn in the power struggle between her husband the Duke of *Zamorna and father Northangerland. The medley of scenes also includes a satiric portrait of a Wesleyan Methodist meeting in the Slugg Street Chapel, Verdopolis, with Mr *Bromley the preacher and his guest, the hypocritical 'Mr Ashworth' (alias Northangerland). Despite the mockery of its outward practice, however, Charlotte's serious concern with Calvinist doctrine at this time is shown in Warner's earnest assessment of Zamorna as 'numbered with the everlastingly condemned'. See also ROE HEAD JOURNAL, THE; METHODISM; RELIGION.

Alexander EW, pp. 148–51.
Gérin Five Novelettes, pp. 31–82.

Pastoral Visitor. A short-lived, monthly magazine, similar to Revd John *Buckworth's *Cottage Magazine* and Revd W. Carus *Wilson's *Friendly Visitor*. Like its counterparts, the *Pastoral Visitor* was established in response to increasing literacy among the poor and was aimed at a rural working-class audience. It was edited by Revd Patrick Brontë's friend Revd William *Morgan and published from January 1815 until December 1816. Mr Brontë was a frequent contributor, his most notable piece being a three-part account of the process of conversion (July, September, and October 1815; printed in BST (1998), 19. 6. 271–5). Mr Brontë's book *The *Cottage in the Wood* (1815) was favourably reviewed by Morgan in the *Pastoral Visitor* in August 1816. CB

Patchett, Elizabeth (1796–?1870s). Together with her younger sister Maria, Elizabeth Patchett established a school at *Law Hill, Halifax, where Emily Brontë was employed from late September 1838 until March 1839. By this time Maria had married and gone to live in Dewsbury with her husband Titus Senior Brooke (see BROOKE FAMILY OF DEWSBURY); and their brother was a respected *Halifax banker, with connections among professional people and the local landed gentry from whom Elizabeth's pupils derived. According to former pupils, the 42-year-old Elizabeth (as she was when Emily met her), although strict, was a beautiful woman, keen walker, and skilful horsewoman. Together with her pupils, she patronized local concerts and museums in Halifax, and attended the local church of St Anne's, Southowram, where a Mr John Hope officiated. In December 1842, Elizabeth Patchett married John Hope and went to live in the vicarage. As director of Law Hill, Elizabeth Patchett was noted for her liberal way of living and was later highly offended by the comments made by Charlotte Brontë and repeated by Elizabeth Gaskell in her biography about the 'hard labour' and 'slavery' encountered by Emily in Miss Patchett's employment; as a consequence she refused to give information on Emily's life at Law Hill, although she lived well into the 1870s.

Pearson, Mary, the eldest of nine children of John Walton, an innkeeper at Ovenden Cross, just outside Halifax on the Keighley Road, where Branwell Brontë boarded for a short time in the autumn of 1846. Mary Walton (as she was then) was about 20 at the time, since she was apparently running the public house, and was obviously intrigued by the entertaining Branwell, although this was the period when he was drowning his sorrows in drink, after the débâcle with Mrs Lydia *Robinson. Branwell made a number of entries in her Commonplace Book, a personal album in which she collected written contributions and sketches from friends and relatives, and pasted in various memorabilia (MS in Ransom HRC, Texas). His contributions are a mixture of verse and pen-and-ink sketches: a testament to his distempered state of mind at the time. The six illustrations include a head-and-shoulders portrait of 'The Results of Sorrow' (the imaginary projection of an older Branwell); a graveyard scene of a tombstone with the words 'I implore for rest' and Haworth church in the background; a vigorous portrait of 'Alexander Percy' (Duke of *Northangerland), a male corpse on a bier below lines from Lord *Byron; a self-portrait and a weeping man kneeling on a rock and looking out to sea at a sinking ship. Interspersed are several sonnets signed with Branwell's pseudonym 'Northangerland', and several newspaper cuttings stuck in by Mary, including Branwell's published poems 'Penmaenmawr' and 'Letter from a Father on Earth to his Child in her Grave' (Neufeldt BBP, pp. 276–8 and 280–1). The illustrations, manuscript inscriptions and sonnets, and an inscription by Mary Pearson to her son explaining the circumstances of Branwell's entries, can be found in Alexander & Sellars, pp. 355–9.

Pearson family, in *Shirley*. Mr Pearson, a wool merchant, lives with his wife and three daughters in *Whinbury, where he has a partnership with Christopher Sykes (see SYKES FAMILY) in a cloth-dressing business. Though their dressing shop is burnt by machine-breakers, the partners do nothing to pursue the miscreants, earning the contempt of Robert Gérard *Moore. In another attack, Mr Pearson is shot at in his own house, but unhurt (an incident possibly suggested by the report in the *Leeds Mercury* (25 Apr. 1812) of a shot fired at a constable as he was retiring to bed at his home near Huddersfield); Moore points to the shooting as evidence that submission to the machine-breakers will not bring safety. Pearson's oldest daughter Anne draws Caroline *Helstone's ire for her criticism of Robert Moore as 'some sort of a sentimental noodle' (p. 175). Anne's siblings Kate and Susan are of school age, and friendly with Rose and Jessy Yorke (see YORKE FAMILY).

HR

Pelet, François, in *The Professor*, the mild-mannered schoolmaster, possibly modelled on Joachim-Joseph Lebel of the *Athénée Royal, Brussels, who engages William *Crimsworth as a teacher, and acts as a foil to him. He mockingly advises William to be 'good' when he teaches Zoraïde Reuter's pupils, yet suggests he might marry either Zoraïde (who is secretly Pelet's own fiancée) or a rich schoolgirl. Having discovered Pelet's duplicity, William rejects his friendship, and despises his drunken fury over Zoraïde's supposed attraction to William. Suspecting that Pelet's and Zoraïde's loose morals will make their marriage an invitation to adultery, William resigns his post.

Pelham, Sir Robert Weaver, an expatriate Englishman, politician, and landowner from Wellington's Land, in the *Glass Town and Angrian saga; formerly engaged to Mary Henrietta Percy but rejected by her in favour of the Duke of Zamorna. Because of his inherited wealth, he is courted by all political parties before becoming a leader of the Moderates in Verdopolis.

Pendlebrow. See PENDLETON.

Pendle Hill (1,831 feet) is a landmark on the boundary between Lancashire and Yorkshire, England, an area famous for its association with the Lancashire witch trials of the 17th century. Its name has been used for the Lancashire borough of Pendle and also features in the Brontë juvenilia as *Pendleton, Pendle Farm, and Pendlebrow.

Pendleton, in the Warner Hills, province of *Angria. Colne-moss Tarn, home of the Hastings family, is in Pendleton, and Pendle Farm where Henry and Elizabeth Hastings lived as children lies at the foot of the Warner Hills. In *Henry Hastings* Charlotte Brontë characterizes the area as rough moorland country with 'no good society' and 'such stony roads'. The village of Boulshill lies nearby. Two distinctive mountains dominate the landscape: Pendlebrow and Boulshill, both derived from peaks in the Pennine Range, England (*Pendle Hill and Boulsworth Hill). There is also a village of Pendleton in Lancashire.

Peninsular War (1807–14). The Iberian peninsula (comprising Spain and Portugal) was the location of Britain's main military contribution to the Napoleonic Wars of 1802–15. It played a major part in the defeat of France, sapping French resources and dispelling the popular myth of Napoleon's invincibility. The French invasion of the peninsula also meant that many in Britain who had previously supported Napoleon's fight against the tyranny of old regimes, now saw him as an aggressor for the first time. The British conception of the war was increasingly one of liberty against tyranny.

Although the war was over before the births of Charlotte and her surviving siblings, the Brontës' childhood reading and political attitudes were informed by these recent events and by Revd Patrick Brontë's intense interest in military affairs. In particular they read about the exploits of the British forces under the Duke of *Wellington (still 'Arthur Wellesley' at the time), who had been sent to support the Spanish in repelling the French invasion and overthrowing the establishment of Napoleon's brother, Joseph Buonaparte, on the Spanish throne. The victories of Sir John *Moore at Corunna (1809) and of Wellington at Vimiero (1808), Oporto, Talavera (1809), Salamanca (1812), and Vittoria (1813) were widely celebrated in Britain in poems, journals, newspapers, and biographies. Samuel Taylor *Coleridge wrote articles on the war for the *Courier* (1809–10). *Byron's famous poetic account of the war in *Childe Harold's Pilgrimage*, canto 1 (1812), was based on his visit to the peninsula in 1809. The war provided the subject for Sir Walter *Scott's narrative poem *The Vision of Don Roderick* (1811; owned by Charlotte), and *Southey's *Roderick* (1814). Reports from a variety of other sources—including *Blackwood's Edinburgh Magazine*, John Malcolm's *Tales of Field and Flood* (1829), *The United Service Journal and Naval and Military Magazine* (July 1829), and Scott's *Life of Napoleon Buonaparte* (1827)—also fired the imaginations of the young Brontës and provided material for their early juvenilia. In *'Tales of the Islanders', volume 2, for example, the fictional Wellington narrates an adventure that occurred after the Battle of Salamanca (Alexander *EEW*, 1. 106–9). See also GLASS TOWN AND ANGRIAN SAGA; BERESFORD, THOMAS; BELLINGHAM, JAMES EVERARD; BADEY (BADY, BADRY, BADHI), DR HUME; DELANCY, ALEXANDER; NAPOLEON (FICTIONAL); SOULT, ALEXANDER (YOUNG SOULT THE RHYMER); WELLESLEY, ARTHUR JULIUS (LORD ALMEIDA).

Penistone Crags (also Penistow Crags or Craggs), the rocky outcrop on the summit of the moors a mile and a half above *Wuthering Heights and four miles further from *Thrushcross Grange. A favourite childhood site of Catherine *Earnshaw and Heathcliff; in her later delirium, Catherine recalls the Fairy cave under Penistone Crags which, years later, her daughter determines to visit. The young Catherine is fascinated by the glow of the crags in the setting sun and her secret excursion on her pony Minny leads to her first encounter with Wuthering Heights. *Joseph loads lime, used in the Pennines to counteract the acidity of the soil, 'on the farther side of Penistone

Crag'. There is a Penistone Hill near Haworth and the crags have been identified as *Ponden Kirk, which also has a 'cave'.

Penistone Quarry was situated near the Haworth Parsonage and provided millstone grit for local buildings. Elizabeth Gaskell records walking with Charlotte Brontë on Penistone Moor (Wise & Symington, 4. 89). See PENISTONE CRAGS; PONDEN KIRK.

pensionnat Heger. See HEGER, PENSIONNAT.

Penzance, seaport and market town on the north-west side of Mount's Bay, Cornwall; home of the *Branwell family. Its mild climate made it an attractive resort for invalids. The bay was usually thronged with fishing boats and other vessels exporting tin and copper from the local mines, china clay, and pilchards. The Branwells imported and sold luxury goods such as tea, wines, and brandy. Maria Branwell Brontë's father owned a quayside warehouse, a brewery, the Golden Lion Inn, and Tremenheere House, and the family had been prime movers in building the Wesleyan chapel near their house (still extant) at 25 Chapel Street.

Pequena, capital city of the province of Northangerland in the kingdom of *Angria. A strategic location for the defence of Verdopolis during the *War of Encroachment and the attack by Napoleon in the early Glass Town and Angrian saga.

Percy, Alexander Augustus. See NORTHANGERLAND, DUKE OF (ALEXANDER PERCY ROGUE (ROUGUE), LORD ELLRINGTON (ELRINGTON)).

Percy, Edward, disowned eldest son of the Duke of *Northangerland, brother of Mary Percy, and hence brother-in-law to the Duke of *Zamorna. Both his physical appearance (his athletic physique, his auburn hair, and penetrating blue eyes) and his character (in particular the unprincipled ambition and violent energy) recall that of his father. He is referred to as 'Young Rogue', suggesting that he derives from the *Young Men's Play. Like his father 'Old Rogue', he becomes an antagonist of the Duke of Zamorna, but his chief role in the *Glass Town and Angria saga lies in the subtheme of two rival brothers. The story of Cain and Abel was to haunt Charlotte and Branwell Brontë's writing, culminating in The *Professor, where the history and relationship of Edward *Crimsworth and William *Crimsworth is essentially that of the Percy brothers (Alexander EW, 221–4). In Shirley, too, the characters of and relationship between Robert Gérard *Moore and Louis Gérard *Moore owe much to these juvenile characters, whose relationship may have originated in a local Yorkshire situation (see HEATON FAMILY).

Both Edward and his younger brother Captain Sir William *Percy are disowned by their father at birth and given to *Sdeath to be destroyed. Sdeath simply leaves them in obscurity but, determined to work their way back into society, they begin a woolcombing business. Mean and ruthless towards William, whom he employs as a clerk in his counting house, Edward soon becomes a 'celebrated eastern Merchant', with mills and factories along the *Olympia River in Angria. His rapid rise is recorded in Branwell's The *Wool is Rising: he saves the Duke of *Fidena's life, marries Lady Maria *Sneaky (after fighting a duel with the Marquis of *Ardrah), founds *Edwardston, becomes an Angrian MP and magistrate for the province of Zamorna, then Lord Viscount Percy and secretary of trade in Angria. Although Edward Percy's early friendship with Zamorna gradually declines into 'extreme coldness', Zamorna continues to promote him because Percy is necessary to Angria's well-being.

Percy, Lady Helen, mother of the Duke of *Northangerland, grandmother and confidante of Mary Henrietta *Percy, Duchess of Zamorna, Queen of Angria, in the *Glass Town and Angria saga.

Percy, Henry, disowned youngest son of the Duke of *Northangerland, who arranges for his murder while on the ship Mermaid, off Otaheite, in the South Sea Islands (recorded in 'Stanzas on the Fate of Henry Percy' in *'Corner Dishes'). He was betrothed while still a child to Marian *Hume.

Percy, Lady Maria Henrietta (Mary Wharton), daughter of Lord George Wharton of Alnwick, second wife of Alexander Percy (Duke of *Northangerland) and mother of Edward, William, Henry, and Mary Percy, in the *Glass Town and Angrian saga. She was a close friend of Marian Hume's mother. Living at Percy Hall in Wellington's Land, she and Percy were idyllically happy, but Lady Maria died of consumption, aggravated by the distressful loss of her three sons who were banished from her at birth because of her husband's unnatural aversion to male offspring. Her grave is a favourite meeting place for her daughter and the Duke of Zamorna when they are courting.

Percy, Mary Henrietta, Duchess of Zamorna, Queen of Angria, third wife of the Duke of *Zamorna and daughter of the Duke of *Northangerland and his second wife Lady Maria Henrietta *Percy (Mary Wharton), in the *Glass Town and Angrian saga. She is raised as a beloved only child by her father in Wellington's Land, following the death of her mother and assumed deaths of her three brothers. Her engagement to

Sir Robert *Pelham is broken when Zamorna—the Verdopolitan Byron whose poetry she has read—pursues and marries her. Mary is of middle height and delicate complexion, with auburn curls and hazel eyes. She has an open nature yet is jealous, capricious, and has a natural aristocratic exclusiveness. Her triumph as the new queen of Angria is celebrated in *High Life in Verdopolis and the christening of her twin sons in *'My Angria and the Angrians': Victor Frederick Percy *Wellesley (Marquis of Arno), and Julius Warner di Enara *Wellesley (Earl of Saldanha). Later she has a daughter Maria and another son, Arthur (although in A *Leaf from an Unopened Volume Charlotte Brontë had originally planned five sons for Zamorna and Mary). She confides in her grandmother, Lady Helen Percy, her increasing unhappiness with Zamorna's duplicity (see SPELL, AN EXTRAVAGANZA, THE) and neglect. As the Angrian situation deteriorates, Zamorna uses Mary as a pawn in his power struggle with her father Northangerland. He refuses to acknowledge her so long as her father plots against him and Mary is left to die in exile at Alnwick House.

Branwell Brontë first introduced Mary Percy as a more complex partner for Zamorna but Charlotte quickly adopted her and resisted Branwell's efforts to dispose of her. Although Mary dies in his stories, Charlotte transforms these reports into rumour and Mary revives on hearing of Zamorna's return from exile during the Angrian wars. Reconciliation follows but Mary's illness has made her moody and apprehensive. She becomes 'a haughty jealous little Duchess' and her relationship with Zamorna degenerates into domestic comedy, particularly when he pursues Mary's young half-sister Caroline *Vernon.

Percy, Captain Sir William, disowned second son of the Duke of *Northangerland, brother of Edward, Mary, and Henry Percy, in the *Glass Town and Angrian saga.

The antagonism between William and his elder brother Edward *Percy is the first instance of the two rival brothers' theme that is explored throughout the juvenilia and into Charlotte Brontë's novels The Professor and Shirley. Assumed dead by their father, who arranged for their murder by *Sdeath, the Percy brothers work in the wool industry; but the antipathetic natures of the two ensure that William, the more sensitive and less aggressive, is dominated by his tyrannical brother. William works as a clerk in Edward's counting house until he is able to quit commercial life for the military. As Captain William Percy, he marries Lady Cecilia Seymour, a cousin of the Duke of Zamorna, and buys *Elm-grove Villa from the Duke of Fidena. This marriage is soon forgotten, however, and William pursues his military career as an Angrian officer of the 10th Hussars and secret agent for Zamorna, doggedly pursuing the reprobate Henry *Hastings.

Thin and pallid, urbane and cynical yet idealistic, he is something of a misanthropist and observer of life, finding the plain Elizabeth *Hastings more fascinating than the many Angrian beauties. The indifference William has always affected towards Edward's brutality masks a deep sense of hurt and a yearning for love. He believes he has found a soulmate in Elizabeth Hastings but pride prevents him offering her more than an illicit relationship. He becomes the ideal friend and correspondent for the narrator of Charlotte's later novelettes, Charles Townshend (see WELLESLEY, LORD CHARLES ALBERT FLORIAN) (a relationship preserved in the opening chapter of The Professor: Alexander EW, 221). In The Duke of Zamorna they become joint narrators, as Percy's letters furnish Townshend with his story (Alexander EW, pp. 180–4). In *Henry Hastings, Sir William Percy's diary assists Townshend's narration.

Percy Hall, family home of the Percy family in Wellington's Land, 20 miles east of Wellington's Glass Town, in the *Glass Town and Angrian saga; bought in 1792 by Lord Edward Percy, father of the Duke of *Northangerland. The Hall remains the home of Northangerland's mother Lady Percy after the murder of his father.

Peterloo Massacre, 1819, one of the political events that caught the imagination of the young Brontës. Together with the *Luddite Riots and contemporary *Chartism, it informs the political events of Charlotte's and Branwell's writing in particular. On 16 August 1819, a crowd of about 50,000 gathered at St Peter's Fields, Manchester, to hear the main Radical orator Henry Hunt speak on parliamentary reform. The crowds were orderly but the magistrates panicked and sent incompetent yeomanry cavalry to arrest Hunt and disperse the assembly. Nine men and two women were killed and about 400 wounded. Within days, the term 'Peterloo' came to signify the horror, disgust, and fury of the radicals towards their social superiors—a deeply ironic reference to the victory over the French at Waterloo four years before which the government had represented as the defeat of French authoritarianism by Britain's free institutions. Instead of condemning the violent suppression of free speech, the Tory government supported the magistrates' decision and clamped down on all forms of meetings and the publication of seditious pamphlets. The son of the editor of the *Leeds Mercury, Edward *Baines, observed the Peterloo Massacre and his report in the issue for 16 August 1819 blamed both the organizers of the event and the officers of the yeomanry for the disaster. His eyewitness account of 'the military assault on the unarmed and peaceful multitude' appears in his biography of his father: *The Life of Edward Baines* (1851).

We have no evidence of Revd Patrick Brontë's opinion of the event which occurred during the fraught period of his contested appointment to the curacy of Haworth. We know, however, that he supported 'Temperate reform' (see REFORM BILL, 1832). His children were clearly aware of the event when they began writing ten years later, since insurrection, orators, and authoritarian suppression frequently occur in the *Glass Town and Angrian saga. 'Peterloo' is recalled particularly in Charlotte's novelette *Stancliffe's Hotel* when angry crowds mass in the city of Zamorna to confront their king, Arthur Wellesley, Duke of Zamorna, who has been consorting with the hated Northangerland who caused havoc in their country. As the crowd surges forward in protest, Castlereagh, Earl of Stuartville, is ordered to disperse them with the cavalry and Zamorna reacts by threatening to deprive the city of its corporate privileges. Zamorna is now seen as 'the Czar', with no obvious disapproval by either the narrator Charles Townshend or the author Charlotte.

pets owned by the Brontës. Haworth Parsonage was always full of animals, especially after Elizabeth *Branwell's 'reign at the Parsonage' (Smith *Letters*, 1. 600). There were usually more than one dog (*Grasper, *Keeper, and *Flossy in particular) and an assortment of cats (including *Tiger, Tom, Snowflake, and probably Rainbow and Diamond). Other pets come and go: a merlin hawk *Nero rescued on the moors by Emily and painted by her, two pet geese Victoria and Adelaide (named after the Queen and her aunt), a canary Dick and 'Jasper pheasent' (*Diary Paper of 24 Nov. 1834). On 1 July 1841, Charlotte noted that the tabby cat 'little black Tom is dead' (Smith *Letters*, 1. 258–9) but other than this reference Charlotte seldom notes the animals except in reference to her sisters. When she is homesick in Brussels, for example, she recalls Emily supervising her cooking and watching to see that she saves 'the best pieces of the leg of mutton for Tiger and Keeper' (Smith *Letters*, 1. 331). Nor does Branwell show much interest in pets, apart from using a dog when hunting on the moors; both he and Charlotte appear more interested in the literary effect of animals (see ANIMALS AND BIRDS IN THE WORKS OF THE BRONTËS). Most references to Brontë pets occur in Emily and Anne's Diary Papers. Apart from Revd Patrick Brontë's dog Grasper, the pets appear to have belonged to the two younger sisters, who cared for them, especially Emily who is

usually the one responsible for feeding them. The Diary Papers are our chief source of knowledge of the Brontë pets. When Emily writes of family members she always includes the pets: 'Victoria and Adelaide are ensconced in the peat-house— Keeper is in the kitchen—Nero in his cage' (*Diary Paper of 30 July 1841). Their loss and acquisition are as important as any happenings to her family: 'We have got Flossey, got and lost Tiger—lost the Hawk. Nero which with the geese was given away and is doubtless dead for when I came back from Brussels I enquired on all hands and could hear nothing of him—Tiger died early last year— Keeper and Flossey are well also the canary acquired 4 years since' (*Diary Paper of 30 July 1845). Despite her intense attachment to the pets, however, Emily's matter-of-fact tone indicates her characteristic resignation to adverse events in the natural world (shown in her devoir 'The *Butterfly'). Elizabeth Gaskell notes that Emily was drawn to the 'fierce, wild, intractability' of animals (Gaskell *Life*, 1. 308), which may explain her particular love for the mongrel Keeper (the model for the dog *Tartar in *Shirley*). Anne too is concerned about the pets, as her *Diary Paper written at Scarborough attests. 'We have got Keeper, got a sweet little cat and lost it, and also got a hawk. Got a wild goose which has flown away, and three tame ones, one of which has been killed' (30 July 1841). On 31 July 1845, she refers to 'little Dick hopping in his cage', presumably the canary. Ellen Nussey recorded that the Brontës' 'love of dumb creatures made them very sensitive of the treatment bestowed upon them, for any one to offend in this respect was with them an infallible bad sign, and blot in their disposition' (Smith *Letters*, 1. 600).

'Philosopher, The' (3 Feb. 1845); 56 lines by Emily Brontë, from the Honresfeld MS (see LAW COLLECTION). It was published by Emily in *Poems 1846, under the title 'The Philosopher', although Hatfield notes that 'The Philosopher's conclusion' is pencilled in Emily's hand at the head of the manuscript poem (Hatfield *EBP*, p. 221). The *Athenaeum* (July 1846) praised this poem as an example of Emily's 'evident power of wing' (Allott, p. 61).

The poem is a dialogue between a 'seer' and a philosopher, with a 'Space-sweeping soul' rather like *Byron's Manfred. The philosopher seeks reconciliation of his internal conflict of 'Three Gods . . . warring night and day' (possibly his heart, soul, and mind, as suggested by Barker (*The Brontës: Selected Poems* (1985), 139); although the final lines suggest 'power and will' as conflicting elements). He has explored heaven and hell, earth and air, but desires oblivion ('senseless rest') because he has failed to experience the transcending and transforming vision seen by the seer. His haunting refrain embodies a rejection of the conventional Christian heaven (and hell) for death 'without identity':

> No promised heaven, these wild Desires
> Could all or half fulfill—
> No threatened Hell— with quenchless fires
> Subdue this quenchless will!

Such oblivion, however, contrasts with Emily's view of death as a release of the soul from the chains of life into eternal liberty. Roper suggests that Emily was influenced by the engraving of John *Martin's painting *Sadak in Search of the Waters of Oblivion*, in *The Keepsake* (1828) (Roper *EBP*, p. 266). The accompanying tale ('The Deev Alfakir') and poem ('Sadak The Wanderer: A Fragment' by *Shelley'), both tell of Sadak, a philosopher and world-weary explorer for whom the waters of Oblivion serve as a Holy Grail (see Christine Alexander, ' "The Burning Clime": Charlotte Brontë and John Martin', *Nineteenth-Century Literature* (1995), 50).

> Davies, Stevie, *Emily Brontë: Heretic* (1994), 220.
> Gezari *EBP*, p. 7.
> Roper *EBP*, p. 164.

Philosopher's Island (Isle), 600 miles from the African coast, where the young nobility of the Glass Town receive their early schooling under the guidance of *Manfred, president of the University and also head of a secret society in the early *Glass Town and Angrian saga. The university (often referred to as a college) is in a fortified castle, situated in a deep valley of the Gordale Mountains in the centre of this barren island of heath and forests. The university is similar to the *Palace School in the *Islanders' Play.

Phoebe, a pointer in *Shirley* belonging to Sam Wynne (see WYNNE FAMILY). Phoebe appears to Shirley Keeldar to have been ill-used by her master, who often beats his dogs; she attempts to coax the dog into her house, but is bitten for her pains. Shirley cauterizes the wound herself with a hot iron, and despite fears that the dog may be rabid, tells no one of the incident until it is drawn from her three weeks later by Louis Gérard *Moore. The episode parallels an event in Emily Brontë's life, as told to Mrs Gaskell by Charlotte Brontë and recounted in the *Life*: '[Emily's] calling to a strange dog, running past, with hanging head and lolling tongue, to give it a merciful draught of water, its maddened snap at her, her nobly stern presence of mind, going right into the kitchen, and taking up one of Tabby's red-hot Italian irons to sear the bitten place, and telling no one, till the danger was well-nigh over, for fear of the terrors that might beset their weaker minds' (1. 308–9).   HR

phrenology is the pseudo-scientific theory that skull contours indicate underlying areas of the brain ('organs') responsible for an individual's 'propensities' and talents. Though the concept of localization within the brain is correct, skull thickness varies, and its surface does not reflect the topography of the brain. Franz Joseph Gall (1758–1828) expounded his theory of 'cranioscopy' in lectures in Vienna from 1796, and in works written with Johann Kaspar Spurzheim (1776–1832). The Austrian government banned Gall's lectures in 1802 because they implied determinism. In England there was a popular 'rage for phrenology' from about 1800, despite Peacock's caricatured 'Mr Cranium' in *Headlong Hall* (1816) and serious criticism in, for example, 'Anti-Phrenologia' (*Blackwood's Edinburgh Magazine*, Jan. 1823). In 1818 George Combe (1788–1858) began a series of influential writings in defence of phrenology. *Mechanics' Institutes acquired popular phrenological manuals and offered lectures on the subject.

The Brontë siblings were evidently intrigued by the impossibly precise phrenological 'maps' of the brain. In her novels Charlotte praises those whose intellectual and moral faculties (in the 'superior' part of the head) predominate over their 'animal propensities' at its base. The jargon of phrenology is used emotively in *The Professor*, where Juanna Trista has 'the same shape of skull as Pope Alexander the sixth; her organs of benevolence, veneration, conscientiousness, adhesiveness were singularly small, those of self-esteem, firmness, destructiveness, combativeness preposterously large' (ch. 12). Spurzheim had analysed the Pope's 'cerebral organization' as 'despicable in the eyes of a phrenologist'. In contrast, the 'superior part' of Frances *Henri's head is 'more developed, the base considerably less' (ch. 14), and William *Crimsworth possesses 'superior' organs such as 'ideality . . . conscientiousness' (ch. 3). In *Jane Eyre* phrenology helps to define the tensions and power contests inherent in complex characters and relationships. Sally Shuttleworth's analysis of the novel, emphasizing Combe's 'theory of innate, unrealized capacity' and the 'psychological exhilaration to be obtained from faculty exertion', sets these against more deep-rooted contemporary 'fears of social turbulence, and "fiendish" female behaviour' (*Charlotte Brontë and Victorian Psychology* (1996), 156–7). In *Shirley*, Hiram *Yorke lacks the 'organs' of veneration and comparison, and has too little benevolence and ideality: the consequences of these deficiencies are presented in detail. Here the alleged 'organs' are little more than the main headings of a traditional brief character study (ch. 4). Helstone's mocking comparison of Sweeting with his 'enormous organ of Wonder' with Malone who 'has none' (ch. 1) and an allusion to Shirley's small 'organ of Acquisitiveness' (ch. 22) can both be seen as serio-comic, but not insignificant, devices. In *Villette* perfunctory or mocking phrenological references are used for minor characters such as Rosine. More seriously, Mrs Bretton 'possessed a good development of benevolence, but' her son 'owned a better and larger'. The outward manifestations of Graham Bretton's 'development' are then listed, but immediately qualified by less benevolent or even conflicting characteristics.

In real life, Charlotte and George *Smith, the model for Bretton, experienced phrenological scrutiny by the 'expert' James P. Browne, MD, in June 1851. While Browne's 'estimate' of Charlotte is astonishingly apt, his assessment of Smith has more than the 'small vein of error' Charlotte observed in it; and she urged Smith to use his own will power to 'strive beyond' the standard perceived by the phrenologist (Smith *Letters*, 1. 656–63). Phrenology by itself was not a sufficient guide, as she must have realized when Harriet *Martineau and H. G. Atkinson shocked her by preaching their phrenologically based materialism and agnosticism.

Anne Brontë also uses a phrenological observation as the basis for a moral lesson in *Tenant*, when Mr Arthur Huntingdon laughingly uses his deficient 'organ of veneration' as evidence that God did not mean him to be religious. Helen responds that he is not without 'the capacity for veneration, . . . and conscience and reason' and that 'every faculty, both good and bad, strengthens by exercise' (ch. 23.) Both Anne and Charlotte, in their mature work, see phrenology as the handmaid of moral improvement.

Jack, Ian, 'Physiognomy, Phrenology and Characterisation in the Novels of Charlotte Brontë', *BST* (1970), 15. 80. 377–91.
Shuttleworth, Sally, *Charlotte Brontë and Victorian Psychology* (1996).

physiognomy. Attempts to correlate physical features and character or disposition are at least as old as the ancient theories of 'humours' and temperaments. Though King Duncan in *Macbeth* lamented that 'There's no art to find the mind's construction in the face', *Shakespeare's contemporaries and later writers and artists such as Fielding and Hogarth deliberately exploited physiognomical significance. The Swiss Protestant pastor Johann Kaspar Lavater (1741–1801), seeking traces of the spirit upon human features, wrote *Physiognomische Fragmente*, translated as *Essays on Physiognomy* (1789–98). The Brontës could have read the *Essays*, or Alexander Walker's *Physiognomy Founded on Physiology* (1834), which was

available at the *Keighley Mechanics' Institute. They used physiognomy and *phrenology to sharpen and direct observation of character, not as a substitute for careful study of behaviour.

In their fiction the Brontës use physiognomy to control the reader's intellectual and emotional response. The 14-year-old Charlotte gives the 'little man' flourishing a 'bloody dagger' in 'Visits in Verreopolis' an appropriately 'sharp, wild physiognomy' (Alexander *EW*, 1. 323). In *Jane Eyre* she increases the tension after Richard *Mason's arrival by an ominous description of his 'unsettled and inanimate' physiognomy (ch. 18); and Jane's penetrating gaze, seeing beyond St John *Rivers's classic features to the 'restless, or hard, or eager' qualities indicated by 'his nostril, his mouth, his brow', gives her the power which comes of understanding. Other characters, apart from *Rochester, interpret Jane imperfectly. Miss Temple perceives her 'ardent eyes' and 'clear front' (forehead), but not the contradictions between one trait and another, observed by Rochester. Blanche Ingram boasts that she sees in Jane 'all the faults of the governess class'. Since these would be, from her point of view, pride and independence of spirit, her perception is accurate as far as it goes, but she is blind to Jane's other qualities, and her assessment is perverted by her prejudice.

In *Shirley* Charlotte's interpretations of the *Yorke family are based on long acquaintance with the *Taylor family of Gomersal. The narrator, observing the child Jessy, remarks, 'It is odd that the doll should resemble her mother feature by feature . . . and yet the physiognomy—how different!' (ch. 9). Such assessments require subtlety in the beholder. In *Villette*, M. Paul Emanuel, a skilled physiognomist, assesses Lucy Snowe, fixing on her a prolonged and penetrating scrutiny. His oracular pronouncement arouses curiosity, gives a sense of his power, and links him with Lucy's fate. But when Lucy herself observes that Père Silas cannot be a 'native priest' because 'of that class, the cast of physiognomy is, almost invariably, grovelling', her Protestant prejudice, reflecting the author's, too obviously loads her judgement.

In *Tenant* Anne Brontë skilfully exposes the fallible physiognomical observer. The immature Helen Graham boasts that she is an excellent physiognomist, and cannot believe there is any harm in Mr Arthur Huntingdon's 'laughing blue eyes'. Her aunt rebukes her: 'False reasoning, Helen!', and Anne Brontë underlines her didactic purpose by Helen's casual dismissal of Huntingdon as 'neither a sage nor a saint' (ch. 16).

Graeme Tytler points out in 'Physiognomy in *Wuthering Heights*' (*BST* (1994), 21. 4. 137–46) that Emily's use of it is in line with that of Ann Radcliffe and Sir Walter *Scott. He notes that while both

Lockwood and Ellen Dean characterize people physiognomically, Ellen is the more perceptive of the two. Tytler also emphasizes Emily's awareness of family physiognomy and her dramatic use of it through the observational skills of some of her main characters.

> Shuttleworth, Sally, *Charlotte Brontë and Victorian Psychology* (1996).

Pigtail, a bizarre and vicious tavern keeper in *Paris (in Frenchyland), whose notorious trade in 'Prussian Butter' and in the sale and torture of children for entertainment is part of the underworld in the *Glass Town and Angrian saga. Originally a member of the *Faction Du Mange, his goods were confiscated and he became an outlaw and sometime cattle rustler on the suppression of that party. A very ugly, tall man (possibly deriving from *Our Fellows' Play), Pigtail takes over the tavern of a man he has killed and becomes 'the greatest vendor of white bread and Prussian butter', Glass Town slang for a mould of arsenic and oil of vitriol made to look like bread and prussic acid transformed into a butter. His trade reduces the population of Paris to such an extent that he is brought to trial by *Napoleon, but escapes to the Glass Town Federation to pursue his cruel activities against 'Enfants', assisted by his gang Monsieur Skeleton (or Sheckleton), Young Napoleon, and Eugene. In 'The Enfant' and *'Letters from an Englishman', he specializes in selling stray children to the owners of mills.

'Pious Cottager's Sabbath, The', Revd Patrick Brontë's idealized portrait of a devout peasant family, which was appended to The *Cottage in the Wood. An evangelical homily in unremarkable blank verse, it describes realistically the cottagers' breakfast of 'grit of wholesome oats'; but thereafter all is perfection. The family receive the 'richer banquet' of holy fare 'From the pure Fountain of Eternal life', and their pastor, like *Cowper's in The Task, book 2, is 'the faithful legate of the skies'.

'Pirate: A Tale, The'. Having been executed at the end of the *'Letters from an Englishman', Alexander Rogue (Duke of *Northangerland) reappears as the captain of a pirate ship, resurrected as the result of an agreement between Charlotte and Branwell Brontë (in Charlotte's The *Foundling, Alexander *EEW*, 2(1). 103–25). In this tale by Branwell, in a hand-sewn booklet of sixteen pages (in Bonnell, BPM), dated February 1833, Rogue captures a ship carrying the Earl of Ellrington (spelt 'Elrington' by Branwell; see ELLRINGTON FAMILY) and his daughter Lady Zenobia *Ellrington (a veritable Mme de Staël). Attracted to one another, they marry, with Rogue taking the title of Viscount Ellrington. This is the first

tale to feature Branwell's hero and begins the transformation of Rogue into Percy/Ellrington/Northangerland. VN

> *Miscellaneous Writings*, 1. 170–82.
> Neufeldt *BB Works*, 1. 239–49.

Plato, Revd Patrick Brontë's Newfoundland dog (crossed with a water-spaniel), acquired by him 'in the middle of 1855—for £3-0-0' (Lock & Dixon, p. 481). Plato was taken to Ireland by Nicholls after Mr Brontë's death and died there in 1866 (Lock & Dixon, pp. 530, 535).

'Plead for me'. See 'TO IMAGINATION'.

Plummer, Thomas (b. 1811), a local portrait painter who, at the age of 18, gave Branwell Brontë and probably his three sisters their first art lessons. Apparently Branwell called at his home in Chapel Lane, Keighley, for lessons but it is also likely that he gave some lessons at Haworth Parsonage (Alexander & Sellars, p. 34 n. 40). The 1851 Census records him as a portrait painter living in Keighley. Plummer is often confused with his father (also Thomas Plummer) who was headmaster of the Keighley Free Grammar School from 1804 to 1840 (as in Barker, p. 864 n. 40).

***Poems* by Currer, Ellis, and Acton Bell, 1846.** *See opposite page*

'Poetaster, The. A Drama in Two Volumes', 'by Lord Charles Wellesley, (Charlotte Brontë) (6–12 July 1830). This is the only complete drama written by Charlotte Brontë, although she often included fragmentary dramatic scenes in her magazines or stories, such as 'The Rivals' in 'Visits in Verreopolis' (Alexander *EEW*, 1. 297–327). 'The Poetaster' continues the rivalry between Glass Town's literati, responding to Captain John *Bud's 'The *Liar Detected' and satirizing the Romantic clichés and posturing of Henry Rhymer, who is actually the poet Young *Soult the Rhymer (pseudonym of Branwell Brontë). Volume 1 (MS in Lowell, Harvard) opens with Rhymer in his lonely garret, adopting the attitudes of a Romantic poet and alluding to Keats, *Shelley, *Wordsworth, Samuel Taylor *Coleridge, and the Graveyard poets. This would-be poet subscribes to the view that poetry should 'come spontaneously', yet his hackneyed language, pedestrian rhymes, and fondness for pathetic fallacy belie his pretension to inspirational genius. Rhymer is laughed at when he attempts to seek patronage from Lord Charles and the Marquis of Douro. In volume 2 (MS in Pierpont Morgan), Captain 'Andrew' *Tree's literary efforts are also treated disparagingly by the author, and when he rejects Rhymer, the poetaster murders Tree in a fit of passion (which represents

(*cont. on page 372*)

IN the autumn of 1845 Charlotte Brontë discovered a manuscript 'volume of verse in . . . Emily's handwriting'. The poems stirred her heart like the sound of a trumpet, and with difficulty she persuaded Emily that they deserved publication. Anne quietly produced some of her own compositions, and the sisters arranged a selection of their verse. They chose 21 poems each by Emily and Anne, and 19 by Charlotte, revised them carefully, removing Angrian and Gondal names, made fair copies of their own poems, and arranged them approximately in rotation, usually in the order Charlotte, Emily, Anne. Following advice from Chambers & Co. of Edinburgh, Charlotte asked *Aylott and Jones on 28 January 1846 whether they would publish the poems. The firm agreed to do so at the sisters' expense. In the published work each poem is attributed to 'Currer', 'Ellis', or 'Acton'. In her *'Biographical Notice', Charlotte explained that 'Averse to personal publicity' the sisters had veiled their own names under those of the 'Bells' through 'a sort of conscientious scruple at assuming Christian names positively masculine, while we did not like to declare ourselves women, because . . . we had a vague impression that authoresses are liable to be looked on with prejudice'. On 3 March Charlotte sent 'a draft for £31–10s' and on 25 May a further £5, that probably included the £2 for advertisements mentioned in her correspondence for 11 May, the date she returned a corrected proof sheet. The printer was John Hasler of Crane Court, Fleet Street. Four misprints were listed in an errata slip, and there were others in the contents list, but the volume, published c.22 May, and sold at 4s., was clearly printed and laid out, with generous margins and widely spaced lines. A thousand copies were printed, of which 961 remained unsold when *Smith, Elder and Company bought the stock in September 1848. The earliest bindings, probably those in light or dark green cloth with a geometrical design, are collectors' rarities. Reviews were also rarities: there were three. On 4 July 1846 the *Critic* welcomed the volume's unconventional, 'genuine poetry' as a ray of sunshine in 'this utilitarian age', and the *Athenaeum* recognized the 'instinct of song' in 'the three brothers' though 'in very unequal proportions': Acton's poems required 'the indulgences of affection', but Ellis had 'a fine quaint spirit' and 'an evident power of wing that may reach heights not here attempted'. Currer Bell's muse, exemplified in 'The Teacher's Monologue' ('The *room is quiet'), walked (rather than soared) between the other two. Despite additional praise from the *Dublin University Magazine* (Oct. 1846) for the poems' unobtrusive feeling and unaffected and sincere tone of thought, only two copies of the volume had been sold by 16 June 1847, when the sisters sent copies to writers they admired—Hartley *Coleridge, *De Quincey, *Tennyson, and others—'before transferring the edition to the Trunk-makers' (Smith *Letters*, 1. 531). Happily, it was transferred instead to Smith, Elder, whose reissue of November 1848 sold slowly but steadily: 556 copies were still 'on hand' in April 1856, and Charlotte recouped some of the original outlay, receiving £24 0s. 6d. from Smith, Elder. In 1857, 450 copies were bound, to coincide with the publication of Gaskell's *Life*. See also POETRY BY ANNE BRONTË; POETRY BY CHARLOTTE BRONTË; POETRY BY EMILY BRONTË.

Hargreaves, G. D., 'The Publishing of "Poems by Currer, Ellis and Acton Bell" ', *BST* (1969) 15. 79. 294–300.

Poems by the Brontë Sisters (1846), rprt. with an introduction by M. R. D. Seaward (1978, 1985). Smith *Letters*, 1. 470–5; 2. 117, 138–9.

wishful thinking on the part of the author since Tree is Lord Charles's literary rival). Rhymer, however, is saved from the hangman's noose by the magnanimity of Lord Charles and the timely resuscitation of Tree. He promises to take up a useful occupation and write no more.

The Glass Town poetaster Rhymer is probably based on Thomas Rhymer (1641–1713), poet and critic, known especially for his *Short View of Tragedy* in which he condemned *Shakespeare's *Othello*. The Drama itself is based on Ben Jonson's *The Poetaster, or His Arraignment* (1601) in which he attacks the poetry of Thomas Dekker and John Marston, identifying himself with Horace at the top of a hierarchy of poets. The Glass Town character General Bobadill, who appears in 'The Poetaster', is based on the boasting, cowardly soldier Bobadilla in Jonson's play *Every Man in his Humour* (1598).

Alexander *EEW*, 1. 179–96.
Monahan, Melodie (ed.), 'Charlotte Brontë's The Poetaster: Text and Notes', *Studies in Romanticism*, 20 (1981), 475–96.

poetry by Anne Brontë. *See opposite page*

poetry by Branwell Brontë. *See page 377*

poetry by Charlotte Brontë. *See page 382*

poetry by Emily Brontë. *See page 386*

poetry by Revd Patrick Brontë. *See page 392*

politics, British, 1800–1850. Revd Patrick Brontë and his family took a keen interest in politics and politicians. Mr Brontë's political views, those of an enlightened Tory with a strong social conscience, influenced his prose tales and tracts, and his many letters to local newspapers. He and Branwell took a prominent part in local election meetings in July 1837. Charlotte told Mary Taylor that she had taken an interest in politics since she was 5 years old, and Charlotte and Branwell's early writings display their eager political partisanship and their ability to satirize plausible or bombastic political oratory. In the 18th century the great landowning aristocracy and wealthy middle class were on the whole associated with Whiggism, and the squirearchy and Anglican clergy with the Tories. But in Parliament party alignment only began to take shape when William Pitt the younger became prime minister in December 1783 and led a new Tory party generally representing the views of the country gentry, merchants, and administrative officialdom, and opposed by Foxite Whigs, supported by Dissenters, industrialists, and reformers. The division was not clear-cut: Pitt began as a reformer, but the parliamentary reform bill of 1785 was not passed. Pitt had advocated Catholic Emancipation, which should have formed part of the

agreement leading to the Act of Union with Ireland in 1800, but was blocked by George III. The French Revolutionary War made Pitt reactionary, and led many moderate Whigs to desert Fox and support Pitt. The Combination Act of 1800 (not repealed until 1824), which forbade working men to form unions, followed a series of repressive Acts designed to stamp out revolutionary ideas. 'Corresponding Societies' which advocated reform were attacked, public meetings made illegal unless licensed by a magistrate, and any attempt to change the British Constitution was made an act of treason. Pitt resigned office in March 1801, but maintained communication with the prime minister Henry Addington (1757–1844, created Viscount Sidmouth 1805) until 1803, when they quarrelled. Pitt returned to office in May 1804. As a war measure he had introduced an income tax in December 1798, and in February 1805 he increased the property tax, raising a loan of £20,000,000. The news of Napoleon's victory at Austerlitz in December 1805 reached Pitt when his health had already broken down, and he died six weeks later. There had been one notable reform in this period: in 1802 Sir Robert Peel (1750–1830, MP for Tamworth and father of the future prime minister) had introduced a Factory Act designed to safeguard the health of apprentices and other factory workers. Despite the March 1807 Act of Abolition of the Slave Trade (see SLAVERY), on the whole government from late 1807 onwards was reactionary and repressive. Sidmouth in particular, as home secretary 1812–21, became identified with vicious coercive measures. In 1806 and 1807 Napoleon had attempted to ruin British trade by his Berlin and Milan decrees, forbidding neutral countries to trade in British goods. In response the British issued orders-in-council decreeing the blockading of foreign ports. The United States then placed an embargo on trade with both Britain and France, hoping to make them lift their edicts. The result was severe depression in British trade, and hardship for both employers and workers. In *Shirley* Robert Gérard *Moore abhors the orders-in-council, Castlereagh, and the war party, because they ruin and baffle him (ch. 2). Between 1790 and 1813 the cost of living rose by 87 per cent, and hand-loom weavers, competing against the power-loom, were especially hard-hit: hence the *Luddite riots, organized on a quasi-military basis—a main theme in *Shirley*. The government, influenced by Lord Castlereagh and Sidmouth, quelled the risings by armed force, made framebreaking a capital offence, and passed a new Watch and Ward Act in 1812 to tighten local security. When in 1815 Tory landlords saw the price of their corn fall by a half owing to foreign imports, Parliament passed the first Corn Law, imposing

(*cont. on page 376*)

FIFTY-NINE poems are attributed to Anne Brontë in Edward Chitham's edition of 1979. A substantial number of these were published during her lifetime: 21 in *Poems* 1846, 'Oh, they have robbed me of the hope' in *Agnes Grey* (ch. 17; Dec. 1847), 'Farewell to thee!' in *Tenant* (ch. 19; June 1848), 'The Three Guides' in *Fraser's Magazine* (Aug. 1848), and 'Believe not those' in *Fraser's* (Dec. 1848), reprinted in the *Leeds Intelligencer* (30 Dec. 1848). When Charlotte prepared two of her sisters' novels for republication in December 1850, she added the *Fraser's* poems and six others by Anne, altering or abridging them to present her sister in a favourable light, and adding to 'Why should such gloomy silence' the inappropriate title 'Domestic Peace'. Charlotte's much-revised version of eight stanzas from Anne's last, most moving, and sombre poem, 'A dreadful darkness', was for many years the only known text. It is misleading, for where Anne wrote 'O Thou hast taken my delight | & hope of life away', Charlotte printed 'Thou, God, hast taken our delight, Our treasured hope away', removing from this stanza its intense personal suffering.

It is fortunate, then, that most of Anne's poems can be found in manuscript, and that Edward Chitham's edition is manuscript-based. T. J. *Wise dispersed the manuscripts for profit, as he did those of Anne's siblings. Most were Anne's fair copies. Her only surviving rough drafts are the undated 'A prisoner in a dungeon deep' (Bonnell BPM MS 132), and her last poem, 'A dreadful darkness' (1849; Bonnell BPM MS 137)— a manuscript that bears witness to Anne's agonizing search for words adequate to this ultimate trial of her faith. The dark mist that surrounds her was first 'rolling', then 'gathering', and finally 'whelming' or 'blinding'. In line 23, Anne submitted her 'bleeding' or 'breaking' heart to God's will. She made no final choice, for there was no fair copy. Fair copy manuscripts of her other poems can be found in Pierpont Morgan; Berg, NYPL; Huntington; BL; and Bonnell BPM (MSS 132, 134, 135, 136, and 137), together with nine lines beginning 'Not only for the past' in her manuscript music book (Bonnell BPM MS 133). Ransom HRC, Texas, has a typed transcript of a now-missing manuscript of poems originally written between 1836 and 1838. The inaccessible Law Collection has, or had, a manuscript fair copy containing ten poems dated 1840 and 1844–5. This is reproduced as an excellent facsimile in the Shakespeare Head *The Poems of Emily Jane Brontë and Anne Brontë* (1934), 331–56.

Among Anne's poems some 25 are concerned with the imaginary land of *Gondal; fifteen are primarily religious; nine almost certainly express her feelings for the curate Revd William *Weightman, though he is never named; and a significant number are lyrics responding to the natural world. Some of the most memorable poems reveal Anne's passionate reaction to her 'exile' as a governess, and her deep emotional attachment to her home. Her longest poem, *'Self-Communion', shows how clearly she could analyse her own personality, and how candidly she could acknowledge with pain the fading of 'early friendship's pure delight'—presumably her fondness for Emily—as she realized that what her 'soul worshipped' was 'slighted, questioned, or despised' (Chitham *ABP*, p. 157).

The Gondal poems, set in the exotic imaginary land invented by Emily and Anne, tell of the loves, griefs, and imprisonments of glamorous ladies and feuding warriors. Anne's earliest surviving Gondal poem was written in December 1836, her last as late as October 1846 seven years after Charlotte's *Farewell to Angria*. Many are attributed to 'Gondalian' heroes or heroines. 'A Voice from the Dungeon' is by Marina Sabia; 'The Captive's Dream', 'The North Wind', and 'The lady of Alzerno's hall' by Alexandrina Zenobia; 'Parting Address' and 'Mirth and Mourning' by Zerona. Similar names recur in Emily's Gondal poems, which have similar themes. Like Byron's protagonists, Anne's dramatis personae are typically parted lovers, banished exiles, or—most often—prisoners consigned by their enemies to gloomy dungeons. Of this genre are the early 'A Voice from the Dungeon', 'The Captive's Dream', 'The North Wind', and the later pair of poems written in July 1846, 'Mirth and Mourning', in which Zerona grieves for her imprisoned lover, and 'Weep not too much', where the prisoner, comforted by the knowledge that Zerona is free, assures her that his 'soul partakes' of Nature's bounty with her. Many of Anne's Gondal poems are unimpressively monotonous in content and clichéd in style. We hear of 'purling' crystal rills, sighing gales, zephyrs waving verdant trees, wild winds howling. The heroes and heroines have raven curls, or snowy necks and 'sunny' hair. Occasionally Anne achieves a successful pictorial, if melodramatic, effect, reminiscent of the poems and illustrations in ladies' 'Keepsakes' and 'Albums'. Alexandrina dreams of her lover: 'And O I thought he clasped his wasted hands, | And raised his haggard eyes to Heaven, and prayed | That he might die' ('The Captive's Dream'). In the same poem a memorable phrase conveys the frustration of nightmare: 'And the dear name I vainly strove to speak, | Died in a voiceless whisper on my tongue'.

Sometimes, too, when Gondalian imaginings may reflect personal experience, a more naturalistic, simpler style conveys powerful emotion in revelatory, moving poems like 'Maiden, thou wert thoughtless once' (1 Jan. 1840), or 'The Consolation' (7 Nov. 1843). In the former, the Gondalian Olivia Vernon seems to voice the fluctuations of Anne's hope and distress when William Weightman left Haworth at the end of December 1839 for his New Year holiday. 'We heard without approaching steps,' she writes, 'But O my spirit burned within, | My heart beat thick and fast. | He came not nigh—he went away | And then my joy was past' (Chitham *ABP*, p. 72). Charlotte later described the attraction between the 28-year-old curate and 22-year-old Anne in a letter of 20 January 1842 (Smith *Letters*, 1. 279). Perhaps for Anne the attraction was all the stronger because after a brief period of about three months, from late January until late April 1840, she was seldom at home when Weightman was in Haworth. A poignant poem written at *Thorp Green Hall on 28 August 1840 conveys her intense emotion. Anne is lonely, tired of weeping, sick of woe, and longs for the unnamed friend: 'Wilt thou not come to me?' The poem makes a strong impact by its direct, repeated appeals, unadorned style, and terse quatrains. Possibly the poems used in *Agnes Grey* and *Tenant* ('Oh, they have robbed me of the hope' and 'Farewell to thee! but not farewell'; Chitham *ABP*, pp. 75–6) were originally written with Weightman in mind. Both recall a loved, smiling or laughing face and a musical voice which gives delight. In this they resemble 'I will not mourn thee, lovely one', written in December 1842, after Weightman's death in September that year. Anne pays tribute to the loved one's endearing qualities, effectively contrasting his smiling brightness with stern and frowning death, and the music of his voice with silence. Her endeavour to see his early death as a blessing is touchingly modified in the last stanza by her admission that she 'still must mourn' the loss of the 'pleasures buried' in his tomb. 'Yes, thou art gone' (Apr. 1844) may also recall Weightman and his kindness, now 'frozen' in the tomb beneath the church floor. 'Night' recalls 'the form it was my bliss to see, | And only dreams can bring again | The darling of my heart to me' (early 1845; Chitham *ABP*, p. 110). Finally, in 'Severed and gone, so many years!', Anne declares that the earth is sweeter, men more true, because the beloved one lived, and gave goodness to the world. Interestingly, she concludes that he lives in her heart, 'and not in mine alone' (Apr. 1847; Chitham *ABP*, p. 141).

Several of the 'Weightman' poems have an important spiritual dimension. He was 'so near divine', he fixed his brightest hopes on heaven, and 'freed from sin, and grief, and pain' he now drinks 'the bliss of heaven'. Religion was a vital part of Anne's life and thought, and her personal religious poems impress by their minute self-scrutiny, unflinching search for religious truth, and declarations of hard-won faith. Those which she regarded as hymns are sincere exhortations to Christian perseverance. Like the Wesleys, John Newton, and *Cowper, she 'wrestled with God' in earnest prayer, facing her doubts, finding courage in the teachings of the New Testament, and (unlike Cowper) rejecting *Calvinism, clinging to her trust in the doctrine of *universal salvation. Some of her most significant religious poems (*'Believe not those who say', *'Confidence', *'To Cowper', 'The *Three Guides', and 'A *dreadful darkness closes in') are treated separately. Others take the form of prayers, such as her desperate plea for either an early death or the strength to bear her 'load of misery' in 'O God! if this indeed be all', written just before she left Thorp Green in 1845. Like Cowper, the sensitive Anne can at times sink into a slough of despond; she accuses herself of spiritual lethargy in 'Despondency', for her faith wavers; but in the end she can still pray to Jesus to save her. Her images here, deriving from Bunyan, the Bible, and the Prayer Book, give a timeless dimension to her poem. But equally sincere is her expression of Christian joy, 'In Memory of a happy day in February' (1842), a rapturous poem of trust. In 'My God! O let me call thee mine!', Anne perhaps consciously echoes Charles Wesley's 'My God! I know, I feel thee mine'. Her hymns are very much in the evangelical tradition. In other poems, her use of dialogue in exploring religious faith, as in 'The Three Guides', recalls the technique of George Herbert's beautiful poem 'Love bade me welcome', his 'Dialogue-Anthem' between Christian and Death, and such well-known hymns as Philip Doddridge's 'See Israel's gentle Shepherd stand'.

Anne was also a nature poet. She observed the natural world minutely, described it evocatively, and believed that 'A fine and subtle spirit dwells | In every little flower'. Her 'bluebell', in the poem of that name, is the harebell, which hangs on a delicate curved stem. It is very aptly described as 'a little trembling flower', recalling for her happy times which 'never may return', now that she spends a 'thankless life' amid heartless crowds. Her emotional response is evident also in 'That summer sun', where she prefers the 'landscape drear' of home to the sunny summer, flowers, and 'thick green leaves' surrounding her at Thorp Green. But she can also find nature exhilarating. 'My soul is awakened, my spirit is soaring' is exceptional in its empathy with wild, roaring wind, and scudding clouds, 'whirlwinds of spray' and dashing waves. She uses a vigorous, rapid, anapaestic metre and lively onomatopoeic effects in this very successful short poem. At other times, though she finds the 'smile of early spring' sweet, she looks beyond nature to its Creator, seeing 'his wisdom and his power' in his works; but 'most throughout the moral world' she sees his glory shine.

Her strong response to the natural world, her awareness of the associations it has for her with human and spiritual life, and her deep concern with 'the human heart by which we live', are akin to the ideas of the Lake Poets, especially those of Wordsworth. She finds 'silent eloquence' and 'sweet feeling' in every little flower, as Wordsworth avows his faith that 'every little flower enjoys the air it breathes' in 'Lines Written in Early Spring'. Anne's recollections of childhood and its lost happiness may recall Wordsworth's 'Heaven lies about us in our infancy'; and her poem entitled 'Dreams' opens with the line 'While on my lonely couch I lie', a variant of Wordsworth's 'For oft, when on my couch I lie' in 'I wandered lonely as a cloud'.

We know, too, that the Brontës regarded Southey as a fine poet. Anne's 'My soul is awakened' echoes in its rhythm Southey's 'The Cataract of Lodore', as well as several of Moore's poems. She had a good ear, and considerable skill in the manipulation of metre. While the staple of her work is Common Metre (iambic stanzas with four lines of eight and six syllables alternately, usually rhyming abab), she also uses a variety of six- and eight-line stanzas and other forms. In 'Self-Communion', one of her most compelling poems, she varies her short lines with unobtrusive art, grouping them irregularly, adapting her rhyme-schemes, and using initial trochees instead of iambs to mark key points in her dialogue.

In her best poems, Anne does not require 'the indulgences of affection' that the critic of the *Athenaeum* patronizingly bestowed upon her in July 1846; her work deserves and repays critical attention.

Chitham *ABP*.

Frawley, Maria, *Anne Brontë* (1996).
Gérin, Winifred, *Anne Brontë* (1959).
Thormählen, Marianne, *The Brontës and Religion* (1999).
Wise, T. J., and Symington, J. A., *The Poems of Emily Jane and Anne Brontë* (1934).

heavy duties on corn and prohibiting the import of foreign corn until the price of English wheat reached 80s. a quarter. This measure coincided with high unemployment, and poor relief rose to nearly £8,000,000 in 1816; yet it did not benefit farmers or landlords in the long run. By 1820 they too were raising cries of distress, and the corn laws remained a highly contentious issue until they were repealed in 1846. From 1816 a Radical party advocating parliamentary reform became active, its leaders including William Cobbett and Henry Hunt (1773–1835). In November 1816 a Bermondsey crowd demanded universal suffrage, and soon afterwards riots were reported from the Midlands and Glasgow. The government, fearing revolution, suspended the Habeas Corpus Act in 1817, and arrested the reformist leaders. Henry Hunt was imprisoned for his part in the Manchester meeting of 1819 which resulted in the *Peterloo Massacre by government troops. Panic legislation was put through in the Six Acts—the 'Gag Acts' of 1819–20, forbidding large public meetings without official permission, imposing heavy duties on newspapers, and permitting magistrates to search private houses for arms. After Castlereagh's death in 1822, a less reactionary policy was introduced by Tory reformers, including George Canning, Wil-

liam Huskisson, and Robert Peel (1788–1850). Peel abolished capital punishment for a large number of crimes, improved legal procedure and prison conditions, and in 1829 established a new Metropolitan police force. With the Duke of *Wellington he passed the Catholic Emancipation Act of 1829, believing that without it Ireland would erupt in civil war. The *French Revolution of 1830, in the same year as the death of George IV and the English elections of July when Wellington was returned to power, helped to stir Whigs and Radicals to new activity. The resulting agitation for a more representative parliament led to the *Reform Bill, 1832. The Tories Peel and Disraeli supported pragmatic reforms, while the theoretically liberal Lord John Russell reacted with illiberal intolerance towards so-called Papal Aggression. Peel's social reforms included the passing of the Mines Act of 1842 prohibiting women and girls and boys under 10 from working underground, and a second Factory Act (1844) limiting the hours of children under 13 to six and a half hours, and of women to twelve hours. His economic reforms included reduced duties on many goods and the abolition of duty on more than 250 others. In 1846 he repealed the Corn Laws—a repeal for

(*cont. on page 381*)

BRANWELL Brontë published at least eighteen poems and one prose piece in his lifetime and was in print five years before his sisters. (Barker, p. 993 n. 18, suggests that 'SPEAK KINDLY', *Halifax Guardian* (19 Sept. 1846), may also be by Branwell. The absence of a signature and the fact that the poem's sentiments are quite uncharacteristic for Branwell in 1846 make the attribution doubtful.) Eighteen of these publications appeared before his sisters published their volume of poems in 1846. He published in local newspapers: the *Leeds Intelligencer*, the *Halifax Guardian*, the *Bradford Herald*, and the *Yorkshire Gazette*. Having poetry published in the Yorkshire newspapers in the 1840s was no mean achievement; it placed one in the company of highly respected poets. These newspapers were very proud of their poetry columns, which were a regular feature. They published not only the works of such local worthies as Thomas Crossley, Robert Story, James Montgomery, and John Nicholson, but also poems by such established figures as *Wordsworth, *Tennyson, *Shelley, *Southey, Hood, Leigh Hunt, and Longfellow. The *Halifax Guardian*, in which Branwell published the largest number of his poems, twelve between 1841 and 1847 in addition to one article in prose, welcomed contributions of 'Original Poetry' but did not hesitate to reject material which it considered beneath the high standards of which it boasted, and printed stinging rebukes to poor souls who had presumed to send in 'feeble verses' for publication. The respect which the *Guardian* accorded him is revealed by the article on Thomas *Bewick. It is the only piece of art/literary criticism to appear in the *Guardian* during 1841–2, though it published poetry regularly during that time. His last published work, a poem fittingly titled 'The end of all', appeared on 5 June 1847, just four months before the publication of *Jane Eyre*. Given that his sisters' 1846 volume of poems sold only two copies in its first year, it is safe to say that Branwell's poems enjoyed a significantly wider readership.

From the age of 11 Branwell saw himself as a published author and editor. He saw himself as a critic, dramatist, historian, conversationalist, editor, publisher, but preeminently as a poet—in short as the great man of letters he saw exemplified by Christopher *North and James *Hogg in *Blackwood's Edinburgh Magazine*, particularly in the 'Noctes Ambrosianae'. Like Charlotte he believed that he had been called to a life of literature, though clearly not with the modest aspirations she expresses in her poem 'The Violet'. By the end of 1837 (at the age of 20) he had put together three 'collected' manuscript volumes of poems (five if one includes Young Soult's two volumes), and after major disasters and crises, such as the Bradford failure, the dismissals at *Broughton-in-Furness, *Luddenden Foot, and *Thorp Green Hall, he consistently tried to redeem himself with feverish efforts to get his work (mainly poetry) published. Unlike Charlotte, who largely ceased to write poetry after she abandoned the Glass Town and Angrian saga in 1839, Branwell never relinquished his belief that his first calling was that of poet. Percy (see Duke of *Northangerland), it should be remembered, was an accomplished poet, as were other significant Angrian personae in Branwell's chronicles such as the Duke of *Zamorna, Henry *Hastings (the poet of Angria), Warner Howard *Warner, Lord Richton (see FLOWER, CAPTAIN SIR JOHN), and Charles *Wentworth. Most of Branwell's early writing, up to the end of 1830, was in verse, and after 1839, when he abandoned the Angrian material on which he had really run out of steam two years earlier, his only prose pieces were his article on Bewick and his unfinished novel.

From the outset, Branwell, like Charlotte, very self-consciously played the role of poet. A poem he composed jointly with Charlotte at the age of 12 ends:

> & such a charming dogge[re]l
> as this was never wrote
> not even by the mighty
> & high Sir Walter Scott

In his first 'edition' of poems—'A Collection of Poems by Young Soult the Ryhmer' [*sic*], the poet of Glass Town (1829)—he includes an elaborate commentary by Moses Chateaubriand, who notes on the 'Ode to Napoleon', 'This poem is [in] an exceedingly rambling and irregular metre and contains a great many things for which he ought to be punished' (Neufeldt *BB Works*, 1. 60). While most of Charlotte's early poems were in quatrains and very regular metre, and she did not begin to experiment with verse form and metrics until 1830, Branwell was much more venturesome from the outset. Of the fourteen poems on which he may have collaborated with Charlotte, thirteen are in quatrains, one is in blank verse. Of the nineteen early poems of his own, eleven reflect her use of quatrains, but employ three different rhyme patterns (sometimes two in one poem) and quite irregular metrical patterns in which he not only varies the number of feet per line, but also combines different types in one line, principally iambs and anapaests. They also include a five-line stanza, with the fifth line a repeated refrain, blank verse, a carefully constructed ode (reflecting his schooling in the classics), and a blank verse drama, something Charlotte was not to attempt for another year. While most of the poems in Young Soult's two volumes are of the noisy Byronic/apocalyptic variety, 'Song 2' shows him to be capable not only of a quieter, more meditative strain, but also of adopting at the age of 12 an adult's retrospective point of view. Some of Branwell's irregularities result from inexperience and lack of discipline, but it is also evident from 'Chateaubriand's' comments that the experimentation was deliberate and not always to Charlotte's taste. She comments on Young Soult's two volumes: 'His poems exhibit a fine imagination, but his versification is not good. The ideas and language are beautiful, but they are not arranged so as to run along smoothly, and for this reason I think he should succeed best in blank verse' (Alexander *EEW*, 1. 127). While Young Soult's romantic posturing is the subject of several satirical comments by Charlotte (see Neufeldt *CBP*, p. 397; Alexander *EW*, pp. 64–6; Alexander *EEW*, 1. 127, 180 ff., 309), the description of Young Soult composing in the face of an oncoming storm in volume 2 of **'Letters from an Englishman'* indicates that Branwell was quite capable of laughing at his poetic posturings.

Between May 1832 and November 1834 Branwell put together the first volume of compositions with himself as author: five poems, all fair copies now in longhand instead of his earlier print writing. Although three of the poems are related to Glass Town, they are not part of a prose chronicle but meant to stand on their own. All the poems show a strong classical influence: the first, a long narrative in rhyming couplets, reminiscent of Pope's translation of the *Illiad* but also clearly influenced by **Milton's Paradise Lost*; two odes, one with a very complicated rhyme scheme, and one on the Battle of Thermopylae, a subject that fascinated Branwell (see Neufeldt *BB Works*, 2. 3–6, 10–16); and a lengthy Byronic reminiscence by Percy in exile, which raises such philosophical questions as 'Oh what is man? a wretched being I Tossed upon the tide of time'.

Between December 1835 and May 1838, Branwell put together a second manuscript volume of at least 60 pages, containing fair copies of eight poems (some unfinished). The first two poems were early drafts of Books I and II of 'Misery', the first work he submitted for publication, to *Blackwood's Edinburgh Magazine* in 1836, and the first work signed 'Northangerland', the pseudonym he was to use for all but one of his published works and for several intended for publication. Again the poems are signed and dated by Branwell, and though in most cases related to Percy, intended to stand on their own. The poems are dark and melodramatic, dealing with loss of innocence, betrayal, desertion, and death, and the resultant sense of loss, anguish, despair, damnation, loss of hope, and loss of belief in God, heaven, and hell.

Between March 1837 and May 1838, when he left for Bradford to try his hand at portrait painting, Branwell compiled his most important manuscript volume of poems. Into it he entered (1) revisions of 26 earlier poems; (2) eight new poems; (3) translations of six odes of Horace. All but two of the revisions have an Angrian source but have been divorced from their original context, and whoever their original 'Angrian author', the revised versions are 'corrected', 'altered', 'enlarged', and 'transcribed' by 'P. B. Brontë'. All are fair copies in longhand rather than the usual minute print writing, and many have pencilled emendations, suggesting that Branwell continued to rework them in hope of publication, but none was ever published. He was more fortunate with the eight new poems, five of which were published in whole or in part (see Neufeldt *BB Works*, 3. 178–84, 194–207).

In April 1840, he sent Thomas *De Quincey revised versions of five of the six translations of Horace's Odes, along with a revised version of *'Sir Henry Tunstall' (the first version was composed while he was at Bradford in 1838) part of which was later published (see Neufeldt *BB Works*, 3. 370). Five days later he sent to Hartley *Coleridge a revised version of 'At dead of midnight—drearily', along with revised versions of two of the translations, followed in June, at Coleridge's invitation, by his translation of the whole of Book 1 of Horace's Odes (except for no. 38: see 'ODES OF HORACE, THE').

In August 1841, while he was clerk in charge at Luddenden Foot, he began to enter drafts of new poems into a small notebook. Most of the poems are related to a very ambitious project he seems to have envisaged: a series of poems about a group of historical figures—mainly men of letters—who had achieved human greatness in the face of adversity, a theme well summed up by the title he eventually gave to the second version of his poem on Admiral Nelson, 'The Triumph of Mind over Body' (the only revision of an earlier work in the notebook). Two lists of persons potentially to be written about total 23. Eight of these—Alexander the Great, Galileo, Tasso, Milton, Samuel Johnson, Cowper, Burns, and Nelson—figure in poems written in 1841. If not in real life, then in imagination he felt himself closely allied to his heroes, and in chronicling their achievements, he would in a small way share in their triumph. He clearly believed that he still had a future as a poet, and was writing with an eye to publication. Unfortunately, only one poem from the notebook, 'On Landseer's Picture', was ever published.

However, even before he began the notebook, on 5 June 1841, his poem 'Heaven and Earth' appeared in the *Halifax Guardian*, under the pseudonym 'Northangerland', the first of the eighteen poems he was to publish by 1847. The poems fall into two groups: the eleven published in 1841–2, before Branwell's departure for Thorp Green, and the seven published after his return from Thorp Green in 1845. Four of the poems in the first group are new, six are revisions of new poems entered into the two notebooks he was using in 1837–8, and only one is recycled from an Angrian chronicle. In the second group, six are new, and one is a revision of a new poem in the 1837–8 notebooks.

The eleven poems Branwell published in 1841–2 are various in both theme and form. Thematically, they range from expressions of traditional piety to political satire, but the predominant mood is well expressed by the subtitles given to two of his sonnets: 'On the callousness produced by cares' and 'On Peaceful Death and Painful Life' (Neufeldt *BB Works*, 3. 366, 369). The progression from childhood to adulthood, from innocence to experience, is painful, and results in the hardening of the heart and the loss of the capacity for empathy. Life is essentially the experience of loss and care, 'So seize we the present, | and gather its flowers; | For—mournful or pleasant— | 'Tis all that is ours' (Neufeldt *BB Works*, 3. 372) The same mood is continued in 'Sir Henry Tunstall', which Branwell sent to *Blackwood's* in September 1842 after the last poem published in 1842, and in 'The Triumph of Mind over Body', of which he prepared a fair copy, signed 'Northangerland', at the same time, obviously with the intention of submitting it for publication. The latter, according to his friend Francis *Grundy (Grundy, p. 79), was also the poem he sent to James and Harriet Martineau and to Leigh *Hunt at this time, who all spoke very highly of it. Some of the credit for all this activity must be given to the influence of the circle of his artistic friends in Halifax— the brothers Francis *Leyland and Joseph Bentley *Leyland, the artist John Wilson Anderson, the poets William *Dearden, John Nicholson, William Heaton, and possibly Thomas Crossley—who read their manuscripts to one another for criticism. Its culmination was the article about Bewick, his last publication in this period, which is as much about Branwell defining his own aesthetic beliefs and principles as it is about explaining the attraction of Bewick's engravings.

The second group of published poems (1845–7) continues the mood of loss and disillusionment, but adds the attractiveness of the oblivion of death as a release from the painfulness of existence. (The unpublished sonnet 'When all our cheerful hours seem gone forever' which he sent to J. B. Leyland in April 1846 encapsulates the mood perfectly.) The same note of loss and disillusionment pervades even poems written while Branwell was at Thorp Green—for example, 'Oer Graftons Hill the blue heaven smiled serene'—some of which Branwell was clearly preparing to send out for publication (see Neufeldt *BB Works*, 3. 409–19), but the attractiveness of death does not become apparent until late 1845 and is related to the growing erosion of Branwell's hopes of marrying Mrs Robinson. His first poem to make reference to her, 'I saw a picture, yesterday', written at Thorp Green, portrays Branwell happy in his affection for her. In 'Lydia Gisborne' (Mrs Robinson's maiden name), written in the late summer or autumn of 1845, after Branwell's dismissal but before the death of Mr Robinson and the collapse of Branwell's hopes, the note of anguish, loss, and disillusionment is reinforced by Branwell's comment to Leyland the day after his return from his trip to Wales: 'I found during my absence that wherever I went a certain woman robed in black, and calling herself "Misery" walked by my side and leant on my arm as affectionately as if she were my legal wife' (Wise & Symington, 2. 57). Branwell's next poem, 'Real Rest', introduces the theme of the attractiveness of death.

'Lydia Gisborne', beginning 'On Ouses grassy banks——', dated 1 June 1846, again traces the collapse of his dreams, reinforcing the theme with a sketch of a stone with 'Memoria' engraved upon it, and a gravestone with the inscription 'EHEV' [Alas!] (an echo of Horace's ode 'Eheu fugaces'). Toward the end of 1846, Branwell wrote two poems depicting historical figures facing despair and death, with the word 'Lydia' appearing in the margin of the second with a sketch of a tombstone (see Neufeldt *BB Works*, 3. 492–7). On 5 June 1847 he published his last poem, 'The end of all', a reworking of a poem about Percy at his wife's deathbed from the 1837 manuscript volume. It was his last significant composition.

After his meeting with Hartley Coleridge in May 1840, Branwell showed signs of a growing maturity as a writer that manifested itself in a number of ways. As his verse became more introspective and reflective he began to demonstrate a greater interest in the social issues of his time. In his poem 'At dead of Midnight, drearily' (Apr. 1840) he explores the double standard for males and females regarding adultery. In his poem on Admiral Nelson ('The Triumph of Mind over Body', 1842) he provides an idealized version of Nelson's heroism and death, but also the grim realism of his children's indifferent discovery of their father's bones in the churchyard. In the unfinished poem 'Morley Hall' (1846) the speaker lashes out against the destructive impact of commercialism and industrialization on Lancashire (a topic also dealt with in Branwell's unfinished novel *And the Weary are at Rest*). There is also evidence of a growing discipline in his writing, beginning with the careful revisions in his 1837 notebook. He produced three and even four versions of some poems he composed after 1838. It is worth noting, too, the number of sonnets among his published poems, a form that requires a high degree of skill and discipline. By the time he left for Thorp Green in 1843 he was well on his way to establishing himself as a regular contributor and local poet of note in the Yorkshire newspapers. Had he been able to maintain the momentum he built up in 1841/2, he might well have achieved a stature equal to that of his poet friends in the Halifax circle, all solidly established regional poets who had to earn a living outside their literary activities. Ironically, Branwell's move to Thorp Green to earn a living destroyed that momentum.   VN

du Maurier, Daphne, *The Infernal World of Branwell Brontë* (1960).
Gérin *BB*.
Neufeldt *BBP*.
Winnifrith, Tom (ed.), *The Poems of Patrick Branwell Brontë* (1983).

which the Anti-Corn Law League had been pressing since the economic crisis of 1838–9. See also CHARTISM.

Politics of Verdopolis, The, narrative by Branwell Brontë of eighteen pages, in eight chapters, in a hand-sewn booklet (MS in Bonnell, BPM), completed in November 1833. In the continuing metamorphosis and development of his protagonist, Branwell has transformed Rogue (spelt 'Rougue' by Branwell) into 40-year-old Alexander Percy, marking the first use of 'Percy' in connection with Alexander Rogue/Ellrington, and his descent from the Percys of Northumberland at Alnwick which

was continued in *The *Life of Feild Marshal the Right Honourable Alexander Percy* [*sic*] (see also Alexander *EEW*, 2(1). 262–7). Percy's first wife Mary Henrietta died eighteen years ago, leaving in Percy's care a daughter Mary, sequestered in his country estate *Percy Hall, but now to be introduced into *Verdopolis society. The plan is interrupted by the dissolution of parliament, Percy's activities in trying to get his associates elected, and the description of the election campaign. In the process, Sir Robert Weaver *Pelham is introduced and becomes one of Percy's candidates and Mary's fiancé. Pelham is elected and the narrative

(*cont. on page 385*)

CHARLOTTE's extant English poems number more than 200, not counting the many drafts and trial lines. By the time she wrote to Robert *Southey on 29 December 1836 asking for his opinion of her poetic talents and telling him of her ardent desire 'to be for ever known' as a poetess, she had written well over a hundred. Most concerned the *Glass Town and Angrian saga, and the earliest (24 July–9 December 1829) were written for Charlotte and Branwell's 'Blackwood's Young Men's Magazine', attributed to *'UT' or 'WT' ('Us Two' or 'We Two'), 'CB' or 'Charlotte Bronte'. ('Interior of a Pothouse by Young Soult' (Neufeldt CBP, p. 5) is probably by Branwell Brontë.) Of these short lyrics, all except the last ('Harvest in Spain') were in rhyming quatrains. From 1830 onwards short pieces were interspersed with immensely long poems, and were attributed either to Charlotte or her fictional characters or to both: thus the 276 lines of 'The Evening Walk' of 28 June 1830 are by 'Marquis of Douro C. Brontë'. 'Miss Hume's Dream' (29 June 1830) is by 'Islander lord C Wellesley', and 'Song' ('Some love sorrows', 27 Aug. 1830) is by Charles Wellesley. The most frequent 'signature' in 1830 is that of Douro (Duke of *Zamorna). Charlotte soon began to experiment with a variety of styles, metres, and forms, including dramatic monologues and verse dramas. An untitled scene in 181 lines of formal blank verse (Neufeldt CBP, p. 79; Dec. 1830) is a tense encounter between Lady Zenobia *Ellrington, Marian *Hume, and Lord Arthur (Zamorna), imagined as taking place on a stage. Other poems written before the end of 1836 are rhetorical or meditative speeches by Angrian characters. Zamorna gives a bravura display of Byronic angst and defiance as he recounts the enacting of the 'mutual doom' between himself and his father-in-law and enemy the Duke of *Northangerland, in 576 lines in the Don Juan stanza form (19 July 1836). Charlotte also produced several songs, in styles appropriate to their singers, like the roistering 'Let us drive care away' of May 1833: twelve lines sung by 'a group . . . partying at Lord Caversham's mill' (Neufeldt CBP, p. 109). In contrast, she wrote romantic, non-Angrian minstrel-like songs, probably inspired by Sir Walter *Scott, for King Richard and Blondel (27 Dec. 1833; Neufeldt CBP, p. 124), and a heroic, bombastic 'National Ode for the Angrians', in doggerel metre, grandly attributed to 'Arthur Augustus Adrian Wellesley | July 17th 1834 C Bronte' (Neufeldt CBP, p. 151).

Charlotte's first intensive period of verse-writing was from July 1829 to the end of 1830, when she wrote 64 poems and an amusing play, 'The *Poetaster', a lively allusive satire on Branwell's literary pretensions. She also made an astonishingly competent *'Translation into English Verse of the First Book of M. Voltaire's Henriade', completed 11 August 1830. Between January 1831 and May 1832 she wrote only three poems, all of them while she was on holiday from *Roe Head; 1833–4 witnessed a great surge in her poetic activity, inspired by the newly created kingdom of Angria, and centring on Zamorna, Marian, Mary *Percy, and Northangerland. Only four of the 33 poems (2,200 lines in total) do not relate to Angria. The three poems written in 1835 include the seminal poem on the Brontës' childhood vision, *'We wove a web in childhood' (19 Dec. 1835). January 1836 was a triumphantly productive month, when Charlotte wrote six poems, including another significant visionary poem, 'Long since as I remember well'—432 lines concluding with a farewell stanza, 'Dreamer awake', and a further 322 lines of vivid Angrian reverie, beginning 'But once again, but once again | I'll bid the strings awake' (Neufeldt *CBP*, pp. 171, 184) (see ROE HEAD JOURNAL, THE). The short spring holiday from Roe Head allowed her to write three poems, the first being a light-hearted song, 'I've a free hand and a merry heart'. In the July holiday Charlotte composed the long Byronic poem, 'And when you left me' (Neufeldt *CBP*, p. 194). A haunting three-stanza poem followed in October 1836, when Charlotte 'dived' into the depth of her thoughts, into what seemed a 'vast realm of death' (Neufeldt *CBP*, p. 209).

We do not know which of her poems Charlotte sent to Southey; but they convinced him that she possessed 'in no inconsiderable degree . . . the faculty of verse'. Though he advised her not to versify 'with a view to distinction', he did not forbid her to write; and 1837 proved to be a prolific year. She continued to write verse both before and after receiving his letter of 12 March 1837, putting her teaching duties first, but delighting to indulge her muse when she was at leisure. She completed a long poem of 439 lines by 9 January 1837, and 48 further poems by the end of January 1838, fifteen of which she thought worthy of revising for publication alongside her sisters' work in *Poems* 1846. Some of these were Angrian, but capable of transformation into 'public' poems; others were already accessible. The year 1838 was difficult for her. She suffered from acute depression in the spring, and had to go home to recuperate: all but one of her poems that year were Angrian, written either in the January or June–July holidays. Only six poems survive from 1839 until February 1842, at which time she and Emily went to Brussels. It is possible that the undated poem 'On its bending stalk' (Neufeldt *CBP*, p. 272) refers to Martha *Taylor's death on 12 October 1842. In 1843, when she was alone in Brussels, Charlotte copied revised versions of earlier poems into an exercise book: 'Parting' and 'Life' were both eventually published in 1846; and the first part of 'Gilbert', with its garden 'in a city-heart', was probably written in 1843. She also translated French and German verses into English, and German and English verses into French (see NOTEBOOKS (CAHIERS)). No poems survive from 1844, and only five from 1845. Two of them use aspects of her experience in Brussels: 'At first I did attention give', where the pupil's rival alienates the master and wins his love for herself (the first part of this poem was to be adapted for use in *Jane Eyre*) and a draft of the related poem 'I gave, at first, attention close' (Neufeldt *CBP*, pp. 274, 276). From the autumn of 1845 until January 1846 she was probably revising existing poems for publication in the sisters' *Poems* 1846. In that year also she revised 'I gave at first, Attention close' for *The Professor*. It is an adaptation of her experience as the pupil of M. Constantin *Heger, with a wish-fulfilment ending in which the master holds his pupil fast before letting her cross the sea, and bids her 'when deceived, repulsed, opprest, | come home to me again!'. Of the five poems written or revised in 1847, two were used in *Jane Eyre*: 'My feet they are sore' and 'The truest love'. An intensely bitter poem, 'He saw my heart's woe discovered my soul's anguish', probably written in December 1847, conveys Charlotte's sense of betrayal and despair when Heger failed to respond to her pleas for continuing friendship and correspondence. She prays that heaven will 'heal the wound'. In December 1848 her grief for Emily was expressed in the fragment 'Not many years', and *'My darling, thou wilt never know'. The tragedy of Anne's death in 1849 was conveyed in Charlotte's last surviving poem, *'There's little joy in life for me'.

The manuscripts of the Brontës' poems are widely scattered, largely owing to the unscrupulous activities of T. J. *Wise, who not only sold them to many different purchasers in Britain and the USA, but separated the leaves of single poems, and of drafts of the same poem. In his bibliographies he sometimes attributed material to the wrong author, or omitted it altogether. Victor Neufeldt lists the following locations in his manuscript-based edition of Charlotte's poems (1985): Library of Roger W. Barrett, Chicago; Beinecke, Yale; Berg, NYPL; BL; BPM; Brotherton; University Library, State University of New York at Buffalo; Houghton, Harvard; Huntington; University of Missouri Library, Columbia; Pforzheimer NYPL; Pierpont Morgan; Ransom HRC, Texas; Library of William Self; Taylor, Princeton; Wellesley College; and the now inaccessible *Law Collection, part of which was transcribed by Davidson Cook, whose copies can be seen at the BPM, as can copies by C. W. Hatfield of other poems. A manuscript poem allegedly by Charlotte, 'This is Thy Natal Day' (Neufeldt *CBP*, p. 333), is likely to be a forgery. Most of the manuscripts are in minuscule script, in either pencil or ink, often difficult to read, sometimes much revised—providing for example two or more uncancelled variant readings of words, phrases, or lines. Thus in 'A Traveller's Meditations' (Bonnell BPM MS 86; Neufeldt *CBP*, p. 57) the editor must decide whether to read 'checked' or 'created' in line 26, 'night' or 'might' in line 41, 'towers' or 'lowers' in line 45; in addition Charlotte may or may not have deleted incomplete words in lines 2 and 37, and she seems to have written 'thought' by mistake for 'though' in line 69.

Though Charlotte disparaged her poems in a letter to Elizabeth Gaskell of 26 September 1850 as 'chiefly juvenile productions; the restless effervescence of a mind that would not be still' (Smith *Letters*, 2. 475), they remain of great interest as evidence of her precocious and adventurous manipulation and love of words, her developing ability to express emotion, her fascination with exotic characters and scenery, and her absorption of the techniques, images, and vocabulary of the poets whose work excited her. Her early Glass Town poems can be highly descriptive and romantic, evoking picturesque landscape, or high-flown in their grandiose appeals to liberty and patriotism, or (occasionally) agreeably self-mocking. She is fascinated by light, and plays endless variations on its brilliance, splendour, glory, sparkle, glow, or glitter—often recalling the palaces and landscapes in James *Ridley's *Tales of the Genii*, or in the *Arabian Nights*. She has read Sir Walter *Scott and *Milton too, and in some poems echoes both the words and metre of *L'Allegro* and *Il Penseroso*; she loves Miltonic words like 'harbinger', 'ebon', 'conglob'd', 'darkling', 'tenebrious' [*sic*] and uses them often to elevate her style. By December 1830 she has read *Comus*, and her verse drama, ''Tis eve; how that rich sunlight streameth', recalls the Lady's opening soliloquy in that poem. Thomson and Gray are other exemplars in her evocation of forest and twilight. *Byron is one of her masters in style, metre, tone, and topic—not least when she describes the ocean she had never seen in real life—though again it is Milton's phrase, the ocean 'swinging slow with sullen roar', which reverberates most often. By 1831 she had probably read Samuel Taylor *Coleridge's *The Ancient Mariner* and *Wordsworth's early poems, and there are Keatsian echoes in the remarkable blank verse poem of 9 December 1829, 'Harvest in Spain', and in the 'Lines written beside a fountain' of 7 October 1833. Thomas *Moore's influence is detectable in her songs—see, for example, the 'Seranade' of June 1833—and in some of her oriental touches. *Shakespeare's *A Midsummer Night's*

Dream, known to her at an early date, is recalled in some of the fairy scenes in her descriptive poems. Thus there is almost always a rich verbal texture in her poems; but her control of their style and structure is often insecure, except when she fair-copies or revises them. Her long, unrevised poems meander rather than progress; her shorter ones may switch disconcertingly, though sometimes entertainingly, from one approach to another. Thus in March 1834 'Gods of the old Mythology' suddenly tires of its ornamental description of the deities and turns to mockery: 'And my lyre like a sparrow with a sore throat has a most unearthly tone' (Neufeldt *CBP*, p. 131). But 'Richard Cœur de Lion and Blondel' (Neufeldt *CBP*, p. 124) in her 'public' volume of poems is competently structured, and trial lines for 'The moon dawned slow on the dusky gloaming' (p. 128) show how effectively Charlotte could improve the phrasing and metre of such Angrian poems. Comparison of the draft and final versions of the poems used in the 1846 collection reveals much tactful pruning and reshaping: see, for example, the three versions of 'Mementos' (Neufeldt *CBP*, p. 316). The eloquent dramatic monologue 'Pilate's Wife's Dream' in *Poems* 1846 may also have been improved by revision, though no more than a fragment of an early draft survives. Other poems of special interest are 'The cloud of recent death' (see LINES ON THE CELEBRATED BEWICK); *'The room is quiet'; *'There's no use in weeping'; and Charlotte's contribution to Emily's 'Silent is the house' (see 'JULIAN M. AND A. G. ROCHELLE').

Barker, Juliet R. V. (ed.), *The Brontës: Selected Poems* (1985).
Chitham, Edward, and Winnifrith, Tom (eds.), *Selected Brontë Poems* (1985).
Neufeldt *CBP*.

closes with the description of a party at which Mary is introduced into society. Also appearing for the first time in Branwell's work is Quashia *Quamina, leader of the Ashantees, who threaten Verdopolis and Angria, and who will aid Percy in his insurrection in Angria and the French invasion of Angria.   VN

Alexander & Sellars, p. 305 (illustrations).
Neufeldt *BB Works*, 1. 333–64.

Ponden House (often referred to as 'Ponden Hall'), Stanbury, home of the *Heaton family from 1513. Rebuilt in 1801 (as the date above the lintel declares; cf. also the date at the beginning of *Wuthering Heights*), it was often a stopping place for the Brontës on their walks. The Brontë children took shelter there in 1824 during the dramatic eruption of bog on the moor at Crow Hill. Robert Heaton, one of the trustees of the church lands at Haworth, had nominated Revd Patrick Brontë to the cure of Haworth. The families were on good terms and it is likely that the Brontës occasionally borrowed books from the substantial library at Ponden House. Many of the books cited by the Brontës in their early writings were in the Ponden House collection that was eventually sold to an American library in 1899: for example, Samuel Johnson's *Lives of the Poets*, Gilbert White's *Natural History of Selborne*, Pope's translation of the *Iliad*, and even a first folio of *Shakespeare (see *Catalogue of Books Contained in the Library of Ponden Hall* (Keighley, William Weatherhead, [1899]), in BPM). Recent critics such as Barker (p. 148) have questioned the use of this library by the Brontës, but there are few local sources from which the 12-year-old Branwell would have gained a working knowledge of the vicomte de Chateaubriand's *Travels in Greece, Palestine, Egypt, and Barbary* (1812). John Hewish points out that Emily's 'occult knowledge of property law in *Wuthering Heights*' could have been derived from Ponden House law books, written for laymen, such as Runnington's *Ejectment* and Lovelass's *The Laws Disposing of a Person's Estate* (*Emily Brontë: A Critical and Biographical Study* (1969), 35). Ponden House is thought to have inspired aspects of *Thrushcross Grange in *Wuthering Heights* (see, for example, Gérin *EB*, pp. 31–2).

Ponden House (Hall) should not be confused with 'Ponden Old Hall' built later in 1634; this Heaton dwelling, opposite Ponden House, was neglected in the Brontës' time and has recently been rebuilt from ruins as a modern stone house. Early pen-and-ink sketches of both dwellings can be found in Whiteley Turner, *A Spring-Time Saunter* (1913). They are situated a mile and a half from Stanbury and a further mile from Haworth. The
(*cont. on page 393*)

W RITING poetry was an intensely personal experience for Emily Brontë. The dramatic urgency she expressed in lyric and ballad form suggests a restless search for self and 'a world elsewhere' that she would have preferred to have remained a secret, even from her family. In the late summer of 1845, Anne records in her *Diary Papers her awareness of Emily's poetry but she has not dared to ask Emily about its content. Charlotte's discovery the following autumn of 'a MS. volume of verse in my sister Emily's handwriting' (Smith *Letters*, 1. 446) violated Emily's fierce sense of privacy. Charlotte tells of her efforts to placate Emily's anger and to persuade her 'that such poems merited publication'. The result was the joint publication of *Poems* 1846, which included the 21 poems Emily published during her lifetime. Despite Emily's own public contempt for her 'rhymes' (as she called them; Smith *Letters*, 2. 119), Charlotte's conviction of their 'sterling excellence' has stood the test of time. A number of Emily's poems are regarded among the finest written in the 19th century, and she is usually ranked with Elizabeth Barrett Browning, Christina Rossetti, and Emily Dickinson as one of the pre-eminent women poets of the period.

There are about 200 known poems and fragments by Emily Brontë, of which approximately 168 exist in manuscript. Almost all these belong to the pre-*Wuthering Heights* period of 1836 to 1845. Her earliest dated poem is 12 July 1836 ('Will the day be bright or cloudy?') and her last poems were written in 1846 and 1848: *'No coward soul is mine'; and two versions of 'Why ask to know the date—the clime?' (Roper *EBP*, pp. 31, 183–93). One poem, 'Stanzas', beginning *'Often rebuked, yet always back returning', is of uncertain authorship, although Charlotte included it with the seventeen poems by Emily that she published in her selection of 'Literary Remains' that accompanied her 1850 edition of 'Wuthering Heights' and 'Agnes Grey'. Charlotte substantially revised and retitled most of these poems and editors now print Emily's version from her manuscript (except in the case of 'Often rebuked'). Charlotte made it clear in her prefatory note to 'Selections from the Poems by Ellis Bell' that 'It would not have been difficult to compile a volume out of the papers left by my sisters', and she spoke of having 'culled from the mass only a little poem here and there'. This indicates a substantial output, and, although it is possible that Charlotte may have thrown away many of the prose manuscripts, scholars now generally agree with Edward Chitham's view that her 'cull' did not include destruction of the poems (Chitham *ABP*, pp. 26–8): it appears that we still have most of the poetry that Charlotte perused after Emily's death.

The poetry manuscripts fall into three major groups: the Ashley Notebook, a fair copy of poems written between August 1837 and October 1839; the Gondal Notebook that Emily headed 'Gondal Poems'; and the E.J.B. Notebook (signed 'E.J.B'), often referred to as the 'Honresfeld MS' since it is part of the *Law Collection. The Gondal and E.J.B. notebooks both date from 1844. The Ashley and Gondal notebooks are available to scholars in the BL. Other repositories of manuscript poems and fragments include Bonnell, BPM; Bonnell, Pierpont Morgan; Berg, NYPL; Ransom HRC, Texas; Taylor, Princeton (see MANUSCRIPTS AND MANUSCRIPT COLLECTIONS). With the exception of the Ashley Notebook, which is in longhand, all Emily's poetry is written in her minuscule hand. Most of her poems are untitled, except for the titled poems she published in 1846, and the titles Charlotte allotted in her 1850 edition remain in common use (such as 'The *Visionary' and 'The Two Children'). At the head of many untitled and some titled poems appear the names and initials of speakers, the dramatis personae of Gondal. Many poems also have composition dates attached and six poems contain Gondal dates indicating a separate earlier chronology for the saga (Roper *EBP*, p. 303).

Well over half (and possibly all) of Emily's poetry was conceived within the frame of her imaginative world of Gondal. Since no related prose evidence survives (apart from the Diary Papers), Emily's poetry represents the most complete record we have of the *Gondal saga. The controversial division of her poems into 'personal' and 'Gondal' categories (a division thought to have been suggested by Emily herself when she named one of her manuscript notebooks 'Gondal Poems') has largely shaped their critical reception, not always with constructive results. It is an issue, however, central to any discussion of Emily's poetry. Since about 1941, when Fannie Ratchford first proposed her 'reconstruction' of the Gondal saga from Emily's surviving poetry and diary fragments in *The Brontës' Web of Childhood*, critics have stressed the importance of a distinction between Emily's Gondal and non-Gondal poetry, arguing that the latter is inherently superior because it represents a genuine personal statement.

In *Gondal's Queen* (1955), Ratchford arranged all Emily's poetry as an epic—'the life story of A.G.A., from dramatic birth, through tempestuous life, to tragic death' (p. 27)—to show Gondal's prefiguring of *Wuthering Heights*. This purely Gondal reading of Emily Brontë's poems appeared to reduce their significance for many readers, confining them within a self-indulgent childhood fantasy world. Derek Stanford, for example, condemned Emily's Gondal verse as 'Byronic melodrama' and 'pseudo-martial rubbish' (Spark and Stanford, *Emily Brontë: Her Life and Work* (1953), 143–4). Such critics felt the need to clearly divide Emily's poetry into Gondal and non-Gondal categories, and so rescue some of the poems as personal romantic statements. However, the reading of any of the poems as autobiography is fraught with its own dangers of misinterpretation. 'No coward soul is mine', for example, was retrieved from its civil war context in *Gondal's Queen*, and reinstated as one of Emily Brontë's most personal statements. Many critics today still feel that all her best poems 'seem to stand better without Gondal references' (Chitham, Edward, and Winnifrith, Tom (eds.), *Selected Brontë Poems* (1985), 25).

Emily herself had suggested the division of her work when, in February 1844, she began copying her poems into two notebooks, one without a heading, but initialled 'E.J.B.' (E.J.B. Notebook) and the other headed 'Gondal Poems' (Gondal Notebook). In the Gondal Notebook the verse appears to follow a chronology and to be grouped around certain characters, whereas the E.J.B. Notebook includes essentially personal lyrics with no specific Gondal references. From 1844 on, Emily added new poems to each notebook, ostensibly making a distinction between Gondal and non-Gondal verse although this is by no means clear. She continued her transcriptions until 13 May 1848, showing a continuing interest in Gondal right through the publication of *Poems* in 1846 and *Wuthering Heights* in 1847. When she came to select poems for publication in 1846, after Charlotte's dramatic discovery of one of her manuscript notebooks, she chose fifteen poems from the E.J.B. Notebook and six from the Gondal Notebook, removing any obvious references to her epic world.

Emily Brontë's third surviving notebook of poems, known as the Ashley MS, including sixteen early poems, contains both 'personal' and Gondal poetry. One poem in particular ('O Dream, where art thou now?') was transcribed without change into the E.J.B. Notebook and four others were copied into the Gondal Notebook ('Lord of Elbë, on Elbë hill', 'O wander not so far away!', 'To the Blue Bell', and 'From our evening fireside now'). If we agree that Emily Brontë only began to categorize her work after 1844, then at least some of the poems we see as personal lyrics seem to have had Gondal origins or at the very least were undistinguished from them in Emily's mind. Furthermore, the easy conversion of six Gondal poems into personal lyrics for publication in 1846 suggests a more unified vision for all Emily Brontë's poetry.

Apart from their odd references to Gondal persons, places, and episodes, most of the poems in the Gondal Notebook are lyrics, similar to those in the E.J.B. Notebook. In some cases, the simple removal of a Gondal heading is all that would be required to place a Gondal Notebook poem with those of the E.J.B. Notebook. This is exactly what Emily did for the 1846 publication of *Poems* when she 'deGondalized' such poems as 'Song' (beginning 'The linnet in the rocky dells') by removing the initials of the speaker. Nor is it hard to imagine that many of the poems classified as 'personal' might have originally been spoken by Gondal characters, whose views reflect those of their creator (*'Shall Earth no more inspire thee', for example); certainly a number of these personal poems either discuss the source of Emily's imaginative experience ('Alone I sat' and 'I'll come when thou art saddest') or directly address her 'God of Visions' (as in *'To Imagination' or 'Plead for Me').

Several recent critics endorse this view that a distinction between Gondal and non-Gondal poems is not clear-cut or even necessary for an appreciation of Emily's oeuvre. Derek Roper, in particular, shows most convincingly that by discarding the assumption that poems in the E.J.B. Notebook must relate directly to Emily's own experience and by comparing poems of similar date in the Gondal Notebook, four poems in the E.J.B. Notebook (that describe a love affair and have therefore led to a variety of speculation about both the identity and nature of Emily Brontë's supposed lover) are actually closely related to several poems in the Gondal Notebook ('Emily Brontë's Lover', *BST* (1993), 21. 1 & 2. 25–31). When Roper's method is applied to other poems in the E.J.B. Notebook they begin to be less enigmatic. 'Well some may hate and some may scorn', for example, need not refer specifically to a dead person in Emily Brontë's experience. Such poems can be seen as dramatic lyrics, spoken by imagined characters at particular moments in time. The situations they spring from may derive from Gondal or some other imaginative experience, with which Emily is able to identify. Derek Roper stresses that the value of these poems 'does not lie in Emily's mining of her own depths, but in the way they express and explore powerfully imagined situations'.

Lyn Pykett, while still maintaining the Gondal and non-Gondal division, sees a common theme at the heart of all Emily Brontë's poetry, the desire for 'a unified sense of the self, together with a simultaneous awareness and fear of the self's diffusion and fragmentation' (*Emily Brontë* (1989), 66). It is certainly more constructive to view Emily's poetry as the product of a single imaginative source. Distinctions between the dramatic personae of the Gondal poems and the lyric 'I' of the so-called non-Gondal verse are blurred in the varied voices through which Emily was able to explore particular imaginative situations and to articulate both her characters' and her own concerns.

Emily's poetry is essentially dramatic. There is an urgency in the lyric voice and narrative ballads that moves the listener on. Her poetry is activated by dramatic confrontations between characters or between points of view or conflicting emotions. 'The Philosopher', for example, is a dialogue between a 'seer' and a philosopher who has failed to reconcile his internal conflict through visionary transcendence. The seer's description of the unifying vision the philosopher has failed to experience, raises the cry of the philosopher to a pitch of agony as he stretches his hands towards oblivion to end his 'cruel strife'. In 'The Night-Wind' two voices oppose each other in alternate stanzas: the night-wind trying to persuade the poet to surrender to the sensuous music of nature. *'Julian M. and A. G. Rochelle' (which includes 'The Prisoner') is typical of Emily's Gondal poems dramatically situated in dungeons that symbolize the living death of the speaker. This long ballad has a complex narrative structure in which the speaker's present situation and story frame an earlier dramatic conversation, a technique Emily was to hone in *Wuthering Heights*.

Her monologues are not less dramatic. The lover Fernando de Samara, discarded by 'Gondal's Queen', cries out against his captor who will 'spare my life, to kill my mind' and, like Heathcliff, takes comfort in imagining that if there is a God A.G.A. will suffer a similar 'hell' ('Written in the Gaaldine Prison Caves to A.G.A.'). The insistent voice of the wind that speaks as a spirit of nature in 'Shall Earth no more inspire thee', confidently importunes the listener in a series of questions and short resolute statements:

> I've watched thee every hour—
> I know my mighty sway—
> I know my magic power
> To drive thy griefs away—

The staccato lines, present tense, repetition, regular rhyme and rhythm carry the urgency of the voice. So distinctive is Emily's method of representing internal conflicts dramatically as colloquies, that editors have been persuaded that separate fragmentary verses on the same manuscript page may constitute a complete poem, although their structure as speaker and respondent is not obvious (see Gezari *EBP*, p. 22). As Gezari points out, there is precedent for this in Emily's paired poems printed as one in 1850 by Charlotte and titled 'The Two Children' (p. 277). Here, a girl 'with sunbright hair' becomes the 'kindred kindness' of a 'melancholy boy' who anticipates Heathcliff. (See Chitham *Birth of WH*, pp. 53–4, for further information about Emily's poetic method, including the fascinating note that descriptions of weather and time of year in the poems are generally consistent with the manuscript date.)

The dialectical structure of the poems gives the constant impression of movement and adds to the musical quality for which Emily's poetry is known. When Charlotte first read her sister's poems, she thought them 'condensed and terse, vigorous and genuine', and noted: 'To my ear, they had also a peculiar music—wild, melancholy, and elevating' ('Biographical Notice', in *Wuthering Heights* (Clarendon edn.), app. 1, pp. 435–6). The beautiful elegy, 'The linnet in the rocky dells', spoken by the faithful Captain of the Guards over the grave of the murdered Augusta, Queen of Gondal, expresses in the simplicity of its language both a deep grief and a sense of peace and harmony in nature after the violence of life. This has been seen as the culmination of Emily's early lyric achievement (up to 1844), a song that might have been set to music by Schubert (Barnard, *Emily Brontë* (2000), 62). Emily's skill as a talented musician (see MUSIC) is seen in her ability to express emotion in words and speech patterns. Critics have remarked on her awareness of the sound-values of words, shown in her use of alliteration and repetition, as in *'Remembrance'. Her regular rhythms are often very successful ('Remembrance' and 'Julian M. and A. G. Rochelle') although some critics argue that her fluency is a limiting feature of her poetry, unadventurous and reflecting the conventional ballad metres of Scott (Lloyd Evans, *Everyman Companion to the Brontës* (1985), 239). Critics also note the numerous banalities of cliché and bombastic outbursts of Gondal characters. 'Far, far away', for example, has all the lurid melodrama of a John Martin painting. The lonely speaker calls on a 'shade' ('Deserted one! thy corpse lies cold | And mingled with a foreign mould—') to commune with her. As she recalls his image (identified as P. B. Shelley by Chitham *EB*, pp. 132–4), the speaker assumes the sorrow of his 'blighted name' and his tears that 'deluge my heart like the rain | On cursed Gomorrah's howling plain—'.

Although not always convincing, the invented characters and situations enabled Emily to return repeatedly to themes that preoccupied her: mutability in nature and time, isolation, exile, and death. Poems express the vitality of the natural world ('High waving heather 'neath stormy blasts bending'), its cyclic continuity ('Death that struck While I was most confiding'), sometimes its destructive changefulness ('A Day Dream'), and often its Wordsworthian role as a source of vision ('A little while, a little while'; 'Shall Earth no more inspire thee'). In 'I see around me tombstones grey', the speaker's heaven is the earth, where at death we share with nature 'A mutual immortality'. Again, in 'Shall Earth no more inspire thee', conventional views of heaven are rejected in favour of a heaven as near as possible to 'this Earth'. In this poem Nature calls the poet away from the 'fond idolatry' of her visionary world.

Emily's personification of imagination as a visitant 'God of Visions' ('Julian M. and A. G. Rochelle'), a 'Benignant Power' heralded by the west wind that brings life not only to the defeated or imprisoned Gondal recipients but also to the poet, is the subject of many of her poems. Most famous is the recurring visionary experience of the prisoner in 'Julian M. and A. G. Rochelle' where 'a messenger of Hope' brings relief from a 'living grave'. In 'I'm happiest when most away', the speaker exults in the release of 'my soul from its home of clay' and her ability to become 'only spirit wandering wide | Through infinite immensity'. In pantheistic mode, the wind in 'Aye there it is! It wakes tonight' kindles a spirit that infuses all:

> A universal influence
> From Thine own influence free—
> A principle of life intense
> Lost to mortality—

Such liberation from mortal existence prefigures death itself, when 'Thy prisoned soul shall rise'. This foretaste of death and the afterlife embodies an experience that was particularly important to Emily herself and her ability to convey it is one of her great achievements as a poet. Margaret Homans (*Women Writers and Poetic Identity* (1980), 124) suggests, however, that the transcendence achieved in such poems is at the expense of the annihilation of the self, either in death or by yielding to an external visionary source, whereas for male poets such transcendence would be achieved through the intensification of subjectivity, an affirmation of the self. She sees this as one of the problems for a woman poet if she chooses, like Emily, to speak from within a Romantic discourse. Thus Emily's many explorations of visionary possession imply that she was 'self-consciously developing a myth of the imagination' (p. 109) in order to negotiate her role as poet.

When Emily first conceived of herself as a poet, it is impossible to say. Her early habit of keeping her personal views close to her breast and her poetry secret even from Anne, and her later tenacious defence of her personal space, suggest that she may have thought of herself as a poet from at least her teenage years. In 1835, Branwell satirized the 16-year-old Emily's view that 'to seek true poetry it is necessary to shut oneself out from Humanity from the stir and bustle of the world from the commonplace weari-someness of its joys sorrows and greatnesses to look in solitude into one's own soul and conjure up there some visionary form alien from this worlds fears or sympathies' [sic] (Neufeldt BB Works, 2. 149). The subsequent pattern of Emily's poetic practice and the conscious ordering of her life to reflect this 'manifesto', suggests that it is an accurate representation of an opinion she deliberately sought to follow.

She read both contemporary and early English poets, and the Bible. Her poems show evidence especially of Sir Walter *Scott's medieval romances, *Milton's Paradise Lost, *Byron's lyrics and narrative tales, *Wordsworth's nature poetry, Samuel Taylor *Coleridge's use of the supernatural, *Shelley's pantheism, Keats's attitude to death, the poetry and thought of Blake (see Gezari EBP, p. 277), and writers who contributed to *Blackwood's Edinburgh Magazine, such as David *Moir and James *Hogg. When possible, she extended her knowledge of the works of European and Classical figures like *Hoffmann, Goethe, Horace, *Virgil, and Epictetus (see 'OLD STOIC, THE'). There is evidence that at the age of 20 she was learning Latin in order to read Horace in the original and the text she chose (Ars Poetica) indicates a special interest in the nature of poetry and the role of the poet. Edward Chitham believes that it is from this date (1838) that Emily became seriously interested in poetry (Chitham Birth of WH, pp. 27–32). Her earliest notebook collection of poems (the Ashley MS) dates from late 1839 (Roper EBP, p. 17). This and her later revision and transcription of poems (beginning 1844) into the two fair-copy volumes suggests at least an intention to preserve her work. It is possible that she may have had publication in mind well before Charlotte suggested the issue, which Emily with her usual perverseness may have felt obliged initially to reject. Once she had agreed, Emily set about revising and titling her poems as diligently as her sisters for publication (see POEMS BY CURRER, ELLIS, AND ACTON BELL, 1846). See also HATFIELD, C. W.

Barker (ed.), The Brontës: Selected Poems (1985).
Gezari EBP.
Hatfield EBP.
Homans, Margaret, Women Writers and Poetic Identity: Dorothy Wordsworth, Emily Brontë, and Emily Dickinson (1980).
Poems 1846.
Peeck-O'Toole, M., Aspects of Lyric in the Poetry of Emily Brontë (Amsterdam, 1988).
Pykett, Lyn, Emily Brontë (1989).
Roper EBP.
Smith, Anne (ed.), The Art of Emily Brontë (1976).

R EVD Patrick Brontë published three small volumes of verse, several short poems associated with his two prose tales, and a quantity of occasional verse. *Winter Evening Thoughts: A Miscellaneous Poem* (London and Wakefield, 1810), written in response to the Day of National Humiliation for the war against France appointed for 28 February 1810, appeared anonymously while he was a curate in Dewsbury. He thought well enough of it to send a copy inscribed 'By P. Brontë. B.A.' to his evangelical friend Revd John Nunn, who would sympathize with his aim so to mingle 'the *Profitable* and *Agreeable*' that he might 'reclaim but *one*, from the error of his ways'. He adapted his poem, retitled 'Winter-night Meditations', for inclusion in *Cottage Poems* (Halifax, 1811), published under his own name as 'Minister of *Hartshead-cum-Clifton'. The twelve poems in this collection reflect Mr Brontë's friendship with Revd John *Buckworth. The somewhat fulsome good wishes for Buckworth's health in the opening poem are combined with a didactic emphasis on the Christian's pilgrimage along the 'short, but narrow way' to 'realms of endless day'. All the poems are designed to instruct. As he explains in his 'Advertisement', he intermingles moralizing 'chiefly designed for the lower classes of society' with poems for 'readers of a different description' for variety's sake, and so as to 'shew to all, that he, who would be truly happy, must be truly religious'. A more ambitious volume followed, with the same ascription: *The *Rural Minstrel: A Miscellany of Descriptive Poems* (Halifax, 1813). Aiming once again both to please and profit, Mr Brontë regards it as his duty to employ God-given poetical talents 'to promote the best interests of mankind' and so to counteract the insidious extension of the devil's empire—for 'the vigilant enemy of souls' has used poets to corrupt men through their pleasure in verse. In their mingling of natural description, meditation, and homily, the verses are closely akin to the 18th-century genre of moralized nature poems, especially those of *Goldsmith, Thomson, Gray, Collins, *Cowper, and the 'Graveyard' poets Blair and Edward Young, whose lineage can be traced back, in part, to the shorter poems of *Milton. There are echoes too of Wesleyan and other evangelical hymns. Four poems are appended to Patrick's prose tale *The *Cottage in the Wood* (Bradford, 1815): 'The *Pious Cottager's Sabbath', 'The *Nightly Revel', and epitaphs on two characters in the prose story, Mary and William Bower. He used songs to enhance the romantic aura of his heroine and the pathos of the distracted maiden, 'poor Ellen', in *The *Maid of Killarney; or, Albion and Flora: A Modern Tale; in which are interwoven some cursory remarks on Religion and Politics* (London, 1818). Possibly he knew that Sir Walter Scott used such songs in his Waverley novels; and he might recall Goldsmith's 'ballad' 'Turn, gentle Hermit of the dale', in *The Vicar of Wakefield* (1766). On 12 September 1821 the terrifying bog-burst, landslip, and flooding on the moor at Crow Hill, 4 miles from the Parsonage, caused him intense anxiety, for his three younger children were out walking with their nurse Sarah Garrs. Hearing the explosion, he set out to look for them, and found them hiding terrified under Sarah's cloak in a porch. He regarded the event as an earthquake, for it caused a 7-foot-high torrent of mud, peat, and water. Letters to the *Leeds Intelligencer*, the *Leeds Mercury*, a sermon, and a poem, testified to his awed belief that God had sent the eruption as a warning to a guilty world to repent of its evil ways and join those of 'pious heart' in the paths of virtue leading to heaven, where 'seraphic choirs' sing God's praise with 'sweet, triumphal, loud, immortal sound!' The poem *The Phenomenon* (Bradford, 1824) was 'Intended as a Reward Book for the Higher Classes in Sunday Schools'. It is an ornate set-piece, designed to impress its readers with its edifying message, which transforms the moors into plains and hills, the wind into an incumbent blast, and the 'sportive fishes' of the opening lines into 'The finny tribe' which sink in 'muddy suffocation'. Nevertheless it retains some of the reality of the local scene in, for example, the 'crackling moorcock' flying over the common, and the 'deep-mouth'd oaths and jests' of the 'sturdy swains' striding on to their 'employ' before the eruption. Mr Brontë's occasional verses include his 'Church Reform' concerning the ejection of the village housewives from the churchyard where they had dried their garments on wash days, and his kindly meant pious words of wisdom in Miss Thomas's album, 'composed hastily, and off hand—but they may serve as a kind memento' (see Lock & Dixon, pp. 365, 343–4).

Mr Brontë's more deliberately crafted poems exemplify the neoclassical principles advocated by Samuel *Johnson: 'The business of a poet' says Imlac in *Rasselas*, 'is to examine, not the individual, but the species; to remark general properties and large appearances'. Thus in Mr Brontë's poems most people are types: the pious cottager, the virtuous maiden, and the devout pastor, contrasted with the rich man corrupted by idleness, the city prostitute, and the foppish, affected preacher. In the domestic and natural world, the cottager has a neat 'humble cot', and lives by his rustic labour while his womenfolk spin or weave, or a 'wretched shed' and naked babes. Outside run tinkling brooks or purling rills, not brawling becks; 'Luna's lovely rays' cast their light where 'Philomel' sings in umbrageous groves, the voice of 'Chanticleer' wakes the cottagers, and spreading plains are musical with poetic larks, linnets, and blackbirds. No crows or lapwings haunt unpoetic moors, though there are 'moorcock' in *The Phenomenon* and we hear of 'wild fowl, aloft on the gale, Loud gabbling and screaming' in a land of 'lakes, bogs, and marshes' in 'The Irish Cabin' in *Cottage Poems*. Mr Brontë disarmingly uses the trope of the 'rustic muse' striking 'uncouth strings' to explain that he tells his tale 'with awkward grace' in his 'Epistle' to John Buckworth. Unfortunately some of the metrical and stanzaic forms in *Cottage Poems* are distinctly uncouth in his hands, but his skill on the whole improves in *The Rural Minstrel* and the later poems.

Brontëana,
'Cottage Poems', rprt. in *The Life and Works of Charlotte Brontë and her Sisters* (Haworth edn., 1900) 4. 485–541.

name 'Ponden' derives from 'pond', a marshy pond, and 'dene', a narrow clough or cleft. In 1870, the Worth valley up to Ponden House was flooded to form Ponden reservoir, so changing the lower aspect of the valley as the Brontës knew it.

Ponden Kirk, a millstone grit landmark at the head of Ponden Clough, on the moors above *Stanbury; represented in *Wuthering Heights* as *Penistone Crags. There is a tradition that anyone passing through the tunnel in the Kirk (the 'Fairy cave' of the novel) will marry within the year. Hareton Earnshaw shows the younger Catherine

Linton 'the mysteries of the Fairy cave, and twenty other queer places' (*Wuthering Heights*, ch. 18).

Poole, Grace, in *Jane Eyre*. When Jane hears strange laughter at *Thornfield Hall, she is led to believe that it emanates from a servant, Grace Poole, allegedly employed to sew and assist with housework, but emerging for only one hour each day from her third-storey room. After Jane has rescued *Rochester from his burning bed, he implies that Grace was the culprit but does not dismiss her. Jane wonders if the staid, plain, coarse-faced servant has Rochester in her power after an earlier amour. She overhears a conversation about the high wages Grace receives for a mysterious and unenviable task. When Rochester reveals his mad wife after the interrupted wedding, Grace is revealed also as her keeper, helping him to restrain the violent Bertha. Later Rochester explains that he had hired Grace from the Grimsby Retreat to guard his wife. He plans to shut Thornfield, leaving Grace there with her son to help her, while he travels abroad with Jane. But after Jane's secret departure, Grace again succumbs to her one failing: drinking too much from her private bottle of gin. Bertha takes her keys, and starts the fire which destroys Thornfield.

Poor Laws. Under the 'old' Poor Law, dating from 1597 to 1601, each parish levied a poor rate and appointed overseers of the poor. Able-bodied poor had to work in the workhouse, 'sturdy beggars' were sent to the house of correction, the sick and aged were relieved in almshouses or their own homes, and children were apprenticed. Gilbert's Act of 1782 encouraged outdoor relief, and the Speenhamland system of 1795, by which relief was given in proportion to the price of corn and number of children in the family, meant that employers paid low wages, knowing they would be supplemented. Since the population was rapidly expanding, the burden on the parishes was great. The 1834 Poor Law report proposed relief only in workhouses, where the paupers' conditions should not be better than those of the lowest paid independent labourer. The resulting Poor Law Amendment Act provided for 600 unions of parishes, each with a Board of Guardians elected by ratepayers, and a London-based central administration. The rules of the new Union workhouses, with their spartan diet, hard labour, and separation of husbands from wives, aroused violent objections, especially in the industrial north. *The Times* (27 Feb. 1837) reported that so many people attended a meeting called by Revd Patrick Brontë to petition for repeal of the Act that they had to adjourn to the street instead of the church Sunday school. Mr Brontë inveighed against the Act as 'a nose-hewing, finger-lopping quack, a legal deformity'. Abraham Wildman, a Keighley Chartist, criticized the workhouse clothes 'which a respectable scarecrow might be ashamed to wear', the taskwork of 'grinding in "gangs!"' for 'slave masters', and the 'Lilliputian' diet. Other speakers, including Revd William *Hodgson, found the law unjust and contrary to the Scriptures. Branwell Brontë read and moved the petition, which was sent for presentation to both houses of Parliament.

Popplewell, Eliza, née Brown (1831–1901), sister of Martha *Brown. She probably helped at Haworth Parsonage in September 1849 and November 1850 when Martha was seriously ill. She was hired again from 1 February 1861 while Martha looked after Revd Patrick Brontë in his last illness, and she attended his funeral. After Martha's death Eliza received a share of her Brontë relics, including several drawings: Charlotte's 'Kirkstall Abbey' (10 Oct. 1832), Emily's 'St Simeon Stylites' (4 Mar. 1833), and Anne's 'Church surrounded by trees' (29 Aug. 1828) and 'Cottage with trees' (7 Apr. 1829), all now at BPM (see Alexander & Sellars, pp. 203, 375, 396; and for other items possibly owned by Eliza, pp. 278, 316).

'Portrait: King Harold before the Battle of Hastings' ('Portrait: Le Roi Harold avant la Bataille de Hastings'). *Devoir by Emily Brontë (June 1842; MS in Bonnell, BPM) that challenges conventional views of the king who lost to William the Conqueror in 1066. According to M. Constantin *Heger, she wrote it in response to his lecture on Victor *Hugo's 'portrait' of Mirabeau. Heger's lesson may also have stressed the transformation of a fallible man into a hero, since this is the theme that emerges here and in Charlotte's matching 'Portrait: Peter the Hermit' (23 June 1842; see DEVOIRS). Emily ignores the Anglo-Saxon defeat; she represents Harold, alone before the battle, as a ruler whom death alone can vanquish. Heger later gave Elizabeth *Gaskell a much-revised copy of the devoir (in Rylands), which she cited as superior to Charlotte's. Charlotte may later refer to it obliquely when she has Frances Evans Henri of *The Professor* write a devoir on King Alfred. SL

Chitham *Birth of WH*, pp. 62–4.
Lonoff, pp. 96–117.

'Portrait: Le Roi Harold avant la Bataille de Hastings'. See 'PORTRAIT: KING HAROLD BEFORE THE BATTLE OF HASTINGS'.

portraits by the Brontës. *See opposite page*

portraits of the Brontës. In their youth the Brontës drew self-portraits and portraits of each other, the two most famous being 'The *Brontë Sisters' and *'Emily Jane Brontë' by Branwell Brontë (see PORTRAITS BY THE BRONTËS). Apart from these amateur works, the only authenticated painting made of any of the sisters in their lifetime is the famous coloured chalk drawing of Charlotte (June 1850) by George Richmond (1809–96), the celebrated London society artist (NPG). The portrait was commissioned by George Smith as a gift for Revd Patrick Brontë, at a cost of 30 guineas, the same price charged by Richmond for Elizabeth *Gaskell's portrait the following year. Richmond was known for the softening and smoothing effect he gave to the sitter's face. A second copy was
(*cont. on page 397*)

CHARLOTTE Brontë told her publisher that there were no known likenesses of her sisters, yet both she and Branwell had made competent family portraits during their late adolescent years. The most famous are the two portraits by Branwell, which each tell their own story and are now in the National Portrait Gallery, London: 'The *Brontë Sisters' and *'Emily Jane Brontë'. Both were originally family group portraits made by the 17-year-old Branwell as practice for his profession as a portrait painter. When shown 'The Brontë Sisters' by Charlotte, Elizabeth Gaskell described it as a 'rough, common-looking thing', but acknowledged its likeness to Charlotte (Chapple & Pollard *Gaskell Letters*, p. 27). Tracings and an early photograph survive of the original second 'Gun Group' portrait that was destroyed by Revd A. B. *Nicholls after Charlotte's death. He preserved only the fragment showing Emily, as a good likeness, hence the title 'Emily Jane Brontë'.

We have a clearer idea of what Anne looked like as a young girl than we have of her sisters, since she appears to have been an obliging model. There are four drawings of Anne by Charlotte in both pencil and watercolour made between 1833 and 1835 (Alexander & Sellars, pp. 210–11, 230, 241); the delicate pencil portrait of Anne in profile (17 Apr. 1833) and the oval watercolour profile portrait (17 June 1834) have been reproduced many times. The images corroborate textual portraits such as Ellen Nussey's endearing description of Anne's 'very pretty light brown' hair and 'lovely violet blue eyes, fine pencilled eye-brows, and clear, almost transparent complexion' (Smith *Letters*, 1. 598). Anne herself seems to have preferred illustrating children, such as the watercolour of a child that she gave as a present to her employer's maid when she was a governess for the Robinsons (Alexander & Sellars, pp. 415–16, pl. xx). Several of her drawings may be of the adolescent Robinson girls, although it is possible that one may be a self-portrait, made from Anne's reflection in a mirror on 24 June 1842 (pp. 411–12). Emily preferred to paint her pets; she made only rough pen-and-ink sketches of herself and Anne in her *Diary Papers. There are two portrait copies from engravings by Emily, 'Woman's Head with Tiara' and 'The North Wind', both possibly associated with *Gondal (p. 384, pl. LIII, and pp. 325–6).

We know that Charlotte first intended to become an artist; her pictures of Anne and the many small, delicate, and often oval watercolours suggest that she thought of becoming a miniaturist. Her numerous exercises in drawing classical heads or portraits from engravings in *annuals or illustrations to Byron's poetry form a large part of her oeuvre. In October 1830 she copied a miniature of her deceased mother: both copy and original survive (BPM). There is a similar miniature by Charlotte that may be of her aunt Elizabeth *Branwell made about the same time. During the years 1837–9, Charlotte made several likenesses of schoolfriends and in February 1840 she drew her father's curate William Weightman, her most accomplished portrait (Alexander & Sellars, p. 255 and pl. XLIX).

Many portraits by Charlotte and Branwell of Glass Town and Angrian heroes and heroines, chiefly in pencil or pen and ink, show the close association of the visual and verbal in the imaginations of the Brontës. They illustrated the Dukes of *Zamorna and *Northangerland at various stages of their lives, and Charlotte in particular drew an array of beauties to partner them. One Angrian poet is actually copied from an

Branwell Brontë's self-portrait, c.1840.

engraving of Byron from the *Literary* *Souvenir*, and there are drawings of heroines based on portraits of Byron's friends like the Countess of *Blessington and the Countess of Jersey.

The most important and professional portraits, as one would expect, are those by Branwell. He had lessons with William *Robinson, who had studied with the pre-eminent 19th-century portrait painter Sir Thomas Lawrence at the *Royal Academy of Arts. He had a studio in *Bradford from May 1838 to May 1839, and although his business was not a success, the images of a number of local dignitaries, Brontë friends and acquaintances have been preserved in large oil paintings on canvas or wood by Branwell. He also made pencil sketches of colleagues when he worked as a railway clerk. Francis *Leyland noted that Branwell's portraits showed excellent draftsmanship and the ability to produce 'admirable representations' of people, but he failed in his career because he lacked the technical skill and knowledge (Leyland, 1. 135). Apart from those of the Kirby family, Margaret Hartley, and one of his friend John Brown (Alexander & Sellars, pls. xxix–xxxii), however, the pictures show little indication of the sitters' characters. It is his self-portraits that catch the imagination of the viewer (mostly in letters to Joseph Bentley *Leyland). They are a poignant record of his later disillusionment and decline: they relentlessly caricature his long nose, his haggard look following his disappointment in love, his drinking with cronies, his sense of guilt (one portrait shows him with a noose round his neck), and the inevitable death he foresees (there are several sketches of himself as a corpse).

made for George Smith at the same time. Many engraved versions have been made of this portrait, the first, by J. C. Armytage, appearing in 1857 in Gaskell *Life*. There is also a contemporary portrait medallion of Branwell Brontë, cast in 1845 by his friend Joseph Bentley *Leyland and described by Francis *Leyland as 'a life-sized medallion . . . in very high relief and the likeness was perfect' (frontispiece to Gérin *BB*); and a profile silhouette of Branwell (illustrated in Gérin *BB*, after p. 258).

A small circular chalk portrait thought to be of Charlotte at about 26 years of age (*c*.1843) has recently come to light, in private hands (*BST* (2002), 27. 3. 259–60); it may have been drawn by Mary Dixon in Brussels, early 1843 (Smith *Letters*, 1. 313). Charlotte also had her photograph taken, probably on honeymoon in Ireland (June 1854) at the same time as her husband (Revd A. B. Nicholls photo illustrated in Rebecca Fraser's *Charlotte Brontë*, (1988), opposite p. 341). A glass negative from the studio of Sir Emery Walker and listed in his index as 'from a carte-de-visite of Charlotte Brontë, taken within a year of her death', may have been made from this photograph (NPG); and a carte-de-visite photograph in the BPM appears to have been made from this negative (*BST* (1986), 19. 1 and 2. 27–8). The question of photographs of Charlotte is a contentious issue (see *BST* (1996), 21. 7. 293–302; and *BST* (1977), 22. 138–144, for a debate on other possible photos).

Soon after Charlotte's death, John Hunter *Thompson, a friend of Branwell's who was active in the 1850s as a portrait painter, made a painting of her (BPM; illustrated in Fraser *CB*, after p. 340). Since then there have been a number of impressionistic portraits based on those of Richmond and Branwell.

The BPM has an interesting oil portrait of Patrick Brontë as a young man, attributed to John *Bradley (illustrated in Jane Sellars, *Charlotte Brontë* (1997), 12); and several photographs of Mr Brontë taken in the late 1850s (illustrated in Robert Barnard, *Emily Brontë* (2000), 101; and Margot Peters, *Unquiet Soul* (1975), opposite p. 223). In October 1830, Charlotte made a watercolour copy of a miniature portrait of her mother, Maria Branwell Brontë, both of which survive in the BPM (Alexander & Sellars, pp. 174–5). There was apparently a companion miniature of Mr Brontë that has since disappeared, but an oval portrait of him, made in 1809 for an old college friend John Nunn, then curate at Shrewsbury, survives in the BPM (illustrated in Alexander *EW*, p. 14). There are also oval portraits of Maria Branwell Brontë and Elizabeth Branwell as young girls and portraits of their parents, plus a profile silhouette miniature of Elizabeth Branwell (BPM; all illustrated in *BS* (2002), 27. 17–25).

From 1954 until 1987 an oil portrait of a thin-faced elderly lady in lace cap and collar believed to be an image of Elizabeth Branwell hung in Haworth Parsonage and was reproduced in a number of books on the Brontës (see Brian Wilks, *The Brontës* (1975), 56); this has now been proved beyond doubt to be a misattribution. Readers should also be warned against several bogus portraits of Emily in early publications, in particular the images reproduced in J. Alex. Symington's *Catalogue of the Brontë Museum and Library* (1927), 139; and in Clement Shorter's 'Relics of Emily Brontë', *The Woman at Home* (Aug. 1897), 910.

postal service. See COMMUNICATIONS.

post-colonial theory has been applied, often controversially, to the Brontës' writings, especially to *Jane Eyre* and *Wuthering Heights*. Post-colonial theory argues that the major literary texts of the West written during the long period of European expansion contributed significantly to the ideological work of empire and that, by adopting new analytic methods and perspectives, we can better understand the cultural power of these texts. Edward Said, a widely known post-colonial critic, identifies the novel as the literary form most responsible for developing the ideology of empire in the 19th century and for helping Europeans (and their Anglo-American counterparts) to create their own national identities by constructing 'the colonial other' against which they defined themselves. Said demonstrates that the hierarchy of binary oppositions upon which empire depends—that of the metropolitan centre and the colonial periphery, for example—not only informs these texts but also, paradoxically, is reversed by the very texts it informs. In Charles Dickens's *Great Expectations*, for example, the success story of the poor English boy who aspires to be a gentleman in the metropolitan centre of London, is made possible by the existence of the far-flung colonies, which provide him with opportunities for success: Pip's early 'expectations' come from a fortune amassed in the penal colony of New South Wales, while his later, more modest living is made in Cairo, at the 'Eastern Branch' of an English business firm. The cultural periphery of Dickens's fictional world is thus made central to the workings of the plot; the myth of the English bourgeois gentleman depends on unacknowledged influence of the colonial other.

Of particular importance to Brontë studies are the debates that have occurred at the intersections of feminist and post-colonial theory. Gayatri Spivak's essay 'Three Women's Texts and a Critique of Imperialism' was the first to bring that debate to bear on the Brontës. Calling *Jane Eyre* 'a cult text of feminism', Spivak challenges readings of the novel which are based on an 'isolationist admiration for the literature of the female subject

in Europe and Anglo-America' (*Critical Inquiry*, 12 (1985), 511) and on an unquestioned valorizing of 'feminist individualism'. According to Spivak, the perspective of 'high feminism' ensures that we see 'nothing [in *Jane Eyre*] but the psychobiography of the militant [European] female subject' (p. 512) in spite of the prominent nativist presence in the text. Spivak shows that Jane's success story is articulated within a discursive field of 'imperialist axiomatics' (p. 515): tropes and figures whose textual meaning depends on an unexamined (because unconscious) acceptance of imperialist ideology. In *Jane Eyre*, as in all 19th-century British literature, Spivak maintains, 'imperialism . . . was a crucial part of the cultural representation of England to the English', and feminist readings that fail to recognize its role in Brontë's novel unfortunately 're-produce the axioms of imperialism' (p. 511).

Spivak's article provoked a spirited response from Laura E. Donaldson, who argues that Jane's discourse employs the metaphor of racial difference in relation to Jane herself as well as in relation to Bertha; 'thus, the trope of "race" not only evokes Jane's subjection in, yet resistance to, patriarchy, but also demands that one read Jane and Bertha as oppressed rather than opposed sisters' ('The Miranda Complex: Colonialism and Feminist Reading', *Diacritics*, 18 (1988), 75). Mary Ellis Gibson's earlier essay, 'The Seraglio or Suttee: Brontë's *Jane Eyre*', maintains that Charlotte's use of metaphors associated with empire—references to 'suttee' and seraglio in particular—creates 'a criticism of domination in domestic relationships' which the reader interprets as a critique of British imperialism itself (*Postscript*, 4 (1987), 1). In the early nineties, more subtle readings of Charlotte's text were made possible by a growing body of work on the history of British women, and British women's writing, in relation to the subaltern women of the British colonies. Suvendrini Perera's *Reaches of Empire* (1991) develops insights from Spivak's critique by showing that 'the vocabulary of oriental misogyny' (p. 80) formed an important part of the discourse of Victorian feminism. In *Jane Eyre*, for instance, the oppression of women is often signified by 'Eastern' allusions to such things as polygamy and sati, which are presented as 'incontrovertibly alien and repugnant practices of inferior cultures' (Perera, pp. 81–2). Though such allusions may imply an 'international sisterhood of suffering' within global patriarchy, they simultaneously enforce the racist assumptions of imperialist ideology. The novel's 'slender consciousness of a wider female oppression seems always to be repressed or denied', Perera maintains, 'by the objectification of the colonized or imagined "oriental" female subject'—most prominently, of course, in Bertha Mason, the 'racial

Other incarnate' (p. 82). Other post-colonial readings of *Jane Eyre* are included in Jenny Sharpe's *Allegories of Empire* (1993) and in essays by Joyce Zonana ('The Sultan and the Slave: Feminist Orientalism and the Structure of *Jane Eyre*', *Journal of Women in Culture and Society*, 18 (1993), 592–617), Elsie Michie ('From Simianized Irish to Oriental Despots: Heathcliff, Rochester and Racial Difference', *Novel*, 25 (1992), 125–40), Susan Zlotnick ('Jane Eyre, Anna Leonowens, and the White Woman's Burden: Governesses, Missionaries, and Maternal Imperialists in Mid-Victorian Britain', *Victorian Institute Journal*, 24 (1996), 27–56), and Sue Thomas, 'The Tropical Extravagance of Bertha Mason', *Victorian Literature and Culture*, 27. 1 (1999), 1–17).

The fullest treatments of the Brontës from a post-colonial perspective are those included in Firdous Azim's *The Colonial Rise of the Novel* (1993) and Susan Meyer's *Imperialism at Home* (1996). Azim, like Spivak, criticizes the 'implicit imperialism' (p. 145) within the tradition of feminist literary criticism on the Brontës, and she faults Brontë critics generally for failing to notice 'the theme of colonial adventure that lies at the heart of the juvenilia' (p. 138). Azim's work is most original and enlightening in its claim that Charlotte gradually developed 'the most important formal device that accrues to the novel [as a literary form] . . . the narrative subject' (p. 145) by repeatedly invoking in her juvenile writing a racial Other (in figures like Quashia Quamina) against which that subject could be defined. Meyer also discusses Charlotte's early writing, but discovers an ideological shift away from imperialism in the 'African Tales' as Brontë's metaphorical use of 'race' gradually revealed to her the similarities between the oppression of women and the subjugation of colonized peoples. See EMMA.

Post-colonial readings of *Wuthering Heights* have largely focused on the depiction of Heathcliff as a 'racial other' and have interpreted the novel within the context of slavery, Irish immigration, and/or the 'problem' of the gypsy population in Yorkshire. Maja-Lisa Von Sneidern ('*Wuthering Heights* and the Liverpool Slave Trade', *ELH* 62 (1995), 171–96), for example, places Emily's story within the history of the Liverpool slave trade, while Terry Eagleton identifies Heathcliff as a starving Irish immigrant whose disruptive influence 'dramatizes . . . a ruling-class fear of revolution from below' (*Heathcliff and the Great Hunger* (1995) 19–20) and beyond the shores of England. Two articles published in the late 1980s by Christopher Heywood offer information about the controversies over slavery that were current in Yorkshire during the Brontës' youth ('Yorkshire Slavery in *Wuthering Heights*', *Review of English*

Studies, NS 38 (1987), 184–98, and 'Africa and Slavery in the Brontë Children's Novels', *Hitotsubashi Journal of Arts and Sciences*, 30 (1989), 75–87). More recently, Christine Alexander has analysed the Brontës' appropriation and construction of 'Africa' within their childhood 'play' ('Imagining Africa: The Brontës' Creations of Glass Town and Angria', in P. Alexander, R. Hutchinson, and D. Schreuder (eds.), *Africa Today: A Multi-Disciplinary Snapshot of the Continent* (1996), 201–19, and Sue Thomas has historicized Bertha Mason in 'The Tropical Extravagance of Bertha Mason', *Victorian Literature and Culture* 27. 1 (1999), 1–7. Taking a somewhat different approach in 'Imperialist Nostalgia and *Wuthering Heights*' (in Linda H. Peterson (ed.), *Wuthering Heights* (1992), 428–49), Nancy Armstrong considers the role *Wuthering Heights* played in the process of 'internal colonization' that was taking place in England during the first half of the 19th century.   CB

Azim, Firdous, *The Colonial Rise of the Novel* (1993).

Meyer, Susan, *Imperialism at Home* (1996).

Spivak, Gayatri Chakravorty, 'Three Women's Texts and a Critique of Imperialism', *Critical Inquiry*, 12 (1985), 243–61.

Postlethwaite family, of Broughton House in Broughton-in-Furness, a small market town in Lancashire, in the southern Lakeland district of England, where Branwell Brontë was employed as a tutor from January to June 1840. His 50-year-old employer Robert Postlethwaite (1786–1859), descended from a family of mercers, was a magistrate (until 1847) although Branwell described him in a letter to John Brown as 'a retired County magistrate, a large landowner, and of a right hearty and generous disposition' and his wife Agnes as 'a quiet, silent, and amiable woman' (Gérin *BB*, p. 163). Branwell lived away from his employers, boarding at High Syke House, the home of the surgeon Edward Fish. He enjoyed considerable freedom, taking walking excursions in the countryside and visiting local public houses (see his annotated copy of James Thorne's *Rambles by Rivers* in BPM).

Branwell's pupils, aged 12 and 11 respectively, were John (1828–86), who later studied at Trinity College, Cambridge, and was ordained as an Anglican priest, and William (1829–1908), who became a magistrate and High Sheriff of Cumberland, before emigrating first to New Zealand (1872) and then to California (c.1903). It is unclear how much effect Branwell had on these bright young boys, since he is said to have neglected his pupils in the pursuit of his literary efforts that were encouraged by Hartley *Coleridge whom he visited for a day in May. Winifred Gérin quotes an unidentified source that describes Branwell's 'spending most of their lesson time in sketching and making up stories in connection with his pictures' (Gérin *BB*, pp. 163–9). A pencil drawing by him of Broughton church survives from this period, on the reverse of which is a boldly sketched self-portrait (see Alexander & Sellars, p. 336). The church is situated in the valley immediately below the main street and has a magnificent view of distant Black Combe, the subject of Branwell's sonnet 'Black Comb' [*sic*] (Neufeldt *BBP*, p. 208), inspired by *Wordsworth's poem 'View from the top of Black Comb'. Branwell was also working on his translation of *The *Odes of Horace* at this time. Branwell was dismissed in disgrace, after being found absent and 'visibly the worse for drink', and returned home in June 1840 (see Timothy Cockerill, 'A Brontë at Broughton-in-Furness', *BST* (1966), 15. 76. 34–5). A further cause for dismissal has been cited in Barker (pp. 334–5): Branwell may have fathered an illegitimate child at this time, who is said to have died soon after birth.

Press, the. Revd Patrick Brontë and his family took a keen interest in the news of the day. The 19th century saw a great increase in the number of newspapers published, and a widening of their readership. During the Napoleonic Wars people of all classes were eager for news, but the high cost of newspapers meant that one copy might be seen by dozens of people, through illegal hiring-out, informal clubbing together, or in coffee houses, public houses, and reading rooms. A paper tax and the government stamp meant that each paper cost 6*d.* in 1800; when the stamp duty rose to 4*d.* after 1815, the newspaper cost 7*d.* Radical newspapers which evaded stamp duty could be prosecuted: between 1816 and 1834 there were 183 prosecutions for seditious or blasphemous libel, but few after 1824, since the authorities realized prosecution advertised the author. In 1815 252 newspapers circulated in the United Kingdom, some being meagre local news-sheets, others well-established London papers, with broad and well-informed news coverage, such as the conservative *Morning Post* (1772–1937), the *Morning Chronicle* (1769–1862, a Liberal paper until it was bought in the Peelite Conservative interest in 1848), the Liberal *Morning Herald* (founded 1780, Conservative from the 1830s onwards), the *Courier* (founded 1792, originally Liberal, but changing political alignment several times later), and the Radical *Globe* (1803–1921). Except for the *Herald*, these papers all reviewed most of Charlotte's works favourably, though, as was customary, such 'reviews' might consist of a very brief critique followed by long excerpts from the works concerned. From *c.*1825 newspaper reading rooms were provided in *Mechanics' Institutes, lyceums,

and athenaeums. In 1829 the Brontës were lent copies of the jingoistic Tory paper *John Bull* by Revd Jonas Driver. They also took the *Leeds Mercury* and *Leeds Intelligencer.* Revd Patrick Brontë published letters in both these papers and in the *Bradford Observer* and *Halifax Guardian;* Branwell published poems in the last three, and in the *Bradford Herald.* Reviews and/or articles about the Brontës were published in such provincial papers. The *Glasgow Examiner, Manchester Examiner,* and *Scotsman,* all papers of high repute, also published significant favourable reviews of the Brontës' works. Some of the harshest reviews appeared in the *Mirror of Literature, The Sunday Times,* and, notoriously, in *The Times,* founded in 1788, which towered above all other British papers in coverage, circulation, and authority, and which made Charlotte cry by its review of *Shirley* on 7 December 1849. *The Times* reached more readers than any other paper worldwide, and its verdict was therefore to be feared: its circulation in 1817 had been 6,000–7,000; in 1840, 18,500; by 1861 it was to reach 70,000. Its price fell from 7*d.* in 1815 and 4*d.* in 1855 to 3*d.* in 1861, for in 1855 stamp duty was abolished, and in 1861 the paper duty was repealed.

Altick, Richard D., *The English Common Reader* (1957).

prints. During the early 19th century there was a revolution in engraving, which allowed for reasonably priced books with steel engravings to reach middle-class families like the Brontës. This was the Brontës' first experience of art, the close examination of prints that would then be meticulously copied. Charlotte Brontë's schoolfriend Mary Taylor recalled that 'Whenever an opportunity offered of examining a picture or cut of any kind, she went over it piecemeal, with her eyes close to the paper, looking so long that we used to ask her "what she saw in it". She could always see plenty, and explained it very well' (Gaskell *Life*, 1. 109). She was skilled in translating pictures and it was through pictorial media that she first conceived of her own imaginary world. Characters in Charlotte's novelettes browse through books of engravings by Edward *Finden, discussing (as she and her siblings must have done many times) the character traits revealed by a particular portrait of one of the Glass Town and Angrian heroes.

The chief forms of the reproductive print in the early 19th century were line engraving and mezzotint engraving, but new methods were introduced to imitate more closely techniques of painting and drawing. Aquatint, stipple, lithography, and colour printing were pioneered in the late 18th century and all received impetus from the London art publishers Rudolph Ackermann and John Boydell. Thomas *Bewick revolutionized the early art of wood-engraving, used particularly in cheap popular publications like the *Penny Magazine*. The introduction in the early 1820s of steel mezzotints (rather than the softer copper plates already in use) meant not only that more copies could be printed from a single plate and the price reduced, enabling people on limited incomes—like Revd Patrick Brontë—to own their favourite pictures, but also that rich velvety blacks and strong contrasts of light and dark could be produced, favouring artists of spectacle like John *Martin. At first the new engraving techniques were employed on famous paintings by Renaissance masters like Raphael and Leonardo da Vinci, and then on works of contemporary painters such as J. M. W. Turner, John Martin, Benjamin West, David Wilkie, Edward Burney, Thomas Stothard, Sir Thomas Lawrence, C. R. Eastlake, William *Etty, and others. The Brontë home contained a number of such engravings on its walls, including five large mezzotint prints by Martin. Branwell's favourite image was William Woollett's engraving of Benjamin West's painting of 1771, *The Death of General Wolfe*, a copy of which was said to hang in his bedroom at Haworth Parsonage (Gérin *BB*, p. 25). In 1850 George Smith sent Charlotte an engraving of the Duke of Wellington, which she called 'a treasure' (Smith *Letters*, 2. 434; illustrated in Charles Lemon, *Early Visitors to Haworth* (1996), 38), and on 26 February 1853 she received from Smith an engraving of Samuel Laurence's drawing of Thackeray, that she hung with Wellington 'for companion' and her own portrait by Richmond 'for contrast' (Wise & Symington, 4. 47; illustrated in Fraser *CB*, after p. 340). See also PORTRAITS OF THE BRONTËS.

Such 'Works of Art' could be bought from local booksellers or sent for from firms like Ackermann & Co. (Alexander & Sellars, pp. 14, 138). The most expensive items listed in Ackermann's catalogues were portfolios containing as many as 50 facsimile sketches, such as Samuel Prout's views made in Flanders and Germany, on sale for £6 6s. on India paper or £5 5s. on 'tinted grey touched with white'. Individual prints of popular paintings of the day such as Landseer's 'High Life' and 'Low Life', anthropomorphic studies of dogs that were probably admired by Emily Brontë, were available for 9s. Also on Ackermann's list were genre subjects, portraits, historical subjects, and a long list of sporting and animal prints. The most humble items advertised were large collections of unspecified drawings and prints for 'Scrap Books and Albums'. Ackermann's also offered 'Drawings Let Out to Copy' of figures, landscapes, flowers, and fruit for a yearly subscription of 4 guineas. Many such prints were used by the Brontës and their school friends at Roe Head as models for art exercises. A finely executed pencil drawing of a girl in a large

hat made by one of Charlotte's contemporaries in the *Roe Head Album is typical of the engravings used in drawing lessons. This particular image is taken from a plate, engraved by George T. Doo from a painting by Sir Thomas Lawrence, that was advertised in the *Forget Me Not* annual of 1829.

The Brontës had access to a substantial amount of visual material, their chief source being engravings in *annuals and illustrated books (see BOOKS OWNED BY THE BRONTËS; BOOKS READ BY THE BRONTËS). Engravings in *Forget Me Not*, *Friendship's Offering*, and the *Literary Souvenir* in particular were copied by the Brontës in pencil and watercolour. Engravings of works by fashionable artists increased the demand for these decorative little books, so adding to the dissemination of art works to remote places in the provinces. Travel books and volumes of popular poetry also provided prints to copy, the Brontë favourites being Allom's *Picturesque Rambles in Westmorland, Cumberland, Durham and Northumberland*, and Finden's *Illustrations of the Life and Works of Lord Byron*. See ART OF THE BRONTËS; BYRON, LORD.

'Prisoner' (A Fragment), The. See 'JULIAN M. AND A. G. ROCHELLE'.

***Professor, The. A Tale*, and related manuscripts.** See page 402

Protestantism, a term now loosely applied to non-Roman Catholic western Christians who wish to see individuals directly responsible to God. They reject the idea that people are brought back to God partly through their own merits and efforts and partly through the mediation of a sacramental and clerical system. Non-*Calvinist Protestants leave as an insoluble mystery the problem of why all are not saved despite the existence of a saviour God, and concentrate on his love in sending his own son to suffer for mankind. All the Brontës would know that *Milton, well aware of this theological impasse, emphasized the Son's divine mission, and relegated endless arguments about 'Providence, Foreknowledge, Will, and Fate' to the fallen angels, who find 'no end, in wand'ring mazes lost'. Charlotte Brontë, temperamentally and by upbringing a Protestant, and thoroughly acquainted with *Paradise Lost*, shared for a brief period in 1836–7 the torture of wrestling with Calvinist ideas of 'Fixt Fate'. In her mature writings, especially in *Jane Eyre*, she stresses the individual will, but also shows Jane's gradual spiritual growth, from her 'untaught, rebellious' childhood to responsible maturity, when she has to be sure that her actions are consistent with God's will. *Rochester has to recognize that if Jane is seized against her will, she will 'elude his grasp like an

(*cont. on page 406*)

A novel by Charlotte Brontë, posthumously published 1857. On 5 February 1851
Charlotte wrote to her publisher, George Smith, wryly acknowledging that *The
Professor* 'now had the honour of being rejected nine times . . . . Few, I flatter my
self—have earned an equal distinction.'

Composition

Charlotte probably began to write *The Professor* in the autumn of 1844, the year of her
return from *Brussels. While there she had devised a scheme for a magazine tale to be
set '30 to 50 years ago', involving loss of relatives, crosses in the affections, 'Going
abroad & Return', a 'Rival or Rivaless', and 'Villains' (Bonnell BPM MS 118–1). With
her experience as both teacher and pupil vividly in mind, she chose to set the greater
part of her novel in Brussels, but to place the 'Going abroad & Return' within an
English framework. As she herself had turned her back on the 'slavery' of being a
subordinate—a governess hard-driven by employers—and had hoped she and Emily
might 'take a footing in the world afterwards' in their own school, so her hero was to
rebel against varieties of servitude.

Manuscript

The manuscript of *The Professor*, now in the Pierpont Morgan Library, is Charlotte's
fair copy, written neatly in ink, with comparatively few authorial revisions: Charlotte
made about 280 alterations of words or phrases in the 340 pages, showing a careful
concern for the *mot juste* and the finer points of character and feeling. Heavy deletions
in dark ink were made by Revd A. B. *Nicholls when he edited the novel for publication in 1857, cutting out for example the profane use of the word 'God': 'God damn
your insolence!' becomes 'Confound your insolence!'.

Sources and context

The manuscript reveals that Charlotte had turned first to a story she had begun in
about 1840. It centred on the fraternal antagonism integral to the *Glass Town and
Angrian saga, as developed in, for example, Branwell's *The *Wool is Rising* (1834).
There Edward *Percy and William *Percy work their way up from a small
woolcombing shop to large-scale manufacturing. Edward tries to bully his spirited
but weak brother and his assistant Timothy Steaton—the Timothy *Steighton of *The
Professor*. In Charlotte's *The *Spell* (1834), William Percy usually pretends indifference
to the brutality of Edward, who (like Edward *Crimsworth) threatens him with a gig-
whip; but William soon abandons his unbearable servitude as a clerk in the woollen
mill to join the army. In Charlotte's fragmentary novel *Ashworth* (1840), the materialistic Edward Ashworth is the master in his mill and counting house. In his youth
he had violently thrashed his cooler, taciturn brother William, who had not been well
liked by his schoolfellows at Harrow, and had found no 'very sentimental Orestes and
Pylades' sort of friendship among them. The allusion is retained in the opening
paragraphs of *The Professor*, which Charlotte originally entitled *The Master*. They

introduce a chapter of *Ashworth*-like material which Charlotte adapted to her new novel simply by revising its first and last pages, where the paper and handwriting differ from the remainder of the chapter, which is written in the bold hand she often used in *c*.1840. This old material is now presented somewhat ineptly as a letter from William *Crimsworth to a friend, who thenceforth vanishes from the story. Charlotte then developed the two brothers' motif for the next five chapters, endowing William, her first-person narrator, with many of her own traits, and introducing the young radical Hunsden Yorke *Hunsden to stimulate William into abandoning his clerkship and seeking a new career in Belgium. Charlotte's personal emotion is evident in the sudden burst of eloquent rhetoric in the opening paragraphs of chapter 7. From then on the narrative becomes more fluent, and the characterization more subtle, especially in the portrayal of Mlle Zoraïde *Reuter, with her outward *bienveillance* and concealed craft. She, if anyone, is the 'Rivaless' of the magazine scheme, and possibly, along with some of her pupils, one of the 'Villains'. William, Frances *Henri's beloved master, somewhat incongruously acquires traits of an idealized M. Constantin *Heger; and Charlotte's desperate pleas for an adequate response from Heger find vicarious fulfilment in the happy union of her hero and heroine.

Attempts to publish

On 6 April 1846 Charlotte wrote to *Aylott and Jones, who were about to publish *Poems* by 'Currer, Ellis, and Acton Bell', to ask if they would also consider publishing the three separate novels the 'Bells' were preparing. They refused, but offered advice, and presumably suggested likely publishers for the novels, *Wuthering Heights*, *Agnes Grey*, and *The Professor*. The last leaf of the *Professor* manuscript is dated 27 June 1846, and the other novels must have been fair copied by early July. Henry *Colburn, to whom Charlotte offered the manuscripts on 4 July, must have rejected the offer. By the time T. C. *Newby accepted *Wuthering Heights* and *Agnes Grey* in July 1847, *The Professor* had perhaps been separated from them. Charlotte received it back, curtly rejected by some publisher, on Tuesday 25 August 1846, when her father was operated on for cataract. From the dreary *Manchester lodgings where she was looking after him, she sent off the manuscript to another London publisher, and forthwith began to write *Jane Eyre*.

On 15 July 1847, after a sixth rejection, *The Professor* was sent to *Smith, Elder and Company. Their reader, W. S. *Williams, responded with a courteous two-page letter, refusing the manuscript, but discussing its merits and demerits with a discrimination which cheered its author, and promising to give careful attention to a three-volume work. Thereupon Charlotte suggested that *The Professor* might be published without 'serious risk' if the more exciting three-volume novel she was then writing speedily followed it. Smith, Elder rejected the idea, but asked to see the new work. So *Jane Eyre* was sent to them on 24 August 1847, and appeared, an immediate best-seller, on 19 October. But when the manuscript of *The Professor* was returned, at Charlotte's request, it was accompanied by the condition that she was not to publish it or any other work until after the appearance of the two books of which Smith, Elder were to have the refusal. They also suggested that her next work might be in serial form. Charlotte rejected this idea, and said that she had made three unsatisfactory commencements of a new novel, but would prefer to recast *The Professor* in three-volume form. Admitting its faults—a feeble beginning, a lack of incident and general attractiveness—she still considered the middle and latter portions as good as she could write. Two fragmentary attempts at recasting survive. Bonnell BPM MS 109 is a preface introducing William Crimsworth as the writer of an autobiography, rejected by various publishers, which he has entrusted to a narrator 'for correction and retrenchment'. Having ruthlessly cut out the first seven chapters, the narrator offers a brief summary of the Crimsworth brothers' upbringing, and of William's decision to 'put his neck under the yoke' of his stepbrother, the manufacturer Edward Crimsworth. The fragment ends with the narrator's unfulfilled promise to describe their first interview.

A longer fragment, 'John Henry' (see SHIRLEY: 'JOHN HENRY'), in Taylor, Princeton, represents a more sustained recasting. It was evidently written before *Shirley*, for the brothers are renamed Moore, the surname used for Robert and Louis in that novel. The fragment ends abruptly after a single paragraph of chapter 3.

Having abandoned these unsatisfactory new beginnings, Charlotte set aside *The Professor* and concentrated on *Shirley*, which was published on 26 October 1849. According to Mr Nicholls, shortly after that date she wrote a preface 'with a view to the publication of "The Professor" ', but it was not until early 1851 that she offered that much-rejected manuscript to her publisher once more. The pencil draft of her preface is now in Pierpont Morgan. On the back of it she calculated the number of extra pages needed to expand the novel into a full-length work, and jotted down two incomplete paragraphs hinting at a fuller development of Hunsden's role, and a new episode concerning the 'fête day of Mlle Pauline'. On 5 February 1851 Charlotte conceded that George *Smith's equivocal response to her attempted revival of the novel amounted to a rejection, and she reclaimed the manuscript.

Publication

After Charlotte's death, George Smith suggested that Elizabeth *Gaskell might read and give her opinion on *The Professor*. He and Nicholls thought too much of it had been embodied in *Villette* for it to be worth publication. But Sir James *Kay-Shuttleworth, having helped Elizabeth Gaskell by wresting the manuscript from a reluctant Nicholls, was keen to edit and publish it. Gaskell thought it a 'curious link' in Charlotte's literary history, but considered Nicholls should edit it, removing any coarseness or profanity which might disfigure Charlotte's pure image. She was disappointed by Nicholls's limited censorship (*Professor* (Clarendon edn.), pp. xxix–xxxviii). Smith, Elder published the novel as *The Professor, A Tale*, on 6 June 1857 in two volumes at 21s. Their text, based on Charlotte's clearly written manuscript but introducing conventional, standardized punctuation, was not completely accurate in substantives, and did not reproduce Charlotte's sporadic and idiosyncratic use of capital initials for abstractions. Two and a half thousand copies of the first edition were printed, but sales were moderate, despite the interest aroused by publication of Elizabeth Gaskell's *Life* of Charlotte on 27 March 1857. Initially Mudie's Circulating Library took 300 copies, then 250 more in the next year. In 1859 719 copies were bound as two volumes in one, and sold to retailers at 3s. 6d. instead of 15s. In 1860, 68 of the 98 copies returned by Scribner's were rebound. The cheap 2s. 6d. Yellow Back reprint of 1860, which included poems by the three sisters, 'Now first collected', sold well. Out of the 5,000 copies printed, 1,348 remained on hand in June 1861, but sales warranted new printings of 1,000 in that year and in 1862.

Plot

After leaving Eton, the orphaned William Crimsworth rejects the suggestions of his aristocratic uncles that he should become a clergyman and marry his cousin Sarah. He decides to become a manufacturer like his father. Received coolly by his brother Edward, a prosperous mill owner, he becomes an office clerk at the mill. At Edward's luxurious home he meets the young radical Hunsden, who later publicly condemns Edward's tyrannous behaviour. Thereupon Edward threatens William with violence and dismisses him. We later learn that Edward became bankrupt, but recovered to become richer than ever. William travels to Brussels, bearing a recommendation from Hunsden to a Mr Brown, through whom he obtains a teaching post in François *Pelet's school for boys. William earns a good reputation, and is invited by Mlle Reuter to give additional lessons at her school. He soon realizes that she aims to discover his weak points in order to gain power over him. He almost falls in love with her, but is disillusioned when he overhears her talking with Pelet, who is evidently her fiancé, and exulting over her conquest of William. Meanwhile the orphaned Frances Henri, who attends William's classes in order to perfect her English, arouses his warm interest. The jealous Mlle Reuter dismisses her, but William searches until he finds her, weeping over her aunt's grave. An idyllic visit to her lodgings confirms their mutual attraction. Through the father of a pupil whom he had rescued from drowning, William becomes a professor of English in a college. Frances also obtains a good teaching post, and William proposes marriage. She accepts, but insists that she must still teach. The school that they eventually set up prospers, and they retire with their son Victor to England, where their friendship with Hunsden continues.

Reception

Almost all reviewers referred to the special history of the novel's publication and to the tragic events revealed in Gaskell's *Life*. Some, like the *Sun, Lady's Newspaper,* and *National Review,* felt that these precluded very severe criticism. Others found in the novel a curious interest as a stage in Charlotte's development, but few wrote wholeheartedly in its favour. The *Critic, Athenaeum, Blackwood's, Leader, Press,* and *Observer* condemned it variously as crude, unequal, slow, dull, tame, lacking dramatic interest, unity, or arrangement, unnatural or unreal, threadbare, coarse, disagreeable, jejune, and pervaded by egotism. All these journals, however, praised the portrayal of Frances and tended to disparage William as unworthy of her. Damning reviews appeared in the *Morning Herald* (18 June 1857) and *Morning Post* (7 Sept. 1857). The *Herald* was unusual in condemning all Charlotte's novels as destitute of 'various and attaching incident', *The Professor* being exceptionally meagre in this respect, while it shared with the other works the insularity which had made them popular with English readers. Posterity's judgement of them would be much less favourable. The *Post* found similar faults, observed that for Charlotte a 'moral leprosy' tainted all foreigners, and doubted whether *The Professor* should have been published at all, for the hateful characters and the vicious antipathy between the brothers served no moral purpose. More favourable reviews appeared in *The Economist, Examiner, Saturday Review, Guardian, Dublin University Magazine,* and *Eclectic Review.* Even the *Spectator* (20 June 1857) conceded that *The Professor* was more worthy of attention than the mass of novels, and praised Pelet and Mlle Reuter. Other friendly reviewers detected suppressed power and accurate observation, despite the clumsy construction and morbid taste for the disagreeable. Most appreciated the Brussels chapters and the charming heroine. Opinions were divided on William Crimsworth and Mlle Reuter, who was pronounced to be either admirably conceived or unnaturally bad. Hunsden baffled or intrigued reviewers, who commented on his curious, almost flirtatious, relationship with William.

Later editions

The Haworth edition (1900) has a brief introduction by Mrs Humphry Ward, a text based on the first edition, Charlotte's fragmentary story *Emma, selections from poems by the Brontës, including Mr Brontë's *Cottage Poems, and illustrations. The Clarendon edition (Oxford, 1987), based on Charlotte's holograph manuscript, has an introduction and textual and explanatory notes by Herbert Rosengarten and Margaret Smith. It includes a manuscript-based text of *Emma*, and indexes of quotations and allusions in Charlotte's novels. The World's Classics edition (Oxford, 1991), edited by Margaret Smith and Herbert Rosengarten, reprints the Clarendon texts, and has a critical introduction, note on the text, and select bibliography. The Penguin edition (1989) has a good critical introduction by Heather Glen.

Duthie *Foreign Vision.*

Glen, Heather, *Charlotte Brontë: The Imagination in History* (2002), ch. 2.

Linder, C. A., *Romantic Imagery in the Novels of Charlotte Brontë* (1978).

Wheeler, M. D., 'Literary and Biblical Allusion in "The Professor"', *BST* (1976), 17. 86. 46–57.

essence'; later, tempted to 'rush down the torrent' of St John *Rivers's will, she prays for guidance, hears Rochester's voice ('no miracle', but the 'work of nature'), and exerts her will to refuse St John. Such assertions provoked Elizabeth *Rigby's notorious condemnation of *Jane Eyre* as antichristian. Protestant emphasis on 'the priesthood of all believers' was an important element in the creeds of Revd Patrick Brontë, Charlotte, and Anne. In contrast to the Catholic emphasis on hierarchical priests who can, under God, grant or withhold absolution and impose penance, and on the high virtue of the separated life of celibate monks and nuns, Protestants affirm that all believers may share in spreading the word of grace, though ministers are expected to study the Scriptures, offer pastoral guidance, and administer the sacraments. Mr Brontë expected his family to teach in the Sunday school, and probably also to take some pastoral care for their scholars. One of Charlotte's bêtesnoires in Catholic Brussels and in the novels set in Belgium was the priestly control of education, taken to an extreme in 'Sylvie' of *The Professor*, who had given up 'her independence of thought and action into the hands of some despotic confessor' and had become a 'pale, blighted image . . . whence the soul had been conjured by Romish wizard-craft' (ch. 12). See RELIGION.

Thormählen, Marianne, *The Brontës and Religion* (1999).

Prunty. See BRONTË FAMILY.

Pryce, Revd David (1811–40), BA Trinity College Dublin, summer 1838, ordained deacon December 1838. The name is spelled 'Bryce' in Wise & Symington (1. 184, 197), and Charlotte Brontë uses the spelling 'Price'. He was curate to Revd William *Hodgson at Colne, Lancs., and visited Haworth with him in July or August 1839. Charlotte responded readily to his witty, lively, ardent talk until he became too flattering. A few days later she was astonished to receive from him a proposal of marriage, which she refused. Mr Hodgson's daughter recalled a longer correspondence, and abandonment of the idea of marriage because he was consumptive. Charlotte was shocked and saddened by his death at Trawden, Lancs., in January 1840.

Pryor, Agnes, in *Shirley*, former governess and now companion to the heiress Shirley *Keeldar. Reserved, formal, and of a somewhat nervous disposition, Mrs Pryor is about 40 years of age, with 'a form decidedly inclined to embonpoint' (p. 219). In Shirley's words, 'of all the high and rigid Tories, she is queen; of all the stanch churchwomen, she is chief' (p. 220). She accompanies Shirley when the latter takes up residence at *Fieldhead, and is soon introduced to Caroline *Helstone, the Rector's niece, in whom she quickly takes a warm interest. When Caroline speaks of the possibility of becoming a governess, Mrs Pryor attempts to dissuade her by describing her own experiences as a governess with the Hardman family, who had treated her with disdain and unkindness. She nurses Caroline through her illness, using the opportunity to reveal that she is Caroline's mother: she had been married to James *Helstone, the Rector's brother, but fled because of his cruelties. To help conceal her identity she had adopted the name 'Pryor', a name in her mother's family. She had left Caroline to Revd Matthewson *Helstone's care because she feared that the child, who had inherited her father's 'fair outside' and elegance, must also have inherited his perversity and would need a firmer upbringing than she could provide. The revelation of Mrs Pryor's real identity allows for a touching reunion between mother and daughter, but her reasons for having abandoned Caroline are less than convincing, leading G. H. *Lewes to an overwrought attack on the author: 'Currer Bell! If under your heart had ever stirred a child, if to your bosom a babe had ever been pressed . . . never could you have imagined a falsehood such as that!' (*Edinburgh Review*, 91 (Jan. 1850)). Mrs Pryor owes some of her qualities to Margaret *Wooler (1792–1885), Charlotte's former teacher and mentor at *Roe Head school; according to Ellen *Nussey, Miss Wooler was 'short and stout, but graceful in her movements, very fluent in conversation and with a very sweet voice' (Shorter *Circle*, p. 261). Mrs Pryor's maiden name, Agnes Grey, and her profession as a governess in a family, are allusions to the eponymous heroine of Anne Brontë's first novel. Her account of her treatment at the hands of the Hardman family (*Shirley*, ch. 21) includes passages adapted, with an overlay of heavy irony, from Elizabeth Rigby's unkind review of *Jane Eyre* in the *Quarterly Review* (Dec. 1848) (see SHIRLEY: 'A WORD TO THE "QUARTERLY" '). HR

pseudonyms used by the Brontës. All four Brontës published under pseudonyms, a continuation of their childhood habit of writing in fictitious authorial voices. Charlotte, Emily, and Anne adopted gender-neutral pseudonyms when they published their first book, *Poems* by Currer, Ellis, and Acton Bell 1846, and they subsequently published all their novels under these pen names, even *Villette* (1853), which was released long after Charlotte's identity had become widely known. Emily was apparently especially anxious to keep her actual identity secret. In 1848, Charlotte warned W. S. *Williams not to refer to her sister except by her pseudonym because it was 'against every feeling and intention of "Ellis Bell" ' to be known in her own person outside her small circle of family and close friends (Smith *Letters*, 2. 94). Charlotte herself used her pseudonym in professional correspondence with people she had not actually met; 'Currer Bell', she explained to Williams in 1848, 'is

the only name I wish to have mentioned in connection with my writings' (Smith *Letters*, 2. 51). The one piece of professional correspondence from Anne still extant is signed pseudonymously (Smith *Letters*, 2. 160–1), as was her poem 'The Narrow Way', which appeared in *Fraser's Magazine* and the *Leeds Intelligencer* in 1848. Nearly all Branwell's publications appeared in provincial newspapers under his favourite pseudonym, *Northangerland.

The Brontës adopted pseudonyms for several reasons. Emily may simply have been averse to any publicity at all, while Charlotte wished to keep her authorial identity a secret in Yorkshire because, as she explained to Williams, it 'would fetter me intolerably' to be 'ever . . . conscious in writing that my book must be read by ordinary acquaintances' (Smith *Letters*, 2. 51). Also, as Charlotte recalled in her 1850 *'Biographical Notice', she and her sisters adopted gender-neutral pseudonyms because they 'had a vague impression that authoresses are liable to be looked upon with prejudice'. Furthermore, pseudonymity and anonymity were common authorial practices in the first half of the 19th century—indeed, they were the rule rather than the exception in periodicals, where all Branwell's publishing occurred—so that the Brontës were following an established convention in taking on fictitious identities. And finally, signing fictitious names to their work was a longstanding habit for all four of the Brontës, who had learned this convention from the books and magazines they read as children and had adapted it to the 'plays' they wrote together when young. Charlotte's favourite juvenile pseudonym was Charles Townshend (originally Lord Charles Albert Florian *Wellesley) or, more ambiguously, 'CT', as she called herself when writing to Hartley *Coleridge in 1840. At 13, she had adopted the prose persona of Captain 'Andrew' *Tree and was signing her poems as Arthur Wellesley, the Marquis of Douro (later Duke of *Zamorna). At the same time, Branwell was writing prose as Captain Sir John *Flower (later Viscount Richton) and composing poetry in the figure of Young *Soult the Rhymer. Other pseudonyms Branwell used before he settled on 'Northangerland' are Captain *Bud, the historian; Captain Henry *Hastings, the national poet of Angria; and Charles *Wentworth. Evidence from Emily and Anne's poems suggest that they, too, followed the same practice. CB

Judd, Catherine A., 'Male Pseudonyms and Female Authority in Early Victorian England', in J. O. Jordan and R. L. Patten (eds.), *Literature in the Marketplace* (1995), 250–68.

psychoanalytic approaches. Since Sigmund Freud (1856–1939) first articulated the principles of modern psychoanalysis in the early 20th century,

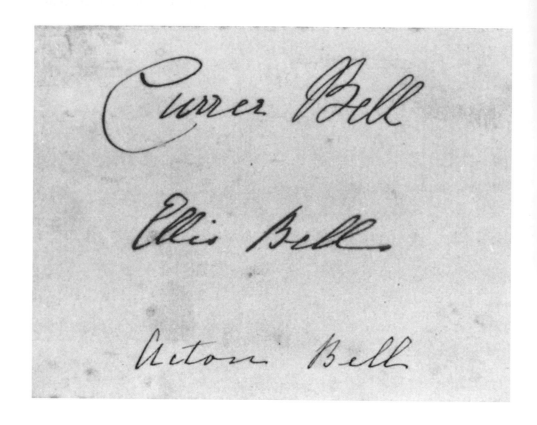

The signatures of 'the Bells', pseudonyms of the Brontës, July 1846.

his theories have been elaborated, contested, and reformulated by numerous thinkers within the field of psychology, including those with strong interests in literature. In recent years, the most important modifications of Freudian thought, with respect to literary criticism, have been made by French psychoanalytic theorist Jacques Lacan and by feminists who have revised Lacan's ideas as well as those of Freud. In its various permutations, psychoanalytic criticism has been one of the most productive approaches to the study of the Brontës' lives and writing.

Three fundamental principles of Freudian psychoanalysis are (1) that the psyche is divided into two primary structures, the conscious and unconscious; (2) that human behaviour is significantly determined by unconscious motivation; and (3) that the economy of the psychic system is maintained by 'defence mechanisms' which allow for the controlled flow of psychically charged material. The upsurging into consciousness of material that has been repressed into the unconscious occurs, according to Freud, by way of such things as dreams, fantasies, and works of art, including literature. Literary texts, therefore, can be interpreted according to psychoanalytic methods in the same way that dreams can. In *The Interpretation of Dreams* (1900), Freud models this interpretative process and presents a catalogue of typical dream stories along with what he takes to be their latent content or 'hidden meaning'; this catalogue has given literary critics powerful tools for interpreting literature.

Also of great importance to literary studies is Freud's articulation of the stages of psychosexual development within the context of the 'family romance', especially as the Oedipal process has been more recently elaborated by Lacan and by feminist psychoanalytic theory. Taking infantile sexuality as a given, Freud traces the child's development from an initial state of undifferentiated oneness with the mother to an anxious, unconscious recognition of the need to separate from her and redirect sexual drives elsewhere; this recognition is produced in the child by the intervention of the father (the phallus) and through cultural proscriptions against incest. During this process, the child's ego is formed by the opposing pressures of the id (instinctive drives, including the sex drive or 'libido') and the superego (unconscious, internalized proscriptions acquired from external sources such as family and society). Lacan elaborates Freud's developmental scheme by adding a 'mirror stage' (also referred to as 'the imaginary') in which the child first sees himself seeing himself. In this stage the child learns to think of himself as both a subject (one who sees) and an object constituted by 'the gaze' of another.

Perhaps of even greater significance for literary theory and interpretation is Lacan's claim that the child's acquisition of language occurs during the period of separation from the mother. Powerfully driven to renounce his mother by the prohibiting 'Law of the Father' and its internalized representative, the superego, the boy child experiences words as compensation for his great loss. The girl child's process of separation from the mother and entry into language and culture, as articulated by Freud and Lacan respectively, has been problematic for feminist psychoanalytic theorists, who have revised the theories of their male counterparts. Lacan reasons that girls are not driven into language acquisition (which is the key to entering culture) as forcefully as boys are, because girls do not fully renounce their identification with their mothers, as boys must do. Feminists do not agree with Lacan's assertion that this is a great 'tragedy' for girls, however. They point out that girls not only *do* learn to use symbolic language like their brothers but they also retain facility with the pre-symbolic language by which they communicated with the mother in early infancy—a preverbal system of sounds and gestures which the boy child forgets when he separates from mother and accepts the Father's 'Word' in her place.

Given the entrenched position of biographical criticism within Brontë studies in the early 20th century, it is not surprising that the first psychoanalytic critics were more interested in the Brontës' lives and personalities than their writings. Lucile Dooley's article 'Psychoanalysis of Charlotte Brontë, as a Type of the Woman of Genius' (*American Journal of Psychology*, 31 (1920), 221–72) and Rosamund Langbridge's book *Charlotte Brontë: A Psychological Study* (1929) are representative. With the rise of formalism and American New Criticism in the 1940s, however, text-oriented psychoanalytic study of the novels gradually became more common. In 1958, Robert Heilman showed how Charlotte modified the conventions of the Gothic romance in order to explore psychological 'depths and intensities' that were new to narrative fiction ('Charlotte Brontë's New Gothic', in McNees, 4. 160). The following year, Robert A. Colby observed that *Villette* plumbs the depths of the unconscious mind, expresses instinctual passions through dream-like symbols, and anticipates the modernist technique of stream of consciousness (a concept elaborated by psychologist William James [1842–1910] before it was adopted by literary criticism) in its narrative presentation of 'the life of the mind' ('*Villette* and the Life of the Mind', *PMLA* 75 (1960), 410–19). A decade later, in *The Inner Structure of 'Wuthering Heights': The Study of an Imaginative Field* (1969), Elisabeth

409

Van de Laar analysed *Wuthering Heights* to show that the novel is structured by a system of images which, in their relationship to each other, function like elements in a dream: they mobilize pent-up psychic energies for deployment in a dynamic relationship which provides both release and gratification. The novel, in short, is structured *and* operates like the psyche.

In 1973, Nina Auerbach noted that the 'language of images' in the Brontë novels anticipates, while it excels, the language of the psyche provided by modern psychiatry ('Charlotte Brontë: The Two Countries', *University of Toronto Quarterly*, 42 (1973), 328). But for some psychoanalytic critics this has not redounded to the Brontës' artistic credit. Charles Burkhart, for example, claims that Charlotte wrote about sex and 'flirt[ed] with the sado-masochistic' without knowing that she was doing so (*Charlotte Brontë: A Psychosexual Study of her Novels* (1973), 58). Thomas Moser's 'What's the Matter with Emily Jane? Conflicting Impulses in *Wuthering Heights*' (*Nineteenth-Century Fiction*, 17 (1962), 1–19) is perhaps the best-known essay of this kind because in 1971 feminist critic Carol Ohmann took Moser to task for what she called the sexual prejudice of his article ('Emily Brontë in the Hands of Male Critics', *College English*, 32 (1971), 906–13). Moser's Freudian reading of *Wuthering Heights* interprets Heathcliff as a tantalizing 'embodiment of sexual energy' (in other words, the libido) which Emily tried to cover up in the second half of her novel by replacing the sexually charged romance of Cathy and Heathcliff with the tepid courtship between Hareton and Cathy's daughter. Having discovered a profound Freudian truth, according to Moser, 'Emily Brontë . . . tried to disguise [that] truth from herself' (p. 89).

In general, however, psychoanalytic criticism has not patronized the Brontës in this manner. Indeed, in his book on the theme and representation of sexuality in Charlotte's writing, *Charlotte Brontë and Sexuality* (1984), John Maynard does quite the reverse: he contends that Charlotte's insights about family romance anticipate Freud, as does her recognition of the ways in which psychosexually charged material can be used in narratives just as it is in dreams; that is, through mechanisms such as displacement and over determination. Moreover, he claims that, through the direct presentation of consciousness in *Villette*, Charlotte explores the nature of human sexual experience with remarkably perceptive intuition and great literary skill. Similarly, Janice Carlisle's essay 'The Face in the Mirror: *Villette* and the Conventions of Autobiography' (*ELH* 46 (1979), 262–89) shows how Lucy Snowe depends on Freudian defence mechanisms such as displacement, projection, and regression in narrating her painful story. Carlisle demonstrates that features of Lucy's narration which had seemed problematic to some critics are actually in keeping with the narrator's personality and consistent with Freud's theory about repression and distortion of psychologically sensitive material. Juliet Mitchell's 1966 essay '*Wuthering Heights*: Romanticism and Rationality' (repr. in her *Women: The Longest Revolution*, 1984) likewise asserts that the supposed obscurities of *Wuthering Heights* are 'fully intelligible' when viewed from a psychoanalytic perspective. According to Mitchell, the novel's greatest mystery, Cathy and Heathcliff's troubled relationship, is explained by the protagonists' respective traumatic separation experiences in early life (Cathy's mother dies, and Heathcliff is orphaned). Philip Wion presents a modified version of the same Freudian analysis, arguing that Heathcliff, who appears at the Heights immediately before Mrs. Earnshaw dies, becomes a mother surrogate from whom Cathy never successfully separates ('The Absent Mother in *Wuthering Heights*', in Linda H. Peterson (ed.), *Wuthering Heights* (1992), 315–29). In the same vein, books by Robert Keefe (*Charlotte Brontë's World of Death*, 1979) and Helene Moglen (*Charlotte Brontë: The Self Conceived*, 1976) maintain that all Charlotte's writings are informed by anxiety about the loss of her mother. Moglen contends that all Charlotte's orphan-protagonists struggle to find effective surrogate mothers and fail to achieve full psychic integration because they do not reach the final phase of psychosexual development for women: the discovery of 'the mother that dwells within' (p. 238), an argument repeated in Marianne Hirsch's 1994 essay 'Jane Eyre's Family Romances' (in Margaret R. Higonnet, (ed.), *Borderwork: Feminist Engagements with Comparative Literature* (1994), 162–85).

Moglen's feminist emphasis on the Brontë heroine's relationship to the mother anticipates later feminist psychoanalytic readings, such as Jean Wyatt's essay, 'A Patriarchy of One's Own: *Jane Eyre* and Romantic Love' (*Tulsa Studies in Women's Literature*, 4 (1985), 199–216), which reinterprets the romantic ending of *Jane Eyre* (Jane's reunion with Rochester) as a fantasy of fusion with the mother. While contributing to the body of criticism on 'the absent mother' in the Brontë novels, Wyatt's article actually focuses primarily on father–daughter incest, and she attributes the persistent appeal of *Jane Eyre* for young women to its success in representing that forbidden relationship while at the same time questioning patriarchal authority and guarding against a too explicit revelation of the taboo desire that informs Jane's passion. Earlier essays by David Cowart ('Oedipal Dynamics in *Jane Eyre*', *Literature and Psychology*, 31 (1981), 33–8) and David Smith ('Incest Patterns in Two

Victorian Novels', *Literature and Psychology*, 15 (1965), 135–62) also identify father–daughter incest as a central feature of *Jane Eyre*, but they lack the theoretical richness of Wyatt's analysis, which draws not only on Freud but also on the work of Norman Holland and Nancy Chodorow, whose 1978 book, *The Reproduction of Mothering*, has been very important to feminist revisions of Freud's notion of the family romance and to Lacan's assertions about girls' relationship to language.

The enriched theoretical context of Wyatt's essay is typical of most psychoanalytic criticism written since the early eighties and can be found in some earlier works informed by Continental theories about gender, language, and subject formation. For instance, in her analysis of the father–daughter dynamic in Charlotte's life and fiction, Diane Sadoff relies on the work of French feminists Luce Irigaray and Julia Kristeva to adapt Lacan's theory of 'the gaze' (by which the individual [male] subject is constituted in the mirror stage) to show that 'what critics often identify as masochism in Brontë's fiction . . . [is actually] the structural repetitions and transformations of the father-daughter bond' (*Monsters of Affection: Dickens, Eliot, and Brontë on Fatherhood* (1982), 132) from which Charlotte and her protagonists attempt to free themselves by 'assuming the uses of language normally reserved for men in her phallocentric culture' (p. 159). By mastering language, says Sadoff, Brontë and her heroines hope to reclaim self-mastery from the usurping authority of a punishing and approving Master father-figure who is the object of the daughter's anger as well as her desire. Margaret Homans, another feminist psychoanalytic critic, is interested in the problem of literary 'figuration' and 'representation' in relation to psychoanalysis and women's writing. Her work therefore combines Lacanian views of language and gender with feminist theories about motherhood, women's language, and feminine identity. In her essay 'Repression and Sublimation of Nature in *Wuthering Heights*' (*PMLA* 93 (1978), 9–19), Homans argues that nature stands for 'the repressed' in Emily's novel and therefore cannot be presented literally (just as we never see Cathy and Heathcliff actually present in nature); instead, nature is sublimated into metaphors used to describe the characters, to structure the novel, and so on. Material nature is thus repressed and put to literary use: nature is made to serve culture 'in the Name of the Father', which is 'the Word'. In a later work, *Women Writers and Poetic Identity* (1980), Homans notes Emily's 'refusal to choose between "feminine nature" and "the masculine Word"', and in yet another work, *Bearing the Word: Language and Female Experience in Nineteenth-Century Women's Writing* (1986), she

shows how *Wuthering Heights* presents two different accounts of the girl child's relationship to language: Catherine Earnshaw will not renounce her affiliation with the literal (nature, the material, and the maternal) and refuses to speak (or, more precisely, to write) the figurative language which the Law of the Father demands; whereas her daughter reluctantly accedes to patriarchal law, learns to speak through figuration, and makes a successful entry into culture as her mother did not. (The scene where the second Catherine teaches Hareton to read near the end of the novel is the key to such interpretations.)

In *A Future for Astyanax: Character and Desire in Literature* (1976), Leo Bersani was the first critic to interpret *Wuthering Heights* by combining deconstruction with psychoanalytic ideas about identity formation within the family unit. Contending that the individual gains identity by his relation to, yet difference from, his siblings, Bersani claims that Cathy and Heathcliff's passion is a 'fascination with self as other . . . [with the] radical open-endedness of being', and that Emily's novel 'explodes the myth of [the unified] personality' (p. 214), which Lacanian theory also rejects (as does French psychoanalytic theory generally). In his 1985 book *Emily Brontë*, James Kavanagh analyses the family in *Wuthering Heights* as a socio-economic unit in transition from being a structure of relationships that functioned in support of an older, agrarian culture to 'an arena of psycho-sexual struggle' which forms the social subjects necessary for modern capitalist economy. In a manner that has become increasingly common for psychoanalytic critics, Kavanagh joins Freudian notions about family romance and Lacanian ideas about 'the imaginary' with cultural theory about the reproduction of social subjectivities to provide what is fundamentally a structuralist reading of *Wuthering Heights*. That is, he explains the formal features of the text by relating them to what Frederic Jameson calls the text's 'libidinal apparatus': the unconscious force that drives the narrative just as the psychic unconscious drives human behaviour. In a similar fashion, Beth Newman ('The Situation of the Looker-On: Gender, Narration, and Gaze in *Wuthering Heights*', *PMLA* 105 (1990), 1029–41) provides an impressively rich interpretation of Emily's novel, using Freudian and Lacanian psychoanalytic theory in order to demonstrate how the modern gendered subject and literary techniques which we today call 'point of view' developed simultaneously in conjunction with the emergence of the bourgeois family and the evolution of the novelistic genre in the 19th century.

Writing on *Villette* in *Women Writing about Women* (1979), Mary Jacobus also makes use of

Lacanian theory to argue that the novel is not only 'about repression' but also is 'formally fissured by its own repressions' (p. 673); just as the psyche and language are similarly structured, so Brontë's text is structured like the psyche and operates through formal devices comparable to Freudian defence mechanisms (displacement, for example, finds its textual equivalent in metonymic substitution). Five years later, Christina Crosby developed Jacobus's claim that *Villette*'s ostensible realism is destabilized by its 'incompletely repressed Romanticism' ('Charlotte Brontë's Haunted Text', *Studies in English Literature* 24 (1984), 673). Crosby offers a deconstructionist reading of this 'radical' text, which, she claims, subverts the very oppositions upon which identity is based, according to psychoanalysis: the contrast between the supposed deep 'truth' of interiority (the unconscious) and the distortions of surface representation. Crosby's astute analysis is the precursor of the work of later critics such as John Kucich ('Passionate Reserve and Reserved Passion in the Works of Charlotte Brontë', *ELH* 52 (1985), 13–37), Janet Gezari (*Charlotte Brontë and Defensive Conduct*, 1992), Nicholas Dames ('The Clinical Novel: Phrenology and *Villette*', *Novel*, 29 (1996), 348–59), and Sally Shuttleworth (*Charlotte Brontë and Victorian Psychology*, 1996), who are interested in the relevance of psychology to the study of the Brontës' lives and writings but contest, either implicitly or explicitly, the principles upon which psychoanalytic criticism is based. These critics veer away from traditional psychoanalytic approaches and write analyses that are informed by the work of Michel Foucault and by the perspectives of *cultural criticism and the New Historicism.   CB

Homans, Margaret, *Bearing the Word: Language and Female Experience in Nineteenth-Century Women's Writing* (1986).

Kavanagh, James, *Emily Brontë* (1985).

Maynard, John, *Charlotte Brontë and Sexuality* (1984).

publishing 1800–1860. The young Brontës were familiar with the idea of writing for publication from their childhood. Five books by their father had been published by the time Charlotte was 2 years old, the first four by local firms, and the fifth, The *Maid of Killarney*, by Baldwin, Cradock, and Joy of Paternoster Row, London. As in the 18th century, publication on a small scale, especially when undertaken at the author's expense, could still be a sideline for a printing firm, who would also sell the book. Revd Patrick Brontë's *Cottage Poems* (1811) was sold by the printers P. K. Holden of Halifax, and by B. Crosby & Co., of Stationers' Court, London, F. Houlston and Son, Wellington, 'and by the Booksellers of Halifax, Leeds, York,

&c.'. Like his fellow clergymen Thomas Allbutt (see ALLBUTT FAMILY), Revd John *Buckworth, and Revd William *Morgan, Mr Brontë was contributing to the vast contemporary output of religious and morally 'improving' literature. The number of publications of all kinds was increasing rapidly. In the first half of the 18th century new books had been published at an average rate of 93 per annum, compared with almost 600 per annum from 1800 to 1825. Charles Knight, in *The Old Printer and the Modern Press* (1854), 260–2, calculated that of the 45,260 titles published 1816–51, 10,300 were works on divinity, as against 3,500 works of fiction, 3,400 drama and poetry, and 2,450 science. The 'Bells'' *Poems* 1846 was published by *Aylott and Jones, who specialized in religious books.

Publications for 'intelligent artisans' who wished to better themselves also formed a large part of the market. In 1826 Henry Brougham and others founded the Society for the Diffusion of Useful Knowledge, whose scientific and utilitarian 'Library of Useful Knowledge' appeared in fortnightly parts at 6*d*. each. In 1832 William Chambers began to reach a wide audience with his *Chambers's Edinburgh Journal* which aimed to inform more than to entertain, but offered more varied topics than Charles Knight's *Penny Magazine*—from 'Literary and Scientific subjects' to essays on trade, commerce, and emigration—and provided a sweetmeat in the form of a weekly short story, ' "a nice amusing tale . . . no ordinary trash about Italian castles, and daggers, and ghosts in the blue chamber, and similar nonsense, but something really good" ' (R. D. Altick, *The English Common Reader* (1957), 333). Charlotte Brontë refers in passing to Chambers's *Journal*, and it was one of the series taken (like the *Penny Magazine*) by the *Keighley Mechanics' Institute. It was to 'the Messrs Chambers of Edinburgh' that Charlotte applied for advice on bringing out *Poems* 1846. John Cassell (1817–65), founder of the House of Cassell in 1848, also had educational ideals. His journal, the *Standard of Freedom* (1848–51), which included a very favourable review of *Jane Eyre*, his *Cassell's Illustrated Family Paper*, *Cassell's Elements of Arithmetic*, *Cassell's Classical Library*, *Working Man's Friend*, *Popular Educator*, and the like, all reflected his policy of publishing worthwhile reading for the working man. Murrays, Longmans, and *Smith, Elder and Company also had significant lists of educational works, textbooks, grammars, dictionaries, histories, and serious books of travel, though their publishing had a broader base, and was not specially directed at a working-class readership.

At the opposite end of the publishing spectrum were the works of 'ordinary trash about Italian castles' spurned by William Chambers. These were pre-eminently the 'New and Entertaining Novels' printed for William Lane at the Minerva Press, Leadenhall-street, from 1790 until his death in 1814, and continued under the same imprint until 1820. Exploiting the *Gothic vogue made famous by Mrs Ann Ward Ratcliffe, they were best-sellers, much in demand in circulating libraries, and had numerous progeny in the *annuals, ladies' magazines, and the like, well into the 1830s. Charlotte refers mockingly to the Gothic vogue in a letter of December 1840, but the Brontës had been fascinated by it as children, as they had been with the works of Sir Walter *Scott. Scott's *Lay of the Last Minstrel* had been published by Longmans in association with Archibald Constable of Edinburgh, who also published many of Scott's other poems and novels until 1826. They had been printed by James Ballantyne, whose bankruptcy in January 1826 disastrously involved Constable and Scott himself, and to a lesser degree Hurst and Robinson, the publishers associated with Constable. In 1827 Robert Cadell (1788–1849), jointly with Scott, bought the copyrights in his novels, and thereafter Cadell published the later editions. In 1851 the publishers Adam and Charles Black of Edinburgh bought the Scott copyright.

Longmans was one of the oldest and most respected publishing firms in the country. Founded by Thomas Longman (1699–1755), it was owned successively by his nephew Thomas Longman II (1730–97), and Thomas II's son Thomas Norton Longman (1771–1842), who succeeded to the business in 1797. After he had taken Thomas *Moore's friend Owen Rees into partnership, the firm became one of the greatest in London, publishing for *Wordsworth, *Southey, Scott, and Moore. In 1826 T. N. Longman became the sole proprietor of the *Edinburgh Review*. He was succeeded by his sons Thomas (1804–79), who became head of the firm in 1842, and William (1813–77). Like Murrays, they published many school textbooks, and Charlotte commented rather sourly on their complaints in April 1851 that the government was infringing their trade rights by its publication of Irish school-books. From the mid-19th century Longmans also supported the 'woman's movement', publishing a work by Anna Jameson advocating a larger share of social work for women in 1856, and J. S. Mills's *Subjection of Women* in 1869.

Murray's publishing house was founded by John Murray I who first set up as a bookseller and stationer in Fleet Street in 1768, and began publishing in a small way. It was his son John Murray II (1778–1843) who made the firm great, and changed the relationship between authors and publishers by his enterprise and generosity. He was the London agent for Constable from 1803 until 1808, when he shared in the publication of Scott's *Marmion*, and again from 1810 to 1813. In 1809 he started the *Quarterly Review*, to which Scott, Southey, and later *Lockhart contributed. Before he moved in 1812 to Albemarle Street (where the firm still is) Murray had met *Byron, and published the first two cantos of *Childe Harold*. He remained Byron's publisher and friend, and in 1826 bought the remaining copyrights in his works. He also published Jane Austen's *Emma*, *Persuasion*, and *Northanger Abbey*, and in 1816, with William Blackwood, published the first series of Scott's *Tales of my Landlord*. Crabbe, George Borrow, and other famous writers were welcome guests in his drawing room, where the fireplace in which Byron's controversial 'Memoirs' were destroyed can still be seen. The third John Murray (1808–92) initiated the famous series of guide-books, and published many travel books and educational works. In 1917 John Murray IV (1851–1928; KCVO, 1926) took over the firm of Smith, Elder.

By 1830 John Murray II was disenchanted with his publishing ventures in poetry and fiction; he had lost heavily through his generosity to Crabbe, and he transferred the copyright in the novels he had published to Richard Bentley. Longmans had taken four years to sell 500 copies of Wordsworth's 1820 volume, and published few poets thereafter. Edward Moxon (1801–58), who had worked for Longmans, became the best-known publisher of poetry. He had a distinguished list, which included Southey, Wordsworth, *Tennyson, Browning, Landor, and Coventry Patmore; but he found that poetry rarely sold well. His carefully produced volumes were respected, and in January 1846 Charlotte Brontë wished the 'Bells'' poems to resemble in their format 'Moxon's last edition of Wordsworth'.

Blackwood's of Edinburgh, founded by William Blackwood (1776–1834) in 1804, and continued by the Blackwood dynasty thereafter, published separate works by *De Quincey, James *Hogg, John *Wilson, and John Galt, as well as their contributions to the famous *Blackwood's Edinburgh Magazine*. Branwell Brontë pleaded in vain to be one of their authors. Unlike Murrays and Longmans, they continued to publish fiction throughout the century: Susan Ferrier's *Marriage* (1818) brought her fame, and Blackwood's also published her *Inheritance* (1824). Samuel Warren and *Bulwer-Lytton were among their authors, and it was John Blackwood (1818–79) who published all but one of George Eliot's novels, for she returned to the firm after Smith, Elder's expensive venture with her *Romola* in 1863.

Novel-publishing, rather in the doldrums in the early 1830s, was given a new lease of life by *Dickens's best-selling *Pickwick Papers*, published in

20 monthly parts in 1836–7 by Chapman and Hall. Part-publication, in Dickens's hands, became a fine art and a profitable commercial venture: *Pickwick*'s monthly circulation rose in a year from 500 to 40,000. The printers of *Pickwick* were Bradbury and Evans, who also had the money-spinning *Punch* as an anchor. They expanded rapidly in the 1840s to combine printing and publishing, for a large printing house with the latest steam-powered stereotyping machines was needed for part-publication. By 1846 they were Dickens's publishers, and they went on to publish W. M. *Thackeray's *Vanity Fair*, *Pendennis*, and *The Newcomes*. Charlotte Brontë declined to attempt either part-publication or serial publication in a magazine, believing that she lacked the constant flow of inspiration needed to make either method a success. All the Brontës' novels published during their lifetime appeared in the dominant Victorian 'three-decker' format, *Wuthering Heights* and *Agnes Grey* forming respectively two-thirds and one third of an incongruous three-volume publication. The format suited the circulating libraries because they could issue single volumes of a popular work, and because the high price (31s. 6d.) meant that, as the publishers' main market, they were the virtual arbiters of taste and morality in fiction. Like Emily and Anne Brontë, new novelists sometimes had to contribute to the cost of publication, theoretically gaining a share of the profits after the sale of a specified number of copies; but T. C. *Newby did not honour his agreement for *Wuthering Heights* and *Agnes Grey*. There were many other publishers of fiction. By 1855 they were almost all, like publishers in general, in either Edinburgh or London. In that year *Hodson's Booksellers, Publishers and Stationers Directory* listed 369 publishers in London (many of them in Paternoster Row, Fleet Street, and Holborn), but only one in Leeds. *Colburn (d. 1855) and Richard Bentley (1794–1871) had vied with each other in the three-decker market, and were notorious for puffing their own publications in their respective journals. Dickens had been briefly the editor of *Bentley's Miscellany* (1837) in which *Oliver Twist* and *Barnaby Rudge* were published, but returned to Chapman and Hall for *Nicholas Nickleby* (1838–9). Thackeray also produced (mainly pseudonymous) fiction for magazines including *Bentley's Miscellany* and *Fraser's Magazine*. He was to become, briefly, the editor of the *Cornhill Magazine*, for which he wrote *Lovel the Widower*, *The Adventures of Philip*, and the unfinished *Denis Duval*. Edward Chapman and William Hall commenced publishing at 186 Strand in 1830, produced a 'library of fiction' which included one-volume reprints, and acquired a distinguished list of novelists and other writers, notably *Carlyle, Dickens, Elizabeth *Gas-

kell, Anthony Trollope, and George Meredith, the firm's reader from 1860.

From the 1830s onward Henry George Bohn, Charles Tilt, and David Bogue published reasonably priced series of reprints, and from the 1840s more publishers than ever copied Colburn and Bentley's practice of issuing 6s. reprints of their novels. In 1846 the Irish firm of Simms and McIntyre issued the first of its Parlour Novelist series at 2s. in wrappers and 2s. 6d. in cloth. It is likely that the copies of Jane Austen's *Sense and Sensibility* and *Pride and Prejudice* sent to Charlotte by Smith, Elder in March 1850 were cheap 1s. volumes in Routledge's Railway series. The era of the cheap paperback and the 'railway novel' had begun.

See also CONTEMPORARY WRITERS, BRONTËS' CONTACTS WITH AND ATTITUDES TO.

pugilism, Brontë interest in. Boxing was a fashionable sport which embraced all classes in the early 19th century and was practised by Brontë heroes like *Byron and John *Wilson (the 'Christopher North' of *Blackwood's Edinburgh Magazine*). The latter was described in *Fraser's Magazine* (Apr. 1831), to which the Brontës subscribed, as 'a sixteen stoner who has tried it, without the gloves, with the Game Chicken, and got none the worse'. About this time Branwell developed a passion for the sport, probably encouraged by his increasing contact with local Haworth youth once Charlotte went to school at *Roe Head. Francis Leyland reports that Branwell became a member of the Haworth boxing club, where the 'fancy' (those who frequent the boxing ring) amused themselves with sparring in the upper room of a local building, possibly the *Black Bull. Benjamin Binns (see BINNS FAMILY) tells how Branwell used to send him to the Shake Hands beerhouse between Keighley and Oakworth every Sunday to collect *Bell's Life in London* (*Bradford Observer* (17 Feb. 1894), 6), the sporting weekly edited by Pierce Egan. Leyland notes that Branwell eagerly read this and other sporting papers of the day (Leyland, 1. 117); it also features in Branwell's unfinished novel *And the Weary are at Rest* (Neufeldt *BB Works*, 3. 429). *Blackwood's* carried extracts from Egan's classic *Boxiana; or Sketches of Ancient and Modern Pugilism* (1819–22), including detailed reports of prize fights at the Castle Tavern, Holborn, London, in the colourful language of the ring. These Branwell transposed into his early writing in fights amongst Glass Town's *'Rare Lads' and their equally enthusiastic aristocratic supporters (for example, Arthur *O'Connor).

Charlotte's early writing reflects Branwell's enthusiasm for the sport, mimicking his banter and use of 'fancy' terms. In *'Corner Dishes', for example, the young Duke of Zamorna patronizes Maurice *Flannagan, a Glass Town pugilist, making him his private secretary so he can spar with him when he wants. Zamorna himself is known as 'Young Wildblood, the Swashing Swell, Handsome Spanker, and such like amongst the officials and the Fancy' (Alexander *EEW*, 2(2). 104–5). Branwell's 'Luddenden Foot Notebook' with its sketch of two boxers (Alexander & Sellars, p. 342) shows that he continued his interest in pugilism amongst colleagues working for the Manchester–Leeds railway (April 1841–March 1842). Both John Brown and Joseph Bentley Leyland also shared his interest in pugilism which continued throughout his life. As late as 1845, he was still following the 'Fancy' and drawing sketches of celebrated pugilists, adorning a letter to Leyland with images of 'Bendigo' (William Thompson) and Benjamin Caunt, who became champion of England in April 1838, by defeating Bendigo after 75 rounds. The image (Alexander & Sellars, p. 348) alludes to the unfair return fight on 9 September 1845, in which Bendigo retrieved his title (see SLAVERY). 'Ben Caunt' is also referred to in Branwell's *And the Weary are at Rest* (Neufeldt *BB Works*, 3. 454).

> Heywood, Christopher, ' "Alas! Poor Caunt": Branwell's Emancipationist Cartoon', *BST* (1995), 21. 5. 177–85 (includes portraits of Bendigo and Caunt).

Pusey, Revd Dr Edward Bouverie (1800–82), a leader of the *Oxford Movement and one of the authors of *Tracts for the Times*; regarded as a bête-noire by the Brontës. He remained within the Anglican communion, but deplored ultra-Protestant tendencies, insisted on the real presence of Christ in the Eucharist, advocated frequent services, and aimed to restore spirituality and dignity to churches which had too often declined into casual slovenliness. He proposed the establishment of celibate monastic orders, founded and paid for St Saviour's, Leeds, and helped to found in London the first Anglican sisterhood. Pusey himself deprecated ritualism and elaborate vestments, but 'Puseyism' became associated with High Church practices (long white surplices, altar-cloths of different colours according to the church's year, red type 'rubric' in service books) deplored by Evangelicals as dangerously close to 'Romanism'. The threat of 'Papal Aggression' in 1850–1 increased Evangelical distrust of Puseyites, described by Lord John Russell in November 1850 as 'enemies within the gates, indulging in their mummeries of superstition'. Revd Patrick Brontë agreed, writing to Revd A. P. Irwine on 15 April 1851 of Puseyism's 'subtle poison'. Charlotte distrusted and, in most of her writings before 1852, mocked Puseyism. In her letter to Hartley Coleridge of December 1840, she claimed that she might have introduced a Puseyite into her story, *Ashworth, and polished off the high church 'with the best of Warren's jet blacking' (Smith *Letters*, 1. 240). In *Shirley* she makes fun of the future 'pre-ordained, specially sanctified . . . successors of the apostles, disciples of Dr. Pusey and tools of the Propaganda' (ch. 1). She and Mr Brontë enjoyed reading a light-hearted 'squib', *A Paper-Lantern for Puseyites* published in 1843 and reissued in 1850 (Smith *Letters*, 2. 493–4, 522–4). More seriously, Charlotte affirmed in April 1840 that although her conscience would not let her be a Puseyite, she strongly objected to intolerant abuse of Puseyism; and while in 1854 she regretted Revd A. B. *Nicholls's rigid Puseyism, she accepted that he was a good man, 'always reliable, truthful' and worthy of respect.

Q

Quamina, Kashna (Cashna), the 'mild and good' king of the *Ashantee when the *Twelves landed in west Africa, in the *Glass Town and Angrian saga. He made an alliance with the Twelves, traded with them, and lived in mutual peace. His son is the warlike Sai-Too-Too *Quamina, father of Quashia *Quamina.

Quamina, Quashia, son of Sai-Too-Too *Quamina, the warlike king of the *Ashantee in the *Glass Town and Angrian saga. When his father dies at the Battle of *Coomassie, he is adopted by the Duke of Wellington and brought up with his own sons. The account of his discovery beside his dying mother and her song of vengeance is told in 'The African Queen's Lament' and his early career and first attack against the Glass Town in The *Green Dwarf (Alexander EEW, 2(1). 3–6, 178–80). Despite his 'golden fetters', literary education, and kind treatment, we are told that his evil nature gets the better of nurture and he becomes leader of the Ashantees, inciting them to rebellion against the Federation with the help of the famous brothers and old counsellors of his father, Eredi and Benini.

The name 'Quashia' is generic for 'Black', from West African *Kwasi*, later to become the West Indian racist epithet 'Quashee'. It embodies all the European literary clichés of the African: initially fascinating, physically powerful, uncontrollably passionate, and treacherous. From noble savage ('a perfect Othello' he is called by Branwell Brontë), Quashia Quamina degenerates (in Charlotte's stories) into a lascivious drunken murderer. Thus he is characterized as bold, irritable, active and daring, but also deeply treacherous. In particular he becomes the enemy of the Duke of *Zamorna and his new kingdom of *Angria, partly because of his early infatuation for Mary *Percy (now Zamorna's wife) in Wellington's Land and partly because the two were rivals as boys, although Quashia was ten years older. Allied with the Duke of *Northangerland in the Angrian Wars, he savagely murders Zamorna's son Ernest

'Fitzarthur' Wellesley, and sacks *Adrianopolis. His erotic wallowing in Mary's boudoir in Zamorna's palace is the climax of his triumph (see ROE HEAD JOURNAL). When Quashia (and Northangerland) are finally defeated, he flees to the southern wastes of Etrei, but re-emerges as Northangerland's crony once again in Frenchyland, where Northangerland is in exile. He is constantly drunk and speaks in a fantastic pseudo-biblical language. Having failed with Mary Percy, Mr Quashia Quamina Kashna (as he now is) makes a bid for Northangerland's other daughter, Caroline *Vernon, but fails in this and in his attempt to become an MP. Charlotte Brontë intended Quashia to meet the ignominious death of a 'barbarous monarch' brought to the capital by the emperors of ancient Rome. He was to be marched captive through the streets of Adrianopolis in Emperor Adrian's (Zamorna's) procession before being guillotined (Alexander EEW, 2(1). 326). He is seldom noble in Branwell's manuscripts and becomes simply a pathetic drunken black scoundrel. In *And the Weary are at Rest, Quashia is mocked bitterly as an agent of evil about to become a Wesleyan convert; he becomes a symbol of the perfidiousness of the slave trade that has corrupted English society itself (Neufeldt BB Works, 3. 444–5). See also AFRICA; POST-COLONIAL THEORY.

Quamina, Sai-Too-Too, the warlike king of the *Ashantee, son of the peaceful Kashna *Quamina and father of Quashia *Quamina, in the *Glass Town and Angrian saga. As a youth he is captured by the *Twelves; later as King, 'headstrong & revengeful', he ignores his father's treaties with the Twelves, wages war against them and is defeated at the Battle of *Coomassie. 'The African Queen's Lament' describes the death of his wife and her prophecy of their son's vengeance (Alexander EEW, 2(1). 3–6).

Quarterly Review. A Conservative review founded by John Murray in 1809 to counter the increasing influence of the Liberal Edinburgh Review. Robert *Southey and Sir Walter *Scott (two writers admired by the young Brontës) contributed heavily to early issues of the Quarterly Review, which was initially edited by William Gifford, upon whom the children modelled a character in their juvenile stories. From 1826 to 1853 the Quarterly was edited by J. G. *Lockhart, previously one of *Blackwood's Edinburgh Magazine's most important writers, and another figure well known to the Brontës. In December 1848, the Quarterly published a review which described Jane Eyre as 'pre-eminently an anti-Christian composition' pervaded by a 'tone of ungodly discontent'. The anonymous reviewer, Elizabeth *Rigby, also asserted that if the novel had not been written by a man, then the author must be a woman who had 'long forfeited the society of her own sex'. Appearing in the wake of Emily's funeral and just as the seriousness of Anne's illness was becoming evident, this review hurt and angered Charlotte, who eventually responded with a satiric 'Word to the "Quarterly"', written for inclusion with her next novel, *Shirley*, but declined by her publishers (see SHIRLEY: 'A WORD TO THE "QUARTERLY"'). A voice for Conservative values throughout the 19th century, the *Quarterly* is also infamous for having published John Wilson Croker's notoriously harsh 1818 review of John Keats's *Endymion*.

CB

Quashia. See QUAMINA, QUASHIA.

R

Rachel (actress) (born Elisa Félix, 1820–58). George *Smith took Charlotte to St James's Theatre in London to see the famous actress Rachel in Scribe and Legouvé's *Adrienne Lecouvreur* on 7 June 1851, and as Camille in a version of Corneille's *Horace* on 21 June 1851. The daughter of impoverished German-Jewish parents, Rachel was acclaimed as a student-actress in 1833–6, and made her début at the Comédie-Française in 1838. Her first London performance in 1841 made an extraordinary impact, as did her performance there as Adrienne on 8 July 1850. Charlotte, who portrayed her as *Vashti, found her unforgettable, and shuddered at her as a fiend incarnate.

Rachel (fictional), Helen *Huntingdon's childhood nurse, her maid and most loyal friend in *Tenant*. As a faithful servant (possibly modelled on the Brontës' servant Tabitha *Aykroyd), she is keenly perceptive, and fiercely protective of Helen and her son. Though Helen cannot pay her, she accompanies Helen to Wildfell Hall, and nurses Arthur.

Radcliffe, Mrs Ann. See GOTHIC NOVELS.

railways. In the late 1820s steam locomotives began to replace horses or stationary engines on the primitive railways used by mines and quarries. Hauling carriages instead of wagons, they were soon used also to transport passengers. Development was at first gradual, but accelerated rapidly: 54 Railway Acts were passed in 1825–35, with a projected coverage of 500 miles, including the 112-mile London–Birmingham–Preston line which eventually opened in 1838. But in just two years, 1836–7, 39 Acts permitted the construction of a further 1,000 miles of track, including the Manchester–Leeds railway, with a tunnel nearly 2 miles long. Both these railways were used by the Brontë family. From 1844, with the emergence of 'railway kings' such as George *Hudson, the proliferation and amalgamation of lines facilitated longer, more rapid journeys, especially from the north-east and north-west, and southwards through the mid-

lands. Railway operators also imperilled travellers' lives through their urge for speed and frequency, and their inadequate braking and signalling systems. Drivers worked dangerously long hours, and the ever-present fire risk intensified the horror of fatal collisions in tunnels. Investment in railway shares had its own hazards, as Charlotte realized. In April 1845 at the height of the 'Railway Mania' the Brontës' investments were not in immediate danger, despite the continual fluctuation in share prices, for they had got on 'very decently', guided by Emily, and had avoided all 'mere speculative buying-in and selling-out' (Smith *Letters*, 1. 390). But by August 1845 thousands of speculators had been ruined, and the Brontës' shares in the York and North Midland railway were precarious. During the railway panic of 1847–8, their investments were again at risk, largely owing to Hudson's malpractices. Charlotte was fortunate, for her publisher, George Smith, shrewdly reinvested her money in safer securities (see FINANCES OF THE BRONTËS).

Charlotte's first railway journey was the prelude to her first, awestruck, sight of the sea. In September 1839 she travelled by coach from Keighley to Leeds, and thence, with Ellen Nussey, took the 20-mile, one-and-a-half-hour train journey from Marsh Lane station to Selby—the first line connecting with Leeds, begun in October 1830 and opened for passengers in September 1834. A light hired carriage (a 'fly') took them on to Driffield, from where they travelled by post-chaise to *Bridlington on the coast. In 1842 a train journey initiated the stay in Brussels which so profoundly affected Charlotte's life and work. On 8 February 1842 Charlotte and Emily with their father, escorted by Mary *Taylor and Joseph *Taylor, left Leeds on the 9 a.m. train to reach Euston station in London eleven hours later. After sightseeing in London for three days, they took the steam-packet (part of a regular service which carried passengers, goods, and mail) from London Bridge wharf to Ostend ('Boue-Marine' in *Villette*) and a 'diligence'—a swift horse-drawn coach—from there to Brussels, arriving on 14 February. Train journeys between London and Leeds were involved in the sisters' hasty return to England (5–8 November 1842) after Elizabeth *Branwell's death, in Charlotte's return journey alone (27–9 January 1843), which included rail travel from Ostend to the Gare du Nord in Brussels, and in her departure thence, disturbed and depressed by the parting from M. Constantin *Heger, on 1 January 1844. In 1845 Charlotte used the train between Leeds and *Sheffield, in conjunction with the horse-drawn omnibus which plied between Sheffield and *Hathersage, where she stayed with Ellen Nussey at Revd Henry *Nussey's vicarage—

gaining impressions of scenes and names recalled in *Jane Eyre*.

Meanwhile, probably in May 1840, Anne Brontë had begun her journeys to and from *Thorp Green Hall, reached by a combination of road and rail journeys. She was joined there by Branwell in January 1843. He had previously been a railway clerk, first at *Sowerby Bridge station on the incomplete Manchester and Leeds line from 31 August 1840, and then from 1 April 1841, clerk-in-charge at *Luddenden Foot, on a part of the line used mainly for goods traffic. He returned home, depressed and ill, on 31 March 1842. On 22 May 1842, however, anxious for an active life, he asked his friend Francis *Grundy if he had any chance of a situation, 'under English Engineers, on one of the lines commencing abroad, either in Russia—Sweden—Belgium—France—or the Sardinian Dominions' where his 'gentleman's education' might be turned to account. Unfortunately for Branwell, no such post materialized. After his dismissal from Thorp Green in July 1845, Branwell applied unsuccessfully on 23 October 1845 for the post of secretary to the 'Manchester and Hebden Bridge and Keighley and Leeds and Carlisle Junction Railway'—a proposed link-line which would have passed through Haworth, and which, like innumerable other projects, was not given permission to proceed. The Aire valley line from Leeds was to be of considerable use to the Brontës. The railway from Leeds to Shipley, opened in July 1846, was extended to Keighley and opened on 16 March 1847. The Brontës and their visitors could now walk or hire a gig to cover the 4 miles or so between the village and Keighley station. Ellen Nussey made her 'first visit to Keighley by rail' to visit the Brontës in mid-July 1847. The 'small Stationhouse'—a temporary structure—at Keighley received the precious manuscript of *Jane Eyre* for despatch by rail to London. In July 1848 Charlotte and Anne were able to 'whirl' up to London by the night train to identify themselves to their respective publishers: for Charlotte it was the precursor of several momentous visits: to London, to Windermere in the *Lake District, and to *Edinburgh. Her only significant use of railways in her novels occurs in *The Professor*, which begins before 'the days of trains and railroads', but ends with Edward Crimsworth recouping his fallen fortunes, 'getting richer than Croesus by railway speculations'. It was perhaps characteristic of Anne and Emily that they spent much time during their excursion to York in July 1845, by this very modern form of transport, absorbed in the adventures of their *Gondal characters. The last journey in Anne's life, also made partly by train, enabled her to have the 'overpowering pleasure' of revisiting York Minster.

Ramsden, Timothy, in *Shirley*, a prosperous corn factor, owner of Royd corn mill, 'a stout, puffy gentleman, as large in person as he was in property' (p. 347). He is one of Robert Gérard *Moore's allies in the defence of *Hollow's Mill against the *Luddite machine-breakers.   HR

Rand, Ebenezer, from January 1844 to ?April 1845, master of the *Haworth National School, opened in the Sunday school building at the instigation of William Scoresby, Vicar of Leeds, with the co-operation of Revd Patrick Brontë. Mr Rand trained at St Mark's College, London, opened 1841. The examination of the school's 160 pupils in July 1844 showed progress in learning and good manners under the tutelage of Rand and his wife, the schoolmistress Sarah Ann. The Rands moved with their baby son to Dukinfield, Cheshire, and later to Ipswich. Charlotte and Mr Brontë liked and kept in touch with them.

'rare lads' (or 'rare apes'), terms of approbation used loosely by the Glass Town 'heavies' to refer both to themselves and to others, usually those destined to be the victims of their midnight *body-snatching raids. They constitute the 'low life' of the *Glass Town and Angrian saga: petty thieves, poachers, and brawlers like Tom Scroven and Dick Crack-Skull. Many, like Richard (Young Man) *Naughty, are used by the Duke of Northangerland in his illegal and revolutionary activities; and Ned *Laury later reforms, and rejects his 'rare lad' days.

Ratcliffe, Tabitha, née Brown (1834–1910), fourth daughter of John *Brown, and sister of Martha *Brown. At the age of 16 she was a worsted weaver. In December 1861 she married Robert Ratcliffe, brother of the first verger of Haworth, appointed 1875. After Martha Brown's death in 1880, all Martha's effects, including items given to her by the Brontës and Revd A. B. *Nicholls, were divided equally among her five sisters. Thereafter Tabitha sold drawings by Charlotte and Emily Brontë to various collectors, including Dr Dobie, William *Law, and J. Roy *Coventry (see Alexander & Sellars, esp. pp. 432–42). See also BROWN FAMILY.

Rawfolds Mill, Cleckheaton, near Liversedge, owned by William Cartwright (1775–1839); one of the many clothweaving mills of West Yorkshire at the time of the Brontës. Robert Gérard *Moore's *Hollow's Mill in *Shirley* and the *Luddite riots which culminate in a night attack on the mill (ch. 19), are based partly on Rawfolds Mill, which was attacked by Luddites on 11 April 1812. The mill of the *Taylor family of Gomersal at Hunsworth, which Charlotte had visited, was probably the closer model for the actual building, but the events are those associated with Rawfolds. Revd Patrick Brontë was incumbent of nearby *Hartshead at the time and the route of the attack went past Charlotte's school at *Roe Head. The mill no longer exists, although one shed was incorporated into the present Rigby's Wire Works.

Shirley (Clarendon edn.), app. A (illustration and excerpts from Leeds Mercury, 1812).

reader reception. See RECEPTION HISTORIES.

reading public. Coined in 1816 by Samuel Taylor *Coleridge, the phrase 'reading public' referred to the increasingly large body of 'common' readers who, by the early 19th century, had become the effective judges of authors and their writings. The term reflects the rise in literacy rates that began in the late 18th century as well as other changes in literary culture that occurred as the long transition from patronage to market economy slowly completed itself during this period. In his Lives of the Poets (1781), Samuel *Johnson welcomed the emergence of this new class of unlearned readers by whom 'must finally be decided all claim to poetical honours' (4. 485), but, in fact, most literary professionals, including Johnson himself, were more than a little anxious about the rise of the 'common reader'. Coleridge, for example, thought the phrase he had coined was a contradiction in terms, a 'misgrowth' produced by a promiscuous literary culture: 'We have now a READING PUBLIC—as strange a phrase methinks as ever forced a splenetic smile on the staid countenance of Meditation' (The Statesman's Manual, 1816). By the 1840s the power of the reading public was effectively consolidated, so that an author like Charles *Dickens could become enormously successful by appealing to and manipulating this large market. Dickens is the example par excellence of such success rather than a typical author of the period, however. Wilkie Collins's cautious optimism about the potential of common readers to be the mainstay of literature is probably more representative of the attitude of literary professionals at mid-century: 'A reading public of three millions which lies right out of the pale of literary civilization, is a phenomenon worth examining,' Collins observed. 'It is perhaps hardly too much to say, that the future of English fiction may rest with this Unknown Public' (Household Words, 18 (Aug. 1858)).

Fictitious authors in Charlotte's juvenilia frequently address their equally fictitious readers ('the reading public of Verdopolis') in prefaces attached to their works, and this reflects the Brontë children's early familiarity with the conventions and controversies in the changing literary economy of their time. As mature authors, Charlotte and Anne continued to think of the public as an important component in their professional experience. Thanking 'the Public, for the indulgent ear it has inclined to a plain tale with few pretensions' in her preface to the second edition of Jane Eyre, Charlotte adopted a fairly restrained stance of respectful politeness toward her readers, but in preparing a preface for The Professor, she took a far more ingratiating approach. Acknowledging that the novel had been rejected by numerous publishers, she asserts that in facing the tribunal of public opinion, it now faces its 'worst struggle and strongest ordeal'; 'but it takes comfort', she concludes with humility, and 'mutters under its breath—while lifting its eye to that of the Public,

He that is low need fear no fall.'

In 'A Word to the "Quarterly" ', which Charlotte wrote for inclusion with Shirley (see SHIRLEY: 'A WORD TO THE "QUARTERLY" '), she again addresses the reading public 'respectfully', but in an unsuccessful attempt at satire, she also refers to the 'too fastidious public', an epithet that was probably somewhat out of fashion by this time. Like Charlotte, Anne publicly expressed her hope to 'gain the public ear', but she addressed her audience rather more defiantly. In the preface to the second edition of The Tenant of Wildfell Hall, she declares that she does not write 'to ingratiate [her]self with the Press and the Public', and she dismisses questions about the anonymous author's gender by insisting that it 'cannot greatly signify to those who know him only by his works'. CB

Real Life in Verdopolis is a 36-page narrative (MS in Brotherton), in two volumes, completed September 1833, in which Branwell Brontë begins to develop several ongoing themes revolving around Alexander Rogue (Rougue) (Duke of *Northangerland). Rogue and his followers (the Democrats) riot and burn down the prison in *Glass Town to cover a gaolbreak for five prisoners who could implicate him in court. The riot is put down by government troops led by the Marquis of Douro (later Duke of *Zamorna). Although Rogue and Douro are close friends, president and vice-president of *Elysium, a secret male club for the wealthy and aristocratic, they engage in a boxing match that leaves both senseless on the floor (see PUGILISM, BRONTË INTEREST IN). We see Rogue at the headquarters of his vast robbery enterprise in a secret cavern in the mountains, but also as leader of the Democrats opposed to the Aristocrats, Douro's party, and for the first time posing as a Methodist preacher (see ASHWORTH, BROTHER).

We are introduced to Rogue's chief co-conspirator, Hector *Montmorency, and his daughter Lady Julia, and to Frederic Stuart, Viscount *Castlereagh, and General *Thornton Wilkin Sneaky, rivals for her hand, who fight a duel. Meanwhile Castlereagh is fleeced of thousands of pounds at the Elysium, and is betrayed by Montmorency, who, having promised him his daughter, sends her off to be married to Thornton. The latter, associated with Rogue's robbery enterprise, which has been uncovered, gives up Lady Julia to Castlereagh in return for a pardon. Castlereagh becomes Douro's close friend and secretary of the Foreign Office. VN

Collins, Robert G. (ed.), *The Hand of the Arch-Sinner* (1993) pp. 120–211.
Neufeldt *BB Works*, 1. 266–332.

reception histories. In the simplest sense of the term, 'reception history' denotes a retrospective account of the critical responses to a literary text, or body of texts, over time. Brief reception histories of the Brontës' writings—especially *Wuthering Heights*, *Jane Eyre*, and *Villette*—are available today in the numerous different casebook studies that have been published on Charlotte and Emily's novels in the last twenty years.

The earliest extensive historical survey of criticism on the Brontës is found in Miriam Allott's introduction to *The Brontës: The Critical Heritage* (1974), a collection of reviews and commentaries (many in extract form) written from 1846 to 1900. Her indispensable book and intelligent editorial commentary have provided more than a starting point for the many more recent reception histories, which bring her account up to date and typically provide brief discussion of the various critical approaches that have been taken to the interpretation of the Brontës' writing over time. Also useful is a collection of reviews, recollections, memoirs, and critical essays on the Brontës, edited by Eleanor McNees in 1996 as part of Helm Information's Critical Assessments series. McNees provides limited editorial commentary, however, so readers are left to develop their own overview of the history of Brontë criticism from the numerous and quite diverse samples included in this four-volume collection. An important reference work concerning the reception of the Brontës' work is the *Cambridge Bibliography of English Literature*, vol. 4 (1999), edited by Joanne Shattock, which contains a useful listing of reviews and criticism in an article on 'The Brontës' compiled by Christine Alexander and H. J. Rosengarten.

The most interesting, and arguably most significant, reception histories are those which not only give an account of critical responses to a work (or group of works) but also provide an illuminating analysis of such critical reviews. The rise of feminism in the 1970s drew attention to the need for studying the history of criticism on women's writing, and Ruth Gounelas's 1984 essay, 'Charlotte Brontë and the Critics: Attitudes to the Female Qualities in her Writing' (*Journal of the Australasian Universities' Language and Literature Association*, 62 (1984), 151–200), attempts to describe changing critical attitudes toward the 'female qualities' in Charlotte's writing. Gounelas divides this critical history into three phases: an early period, from 1847 to the early 1850s, when the author's gender was a prominent and problematic factor in reviews by critics such as George Henry *Lewes, Elizabeth *Rigby, and Harriet *Martineau; a long middle period when, according to Gounelas, Charlotte's gender didn't seem to matter to critics including Leslie Stephen, David Cecil, and Virginia Woolf; and another long period beginning in the 1960s when the fact 'that Brontë wrote so demonstrably as a woman' began to attract positive critical interest in her work (p. 161). More subtle analyses of gender issues in early reviews of the Brontës' writing have been offered by Nicola Diane Thompson in *Reviewing Sex: Gender and the Reception of Victorian Novels* (1996) and by Catherine Malone, whose article on the reception of *The Professor*, ' "We Have Learned to Love Her More than Her Books": The Critical Reception of Brontë's *Professor*' (*Review of English Studies* NS 47 (1996), 175–87), draws on sixteen reviews not included in Allott's collection; moreover, Malone presents an enlightening discussion of the way in which the responses of professional reviewers and general readers were influenced by the timing of the book's release in relation to the publication of Elizabeth *Gaskell's *The Life of Charlotte Brontë*.

Given the fairly recent emergence of *cultural criticism and new historicism as well as the development of the discipline of book history (which includes historical study of reading practices and audience formation), it seems likely that more theoretically sophisticated and/or comprehensive histories of readers' responses to the Brontës' writing will one day be available. Malone's article makes a beginning in its discussion of reading practices and a recent article by Haruko Iwakami surveys the Japanese reception of *Jane Eyre* (*BS* (2002), 27. 2. 91–9) See CRITICAL RECEPTION TO 1860; CRITICISM 1860–1940; CRITICISM FROM 1940. CB

Redhead, Revd Samuel (1778–1845), amiable evangelical friend of Revd Patrick Brontë, fellow member of Bradford Auxiliary Bible Society and Church Missionary Association. After Mr Brontë's resignation on 21 October 1819 from his controversial appointment to Haworth, Revd Henry *Heap appointed Redhead. On 31 October the congregation 'stomped' out, shouting and hooting, when Redhead entered the pulpit; on 7 November uproar continued within and outside the church; and on 14 November indecency, impiety, and insults caused him to leave without preaching a sermon. He resigned on 15 November, and in 1822 began a long, faithful ministry at Calverley. Yet Haworth welcomed him on 21 July 1844, when he good-humouredly reminded the congregation of previous events.

Barker, ch. 3.
Lock & Dixon, ch. 11.

Red House, Gomersal, Cleckheaton, West Yorkshire, named from its unusual red brick construction which sets it apart from the surrounding houses of local stone; the model for *Briarmains in Shirley.* Built in 1660 by William Taylor, it was owned by the Taylor family until 1920 and is now administered by the Kirklees Metropolitan Council as an example of a prosperous middle-class home of the 1830s, when Charlotte Brontë stayed there with her friend Mary *Taylor. Charlotte's description of the parlour of Briarmains in *Shirley* is typical of the original house: 'The most cheerful of rooms . . . there was no splendour, but there was taste everywhere'. The french windows (no longer there but described in *Shirley*, ch. 9) opened onto the lawn and were a particular feature. At the Red House, Charlotte encountered, possibly for the first time, original paintings that Joshua Taylor, a cloth manufacturer, had bought on his business travels to the Continent (see Alexander & Sellars, p. 25), as well as imposing family portraits in the elegant entrance hall. The literary interests of this cultured, Nonconformist family are also reflected in two stained-glass windows in the dining room, each with a central roundel depicting painted heads of Milton and Shakespeare (referred to in *Shirley*, ch. 9). See also MUSEUMS.

Redman family. Joseph Redman (christened 16 May 1796) was Haworth parish clerk at the time of the Brontës. He married Betty Ogden in February 1817. They had a son John and daughter Martha (christened April 1827), who at 23 was listed in the 1851 census as a powerloom weaver at Haworth. She married William *Widdop and often did the washing for the Brontës; their son married Ellen Greenwood, daughter of John *Greenwood (stationer) of Haworth.

red room, in *Jane Eyre.* The child Jane Eyre is locked in this cold, silent, darkened room at Gateshead Hall as a punishment for attacking her cousin John Reed. Though predominantly red and white, the room is also associated with the shades of death, for Jane's uncle Mr Reed died there, and it becomes for her a place of disturbing terror, crisis, and self-recognition. The colour of the room and Jane's trauma within it, following her infliction of a bleeding wound on John Reed, have led critics (for example Sally Shuttleworth, *Charlotte Brontë and Victorian Psychology* (1996), chs. 5 and 8) to associate it with the onset of menstruation.

Reed, Mrs Sarah, Jane Eyre's aunt. She hates her orphaned niece, despite promising her dying husband to treat Jane as her own child. Condoning her son's cruelties, she punishes Jane for retaliating against him. When Jane screams in the *red room, Mrs Reed accuses her of underhand tricks, thrusting her back pitilessly. After Jane's illness, Mrs Reed separates her rigidly from her own children. Momentarily troubled when Jane asks what her uncle Reed would say, Mrs Reed rallies, striking her violently; then, longing to be rid of her, arranges for her to go to *Lowood, previously warning Revd Robert *Brocklehurst that she is deceitful. Only when Jane vows to tell of her cruelty does Mrs Reed beg her to speak of her as her 'best friend'. Later, worried into ill health by her son's dissipation and debts, she refuses to give him the estate, and has a stroke when she hears of his suicide. On her deathbed she confesses that she had told Jane's uncle John Eyre, who wished to make her his heir, that Jane had died at school of typhus. Though Jane seeks reconciliation, Mrs Reed is inexorable.

Reed family, in *Jane Eyre.* Jane's cousins Eliza, John, and Georgiana Reed, all older and taller than Jane, are encouraged by their mother, Mrs Sarah *Reed, to keep aloof from her. Fourteen-year-old John, a stout, heavy, greedy, unwholesome-looking bully, is never punished for his cruelty to animals, or his rude violence to his mother; but when he strikes Jane and throws a book at her (as Mrs *Sidgwick's son John had thrown a Bible at Charlotte) Jane is cruelly shut in the *red room for retaliating against 'her young master'. He fails his college examinations, and ruins his health and the estate by dissipation and gambling instead of studying law. After Mrs Reed has twice paid his debts to get him out of prison, she refuses to give up all to him, and he commits suicide.

Eliza, the elder sister, embodies judgement untempered by feeling. She concentrates on making money, despises the frivolous Georgiana, spies on her, and betrays her plan for elopement. She is thin, sallow, severe, and ascetic, imposing on herself a rigid routine of work and prayer, and devout in her attendance at the new Tractarian church. Little moved by her mother's death, she secures her own fortune, moves to a French nunnery, and becomes a Catholic and the superior of her convent, which she endows with her fortune.

At 11 Georgiana is a fairy-like girl with long golden curls and blue eyes; but she is spoilt, vain, and a liar. Later, plump, fair, stylishly dressed, idle, and self-centred—embodying feeling without judgement—she boasts of her brilliance and her titled 'conquest' during the London season, and, indifferent to her mother's griefs and illness, still hopes for future dissipations. She eventually makes an 'advantageous match with a wealthy worn-out man of fashion'.

Reform Bill, 1832, a Whig measure proposed by Earl Grey (1764–1845) and framed principally by Lord John Russell, designed to remove inequities of parliamentary representation and franchise. The great urban populations of the north of England were grossly under-represented, and the franchise was unjustly distributed and limited: 200 'pocket' boroughs belonged to patrons, and in others the few voters could be bribed by local landowners. Grey's first Reform Bill of 1831, proposing extension of the franchise, removal of 168 seats, and creation of 97 new seats, was carried by a majority of one at its second reading on 23 March, amidst intense excitement, but defeated by the Tories in committee in April. On 28 April Revd Patrick Brontë deplored the defeat, and defended the 'cause of Temperate reform' on the grounds that unscrupulous popular leaders would stir up insurrection. Parliament had meanwhile been dissolved, and a new general election gave the reformers a larger majority. Grey shepherded his Bill safely through the Commons in September 1831, only to have it defeated by the Lords on 8 October. There were countrywide riots, Grey resigned, the Duke of *Wellington failed to form a ministry, and Grey returned to office. When the Lords obstructed the passage of his third Bill, Grey resigned on 9 May 1832, but returned to office with King William's promise to create new Whig peers. Wellington advised his followers not to vote, and the Bill was passed at its third reading on 4 June 1832. On 17 May 1832 Charlotte Brontë wrote of her 'extreme pleasure' at the rejection of the Bill and the 'expulsion or resignation of Earl Grey' (Smith *Letters*, 1. 112–13). Although her letter is addressed to her brother Branwell, it seems not to have been sent to him, and it may have been a school exercise, not insincere, but perhaps designed to please her teachers at *Roe Head.

Regina, Battle of, in *Sneaky's Land, in the *Glass Town and Angrian saga; between Rogue's (Duke of *Northangerland) revolutionary forces under Captain O'Connor and the Royal Armies of the four kings of the *Glass Town (Verdopolitan) Federation.

Reid, Sir Thomas Wemyss (1842–1905), knighted 1894; chief reporter, *Leeds Mercury* from 1866, editor 1870–87; manager of Cassell's, publishers, thereafter; biographer of W. E. *Forster 1888, Lord Houghton (Richard Monckton

*Milnes) 1890, and others. In his *Charlotte Brontë* (1876, 1877) he used information provided by Lord Houghton and Ellen *Nussey. Ellen met him early in 1876, and they planned that he should weave some of Charlotte's letters into a sketch of her life. On 10 May 1876 Ellen suggested he might enlarge it into a memoir, without the besmirching history of her brother. Reid's preliminary sketch, acknowledging Ellen's help, appeared in *Macmillan's Magazine* (Aug.–Oct. 1876). She had told him about her family's homes, the *Bolton Priory excursion, and Revd A. B. *Nicholls's friend, Sutcliffe Sowden, but in a biased and inaccurate way, for her letters to Reid showed a venomous hostility to Nicholls and Revd Patrick *Brontë. Though Reid played down Branwell's impact on Charlotte's 'pure' life, he presented her experience in *Brussels as the arena for a sharp contest with temptation. Nicholls objected to the obscurity of Reid's comments on Charlotte's single failure of duty, when she 'allowed inclination to blind her' to the right path. In his revised edition in book form (1877), Reid noted that Charlotte herself confessed this failure. But he retained references to Charlotte's analysis of her feelings for James *Taylor ('Mr X') despite Nicholls's objections and bitter regret that he had not asked Ellen to destroy the relevant letters. Reid's biography is still of some value; he reminds one, for example, of occasions when Charlotte showed 'the happy levity of youth'; but he repeated myths about Mr Brontë's neglect of his wife, and added comments derived from Ellen on his vanity and injustice; and too many of his extracts from Charlotte's letters are inaccurate or misleading in other ways.

religion. Between 1800 and 1830 adult membership of the *Church of England in England and Wales (measured by the number of Easter communicants) declined from about 10 per cent of the population to just over 7 per cent, whereas the total membership of the Dissenting churches rose steadily from about 3.5 per cent to almost 6 per cent, the most rapid rise being that of the *Methodists. Roman *Catholics also increased from under 2 per cent to over 3 per cent, and their numbers, swelled by the influx of Irish workers, continued to rise in the next three decades. In contrast, the percentage of Unitarians and Quakers, never large, steadily diminished from 1800 onwards. In 1830, then, Anglicanism was a minority religion compared with the total of non-Anglicans, though its membership was not evenly distributed geographically or socially. In the next two decades all denominations except Unitarians and Quakers saw a marked rise in membership. The Church of England recovered some lost ground, partly through church reforms, including the creation of new parishes in the great northern industrial cities, partly through the new impetus given by the *Oxford Movement, and partly through its realization that it could not simply remain on the defensive against the rise of the *Dissenters. New Anglican churches and schools were built, ministers like Revd J. B. *Grant (Revd Joseph *Donne) raised funds, and Revd Patrick Brontë helped to establish the Haworth Sunday school and day school. Mr Brontë, defending the rights of the established Church, quarrelled with the militant Baptist Mr Winterbotham in 1834 and 1835, and on 26 May 1845 Charlotte wrote to the former Haworth schoolmistress: 'It does not appear that the number of children increases much—however I think it is very well that it does not diminish—considering the unceasing opposition of the Methodists and Dissenters' (Smith *Letters*, 1. 398).

In 1851 the Census totals for church attendance in England and Wales were 48.5 per cent Church of England, 3.5 per cent Roman Catholic, and 48.0 per cent other denominations, of whom about half were Methodists and 20 per cent Baptists. However, Anglicans were again on the defensive, reacting hysterically against the so-called 'Papal Aggression' initiated by the Pope's elevation of *Wiseman to the cardinalate and creation of Catholic bishoprics in England. The *Leeds Intelligencer* had published Mr Brontë's 'A Tract for the Times', alleging that the whole fabric of the established Church was 'shaken to its very centre' and threatened to fall, because people no longer looked on it as 'the bulwark of *Protestantism, but a Romish nursery' (19 Oct. 1850). In Yorkshire the Catholic 'threat' was numerically weak, compared with the strong Catholic presence in Lancashire, Cheshire, the west midlands, and north-east; but Yorkshire Dissent was well established, especially in the industrial towns. Wesleyan Methodist, Baptist, and Congregational adherents were predominantly artisans. Primitive Methodism also attracted artisans, but its members included more colliers, miners, and labourers than the other Dissenting churches. Thus we have Branwell Brontë's crude satire of Methodism and Charlotte's perception of Dissent in *Shirley* as an inviting field for hypocritical, ignorant, venial 'shepherds' to prey on their semi-literate flocks. Charlotte's scorn was in part a defensive reaction on behalf of the Church of England, which retained her loyalty despite her knowledge of its faults, and which had inherited the dignified orders of service, prayers, and readings laid down in the *Book of Common Prayer.*

Meanwhile casual and migrant workers and slum dwellers might remain untouched by religion. Disraeli, using the evidence of the 1841–2 Royal Commission for the Investigation of Employment of Children in Mines and Factories, por-

trayed 'Wodgate' in *Sybil*—the Black Country near Wolverhampton where many children had never heard of Christ or heaven. The equivalent in Haworth might be Brandy Row, behind Main Street, though conscientious curates like Revd William *Weightman (and Anne's Edward *Weston) visited the poorest of their parishioners. Mr Brontë's practical Christianity was reflected in his efforts on behalf of the unjustly accused William Nowell in Dewsbury, his persistence in seeking a better water supply and efficient drainage for Haworth, and his letters to newspapers on matters of wider social concern, such as the fire risk from children's cotton clothing, and the inequities of criminal law.

Social concern was a mark of the evangelical wing of the Church of England, to which Mr Brontë belonged. Critics of the evangelicals, like Dickens and Thackeray, condemned the Mrs Jellybys who pitied African 'natives' and ignored the needs of their own families and the English poor, but Mr Brontë retained his respect for the Claphamite evangelicals, who included Revd Charles *Simeon, and was a close friend of socially aware evangelical ministers like Revd John *Buckworth and Theodore *Dury. Unfortunately he also sent four of his children to *Cowan Bridge school, where the evangelical patrons included Wilberforce, Hannah More, and Dury. Its founder, Revd W. Carus *Wilson was also an evangelical; but unlike Mr Brontë, he was a *Calvinist who predicted hellfire for unrepentant children.

Mr Brontë's Christianity was an orthodox Trinitarianism based on the *Bible and summed up in the Apostles' Creed. He emphasized the possibility and need for conversion from sin, and Christ's commandment to 'love one another'. He preached, in moral tales such as The *Cottage in the Wood, that religion was the only source of true happiness. Like Charlotte, he clung to the belief that all things would work together for good to those who love God, despite his terrible afflictions and bereavements. Hell was real to him. He preached that sinners must repent if they were not to be condemned to its flames, and interpreted the Crow Hill bogburst as God's dire warning of the gruesome fate awaiting the wicked. But he also emphasized Christ's love and mercy to all believers. He did not underestimate the difficulties in the way of faith, and he did not believe that conversion was instantaneous. In 'On conversion' (*Pastoral Visitor*, July, Sept., Oct. 1815), he expounded his message in simple terms for the cottage reader, dramatizing it as the experience of the narrator, who admits that he has done no enormous crime, but has often been tempted by 'Satan' who subtly tries to persuade him that he is being 'righteous overmuch'. But now he understands that if he continues to watch, pray, and read the Bible, he will conquer sin and then, saved by Christ, 'plucked as a brand out of the burning', will seek to save his fellow mortals (*BST* (1988), 19. 6. 271–5).

Though none of his children accepted the Christian faith on such simple terms, its essentials formed the basis of Anne's and Charlotte's beliefs, and probably those of their sister Maria, modified by their unorthodox faith in the doctrine of *universal salvation. Mr Brontë was not a model Christian, but he was sincere and he knew how to forgive. He cared for his prodigal son, even though Branwell seemed to have cast Christianity aside. On his deathbed Branwell prayed softly, and 'to the last prayer which [his] father offered up at his bedside, he added "amen"'. 'The remembrance of this strange change now comforts my poor Father greatly,' Charlotte wrote to W. S. Williams on 6 October 1848. She too emerged from the ordeal with her faith renewed: 'I felt as I had never felt before that there was peace and forgiveness for him in Heaven' (Smith *Letters*, 2. 124). Less admirably, Mr Brontë's pride in his daughter's fame led him to a furious rejection of Revd A. B. *Nicholls's proposal, and to an unchristian antipathy. After he had finally consented to the marriage, he came to respect and trust his 'beloved and esteemed' son-in-law.

Charlotte's writings demonstrate the importance of religion to her. She believed that the Christian's faith in God's Providence might be tested by suffering, but that such ordeals ultimately strengthened faith. 'Manfully, fearlessly, | The day of trial bear', she wrote in her poem 'Endurance', and in 'The Teacher's Monologue' she prayed, 'Then aid me, Reason, Patience, Faith, | To suffer to the end.' Christian faith is integral to *Jane Eyre*, where some of the most dramatic scenes are essentially religious. At the nadir of her experience, alone on the heath after leaving Thornfield, Jane prays for Mr Rochester, and looking up at the night sky, feels 'the might and strength of God': 'Sure was I of his efficiency to save what He had made' (ch. 26). Rochester, too, receives assurance of God's mercy: he has prayed for death, but instead hears Jane's call, and when she returns to him, he thanks God that 'in the midst of judgment he has remembered mercy' (ch. 37). Charlotte associated prayer with heroes as well as devout clergymen and parishioners. The hardy warriors of the Scottish brigade in her devoir 'La Prière du soir dans un camp' listen to the Lord's Prayer, 'faithful to the simple and stern forms of the Christian faith'. Her heroic martyr figures—the tortured Protestant Anne Askew, Pierre l'Hermite in another devoir, the Missionary in her poem of that name, Helen Burns and St John *Rivers in *Jane Eyre*—are all envisaged as 'enduring to the end', strengthened by their prayers. In *Villette* M. Paul is

a 'Christian Hero', obeying Christ's commands to succour the weak, praying as simply as a child, and in the end laying down his life as a result of a sea voyage undertaken at the behest of his priest on behalf of the undeserving Mme Walravens. The Christian's duty of pastoral care is exemplified in M. Paul's good works, and in those quietly performed by Miss Ainley in *Shirley*, who helps Caroline to find some satisfaction in imparting pleasure or allaying suffering.

Charlotte, like her siblings, saw clearly the faults of the visible Church and its ministers. Timothy *Steighton in *The Professor*, Revd Robert *Brocklehurst in *Jane Eyre*, and the *curates in *Shirley*, are the victims of her sharp satire because they bring the Church into disrepute by their extremism, pettiness, hypocrisy, or absurdity. William *Crimsworth voices her opinion that 'a good clergyman is one of the best of men', but he must have 'the peculiar points which go to make a good clergyman', if he is not to mistake his vocation. Revd Matthewson *Helstone in *Shirley* should have been a soldier; Revd Peter *Malone is too unworthy of the ministry for his sins to be described. One touchstone for the truly good clergyman is his response to Christ's commandment 'Suffer the little children to come unto me.' Brocklehurst signally fails; in contrast, the kindly Revd Cyril *Hall in *Shirley* welcomes the Farrens' children as they come about his knee, addresses them affectionately as 'bairns', and arranges help for their needy parents.

Though Charlotte mocked religious extremists (for example in *Passing Events), and detested those whose show of religion masked worldly self-seeking, like Mme *Beck in *Villette*, she acknowledged that there could be different perceptions of God's nature. Her own adolescent fears that Calvinism might be true made her sensitive to those who found faith difficult, or who stood apart from mainstream denominations. She read W. S. *Williams's views on the 'providence of God and the nature of man with interest', agreed with much of what he said, and did not attempt to bias him where she differed. On ?18 October 1848 she told him that 'Thought and conscience are, or ought to be, free; and at any rate, if your views were universally adopted there would be no persecution and no bigotry.' But she felt mankind was 'not yet fit to receive' Williams's Emersonian views, for 'man as he now is, can no more do without creeds and forms in religion than he can do without laws and rules in social intercourse' (Smith *Letters*, 2. 129). She was attracted to F. D. Maurice's liberal theology; she wrote to James Taylor on 15 November 1851 that if she had a choice of preachers in London, it was Maurice whose ministry she would frequent (Smith *Letters*, 2. 718). She did not allow the difference in faith to spoil her friendship with the Unitarian *Gaskell family. She also described unconventional epiphanic scenes such as that in *Shirley*, where the 'Bridal Hour of Genius and Humanity', a non-Christian religious fable, uses religious terms such as the 'Dayspring from on High', and the central figure, Eva, has her religion, for 'all tribes held some creed' (ch. 27).

Anne's evangelical faith, attained after the kind of rigorous self-scrutiny embodied in her religious *poetry, entailed a strong conviction that she must do good, and teach Christ's message. In May 1845, agonized because she had no power 'to quell vice and sin', she turned to prayer, asking God to call her soon, or to give her strength to bear the misery of her powerlessness ('O God! if this indeed be all'; Chitham *ABP*, p. 111). In writing *Agnes Grey* and *Tenant* she endeavoured to strengthen the faith of others and to help them to avoid sin and its consequences. The reissue of her poems, with those of her sisters, in 1848, gave her welcome proof that her writing could be heeded, for Revd David *Thom wrote that he too believed in universal salvation. On 30 December 1848 she admitted that in *Tenant* she had given 'as many hints in support of the doctrine' as she could 'venture to introduce into a work of that description', but she feared lest the 'infatuated slave of Satan' might take such assurance of ultimate salvation as a licence to sin (Smith *Letters*, 2. 160–1).

Anne retained her faith during her last illness. In January 1849, amid the 'dreadful darkness' of knowing that Death might be 'standing at the gate', she still prayed, 'So let me serve Thee now.' On 5 April 1849, dangerously ill, weak, and thin, she contemplated her death without horror, and continued to think of the good of others. She told Ellen Nussey on 5 April 1849 that she could quietly resign herself to death if Ellen would be a sister to Charlotte in her stead: 'But I wish it would please God to spare me not only for Papa's and Charlotte's sakes, but because I long to do some good in the world before I leave it' (Smith *Letters*, 2. 195).

The knowledge that her novels had been read by a wide audience perhaps gave her some satisfaction. The moral and religious lessons in *Agnes Grey* are both implicit and explicit. Agnes's naïve belief that she will immediately know how to make 'Religion lovely and comprehensible' to her pupils is convincingly refuted by her experiences in the Bloomfield household; and Anne's message is clearly that the parents and other relatives are at fault: Christian nurture is their primary responsibility. Like Charlotte, Anne also brilliantly exposes the pretensions of those who arrogantly claim religious virtue. 'I'm one of the pious ones, Miss Grey!' claims the senior Mrs Bloomfield, with 'a very significant nod and toss', and 'I glory in it'

(ch. 4). The dire results of worldly upbringing in the Murray family are displayed in Rosalie's heartless cottage-visiting to impress Mr Weston and in her mercenary marriage with the roué Sir Thomas. In contrast Agnes and Weston exemplify in their marriage the happiness of a shared evangelical Christianity, keeping in mind 'the glorious heaven beyond'.

The Tenant of Wildfell Hall is even more obviously didactic. Anne wished to tell the truth, and had the 'courage to dive for it', as she explained in her preface to the second edition, despite the 'scorn and obloquy' she might incur 'for the mud and water' in which she had to plunge. She represented vice and vicious characters as they were, because she believed it was her Christian duty to do so, in the hope of saving the rash and thoughtless from the error of their ways. Her evangelical conviction is the driving force of the novel: 'Such humble talents as God has given me I will endeavour to put to their greatest use; if I am able to amuse I will try to benefit too; and when I feel it my duty to speak an unpalatable truth, with the help of God, I *will* speak it.'

The contrast between Anne and Emily is marked. For Emily, religion concerned God and herself. Haworth villagers reported that she did not teach in Sunday school, and did not attend church regularly. Yet her poems reveal intense personal vision of the divine. When she is saddest, 'Hid alone in the darken[e]d room', the spirit comes to 'bear [her] soul away', and she feels strange sensations, forerunners of a 'sterner power'. In exquisitely beautiful lines, she describes the mystical experience of divine visitation: 'He comes with western winds, with evening's wandering airs . . . And visions rise and change which kill me with desire. . . . Then dawns the Invisible, the Unseen its truth reveals.' The return of the soul to the body is agonizing, when 'the pulse begins to throb, the brain to think again, | The soul to feel the flesh and the flesh to feel the chain' ('Julian M. and A. G. Rochelle'). In *Wuthering Heights* Cathy, tired of being enclosed in the 'shattered prison' of her body, longs 'to escape into that glorious world' where Heathcliff will be with her, for 'he's in my soul'. But Emily imagines no conventional heaven for them; their spirits remain on earth, 'near the church, and on the moor, and even within this house'; and their graves are last seen under a benign sky, as Lockwood wonders 'how any one could ever imagine unquiet slumbers for the sleepers in that quiet earth'. Emily's wrath is reserved for narrow-minded canting hypocrites like the servant *Joseph, who oppress children in the name of religion, and the fanatics who, blind to the 'thoughtful Comforter' who inspires Emily, remain 'wretches uttering praise, | Or howling o'er their hopeless days, | And each with Frenzy's tongue' ('My Comforter').

In some of her early writings Emily interprets suffering as the seed of the 'divine harvest'. Her devoir 'Le *Papillon', written in 1842, faces the 'inexplicable problem' of Nature and humanity. Within the flower lies the caterpillar which has made its petals wrinkled and faded. It is a 'sad image of the earth and its inhabitants! . . . why was man created? He torments, he kills' (Lonoff, pp. 176, 178). Yet as the ugly caterpillar becomes a beautiful butterfly, so this earth is the embryo of a new heaven and a new earth. But two poems written towards the end of Emily's life, 'Why ask to know the date—the clime?' (14 Sept. 1846) and the revised version of its opening lines written in May 1848, depict a grim, apparently irredeemable world, in which humanity, 'Crushing down Justice, honouring Wrong', mocks heaven 'with senseless prayers For mercy on the merciless'.

Branwell's nearest approach to a sense of the divine came, perhaps, through sacred music. As a member of the committee for the installation of the new organ in Haworth church in March 1834, he requested that Handel's 'I know that my Redeemer liveth' from Messiah should be played. In *'My Angria and the Angrians' Charlotte teasingly exaggerated his ecstatic response to its performance. Branwell's flute book included arrangements of church music, and, according to Francis *Leyland, he was especially fond of Handel's Samson and the masses of Haydn and Mozart. He retained this love of sacred music, but in most other respects reacted against his religious upbringing, and became fascinated by the glamour of wickedness. Charlotte had joined in the creation of the diabolic Northangerland in their early writings, but did not identify herself with him, whereas Branwell chose the name 'Northangerland' as his authorial pseudonym, and parodied evangelical services by making Percy, alias Northangerland, both preacher and organist at the 'Sanctification Chapel'. In the eloquent rhetoric of his poem 'Azrael', Branwell proclaimed the rebel spirit's perversion of the nature of God, who 'though he loves our race so well . . . hurls our spirits into Hell'. In 'At dead of midnight' Branwell exploited in romantic fashion the idea of the sinful woman facing Eternity, and imagining her sentence: 'Depart, lost Spirit, into Hell.' In real life, he and his drinking companions jestingly used diabolic nicknames, 'the Devil's Thumb', the 'Devil in Mourning', and 'him who will be used as the tongs of Hell' (Barker, p. 323, quoting a letter of 13 March 1840). In June 1846, separated from his beloved Lydia Robinson, and in despair, he depicted himself burning in the flames of hell, and as late as January 1848 he kept up the idea of a 'hell-fire club', juxtaposing a drawing of himself with a hangman's rope round his neck with an apparently devilish drinking scene. Yet sometimes he searched his conscience, recognized his waste of talents, and prayed for a clearer vision. His poem written at Luddenden church on 19 December 1841 asked God to give him 'the stern sustaining power | To look into the past | And see the darkly shadowed hour | Which I must meet at last' (Neufeldt BBP, p. 219).

In his Luddenden notebook he interspersed the repeated name of Jesus with more mundane jottings. Perhaps it was this undercurrent of awareness of sin and salvation that led him to pray softly on his deathbed, touched by his father's prayers.

'Remembrance' (3 Mar. 1845); 32 lines in eight quatrains by Emily Brontë, from the Gondal Poems manuscript notebook where it appears with the title 'R. Alcona to J. Brenzaida'; published by Emily in Poems 1846, with the Gondal names removed. The poem is a lament by Rosina *Alcona for Emperor Julius *Brenzaida, who as emperor of Gondal was assassinated fifteen years earlier. She recalls her 'only love', now buried in *Angora in the north of Gondal (the manuscript was changed from 'Angora's shore' to 'northern shore' for publication); and she asks forgiveness if she forgets him while 'the world's tide' is bearing her along. Her 'life's bliss' was buried with him, yet she has learnt to live 'without the aid of joy'. By sheer force of will she has checked suicidal feelings and 'useless passion'. Even now, however, she dare not 'indulge in memory's rapturous pain' lest she lose the courage to live in this 'empty world'. Her speech celebrates the power of the human heart to transcend the barriers of death in remembrance of a loved one and to survive such grief. It also explores the complexities of memory, subject to 'Time's all-wearing wave', and the constant change in life that would erode a permanent Love.

The haunting rhetorical questions, alliteration, and repetition of phrases and words make this one of the most musical and most anthologized of Emily's poems. F. R. Leavis called it 'the finest poem in the nineteenth-century part of The Oxford Book of English Verse' (cited in Gezari EBP, p. 228) and spoke of its emotional intensity. The skilful use of feminine rhymes was noted by C. Day Lewis, who found the rhythm powerful and appropriate: 'It is a dragging effect, as of feet moving in a funeral march; an andante maestoso: it is the slowest rhythm I know in English poetry, and the most sombre' ('The Poetry of Emily Brontë', BST (1957), 13. 67. 91). Chitham notes the influence of Thomas *Moore's Irish Melodies in the phrase 'Cold in the Earth', also echoed in Anne's poem

'Night', written at about the same time (Chitham *ABP*, p. 183).

Gezari, J., 'Fathoming *Remembrance*: Emily Brontë in Context', *ELH* 66. 4 (1999) pp. 965–9.
Roper *EBP*, p. 166.

reputation of the Brontës' works. The Brontës' literary reputation today rests on the three novels Charlotte published during her lifetime; on *Wuthering Heights* and a handful of Emily's poems; and, to a lesser extent, on Anne's second novel, *The Tenant of Wildfell Hall*. *Agnes Grey* and *The Professor* are read by those interested in the Brontës, but they have never had wide appeal, nor have they attracted a great deal of critical attention. Branwell is still the least appreciated of the four Brontës. Among the sisters, Anne has always been rated lower than Emily and Charlotte, though recent work suggests she may now be emerging as the most admired of the three women authors.

By early 1848, just months after the publication of *Jane Eyre*, *Agnes Grey*, and *Wuthering Heights*, all three of 'the Bells' were a source of public curiosity and literary gossip. *Jane Eyre* caused a greater sensation than the other novels, however, and Emily's and Anne's early deaths ensured that Charlotte's reputation would eclipse theirs at least temporarily. After Charlotte's death in 1855, the success of Elizabeth *Gaskell's *The Life of Charlotte Brontë* reinforced that reputation, which remained strong until the last decades of the century.

By the 1880s, the Brontës (Charlotte in particular) were starting to seem rather old-fashioned to many readers. Margaret Oliphant dismissed *Jane Eyre* and *Villette* as novels to be read 'at the spa or seaside' (*Blackwood's Edinburgh Magazine*, 141 (1887), 758), and Charlotte's reputation continued to decline, receiving its worst blow in 1934, when Lord David Cecil pronounced her novels 'formless, improbable, humourless, exaggerated, [and] uncertain' ('Charlotte Brontë', *Early Victorian Novelists*, in McNees, 1. 398). By contrast, in another essay in the same volume, Cecil accelerated the steady rise in Emily's reputation that had begun in 1900 when Mrs Humphry *Ward declared in the introduction to the Haworth edition of *Wuthering Heights* that 'Emily's genius [was] . . . greater' than Charlotte's (McNees, 2. 242). In 1926, Charles Percy Sanger's ground-breaking article on 'The Structure of *Wuthering Heights*' (McNees, 2. 71–82) provided conclusive evidence of Emily's literary skill, and Cecil's later essay elaborated a structuralist reading in line with Sanger's claims about the novel's remarkable coherence. With the emergence of formalism and the New Criticism as the dominant modes of literary analysis at mid-century, Sanger's and Cecil's assessments were

decisive: by 1940 the two sisters had exchanged places, Charlotte's reputation having sunk as low as it has ever gone and Emily's having risen to its greatest height.

The next development to influence the Brontës' reputation with academics as well as general readers was the women's movement in the 1970s and the proliferation of feminist literary criticism that accompanied it. Printed in its entirety in the *Norton Anthology of Literature by Women*, edited by Sandra Gilbert and Susan Gubar (1985, 1996), *Jane Eyre* rapidly emerged as a favourite text with feminist readers, while *Villette*, and to a lesser extent *Shirley*, attracted considerable attention as well. Emily's reputation did not suffer from this dramatic revival of interest in Charlotte's work, and a staggering amount of criticism has been published on *Wuthering Heights* since the early seventies.

Both *Jane Eyre* and *Wuthering Heights* remain widely read by professional and leisure readers alike. *Villette*, generally considered Charlotte's most mature work, is still admired by experts and enjoyed by many other readers, while *Shirley* and *The Tenant of Wildfell Hall* command greater critical interest and respect today than ever before.   CB

Winnifrith, Tom, 'Charlotte and Emily Brontë: A Study in the Rise and Fall of Literary Reputations', *Yearbook of English Studies*, 26 (1996), 14–24.

'Retrospection'. See 'WE WOVE A WEB IN CHILDHOOD'.

Reuter, Mlle Zoraïde, in *The Professor*. Like Mme *Beck in *Villette*, Mlle Reuter is modelled on Mme *Heger, and acts as a foil to the morally upright, sincere heroine. Charlotte skilfully uses images of predation, insidious penetration, and entrapment to enhance the threat she poses to William *Crimsworth's integrity, and to create dramatic tension. Though superficially attractive, Zoraïde is a 'wary general', intent on power achieved by discreet manipulation. She glides cat-like after her prey, or sits serenely in wait, surveying those she wishes to understand and control. In conversation with Crimsworth, whom she engages as a teacher, she talks with seeming casualness, seeking out his weak points so that she may 'set her foot' upon his neck. Aiming to win his respect, affection, and finally, love, she uses cool reason to shape her strategy. When he baffles her craft, she affects motherly concern, and leads him into the sensuous delights of her pretty garden until he is on the brink of love. Abruptly disillusioned when he overhears her exulting over her conquest of him to M. François *Pelet, her fiancé, William becomes coldly scornful. Fascinated, she tries to lure him back by feigning concern for Frances *Henri's welfare, and by flattering him; but he sees through her 'plating of pretention'. Becoming jealous of William's interest in Frances, she pretends a benevolent desire to further the girl's career, and dismisses her regardless of Frances's need to earn money. William glimpses her 'hard, dark, inquisitive' look when he tries to discover Frances's address, which she pretends not to know. Then, having fallen into a snare of her own laying by arousing Pelet's suspicion of her 'besotted' desire for William, she is brought to her senses by William's resignation, and recaptures and marries Pelet. The Pelets find consolation for the discords of their marriage in the prosperity of their schools.

'Revenge: A Tradgedy, The' [sic]. See VERSE DRAMA BY BRANWELL BRONTË.

Rhymer, Henry. See SOULT, ALEXANDER (YOUNG SOULT THE RHYMER).

Rhys, Jean. See SEQUELS AND 'INCREMENTAL LITERATURE'.

Richardson, Samuel (1689–1761), author of *Pamela; or Virtue Rewarded* (1740), *Clarissa Harlowe* (1747, 1748), and *Sir Charles Grandison* (1754). Anne and Charlotte Brontë knew the works of Richardson well enough to refer to them *en passant*, and some early reviewers saw Rochester's wooing of Jane Eyre as a variant of 'Mr B's' attempted seduction of the virtuous heroine in *Pamela*. But the careful, smug Pamela has little in common with passionate Jane, and Charlotte insisted that Rochester was a good man trapped by scheming relatives, not an unprincipled rake to be superficially reformed by marriage. Charlotte had written flippantly to Hartley *Coleridge in December 1840 about the immensely long 'Richardsonian Concern' her juvenile tale (a variant of *Ashworth*) might have become: 'Mr West should have been my Sir Charles Grandison—Percy my Mr B—and the ladies should have represented—Pamela, Clarissa Harriet Byron &c.' Certainly the *Glass Town and Angrian saga, like Richardson's novels, is voluminous and often preoccupied with high society and its manners. The last quality Charlotte perhaps found both appealing and amusing, for in *The Professor* Hunsden Yorke *Hunsden bows on Frances *Henri's hand 'absolutely like Sir Charles Grandison on that of Harriet Byron' (ch. 24). But she mocks Richardson's Harriet singing 'her own praises as sweetly as a dying swan' (Smith *Letters*, 1. 239), and in her 'A Word to the "Quarterly"' (see SHIRLEY: 'A WORD TO THE "QUARTERLY"') calls Richardson an 'idiot (inspired or otherwise)' (Smith *Letters*, 2. 243). Anne Brontë had perhaps pondered more seriously on Richardson's attitude to marriage, for in *Agnes Grey*, like Pamela, she

dismisses the notion that 'reformed rakes make the best husbands', and shows Rosalie *Murray bitterly repenting her marriage to Sir Thomas Ashby. In *Tenant*, Helen rashly thinks she can recall Huntingdon to 'the path of virtue', as Clarissa hopes to reclaim Lovelace.

'Riches I hold in light esteem'. See 'OLD STOIC, THE'.

Richton, Viscount. See FLOWER, CAPTAIN SIR JOHN.

Ridley, James, *Tales of the Genii* (1764), published under the pseudonym of 'Sir Charles Morell', one of the many pseudo-oriental collections of stories inspired by 18th-century English translations of Galland's French translation of the *Arabian Nights*. Jane Stedman argues persuasively that the Brontës read one of the cheap 19th-century editions of this didactic work made palatable by 'romantic enchantment' ('The Genesis of the Genii', *BST* (1965), 14. 75. 16). In particular, the Brontë children's conception of genii as guardians, who are female as well as male, is closer to *Tales of the Genii* than to the *Nights*. The fabulous world of the genii, however, with their palaces of gold and precious stones, owes as much to the Book of the Revelation in the *Bible as it does to either of these two popular sources. See GENII, CHIEF (LITTLE KING AND QUEENS).

Rigby, Elizabeth (1809–93; after 1849, Lady Eastlake), from 1842 the only female contributor to the influential *Quarterly Review*. Her anonymous December 1848 review of *Jane Eyre*, while acknowledging the novel's power, judged Jane vulgar, 'undisciplined', and 'unregenerate'; Rochester coarse and brutal; and the novel itself anti-Christian and socially disruptive. If the novelist was female, Rigby concluded, she must have 'long forfeited the society of her own sex'. In passing, Rigby castigated the writings of Acton and Ellis as coarse and 'heathenish'. Charlotte penned a sarcastic 'Word to the "Quarterly"' to preface *Shirley*, but her publishers rejected it (see SHIRLEY: 'A WORD TO THE "QUARTERLY"'). Her character Agnes *Pryor allusively reproves Rigby (as 'Mrs Hardman') by describing employers' contempt for *governesses.

BT

Allott, pp. 105–12.
Lochhead, Marion, *Elizabeth Rigby, Lady Eastlake* (1961).
Smith *Letters*, 2. 241–5 (for 'A Word to the "Quarterly"').

Ringrose, Amelia. See TAYLOR, AMELIA.

Ringrose family. Christopher Leake Ringrose (b. 1791), the father of Amelia Ringrose (see

TAYLOR, AMELIA), was the son of John and Rebecca Ringrose of Cottingham, Yorks. He and his brother William (?1779/80–1845) were wealthy shipowners; hide, bark, and bone importers; corn merchants; and factors based in Hull, Yorks., and trading with Holland. He married Mary Ann Boyes in Hull in March 1818. At least four of their children were born in Rotterdam, where also the eldest son, Christopher, married Euphemia Knowles in November 1845. Another son, F. Philip Ringrose, became his father's trading partner. The family lived at Tranby Lodge, Hessle, Hull, from 1841. Charlotte Brontë's impression, deriving from Ellen Nussey's descriptions, was that Mr Ringrose was coarse and unfeeling, and his wife was selfishly absorbed in cravings and indulgences. She sympathized with the daughters Amelia and Margaret Rosetta (b. 1830), who had to nurse their mother in her last illness, and implied that they had many frailties and vices to forgive when she died in March 1850; but, as with Branwell Brontë, Charlotte acknowledged the 'oblivion of faults which succeeds to Death'. Charlotte met the pretty Rosetta, an engaging person whom she compared to Martha *Taylor, but on occasions 'wretched and unsisterly' after her marriage to John Dugdale, merchant, of Eccles, in January 1851. Charlotte probably met briefly another sister, Clara (b. ?1834), who attended *Oakwell Hall school in 1849. Ellen Nussey visited Clara there, and knew also a younger sister Laura (b. ?1836). Charlotte mentions a schoolboy brother who in 1845–8 was probably a pupil of John Gorham, one of Ellen's Sussex acquaintances.

Ritchie, Lady. See THACKERAY, ANNE ISABELLA.

Rivers, Diana and Mary. Jane Eyre first sees the two sisters through the window at *Moor House. They are absorbed in the study of *Schiller's 'Die Räuber', and Diana's 'dark and deep eye' sparkles as she relishes the grandeur of his visionary words. Both are slender and fair-complexioned, with faces full of distinction and intelligence. Mary's pale brown hair is smoothly braided, Diana's darker tresses cluster in thick curls. Mary is gentle, reserved, and calm, speaking with undemonstrative sincerity; Diana has a remarkable countenance 'instinct with power and goodness', and is more forthright, vivacious, and authoritative than her sister; but both pity the destitute Jane, tend her carefully, and hope they may be able to benefit her permanently. As she recovers, Jane finds their tastes and characters wholly congenial. In many ways they resemble Emily and Anne Brontë. They have travelled to London and other towns, but they love their secluded, ancient home and the surrounding moors and hills; within the house, where both have been nursed by *Hannah, they like to sit in her scrupulously clean kitchen, and

prepare their own meals if they wish. Widely read and talented, they intend, like Anne, to earn their own living as *governesses, but are unhappy to leave their home for the fashionable city where their employers will regard them merely as humble dependants. Saddened by their brother St John's intention to become a missionary in India, they hope he may stay in England if he marries Jane, and deplore his assumption that she could live in the killing climate of India. Jane's shared legacy rescues them from governess-servitude; and after she marries Rochester, they both make happy marriages, Diana to the gallant Captain Fitzjames, Mary to the worthy Mr Wharton, a college friend of her brother's.

Rivers, St John, the young minister at *Morton, handsome, tall, and slender, with classical Greek features, fair hair, and blue eyes, in *Jane Eyre*. He allows Jane Eyre to take shelter in *Moor House, interrogates her like a 'penetrating young judge', and promises to find work for her. Jane detects beneath his icy outward control a restless perturbation: zealous, diligent, and pure, he is brooding rather than content. His sermons astonish by their power, yet do not touch the heart, conveying stern Calvinistic doctrines of election, predestination, and reprobation.

After Jane has become the mistress of a school he has established in Morton, she elicits from him a confession that he had once yearned for worldly distinction, but became convinced that God called him to use his talents as a missionary and to overcome the human weakness of his passion for Rosamond *Oliver. Believing it salutary for him to express his feelings, Jane encourages him to look at her portrait of Rosamond and indulge in imagined bliss, which he afterwards declares is delusive: Rosamond could not share his ambition to better the human race. Like Henry *Martyn he cannot relinquish a great work which is his foundation for 'a mansion in heaven'.

As he covers Rosamond's portrait, he notices the name 'Jane Eyre', and realizes Jane is the heiress of his uncle John Eyre's fortune. She shares her bequest with her cousins but continues to visit the school, and to study. St John believes she will be a suitable helpmeet, asks her to study Hindustani to confirm his own knowledge of it, and to marry him. The 'iron shroud' of his despotic will seems to close round her; but she cannot accept the idea of a loveless marriage, and offers to go with him, unmarried, as an assistant. Rejecting her offer as impracticable, he promises to arrange for her to assist a missionary's wife, so as not to 'dishonour' her word: but Jane, denying such an obligation, insists she must know *Rochester's fate before deciding. St John's prayers show he fears her earthly love will lead to eternal damnation; and, tempted to 'rush down the torrent of his will', Jane prays intensely, hears Rochester's call, and dismisses St John. He goes to India to labour for his race with indefatigable devotion, and welcomes an early death as the attainment of his 'incorruptible crown'. Some of his characteristics resemble those of Revd Henry *Nussey.

Roberson, Revd Hammond (1757–1841), friend of Revd Patrick Brontë; BA Cambridge 1779, MA 1782; ordained deacon 1779, and licensed as curate to *Dewsbury; resigned curacy 1788; opened a boys' school at Squirrel Hall, Liversedge, 1783, which he transferred to Heald's Hall, Liversedge, 1795; vicar of *Hartshead 1785–1803; perpetual curate of Liversedge from 1812. He built Christ Church, Liversedge, consecrated 1816, and rode, armed with a sword, to help defend Rawfolds Mill during the *Luddite riots. Charlotte, who saw him once in her girlhood, was struck with his stern, martial air, and based Revd Matthewson *Helstone in *Shirley* on him.

Robinson, Agnes Mary Frances, later (1888) Mme Darmesteter, later (1901) Mme Duclaux (1857–1944); author of *Emily Brontë* (1883), *Grands Écrivains d'Outre-Manche: Les Brontë . . . Rossetti* (1901), and many other books. In her preparation for *Emily Brontë* she stayed in Haworth with Amos *Ingham, the Brontës' doctor, and talked to others who had known them: Mrs Wood, William Wood, the *Brown family, and Mrs Tabitha *Ratcliffe. Sir Thomas Wemyss *Reid, J. H. Ingram, and Sidney Biddell collected information for her, and Ellen Nussey provided recollections and manuscript notes. Robinson was heavily influenced by Ellen's tendency to stress the sisters' noble purity, and adopted some of her romanticized versions of events: the 'two suns' (the parhelion which Ellen saw on Haworth moor in July 1847) become three, and Ellen tells the sisters, with Emily standing high 'on a heathery knoll', that they are 'the three suns'; Emily responds with 'a very soft and happy smile'. More convincing, because she had the stories from the Brown family, are her descriptions of Emily falling as she went to feed Floss and Keeper, and finally being too weak to pick up her comb. Robinson had seen 'that old, broken comb, with a large piece burned out of it'. She does not deny Emily's 'violent genius' or passionate spirit, and she writes well of Emily's 'terse, fiery, imaginative style' in *Wuthering Heights* and her 'strenuous' verse. But in order to rescue her from any taint of kinship with the 'morbid passions' of her characters, Robinson darkens the character of Branwell, exaggerating his morbidity and sordid lack of principle as material for the novel. She also follows Elizabeth *Gaskell in accepting stories of Revd Pat-

rick Brontë's violence, and adds to them Ellen's accusations that he was vain, and that Maria Branwell's engagement to him was not as happy as it ought to have been.

Robinson, Revd Edmund (1800–46), employer of Anne and Branwell Brontë. He matriculated at Balliol in 1817, graduated BA 1820, and MA 1823, when he became, nominally at least, curate to the vicar of Great Ouseburn, Yorks. He had inherited *Thorp Green Hall and the manorial rights of Little Ouseburn from his father. His marriage to Lydia Gisborne was followed by the birth of five children, whom he christened in Little Ouseburn church. He gave generously to charities, loyal servants, and his family, though he altered his will after his daughter Lydia eloped with an actor, to prevent her benefiting from his own marriage settlement. He frequently gave his wife costly presents, and there is no convincing evidence that he was unkind to her, despite Branwell's allegations and sneers about him as 'an eunuch-like fellow' who slept apart from her. He might, however, have been sick and emaciated by 1843, for he died on 26 May 1846 from 'Dyspepsia many years Phthisis 3 months'. His wife lavished endearments on her departed 'Angel Edmund', and obituaries recorded his parishioners' great esteem. He appointed her a trustee and executor of his will, and joint guardian of her children with her brothers-in-law Archdeacon Charles Thorp and William Evans MP. Branwell's assertion that the will had been altered to disinherit her if she communicated with him was untrue. She must have convinced her husband of her own probity, whether or not his dismissal of Branwell involved her in any way.

Robinson, Mrs Lydia (1799–1859), daughter of Revd Thomas Gisborne (1758–1846) of Yoxall Lodge, Staffs., an evangelical writer and adherent of the Clapham Sect, which included William Wilberforce and Thomas Babington, Gisborne's brother-in-law. Lydia's marriage in December 1824 to Revd Edmund *Robinson, on whom Gisborne settled £6,000 for life, must have seemed appropriate. She was a small, pretty woman with a darkish skin and bright eyes, as Branwell Brontë's description and her portrait show (see *BST* (1981), 18. 91. 28–9). Her attitude to her children and their governess, Anne Brontë, may be reflected in Mrs *Murray's exhortation to Agnes *Grey to identify herself with the reputation of her 'young ladies for elegance and propriety', which should be of more consequence to the governess than her own, and in Mrs Murray's encouragement of her daughter Rosalie's marriage to a wealthy man regardless of his character. Though concerned for all her children, and positively fond of Mary and of her son Edmund, Mrs Robinson was willing to leave the girls in their grandmother's care while she stayed at Great Barr. Her attitude to her husband cannot be clearly discerned: immediately after his death she wrote fondly of her 'angel Edmund', and gave money to the poor 'for Edmund's precious sake'. But two years later, according to her younger daughters, she was anxious to get them husbands of any kind so that she might be free to marry Sir Francis Edward *Scott of Great Barr, whose infatuated slave she appeared to be.

We have only Branwell's word, and some rumours, for Mrs Robinson's being 'damnably too fond of' him during his tutorship at *Thorp Green Hall, and 'insane' with remorse after her husband's death for her conduct towards him. There is no evidence that Mr Robinson distrusted his wife. His will stipulated that she should be one of the guardians of her children, and that during her widowhood other trustees should attend to her wishes in the management of the estate and the execution of the trusts. The provision that if she remarried she would lose her income from the estate was a normal one, with no specific reference to Branwell. In the *Life*, Elizabeth Gaskell, on the authority of Revd Patrick Brontë and Charlotte, who believed Branwell's stories, portrayed her as a wicked seducer; but investigations by George *Smith's legal advisers found no foundation for this portrayal. Elizabeth Gaskell's lawyers published a retractation of the imputations in *The Times* (30 May 1857) and *Athenaeum* (6 June 1857), all unsold copies of the first and second editions of the *Life* were withdrawn, and a revised third edition produced. Far from showing an 'inextinguishable' love for Branwell, as he had alleged, Mrs Robinson married the rich Sir Francis Edward Dolman Scott (?1797–1851) at a private ceremony in Bath on 8 November 1848, only three months after his first wife died. She outlived him, and died at her Mayfair home in June 1859 of liver disease. She left everything to her son except her jewellery, which was to be divided among her three daughters.

Robinson, William (1799–1838), successful Leeds portrait painter who gave lessons to Branwell Brontë. Robinson studied first under Joseph Rhodes, sen., a watercolourist in Leeds, and then in London in 1820 as a free pupil of Sir Thomas Lawrence (1769–1830), the greatest English portrait painter of the early 19th century and president of the *Royal Academy of Arts, 1820–30. He was introduced to Fuseli and other famous artists, and studied at the Royal Academy before returning to Leeds in 1823. Among his more famous sitters was the Duke of Wellington, whose portrait Robinson painted for the United Services Club, London. His self-portrait, now in Leeds City Gallery, is reproduced in *BST* (1985), 18. 95. 342. Despite his talent

and eminence, however, Robinson died at 39 leaving his wife and six children destitute. He had exhibited at the Bradford Artists' Society of Painting and Sculpture in 1827, and at the Leeds exhibitions of the Royal Northern Society for the Encouragement of the Fine Arts from 1823 on, contributing fourteen paintings in 1833. The Brontës first saw Robinson's work at the 1834 summer exhibition in Leeds. Revd Patrick Brontë seems to have engaged Robinson's services soon after for a few lessons for Branwell at the Parsonage at 2 guineas a visit; and then in mid-1835 for a course of lessons at Robinson's studio in Leeds terminating on 11 September (Alexander & Sellars, p. 26). On 16 November, Mr Brontë requested a further ten weekly lessons, with the clear intention of preparing Branwell for a similar career to that of Robinson, citing the importance of anatomy in painting and his continued intention to send his son to the Royal Academy (*BST* 1996), 21. 7. 323–6). Francis Leyland tells how Branwell stayed at an inn in Briggate for this purpose but occasionally took his master's pictures home to Haworth to copy (Leyland, 1. 174). At Robinson's studio Branwell first met fellow pupil J. H. *Thompson. There is no evidence that the Brontë sisters participated in any of these lessons. Nor is there evidence of further contact with Robinson after Branwell's plans to study at the Royal Academy were abandoned and he set up his own studio in Bradford (see *BST* (1996), 21. 7. 323–6; Alexander & Sellars, pp. 78–9); BS (2003), 28. 2. 161–6.

Robinson family of Thorp Green, where Anne Brontë was employed as a governess. Lydia Mary Robinson (b. 1825), eldest daughter of Revd Edmund *Robinson, may have ceased being Anne's pupil in 1843. She made a Gretna Green marriage in October 1845 to an actor, Henry Roxby of the Theatre Royal, *Scarborough. Though her father changed his will on 2 January 1846 to prevent her inheriting anything directly from him, she received some money from the family trustees, and bequests from her mother and brother.

Elizabeth Lydia Robinson ('Bessy', 1826–82), Anne's pupil 1840–5, like her younger sister Mary, eventually became fond of her. Early in 1848 she became engaged to a Mr Milner, without a 'spark of love' for him. In November 1848 he threatened her with an action for breach of promise, and in December with publication of her letters. In January 1849 her mother paid the family lawyer, Henry Newton, £85 19s. 5d. for a settlement in Chancery, and £6 5s. 4d. for private negotiations with Milner. In November 1851 Bessy married William Jessop, an ironmaster of Butterley, Derbys., at Great Barr, near Birmingham.

Mary Robinson (1828–87) was, according to her mother, a good girl, but like the equally stylish and attractive Bessy, showed 'levity and giddiness' during a visit to Anne in December 1848, after her loveless marriage to Henry Clapham of Aireworth House, Keighley, in October. They had one daughter, but Clapham died in 1855, and Mary later married Revd George Hume Innes Pocock, Vicar of Pentrich, Derbys.

The Robinsons' daughter Georgiana Jane, christened August 1838, died March 1841. Their son Edmund (1831–69) was probably Anne's pupil before Branwell became his tutor in January 1843. The theory that information from Edmund caused Branwell's dismissal in 1845 is unproven. Edmund's new tutor, Revd Theophilous Williams of Charlton Mackwell, commended his 'purity and innocence', but added that his inferior mental acquirements were his infelicity rather than his fault. His matriculation at St Mary's Hall, Oxford, in March 1851, was not followed by graduation. His father left him his capital estate in trust, and he sold Thorp Green to Henry Stephen Thompson of Kirkby Hall in 1866. He drowned in the River Ure in February 1869 when a boat overturned.

Rochelle, A. G., a fair-haired girl whose parents are dead, in the *Gondal saga. When she is imprisoned, she is looked after by her former playfellow Julian M. who grows to love and pity her. She is the speaker and protagonist of Emily's poem 'The Prisoner' (see 'JULIAN M. AND A. G. ROCHELLE'), whose visions grant her liberty from the 'chains' of the flesh and her present situation. See also ALMEIDA (ALMEDA), AUGUSTA GERALDINE.

Rochester, Bertha, in *Jane Eyre*. Edward Fairfax *Rochester, by his father's connivance with the Mason family, was encouraged to marry the handsome Bertha Antoinetta Mason, daughter of a wealthy merchant of Spanish Town, Jamaica. Dazzled by her appearance, seldom seeing her alone, Rochester thought he loved her, but after marriage discovered that her family was tainted by madness and that she was gross, intemperate, and unchaste. After four years of marriage, Bertha became prematurely mad. Revolted and despairing, Rochester contemplated suicide, but decided instead to return to Europe, leave Bertha securely guarded at *Thornfield Hall, and seek a new life.

Jane Eyre believes that the preternatural laughter echoing through the third storey at Thornfield is Grace *Poole's. A demoniac laugh outside Jane's room precedes her discovery that Rochester's bed curtains have been set on fire. Later Jane hears shrieks in the room above hers, and has to tend the wounded Richard *Mason, while snarls and groans resound from the 'side-den'. Bertha had sucked Mason's blood. Two nights before Jane is to marry Rochester, a light wakes her, and a ghastly woman, with swollen, blackened lineaments and savage fiery eyes, emerges from the closet where Jane's wedding garments hang. The woman throws the wedding veil over her own head, then tears it in two, and tramples on it. Jane faints as the 'lurid visage' leans over her. When the lawyer and Richard Mason reveal that Rochester's wife still lives, he takes Jane and his accusers to see the secret room, where Bertha attacks him viciously until with Grace's help he subdues her. After Jane leaves Thornfield, Bertha escapes again, fires the hangings in the next room and the bed in Jane's room, and climbs up to the roof. As Rochester approaches to rescue her, she leaps over the battlements to her death. See also SCOTT, SIR WALTER; GOTHIC NOVELS; SEXUALITY; MYTH AND SYMBOL; FAIRY TALES; FEMINIST APPROACHES; POST-COLONIAL THEORY; PSYCHOANALYTIC APPROACHES.

Rochester, Edward Fairfax. In *Jane Eyre*, Jane first meets Rochester when his great black horse Mesrour slips on ice; with her help he reaches and remounts his 'tall steed'. Because he is granite-faced and grim rather than handsome, Jane is at ease with him. At Thornfield he interrogates her, finding her piquant and refreshing. Though proud and masterful, he respects her unflattering honesty and, though not 'a general philanthropist', has a conscientious concern for his ward, Adèle *Varens. In Byronic fashion, he admits his sins and regards himself as cursed—for ever denied true happiness, and therefore justified in getting pleasure at any cost. After Jane has rescued him from the burning bed ignited by the mysterious visitant from the third storey, he comes close to declaring his love for her. Nevertheless, to make her jealous, he pretends he is to marry Blanche *Ingram. Jane suffers, realizing that despite his constant attendance on Blanche and charade wedding with her, he sees all her defects. Disguised as a gipsy, he tells Blanche that his wealth is less than she fancied. He detects in Jane passion held in check by conscience and reason—qualities he vows to respect. Richard *Mason's arrival shocks him, for a single word might destroy all his plans. But he keeps Jane ignorant of his connection with Mason, and sends him away after the madwoman's midnight attack. He welcomes Jane on her return from *Gateshead Hall, and at midsummer proposes marriage to her, acknowledging the equality she has claimed. Yet after her acceptance he is more amused than distressed by her rebellion against his loading her with gifts as if she were a slave in his seraglio. He reacts with fury and despair to Mason's interruption of the wedding. Recklessly acknowledging his intention to be a bigamist, he reveals the 'disgusting secret' of his marriage to the former Bertha Mason (see ROCHESTER, BERTHA), and invites all present to see his brute-like partner. Afterwards, in bitter remorse for causing Jane to suffer, he asks her forgiveness; she in her heart forgives him, but insists she must leave him. He assures her that she can still be his wife 'both virtually and nominally', and tells her how, defrauded into marriage with Bertha, he had placed her securely at Thornfield, had wandered through the Continent in a vain search for a 'good and intelligent woman' whom he could love, and had found the company of merely sensual mistresses degrading. He had found his ideal in Jane, and, convinced that his marriage to Bertha was a mere mockery, had resolved to marry his 'better self'. Jane's secret departure left him desolate; yet after he had been blinded and maimed in the fire at Thornfield, he perceived the working of divine justice in chastising his sins, ultimately tempered by mercy in the strange call which reunited him with Jane, and in the partial recovery of sight which enabled him to see his firstborn son. Rochester's antecedents include· *Richardson's 'Mr B', Lord *Byron, and the Duke of *Zamorna. See also SEQUELS AND 'INCREMENTAL LITERATURE'.

Stoneman, Patsy, *Brontë Transformations* (1996).

Roe Head, Mirfield, an 18th-century house named after the hamlet of the same name on the northern edge of Mirfield, overlooking *Dewsbury and the Calder valley, 20 miles from Haworth; where the Brontë sisters went to school and where Charlotte Brontë was employed as a teacher. It had been rebuilt in 1740 for the Marriotts, local coal owners, and since 1830 had been a girls' boarding school run by Miss Margaret *Wooler and three of her sisters. Revd Patrick Brontë, who had held two curacies in the area, had a number of friends nearby including Charlotte's godparents, the *Atkinsons, who lived at Green House, Mirfield. At Roe Head Charlotte made her own lifelong friends Mary *Taylor and Ellen *Nussey. The school had only ten pupils, the daughters of the new manufacturing families that figure so prominently in *Shirley*. The curriculum offered literacy and the rudiments of language, history, *geography, arithmetic, and the 'extra' *accomplishments of French, music, and drawing. Many of the Brontës' drawings and paintings made at Roe Head are still extant and a surviving *Roe Head Album reflects the accomplishments and taste of their schoolfellows (see ART OF THE BRONTËS). The girls had their lessons in one of the large front rooms, with large bay windows that look across the park of neighbouring Kirklees Hall and down the valley. Charlotte's and Anne's drawings of the school building show the unusual double-bowed frontage, the long sweeping drive, and the extensive grounds (Alexander & Sellars, pp. 191–2, 339–40).

Charlotte attended the school from 17 January 1831 until mid-June 1832. She returned as a teacher in July 1835, remaining until December 1838. Emily Brontë attended for three months from 29 July 1835 until late October, when Anne replaced her as a pupil (both their fees being paid by Charlotte's teaching). Anne left in about December 1837, although it is possible she returned for a month or so in early 1838, or even longer (Smith *Letters*, 1. 175 n. 4). Charlotte (and possibly Anne) accompanied Miss Wooler when she moved the school from Roe Head to *Heald's House, Dewsbury Moor, in late February/early March 1838, but left on 23 May after suffering illness and depression. Charlotte then returned before 24 August, and remained at Dewsbury Moor until 22 December 1838 (Smith *Letters*, 1. 180, 184). Miss Wooler retired at the end of 1838 and her sister Eliza took over its management, but failed to make a success of the school. Roe Head, which still survives, was subsequently extended to provide accommodation first for the Verona Fathers and, more recently, for Hollybank School for students with special needs.

Pobjoy, H. N., *A History of Mirfield* (1969).

Roe Head Album. Originally owned by a mysterious 'F. R.' (a pupil or teacher at *Roe Head) and dated 'Dewsbury, Feby 26th 1831', this album of drawings, paintings, and poems is noteworthy for the artistic contributions of three pupils at Miss Margaret *Wooler's school at Roe Head, near *Mirfield, Yorkshire: Charlotte Brontë and her friends Mary and Martha Taylor. It is also more generally significant as evidence of art education in such small private schools for girls and the way it reinforced gender stereotypes of the period.

The album, now in the BPM, descended through the *Allbutt family: Dr George Allbutt and his wife Anna Maria Brooke. They may have acquired it through Revd Thomas Allbutt of Dewsbury and his wife Marianne Wooler, who taught at her sister's school, or through a member of the *Brooke family of Dewsbury. The album is a substantial volume of about 190 pages, many blank, in a dark green cover with an elaborately embossed floral design and the maker's name, 'De La Rue and Co. London', in raised letters along the left edge of the front cover. On the spine the words 'Album' and 'London' are embossed in gold; and the inside covers and flyleaves are of pink imitation moire silk card. Many of the pages are of different colour and texture, examples of quality paper that might be purchased in London from Ackermann's Repository of Arts or Lackington's Temple of the

Charlotte Brontë's crayon drawing of Roe Head school, c.1831–2, inscribed by Mr Brontë on the mounting below the drawing, 'By my D[ea]r Daughter Charlotte | P Bronte Min[iste]r of Haworth'.

Muses that also sold painting materials and papier mâché products for women to decorate. Some of the papers have decorative gold borders, ready-made printed frames for friends to insert their paintings. Although now worn and in disrepair, the album was an object of value, not least because of its elegant appearance.

There are nineteen drawings, ten in watercolour (one of which is possibly tempera) and nine in pencil, interspersed with a variety of conventional verses, a few original but the majority copied from the Bible or from fashionable poets. The owner's initials 'FR' appear beneath the 'Prologue' to the volume, a sententious piece in rhymed couplets that asks for only 'chaste and sober prose', particularly religious verse that might 'instruct the mind, & mend the heart'. Charlotte's contribution to the album was a pencil drawing, made just before she left Roe Head as a pupil in May 1832 and titled 'St Martin's Parsonage' (pp. 200–1). It is clearly copied from an engraving since she never visited Birmingham. The remaining contributions are the productions of her fellow pupils, providing us with valuable knowledge of the girls at Roe Head: a landscape of Caernarfon Castle, a watercolour copy of Raphael's *Madonna della sedia* and of a ruined church by Mary and Martha Taylor; decorative flowers by J. Brooke; a detailed illustration of a music book by A. M. Kitson; a primrose similar to one by Charlotte; a sketch of the St Gothard Pass; and others that are tantalizingly signed only with initials.

The album clearly reveals the method of instruction followed by both Charlotte Brontë and her teachers. The illustrations are all careful copies of contemporary prints, chiefly engravings from the fashionable *annuals and sets of plates sold by print-sellers like Ackermanns. 'Ludlow Castle, Shropshire', for example, a pencil drawing signed with the initials 'S.C.', possibly Susan Carter (see CARTER FAMILY), several of whose drawings survive from the time she was an art teacher at Roe Head, is clearly copied from an engraving of the type found in the annuals. It was probably executed at school as an exercise, since Charlotte made a similar copy there in 1831 (Alexander & Sellars, p. 193). It was common practice for the teacher to draw with the pupils or to duplicate the original for pupils to copy. All the dated drawings in the Roe Head Album were made about this time and bear a striking resemblance to Charlotte's own artworks surviving from her brief period as a pupil at the Woolers' school.

Roe Head Journal. This is a series of six fragmentary semi-autobiographical manuscripts written by Charlotte Brontë between 1836 and 1837, while she was a teacher at Margaret *Wooler's

school at Roe Head. They provide a valuable record of her efforts to cling to her imaginary Angrian world during what she calls 'this wretched bondage': her life as a teacher. The manuscripts (in Bonnell, Pierpont Morgan and BPM) are written in Charlotte's minuscule script and vary in length from one to seven pages. They are customarily referred to by their first lines as follows:

'Well here I am at Roe Head' (4 Feb. 1836)
'Now as I have a little bit of time' ([5 Feb.] 1836)
'All this day I have been in a dream' (11 Aug.–14 Oct. 1836)
'I'm just going to write because I cannot help it' [c.Oct. 1836]
'My Compliments to the weather' [c.Mar. 1837]
'About a week since I got a letter from Branwell' [c.Oct. 1837]

The *Glass Town and Angrian saga had reached a crisis when Charlotte was obliged to go to Roe Head at the end of July 1835. She was desperate for news from home of the battles Branwell was concocting and the subsequent fate of her heroine Mary Henrietta *Percy. In moments of quiet, while supervising her pupils' preparation or while alone in the dormitory, Charlotte's thoughts would wander back to Haworth with its Angrian associations. A gust of wind or the sound of distant church bells would initiate an Angrian vision which she would jot down on scraps of paper: disconnected images of the war-torn banks of the *Calabar River and the rebel Quashia *Quamina desecrating Mary Percy's quarters in the palace at *Zamorna; the Duke of Zamorna and Henry Fernando di *Enara relaxing in a Claudian landscape at *Hawkscliffe; news from Mr Saunderson (John *Sneaky) of the fighting in Angria; the unimaginative Angrian beauty Jane *Moore in a moment of uncharacteristic reverie on her dead sister Harriet; Mary Percy reading a letter from her exiled father the Duke of *Northangerland; and Dr Brandon, a character not otherwise associated with Angria, thinking of a young woman Lucy and her reaction to the operation he has just performed. Each of these visions is framed by Charlotte's thoughts of her frustrating personal situation and the relief that this mental escape provides. The interruption of her visions by some unsuspecting pupil produces a reaction of physical violence: 'I thought I should have vomited' (*Jane Eyre* (Norton, 3rd edn.), 404).

Three long poems, written during her first school holidays in December–January 1835, show a similar movement between autobiographical and imaginary sequence: *'We wove a web in childhood' (19 Dec. 1835), sometimes titled 'Retrospection'; 'Long since as I remember well' (Jan. 1836); and 'But once again, but once again' (19 Jan. 1836). Like the prose fragments, the poems trace a series of Angrian visions that Charlotte experienced in odd moments during the school day, visions which bring excitement to her dreary routine as she shares vicariously the life of her imaginary characters. As she pictures the Duke of Zamorna leaning against an obelisk, she is captivated: 'I had really utterly forgot where I was and all the gloom and cheerlessness of my situation' (Alexander *EEW*, 2(2). 385).

The poems, together with the *Roe Head Journal*, provide the corollary to Charlotte's sometimes hysterical correspondence with Ellen Nussey at this time (see Smith *Letters*, 1. 143, 153–6). The letters suggest a religious crisis, while the *Roe Head Journal* reveals a further conflict between Charlotte's absorbing and sustaining Angrian dreamworld and her sense of its idolatrous nature. The sensual world of Angria had become a sinful pleasure for the young Christian woman. See PASSING EVENTS.

Because the *Roe Head Journal* fragments were written in moments snatched from a busy routine, Charlotte's handwriting is particularly rough, with few corrections, crooked lines, and dashes in lieu of punctuation. Not only is Charlotte writing quickly but she describes how she writes with her eyes closed to maintain her vision. Here, her creative process is described in biblical phrases and is essentially trance-like, suggesting the visionary inspiration of the Romantic poets she knew so well. This, however, was not always her characteristic practice; most of her juvenile manuscripts, especially the earlier ones, show a high level of polish in the care taken with title-pages, signatures, and frequent corrections. Generally, her manuscripts are intended to be finished copies, modelled on published volumes. Charlotte's later manuscripts do show an increase in dashes and are often untitled, but it is erroneous to base an interpretation of her creative process on these numerous dashes and the writing experience described under difficult circumstances at Roe Head (as in Sandra M. Gilbert and Susan Gubar's *The Madwoman in the Attic* (1979), 311–12). Charlotte's method of imagining and describing scenes was honed in childhood, but she was not a trance-writer.

> *Roe Head Journal* (complete text), in *Jane Eyre*, ed. Richard Dunn (Norton, 2nd edn., 1987; 3rd edn., 2001).

Rogue (Rougue), Alexander. See NORTH-ANGERLAND, DUKE OF (ALEXANDER AUGUSTUS PERCY, ROGUE (ROUGUE), LORD ELLRINGTON (ELRINGTON)).

'Romantic Tale, A'. See 'TWO ROMANTIC TALES'.

'room is quiet, The', by Charlotte Brontë; published in *Poems* 1846 as 'The Teacher's Monologue' (draft MSS, pt. 1, 15 May 1837, Bonnell BPM, 94; pt. 2, 12 May 1837, Bonnell, BPM 98, both written at *Roe Head, and revised for publication). Charlotte recalls her beloved home beyond the distant hills, and contemplates transience, fearing that even her home may soon be desolate. A questioning couplet is followed by more formal eight-line stanzas ending philosophically with a prayer for 'Reason, Patience, Faith'.

> Neufeldt *CBP*, p. 308.

Rosendale (Rossendale), Marquis of. See SNEAKY, JOHN AUGUSTUS, JUN.

Rosendale (Rossendale) Hill on the outskirts of Coomassie in *Sneaky's Land, in the *Glass Town and Angrian saga. Frederick Guelph, Duke of York and first King of the Twelves, is slain at the Battle of Rosendale Hill, the Glass Town 'Battle of Marathon' and part of its early mythology.

Rosier, Eugene, the Duke of Zamorna's French page in the *Glass Town and Angrian saga, a dark, foreign-looking youth of 15, who is in love with Harriet, a serving girl at *Wellesley House. Rosier is indicative of Zamorna's penchant for foreigners, a trait disliked by the Angrians.

Rosina. See ALCONA, ROSINA.

Ross, Edward Tut, Marquis of Harlaw (Harlow), son of Captain John *Ross, King of Ross's Land, in the *Glass Town and Angrian saga. He is the friend of the Marquis of *Ardrah and home secretary in his Verdopolitan government. Like Ardrah, he is associated with the 'Northern Review', in writing falsehoods about the Duke of Zamorna and the ladies of Angria.

Ross, Sir James Clark (1800–62), Scottish polar explorer and naval officer like his uncle Sir John *Ross whom he accompanied at sea from the age of 12, conducting surveys of the White Sea and the Arctic. He sailed with Sir William Edward *Parry on four Arctic expeditions (1819–27) that the young Brontës read about in *Blackwood's Edinburgh Magazine* (Alexander *EW*, p. 28), inspiring Anne to adopt him (together with his uncle) as her leading character in the *Young Men's Play and the *Glass Town and Angrian saga (see ROSS, CAPTAIN JOHN (FICTIONAL)). From 1829 to 1833 he was joint leader with his uncle of a private expedition and in 1831 he located the magnetic north pole. He made a magnetic survey of Britain, led an expedition to the Antarctic (1839–43) where he discovered Victoria Land and the volcano Mt Erebus, wrote his *Voyage of Discovery* (1847), and made his final expedition searching for Franklin in Baffin Bay (1848–9). Ross Island, the Ross Sea, and Ross's Gull are named after him.

Ross, Captain John (fictional), King of Ross's Land (Rossesland), friend and ally of Sir William Edward *Parry, and father of Edward Tut Ross, Marquis of Harlaw, who is friendly with Parry's son, in the *Glass Town and Angrian saga. Ross's gluttony during a visit to his friend horrifies Lord Charles Wellesley in 'A Day at Parry's Palace' (see 'YOUNG MEN'S MAGAZINE'). Captain John Ross is Anne Brontë's chief man in the Young Men's Play, replacing the original 'Waiting Boy' soldier. The friendship between the two kings, Ross and Parry, and between their sons, reflects the close early association between Emily and Anne. Like Parry, Ross is based on two famous Arctic explorers, uncle and nephew, whose exploits were reported in *Blackwood's Edinburgh Magazine* during the 1820s (see ROSS, SIR JOHN; ROSS, SIR JAMES CLARK).

Ross, Sir John (historical) (1777–1856), Scottish Arctic explorer and naval officer who served with distinction in the Napoleonic Wars. He is the uncle of Sir James Clark *Ross who is generally thought to be the model for the fictional Captain John *Ross nominated by Anne Brontë as her 'chief man' in the *Young Men's Play and the *Glass Town and Angrian saga. It is likely, however, that a combination of uncle and nephew, whose exploits were reported together in *Blackwood's Edinburgh Magazine*, inspired the 9-year-old Anne's character. In 1818 he led an expedition that included his nephew and Parry, in search of the north-west passage; and on his 1829–33 expedition, led jointly with his nephew, he discovered and named Boothia Peninsula, King William Land, and the Gulf of Boothia.

Barnard, Robert, *Emily Brontë* (2000), 17 (illustration).

Ross's Land (Rossesland), ruled by Captain John *Ross, one of the four kings of the Glass Town Federation and, like *Sneaky's Land, associated with Scotland and Highland scenery. The capital city is Ross's Glass Town (Rosstown).

Royal Academy of Arts (RA), established in *London in 1768 by Royal Charter, with Sir Joshua Reynolds as its first president. Like its Continental precursors, the RA aimed to raise the status of the fine arts and foster a national school of art through the instruction of young artists, the provision of objective criteria for the arts (articulated in part through Reynolds's *Discourses* 1769–1790), and the establishment of an annual exhibition of new art. By the time Branwell Brontë considered entering the Academy schools in 1835, the RA was housed in Somerset House (whose architecture was pronounced 'Tolerable' by the 10-year-old Branwell in his copy of *A Description of London* by William Darton (1824): see Alexander & Sellars, app. 1). In

1837 it moved to the new National Gallery Building and in 1868 to Burlington House. The RA became the arbiter of 'High Art', whose judgements were based on recognized canons of good taste and whose standards were founded on the distinction between genius and mere imitation, as practised by amateurs like the Brontës (see ART OF THE BRONTËS). During the 19th century the RA's supremacy was repeatedly challenged by individuals (like John *Martin) and groups (such as the Water-Colour Society and the British Institution), and its cautious approach to change provoked the charge of conservatism. The Brontës were aware of its prejudice against Romantic artists like Constable and Martin, and against women artists (who were not elected until 1922, although they could attend some classes). Nevertheless, like most families with aspiring artists, they held the RA in high respect and were familiar with the work of its members through reviews in *Blackwood's*, *Fraser's*, and local newspapers, and through engravings in *annuals and elsewhere. Charlotte, for example, made a copy of an engraving of *Solitude at Dawn* by Fuseli (RA professor of painting 1799–1805, and 1810–25), which was exhibited in the RA (1823) and reviewed in *Blackwood's* in July of that year (see 'Lycidas', 4 Mar. 1835, in Alexander & Sellars, p. 238).

The idea that Branwell might study at the Royal Academy was mentioned by Charlotte in a letter to Ellen Nussey on 2 July 1835 (Smith *Letters*, 1. 140), and again on 6 July by Revd Patrick Brontë in a letter to Mrs Elizabeth *Franks (Wise & Symington, 1. 130). An undated draft letter from Branwell to the secretary of the RA survives, enquiring how to apply and whether he can present himself in August or September (Alexander & Sellars, p. 76). In mid-1835 and again at the end of the year, Branwell received two series of ten weekly lessons from William *Robinson, who had studied at the RA under Sir Thomas Lawrence (president 1820–30), with the intention of preparing Branwell for a similar career as a portrait painter. Mr Brontë was anxious that Branwell should 'improve himself, in Anatomy, which is the grammar of painting, & also make some farther progress in Classics, and consequently defer his journey, to London, till next Summer—When, God willing—I intend he shall go' (16 Nov. 1835; *BST* (1996), 21. 7. 324; see also Wise & Symington, 1. 132). There is, however, no firm evidence that Branwell ever went to London or presented drawings for admission as a student. Branwell's fictitious tale of Charles *Wentworth's disastrous visit to London in his 'History of Angria' has been seen as an autobiographical account of his trip (Gérin *BB*, pp. 99–110); but this, and the unauthenticated reports of his trip by his friends Francis *Leyland

and Francis *Grundy, may simply be the result of Branwell's vivid storytelling based on an intimate knowledge of London gained from his early reading. Leyland notes that potential probationers were required to present a portfolio of drawings 'from the skeleton' and 'from the antique' (Leyland, 1. 142–3) but no such drawings exist among Branwell's extant art works. Nor is there any evidence at the RA of an application by Branwell, and Barker points out that once he met Robinson he would have realized that his plans were premature, since he did not have the required portfolio (Barker, pp. 227–8). Gaskell believed Branwell never made the trip to London; Ellen Nussey told her: 'I do not know whether it was conduct or want of finances that prevented Branwell from going to the Royal Academy. Probably there were impediments of both kinds' (Shorter Circle, p. 15). A letter written by Branwell late in life (24 Jan. 1847) appears to confirm this now generally accepted view that he never attempted to fulfil his dream of entering the RA schools and visiting the British Museum: 'I used to think that if I could have for a week the free range of the British Museum—the Library included—I could feel as though I were placed for seven days in Paradise, but now, really, dear sir, my eyes would roam over the Elgin marbles, the Egyptian saloon and the most treasured volumes like the eyes of a dead cod fish' (Symington, J. A., and Hatfield, C. W., *A Complete Transcript of the Leyland Manuscripts* (1925), 39–42).

Royal Northern Society for the Encouragement of the Fine Arts, established in 1800 to foster the Fine Arts in the northern provinces of England, mainly by holding annual exhibitions in which artists from London exhibited alongside local artists. The young Brontës would have been aware of the importance of this cultural event through their first art teacher, John *Bradley, who regularly exhibited during the 1820s. They may have first encountered such names as Richard Westall, William Turner, William Mulready, and Sir Thomas Lawrence in the exhibition catalogues. There is no evidence, however, that they visited the exhibition before the summer of 1834, when Charlotte herself submitted two of her detailed pencil copies of engravings for exhibition, 'Bolton Abbey' and 'Kirkstall Abbey', famous views of two local landmarks (Alexander & Sellars, pp. 52, 228–9). The 1834 catalogue records that alongside such amateur works were landscapes by Copley Fielding, Alexander Nasmyth, John Linnel, Robert Macreth, and others; historical paintings by H. Fradelle; seascapes by Carmichael; animal paintings by Schwanfelder; portraits by William *Robinson; and sculpture by Joseph Bentley

*Leyland. In 1835 Robinson, who had exhibited regularly from 1823 on, was engaged to give Branwell a course of lessons in painting.

Rural Minstrel, The (Halifax, 1813). In this volume Revd Patrick Brontë intends to please and profit by moral instruction, as in his *Cottage Poems, but in the 'irregular metre' suitable for descriptive poems: the English Pindaric ode, sometimes using rhyme, but irregular in the number of stanzas, lines, and stresses. He is more at ease in this unconstricting mode. 'The Sabbath Bell' deploys the clichés of 18th-century moralized nature poems with some skill: the solemn bell and ancient tower remind mortals of the final sentence to 'never-ending woe' or 'Eden's amaranthine shades'. 'Kirkstall Abbey: A Fragment of a Romantic Tale' is a night scene with the obligatory ruined tower, inlaid by moonlight with 'sable ebony, and silver white'. But this ruin is real, and Mr Brontë's visits there with Maria Branwell *Brontë give a new warmth. He imagines celestial regions where 'all the soul' will be love. This poem and the next have faint echoes of *Milton's shorter poems. The 'Lines, addressed to a lady, on her birth-day', written for Maria, have a pleasant sweetness despite the clichés of poetic diction, for he invites her to walk where 'The modest daisy, and the violet-blue, | Inviting, spread their charms for you'. 'The Epitaph' begins clumsily and develops conventionally, borrowing phrases from *Goldsmith's The Deserted Village for its 'lowly cot, that mouldering falls, | Whilst the long grass o'ertops the walls'. A successful, atmospheric 'Winter'; an evangelical, sentimental poem of 'Rural Happiness'; and an unconvincing moral exercise in curious jerky lines, 'The Distress and Relief' follow—the last making much of man, the 'helpless worm's', feeble cry. 'The Christian's Farewell' is an unoriginal deathbed poem with a bathetic ending, but 'The Harper of Erin', Mr Brontë's grand finale, uses an effective framework setting 'on Killarney's shore' for its evocation of divine visions and immortal harps.

Ruskin, John (1819–1900), eminent critic of art, architecture, and society. Charlotte Brontë delighted in all Ruskin's works, his eloquent forceful prose and his earnest content, likening him to 'a consecrated Priest of the Abstract and Ideal' and appreciating his deep 'reverence for Art' (Smith Letters, 2. 546). She read the first two of the five volumes of his Modern Painters, published by *Smith, Elder (1843–60) and given to her by George Smith. These two volumes (1843 and 1846), which she read during the summer of 1848, gave her immense pleasure and made her feel how 'ignorant' she had previously been 'in judging of art': 'this book seems to give me eyes' (Smith *Letters*, 2. 94). Ruskin had begun the work as a vindication of the genius of J. W. M. Turner and his 'glowing descriptions' of Turner's paintings made Charlotte long to see them (something she accomplished in December 1849, when she saw two Turner exhibitions in London). Since her youth, she had admired *prints of Turner's paintings, at least one of which she had copied and exhibited (see FINDEN, EDWARD AND WILLIAM), but Ruskin pointed out the inability of steel engravings to imitate 'the depth and delicacy' of the original colours (Smith *Letters*, 2. 96 n.). He also argued that art was a means to social good and further developed this idea in *The Seven Lamps of Architecture* (1849) and its sequel *The Stones of Venice* (1851–3), both illustrated by Ruskin's own drawings. In December 1850, Ruskin sent Charlotte his popular Christmas book, 'a divine fairy tale' entitled *The King of the Golden River; or The Black Brothers, A Legend of Stiria* (Smith *Letters*, 2. 541 and 546). Charlotte and her father agreed with Ruskin's attack on the Puseyites in his pamphlet *Notes on the Construction of Sheepfolds* (1851) (see

PUSEY, EDWARD BOUVERIE; and Smith *Letters*, 2. 584 n.); she read his early defence of the Pre-Raphaelites (681 n.); and she shared a liking for Ruskin with Elizabeth Gaskell, sending her her copy of *The Stones of Venice*.

Rydings, in Birstall Smithies, was Ellen *Nussey's home from c.July 1826 to June 1836, when it belonged to her uncle Richard Nussey. The lease of Rydings Hall and estate was acquired by her great-grandfather George Nussey in two stages in and after 1711 and sold by his son Joshua in 1776; but in 1791 her great-uncle Richard Walker (1749–1817), a royal apothecary, purchased the estate and began renovations. He added the battlements which helped Charlotte Brontë to imagine *Thornfield Hall, as did the fine chestnut and thorn-trees, the rookery, and the plantations and fruit garden where she sought seclusion from other visitors.

Ryecote Farm, home of the *Wilson family in *Tenant*, managed by Richard *Wilson, the eldest son and a gentleman farmer like Gilbert Markham.

St Clair, Lord Ronald Roslyn, Earl, a highland chieftain of Clan Albyn in the Branii Hills, with a castle on Mt Elimbos, in the *Glass Town and Angrian saga. A friend and contemporary of the Duke of *Wellington, he is prime minister of the Verdopolitan Federation and Leader of the House of Lords during the *War of Encroachment. Executed by Rogue (Duke of Northangerland) because he and his party (The Aristocrats) withhold financial support from the army, he is 'made alive' again in true Glass Town style. The story of his courtship, his disguise as 'Mr Leslie', and marriage to Lady Emily Charlesworth is told in *The *Green Dwarf*. Their daughter Lady Flora Roslyn is rejected by Warner Howard *Warner as a possible bride because of her lack of dowry.

In *The Lay of the Last Minstrel*, Sir Walter *Scott tells of the noble St Clairs, often called the St Clairs of Roslin (they built Roslin Chapel in 1446 on their lands in Midlothian) and also the Earls of Orkney (where they built the Castle of Kirkwall). James St Clair Erskine, Earl of Rosslyn, was a member of the historical Duke of Wellington's cabinet in 1830. Charlotte Brontë has a similar character, Lord Rosslyn, in the Duke's cabinet in the Islanders' Play (Alexander *EEW*, 1. 141).

St Michael's Cathedral, with its impressive dome, is a landmark in Verdopolis, in the *Glass Town and Angrian saga. Coronations are performed here and it is the burial place of the Glass Town aristocracy, rather like Westminster Abbey although its architecture resembles St Paul's, London. The name probably derived from Haworth parish church of St Michael's and All Angels, of which Revd Patrick Brontë was the incumbent.

St Pierre, Zélie de, in *Villette*, teacher at Mme *Beck's pensionnat; possibly based on 'Mlle Blanche' at the Pensionnat *Heger. She is a Parisian, externally refined, but really a corrupt, unprincipled, callous epicure, profligate in outlook; sallow, with ice cold eyes and thread-like lips which smile only to display her perfect teeth. Though she hates work, she keeps perfect order, and is valued by Mme Beck as a useful tool. She attempts to please M. Paul *Emanuel, whom she would like to marry, though she suspects he knows her secret 'barrenness'; and she maliciously insinuates that Lucy thinks his birthday too frivolous to warrant a gift.

Sai Too-Too. See QUAMINA, SAI-TOO-TOO.

sales of Brontëana. On 1 and 2 October 1861 Revd A. B. *Nicholls put up for sale the remaining contents of Haworth Parsonage after selecting items he wished to take to Ireland. The buyers were mainly local people. The large number of carpets offered for sale, along with 'Bed Hangings', 'Window Hangings', and 'Cornice and Curtain', show how much Charlotte had added to the comfort of the Parsonage since Ellen Nussey first saw it in 1833, lacking 'drapery of all kinds', with 'not much carpet any where'. The furniture included six chairs, a dining table, a card table, and drawers, all in mahogany. A 'Camp Bedstead' bought for 7s. 9d. was perhaps the narrow bed visible in Emily's *Diary Paper of 30 July 1845. The sofa bought for £3 12s., now in the Parsonage dining room, was traditionally Emily's deathbed. Most of the pictures sold cheaply; but prints of John *Martin's *Belshazzar's Feast* (now in BPM), *Joshua and the Sun*, *Passage of the Red Sea*, and *Deluge* totalled £2 6s. 6d. The books which fetched the highest prices were two three-volume editions of *Jane Eyre*, one bought by Mr Wildman for 15s., the other by John Cragg, the auctioneer, for 10s. 6d.; Mr Cragg also paid 1s. 6d. for the Brontës' *Poems* 1846, which is now an extremely expensive rarity. 'Sermons' fetched very little, for Mr Kay obtained six for 4d.; and M. Constantin *Heger's gift to Charlotte, a German Testament now at BPM, went for 8d. to Elijah Craven. The total takings were £115 13s. 11d., of which Nicholls received £91 in cash (see *BST* (1965), 14. 75. 46–50).

Martha *Brown's sister Ann and her husband Benjamin Binns bought several items at the 1861 sale. On 26 and 27 January 1886 some of these, along with articles inherited by or given to Mrs Binns, were sold at Saltaire, near Leeds. The 44 lots of Brontëana included drawings, paintings, a few letters, books, and clothing. At the well-attended sale Emily's watercolour of *Flossy, misattributed to Charlotte, was acquired, with Charlotte's 'Study of Eyes', 'Amelia Walker', 'Laughing Child', 'Crying Child', and other lots, by Alfred *Gledhill, who later sold them to Martha Brown's cousins Robinson and Francis Brown.

After Ellen Nussey's death at Moor Lane House, Gomersal, in November 1897, the contents of the house were sold by auction on 18 and 19 May 1898. Though Ellen had sold almost all Charlotte's letters to T. J. *Wise, she had retained some Brontë drawings and jewellery, and correspondence about the Brontës. Her transcripts of parts of Charlotte's letters, bought by Alice *Needham, are now in the BPM. The drawings included those in Alexander & Sellars, pp. 249, 253. An ornately decorated tea caddy given by Charlotte to Ellen was sold, and later, in 1928, given to the BPM (*Sixty Treasures*, ed. J. R. V. Barker (1988) 57).

On 2 July 1898 Sotheby's auctioned Robinson and Francis Brown's collection of Brontëana, formerly displayed in their unsuccessful 'Museum of Brontë Relics' at 123 Main Street, Haworth. The Brontë Society acquired ten of the 30 drawings on offer; nineteen unsold paintings remained with the Brown family until 1950, when the Society bought them from Francis Brown's daughter Gladys Jane Brown.

On 26 July 1907, after Mr Nicholls's death, Sotheby's sold on behalf of his widow 58 lots of Brontëana. Mrs Nicholls had previously given away various items, but many books, manuscripts, and drawings remained. C. K. *Shorter's *Charlotte Brontë and her Circle* (1896) had aroused an avid interest in both British and American collectors and booksellers, and the sale raised £718 2s., with comparatively high prices paid for signed or inscribed books. Maggs paid £6 for Charlotte's copies of *Voltaire's *La Henriade* and *Bernardin de Saint-Pierre's *Paul et Virginie*, and £9 for a collection of her schoolbooks. The sale included fifteen lots of manuscripts: early writings, draft letters, letters to Charlotte, Nicholls's transcripts of her poems, and her pencil draft of a preface to *The Professor*. Many of these were eventually acquired by American libraries. Lot 35, Charlotte's paintbox, was bought by the Brontë Society for £4 4s., and Lot 32, Emily's writing desk, was later acquired by Henry *Bonnell, and bequeathed to the BPM. George *Smith's son-in-law Reginald Smith bought Charlotte's writing desk, afterwards bequeathed to the BPM by Alexander Murray Smith.

On 19 June 1914 Sotheby's sold for Mrs Nicholls for a total of £613 14s. pieces of furniture formerly at Haworth, Brontë books, notebooks used in Brussels and afterwards, manuscripts including *Emma*, poems, fifteen tiny booklets of early writing, and Emily and Anne's *Diary Paper of 24 November 1834 (now BPM MS Bonnell 131). After Mrs Nicholls's death in 1915, the last of the Nicholls collection was sold at Sotheby's on 15 December 1916, along with the property of J. H. Dixon of Harrogate. Lot 664, Anne's autograph music book, is now BPM MS Bonnell 133. The Brontës' piano, sold for £5 5s. in 1861 to John Booth of Oxenhope, was offered for sale among Dixon's property, then withdrawn by his widow, who was dissatisfied with the bidding, and presented by her in 1917 to the BPM.

On 18 June 1928 an American collector, Cecelia Eareckson, purchased several Brontë books, an album with watercolours by Charlotte, and Emily's drawing of the dog *Grasper at Sotheby's sale of Shorter's library. She generously gave these to the BPM in October 1986. Of the many subsequent sales of Brontëana in Britain and the USA, the most important was probably Christie's sale in New York on 25 March 1980 on behalf of the Grolier Club, offering a devoir by Emily, three prose manuscripts by Branwell, and letters by Charlotte. The Brontë Society purchased 44 of Charlotte's letters for approximately £70,000, and subsequently acquired the devoir (Lonoff, p. 140: devoir no. 12) from the purchaser at the sale. See also MANUSCRIPTS AND MANUSCRIPT COLLECTIONS.

Alexander & Sellars.
Annotated sale catalogues at BPM.

Samara, Fernando de, a guitar player, different in temperament from the usual inhabitants of *Gondal. Although he pledges his love to the daughter of the family of Areon Hall in Exina, where he is raised, A.G.A. steals his heart, has an affair with him, and, when she tires of him, sends him to a dungeon in the Gaaldine Caves. He escapes but after looking at A.G.A.'s miniature, he commits suicide, his heart still ruled by 'the Tyrant'.

Sand, George (1804–76). Pen name of Aurore Dupin, baroness Dudevant, a prolific French Romantic novelist also noted for her love affairs. Enid Duthie speculates that Charlotte Brontë read Sand's works by the early 1840s; certainly she read them later, since she comments on Sand's nature and her 'poetry' in letters to George Henry Lewes. Though these judgements are not unmixed with criticism, on the whole she admires Sand's work, especially *Consuelo* (1842–3) with its outwardly 'conventual', inwardly passionate, heroine.
SL

Duthie *Foreign Vision*, pp. 16–18.
Smith *Letters*, 2. 10, 485.

Sarah, in *Shirley*, housemaid to Robert Gérard *Moore and Hortense Gérard *Moore at *Hollow's Cottage. Pert, fresh-faced, with 'plentiful tresses of . . . yellow hair' which she refuses to cover, she has many admirers, including Moore's employee Fred *Murgatroyd and the preaching tailor Moses *Barraclough. She expresses native English contempt for the strange foreign ways imported by her Belgian mistress, Hortense Moore, especially Hortense's cooking.
HR

Scarborough on the East Yorks. coast was in the mid-19th century a fashionable seaside resort and spa. An elegant iron bridge, built across the Mill-beck ravine in the south bay in 1827, provided a pleasant walk from the streets of Georgian and Regency houses to the spa with its chalybeate and saline springs, esplanade, and gardens. The fine sands of the south bay curve towards the harbour, which is edged by the clustering houses of the old town, below a high promontory crowned by a ruined castle and by St Mary's church and church-yard. The town was Anne Brontë's model for 'A——' in *Agnes Grey* (chs. 21, 24, 25), and it fig-ures briefly as *Cliff-bridge in Charlotte's *Shirley* (ch. 11). Anne grew to love it when she accompan-ied the *Robinson family there for the summer holidays, which they regularly spent in 'William Wood's Lodgings . . . patronized by the Nobility and Gentry' at The Cliff, a high building on St Nicholas Cliff, where the Grand Hotel, built in 1867, now stands. In the 1840s Wood offered thir-teen apartments with between five and fifteen beds, reception rooms, and usually a housekeeper's room. Branwell also visited Scarborough with the Robinsons, and mentioned its 'little Circular Mu-seum' in *And the Weary are at Rest* (see also Gérin *BB*, p. 229).

In the spring of 1849 the fragile Anne, emaciated with TB, longed to go to Scarborough in the hope of improvement. Charlotte and Ellen Nussey chose to take her to pleasant, familiar rooms at no. 2 The Cliff rather than to Margaret *Wooler's house on the 'bleak, steep' coast of the north bay. Anne died peacefully at The Cliff on 28 May. Her funeral took place on 30 May at Christ Church, Vernon Road, since St Mary's was being rebuilt, but she was bur-ied in St Mary's churchyard, where her grave may be seen.

Scatcherd, Miss. This irritable teacher of his-tory and grammar at *Lowood, in *Jane Eyre*, con-stantly scolds Helen *Burns, and punishes her for trivial offences or untidiness by making her stand alone in the middle of the schoolroom, flogging her, making her wear an 'untidy badge', or attach-ing a phylactery-like board labelled 'Slattern' to her forehead. Unlike Miss *Temple she never com-mends Helen's merits, and she arouses Jane's in-dignant fury by her cruelty. See also ANDREWS, ANNA.

Schiller, Friedrich von (1759–1805), German dramatist, poet, and historian; a seminal figure in the German Romantic movement. Charlotte Brontë read his *Ballads* in 1843 at the Pensionnat *Heger and translated at least six into English and French (see NOTEBOOKS (CAHIERS)). Allusions to Schiller's work occur in three of her novels. His books appear on Hunsden Yorke *Hunsden's shelves in *The Professor* (ch. 4). Diana and Mary *Rivers of *Jane Eyre* are reading his play *Die Räuber*

(*The Robbers*), when Jane first sees them (ch. 28); she herself is later reading Schiller when St John *Rivers urges her to give up German for Hindu-stani (ch. 34). Paulina Mary *Home of *Villette* reads his *Ballads* 'beautifully', translates them flu-ently, and memorizes several; she and Lucy Snowe discuss one of her favourites, 'Des Mädchens Klage' ('The Maiden's Lament', ch. 26). Several critics have detected affinities between Emily's poems and German Romanticism; it is possible that she read Schiller in translation, as his works were ad-mired and available in England, but no direct evi-dence exists.   SL

Neufeldt *CBP*, pp. 357–70, 48–90.

Scoresby, Revd William (DD, FRS, 1789–1857), son of a Whitby sea-captain; distinguished Arctic voyager and scientific writer. Ordained 1825, he ministered in Bessingby, near *Bridlington, in Liverpool, and Exeter, before becoming vicar of *Bradford 1839–47. He angered Dissenters by in-sistence on church rates, and antagonized some colleagues. But he urged the establishment of more Anglican Sunday and day schools, including *Haworth National School. On 9 January 1844, he asked Revd Patrick Brontë, for the sake of the poor children of Haworth who were under his spiritual care, to call a church trustees' meeting to arrange for the appointment of an Oxford or Cambridge graduate at the Haworth Free Grammar School. In July 1844 he nominated Revd J. B. *Grant as master of the grammar school to replace the Methodist Mr Ramsbottom. During a visit to Canada in 1847 he told Joseph Abbott of the Brontës' bereavements, and in September 1855 he told Elizabeth Gaskell 'many curious anecdotes about the extraordinary character of the people round Haworth' (Chapple & Pollard *Gaskell Let-ters*, 872).

Scott, Sir Francis Edward Dolman (?1797–1851), married Mrs Lydia *Robinson's cousin Cath-erine Julia née Bateman, niece of Revd Thomas Gisborne. From March 1847 Lydia lived at the Scotts' home, Great Barr Hall, near Birmingham. Lady Scott died on 4 August 1848 and by 18 August Lydia was allegedly the wealthy Sir Edward's 'in-fatuated slave'. They married at a private ceremony in Bath on 8 November 1848, and planned to win-ter abroad, Sir Edward's yacht meeting them at Marseilles. He bequeathed to Lydia £600 a year, his house in Bryanston Square, London, and the family diamonds during her lifetime, to pass to his heir by his first wife.

Scott, Joe, in *Shirley*, the overlooker at *Hollow's Mill. He is sent by Robert Gérard *Moore with three others (*Murgatroyd, Pighills, and Sykes) to collect new frames and shears, but on their return they are waylaid on *Stilbro' Moor by a gang of machine-breakers led by Moses *Barraclough. Joe is a type of the sharp-witted, self-educated northern working man, one of the 'manufacturing lads i' th' north' (p. 68) who takes pride in his station and asserts a native superiority over southerners. As a mill overlooker he is rigid in applying workplace rules, but never cruel like the 'Child-torturers, slave masters or drivers' whom the novelist declines to portray (p. 71). His young son Harry hangs about the mill performing odd jobs. Though a mill mechanic, Joe sides with the masters in their dispute with the workers, assisting Moore both in the capture of Barraclough and the defence of Hollow's Mill. He also embraces the traditional view of woman's place in society, for which he is roundly condemned by Shirley and Caroline (ch. 18). Joe Scott is the descendant of a recurring character in the Brontës' writing, first seen as Timothy *Steaton (Steighton), an obsequious or scoundrelly assistant to Edward *Percy and Captain Sir William *Percy in the juvenilia, then named Timothy *Steighton, a counting-house clerk to mill owner Edward *Crimsworth in The *Professor, and subsequently appearing as John Henry Moore's bookkeeper Tim Steele in the fragment 'John Henry', where he is said to be 'a joined Wesleyan Methodist and an eminent class leader', attributes that in Shirley are transferred to Moses Barraclough.   HR

Scott, Sir Walter (1771–1832), Scottish novelist, poet, critic, historian, antiquarian, and biographer whose works had a profound effect on the Brontës. One of the most important early practitioners of the historical and regional novel, his work raised the cultural status of prose fiction and exerted a far-reaching influence throughout the 19th century. He rose to fame as a poet with the publication of his collection of Minstrelsy of the Scottish Border (1802–3) and his narrative poem The Lay of the Last Minstrel (1805), repeating his success in Marmion (1808), The Lady of the Lake (1810), Rokeby (1813), and The Lord of the Isles (1815). The young Brontës were avid readers of all his poetry, particularly The Lay of the Last Minstrel, much of which they knew by heart from their father's edition of 1806 that had purchased while a student at St John's College, Cambridge. His copy of George Allan's Life of Walter Scott (1834) provoked an interest in Scott's life, and in December 1827, at the age of 9, Emily Brontë named Scott as her particular hero in the *Islanders' Play (Alexander EEW, 1. 22). After reading his Tales of a Grandfather, given to the Brontë children by their aunt the following year, Emily added Scott's son-in-law John Gibson *Lockhart and his grandson Johnny Lockhart to her 'chief men' (p. 6). In 1838, Charlotte was given a volume

containing Scott's The Vision of Don Roderick (1811) and Rokeby for her services as a teacher at Margaret Wooler's school; and while in Brussels, she translated extracts from Scott's poetry as language exercises (Lonoff, p. 254).

In July 1834, Charlotte recommended a list of authors to Ellen *Nussey, enthusiastically stating, 'For Fiction—read Scott alone all novels after his are worthless' (Smith Letters, 1. 130–1). Scott had embarked on his career as a novelist with his highly acclaimed Waverley (1814) and then followed up with a series of historical novels set in Scotland: Guy Mannering (1815), The Antiquary (1816), The Black Dwarf and Old Mortality (both 1816 and constituting the first series of Tales of my Landlord), Rob Roy (1817), The Heart of Midlothian (1818; second series of Tales of my Landlord), The Bride of Lammermoor and The Legend of Montrose (1819; third series of Tales of my Landlord). With these novels of Scottish history, Scott found that he had created a public appetite for historical fiction that he felt bound to satisfy. He was also driven by the state of his finances: he was a partner in a publishing firm hovering on bankruptcy from about 1813 and he had purchased his country house Abbotsford in 1811. Thus he turned to themes from English history and elsewhere and wrote Ivanhoe (1819), The Monastery and The Abbot (both 1820), Kenilworth and The Pirate (both 1821), The Fortunes of Nigel (1822), Peveril of the Peak, Quentin Durward, and St Ronan's Well (all 1823), Redgauntlet (1824), Tales of the Crusaders, The Betrothed, and The Talisman (all 1825), Woodstock (1826), and a number of lesser-known novels.

It is remarkable how many of these novels are alluded to in the Brontës' own novels. There are direct quotations from Waverley, The Black Dwarf, The Heart of Midlothian, Ivanhoe, Kenilworth, Old Mortality, The Pirate, and The Talisman (see The Professor, pp. 333–4). References range from quotation and the use of place names and characters to general similarities like the blend of romantic elements with realistic regional landscape. In her poem 'A sudden chasm of ghastly light' (14 Oct. 1837), for example, Emily refers to Tyndarum, a Scottish place name mentioned several times by Scott in his Legend of Montrose (ch. 17) (Roper EBP, p. 227). Again, her poem 'The Prisoner' echoes the same novel (Roper EBP, p. 271); and the regular rhythms of much of her poetry reflect the conventional ballad metres of Scott (Gareth and Barbara Lloyd Evans, Everyman Companion to the Brontës (1982), 239). Minna, the heroine of The Pirate, probably inspired the name of the Angrian heroine Mina *Laury; and Branwell's story of the same name was probably inspired by Scott's novel (and Byron's 'The Corsair'). Minna's portrait in the first edition of The Pirate is signed by William *Etty, who illustrated a number of Scott's novels and who also becomes a fictional artist in Angria. Charlotte would have encountered (among other places) the name 'Keeldar', given to the heroine of Shirley, in Scott's poem 'The Death of Keeldar'. Branwell's writing is punctuated throughout by allusions to Scott, from old Scottish dialect to references to Dr Jonas Dryasdust, the antiquarian recipient of several prefaces to Scott's novels (see, for example, Neufeldt BB Works, 2. 370; 3. 464). Even in his published essay on Thomas *Bewick, Branwell refers to Old Mortality and Heart of Midlothian. Much of the Brontës' penchant for German Romanticism, Gothic novels, Scottish border ballads, regional dialect, the evocation of landscape, chivalrous war, and romantic love, had been fostered by their addiction to Scott's poetry and novels. Even his Tory vision of history, reinforced in the pages of Blackwood's Edinburgh Magazine to which Scott also contributed, helped to consolidate Revd Patrick Brontë's legacy to his children. Scott's Life of Napoleon (1827) was familiar to them all by June 1829 (Alexander EEW, 1. 28), and may have inspired a joint poem on *Napoleon by Charlotte and Branwell (Neufeldt BB Works, 1. 33). Scott's Tales of a Grandfather was particularly influential in the Brontës' early writing. Its 'general view of Scottish History, with a selection of its more picturesque and prominent points' depicts a series of exciting and violent stories, especially those of the civil wars in Scotland 1570–3, material upon which the violence of *Gondal with its struggles for power and love, its revenges, assassinations, and battles might be based. Tales probably provided the Brontës with their first taste of Scottish history, including the legend of the Percys of Alnwick Castle (see ALNWICK HALL; NORTHANGERLAND, DUKE OF) and probably inspired Charlotte's enthusiasm for *Mary Queen of Scots, who features in much of the book and is perhaps the main prototype of Emily's 'Gondal's queen', the passionate A.G.A. Winifred Gérin argues that it was in Scott's heroines, like Diana Vernon and Flora MacIvor, that Emily found the prototype for her ideal of strong, 'beautiful and uncontrolled' womanhood and also found her model for the 'weakling character' of most Gondal heroes (Gérin EB, pp. 26–8).

The Brontë juvenilia owe much to Scott's poetry, his novels, and the ballads he collected and imitated. Charlotte's The *Green Dwarf. A Tale of the Perfect Tense, for example, imitates Scott both in title and in form, drawing on the concept of historical romance and the theme of abduction (Alexander EW, p. 97). There is a prevalence of Scottish names among Gondal characters and much of the landscape of Gondal with its lakes, snowcapped Highland mountains, glens, castles, and wandering deer or its green valleys and wooded hills reflects that of Scotland. The *Glass Town and Angrian saga echoes similar features in the kingdoms created by Emily and Anne, and the 'Scottish' region of Angria draws on descriptive passages from Scott's novels. Branwell admired Scott's ability to conjure the moving associations of ordinary valleys and monotonous moorland—much like Branwell's own Yorkshire homeland—without recourse to the sublime or beautiful in Nature. He singles out the opening of Old Mortality as the most beautiful he has read, with its description of 'lone vales of green Bracken' and 'Linnet peopled Hills' (Neufeldt BB Works, 3. 186). The landscape reminds him of his own with its lonely farmhouses 'on the confines of the heath' and he conjures from it the Angrian landscape surrounding Darkwall Manor, home of the *Thurstons. The Angrian Airdmore is based on 'Aird' in Ayrshire, Scotland, described in Tales of a Grandfather and the Darkwall *Gytrash resembles not only the spectre of *Ponden House, near Haworth, but also Scott's evocation of such spirits in his novels and poems. Barker (p. 501) finds it 'ironical' that Wuthering Heights should be regarded as the archetypal Yorkshire novel yet owe more to Scott's Border country than to the Yorkshire moors. She cites Rob Roy (1817), in particular, as the model for Emily's novel, with its setting among the uncouth and quarrelsome Osbaldistones, who spend their time drinking and gambling. She suggests that Heathcliff is a re-creation of the cruel outlaw Douglas (see also MOIR, DAVID), that his unusual name recalls that of the surly Thorncliff, and that he mimics Rashleigh Osbaldistone in his sinister hold over the Earnshaws and Lintons and his attempts to seize their inheritances. Pinion too believes Scott's influence is 'unmistakable', citing The Black Dwarf as the source for Cathy's delirious view of Nelly as an old witch 'gathering elf-bolts to hurt our heifers' (A Brontë Companion (1975), 207). The Black Dwarf, The Bride of Lammermoor, Redgauntlet, The Antiquary, St Ronan's Well, and Kenilworth have also been cited as sources for Wuthering Heights (Florence Dry, The Sources of Wuthering Heights (1937), 7–8; Q. D. Leavis, 'A Fresh Approach to Wuthering Heights', in Collected Essays, ed. G. Singh (1983), 1. 272; and two articles by Rose Lovell-Smith in BST (1994), 21. 3. 79–87 and 4. 117–24). Jacques Blondel believes that Emily largely learnt her trade as a novelist from 'the Scottish master' (Emily Brontë: Expérience spirituelle et création poétique (1955), 271). In his 1981 introduction to the World's Classics edition of Wuthering Heights, Ian Jack points to an impressive list of similarities between Emily's novel and Waverley, particularly Lockwood's arrival at the Heights and his resemblance to Scott's typical young heroes— observant and educated yet also ignorant—who travel into a more primitive and violent society.

Scott's narrative method made a deep impression on all the Brontës. Charlotte's early writing in particular indicates a debt to his invention of a fictional storyteller who establishes an initial relationship with his audience. 'The Duke of Zamorna', for instance, is narrated by Charles Townshend (see WELLESLEY, LORD CHARLES ALBERT FLORIAN) who, like Scott's provident legatee of *Tales of my Landlord*, presents relics from the past to the reader as a pretext for his story (Alexander *EW*, 180–1). Carol Bock argues that this adoption of Scott's 'character of masquerade' eventually had an 'inhibiting influence on Brontë's development as a writer' ('Charlotte Brontë's Storytellers: The Influence of Scott', in McNees, 4. 539). In 1833 Charlotte included a critique of *Kenilworth* in a letter to Ellen Nussey, pronouncing it 'a splendid production more resembling a Romance than a Novel and in my opinion one of the most interesting works that ever emanated from the great Sir Walter's pen' (Smith *Letters*, 1. 121); and in 1848 it was Scott alone whom she cited in a negative reference to antecedents for her own fiction: 'Were I obliged to copy any former novelist, even the greatest, even Scott, in anything, I would not write' (Smith *Letters*, 2. 118). Her protest paradoxically betrays not only the depth of her own engagement with Scott, but also that of Emily and Branwell. They appear to have read almost all Scott's poetry and his many novels, and because so much of his writing is repetitive in what Ian Jack calls a 'remarkable similarity of pattern', it is not hard for a Scott reader to add further Brontë resemblances to those cited above. See also HOFF-MANN, ERNST THEODOR AMADEUS.

'Scrap Book, The. A Mingling of Many Things', 'Compiled by Lord C A F Wellesley' (19 Mar. 1835), a manuscript of 31 pages in minuscule script (BL), including one poem and nine prose items by Charlotte Brontë and one poem by Branwell. These miscellaneous items have been dismissed as 'pages of wearisome and absurd newspaper and platform oratory' (Fannie Ratchford, *The Brontës' Web of Childhood* (1941), 99), yet they can be seen as writing exercises: portraits of characters; analyses of their motives; drafts of dialogues, speeches, and incidents. The Duke of *Zamorna's 'Adress [sic] to the Angrians' is a dramatic defence of his political position, written as an open letter to his subjects: an exercise in persuasive rhetoric. This contrasts with the more formal tone of his following speech 'At the opening of the first Angrian Parliament'. Other items

assume different voices. The Marquis of *Ardrah, Zamorna's enemy, is responsible for the extract from the 'Northern Review'; here Charlotte is sarcastic about her hero's lust for military fame and his reckless disposal of his troops. 'A Brace of Characters' is a rare analysis of two children (John Augustus *Sneaky, Jun. and Ernest Edward Gordon *Wellesley), demonstrating, among other things, Charlotte's knowledge of Scotland and of *Shakespeare's history plays. 'A Late Occurrence' is a lively episode of Angrian scandal, involving the divorce of Edward *Sydney and Lady Julia *Wellesley, and exposing Zamorna's influence in the affair; and Lord Charles continues his portraits in another fragment analysing Zamorna and Edward *Percy from different perspectives.

By now, writing had become an obsession for the 19-year-old Charlotte. Her output is various and indiscriminate as she herself recognizes in the subtitle 'A Mingling of Many Things'. When she fails to construct a plot for a novelette, the larger plot of the *Glass Town and Angrian saga provides the framework for such fragmentary exercises. She is under no illusion that these are any more than literary excursions, frail barks 'freighted purely with a dish of Syllabub' (Alexander *EEW*, 2(2). 84). *'Corner Dishes' is a similar volume.

Alexander *EEW*, 2(2). 294–377.

Scruton, William (1840–1924), Bradford antiquarian and writer, member of the *Brontë Society committee from 1894. In January 1885 he introduced himself to Ellen Nussey as a Moravian with a collection of Brontë items who would like to buy an autograph letter by Charlotte. Ellen agreed to give him one, if she could find one, in gratitude for his 'little work' on Charlotte's birthplace: *The Birthplace of Charlotte Brontë* (1884). His informative illustrated book *Thornton and the Brontës* (1898) provides a historical sketch of Thornton, a section on Revd Patrick Brontë's ministry there, selections from the Brontës' poems, and reminiscences of the family by people who had met them. Scruton himself, during a visit to Martha *Brown on 15 June 1879, had seen the Brontë mementoes which she delighted to exhibit, including a portfolio of drawings, and heard her 'peculiarly vivid' recollections of life at the parsonage. 'Very touching was her narrative of the last moments of the brave and patient' Charlotte (*Yorkshireman Royal Summer Number* (1882), 13–14). Scruton had also known the *Taylor family of Gomersal, and he wrote *Pen and Pencil Pictures of Old Bradford* (1889) and 'Reminiscences of the late Miss Ellen Nussey', *BST* (1898), 1. 8. 23–42. 8.

sculpture does not figure notably in the Brontë works, unless we include the 'wilderness of crumbling griffins and shameless little boys' surrounding the door of Wuthering Heights (ch. 1), but it did provide Charlotte with a memorable metaphor for Emily's composition of *Wuthering Heights*. At the end of her Preface to the second edition of the novel (1850), Charlotte describes the writer as a 'statuary' (sculptor) who 'found a granite block on a solitary moor . . . With time and labour, the crag took human shape; and there it stands colossal, dark, and frowning, half statue, half rock'. The half-human 'statue' is, of course, Heathcliff.

The Brontës themselves, however, have been depicted in sculpture. Branwell Brontë's friend Joseph Bentley *Lcyland made a bust of him (1845) and also a stone medallion portrait (1846) which is now in the BPM. The Brontë sisters inspired a bronze group statue by Jocelyn Horner in 1951, which now stands in the garden of the BPM. The group shows each sister rapt in her own thoughts; Charlotte, with neat collar and smooth hair, looks down with a slight frown; Emily, much taller and with bare, gaunt shoulders and wild hair, stares before her with half-opened lips; Anne, in profile, looks up and seems to be starting forwards. Charles Lemon records that 'Jacob Epstein saw the group in London after casting and described it as a fine piece of work' (*Centenary History of the Brontë Society* (1993), 51). PS

Sdeath (S'Death, S'death), Robert Patrick, the hideous red-haired minion of the Duke of Northangerland in the *Glass Town and Angrian saga, and a reincarnation of Chief Genius 'Brannii Lightning' (Branwell Brontë, whose first name was Patrick like his father's; see GENII, CHIEF). His name is derived from the oath 'God's death': he is a Mephisphelean figure, who mockingly quotes Scripture and executes evil. His Christian name may owe something to Dr Robert Knox, the surgeon involved in *bodysnatching, an activity especially delightful to Sdeath. Captain of the pirate ship *The Rover*, and sometime servant and alter ego of the young Northangerland (then 'Rogue'), he is impervious to any attempts to destroy him. His evil relationship with Northangerland (and with his father before him) owes much to James *Hogg's study of evil possession and double personality in *Confessions of a Justified Sinner* (1824). His supernatural powers derive from his early association with his author (Chief Genius Brannii). He reappears in *Ashworth* as a jockey and drover, who is deserted by his gang at the Doncaster Races—'laid up in lavender' because of fraud.

'Search after Happiness, The', 'A Tale by C. Brontë' (28 July–17 Aug. 1829; MS in BL Ashley). A story only obliquely related to the *Glass Town, 'The Search after Happiness' (spelt 'Hapiness' on the title-page but not elsewhere in the manuscript) mirrors Samuel *Johnson's *Rasselas* (1759) in the hero's discontent with life, his search for happiness in a fantasy land, and his eventual recognition that his goal lies not in wandering but with loved ones at home. Henry O'Donell, joined by the Frenchman Alexander Delancy, passes through a subterranean tunnel into a land of liquid mountains, black forests, and vivid skies streaked by lightning, scenes reminiscent of the landscapes of John *Martin. A chance meeting with an old man who has experienced 'dreadful scenes of magic' allows the young author to further hone her descriptive skills in fantastic imaginative scenes, this time recalling James *Ridley's *Tales of the Genii* (by 'Sir Charles Morell', 1820). O'Donell and his friend dwell content in an isolated valley until the memory of his beloved ruler the Duke and his young sons awakens his longing for home. Promising servitude to a Genius, he is transported home, free to live in the Glass Town for the remainder of his life; and Delancy is similarly mysteriously conveyed to *Paris, where he becomes a rich merchant and a favourite with the Emperor *Napoleon.

Alexander *EEW*, 1. 42–53.

Secret and Lily Hart, The 'Two Tales by Lord Charles Wellesley' (Charlotte Brontë) (7 Nov. 1833), focusing on the domestic life of Charlotte's hero the Marquis of Douro and his wife Marian, and the secret romance of his friend Prince John Sneaky, Duke of *Fidena. The manuscript is a hand-sewn booklet of sixteen pages written in minuscule script (Ellis Library, University of Missouri-Columbia). The two stories are an excellent example of the interrelation of Charlotte's early writings, which in turn are interwoven with those of Branwell (see Alexander *EW*, pp. 107–8). The detached ironic voice of the narrator Lord Charles emerges intermittently to impose some control on the emotionally charged melodramatic material.

The Secret is an elaborate hoax by the scoundrel Edward *Percy and the governess Miss Foxley to extort money from the credulous Marian *Hume. Marian is led to believe that a childhood betrothal is still valid, that her marriage to Douro is illegal, and that her father is not Alexander Hume but her husband's enemy Alexander Percy. The plot involves blackmail, incest, and bigamy; and Marian—Charlotte's most innocent and pathetic heroine—is made to suffer at the hands of her autocratic husband and those of the terrifying former pirate Alexander Percy.

Lily Hart records the courtship and clandestine marriage of John Sneaky, Duke of Fidena, and Lily *Hart, a poor seamstress who helped her mother care for the wounded Fidena during the Great Rebellion of 1831, led by Rogue (Duke of

*Northangerland). The tale is an example of the working relationship between Charlotte and Branwell: she is aware of her brother's initiatives in the Glass Town political plot but pursues her own interest in personal relationships.

Alexander *EEW*, 2(1). 269–315.
Alexander *EW*, pp. 107–10.
Holtz, William (ed.), *Two Tales by Charlotte Brontë 'The Secret' & 'Lily Hart'* (1978).

Segovia, Augusta (or Maria) di, the beautiful, imperial, part-Italian first wife of the Duke of *Northangerland (then Alexander Percy), in the *Glass Town and Angrian saga. Her home is Jordan Villa in Senegambia (*Wellington's Land). The young Percy is bewitched by her brilliance and passion, and she squanders her brother Lord *Jordan's fortune on him. They have one child, unacknowledged by Northangerland, who becomes the artist Sir William *Etty. A type of Clytemnestra, she arranges the murder of her father-in-law so that her husband should inherit his money and is then poisoned herself by her accomplices for withholding their payment.

Selden House, the Duke of Northangerland's residence in *Ross's Land (Rossland), in the *Glass Town and Angrian saga.

'Self-Communion' ('The mist is resting'), poem by Anne Brontë (Nov. 1847–17 Apr. 1848). A dialogue between the self and a wise spiritual mentor, remarkable in its revelatory self-scrutiny and fine-drawn analyses of character, feeling, and belief. The dialogue form enhances the dramatic tensions through which Anne achieves spiritual strength to 'press forward . . . labour and love'. Lines 178–207 probably describe Anne's painful growing apart from Emily. Biblical images (the 'way', watching and praying, arming for the fight, seeking treasure in heaven) extend the significance to all Christian pilgrims.

Chitham *ABP*, p. 152.

self-portraits. See PORTRAITS BY THE BRONTËS.

Senegambia. See WELLINGTON'S LAND (WELLINGTONSLAND).

sequels and 'incremental literature' have mostly accumulated around *Jane Eyre* and *Wuthering Heights*, though the lives of the Brontës have attracted a mass of writing on the borderline between fact and fiction. Although a 'sequel' would seem to be a well-defined category, clearly announced in titles such as *Return to Wuthering Heights* (Anna L'Estrange), defining 'incremental literature' is much more difficult. For readers who know *Jane Eyre*, it is impossible to read *Wide Sargasso Sea* (Jean Rhys) without recognizing

the names—'Bertha Antoinette Mason', 'Grace Poole'—which identify this as the story of Rochester's mad wife; for other readers, however, it is an independent story. Then there are texts which discerning critics have seen as 'reworkings' of Brontë novels but which bear very distant relationships to them (as *The Story of an African Farm* (Olive Schreiner) does to *Wuthering Heights*), or texts which make fleeting but interesting references to the Brontë novels (as Jeanette Winterson does in *Oranges are not the only Fruit*), or which bear a generic resemblance to the originals (as Mills and Boon romances do to the plot of *Jane Eyre*).

As with stage plays, it was *Jane Eyre* which attracted immediate attention from other writers. Margaret Oliphant, in a review of 1855, blamed *Jane Eyre* for a new fashion for love stories by women writers in which the traditional courtship-and-marriage plot is complicated by the independence of the heroine and her resistance to male dominance. In Dinah Mulock Craik's *Olive* (1850), for instance, the heroine earns her own living and rescues the hero from a fire in which he is badly injured, so that he has to depend on her for support. Mrs E. J. Burbury's *Florence Sackville* (1851) announces this preoccupation in its subtitle: *Self-Dependence*. A curiosity of this period is 'Kitty Bell, the Orphan', a story closely following the plot of *Jane Eyre* which appeared inset within the 'governess' novel *Mary Lawson* (apparently a translation of work by the French novelist Eugène Sue) which appeared in weekly parts in Reynolds's *London Journal* during 1850–1. The origin of 'Kitty Bell' is still somewhat of a mystery: almost certainly not the work of Sue, it clearly attempts to exploit the current sensation surrounding *Jane Eyre*. A reviewer of Julia Kavanagh's *Nathalie* (1850) confirmed that 'Whatever be the world's verdict on *Jane Eyre* . . . certain it is, that she has been foundress of a family; and we cannot but think that "Nathalie" would hardly have been born had not Currer Bell's daughter been her ancestress' (*Athenaeum*, 1203 (6 Nov. 1850), 1184). In 1867 Oliphant was holding *Jane Eyre* responsible for the more tangible sexuality of women's novels in the 1860s, representing Charlotte Brontë as 'the only begetter of the new palpitating heroines who excitedly await the heroes' "flesh and muscles . . . strong arms . . . and warm breath" in the sensational pages of Annie Thomas, Miss Braddon, Rhoda Broughton and "Ouida"' (*Blackwood's Edinburgh Magazine*, 102 (Sept. 1867), 257–80); in 1887 she was still repeating this judgement (*Blackwood's*, 141 (Jan. 1887), 389–90).

Henry James's *The Turn of the Screw* (1898) is a widely recognized reworking of the *Jane Eyre* plot, in which a lonely governess, fixated on her

The *Jane Eyre* plot has become a paradigm for popular romance fiction, illustrated here in the cover for the Woman's World Library No. 347.

employer, is distressed by a mystery concealed in the house where she takes care of her master's wards. The relationship between the two novels is mutedly acknowledged when the heroine wonders 'Was there a "secret" at Bly? . . . an insane, an unmentionable relative kept in unsuspected confinement?' (ch. 4). It is, however, a critical relationship, since James's heroine is shown to be misguided or inadequate in the role thrust upon her, of taking responsibility for herself and her pupils. Obsessed by the possibility that the children are sexually corrupted, she inadvertently causes them harm. The (just) post-Freudian awareness of infant sexuality and of feminine repression in this novel acts as a critique of Jane Eyre's Victorian self-possession. The novel has attracted a lively critical debate, some of it with Brontë references.

From the First World War onwards, however, in the era of growing women's emancipation, it was women writers who looked back apprehensively at the love-and-marriage structure of Jane Eyre. Elizabeth von Arnim's Vera (1921) shows its orphan heroine, Lucy, swept off her feet by an older husband, only to find herself trapped by his sterile egotism. Gradually she identifies herself with his first wife, Vera, who passed the time by reading Wuthering Heights, and died by leaping from an upper floor. Rosamond Lehmann's The Weather in the Streets (1936) has a lonely, semi-independent heroine who falls in love with her social superior, who has a neurotic and invalid wife. This bleakly modern treatment of the triangle situation includes the heroine's forced abortion. Winifred Holtby's South Riding (1936) announces its critical relation to Jane Eyre when the heroine suddenly meets an older, landowning man, riding a black horse; we are told that 'into Sarah's irreverent and well-educated mind flashed the memory of Jane Eyre and Mr Rochester'. Against her will, she grows to love Mr Carne and pity his relationship with his mad wife; like Holtby, however, Sarah believes passionately in education as liberation for women, so that Jane's stifling occupation as a governess becomes an energetic public battle for Sarah as the headmistress of a girls' school.

The best-known of this group of novels is Daphne du Maurier's Rebecca (1938), in which the heroine is rescued from a thankless job as a rich woman's paid companion by marriage to a landowning hero; having got her man, however, she discovers that her victory is hollow. He, and Manderley, his home, are possessed not by a madwoman in the attic but by a dead wife who, if not mad, was bad, and effectively 'haunts' the heroine through the housekeeper, Mrs Danvers. Modern readers of this novel often find that their sympathies are with the dead wife, Rebecca, rather than with the spiritless heroine. It is interesting that in the 1940 film of Rebecca, the nameless heroine was played by Joan Fontaine, who was to make a subservient Jane Eyre in the 1944 *film.

Brontë references proliferate in the novels of Elizabeth Taylor, published during the forties, fifties, and sixties. In At Mrs Lippincote's (1945), a little boy 'makes friends' with Mrs Rochester, whom he imagines shut in the tower of their house. A more extended relationship exists with Palladian (1946), which has a modern young heroine who nevertheless takes a post as governess in the house of a widowed employer. Like Sarah Burton in South Riding, Cassandra is quite aware of the parallels between her situation and Jane Eyre's. Before she even arrives at Cropthorne Manor, she nourishes 'a very proper willingness to fall in love, the more despairingly the better, with her employer'. As in Rebecca, her 'rival' is already dead, and Taylor makes explicit the chilly implications of Rebecca's conclusion; in these novels, getting your man is not happy ever after but only 'a new servitude'. A similar atmosphere prevails in Iris Murdoch's The Unicorn (1963), in which Marian Taylor goes as governess-companion to, in this case, the madwoman herself, who has attempted to kill her husband. This complex and self-consciously literary novel ends with Marian contemplating a public career instead of a future in love. Margaret Drabble's The Waterfall (1969) is another self-consciously referential novel, though its heroine, Jane, identifies herself with Charlotte Brontë rather than Jane Eyre, representing herself to herself as suffering 'in some Brussels of the mind'. Like Charlotte Brontë, Jane Gray extricates herself from her 'romance plot' by writing. In these sophisticated and individual novels, Jane Eyre appears as what Umberto Eco calls an 'intertextual archetype'. Jane Eyre also, however, provides the paradigm for the popular genre of 'Gothic' romances for women. One of the earliest of these is Mistress of Mellyn, by Victoria Holt (1961), which tells of a governess who is courted by her employer, only to suffer a series of terrifying experiences which lead her to believe not only that he is trying to kill her, but that he already killed his first wife. The plot culminates with our heroine locked in a cell with the decayed body of the first wife; but all is well when the villain is revealed to be another woman. The implicit horror of the Jane Eyre plot is exploited by some feminist rewritings such as Clare Boylan's 'Jane Eyre Revisited: An Alternative Ending', which shows Jane as the latest in a series of wives to be locked up in the attics of Thornfield Hall (Good Housekeeping (Jan. 1990), 136–40). The basic plot, however, continues to be reproduced in romances of the Mills and Boon type, where a young woman meets an older, more powerful man with a secret past and, after apparent hostility, his neediness is revealed. In Catherine George's *Devil Within* (1984), the governess heroine explicitly dissociates herself from her conception of Jane Eyre as a prudish Victorian; the impeded-courtship plot, however, persists. There has been extensive feminist debate about the popularity of romance fiction, from Germaine Greer's *The Female Eunuch* (1970), which sees women readers as dupes of an ideological plot, to Janice Radway's *Reading the Romance* (1984) and Tania Modleski's *Loving with a Vengeance* (1984), which present romance fiction as women's way of asserting that men need to be feminized before they can have meaningful relationships with women. The same debate prevails over *Jane Eyre* itself, with readers who deplore Jane's capitulation to marriage in opposition to those who stress the companionate nature of that marriage.

The most distinguished of *Jane Eyre* derivatives, however, diverts our attention away from the Jane-and-Rochester plot. This is Jean Rhys's novel *Wide Sargasso Sea* (1966), which tells the story of the first Mrs Rochester, the Caribbean heiress to whom Rochester was married at the insistence of his father and brother. Herself born in Dominica, Jean Rhys found herself both fascinated by *Jane Eyre* and repelled by its depiction of the mad Creole. She determined to bring this marginalized figure into the centre, giving her a different name—Antoinette, which is Bertha's middle name in *Jane Eyre*—and her own history. After many years of pondering on how best to write this story, Rhys decided to present the novel in the form of three extended monologues; the first and last are by Antoinette, and the central one by an unnamed but recognizable Rochester. A beautiful, sparely written novel, *Wide Sargasso Sea* is set in the period immediately after the emancipation of British slaves in 1834, when Antoinette's family is isolated equally from their former slaves and from their former slave-owning friends by their new poverty. In this situation women become themselves commodities; Antoinette's widowed mother remarries to survive, and Antoinette herself is married to Rochester by her new stepfather. Educated in a convent, she is a docile creature who readily accedes to Rochester's bewildered sexual frenzy, only to find herself rejected for 'intemperate' and un-English behaviour. Rochester, defining himself as a victim of the elder men in both families, uses his power over Antoinette in order to assert his bruised manhood. Certifying her mad, he returns to England and locks her up in the attic. As a dreamy, lonely girl, Antoinette had filled her mind with images of the luxuriant gardens of her father's estate, and was happiest in the company of Christophine, her black nurse, and Tia, her black friend. Her 'mad' reveries at Thornfield recur to the flowers and the scents of her vivid youth, and she uses flame to resurrect its lost colour. Anticipating her fall from the battlements in a riot of flame, she imagines her friend Tia waiting.

Wide Sargasso Sea permanently altered the reception of *Jane Eyre*. Delbert Mann's popular film of *Jane Eyre* (1970) shows a new kind of Bertha—pretty, young, dreamy—in place of the raging maniac of previous representations. In 1979 Sandra Gilbert and Susan Gubar's *The Madwoman in the Attic* reorientated critical readings, not only of *Jane Eyre*, but of 19th-century women's writing in general. Gilbert and Gubar argue that Bertha Mason represents the rage and sexual frustration which decorous heroines could not acknowledge; but her presence in the novel signals that the repressed is waiting to return. *Wide Sargasso Sea* has itself produced a lively critical debate, ranging from feminist celebration of 'sisterhood' between Antoinette, Jane and Tia to a post-colonial insistence that 'sisterhood' between the white European Jane and the white Creole Antoinette still excludes the black Caribbean woman. In a further intertextual chain, writers are now including material from *Wide Sargasso Sea* in dramatizations of *Jane Eyre* (see THEATRE ADAPTATIONS AND BIOGRAPHIES).

Jean Rhys, however, was not the only novelist to attempt the story of the first Mrs Rochester. In *The Quiet Stranger* (1991), the Scottish writer Robbie Kydd tells the story of Richard Mason, Bertha's brother, which includes that of his sister. Set in Tobago and Trinidad, this is a learnedly researched novel which tries to make its dates comply with those of *Jane Eyre*, rather than using the post-emancipation period as in *Wide Sargasso Sea*. Beginning in the late 18th century, the story of *The Quiet Stranger* is almost independent of *Jane Eyre*; its main focus is on the surprising love affair between Richard and a black slave girl called Betsy, who proves to be descended from dispossessed royalty, and develops into a powerful and courageous woman. Richard's sister Bertha is presented as a volatile but enterprising young woman who runs her own sugar plantation and rides with daring bravura. She is tricked into marriage with a brutal version of Rochester, incompatible with Charlotte Brontë's hero. Where Rhys's Rochester becomes hard through his own bewilderment and suffering, Kydd's simply is a heartless brute who imprisons his wife to punish her failure to conform to expected standards of femininity. Jane Eyre is also a calculating adventuress who blocks Richard's attempts to save his sister.

D. M. Thomas's *Charlotte: The Final Journey of Jane Eyre* (2000) is a more sophisticated novel in which a postmodern consciousness presents us with layers of textual interpenetration. The novel begins as a continuation of Jane Eyre's autobiography, after the early death of Rochester. Their marriage is unconsummated, his affairs in disorder, and Jane leaves in search of a possible heir (son of Bertha and Edward) in Martinique. This text then appears to have been written by Miranda Stevenson, a present-day lecturer who is in Martinique to deliver a paper beginning 'Charlotte Brontë was an extraordinary liar'. 'Lying' is explained as a necessary quality in writers who use 'their own lives, their own emotions' as 'their material'; 'they distort them, twist them, partly to make a fiction, partly because they themselves are half-unconscious of the personal realities'. Charlotte, it is implied, could easily have made different stories from the same material, and accordingly, Jane's new story later appears to be a 'genuine' Brontë manuscript. There is no way of assessing the conflicting truth-claims, but the three interwoven stories—of Jane, of Charlotte, and of Miranda—echo each other's strong Oedipal resonances. Charlotte is described as living with 'her father—her first husband' (ch. 12), while Miranda appears to have written the story of Jane's inability to rouse a Rochester obsessed with his first wife in order to dissuade her own father from marrying again. Miranda then impersonates her mad Cornish mother (who died by jumping off a cliff) and in Martinique re-enacts her promiscuity, to please her purblind father. In Jane's new story, the Martiniquan heir to Edward and Bertha proves to be a coal-black throwback, with whom Jane experiences true passion before her early death in pregnancy.

Jane Eyre has influenced a wide range of readers. In I Know Why the Caged Bird Sings (1970), the black American writer Maya Angelou remembers how, as a child, she saw her black friend Louise as being like Jane Eyre, despite the differences in their situations. The Zimbabwean writer Tsitsi Dangarembga also shows the Brontë novels as influential on her young heroine, Tambudzai, in Nervous Conditions (1988): 'plunging into these books . . . I was filled with gratitude to the authors for introducing me to places where reason and inclination were not at odds'. Jeanette Winterson's youthful persona in Oranges are not the only Fruit (1985) is also brought up on Jane Eyre, this time in a version edited so that Jane marries the missionary St John Rivers. When Jess grows up, she sets herself to rewrite the romance plot to include passionate love between women. Each of these novels describes an encounter between Jane Eyre and a young, female reader, but is intended for adult readers. One novel intended for young readers is Sheila Greenwald's It all began with Jane Eyre or

The Secret Life of Franny Dillman (1980), the story of a young teenager who tries to restructure her life on the Jane Eyre model. Hilarious complications ensue, and she is eventually persuaded to write a story based on these real-life events, so that escapism and fantasy turn to analysis and creativity.

Wuthering Heights did not inspire its immediate readers to imitate its plot or characters, and it is not until Olive Schreiner's The Story of an African Farm (1883) that a possible influence can be detected. Elaine Showalter, in A Literature of their Own, writes that 'the central situation of the persecuted orphan, Waldo, who falls in love with his childhood ally, Lyndall, has reminded many readers of Wuthering Heights' (ch. 7). Other aspects of the story, however, depart radically from Emily Brontë's plot; in particular the feminist aspirations of her heroine. From the Modernist period onwards, there are many incidental references to Wuthering Heights, for instance in H.D.'s Bid Me to Live (written 1927; pub. 1960) or Elizabeth Taylor's novels At Mrs Lippincote's (1945) and The Sleeping Beauty (1953). Sylvia Plath, in her poem 'Wuthering Heights' (1961), feels the oppression of its landscape ('The sky leans on me') but is also aware that the seduction of romantic love is ambiguous: 'the roots of the heather . . . invite me I To whiten my bones among them' (Ted Hughes (ed.), Collected Poems (1981), 167–8). V. S. Naipaul's novel Guerrillas (1975) includes references to both Jane Eyre and Wuthering Heights: it has characters called Jane and Roche, a house called Thrushcross Grange, and a backstreets would-be leader who is inspired by Heathcliff's imaginary genealogy as son of an Indian princess and the emperor of China.

Q. D. Leavis, in her essay 'A Fresh Approach to Wuthering Heights' (1969), makes an extended comparison between Emily Brontë's novel and Henri-Pierre Roché's Jules et Jim (1953), later filmed by François Truffaut (1962). Like many of the stage and film versions of Wuthering Heights, Jules et Jim focuses on the sexual jealousies involved as modern 'liberated' ideas break down in a triangular relationship between one woman and two men. In the 1970s more popular writers began to 'take liberties' with Emily's novel. Jeffrey Caine's Heathcliff (1977) is a picaresque account of Heathcliff's 'absent' years. In this version, he is taken up by a highwayman, educated by a lady, and narrowly escapes hanging before returning to Wuthering Heights. Anna L'Estrange's Return to Wuthering Heights (1978) is a family saga which tells the fortunes of the second generation, and of their descendants, as they are integrated into the industrial development of West Yorkshire and of imperial trade. Though Heathcliff is dead, he lives on not only in memory but also in the persons of an illegitimate son and grandson. John Wheatcroft's *Catherine, Her Book* (1983) is a resourceful extension of Catherine's diary paper. During her illness, after her marriage to Edgar, Catherine whiles away the time by writing at length the story of her relationship with Heathcliff. Carefully based on researches into 18th-century and local dictionaries and religious tracts as well as a developed post-Freudian consciousness, Wheatcroft reconstructs the child Catherine's early sexual union with Heathcliff, and her painful piecing together of the awful truth that he is her half-brother; her marriage to Edgar is, therefore, her self-sacrifice to save Heathcliff, and herself, from eternal damnation.

The most imaginative of recent reworkings of *Wuthering Heights* is Jane Urquhart's novel *Changing Heaven* (1990). A split narrative brings Ann, a modern Canadian academic, to Haworth, while on Haworth moor the ghost of Emily Brontë has an extended conversation with the ghost of Arianna Ether, a balloonist wrecked on the moor at the turn of the 20th century. Ann's childhood obsession with *Wuthering Heights* leads her to misconstrue her real relationships with men, while Emily is busy abrogating responsibility for having made a 'practically unkillable' myth in the shape of Heathcliff, and Arianna describes a lover who is destructively obsessive about her 'perfect womanhood'. The novel ends with Emily fading into the landscape, while Ann settles for a local storyteller. The novel is beautifully written, with pervasive half-quotations woven richly into a subtle and humorous text. It is also historically accurate, with an unsentimental view of what Haworth is and was like for the people who earned their living there.

The most spectacular of the incremental literature, however, is Lin Haire-Sargeant's *Heathcliff: The Return to Wuthering Heights* (1992), which recounts how Heathcliff, during his 'missing years', was adopted by Mr Rochester (from *Jane Eyre*), and proves to be the son of Bertha Mason, born in a Liverpool madhouse. The plot has sensational inventions such as Heathcliff's 'gelding' of Edgar, and although the two plots are ingeniously made to fit together, there is a stubborn difference of ethos between the novels which makes Heathcliff's movement between the two worlds unconvincing. The novel also makes play with a post-modern awareness of pervasive textuality to destabilize normal distinctions between fact and fiction. Beginning with a conversation between Charlotte Brontë and Mr Lockwood, it ends with Charlotte and Emily visiting Nelly Dean. What could have been playful elaboration, however, is undercut by a failure of literary tact. Emily's alter-

native ending for *Wuthering Heights*, in which Heathcliff rescues Catherine from her deathbed to an idyll in the New World, is written in a style which is lurid rather than intense, drawing on conventions of modern romance fiction.

Maryse Condé's *Windward Heights* (1998) also has a New World setting. Set in Cuba, Guadeloupe, and Dominica at the end of the 19th century, it takes a life of its own from the multiracial, multilingual islands of the Caribbean. The central character, Razyé, is black, and has a name which means heath or scrubland, which is where he was discovered; his soulmate is a burnt-sugar-coloured Cathy, who marries Aymeric de Linsseuil, a liberal plantation owner. The novel has an extraordinary social breadth, with not only more characters, but more narrators than *Wuthering Heights*; the effect is to tell the story of a whole society, through which the tale of Razyé and his Catherine runs like a thread. While Emily Brontë's narrators suggest and skirt around the central mystery of their relationship, however, the tellers of *Windward Heights* dispel mystery; the relationship here is emphatically sexual, so that the younger Catherine is born black, resembling though not knowing Razyé, whose son she meets and marries, and this involuntary incest provides the tragic catastrophe. Condé's novel has a story, an ethos, and a setting of its own, and leaves the reader wondering exactly why *Wuthering Heights* is there as its pretext. The relation between the novels seems destructive rather than dialogic, the Caribbean novel implying that its British original is too ethereal, too restricted, too sexually inexplicit.

As well as their novels, the Brontë lives have seduced innumerable writers to embroider and extend their stories. Many so-called biographies are more invention than record; the texts mentioned here, however, are those which show an idiosyncratic or imaginative response to the well-known 'facts'. Many later creative writers were fascinated by the Brontë writings and tried to orientate themselves in relation to these 'other' lives. Matthew Arnold dubbed the sisters 'unquiet souls!' in his poem 'Haworth Churchyard' (1855), while Emily Dickinson wrote a number of poems in response to the life of Charlotte Brontë (Thomas Johnson (ed.), *The Poems of Emily Dickinson*, 3 vols. (1955), nos. 312, 593, & 1562). One of these includes the stanza: 'Her losses make our Gains ashamed— | She bore Life's empty Pack | As gallantly as if the East | Were swinging at her Back' (no. 1562). By 1897, Harriet Spofford had a more morbid fascination with the successive deaths of the sisters, writing a poem called 'Brontë' with the refrain 'There are two ghosts ... there are three ghosts upon the stair!' (*In Titian's Garden and Other Poems* (1897), 39–42). Virginia Woolf wrote her very first published essay on 'Haworth. November 1904', and May Sinclair, not content with a eulogistic biography of *The Three Brontës* (1912), also wrote a much more sardonic novel, *The Three Sisters* (1914), which gives a brutally Freudian interpretation of the behaviour of three sisters isolated in a country parsonage with a widowed and repressed father. The fact that the Brontës, in the teens of the century, were becoming objects of lurid curiosity is shown by C. L. Graves's poem 'To Charlotte Brontë' (1917), in which he speaks of 'Sensation-mongers, strident and voracious . . . Raking the rag heaps for unprinted matter', and by the 1920s there was a great spate of semi-biographical novels and plays. A notable contribution to this flood of emotive writing is J. A. Mackereth's long poem *Storm-Wrack: A Night with the Brontës* (1927), which represents Emily, on a mission to rescue Branwell from the Black Bull, as 'Waiting, watching, hounded there, | With senses straining, with tortured hair . . .'.

An imaginative and independent novel from this period is Rachel Ferguson's *The Brontës Went to Woolworth's* (1931), which tells the story of a family of sisters who live modern, independent lives as a journalist and an actress, while the youngest is still taught by a governess. Resistant to what seems to them the Victorian gloom of the Brontës, they nevertheless live a fantasy life which is parallel to the Brontës' own. Eventually, after the fright of feeling that they might be sucked back into the stifling emptiness of Victorian women's lives, they assert themselves by incorporating the Brontës into their own fictions—hence the Brontës go to Woolworth's. Elizabeth Taylor, in her novel *A Wreath of Roses* (1949), also shows female friends imagining literary tea parties in which Charlotte 'told Ivy how much she gave for her lace shawl in Bradford', while 'Emily wouldn't come in at all. She just stood up the road and eyed the gate' (ch. 2).

Stella Gibbons, like Rachel Ferguson, earned her living as a journalist, but where Ferguson's novel is whimsical in tone, Gibbons's *Cold Comfort Farm* (1932) is a tribute to 'The Higher Common Sense'. Its thoroughly modern heroine, Flora Poste, takes in hand a whole family of tragic cousins, solving their problems by a mixture of humour and practicality. Cousin Seth, a very good-looking latter-day Heathcliff, is sent off to Hollywood, while Elfinc is transformed from a kind of dryad into a county wife. Among Flora's encounters in the novel is one with a Mr Mybug, a fictional version of the critics who, at about this time, were busy debating whether Branwell wrote *Wuthering Heights*. Flora attributes Mybug's obsession to male inability to accept female creativity. Another delightful product of the irreverence of this period is

F[rances] B[ickley]'s 'Christmas Dinner at Haworth Parsonage', which includes lines such as these (from Anne): 'Charlotte, I sometimes wish we had a mother, | For then perhaps our sister would not wuther' (*Punch* (25 Dec. 1935), 708). Parodic impulses continue throughout the 1980s and 1990s. *Withering Looks*, performed by Lip Service in Buxton in 1989 and on a number of occasions and locations since, is a rollicking parody of the Brontë lives and works in which two actresses, assisted by various bonnets on sticks, take the parts of all the Brontë family and the fictional characters. Focusing on the impracticality of romantic intensity, they manage to compress the plot of *Wuthering Heights* into a hectic two minutes.

Much of the most imaginative writing around the Brontë lives has been done for children. Pauline Clarke's *The Twelve and the Genii* (1962) is an enthralling adventure based on the modern rediscovery of Branwell's toy soldiers, which were the origin of Angria and Gondal. The story, though addressed to quite young children, is thought-provoking in the questions it asks about imagination and agency. Jane Amster's *Dream Keepers* (1973) deals with the fantasy worlds in the form of an imaginative biography of the young Brontës, presented as a 'spirited band of sceptics', while Glass Town is dramatized in two plays, Noel Robinson's *Glasstown* (1974) and *The Glasstown Confederacy* (1993) by Melanie Postma, Sally Dunbar, and Timothy Clarke. Robert Swindells's *Follow a Shadow* (1989) has a teenage hero who is more interested in drinking and stealing from his granny than in imaginative adventures, but the story turns into a moral tale when the ghost of Branwell Brontë leads Tim and his friends out of a dangerous snowstorm on Ponden Moor. Tim's uncanny experience begins when he realizes that he looks just like Branwell; similarly, in Jane Gardam's novel *The Summer after the Funeral* (1973), Athene Price realizes that she looks just like Emily. Gardam's novel, though written for the same age group, is more sophisticated and challenging than Swindells's. Athene, the dutiful daughter of a parson, is encouraged by her likeness to Emily to take risks, but also to take her place in her family as an individual. Garry Kilworth's novel, *The Brontë Girls* (1995), describes how a reclusive couple decide to bring up their three daughters in isolation from the modern world on an island in the Essex marshes. Mr Crastor announces his disaffection from the 20th century by calling his island 'Haworth Farm' and his daughters Charlotte, Emily, and Anne. The benefits and disadvantages of 19th- and 20th-century life are explored through Emily's friendship with a boy called Chris; her wide reading is set against his technological expertise, but the main advantage of the present day is the added protection given to children by the law.

It was inevitable that the rich field of Brontë biography should have yielded some crime writing. Robert Barnard's *The Missing Brontë* (1983) shows his detective-hero, Perry Trethowan, on the track of a lost manuscript, impeded by a literary collector, a sour academic, a millionaire, and a suspicious cleric. Barnard's writing is clever and basically innocent; not so James Tulley's *The Crimes of Charlotte Brontë* (1999), which presents its thesis, that Charlotte and Arthur Bell Nicholls contrived to murder the other members of her family, with apparent scholarly authentication. The book made a flurry in the press, but its basic premiss—that three deaths in a year in a single family must be suspicious—betrays ignorance of the sad facts of Victorian life and death.   PS

> Stoneman, Patsy, *Brontë Transformations: The Cultural Dissemination of 'Jane Eyre' and 'Wuthering Heights'* (1996).
> —— 'The Brontës in Other People's Childhoods', *BST* (1998), 23. 1. 3–16.

Seringapatan, an elderly veteran in the Islanders' Play, named after Seringapatam [*sic*], the district in India where the Duke of *Wellington first gained military success. Formerly under Wellington's military command, he lives in one of the soldiers' cottages in the great park of *Strathfieldsay. He is characterized as a 'bookish neighbour', with a nose like an eagle's beak, an eye 'of true Milesian origin', an enormous mouth stretching from ear to ear, grizzled grey hairs plaited into a long queue, muscles like those of Hercules, and the bones of a mammoth. The description of his cottage kitchen is equally picturesque and recalls that of the Brontës' own home (Alexander *EEW*, 1. 198).

sermons and tracts by Revd Patrick Brontë. Revd Patrick Bronte published two sermons, the first 'In Reference to an Earthquake, And Extraordinary Eruption of Mud and Water' (Bradford, 1824), the second *A Funeral Sermon for the late Rev. William Weightman, M.A.* (Halifax, 1842). Two other sermons remain in manuscript, one on baptism, based on Matthew 3: 11 (Pierpont Morgan MA 2696, fos. 10–12), and the other on conversion, based on Romans 2: 28–9 (BPM BS 150). For his articles 'On Conversion' in *The Pastoral Visitor* for 1815, see *BST* (1988), 19. 6. 271–5. The sermon on the eruption (the Crow-Hill bog-burst, 2 Sept. 1824), which he preferred to think of as an earthquake, was preached on 12 September 1824, and reprinted in the *Cottage Magazine* (Jan. 1828). (For his related poem *The Phenomenon*, see POETRY BY REVD PATRICK BRONTË.) His sermon text, from Psalm 97: 4–5, prefigures his use of the terrifying event and its devastating results as a div-

ine warning to mankind to repent. The title-page quotation from Cowper's *The Task*, 2. 53–61, recalls the poet's dramatic description of Sicilian earthquakes, which seemed 'To preach the general doom'. Since Mr Brontë's primary audience is the 'poorer classes in Haworth', he tries to explain the causes of earthquakes in terms familiar to them, such as the explosive expansion of water in an overheated boiler. He effectively evokes the 'profound calm' before the storm, the strongly 'electrified' sultry heat, 'copper-coloured, and hazy, lowering gloom'; reveals his anxious concern for his children, out walking on the moors; and gives an eyewitness account of the deep cavities, breached bridges, uprooted trees, and prostrate walls left behind by the rapid torrent of mud and water which was, for him, an irresistible instrument to execute the judgements of the Omnipotent. His account of giddy, frivolous, or grumbling sightseers acts as a foil to his solemn biblical peroration.

He wrote a deeply felt, touching funeral sermon for Revd William *Weightman, his 28-year-old curate who died on 6 September 1842 of cholera caught through visiting sick parishioners. Restrained, dignified, scrupulously fair, admirable in its clear, orderly, well-cadenced style, it pays tribute to Weightman's Christian faith, pastoral care, preaching, and personality, revealing much about Mr Brontë's own faith. Poignantly, too, he recalls that 'we were always like father and son'. Like Weightman, he emphasizes the love of God, and wishes others to 'rejoice in the glad tidings of salvation'. His tribute is the more convincing because he admits that Weightman, a good classical scholar, had sometimes preached sermons 'above the reach of ordinary capacities'; but, on Mr Brontë's advice, had good-naturedly endeavoured to adapt them for the 'most illiterate' of his congregation. Mr Brontë visited Weightman twice a day and 'joined with him in prayer' during his illness; and his grief for the loss of the young man is balanced by reflection on his tranquil deathbed: 'I may truly say, his end was peace, and his hope glory'.

In 1835 Mr Brontë published a political 'treatise', *The Signs of the Times*, and in 1836 *A Brief Treatise on the Best Time and Mode of Baptism*, both printed in Keighley; his *A Tract for the Times* appeared in the *Leeds Intelligencer* (19 Oct. 1850). The first of these was Patrick's defence of the established Church, following the Whigs' return to office in 1835 and their proposals for its disestablishment. He pointed out that a sign of the times was a 'restless propensity towards change' which had produced assaults on government-established religions as anti-scriptural. He argued that a government should make religious provision for the people, as a father would for his children, providing it was adapted to the wants of the community, and that 'all religions are tolerated, and that there is full liberty of conscience'. He regretfully admitted that other churches as well as Catholics had persecuted men for their faith, but believed that with a few exceptions, toleration was now general. To avoid 'collision' between the churches, he considered tithes should be fairly commuted, and church rates abolished in their present form. A second 'sign' was the call for total abolition rather than commutation, and for the 'violent appropriation' of established church property by Act of Parliament. Mr Brontë argued that if the original Acts of entitlement could be arbitrarily rescinded, a precedent would be set for removing 'our great charter of liberty'. The modern 'March of Intellect' had lost sight of true religion: poor attendance no more justified the destruction of a church building than poor response to missionary endeavours justified their withdrawal. Admitting that the established Church was imperfect, he advocated judicious reform. The conviction that we were 'wiser than our forefathers' was another 'sign', which he countered by eloquently defending the excellence of great classical writers and the Bible. Admitting that printing had diffused knowledge widely, he observed that more people 'know a little, but fewer know much'. Finally he deplored the sign of party violence in the recent elections, and recommended that people should join societies which encouraged mental power, not physical force.

His treatise on infant baptism is a somewhat tedious contribution to an ongoing dispute with 'Peter Pontifex', alias Moses Saunders, minister of the Haworth Strict Baptist church. Having pointed out condescendingly that if Saunders had, like Anglican ministers, studied the Classics, he would not have made elementary mistakes in Latin, Mr Brontë argues that though infant baptism is not specifically decreed in the Scriptures, it is no more improper than the admission of women to communion, of which both Saunders and he approve. With an attempt at humour, he advises Saunders not to quarrel with the ladies of Haworth in his arguments about 'dipping' as a form of washing; but then more seriously affirms that if through parental neglect or unsound views, children die unbaptized, the 'infinitely merciful Saviour' will not shut them out of his kingdom.

A Tract for the Times was Mr Brontë's response to the so-called 'Papal Aggression' which alarmed English Protestants after the Pope's appointment of Nicholas *Wiseman as cardinal-archbishop of Westminster in August 1850. He declared that 'the whole fabric of our establishment' was shaken to its centre, and warned Catholics and other Dissenters that if through their actions, the Church of England was overthrown, people would look not to religion but to the Goddess of Reason, as they had during the French Revolution.

Brontëana.

servants of the Brontës. Apart from Maria Branwell Brontë's nurse, who was dismissed by Revd Patrick Brontë after his wife's death for 'reasons which he thought sufficient', the Brontës' servants were devoted to the family, who were equally loyal to them. Martha *Brown's tribute is characteristic. She praised Mr Brontë's kindness, and wrote 'From my first entering the house . . . I was always recognised and treated as a member of the family' (William Scruton, *Thornton and the Brontës* (1898), 129). Tabitha *Aykroyd and Martha served the family for many years, Tabby from 1824 until her death on 17 February 1855, with an unavoidable absence through illness 1840–3. Martha was giving occasional help at Haworth Parsonage before July 1841, by which time she had become a full-time servant there and remained until Mr Brontë's death in 1861, when she accompanied Revd A. B. Nicholls to Ireland and stayed there for about a year. They were preceded by Sarah and Nancy Garrs in *Thornton; and other named or unnamed helpers—remarkably few in number—gave occasional help at the Parsonage. They included 'Sally Mosley . . . washing in the back-kitchin' (*sic*) in Emily's *Diary Paper of 26 June 1837, Martha's sister Eliza and her cousin Sarah Wood, Martha *Redman, and Hannah Dawson who was with the family at the time of Charlotte's death.

After Elizabeth *Branwell left Thornton at the end of July 1816, help with the growing family was essential. Mr Brontë applied to the Bradford School of Industry in Kirkgate, where about 60 girls of poor parents were taught to sew, knit, and read, and to earn a minute reward of a penny halfpenny per quarter if they attended the parish church regularly, learnt their collects and psalms, and always had their sewing implements to hand (Barker, p. 72). Twelve-year-old Nancy Garrs, one of the twelve children of Richard Garrs, a shoemaker, of Westgate, Bradford, was selected. In 1885 Nancy Wainwright, as she then was, recalled very clearly her experience as nurse to the Brontë children. When her sister Sarah was engaged as a nursemaid in 1818, Nancy became the cook, and both girls accompanied the family to Haworth. Nancy recalled Charlotte's kindly disposition, but remembered also that 'When "distinguished" visitors came' it was difficult to keep her 'from silently stealing into the drawing-room, and when they had gone she would criticise their appearance, manner, and speech with such cleverness that her father would often laugh heartily in spite of the utmost efforts to restrain himself'. She thought Branwell wilful, but 'a good lad enough . . . until the serpent beguiled him'; he had been 'made out to be a good deal worse than he really was'. 'She could "manage him" better than any one else when his fits of fury were on him' (J.B. in *Pall Mall Budget* (1885); newspaper cutting in BPM) and he seemed to have a real affection for her. According to Sarah Garrs, she and her sister left the Parsonage some months after the deaths of Maria and Elizabeth Brontë in 1825. Mr Brontë gave them £10 each as parting presents, and recommended Sarah to a post which involved travelling for two years with a wealthy widow and her daughter; but Sarah's mother objected, and she returned to Bradford, where she became an apprentice to a dressmaker. Both sisters were incensed by Elizabeth Gaskell's *Life*, which alleged that Mr Brontë's not letting his children eat meat was through 'no wish for saving, for there was plenty and even waste in the house, with young servants and no mistress to see after them' (*Life*, 1. 48–9). The source of this and other misleading statements about the Brontë household was the dismissed nurse employed during Mrs Brontë's last illness. She had moved to Burnley, near Gawthorpe, and had passed on her biased opinions to Lady Kay-Shuttleworth, who in turn reported them to Elizabeth Gaskell. The passage was omitted from later editions when Nancy and Sarah Garrs complained, and Mr Brontë wrote a testimonial for them on 17 August 1857, stating that they were kind to his children, 'and honest; and not wasteful, but sufficiently careful in regard to food, and all other articles committed to their charge' (Wise & Symington, 4. 226). Nancy said that Mr Brontë himself had been 'outrageously misrepresented', for 'A kinder master . . . never drew breath'. 'She was one of the chief mourners' at his burial on 7 June 1861 (J.B. in *Pall Mall Budget*, 1885). Nancy died in 1886. Her sister Sarah, born in 1806, married William Newsome of Bradford in 1829. Following his emigration to America in 1841, she and their four children travelled to join him in 1843. She died in Iowa City in September 1899, having previously given 'Marion Harland' (Mary Virginia Terhune) much information for *Charlotte Brontë at Home* (1899). Sarah claimed that her family was of French descent, so that her name was really De Garrs, elevated her position as nurse to the Brontë children to that of governess, and recalled that she and her sister were always treated as superiors in their presence. She became the children's 'playmate, friend, and guardian', and patiently helped them to acquire skill in needlework. She praised Charlotte's clean, neat sewing, and described her as a 'thoughtful, neat, womanly child'. On the afternoon of the bog-burst of 12 September 1824 which so alarmed Mr Brontë for his children's safety, Sarah and Nancy had taken them out on the common. Afterwards he learned that the frightened children had hidden themselves under Sarah's apron, as they sheltered in a porch. Their usual behaviour was not 'grave and silent beyond their years', as Mrs Brontë's former nurse had alleged (Gaskell *Life*, 1. 48). Sarah recalled that 'Their fun knew no bounds. . . . they enjoyed a game of romps, and played with zest'. Sarah had joined in one of their games 'as an escaping prince', and the children were 'loyal and true' to her when Mr Brontë asked questions about the branch she had broken during their play. A touching letter from Mr Brontë to Sarah on 12 June 1855 expressed thanks for her 'kind letter', told her about the 'clever books' his daughters had written and the sad deaths of his whole family, and mentioned that 'My children, and I, often thought and talked of you' (L. A. Herbert, 'Charlotte Brontë: Pleasant Interview with the Governess of this Famous Author', n.d.; typescript in BPM). The kindness of the Brontës extended to Sarah's brother Henry (b. 1827), an aspiring poet, whom Charlotte advised and encouraged.

sexuality. Despite its large families the Victorian period has long been identified with sexual repression, partly because the Victorian middle classes observed high standards of decorum in contrast to Regency laxity. Yet mid-Victorian writers represented sexual matters with surprising frankness, though their methods were often metaphorically suggestive or euphemistic. Sarah Stickney Ellis, for example, in her popular conduct book *The Wives of England* (1843), admonishes candidly that wives should not reject husbands' physical overtures by pleading petty illness, while she refers abstractly to women's sexuality as 'the richest jewel in their bridal wreath'. Though officially naive about sex Victorian women confronted biological facts in both life and art. *Tennyson's *The Princess* (1847) humorously associates women's domestic responsibility for nursing with sexual knowledge when maidens sworn to celibacy rapidly pair off amorously with their patients. Though W. M. *Thackeray's 1840s art reviews in *Fraser's Magazine* express reservations about the candour of painters' nudes, his own *Vanity Fair* (1847–8), aimed at a family audience, contains sexual implications in the image of Becky Sharp as a siren (ch. 64). Poetry such as Tennyson's frequently conveyed powerfully erotic feeling through imagery and metaphor.

Woman's libidinal nature was much debated at mid-century. While conceding the existence of lower- and upper-class amorality, conduct literature, clerical and educational tracts, and numerous medical studies minimized or denied the sensuousness of 'good' (middle-class) women, characterizing them as 'sexually anaesthetized'. Some physicians and social scientists disputed this assumption, however, and diaries such as Charles Kingsley's and personal letters testify to mutually satisfying sexual relationships among middle-class Victorians. A sexual double standard prevailed nonetheless. In medical practice and literature Victorians frequently associated expressions of female sexuality with madness. Although sexuality was considered more 'natural' and less dangerous in men, even they were warned that sexual indulgence could debilitate them physically and mentally. Fear of women's sexuality registers in the culture's preoccupation with prostitution, a much-discussed social evil usually attributed not to women's poverty or male desires, but to women's moral depravity.

Sexual latitude uncharacteristic of the period permeates the Brontës' early writings. Charlotte and Branwell depict unprincipled seductions, multiple lovers, mistresses, illegitimate children, infatuated women pursuing men—a range of subjects also suggested in the poetry representing Emily and Anne's Gondal writings. In Angria women are often sexually aggressive, and both rogues and heroes transgress Victorian bourgeois sexual mores. Although Charlotte cautioned Ellen *Nussey on 4 July 1834 to 'choose the good and avoid the evil' (Smith Letters, 1. 130–1) from readings she proposed, Charlotte herself had read them all, including *Shakespeare's comedies and *Byron's Don Juan—along with earthy 18th-century novelists. Tom Winnifrith links the 18th-century tradition of sexual frankness with the Brontës' unselfconscious treatment of passion (Winnifrith, Tom, The Brontës and their Background (1973), pp. 86 ff.).

As contemporary reviews reveal, the Brontës' novels shocked many readers with their general 'coarseness', which included sexual material (see Winnifrith Background, pp. 110–38). Rochester's narrative of his illicit sexual history to the teenaged Jane Eyre, for example, contributes to the novel's 'indifference to vice' (Anne Mozley, Christian Remembrancer (Apr. 1853), 401), much as Arthur Huntingdon's flagrant adultery with Lady Lowborough contributes to the 'sensual spirit' of Tenant, in which the heroine deflects unwanted amorous advances with her artist's palette-knife. Both novels were said to dwell on the 'grosser and more animal portion of our nature' (Rambler (Sept. 1848), 65–6).

Charlotte's novels pointedly challenge prevailing decorum, prompting John Maynard to judge that she 'offers the fullest and most sophisticated discussion of sexual issues of any major Victorian writers before Hardy' (Charlotte Brontë and Sexu-ality (1984), p. viii). Though Jane Eyre evokes familiar stereotypes by linking Bertha Mason's madness to her sexual promiscuity, it also critiques characters such as St John who repress desire. Most dramatically, it depicts the 'good' heroine as intensely passionate, guided as much by love as by reason. Jane's reference to her son at the end of the novel, rather than demonstrating that at last she has conformed to Victorian veneration of motherhood as woman's highest calling, establishes that she is finally 'flesh of [Rochester's] flesh' both spiritually and physically—and that his virility has not been diminished along with his eyesight. Villette's focus on female desire prompted Harriet *Martineau to criticize Charlotte's heroines for their excessive preoccupation with love (Daily News (3 Feb. 1853), 2), a position echoed more mildly in Thackeray's discomfort with a heroine in love with two men at once (to Lucy Baxter, 11 Mar. 1853). Charlotte countered Martineau's complaint: 'if man or woman should be ashamed of feeling such love, then is there nothing right, noble, faithful, truthful, unselfish in this earth' (to Martineau, n.d.; Wise & Symington, 4. 42). She also affirmed the appropriateness of her subject matter by judging Jane *Austen's work inadequate: in a letter to W. S. Williams of 12 April 1850 she declared that 'the Passions are perfectly unknown to her . . . what throbs fast and full, though hidden, what the blood rushes through, what is the unseen seat of Life' (Smith Letters, 2. 383).

Though Anne's heroines are more conventionally reticent, Emily's Catherine Earnshaw harks back to the passionate excesses of characters in the Brontë juvenilia. The profound emotions of Catherine and Heathcliff exceed familiar categories and are difficult to label sexual, however. The characters most closely approximate consummation of physical desire in their single passionate embrace when Catherine is conspicuously pregnant with Edgar Linton's child and nearly dead from starvation. Whatever sexuality inheres in their bond is sublimated in a total, ineffable union. Even so, the intensity of their feeling pulsates through the novel, rather like a physical electricity investing the work with a sexual aura.

BT

Gay, Peter, The Bourgeois Experience, Victoria to Freud, 2 vols. (1986).

Mason, Michael, The Making of Victorian Sexuality (1994).

—— The Making of Victorian Sexual Attitudes (1994).

Maynard, John, Charlotte Brontë and Sexuality (1984).

Showalter, Elaine, The Female Malady: Women, Madness, and English Culture, 1830–1980 (1985).

Seymour family, relations of the Duke of *Wellington in the *Glass Town and Angrian saga. The Earl and Countess Seymour (sister to the Duke) have one son, Fitzroy, and six daughters: Cecilia, Georgiana, Catherine, Agnes, Eliza, and Helen, all tall haughty blondes who are infatuated with their cousin the Duke of Zamorna. Cecilia marries Captain Sir William *Percy.

Shakespeare, William. The Brontës knew the works of Shakespeare almost as well as they did the Bible, and their works and letters are rich in Shakespearian echoes and allusions, sometimes enhancing irony or sorrow, sometimes showing a lively appreciation of comedy. Uniquely, they are used at length to elucidate and moralize on the character of Robert Gérard *Moore in *Shirley* (ch. 6), when Caroline persuades him to read from *Coriolanus* and to recognize his own faults and virtues registered there. The Brontës responded to Shakespeare's language and to his dramatic power through their reading, for until 1849 none of them, as far as we know, had seen the plays acted. In December that year Charlotte saw the famous William Macready (1793–1873) in *Macbeth* and *Othello*. She thought the performances were travesties: 'The stage-system altogether is hollow nonsense . . . the actors comprehend nothing about tragedy or Shakespeare and it is a failure' (Smith *Letters*, 2. 344). We do not know what she thought of the performance of *Twelfth Night* in Manchester on 25 April 1853, but it was not well reviewed (*BST* (1968), 15. 78. 242–3). She and Branwell were precocious readers of the plays, perhaps from as early as 1829, when Charlotte referred to the 'Spirit of Cawdor' (Alexander *EEW*, 1. 64) and Branwell wrote 'Laussane' (see VERSE DRAMA BY BRANWELL BRONTË), a dramatic poem in blank verse (Neufeldt *BBP*, pp. 37–46). In 1830 there are echoes of the tragedies in Branwell's *Caractacus* (see VERSE DRAMA BY BRANWELL BRONTË), and in 1833 Charlotte introduced a soliloquizing porter in *The *Green Dwarf*. References to *Macbeth* occur frequently in the early works, appropriately enough in stories often concerned with contests for power, dire temptations, violence, and remorse. Words and lines from *Macbeth*, *Hamlet*, *Othello*, *King Lear*, and the English and Roman history plays haunted Charlotte's imagination, and references to them then and later outnumber those to the comedies except for *A Midsummer Night's Dream*, which was evidently a favourite. Echoes of *Macbeth* are especially potent in *Jane Eyre*, where they enhance the motif of ill-fitting or inappropriate robes (Rochester's disguise, the silk dresses he wishes to buy for Jane, her bridal gown) and the concealed tragedy of the madwoman. Charlotte's personal tragedy of mental agony after

her sisters' deaths reverberates in a letter to W. S. Williams of 25 June 1849: 'Labour is the only radical cure for rooted sorrow' (Smith *Letters*, 2. 224) echoes Macbeth's question to the Doctor, 'Canst thou not minister to a mind diseased'. Anne Brontë had known Shakespeare's plays equally well. *Tenant* is rich in apposite allusions to both comedies and tragedies, the tragedies increasingly dominant as Helen Huntingdon's fate darkens. As in *Macbeth*, Huntingdon's vices 'sit loose upon him, like a cloak' (ch. 32), and Grimsby curses women with their 'false, fair faces' (ch. 33), recalling *Macbeth* 1. 7. 81. Shades of *Hamlet* accompany Huntingdon's deathbed, as Helen's faith asserts that his 'erring spirit' may attain bliss beyond the 'purging fires' (ch. 49). Emily Brontë's rare allusions or echoes derive almost exclusively from the dark tragedies, perhaps most memorably in Heathcliff's Hamlet-like gazing on Cathy's face in the opened coffin, and in some of her poems. In 'A Day Dream' the music and imagery of Coleridge's 'The Ancient Mariner' mingle strangely with the Shakespearian 'unreal mockery' of stanza 7.

'Shall Earth no more inspire thee' (16 May 1841); 28 lines by Emily Brontë, from the Honresfeld MS (see LAW COLLECTION); published by Charlotte in 1850 with the comment 'The following little piece has no title; but in it the Genius of a solitary region seems to address his wandering and wayward votary, and to recall within his influence the proud mind which rebelled at times against what it most loved.' The interlocutor is confident of the power of Nature over the listener; since there is no reply, there is no protest against Nature's soothing power. Homans argues that the wind that brings Emily's visionary influence has so successfully pre-empted the poet's voice as to become the only speaker (*Women Writers*, p. 127), but as Gezari points out (Gezari *EBP*, p. 130), the speaker of the poem is not a masculine wind but a feminine Earth. Although the 'fond idolater' may be a Gondal character, Emily's own pantheistic sentiments and 'proud mind' are reflected here. The famous lines

> Few hearts to mortals given
> On earth so wildly pine
> Yet none would ask a Heaven
> More like the Earth than thine—

are echoed in Catherine Earnshaw's dreams in *Wuthering Heights* (ch. 9), where 'heaven did not seem to be my home; and I broke my heart with weeping to come back to earth'.

Gezari *EBP*, p. 130.
Homans, Margaret, *Women Writers and Poetic Identity: Dorothy Wordsworth, Emily Brontë, and Emily Dickinson* (1980), 104–61.
Roper *EBP*, p. 121.

Sheffield, Yorks., had been for centuries the principal centre for the manufacture of cutlery, and by 1840 was exporting 'to all parts of the habitable globe'. Its many foundries and factories produced much smoke, but it is close to the hilly open moorlands of Derbyshire. On *c.*3 July 1845 Charlotte Brontë travelled by train from Leeds to Sheffield, and then by horse omnibus to *Hathersage, returning on 26 July by the same means. She probably imagined Rosamond *Oliver in *Jane Eyre* dancing in the handsome Norfolk Street Assembly Rooms with officers stationed in Sheffield since the *Luddite riots of 1811–12.

Shelley, Percy Bysshe (1792–1822), major Romantic poet and proponent of radical social change, revered by the young Brontës. He expressed revolutionary principles and philosophical idealism in poetry, which championed individual liberty as the wellspring of social good and universal joy. The Brontës had a copy of Mary Shelley's 1839 edition of her husband's *Poems* but seem to have known some of his works earlier, perhaps stimulated by Thomas *Moore's *Letters and Journals of Lord Byron, with Notices of his Life* (1830). As Chitham demonstrates (Chitham *ABP*, pp. 181, 177), Shelley's influence is evident in Anne's poetry (echoes, for example, in 'What though the sun had left my sky' (Poem 33 in Chitham *ABP*) and 'The Captive Dove'), but it figures even more conspicuously in Emily's works. Her watercolour of Ianthe as 'The North Wind' (1842) copies an engraving from Thomas Moore's *Life of Byron* and, as Alexander notes (Alexander & Sellars, pp. 386–7), traces back to a maiden granted visionary power in Shelley's early poem 'Queen Mab' (1813). Emily's views on love and marriage, God, and the soul bear the impress of Shelley's philosophy. More specifically, her poetic preoccupation with the imprisoned soul has affinities with Shelley's *Epipsychidion* (1821), which advances a theme central to *Wuthering Heights*: the love between soulmates that transcends earthly limits. Catherine's impassioned declaration 'I *am* Heathcliff' recapitulates and surpasses *Epipsychidion*'s 'I am not thine: I am a part of *thee*' (line 52). In *Shirley* Charlotte captured Emily's Shelleyan passions in the eponymous heroine's idealism, social conscience, and rebelliousness against oppressive institutions.   BT

Chitham *EB*.
Chitham, Edward, 'Emily Brontë and Shelley', in Chitham, Edward, and Winnifrith, Tom, *Brontë Facts and Brontë Problems* (1983).

Shibden Hall, the elegant half-timbered stone mansion that lies in the Shibden Valley below *Law Hill, Halifax. Like nearby *High Sunderland Hall it is thought to have contributed to the setting of *Wuthering Heights*. Phyllis Bentley points out that the relative situation of Shibden Hall in the valley and High Sunderland on the moors corresponds to that of Thrushcross Grange and Wuthering Heights (*The Brontës and their World* (1969), 53–4). Both are within walking distance of Law Hill.

Shirley. A Tale, and related manuscripts.
See page 461

Shorter, Clement King (1857–1926), prolific journalist and editor. He was born in London, and in 1896 married Dora Sigerson (d. 1918). His second wife, whom he married in 1920, was Doris Banfield, by whom he had one daughter. From 1877 to 1890 he was a clerk at Somerset House, and from 1891 to 1900 he edited with enthusiasm the *Illustrated London News*. In 1893 he founded the *Sketch*, which he edited until 1900, when he founded the *Sphere*, an illustrated weekly. In 1903 he founded the *Tatler*. As well as numerous editions of the Brontë works, he published among other books *George Borrow and his Circle* (1913) and an edition of Sir Walter Scott's Waverley novels. In August 1889 he visited Ellen *Nussey and acquired some biographical information about Charlotte for his introduction to the Camelot *Jane Eyre*. In September 1890 he offered to assist Ellen's friend Sir George Morrison in editing Charlotte's *letters. Ellen told him his assistance was not needed then, but in June 1892 she finally turned to him. He warned her that Revd A. B. *Nicholls owned perpetual copyright, and would prevent separate publication of the letters; but Shorter would be willing to write a biography instead. In October 1892 he told Ellen that a friend of his would pay her £100 for her letters, and would not object to Shorter's writing the biography. The 'friend' was T. J. *Wise, who persuaded Ellen that he wished to keep the letters safe for posterity in his library, which he intended to bequeath to the South Kensington Museum. She sold them to him for £125 on that understanding, and was horrified to discover in 1895 that he was already selling them piecemeal. She still trusted Shorter, and had already sent him an annotated copy of the incomplete Joseph Horsfall *Turner edition of Charlotte's letters. In March 1895, realizing that he needed new material, Shorter visited Mr Nicholls in Ireland, won his trust, and gained access to almost all his Brontë manuscripts. On 23 November 1895 Shorter bought from him for £125 the copyright in all Charlotte's manuscripts that passed through his hands, over which Nicholls had any rights, or which he received from Ellen Nussey. Shorter also bought on Wise's behalf many of the precious manuscripts; others he was allowed to
(*cont. on page 470*)

NOTWITHSTANDING the success of *Jane Eyre*, Charlotte Brontë was very anxious to avoid a repetition of the charges of melodrama and improbability that had been levelled at her by reviewers of her first published novel. In *Shirley* (1849) she set out to write 'Something real, cool, and solid . . . something unromantic as Monday morning' (*Shirley*, p. 7). To this end she drew her materials from history and from life. The plot is partly based on the *Luddite riots of 1812 in the West Riding of Yorkshire. The setting and characters correspond closely to the West Riding of Charlotte's own experience, and indeed—despite her assertion to Ellen Nussey on 16 November 1849 that 'we only suffer Reality to *suggest*—never to *dictate*' (Smith *Letters*, 2. 285)—she drew heavily on her own circle of acquaintance to populate the pages of the novel. This reliance on real life was to be both a strength and a weakness: a strength in that Charlotte Brontë is at her best in depicting the hard realities of Yorkshire life, the eccentricities of its people, and the sweeping beauties of its landscape; but the tragedies that afflicted her family during the novel's composition also found their way into the book, distorting its narrative structure and turning what had begun as a study of regional life into, at least in part, a veiled tribute to her deceased sisters Emily and Anne. Despite its flaws, however, *Shirley* remains one of the greatest of English regional novels and presents some of the most memorable characters in English fiction.

Composition

The writing of the work that was to become *Shirley* was under way by February 1848; on the 15th of that month Charlotte Brontë told W. S. *Williams that her next book was making slow progress, for 'it is not every day, nor even every week that I can write what is worth reading' (Smith *Letters*, 2. 27). Notwithstanding this cautionary note, the work proceeded steadily through the spring and summer of 1848, and Charlotte had almost reached the end of volume 2 when her brother Branwell died suddenly on 24 September. Despite the rift between them caused by his drug abuse and drunkenness, Charlotte was deeply affected by his death, and even more by the subsequent onset of Emily's fatal illness. She herself entered a period of illness and depression that disrupted her writing, and that intensified with Emily's death from consumption on 19 December 1848. More tragedy was to come: Anne now fell prey to what was to be her final illness, and much of Charlotte's energy was dedicated to caring for her dying sister. Yet her sense of obligation to her publisher Smith, Elder led Charlotte to continue working; she sent volume 1 to the publisher on 4 February 1849, and, despite the difficulty of composition in such trying circumstances, managed to finish volume 2 before Anne died on 28 May 1849. Soon after Anne's death Charlotte commenced the third volume, beginning with the chapter entitled 'The Valley of the Shadow of Death', which, in describing Caroline's grave illness and recovery, offers mute testimony to the author's painful emotional engagement with her character's plight and her own feelings of grief and loneliness.

Charlotte sought and found relief from her pain in her work: as she would write to W. S. Williams, on 29 August 1849, 'the occupation of writing [the novel] has been a boon to me—it took me out of dark and desolate reality to an unreal but happier

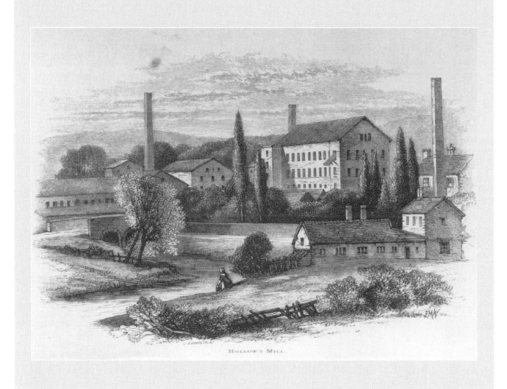

HOLLOW'S MILL.

Hollows Mill by Edmund Morison Wimperis from the first illustrated edition of *Shirley*, Smith, Elder & Co., 1872.

region' (Smith *Letters*, 2. 241). Begun in early June 1849, volume 3 was finished by 29 August, and the completed manuscript was collected from the Parsonage by James Taylor on 8 September. After flirting briefly with other titles ('Fieldhead', 'Hollows Mill'), Charlotte settled on 'Shirley' as the title because, she wrote to Williams on 21 August, 'Shirley, I fancy, has turned out the most prominent and peculiar character in the work' (Smith *Letters*, 2. 237). Charlotte also composed a preface, 'A Word to the "Quarterly" ' (see section below), in which she sought to retaliate for the unfriendly review of *Jane Eyre* by Elizabeth Rigby that appeared in the *Quarterly Review* (Dec. 1848); however, George Smith and W. S. Williams objected to its tone, Charlotte declined to revise it, and it remained unpublished.

'A Word to the "Quarterly" '

In the December 1848 issue of the *Quarterly Review*, Elizabeth *Rigby (1809–93), who was soon to marry the painter Charles Eastlake (1793–1865), gave an unfavourable review of *Jane Eyre*. In its defiance of social custom and its strong assertion of the heroine's individual will, the novel seemed to her 'pre-eminently an anti-Christian composition' likely to do harm to governesses, 'that class of ladies whose cause it affects to advocate' (and for whose plight, in fact, Rigby does express some sympathy). 'It is true,' wrote Rigby, 'Jane does right, and exerts great moral strength, but it is the strength of a mere heathen mind which is a law unto itself. . . . We do not hesitate to say that the tone of mind and thought which has overthrown authority and violated every code human and divine abroad, and fostered Chartism and rebellion at home, is the same which has also written Jane Eyre.' The harshness of the review deeply hurt Charlotte Brontë, who sought to offer a riposte in the form of a satiric preface to her next published novel, *Shirley*. In 'Preface: A Word to the "Quarterly" ', a six-page holograph manuscript in the Seton-Gordon Collection at the BPM, Currer Bell, describing himself as 'an old bachelor', mockingly identifies the *Quarterly*'s reviewer as 'an Old Woman' and with a rather ponderous irony takes her to task for attacking the novel's supposed revolutionary tendencies. The Preface also satirizes the review's preoccupation with the novel's evident misrepresentation of the domestic arrangements in upper-class households; Currer Bell claims to have made 'personal inquiry of Miss Blanche Ingram's maid about the material of her lady's morning-dress'. Currer Bell concludes with a polite invitation to the reviewer to visit him at 'Hay-lane Cottage[,] Hay, Millcote'. Charlotte sent the manuscript of her preface to her publisher Smith, Elder on 29 August 1849. It appealed to neither George Smith nor W. S. Williams, and when the author declined to make any changes, the matter of a preface to *Shirley* was dropped. Charlotte still enjoyed some revenge, however, for in her portrait of the Hardmans (*Shirley*, ch. 21) she quotes freely from Rigby's review to convey what she saw as the cruel indifference of the moneyed classes to the poverty and isolation of governesses in their employ.

Manuscript and early editions

The manuscript of *Shirley* that Charlotte sent to the printers is contained in three quarto volumes that form part of the George Smith Bequest in the British Library (Add. MSS 43477–9). Like the fair copy of *Jane Eyre*, the handwriting is neat and clear, but there are many more textual revisions in this novel than in the manuscript of its predecessor, reflecting perhaps the difficult circumstances under which much of

Shirley was written, and the emotional struggles of its author. Among manuscript alterations may be noted the occasional correction of names ('Elizabeth' corrected to Caroline, 'Warner' changed to Pryor) that suggest the possibility of an Angrian provenance for some of the characters. Deleted in the second volume is an explicit reference to the *Quarterly Review* of *Jane Eyre* from which Charlotte drew for Miss Hardman's criticism of Mrs Pryor and governesses in general (*Shirley*, ch. 21). In the third volume, Charlotte excised a passage in French and replaced it with Shirley's essay 'La Première Femme Savante', translated into English 'on pain of being unintelligible to some readers' (*Shirley*, ch. 27). Further substantive changes were made in proof, including the removal of an invitation to the reader, in the novel's final chapter, to correspond with the author via 'a note addressed Mr Currer Bell Hay-Lane Cottage, Hay, near Millcote'—the same lane in which Jane *Eyre first meets Mr *Rochester. The proof corrections completed, *Shirley. A Tale. By Currer Bell, Author of 'Jane Eyre'* was issued by Smith, Elder and Co. on 26 October 1849 in three volumes at 31s. 6d. For this novel Charlotte was paid £500, the same amount she had received for *Jane Eyre*, and she promptly asked George Smith to invest the money for her in bank annuities (the 'Funds'): see her letters to Smith, 14 and 22 September 1849 (Smith *Letters*, 2. 253, 262).

The novel's second edition, published in one volume in November 1852 (though dated 1853) and priced at 6s., incorporates revisions Charlotte sent to the publisher in March 1852, as well as printing-house corrections of misprints, and changes designed to make the punctuation more consistent and conventional. Revisions that can be attributed with some confidence to the author include the omission of notes on French poetry in the chapters 'Coriolanus' and 'The First Blue-Stocking'. Other early editions include a 'Copyright Edition' in two volumes issued by Bernhard Tauchnitz of Leipzig in 1849; and a one-volume edition dated 1850, published by Harper & Brothers of New York in November 1849; neither edition has textual significance, the author having had no hand in their preparation.

Sources and context
Following criticism by some reviewers, notably George Henry *Lewes, that *Jane Eyre* had been too sensational and melodramatic, Charlotte sought for her new work a story that would be 'unromantic as Monday morning', and turned to the novel that had already been declined by seven publishers, namely *The Professor*. Her hope was to recast and extend the story so that it would meet the requirements of the 'three-decker' form preferred by the circulating libraries. The undated fragment 'John Henry' (see section below) may represent such an attempt; almost certainly composed after the rejection of *The Professor* and before the publication of *Shirley*, it presents a harsh mill owner named Moore who is aided in his business by a rough-spoken Yorkshireman and who maltreats his sensitive younger brother. In this and other respects one may see a reworking of the first part of *The Professor* and characters whose origins can be traced back to the *Glass Town and Angrian saga. For the historical elements of her plot, set in West Yorkshire at the time of the Luddite troubles, Charlotte relied heavily on the files of the *Leeds Mercury* for 1812–14; at the same time, she would have been familiar with the main events of the period through the recollections of her father, who had been curate at Hartshead from 1811 to 1815 and had witnessed some of the Luddites' activities. Elizabeth Gaskell (*Life*, 2. 114)

adds that Charlotte would have heard stories about this period from her teacher Margaret *Wooler, whose Roe Head school at Mirfield was situated in the heart of the wool-manufacturing district affected by the industrial disturbances. Charlotte may have been inspired to write about the economic and political troubles of West Yorkshire because of the Chartist agitation that in the England of 1848 was fed by an industrial slump and high unemployment (see CHARTISM). She chose to develop this topic by turning to its manifestation in the past because, as she was to tell George *Smith on 30 October 1852 in connection with *Villette*, 'I cannot write books handling topics of the day; it is of no use trying' (Wise & Symington, 4. 14). Frightened of 'meddling' in a world she did not know, she declined to produce a 'factory novel' of the kind she condemned in the work of Mrs Trollope in a letter to Williams of 28 January 1848 (Smith *Letters*, 2. 23).

'John Henry'

The manuscript of the untitled and undated fragment known as 'John Henry', now in the collection of Robert H. Taylor at Princeton, contains two completed chapters and the first paragraph of a third. Under the title 'The Moores: An Unpublished Fragment', it was first transcribed and published by W. Robertson Nicoll as an appendix to his edition of *Jane Eyre* (1902); a more detailed transcription appears in appendix D of the Clarendon edition of *Shirley*.

John Henry Moore and his new wife (in the manuscript first called Sarah Julia, then Hannah Julia) are described at their residence in Aspen Place, on the outskirts of the industrial city of Everintoyle. John Henry is a rough and tyrannical mill owner who places more value on his bookkeeper Tim Steele than on his wife. He receives a letter from his younger half-brother William Calvert Moore, currently working as sub-editor of a Dissenting journal, the *Westhaven Oracle*, who wants to escape the plans of his family and patrons for him to become a preacher in a new chapel and marry the daughter of a Dissenting clergyman, Dr Greatorix (first called Dr McShane). William asks his brother's help; John Henry grudgingly offers him a position as a clerk. William arrives while Miss Alicia Wynne, a friend of Mrs Moore's and the ambitious daughter of a local landowner, is visiting Aspen Place. After the evening meal Alicia attempts to exercise her charm over William, but he sees her for what she is, selfish and grasping. The fragment concludes in the back parlour, where Mr Moore is meeting with Tim Steele, 'a joined Wesleyan Methodist and an eminent class leader' (*Shirley* (Clarendon edn.), app. D, p. 835).

Several details of the fragment suggest that this was an attempt to revise *The Professor*, and possibly a first attempt at the work that was to become *Shirley*. In the brothers John Henry Moore and William Calvert Moore—the first a forceful and single-minded mill owner who defies opposition, the latter a quiet intellectual who disdains social climbers and hypocrisy—we see the lineaments of Edward and William Crimsworth, whose mutual antagonism leads the younger brother to begin a new life as a teacher in Brussels. (See Alexander *EW*, ch. 29, for a discussion of the motif of the rival brothers in Charlotte's early stories.) In *Shirley* Robert and Louis Moore retain some likeness to their predecessors—Robert is an ambitious manufacturer, Louis a reticent tutor—but their rivalry is muted and overlaid by affection. Other characters in 'John Henry' look forward to *Shirley*: thus, John Henry's dislike of pretence and affectation, an echo of Hunsden's in *The Professor*, anticipates Hiram

Yorke's directness of speech and manner, and his wife's bluntness looks forward to a similar quality in *Shirley*'s Mrs Yorke. Hannah Julia also suggests some of the features of the harsh but good-hearted Hortense Moore, Robert's and Louis's sister. Miss Wynne's name, and the name of her home at De Walden Hall, reappear in *Shirley*. John Henry's bookkeeper Tim Steele is a precursor of Robert Moore's overlooker Joe Scott (Tim is first described as an 'overlooker', then the word is deleted and replaced by 'book-keeper'). The name 'Helstone' appears in the manuscript as the name of the Moores' home, but is deleted in favour of Aspen Place; a few lines later it appears again as the first version of John Henry's surname, but at once gives way to Moore. In the second chapter, speaking to Miss Wynne, Mr Moore refers to their common working-class origins, and alludes to 'Billy Moore [his] old grandsire' who was in-volved in an illegal affair that landed Jacky Whin in York Castle; this is doubtless a reference to the Luddite riots that form the historical subject of *Shirley*, and that culminated in the arrest, imprisonment, and execution of some the rioters in York Castle.

Plot

In *Shirley*, Robert Gérard *Moore, half English, half Belgian, has lived for two years in *Briarfield in the West Riding of Yorkshire, where he has rented a cloth mill in hopes of restoring his family fortunes, hard hit by the French Revolution. At the time the narrative begins (mid-February 1811), the country is suffering from the restraints on trade caused by the war and government regulation. In an effort to boost his business, and in line with his progressive outlook, Moore purchases some of the new frames and shears 'which, greatly reducing the number of hands necessary to be employed, threw thousands out of work, and left them without legitimate means of sustaining life' (p. 37). For this Moore is hated, and his new frames are smashed en route to his mill. In his opposition to the Luddites, Moore is aided by the Tory parson Revd Matthewson *Helstone, Rector of Briarfield, and by Revd Peter Augustus *Malone, Helstone's boisterous Irish curate. Moore's foreman Joe *Scott, who had been over-powered by the frame-breakers, is rescued by Hiram *Yorke, a freethinking Yorkshire merchant and mill owner who lives at *Briarmains with his wife Hesther and six children. Yorke is implacably opposed to everything Helstone stands for. Some of his animosity derives from their rivalry when younger for the hand of Mary *Cave, a contest won by the Rector; once married, Helstone had neglected Mary, leading to untrue stories about his abuse of her that, upon her untimely death, fed Yorke's hatred of the Rector.

Despite attempts to intimidate him, Robert Moore defies his enemies, and in a confrontation with protesting millworkers he has Moses *Barraclough, a leader of the frame-breakers, arrested. He harshly rejects the pleas for compassion by William *Farren, an unemployed millworker in desperate straits, though he secretly arranges with Hiram Yorke to find Farren work. Moore lives in *Hollow's Cottage with his sister Hortense Gérard *Moore, who teaches French to their 18-year-old cousin Caroline *Helstone, the ward of Revd Matthewson Helstone. Mr Helstone discourages his niece's attempts to find out more about her deceased father and her absent mother, and rejects any suggestion that she look for employment as a governess. Caroline spends many evenings at Hollow's Cottage, and her obvious feelings for Robert seem reciprocated; however, Robert soon represses what he regards as 'weakness', and becomes cooler towards Caroline. The distance between them grows when Mr Helstone, angered by Moore's opposition to England's war with France, forbids Caroline to continue visiting her cousins; she obeys, but deprived of Moore's companionship and unable to adopt any profession, she enters a period of emotional and physical decline.

In May (1811), Caroline meets Shirley *Keeldar, a 21-year-old heiress who has arrived to take possession of her home at *Fieldhead. She is accompanied by her former governess and now companion Mrs Agnes *Pryor, a rather timid and retiring woman in her early forties who is rigidly Tory and High Church. Shirley by contrast is mercurial and aggressively independent. She soon establishes herself as a force in the neighbourhood, and strikes up a warm friendship with Robert Moore, her tenant at Hollow's Mill. Caroline, by now an intimate of Shirley's, becomes melancholy as she sees Robert's interest in Shirley grow; indeed, a union between these two seems more and more likely. In early June, the growing unrest among the working people of the district culminates in an attack on *Hollow's Mill by a band of desperate men who, in a bloody battle witnessed by Caroline and Shirley, are repulsed by Moore and his allies, leaving one man dead and five or six wounded.

Over the summer that follows, Moore pursues the leaders of the riot and Shirley's attention is fully occupied by her former guardian Mr *Sympson and his family who have descended on Fieldhead for a prolonged visit. Caroline becomes increasingly lonely and melancholy and falls prey to a dangerous fever; upon news of her illness, Mrs Pryor comes to the Rectory to take care of her, and reveals that she is Caroline's mother. She explains that after the death of her profligate husband James *Helstone, she had given Caroline into the care of Matthewson Helstone, taken on an assumed name, and become governess to Shirley Keeldar. Following her recovery, Caroline befriends Louis Gérard *Moore, Robert's younger brother who is staying at Fieldhead with the Sympson family. Now tutor to Mr Sympson's crippled son Henry, Louis had also tutored Shirley several years earlier when the latter had lived with her guardian. Mr Sympson attempts to find a husband for Shirley among the local gentry, but she fiercely asserts her independence and rejects several candidates, including a young baronet, Sir Philip Nunnely. For a time she is subdued by fears that she may have been bitten by a rabid dog, but Louis calms her troubled spirit and helps her to regain her self-confidence. Through extracts from Louis' diaries the reader learns of his passionate love for the heiress, first aroused when she was his pupil, but carefully hidden.

Robert Moore, meanwhile, spends several months away from Briarfield, first in Birmingham in connection with the capture, trial, and sentencing to transportation of the four ringleaders of the riot at Hollow's Mill, then in London. In October he returns, and riding back to Briarfield in the company of Hiram Yorke, he reveals that he had proposed marriage to Shirley Keeldar, who had angrily rejected him and reproached him for his insincerity. From this experience he has emerged chastened, resolved never to marry for mercenary motives. His travels have also taken him 'where there was no occupation and no hope' (p. 616), and taught him a new compassion for the sufferings of the poor. In the midst of his confessions he is ambushed and shot by a half-crazed Antinomian weaver, Michael *Hartley. Seriously wounded, he is taken to the Yorkes' home at Briarmains and nursed back to health. Mrs Yorke forbids all access, but with young Martin Yorke's help, Caroline manages to evade her and visit her convalescing cousin. On his recovery Moore admits to Caroline that he had wanted to marry Shirley for her money, asks Caroline's forgiveness, and expresses his love for her. Shortly before Christmas (1811), Louis Moore finally gives voice to his love for Shirley, a love that she returns; the revelation of their feelings brings a confrontation with the outraged Mr Sympson, who is ejected from Fieldhead by an aroused Louis. The narrator jumps to mid-June 1812, noting the rescinding of the Orders in Council that had strangled trade and whose removal now promises the return of prosperity. Robert Moore drops his plans of emigrating to Canada, and in mid-August he and Caroline are married in a double ceremony with Louis and Shirley.

Reception

Given the huge success of *Jane Eyre*, it was perhaps inevitable that Currer Bell's new novel would be measured alongside its predecessor. Certainly Charlotte anticipated such comparisons, and in her choice of subject sought to appease those critics, especially George Henry Lewes, who had found fault with *Jane Eyre* on the grounds of its sensationalism. The first reviewers of *Shirley* did indeed draw comparisons, but to the writer's chagrin many found fault with the 'real, cool, and solid' material that comprised the substance of her new work, and looked back nostalgically to the excitement provoked by the earlier novel. 'Well do we remember how we took up *Jane Eyre* one winter's evening', reminisces the anonymous reviewer (probably William George Clark) in *Fraser's Magazine*, 40 (Dec. 1849), recalling his initial intention 'to be as critical as Coker'; 'But as we read on we forgot both commendations and criticism, identified ourselves with Jane in all her troubles, and finally married Mr. Rochester about four in the morning.' The reviewer describes how he shut himself up with *Shirley* in keen anticipation of a similar experience—but then fell sound asleep. The *Atlas* (3 Nov. 1849) notes how eagerly the reading public has awaited Currer Bell's new book—'never has the third volume of that indescribable fiction been laid down without a longing after more fruit from the same tree'—and the reviewer is willing to grant the new book some superior qualities ('*Shirley* is a more womanly book than *Jane Eyre*, and on the whole more pleasing'); nonetheless, he laments that *Shirley* does not exercise the 'irresistible spell' that was cast over *Jane Eyre*'s readers. The *Weekly Chronicle* (10 Nov. 1849) finds *Shirley* a worthy successor to *Jane Eyre*, but lacking the intensity and excitement of the earlier work. Paradoxically, the *Church of England Quarterly Review*, while allowing that *Jane Eyre* is superior in interest and excitement, prefers *Shirley* because it 'enlists the purer sympathies of our nature, instead of appealing to its baser passions' (Jan. 1850).

Charlotte noted the comparisons, writing to W. S. Williams on 15 November 1849 that 'from the tone of the Newspapers it seems that those who were most charmed with *Jane Eyre* are the least pleased with *Shirley* . . . while those who spoke disparagingly of *Jane Eyre*—like *Shirley* a little better than her predecessor. I suppose its dryer matter suits their dryer minds' (Smith *Letters*, 2. 282). She was angered by the critics' continuing preoccupation with Currer Bell's identity and gender, and their condescending assertions that *Shirley*'s author must be a woman; 'that Currer Bell is petticoated will be as little doubted by the readers of her work as that Shirley Keeldar is breeched', stated the *Daily News* (31 Oct. 1849). 'Why can they not be content to take Currer Bell for a man?' exclaimed Charlotte to James *Taylor on 6 November 1849 (Smith *Letters*, 2. 280). More disturbing was the diatribe levelled against *Shirley* by *The Times* (7 Dec. 1849), whose anonymous reviewer, after praising *Jane Eyre* as a 'remarkable production', pronounces its successor to be a work that 'bears no likeness to actual life, and affords no satisfaction or pleasure to those who survey it'. The chief grounds of the reviewer's displeasure are what he calls its 'artificial and unnatural history' and its unrealistic characters, none of whom is exempted from the reviewer's sarcasm ('As for Miss Shirley, her metaphysical acumen and argumentative prowess are beyond all praise, whilst the dialectics of the precocious 12 year old [Rose Yorke] would do honour to John Stuart Mill himself').

Few of the early reviews were as condemnatory as that in *The Times*. Many critics, while acknowledging some deficiencies in the creation of character or occasional stiffness in the dialogue, praised *Shirley*'s moral strength and its handling of important themes, the author's ability to convey the interior life of her characters, and her skill in rendering historical events in realistic and dramatic fashion. A. W. Fonblanque, reviewing *Shirley* on 3 November 1849 for the *Examiner* (the journal he had edited from 1830 to 1847), like *The Times* reviewer finds the characters to be creations of intellect, not flesh and blood; at the same time, he is moved by the power and intensity of the novel's 'graphic delineation and expression. . . . There are scenes which for strength and delicacy of emotion are not transcended in the range of English fiction.' William Howitt, who had favourably reviewed *Jane Eyre*, finds in *Shirley* evidence of 'real genius'; he notes similarities to Elizabeth Gaskell's *Mary Barton* (1848) (something which Charlotte herself had drawn to her publisher's attention in her letter to Williams of 1 Feb. 1849 (Smith *Letters*, 2. 174)), but in his view the likeness in no way detracts from the originality of the later novel (*Standard of Freedom*, 10 Nov. 1849). He draws a shrewd distinction by pointing out that the two writers 'regard life from a very different point of view. . . . the author of *Mary Barton* is obviously more at home amongst the "hands," the author of *Shirley* amongst the masters'. The review that gave Charlotte the most satisfaction was that by Eugène Forçade in *Revue des deux mondes*, 4 (15 Nov. 1849), which praises the novel's rebelliousness ('l'esprit d'insoumission', p. 719) and its examination of the place of women in English society. Forçade was one of the few critics to treat the novel's social ideas seriously, without condescension or patronizing remarks about the author's feminine identity.

Forçade's review was in stark contrast to that by George Henry Lewes in the *Edinburgh Review* (Jan. 1850). Like most other reviewers, Lewes laments the disappearance of the power and the passion that imbue *Jane Eyre*. He is willing to allow that *Shirley* shows remarkable powers of intellect, and that Currer Bell can capture minor characters with 'a few brief vigorous touches'; but most of the review is a stern catalogue of the work's failings, from a perceived lack of plot unity and coarseness of tone to the 'want of truth' in the depiction of Caroline Helstone and her mother Mrs Pryor. *Shirley*'s heroes, the brothers Moore, are sordid and disagreeable, while the three curates are 'offensive, uninstructive, and unamusing'. Charlotte might have accepted these strictures with more equanimity—Lewes, after all, professed himself to be one of her greatest admirers—were they not accompanied by needless revelations about her gender and her status ('the authoress is the daughter of a clergyman!' exclaims Lewes in the review), and by a caustic attack on her failure to understand the nature of maternal feeling. Charlotte, who had entered into a friendly correspondence with Lewes after the publication of *Jane Eyre*, felt betrayed: 'I can be on guard against my enemies,' she wrote to him bitterly on *c*.10 January 1850, 'but God deliver me from my friends!' (Smith *Letters*, 2. 330). She was hurt, she told Lewes on the 19th, 'because, after I had said earnestly that I wished critics would judge me as an *author* not as a woman, you so roughly—I even thought—so cruelly handled the question of sex' (Smith *Letters*, 2. 332–3).

The judgement of later 19th-century readers did not greatly differ from the initial critical response. Though armed by Gaskell's *Life* with a new understanding of the writer's difficulties in composing the work, critics continued to dwell on the inconsistencies and improbabilities of plot, the weaknesses of characterization, the lack of the kind of excitement provided by *Jane Eyre*. Even among her most dedicated admirers, *Shirley* was perceived as an uneven work adding little to Charlotte Brontë's reputation. Swinburne, in an otherwise positive survey of Charlotte's work, finds *Shirley* 'the most unequal and least fortunate of her three great books. . . . a notable example of failure in the central and crucial point of masculine character' (*Charlotte Brontë, A Note*, 1877). Augustine Birrell judges it to have 'passages of great daring and beauty', but concludes that it is 'inferior alike to its predecessor and its successor' (*Life of Charlotte Brontë* (1887), 122–3). In her introduction to the Haworth edition (1900), Mrs Humphry Ward does not attempt to defend *Shirley* from accusations of deficiencies in plot structure or the creation of male characters; indeed, she sharply criticizes the middle chapters (chs. 14–17) as contrived and clumsy, and exempts only Mr Helstone and Martin Yorke from the charge that the male characters have no 'convincing veracious quality' ('Introduction', p. xxii). Instead, she believes the novel's strength to lie in the depiction of its female characters, which ring with a truth denied to the male figures because they are 'spirits born of [the author's] own essence'; Caroline, Shirley, and Mrs Pryor embody 'delicacy, wildness, family affection . . . the three aspects of Charlotte's personality, Charlotte's genius' (p. xxvii). For all its faults, concludes Mrs Ward, *Shirley* marked a necessary growth in the author's insight and understanding, a maturing of vision that would make possible 'the brilliant, the imperishable *Villette*' (p. xxviii). HR

Brontë, Charlotte, 'John Henry', in *Shirley* (Clarendon edn.), app. D.

—— 'A Word to the "Quarterly" ', in *Shirley* (Clarendon edn.), app. C, and Smith *Letters*, 2. 242–5.

Eagleton, T., 'Class, Power and Charlotte Brontë', *Critical Quarterly*, 14 (autumn 1972), 223–35.

Glen, Heather, *Charlotte Brontë: The Imagination in History* (2002), ch. 6.

Korg, Jacob, 'The Problem of Unity in *Shirley*', *Nineteenth Century Fiction*, 12 (Sept. 1957), 125–36.

Rosengarten, Herbert, 'Excerpts from the *Leeds Mercury*, 1812', in *Shirley* (Clarendon edn.), app. A.

Wroot.

borrow on condition that he returned them, for in January 1896 Nicholls discovered that Wise had already sent a particularly sensitive letter for sale at Sotheby's. Though Shorter did not have access to Charlotte's letters to M. Constantin *Heger, George *Smith, or Elizabeth *Gaskell for his *Charlotte Brontë and her Circle* (1896), it was a substantial achievement. He listed the Brontës' juvenilia, provided facsimiles of some of the diary papers, and printed very fair transcriptions of Charlotte's letters to Laetitia Wheelwright (see WHEELWRIGHT FAMILY) and of some to W. S. *Williams. In reproducing the correspondence with Ellen, he was too often hampered by her previous editing, since Wise had sold many of the originals. Shorter printed a number of Charlotte's letters to George Smith in his notes to the Haworth edition of the *Life* (1900), but was not allowed to use them for *The Brontës: Life and Letters*, 2 vols. (1908) (see Smith *Letters*, 1. 52–70).

Shuttleworth, Sir James and Lady Kay-.
See KAY-SHUTTLEWORTH, SIR JAMES; KAY-
SHUTTLEWORTH, JANET, LADY.

Sidgwick, John Benson (1800–73), principal
partner in High Mills, Skipton, Yorks. He and
his family lived at Skipton Castle Gatehouse in
winter and at *Stonegappe in summer; they
moved to West Riddlesden Hall in 1854. Charlotte
Brontë, as temporary governess at Stonegappe,
liked Mr Sidgwick, whom she thought kinder,
less condescending, with less 'profession' than his
wife, and not so excessively indulgent to his children. He seemed to her an ideal Conservative
gentleman as (like the Duke of *Zamorna in
*Caroline Vernon) he strolled through his fields
with his magnificent Newfoundland dog. He built
a new church at *Lothersdale, opened October
1838.

Sidgwick, Mrs Sarah Hannah, née Greenwood (1803–87), of *Stonegappe, *Lothersdale.
The daughter of John Greenwood (1763–1846) of
Knowle House, Keighley (see GREENWOOD FAMILY
OF HAWORTH AND KEIGHLEY), she married John
Benson *Sidgwick in January 1827. Charlotte
Brontë, her temporary governess in 1839, found
her unjust and unsympathetic, resentful of complaints about her children, and tyrannical in her
demands for 'oceans of needlework'. Unlike most
other people, Charlotte thought her 'fussily affable' and condescending rather than amiable. She
once rebuked Charlotte's depression so harshly
as to make her cry. Others thought the *Sidgwick
family generous and considerate, and their great-
nephew A. C. Benson (1862–1925) praised Sarah's
'sweet face' and 'gentle cordiality'.

Sidgwick family. Charlotte Brontë was governess to two of the children of John Benson
*Sidgwick and Sarah Hannah *Sidgwick from
May to July 1839. They were Mathilda (b. 1832) and
John Benson (b. August 1835); these two and
the older children Margaret (b. 1827) and William
(b. 1829) were christened at Kildwick, Yorks. A
fifth baby, Edward (b. 18 August 1839), was christened at *Lothersdale. According to Gérin (Gérin
CB, p. 142), their last son was Charles (b. 1845).
Thus Mrs Sidgwick was heavily pregnant during Charlotte's governess-ship. According to A. C.
Benson, Charlotte had 'no gifts for the management of children, and was also in a very morbid
condition the whole time', though the young
'Benson Sidgwick . . . certainly on one occasion
threw a Bible at Miss Brontë' (Life of Edward White
Benson (1899), 1. 12). Charlotte told Elizabeth Gaskell that she had 'been entrusted with the care of' a
little boy 'during the absence of his parents . . . and
particularly enjoined to keep him out of the stable-
yard. His elder brother . . . tempted the little fellow
into the forbidden place. She followed, and tried to
induce him to come away; but, instigated by his
brother, he began throwing stones at her, and one
of them hit her so severe a blow on the temple that
the lads were alarmed into obedience.' Afterwards,
she told their mother that her wound was caused
by an accident, and the children honoured her for
not 'telling tales'. She gradually gained their affection thereafter, and 'one day, at the children's dinner, [Benson] . . . in a little demonstrative gush,
said, putting his hand in hers, "I love 'ou, Miss
Brontë." Whereupon, the mother exclaimed, before all the children, "Love the *governess*, my
dear!" ' (Gaskell *Life*, 1. 190–1).

Sidonia, Lord Alfred, the fair-haired, blue-eyed
lover of the dark A.G.A. in the *Gondal saga. He
appears to have married her, since their pictures
hang side by side in his ancestral home. In his infatuation with A.G.A. who is disliked by his
people, Sidonia neglects his fair-haired daughter.
He dies in England but his ghost haunts Aspin
Castle in Gondal.

Silas, Père, in *Villette*, the kindly, devout French
priest to whom Lucy *Snowe confesses her mental
torment during the long vacation, as Charlotte
had confessed in the church of Ste Gudule in August 1843. He wishes to convert Lucy to his faith,
but though grateful to him, she remains staunchly
Protestant. He helps Dr John *Bretton take her to
*La Terrasse. As M. Paul *Emanuel's spiritual
mentor, he seeks to separate Paul from the heretic
Lucy, assuring her that Paul is faithful to the memory of his Catholic love, Justine Marie Walravens.
He helps to arrange Paul's voyage to the West Indies.

'Silent is the house'. See 'JULIAN M. AND A. G.
ROCHELLE'.

Simeon, Revd Charles (1759–1836). Revd Pat-
rick Brontë heard Simeon preach at Holy Trinity,
Cambridge, where, as the incumbent from 1783
until his death, he ensured the continuity of the
evangelical tradition in the university. His missionary projects had been discussed with Mr
Brontë's benefactors *Wilberforce and Henry
Thornton in 1797, he helped to found the *Church
Missionary Society, and was a subscriber to
*Cowan Bridge school. In 1848 Mr Brontë wel-
comed Ellen Nussey's loan of William Carus's
Memoirs of the Life of the Revd Charles Simeon
(1847), and was 'very much interested in reading
the book—there is frequent mention made in it of
persons and places formerly well known to him'
(Smith *Letters*, 2. 104).

Simpson, Jeremiah ('Macterrorglen'), a banker and associate of Montmorency, he is a creditor of the young Alexander Percy (Duke of Northangerland) and Augusta di Segovia in the *Glass Town and Angrian saga. As Sir Jehu Macterrorglen, with unruly Scots troops, he leads the Verdopolitan Reform Army, supported by the Marquis of *Ardrah and the Navy, in the war against the Federation and Angria (in the Angrian Wars). When Ardrah is defeated he joins Lord Jordan and Quashia Quamina in support of Northangerland, occupies Angria, and captures and court-martials the Duke of Zamorna after his defeat at the Battle of *Edwardston. Under Macterrorglen, the province of Zamorna becomes a scene of 'never ending cruelty and horror'. After his defeat at Evesham, Macterrorglen is hunted down by Captain William Percy and the Angrian Government Police. The character Jeremiah Simpson reappears in a later fragmentary manuscript by Charlotte Brontë, as 'a linen-draper who had large acquaintance in the world of fashion & . . . had the reputation of a most thorough-paced & subtle scoundrel' (*Ashworth).

'Sir Henry Tunstall', Branwell Brontë's important narrative poem begun in Bradford on 31 July 1838 (MS in Emily's hand: BL); revised as 'Sir Henry Tunstall' at Broughton-in-Furness and dated 15 April 1840 (Houghton, Harvard); and further revised in 1842 and signed 'Northangerland' (National Library of Scotland). The early version was misattributed to Emily (who had copied the poem) and called 'The Wanderer' by T. J. *Wise. Branwell recognized this as one of his best poems, choosing to send the first revision for comment to Thomas *De Quincey on 15 April 1840, and the final version to *Blackwood's Edinburgh Magazine on 6 September 1842. 'Sir Henry Tunstall' is significant for its literary merit and for what it reveals of Branwell's state of mind and emotional development. Written after the 'Caroline' poems of 1837 (SEE POETRY OF BRANWELL BRONTË), this work expresses Branwell's philosophy of loss and the consoling power of memory. Winifred Gérin discusses in detail the narrator's gradual recognition of the 'sad inevitability of change' (Gérin *BB*, pp. 153–9), in the experience of his own absence and return to his birthplace and in his final acceptance of the death of his sister Caroline. After sixteen successful years of military service in India, Sir Henry *Tunstall returns to his parents, sister, and children, a changed man both physically and spiritually and unable to respond to his home and family as before. With sorrow he recognizes (as Branwell himself must have done) that the old familiar circle has 'lost him beyond recall'.

Neufeldt *BB Works*, 3. 233–45; 273–85; 377–89.

slavery. By the Treaty of Utrecht (1713), Spain gave to Great Britain the monopoly of the slave trade with Spanish America, which continued until 1807. In Britain William Wilberforce, one of Revd Patrick Brontë's benefactors, became parliamentary leader of the abolitionist cause in 1787, and was supported by members of the Clapham Sect and by evangelicals such as Revd Charles *Simeon. Mr Brontë would undoubtedly have supported the cause. In March 1807 the Act of Abolition of the Slave Trade prohibited dealing and trading in slaves and their transportation by British subjects or in British ships. It did not abolish slavery in the British dominions, and the anti-slavery movement continued, its icon being Josiah Wedgwood's medallion of 1787 showing a kneeling slave, his chained hands raised in supplication, encircled by the words 'Am I not a man and a brother'. Branwell Brontë showed his familiarity with the medallion in a letter to Joseph Bentley Leyland of 10 September 1845, where he depicted the pugilist Benjamin Caunt raising his chained hands to a triumphant slave-driver, Bendigo (William Thompson), Caunt's victor in a disgracefully unfair match on 9 September 1845 (see *BST* (1995), 21. 5. 177–85). Branwell also took the title of *And the Weary are at Rest from a verse in Job 3, well known in a version of the words used in an emancipationist poem, 'The Sorrows of Yamba'. This was reprinted in a magazine for children produced by Mr Brontë's friend Theodore Dury (see DURY FAMILY): the *Monthly Teacher*, 2 (1830), 32–6. In 1827 Dury had been visited by his friend Wilberforce in Keighley, where Mr Brontë might have met him. Though slavery was abolished in the British dominions by an Act of 1833 freeing all British-owned slaves from 1 August 1834, with provision for a period of apprenticeship, slavery continued in the southern states of America. In a letter to George Smith of 30 October 1852 (Wise & Symington, 4. 14) Charlotte Brontë metaphorically veiled her face before such a mighty subject as that handled in *Uncle Tom's Cabin* (1851–2).

Smith, Elder and Company, publishers of Charlotte Brontë's novels and of some later editions of Emily's and Anne's works, founded by two young Scotsmen, George Smith (1789–1846) and Alexander Elder (1790–1876). In 1816 they opened a booksellers' and stationers' shop in Fenchurch Street, London, and in March 1819 expanded into publishing. In 1824 after Smith's marriage in October 1820 to Elizabeth Murray, and the birth of his children Eliza (?1822) and George (1824), the firm moved to 65 Cornhill. It was joined by the brilliant but unreliable Patrick Stewart (d. 1852), through whose guardian, Aeneas Mackintosh, Smith, Elder developed an Indian agency. At first they exported books and stationery to East India Company officers; later they sent out goods even further afield, ranging from surveying instruments to ladies' bonnets. The agency also provided banking facilities, and from *c*.1837 to 1850 an Eastern postal service on the overland route pioneered by Lieutenant Thomas Waghorn (1800–50). Early publications included **Friendship's Offering*. From 1831 the firm imitated Bentley and Henry **Colburn's Standard Novels* series in the 6*s*. volumes of their *Library of Romance*, which ended unprofitably in 1835 after fifteen volumes. They also published expensively produced collections of engravings (1836), and finely illustrated reports of government-sponsored expeditions—notably the *Zoological Report of the Expedition of HMS 'Beagle'* (5 vols., 1840) supported by a government grant of £1,000, with lithographic plates by Charles Joseph Hullmandel. During a visit to Hullmandel and Walter the younger George Smith met their clerk, W. S. **Williams, whom Smith engaged in 1845 as a literary adviser.

In April 1843 Smith, Elder published the first volume of **Ruskin's Modern Painters*, which in 1848 gave Charlotte new insights into art in general and J. W. M. Turner in particular. By courtesy of her publishers Charlotte saw and admired several other works by Ruskin, who was later to become dissatisfied with Smith, Elder. After 1878 he transferred his work wholly to George Allen.

Despite the appointment of managers, the firm lacked a consistent policy, and experienced more disaster than success until 1843, when the 19-year-old George **Smith took temporary control of the publishing side. His first venture was Richard H. **Horne's *A New Spirit of the Age*. The firm produced many works by Leigh **Hunt, some of them sent as gifts to Charlotte. After his father's death in August 1846, the younger George Smith took full responsibility. By 1848 he had discovered that Patrick Stewart had defrauded the firm of thousands of pounds, and after the retirement of Alexander Elder, Smith alone had to restore the firm to solvency. Despite the crisis, they completed Sir John Herschel's costly *Results of Astronomical Observations . . .* (1847), advertised along with *Jane Eyre* in their list for October 1847. Charlotte was 'glad and proud' to hear that Herschel had praised her novel. Smith, Elder's acceptance of *Jane Eyre*, published on 19 October 1847, was fortunate for both firm and author. Rapidly succeeding editions brought them profit, renown, and the prospect of lucrative future publications: *Shirley* (1849), Charlotte's edition of her sisters' works (1850) with its **'Biographical Notice', *Villette* (1853), Elizabeth **Gaskell's *Life* (3 edns., 1857), *The Professor* (1857), W. M. **Thackeray's 'Last Sketch', introducing Charlotte's fragment **Emma* in the **Cornhill Magazine* for

April 1860, sundry poems by the 'Bells' in the *Cornhill* thereafter, and good collected editions of the Brontës' works like the Haworth edition (1899, 1900). When Gaskell's *Life* brought the publisher into a 'hornet's nest' of threatened libel actions and controversy, Smith rather enjoyed the challenge, and was rewarded by large sales of the third edition and the huge number of copies of Charlotte's novels printed in 1857 and 1858. Charlotte's letters to members of the firm praise their shrewdness, scrupulous honesty, efficiency, and patience with her slow progress in writing *Villette*—for which, however, she considered herself underpaid. But she was grateful for their generous loans and gifts of books, for Smith's help with her investments, and (with some reservations) for his introductions to Thackeray and other literary lions.

Though Smith, Elder's lists included a fair number of now-forgotten books, they published works by, for example, Matthew **Arnold, the Brownings, George Eliot, Elizabeth Gaskell, **Tennyson, Thackeray, and Trollope. Their serialization of fiction in the *Cornhill*, founded in 1860, provided opportunities for both new and established authors, most of them paid with great generosity. George Eliot was initially offered £10,000 for serial publication of *Romola*. Other events in the firm's history were James **Taylor's failed attempt to establish a profitable branch, Smith, Taylor and Company, in Bombay between 1851 and 1856; the establishment of their own printing offices in London in 1855; the foundation of a new evening paper, the *Pall Mall Gazette*, in 1865; the separation of the publishing department under Smith at 15 Waterloo Place from the agency and banking business under H. S. King at Cornhill in 1868; and Smith's crowning achievement, the founding of the *Dictionary of National Biography* in 1882. During his son-in-law Reginald Smith's period of office from 1899, the firm gradually lost its earlier prestige, and was disposed of to John Murray in May 1917.

[Huxley, Leonard], *The House of Smith Elder* (1923).

Smith, Mrs Elizabeth, née Blakeway (?1831–1914), daughter of a London wine merchant, John Blakeway; wife of George **Smith, who met her at a ball in April 1853, loved her at first sight, and married her in February 1854. Elizabeth Gaskell described her as a 'very pretty, Paulina-like little wife' (see HOME, PAULINA MARY (POLLY)) (1856). Helen Allingham exhibited her portrait as *Spring Days* (1877), Alexander Munro sculpted a portrait bust, and she remained beautiful in old age. A gracious hostess, with literary taste, she supported Smith's business ventures and took a kindly interest in the tenants of his Whitechapel model dwellings. She edited *George Smith: A Memoir...* (1902), and helped to ensure the continuity of the *DNB*.

Smith, Mrs Elizabeth, née Murray (1797–1878), mother of George *Smith; the shrewd, vivacious model for Mrs Louisa *Bretton. Her resourcefulness, humour, and optimism sustained George in 1848, when he discovered that Patrick Stewart had cheated *Smith, Elder and Company of at least £30,000. A serene, kindly hostess to Charlotte Brontë in London, and a correspondent who elicited Charlotte's own sense of fun, she observed Charlotte keenly when she was in George's company, agreeing perhaps reluctantly to their meeting in Edinburgh. She approved of his engagement to Elizabeth Blakeway, hinting gently to Charlotte in November 1853 about his 'important step in life'.

Smith, George (1824–1901), publisher of Charlotte Brontë's novels; son of one of the founders of *Smith, Elder and Company, George Smith (1789–1846) and his wife Elizabeth, née Murray (1797–1878). Soon after his birth the family and firm moved to 65 Cornhill, London. Intelligent but unruly at school, George was taken into his father's office in 1838 and apprenticed to the third partner, Patrick Stewart, whose guardian was the head of Mackintosh and Company of Calcutta. Rapid expansion into exports and postal and banking arrangements with India and the Far East was to follow. The younger George Smith gained a thorough practical training in all aspects of the firm's trade. Their publication of the first volume of *Modern Painters* in 1843 began Smith's 30-year personal and professional connection with *Ruskin. He was soon given control of the publishing department, and began to improve the firm's profits by shrewd reorganization and the successful publication of Richard H. *Horne's *A New Spirit of the Age* and Leigh *Hunt's *Imagination and Fancy* (1844). Following his father's illness and death in 1846 he became responsible for both firm and family, and was delighted when, in 1847–8, the best-selling *Jane Eyre* increased both prestige and profits. Charlotte first met the young, handsome, energetic head of Smith, Elder in July 1848, when she and Anne made themselves known to their respective publishers. She admired Smith, but at first did not particularly like him: better understanding and warm friendship came later, after she stayed with the Smiths in December 1849. Her impressions of mother and son were later used in *Villette* in her portrayal of Dr John *Bretton and Mrs Louisa *Bretton. The breach between them came in 1853, when after a long silence on his part, Charlotte discovered that he was engaged to the beautiful Elizabeth Blakeway, whom he married in

February 1854. Smith later told Mrs Humphry Ward that he was never in love with Charlotte, for he could not have loved a woman without 'some charm or grace of person' (Gérin *CB*, p. 436 n. 2). Through his connection with Charlotte, Smith came to know Harriet *Martineau, Elizabeth *Gaskell, and W. M. *Thackeray, and published several of their works. Thackeray's daughter Anne recalled Smith's kind-hearted practical help to her and her sister after their father's sudden death.

Until 1853 Smith worked excessively long hours, for by 1848 he had discovered that Patrick Stewart, then in charge of the foreign department, had defrauded the firm of more than £30,000. Smith undertook to meet all the firm's liabilities, and by strict economy and unremitting labour, and with the support of his mother, finally did so. New branches were established in Bombay, Java, and West Africa, and exports included surveying instruments and electric telegraph plant. In 1853, when the pressure of work was affecting Smith's health, Henry Samuel King joined the firm as a partner. In 1855 Smith, Elder took over the printing firm of Stewart and Murray, who had printed the early editions of Charlotte's works, and until 1872 printed many of their own books, magazines, and newspapers, including the *Overland Mail* and *Homeward Mail*, supplying home news for readers in India and Indian news for readers in Britain. The dislocation of the firm's Indian business caused by the Indian Mutiny of 1857 and the transference of the government of India to the crown in 1858 caused Smith to diversify his trading operations. At home his payments to contributors to his *Cornhill Magazine*, founded in January 1860, were both generous and shrewd, for they secured the services of famous writers and artists, many of whom were entertained at the Smiths' Friday dinners in Oak Hill Lodge, Hampstead. On 7 February 1865 the first number of Smith's evening newspaper the *Pall Mall Gazette* appeared. After a slow start, its circulation improved, and by 1868 it was a profitable success. He remained in charge of the firm's publishing department, which was transferred to 15 Waterloo Place in January 1869, detached from the Cornhill agency and banking business, and in 1872 inaugurated a department of medical literature. From 1870 to 1879 he was also a partner in a shipping firm, and in 1873 formed a company to import Apollinaris water—a business profitably disposed of in 1897 after yielding an immense income. Smith's typescript 'Recollections', in the National Library of Scotland, include unflattering remarks about Charlotte's vanity, not printed in his articles about her in the *Cornhill Magazine*. Smith's greatest achievement was the creation of the *DNB*, undertaken not for profit but as a contribution to literature and in the public

George Smith as a young man.

interest. From 1882 to 1900, under the editorship of Leslie Stephen until 1891, and of Sidney Lee thereafter, the 60 quarterly volumes were punctually produced, earning well-deserved praise for all concerned. The honorary degree of MA was conferred on Smith by the University of Oxford in 1895. In January 1901 he underwent an operation, did not regain strength, and died in April at Byfleet near Weybridge.

Lee, Sir Sidney, Memoir in *DNB* (suppl.), vol. xxii, pp. [xi]–xlix.

Smith, Revd James William (b. ?1815), Revd Patrick Brontë's curate March 1843–October 1844; model for Revd Peter Augustus *Malone; possibly the James Smith admitted to Trinity College Dublin 1832, BA 1837, MA 1840. He took occasional services at Haworth after moving to Keighley in 1844. His curacy at Eastwood, Keighley, was confirmed in February 1846. Ellen Nussey alleged he drank to excess with Mr Brontë. Charlotte thought him fickle, mercenary, and dishonest, because by February 1848 he had absconded, misappropriated £5 given for charity, and left other debts. He may have been drowned at sea, or have emigrated to Canada. Revd J. C. *Bradley defended his character.

Smith, John Stores (1828–?93), author of *Mirabeau: A Life History* (2 vols., 1848) and *Social Aspects* (1850), both sent to Charlotte Brontë. He was born in Hulme, Manchester; educated at Manchester Grammar School; and was managing director of Sheepbridge Coal and Iron Company, Derbys. He admired and aped the style of Carlyle. Charlotte appreciated his talent, but decried his Carlylese and exoneration of Mirabeau's vices. He travelled from Halifax in September 1850 to see her, and admired the 'strange lustre and intensity' of her eyes. He recalled Revd Patrick Brontë as erect and handsome, though (Smith falsely alleged) 'quite blind'.

Smith, John Stores, 'A Day with Charlotte Brontë', in Shorter, C. K., *The Brontës: Life and Letters* (1908) app. 6.

Smith family (relatives of George Smith). George Smith sen. (1789–1846), a Scotsman, was co-founder with Alexander Elder of Smith and Elder, booksellers and stationers, 158 Fenchurch Street, London, in October 1816. The firm, later *'Smith, Elder and Company', expanded immensely after George *Smith jun. (1824–1901) took over major responsibility from August 1846. His siblings were Eliza (?1823–80), who accompanied her brothers and Charlotte Brontë in Edinburgh in July 1850; Sarah (b. ?1831), who died of TB in or before 1865; Alexander ('Alick', b. ?1835), described as a 'Bookseller' in the 1851 Census, who

went to Bombay, presumably to work for the Indian branch of the firm, in summer 1852; and Isabella, (b. ?1838), described by Charlotte on 17 December 1849 as 'good, quiet, studious little Bell' (Smith *Letters*, 2. 307). Largely in Isabella's interest, George Smith erected a block of model dwellings for the poor in George Yard, Whitechapel, in 1880.

George Smith jun.'s sons were George Murray Smith, who married in 1885 Ellen, daughter of Edward Strutt (1st Lord Belper, 1801–80); and Alexander, partner in the firm 1890–9, who married in 1893 Emily Tennyson Bradley, daughter of Dr George Granville Bradley, Dean of Westminster. His eldest daughter, Elizabeth Alexandrina Murray Smith, married in 1878 Henry Yates Thompson (1838–1928), book and manuscript collector. She lent original letters from Charlotte to Wise & Symington for their edition; as also did his third daughter, who married in 1893 Reginald J. Smith KC, partner in the firm 1894 until his death in 1916. George Smith's second daughter was Ethel Murray Smith.

Mrs Elizabeth Seton-Gordon, George Smith's granddaughter, gave a collection of Charlotte's letters and other documents to the BPM in 1974; she bequeathed the remainder of her Brontëana (received in 1986) to the BPM, and many of Smith's papers, including documents relating to the *Cornhill Magazine*, to the National Library of Scotland.

Sneaky (Sneakie, Sneachi, Sneachie), Alexander, King of Sneaky's Land; one of the four kings of the *Glass Town Federation. One of the original *Twelves of the Young Men's Play, Sneaky replaces *Napoleon as Branwell's chief man and Napoleon retires to Frenchyland. Throughout the *Glass Town and Angrian saga, Sneaky is the close associate of the Duke of *Wellington, reflecting Branwell and Charlotte's partnership. A tall old gentleman of 60, with piercing grey eyes, Sneaky is characterized by his dour 'Scots' heritage. His residence in Sneaky's Glasstown is the Palace of St Mary, and he owns Elimbos Palace on the upper reaches of the Niger in Fidena. His eldest son the Duke of *Fidena has his father's upright moral character but the early dissipation of the youngest, General *Thornton, led to his disowning him. Sneaky's two daughters, Edith and Maria, are proud beauties of the Duke of Zamorna's set.

Sneaky (Sneakie, Sneachie), Lady Edith, Princess Royal, daughter of Alexander Sneaky, King of Sneaky's Land, and sister of Fidena, Maria, and Thornton, in the *Glass Town and Angrian saga. The tall and stately Edith marries Lord Frederic *Lofty, Earl of Arundel; and like her sister is passionately devoted to the Duke of Zamorna and Angria.

Sneaky (Sneakie, Sneachie), John Augustus, Jun. Marquis of Rosendale (Rossendale), eldest son of the Duke and Duchess of *Fidena and godson of the Duke of Zamorna, in the *Glass Town and Angrian saga. A detailed description of his appearance and character at 6 years old occurs in 'A Brace of Characters' (Alexander *EEW*, 2(2). 327–40).

Sneaky (Sneakie, Sneachie), Prince John Augustus. See FIDENA, PRINCE JOHN AUGUSTUS SNEAKY, DUKE OF.

Sneaky (Sneakie, Sneachie), Lady Maria, daughter of Alexander Sneaky, King of Sneaky's Land, and sister of Fidena, Edith, and Thornton, in the *Glass Town and Angrian saga. A tall dark beauty, known for her wit, coquetry, and haughty manner. After flirting with the Duke of Zamorna for some years, she marries the equally strong-willed Edward *Percy, the disowned eldest son of the Duke of Northangerland and an industrialist who becomes the Angrian minister of trade.

Sneaky (Sneakie, Sneachie), General Thornton Wilkin (or Wilson). See THORNTON, THORNTON WILKIN SNEAKY, GENERAL.

Sneaky's Land (Sneakysland, Sneachiesland), one of the four kingdoms of the *Glass Town Federation, ruled by Alexander *Sneaky. His son, the Duke of *Fidena, is named after the capital city of *Fidena. In the early *Glass Town and Angrian saga, Rogue (Duke of *Northangerland) leads a rebellion in Sneaky's Land, captures and burns Fidena, but is eventually defeated by Sneaky and his son, with help from the forces of Parry, Stumps, and the Duke of Wellington.

Snowe, Lucy. In *Villette* Lucy looks back on and interprets her life and relationships. The tensions resulting from her roles as narrator, observer, and participant create a powerful psychological drama, and the conflicting, inadequate interpretations of Lucy by other characters sharpen her self-knowledge. To Dr John Graham *Bretton she is a being 'inoffensive as a shadow' but to M. Paul *Emanuel she seems too 'fiery' and 'coloury', unamenable to control. It is this fire which convinces him, and Lucy, of their real affinity. But the reader does not readily identify with her. Whereas Jane Eyre is seen from the beginning as fiery and spirited, Lucy introduces herself in the peaceful surroundings of Mrs Louisa *Bretton's house, where she observes the Brettons dispassionately, and at first detaches herself from the disturbing emotions introduced by Paulina *Home's arrival. The child's misery has to become extreme before it arouses Lucy to active sympathy. This pattern of cool observation and control yielding to warmth and expression recurs. Yet expression is also constantly frustrated, either by Lucy's exertion of reason, or by overmastering circumstances. In a letter to W. S. *Williams of 6 November 1852 Charlotte wrote: 'A *cold* name [Lucy Snowe] must have; partly, perhaps, on the *lucus a non lucendo* principle—partly on that of the "fitness of things," for she has about her an external coldness' (Wise & Symington, 4. 18). Thus Lucy acquiesces in her limited life with Miss *Marchmont: 'I would have crawled on with her for twenty years . . . I must be goaded, driven, stung, forced to energy' (ch. 4). Lucy 'clings' to Miss Marchmont, only to be thrown once again into the world by her death. At the pensionnat Lucy remains detached until M. Paul compels her to act in the 'vaudeville': 'A keen relish for dramatic expression had revealed itself as part of my nature . . . it would not do for a mere looker-on at life' (ch. 14)—and so Lucy locks up her longing. During the long vacation, crushed by a 'deadly paralysis' she pours out her 'long pent-up pain' in confession, and is solaced. The indirect result is renewed contact with the Brettons, and the gradual growth of a new strong feeling for Graham. The pattern recurs in the letters she writes to him: first a letter warm with feeling, which she puts aside, then one dictated by Reason, which she sends. Graham's fascination with Paulina leads to Lucy's symbolic burial of his letters. It remains for M. Paul to kindle Lucy's inner fire. Before she knows him well she sees him as a 'spy', intruding on her grief after she returns from her stay with the Brettons; but he is perceptive, seeing her as an 'untamed' creature 'viewing with a mixture of fire and fear the first entrance of the breaker-in' (ch. 21). His persevering attempts to draw her into conversation fail, but cause her to weep—the expression of feeling that she needs. It is the beginning of their mutual understanding: jealousy, irascibility, and imperiousness on his part rouse Lucy to indignant or amused response, but his real kindness and magnanimity win her love. The climax comes when Lucy's jealousy of Justine Marie impels her to an outburst which convinces Paul of that love. The final check—his death at sea—is inevitable, given the pattern of Lucy's experience: for her there will be no fruition.

Sofala (Soffala), one of the Duke of *Zamorna's many early mistresses who proliferate as the *Glass Town and Angrian saga progresses. She appears to have been a 'Negress' or 'Moorish lady', who was forsaken by the 18-year-old Douro (Duke of Zamorna) on the shores of Hemiad and buried in the desert. She prays that her son may shame his false father: he is the hideous dwarf *Finic, who is Zamorna's mysterious servant. Sofala's brother Stungaron unsuccessfully tries to murder Zamorna.

Something about Arthur, 'Written by Charles Albert Florian Wellesley' (1 May 1833), is, as the title suggests, a tale designed by Charlotte Brontë's favourite narrator to expose his older brother's vices (MS in Ransom HRC, Texas). Arthur Wellesley, Marquis of Douro (later Duke of *Zamorna), is no longer the perfect Glass Town hero: he now displays a ruthless pursuit of ambition and a petulant stubbornness, and indulges in his first love affair.

Following the example of Sir Walter *Scott, the tale begins with a moral maxim admonishing those who associate with the lower orders of society. Thus Lord Charles frames his story with an account of his own penitent return 'like the Repentant Prodigal to my father's house' after a voluntary six-month exile on the streets of *Glass Town. He is provoked by the hostile attitude of his tutor to his truancy into recalling his older brother's similar association with vice. The 15-year-old Douro had been persuaded by the Baron of *Caversham to enter his stallion Thunderbolt in the grand Verdopolitan horse race; but meanwhile Caversham had bribed the jockey to guarantee that the horse did not win. Mortified by what he sees as his dishonour in losing, Douro shoots his horse and plans revenge on Caversham. With the help of Sergeant Edward (Ned) *Laury he leads a band of *'Rare Lads' on a silent march to burn Caversham's mill—prefiguring the mill attack in *Shirley*, based on the *Luddite riots (Alexander *EEW*, 2(1). 26). Douro is wounded but nursed back to health by Mina *Laury, who makes her first appearance here in the juvenilia. Their ensuing romance is interrupted by the Duke of *Wellington, but the peasant girl Mina remains the oldest and most faithful of Douro's mistresses.

Alexander *EEW*, 2(1), 7–40.
Alexander, Christine (ed.), *Something about Arthur, by Charlotte Brontë* (1981).

Sophie, Mlle, the most likeable of the three teachers at the Pensionnat *Heger; probably an old maid of 'no particular character'. Perhaps her own honesty is implied in her intense dislike of the 'heartless, insincere, and vindictive' Mlle Blanche (Charlotte to Ellen Nussey, May 1842; in Smith *Letters*, 1. 284). Though Charlotte did not make an intimate friend of Mlle Sophie, she was consistently friendly enough for Sophie to write an affectionate, elaborately polite note to her 'bonne Charlotte' on 17 December 1843 accompanying the farewell gift of a little box 'en souvenir de moi' and assuring her that more than one person would be thinking of her.

Soult, Alexander (Young Soult the Rhymer), Marquis of Marseilles, Duke of Dalmatia, a pseudonym of Branwell Brontë in the early juvenilia. Known as 'Young Soult the Rhymer' or 'Henry Rhymer', his extravagant enthusiasm is satirized by Lord Charles *Wellesley in 'The *Poetaster', but despite his unconventional, 'harebrained' manner he becomes a celebrated poet, patronized by the Duke of *Zamorna and later made Angrian ambassador to Verdopolis. Soult originates from the *Young Men's Play, where he is the son of Napoleon's general, Marshal Soult. Zamorna (as Douro) and Lord Charles Wellesley rescue him from a destitute position in a French tavern where he is trying to live as a poet. In Verdopolis he lives at *Waterloo Palace and finds fame and fortune. The historical Marshal Soult was Wellington's opponent in the *Peninsular War and again at Waterloo, under *Napoleon.

Southern College. See PALACE OF INSTRUCTION.

Southey, Robert (1774–1843), biographer, essayist, editor, poet; Poet Laureate from 1813. The young Brontës admired Southey and echoed him in their juvenilia. Charlotte recommended the 'greater part' of his poetry and his *Life of Nelson* (1813) to Ellen *Nussey on 4 July 1834 (Smith *Letters*, 1. 130). On 29 December 1836 Charlotte solicited Southey's opinion of her poetry (in a letter, not extant, which he characterized as 'flighty' to Caroline Bowles, 27 March 1837 (Smith *Letters*, 1. 171)). Southey's 12 March 1837 reply (which quoted some of her extravagant praise of him) acknowledged that she had 'the faculty of Verse' but warned her to write for personal benefit rather than professional ambition: 'Literature cannot be the business of a woman's life: & it ought not to be. The more she is engaged in her proper duties, the less leisure will she have for it, even as an accomplishment & a recreation' (Smith *Letters*, 1. 166). She responded on 16 March, 'I trust I shall never more feel ambitious to see my name in print; if the wish should rise, I'll look at Southey's letter, and suppress it', and on the wrapper of his approving reply (22 March) she wrote, 'Southey's Advice To be kept for ever' (Smith *Letters*, 1. 170). Years later Charlotte described Southey's admonitory letter as 'kind and admirable'; though 'a little stringent . . . it did me good' (Gaskell *Life*, 1. 172). Reading his biography and letters, she praised his domestic devotion and unworldliness (to W. S. Williams, 12 Apr. 1850; Smith *Letters*, 2. 382–3).   BT

Storey, Mark, *Robert Southey: A Life* (1997).

Sowerby Bridge, a populous village *c*.3 miles west of *Halifax, with iron foundries, chemical works, textile and corn mills, in the Calder valley. From 31 August 1840 until 31 March 1841 Branwell Brontë was assistant clerk-in-charge at Sowerby Bridge railway station on the Leeds and Manchester railway, of which the Hebden Bridge–Normanton section opened on 5 October 1840. Barker (p. 347) notes an unreliable local tradition that he lodged in the Pear Tree Inn, then no more than a beerhouse, in Sowerby street. Rail traffic increased from six to 24 trains per day by 1 March 1841, but Branwell had time to visit and make friends in Halifax.

Spell, An Extravaganza, The, 'By Lord Charles Albert Florian Wellesley' (Charlotte Brontë) (21 June 1834; MS in BL); novella in the *Glass Town and Angrian saga, 'fabricated' by the narrator in revenge against his elder brother in order to expose the Duke of *Zamorna's 'hypocritical, close, dark, secret, half-insane character'. Charlotte employs the motif of the doppelgänger to explore the increasingly complicated personality of Zamorna. She creates a twin brother, Ernest, to account for his multiple interests and relationships, including an early marriage to Lady Helen Victorine, Baroness *Gordon, the mother of 'Fitzarthur' (Ernest Edward Gordon *Wellesley) whose relationship to Zamorna has been hinted at in a number of earlier stories. In *The Spell*, Zamorna's twin brother is married to a Scottish woman resembling *Mary Queen of Scots (Mary Stuart). This couple live in secret since a spell was placed on the twins at birth, dictating the death of one of them if they are ever seen together. Zamorna's new wife Mary *Percy becomes jealous of this Scottish woman whom she believes to be a mistress of Zamorna and mother of his son Ernest. The plot involves the twins' ingenious efforts to keep their lives separate, but Mary's curiosity causes the secret to be revealed, bringing Zamorna to the brink of death.

The subtitle suggests that Charlotte may have intended *The Spell* to be a burlesque of Romanticism. She was conscious of the wildness, the Gothic elements, and supernatural fantasy of the composition; and the note at the end (signed 'C Brontë' rather than by her narrator) shows her struggling to explain the complexity of character. The motto underlines this search for interpretation: 'I give you the raw material, Words; to your own ingenuity I leave the eliciting of the manufactured article, Sense'. Despite the melodramatic material, Charlotte is critical about the shape of both content and form of this story, as Lord Charles cynically suggests when he ends his 'novel' with the requisite marriage. See also BYRON, LORD.

Alexander *EEW*, 2(2). 149–238.

MacLean, George Edwin (ed.), *The Spell: An Extravaganza. An Unpublished Novel by Charlotte Brontë* (1931).

Staël, Anne Louise Germaine Necker, Mme de (Baroness of Staël-Holstein) (1766–1817), referred to by *Byron as the greatest mind of her times; a noted intellectual and writer who received, in her Paris salon on the eve of the Revolution, the most progressive elements in French society. She emigrated to England in 1793 where she was surrounded by *Talleyrand and other French *émigrés*, returned to Paris 1795, and was exiled by *Napoleon Buonaparte, first from Paris and then from France, partly because of her friendship with men like Bernadotte (see PARIS (IN FRENCHYLAND)). She was again exiled in London, where the publication of *De l'Allemagne* (1810), on Germany and Romanticism, made her especially popular. She first met the Duke of *Wellington, whom she regarded as a heroic liberator, in 1814 in her reconstituted Parisian salon (he was then ambassador to the reinstated French court of Louis XVIII), and they subsequently became friends and correspondents. Charlotte Brontë often refers to Lady Zenobia *Ellrington as the Verdopolitan de Staël; and probably read at least de Staël's famous romance *Corinne* (1807), among the French novels she borrowed from the *Taylor family of Gomersal.

Stanbury, a farming hamlet just over 1 mile west of Haworth, on raised ground within the deep Aire valley. In the Manor House, dating from 1753, lived Stephen Taylor and his sons (see TAYLOR FAMILY OF STANBURY), all of them trustees of Haworth church when Revd Patrick Brontë was appointed. The old Haworth three-decker pulpit, still stored in the Manor barn in 1915, has been re-erected in Stanbury church. Revd A. B. *Nicholls, who had pastoral responsibility for Stanbury, obtained charity funds to build a schoolroom there, opened in September 1848, which could be used as a chapel-of-ease on Sundays.

Stancliffe's Hotel, in Thornton Street, city of Zamorna, Angria; named after the Angrian family name of the Duke of Arundel. Opposite the Court House, the hotel is Zamorna's premier inn and Mrs Stancliffe is known for her regal catering. It is the setting for the opening of Charlotte Brontë's novelette of the same name.

Stancliffe's Hotel, beginning 'Amen! Such was the sound. . .' (28 June 1838), an untitled Angrian novelette written by Charlotte Brontë in minuscule script on 34 loose sheets of paper (MS in BPM); the name was first used by Christine Alexander in *EW*, p. 171. The story is typical of Charlotte's episodic writing at this time, crowded with

Staningley Hall

characters and scenes that give us a panoramic view of Angria life. *Stancliffe's Hotel* is important in the *Glass Town and Angrian saga for its description of Lord Macara *Lofty's opium addiction, for the introduction of the heroine Jane *Moore, for Charlotte's changing attitude to the Duke of *Zamorna in both his public and private roles, and for the presentation of the city of Zamorna as a thriving industrial town. Although ostensibly in Africa, Charlotte's settings and background events are now based on a more realistic portrayal of the commerce and politics of England in the 1830s (Alexander *EW*, p. 177). The narrator Charles Townshend (see WELLESLEY, LORD CHARLES ALBERT FLORIAN), a self-opinionated young dandy of 20, plays an active part in his picaresque tale as he takes the reader on a journey through the new kingdom of Angria.

The opening episode involves a comic satire on *Methodism, as Charles reports on a visit to Ebenezer Chapel in Verdopolis. The remainder of the story centres on Stancliffe's Hotel in the province and city of *Zamorna, in Angria. Here Charles stays and meets his old friend Captain Sir William *Percy, who has distinguished himself in the recent Angrian war and who now describes his relations with the various Angrian powerbrokers, members of Zamorna's coterie. It is in this story that the similarity between Percy and Townshend is emphasized: the first hint of their later conflation as narrators culminating in William *Crimsworth in *The Professor* (Alexander *EW*, p. 174). The two young fops visit the Angrian beauty Jane Moore but are repulsed by her (she has her sights set on General Lord Edward *Hartford). Zamorna has again been staying with his old enemy Northangerland, hated by the Angrian population. His arrival in Zamorna city provokes protest from 'mad mechanics and desperate operatives' (see LUDDITE RIOTS) and a riot ensues when Lord Castlereagh is ordered to disperse them with cavalry in a charge that resembles the *Peterloo Massacre (Alexander *EW*, pp. 177–8).

Alexander, *EW*, pp. 171–8.
The Times, 14 Mar. 2003.

Staningley Hall, the stately home of Helen *Huntingdon before her marriage in *Tenant*, owned by her uncle, Mr *Maxwell. On his death, she inherits the property, and after her marriage to Gilbert Markham, the couple choose to live at Staningley, together with Helen's son and Aunt Maxwell.

'Stanzas'. See 'OFTEN REBUKED, YET ALWAYS BACK RETURNING'.

Steaton (Steighton), Timothy, an obsequious evangelical clerk in the *Glass Town and Angrian saga, who reappears as Timothy *Steighton in *The Professor*. Son of the Duke of Northangerland's steward who manages 'things' for him (such as the murder of Henry *Percy), Timothy repeats his father's relationship with his master and follows the fortunes of Northangerland's sons, Edward and William Percy, as they work first in the woolcombing industry and then in a counting-house.

Steighton, Timothy, in *The Professor*. Edward *Crimsworth's senior clerk is about 35, has a sly, heavy face, and resembles Timothy *Steaton in the Angrian *Passing Events and Tim Steele in 'John Henry'. A Methodist, but an 'engrained rascal', he is Edward's spy on William *Crimsworth, whose alleged piety baffles him.

Stilbro', the large manufacturing town in *Shirley* lying to the east of *Briarfield, across Stilbro' Moor. It is to Stilbro' that Robert Gérard *Moore sends for two wagonloads of frames and shears for his mill. The frame-breaker Moses *Barraclough is sent to Stilbro' gaol for his part in the destruction of Moore's frames in 'the battle of Stilbro' Moor'. It is on the Stilbro' road that Robert Moore is shot by his would-be assassin Michael *Hartley, as he is returning to Briarfield after a dinner at the George Inn in Stilbro'. Given that the furnaces of Stilbro's ironworks cast a glimmer visible to the east of Briarfield (*Shirley*, ch. 2), it would appear that Charlotte's model for Stilbro' was the industrial town of Leeds, lying 6 or 7 miles to the east of Birstall (Briarfield). The *Stilbro' Courier* newspaper may have been suggested by the *Leeds Mercury*, the local paper read by the Brontë family, whose back files provided Charlotte Brontë with much of the historical material she used in *Shirley*. However, F. B. Pinion (*A Brontë Companion*, 1976) argues that Stilbro' must be *Huddersfield, noting that William Cartwright, the model for Robert Moore, was shot at as he was returning to *Rawfolds Mill from Huddersfield, which lies several miles to the south-west of Birstall. Pinion adds that 'Huddersfield had its Cloth (or Piece) Hall, and the George Inn was an important coach station' (p. 327). He attributes the apparent inconsistencies in the location of Stilbro' to Charlotte's wish to conceal Huddersfield's identity, though he does not explain why she should take such a step. It is more likely that Stilbro' is simply an amalgam of features taken from both Leeds and Huddersfield, adapted for the purposes of the novel. HR

Stonegappe, a substantial three-storey house set on a hillside in Lothersdale, near Skipton, Yorks., with panoramic views towards the River Aire. Charlotte Brontë took a temporary post there as governess from May to July 1839 in the family of

John Benson *Sidgwick and his wife Sarah Hannah *Sidgwick, née Greenwood. Charlotte thought the countryside and the grounds 'divine', but, preoccupied with her unruly pupils, she could not enjoy the beauty of the pleasant woods, winding white paths, and green lawns. Surrounded by strange faces, like Jane *Eyre at *Thornfield Hall, she felt shy, and found it dreary to look on and listen.

'Strange Events'. See 'YOUNG MEN'S MAGAZINE'.

Strathfieldsay, English country estate of the Duke of *Wellington in the *Islanders' Play; modelled on the historical Duke's estate of Stratfield Saye in Hampshire, England. In the *Glass Town and Angrian saga, Lord Charles Wellesley creates a similar estate for the Duke, Strathelleraye, in his 'fictitious' story *'Albion and Marina'.

structuralist approaches. Broadly defined, structuralism is a way of explaining how the human mind makes reality knowable. Structuralists contend that individual phenomena do not have inherent meaning and that reality is not understood in a piecemeal fashion; rather, the mind knows by organizing individual phenomena in structural relationships to one another. Thus, known reality is structured phenomena: the world organized by an abstract system which anthropologist Claude Levi-Strauss (b. 1908) called the mind's 'logic of the concrete'. Levi-Strauss studied various cultural phenomena, including myths, as the manifestations of this structuring process of the mind, showing how the recurring patterns in myth can be traced back to an underlying, two-part structure that makes meaning through contrast: good–evil, sun–moon, male–female, and so on. Linguist Ferdinand de Saussure (1857–1913) similarly defined language (*langue*)—as opposed to individual utterances of speech (*parole*)—as the structure (or grammar) by which discrete, inherently meaningless elements (phonemes, words, and so on) are organized to produce meaning. The ideas of Saussure and Levi-Strauss, the founding figures of structuralism, have had inestimable impact on the study of literature, and in varying degrees they inform every critical approach discussed in this Companion.

With respect to literary criticism, structuralism produced a reaction against older methods of analysis such as philology, which took a historical, arguably atomistic approach to the study of literature. Instead, structuralism encouraged the development of analytic methods that were synchronic and that focused on the structural elements of literary texts. Overlapping with various schools of formalism and with the American school of the New Criticism (both are sometimes subsumed under the broader designation of structuralism), structuralism drew critical attention to the ways in which a text's formal features—for example, its image patterns or its deployment of characters or its narrative perspective—provide its underlying structure and *modus operandi*. Specialized fields such as narratology (the systematic study of the structures and codes by which narratives function) grew out of this broader approach and began to influence critical readings of the Brontës' writings by about the middle of the 20th century. The 1960s are the high-water mark for such criticism, and, in its various ramifications (reader-response criticism and deconstruction, for example), structuralism continued to influence critical work on the Brontës throughout the eighties and nineties.

Lord David Cecil's seminal essay on *Wuthering Heights* is essentially a structuralist reading of the novel since it claims that Emily understood the cosmos as conforming to an underlying dual structure of complementary forces, 'the principle of storm' and 'the principle of calm' ('Emily Brontë and *Wuthering Heights*', in McNees, 2. 105), and that virtually all the elements of her story—characters, settings, image patterns, even the division of the novel into two parts—can be analysed according to that structural scheme. Several similar readings of *Wuthering Heights* followed in the 1950s, most notably Dorothy Van Ghent's 'The Window Figure and the Two Children Figure in *Wuthering Heights*' (*Nineteenth-Century Fiction*, 7 (1952), 189–97). The 1950s also saw the publication of numerous essays, including articles in *Nineteenth-Century Fiction* by John K. Mathison ('Nelly Dean and the Power of *Wuthering Heights*', 11 (1956), 102–29); Carl R. Woodring ('The Narrators of *Wuthering Heights*', 11 (1957), 298–305), and James Hafley ('The Villain in *Wuthering Heights*', 13 (1958), 199–215) on the narrative method of *Wuthering Heights* (the function of the narrative frames and the two narrators), a perennially productive line of criticism that led to later readings which variously describe the novel's 'ambiguity', 'indeterminacy', and 'writerly-ness' (see DECONSTRUCTIONIST APPROACHES). In 1969 Elisabeth Van de Laar published her comprehensive study of *The Inner Structure of 'Wuthering Heights'* which combined structuralist analysis with psychoanalytic theory to show that the novel is structured by a system of connected images which function in relation to each other just as related elements in a dream operate together (see PSYCHOANALYTIC APPROACHES).

Charlotte's novels were initially less attractive to structuralist critics than Emily's, in part because Cecil had dismissed Charlotte's work as formless in the same book in which he celebrated the artistic unity of *Wuthering Heights*. But the 1960s saw the publication of numerous articles and several books which show how Charlotte's stories are also susceptible to this kind of analysis. Three books were especially influential in demonstrating the artistry of her work: Robert Martin's *The Accents of Persuasion* (1966), Earl Knies's *The Art of Charlotte Brontë* (1969), and Wendy Craik's *The Brontë Novels* (1968), the last being one of the few critical works to consider Anne's novels seriously on their own terms. Like the many interpretations of *Wuthering Heights* that built upon Cecil's early analysis, numerous readings of Charlotte's novels in the sixties traced patterns of contrasting images that make up the aesthetic fabric of her stories. *Jane Eyre*, for instance, was repeatedly shown to be organized through multiple oppositional pairs that represent the central character's conflicted affective experience: fire–water, red–white, Rochester–St John, the Reeds–the Rivers, Helen–Bertha, and so on. Articles by Eric Solomon ('*Jane Eyre*: Fire and Water', *College English*, 25 (Dec. 1963), 215–17), Donald Ericksen ('Imagery as Structure in *Jane Eyre*', *Victorian Newsletter*, 30 (Fall 1966), 18–22), and David Lodge ('Fire and Eyre: Charlotte Brontë's War of Earthly Elements', in *The Language of Fiction* (1966), 114–43) are representative. In 1978, Cynthia A. Linder's *Romantic Imagery in the Novels of Charlotte Brontë* demonstrated that the patterns of imagery that structure Charlotte's novels derive from the structure of Romantic ideology. The importance of Linder's work with respect to structuralist thought lies not so much in her identification of specific images that appear in both Charlotte's novels and in the works of her Romantic predecessors, but rather in her argument that these image patterns originate from the structure of Romantic thought itself. In this way, Linder's work is similar to Terry Eagleton's 1975 Marxist study of the Brontës, a book that is otherwise quite different. Eagleton claims that the 'categorical structures' of the Brontës' fiction—and of the writers' imaginative consciousnesses as well—derived from the 'tensions and alliances between the two social classes which dominated [their] world: the industrial bourgeoisie, and the landed gentry or aristocracy' (*Myths of Power: A Marxist Study of the Brontës* (1975), 4); in other words, the aesthetic structure that underlies their novels is ideologically rooted in the socio-economic situation of their time and situation. As the example of Eagleton's book illustrates, structuralist analyses need not necessarily focus exclusively (or even primarily) on literary devices when identifying the formal features that structure a work; nor do they necessarily maintain a highly text-focused perspective in their criticism.

Indeed, criticism that relates a text's structure to a more comprehensive extra-textual structure—such as the author's or a group's consciousness, or a particular ideology, or a particular genre, or the entire framework of all literary texts considered as a self-contained system (or structure)—is, arguably, more in the spirit of structuralist thought than the more narrowly focused, single-text-oriented interpretations that dominated literary criticism in the sixties and seventies.

As with *Wuthering Heights*, structuralist approaches to Charlotte's novels (and, in a few notable instances, Anne's) produced many readings focusing on narrative method; for *Villette* especially, such analyses eventually led in the eighties and nineties to interpretations that argue for the thematic centrality of the question of interpretation itself. See DECONSTRUCTIONIST APPROACHES. Jerome Beaty is one of the few Brontë critics who have continued to develop analyses that are in line with structuralism, that take into account the theoretical and methodological problems raised by (and within) structuralism, and yet do not ultimately accept the conclusions that latter-day structuralists (that is, deconstructionists) logically draw. Building on Bakhtinian ideas about narrative's polyphonic nature, on the work of reader-response narratologists such as Wolfgang Iser, on notions of intertextuality, and on the temporal formalism of Meir Sternberg, Beaty's *Misreading 'Jane Eyre': A Postformalist Paradigm* (1996) discusses Charlotte's novel in a way that freshly illuminates not only the text itself but also its position within 'intraliterary history' (the texts that predate and were contemporary with *Jane Eyre*) and 'extraliterary history' (in relation to, for instance, contemporary debates about the role of the governess in early Victorian England). Moreover, Beaty shows how a highly text-oriented reading of the novel, far from effacing those extra-textual issues, in fact necessarily deflects the act of reading from its textual orientation toward those relevant extra-textual arenas of knowledge and experience.

CB

Beaty, Jerome, *Misreading 'Jane Eyre': A Postformalist Paradigm* (1996).

Stuartville, the Angrian country seat of Viscount *Castlereagh and Lady *Castlereagh near *Edwardston, in the province of Zamorna, Angria, in the *Glass Town and Angrian saga.

Stumps' Island (Isle), later referred to as Stumpzland, off the coast of Glass Town, near *Monkey's Island; founded by the veteran Stumps, one of the original *Twelves. Both islands are a popular resort with the older inhabitants of Verdopolis; the Duke of *Northangerland retreats to the seclusion of Stumps' Island to plan his Angrian coup. The capital is Frederic's Town.

stylistic analysis and criticism. Stylistics is a systematic and objective study of texts which adapts the methods and principles of linguistics to the analysis of literature. Stylistics developed out of the much older discipline of rhetoric, evolving hand-in-hand in the mid-20th century with other approaches that emphasize the analysis of formal elements in literary texts like those of the Brontës: formalism, New Criticism, structuralism, semiotics, and poetics. Stylistics typically does not produce an interpretation of the text, as the New Criticism does; rather, like formalism and structuralism, stylistic criticism is centrally concerned with the modes of signification that texts employ. In stylistics, this entails the taxonomic study of the significant linguistic features by which the text operates; stylistic analysis of a particular work will examine features such as diction, imagery, sound, syntax, rhythm, metaphors, and other figures, identifying and classifying them in a systematic fashion derived from the theories and concepts of modern linguistics.

A broader application of stylistics that is quite common in literary studies is the examination of a writer's entire oeuvre (or a significant portion of it) in order to identify the particular linguistic features and literary devices which constitute his or her distinctive style; this approach may also be used to explain how a writer's style is related to his or her sensibility, world view, or consciousness. Stylistic analysis has also been applied more broadly to groups of writers or bodies of literature which are shown to have sets of linguistic features in common and thus can be said to share a generic style. In this way, stylistics may identify the style of, say, a particular national literature, or that of literary texts written in a particular period of time, or of authors united by a specific sense of the purpose of their writing in relation to their readers (John Holloway's *The Victorian Sage: Studies in Argument* (1953) is a good example of the latter).

Under the impact of deconstruction and other Continental theories, and in face of the growing need to understand literature in its cultural contexts, stylistics has developed in the last two decades in ways that mirror the development of literary criticism as a whole. As structuralism evolved, stylistics developed in conjunction with narratology, or narrative poetics, and came to share its concern with the reader's role in the processes of signification. Out of this interest came the sub-field of pragmatics, the study of styles of reading response which develops its analytic methods and goals from those of its parent discipline and

which is allied to the speech act theory of J. L. Austin (1911–60) and his followers. The term stylistics is less often used in literary studies today than it was twenty years ago, and the lengthy taxonomic studies like those common in the 1970s are less commonly seen today. But many contemporary critics continue to make use of stylistic analyses within their own, more broadly focused studies of literary texts, and stylistic criticism itself has contributed to the development of culturally contextualized studies of language and literature such as sociolinguistics and discourse theory.

Though the writings of all three Brontë sisters have received attention from stylistic critics, Charlotte's novels have attracted the most thorough and sophisticated study of this kind. Margot Peters's *Charlotte Brontë: Style in the Novel* (1973), the only book on this topic, looks closely at Charlotte's use of emphatic adverbs, syntactical inversion, 'the language of antithesis', and 'courtroom language', concluding that her style is characterized by 'tension': hers is 'a prose vitalized by the unresolved battle of its conflicting parts' (p. 156). Peters argues, moreover, that this style derives naturally from the 'neurotic personality' of the author, who was torn by a 'continual but unresolved conflict of opposing drives' (p. 156), and that it speaks to any reader of the modern age who recognizes the validity of 'the divided self' (p. 164). Similarly, in *Styles in Fictional Structure: The Art of Jane Austen, Charlotte Brontë, and George Eliot* (1971), Karl Kroeber finds that 'conflict' or 'contrast' are the key words for describing the distinctive style of Charlotte's writing. Studying her use of metaphor and the relationship between imagery and narrative point of view in her novels, Kroeber observes that the language of her writings is perfectly suited to her overarching theme: 'the vital rivalry between what an individual intrinsically is and what his social role presses him to become' (p. 192). Such stylistic analyses of Charlotte's novels conform to many readings offered from other approaches—for example, structuralism and psychoanalysis—and provide textual evidence by which such interpretations may be supported and elaborated. In more recent issues of the journal *Style*, Laurel J. Brinton ('The Historical Present in Charlotte Brontë's Novels: Some Discourse Functions', *Style*, 26 (1992), 221–44) has updated Edgar F. Shannon's short article, 'The Present Tense in *Jane Eyre*' (*Nineteenth-Century Fiction* 10 (1955–6), 141–5) on Charlotte's use of the historical present, and Elizabeth Preston has challenged feminist readings of *Villette* by re-examining the text's handling of unreliable narration ('Relational Reconsiderations: Reliability, Heterosexuality, and Narrative Authority in *Villette*', *Style*, 30 (1996), 386–408).

Wuthering Heights has received slightly less attention from stylistics than Charlotte's work. By the end of the 19th century, assessments of Emily's novel often emphasized the peculiarly poetic quality of Emily's language and noted its resemblance to that used in the plays of Shakespeare. G. D. Klingopulos echoed this opinion in 1947 ('The Novel as Dramatic Poem II: *Wuthering Heights*', *Scrutiny*, 14 (1947), 269–86), and in 1964 Vincent Buckley arrived at the same conclusion by analysing the novel's 'great speeches' within the context of its surrounding 'staple prose'. Focusing on pace and rhythm, Buckley notes that Emily's controlled prose style creates 'emotional intensity . . . by . . . refus[ing] to inflate it' ('Passion and Control in *Wuthering Heights*', *Southern Review*, 1 (1964), 7). In an earlier, influential essay by Mark Schorer, 'Fiction and the Matrix of Analogy' (*Kenyon Review*, 11 (1949), 544–50), Schorer identifies two patterns of language use in *Wuthering Heights*: first, the deployment of particular categories of metaphors (the elements, the landscape, and images of animals); and second, the repetition of 'verbs of violent movement and conflict' matched by 'metaphors that *demand* rest' (McNees, 2. 184, 186). There are significant similarities between Schorer's stylistic analysis and a number of structuralist readings of *Wuthering Heights*, for example Elisabeth Van de Laar's *The Inner Structure of 'Wuthering Heights'* (1969), and, indeed, stylistic analysis is often a crucial component of structuralist interpretations. Susan L. Ferguson's article on dialect in *Wuthering Heights* is characteristic of stylistics' more recent efforts to understand such linguistic features in connection to both the sociolinguistic context in which the novel was written and to the 'ficto-linguistic system' which the narrative constructs ('Drawing Fictional Lines: Dialect and Narrative in the Victorian Novel', *Style*, 32 (1998), 1–17).

Anne's writing has received little serious attention in the way of stylistics analysis, which is surprising since her style has received lavish praise from critics such as George Moore (*Conversations at Ebury Street*, 1924), Derek Stanford (*Anne Brontë: Her Life and Work*, coauthored with Ada Harrison, 1959), and P. J. M. Scott (*Anne Brontë: A New Critical Assessment*, 1983). However, the appearance of a number of articles on 'layered narrative' in *The Tenant of Wildfell Hall* over the last twenty years (for example, N. M. Jacobs, 'Gender and Layered Narrative in *Wuthering Heights* and *The Tenant of Wildfell Hall*', *Journal of Narrative Technique*, 16 (1986), 204–19)) suggests that more work in this area might profitably be done.   CB

Sugden, in *Shirley*, the constable from *Whinbury whom Robert Gérard *Moore summons to arrest Moses *Barraclough for leading the assault on his men at Stilbro' Moor and breaking the machinery intended for his mill. He takes Barraclough to prison in *Stilbro'. Sugden was a common name in the West Riding; Charlotte Brontë's letters include numerous references to Sugdens of Keighley, while Daniel Sugden (d. 1846) was landlord of the Talbot Inn at Halifax and a friend of Branwell's (see Smith *Letters*, 1. 224; 2. 7).
                    HR

Sunderland, Abraham Stansfield (1800–55), the Keighley organist who taught the young Brontës music on their small cabinet piano, from about late 1833 when it was acquired, at least until the end of 1834 (*Diary Paper of 24 November 1834, signed by Emily and Anne) when Charlotte gave him one of her drawings (Alexander and Sellars, pp. 209–10). He also gave Branwell flute and organ lessons, the flute lessons possibly beginning as early as 1828 since Branwell wrote an early story on music manuscript paper at this date (Neufeldt *BB Works*, 1. 2). In January 1834 when Haworth held a music festival, Sunderland conducted the orchestra and choirs for the sacred music section, with Thomas *Parker as principal soloist. He also organized and presided over the concert celebrations for the opening of the organ in Haworth church (March 1834), an event satirized by Charlotte (Alexander *EEW*, 2(2). 251–2). Here and elsewhere in the Brontë juvenilia, he is caricatured as Mr Sudbury Figgs, friend of Mr John *Greenwood.

Supplehough, in *Shirley*, a Dissenting preacher whose zeal is reflected in his willingness to brave a wet night to preach 'at Milldean opposition shop' (p. 17), and whose success in baptizing sixteen adult converts in one day is contrasted by Revd Matthewson *Helstone to the idleness and ineffectual conduct of the three Anglican curates Revd Peter *Malone, Revd Joseph *Donne, and Revd David *Sweeting (ch. 1).   HR

Swarcliffe Hall, a stately, rambling house, looking down towards Birstwith in the Nidd valley, Yorks., had been bought and rebuilt in 1805 by the mill owner John Greenwood (1763–1846) (see GREENWOOD FAMILY OF HAWORTH AND KEIGHLEY), father of Charlotte Brontë's employer Mrs Sarah *Sidgwick, as a summer residence. In July 1839 Charlotte was too exhausted and depressed to enjoy the beautiful countryside, for while the house was filled with cheerful company, she had to amuse and instruct turbulent children. She used her experience as an outsider there and at *Stonegappe in *Jane Eyre*. After John Greenwood's death the house was enlarged by Mrs Sidgwick's brother Edwin Greenwood (1798–1852).

Sweeting, Revd David, the least offensive of the three curates in *Shirley*. Mr Sweeting is mocked for his diminutive stature and his flute-playing by his two companions. He is curate to Revd Cyril *Hall, vicar of *Nunnely. His ambitions include marriage to the vast and ponderous Dora *Sykes. His essentially good nature brings him Shirley *Keeldar's friendship, and protects him from the attentions of Shirley's dog *Tartar, which attacks the other curates (ch. 15). At the end of the novel we learn that Mr Sweeting does indeed marry Miss Dora Sykes, 'the most splendid and the weightiest woman in Yorkshire' (p. 723), on the occasion of Mr Sweeting's induction into a comfortable living. Sweeting's original was Revd James Chesterton *Bradley. Wroot (p. 134) notes that the name 'Sweeting' appears in a notebook used by Charlotte Brontë during a visit to Manchester in 1846.
HR

Swift, Jonathan (1667–1745), dean of St Patrick's, Dublin, and satirist. Swift's *Gulliver's Travels* (1726) appealed strongly to the Brontës. Their 'Magazine' advertised 'Tales of Captain Lemuel Gulliver in Houynhmhm Land' (Alexander *EEW*, 1. 61), Mirza is conveyed, wrapped in a leaf, to a tent full of giants in *'Tales of the Islanders', volume 4, and in 'Strange Events' (see 'YOUNG MEN'S MAGAZINE') an enormous hand raises Lord Charles to the ceiling (Alexander *EEW*, 1. 258). Jane Eyre's misery changes her usual childish delight in Swift's 'real-seeming' land into fear of 'eerie and dreary' regions, and Eliza Reed's sharp verdict on the 'vain and absurd animal' Georgiana is Swiftian (see REED FAMILY). Frances *Henri ties up coins in a 'Lilliputian' packet, and William *Crimsworth compares Belgian fields to 'Brobdingnagian' kitchen gardens.

Sydenham Hills, in Angria, in the *Glass Town and Angrian saga. They can be seen from Zamorna and from Hawkscliffe Forest. They take their name from an old family in the area, whose descendants are now magistrates, parliamentary members, and factory owners.

Sydney, Edward Geoffrey Stanley (also Prince Edward of York and Lord Strafford), in the *Glass Town and Angrian saga. Initially patronized by the Marquis of Douro (Duke of *Zamorna) when he arrives in Verdopolis from England to seek his fortune, Sydney becomes a talented debater and parliamentarian, who boosts Zamorna's opposition to Alexander Rogue (Duke of *Northangerland). Hero of 'The *Foundling', Sydney discovers that he is actually the son of the late Frederick Guelph, Duke of *York and King of the Twelves. He marries Zamorna's cousin Lady Julia *Wellesley and their antipathetic characters become a major source of domestic comedy in the juvenilia, until their marriage ends in divorce. Sydney's delicate English constitution, seriousness, diligence, and parsimony are the target of satire, yet his political career thrives. He becomes Home Secretary and Leader in the Commons. While Zamorna is away with the army fighting the French in the *War of Encroachment, Sydney takes the opportunity to break with him and supports the government against the army. Zamorna's revenge is to shatter Sydney's already fragile marriage (recorded in 'A Late Occurrence', in 'The *Scrap Book'). During the Angrian wars, Sydney (now Lord Strafford) supports the Marquis of Ardrah and Northangerland.

Sydney, Lady Julia. See WELLESLEY, LADY JULIA.

Sykes family. Christopher ('Christie') Sykes is a manufacturer and wool merchant in *Shirley* who lives in *Whinbury with his wife, son John, and six daughters. He is 'a tall stout man of about fifty, comely of feature, but feeble of physiognomy', requiring the ingestion of 'Hollands-and-water' to make him 'at least *word*-valiant' (p. 145). He is a partner with Mr Pearson (see PEARSON FAMILY) in a cloth-dressing operation in Whinbury which has been attacked by machine-breakers led by Moses *Barraclough, and he joins with Robert Gérard *Moore and Constable *Sugden in Barraclough's arrest at *Hollow's Mill. He also assists in the later defence of the mill against *Luddite rioters. Mrs Sykes, 'a tall bilious gentlewoman' (p. 122), and three of her buxom daughters (Harriet, Hannah, and Mary) take tea at the Rectory (ch. 7), a comic scene in which Charlotte Brontë mocks the superficiality and triviality of 'English country ladies'; that is, socially ambitious women of the provincial middle class. A fourth daughter, the vast and ponderous Dora Sykes, is admired by the little curate Revd David *Sweeting; at the novel's conclusion they are married 'under the happiest auspices, Mr. Sweeting having been just inducted to a comfortable living, and Mr. Sykes being in circumstances to give Dora a handsome portion' (p. 723). The Sykes family is probably based on the *Brooke family of Dewsbury and their friends the Hallileys.

The Sykes referred to in chapter 2, who is with Joe *Scott when the wagons are attacked, appears to be an employee of Moore's and not related to Christopher Sykes.
HR

Symington, John Alexander (1887–1961), civil servant, editor, collector, bibliographer, bookseller, and part-time librarian to Lord Brotherton; life member of the Brontë Society from 1924, member of the Brontë Society Council (1925–30); honorary

Symington, John Alexander

curator of the Brontë Collection (1926–29), librarian, bibliographical secretary, and editor of *BST* (1926–9). After an early career in his father's antiquarian bookshop in Harrogate, Symington worked in the Leeds Employment Exchange. He had a surprising range of book-related experience, even before he met his patron Lord Brotherton. He had worked as assistant in the reference department of the Leeds Public Libraries, as a part-time English student at the fledgling University of Leeds and then library assistant there, as contributor to the *Yorkshire Weekly Post* and other newspapers, as author of books with local Yorkshire associations and, in the tradition of his father, as buyer, seller, collector, and editor of books and manuscripts. Brotherton was impressed with this industrious self-made man, like himself, and in 1923 he offered him a part-time post as librarian at Roundhay Hall. Symington gave the impression that his patron sat back while he 'made' the Brotherton Collection, a myth he circulated after Brotherton's death when his reputation had fallen under a cloud. He was instrumental, however, in shaping the Brontë section of the Brotherton collection, including the acquisition of Branwell Brontë's letters to Joseph Bentley *Leyland and Charlotte's to Amelia *Taylor. He obtained as many as he could of C. K. *Shorter's papers and continued to produce limited editions of unpublished manuscripts, including Branwell's *And the Weary are at Rest* (1924). He contributed a transcript of the Leyland letters to *BST* for 1925.

Symington 'turned the Brontë Society's collection from a cabinet of curiosities into an attractive, rationally laid out museum' (Smurthwaite, p. 122). He supervised the unpacking and installing of the Bonnell Collection in the Brontë Museum in 1929 (see BONNELL, HENRY HOUSTON). He was in contact with the still-honoured T. J. *Wise, and with the devoted Brontë scholar C. W. *Hatfield, who helped to prepare Symington's illustrated 200-page *Catalogue of the Museum & Library* at Haworth (1927). Symington must have seemed the obvious person to edit the Shakespeare Head *The Brontës: Their Lives, Friendships and Correspondence* (4 vols.) which eventually appeared in 1932. But in 1930 Symington was *persona non grata* to Brontë Society Council members, who had discovered that certain items were missing from the Museum. Symington resigned from his various posts at the 1930 annual meeting. The society's co-operation in the production of the correspondence was secured only when Wise was brought in as a nominal fellow-editor or rather as a famous name, for he did very little for the edition. Symington fortunately had the assistance of the conscientious Hatfield and, aware of the need for accurate texts, he obtained photostats

of Brontë letters in the Huntington and Pierpont Morgan collections, and the New York and Buffalo Public Libraries. Hatfield's friend Davidson Cook provided transcripts of some manuscripts in the *Law Collection, and Sydney Cockerell transcribed the Wooler letters in the Fitzwilliam Museum, Cambridge. The new edition improved on Shorter's edition of 1908, which Symington used as a basis. But he did not have access to all the manuscripts dispersed by Wise, nor to the originals of Charlotte's letters to Mrs Gaskell. He retained some of the censored and abridged letters Ellen Nussey had supplied to Shorter, failed to rewrite Shorter's error-prone introduction, took on trust unreliable transcripts by Wise, Bonnell, and other copyists, and failed to indicate his sources. Later, with much help from Hatfield, Davidson Cook, Adrian Mott, Marian Wood, and Helen Kilburn, Symington transcribed some documents and arranged for facsimiles of others in the Shakespeare Head *Miscellaneous and Unpublished Writings of Charlotte and Patrick Branwell Brontë* (2 vols., 1936). He also compiled a bibliography of Brontë works and Brontëana, but it was not ready for publication at the outbreak of the Second World War, and was not published until 2000, when Ian Hodgkins & Co were permitted to use the title *The Shakespeare Head Bibliography*.

Leeds University was understandably wary of employing Symington, despite Brotherton's 'memorandum' that he should be the first 'Brotherton Librarian' when the collection passed to the University. Wise assured the University that Symington was 'honest', a nice irony in view of later revelations about Wise himself. Symington, with his two assistants, was duly appointed to a full-time position but remained at Roundhay Hall with the collection for some time. He continued his idiosyncratic practices: charging scholars for transcripts he made of manuscripts, keeping valuable books in his own home, building up his own substantial collection under the auspices of Wise, indulging in high-handed litigious behaviour, and generally making himself unpopular with his new and prospective employers. His intimate dealings with Wise did not help his reputation when Wise was exposed in 1934. Nevertheless, in November 1935, he went with the collection to the new Brotherton Library; but his lack of tact and ingrained unorthodox practices meant that his days were numbered. Furthermore, it is now clear that some material still in the Symington collection (chiefly at Rutgers University) should properly belong in the Brotherton. John Smurthwaite has argued in *The Life of John Alexander Symington* (p. xii), that his subject was a talented self-made man lost in a world of exclusive professionalism, that saw him as 'an upstart tradesman'. His dubious practices compromised his considerable achievements and caused his dismissal at the beginning of 1938. He could find no further work as a librarian but continued his bookselling with a wartime spell at the Ministry of Food. He had eventually to offer his private collection of manuscripts and books for sale. Rutgers University was the principal purchaser.

Lemon, Charles, 'John Alexander Symington (1887–1961) and the Brontë Society', *BST* (1997), 22. 113–26.
Smurthwaite, John, *The Life of John Alexander Symington, Bibliographer and Librarian, 1887–1961: A Bookman's Rise and Fall* (1995).

Sympson family. In *Shirley*, Mr Sympson, Shirley *Keeldar's uncle and one of her guardians until she attains her majority, lives at Sympson Grove, ——shire, where Shirley spent two years of her early youth. He, his wife, their daughters Gertrude and Isabella, their crippled 15 year-old son Henry, and Henry's tutor Louis Gérard *Moore, descend on *Fieldhead for a visit. The Sympsons are 'Church people', but they adhere to narrow principles and intolerant views. Mr Sympson is 'a man of spotless respectability, worrying temper, pious principles, and worldly views'; his wife is 'a very good woman', but raised on 'a narrow system of views' (p. 511). Isabella and Gertrude have received the best education, learned 'principles and opinions . . . which could not be mended', and feel abhorrence for any deviations from the accepted norms (p. 512). Only Henry, infatuated with his older cousin, obtains Shirley's affectionate regard. Mr Sympson attempts to arrange suitable marriages for his niece, but is shocked by her rejection of his chosen suitors (Sam Fawthrop Wynne (see WYNNE FAMILY), Sir Philip *Nunnely), and attributes her rebelliousness to the poisonous effect of her reading French novels. Following a violent confrontation with Louis Moore, Mr Sympson finds himself expelled from Fieldhead, and the rest of the family follows. Like the *Ingram family in *Jane Eyre*, the Sympson family embodies Charlotte Brontë's view, developed from her experience as a governess, of the snobbery and cold selfishness of the English middle and upper middle classes, the essential vulgarity of people ruled by the superficies of wealth and station. Only young Henry, 'little, lame, and pale' (p. 512), is exempted from criticism by virtue of his idealism and his adoration of Shirley.　　HR

T

'Tales of the Islanders', volumes 1–4, written between 31 [*sic*] June 1829 and 30 June 1830, is Charlotte Brontë's first extended attempt at storytelling, involving both political allegory and fairytale. It is the only surviving document relating to the *Islanders' Play and was originally a series of four miniature hand-sewn booklets in brown paper covers, each signed, dated, and written in Charlotte's minuscule script (MS in Berg, NYPL; the pages are now separated, mounted, and rebound in one volume). The adventures deal almost exclusively with Charlotte's chief men, the Duke of *Wellington and his two sons, tracing the play from Charlotte's point of view and illustrating her early interests in fantasy, ghost stories, the supernatural, and events relating to the Duke of Wellington. A number of episodes involve characters narrating tales to a fictitious audience, such as Douro's and Wellesley's Tale to Little King and Queens and the Duke's household: *Seringapatan, Old Man Cockney (steward), Gamekeeper, Jack-of-all-trades, and Orderly-man, all veterans of the fictitious Duke's early campaigns and now living in soldiers' cottages on his estate. The Brontës themselves are involved not only as creators but as actors within the play, in the roles of Little King and Queens (see GENII, CHIEF), although they are also referred to by their own names. For Emily's special interest see ISLANDERS' PLAY.

Volume 1 ('31 June [*sic*] 1829')
Chapter 1 describes the origins of the Islanders' Play in four islands off the coast of Britain, but these islands are soon replaced by Vision Island, 'a beautiful fiction' with the sublime and magical scenery of fairyland. Here the *Palace School, an institution for a thousand young nobles, becomes the focus with particular provision being made for naughty children, locked in cells in a subterranean dungeon. There are special guards 'for threshing the children' and to restrain Branwell's use of his large black club, Charlotte keeps the key to the dungeon and Emily the key to the cells. There is no doubt that the Islanders' Play, despite

a school rebellion, was too tame for Branwell and he withdrew to concentrate on the *Young Men's Play in October 1829.

The Duke of Wellington (who in real life had been prime minister of England since January 1828) is honorary governor of the school and his duties are carried out by his sons the Marquis of Douro (see ZAMORNA, DUKE OF) and Lord Charles *Wellesley. Chapters 3 and 4 relate fantastic adventures based on political events and involving these three characters. For example, Ratten (son of Edward *Baines, the Whig editor of the *Leeds Mercury*) tries to poison the Duke who had 'obscured the bright dawn of Whiggish intellect!' but he is saved by the reverent touch of a 'Giant of Clouds', his creator Charlotte who is responding to Whig criticism of Wellington in the *Leeds Mercury*.

Volume 2 (2 December 1829)
Preoccupied by 'the great Catholic Question', the Duke and the Brontës themselves neglect the Palace School until an urgent letter arrives from Lord Charles informing them of the School Rebellion. The chief instigators are Emily's characters including Johnny Lockhart (see LOCKHART, JOHN GIBSON) and Princess Vittoria. Various factions (based on contemporary politics surrounding the future Queen *Victoria: see Alexander *EW*, pp. 48–9) battle for supremacy until the Duke arrives in a balloon from his estate of *Strathfieldsay and quells the rebellion with a single autocratic threat (see Alexander *EW*, pp. 48–9). The young Brontës responded passionately to events preceding the Catholic Emancipation Act of 1829. They followed their father (and Wellington) in his conditional support for Catholics, provided they might be legally removed from places of trust or influence if danger threatened.

After the rebellion, the Brontës tire of the Palace School, send the nobles home, and leave the island to fairies, signifying the withdrawal of all except Charlotte from the Islanders' Play. She continues to compose stories within the frame of this play, concentrating on political allegory set in England at *Strathfieldsay, the Horse Guards, and No. 10 Downing Street. Wellington becomes St George slaying the dragon of bigotry that pursues Roman *Catholicism in Ireland (ch. 4). Chapter 5 relates a traveller's tale of the wickedness of Roman Catholicism in southern Ireland and the value of searching the Bible for oneself.

Volume 3 (8 May 1830)
After a comical scene in which the Duke of Wellington is surrounded by his ineffectual Tory cabinet, based closely on the contemporary political scene, the Duke is called away by a mysterious message in blood to rescue his son Douro, whom he finds (with the help of Seringapatan, an old veteran

on his estate) in a vast cavern after a long journey through romantic scenery of precipices and cataracts. A genie transports the Duke and his son home but Douro's sufferings are 'indescribable'. This curious amalgam of political cynicism and fairytale characterizes all Charlotte's early stories, including the subsequent chapters of 'Tales of the Islanders'. The detailed description of landscape, the interior of Seringapatan's cottage, and the creating of an atmosphere of anticipation is of more interest to Charlotte than the structure of her tale, with its feeble *deus ex machina* ending.

Volume 4 (30 July 1830)

Little Queens disguise themselves as three Old Washerwomen who seek employment at *Strathfieldsay, but their stay is fraught with quarrels incited by Little King (Branwell), who does no work but has a 'constant disposition to all kinds of mischief'. Already Charlotte's amused and patronizing attitude to Branwell's wayward behaviour and posturing is well established and forms much of the comedy of her early writing. Her attitude reflects his privileged position in the Brontë household, for he acts more like 'an evil brownie than a legitimate fairy'.

In the final tale, Lord Charles relates the story of Mirza, a Moslem woodcutter in the Caucasus, and his strange adventures amongst huge birds who nurse him and huge female forms who sacrifice him to their mountain god: a tale-within-a-tale that combines elements from the *Arabian Nights* and *Swift's *Gulliver's Travels*.

> Alexander *EEW*, 1. 21, 48–9, 99, 140, 196.
> Alexander, Christine, *et al* (eds.), *Tales of the Islanders by Charlotte Brontë*, vol. 1 (2001); vol. 2 (2002); vols. 3 and 4 (forthcoming).

Talleyrand (1754–1838), the famous French diplomatist and statesman under both *Napoleon and Louis XVIII. By 1829 when he enters the *Glass Town and Angrian saga as a fictitious character from Branwell's *Paris, he had all but retired, although he later became ambassador to London for King Louis Philippe.

Tartar. In *Shirley*, Shirley *Keeldar's 'black-muzzled, tawny dog' (p. 309), a cross between a mastiff and a bulldog, is constantly at his mistress's side and defends her from the unwanted attentions of the vain and blustering curates Revd Peter Augustus *Malone and Revd Joseph *Donne (ch. 15). Tartar shows 'a singular partiality' for the tutor Louis Gérard *Moore who, alone among Shirley's acquaintance, can command the dog's obedience. Mrs Gaskell states that Charlotte modelled Tartar on Emily's bulldog *Keeper, which, like his fictional counterpart, was friendly unless struck with a stick or a whip (*Life*, 1. 309). Keeper joined the

Brontë household in 1838, rapidly attaching himself to Emily; on one occasion Emily rescued him from a savage attack by another dog, an incident used by Charlotte Brontë to illustrate Shirley's unflinching courage and her attachment to Tartar (pp. 401–2; Gérin *EB*, pp. 146–7). HR

Taylor, Amelia (b. 1818), daughter of Christopher Leake *Ringrose, and friend of Ellen Nussey and Charlotte Brontë. Her engagement to marry Ellen's brother George was broken off *c.*1845 owing to his incurable mental illness. In October 1850 she married Joseph *Taylor, whose efforts to improve her uncultivated mind amused Charlotte. She became almost totally absorbed in tending Joe and her daughter Emily Martha ('Tim', 1851–8), who endeared herself to Charlotte, her honorary 'grandmamma', and Revd Patrick Brontë. Charlotte visited Scotland with the Taylors, and though often wearied by Amelia's egotistical fretfulness, valued her affectionate nature, and came to care wholeheartedly for her. Charlotte's letters to Amelia were sold at Sotheby's on 26 March 1923, as the property of 'Mrs Helmsing, Woodcroft, Beverley', (a descendant of Amelia's sister Laura) and were acquired by the Brotherton Library, Leeds.

Taylor, James (?1817–74), a Scotsman, *Smith, Elder and Company's manager, controlling 40 clerks by his 'iron will'. His enthusiasm for *Jane Eyre* stirred George *Smith to read it. He chose some of the books sent by the firm to Charlotte, and lent her the *Athenaeum* and several serious biographical and social works. Charlotte respected but did not act on his criticisms of *Shirley*, and he collected the manuscript from Haworth on 8 September 1849. He was small, with red hair and beard, and seemed to Charlotte 'rigid, despotic and self-willed . . . he has a determined, dreadful nose in the middle of his face which when poked into my countenance cuts into my soul like iron—Still he is horribly intelligent, quick, searching, sagacious' (Smith *Letters*, 2. 299). Later he sent her a copy of the *Palladium* (Sept. 1850) in which Sydney Dobell praised *Wuthering Heights*—a well-conceived gesture, after which Charlotte observed in him 'spirit and sense'. Her respectful letters probably encouraged him to hope she would receive him kindly on his farewell visit in April 1851 before leaving England to establish 'Smith, Taylor & Co.' in Bombay. Elizabeth Gaskell alleged that he made Charlotte an offer of marriage, and quoted her letter to Ellen Nussey of 9 April 1851 admitting 'Friendship—gratitude—esteem' for him, counteracted by her recoil in his presence: 'I did not want to be proud nor intend to be proud—but I was forced to be so' (Smith *Letters*, 2. 1). There may not have been a formal proposal, though Revd Patrick Brontë favoured 'a prospective union, deferred for 5 years'. Charlotte remained convinced that 'if Mr. T—— be the only husband Fate offers to me—single I must always remain'. Taylor's two letters to her from India (15 September and 2 October 1851), and her reply of 15 November, closed their correspondence. Yet the lack of letters from him made her suffer the pain of 'absolute uncertainty', and she wrote miserably on 1 July 1852 that all was 'silent as the grave'. Taylor had probably returned to England by 6 December 1856, when Elizabeth Gaskell thanked George Smith for sending his letters for use in the *Life*. 'Smith, Taylor & Co.' was unsuccessful, and was eventually closed. In England Taylor 'engaged in mercantile pursuits'. He married Annie, widow of Adolph Ritter of Vienna, at St John the Evangelist, St Pancras, in October 1862, but the marriage was not happy, and he left no family. A succession of posts in India followed his return to Bombay in 1863: editor of the *Bombay Gazette*, then of the Bombay *Saturday Review*, from which he resigned, having perhaps been 'too independent to be successful'; an active and outspoken secretary to the Bombay Chamber of Commerce from 1865; honorary secretary to the Bombay Branch of the Royal Asiatic Society from 1868 when he 'was so fond of doing things in his own way, that he almost ignored . . . the Managing Committee'; registrar of Bombay University for 3 years from 1868, and sheriff of Bombay from January 1874. The indirect cause of his death on 29 April 1874 was a fracture of the right leg in March, caused by his tripping over the matting of the Bombay Club billiard room. After an impressive funeral in Bombay cathedral in April he was buried in the Sewree cemetery, regretted as a man 'identified' with Bombay, whose qualities had 'secured him the esteem of all who knew him'.

> Cory, Charlotte, 'Letter from Bombay', *Times Literary Supplement* (16 Aug. 2002), 13–14, with portrait.
> Smith *Letters*, vol. 2, pp. liii–lv: 'Biographical Note'.
> *Times of India* (30 Apr. 1874), 2 (obituary).

Taylor, Joseph ('Joe') (?1816–57), Mary *Taylor's brother, a clever practical and theoretical chemist whose character suggested Martin Yorke (see YORKE FAMILY) and Hunsden Yorke *Hunsden in *Shirley*. Charlotte Brontë asked for his comments on parts of the *Shirley* manuscript before publication. He and his brother John carried on the family business as woollen manufacturers and merchants at *Hunsworth Mill, travelling extensively on the Continent in the course of trade. By April 1850 they were prosperous enough to convert their loan of £300 to Mary into a gift, and lend her a further £100. A curious mixture of kindness and callousness, principles and pragmatism, Joe shocked Charlotte in 1845 by his apparent loss of his early idealistic radicalism,

for he courted the wealthy Isabella Nussey, audaciously avowing the views of 'any hackneyed Fortune-Hunter' (Smith *Letters*, 1. 392). His eventual marriage to Amelia Ringrose (see TAYLOR, AMELIA) seems not to have been primarily for money, despite her father's wealth. Amelia was devoted to him, and they both cosseted their delicate little daughter Emily Martha ('Tim', 1851–8). Yet he could show a strange Gradgrind-like hardness, as Elizabeth Gaskell wrote to John Forster in May 1854: to prove that cruelty was natural, he showed the 2-year-old child a dead robin, said her tears were nonsense, and she would enjoy eating it; another day he told his invalid wife he was glad the child would die, for life would only be a trouble to herself and them, and death would spare her much (Chapple & Pollard *Gaskell Letters*, 282–3). By that date his own liver disease was probably well advanced. Charlotte was grieved to hear of his serious illness in December 1854, for, as she wrote to Amelia Taylor, she had known him 'above twenty years and differed from him and been enraged with him and liked him and cared for him as long' (Wise & Symington, 4. 163).

Taylor, Martha (1819–42), original of Jessy Yorke (see YORKE FAMILY), in *Shirley*; favourite child of Joshua Taylor (1766–1840), who loved to hear her sing, and called her 'Patty lass'. She was not pretty, but piquant, full of variety, 'rudely outspoken, lively, and original, producing laughter with her own good-humour and affection' (Shorter *Circle*, pp. 234–6). Charlotte Brontë first met her at *Roe Head, where little 'Miss Boisterous' would sometimes dare her teachers face to face. She was attractive to men, a chatterbox, a gossip, and occasionally petulant; but Charlotte delighted in her company, was amused by her 'adventures', and intensely grieved by her death from cholera at the Château de *Kœkelberg in October 1842.

Taylor, Mary (1817–93), one of the *Taylors of Gomersal, a close friend of Charlotte Brontë. The elder daughter of the cloth manufacturer Joshua Taylor, she was the original of the 'fine, generous' and intellectual Rose Yorke (see YORKE FAMILY) in *Shirley*. She and her sister Martha *Taylor met Charlotte in 1831 as fellow pupils at *Roe Head school, and thought her plain, shy, nervous, and oddly dressed. Mary by contrast was pretty and energetic, clever and intolerant, hard-working but 'quietly rebellious' if she chose not to obey instructions. She and her sister had adopted the furious radical and republican principles of their father. Charlotte delighted in both of them, and Branwell Brontë was attracted to Mary 'till he began to suspect that she cared more for him and then instantly conceived a sort of contempt for her'. Charlotte, looking on, understood Mary's remorse, as she wrote to Ellen Nussey on 20 November 1840, after she realized that her 'noble, warm—generous—devoted and profound' feelings 'too freely revealed—too frankly bestowed' had not been estimated at their real value. Charlotte considered her 'truly noble—she would *die* willingly for one she loved'; but her conduct during a visit to Haworth had been 'wrought to a pitch of [such] great intensity and irregularity' that 'Mr *Weightman thought her mad' (Smith *Letters*, 1. 234; conjectural reading of a deleted passage). Because Mary bitterly regretted this too frank revelation of her feelings, and deeply resented the response to it, she became more defiantly insistent on women's right to an independent and self-supporting life.

After her father died in December 1840 Mary travelled on the Continent for a time with her brother John, Martha was sent to school in *Brussels, and their youngest brother Waring emigrated to New Zealand in November 1841. When Mary returned to visit Yorkshire, she did not stay with her dour, disagreeable mother, but with her brothers Joseph and John at their cottage next to Hunsworth Mill. She actively encouraged Charlotte to go abroad in search of education and the means of attaining an independent career. Her lively mind and iconoclastic temperament are shown in the letters she wrote to Ellen *Nussey in 1842 from the school at the Château de *Kœkelberg, Brussels, where she had joined her sister Martha. Charlotte and Emily Brontë's visits there relieved their feelings of isolation in Belgium, and they were greatly shocked and distressed by Martha's death on 12 October 1842.

By 1843 Mary's 'resolute and intrepid proceedings' had taken her to Hagen in Germany to teach 'nice dull' German boys and to have piano lessons from Friedrich Halle, the father of Sir Charles Halle. After a brief visit to England and a happy reunion with Charlotte and Ellen in May 1844 Mary returned to Germany. There she became lonely and disillusioned, and she resolved to follow her brother Waring to New Zealand. She left England in March 1845 and arrived in Wellington on 24 July. She helped her brother to run his general store in Herbert Street, offered 'Instructions on the Piano Forte', and built a five-roomed house with a shop which she at first let and later lived in with her cousin Ellen Taylor. She threw herself energetically into the work of making her business prosper, bought a cow, began writing a novel, longed to 'hallack' about the country, and grumbled about the ignorance of middle-class women: 'You are thrown entirely on the men for conversation' (Smith *Letters* 2. 88, 89).

After Ellen Taylor's death from tuberculosis in December 1851 Mary carried on alone. She kept in touch with Ellen Nussey and Charlotte, found

Shirley more interesting than *Jane Eyre*, and commented, 'What a little lump of perfection you've made me!' She was angered by what she called Charlotte's 'sacrifices' to Revd Patrick Brontë's wishes, and after Charlotte's death wrote two long letters of recollection of her which were incorporated in Elizabeth *Gaskell's *Life*. In 1859 Mary invested £400 in land in Wellington before leaving it on 20 May, probably for the 'hallacking' around the country that she had promised herself.

On her return to Yorkshire she lived in Gomersal and wrote articles on 'The First Duty of Women', published as a series in the feminist *Victoria Magazine* between 1865 and 1870, and as a book in 1870. She argued that women should feel neither indignity nor hardship in working for their living; they should not let themselves be 'driven into matrimony'. In 1875 she contributed to *Swiss Notes by Five Ladies*, an account of an expedition in Switzerland by four young women, with Mary as 'the originator, *chaperone*, and moving spirit'. Her novel, *Miss Miles: A Tale of Yorkshire Life Sixty Years Ago* (1890), portrays the contrasting lives of four women, each in her way struggling against the limitations imposed upon her by convention. Though the novel lacks narrative cohesion, it is redeemed by its sympathetic insight and its portrayal of the independent, talented, and lively Sarah Miles.

Mary destroyed all but one of Charlotte's letters to her, but later wished she had kept them. The surviving letter, that of 4 September 1848, is Charlotte's graphic account of her whirlwind visit to London with Anne in July 1848. It is regrettable that no other letters to this unconventional, intelligent friend survive, for Charlotte shared some of Mary's intellectual interests and respected her independence of mind. Mary's own letters to Charlotte and Ellen reveal much about their relationship as well as about Mary's pioneering life in New Zealand. Joan Stevens prints 34 letters, of which six are from Martha Taylor, and reconstructions of Mary's two letters to Gaskell written in 1857. The complete manuscript of her letter to Gaskell of 30 July 1857 (Stevens's letter 30) and of a letter to Ellen Nussey of 28 January 1858 are in the BPM. The second of these is printed in the Horsfall Turner suppressed edition of Charlotte's letters, pp. 382–4.

Bellamy, Joan, *'More Precious than Rubies': Mary Taylor, Friend of Charlotte Brontë, Strong-Minded Woman* (2002).

Stevens, Joan, *Mary Taylor: Friend of Charlotte Brontë* (1972).

Taylor family of Gomersal, well-known to Charlotte Brontë through her friend Mary *Taylor. Their home, the *Red House (*Briarmains), was built by an ancestor, William Taylor, in 1660. His great-grandson, John Taylor (1736–1805), built the

*Hunsworth woollen mills on the River Spen in 1780–5, and prospered as a manufacturer and exporter of army cloth. The characters of his eldest son Joshua (1766–1840) and Joshua's wife Anne, née Tickell (?1781–1856), suggested those of Hiram and Hesther Yorke (see YORKE FAMILY) in *Shirley*. Joshua's private bank failed in 1825. Despite efforts to satisfy his creditors, Joshua left property encumbered by debts to his sons. Charlotte portrays the eldest, Joshua (1812–80), as Matthew Yorke. He was said to be a theoretical chemist, well read, but eccentric in later life. By 1856 he had paid all his father's creditors or their representatives. He married Jane Lister Charlesworth (?1815–87), a *Moravian adherent, and had four sons and a daughter; the family left the Red House in 1845. He gave no financial help to his sister Mary. His brother John (1813–1901; 'Mark Yorke') moved with Joseph *Taylor to a cottage near Hunsworth mill in 1840, and like him travelled extensively on business. Though Charlotte imagined he was 'interested' in Ellen Nussey at various times, she liked him less than Joseph, and in 1843 mentioned a deplorable change in him, only to be expected from his mode of life; but both he and Joseph helped their sister Mary financially, and she in turn bequeathed him an annuity. He emigrated to New Zealand in 1860, bought a sheep-run in Hawkes Bay in 1868, later lived on Waring Taylor's property at Shannon, Wellington province, and died unmarried. Mary Taylor's youngest brother William Waring Taylor (1819–1903) emigrated to New Zealand in 1841, leaving on the *Martha Ridgway* in November and arriving in Wellington in April 1842. He set up shop in Herbert Street, where he dealt in land, wool, cattle, and general goods. He helped Mary in many practical ways. In February 1848 he married Mary, daughter of Dr Frederick John Knox (brother of the anatomist and ethnologist Robert Knox, 1791–1862). Some of their descendants still live in New Zealand.

Taylor family of Stanbury, influential landowners living at the Manor House, *Stanbury; trustees of the Haworth church lands. Stephen Taylor (1772–1831), a woolstapler and farmer, was related to Mercy Kaye of Allerton Hall near *Thornton, whom Revd Patrick Brontë knew. It was to him that Mr Brontë wrote in July 1819 about his controversial appointment to Haworth by the Vicar of Bradford. He learned from Taylor that the trustees insisted that the nomination was their right, though they had no personal objection to Mr Brontë. Once a compromise was reached by which the Trustees shared nomination with the Vicar, Stephen Taylor was co-operative, and sent two carts to transport the Brontës' household

goods to Haworth in April 1820. Branwell's portrait of Stephen's daughter Maria (1808–75; later Mrs James Ingham) in *c*.1838–9 indicates the friendly relationship between the families, as does Charlotte's note to Maria of September 1839. Stephen's widow Mary, née Wright (m. February 1797) continued to befriend the Brontës, inviting them to visit her at the Manor House, and being invited by Charlotte to meet the schoolmaster Mr Ebenezer *Rand at the Parsonage on 19 July 1844.

Stephen Taylor's sons George (1801–65), woolstapler, landowner, and churchwarden; John (1812–?80); and Robert (1815–90) also attended vestry meetings. George, a widower since July 1842, was thanked by Mr Brontë for his 'friendly and open conduct' in June 1832, witnessed Elizabeth *Branwell's will in April 1833, and on 29 February 1844 was asked by Mr Brontë to 'divert' Enoch Thomas, who was possibly suffering from melancholia, by inviting him to a tea party. As a member of the Haworth *Mechanics' Institute, George Taylor helped to ensure that *Shirley* was ordered for the library. He and his mother and 'Miss Taylor'—perhaps his daughter—received Charlotte's wedding cards in June 1854.

Teale, Dr Thomas Pridgin (1800–67), MRCS 1823, Hon FRCS; FLS; elected surgeon to the Leeds General Infirmary in June 1833 by a large majority; lecturer in anatomy and physiology, Leeds School of Medicine; Hon. Curator in Zoology, Leeds Philosophical and Literary Society, and author of treatises in the *Provincial Medical Journal*. In early January 1849 he examined Anne Brontë, using a stethoscope, diagnosed an advanced stage of pulmonary TB, and advised that she must stay indoors in an even temperature during the winter. Dr John Forbes knew Mr Teale and approved his advice and prescription for Anne.

telegraphy. See COMMUNICATIONS.

television and radio adaptations. The 1931 BBC radio dramatization of *Jane Eyre* by Barbara Couper and Howard Rose was repeated up to the early 1940s and in 1972. Rochester was played in 1932 by Milton Rosmer (who played Heathcliff in the 1920 silent film) and in 1946 by Reginald Tate, who played Rochester in Helen Jerome's version on stage in 1936 and on BBC television in 1937, with Curigwen Lewis as Jane. American television saw *Jane Eyre* in 1939, with Flora Campbell and Dennis Hoey; Charlton Heston was Rochester for CBS in 1949, Kevin McCarthy in 1952, and Zachary Scott in 1961. For NBC, Robert Esson adapted the novel for a colour broadcast in 1957, with Joan Elan and Patrick Macnee as Jane and Rochester. In Britain, Constance Cox's six-part BBC TV serial, with Stanley Baker and Daphne Slater, was broadcast in 1956, 1963, and 1965. In 1973 Robin Chapman adapted the novel in four hourly episodes for BBC TV; Jane and Rochester were played by Sorcha Cusack and Michael Jayston.

Probably the best television adaptation to date was Julian Amyes's 1983 production in colour for BBC TV, dramatized by Alexander Baron in eleven episodes, with Zelah Clarke and Timothy Dalton (who had played Heathcliff in Robert Fuest's 1970 film of *Wuthering Heights*). The leisurely pace allowed sensitive attention to be paid to Charlotte Brontë's dialogue, and both principal actors were subtle and humorous in their delivery; reviewers, however, were fixated on Timothy Dalton's sexy reputation as James Bond. The 1997 LWT feature version directed by Robert Young, by contrast, had a screenplay by Kay Mellor with sensationally Gothic sequences. Samantha Morton was an appealing Jane, but a voice-over set her motives in a Mills-and-Boon-like paradigm, while Ciaran Hinds played Rochester as a stage villain with a vulgar, surly temper. Charlotte Brontë's *Villette* was serialized for BBC TV in 1957, with Jill Bennett and Michael Warre, and in 1970, with Judy Parfitt and Peter Jeffrey; it was also adapted for BBC Radio by Valerie Windsor in 1990.

Barbara Couper, the adaptor of *Jane Eyre*, also adapted *Wuthering Heights* for BBC radio in 1934, with Milton Rosmer, who had played the part in the 1920 silent film, as Heathcliff. In 1948 the novel was televised in a studio-bound BBC production of John Davison's 1937 stage play, with Kieron Moore and Katharine Blake in 18th-century costumes. More naturalistic versions appeared in 1953, with Richard Todd and Yvonne Mitchell; in 1962, with Keith Michell and Claire Bloom; in 1967, with Ian McShane and Angela Scoular; and in 1978, with Ken Hutchinson and Kay Adshead. The 1978 version was learnedly reviewed for *Radio Times* by Claire Tomalin (24 Sept. 1978). ITV belatedly produced an unconvincing version in 1998, with Orla Brady and Robert Cavanagh. An oddity is the Monty Python's Flying Circus semaphore version of *Wuthering Heights* (1989), which shows Catherine and Heathcliff on opposite hilltops, signalling their desire with semaphore flags. This immensely funny item indicates the thoroughness with which *Wuthering Heights* has passed into the general culture; reduced to minimal elements, it remains recognizable.

The only other Brontë novel to attract radio or television attention is *The Tenant of Wildfell Hall*, which was adapted by Peter Hanvey for Irish Radio 1970. Christopher Fry, who was to write the biographical series The Brontës in 1973, had already dramatized *Tenant* in four parts for BBC2 in 1968–9, with Janet Munro as Helen and Corin Redgrave as Huntingdon, and this was broadcast again for Irish Television in 1973. The 1996 BBC TV version adapted by David Nokes and Janet Barton, with Tara Fitzgerald as Helen, Rupert Graves as Arthur, and Toby Stevens as Gilbert, provoked much debate about the status of Anne as 'the other one' and about the feminist content of the novel. David Nokes wrote that the novel is 'Now hailed as a feminist classic' (*Times Literary Supplement*, 26 Apr. 1996), while the *Daily Mail* classed the serial as a 'Bodice Ripper' (6 Sept. 1996). In 1973 Christopher Fry made the television *biography The Brontës of Haworth* (1973). See FILM ADAPTATIONS AND BIOGRAPHIES; THEATRE ADAPTATIONS AND BIOGRAPHIES. PS

Nudd, Donna Marie, 'Bibliography of Film, Television and Stage Adaptations of *Jane Eyre*', BST (1991), 20. 3. 169–72.

Stoneman, Patsy, *Brontë Transformations: The Cultural Dissemination of 'Jane Eyre' and 'Wuthering Heights'* (1996).

temperance. Churches introduced 'abstinence pledges' as early as 1800, and a temperance movement founded in USA in 1808 spread rapidly. An Ulster Temperance Society was formed in 1829, initiating a movement that spread through Ireland, Scotland, and the rest of Britain. Most British temperance movements did not favour prohibition, but after 1853 the Methodist Church increasingly promoted total abstinence among its members. Revd Patrick Brontë, supported by Haworth Dissenters and the Keighley ministers Theodore *Dury and James Bardsley, inaugurated a Haworth Temperance Society at a meeting which he planned to hold at the Haworth National School on 17 November 1834. So many people came that the West Lane Methodist Chapel was used instead. Mr Brontë became president of the Society, and the Baptists Moses Saunders and John Winterbotham, with Branwell Brontë, were appointed secretaries. A 'considerable number' of people signed the pledge to 'abstain from Distilled Spirits, except for Medicinal Purposes'. In 1850, during his inspection on behalf of the General Board of Health, Benjamin Babbage found that Haworth's consumption of beer and spirits was below the average, and directories record the existence of a Haworth temperance hotel in 1853.

Temple, Miss Maria, the superintendent at *Lowood, modelled on Miss Ann *Evans, in *Jane Eyre*. Tall, erect, and stately, she has benignant brown eyes, dark brown hair, and a pale large forehead. Jane Eyre responds with love and awe to her kindness (shown especially to Helen *Burns), her refinement, wide knowledge, and humanity in ordering extra food for the hungry pupils despite school regulations. She clears Jane of Mr Brocklehurst's unjust accusation of deceitfulness. To her Jane owes her best acquirements and the solace of her friendship and society. She leaves the school to marry Revd Mr Nasmyth.

Tenant of Wildfell Hall, The. *See opposite page*

Tennyson, Alfred, Lord (1809–92), leading Victorian poet, Poet Laureate from 1850, baron from 1884. As 'Currer Bell' Charlotte Brontë sent Tennyson a copy of *Poems* 1846 in June 1847, with the sisters' standard acknowledgement of 'pleasure and profit' from his works. In July 1848 Charlotte and Anne brought a volume of Tennyson's poetry from London, probably for Emily. Though many topics in his collections (from 1830 onwards), *The Princess* (1847) and *In Memoriam* (1850), share Charlotte's interests—sexual desire and repression, madness, gender inequities, religious faith—she disliked his poetry's control. She abandoned *In Memoriam* halfway through, writing to Elizabeth Gaskell on 27 August 1850 that it was 'beautiful' but 'monotonous'—too 'measured' to convey 'bitter sorrow, while recent' (Smith *Letters*, 2. 457).   BT

> Martin, Robert B., *Tennyson: The Unquiet Heart* (1980).

Thackeray, Anne Isabella ('Anny'), later Lady Ritchie (1837–1919), elder daughter of William Makepeace *Thackeray, Charlotte Brontë's literary hero. Because of their mother's mental illness, Anne and her sister Minny spent their early life with grandparents in Paris and returned to their father in 1846. She married her cousin Richmond Ritchie in 1877 and had two children. Anne Thackeray became a novelist in her own right and is particularly famous for her biographical records of great Victorian writers she had known, notably *Records of Tennyson, Ruskin and Robert and Elizabeth Browning* (1892) and *Chapters from Some Memoirs* (1894). It is in the latter work that her brilliant description of the first occasion on which she met Charlotte Brontë is preserved (quoted in Wise & Symington, 3. 48–50; and Smith *Letters*, 2. 754–6). Anne Thackeray was only a girl at the time when Charlotte was brought by George Smith to a dinner party at Thackeray's house in Young Street, Kensington, London, on 12 June 1850. She watched at the window as the guests arrived and her huge father escorted 'a tiny, delicate, serious, little lady, pale, with fair straight hair, and steady eyes' into the house: 'She enters in mittens, in silence, in seriousness; our hearts are beating with wild excitement.' She records Charlotte's 'little *barège* dress, with a pattern of faint green moss', and the general amusement when Thackeray stooped to offer 'the great Jane Eyre—the tiny little lady' his arm, 'for, genius though she may be, Miss Brontë can barely reach his elbow'. She recalls, too, Charlotte's intense interest in Thackeray's conversation

but her inability to perform for his invited guests. Charlotte preferred the company of Miss Trulock, the children's governess, to that of the society ladies and the evening was such a gloomy embarrassment that Thackeray quietly stole away to his club the minute Charlotte left. A year later, the 13-year-old Anne Thackeray probably met Charlotte a second time when she accompanied her grandmother Mrs Carmichael-Smyth on a visit to Charlotte at the home of George Smith, the day after Thackeray's lecture on 29 May 1851 (Smith *Letters*, 2. 629 n. 3).

Thackeray, William Makepeace (1811–63), novelist, journalist, and editor of George Smith's *Cornhill Magazine* (1859–62). From the 1847–8 publication of *Vanity Fair* Thackeray came to be regarded as *Dickens's main rival, widely thought to surpass Dickens in realism and stylistic polish. Reviewers frequently compared Charlotte Brontë's works to Thackeray's, judging that they both exposed hypocrisy and detested the contemporary 'predominance of the husk over the kernel'. Reviewers also contrasted their methods: Thackeray described 'what is', Charlotte 'what is not' (*Oxford and Cambridge Magazine*, June 1856), he painting social life from detailed observation, she creating a realm from the imagination. To some Thackeray seemed more malicious, she more genial (*North American Review*, Oct. 1857), yet others regarded Thackeray as superior in depicting human experience in its sunnier moments.

Reading *Jane Eyre* as he was completing *Vanity Fair*, Thackeray confessed he could not put the book down despite his pressing printers' deadlines. He guessed that the author was a woman who 'knows her language better than most ladies do, or has had a "classical" education'. Praising the principal characters and remarking that 'some of the love passages made me cry', he declared to W. S. Williams on 23 October 1847 that the novel was 'the first English one . . . that I've been able to read for many a day' (Wise & Symington, 2. 149). Charlotte had read some of Thackeray's pseudonymous work in *Fraser's Magazine* and *Punch*, including 'The Snobs of England' (to Ellen Nussey, 28 December 1846; in Smith *Letters*, 1. 509, 510 n.). She loved *Vanity Fair*, which she read in monthly instalments (serialization began in January 1847); the novel was incomplete when Charlotte dedicated the second edition of *Jane Eyre* to Thackeray in December, prompted by his admiring note to her. The dedication created embarrassment: though wholly ignorant of his personal circumstances, Charlotte had seemed to allude to them, for Thackeray's mentally ill wife had been confined for years. The coincidence spawned rumours that the

(*cont. on page 503*)

A NNE Brontë's second and last novel, *Tenant* was published under her pseudonym Acton Bell, in June 1848. Conceived under a powerful sense of duty, it is an unsentimental depiction of individual excess and its contagion for family, friends, and society, and a plea for the independence of women and equal education for the sexes. Despite contemporary criticism of what Charlotte Brontë called an unfortunate choice of subject, the novel was a success with the public and went into a second edition in less than two months. Yet perhaps because it is always compared with two of the greatest 19th-century English novels, *Jane Eyre* and *Wuthering Heights*, *Tenant*—whose realism and clear moral vision challenge the romanticism of her sisters' works—remains undervalued.

Composition

We know that even before her first novel *Agnes Grey* had been accepted for publication by the London firm T. C. *Newby (July 1847), Anne had begun writing her second novel; but beyond this it is impossible to make more than a few observations on its composition, since there is no surviving manuscript and no authorial comment.

The three sisters had difficulty in finding publishers for their first novels but this lack of success and repeated rejection failed to halt their ambition to write. We know that in August 1846, Charlotte began writing *Jane Eyre*, which she was to finish approximately a year later. Following the lead of Herbert Rosengarten (*Tenant*, p. xiii), it seems reasonable to assume that Anne and Emily also began writing their second novels about this time, during the summer of 1846, and that they took shape over the same period of time. The first draft of *Tenant* was probably concluded on 10 June 1847, the fictional date at the end of Gilbert *Markham's letter to J. *Halford which forms the frame of the novel. In November 1847, Anne was busy working on the final proof-sheets of *Agnes Grey* and it is possible that she completed her fair copy of *Tenant* during the following December. This would allow Newby six months for typesetting and proofs, before the novel was published on or about 27 June 1848.

Of all the Brontë novels, *Tenant* appears to have benefited most from the Brontës' collaborative writing experience. It was their habit to discuss ideas each evening in the sitting room of the Parsonage, often pacing up and down as they talked over their plots. Elizabeth *Gaskell records that 'Once or twice a week, each read to the others what she had written, and heard what they had to say about it' (Gaskell *Life*, 2. 11). *Tenant* is both more expansive and more sophisticated in form than *Agnes Grey*, and the similarity of tone and narrative technique to *Wuthering Heights* suggests that Anne was not slow to learn from her sister's work.

It is likely, too, that Charlotte's later objections to what she considered Anne's mistaken choice of subject were voiced during these early discussions (*'Biographical Notice'), but Anne was determined to speak the 'unpalatable truth'. Her preface to the second edition (22 July 1848) makes a strong plea for realism in the novel. Responding to critical accusations of 'a morbid love for the coarse, not to say the brutal' (*Spectator*, 8 July 1848), she acknowledges that the most agreeable course for a writer of fiction would be 'to represent a bad thing in its least offensive light'. But this would be a dereliction of the writer's moral duty: 'O Reader! if there were less of this delicate concealment of facts—this whispering "Peace, peace," when there is no peace, there would be less of sin and misery to the young of both sexes who are left to wring their bitter knowledge from experience' (*Tenant* (Clarendon edn.), p. xxxviii).

In this same preface, Anne also addresses the question of an author's identity, and, of readers' expectations, based on the author's presumed gender. The sex of an author is irrelevant to the quality of a novel: 'All novels are or should be written for both men and women to read, and I am at a loss to conceive how a man should permit himself to write anything that would be really disgraceful to a woman, or why a woman should be censured for writing anything that would be proper and becoming for a man.'

Manuscript and early editions

The manuscript of *Tenant* has not survived. With the publication of *Agnes Grey*, Thomas Newby had secured the first refusal of Anne's second novel and with the good sales of *Agnes Grey* she saw no reason to deny him *Tenant*, despite Charlotte's advice to the contrary. Thus *Tenant* by 'Acton Bell' was published by Newby in three volumes on or about 27 June 1848. Herbert Rosengarten points out that the work appeared in the 'Alphabetical List of New Works' in the *Publishers' Circular* for the week ending 1 July 1848, with the announcement: 'TENANT (THE) OF WILDFELL HALL. By Acton Bell. 3 vols. post 8vo. pp. 1064, boards, 31s. 6d.' (*Tenant* (Clarendon edn.), p. xix). A second edition (technically, a second issue) followed in early August consisting of 'unused sheets of the first edition with an emended title page and the addition of a preface [and] a small number of corrections [in] the unbound sheets, mostly on single-leaf cancels' (*Tenant* (Clarendon edn.), p. xxii).

The terms of Newby's agreement with Anne were more generous than his previous cost-sharing publication of *Wuthering Heights* and *Agnes Grey*. This time he required no contribution from the author and offered to pay Anne on a sliding scale, as Charlotte explains in a letter to W. S. *Williams when *Smith, Elder and Company were exploring the idea of republishing *Wuthering Heights*, *Agnes Grey*, and *Tenant* (Smith *Letters*, 2. 465). Newby agreed to print 500 copies and to pay Anne £25 at the time of publication, a second £25 on the sale of 250 copies, £50 on the sale of 400 copies, and another £50 when the edition had sold out. Anne received only two instalments of £25 yet the edition had sold out by early August when the second edition appeared. Not until well after Anne's death, in March 1854, did Newby send a further £30 to Charlotte, probably at the instigation of George *Smith who would have been aware that Newby had sold the copyright of *Tenant* to Thomas Hodgson, who published a corrupt text in his Parlour Library edition of February 1854. Ever distrustful of Newby, Charlotte had added with her thanks to Smith: 'Should there be any difficulty in cashing the cheque at the Keighley Bank—I will let you know' (Christine Alexander, 'Newby's Chicanery', *N & Q* NS 42 (June 1995), 189–91).

With *Tenant*, Newby continued the duplicitous advertising he had begun with *Wuthering Heights* and *Agnes Grey*, conflating the names of the three Bell authors and capitalizing on the best-selling *Jane Eyre*. For example, he advertised *Tenant* 21 times in the *Morning Herald* (July and August 1848) (Geoffrey Larken, 'The Shuffling Scamp', *BST* (1970), 15. 80. 400–7), often implying that Acton Bell alone had written all the Bell novels and cleverly misquoting favourable notices from false sources. In the *Athenaeum* (10 June 1848), 'Mr. Acton Bell's New Novel' was linked with a selection of

'Opinions of the Press on Mr. Bell's first Novel', suggesting that this was *Wuthering Heights* and linking it to *Jane Eyre*. Newby overreached himself, however, when he dishonestly presented *Tenant* to an American publisher as the latest work by 'Currer Bell', the author of *Jane Eyre*. Since Charlotte's next novel had been promised to Harper Brothers of New York by her English publishers Smith, Elder, the American firm was understandably displeased and wrote to Smith, Elder complaining about 'false play'. Smith, Elder in turn wrote to the 'Bells' 'in alarm, suspicion and wrath' for clarification (Smith *Letters*, 2. 111–12). The sisters were annoyed at the aspersion on their integrity, and Anne and Charlotte immediately set out for London (7 July 1848) to confront Newby with his lie and to prove their separate identity to Smith, Elder. Yet Harper Brothers, already misled by Newby, had secured *Tenant* and published the first American edition on 28 July as 'By Acton Bell, Author of *Wuthering Heights*'.

Newby could hardly be accused of tardiness in the production of *Tenant*, as in the case of *Wuthering Heights* and *Agnes Grey*, but Anne's second novel did suffer the same general shoddiness of production as the earlier works, which Charlotte complained 'abound in errors of the press' (Smith *Letters*, 1. 575). Herbert Rosengarten points out careless errors in spelling, punctuation, and capitalization, and even a number of substantive errors which may derive from misreading Anne's handwriting or the common practice by some printers of having an apprentice read out copy to the compositor (*Tenant* (Clarendon edn.), p. xxiv). Modern editors might draw conclusions about Anne's preferences from her 'Author's Own Copy' of the first edition of *Tenant* (preserved in Parrish, Princeton), although it is not absolutely certain that the 34 pencil corrections in volume 2 are in Anne's hand.

When, in September 1850, Charlotte discussed with her publishers Smith, Elder the possibility of a new edition of *Wuthering Heights* and *Agnes Grey*, she excluded *Tenant*, considering it 'hardly . . . desirable to preserve' a work whose subject was so distasteful (Smith *Letters*, 2. 463). Even if they disagreed with Charlotte's judgement, Smith, Elder would have had difficulties over copyright, since Newby had bought *Tenant* outright (unlike *Wuthering Heights* and *Agnes Grey*). In about 1854, Newby sold the copyright of *Tenant* to Thomas Hodgson, on whose one-volume Parlour Library Edition most British editions of *Tenant* over the next century were based. From Hodgson copyright passed to Darton & Co. before at last being purchased in 1859 by Smith, Elder & Co. who, nevertheless, still followed the text of the corrupt Parlour Library edition, which omits chapter headings and the first four pages of the novel (the letter to J. *Halford) thus destroying its initial epistolary structure. American readers were more fortunate, since successive editions under the Harper imprint (1857, 1858, and 1864) carried the complete text of 1848.

Sources and context

Anne's preface to the second edition of *Tenant* explains her motives for handling the violent and passionate subjects that appeared so disagreeable and incongruous 'with the character—tastes and ideas of the gentle, retiring, inexperienced writer', as Charlotte put it to W. S. Williams (Smith *Letters*, 2. 463): 'My object in writing the following pages, was not simply to amuse the Reader, neither was it to gratify my own taste, nor yet to ingratiate myself with the Press and the Public: I wished to tell the truth, for truth always conveys its own moral to those who are able to receive it' (*Tenant* (Clarendon edn.), p. xxxvii).

She was spurred on by a powerful sense of duty to warn against such 'vice and vicious characters' as she portrays in the novel with scrupulous fidelity. She admits that the 'unhappy scapegrace' Mr Arthur *Huntingdon and his profligate companions are an extreme case, but assures her readers that 'such characters do exist, and if I have warned one rash youth from following in their steps, or prevented one thoughtless girl from falling into the very natural error of my heroine, the book has not been written in vain'.

As in the case of *Agnes Grey*, the moral purpose and content of *Tenant* are closely allied to Anne's personal experiences as a governess living in the household of her employers. *Tenant*, however, reaches further into 'some very unpleasant and undreamt of experience of human nature' (Diary Paper, 31 July 1845) encountered by Anne at *Thorp Green Hall, where she was employed by the *Robinson family from May 1840 until June 1845. Although unhappy there and planning to leave by December 1841 (see DIARY PAPERS), Anne was so valued by the Robinsons that they persuaded her to return and she eventually won the respect and affection of the two younger girls. When Branwell arrived to become tutor to young Edmund Robinson in January 1843, however, Anne became the silent witness to behaviour that she found particularly distressful. Always reckless and unstable, Branwell became convinced that Lydia Robinson was in love with him and responded accordingly. Apart from Branwell's often-unreliable assertions, his sudden dismissal by Revd Edmund Robinson in July 1845, and Anne's obvious agitation and lack of contradiction, there is little evidence about an illicit affair. However, Elizabeth Gaskell wrote to George Smith on 29 December 1856 that Lydia Robinson was at fault: 'bad as Branwell was,—he was not absolutely ruined forever, till she got hold of him, & he was not the first, nor the last' (Chapple & Pollard, *Gaskell Letters* 432). In the *Life* (1st and 2nd edns.), Gaskell told the story of Branwell's 'seduction' as she had heard it from Charlotte and Revd Patrick Brontë, but she was compelled by a threat of legal action to publish a retraction of 'every statement' imputing any breach of 'conjugal . . . duties' (see Smith *Letters*, 1. 413–14 n.).

Anne gave notice and 'escaped' from Thorp Green before Branwell's dismissal, but at home she was still subject to her brother's downward slide into drink, drugs, and despair as he gradually realized that Lydia Robinson would not marry him. Together with the rest of her family, Anne was forced to cope with the self-indulgence of an undisciplined character and the effect it had on those surrounding him. *Tenant* is a testament to this painful family tragedy of a son's degeneration, 'the terrible effects of talents misused and faculties abused' ('Biographical Notice'). Characters like Lord *Lowborough with his constant debts, his recourse to laudanum, his apoplectic fits after drinking bouts, and his belief that the false Annabella's love will save him from eternal damnation (ch. 22), vividly recall Branwell. Charlotte wrote of Anne: 'She brooded over it till she believed it to be a duty to reproduce every detail (of course with fictitious characters, incidents, and situations) as a warning to others.'

Thus not only the realistic portrayal of degenerate behaviour but also the judgements of Helen *Huntingdon about the necessary education of her son are informed by Anne's own experiences and by frequent discussion at Haworth Parsonage. With reference to Branwell's lack of 'self-government', Charlotte had told Margaret *Wooler, about the time Anne began writing *Tenant*, that boys 'are not half sufficiently guarded from temptation—Girls are protected as if they were something very frail and silly indeed while boys are turned loose on the world as if they—of all beings in existence, were the wisest and the least liable to be led astray' (Smith *Letters*, 1. 448). Anne's experience in drawing and painting also plays a major role in the life of her heroine, especially in her sensitive response to natural foliage and to the sea as subjects for illustration. Helen Huntingdon's accomplishment and hobby becomes her livelihood—something Charlotte, if not Anne, had seriously contemplated (see ART OF THE BRONTËS). So too the unorthodox belief in the doctrine of *universal salvation to which Helen clings during her dark times nursing her debauched husband, had been part of Anne's own private belief since her schooldays at *Roe Head when she suffered a period of religious depression and was comforted by 'the sweet views of salvation, pardon, and peace in the blood of Christ' (*BST* (1898), 1. 8. 27) brought to her by the *Moravian minister Revd James *La Trobe. As in the case of other Brontë novels, the neglected *Wildfell Hall is typical of the old stone houses on the edge of the Yorkshire moors, exposed to the weather and associated with 'ghostly legends and dark traditions'. The garden too is derelict, its topiary misshapen into a 'goblinish appearance' (ch. 2) that reinforces the *Gothic features of the novel and the suggestion of natural analogues to human behaviour that we find in *Wuthering Heights*. This may owe something to Anne's early collaboration with Emily in the lurid plots of *Gondal, although there is little other evidence of her early writing in *Tenant*. Branwell also describes a loveless marriage in his tale of the *Thurstons of Darkwall Manor.

Two letters from Charlotte to Ellen Nussey suggest a further source for Helen Huntingdon's flight from her debauched husband, in the experiences of a woman known to the Brontë family. In 1840, Patrick Brontë had advised a Mrs Collins, wife of a Keighley curate, to escape from 'her wretched husband's drunken, extravagant, profligate habits' (Smith *Letters*, 1. 231). Six and a half years later, in April 1847, when Mrs Collins again visited the Haworth Parsonage, Anne would have heard the frankly told 'narrative of her appalling distresses' at the hands of 'that wretched and most criminal Mr Collins' (Smith *Letters*, 1. 521). Although left destitute with two small children and suffering from venereal disease, Mrs Collins managed to regain a respectable position in society and ran a lodging house in *Manchester to provide for herself and her children, so preserving them from the corrupting influence of their father.

There are also literary analogues for the plot of *Tenant*, especially for the incompatible marriage between a self-indulgent husband and his highly principled, religious wife. Annabella Milbanke's marriage to Lord *Byron, her naive belief that she might save him from himself (cf. Helen's ideal 'to do my utmost to help his better self against his worse', ch. 20), and the riotous behaviour and gambling of Byron and his cronies was well known to the Brontës through such sources as Thomas *Moore's *Life of Byron*. Literary precedents are evident in the text of *Tenant* itself, in allusions to *Shakespeare's plays, to *Richardson's novels (cf. Clarissa Harlowe's 'secret pleasure' in the idea that she might reclaim the rake Lovelace with Helen's similar pious hope), and to such poets as Gray, Young, *Cowper, Sir Walter *Scott, and *Wordsworth. Huntingdon's dissolute friend Wilmot recalls the poet and libertine John Wilmot, second Earl of Rochester (as does Charlotte's Edward *Rochester in *Jane Eyre*); and Helen's Aunt *Maxwell's language echoes the rhetoric of *Methodist preachers, possibly from the Wesleyan Methodist literature of the Brontës' own Aunt Elizabeth

*Branwell. Above all, Anne's intimate knowledge of the *Bible enriches the language of *Tenant*.

Plot

The narrative begins by surveying a twenty-year period, in which Gilbert Markham tells in a series of letters to his brother-in-law, J. Halford, Esq., the story of his courtship of Helen Huntingdon. Within these letters, which frame the novel and conclude on 10 June 1847, we read the interpolated narrative of Helen's journal that covers the events of her life before she meets Gilbert and explains her situation and behaviour at Wildfell Hall.

Gilbert Markham, a young farmer of respectable yeoman stock, lives with his gossipy mother, pretty sister Rose, and sulky adolescent brother Fergus, at *Linden-Car. He falls in love with Mrs Graham (the name of Helen's mother which Helen assumes to preserve her anonymity), a beautiful young widow who has newly arrived in the neighbourhood with her son Arthur. She is the tenant of the gloomy mansion Wildfell Hall, whose Gothic setting and atmosphere reinforce the mysteriousness of her seclusion and her strange familiarity with her landlord Mr Frederick *Lawrence. Helen is a talented artist, an independent woman who sells her paintings to support herself and her child. Her quiet superiority, unconventional opinions and personal reticence intrigue Gilbert but also give rise to malicious gossip in the small country community of *Lindenhope, which includes the *Millward and *Wilson families.

Helen's protectiveness towards 'little Arthur' exacerbates her difference, but also provides the author with an excuse to discuss the very different education accorded to girls and boys, which she sees as detrimental to both sexes. Gilbert says that girls need more protection and guidance than boys, but Helen can see no reason to assume that boys should be better able to withstand temptation than girls. She has taught her son to dislike 'tempting liquors' (ch. 4), much to the merriment of Gilbert and his mother who believe that to bring a boy up in cloistered virtue (ch. 3) will make a 'milksop' of him. Mr *Millward, the village parson whose daughter Eliza had previously bewitched Gilbert, declares it is 'criminal' and 'contrary to Scripture and reason' to teach a child to despise 'the blessings of Providence'. Mr Lawrence, however, quietly observes that laudanum may fall into this category, yet it is better to abstain from it, even in moderation. Despite the didactic element in these scenes, they are wryly comic and reflect the parochial nature of a small village community.

Mrs *Markham's views on the role of the sexes in marriage are further cause for debate. Her advice to her son that 'it's your business (as a husband) to please yourself, and hers to please you' is the conventional view challenged verbally by Gilbert's sister Rose and implicitly by Helen Graham's behaviour. Helen's views on marriage (when she takes over the narrative in her journal) are as eloquent as they are on the education of children.

Gilbert Markham's relationship with Helen and consequently our knowledge of her character and situation, ebbs and flows with remarkable credibility as he feigns excuses to visit her and her son Arthur. Arthur's joyful response to Gilbert's 'beautiful black and white setter' Sancho, and Gilbert's genuine delight in his young friend assist in drawing them together. He refuses to credit aspersions against Helen's character until he overhears Helen and Lawrence in intimate conversation. Gilbert's ungovernable jealousy provokes a violent assault on Lawrence, a former friend; and Helen, distressed at the rupture of her friendship with Gilbert and eager to clear her name, entrusts him with her lengthy private journal that reveals the truth about her past.

The main story of Helen's struggle as wife and mother (chs. 16–44), is recorded in her journal from June 1821 to October 1827. Together with Gilbert Markham, we learn that she is actually Helen Huntingdon, the fugitive wife of a debauched man still living. Six years earlier, despite warnings from her prudent aunt Mrs *Maxwell (who with her husband acts as Helen's guardian), the 18-year-old Helen marries the charming but reckless Arthur Huntingdon who, despite an initial period of happiness and his young wife's efforts to save him, relapses into drinking, debauchery, and infidelity. He is governed by his appetites, formed by parental indulgence, and his weaknesses are exacerbated by the leisured mode of life expected of a country gentleman. Before the marriage, the handsome Huntingdon provides for the young Helen a fascinating contrast to her older suitors, the aptly named, smug Mr *Boarham and the wealthy but 'worthless old reprobate' Mr *Wilmot. Helen naively believes that by separating the sins from the sinner, her love will enable her to reform Huntingdon: 'if I hate the sins I love the sinner, and would do much for his salvation . . . I would willingly risk my happiness for the chance of securing his' (ch. 17). Once mistress of his *Grassdale Manor, however, she realizes that she was idealistic and 'wilfully blind'; but she determines that 'whatever I ought to have done, my duty, now, is plainly to love him and to cleave to him' (ch. 23). The challenge proves intolerable when her husband, jealous of the attention Helen bestows on their son, begins to systematically corrupt the child with drink, foul language, and maternal disrespect, in an insidious effort to manipulate his mother (ch. 30). Young Arthur's training in 'manhood' becomes a source of amusement to his father and his drinking companions *Mr Grimsby, *Walter Hargrave, *Ralph Hattersley, and Lord Lowborough (whose painful experiences parallel those of Helen and whose redemption provides a contrast to Huntingdon's corruption). Huntingdon also amuses himself in an affair with Lowborough's unprincipled wife Annabella *Wilmot. When Helen discovers the double adultery, she insists that her marriage shall exist only in name, refusing to play the submissive wife to her profligate husband. She feels she is losing her instinctive horror of vice and finds herself in moral danger when the 'keen, crafty, bold' but attractive Walter Hargrave (brother of her friend Millicent who has married Hattersley) tempts her to revenge herself on her unfaithful husband. Her initial plans to flee their corrupting influence and protect her child are thwarted, but after Huntingdon uses his son as an excuse to engage his mistress as a 'governess', Helen's brother Mr Lawrence and her loyal servant *Rachel succeed in arranging their escape.

Helen, Rachel, and 'little Arthur' seek refuge at Wildfell Hall, owned by Mr Lawrence. There she plans to earn a living from her hobby of painting, which has been a source of consolation throughout her trials. Her journal ends where the novel begins, with her new residency at Wildfell Hall and with a sarcastic reference to the 'fine gentleman and beau of the parish', Gilbert Markham, whom she has just met.

Shortly after the revelation of her secret, Helen courageously returns to nurse her dying husband who welcomes her with scorn but then sinks into pitiful dependence on her physical and spiritual strength. Christian commitment is an integral part of

Helen's character. She firmly believes that, although her husband cannot repent, 'through whatever purging fires the erring spirit may be doomed to pass—whatever fate awaits it, still, it is not lost, and God, who hateth nothing that He hath made, *will* bless it in the end!' (ch. 49).

The newly widowed Helen has inherited her uncle's Staningley estate and now holds her husband's estate in trust for her son. With the death of Huntingdon, the way is left clear for Gilbert Markham to renew his suit, but several episodes of suspense, caused by Gilbert's gaucheness and feelings of inferiority towards the wealthy Helen and his mistaken assumptions about the marriage of Lawrence (to Esther *Hargrave whom Helen has encouraged not to marry without love), delay their union. Finally, after a brilliantly written scene in which Gilbert's usual lack of perception, and 'scruples of false delicacy and pride' (so disappointing to critics of the novel), are overcome by Helen's offer of herself through the symbol of a white Christmas rose, Helen and Gilbert are married in August 1850. The heroine of *Tenant*—a principled, religious, and intelligent woman—teaches her narrator husband and his reading audience that 'the greatest worldly distinctions and discrepancies of rank, birth, and fortune are as dust in the balance compared with the unity of accordant thoughts and feelings, and truly loving, sympathizing hearts and souls'.

Reception

Anne Brontë's determination to portray scenes of dissipation with uncompromising faithfulness, to defend a married woman's rights and to present an argument for moral equality between the sexes struck the first readers of *Tenant* with amazed incredulity and brought mixed reactions. The public reacted with excitement to the startling unsentimental plot, pushing sales well beyond the expectations of author or publisher. Here was a challenge to the concept of the dutiful Victorian wife in the unconventional behaviour of a woman who believed it her right to think and act according to her conscience, unendorsed by the law. In 1848, a wife had no legal rights to her children or to her property. The heroine's actions were both controversial and illegal. Yet it was the slur on English society rather than Helen Huntingdon's actions that brought accusations from the critics of an 'objectionable' subject and 'a coarseness of tone' (*Spectator* (8 July 1848); in Allott, p. 249). The *Literary World* (12 Aug. 1848) sprang to the defence of upper-class society: 'Is it characteristic of "English Respectabilities"—the landholders, common law men, or gig-keeping classes—to unite manners and principles like those of Huntingdon to property and position like his—or intelligence and taste like that of Markham to his clownishness?' (Allott, p. 259). Although the realism of *Tenant*'s scenes and characters was not acknowledged, there was praise for its 'vigor of thought, freshness and naturalness of expression' and the 'vividness and fervor' of the author's 'intense realization' of imaginative scenes. Contrary to Charlotte Brontë's 'Biographical Notice' of 1850, in which she states that *Tenant* had an unfavourable reception, a number of reviewers defended the work against charges of immorality (Allott, pp. 260–1) and the *Athenaeum* recommended it as 'the most interesting novel which we have read for a month past' (Allott, p. 251). The *Morning Herald* (3 July 1848) pronounced it 'a thorough racy English novel' and the *Manchester Examiner* (8 July 1848) enthusiastically wrote: 'Mr. Bell has managed to frame a tale, which we defy the most *blasé* novel reader to yawn over' (Smith *Letters*, 2. 97).

The debate on the sex of the author or authors of the 'Bell' novels was still raging. *Sharpe's London Magazine* (Aug. 1848), found the enigma further complicated by the appearance of *Tenant*. Whereas there are 'a thousand trifles' indicating a woman's mind and no man would have made his sex appear so 'disgusting and ridiculous', yet 'a bold coarseness, a reckless freedom of language' and a familiarity with 'the worst style of *fast* men' suggest no woman would have written the book. The reviewer concludes that 'it may be the production of an authoress assisted by her husband, or some other *male* friend' (Allott, p. 265). Charles Kingsley was convinced that 'Acton Bell' was a woman since the 'unnecessary coarseness' that makes the novel unfit for girls, is 'just such as a woman, trying to write like a man, would invent' (*Fraser's Magazine*, Apr. 1849). Yet he boldly defended the author's courage in realistically exposing 'this smug, respectable, whitewashed English society', and felt society should be grateful to those 'who dare to show her the image of her own ugly, hypocritical visage' (Allott, pp. 270–3). See CRITICAL RECEPTION TO 1860; CRITICISM 1860–1940; CRITICISM FROM 1940.

Carnell, Rachel K., 'Feminism and the Public Sphere in Anne Brontë's *The Tenant of Wildfell Hall*, *Nineteenth-Century Literature* 53: 1, 1–24 (1998).

Hargreaves, G. D., 'Incomplete Texts of *The Tenant of Wildfell Hall*', BST (1972), 16. 82. 113–17.

—— 'Further Omissions in *The Tenant of Wildfell Hall*', BST (1977), 17. 87. 115–21.

Langland, Elizabeth, *Anne Brontë: The Other One* (1989).

Nash, Julie, and Suess, Barbara A. (eds.), *New Approaches to the Literary Art of Anne Brontë* (2001).

Scott, P. J. M., *Anne Brontë: A New Critical Assessment* (1983).

Thormählen, Marianne, 'The Villain of Wildfell Hall: Aspects and Prospects of Arthur Huntingdon', *Modern Languages Review* 88, 839–40 (1993).

—— *The Brontës and Religion* (1999).

governess of Thackeray's daughters had written *Jane Eyre*.

In a letter to W. S. Williams of 28 January 1848, Charlotte called Thackeray 'that greatest modern Master' (Smith *Letters*, 2. 23). She revered Thackeray's artistic fidelity to life, his imaginative control and avoidance of melodrama. She wrote to W. S. Williams on 11 December 1847 that she recognized Thackeray as a 'keen, ruthless satirist' in 'his war against the falsehood and follies of "the World"' (Smith *Letters*, 1. 571), and on 11 March 1848 that in his fresh, dynamic illustrations he was Truth's 'high-priest' (Smith *Letters*, 2. 41). She eventually expressed disappointment in Thackeray's depiction of women, however. For *Rebecca and Rowena* (1849), she declared to Elizabeth Smith on 9 January 1850, he should be 'tried by a jury of twelve matrons' (Smith *Letters*, 2. 327), and she told George *Smith on 14 February 1852 that she judged the first volume of the *History of Henry Esmond* (which Smith sent her in manuscript, 7 February) 'unjust to women' (Wise & Symington, 3. 314). She also 'grieved' that 'the Great Doubter and Sneerer' (rather than the idealist in him) usually guided his pen (to W. S. Williams, 10 Jan. 1850; in Smith

Letters, 2. 328), and that his fiction treated vice too lightly (to George Smith, 26 Mar. 1853 [mistakenly given as to Williams, May 1853], in Wise & Symington, 4. 67). Thackeray in turn found the subject of *Villette* 'vulgar' and disapproved of the heroine: 'I don't make my *good* women ready to fall in love with two men at once' (to Mrs Carmichael-Smyth, 28 March 1853). He linked the novel's disturbing depiction of female passion to Charlotte's frustration as 'a noble heart longing to mate itself and destined to wither away into old maidenhood with no chance to fulfil the burning desire' (to Lucy Baxter, 11 March 1853).

Their actual meetings (the first in December 1849) proved mutually unsatisfying. During her June 1850 visit to London Thackeray disappointed Charlotte by speaking of his art in an ironic, cavalier vein, and when he entertained Charlotte at a dinner in his home, her reserve considerably dampened the evening's mood. In London again in May–June 1851, she delighted in his lecture series on 18th-century English humorists but disapproved of his levity in referring to young men's dissipations. She also abhorred his habit of calling attention to her in public and referring to her as

'Jane Eyre'. She scolded him roundly for these transgressions and for what she considered his toadying to aristocrats. Apart from her dissatisfaction with the man, she maintained her regard for his art, and she hung an engraving of Thackeray in the Parsonage dining room (with another of the Duke of *Wellington and George Richmond's portrait of herself (see PORTRAITS OF THE BRONTËS)— all gifts from George Smith).

Thackeray published Charlotte's last piece of writing, the novel fragment *Emma, as 'The Last Sketch' in the *Cornhill* (Apr. 1860), prefacing it with a graceful tribute to her 'burning love of truth', her bravery, simplicity, 'indignation at wrong', 'eager sympathy', 'pious love and reverence', and 'passionate honour'. Over the following eighteen months he also published in the *Cornhill* two poems by Charlotte, 'Watching and Wishing' and 'When Thou Sleepest', and one by Emily, 'The Outcast Mother' (Neufeldt *CBP*, pp. 248, 231; Roper *EBP*, p. 85 as 'A Farewell to Alexandria').　　　BT

Carey, John, *Thackeray: Prodigal Genius* (1977).
Monsarrat, Ann, *An Uneasy Victorian: Thackeray the Man, 1811–1863* (1980).

theatre adaptations and biographies. Adaptations of the Brontë novels began almost immediately with stage versions of *Jane Eyre*, the first of which (*Jane Eyre or The Secrets of Thornfield Manor*, by 'John Courtney'—the pseudonym of the actor John Fuller) appeared in 1848 at the Victoria Theatre. In 1856 a version by John Brougham was performed and printed in New York. A German version by Charlotte Birch-Pfeiffer had already been performed in New York in 1854, and appeared again in 1856, 1870, 1882, and 1884. The play was printed in a dual-language version entitled *Jane Eyre or The Orphan of Lowood* (*Die Waise Von Lowood*) in New York in 1870. An anonymous version bearing strong resemblances to this was performed at the Surrey Theatre in London in 1867 and another possibly plagiarized version by 'Mme von Heringen Hering' appeared at the Theatre Royal, Coventry, in 1877. Clifton W. Tayleure's American play, another version of Birch-Pfeiffer, was performed in St Louis, Washington, Boston, Chicago, and New York between 1871 and 1882, and there were also American versions by J. S. Houghton (1874), Anna E. Dickinson (1876), and Charlotte Thompson (1883). Miron Leffingwell's 1909 American version also owes something to Birch-Pfeiffer. In Britain, two versions appeared in 1879: that by T. H. Paul was performed at the Adelphi Theatre, Oldham; *Jane Eyre or Poor Relations*, adapted by James Willing [J. T. Douglass] and Leonard Rae, was performed at the Royal Park Theatre, London. A version by W. G. Wills appeared at the Globe Theatre, London, in

1882. The plays differ greatly from one another even at the level of plot, with the Courtney play poking fun at authority for the benefit of an audience of costermongers, while the Birch-Pfeiffer group present Rochester as a saintly figure whose madwoman in the attic is not his wife, but an object of charity. The later group of British plays (1879–82) focus more on Jane's sexual vulnerability, making her the object of attentions by John Reed and Mr Brocklehurst. The British plays exist at present only in manuscript, although an edition by Patsy Stoneman is in preparation.

Two American versions of *Jane Eyre* appear under the title *The Master of Thornfield*: by W. H. C. Kirkbride in 1915, and by Rose Bachelis Shomer and Miriam Shomer in the 1920s; the title was used in England by Dorothy Brandon (1944). A British play by Phyllis Birkett was performed in Keighley in 1929, and in London in 1931. Birkett herself played Bertha 'with tremendous gusto' (*Yorkshire Post*, 25 Sept. 1931). An interesting feature of Birkett's play is the interpolation of a scene between Bertha and her brother showing that Richard had cheated Bertha of her inheritance. Helen Jerome's version was first performed at Birmingham Repertory and subsequently at the Queen's Theatre, Shaftesbury Avenue, in 1936, with Curigwen Lewis and Reginald Tate as Jane and Rochester; it appeared in Leeds in 1937, in Liverpool in 1938, and was also performed on British television in 1937. Although much of Jerome's dialogue is drawn from the novel, the text scarcely lives up to its subtitle, 'A Drama of Passion'; on the other hand, a Liverpool reviewer comments on the startling effect of seeing a woman not as the object, but the subject of desire (*Liverpool Echo*, 11 Mar. 1938). The staging seems to have sensationalized the triangle situation, with the two women facing each other over the sleeping Rochester. Katharine Hepburn played Jane in Jerome's play in a tour including Boston, Chicago, Cleveland, Pittsburgh, and Washington (DC) during 1936–7, and Tony Miner compares her favourably with 'Joan Fontaine, in the film', who 'showed the governess as mousy, beaten, shy, yet bold'. By contrast 'Kate . . . played the role with a quiet wit, a delicate charm and . . . a certain sharp intelligence. It was the very best portrayal of the role I have seen, on stage or screen' (quoted in Charles Higham, *Kate* (1975), 83). Nevertheless, Hepburn found Jerome's dialogue lacking in dramatic flexibility and the two women quarrelled over Jerome's refusal to revise it; the play never reached Broadway. The play continued to be performed regularly in Britain and America into the 1980s.

Other adaptations from this period include those by Pauline Phelps (Iowa, 1941), Dorothy Brandon (*The Master of Thornfield*, Oxford, 1944),

Jane Kendall [Anne Martens] (Chicago, 1945) and Huntingdon Hartford (New York, 1956). Constance Cox's 1959 version, which was also adapted for BBC TV, was performed in Canterbury in 1972 and Wigan in 1973. Brian Tyler's play went on tour, including London and Nottingham, in 1964. John Cannon's 1973 version, performed in Crewe, showed a drooling, sexually uninhibited Bertha; interestingly, when the play was revived at the Wyvern Theatre, Swindon, in 1982, the 'maniac' of the earlier cast list had become 'the madwoman', possibly reflecting the intervening appearance of Sandra Gilbert and Susan Gubar's *The Madwoman in the Attic* (1979). In 1978, *Jane Eyre* was performed in Japan, directed by Kazue Kontaibo. Lionel Hamilton's 1978 adaptation later appeared at nine locations on tour in 1989. Other adaptations were by Christopher Martin (Stoke-on-Trent, 1983), Jonathan Myerson (Harrogate and York, 1984), Sheila Haughey (Cheltenham, 1985), Peter Coe (Chichester, 1986), Annette Marten (Michigan, 1989), and Judy Yordon (Indiana, 1989). Sylvia Wharton's *The Childhood of Jane Eyre* was performed in Keighley in 1985 and *Young Jane Eyre* in Minneapolis in 1988. Charles Vance's England Touring production appeared in eleven venues during 1985, with an elaborate scholarly programme aimed at an educational market, and reappeared in Bradford in 1996, billed as 'newly adapted for the stage'. Willis Hall's play was performed in Sheffield in 1992 and in York in 1993; Sally Hunt's in Leeds in 1993.

A new departure was Fay Weldon's adaptation, directed by Helena Kaut-Howson, performed at Birmingham Repertory Theatre in 1986 and, in a completely rewritten form, at the Leeds Playhouse in 1988. This production took advantage of the open staging of the Playhouse to present fluid movements and striking effects of lighting and music in which the vivid reds of Bertha's dress and the fire at Thornfield contrasted with the monotone grey of the set. The Brontë family were on stage throughout, commenting on Charlotte's developing story. Charlotte and Jane merged into one another and the Lowood girls (and sometimes Jane and Adèle) were represented by life-sized dolls who indicated the dreary conformity of Victorian life for women. Interviews with Weldon and Kaut-Howson show that the Gilbert-and-Gubar conception of Bertha's role as representative of repressed anger and sexuality in the text had now become orthodox, and reviewers described the play as 'a feminist fairy-tale' (*Daily Express*, 8 Dec. 1993). Weldon's adaptation was subsequently performed in Dublin (1990), Pitlochry (1992), and London (1993).

Polly Teale's 1999 adaptation was also acclaimed as a 'daring' and 'potent' piece of drama: 'using a dazzling theatrical vocabulary, this is not only magnificent and exciting acting, it's also daring in its interpretation' (*International Herald Tribune*); 'What's impressive is that, once again, the company have managed to put the interior life of a book on stage as well as its narrative. Adaptations of this quality can't be dismissed as a poor second to reading the book' (*Time Out*). Teale's play was performed by the Shared Experience Theatre Company at the West Yorkshire Playhouse in Leeds; the Yvonne Arnaud Theatre, Guildford; and the New Ambassadors Theatre, London.

The increasing interest in the first Mrs Rochester had already been seen in a radio play by Michelene Wandor called *A Consoling Blue*, broadcast in 1985, which combined elements from *Jane Eyre* and from Jean Rhys's novel *Wide Sargasso Sea* (1966) (see TELEVISION AND RADIO ADAPTATIONS; SEQUELS AND 'INCREMENTAL LITERATURE'), and 1988 saw the stage performance in Cardiff of *Shadow in the Glass*, a play also based on the two novels and written by Valerie V. Lucas and David D. Cottis. In 1990 the idea reached London when Monstrous Regiment performed Debbie Shewell's *More than One Antoinette* at the Young Vic Theatre. The feminist direction of this play is indicated by the fact that Jane's marriage to Rochester becomes a self-inflicted punishment for Antoinette/Bertha's sufferings.

Judith Adams adapted *Villette* for the stage in a version performed at the Crucible Theatre, Sheffield, in 1997. The programme contextualized the play by quotations from Christina Rossetti and Emily Dickinson, and from modern feminist literary theory. *The Tenant of Wildfell Hall* was dramatized by Kenneth Hillmer in 1969 and by Lisa Evans in 1995. Evans's version was directed by Gwenda Hughes for the Birmingham Repertory Theatre and was also performed at the New Vic, Newcastle under Lyme, in 1998; the play was presented in the context of the Victorian fight for women's rights.

Unlike *Jane Eyre*, *Wuthering Heights* did not attract Victorian adaptors, and the first stage version was probably that performed at the Little Theatre, Sheffield, at some date after 1929. The structure included the second generation of characters and the programme included a family tree and a quotation from Charles Simpson's *Emily Brontë* (1929), commenting on the symmetry of design in the novel. Randolph Carter's 1933 adaptation was performed at various locations in the eastern States of America during the 1930s and on Broadway in 1939. The version by Mary Pakington and Olive Walter had a similar history in England, being performed in Croydon in 1933, at the Royalty Theatre, London, in 1934 and in an England Touring Production throughout the 1930s and in 1947. It seems to have been in the style of a 19th-century melodrama, with intensified emotion and ethical polarization. At the Manchester Repertory Theatre (1935, where the assistant stage manager was Miss Joan Littlewood), and at the Theatre Royal, Huddersfield (1937), the performance also included incidental light music.

One of the best-known dramatizations of *Wuthering Heights* was that by John Davison, first performed in 1937 and in at least nine locations between then and 1957, with a revival in 1986. Reginald Tate, who played Rochester in Helen Jerome's 1936 stage play of *Jane Eyre*, played Heathcliff in Davison's play, probably in 1937. Despite its popularity, Davison's play reduces the originality of the novel by presenting Catherine as a coquette, who exploits her feminine helplessness(!) to make Heathcliff her servant, and uses her relationship with Edgar to make him jealous. A version adapted by Ria Mooney and Donald Stauffer was performed at the Dublin Gate Theatre in 1939; this time the incidental music was heavyweight, including Beethoven, Tchaikovsky, Bach, and Wagner. Various ephemeral versions from the next decades include C. F. Mynhardt's *Helshoogte*, a drama in Afrikaans performed in Pretoria c.1941–2, Beppe Fenoglio's *La Voce nella tempesta* (*The Voice of the Storm*), written before 1960, and a version by Jay Nivison performed in Durban in 1975.

Constance Cox, who adapted *Jane Eyre* for television in 1956 and for the stage in 1959, adapted *Wuthering Heights* for a stage performance in Bolton in 1984, and the same year saw the first performance in Cambridge of a version by Vince Foxall which was also produced in at least five other locations up to 1990. Foxall's text included some of Emily Brontë's poetry, and indicates a general tendency at this time to place the text in a 'high-brow' context. The year 1988 saw two new dramatizations; that by John Boyd, produced at the Lyric Theatre, Belfast, evoked comparisons with Shakespearian tragedy and was commended for its 'use of Mahler's Fifth Symphony to intensify the melodramatic atmosphere' (*Belfast Newsletter*, 18 Feb. 1988), while that by Charles Ivan [Charles Vance] at the Alhambra Theatre, Bradford, quoted Lord David Cecil's eulogistic 1934 essay on Emily Brontë. Cecil's phrase 'children of storm' was also prominent in Michael Napier Brown's version, first performed in Northampton, and revived at the Grand Theatre, York, in 1994. Although this performance had genuine Yorkshire speakers and shabby costumes, the set, lighting, and generous use of recorded music combined to create an iconic image of the doomed lovers on the hilltop. While Vance's play was described as 'Victorian melodrama', Chris Martin's 1989 version at the New Victoria Theatre, North Staffs, was described

as 'naturalistic' (*Guardian*, 6 May 1989), and the 1990s saw less culture-bound performances by resourceful low-budget touring companies. The Snap Theatre Co. performed Lynn Robertson Hay's lively version in a variety of college venues in 1993, while William Ash's version was performed by Good Company throughout 1994. Three of the actors in this production—Jason Riddington (Heathcliff), Caroline Milmoe (Cathy), and Nigel Pivaro (Hindley)—were well known to audiences from television appearances in *Casualty* and *Coronation Street*. Jeremy Raison's adaptation, also performed in 1994, at Chester Gateway Theatre, was notable for having a black actor, Patrick Robinson (also familiar from *Casualty*), playing the part of Heathcliff. Gerry Dempsey wrote that 'his dreadlocked presence subtly alters the tone and emphasis of the play . . . The conflict is suddenly racial, not social, and Heathcliff is a different kind of victim'. Robinson was described as 'an actor of towering presence' well supported by a 'spooky' set and music composed by Corin Buckeridge (*Daily Express*, 29 Mar. 1994).

The Brontë lives have also inspired many stage plays, including those by M. B. Linton (*The Tragic Race*, 1926), Isabel Clarke (*Haworth Parsonage*, 1927), Oscar W. Firkins (*The Bride of Quietness*, 1932), Clemence Dane (*Wild Decembers*, 1932), Alfred Sangster (*The Brontës*, 1933), Mary D. Sheridan (*The Parson's Children* and *The Parson's Wife*, 1933), Rachel Ferguson (*Charlotte Brontë*, 1933), John Davison (*The Brontës of Haworth Parsonage*, 1934), Ella Moorhouse (*Stone Walls*, 1936), Edward Purchase (*The White Flame*, 1937), Elizabeth Goudge (*The Brontës of Haworth*, 1939), Martyn Richards (*Branwell*, 1948), Robert Gittings (*The Brontë Sisters*, 1955), Margaret Compton (*Shadows of Villette*, 1950s?), Winifred Gérin (*My Dear Master*, c.1955), Richard Crane (*Thunder*, 1976), Bettine Manktelow (*Branwell*, 1977), Beverley Cross (*Haworth*, 1978), Douglas Jackson (*Episode*, 1978), Anthony Hunt (*Brontë Seasons*, 1985), Lesley Alexander (*A Tender Fire*, 1988), Lee Bollinger (*The Gales of March*, 1989), and S. Robertson-Brown (*Emily*, 1994). PS

Nudd, Donna Marie, 'Rediscovering *Jane Eyre* through its Adaptations', in Diana Hoeveler and Beth Lau (eds.), *Approaches to Teaching Jane Eyre* (1992).
—— 'Bibliography of Film, Television, and Stage Adaptations of *Jane Eyre*', *BST* (1991), 20. 3. 169–72.
Stoneman, Patsy, *Brontë Transformations: The Cultural Dissemination of 'Jane Eyre' and 'Wuthering Heights'* (1996).

'There's little joy in life for me', by Charlotte Brontë (21 June 1849); published under the title 'On the Death of Anne Brontë', *The Woman at*

Home (Dec. 1896). The draft manuscript has many uncancelled variants. Charlotte's mood after Anne's death is one of exhaustion and contemplation of future 'weary strife' rather than the wrenching memory of agony associated with Emily; but the poem is complex, for 'Calmly to watch' conflicts with Charlotte's 'longing', and her fervent thanks for Anne's peace contrast with her personal sensation of being 'benighted' and 'tempest tossed'. Compare *'My darling, thou wilt never know'.

Neufeldt *CBP*, p. 342.

'There's no use in weeping', by Charlotte Brontë; in *Poems* 1846 as 'Parting', a revised version of manuscripts in Pierpont Morgan and Bonnell, BPM MS 113. Written at Haworth, 29 January 1838, just before returning to Margaret *Wooler's school, it is a spirited declaration of personal loyalty and love, defying the cold outer world which separates the family physically but cannot destroy its close bonds or the memories it shares. The opening lines have a song-like rhythm, and the poem is finely phrased and structured.

Neufeldt *CBP*, p. 329.

'There was once a little girl' is the first line of Charlotte Brontë's earliest extant manuscript (BPM B78), composed when she was about 10–12 years old for her youngest sister Anne (*c*.1826–8). Written in bold childish script on sixteen tiny pages (5.6 × 3.6 cm) and enclosed in a cover of white, grey, and blue spotted wallpaper, this is the first of the famous little hand-sewn booklets of the Brontës' *juvenilia. The story is a mixture of fact and fiction, describing how 'Ane', the only child of rich parents, is taken by her mother to visit a fine castle near London. When she travels with her parents in a ship, however, her mother becomes ill and Ane attends her 'with so much care', administering the required medicine. Charlotte illustrated the story with tiny watercolour paintings of a house, a castle, a rowing boat, a sailing boat, a lady walking a dog, and the mother's sickroom (illustrated and described in detail in Alexander & Sellars, pp. 1–6).

Alexander *EEW*, 1. 3.

Thom, Revd David (b. *c*.1795), minister of the Scotch church, Rodney Street, Liverpool, and then of Bold Street chapel, Liverpool; a leading proponent of the doctrine of *universal salvation. He wrote *The Assurance of Faith: or Calvinism Identified with Universalism* (2 vols., 1828), *Dialogues on Universal Salvation and Topics Connected Therewith* (1838; 2nd edn. 1847; 3rd edn. 1855) and other works. He had probably read the Smith, Elder 1848 reissue of *Poems* 1846 and perhaps *Tenant*, for he wrote flatteringly to Anne Brontë in late 1848. She was delighted to find an 'able and ardent' advocate for the Universalism she had cherished from her childhood.

'Thomas Bewick', published in the *Halifax Guardian* (1 Oct. 1842) (no surviving manuscript), and signed 'NORTHANGERLAND', is the only piece of art/literary criticism Branwell Brontë is known to have written and his last publication before leaving for *Thorp Green Hall. In it he attempts to define and articulate his own aesthetic beliefs and principles. Ostensibly analysing what, in comparison to the work of more modern and popular engravers, makes Bewick's engravings so powerful and attractive for him, Branwell, in trying to define the nature of the 'quiet poetry' he finds in Bewick's work, reveals as much about his own taste in poetry as about his taste in art. The influence of *Wordsworth is readily apparent when Branwell says of Bewick, 'the designer must have been imbued with a feeling in unison with nature, and far removed from the Chinese exactness of a mere copyist', and 'Let us then give honour to those who have so far extended the range of our sympathies, and compelled us to understand both what our feelings are, and in what manner to express them.' See also NATURAL HISTORY AND THE BRONTËS. VN

Neufeldt *BB Works*, 3. 397–400.

Thomas family of Haworth, descendants of John Thomas (*c*.1769–1841), one of Revd Patrick Brontë's churchwardens in 1820. His son William Thomas sen. (1789–1875), butcher, wine and spirit merchant, landowner, owner of Hollings Mill, Stanbury, from 1849, let the mill to his son William (1814–86), after whose bankruptcy in 1853 it was taken over by two other sons, James (1812–88) and Richard Roberts (1819–76). James and Richard were landowners and in charge of the wine business before 1850, supplying port and sherry to the Parsonage. In 1850 the Thomases assisted in the Public Health Enquiry, but in April 1851 William sen. and Richard objected to inclusion in the improvement scheme, since their property was well supplied with water. Branwell painted William Thomas jun.'s portrait in *c*.1838–9. William sen.'s younger brother Enoch (1811–48) was Branwell's drinking companion, nicknamed the 'Devil's Thumb'. A property-owner, listed as a butcher in 1830, by 1837 he was tenant-landlord of the King's Arms, then from 1841/2 landlord of the *Black Bull. In February 1844 his mind was disordered by 'very severe and great affliction', as Revd Patrick Brontë told George Taylor (Lock & Dixon, p. 340). Probably an alcoholic, he died in March 1848 from dropsy and chronic inflammation of the liver. A family autograph book, letters to the Thomases from Charlotte and Mr Brontë, and 'R. Thomas's' inclusion in Charlotte's wedding-card list in 1854 indicate a friendly relationship.

Thompson, John Hunter (1808–90), a fellow pupil with Branwell Brontë of the portrait painter William *Robinson in Leeds. Branwell met Thompson again in Bradford when he joined a circle of young struggling artists there. Thompson worked as a professional painter from the premises of Mr Aglen, a carver and gilder, and subsequently from the George Hotel at Bradford. Like Branwell, Thompson was the son of an Ulsterman, a noted raconteur, and fond of good conversation. He was probably Branwell's closest friend in Bradford and even finished one of Branwell's portrait commissions for him after he left Bradford (Alexander & Sellars, p. 332). Unlike Branwell, Thompson seems to have made a reasonable living in the Bradford area painting portraits—a fact that rather belies the usual belief that Branwell's prospects suffered from competition with the new craze for photo portraits.

Thornfield Hall, in *Jane Eyre*. In Thornfield Hall Jane hears demoniac laughter from the third storey, teaches her young pupil Adèle *Varens, falls in love with her 'master', *Rochester, rescues him from the bed set alight by his mad wife, and looks on with pain at the house-party charades where he 'marries' Blanche Ingram. In an eerie tapestried room in the third storey she tends Richard *Mason, and in her own room sees the terrifying Bertha *Rochester tear her bridal veil. In the Eden-like garden Jane accepts Rochester's proposal, and in Hay church just beyond the gates their wedding is broken off. Rochester takes Jane to see Bertha, snatching and growling like a wild-maned animal in her secret room. Afterwards, in the library, he pleads with Jane to become his 'wife'; but she 'rends her heart-strings' from him, leaving Thornfield in the early dawn. Only after the hall has become a ruin, blackened by the fire which destroyed the madwoman who kindled it, can Jane seek out and marry the maimed Rochester.

Charlotte's visionary imagination created Thornfield from many sources: *Gothic novels by Ann Radcliffe and her imitators; the works of Sir Walter *Scott, especially *Ivanhoe*; *fairy tales; and the sad reality of madwomen living in the upper storeys of local houses, as Martha Greenwood apparently did within forbidding grey stone walls at Spring Head, half a mile from the Parsonage. Aspects of other houses Charlotte had seen or visited helped to give Thornfield a vivid material presence: Ellen Nussey's early home, the battlemented *Rydings; *North Lees Hall, also battlemented, near Hathersage—home of some of the Eyre family; and possibly the picturesque Jacobean mansion *Norton Conyers near Ripon or Thurland Castle near *Tunstall (see *BST* (2000), 25. 2. 146–53).

Secluded by lonely hills, the battlemented grey walls of Thornfield rise against the background of a rookery, and its lawns are separated by a sunk fence from a great meadow in which mighty thorn-trees grow. Within, Jane's room, like Mrs Fairfax's, is small and cheerful; but at the heart of the house are stairs rising to a long, cold gallery from a vault-like hall. Upstairs are large front chambers; and above them the dark, low rooms of the third storey, where strange old furniture, embroideries wrought by fingers now turned to coffin dust, and effigies of flowers form a 'shrine of memory', reinforcing the notion of Gothic haunting. Jane first hears the 'mirthless laugh' of the madwoman in a corridor like that in 'some Bluebeard's castle'; and though the return of Rochester and the house party fill the house with life, reminders of its evil mystery recur, especially when Rochester, Macbeth-like, defies his destiny, glaring at the battlements, and when Jane dips her hand in blood and water, tending the wounded Mason as the shadows darken, and the 'devilish face of Judas' seems to grow out of the panelled cabinet. The chestnut-tree in the garden writhes and groans before it is split by lightning; and images of mutilation and death climax in Thornfield's final shattered walls and silent ruin.

Thornton, a moorland township 4 miles west of *Bradford, birthplace of Charlotte, Branwell, Emily, and Anne Brontë. Revd Patrick Brontë, perpetual curate there from May 1815 to April 1820, ministered also to the nearby villages Allerton, Clayton, Denholme, and Wilsden. Many inhabitants were quarry-workers, hand-loom weavers, or farm labourers. The small, stone-built parsonage (still extant) faced busy Market Street, but had a yard and barn to the rear. Mr Brontë renovated the now ruinous 'Old Bell Chapel' (1612) in which he preached. Nearby 17th-century houses included Thornton Hall, Leventhorp Hall, and *Kipping House, home of the *Firth family.

Thornton, Thornton Wilkin (or Wilson) Sneaky, General, younger brother to the Duke of *Fidena, the Princesses Edith and Maria Sneaky, and second son of the King of Sneaky's Land, in the *Glass Town and Angrian saga. In earlier stories he is simply called Thornton Wilkin (or Wilson) Sneaky. Known for his honesty, his 'hearty' frank countenance and stout figure, there are constant hints in the saga that he has been 'shamefully wronged'. His Sneaky heritage is never mentioned and his family disown him because of his early 'immoral' conduct, which seems to amount to drunkenness, membership of the *Elysium and association with Rogue (Northangerland). He also fought a duel with Viscount *Castlereagh over Lady Harriet Montmorency but lost to his rival.

Thornton and his brother Fidena, whose characters are antipathetic, are not on speaking terms although both claim the friendship of the Duke of Zamorna. He obliges Zamorna by assuming guardianship of his troublesome young brother Lord Charles Wellesley. Thornton's amusing efforts to control Lord Charles add to the comedy of the Glass Town and Angrian saga, as does his broad dialect which is scorned by Zamorna's dandified friends. He becomes a respected general in the *War of Encroachment, a member of the Council of Six, and a distinguished military leader in the campaign against the Ashantees, later assuming command of the Angrian Army. His financial fortunes also rise. As owner of Thornton Hotel in Verdopolis and Girnington Hall in the Verdopolitan Valley, he marries the equally boisterous and fun-loving Lady Julia *Wellesley after her divorce from Edward Sydney. See also ASHWORTH.

Thornton Hotel, residence of General Thornton in Ebor Terrace, *Verdopolis, in the *Glass Town and Angrian saga.

Thorp Green Hall, 10 miles north-west of *York, was the home of the *Robinson family until 3 March 1847. Anne Brontë was a governess there from c.8 May 1840 to June 1845, and Branwell was a tutor from January 1843 to July 1845. It was an attractive Georgian house with a portico, long windows, and a conservatory, set in 11 acres of grounds, and staffed by three male and seven female servants. Anne probably described it as *Horton Lodge in Agnes Grey. The spacious dining room, drawing room, and library were luxuriously furnished, and their walls hung with valuable paintings—unlike the schoolroom (probably on the second floor) with its drugget, old hearth rug, and painted bookshelves, though even here there were 20 pictures. Anne herself drew and painted while she was at Thorp Green (see for example Alexander & Sellars, no. 358 on p. 411). The library, schoolroom, and several other rooms housed a substantial collection of classical, theological, and other works.

The outbuildings included a dairy, and there was stabling for fourteen horses. Mr Robinson had shooting rights over nearly 2,000 acres of land. The hall was set in a rich, fertile, well-wooded area, about a mile and a half from Little Ouseburn, where Mr Robinson was lord of the manor. It was a little more than half a mile from the banks of the Ouse, where at Whitsuntide 1845 Branwell had hoped love would keep his 'heart beside' his beloved Mrs Robinson (see his poem 'Lydia Gisborne': 'On Ouse's grassy banks'). The hall was destroyed by fire in the early 20th century, but the 14th-century timbered building in the grounds, where Branwell lodged, still survives.

Gérin BB, photographs between pp. 194 and 195.

'Three Guides, The' ('Spirit of earth!'), by Anne Brontë (11 Aug. 1847). A carefully crafted poem devoting nine stanzas each to the spirits of Earth, Pride, and Faith. Earth's cold rationality, which dismisses divinely inspired thoughts, and fascinating but treacherous Pride, which destroys its votaries, are rejected. Instead, Faith is invoked as a divine guide, comforting and leading the soul through the narrow way to heaven. Strongly emotive words, and echoes of *Bunyan and the *Bible (especially Psalm 23 and Matthew 7: 14) convey Anne's devout, intimate faith, while the simply rhymed eight-line stanzas aid the clearly structured thematic development.

Chitham ABP, p. 144.

Thrushcross Grange, home of the *Lintons near *Gimmerton in Wuthering Heights; situated in a cultivated valley and surrounded by an extensive sheltered park, it forms a strong geographical and social contrast to *Wuthering Heights. Although we are given little architectural information on the Grange, we are told it is 'a splendid place', richly carpeted and decorated in gold, silver, and crimson. The estate becomes the property of *Heathcliff as a result of his sustained strategy for revenge, but finally reverts to Linton's daughter Catherine, and she and Hareton Earnshaw plan to live there when they marry. The Grange has been traditionally associated with *Ponden House and its setting may also owe something to that of *Shibden Hall, although it is largely an imaginary amalgamation of all substantial Georgian country houses.

Thurstons of Darkwall Manor, in Branwell Brontë's fragment of Angrian narrative composed on 30 December 1837, and later revised in his unfinished novel *And the Weary are at Rest (c.1845). The Thurstons are 'the object of awe and tale telling to the parish', since they are seldom in the district of their oldest family land. The present occupant is William Thurston, a man 'more addicted to vice than virtue', who usually lives at Thurston House near *Edwardston. He has married Maria, 'a Lady of good family from nobody knew where and a sight of Mrs Thurston was much more frequently wished for than obtained' (Neufeldt BB Works, 3. 188). She had met Alexander Percy when she was 14 and when he accompanies her husband

and his cronies to Darkwall Manor, she is again fascinated by him. In Branwell's later work, Maria's marriage is loveless and lonely and she is tempted to betray her marriage vows, a situation faced by Helen *Huntingdon in *Tenant*. Details of a scandal between Percy and Maria are also referred to in Charlotte's story *Ashworth* (1840–1).

The Thurstons and their manor resemble the *Heaton family of *Ponden House, near Haworth, and it is possible that, in his early manuscript, Branwell may have deleted the phrase 'Mr Heaton's Pondens at Yorkshire' although transcription is uncertain (MS in Bonnell, BPM). The Ponden House ghost also suggested the Darkwall *Gytrash, a spectre in the form of a hideous, often headless, dwarfish man, whose visitations were 'connected in all mens minds with the fortunes of the family he hovered round and evil omens were always drawn on such occasions and if tradition spoke true fullfilled upon them' (Neufeldt *BB Works*, 3. 187–8). Some biographers note that this headless man is said to be Henry Cass or Casson, a malignant figure in the Heaton legend at the time of the Commonwealth, who was the cause of a bitter inheritance feud and disposition similar to that in *Wuthering Heights* (Gérin *EB*, p. 31). Apparently he also appeared as a flaming barrel which rolled down the hillside and disappeared through the garden wall.

Tiger, one of several Haworth Parsonage cats and a fixture during the years of Emily and Anne's *Diary Papers. Tiger is probably the cat that features in Emily's sketches of the Brontë *pets (Alexander & Sellars, pp. 309–92).

'To Cowper' ('Sweet are thy strains'), by Anne Brontë (10 Nov. 1842). As a child Anne recognized her own sins, sorrows, hopes, and fears in *Cowper, and wept for herself, knowing nothing of his prolonged, torturing despair; but now she trusts that he must be at home with God, for God is love. If Cowper's pure life had ended in damnation, Anne fears for her own fate. Anne's personal involvement is reflected in highly emotional, extreme words, searching questions, and in the crucial, disturbing conditional clause of the conclusion. See also CALVINISM; UNIVERSAL SALVATION, DOCTRINE OF.

Chitham *ABP*, p. 84.

'To Imagination' (3 Sept. 1844); 36 lines by Emily Brontë, from the Honresfeld MS (see LAW COLLECTION). Published by Emily in *Poems* 1846, under the title 'To Imagination' and immediately following the poem 'How clear she shines', which apostrophizes the less substantial faculty of Fancy (a distinction that echoes Samuel Taylor Coleridge). After the long weary day, the speaker is called by an imaginary voice denoted as 'my true friend'. Despite Reason's assertion of the vanity of 'the world within', it is doubly prized since there—without guile, hate, doubt, and suspicion—'thou, and I, and Liberty, | Have undisputed sovereignty'. Nature's 'sad reality' can be replaced by this friend's 'divine voice' that whispers of 'new glories' and brighter worlds. The speaker is not so naive as to trust to this 'phantom bliss', yet its divine power is welcomed as a 'Sure solacer of human cares | And sweeter hope, when hope despairs!'. Although this poem may have a Gondal context, Emily's own contempt for society and her practice of retreat into her dreamworld is reflected here. Compare also the similar poem 'Plead for Me' (14 Oct. 1844; Roper *EBP*, p. 155) where the speaker calls on her 'God of Visions' to explain why she has chosen this 'phantom thing' over 'the common paths that others run'.

Gezari *EBP*, p. 19.
Roper *EBP*, p. 153.

Tom, one of the Haworth Parsonage *pets, a tabby cat who according to Ellen Nussey was 'everybody's pet, it received such gentle treatment it seemed to have lost cat's nature and subsided into luxurious amiability and contentment' (Smith *Letters*, 1. 600).

Top Withins, a site high on Haworth Moor, near the Pennine Way and commanding extensive views of the surrounding countryside. It is the site of High Withens, an Elizabethan farmhouse owned for many years by the *Heaton family and derelict even in Emily Brontë's time. It was said by Ellen Nussey to be the original site for *Wuthering Heights. The building is now a ruin that has been recently restored to preserve what stones remain. There were formerly three isolated farmhouses, known as Low, Middle, and High Withens. The name comes from a dialect word used especially in Yorkshire and Lancashire: to 'whither', 'wither', or 'wuther' (hence 'whithering', 'withering', and 'wuthering'), meaning to tremble, shake, shiver, flutter, or—in the case of wind—to bluster or rage (Joseph Wright, *The English Dialect Dictionary*, 6 vols., 1898–1905).

Tower of All Nations, the great towering landmark in *Verdopolis, residence of *Crashey (Crashie), 'the great patriarch' in the *Glass Town and Angrian saga; modelled on the Tower of Babel. It rises 6,000 feet above the city and has dungeons and subterranean caverns which reach through underground passages 1,000 miles in length to the haunted hills of *Jibbel Kumri.

Townshend, Charles. See WELLESLEY, LORD CHARLES ALBERT FLORIAN.

translated poems. See NOTEBOOKS (CAHIERS).

'Translation into English Verse of the First Book of M. Voltaire's Henriade . . ., A' (MS in Houghton, Harvard). In May 1830 the 14-year-old Charlotte Brontë bought a copy of *Voltaire's epic poem *La Henriade* (1728) for 3*s*. On 11 August, as she noted on the title-page, she finished her translation of the first of its ten cantos, which concerns the expedition of Henri of Navarre to the court of Queen Elizabeth in 1589. She transposed Voltaire's alexandrines, the characteristic metre of French poetry, into rhyming couplets of iambic pentameter and, while remaining fairly close to the original, emphasized its passions and its hero's admiration for England. Her 457-line version testifies to her budding interest in French culture and her reading knowledge of the language. SL

> Duthie, Enid L., 'Charlotte Bronte's Translation: The First Canto of Voltaire's *Henriade*', *BST* (1959), 13. 69. 347–51.
> Neufeldt *CBP*, pp. 343–52.

translations of Brontë works. The BPM has translations of the Brontës' works into 43 different languages. *Jane Eyre* and *Wuthering Heights* have been most often translated, and have appeared in almost all the main European languages, including French, German, Finnish, Swedish, Serbo-Croat, Czech, Hungarian, Italian, and Portuguese. *Tenant* was translated into Dutch as early as 1849. Since the 1950s the Brontës' oeuvre has become well known in the Far East, principally in Japan and China, where it is read both in English and in translation. Selected parts of *Jane Eyre* were translated into Japanese by Futo Mizutani in 1896. Since then, there have been Japanese translations of all the sisters' novels; selections from the poems of Branwell, Charlotte, Emily, and Revd Patrick Brontë; and Elizabeth Gaskell's *Life*. Acquisitions by the BPM in 1998–9 included translations into Chinese of poems by Emily and Charlotte, juvenilia, and all the novels except *Agnes Grey*. In Europe translation began very soon after the publication of the first English editions. Hachette published French translations of *The Professor* in 1858, and *Agnes Grey* (attributed to Charlotte) and *Shirley* in 1859. The first French translation of *Jane Eyre*, abridged and probably unauthorized, was by Émile Dauran-Forgues, a well-known critic and translator, in the Belgian *Revue de Paris* (Apr.–June 1849), reprinted in book form by Hachette, 1855. The translation by Mme Lesbazeilles-Souvestre (1854, published by D. Giraud) had allegedly 'the authorization of the author'. Émile Langlois comments that this was one of the better contemporary translations, 'improved and reprinted seventeen times' (*BST* (1971), 16. 81. 11–

18). A pirated edition of *Villette*, translated into French and dated Bruxelles et Leipzig 1855, could have been read by Mme Zoë *Heger, for her descendants brought a copy to the BPM in August 1953. The first translator of *Wuthering Heights* into French was Théodore de Wyzewa, whose version, *L'Amant*, was published in Paris in 1892. In his preface de Wyzewa explained that he had 'taken the liberty of omitting a few incidental passages which tend to complicate the story' (*BST* (1976), 17. 86. 30). More recent French translations of the Brontë works include Sylvère Monod's *Hurlemont* (1963) and *Jane Eyre* (1966), both published by Garnier Frères, and a sensitive rendering of *Wuthering Heights* by Pierre Leyris (J. J. Pauvert, 1972). An enterprising French translation of selected juvenilia, *Charlotte Brontë; Patrick Branwell Brontë: Choix établi et présenté par Raymond Bellour*, was published by Jean-Jacques Pauvert in 1972. A three-volume edition of the Brontës' works (Robert Laffont, collection 'Bouquins', 1990–2) included translations of all the major novels and selected juvenilia. The three-volume Pléiade edition now in progress, with a similar broad coverage and the addition of poems, has translations by Véronique Béghain, Robert Davrcu, Michel Fuchs, Dominique Jean (the general editor), and Annie Regourd.

In *BST* (1980), 17. 90. 375–8 Dr Heidemarie Ganner notes that there was a very early translation of *Wuthering Heights* into German, published anonymously as *Wutherings-höhe* (Verlags-Comptoir, Grimma & Leipzig, 1851) in the same year as the Tauchnitz edition. No other German translation appeared until *Der Sturmheidhof* by Gisela Etzel was published by Julius Zeitler in Leipzig (1908). Grete Rambach's *Die Sturmhöhe* (Leipzig, 1938) is praised by Dr Ganner as an 'honest attempt at faithfully rendering the original', and she gives a judicious assessment of the faults and virtues of subsequent translations by Gladys von Sondheimer, *Liebe und Hass auf Wuthering Heights* (Zürich, 1945), and Siegfried Land, *Sturmhöhe* (Zürich, 1949). An attractive selection of Emily's poems, with German translations on facing pages, was produced as *Ums Haus der Sturm: Gedichte Englisch und deutsch* (Insel Verlag, Frankfurt and Leipzig, 1998). Thirty poems are translated by Wolfgang Held, retaining the stanza forms and rhyme schemes of the originals. One of the earliest translations of *Jane Eyre* into German appeared in 1856 as *Jane Eyre: Die Waise von Lowood*, a version which was reprinted a number of times. A German translation of *Villette* by August Diezmann (Berlin) appeared as early as 1853. A revival of interest in the Brontës took place in German-speaking countries in the 1970s; recent translations include one by Ingrid Rein (Reclam,

Stuttgart, 1990), and another by Elisabeth von Arx (Ullstein, 1996).

The first Russian version of *Wuthering Heights* was a translation by Nadezhda Volpin, published by Belles Lettres, Moscow, in 1956. A commentary on the problems of idiomatic translation exemplified in this version, and a translation of the prefatory essay, are printed in *BST* (1976), 17. 86. 20–9.

Alexander, Christine, and Rosengarten, Herbert, 'The Brontës', in Joanne Shattock (ed.), *Cambridge Bibliography of English Literature*, 4 (3rd edn., 1999).
De Leo, Maddalena, 'Brontë Books Published in Italy since 1997', *BST* (2002), 27. 1. 79–80.
The Brontë Society of Japan, under the leadership of Hiroshi Nakaoka, published the first Japanese translation of the Brontë works in ten volumes (1995). Nakaoka also translated *The Art of the Brontës* (Alexander & Sellars) in 1999.
Rosengarten, Herbert J., 'The Brontës: Translations', in George H. Ford (ed.), *Victorian Fiction: A Second Guide to Research* (1978), 200–1.
Symington, J. A., *Bibliography of the Works of all Members of the Brontë Family* (2000).

travel by the Brontës. In the 19th century Britain's great ports were crowded with oceangoing vessels, and smaller packet-boats and colliers plied up the coasts or crossed to Ireland and the Continent. In 1812 Maria Branwell *Brontë might well have preferred a voyage by sea from Penzance to Plymouth or some other port before journeying on to Yorkshire, for long-distance land travel by coach could be both slow and perilous. 'Cross turnpike' roads might be impassable, furrowed by deep ruts, or roughly repaired with boulders. Maria's box of possessions 'was dashed to pieces with the violence of the sea' later in 1812, and the *Lady's Magazines* which had belonged to her or Elizabeth *Branwell also suffered shipwreck. Perhaps such associations strengthened the emotional charge of the storm imagery Charlotte Brontë used in her novels. Revd Patrick Brontë's brief return to *Ireland after his ordination may be recalled in *The *Maid of Killarney*, where Albion sees Ireland 'rise out of the ocean like a blue cloud' and Charlotte was to have a smooth voyage to Ireland on her honeymoon journey in 1854. Her earlier sea voyages were made to and from *Brussels in 1842 and 1843. We do not know which boat the Brontës sailed to Ostend in February 1842, but on their return Charlotte and Emily took the steam packet *Wilberforce* from Antwerp. Charlotte described her second journey to Elizabeth Gaskell: 'her sense of loneliness, and yet her strange pleasure in the excitement of the situation, as in the dead of that winter's night she went swiftly over the river to the black hull's side, and was at first refused leave to ascend to the deck' (Gaskell *Life*, 1. 282). This momentous journey—for Charlotte was returning,

alone, to the Pensionnat *Heger—is hauntingly recalled in Lucy Snowe's voyage in *Villette*. Charlotte sailed on 28 January on the *Earl of Liverpool*, 'cleared outwards with cargo' by the Custom House on 27 January 1843, and returned by the same vessel from Ostend on 2 January 1844. Branwell never travelled abroad, though he daydreamed of Far Eastern travels, and in 1842 and 1846 enquired about situations abroad. On his short sea voyage along the Welsh coast from Liverpool in July 1845, he was obsessed with the misery of parting from Mrs Lydia *Robinson. His poem 'Penmaenmawr' recalls that he was 'more troubled than' the restless sea, and fancied that the mountain's 'slaty brow' 'Claimed kindred with a heart worn down by care'.

All the Brontës travelled much by road, either on foot or in some kind of vehicle. Charlotte's horse-riding through the Dunloe Gap near *Killarney in 1854 was exceptional. Mr Brontë did not keep a horse or carriage, and he and his family usually walked or hired a gig to Keighley before journeying onwards by coach, or from 1847, by train. Charlotte's childhood journey by coach from Keighley to *Cowan Bridge school is vividly recalled in Jane Eyre's journey to *Lowood, when she 'appeared to travel over hundreds of miles of road, . . . the country changed; great grey hills heaved up round the horizon'. Afterwards Jane was 'stiff with long sitting, and bewildered with the noise and motion of the coach' (*Jane Eyre*, ch. 5). A more humble vehicle was used for the family's excursion to *Bolton Priory. Ellen Nussey was condescending about their 'conveyance', a 'small double-gig or phaeton', 'no handsome carriage, but a rickety dogcart, unmistakably betraying its neighbourship to the carts and ploughs of some rural farmyard' (T. Wemyss Reid, *Charlotte Brontë: A Monograph* (1877), 30). Branwell 'seemed to know every inch of the way, could tell the names of the hills that would be driven over, or walked over . . . it was an event to each that, they were about to cross part of . . . the Back-bone of England' (Smith *Letters*, 1. 600). In 1839 Branwell visited Liverpool with a friend, one of the Merrall brothers (see MERRALL, HARTLEY), whom he persuaded to buy a copy of Handel's *Samson* and other music. He and his sisters also had to travel to their places of employment, most of which required a coach journey, sometimes completed by a hired or private vehicle for the last few miles, for employers might send a carriage or 'car'—a second-class vehicle, often with two wheels, or if with four wheels, pulled by only one horse. Branwell's journey to *Broughton-in-Furness in 1840 was perhaps completed in this way, for the coach from Kendal would only take him as far as Ulverston. The Brontës' later journeys often included *railway travel; but Charlotte still had to use a gig or coach to complete her journeys to *Birstall to stay with Ellen Nussey, and when she visited the Kay-Shuttleworths in the *Lake District, she was met at Windermere station by her host. When he took his guests sightseeing by carriage, Charlotte longed to get out and wander by herself among the beautiful hills and dales.

Tree, Captain 'Andrew', a Glass Town novelist, who lives at No. 5 Branch Street, Connaught Square, Verdopolis; an early persona of Charlotte Brontë. Both Tree and his son, Sergeant *Tree, lawyer, bookseller and publisher, appear to have Scottish origins. They derive from the *Young Men's Play, where a number of characters had botanical names and addresses. The rivalry between Tree and both Captain John *Bud (Branwell) and Lord Charles *Wellesley (Charlotte) makes for a lively series of Glass Town scandals narrated in articles, novels, and 'fictitious' histories. Lord Charles is especially keen to characterize Tree as a thief, malicious, stunted, and cowardly. See 'INTERESTING PASSAGE IN THE LIVES OF SOME EMINENT MEN OF THE PRESENT TIME, AN'; FOUNDLING: A TALE OF OUR OWN TIMES, THE; GREEN DWARF, THE.

Tree, Sergeant, Glass Town lawyer, bookseller, and publisher, and son of the novelist Captain *Tree. Father and son both appear to have Scottish origins and occasionally Sergeant Tree speaks in Scots dialect. His name appears on the title-page of most Glass Town publications, including the *'Young Men's Magazine'.

Tunstall, Lancs., was Revd W. Carus *Wilson's parish. While Charlotte Brontë was at *Cowan Bridge, the pupils had to walk 2 miles to Tunstall church and back on Sundays, eating their lunch there. The paralysingly cold journey is recalled in *Jane Eyre* (ch. 7) as that to 'Brocklebridge'. The name of Branwell's hero Sir Henry Tunstall may derive from this source.

Tunstall, Sir Henry, hero and narrator of Branwell Brontë's poem *'Sir Henry Tunstall'. After sixteen years away distinguishing himself in military service in India, he returns home to England and his family a disillusioned man, changed in mind and body and feeling alienated from his kindred.

Turner, Joseph Horsfall (1845–1915), antiquarian who edited *Yorkshire Notes and Queries* and produced *Haworth Past and Present* (1879), and the valuable *Brontëana* (1898) containing Patrick Brontë's collected works and Turner's essay on 'The Brontës of Ireland'. Seeking authentic information to counteract 'erroneous notions' about the Brontës, he met Ellen *Nussey in 1885, when she lent him her Brontë letters, which he returned. Subsequently Ellen wished to counteract some of F. A. Leyland's assertions in *The Brontë Family* (1886). She and Turner decided that satisfactory insight into Charlotte's life could 'alone be obtained from her letters', chronologically arranged, and that Turner should have them printed so that Ellen could 'see them in type and make notes . . . but not publish them during her life time' (*Brontëana*, p. ix). On 18 March 1887 Ellen sent selected Brontë letters to Turner, adding that she intended the originals to come to him after her death. Turner arranged for Thomas Harrison & Sons of Bingley to print the letters in instalments, sending Ellen batches of proofs so that she could add notes. Printing continued until spring 1889, by which time Ellen had decided to bequeath her letters elsewhere, and considered that more material should have been omitted. Turner demanded compensation, and much argument followed. On legal advice, she eventually paid him £100 providing he returned all her manuscripts '& 1,000 sheets of the printed letters'. By 16 November 1889 Ellen had received her manuscripts. The sheets were left in her solicitor's office until in 1892, perhaps at the insistence of C. K. *Shorter and T. J. *Wise, all but about twelve copies were burnt. Turner later bought numerous Brontë autographs from Wise. These, and a collection of photographs used in *Haworth Past and Present*, were acquired by the Brontë Society in 1974. In *BST* (1990), 20. 1. 3–11 Juliet Barker used Turner's photograph of the 'Gun Group' portrait of the Brontës to prove that Branwell painted two, not three, group *portraits.

Turner, J. W. M. See RUSKIN, JOHN; FINDEN, EDWARD AND WILLIAM; PRINTS.

'Twelve Adventurers, The'. See 'TWO ROMANTIC TALES'.

Twelves, the, also known as the Young Men. Originally Branwell Brontë's toy soldiers, the Twelves become the founders of the Glass Town Federation. Charlotte's 'A Romantic Tale' or 'The Twelve Adventurers' (see 'TWO ROMANTIC TALES') first describes their exploits and lists them as Marcus O'Donell, Ferdinand Cortez, Felix de Rothsay, Eugene Cameron, Harold Fitzgeorge, Henry Clinton, Francis Stewart, Ronald Traquair, Ernest Fortescue, Gustavus Dunally, Frederick Brunswick, and Arthur Wellesley. A year and a half later, however, Branwell rewrote 'The *History of the Young Men', greatly elaborating Charlotte's account and replacing all except her last two Twelves with characters that were to survive throughout the *Glass Town and Angrian saga: Butter Crashey, Alexander Cheeky, Arthur Wellesley, William

Edward Parry, Alexander Sneaky, John Ross, William Bravey, Edward Gravey, Frederick Guelph, Stumps, Monkey, Traky, and Crackey. Frederick Guelph (Brunswick), Duke of *York, is elected first king of the Twelves, but is replaced by Arthur Wellesley, Duke of *Wellington, when he is slain or decides to return to England (there are two versions of his exit from the saga). Alexander Cheeky (the surgeon) becomes Alexander Hume *Badey, and Alexander *Sneaky appears to have been a combination of Branwell's characters Napoleon and Alexander Percy, although neither of these is referred to as a Twelve. Some of the Twelves become rulers of kingdoms and islands in the Glass Town Federation. All, especially *Crashey (Crashie), are revered as elders and originators of Glass Town. See YOUNG MEN'S PLAY.

Two Nations, the. The personal and social implications of class-division—the coexistence of two separate 'nations' in one country—are recognized in The Professor and in Shirley. Disraeli's 'condition of England' novel of 1845, Sybil: or The Two Nations, had dramatized the concept unforgettably. Using Blue Book evidence he documented the horrors of poverty, ignorance, and squalor, especially in the industrial midlands and the north of England, and showed that both demagogic exploitation of discontent and the selfish indifference of the wealthy were threats to social stability. His aristocratic hero, Egremont, naïvely assuming that England is 'the greatest nation that ever existed', is confronted with the challenging words of Stephen Morley, who affirms that there are 'Two nations; between whom there is no intercourse and no sympathy; who are as ignorant of each other's habits, thoughts, and feelings, as if they were . . . inhabitants of different planets; who are formed by a different breeding, are fed by a different food, are ordered by different manners, and are not governed by the same laws.' 'You speak of—', said Egremont, hesitatingly, 'THE RICH AND THE POOR' (Sybil, ch. 5). The rift had become obvious in the years of depression following the Napoleonic Wars. In the industrial north, capitalist employers were better able to survive the lean years than millworkers who might be laid off without notice, and who were prevented from standing out for better wages by the Combination Acts of 1799 and 1800. Workers might have to accept lower-than-subsistence wages or see themselves permanently displaced by 'scabs': labourers, many of them from Ireland, willing to work for a pittance, and to crowd together in the cellar dwellings of *Manchester, the foul yards and back streets of *Leeds or *Liverpool. In the spring of 1842, almost 1,500,000 people out of a population of 16 million were receiving poor relief. By 1 July 1847, after the Irish

potato famine of 1845–7, at least 300,000 Irish had arrived in Liverpool, where about 75,000 of them, penniless, starving, and afflicted by smallpox and typhus fever, attempted to find a home. The plight of the agricultural workers of the south, as revealed in the Assistant Poor Law Commissioners' reports in 1843, was equally acute: the labourer and his family were condemned to ill health and immorality by their circumstances: their cramped, insanitary, foul-smelling homes, where old and young of both sexes were herded promiscuously together. The split between the underclass and the rich had been exacerbated by what Carlyle called 'the abdication on the part of the governors', and intensified by the migration of the poor northwards in search of work. Disraeli advocated a responsible benevolent paternalism, a new variety of feudal nexus such as that preached by the Young England movement. Though Charlotte disliked Disraeli's novels, she almost certainly read Sybil. In The Professor the radical Hunsden Yorke *Hunsden condemns the injustice of a social system which preserves the 'rotten order' of the aristocracy, while it allows poverty and misery to increase. He sees Frances *Henri first as a 'lady-abbess', then as 'a sort of Swiss Sybil, with high tory and high church principles', enthusiastically admiring the England she does not know. She should see the real England, visit the English poor, and 'get a glimpse of Famine crouched torpid on black hearth-stones', just as Disraeli's Sybil Gerard visited the Warners' 'squalid lair' with its starving inhabitants and its fireless grate (Sybil, vol. 1, pp. xiii, xiv). Charlotte could not be unaware of the local destitution or the reform movements of the *Chartists and the Anti-Corn Law League. The Leeds Reform Association was active, and its meetings were reported in the *Leeds Mercury. On 3 December 1842, when Charlotte was for a short time at home, the Northern Star reported a meeting at Haworth: 'On Wednesday evening last, Mr. Ross, of Manchester, delivered a lecture . . . on the various evils which have been, and are still, afflicting the working classes.' The condition of the poor at the time of the *Luddite riots is integral to the development of Shirley. Charlotte was aware of the pitfalls of exaggerated emotionalism and melodrama, and on 28 January 1848 she assured W. S. *Williams that she would not meddle with 'situations which I do not understand, and cannot personally inspect' lest she should 'make even a more ridiculous mess of the matter than Mrs. Trollope did' in The Life and Adventures of Michael Armstrong, the Factory Boy (1839–40) (Smith Letters, 2. 23). Frances Trollope intended to expose 'the fearful evils of the Factory System', but her work, based on insufficient knowledge, caricatures the mill owners. In Shirley the poor man's plight is voiced by the credible and intelligent working man William Farren, and the mill owner Robert Gérard *Moore's pride and harshness are chastened by his wider experience. In Birmingham and London Moore 'went where there was want of food, of fuel, of clothing; where there was no occupation and no hope', and came to believe that justice required him to be 'more considerate to ignorance, more forbearing to suffering' (ch. 31). Charlotte's view was akin to that expressed in *Mary Barton* (1848), which she had read by 1 February 1849. In her Manchester novel Elizabeth *Gaskell pointed out that amelioration was impossible so long as 'class distrusted class, and their want of mutual confidence wrought sorrow to both' (ch. 15). Charlotte's interest in works on the 'condition of England' continued. She found Charles Kingsley's Chartist novel *Alton Locke* 'wished-for and welcome' in October 1850, and thought Henry Mayhew's *London Labour and the London Poor* (1850–1) opened a 'new and strange world . . . fostering such a future' as she scarcely dared imagine (Smith *Letters*, 2. 573).

Clapham, J. H., 'Work and Wages', in G. M. Young (ed.), *Early Victorian England 1830–1865* (1934), vol. 1.

'Two Romantic Tales', by Charlotte Brontë; includes 'A Romantic Tale' (15 Apr. 1829), and 'An Adventure in Ireland' (28 Apr. 1829) (MS formerly in *Law Collection: see Alexander, Christine, *A Bibliography of the Manuscripts of Charlotte Brontë* (1982)). 'A Romantic Tale', listed in Charlotte's 'Catalogue of my Books' (1830) as

'The Twelve Adventurers', is her first story about the *Young Men and their voyages from England to the west coast of *Africa, their struggle with the Ashantee natives, their eventual settlement, and their building of the *Glass Town. The Duke of *York is elected as king of the *Twelves but replaced by the Duke of *Wellington when he decides to return to England. This story, retold later by Branwell in 'The *History of the Young Men' with various elaborations and changes, establishes the geographical and historical background of the *Glass Town and Angrian saga and the supernatural nature of the Glass Town, with the controlling presence of the four Chief *Genii.

'An Adventure in Ireland', one of the few juvenile stories unrelated to the Glass Town and Angrian saga, recounts a nightmare caused by the Ghost of O'Callaghan Castle and Dennis Mulready's Irish goodnight: 'may the saints keep you from all fairies and brownies'. The first-person narrator and the matter-of-fact description of the Irish scene and accommodation contrasted with the ghoulish dream, suggest that Charlotte has been influenced by the horror tales of James *Hogg and his fellow authors in *Blackwood's Edinburgh Magazine. C. K. *Shorter judged this the only juvenile fragment 'worth anything' because of its lack of 'Wellington enthusiasm' and its indication that the young Charlotte knew something of her father's native land (Shorter, C. K., *The Brontës: Life and Letters* (2 vols.) 1908, 1. 74).

Alexander *EEW*, 1. 18–21.
Alexander *EW*, pp. 29–32.

U

doctrine of Universal Salvation', but surely they did not expect her 'to deny or suppress what I believe the truth!' (Smith *Letters*, 2. 343). No consistent belief in universalism can be deduced from Emily's poems, for she dramatizes the feelings of different protagonists, who may reject eternal punishment ('A God of *hate* could hardly bear | To [watch] through all eternity | His own creations dread despair', or believe that 'The guiltless blood upon my hands | Will shut me out from Heaven' (Roper *EBP*, pp. 100, 111). *Wuthering Heights*'s serene ending perhaps suggests universalism.

Ula, one of the five kingdoms of Gaaldine in the *Gondal saga; ruled by four sovereigns, rather like the four presiding Chief Genii of the *Glass Town and Angrian saga (see Roper *EP*, p. 303).

Unique Society, the, a group of Gondal characters who sail to 'Zedoras strand and Ula's Eden sky' in *Gaaldine. Their names suggest they belong to the noble *Gleneden family: R. Gleneden, Edmund, Mary, and Flora. Their loyalty and preference, however, are for Gondal's 'mists and moorlands drear', and while returning to Gondal they are shipwrecked on a desert island (see DIARY PAPERS: 31 JULY 1845, DIARY PAPER SIGNED BY ANNE).

universal salvation, doctrine of: universalism or apocatastasis, the belief that hell is purgative and therefore temporary, and that ultimately all free moral creatures—angels, men, and devils—will share in the grace of salvation; a tenet held by Origen and others, but opposed by Augustine and his theological successors. *Moravians and Unitarians are sympathetic to the doctrine. When the Universalist Revd David *Thom wrote to Anne Brontë she replied joyfully on 30 December 1848, as to a kindred spirit: 'I have cherished [the belief] from my very childhood—with a trembling hope at first, and afterwards with a firm and glad conviction of its truth' (Smith *Letters*, 2. 160). Mr Thom had probably read the 'Bells'' reissued *Poems* (1848). In 'A Word to the "Elect"' Anne hopes 'That even the wicked shall at last | Be fitted for the skies; | And, when their dreadful doom is past, | To life and light arise'. In *Tenant* (chs. 20 and 49) Helen Huntingdon also hopes that God will bless all 'that He hath made . . . in the end'. Charlotte moved from early fears that extreme Calvinism might be true towards universalism. A reviewer in the High Church *Guardian* (1 Dec. 1847) deplored Helen *Burns's heretical belief that the human spirit would rise 'through gradations of glory'. Helen was sure God would 'never destroy what he created' (*Jane Eyre*, ch. 9). Charlotte wrote to Margaret Wooler on 14 February 1850, saying that she was 'sorry the Clergy [did] not like the

Upperwood House, Rawdon, 6 miles northwest of *Leeds, was inherited by John White (see WHITE FAMILY) from his uncle William Leavens, a wealthy woolstapler. A well-appointed Georgian house, with extensive grounds near *Woodhouse Grove school, it was demolished in the late 19th century to make way for the school's preparatory department, but its portico survives as part of a summer-house. Charlotte Brontë, a governess there from ?early February to 24 December 1841, found the place exquisitely beautiful in spring, and by August, with the children under control, was comparatively happy. She eventually left because she had determined to go abroad.

UT and WT ('Us Two' and 'We Two'), Glass Town signatures commonly thought to refer to Charlotte and Branwell Brontë, yet more likely to denote the joint composition of Charlotte's two author characters Marquis of Douro (Duke of *Zamorna) and Lord Charles *Wellesley. This view is first canvassed in Alexander *EW*, pp. 38–9, and repeated in Alexander *EEW* (textual introduction), where the relevant texts are assumed to have some input by Branwell although the 'voice' is ostensibly that of Charlotte's characters. Neufeldt includes works signed 'UT' and 'WT' in his edition of Branwell's works, assuming that both Charlotte and Branwell composed them, which is also possible though they are all written in Charlotte's hand (Neufeldt *BB Works*, 1. 70–6).

Before the Alexander and Neufeldt editions of the juvenilia, questions of disputed authorship of manuscripts were of concern (Winnifrith, Tom, *The Brontës and their Background*, (1973) p. 18). Given Charlotte and Branwell's close collaboration in the early days of the saga, especially in the production of their *'Young Men's Magazine' where all except one of the disputed texts occur, the question of distinct authorship, regardless of handwriting, seems to some extent irrelevant. The saga was a joint venture. Branwell initiated the monthly Glass Town magazine but Charlotte contributed to it, as evidenced by a copy of her story 'The Enfant' in Branwell's script in the June 1829 issue. When Charlotte took over the editorship, Branwell promised to contribute 'now and then' and no doubt he did with ideas and critical comments, as was the nature of this family saga. (One poem, in which the signature 'UT' has been cancelled and replaced by 'Young Soult', seems undeniably Branwell's contribution.) The precise influence of the siblings on each other, however, has become something of an issue since Barker set out to privilege Branwell over Charlotte in her biography (1994), although this has been challenged by Robin St John Conover ('Creating Angria: Charlotte and Branwell Brontë's Collaboration', *BST* (1999), 24. 1. 16–32). Alexander is also of the opinion that Charlotte's early writings are as innovative as and, in many ways, more mature in their adoption of various genres and allusions than those of Branwell.

'UT' and 'WT' was clearly a puzzle within the *Glass Town and Angrian saga itself. It was one of the games played by the literati (the Duke of Wellington's cronies) who met in Bravey's Inn: recorded in the style of a drama in 'Conversations' (originally called 'Nights' and then 'Military Conversations'), directly inspired by *Blackwood's* famous 'Noctes Ambrosianae'. The Duke's sons are habitually asked to entertain this group with their stories and songs. In Charlotte's magazine for October 1829, General Ramrod says that it has been found out who 'UT' are and asks the Duke of Wellington to guess. He guesses correctly: 'Arthur and Charles Wellesley' (Alexander *EEW*, 1. 74). Other internal evidence supports this verdict. The previous poem (also signed 'UT') in the same magazine, which describes a visit to Geniland situated in the desert, includes the lines 'We both of us must go | So come my brother dear', referring not to Branwell but to one of the Wellesley brothers. This is reinforced by the earlier comments of General Bayonet, who admires a speech by the Marquis of Douro and Lord Charles Wellesley on the subject of the Genii, probably referring to the preceding patriotic poem vowing vengeance on the tyrannical creators of Glass Town (Alexander *EEW*, 1. 57, 59).

It is clear from an examination of the poems and songs signed 'UT' and 'WT' that they all include the experience of the Marquis of Douro and Lord Charles Wellesley, in particular their protest against the tyranny of the genii (i.e. against Branwell's manipulation of the Chief *Genii in particular) and the sovereignty of Wellington over the Glass Town (see, for example, Alexander *EEW*, 1. 57 and 67–8). Further, the poems are all written in Charlotte's hand, all 'published' under her editorship, and both subject matter and style are closer to Charlotte's other writing at that time. Even the single prose fragment—a letter signed 'UT'—which is closer in tone to Branwell's shrill demands as Chief Genii and equally violent threats of vengeance against the genii, is written in the cool tone of Douro to the editor of the magazine, pointing out the wickedness of the tyrannical assumptions of the Chief Genii. The passages here that sound like Branwell probably are by Branwell since they are in quotation marks, which seem to have been previously overlooked by commentators. Thus in the case of the eleven early juvenile works signed 'UT' and 'WT', authorship is more clearly that of Charlotte than of Branwell.

V

Varens, Adèle, in *Jane Eyre*; Jane's pupil, a slight, pale, hazel-eyed child. She is the daughter of Rochester's former mistress, Céline *Varens, who had taught her to dance, recite, and sing inappropriate operatic songs. Like her mother, she adores pretty clothes, and is sometimes wayward; but under Jane's tuition she becomes docile, and her vivacious affection and efforts to please make Jane sincerely fond of her. By contrast Blanche *Ingram treats her spitefully. After her marriage to Rochester Jane finds a suitable school for Adèle, and is rewarded when she becomes a pleasing, grateful, and well-principled companion.

Varens, Céline. Like Louisa *Vernon, Rochester's former mistress in *Jane Eyre* was an opera dancer. She pretended to return his 'grande passion', but he overheard her abusing him to her brainless new lover. Disregarding hysterics, he dismissed her. Though not admitting his paternity, he took into his care Adèle *Varens, the child she abandoned.

Vashti. In *Villette*, Dr John *Bretton escorts Lucy *Snowe to the theatre where the great actress Vashti, modelled on *Rachel, thrills Lucy with the fervid intensity of her acting. Pale, wasted, yet regal in her long, sculptural, death-white robes against a crimson background, she acts out the tragedy as if torn apart by demons. With her hair flung loose, like a maenad or a sinister fallen angel, her looks befit her fall from virtue in real life. Lucy, unlike the coolly curious Bretton, is irresistibly drawn by the magnetism of her genius.

Velino, Battle of, in the *Glass Town and Angrian saga. Velino is a small village in a range of hills of the same name, near *Freetown. The Duke of Fidena's army retreats there during the *War of Encroachment and Velino becomes his headquarters. The battle is a victory for Fidena and the Duke of Zamorna's forces but Lord Frederic Lofty, Earl of Arundel, was thought to have died during it (see HIGH LIFE IN VERDOPOLIS).

Verdopolis, formerly the Great Glass Town, capital of the *Glass Town (Verdopolitan) Federation. Situated on the Bay of Glass Town, at the mouth of the *Niger River and its confluence with the *Guadima River, Verdopolis has a thriving port and is the centre of commerce, government, and 'high life'. It was built when Twelvestown, the original settlement of the *Twelves, was destroyed by fire. As the city develops from its colonial days into a sophisticated mixture of London, Paris, and Babylon, its name changes to 'Verreopolis' (meaning 'the Glass Town being compounded of A Greek & French word to that effect') and is then corrupted to 'Verdopolis'. It boasts a cosmopolitan society ranging from visiting Englishmen and Frenchmen (from the nearby island of Frenchyland), concert artists, authors, painters, and politicians, to degenerate tavern keepers, revolutionaries, and child molesters (see PIGTAIL). The noble families of the various kingdoms all have a residence in Verdopolis. The city skyline is dominated by the *Tower of All Nations and *St Michael's cathedral; its elegant squares and streets are lined with shops and coffee houses; and the public buildings (for example, *Bravey's Inn, *Wellesley House, *Thornton Hotel) are modelled on the ancient cities of John *Martin's biblical paintings and on the neoclassical architecture of London and Paris. Biblio Street, where Sergeant *Tree has his publishing firm, is the Verdopolitan equivalent of Fleet Street, London. Antiquarians, like John *Gifford and Love-dust, live in Quaxima Square. The French quarter has sordid taverns and elegant hotels like D'Aubigné's, where the Duke of *Northangerland takes his pre-Revolutionary breakfast.

Verdopolis develops mythic status: it is 'the emporium of the world', 'the Home of their Fathers, the Queen of the Earth, who looks down on her majestic face mirrored in the noble Niger and sees the far reflection of her valley and her turrets caught by the flashing Guadima and flung with beauty unimaginable on the glass that her harbour gives her' (Alexander *EEW*, 2(2). 221, 241). Verdopolis dominates the scenes of the early stories of the Glass Town and Angrian saga; when Angria is established, its youth migrate to *Adrianopolis, and Verdopolis shares its reputation as 'Babylon' (synonymous with luxury and degeneracy) with the new city.

Verdopolis, Valley of, formerly Vale of the Glass Town or Glasstown Valley, in the *Glass Town and Angrian saga. At the southern tip of the plains of *Dahomey 2 miles from the northern suburbs of *Verdopolis, the wide fertile valley is traversed by the Rivers Niger and Guadima, and contains 'a hundred stately parks and a thousand stately

Mansions', the country estates of the Verdopolitan aristocracy. When the new kingdom of Angria is formed part of the Valley of Verdopolis is subsumed into the province of *Zamorna, Angria.

Verdopolitan Federation. See GLASS TOWN (VERDOPOLITAN) FEDERATION.

Vernon, Caroline, daughter of the Duke of *Northangerland and his mistress, Louisa *Vernon, Marchioness of Wellesley; and heroine of Charlotte Brontë's novelette *Caroline Vernon. She features only in the later *Glass Town and Angrian saga, where her entry ignites yet again the old rivalry between the Dukes of *Zamorna and Northangerland. It also allows Charlotte to explore with cynicism rather than her earlier adulation, the seductive manœuvres of the now-ageing Zamorna. Caroline appears first as an 11-year-old in *Julia, an intelligent girl with dark hair and 'Italian eyes'. She lives at *Eden-Cottage with her mother, who is a prisoner of Zamorna, and seldom sees her father who is in exile. She has never met her half-sister Mary, Zamorna's wife, but is envious of her. Zamorna is Caroline's guardian and responsible for her education. She is 'raw, flighty & romantic', with ambitions to make an impression in life. Zamorna would prefer to keep her 'innocent' but agrees to Northangerland's plan to introduce her to the sophisticated society of *Paris. Her heroes are Lord *Byron, *Napoleon Buonaparte, the Duke of *Wellington, and Lord Edward Fitzgerald. Zamorna, too, becomes one of her pantheon, especially when she learns the true nature of his character from Hector *Montmorency. She becomes infatuated by the idea of Zamorna and powerless to resist temptation when next they meet. Caroline becomes the last in a long line of Zamorna's mistresses.

Vernon, Lord George (or Dance (Danci)), first husband of Louisa *Vernon (née Allen) but constantly cuckolded by his friend Alexander Percy (Duke of Northangerland).

Vernon, Louisa (Marchioness of Wellesley), formerly Louisa Allen, a singer and opera dancer in the *Glass Town and Angrian saga. She marries first Lord George Vernon (or Dance (Danci)), and then the elderly Edward, Marquis of *Wellesley, brother of the Duke of Wellington. Hence her surnames fluctuate bewilderingly between Allen, Dance, Vernon, and Wellesley. The name Vernon was probably suggested by that of Diana Vernon, heroine of Sir Walter *Scott's Rob Roy (see NORTHANGERLAND, DUKE OF).

Although Louisa Vernon is the Duke of Zamorna's contemporary, her second marriage makes her Zamorna's aunt, much to her indignation. Throughout the saga she is the most constant of Northangerland's mistresses, and later briefly becomes mistress of Lord Macara *Lofty. Because of her Parisian intrigues and association with Northangerland, helping to 'revolutionise Africa' and becoming Lady Protectress of Republican Verdopolis, she is condemned to death and sent to the Tower. Later Zamorna imprisons her in *Fort Adrian in Adrianopolis during the Angrian Wars, but she survives to be jealous of her daughter Caroline *Vernon's affair with Zamorna. Rochester's former French mistress in *Jane Eyre*, Céline *Varens, recalls the character of Louisa Vernon: vain and especially proud of her delicate hands, of capricious temper, a loose talker, hysterical and shallow, a consummate actress with the power to fascinate and easily won by frivolous gifts. She reappears in *Ashworth as 'that hussey Miss Allan', connected with Ashworth's name in Yorkshire scandal.

Verreopolis. See VERDOPOLIS.

verse drama by Branwell Brontë. In 1829–30 Branwell composed three 'published' (i.e. published in Glass Town) verse dramas or 'Dramatic Poems' as the 'author', Young *Soult the Rhymer (spelt 'Ryhmer' by Branwell), poet of Glass Town and Branwell's alter ego, termed them. All are in blank verse.

'Laussane: A Trajedy [sic]' (in two acts), a hand-sewn booklet of sixteen pages (in Bonnell, BPM), dated 23 December 1829, and set in 15th-century France, recounts the fortunes of Albert, Count of Laussane, who having offended Count Liliard, has been forced to flee to Spain. Here Laussane encounters a hermit who has also been exiled by Liliard. Together they set out with others whom Laussane recruits to avenge themselves. Disguised as Italians, they manage to get an audience with Liliard and overwhelm him and his knights. As Laussane prepares to stab Liliard, the latter repents, is spared, and returns Laussane's property to him.

'Caractacus' (in two acts), a hand-sewn booklet of twenty pages (in Brotherton), dated 28 June 1830, relates the appearance of the British King Caractacus, before Cartismandua, Queen of the Brigantes, to whom he fled after being defeated by the Romans; his betrayal to the Romans through the scheming of her advisers, Mumius and Icenus, for the reward offered by the Romans; the plotting of Mumius to kill the Queen because she repents the betrayal; the appearance of the captive Caractacus before the Emperor Claudius; and his stout defence in a long speech of his nine-year war with the Romans, which so impresses Claudius that he sets Caractacus free and condemns Mumius to the scaffold.

Victoria (goose)

'The Revenge: A Tradgedy [*sic*]', a hand-sewn booklet of fourteen pages (in BPM), dated 18 December 1830, was to have three acts according to the title-page, but Branwell completed only two. In 14th-century Germany, Count Albert Thura conspires to overthrow the tyrant John, a prince of Germany. Albert is captured by a band of robbers, whose captain, Werner, turns out to be Albert's long-lost son, and they join forces. Act 2 reveals that Lodborg, one of John's knights, in hopes of being granted their estates, had deceived the King into thinking that Werner and Albert were plotting against him. An astrologer appears before the King and Lodborg and foretells the death of both by the sword. Presumably, Act 3 was to have portrayed the fulfilment of the prophecy.   VN

Alexander & Sellars, pp. 293, 296 (illustrations).
Miscellaneous Writings, 2. 405–22.
Neufeldt *BB Works*, 1. 77–91, 98–117, 125–36.

Victoria (goose), one of the Brontës' two tame geese (see PETS OWNED BY THE BRONTËS), named after Queen *Victoria who was of particular interest to Emily.

Victoria, Queen (1819–1901), queen of the United Kingdom of Great Britain and Ireland, and (in 1876) empress of India. Princess Victoria was 18 when she ascended the throne in 1837, the same age as Emily Brontë (b. 30 July 1818) who showed an early interest in this young woman destined for power. Victoria was the only child of George III's fourth son, Edward, Duke of Kent (who died when she was eight months old), and Victoria Maria Louisa of Saxe-Coburg, sister of Leopold, king of the Belgians. The latter took a particular interest in her education and remained a correspondent and 'Continental' adviser, as did Lord Melbourne, prime minister, trusted friend and (thoroughly English) mentor. Her early firmness and grasp of constitutional principles impressed those who worked with her even when they did not agree, including Wellington, Peel, Disraeli, Palmerston, and Gladstone. In 1840, Victoria married her cousin Prince Albert of Saxe-Coburg-Gotha, to whom she was devoted. Together they were strong advocates for family life and middle-class values, producing four sons and five daughters who were to succeed to various European dynasties. The *Great Exhibition (1851), visited by Charlotte Brontë, was masterminded by Prince Albert and finally won him the respect of the British people. Victoria was stricken by Albert's death (1861) and her lengthy seclusion brought her temporary unpopularity. But under Disraeli's administration she rose high in her subjects' favour: her experience, shrewdness, and innate political flair gave her powerful influence in foreign affairs, although she was a strong advocate of constitutional government. Her personal sense of mission underscored the nation's own drive for industrial enterprise and empire, and her name is synonymous with the 19th century in style and achievement. She was the longest reigning monarch in British history.

Emily Brontë appears to have been responsible for Princess Victoria's presence in the *Islanders' Play. The school rebellion in volume 2 of Charlotte's 'Tales of the Islanders' is based on intrigues associated with the accession of the young Princess Victoria (Alexander *EEW*, 1. 102). The earliest map of the Brontë children's play (see Alexander & Sellars, p. 156) indicates a province and city named 'Vittoria' (their spelling of Princess Victoria's name, also the name of one of Wellington's victories in the *Peninsular War). In her *Diary Paper of 26 June 1837, Emily records the preparation for a coronation in Gondal (see GONDAL SAGA), that coincides with Victoria's accession to the throne; her actual coronation was on 28 June 1838. Two pet geese at the Brontë parsonage—Victoria and Adelaide—were named after the Queen and her aunt. There are occasional references to the Queen in Charlotte's letters: she saw the 'little, stout, vivacious Lady' flash by in a carriage in Brussels (Smith *Letters*, 1. 331). But neither she nor Branwell nor Anne seem to have had any particular interest in their monarch.

Victorine, Lady Helen. See GORDON, LADY HELEN VICTORINE, BARONESS.

Villette ('little town') is based on *Brussels, as Charlotte saw it in 1841–3; it is the little capital of a little country, *Labassecour, in *Villette*. Despite the contemptuous name, it has guarded gates, some magnificent streets and squares, a royal palace, grand assembly rooms, a theatre, and art gallery; older, quieter precincts like the rue *Fossette, and an 'old and grim' 'Basseville' with a half-ruinous church and mysterious antique buildings. Around the city are tree-lined boulevards from which the flat fields stretch into the distance. A spacious park lies within the boundaries, not far from Mme *Beck's pensionnat.

***Villette*, and related manuscripts.** *See opposite page*

Vincent, Revd Osman Parke (?1813–85), MA Magdalene College, Cambridge, 1842; friend of Revd Henry *Nussey, and suitor of Ellen *Nussey, who refused him in October 1841. He was still interested in her in 1843 when, on 6 March, Charlotte Brontë sketched herself waving goodbye to the supposedly newly married Ellen as 'Mrs O. P. Vincent', with her bridegroom. But in May 1844 (*cont.* on page 527)

A NOVEL by Charlotte Brontë, 1853. In this mature and complex novel, Charlotte depicts Constantin *Heger, the 'master' who most profoundly influenced her life, as the temperamental, unforgettable Paul *Emanuel.

Composition

After the publication of *Shirley* in October 1849 Charlotte's continuing grief for the loss of her sisters and brother intensified, and she was haunted by the fear—which she had to keep secret from her father—that she too might succumb to the tuberculosis which had killed them. The temporary relief of visits to friends made the solitude to which she returned only more unbearable. She was harassed too by the knowledge that her publishers expected a third novel; yet her frequent depression made periods of creativity fitful and unsatisfying. As she told George *Smith on 30 October 1852, when she sent him the manuscript of the first two volumes of *Villette*, she 'hungered' for some opinion beside her own; she had 'sometimes desponded and almost despaired because there was no one to whom to read a line—or of whom to ask a counsel. *Jane Eyre* was not written under such circumstances, nor were two-thirds of *Shirley*' (Wise & Symington, 4. 13). Soon after her visit to London from 29 November to 14 December 1849, when she had stayed with George Smith and his mother, and met two writers she admired—William Makepeace *Thackeray and Harriet *Martineau— Charlotte was able to relax in the company of Ellen Nussey at home: 'she makes me indolent and negligent—I am too busy talking to her all day to do anything else' (Smith *Letters*, 2. 323). Though it was 'lonesome' after Ellen had gone, Charlotte managed to counteract the 'desolate moments' by seeking employment in writing. A manuscript fragment dated 'Jany 23rd 1850' (Bonnell BPM MS 124–1) survives to show that she had made a tentative beginning on a new story, in which the first-person narrator, like Lucy *Snowe in *Villette*, has retired from 'active life' and decided to write about past events; but unlike the complex Lucy, this narrator, 'Elizabeth Home' (a surname used in *Villette*), declares she is 'sensible, unimaginative', with firm nerves and no morbidity in her nature. Charlotte probably felt the need to make her heroine as unlike her all-too-sensitive self as possible. But the creative impulse soon deserted her: in the silence of the Parsonage a 'heaviness of spirit' dulled her faculties, and by 16 February she could not write another line. Nor had she made any progress by October 1850; her efforts had been 'very vain', she told Ellen on 23 October. She spent the autumn instead working on a new edition, introduced by a *'Biographical Notice', of her sisters' *Wuthering Heights* and *Agnes Grey*, with a selection of their poems. Poignant memories stirred into life by this work, and the close attention she had to pay to the 'storm-heated and electrical atmosphere' of Emily's novel, where 'we seem at times to breathe lightning', were to have an impact on *Villette*, with its exploration of feelings which threaten sanity, and its pervasive storms. But after the publication of her sisters' works on 7 December 1850 Charlotte still found herself unable to make progress with her new work. Early in 1851, goaded and tortured, as she said, by 'a haunting fear that my dilatoriness disappoints others', she apparently suggested to her publishers that she might rewrite and expand the often-rejected *Professor*. Their generous advice to take her own time, and their lukewarm response to

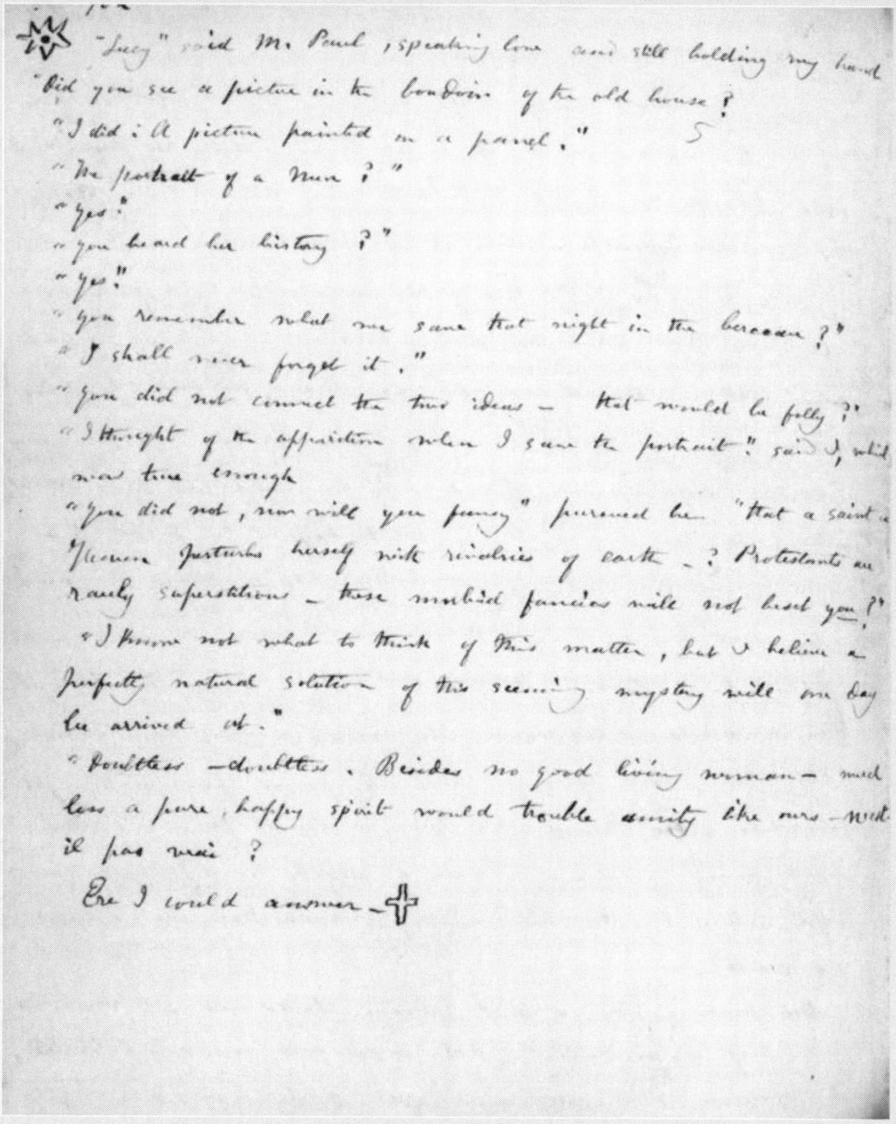

"Lucy" said M. Paul, speaking low and still holding my hand "Did you see a picture in the boudoir of the old house?"

"I did; a picture painted on a panel."

"The portrait of a Nun?"

"Yes:"

"You heard her history?"

"Yes."

"You remember what one said that night in the berceau?"

"I shall never forget it."

"You did not connect the two ideas — that would be folly?"

"I thought of the apparition when I saw the portrait." said I, which was true enough

"You did not, now will you fancy" pursued he "that a saint in Heaven perturbs herself with rivalries of earth — ? Protestants are rarely superstitious — these morbid fancies will not beset you?"

"I know not what to think of this matter, but I believe a perfectly natural solution of this seeming mystery will one day be arrived at."

"Doubtless — doubtless. Besides no good living woman — much less a pure, happy spirit would trouble amity like ours — n'est il pas vrai?

Ere I could answer ✠

A manuscript page of Charlotte Brontë's last novel, *Villette*.

her revival of the *Professor*, led her to lock up the 'martyrized M.S.' 'in a cupboard' by itself. In fact this left her free, if she wished, to shape her experiences in *Brussels in a new way, to use a female narrator, and to develop in depth the characters of the professor (M. Paul *Emanuel, based on M. Constantin *Heger) and the devious directress (Mme *Beck, based on Mme Zoë *Heger). Other material and other characters used in the novel were suggested by Charlotte's experiences in the summer of 1851: Paul Emanuel asks Lucy her opinion of his speech as Thackeray asked Charlotte hers after his lecture on Congreve and Addison on 29 May 1851; and Dr John Graham *Bretton takes Lucy to see the great actress *Vashti as George Smith took Charlotte to see *Rachel in *Adrienne Lecouvreur* on 7 June, and *Les Horaces* on 21 June. In the novel Lucy shrewdly assesses Dr John's character as a 'Cool young Briton' and 'almost callous' judge of the actress as a woman. It may have been after Charlotte met Elizabeth *Gaskell's 'dear but dangerous' little daughter Julia at the end of June that she decided to introduce the child Paulina (Polly) *Home into the early chapters of *Villette*. Two unused and undated fragmentary episodes are extant, the first narrated by the Paulina character, recalling her experiences as a 4- or 5 year-old child who wishes to be always with her father, and the other presenting a child, now called Rosa, passionately devoted to her grimy doll. 'Candace' (a name retained in *Villette*) is a real baby to her, unlike the usurping wax doll which the narrator, Bessie Shepherd, endeavours to put in its place. Bessie resembles Lucy Snowe in her cool observation; she is, Rosa confides to the schoolboy Graham, 'the silentest watchingest girl that ever lived' (Bonnell BPM MSS 124–2, 125–3). There is also a variant manuscript version of Lucy's conversation with the adult Paulina about 'Dr John's' attitude to Ginevra *Fanshawe, comparable to that in chapter 32 of the finished novel, but written when Ginevra's surname was 'Liddell' and the 'Rue Crécy' was named 'Rue de la Reine' (Bonnell BPM MS 125–2). By 20 November 1851 Charlotte had made some progress with the novel, but for almost four months after that, depression and illness, aggravated by mercury poisoning caused by the doctor's medicine, made it impossible for her to write. Her depression arose partly from James *Taylor's failure to write to her again from India: 'All is silent as the grave,' she told Ellen Nussey on 1 July 1852 (Wise & Symington, 3. 341). Winifred Gérin notes that 'The circumstances of [Taylor's] loss—the distance and danger of the voyage from India, and the letters for which she waited and which came no more—became a part of the texture of *Villette*' (Gérin *CB*, pp. 507–8). In spring 1852 the novel progressed far enough for her to begin fair copying the first volume on 29 March. In the summer a deterioration in health and spirits from the end of May onwards meant that the 'power of composition' did not flow; and in August and September she had to force herself to continue despite feeling acutely that she was 'a *lonely* woman and likely to be *lonely*'; life, she told Ellen, was a 'pale blank and often a very weary burden' (Wise & Symington, 4. 6). In the novel Lucy Snowe's moods of despair are described with the intensity of personal experience. Eventually, after a comforting visit from Ellen Nussey in mid-October, a welcome return of the creative impulse enabled Charlotte to complete and send the manuscript of the first two volumes to W. S. *Williams on 26 October 1852. Though George Smith considered that Graham Bretton's changed attitude to Ginevra Fanshawe was too abrupt, and Williams complained of the novel's lack of excitement and inadequate development of Lucy's character, both men were eager to publish, and Charlotte agreed that they could begin to set the manuscript in type immediately.

Their criticism seems to have stimulated her, for she both defended her presentation and continued to write so rapidly that she completed the work by 20 November and forthwith despatched the manuscript of the last volume to her publishers. George Smith's response to the completed manuscript was cool, and she told Ellen that 'something in the third volume sticks confoundedly in his throat' (Wise & Symington, 4. 24), possibly her presentation of Bretton's limitations of character, possibly the implication that M. Emanuel's journey abroad in the interests of 'Mammon'—the selfish avarice of the Beck–*Walravens junta—was not unlike James Taylor's exile to India in the service of *Smith, Elder and Company. Proofs came slowly, and full production was not resumed until early January; Charlotte corrected the remaining proofs at her publisher's London home during her stay there from 5 January until 2 February 1853. Then, since she did not wish her novel to come in the way of Mrs Gaskell's *Ruth*, publication of *Villette* was delayed until 28 January 1853.

Manuscript and early editions

The fair copy manuscript of *Villette* (BL Add. MSS 43480–2) was used in setting up the first edition. Like the manuscript of *Shirley*, it is heavily revised. Charlotte cut out some passages with scissors or a knife, deleted others, and made additions, especially in passages dealing with 'Dr John' in volume 2, and with M. Paul in volume 3, where for example she removed some seven pages from the end of chapter 30. Chapters dealing with Paulina are on the whole least revised, whereas passages closely based on Charlotte's own experience, or concerned with Lucy Snowe's relationship with Dr John and M. Paul, are often much altered. Incomplete proofs of the first edition survive in the Sterling Library of the University of London. Comparison with the manuscript enables one to recognize deliberate authorial revisions in the first edition as published, and to realize that Charlotte did not necessarily proof-read with the manuscript at hand, for she occasionally accepted misprints and adapted their context to suit the new reading. The editors of the Clarendon edition (Oxford, 1984) took this into account in establishing their textual policy. They also adopted emendations deriving from the advance copy of the first edition now in the BPM. This belonged to Revd A. B. *Nicholls, and has his signature, but it includes pencilled corrections and additions in Charlotte's hand (see *Villette* (Clarendon edn.), textual introduction, pp. xxx–xlix.)

The novel was published in the customary three volumes at £1 11*s.* 6*d.* by Smith, Elder & Co. of Cornhill, London, and Smith, Taylor & Co. of Bombay on 28 January 1853. The title-page described it as 'VILLETTE. | BY CURRER BELL, | AUTHOR OF "JANE EYRE," "SHIRLEY," ETC. . . . The Author of this work reserves the right of translating it'. Smith had bought the copyright for £500, the same price as he paid for her previous novels. Charlotte had hoped for more, and thought the transaction 'not quite equitable'. By the end of April 1853 George Smith had arranged for her to receive £100 for a French translation. Mme Heger had read the novel in French, possibly in a pirated edition published in Brussels in 1855, by the time Elizabeth Gaskell visited Brussels in May 1856, and refused to see her in consequence. In July 1853, 233 copies of the first English edition were still 'on hand', and the edition sold slowly thereafter. In June 1855 139 copies remained, and the price to booksellers had been reduced from 22*s.* 6*d.* to 10*s.* 6*d.* Smith, Elder and Smith, Taylor produced a new, cheap edition in October 1855 in a single clothbound volume, uniform with the second edition of *Shirley* and the fifth edition of *Jane Eyre*, to be sold at the retail price of 6s. There is no external evidence that Charlotte had prepared revisions for this edition, but it is possible that some of its substantive variants were hers (see *Villette* (Clarendon edn.), pp. xlvii–xlix and textual notes). In October 1857, after the publication of Elizabeth Gaskell's *Life*, Smith, Elder published a 'new edition' of 15,000 copies, selling at 2s. 6d., followed by the printing of another 5,000 copies in July 1858. The first American edition was published by *Harper & Brothers in New York in 1853, the first Tauchnitz edition in Leipzig, and the first translation into German in Berlin in the same year.

Plot

During a visit to the home of her godmother, Mrs *Bretton, the young Lucy Snowe meets Polly Home, who at first mopes for her father during his absence abroad, but soon becomes devoted to the schoolboy John Graham Bretton. Polly leaves England to join her father, and Lucy returns to her relatives, suffering distress which eventually leaves her solitary and forced to earn her own living. She becomes a companion to the invalid Miss *Marchmont, who intends to benefit her, but dies before doing so. Lucy decides to go abroad. On board the boat to *Boue-Marine she meets Ginevra Fanshawe, who mentions that she is at Mme Beck's school in *Villette. Lucy finds her way there, and is engaged as a nursery-governess, but is soon appointed as an English teacher. She recognizes the English 'Doctor John' called in to attend Fifine and Désirée Beck as Graham Bretton, and discovers that a billet-doux thrown into the pensionnat garden is intended for Ginevra, who prefers its sender, Colonel Alfred *De Hamal, to 'Isidore', alias 'Doctor John'. When M. Paul Emanuel persuades Lucy to act in a play, she discovers but afterwards suppresses her relish for acting. Left virtually alone during the summer vacation, Lucy finds the pensionnat unbearable, and seeks relief in confession to Père *Silas. She becomes lost in the old town, and faints. When she recovers, she realizes that she is being cared for by the Brettons, with whom she later enjoys visits to concerts and art galleries. Graham's attentiveness to her and his subsequent letters arouse Paul's jealousy. In the pensionnat garret she twice sees the figure of a nun. When Graham takes her to see the actress Vashti, an alarm of fire in the theatre leads to general panic, from which he helps to rescue a girl who proves to be Polly, now known as Paulina. Graham is charmed by Paulina; but Mme Beck suspects he is Lucy's admirer, and secretly examines his letters to her. After Lucy has buried them in the garden, the 'nun' reappears. At a gathering of savants Paulina outshines the jealous Ginevra. M. Paul offends Lucy by accusing her of coquetry; but she eventually agrees to call him 'mon ami'. More periods of tension and reconciliation follow. After he has declared an 'affinity' with her, a 'nun' 'blackens out from the tree-boles'. In a happy pastoral interlude M. Paul takes Lucy and the schoolgirls out into the country for a picnic. Afterwards Lucy sees him in grave conversation with Mme Beck, who later sends Lucy on a contrived errand to Mme Walravens, when Père Silas tells her of Paul's continuing devotion to the memory of his dead fiancée, Justine Marie, and to the Catholic Church. She forgives M. Paul for making her undergo an inquisition by two professors, for she has now heard of his real virtues, and is content with his offered 'fraternity'. She resists various attempts to convert her to Catholicism, and Paul, convinced of her sincerity, believes God loves her. Mr *Home permits Paulina's engagement to Graham Bretton, and their subsequent marriage is foreseen as a happy one. But for Lucy there is the shock of Mme Beck's sudden announcement that M. Paul is leaving Europe at the 'urgent summons of duty'. Mme Beck prevents Paul from seeing Lucy when he makes his farewell visit to the school, and ensures that Lucy is given a sleeping-draught on the night of a fête at which he will be present: but the draught does not work, and Lucy, seeing the Beck–Walravens group in the Park with Paul and his god-daughter, Justine Marie Sauveur, believes that he will marry the girl on his return to Europe. On Lucy's return to the pensionnat she finds on her bed a bolster dressed in a nun's habit, left there by Ginevra and De Hamal, who have eloped together. On the following day Paul puts aside Mme Beck, takes Lucy to see the school and house he has arranged for her, and offers her his love as 'his dearest, first on earth'. In the last chapter Lucy describes her happiness, nourished by Paul's loving letters, sent her from abroad; but the novel ends with an Atlantic storm which, it is implied, caused Paul's death at sea—though 'sunny imaginations' may envisage a happier fate.

Reception

Most reviewers found much to praise in *Villette*, considering it better than *Shirley*, and comparable to *Jane Eyre* in its interest. 'Currer Bell', George Henry *Lewes claimed in the *Leader* (12 Feb. 1853), had no rival in 'Passion and Power' except George Sand. Even Harriet Martineau, who found serious faults, observed in the novel 'power, skill and interest' (*Daily News*, 3 Feb. 1853); and the critical Anne Mozley, writing in the *Christian Remembrancer* (Apr. 1853), perceived its 'clear, forcible, picturesque style'. As with Charlotte's other novels, reviewers admired her power, originality, observation, insight into character, and deep feeling. The *Literary Gazette* (5 Feb. 1853) considered that her strength lay not in story but in character, and the *Examiner* for the same date admired her individualized, 'flesh-and-blood' people, and her humour and 'fine sense of the picturesque' in their presentation. Eugène Forçade in the *Revue des deux mondes* (15 Mar. 1853) noted their 'piquant reality', and *Putnam's Monthly Magazine* (May 1853) considered that Charlotte's depiction of ordinary human characters showed her mastery and fusion of elements 'usually considered repugnant to romance'. The character of M. Paul Emanuel was especially appreciated: *Putnam's* noted the skill with which the writer 'melted' the reader's initial dislike of Paul into esteem for him, gradually developing his Rochester-like power 'not grotesquely, but nobly'. Reviewers found Mme Beck an 'original', but differed on her presentation: some thought the aversion mingled with respect that she inspired was cleverly observed, others thought her unnatural. Other faults in the novel were criticized: events were 'strangely managed'; the plot was slight and lacking in unity; some incidents were unnecessary, trivial, or improbable; characters such as Miss Marchmont, introduced early in the story, played no further part in it. Carping critics complained that feelings were strained to an unnecessary pitch, and expressed in violent and ultimately tedious figurative language or in a declamatory and exaggerated style. Characters did not touch the heart, as they did in *Jane Eyre*. The *Eclectic* reviewer thought the dialogue tired the reader by its sameness (Mar. 1853), but Eugène Forçade in an otherwise favourable review found the manner 'harsh, tormented, a little uncouth', marked by abrupt transitions and wayward broken sentences (*Revue des deux mondes*). *Putnam's* noted that the portrait of Rachel was sketched in the lurid 'French melodramatic style'. But the chief difficulty was the character of Lucy Snowe and the suspicion that she reflected the writer's own morbidity. Matthew *Arnold found *Villette* disagreeable, for the writer's mind contained 'nothing but hunger, rebellion and rage' (Allott, p. 201). The *Examiner*, detecting personal experience in Lucy's mind and fate, found her out of harmony with the prevailing 'humour and good feeling' of the novel, deplored her unjustly hard irony, 'morbid wail' and the tragical apostrophes which spoilt the novel's conclusion; the reviewer delivered a brisk sermon on the need for 'Exertion . . . the indispensable condition of all healthy life, mental or bodily'. The *Spectator* unsympathetically noted Lucy's 'savage delight in refusing to be comforted' (12 Feb. 1853). Harriet Martineau, on the other hand, considered that Lucy's 'chronic nervous fever' did not prevent her from acting admirably 'with readiness, sense, conscience and kindliness' (*Daily News*, 3 Feb. 1853), and the *Literary Gazette* decided that Lucy's suffering, inward tenderness, and severe trials earned the reader's sympathy and respect (3 Feb. 1853). The *Eclectic Review* (Mar. 1853) complained that Lucy was clever, but lacked the 'enthusiasm and deep womanly love' which characterized Sir Walter *Scott's heroines. Anne Mozley in the *Christian Remembrancer* also deplored a novel which demanded sympathy for an 'unfeminine' heroine, contemptuous of decorum, unfit for domestic tenderness, and reliant on the 'unscrupulous, and self-dependent intellect'. This was a facet of Lucy's, and Currer Bell's, Protestant prejudice: her religion lacked awe, for though she rejected all guides but her Bible she constantly quoted and played with its sacred pages. Like Elizabeth *Rigby, Mozley linked 'true' womanliness with true Christianity, and found Currer Bell lacking in both, even though she had gained in propriety since she first presented herself in *Jane Eyre* as 'an alien, it might seem, from society, and amenable to none of its laws'. Charlotte, deeply wounded, wrote to the editor of the *Christian Remembrancer* pointing out that there was no cause of seclusion such as the reviewer implied. She was also angered and hurt by Harriet Martineau's review in the *Daily News*, and broke off their friendship in consequence. Martineau had asserted that 'all the female characters . . . are full of one thing, or regarded by the reader in the light of that one thought—love'; the heroine's apparent 'double love' made matters worse: 'it is not thus in real life . . . [readers'] reason and taste will reject the assumption that events and characters are to be regarded through the medium of one passion only'. Charlotte made an angry declaration of faith in response: 'I know what *love* is as I understand it; and if man or woman should be ashamed of feeling such love, then there is nothing right, noble, faithful, truthful, unselfish in this earth' (Wise & Symington, 4. 42).

Allott.

Allott, Miriam (ed.), *Charlotte Brontë: 'Jane Eyre' and 'Villette': A Casebook* (1973).

Duthie *Foreign Vision*.

Maynard, John, *Charlotte Brontë and Sexuality* (1984).

Shuttleworth, Sally, *Charlotte Brontë and Victorian Psychology* (1996).

Vincent married Elizabeth Hale Budd, daughter of the Rector of White Roding, Essex, where Vincent was curate in 1846 and 1847—one of six curacies he held before becoming rector of St Mildred's, Bread Street, London, in 1872.

Virgil (Vergilius Maro, 70–19 BC), Roman author of the *Eclogues* (*Bucolica*), *Georgics*, and *Aeneid*. Of all the classical writers, Virgil was probably the most acceptable to evangelical Anglicans. The *Georgics* were set for Revd Patrick Brontë's college examinations in December 1804. Having had a record of first-class successes in classics by June 1805 he proudly retained his prize books (Horace's *Works* and Homer's *Iliad*) and later acquired Dryden's *The Works of Virgil, translated into English Verse* (1824; BPM bb 64). Within that volume Angrian names (see GLASS TOWN AND ANGRIAN SAGA), figure drawings, and (at the end of book 10) Charlotte's signature, show that the Brontë children had access to it. Mr Brontë instructed Branwell in the classics, and his daughters also acquired some familiarity with them at an early age.

Charlotte includes 'Mantua's glorious swain' inspired by 'heavens own fire' in her parade of great poets in 'The Violet' (10 Nov. 1830). In *Jane Eyre* Helen *Burns (based on the young Maria Brontë) construes a page of 'Virgil' (ch. 8), while in *Shirley* (ch. 31) the heroine defies her worldly uncle as a tyrant who 'stretches out the arm of Mezentius, and fetters the dead to the living'. Her speech gains in drama and potency by this echo of Dryden's translation of *Aeneid* 8. 636–9, 'The living and the dead, at his command, I Were coupled face to face'. In *Villette* (ch. 30) a classical allusion adds to the comic effect when 'Madame Panache' is said to be 'bellicose as a Penthesilea' (queen of the Amazons, in *Aeneid* 1. 491). Charlotte's letter to Sydney Dobell of 8 December 1850 had shown that she recognized, and disclaimed, his flattering allusion to her as a 'Penthesilea mediis in [milibus]' (Smith *Letters*, 2. 527). Lacking formal classical learning, Charlotte nevertheless responded imaginatively to the grandeur and strangeness of the epic mode: the tall funeral pyre, the priestess, and the altars of sacrifice in book 4 of the *Aeneid*, the helmsman who has fallen from the ship's stern in book 6, and the pervasive ideas of fate and 'manifold calamity' contribute to the sombre, intense imagery and mood of her later works, especially *Villette*.

Emily Brontë knew enough Latin to translate and make notes on lines from *Aeneid*, book 1. Edward Chitham comments on the accuracy of her parsing, and her understanding of the need to explore the 'full meaning' of the Latin words (Chitham, *Birth of WH*, 17–23). He suggests that the 'god-like "Sidonian Dido"' of the *Aeneid* may be recalled in Emily's 'Sidonia' and her concept of 'A.G.A.' in her poems, and that Dido's impassioned speeches after Aeneas's desertion may reverberate in the 'emotional heat' of passages in *Wuthering Heights*.

Branwell Brontë, a competent Latinist whose translations of Horace's Odes won praise from Hartley Coleridge, had also attempted at the age of 12 original Latin verse in which the 'heavily Virgilian vocabulary' suggests how much he had 'steeped himself in the Virgilian epic' (Neufeldt *BBP*, p. 369). Like Charlotte, Branwell was familiar with the names of the Greek and Roman deities, and their legendary exploits. An unfinished epic poem in blank verse, beginning 'Not thus, but with the fiery speed all rent', may be by either Charlotte or Branwell (see Neufeldt *BBP*, app. C). It has a mélange of Greek and Latin names: Pentheus, Poseidon, Cytherea, Zeus alongside Bacchus, Mars, Saturn. In style it imitates the grand sonorities and Latinate vocabulary of Miltonic epic, enhanced by specific echoes of the *Aeneid*. Thus book 2 of the Brontë fragment recalls Aeneas' visit to the underworld in Virgil's book 6, for it describes the torments of Typhaeus, Tantalus, and the other Titans. It may well be the work of the precocious Charlotte, who was later to write of the Titans, 'the first men of the earth', in *Shirley* (ch. 18).

'Visionary, The'. See 'JULIAN M. AND A. G. ROCHELLE'.

Vision Island, an enchanted region 50 miles in circumference, ruled over by Little King and Queens (see GENII, CHIEF) in the *Islanders' Play. The *Palace School is situated here but, after the school rebellion, the young Brontës tire of the school and the 'Island of a dream' is left in the hands of fairies.

Vittoria. See VICTORIA, QUEEN.

Voltaire, pseudonym of François-Marie Arouet (1694–1778), famous French writer and philosopher and a key figure of the Enlightenment. Charlotte Brontë translated the first canto of his epic poem *La Henriade* into English (see 'TRANSLATION INTO ENGLISH VERSE OF THE FIRST BOOK OF M. VOLTAIRE'S HENRIADE . . ., A'). SL

Wales. On 29 June 1854 Charlotte Brontë and Revd A. B. Nicholls took their honeymoon journey by train, reaching the walled town of Conway in north Wales via Robert Stephenson's tubular railway bridge (1848). The next day they moved on to Bangor, and from there drove through scenery which Charlotte thought finer than the English *Lake District: the awe-inspiring Llanberis pass, from which they would see Snowdon, and Beddgelert, with its memorial to Llewelyn's faithful hound Gelert. On leaving Bangor on 4 July 1854 they would have spectacular views of the Menai Straits before passing through Stephenson's Britannia railway bridge (1850) to cross Anglesey to Holyhead for the steamer to Dublin.

Walker, Amelia (?1818–92), Charlotte's fellow pupil at *Roe Head; younger daughter of Joseph *Walker II of Lascelles Hall; niece of Mrs Thomas Atkinson (see ATKINSON FAMILY), and daughter of a cousin of Elizabeth *Franks. In 1836 Charlotte described her as pretty, ladylike, and polished, but hideously affected. Charlotte adapted a drawing to resemble her in March ?1831, possibly taught her drawing later, and gave her a copy of an engraving. In late 1850 or early 1851, Amelia wrote Charlotte a letter full of 'claptrap sentiment', asking her for autographs of famous writers. Amelia died in Torquay, leaving a fortune of almost £55,000.

Walker family of Lascelles Hall Joseph Walker I (d. 1774), a Huddersfield merchant, bought the three *Lascelles Halls in c.1751. The property passed to his son Samuel (d. 1809), and then to his grandson Joseph Walker II (?1799–1862) who became a county magistrate in 1829. Charlotte Brontë, a reluctant visitor in July 1836 and January 1839, preferred Joseph Walker II's affable, unaffected daughter Jane (b. ?c.1816) to Amelia *Walker, and thought their brother William (?1816–48) a booby. The family moved to Torquay in 1845, then to the Continent, returning to Torquay by January 1851.

Walravens, Mme, in *Villette*. Like Sidonia, the sorceress in J. W. Meinhold's *Sidonie von Bork, die Klosterhexe* (1847; trans. as *Sidonia the Sorceress*, 1849), or a malevolent fairy, Magloire Walravens descends a 'mystic winding stair' into the shadowed room where Lucy *Snowe awaits her. A shapeless, hunchbacked dwarf, she wears a brilliant blue gown and lustrous jewels. She sends a brusque, ungrateful message when Lucy offers the fruit sent by Mme Beck, who courts her for her wealth. Her West Indian estates, sequestered after the exposure of her jeweller-son's fraud, are now clear. M. Paul *Emanuel, who has nobly protected her despite her opposition to his marriage with her

granddaughter, is sent abroad to restore her estates to prosperity.

Ward, Mrs Humphry, née Mary Augusta Arnold (1851–1920), novelist and president of the Brontë Society (1912–17); granddaughter of Dr Thomas Arnold (see ARNOLD FAMILY), headmaster of Rugby, daughter of his second son Thomas (1823–1900) and niece of Matthew *Arnold. She was born in Hobart, Tasmania, where her father was inspector of schools until 1856, when the family returned to England. She spent two years in private boarding schools and then joined her family in Oxford where her father was now teaching. In 1872 she married Thomas Humphry Ward, an Oxford don and later art critic for *The Times*, who edited Edmund Gosse's *The English Poets* (1880) which included a seminal essay on Emily Brontë. She was acquainted with leading Oxford figures and became first secretary of Somerville College in 1879. The most notable of her 25 novels, *Robert Elsmere* (1888), explores the intellectual and emotional implications of her own spiritual pilgrimage towards her unorthodox religious position which resembled that of her uncle Matthew Arnold. She believed that religious faith need not depend on the historical truth of the Gospel but should concentrate on applying the spiritual truths of Christianity to practical humanitarian work. This she put into practice in 1881 when her family moved to London and she worked on educational programmes for the physically handicapped. She supported higher education for women but became president of the Women's National Anti-Suffrage League (1908). In 1920 she was appointed one of the first seven women magistrates in the UK. Her novels, such as *The History of David Grieve* (1892) and *Helbeck of Bannisdale* (1898), engage with religious issues and others deal with social and political problems. From 1899 to 1900 she edited the famous Haworth edition of the *Life and Works of Charlotte Brontë and her Sisters*; her introductions to these volumes became seminal pieces of criticism. Her memories of her father's family and the

Warner, Warner Howard

Arnolds' home at Fox How, visited by Charlotte Brontë in late August 1850, are recorded in *A Writer's Recollections* (1918), together with accounts of major literary figures she had met, including George Eliot and Henry James. Mrs Humphry Ward's address given during the 1917 centenary year of the Brontë Society was published, together with contributions by Edmund Gosse, G. K. Chesterton, M. H. Spielmann, and Halliwell Sutcliffe, in the 330-page *Charlotte Brontë 1816–1916: A Centenary Memorial* (1917), for which she also wrote the foreword, her last words as president. In her address she speaks of her relationship with her publisher and friend, 'the same Mr George Smith in whose hands, on July 16 [actually July 8], 1848, Charlotte Brontë had placed his own letter as the proof of her identity' (p. 32). She writes too of her aunt's visit to Haworth in 1850 and of her uncle, Matthew Arnold's memory of Charlotte's visit to Fox How and his conversation with her.

Ward, Mrs Humphry, 'Wuthering Heights', *BST* (1906), 2. 15. 227

Warner, Warner Howard, barrister, prime minister of Angria, and head of the oldest and most influential Angrian family of Warners, Howards, and Agars, whose property includes a significant part of Angria in the *Glass Town and Angrian saga. His thousands of tenants include the family of Elizabeth *Hastings. Although he is a wealthy, tough businessman, he values the simple pleasures of life and is scrupulously moral and loyal. During the *War of Encroachment he offers to finance the Verdopolitan Government troops, gives hospitality to the huge casualties at the Battle of Little Warner, criticizes the ruling Aristocrats' Ministry for not supporting the army, and is subsequently made a member of the Council of Six. A contemporary and important ally of the Duke of *Zamorna, his relationship with his monarch is similar to that between the historical Arthur Wellesley, 1st Duke of *Wellington, and Sir Robert Peel, on whom Warner is based. Like his model, Warner is made Zamorna's chancellor of the exchequer and home secretary, then succeeds Northangerland as prime minister of Angria. During the Angrian wars, Warner's speech over Zamorna's butchered son and the 'death' of Mary Percy is a turning point; it echoes throughout the Olympian Hills, rousing the countryside to resist the intruder. His Army of Vengeance joins Fidena's Constitutional troops and victory is assured for Zamorna after the Battle of Ardsley.

Warner marries Ellen *Grenville and they and their daughter, Caroline, live a somewhat reclusive life at their many residences: *Warner Hall, *Warner Hotel, *Warner Palace, Howard Castle (Angria), Woodhouse Cliffe (near *Freetown).

Warner is also a Calvinist, who sees his hereditary 'second sight' or gift of prescience as divinely inspired (see for example HIGH LIFE IN VERDOPOLIS); his clairvoyance is a further precursor to the divinely inspired voices and visions in *Jane Eyre* (ch. 35). Warner's 'womanish' appearance is often mocked (he is called 'a Hermaphrodite') but his 'masculine mind' is much admired. Zamorna characterizes him as 'the brisk gallant little cock' but does not always follow his wise advice.

Warner family, in the *Glass Town and Angrian saga. This is the oldest and most influential Angrian family, consisting of Warners, Howards, and Agars, whose property includes most of Angria province in Angria. The family head is Warner Howard *Warner, who rules his clan with a firm hand and an eye on the family name. Particularly troublesome are his youngest brother Vincent James Warner who shoots Frank Kirkwall, and Revd Henry Warner, whose drunken behaviour costs him the primacy of all Angria. Nepotism, however, ensures that Henry Warner is made primate of Angria province, although he considers it a great misfortune to be a parson. Sir Richard Warner is doctor to the Duke of Zamorna's family in Verdopolis. Warner's sister Theresa and his mother still live at Warner Hall. It is impossible to tell, however, whether the Warner males are brothers or cousins of Warner Howard Warner; narrators of the saga assume that the reader knows. We do know that Charles Warner and John Howard are inseparable cousins. Both are gullible, slow of speech, and have a passion for hunting. They are more at home with their pointers than with women.

Warner Hall (House), country residence of Warner Howard *Warner, premier of the kingdom of *Angria, in the *Glass Town and Angrian saga. Set in a landscape of deep woods and long dark moors in Angria province, Warner Hall is the favourite residence of Warner's mother and is frequented by others chiefly during the hunting season. The residence is generally referred to in the saga with Warner's other family country residence, Howard Castle.

Warner Hills, a ridge of isolated mountains to the north of the Valley of *Verdopolis, later incorporated into Angria in the *Glass Town and Angrian saga. It was the site of the first military engagement in the *War of Encroachment and of a subsequent mutiny in the Glass Town army known as the Mutiny of Little Warner.

Warner Hotel, Ebor Terrace, *Verdopolis, in the *Glass Town and Angrian saga; residence of the *Warner family.

Warner Palace, Warner Howard Warner's splendid residence in Howard Square, Adrianopolis, in the *Glass Town and Angrian saga.

War of Encroachment, in the *Glass Town and Angrian saga. In 1833, the Ashantees, Arabs, and French on the borders of the Glass Town Federation unite against the Federation's Verdopolitan forces. Events are chronicled in Branwell's 'An *Historical Narrative of The "War Of Encroachment"'. Political differences between the kingdoms of the Federation cause difficulty for those fighting at the front but eventually the Dukes of *Zamorna and *Northangerland triumph and claim as the spoils of war the new kingdom of *Angria.

Waterloo Palace, residence of the Duke of *Wellington in Verdopolis, in the *Glass Town and Angrian saga. Named after Wellington's great victory over Napoleon at the Battle of Waterloo.

Weightman, Revd William (1814–42). Weightman became Revd Patrick Brontë's second curate in August 1839, lodging in Haworth at Cook Gate with the Ogden family. He was the son of a brewer in Appleby, Westmorland, and came to Haworth after gaining his licentiate in theology (equivalent to a BA) from Durham University. He was ordained deacon and licensed to the curacy of Haworth in July 1839; in July 1840, he was ordained priest by Bishop Longley of Ripon; and in June 1842, his MA degree was automatically conferred (Smith *Letters*, 1. 212 n. 4).

It is clear from Charlotte's letters that parsonage life was much enlivened by the frequent company of the young Weightman, especially during 1840 when the Brontës were at home. In February of that year, Weightman discovered the sisters had never received a Valentine, so he walked 10 miles to post them each an 'anonymous' verse (Charlotte's response is in Neufeldt *CBP*, p. 271). They playfully named him 'Miss Celia Amelia' and Charlotte made an accomplished pencil sketch of the handsome young man while Ellen Nussey was staying at the parsonage, possibly a preparatory study for a painting she made (Alexander & Sellars, p. 255; Smith *Letters*, 1. 211). Charlotte also made a portrait for Weightman of Agnes Walton, his 'supposed fiancée' from Crackenthorpe, near Appleby (Chitham *ABP*, p. 17–18), with whom he corresponded and with whose family he often stayed on visits home. Weightman was well grounded in classics, having been taught by the professor of Greek at Durham (Smith *Letters*, 1. 212 n. 4), and gave several lectures on classical studies at the *Keighley Mechanics' Institute (April 1840), one of which the Brontë sisters and Ellen Nussey attended. The girls were all a little in love with him: Charlotte was convinced that 'he is a thorough

male-flirt' since 'he has scattered his impressions far and wide', and appeared to flirt with several young women at the same time (Smith *Letters*, 1. 222–4). Anne Brontë is said to have been particularly enamoured of William Weightman but there is little evidence for this. Weightman was charming to all, kind and generous to the poor, and diligent in his clerical duties. Branwell spoke of him as 'one of my dearest friends'. All suffered when Weightman fell ill with cholera, caught while visiting the sick, and died on 6 September 1842, at the age of 28. In his funeral sermon, Mr Brontë acknowledged his love for the young man, saying they had been 'always like father and son' (*Brontëana*, p. 258). Anne's poem *'I will not mourn thee, lovely one', written in December 1842 (Chitham *ABP*, p. 87), suggests her attempts to control her grief for his death. She expresses not only her own but everyone's esteem for the young clergyman with so much promise when she calls him 'our darling'.

Wellesley, Prince Adrian Percy. See WELLESLEY, JULIUS WARNER DI ENARA (EARL OF SALDANHA).

Wellesley, Prince Alexander Ravenswood. See WELLESLEY, VICTOR FREDERICK PERCY (MARQUIS OF ARNO).

Wellesley, Arthur. See WELLINGTON, ARTHUR WELLESLEY, 1ST DUKE OF.

Wellesley, Arthur Augustus Adrian. See ZAMORNA, ARTHUR AUGUSTUS ADRIAN WELLESLEY, MARQUIS OF DOURO, DUKE OF ZAMORNA, KING OF ANGRIA.

Wellesley, Arthur Julius (Lord Almeida), son of the Duke of *Zamorna and Marian *Hume in the *Glass Town and Angrian saga. Like his mother he is delicate and fair, and inherits her consumption. After her death he lives a lonely life with his older half-brother Ernest Edward Gordon 'Fitz-Arthur' *Wellesley, under the care of Mina *Laury at Grassmere Manor. Charlotte Brontë had originally intended Julius to marry his godmother Zenobia Ellrington's daughter Hermione (see LEAF FROM AN UNOPENED VOLUME, A), but he dies while still a baby (see SPELL, THE). He is initially called Arthur Gerald and Lord Rossendale, but these names are abandoned. The title is derived from the frontier fortress town of Almeida in north-east Portugal, situated on a tributary of the River Douro; during the *Peninsular War, Almeida was taken by the French in 1810 but relieved by the Duke of *Wellington the following year.

Wellesley, Lord Charles Albert Florian (later Charles Townshend), the annoying and precocious

A pencil portrait of William Weightman by Charlotte Brontë, February 1840.

young brother of the Duke of *Zamorna in the *Glass Town and Angrian saga. Both feature in the *Young Men's Play and in the *Islanders' Play as sons of the Duke of *Wellington. Charlotte Brontë's favourite persona, he later becomes her cynical narrator Charles Townshend. As author of various satires, literary libels, and tracts (such as 'A Day at Parry's Palace' (see YOUNG MEN'S MAGAZINE), *Something about Arthur and An *Interesting Passage') he is the subject of Captain Bud's 'The *Liar Detected'. Bud, his former friend and mentor, judges him as 'Foolish and Inconsiderate in the extreme But with a few small marks of some sort of a genius'. Impertinent, playful, and giddy, he is the antithesis to his moody, serious brother; and their antagonism becomes the springboard for many of Charlotte's stories. Lord Charles never misses an opportunity to report, create, or elaborate scandal against Zamorna and his coterie, or against his great literary rival in fictional prose, Captain Andrew *Tree, Charlotte's other main narrator.

Lord Charles's spying on his brother's love affairs and political intrigues, and the resulting stories he publishes, become so intrusive that Lord Charles is placed under the guardianship of General *Thornton at Thornton Hotel and Girnington Hall. This, however, increases his appetite for revenge and the scandalous publications continue, such as The *Spell which tries to account for Zamorna's increasingly duplicitous character. While travelling with his brother during Rogue's revolution, he is captured and wounded, but otherwise he plays little part in the action of the saga. He simply follows Zamorna and his coterie.

Lord Charles's role is surveillance and authorship. His satirical writings and urbane attitude as author are often at odds with his young age in the saga, creating a disjunction that the young Charlotte finds difficult to handle (for example, see HIGH LIFE IN VERDOPOLIS). Her later reworking of her narrator as Charles Townshend, who appears for the first time in *Passing Events, is more successful. As Zamorna's brother, he is still granted access to royal palaces but he is less obtrusive and his vindictiveness towards his brother has disappeared. His racy slang and ironic voice, however, remain. Charles is now a self-opinionated young dandy of 20: 'I'm a neat figure—a competent scholar, a popular author, a gentleman and a man of the world—who then shall restrain me?' (Alexander EW, p. 173). The self-confidence and detached irony of this favourite narrator frames most of Charlotte's narratives, and his intermittent commentary reflects her attempt to gain control over her often powerfully emotional material. See also PSEUDONYMS USED BY THE BRONTËS; PETS OWNED BY THE BRONTËS.

Wellesley, Edward (Richard), Marquis of, eldest brother of the Duke of Wellington and father of Julia in the *Glass Town and Angrian saga, a crotchety, gout-ridden old man who is fond of claret and rich food. Soon after his arrival in Verdopolis from England, he marries as his second wife Louisa *Vernon, a former opera singer and mistress of the Duke of Northangerland. He is modelled on the historical Duke of *Wellington's eldest brother, Richard Colley, 1st Marquis of Wellesley (1760–1842), who was an outstanding administrator in Ireland, in the British government, and as governor-general of India, where he assisted his brother's advancement.

Wellesley, Ernest Edward Gordon ('Fitzarthur'), also spelt 'Fitz-Arthur', indicating his position as a morganatic son of the Duke of Zamorna by his first wife Lady Helen Victorine, Baroness *Gordon, who died in childbirth, in the early *Glass Town and Angrian saga. As Baron Gordon he is heir to Douglas Priory, Selden, and Glen-Avon in the 'Scottish' Highlands. He lived first in lonely Alderwood, then with his guardian Mina *Laury at Grassmere Manor and at Douro Villa, and finally at Fort Adrian in Adrianopolis. A quiet boy, he dresses always in black and white, and books are his chief companions. His history, appearance, and character at 4 years old are described in 'A Brace of Characters' (Alexander EEW 2(2). 327–40). He is the epitome of Zamorna in his youth: slender and delicate, with dark brown curls and patrician features. Despite the bravery of Mina Laury, he is brutally murdered by Quashia *Quamina during the invasion of Angria. The name Gordon originated from *Byron's Gordon relatives on his mother's side.

Wellesley, Revd Dr Gerald, brother of the fictional Duke of *Wellington and primate of Wellington's Land in the *Glass Town and Angrian saga. He and his wife Lady Elizabeth live in the Episcopal Palace at Lismore with their daughters Rosamund and Lucy Wellesley, both of whom are under their cousin the Duke of Zamorna's influence despite their parents' disapproval. He is modelled on Revd Gerald Valerian Wellesley, one of the historical Duke of *Wellington's younger brothers.

Wellesley, Lady Julia, favourite cousin of the Duke of Zamorna, whom she idolizes as does her bosom friend Lady Maria *Sneaky, in the *Glass Town and Angrian saga. The heiress of Edward Marquis of *Wellesley (brother of the Duke of Wellington and husband of Louisa *Vernon), Julia is a raven-haired beauty, stout, extravagant, fun-loving, and flashy—'a divine coquette'. She is especially fond of jewels and her trademark is a diamond aigrette and ostrich feathers. She marries first the unsuitable Edward *Sydney and then, after a divorce, General *Thornton, who names his new palace in Adrianopolis 'Julia Palace'. See JULIA.

Wellesley, Julius Warner Di Enara (Earl of Saldanha), also known as Prince Julius of Hawkscliffe and 'Edward', in the *Glass Town and Angrian saga. He is the younger twin son of the Duke of Zamorna and Mary Percy, born 9 October 1834 and christened by Dr Stanhope, primate of Angria (in *'My Angria and the Angrians'). His character at 21 is portrayed in A *Leaf from an Unopened Volume as Prince Adrian Percy Wellesley, a 'tall and noble youth' as the early Zamorna once was, with a love of literature and war.

Wellesley, Rosamund, known as 'the Rose of Woodstock', 'Flower of Fort Adrian', and 'Rosamund Clifford'. She is the daughter of Revd Dr Gerald *Wellesley and one of the Duke of Zamorna's many favourite female cousins who worship him in the *Glass Town and Angrian saga. Clever and sensitive, with brilliant blue eyes, gold hair, and a 'perfectly Roman profile', Rosamund is lured from Wellington's Land by Zamorna to the secluded Angrian location of Scar House, Ingleside, where he undertakes to be her guardian and tutor. After a year as his mistress, shame and neglect drive her to suicide. The plain marble stone over her grave bears the word 'Resurgam', as does Helen *Burns's grave in Jane Eyre (ch. 9) and Branwell's pen-and-ink sketch of 1842 (Alexander & Sellars, p. 345). Her name and dismal fate echo throughout the later Angrian stories as a warning to such heroines as Elizabeth *Hastings and Caroline *Vernon.

Wellesley, Victor Frederick Percy (Marquis of Arno), heir apparent of Angria and Wellingtonsland in the *Glass Town and Angrian saga, following the deaths in childhood of his two eldest half-brothers. He is the elder twin son of the Duke of Zamorna and Mary Percy, born 9 October 1834 and christened by Dr Stanhope, primate of Angria (in *'My Angria and the Angrians'). His character at 21 is portrayed in A *Leaf from an Unopened Volume as Prince Alexander Ravenswood Wellesley, a 'young Apollyon' with more of the evil Percy genes than those of Wellesley.

Wellesley House, Victoria Square, Verdopolis, in the *Glass Town and Angrian saga; built when the Duke of Zamorna (then only Marquis of Douro) was married to Marian Hume. Designed by Edwin *Hamilton in Palladian style, it is seen as the epitome of Douro's elegance, taste, and learning. It is used only during the winter season by Zamorna and his third wife Mary Percy. The River Niger flows by the house and can be seen through the garden shrubbery.

Wellington, Arthur Wellesley, 1st Duke of (historical) (1769–1852), known as the 'Iron Duke', soldier and statesman. He defeated *Napoleon at Waterloo (1815), became British prime minister (1828–9; 1834), and was the particular hero of both Revd Patrick Brontë and his daughter Charlotte. He was born in Dublin, the son of the 1st Earl of Mornington. His career at school, including Eton and a military school at Angers, was undistinguished, but despite lack of means he entered the army as an ensign and gained rapid promotion with the help of his brother Richard Wellesley. From 1796 to 1803 he served with his regiment in India, where his brother became governor-general. Arthur Wellesley was dispatched to deal with Tippu Sultan, 'Tiger of Mysore' (mentioned in the juvenilia), excelling himself in the *Seringapatam expedition and as administrator of the conquered territory (Seringapatan [sic] is a veteran living on the Duke's estate in the Islanders' Play). In 1809 he was made commander-in-chief against the French in Spain and Portugal in the *Peninsular War, following Sir John *Moore's retreat to Coruña and heroic death. Despite various setbacks, Wellesley achieved important victories, including Salamanca (July 1812) which provides the setting for one of Charlotte's tales told by Wellington to his sons (Alexander EEW, 1. 107), and eventually drove the French out of Spain by 1814. He was created Duke of Wellington and showered with honours. Nicknamed the 'Iron Duke', he was respected by his men for coolness and courage, though he avoided fraternizing or courting personal popularity. With Napoleon's escape from Elba, Wellington went from the Congress of Vienna to lead 'an infamous army' to victory at the field of Waterloo (see WATERLOO PALACE), where the French were routed on 18 June 1815, with the help of the Prussians under General *Blücher. For Mr Brontë and his fellow countrymen this was a uniquely important event: it heralded the end of decades of warfare. Wellington was rewarded with the Hampshire estate of *Strathfieldsay, inspiration for the fictitious Duke's similar estate in *'Tales of the Islanders'. Like Nelson before him, he became a symbol of British national identity and the subject of heroic paintings and public statuary. Even in the remote Yorkshire location of Cross-stone, where the little Brontës stayed with their uncle John *Fennell, the dramatic stone obelisk of Stoodley Pike dominates the view across the valley—a visible symbol of Wellington's success at Waterloo.

In 1818 Wellington joined the Liverpool administration, was made constable of the Tower (1826) and commander-in-chief (1827), an office he was confirmed in for life in 1842, and assisted Sir Robert *Peel's reorganization of the Metropolitan Police (1829). With Canning's death in 1827 and the collapse of the Goderich administration, Wellington became prime minister (January 1828), with Peel as home secretary. His reluctance to oppose the Test and Corporation Acts cost him the allegiance of Huskisson (colonial secretary) and the Liberals, and his support for Catholic emancipation (forced by the fear of civil war in Ireland) brought further opposition. His conservative political policy was basically to refrain from weakening established authority and to avoid foreign entanglements, since Britain's army was too small to enforce her will. His non-intervention policies offended most of his party; while his opposition to the Reform Act of 1832 brought widespread unpopularity, including the smashing of his windows at Apsley House on the anniversary of Waterloo. He was now famous as a bastion of ultra-Tory and aristocratic values against the forces of liberal change. In the political crisis of 1834 he again briefly formed a government but abdicated in favour of Peel, serving under him as foreign secretary (1834–5) and later as minister without portfolio (1841–6). Wellington was chosen chancellor of Oxford University (1834) and, as lord high constable of England, he organized the military in London against the Chartists in 1848 (see CHARTISM).

Throughout his life Wellington disdained popularity, disliked democracy, and believed in a strong, disinterested, and just aristocratic government. To many, including *Dickens, he was the quintessence of reactionary Toryism, yet by the time of his death he was almost universally revered (even by Dickens) as 'a great old man' (Dickens, 14 Sept. 1852). His state funeral was conducted with splendid pomp and expense in St Paul's Cathedral with over a million mourners.

The Duke of Wellington's private life was less successful. After a long engagement, he married 'Kitty' Pakenham (1806) and had two sons: Arthur Richard Wellesley, Marquis of Douro (a title given to Wellington in 1812 and derived from the River Douro in Portugal) and Charles Wellesley. Their names and early characters, especially that of the 'wild, rattling, high-spirited' Charles who was 'full of tricks' (Elizabeth Longford, Wellington: Pillar of State (1972), 169), are transferred to the Duke's two sons in the juvenilia, Arthur Wellesley, Duke of *Zamorna, and Lord Charles *Wellesley. Kitty Pakenham (her surname is assumed by Zamorna in *Mina Laury) was pretty when young, but she soon lost her good looks and was well known for her dowdy appearance and unconcern with fashion, a source of constant irritation to the

Duke (Wellington: Pillar of State, pp. 112–13). He also disapproved of his wife's preference for domestic life, her more sympathetic child-rearing, and efforts to aid young people. The secret romance between their 14-year-old son Douro and Elizabeth Hume (daughter of the Duke's surgeon, Dr John Robert Hume, who features as *Badey in the juvenilia) was supported for several years by Lady Wellington until the Duke ended the affair (see 'ALBION AND MARINA: A TALE'). Although Kitty often misjudged situations, her kindness and charity were legendary. Her character becomes that of Lady Catherine, Duchess of *Wellington, in Charlotte's early stories, and the Duke's private life, including his readiness to duel, his sexual peccadilloes, and frequent friendships with fascinating women like Mme de *Staël, also found its way into the juvenilia.

Revd Patrick Brontë had a special passion for Wellington, a fellow Irishman and Tory statesman who embodied Mr Brontë's unfulfilled dream of an heroic army career. As a student at Cambridge, Mr Brontë had followed Wellington's career and hailed him as Europe's greatest military genius and the country's finest patriot. Later, he even sent a letter to Wellington suggesting a novel sighting device for army muskets which he had tried out on a flying bird; but he received a crushing reply (the Duke was suspicious of innovation), reminiscent of Charlotte's own imaginary letter from the Duke in her 'Tales of the Islanders' (Alexander EEW, 1. 25).

Following their father's example, the young Brontës' hero worship of Wellington was fed by the politically biased Tory newspapers and journals (such as the *Leeds Intelligencer, *Blackwood's Edinburgh Magazine, and *Fraser's Magazine), and by the many portraits and engravings of the Duke, some of which the children copied as both art exercises and illustrations of their juvenile characters (see Alexander & Sellars, pp. 218, 226–7). They probably owned a biography of Wellington and certainly one of Napoleon by Walter *Scott (Alexander EEW, 1. 28, 88–9). They had a detailed knowledge of Wellington's military career and followed his political exploits with surprising enthusiasm. Volume 2 of 'Tales of the Islanders' opens with a description of the Brontë household's excitement over 'the Great Catholic Question', their delight in the political 'slander, violence, party spirit and confusion', and their breathless anticipation as their father read aloud the news reports of the Emancipation Bill's passage in the House of Lords where 'the Great Duke in green sash and waistcoat' spoke, according to Mr Brontë, in words that were 'like precious gold'.

Amongst the radical *Taylor family of Gomersal, however, Charlotte was forced to defend her Tory hero and his opposition to the Reform Bill. Mary *Taylor recalled that as a schoolgirl Charlotte worshipped the Duke of Wellington and 'would launch out into praises of [him], referring to his actions' (Gaskell *Life*, 1. 109–10). Every scrap of information on the Duke was stored for entertainment, debate, or appropriation. His adoption of the 4-year-old Salabut Khan, for example, whom he rescued from the Deccan battlefield during the Mahratta Wars in India, becomes the experience of the fictitious Duke's adoption of Quashia *Quamina in the *Glass Town and Angrian saga. The voluminous pages of the juvenilia are peppered with the names of Wellington's political associates (John Charles Herries, Lord Eldon, Viscount *Castlereagh), members of his cabinet (Sir Henry Hardinge, Lord Roslyn, and Sir Robert Peel), his military friends and colleagues (Lord Fitzroy Somerset, General Sir Rowland Hill, General Sir George Murray, Lord William *Lennox, General William Carr Beresford (see BERESFORD, THOMAS)), and numerous family members.

Charlotte found inspiration in her hero throughout her life. He was her 'chief man' in almost all the early plays, and her early writings reveal the extent of her initial hero worship. Although Wellington appears in Branwell's manuscripts, it is Charlotte who moulds him into a distinct character based firmly on the real Duke. His career is continually compared to that of his rival Napoleon, and is marked (according to the 12-year-old Charlotte) 'by the hand of Justice and mercy and not that of oppression and tyranny' (Alexander *EEW*, 1. 93). Years later, at school in Brussels (31 May 1843), she reverted in an essay on Napoleon and genius to a comparison with Wellington, asserting that he is the equal of Napoleon in genius but 'in rectitude of character, in loftiness of aim, he is neither equal nor superior; he is of another species' (Lonoff, p. 278). The essay, ostensibly on 'The *Death of Napoleon', becomes instead a eulogy on the Duke's self-control, righteous pride, moderation, resistance to flatterers and public opinion, and adherence only to the voice of his own upright conscience: 'His character equals in grandeur and surpasses in truthfulness that of every other hero, ancient or modern.'

Friends were well aware of Charlotte's lifelong passion. George Smith sent her a framed portrait of Wellington which she esteemed 'a treasure' (Smith *Letters*, 1. 434); and Harriet *Martineau recalls Charlotte's emotional reaction to part of her *Introduction to the History of the Peace* on Wellington and the Peninsular War. With tears running down her cheeks, Charlotte had said 'Oh! I do thank you! Oh! we are of one mind! Oh! I thank you for this justice to the man!' As Martineau remarked, 'I saw at once there was a touch of idolatry

in the case, but it was a charming enthusiasm' (quoted in Alan Shelston's edition of Gaskell *Life* (1975), 2. 610 n.).

Wellington, Arthur Wellesley, Duke of (fictional). Fictitious character in the Brontë juvenilia, based on the historical Duke of *Wellington, he plays a major role in both the *Young Men's Play and the *Islanders' Play, but is overshadowed by his two sons in the *Glass Town and Angrian saga. In 1826 Charlotte named her toy soldier 'Duke of Wellington' and he continued to be her 'chief man' throughout the early juvenilia, inspiring character and incident based on the military and political exploits of his original. He is described as the epitome of a great general, with 'high stern forehead, noble Roman nose, compressed disdainful lip', and a disposition that is decisive, calm, courageous, and noble-minded: 'Equally irresistible in the Cabinet as in the field' (Alexander *EEW*, 1. 123–4). Much of his character also informs that of his eldest son (also Arthur Wellesley, later Duke of *Zamorna), although this was considerably modified as Charlotte's and Branwell's reading expanded to include such writers as *Scott, *Byron, *Milton, and *Hogg.

Arthur Wellesley appears in *'Two Romantic Tales' and 'The *History of the Young Men' as one of the *Twelves, 'a common trumpeter' who returns to England and after twenty years reappears at the head of a huge army as 'our most Noble General . . . the conqueror of Bonaparte and the deliverer of Europe'. On the abdication of the Duke of York, Wellesley—now Duke of Wellington—is elected king. He becomes king of *Wellington's Land and the senior of the four kings of the *Glass Town Federation. He presides over the conversations in Bravey's Inn, reported in the *'Young Men's Magazine', expelling those who are drunk, and pontificating on women, whose 'proper & native element' is the home. He is the subject of articles discussing his self-control, his spartan habits, his mother the Countess of Mornington, and his return to Glass Town from school at Eton. His white marble palace, set amongst olives, myrtles, palms, almonds, vines, jasmine, lilies, and roses in the Sahara Desert, is the subject of duplicate manuscripts (Alexander *EEW*, 1. 130 and 349). Several stories illustrate his gift of prescience and possession of supernatural powers. In *'Tales of the Islanders' he is the chief governor of the Palace School, although he must delegate authority to his sons since he is preoccupied by political duties (the historical Wellington was prime minister of Britain at the time). In later stories Wellington adopts the role of elder statesman and benevolent but stern father to the increasingly wayward Zamorna. He adopts his enemy's child Quashia *Quamina and raises him as his own son; and he assists Earl *St Clair to prove his innocence in *The Green Dwarf*.

Wellington appears not only as saviour and deus ex machina in numerous short tales, but also as the subject of apparently irrelevant fragments. In 1829, his tomb is described as a mound erected by superhuman agency, over which 'the light of his glory stands fixed in the heavens' to 'eternally illuminate . . . that mighty one' (Alexander *EEW*, 1. 41; the historical Duke did not die until 1852). About a month or so later Charlotte compiled and illustrated a series of 'Anecdotes of the Duke of Wellington' from a variety of sources including John Malcolm's *Tales of Field and Flood* (1829), *The United Service Journal and Naval and Military Magazine* (July 1829), and Walter Scott's *Life of Napoleon Buonaparte* (1827) (Alexander *EEW*, 1. 88–90; Alexander & Sellars, p. 179). And in a curious ritual on 25 September 1829, Charlotte inserted 'a piece of paper burnt at one end' and inscribed 'Charles and Arthur' into 'the Life of the Duke of Wellington', suggesting that the family owned a biography of Wellington which was a revered source book.

Wellington, Lady Catherine, Duchess of. Fictitious character in the *Glass Town and Angrian saga. Like her husband in the saga, she has her counterpart in real life, Catherine or Kitty Pakenham, wife of the Duke of *Wellington, and derives from her much of her character. Lord William Lennox described the historical character as 'amiable, unaffected and simple-minded . . . generous and charitable' (*Three Years with the Duke, or Wellington in Private Life* (1853), 270). The fictitious Duchess dotes on her two sons, Arthur and Charles; adores all young people; prefers domesticity to her husband's public life; and is noted for her charity, her simple dress, and lack of ornamentation. She lives chiefly at the country estate of Mornington in *Wellington's Land. In the Islanders' Play her chief concern is for the servants and the poor. In *'Albion and Marina' she features as the Duchess of Strathelleraye, a character even closer to her original: 'Her mind was composed of charity, beneficence, gentleness, & sweetness. All, both old & young, loved her.' Imitating Kitty Pakenham's liking for Elizabeth Hume, the Glass Town Duchess fosters the romance between Marina (Marian *Hume) and her son Albion (Duke of Zamorna). She also befriends Mina *Laury, whom she trains as a lady's maid and who nurses her until her death on 10 August 1831.

Wellington, Shropshire (now part of Telford New Town), where Revd Patrick Brontë was curate at the neoclassical church of All Saints from early January to December 1809. There he first met his fellow curate, William *Morgan, and, in Madeley, Mary Fletcher, widow of the evangelical John Fletcher. In the rapidly growing town many people worked in iron foundries, nearby coal mines, or limestone quarries; others in the town maltings, corn mills, or timberyard. Though prosperous, the town had poor areas where newcomers in search of work were crammed together. It also had a large Free School, and many coaching inns and shops, including Edward Houlston's bookshop, which in 1811 stocked and sold Mr Brontë's *Cottage Poems*.

Wellington's Land (Wellingtonsland), later called Senegambia, in the west of the Verdopolitan Federation; situated in what is now Senegal, Gambia, Guinea, and Sierra Leone. Although Wellington's Land is called the 'Green Country' or Ireland of the *Glass Town Federation, it also has a 'Lake District' with names like Keswick and Grasmere (Grassmere), reflecting the English Lake District. See GLASS TOWN AND ANGRIAN SAGA.

Wellwood is the *Bloomfield family's house, based on *Blake Hall, in *Agnes Grey*. New but stately, amid 'mushroom poplar groves', it has a large garden, a well at the bottom of the lawn, stables, a farmyard, and a fir plantation. Agnes Grey is a governess there from autumn until the following midsummer.

Wentworth, Charles, a late persona of Branwell Brontë. Wentworth helps to chronicle the history of *Angria and the Angrians in the fragmentary manuscripts of 1836–7. He is troubled by the Calvinist doctrine of predestination, becomes private secretary to Lord Macara *Lofty, and visits Verdopolis as a wealthy 21-year-old Angrian. Winifred Gérin interprets Wentworth's experiences in this Glass Town Babylon as an autobiographical account of Branwell's actual experiences in London, arguing that Branwell made the trip but failed to present his letters of introduction at the Academy Schools (see ROYAL ACADEMY OF ARTS), instead frittering away his time and money like Wentworth on visiting sites he had always associated with Angria (Tower of London, Houses of Parliament, St Paul's, Apsley House, etc.) and in coffee houses (actually the Castle tavern at Holborn) (Gérin *BB*, pp. 99–110). Gaskell believed Branwell never made the trip to London; and Barker, after a thorough examination of all surviving evidence, concludes that 'such a visit was unlikely' and Wentworth should not be interpreted as Branwell's self-portrait (Barker, pp. 230–1). As Barker points out, Wentworth's hasty departure from Verdopolis is precipitated by news of the outbreak of the Angrian wars (see GLASS TOWN AND ANGRIAN SAGA). He enlists in

Northangerland's forces which at this stage in the saga are protecting Angria from the Reformist Ministry in Verdopolis.

Wesley, Revd John (1703–91), evangelist and founder of *Methodism. His devotion to preaching the Christian message of salvation was such that he continued to travel, preach, and write in his 86th year, despite the failing sight which ended his lifelong habit of omnivorous reading. He made some inspired translations of German *Moravian hymns, such as 'Now I have found the ground wherein I Sure my soul's anchor may remain'. Among his *Works* (32 vols., 1792) was a reprint of his popular abridgement of Henry Brooke's *The Fool of Quality: the History of Henry Earl of Moreland*. The young Jane Eyre listens eagerly to *Bessie's tales of love and adventure culled from this volume and from fairy tales and ballads. Wesley was a personal friend of Thomas Tighe, who helped to establish Mr Brontë's career. In 1742 Wesley made the first of several visits to Haworth, where he was welcomed by Revd William *Grimshaw, and where his congregations were so numerous that preaching took place in the churchyard. Later, Tabitha *Aykroyd was a Methodist class leader. Yet in 1837, provoked by the Dissenters' campaigns against church rates, Revd Patrick Brontë endorsed as 'just & excellent' the opinions expressed in *An Earnest Address to the Working Classes . . . by a Poor Man* (1836), where Wesley was described as a 'crafty, ambitious' hypocrite who 'made use of a little Christianity, in order that it might be the better swallowed', and adapted his doctrines 'to the depraved taste of the carnal mind' (pp. 86–7). In contrast, the *Taylors of Gomersal continued the family tradition of friendly tolerance towards Methodists: John Taylor (1737–1805), an admirer and friend of Wesley, welcomed him to the *Red House, and built the nearby redbrick chapel (Briar-chapel in *Shirley*) probably for the dissident 'New Connexion' Methodists. Mrs Yorke (see YORKE FAMILY), modelled on Mrs Taylor, gives her children Wesley's sermons to read, for 'John Wesley, being a Reformer and an Agitator, had a place both in her own and her husband's favour' (*Shirley*, ch. 34.)

West, Arthur Ripley, the potential hero of Charlotte Brontë's fragmentary story *Ashworth*. Son of General West, Arthur appears only briefly when he visits De Capell Hall and converses with Amelia De Capell, her cousin Marian Fairburne, and Mary Ashworth. Yet he displays the same haughty grandeur and magnetism as his prototype the Duke of *Zamorna, King of Angria, in the Brontë juvenilia. A conversation between his father and godfather Mr De Capell reveals that the 21-year-old Arthur Ripley is 'a reprobate' and

has fallen under the dubious influence of Alexander *Ashworth.

West, General, father of Arthur Ripley West and owner of Ripley Towers in Charlotte Brontë's fragmentary story *Ashworth*. He is a 'truculent Tory' and veteran soldier based on the Duke of *Wellington in the *Glass Town and Angrian saga, and a prototype for Mr Helstone in *Shirley*.

Westminster Review. Founded in opposition to the liberal *Edinburgh Review* and the conservative *Quarterly Review*, the *Westminster Review* was established by James Mill in 1824 and became known as the journal of the 'philosophical radicals'. It was edited by John Stuart Mill from 1835 to 1840. George Eliot served as assistant editor from 1852 to 1854. Except for one unenthusiastic review of *Shirley* (Jan. 1850), the *Westminster Review* was consistently positive in its criticism of the Brontës' work. George Henry *Lewes was a regular contributor and wrote highly favourable reviews of *Jane Eyre* (Jan. 1848), which he declared 'the best novel of the season', and *Villette* (Apr. 1853), which he admitted was not entirely successful 'as a novel, in the ordinary sense of the word', but praised lavishly as 'the utterance of an original mind'. George Eliot's famous article 'Silly Novels by Lady Novelists', published in the *Westminster Review* (Oct. 1856), notably exempted Charlotte from the charge that most contemporary novels by women were deficient in 'genuine observation, humour, and passion'. In August 1898, another contributor, Angus Mckay, asserted that Emily 'might have been Shakespeare's youngest sister'.

CB

Weston, Edward, the curate at *Horton church, attended by Agnes Grey and the *Murray family, in *Agnes Grey*. A sincere, effective, evangelical preacher, he is sensible and kind, comforting the poor with his gospel of God's love and with practical gifts. Strongly built, neither handsome nor ugly, he has brilliant brown eyes, a firm mouth, and the look of a thinker. A lover of animals, he rebukes those who are not, regardless of their rank. He values friendship, but believes adversity can strengthen character, and is gently abrupt in finding out Agnes's feelings and tastes. He resists Rosalie's wiles, and criticizes her mercenary mother. When he secures a living near *A——, where Agnes and her mother have set up a school, he seeks her out, becomes a welcome visitor, and proposes to her on the hill overlooking the sea. In their happy marriage, both live 'to the glory of God': Weston works 'surprising reforms' in his parish, and is esteemed by all. He resembles Revd William *Weightman in his evangelical doctrines and his kindness to the poor.

Westwood, battle of. See LEYDEN, BATTLE OF.

Wethersfield, a parish 7 miles from Braintree, Essex, in fertile farmland. Revd Patrick Brontë was the curate of Wethersfield from 1806 until early January 1809. Pleasant old brick or half-timbered houses border the street and village green. A sloping path leads up to the ancient brick and flint-walled church of St Mary Magdalene, whose south door faces Wethersfield Manor. On the opposite side of the green is St George's House, where Mr Brontë lodged with Miss Mildred Davy, and met her niece, Mary *Burder. The Congregational chapel probably attended by the Burders is a little further along the street.

'We wove a web in childhood' ('Retrospection') by Charlotte Brontë (19 Dec. 1835); published in C. W. Hatfield (ed.), *The Complete Poems of Charlotte Brontë* (1923) as 'Retrospection'. This seminal poem, written at *Roe Head, leads into a visionary prose passage where music comes 'thrillingly' almost to the body's ear, and Charlotte sees the Duke of *Zamorna lifting up his 'sable crest'. Brilliant images evoke the youthful dream: the aerial web, the pure spring of inspiration, the biblical mustard-seed and almond rod. Miraculously unfading, the light of the web expands into a glowing sky, the spring into a swelling ocean, the seed into a tree, the almond wand into fruit-fulness. Then, dramatically, Charlotte recalls the heartbreaking, dreary reality of the schoolroom, only to return, spellbound, to the Angrian dream-world. See ROE HEAD JOURNAL, THE.

Neufeldt, *CBP*, p. 165.

Wharton, Mary. See PERCY, LADY MARIA HENRIETTA.

Wheelhouse, Dr John Bateman, surgeon, c.1819–52, MRCS ?1841. Born in Whalley, Lancs., he was in Haworth by February 1843 when he witnessed the second codicil to the will of John Beaver. In December 1848 he married Hannah, widow of Enoch Thomas (see THOMAS FAMILY), and lived with her in a cottage in West Lane. In some crude doggerel verses Branwell satirically defended Wheelhouse from accusations that he was ugly, bad-tempered, and lustful, by invoking hell's curse on his accusers (Neufeldt *BBP*, pp. 298–9). Wheelhouse signed Branwell and Emily's death certificates. He also supported the petition for a better water supply for Haworth. He died of dropsy on 23 March 1852.

Wheelwright family, friends of Charlotte Brontë. Dr Thomas Wheelwright (1786–1861) MD Edinburgh, MRCS 1807, born in Aston, Birmingham, married Elizabeth Ridge in 1821. They had seven children: a son, name unknown; a second son, Charles Thomas (?1826–1908) who emigrated to South Africa and was thrice married; Laetitia Elizabeth (1828–1911); Emily (1829–88) who married Daniel P. Poulter in 1856; Frances ('Fanny', 1831–1913); Sarah Ann (1834–1900); and Julia (1835–42). Dr Wheelwright practised in London until July 1842, when he moved to the Hotel Cluysenaar, rue Royale, *Brussels (Hotel Crécy in *Villette*). The girls were day-boarders at the Pensionnat *Heger, and their parents often invited Charlotte and Emily to visit the Hotel Cluysenaar. Fanny recalled Charlotte as a 'gentle diminutive neat little retiring thing, but a genius even then', kind to her and her sisters, and fond of their mother. Fanny, Sarah, and Julia disliked Emily Brontë, who taught them music during recreation time. Julia's death from typhoid or cholera (accounts differ) might have been caused by the pensionnat's primitive sanitation. Mme Heger wrote sympathetically to the family on the death of their 'little angel'. On their return to England in August 1843 the Wheelwrights lived in Dover and Bath before moving in ?1849 to 29 Lower Phillimore Place, Kensington, where Charlotte visited them, but to their regret never stayed long, preferring to stay at George *Smith's home. She wrote affectionately at intervals to Laetitia, a handsome, strong-willed woman who 'ruled the roast' [*sic*] at home and had some linguistic skill and literary taste. Charlotte described to her the family's tragic bereavements, showed concern for Dr Wheelwright's failing sight, and on her death-bed wrote of Revd A. B. Nicholls's 'tenderest' nursing. The Wheelwrights gave Elizabeth *Gaskell and Clement King *Shorter valuable information about the Brontës, and allowed Shorter to print Charlotte's letters to Laetitia.

Whinbury, a market town close to *Briarfield in *Shirley*, and the largest and most populous parish in the area. The rector of the parish is Revd Dr Thomas *Boultby; his curate is Revd Joseph *Donne. Whinbury is also the home of the *Sykes and *Pearson families, Sykes and Pearson being two cloth manufacturers acquainted with Robert Gérard *Moore and threatened, as he is, by the actions of the machine-breakers. The town on which Whinbury is based is identified by Wroot (p. 85) as *Dewsbury, at the time of the events in *Shirley* a rapidly growing industrial centre, where Revd Patrick Brontë was curate from 1809 to 1811. HR

Whitcross, in *Jane Eyre*. After leaving Thornfield, Jane arrives at Whitcross, a stone pillar where four lonely moorland roads meet in a north-midland county. *Morton is several miles to the north, the nearest town S—— (*Sheffield) 10 miles away. No real place matches the description, though Ernest

Raymond suggests Moscar Cross on the Hallam moors.

Raymond, Ernest, *In the Steps of the Brontës* (1948).

White family of Rawdon. Charlotte Brontë's second period of private governess-ship, from February to 24 December 1841, was spent at *Upperwood House, Rawdon, the home of a former Bradford merchant, John White (?1790–1860), and his wife Jane, née Robson, the 'co-heiress of John Robson, Esq. of Charlton Hall, Northumberland', whom he married in October 1830. White had inherited Upperwood from his uncle William Leavens, a wealthy woolstapler. Charlotte's pupils were Sarah Louisa (b. 1832), later Mrs S. W. Atkinson, and Jasper Leavens (?1834–?60). Both children seemed over-indulged, wild, and unbroken, but apparently well disposed, and their parents were 'good sort of people': Charlotte liked the hospitable Mr White extremely, and tried hard to like his wife. By early May she had got more control over the children, and on 20 July gave each of them a present of a book. By dint of nursing the fat baby (Arthur Robson White, b. ?1840, later the father of Dr Percy Stanhope White of Eccleshill) it had become fond of her, and she of it until its mother made a fool of it and it seemed a 'small petted nuisance'. Charlotte was amused by Mrs White's boasting of her family connections, despite being (Charlotte believed) an exciseman's daughter, with 'bad grammar and worse orthography'. Mrs White angered her by telling her off in a 'very coarse unladylike manner' and by her reluctant granting of a brief holiday. Yet the place was a favourable one, even though the salary of £20 was reduced to £16 by the expense of washing. For the last six months of her stay at Upperwood Charlotte's employers made much of her, urged Revd Patrick Brontë to visit her there, then parted from her with regret, and later invited her to visit them.

Widdop, Mrs Jane Helen ('Ellen') (1851–1924), daughter of the Haworth stationer John *Greenwood and wife of John Heaton Widdop (m. 1876), son of William Widdop and Martha Redman, who used to wash for the Brontës. Her husband was verger of Haworth church for seventeen years (his name is incorrectly recorded on their gravestone in Haworth churchyard as 'Joseph'). Ellen Widdop inherited from her father a painting by Charlotte Brontë (BPM) and ten pencil sketches by Anne (private owner; Alexander & Sellars, pp. 171, 397, 412–15, 420–1). She recalled that as a little girl she used to bring tripe to the parsonage for Revd Patrick Brontë every Friday and was rewarded with a slice of bread, butter, and jam (Lock & Dixon, p. 345). Charlotte Brontë used the names Ellen and Widdop for characters in her writing: see ASHWORTH; 'WILLIE ELLIN'.

Wiggins, Patrick Benjamin, caricature of Patrick Branwell Brontë. He was born at Thorncliffe (*Thornton) but lived most of his life in *Howard (Haworth). He enters the *Glass Town and Angrian saga briefly as colour grinder to the famous painter Sir Edward de Lisle in chapter 5 of The *Wool is Rising, 12 June 1834 (Neufeldt BB Works, 2. 60). Here Branwell laughs at his own pretensions to art, his thick mat of red hair, his face which looks older than his near 17 years of age with its 'freckled visage and large Roman nose', and his inarticulate response when addressed by someone of importance. Three days later Charlotte repeats this description, adding that this 'quizzical little personage' has an 'almost insane devotion to all celebrated characters in Verdopolis', in this case Maurice *Flannagan the boxer and John *Greenwood the organist (Alexander EEW 2(2). 108–9). Branwell's excessive enthusiasms, especially for *pugilism and *music, his habits of exaggeration, boastfulness, and ambition are brilliantly captured by his sister in her extended portrait of Wiggins in *'My Angria and the Angrians' (Alexander EEW 2(2). 245–53) where 'as a musician he was greater than Bach; as a Poet he surpassed Byron; [and] as a painter, Claude Lorrain yielded to him'. Wiggins's dismissal of his three sisters (Charlotte, Jane and Anne Wiggins representing the three Brontë sisters) is an ingenious piece of comic insight and self-deprecation by Charlotte.

Wilberforce, William (1759–1833), prominent in the struggle to abolish the slave trade and slavery in British overseas possessions. An adherent of the evangelical 'Clapham sect' and a graduate of St John's College, Cambridge, he responded to Henry *Martyn's request for financial help for Revd Patrick Brontë in February 1804 by promising that he and Henry Thornton would each give £10 per annum. In 1810 Mr Brontë secured the release of William Nowell, falsely accused of deserting from the army, and a review of the case against him, by asking Wilberforce to request Lord Palmerston's intervention. Wilberforce helped to found the *Church Missionary Society and the *British and Foreign Bible Society, causes actively supported by Mr Brontë, and was a subscriber to *Cowan Bridge School.

Wildfell Hall is a large Elizabethan house, owned by Frederick *Lawrence, in *Tenant*. During the fifteen years in which it has not been inhabited, the Hall and formal garden have fallen into disrepair. Several rooms are made habitable by Mr Lawrence for his sister, Helen *Huntingdon, posing as Mrs Graham. Wildfell Hall is a sanctuary for Helen from her husband and his debauchery. Here she can paint and instruct her child away from the perverting influence of his father.

The house is isolated from the village, 2 miles from Gilbert *Markham's home at *Linden-Car, and 4 miles from the sea. Situated at the top of heathclad Wildfell (a 'fell' being dialect for a high hill, ridge, or mountain), the house has no shelter from the wind except a group of Scotch firs. Its gloomy setting, its disuse, and the mystery which surrounds its occupant lend it a Gothic aspect which emphasizes the plight of its tenant. Wildfell Hall is sometimes identified with *Ponden House; but its surrounding countryside and proximity to the sea are seen as similar to those of *Scarborough and the east coast of Yorkshire, which Anne Brontë loved.

Williams, William Smith (1800–75), literary adviser to *Smith, Elder and Company. His sympathetic criticism and kindly judgement earned him the regard of many distinguished writers, including Charlotte Brontë. He had formerly been an apprentice to the publishers Taylor and Hessey, through whom he met and was kindly regarded by Leigh *Hunt, Hazlitt, and Keats. He felt the 'last kind pressure' of the poet's hand as Keats began his last journey in September 1820. He married Margaret Eliza Hills on 14 January 1826, and at about the same time or just before opened a bookshop. After this closed in 1827 through lack of capital, he became a somewhat inefficient bookkeeper to the lithographic printers Hullmandel and Walter. He wrote reviews and essays on theatrical and literary topics for the *Spectator*, the *Athenaeum*, and other journals. In 1845, at George *Smith's invitation, he took up the more congenial post of literary adviser to Smith, Elder. Charlotte was heartened by his discriminating response to *The Professor* in July 1847. Though her short novel was refused, the firm expressed interest in a three-volume work, and Williams warmly recommended *Jane Eyre* for publication. Charlotte and Anne first met him in London in July 1848—a 'pale, mild, stooping man' who, with George Smith, accompanied them to the Opera House to see Rossini's *The Barber of Seville* on Saturday evening (8 July), and kindly came early on Sunday morning to take them to church: 'he was so quiet but so sincere in his attentions—one could not but have a most friendly leaning towards him—he has a nervous hesitation in speech and a difficulty in finding appropriate language in which to express himself—which throws him into the background in conversation—but I had been his correspondent—and therefore knew with what intelligence he could write—so that I was not in danger of underrating him' (Charlotte to Mary Taylor,

4 September 1848, in Smith *Letters*, 2. 111–15). When Charlotte read his sensitive, well-informed comments on art in *John Bull* for 1 July 1848, she wished he had been their guide to the Royal Academy exhibition. He became one of her most valued correspondents. She shared with him her opinions on the books she read, many of them sent as gifts or loans by the firm. She considered his criticism of parts of *Shirley* with care, and though she refused to alter her satirical treatment of the curates, she was obliged to defer to his (and George Smith's) disapproval of her intended preface, 'A Word to the "Quarterly"' (see SHIRLEY: 'A WORD TO THE "QUARTERLY"'). Some of her most poignant letters on the deaths of Branwell, Emily, and Anne were written to him, and he wrote a long, delicately sympathetic letter of condolence after the death of Emily. Charlotte in turn was sympathetic to his troubled efforts to reconcile orthodox Christianity with Emersonian philosophy. She also took a friendly interest in his anxious concern to establish the older members of his family of eight children in self-supporting careers. She was particularly interested in the daughters who were to become *governesses, offered her advice, and shared his pleasure when Louisa gained a place at Queen's College in Harley Street. She trusted his discretion and judgement when she wrote to him, after she had received two letters written by James *Taylor from Bombay in September–October 1851, asking for his 'advice and information' on Taylor's character. In November 1851 Charlotte exerted herself to provide an introduction to Elizabeth Gaskell for Mr Williams's artist son, Frank, and was delighted when Gaskell agreeably impressed by 'Young Mr. Williams'.

Charlotte's informal, confidential correspondence with Mr Williams seems to have ended in 1853, with her brief, restrained note of 6 December thanking him for the books she was returning, but refusing further loans. It is likely that he wrote to her after this when she became engaged to Revd A. B. *Nicholls in April 1854, for his name is in the list of friends to whom wedding cards were to be sent in June. Their relationship was undoubtedly affected by the coolness between Charlotte and George Smith in 1853–4. Mr Williams remained loyal to Smith, Elder, and friendly with other authors whose work they published, especially with Thackeray and Ruskin. Sir Sidney Lee wrote of him: 'During his association with Smith he did no independent literary work beyond helping to prepare for the firm, in 1861, a "Selection from the Writings of John Ruskin"' (Leonard Huxley, *The House of Smith, Elder* (1923), 56). He was from youth a warm admirer of Ruskin, sharing especially his enthusiasm for J. W. M. *Turner. Williams retired from Smith, Elder in February 1875,

A photograph of William Smith Williams.

and died six months later on 21 August at his residence at Twickenham. His eldest daughter, Margaret Ellen, was the wife of Lowes (Cato) Dickinson, the portrait painter, and his youngest daughter Ann Catherine ('Anna', 1845–1924) became a distinguished soprano singer.

'Willie Ellin' ('I will not deny that I took a pleasure . . .') (May–June 1853), the beginning of an unfinished story in which Charlotte Brontë tried to revive the early chapters of *The Professor*, a novel which Smith, Elder had refused to publish. The central portion of *The Professor* had been recast in *Villette*, and Charlotte was reluctant to abandon the remaining early theme of the rivalry of two brothers. Immediately after the publication of *Villette*, she wrote three fragments relating to Edward and Willie Ellin, each in pencil and first published in *BST* (1936), 9. 46. 3 22:

1. 'I will not deny that I took a pleasure in studying the character of Mrs Widdop', May 1853 (Houghton, Harvard) (see WIDDOP, MRS JANE HELEN).
2. 'In other countries and in distant times—it is possible', 22 June 1853 (Houghton, Harvard).
3. ' "Stop"—said the expectant victim earnestly', c.June 1853 (BPM).

The narrator is Ellin of Ellin Hall, probably the same person as the young child Willie Ellin in the story. He is an orphan deprived of his position as a gentleman and forced by his brutal elder brother Edward to become a shop apprentice. Like his precursors in the juvenilia and later fragments (see Alexander *EW*, pp. 219 24), Edward is 'athletic and red-whiskered', but his character is presented in its extreme form as violently sadistic. When the young Willie runs away to his ancestral home, he is pursued by Edward wielding his gig-whip. A kindly Jewish merchant, Mr Bosas, prevents Willie's punishment, only to delay the inevitable in Edward's brutal attack on his brother in the final scene. The gratuitous violence, the brutalized child, the lonely house, and the housekeeper suggest that Charlotte may have been influenced by her recent rereading of *Wuthering Heights* for the new revised edition of 1850, although such features are not uncommon in the juvenilia.

Wilmot, Annabella, a beautiful, accomplished heiress in *Tenant*, and niece of the rich Mr *Wilmot, a suitor of Helen Lawrence (*Huntingdon). Annabella marries Mr Arthur *Huntingdon's tormented friend Lord Lowborough for his title. He loves her, but she scorns him and begins a shameless two-year affair with Huntingdon. She has two children, a boy and a girl (the latter of whom is not her husband's), but has no maternal feelings. She later elopes with another man to the Continent and Lord Lowborough divorces her. Quarrelling with her lover, she finally sinks into debt and reputedly leads a wretched existence until she dies in poverty and misery.

Wilmot, Mr, a rich old friend of Helen Huntingdon's uncle, and uncle of Annabella *Wilmot in *Tenant*. To Helen he is 'a worthless old reprobate' but he courts her despite her discouragement: she would 'Rather be an old maid and a pauper, than Mrs Wilmot' (ch. 16). It is at Mr Wilmot's party in London that Mr Arthur Huntingdon first declares his admiration for Helen.

Wilson, John (Christopher North) (1785–1854), born in Paisley, Scotland, a prolific contributor to *Blackwood's Edinburgh Magazine*. John Wilson wrote the bulk of *Blackwood's* famous series 'Noctes Ambrosianae' (1822–35), which Charlotte and Branwell Brontë imitated in the miniature versions of *Blackwood's* they created as children. Wilson was known to *Blackwood's* readers as its fictitious editor 'Christopher *North', an elderly but energetic critic of contemporary poets and a poet in his own right. As a young man, Branwell enthusiastically recalled that he had delighted to 'read and re-read [Wilson's articles] while a little child' (Wise & Symington, 1. 133), and Wilson's influence can be seen in the early writing of both Branwell and Charlotte. Wilson enjoyed a distinguished university career at Glasgow and Oxford, where he was recognized as an outstanding classical scholar, poet, and athlete. After graduating, he lived near Lake Windermere and became acquainted with a number of authors, including Thomas *De Quincey, Samuel Taylor *Coleridge, Robert *Southey, and especially William *Wordsworth, with whom he regularly conversed. In 1817, Wilson joined John Gibson *Lockhart and James *Hogg in *Edinburgh on the staff of *Blackwood's Magazine*, helping to write the infamous 'Chaldee Manuscript', which secured the magazine's reputation as a lively and provocative periodical. As a major contributor for many years, Wilson wrote reviews of contemporary poetry and general articles on a wide variety of topics for *Blackwood's* as well as contributing his own prose fiction and poetry. He participated in the magazine's attacks on Leigh *Hunt, John Keats, and 'The Cockney School of Poetry'; savagely reviewed Coleridge's *Biographia Literaria*; supported Percy Bysshe *Shelley; and alternately praised and condemned Wordsworth. Wilson published three sentimental novels in the 1820s. Enormously versatile, the distinctive traits of Wilson's writing are its energy and wild inconsistency of opinion. He served as professor of moral

Wilson, Richard

philosophy at Edinburgh University for many years but wrote none of his own lectures.   CB

Wilson, Richard, alias assumed by Captain Henry *Hastings when he is on the run from the Angrian police.

Wilson, Revd William Carus (1791–1859), model for Revd Robert *Brocklehurst, in *Jane Eyre*, graduated BA 1815, MA 1818 from Trinity College, Cambridge. In October 1815 Revd Charles *Simeon warned him of his excessive Calvinism, for which he was refused orders in 1815. But after ordination in 1816 he became rector of *Tunstall (1816–28) near *Cowan Bridge, where in 1824 he founded the Clergy Daughters' School attended by Maria, Elizabeth, Charlotte, and Emily Brontë 1824–5. Wilson was rector of Whittington, Lancs., 1825–57, and from 1825 to 1857 non-resident perpetual curate of Casterton, to which the school moved in 1833. He succeeded to the Casterton estates in 1851. Proud of his careful supervision of the school, which he regarded as a 'nursery for heaven', he was not intentionally cruel, and endeavoured to remedy its early deficiencies. But many pupils fell ill before the move to Casterton, their stamina undermined by a spartan régime of early rising, long prayers, poor food, and outdoor exercise in all weathers in inadequate clothing. Wilson's publications for children, including *The Child's First Tales* (Kirkby Lonsdale, 1836) and the monthly magazine the *Children's Friend*, inculcate good behaviour by dire warnings of eternal damnation for children struck down by God, without time for repentance, as punishment for their sins. He regarded a good child's death, however painful, as something to thank God for, and a means of encouraging other children to 'seek the Lord', and find salvation, as he was confident the 10-year-old Sarah Bicker had done when she died in pain at the school in September 1825 (*Children's Friend*, Dec. 1826). Elizabeth Gaskell later revised the controversial statements she made about Wilson in *Life* (see Angus Easson's World's Classics edn. (1996), 474–9). Emma Jane Worboise, a pupil at Casterton, later praised Wilson and the school in *Thornycroft Hall* (1864).

Wise & Symington, app. 1.

Wilson, Dr William James, Hon FRCS 1843 (d. 1855), the skilful oculist who removed the cataract from Revd Patrick Brontë's left eye on 25 August 1846 at 83 Mount Pleasant, Boundary Street, *Manchester. His father was a Leeds solicitor. After apprenticeships to surgeons in Lancaster and Chester, he studied at St Bartholomew's, London, and the Infirmary for Diseases of the Eye in Charterhouse Square, gained his MRCS (1813), and soon afterwards moved to Manchester. There he

helped to found the Institution for Curing Diseases of the Eye, and was Honorary Surgeon, Manchester Royal Infirmary 1826–55, with a private practice at 72 Mosley Street.

Wilson family. Mrs Wilson is the widow of a substantial farmer in *Tenant* and 'a narrow-minded, tattling old gossip' (according to Gilbert *Markham, ch. 1), who lives with her two sons and daughter at *Ryecote Farm. The daughter Jane is graceful, elegant, and snobbish, having acquired accomplishments at boarding school. She intends to marry a gentleman and has designs on Frederick *Lawrence, until Gilbert Markham disabuses him of her attractiveness. Like her mother she indulges in gossip, delighting in the supposed scandal about Mrs Graham. She remains unmarried and retreats to the gentility of a country town on the marriage of her elder brother Robert, 'a rough countrified farmer' (ch. 1) who manages the farm. Richard Wilson, the youngest son, is a quiet, studious young man. After graduating from Cambridge, he becomes *Millward's curate, marries Mary Millward, and succeeds him in the parish of *Lindenhope.

Winkworth, Catherine (1827–78), accomplished translator of German hymns, friend of Elizabeth Gaskell. With her sister Susanna (1820–84) she began Greek lessons with William Gaskell (see GASKELL FAMILY), c.1846, and in April 1853 met Charlotte Brontë at the Gaskells' house. Charlotte found her intelligent and sympathetic, and confided to her that her decision to marry Revd A. B. *Nicholls had 'cost [her] a good deal': he was not intellectual, and was a Puseyite. Catherine responded that affection and trustworthiness outweighed such aspects. Her letter to Emma Shaen of 8 May 1854 and Charlotte's to Catherine of 27 July 1854 significantly illuminate Charlotte's relationship to Nicholls.

'Winter Evening Thoughts'. See POETRY BY REVD PATRICK BRONTË.

Wise, Thomas James (1859–1937), bibliographer, collector, and forger. As a young clerk in the commodity-importing firm of H. Rubeck and Company of which he eventually became chief clerk and cashier, he became interested in book-collecting and bibliography, in which he was soon regarded as pre-eminent. In 1900, as vice-president of the *Brontë Society, he gave the Brontë Museum fourteen autograph letters by Charlotte, and he was its president in 1926. In 1917 he produced *A Bibliography of the Writings in Prose and Verse of the Members of the Brontë Family*. Like his other author bibliographies, it was considered definitive. He was president of the Bibliographical Society 1922–4, and his credentials as honorary

544

fellow of Worcester College, Oxford, and honorary MA were displayed in the Shakespeare Head Brontë correspondence (1932) and miscellaneous writings (1936). Yet in 1934, after brilliant detective work by John Carter and Graham Pollard in *An Enquiry into the Nature of Certain Nineteenth Century Pamphlets*, he was implicated in the forgery of some 50 'first-edition' pamphlets issued 1887–1903 containing works by famous writers (notably Elizabeth Barrett Browning's *Sonnets from the Portuguese*, allegedly printed in Reading in 1847), all printed later than their title-page dates by Richard Clay and Sons in London, and authenticated by Wise. Though not directly accused of forgery, Wise was clearly indicated as responsible for the deception. He never admitted his guilt, withdrawing from public discussion on the plea of ill health. More incriminating evidence, and proof of H. Buxton Forman's complicity, emerged after his death. Many of his private printings were piratical, his highly profitable forgeries were given fictitious provenances, he stole leaves from volumes in the British Museum to supply those missing from his own and other collectors' copies, and acted with shameless duplicity towards Ellen *Nussey, and Revd A. B. *Nicholls. By October 1892, when Ellen was anxious to secure a safe depository for her Brontë letters and arrange for at least partial publication, Wise was negotiating with her through C. K. *Shorter, assuring her that he bought *manuscripts for their own sakes, would pay her £100 for her letters (raised to £125 when Ellen hesitated), and would permit Shorter to use them in a biography, for which Ellen would receive two-thirds of the profits. In November he wrote to her directly: he and Shorter wanted the letters to enhance 'the honor & reputation of their gloriously gifted writer', and to keep them safe for 'future generations'; for he intended that at his death his library should go to the South Kensington Museum. By 18 November 1892, when she thanked Wise for his 'enclosure', Ellen had capitulated, and he was later able to produce her receipt for £125, and his cheque counterfoil dated 17 November 1892. On 16 July 1895, having discovered to her great distress that Wise was selling her manuscripts piecemeal, Ellen wrote to him to say she had understood her letters would go to 'Kensington Museum'. He denied that such a bequest had been one of the 'conditions of sale' and alleged that he had told Ellen in January 1893 that he was 'weeding out' letters already printed or 'devoid of interest'. In 1895–6 Wise also bought, through Shorter, many of Mr Nicholls's Brontë treasures. He split up and misattributed many manuscripts to make them more attractive to collectors in Britain and America, so causing endless trouble to later Brontë editors. His Ashworth library is now

in the British Library but not through bequest: it had to be bought.

Wiseman, Nicholas Patrick Stephen, Cardinal (1802–65), Roman *Catholic prelate. After ordination in 1825 he rose rapidly in the Catholic hierarchy, becoming vicar apostolic of the London District in February 1849, archbishop of Westminster in August 1850, and cardinal in September 1850. His intention to restore England 'to its orbit in the ecclesiastical firmament' was satirically interpreted by Charlotte Brontë as going back 'six centuries' to an age of blind obedience to Rome and denial of common sense. She saw Wiseman as a wolf in sheep's clothing, aiming at power; and, after hearing him speak in London on 16 June 1851, she described him to her father as 'a sleek hypocrite' with oily lips and a 'smooth whining manner'. A confirmation service held by him on 22 June 1851 she thought 'impiously theatrical'. Neither she nor Revd Patrick Brontë recognized his scholarship, intellect, and humanitarianism.

Wolfe, James (1727–59), English soldier distinguished in the North American theatre of the Seven Years War for empire (1756–63). Wolfe commanded the expedition for the capture of Quebec in 1759, as part of the British scheme for expelling the French from Canada. The attack on the Marquis de Montcalm's strong position was fraught with difficulty but, after ascending the St Lawrence and eventually scaling the heights of Montmorency at a lightly guarded position, Wolfe reached the plains of Abraham. After a short struggle the French were routed, Montcalm was killed, Quebec capitulated, and the fate of Canada was decided. Benjamin *West's painting *The Death of General Wolfe* (1771), at the moment of victory, made an indelible impression on the young Branwell Brontë. A copy of William Woollett's engraving of West's painting was said to have hung in his bedroom at Haworth Parsonage (Gérin *BB*, p. 25).

women, position of. As workplace and home separated more emphatically and opportunities for upward social mobility increased, Victorians embraced the 'separate spheres' ideology, the view that men and women were physically and spiritually predetermined to inhabit different realms. Active and assertive, men were naturally equipped for the public arena ruled by competition and materialism. Women were the guardians of emotional and spiritual values properly confined in a domestic space protected from the market's corrosive practices. Woman was idealized as the 'Angel in the House', a 'relational creature' who derived her value and purpose from relationships, as daughter, wife, mother. Such works as Sarah

Stickney Ellis's popular conduct books (from 1838) and Coventry Patmore's *The Angel in the House* (1854) extolled the domestic ideal, attributing to women great 'influence'—symbolic capital which assigned them responsibility for the moral condition of a society which denied them political and economic power. The separate-spheres ideology consigned middle-class women to supervising servants, paying social calls, and displaying the family's wealth and rank in their dress and household furnishings. The Brontës' novels clearly address the 'condition of women' by criticizing the separate spheres, confining feminine ideals, and women's limited professional and educational opportunities. Florence Nightingale and Elizabeth Barrett Browning wrote that tormenting idleness made them fear they would go mad.

Throughout the century debates over women's political and legal rights and their educational, professional, and economic opportunities—issues collectively designated 'the Woman Question'—contested the domestic ideal. The 1832 *Reform Bill extended the franchise in national elections to about one man in seven (based on property qualifications), but for the first time pointedly excluded women from the electorate by defining voters as male. Discussion of female suffrage intensified during the *Chartist movement of the late 1840s, when supporters linked women's rights to those of unenfranchised labourers. One rationale for denying women the vote was 'coverture', the concept that a woman was 'covered' by her husband. Marriage was considered woman's appropriate destiny, and motherhood her apotheosis. According to the 1851 census, however, 43 per cent of British women lacked spouses. Such statistics eventually gave rise to the term 'Redundant Woman', with emigration proposed as a remedy for the social 'problem' spinsters represented.

Upon marrying, women essentially forfeited the right to inherit and hold property in their own names. Until 1870, except for inheritance carefully sheltered by a legal settlement (a practice usually confined to the wealthy), a woman's earnings, real estate, and personal property (including her clothing and jewellery) automatically became her husband's, even if she had been deserted or separated from him. Because they legally had no separate identity, wives could not enter legal contracts, sue, or be sued. Custody and *divorce laws disadvantaged women, for fathers had exclusive rights to their children (but could not be forced to provide for them), and men could obtain divorces more easily than women could. Women had few economic alternatives to marrying or depending on male relatives. Labouring-class women found physically rigorous jobs in agriculture, mining, factories, and domestic service: in 1851 over 10

per cent of the female population worked as maids, charwomen, and laundresses. The gruelling hours and conditions in the seamstress trade drove many needlewomen to life on the streets. Victorians judged prostitution a social evil of monstrous proportions, generally attributing the trade to female decadence rather than economic laws of supply and demand (see SEXUALITY). Men's fear of financial competition retarded women's entry into trades. In order to keep women from surpassing their own skills and earning higher wages, male china painters, for example, organized to deny to women entering the field use of maulsticks with which men propped their wrists while painting. Admission requirements and regulations at art schools inhibited women's success in painting and sculpture; women were barred from classes in life drawing, ostensibly to protect their modesty from confronting nude models.

Within the middle classes women's principal options in the first half of the century were *governess, schoolteacher, or lady's companion. Even if becoming a teacher or governess did not involve a humiliating drop in social class, the field offered scant rewards. Many governess positions advertised minimal salaries (or no salary at all) beyond room and board, providing a home for the present but no resources for old age. Governesses' wages often barely met needs for clothing, laundry, and provisions during their limited holidays. Besides low pay, as Charlotte's novels and letters testify, working as a governess might subject a woman to a demoralizing loss of autonomy and respect. Falling into an ill-defined status beneath her employers but above the household servants, she often experienced depressing social isolation as well.

In the first half of the century schooling for middle-class girls was normally limited to home instruction provided by parents or governesses, though private schools such as the charitable *Cowan Bridge School (notoriously immortalized as *Lowood) and Margaret Wooler's school at *Roe Head (where the Brontë sisters studied and Charlotte taught) were available (see EDUCATION). Only after mid-century did girls' schools increase in number and quality, with objectives ranging from training governesses to preparing women to enter universities (a goal attained incrementally over some 75 years from 1869).

Increasingly, authorship provided a financial opportunity for educated women, though many women writers remained anonymous or, like the Brontës, adopted male pseudonyms. As Charlotte suggested in her 1850 *'Biographical Notice', reviewers often applied different standards to women's writing, expecting from them decorous subject matter, 'delicacy', and sentimentality.

Despite this critical double standard and payment practices which favoured publishers, writing, because it could be pursued at home, represented one of the most secure professional opportunities for women.

Writing posed a happy alternative to teaching for the Brontës. After publishing *Jane Eyre* Charlotte wrote to W. S. Williams on 12 May 1848 that she frequently wished 'to say something about the "condition of women" question', though she found the amount of 'cant' on the subject repugnant (Smith *Letters*, 2. 66). Mentioning a *West-minster Review* article on 'Woman's Mission', she wrote to Elizabeth Gaskell on 27 August 1850 that although 'a few Men' with fine sympathies and a strong sense of justice support changing attitudes toward women, 'the amelioration of our condition depends on ourselves'—adding, however, that some 'evils—deep rooted in the foundations of the Social system—' cannot be changed (Smith *Letters*, 2. 457). The Brontës' novels mount a powerful critique of the position of women in mid-Victorian England. Besides examining the painful position of the governess (a topic also in *Agnes Grey* and *Shirley*), *Jane Eyre* exposes the ills of female economic dependency, class barriers to marriage (subjects also addressed in *Shirley*), and associations of female sexual appetite with insanity. Jane protests against the cultural constrictions that deny women outlets for their energies and intellectual abilities, a topic reiterated in *Shirley*'s exposition of the dismal lot of spinsters and limitation of ladies' options to marriage and charity work. *Shirley* links the anger and powerlessness of middle-class women to those of unemployed labourers, and exposes the crass operations of a marriage market in which men woo wealthy women from financial need rather than love. The character Shirley *Keeldar depicts what a woman can be, given autonomy, education, and financial independence: a vibrant being who can equal or surpass men in improving social conditions.

Tenant attacks the legal disabilities of married women with regard to child custody, property ownership, and access to divorce. Helen's work as a painter exemplifies women's disadvantages in the art field in her lack of professional training and need for a male representative to market her work. The novel also exposes the gendered double standards which warp domestic relationships. Rose Markham protests against women's servitude to men's whims and desires, an apparently benign inequality in the Markham household which produces sinister effects in the marriages of Arthur Huntingdon's set.

Shirley examines the difficulties of the heiress (a subject raised in *Tenant*, where Huntingdon pursues Helen's fortune but Gilbert finds it daunting).

Financial freedom to wed the man she loves proves problematic for Shirley, for conventions make it difficult to conceive of partnership uninflected by gender and class hierarchies. Similarly the end of *The Professor* calls into question whether marital equality can flourish amid Victorian idealizations of angelic wives and separate spheres, for William Crimsworth views Frances as an anomaly, in effect as two different women who succeed as wife and professional, and in dealings with his son he reasserts his dominant masculinity.

Like *The Professor*, *Villette* turns to a Continental setting to explore alternative class and gender dynamics which allow greater female autonomy. *Villette* contrasts Polly Home's Angel-in-the-House vapidity with Lucy Snowe's passion and intellectual vigour. Paintings which display the conventional feminine ideal and its sensual opposite Cleopatra, like the apparition of the nun and the mesmerizing but repellent spectacle of *Vashti, represent the madonna–harlot paradigm against which Lucy struggles to define herself anew.

Wuthering Heights, while seeming to create its own realm and unique concerns, challenges the ideological tyranny of separate spheres and the Angel in the House. Unable to resist cultural imperatives of money and rank, Catherine Earnshaw weds Edgar Linton even though other women characters link the traditional female role to subordination, weakness, and death. Social convention cannot accommodate the dynamic equality and unity represented by the ungendered early comradeship of Catherine and Heathcliff, and the narrative traces their divisive attempts to achieve the gender expectations defined for them by society. See also EMIGRATION; POLITICS, BRITISH.   BT

Bodichon, Barbara Leigh Smith, *A Brief Summary, in Plain Language, of the Most Important Laws Concerning Women* (1854).
Helsinger, Elizabeth K., Sheets, Robin L., and Veeder, William, *The Woman Question: Society and Literature in Britain and America, 1837–1883*, 3 vols. (1983).

Wood, William (1808–89), joiner and cabinet-maker who lived and worked at Newell Hill, now known as Lodge Street, just off Main St., Haworth; great-nephew of Tabitha *Aykroyd, the Brontës' servant. William's father, John Wood, was the son of Tabby's sister Susannah Wood. His mother Rebecca died at the age of 25 (1814) and his father then married Martha Greenwood, raising another family including Greenwood Wood (1820–87), who married Sarah, a casual *servant of the Brontës. William Wood carried out repairs at the Parsonage and made several articles of furniture for the Brontës. By his first wife Matty Ogden (*c*.1812–35; m. 1830), he had four children, only one of whom reached adulthood and became the subject of an oil painting by Branwell Bronte: 'John Ogden Wood, 4 April 1836' (the boy and his dog; BPM). He then had nine children by his second wife Ann Altham (*c*.1817–1902). William Wood claimed to be the most familiar with the Brontës of all the local Haworth residents, since 'the Vicar's children were in the habit of coming to his workshop to obtain frames for their drawings: they were too proud to accept them as presents, and they were accustomed to give him a drawing in exchange' (Chadwick, p. 102). At one time he apparently had a drawer stuffed with their little drawings and paintings, some of which still survive (see Alexander & Sellars, p. 111). It was William Wood who made the Brontës' coffins and remarked on the narrowness of Emily's (Smith *Letters*, 2. 158). In 1836, he and Tabby jointly bought three cottages in Newell Hill.

Woodford, Mr Lawrence's residence, some 3 miles outside *Lindenhope in *Tenant*. His family left Wildfell Hall fifteen years before the commencement of the novel, preferring this more modern mansion.

Woodhouse Grove school. In 1811 the Wesleyan Methodist Conference resolved to provide another boarding school in addition to John *Wesley's foundation, Kingswood. Woodhouse Grove school, Apperley Bridge, near *Leeds, was opened in January 1812 to educate boys whose fathers were preachers moving from circuit to circuit every two years, and to provide a trained and educated ministry. The first 'governor' was Revd John *Fennell, whose wife Jane, née Branwell, acted as 'governess'. Her niece Maria Branwell *Brontë met there her future husband, Revd Patrick *Brontë, external examiner in classics for that year and again in 1823. The school is still owned by the Methodist Conference.

Wooler, Eliza. See WOOLER FAMILY.

Wooler, Katherine Harriet (Catherine) (1796–1884), Margaret *Wooler's sister and partner at *Roe Head, where she taught French and other subjects. Said to be intelligent, but a severe disciplinarian and narrow-minded, she 'cut' Mary *Taylor for living alone in Germany, teaching German boys. Charlotte Brontë thought her like Mme Zoë *Heger in mind, degree of cultivation, and character, but unlike in being a soured spinster, disappointed in her hopes of marriage. Though Charlotte suspected insincerity in Catherine's renewed contact with Ellen Nussey in 1851, she thanked her cordially for a kind letter in July 1854, described her honeymoon, and signed herself 'Your old pupil'.

Wooler, Margaret (1792–1885), teacher and friend of Charlotte Brontë. The eldest of eleven children in the *Wooler family of Rouse Mill, Batley, she had a good education, and according to Ellen Nussey lived for six years on the Isle of Wight with an uncle, Dr William Moore, who was 'on the military staff', and his wife. Her nephew, Sir Thomas Clifford Allbutt, described her as 'a woman of unusual brains and accomplishments, especially a fine Italian scholar . . . a keen-witted, ironical, and very independent Yorkshire woman' (Smith *Letters*, 1. 99). Ellen Nussey recollected her as 'short and stout, but graceful in her movements, very fluent in conversation and with a very sweet voice. . . . Miss Wooler was like a lady abbess. She wore white, well-fitting dresses embroidered [*sic*]. Her long hair plaited, formed a coronet, and long ringlets fell from her head to shoulders. She was not pretty or handsome, but her quiet dignity made her presence imposing' (Shorter *Circle*, pp. 261–2). She was tactful in handling the sensitive Charlotte, who from 17 January 1831 to May 1832 was her pupil at *Roe Head, the school she established in 1830, rarely taking more than eight or nine pupils at the same time. Elizabeth Gaskell was told that she had a remarkable knack of making her pupils 'feel interested in whatever they had to learn' which inspired them with a healthy desire for knowledge, and helped them to 'think, to analyse, to reject, to appreciate . . . on Saturdays they went long scrambling walks'. Charlotte recalled in writing *Shirley* the tales of the *Luddite riots which Miss Wooler 'related during these long walks', telling her pupils of 'times when watchers or wakeners in the night heard the distant word of command, and the measured tramp of thousands of sad desperate men receiving a surreptitious military training' (Gaskell *Life*, 1. 113–14). Some of Miss Wooler's traits may be recalled in Mrs Agnes *Pryor. On 29 July 1835 Charlotte returned, at Miss Wooler's invitation, to become a teacher in her old school. Although she was often irritated by the chore of teaching stupid 'dolts', she respected Miss Wooler, and was trusted by her. They had a temporary estrangement at the end of December 1837, when Charlotte accused Miss Wooler of failing to recognize the seriousness of Anne Brontë's illness. Miss Wooler at first thought Charlotte foolish and treated her coldly; but then, hurt by Charlotte's bitter reproaches, she privately gave way to her feelings, 'crying for two days and two nights together', instead of exercising her usual rigid restraint, and told Charlotte that despite her outward coldness she had 'a considerable regard' for her, and would be very sorry to part (Smith *Letters*, 1. 174). Charlotte accordingly returned, possibly with Anne, for another year. Miss Wooler moved her school to *Heald's House in early 1838.

Margaret Wooler, Charlotte Brontë's schoolmistress and friend.

Wooler family

At Christmas 1838, when Charlotte left, Miss Wooler handed over its management to her sister Eliza, though she remained in the house. In 1840 Charlotte tried but failed to get more pupils for the failing school. Towards the end of 1841 she provisionally accepted Miss Wooler's proposal for her to take over and revive the school, but decided instead to further her studies in *Brussels.

Miss Wooler and her sister closed their school at the end of 1841. She would sometimes make her home with her sister Susanna's family, the *Carters, at Heckmondwike, and then go away for a few months to the seaside, either alone or with one of her sisters. Charlotte retained her friendship, wrote 'respectfully and affectionately' to her, and welcomed her visits to Haworth Parsonage. In the spring of 1849 she offered the hospitality of her house in the North Bay at *Scarborough to the desperately ill Anne Brontë, but for Anne's sake warmer lodgings in the South Bay were chosen. Miss Wooler probably attended Anne's funeral in Scarborough on 30 May 1849. Though she had limited means, and gave half her income to charities, she managed to take extended holidays, for example in a Lake District cottage in 1850, and in Ilkley in 1851; she invited Charlotte to join her, and was touched and grateful for Charlotte's attention to her comfort when she stayed at Haworth Parsonage in September–October 1851 for a few days. She found Charlotte's company congenial, and Charlotte in turn became increasingly affectionate towards her, as she recognized her quiet strength of character in making a career for herself without repining. With certain reservations about the bolder aspects of Charlotte's style, Miss Wooler admired her novels. By 1853 she had moved to *Hornsea for a time, and there Charlotte spent a 'happy and pleasant week' with her in October. In June 1854, as one of the few friends invited to Charlotte's wedding, she gave her away when Revd Patrick Brontë decided not to go to the church. In December 1854 Charlotte assured her that all at the Parsonage would be glad to see her, but before any visit could take place, Charlotte became too ill to receive her. After Charlotte's death Miss Wooler chose the letters she lent to Elizabeth Gaskell carefully, burnt one confidential letter which might have hurt the feelings of Revd A. B. Nicholls, and cut off parts of other letters, but 33 of Charlotte's manuscript letters to her, most of them intact, survive in the fine collection given by Sir Clifford Allbutt to the Fitzwilliam Museum in Cambridge.

By 1867 Miss Wooler was living in a separate wing at West House, Dewsbury, the home of her brother Dr William Moore Wooler. After his death in 1873 she lived with her sisters Katherine and Eliza and one of her nieces in *Gomersal, taking

'the greatest interest in religious, political, and every charitable work, being a life governor of many institutions. . . . She made a point of reading the Bible steadily through every year, and a chapter out of her Italian Testament each day. . . . It was always a pleasure, too, if she met with any one who could converse with her in French'. She led 'a quiet and retiring, but useful life' (Shorter *Circle*, pp. 260–1).

Wooler family. Charlotte Brontë's teacher, Margaret *Wooler, was one of a large family, the children of Robert Wooler (1770–1838), corn miller and farmer of Rouse Mill, Batley, Yorks., and his wife Sarah Maud, née Upton (1767–1841). He owned other property and was evidently prosperous, for his children had a good education. His daughter Eliza (1808–84) shared in the teaching at *Roe Head, but probably left before 1838 to look after her parents. At Easter 1838 Miss Wooler had to leave Charlotte in charge of her school because of the illness and death of Mr Wooler. At Christmas 1838 his widow and Eliza (1808–84) moved to the school (by then at *Heald's House) which was to be handed over to Eliza. To her great-nephew, Revd Max W. Blakeley, Eliza seemed rather austere and proper, but he later realized her kindness (*BST* (1952), 12. 62. 113–14). Under her direction the school declined. By November 1840 Charlotte, realizing it was 'in a consumptive state of health', had tried unsuccessfully to find more pupils for it; it was relinquished in 1841.

Charlotte knew Dr William Moore Wooler, LSA 1817 (1795–1873), through his sister Margaret, and as one of the Nusseys' acquaintances. Described in Pigot's *Directory* 1835 as a surgeon at 9 Friar Gate, Derby, he moved to West House, *Dewsbury, before 1844, and was still listed as a practitioner there in 1847. He also owned freehold houses and land on Staincliffe Common, Batley. He married Sidney Maria Allbutt, daughter of the former proprietor of the Lawton pottery, Cheshire, in February 1827, and had two daughters by her. She died of cholera in York in 1832. Ellen Nussey passed on a rumour hinting that Mr Wooler's disturbed state of mind after her death was connected with the ill omen of a white hen seen at her funeral (Smith *Letters*, 117). His second wife was Anne Medley (1812–84) by whom he had two sons (William Upton and Walter Hernaman) and a daughter. In March 1853 Charlotte received a 'long and kind' letter from William Wooler, implying that she was a 'hotter advocate for *change*' and political progress than she really was, and seeking advice on publishing some of his own manuscripts. Charlotte replied cordially, advising him that Smith, Elder dealt chiefly in fiction, not 'works of a graver character', and warning him not to publish at his own risk. He had already published *The Philosophy of Temperance, and the Physical Causes of Moral Sadness* in 1840, and was to publish *The Physiology of Education* in 1859. Charlotte mentions Thomas Wooler (?1803–95) sympathetically as a sufferer from nervous complaints, and on 12 March 1852 hopes foreign travel may help him. Sarah Wooler (b. 1798), previously a private governess in London, was living with Margaret by late 1851, when Charlotte invited her to accompany her sister to Haworth. Charlotte grew fonder of the Woolers as she grew older, and appreciated their kindness. See also WOOLER, KATHARINE; CARTER FAMILY; ALLBUTT FAMILY.

Wool is Rising, or The Angrian Adventurer, The, a narrative by Branwell Brontë of 24 pages in a hand-sewn booklet (in BL), completed 26 June 1834, in which the Duke of *Zamorna is granted his own kingdom of *Angria—for his heroic efforts in defeating the French. He names the Duke of *Northangerland, his father-in-law, prime minister, but the latter immediately begins to plot sedition and rebellion.

At the same time the narrative introduces Edward and Captain Sir William *Percy, Northangerland's sons, who were to have been put to death at birth, but survived because *Sdeath disobeyed his master's orders. Edward has become a successful stuff manufacturer, and enriches himself significantly by investing in the industry and commerce of the new kingdom of his brother-in-law, whom he detests. Meanwhile, he bitterly antagonizes the Marquis of *Ardrah, heir to the throne of Parrysland and First Lord of the Admiralty, while attracting the attention of his fiancée, Lady Maria *Sneaky. Edward pays court to Maria, knowing her prospective marriage to Ardrah is purely a political arrangement. Having become an MP, he defeats Ardrah in a duel, and despite the objections of her family (the royal family of Sneaky's Land), marries the Princess Maria Sneaky. In contrast to the aristocratic settings of Charlotte's fiction, Branwell's narrative is partially set in a counting house.   VN

Alexander & Sellars, p. 313 (illustrations).
Neufeldt *BB Works*, 2. 24–91.

Wordsworth, William (1770–1850), major Romantic poet, revered by the young Brontës; Poet Laureate from 1843. Wordsworth's nature poetry, with its delineation of commonplace beauties and assertion of their transcendental significance, influenced the Brontës' visual arts and writings. In some instances Wordsworth's poetry inspired specific works, such as Charlotte's drawing of Bolton Abbey (*c.*May 1834), a site commemorated by Wordsworth in 'The White Doe of Rylstone',

and Branwell's 1840 sonnet on a view of Black Comb mountain, which responds to Wordsworth's 'View from the Top of Black Comb'. Elsewhere Brontë works echo Wordsworth's cadences and allude to his phrasing and imagery, as in Emily's poetic description of the bluebell (Hatfield *EBP*, p. 97) hiding 'beneath its mossy stone', which gestures to Wordsworth's 'She dwelt among the untrodden ways'. More generally the Brontës' writings display Wordsworth's impress in landscape depictions imbued with mystical meaning, powerful connections between nature's moods and human feeling, expressions of the spiritual benefits of nature, and, to a more limited extent, representations of spiritually aware children who gradually lose their innocence.

Wordsworth remained for Charlotte a literary touchstone for excellence. She recommended his poetry to Ellen *Nussey (4 July 1834), and indicated to publishers *Aylott and Jones that the Bells wanted for their *Poems* the paper quality and type size found in Moxon's latest edition (1845) of Wordsworth's poetry (31 Jan. 1846). The sisters may have sent a copy of *Poems* to Wordsworth in 1847, but evidence is lacking. Earlier, Branwell solicited Wordsworth's opinion of his verse (10 Jan. 1837); he sent 'The Struggles of flesh with Spirit: scene 1—Infancy' ('Still and bright in twilight shining' in Neufeldt *BBP*, p. 120) with a letter that identified Wordsworth as 'a divinity of the mind' and disparaged contemporary poets as not 'worth a sixpence'. Though Branwell's poem echoes Wordsworth's 'Intimations of Immortality' ode, the distinguished poet ignored the youth's brash letter. Throughout her life Charlotte alluded to and quoted from Wordsworth's poetry in her verse, letters, and novels. In *The Professor* Frances Henri progresses beyond her ready liking for Byron and Scott, learning to appreciate Wordsworth's 'deep, serene and sober mind' (ch. 25).

BT

Gill, Stephen, *William Wordsworth: A Life* (1989).

'Word to the "Quarterly", A'. See SHIRLEY: 'A WORD TO THE "QUARTERLY"'.

Wright, Dr William (1837–99), DD, FRGS; born at Finnard, County Down; editorial superintendent of the British and Foreign Bible Society from 1876, and author of *The Brontës in Ireland or Facts Stranger than Fiction* (1893, 1894). Wright gives few facts, and much hearsay embroidered with romantic detail. To provide an Irish source of the *Brontë family's genius, he retails stories involving a Heathcliff-like character. Patrick's father Hugh Brontë becomes a heroic figure, ill-treated as a child by his Aunt Mary's husband, Welsh, a sinister foundling discovered in the hold of a ship returning to Ireland from Liverpool, and adopted by Hugh's grandfather. Later, Welsh persuades Hugh's parents to let him adopt the child, on condition that they are never to seek him. Wright adorns his story with accounts of violent feuds and heroic fights, and describes Hugh's clandestine courtship of the allegedly Catholic 'Alice' McClory. Angus Mason Mackay attacked the book in 'A Crop of Brontë Myths', *Westminster Review* (Oct. 1895), and *The Brontës: Fact and Fiction* (1897). Joseph Horsfall *Turner revealed more of Wright's inaccuracies and inconsistencies in *Brontëana* (1898), 267–304, concluding charitably that 'we are persuaded he has been very much misled' (p. 301). In his preface Wright acknowledged details regarding the Brontës in England given to him by Ellen *Nussey in 1891. He had been given Ellen's address by Horsfall Turner, and toyed with the idea of jointly editing Ellen's Brontë letters or providing an essay on the Brontës' Irish connections for Scribner's. He also offered to place the letters temporarily in his safe or in the Bible House strong room, and then buy them from her for £50, arrange them, and return 'compromising' ones for her to destroy. Ellen's early enthusiasm for his help waned, and on 16 April 1892 he accepted with relief her refusal of his offers. Edward Chitham defends some of Wright's notions in *The Brontës' Irish Background* (1986).

WT. See UT AND WT ('US TWO' AND 'WE TWO').

Wuthering Heights. *See opposite page*

Wuthering Heights, the property of the *Earnshaw family and subsequently of *Heathcliff, in Emily Brontë's novel of the same name. Its neglected, fortress-like appearance and windswept situation stand in stark contrast to *Thrushcross Grange, 4 miles away and concealed from view by the bleak summit that rises behind Wuthering Heights. The name is derived from the local word describing 'the atmospheric tumult to which its station is exposed in stormy weather. Pure, bracing ventilation they must have up there, at all times, indeed: one may guess the power of the north wind, blowing over the edge, by the excessive slant of a few, stunted firs at the end of the house; and by a range of gaunt thorns all stretching their limbs one way, as if craving alms of the sun' (ch. 1). Lockwood notes that the architect had foresight in building narrow windows deeply set into the walls and large jutting stones at the cor-

ners. The property is a working farm and the interior of the house is that of a typical yeoman farmer of the area, although the outside suggests a grander past with its 'grotesque carving lavished over the front', a feature that corresponds closely to the carvings on the door and over the gateway of *High Sunderland Hall. Also above the entrance to Wuthering Heights is the inscription 'Hareton Earnshaw' and the date '1500' (as in the case of *Ponden House which bears the inscription '1801' on the lintel).

Wycoller Hall, Lancs., a 16th-century house in a deep pastoral valley 8 miles west of Haworth, was perhaps recalled by Charlotte Brontë when she created *Ferndean Manor in *Jane Eyre*. Henry Owen Cunliffe, grandson of Elizabeth Cunliffe, who became Elizabeth Eyre by her second marriage, extended it in 1774, but his extravagance left the estate heavily in debt. Divided up, and only partly inhabited, the hall had fallen into picturesque ruin by the mid-19th century, while nearby farms and weavers' cottages, which had flourished when the hamlet was on a busy packhorse route to Yorkshire, were in disrepair.

Wynne family, in *Shirley*, are 'Briarfield gentry' (p. 344), whose status is reflected in the ambitious family monument in *Briarfield churchyard. Mr Wynne is a magistrate; he lives with his wife and three children at De Walden Hall on an estate 'delightfully *contagious*' (p. 345) to the Fieldhead estate, which prompts the family to put forward young Mr Samuel Fawthrop Wynne as a suitor to Shirley *Keeldar. Mr Sam, however, the former 'booby of Stilbro' grammar school' (p. 534), awakens only aversion in Shirley, who rejects his suit outright. Mr Sam's coarseness is joined to brutality: he often flogs his dogs, one of which bites Shirley's arm and draws blood (see PHOEBE). Sam has two sisters, 'the superlative Misses Wynne, of De Walden Hall' (p. 233). Before she wrote *Shirley*, Charlotte Brontë had used the name 'Wynne' in the unfinished story of 'John Henry', in which John Henry Moore's wife is visited by her old school friend Alice, or Alicia, Wynne of De Walden Hall (see SHIRLEY: 'JOHN HENRY'). Alicia's father is a magistrate with landed property 'who had long ago made a point of forgetting that his own father had been a cotton-spinner—and his grandfather a working wool-comber' (*Shirley*, p. 822). HR

E MILY Brontë's only novel is considered to be one of the most powerful and
enigmatic works in English literature. An intense tale of passionate relationships,
set in the windswept Yorkshire moors of the north of England and ranging over two
generations, it has been compared to Tolstoy's *War and Peace* and to Shakespeare's
tragedy *King Lear*.

Composition

Despite the secrecy of much of Emily Brontë's writing, the composition and publication of *Wuthering Heights* was closely linked with the work of her sisters. Early
collaboration in the *Glass Town saga and later partnership with Anne in the *Gondal
saga meant that Emily's writing practice (if not the content of the writing) was
associated with a family atmosphere of literary activity. The *Diary Papers show
that Emily knew what was happening in Charlotte and Branwell's Angrian manuscripts and that she read sections of 'the Emperor Julius's life' and other Gondal prose
to Anne. Elizabeth *Gaskell describes the way the sisters would pace up and down the
sitting-room, discussing their stories and regularly reading chapters to each other
(Gaskell *Life*, 2. 11), a habit that may have started well before the novels. If there was
criticism and debate, it was only to confirm the writer's own judgement. Charlotte
tells how the readings were 'of great and stirring interest to all', but her sisters' remarks
seldom caused her to alter her work, and her comment on Emily's reaction to criticism suggests a similar self-confidence, if not intransigence:

'If the auditor of her work when read in manuscript, shuddered under the grinding influence of
natures so relentless and implacable, of spirits so lost and fallen; if it was complained that the
mere hearing of certain vivid and fearful scenes banished sleep by night, and disturbed mental
peace by day, Ellis Bell [Emily] would wonder what was meant, and suspect the complainant of
affectation' (Editor's Preface to 1850 edn.; in *Wuthering Heights*, p. 443).

The date of composition of *Wuthering Heights* is uncertain; no drafts or fair copy of
the novel survive. In her 'Biographical Notice of Ellis and Acton Bell', Charlotte
explained that although only two copies of their *Poems 1846 were sold, the sisters'
appetites for publication had been whetted and they 'each set to work on a prose tale:
Ellis Bell produced *Wuthering Heights*, Acton Bell *Agnes Grey*, and Currer Bell also
wrote a narrative in one volume [*The Professor]'. Her chronology, recalled some time
after the event and after the deaths of her sisters, is in fact inaccurate. As the editors of
the Clarendon edition point out, *Poems* was published in May 1846, yet Charlotte had
already approached the same publishers (*Aylott and Jones) as early as 6 April 1846
about the possibility of publishing 'three distinct and unconnected tales' which the
sisters were 'preparing for the Press' (*Wuthering Heights*, p. xiii). To approach a
publisher like this, all three novels must have been well on the way to completion.
We know only the completion date of *The Professor*—27 June 1846—but *Wuthering
Heights* and *Agnes Grey* must both have been fair copied by early July, when Charlotte
offered all three manuscripts to Henry *Colburn.

When Charlotte wrote to Aylott and Jones announcing the preparation of the
novels, she spoke of their possible publication 'either together as a work of 3 vols.
of the ordinary novel-size, or separately as single vols' (Smith *Letters*, 1. 461).

Wuthering Heights and *Agnes Grey* were eventually to be published together as three volumes, without *The Professor* which was not published until after Charlotte's death. Charlotte's underestimate here of *Wuthering Heights* as material for one volume rather than two, may mean that Emily had written or planned to write a much shorter novel than the one we now have (see Chitham, Edward, and Winnifrith, Tom, *Brontë Facts and Brontë Problems*, pp. 84–90).

Although the above discussion provides what evidence there is of the novel's composition, there has been much debate and speculation over the years about its genesis. The Clarendon editors conclude that the writing of *Wuthering Heights* 'is not likely to have started before October 1845', since until this date Emily was preoccupied with her Gondal saga. After 9 October (the date of **'Julian M. and A. G. Rochelle') there is a marked interruption in her poetry writing that coincides with the discovery and revision of her poems for publication. From this date until the completion of the novel there are about nine months in which *Wuthering Heights* could have been written. However, as the Clarendon editors concede, this seems too short a time to account for the composition of such a complex novel as *Wuthering Heights* (*Wuthering Heights*, p. xvi). It may be that although Emily began writing her final draft in earnest in October 1845, she had been planning various episodes of *Wuthering Heights* for some time. For example, by 31 July 1845, Anne had begun the third volume of *Passages in the Life of an Individual* (thought by several scholars to be a draft or version of *Agnes Grey*) and, by analogy, it is possible that Emily's 'work on the First Wars' written at the same time and described by Anne as 'the Emperor Julius's life', may be an early version of *Wuthering Heights* (see DIARY PAPERS: 31 JULY 1845, DIARY PAPER SIGNED BY ANNE).

Composition dates as far back as 1837, 1839, and 1843 have been suggested, usually by those seeking to prove that Gondal shows '*Wuthering Heights* in the making' (Ratchford, *Gondal's Queen* (1955), p. 37) or by those who seek to associate Branwell *Brontë with the authorship of the novel (William *Dearden and Francis *Grundy: see also Leyland, 2. 186–9). Common elements in *Wuthering Heights* and Branwell's story about the *Thurstons of Darkwall Manor (1837; based on the *Heaton family legends) reflect the shared 'myth kitty' (J. Hillis Miller, *The Disappearance of God*, 1963) of the Brontës rather than Branwell's hand in the novel's composition. The most detailed thesis is that put forward by Edward Chitham, who argues that composition of *Wuthering Heights* began as early as December 1844. Chitham notes that the real weather at the time of writing corresponds with the fictional weather in *Wuthering Heights*. Basing his argument on this observation, on gaps in Emily's poetry composition when she might have been busy writing *Wuthering Heights*, and on connections with poems written at the same time as *Wuthering Heights*, Chitham constructs an elaborate chronology for the writing and production of the novel. He summarizes his proposed chronology in monthly sections (*Birth of WH*, pp. 173–81), such as 'March 1845' when the snowy weather of the time (verified by almanacs) agrees not only with the poem 'Cold in the earth' (dated 3 March), but also the pervasive snow in the first part of *Wuthering Heights*, especially chapter 3 where Lockwood is forced to lodge at the Heights because of the weather. The argument is that these circumstances suggest the writing of the first chapters at this time. Again, in the entry for 'January–April 1846' Chitham notes that the tone of **'No coward soul is mine' (written 2 January) 'accords with' the section of *Wuthering*

Heights leading up to Catherine Earnshaw's death, as does the 'unusually fine' February weather. The lack of other poetry in these months 'is surely because *Wuthering Heights* is currently an obsession', with the 'white heat' of this section being 'very noticeable'. This of course is circumstantial evidence only and although at times most plausible, 'there can be no complete certainty', as Chitham himself admits (p. 177).

Manuscript and early editions

There is no surviving manuscript of *Wuthering Heights*. Together with the manuscripts of *The Professor* and *Agnes Grey*, *Wuthering Heights* was sent out on a joint search for a publisher sometime after 4 July 1846, when Charlotte wrote to Henry Colburn, one of the most prominent publishers of fiction at the time, to 'request permission to send for your inspection the M.S of a work of fiction in 3 vols. It consists of three tales, each occupying a volume' (Smith *Letters*, 1. 481). An annotation by him on Charlotte's letter suggests he wanted more information about the authors and their works before agreeing to consider their 'tales' (p. 482) but we have no evidence for the decision he made. Charlotte had enquired of Aylott and Jones what publishers would be most likely to look favourably on such works of fiction, and they may have suggested not only Colburn but his rival Richard Bentley, and perhaps the firms of Bradbury and Evans (who published *Pickwick Papers*) and Chapman and Hall (see PUBLISHING 1800–1860). T. C. *Newby and *Smith, Elder and Company, who eventually published the manuscripts, may have been on this recommended list. We don't know how many publishers received and rejected *Agnes Grey* and *Wuthering Heights*, but it took considerable effort and persistence by the sisters to get their novels accepted: 'These MSS. were perseveringly obtruded upon various publishers for the space of a year and a half; usually, their fate was an ignominious and abrupt dismissal' ('Biographical Notice', *Wuthering Heights*, p. 437). If *Wuthering Heights* and *Agnes Grey* continued to accompany *The Professor* until Newby accepted them (without *The Professor*) then each had four rejections after the two from Aylott and Jones (early April 1846) and Colburn (Smith *Letters*, 2. 572 and 573 n. 1).

In July 1847, Thomas Cautley Newby accepted *Wuthering Heights* and *Agnes Grey* for publication on condition that the authors contribute towards the costs. *The Professor*, either separated from them by this time or rejected by Newby, was sent alone to Smith, Elder on 15 July. Although they rejected *The Professor*, Smith, Elder were quick to accept *Jane Eyre* which was published in October, while Emily and Anne were still receiving proof-sheets for their novels from the tardy Newby. Charlotte complained to her publishers of Newby's 'exhausting delay and procrastination', explaining that the first proof-sheets of *Wuthering Heights* and *Agnes Grey* had already been returned to Newby by the beginning of August, before they had even received *Jane Eyre* (Smith *Letters*, 1. 561). Emily and Anne received the last proof-sheets for correction by 17 November and Newby, encouraged by the success of *Jane Eyre*, finally published the two novels in December 1847, *Wuthering Heights* forming the first two volumes with *Agnes Grey* tacked on as a third to make up the requisite 'three-decker' for 31s. 6d. On 14 December, Charlotte reported that the authors had received their six copies from Newby, only to find that 'they abound in errors of the press' (Smith *Letters*, 1. 575). A week later she complained that 'The orthography & punctuation of the books are mortifying to a degree'. The title-page of volume 1 misleadingly announced 'WUTHERING HEIGHTS | A NOVEL, | BY | ELLIS BELL, | IN THREE VOLUMES' and the edition included superfluous commas, inadequate hyphenation, and numerous mis-spellings. Most of Emily's corrections made to the page proofs were ignored by Newby who was both printer and publisher of this first edition.

Newby's shoddy handling of the text was repeated in his handling of the financial and marketing arrangements. He agreed to print 350 copies but only printed 250, and he insisted the authors pay £50 towards costs, to be refunded when he had sold 250 copies, which 'would leave a *surplus* of 100£. to be divided' presumably between himself and the Bells (Smith *Letters*, 2. 464, 473). No money was ever returned, yet the novel was out of print by September 1850. Eventually in March 1854, well after the deaths of the authors and possibly at George *Smith's insistence, Newby sent Charlotte a cheque for £30, probably because he had sold the copyright of *Tenant* to Thomas Hodgson, who published a corrupt text in his Parlour Library edition of February 1854. She called Newby's practice 'a system of petty and contemptible man-oeuvring' by which he throws 'an air of charlatanry' over works under his manage-ment (see 'Newby's Chicanery', *Notes and Queries* NS 42 (June 1995), 189–91). His eagerness to exploit the confusion over the identity of the three 'Bell' authors and to capitalize on the success of *Jane Eyre* (by 'Currer Bell') led to a series of dishonest advertisements. First he advertised *Wuthering Heights* by quoting the review in the *Star* which suggested Currer and Ellis Bell were the same person (*Athenaeum*, 25 Dec. 1847). A month later he again advertised *Wuthering Heights* in the same journal without the author's name and with press notices insinuating that the author also wrote *Jane Eyre*. At the same time (29 Jan. 1848) a large notice appeared in the *Examiner* announcing 'Acton Bell's Successful New Novel Wuthering Heights', to-gether with reviews associating it with *Jane Eyre*. (*Wuthering Heights* (Clarendon edn.), pp. xxi–xxii, has further examples of Newby's advertising and suggests that he may have been genuinely confused at first about the authors' identities.) Newby's deception was repeated in his negotiations with American publishers and led to trouble between Smith, Elder and their American associates, so initiating Charlotte and Anne's famous visit to London in July 1848 to reveal their true identity to their publishers (Smith *Letters*, 2. 111–15).

Harper & Brothers of New York, who had published the first American edition of *Jane Eyre*, published in April 1848 'WUTHERING HEIGHTS. | A Novel. | BY | THE AUTHOR OF "JANE EYRE."' for the price of 75 cents. At the same time they published a cheaper version in two volumes, bound in brown paper covers instead of green cloth, for 25 cents a volume. In 1857 they republished the novel with the correct attribution 'By Ellis Bell'. The first continental edition is the famous two-volume 'Tauchnitz edition' of *Wuthering Heights* and *Agnes Grey* (1851) published in Leipzig.

By September 1850 the English edition of *Wuthering Heights* was out of print and, with Newby appearing to have no claim to copyright, Smith, Elder suggested that Charlotte might revise the work of her sisters for a new edition. Although this was a 'sad' task because of the memories it aroused, Charlotte agreed, and in December 1850 Smith, Elder produced a single-volume second edition, at 6s.: 'A NEW EDITION RE-VISED, WITH | A BIOGRAPHICAL NOTICE OF THE AUTHORS, | A SELECTION FROM THEIR LITERARY REMAINS, | AND A PREFACE, | BY CURRER BELL.' *Wuthering Heights* had originally been presented to the public without preface or introduction. Charlotte proposed 'a brief and simple notice of the authors' to dispel 'all erroneous conjec-tures' about the identity of the authors (Smith *Letters*, 2. 466). She was keen to set the novel in a context and explain how a 'homebred country girl' might produce such a tale of violence and amorality that so shocked the public; and she also proposed to alter the orthography of Joseph's dialect speeches so that this graphic character might not be lost on uncomprehending 'Southerns'. In Joseph's first speech in chapter 2, for example, the first edition reads: ' "Whet are ye for?" he shouted. "T' maister's dahn i' t'fowld. Goa rahnd by th'end ut'laith, if yah went tuh spake tull him."' In 1850 Charlotte altered it accordingly: ' "What are ye for?" he shouted. "T' maister's down i' t'fowld. Go round by th'end ot' laith, if ye went to spake to him."' Further alterations made to the text included the running together of the many short paragraphs of the original, probably to save space; the removal of superfluous commas from Newby's edition; the substitution of more formal punctuation for dashes; and the regularizing of other accidentals, such as exclamation marks. The Clarendon editors, however, believe that despite Charlotte's comments on the original edition, it was probably written in short paragraphs and punctuated erratically. They retain the original brief paragraphs, arguing that their staccato effect often contributes to the drama of the narrative, and correct Newby's punctuation only where it is wrong, misleading, or eccentric (*Wuthering Heights*, pp. xxvii, xxxii). See TRANSLATIONS OF BRONTË WORKS and EDITING HISTORY OF MATURE WORKS for a general survey of later editions.

Sources and context

The imaginative sources of *Wuthering Heights* are clearly evident in Emily Brontë's *poetry. Here we see the power of nature to transport her to rapture or to consideration of human concepts like pain, loneliness and faith (see 'SHALL EARTH NO MORE INSPIRE THEE'; 'OFTEN REBUKED, YET ALWAYS BACK RETURNING'). 'Her sense of nature as a presence and a power in human destiny was all-pervading' (Gérin *EB*, p. 13). In *Wuthering Heights* the natural elements pervade the human drama, from the snowstorm that forces Lockwood to spend the night at the Heights in the opening chapters to the description of the three gravestones among the heath and harebells, under a benign sky, on the closing page. No aspect of the season or time of day is left undocumented. Hareton Earnshaw's birth at midsummer is marked by the gathering of hay in the fields and the young Catherine's growth is measured by natural simile: 'she grew like a larch; and could walk and talk too, in her own way, before the heath blossomed a second time over Mrs. Linton's dust' (ch. 18). Emily's personal experience of the moors gives solidity to her novel of elemental emotion and spiritual quest.

The passionate relationship of Heathcliff and Cathy, forged in childhood, is prefigured in the Gondal saga where relationships of love and hate transgress public and private morality. All the ingredients of *Wuthering Heights* that so shocked the critics when the novel was first published are typical of both Gondal and the Angrian saga, where we also find an amoral tone, scenes of drunken debauchery, casual cruelty, and passionate love. Situations of separation, exile, and imprisonment in the early writings foreshadow those in *Wuthering Heights*. For example, Catherine Earnshaw's dream of being miserable in heaven and being flung out 'into the middle of the heath on the top of Wuthering Heights; where I woke sobbing for joy' is anticipated in Gondal poems such as 'Shall Earth no more inspire thee' and 'I see around me tombstones grey'. Counterparts for Joseph, the religious fanatic, can be found in the later Angrian stories, especially those of Branwell. In the poetry too (*'To Imagination';

'The *Philosopher'; *'Julian M. and A. G. Rochelle') we find Emily's explorations into 'the shadowy regions' of the soul, her quest for a unifying vision.

Emily's own experience of Yorkshire character and dialect, buildings (such as *High Sunderland Hall, *Ponden House, *Shibden Hall, the situation of *Top Withins), and local histories of usurpation like that of Heathcliff which she heard at *Law Hill and locally in the *Heaton family, all contributed to the germ of the novel. Her descriptions are never superficial and show a marked conflation of the general and particular, as in the case of Lockwood's first impressions of *Wuthering Heights. Her early education, her study of Homer and *Virgil, of *Shakespeare, *Milton, Sir Walter *Scott, and the Romantic poets, especially *Shelley, can be mined for echoes of inspiration and allusions. Heathcliff can be seen as a recreation of the dark, brooding Gondal outlaw *Douglas, though he derives as much from other Gothic and Romantic heroes, such as *Byron's Corsair or Manfred, or even Milton's Satan. Emily also had access to novels like James *Hogg's *Confessions of a Justified Sinner*, *Hoffmann's *The Devil's Elixir*, and Mary Shelley's *Valperga* in journals like *Blackwood's* and *Fraser's*. All these might well suggest a character as a principle of evil like Heathcliff; although his darkness and mysterious origins have also led to his identification with the dispossessed 'others' of British imperialism in, for example, Maja-Lisa von Sneidern's 'Wuthering Heights and the Liverpool Slave Trade' (*ELH* 62 (1995), pp. 171–96). Hoffmann's *Das Majorat* (*The Entail*) has also been cited as a source (*Wuthering Heights*, p. 418 n.), as has Bartholomew Simmond's Irish story, 'The Bridegroom of Barna' in *Blackwood's*, November 1840. Critics such as L. Bradner ('The Growth of *Wuthering Heights*', *PMLA* 48 (1933), 129–46) and Edward Chitham (*Birth of WH*) have traced further links with Emily's poetry and early education. (See also GOTHIC NOVELS and GONDAL SAGA for sources.) It need hardly be said, however, that the novel is more a seamless whole than a sum of its parts. It is seen as having a mythic inevitability that is impossible to identify.

Plot

Wuthering Heights is remarkable for the way its tortuous and violent plot is given credibility and subtlety by the shifting narrative viewpoints. The central narrative which spans over twenty years is told by the housekeeper Nelly (Ellen) *Dean and punctuated by intense personal stories of the participants and by *Zillah, a temporary housekeeper from the local village of *Gimmerton. This is framed by the two-year narration of the stranger Mr *Lockwood, who brings us into and takes us out of the world of the novel. Neither of the main narrators, however, is reliable and the reader is plunged into a world of conflict that ranges over two generations and that defies any neat interpretation.

The story opens with the 1801 journal entry of Lockwood, the new tenant of *Thrushcross Grange. He describes a visit to his morose landlord, the gipsy-like *Heathcliff of *Wuthering Heights, an imposing though somewhat neglected farmhouse situated high on the *Yorkshire moors. Despite his unwelcome reception, Lockwood is intrigued and repeats his visit the next day. He receives a hostile reception not only from the dogs but from the inmates of Wuthering Heights, the young Catherine (Heathcliff's daughter-in-law) and the loutish Hareton *Earnshaw, who reflect the isolation of their habitation and its distance from civilization. Lockwood's alienation and misplaced courtesy create the effect of black humour, but there is also a sense of real danger and threat. The landscape is equally inhospitable and Lockwood, having been attacked by the dogs, is forced by a snowstorm to stay the night at the Heights. He is shown to a disused bedroom where he finds the name Catherine linked with those of Earnshaw, Heathcliff, and Linton, scratched in the windowsill, and some books inscribed 'Catherine Earnshaw'. In the margin of one, he reads her account of a wet Sunday 25 years ago when she and Heathcliff had to listen to a sermon by the old servant Joseph in a cold attic, while her brother Hindley and his wife enjoyed themselves downstairs. They are later punished by Hindley for scampering on the moors. Lockwood dreams that he is listening to an interminable sermon that ends in a fight; he wakes and finds a fir tree outside tapping on the lattice window. He dozes again and the knocking becomes nightmare: he breaks the window to stop the noise and his fingers are grasped by a 'little, ice-cold hand!' (ch. 3). As a child's voice cries to be let in, he panics and tries to free himself, savagely rubbing the wrist against the broken pane 'till the blood ran down and soaked the bedclothes'. His cries bring Heathcliff to the room and Lockwood hears his host's anguished cry for Cathy, his 'heart's darling'. Lockwood's perplexity is that of the reader. Returning to Thrushcross Grange in deep snow, he contracts a fever, and to while away his convalescence, he asks Nelly Dean to tell him what she knows of Heathcliff and his strange household. Nelly, who spent her girlhood at the Heights and was in service there and at Thrushcross Grange, takes over the story.

One day in 1771, her master old Mr *Earnshaw returns from *Liverpool with a black-haired orphan, 'as dark almost as if it came from the devil', whom he calls Heathcliff after a son who died. Heathcliff is brought up with Mr Earnshaw's two children Hindley and Cathy *Earnshaw and becomes Earnshaw's favourite, earning Hindley's hatred and forming a powerful bond with dark-haired, dark-eyed Cathy. When Mr Earnshaw dies, Hindley returns from college with a wife, Frances *Earnshaw, and Heathcliff is relegated to the status of a farm-labourer. He and Cathy are still inseparable and spend time together on the moors, *Penistone Crags being their favourite place. One day they trespass into the park of Thrushcross Grange, spying on the affluent young fair-haired *Lintons, Edgar and Isabella. Cathy is bitten by a guard dog while escaping and spends five weeks at the Grange while her ankle recovers, indulging in the comfort and manners of a civilized life. She returns to Wuthering Heights as an elegant young lady, who mocks her former playmate's uncouth appearance. Hindley's wife dies, leaving a son, Hareton, and the heartbroken Hindley begins drinking heavily and further degrades Heathcliff, who vows undying revenge. When Edgar Linton courts Cathy and she agrees to marry him, Heathcliff overhears her tell Nelly that it would degrade her to marry Heathcliff. He slips away and disappears during a furious storm, too early to hear her declare that by accepting Edgar she is betraying her own soul: 'My love for Linton is like the foliage in the woods. Time will change it, I'm well aware, as winter changes the trees. My love for Heathcliff resembles the eternal rocks beneath—a source of little visible delight, but necessary. Nelly, I *am* Heathcliff—he's always, always in my mind' (ch. 9). Three years later, Cathy marries Edgar Linton and becomes mistress of Thrushcross Grange.

The peaceful existence at the Grange is shattered by the sudden return of Heathcliff, who having acquired an imposing stature, education, and wealth by mysterious means, now seeks vengeance. He lodges at the Heights, exploiting Hindley's degeneracy and gradually winning possession by gambling. He encourages Isabella Linton's infatuation for him and elopes with her. He treats her despicably so that she escapes to the south. There she gives birth to a fair-haired son, Linton. Torn by the enmity between Edgar and Heathcliff and weakened by pregnancy, Cathy dies giving birth to a girl, another Catherine. During the next twelve years Catherine grows up beautiful but spoilt. Isabella dies and Heathcliff claims his sickly petulant son Linton, planning to marry him to Catherine before he dies. Edgar objects, but while he is dying Catherine and Nelly are lured to the Heights and imprisoned until the marriage takes place. After Edgar's burial, Catherine returns to the Heights and nurses Linton, who dies leaving everything to his father. Heathcliff is now the possessor of both Thrushcross Grange and Wuthering Heights, but his satisfaction is abated by his obsession with Cathy's ghost and the prospect of spiritual reunion with her. He tells Nelly how he opened Cathy's coffin and held her in his arms; he has loosened the side panel in her coffin so that when he is buried next to her they will merge eternally.

Nelly, having brought the story up to the present time, is replaced again by Lockwood as narrator. He visits the Heights to tell Heathcliff he is giving up the tenancy of Thrushcross Grange. He finds that Catherine has been hardened by circumstances since Nelly's description and that she treats the boorish but handsome Hareton with contempt, though he would like to become friends. In September 1802, on a visit to the area, Lockwood again visits Wuthering Heights, where he finds Catherine teaching Hareton to read and realizes they are in love. They are to be married and to move to the Grange, where life promises this younger generation a happiness denied to the earlier lovers. Heathcliff, thwarted in the end by the vision of Cathy's ghost and fixated by the idea of reunion with her, dies mysteriously in her former bed one night, with the lattice window flapping to and fro. He is buried on the other side of Cathy to Edgar, in the corner of the graveyard closest to the moors. Joseph and the villagers claim to have seen the ghosts of Heathcliff and Cathy, but Lockwood, passing the three graves, wonders how anyone could imagine the dead not sleeping peacefully there amongst the heath and harebells, under such a benign sky.

Reception

No mere synopsis can convey the peculiar power of *Wuthering Heights* and its challenge to both fictional and moral conventions. Early readers were disturbed and shocked, especially by the raw emotions of Heathcliff who places instinct above moral or social obligation; whereas later readers have been fascinated by the enigmatic nature of Heathcliff who seems the embodiment of Romantic values. Even contemporary reviews made allusions to Byron (Heathcliff was compared with the Corsair in the *Examiner*) and parallels were drawn with some German 'Gothic' tales (Allott, p. 32). It is possible that the book would have received little early notice but for the success of *Jane Eyre*, which constantly features as a comparison in early reviews of *Wuthering Heights*. Charlotte's memorial to her sisters in the 1850 edition also did much to raise the profile of the novel and ensure it a favourable reception, although her opinion that the 'very real powers revealed in *Wuthering Heights* were scarcely recognised' is incorrect. In fact, George Lewes commented in his notice of the new edition for the *Leader* that the critics had been 'excessively indulgent' (Allott, p. 291).

We know nothing of Emily's response to contemporary reviews of *Wuthering Heights*, but it appears that she preserved five of them in her writing desk, all dated January 1848 and cut from the *Atlas*, *Britannia*, the *Examiner*, *Douglas Jerrold's*

Weekly Newspaper, and an unidentified paper (J. R. V. Barker (ed.), *Sixty Treasures*, (1988) n. 43). They contain both condemnation and grudging praise. The *Atlas* wrote: 'The general effect is inexpressibly painful. We know nothing in the whole range of our fictitious literature which presents such shocking pictures of the worst forms of humanity', yet also conceded that 'The reality of unreality has never been so aptly illustrated as in the scenes of almost savage life which Ellis Bell has brought so vividly before us' (Allott, pp. 230–1). The *Britannia* found the work 'strangely original . . . but a fragment, yet of colossal proportion, and bearing evidence of some great design' (Allott, pp. 223–6). The *Examiner* found *Wuthering Heights* 'a strange book' but 'not without evidences of considerable power' (Allott, p. 220). *Douglas Jerrold's Weekly* again was appalled by the 'brutal cruelty, and semi-savage love . . . the most diabolical hate and vengeance', yet recognized a 'great power' in the book: 'We are quite confident that the writer of *Wuthering Heights* wants but the practised skill to make a great artist; perhaps, a great dramatic artist' (Allott, p. 228). Sydney Dobell's florid praise in the *Palladium* (Sept. 1850) came too late to be read by Emily. He wrote 'It is the unformed writing of a giant's hand; the "large utterance" of a baby god. . . . There are passages in this book . . . of which any novelist, past or present, might be proud. . . . We cannot praise too warmly the brave simplicity, the unaffected air of intense belief, the admirable combination of extreme likelihood with the rarest originality, . . . The *thinking-out* of some of these pages . . . is the masterpiece of a poet' (Allott, pp. 279–80)—a judgement later endorsed by the poets Swinburne, D. G. Rossetti, and Matthew Arnold. See also CRITICAL RECEPTION TO 1860; CRITICISM 1860–1940; CRITICISM FROM 1940; CULTURAL CRITICISM; FEMINIST APPROACHES; IMAGERY; MARXIST APPROACHES.

Alexander, Christine, and Rosengarten, Herbert J., 'The Brontës', in Joanne Shattock (ed.), *Cambridge Bibliography to English Literature*, 4. *1800–1900* (3rd edn., 1999).
Allott, Miriam (ed.), *Wuthering Heights: A Casebook* (1970; rev edn. 1992).
Bloom, Harold (ed.), *Modern Critical Views: The Brontës* (New York, 1987).
McNees, vol. 2.
Peterson, Linda H. (ed.), *Emily Bronte, Wuthering Heights: Case Studies in Contemporary Criticism* (1992).
Stoneman, Patsy (ed.), *Wuthering Heights: A New Casebook* (1993).

X—— in *The Professor* is the large northern manufacturing town where high black walls enclose Edward *Crimsworth's mill. Like Victorian *Bradford, X—— is in a valley overhung by a 'dense, permanent vapour', dominated by tall mill chimneys vomiting soot, and noisy with machinery, mill-bells, and rattling wagons laden with woollen cloth.

York, on the site of the Roman Eboracum, lies at the confluence of the Ouse and the Foss. Surrounded by ancient high stone walls with elaborate gates or 'bars', and dominated by the great Minster towers, it still retains some narrow medieval streets, where the upper storeys of timbered houses project towards each other. Anne Brontë passed through it regularly en route to *Thorp Green, and enjoyed a journey there with Emily on 30 June 1845. On 24 May 1849 she was carried in a chair from the George Hotel in Coney Street to the Minster on the last visit of her life.

York, Frederick Guelph, Duke of, 'Frederick the Great', first King of the *Twelves in the *Glass Town and Angrian saga; also referred to as Frederic Brunswick. Generous, brave, and commanding, he assumes leadership of the Twelves after their voyage to Africa and leads them in their battles against the *Ashantee. He rescues a Spanish lady Zorayda from the evil genie Danasch, marries her and has a son, Edward *Sydney (*The *Foundling*). York is slain at the Battle of Rosendale Hill, near *Coomassie, by *Sai-Too-Too. Branwell informs the reader that he was allowed to die because 'at the time we let this battle take place (ie in the beggining [sic] of AD 1827) The real Duke of York died of a mortification' (Neufeldt *BB Works*, 1. 158), referring to the second son of George III of England, the Duke of York, Commander-in-Chief. Various Glass Town sites, such as 'Frederick's Crag', are named after the fictitious Duke and he becomes the subject of Glass Town legend. In Charlotte's *'Two Romantic Tales', York is 'made alive' again and decides to return to England, whereupon the Twelves elect Arthur Wellesley, Duke of Wellington, as their new king.

Yorke, Hiram, in *Shirley*, a West Riding cloth manufacturer living at *Briarmains, near *Briarfield, with his wife Hesther and six children (Matthew, Mark, Martin, Rose, Jessy, and an unnamed baby) (see YORKE FAMILY). He is about 55 years old, white-haired, stubborn and sarcastic by nature. Though travelled and well educated (he speaks French and Italian), he likes to lapse into broad Yorkshire and to proclaim his sympathies for the poor and the downtrodden. His radical politics bring him constantly into conflict with the Tory clergyman Revd Matthewson *Helstone, Rector of Briarfield; they were also rivals in youth for the hand of Mary *Cave, and Yorke still bears animosity towards Helstone for having married, then largely ignored, the former love of Yorke's life. Though he rails against the monarchy and the established Church, he belongs to 'the first and oldest' family in the district, and occasionally betrays pride in his lineage. He incurs the wrath of Shirley *Keeldar, formerly his ward, for his criticism of

fellow mill owner Robert Gérard *Moore and Moore's ally the Rector for their treatment of the workers who attack Moore's mill; however, when Moore is the victim of an attempted assassination, Yorke's essentially generous nature is revealed since he takes Moore back to Briarmains to be cared for and nursed until his health is regained.

When *Shirley* was first published, the figure of Yorke was soon identified locally as a fictional version of Joshua Taylor (1766–1840) (see TAYLOR FAMILY OF GOMERSAL), the cultured and cosmopolitan owner of Hunsworth Mill and father of Charlotte's schoolfriend Mary *Taylor. The latter wrote to Charlotte on 13 August 1850 to complain that, though her father's fictional counterpart 'hates well enough and perhaps loves too' (Smith *Letters*, 2. 439), her father would never have advised anyone to marry for money (Yorke hints at Moore's possible marriage into wealth and encourages him to 'profit by a good chance if it offers' (ch. 9) in order to help him meet his debts). In the *Life*, Mrs Gaskell describes Joshua Taylor as 'a man of remarkable intelligence, but of strong, not to say violent prejudices, all running in favour of Republicanism and Dissent' (*Life*, 1. 168). An earlier version of Yorke is Hunsden Yorke *Hunsden, the mill owner in *The Professor* who befriends William *Crimsworth and assists him to escape his brother's tyranny. Phyllis Bentley, herself the author of a novel on the *Luddite riots (*Inheritance*, 1932), called Hiram Yorke 'the finest extant portrait of the West Riding manufacturer' (*The Brontës* (1947), 73).

Charlotte drew upon one episode in Joshua Taylor's history to add a layer of motivation to the depiction of her male protagonist Robert Gérard Moore: Taylor's bank failed during the commercial crisis of 1825; he 'set his mind on paying all creditors, and effected this during his lifetime as far as possible, willing that his sons were to do the remainder, which two of his sons carried out, as was understood, during their lifetime—Mark and Martin Yorke of *Shirley* [i.e. brothers John and Joseph Taylor]' (Ellen Nussey, cited in Shorter *Circle*,

p. 236). Joshua Taylor's grandson Edward Taylor maintained that it was his (i.e. Edward's) father Joshua, the 'Matthew Yorke' of *Shirley*, who 'carried out the payment of his Father's debts, who was brought down by the failure of a cousin—Dixon of Birmingham' (Joan Stevens, 'Sidelights on *Shirley*', *BST* (1969), 15. 4. 306). HR

Yorke family in *Shirley*. The Yorke family corresponds in many respects to the *Taylor family of Gomersal. Hiram *Yorke is married to Hesther, 'a large woman of the gravest aspect' who is perpetually gloomy, a woman with a 'uniformly overcast nature' whose main fault is 'a brooding, eternal, immitigable suspicion of all men, things, creeds, and parties' (ch. 9). She condescends to pay Hortense Gérard *Moore a visit because she approves of Hortense's 'plain aspect, homely precise dress, and phlegmatic unattractive manner. . . . Whatever gentlemen are apt to admire in women, Mrs. Yorke condemned; and what they overlook or despise, she patronized' (ch. 23). Mary *Taylor wrote to Ellen *Nussey on 11 March 1851 that her mother Anne Taylor, née Tickell, upon whom Hesther Yorke was based, wrote to her son Waring in New Zealand 'abusing Miss Brontë for writing *Shirley*' (Smith *Letters*, 2. 586).

Like the real-life Taylors, the Yorkes have six children. Matthew, the eldest, is volcanic in temper, 'an Italian stiletto in a sheath of British workmanship' (ch. 23); Mark, 14 years of age, appears melancholy and phlegmatic; Martin, the youngest of the three (though he is aged 15 in ch. 32), is stubborn and wilful. Martin is infatuated with Caroline *Helstone and assists her to enter *Briarmains unseen so that she may speak with her wounded cousin Robert Gérard *Moore, who is convalescing at the Yorkes' home after the attempt on his life. The three boys were modelled on Mary Taylor's older brothers Joshua (1812–80), John (1813–1901), and Joseph ('Joe') Taylor (?1816–57); the unnamed baby on Mrs Yorke's knee corresponded to the youngest Taylor child, William Waring Taylor (?1820–1903). The narrator in *Shirley* predicts that Martin Yorke will for a time become 'vain, a downright puppy, eager for pleasure, and desirous of admiration' (ch. 9). Charlotte undoubtedly had in mind Joe Taylor's many youthful flirtations, to which she often refers in her correspondence, and which drew her censorious comment to Ellen Nussey on 26 August [1846] that Joe 'has had his fill of pleasure and can with impunity make a mere pastime of other people's torments' (Smith *Letters*, 1. 494). In 1850 Joe Taylor married Amelia Ringrose (1818–1861 or later), who had at one time been engaged to Ellen's brother George Nussey.

Next among the Yorke children is 12-year-old Rose, sharp, precocious, and outspoken. The narrator speaks of her as one whose mind 'is full-set, thick sown with the germs of ideas her mother never knew' (p. 166). Looking into the future, the narrator tells us that Rose is destined to accompany her younger sister Jessy in foreign travel, and to be with her at her premature death; two years later Rose will be 'a lonely immigrant in some region of the southern hemisphere' (ch. 9). Rose Yorke is modelled on Charlotte's friend Mary Taylor (1817–93), whom she first met at *Roe Head school in 1831. Rose's strong views echo those of her original: Mary Taylor told Mrs Gaskell that whenever Charlotte visited the Taylor household during their schooldays together, 'We used to dispute about politics and religion. She, a Tory and clergyman's daughter, was always in a minority of one in our house of violent Dissent and Radicalism. She used to hear over again, delivered *with authority*, all the lectures I had been used to give her at school on despotic aristocracy, mercenary priesthood, etc.' (cited in Gaskell *Life*, 1. 167). After the death in 1840 of her father Joshua Taylor, Mary and her younger sister Martha ('Jessy Yorke') attended a 'Pensionnat des Dames' at *Kœkelberg, near Brussels. In 1845 Mary emigrated to New Zealand, opened a store and lived for a time with her brother Waring, then returned to England in 1860. In Rose's longing to see the world and her determination not to inter her talents 'in the dust of household drawers' (ch. 23), Charlotte portrays Mary Taylor's wanderlust and her belief in the necessity for women to work—'A woman who works is by that alone better than one who does not' (Mary Taylor to Charlotte Brontë, *c.*29 Apr. 1850, in Smith *Letters*, 2. 392). Mary was to publish her views on the importance of independence for women in a series of articles for the *Victorian Magazine*, collected and issued in volume form under the title *The First Duty of Women* (1870). She also published a novel, *Miss Miles: A Tale of Yorkshire Life Sixty Years Ago* (1890).

Jessy Yorke (also spelled 'Jessie') is more outgoing and good-humoured than her older sister; her father's pet, she defies her mother and rules her sister. Though Rose has the advantage in looks, Jessy has the power to charm and attract, and displays spontaneity and an affectionate nature in her relations with Robert Moore and Caroline Helstone. She imbibes her father's radical views, and pertly lectures Caroline on the evils of the war and the established church. However, she is doomed to an early death, and in a very moving passage the narrator speaks of a pilgrimage made 'some years ago' to 'a grave new-made in a heretic cemetery' where 'Jessie lay cold, coffined, solitary' (ch. 23). Jessy was modelled on Mary Taylor's younger sister Martha *Taylor (1819–42). The livelier of the two sisters and her father's favourite child, she was known to her school companions at Roe Head as 'Miss Boisterous', sometimes receiving a box on the ear from Margaret *Wooler for her outspokenness (Ellen Nussey, in Shorter *Circle*, p. 235). With Mary, she attended a 'pensionnat des dames' in Kœkelberg, near Brussels, where after a brief illness she died of cholera on 12 October 1842. She was buried in the Protestant Cemetery on the Chaussée de Louvain, outside Brussels; Charlotte and Emily accompanied Mary on a walk to the cemetery on 30 October 1842, and a sombre Charlotte would later tell Ellen Nussey on 10 November [1842], 'I have seen Martha's grave—the place where her ashes lie in a foreign country' (Smith *Letters*, 1. 302). The Protestant Cemetery is described in William Crimsworth's account in *The Professor* (ch. 19).   HR

York Place, home of Edward *Sydney (Prince Edward of York) and Lady Julia, in Verdopolis, in the *Glass Town and Angrian saga. To Julia the palace is 'a wilderness of Brick & Marble'.

Yorkshire. Until 1974 this vast county, c.104 miles at its widest point between Lancashire and the east coast, and nearly 90 miles north to south between Durham and Derbyshire, was divided into the West Riding, where *Haworth lies, and the smaller North and East Ridings. On the western borders are Pennine fells, moors, and river valleys: dramatic landscapes with the mountain-heights of Ingleborough and Whernside in the north-west, which the Brontës would see on their way to *Cowan Bridge. In the green dales between the lower hills lie ruined abbeys: Jervaulx, Fountains, *Bolton, *Kirkstall, *Kirklees. Between Haworth and Lancashire is high moorland, resembling the brown, heath-clad summit behind *Wildfell Hall, or the distant moors 'broken into dusky dells', evoked in *Wuthering Heights* and in Charlotte's 'Biographical Notice' of her sisters: 'My sister Emily loved the moors. Flowers brighter than the rose bloomed in the blackest of the heath for her.' Wild moorland, the scene of the Luddite frame-breaking in *Shirley*, lay also near *Hartshead. West Yorkshire is a county of rivers, 'becks' (small streams), and waterfalls, whose sounds and movements are delicately evoked in the Brontës' writings. Jane Eyre feels rather than hears the rapid flow of distant becks before she meets Rochester; and Caroline *Helstone hears the beck in the Hollow before the night attack on Robert *Moore's mill. The banks of rivers such as the Worth, Aire, Colne, and Calder were lined with woollen and cotton mills, for it was water power, and later steam power, which drove them, and brought increasing wealth to the West

Riding manufacturers and merchants. Charlotte described aspects of this industrial landscape, and dramatized the relationship between masters and men, in the quintessentially West Riding *Shirley*, and in parts of *The Professor*. Mills, with their chimneys, noisy mill-yards, and counting-houses, figure there, and in some of the Angrian stories (see GLASS TOWN AND ANGRIAN SAGA). The Yorkshire dialect-speakers in these works show how well the Brontës observed the people among whom they lived, such as the Parsonage servant Tabitha *Aykroyd, Haworth woolcombers, millhands, mill owners, and hill-farmers, and others further afield, such as Joshua *Taylor, that cultured, cosmopolitan, brusque Yorkshireman.

The Brontës were less familiar with the North and East Ridings; but Anne and Branwell knew the flat vale of the Ouse, and the cliffs of the North Riding coast near Scarborough. Both kinds of landscape are described in *Agnes Grey*. For Charlotte Scarborough had the sad associations of Anne's death. Later she passed through the North Riding on her rail journey to meet George Smith in *Edinburgh. She and Ellen Nussey had travelled through the Wolds of the East Riding to reach *Bridlington. In 1854 she changed from train to coach in Hull, the fourth biggest seaport in the country, on her way to *Hornsea. She knew little of Hull personally, but would hear much of it as the port used by the Taylors, *Nusseys, and *Ringroses in their trade with European markets.

While the Brontës' writings transcend any simple 'regional' classification, they derive much of their strong individuality from Yorkshire landscapes, speech, and people. See also INDUSTRY AND AGRICULTURE IN YORKSHIRE.

Yorkshire Gazette. This conservative weekly newspaper was read at *Thorp Green Hall, the home of Revd Edmund *Robinson, where Anne and Branwell were employed as teachers. Essentially an agricultural paper, it also included poetry. The *Yorkshire Gazette* printed four of Branwell's poems, signed '*Northangerland', shortly before the Robinsons dismissed him in the summer of 1845.   CB

Young Men. See TWELVES, THE; YOUNG MEN'S PLAY.

'Young Men's Magazine' ('Blackwood's Young Men's Magazine'), a continuation of 'Branwell's Blackwood's Magazine', the Glass Town journal modelled on *Blackwood's Edinburgh Magazine*. The 13-year-old Charlotte took over the editorship in August 1829 and changed the name first to 'Blackwood's Young Men's Magazine', and then to 'Young Men's Magazine' in

August 1830 when she began a 'second series'. Each series includes a monthly number from August to December, the final month having a double issue. The manuscripts are all miniature booklets written in minuscule script, designed to look like newsprint, and located in a variety of repositories (BL; BPM; *Law Collection; Houghton, Harvard). Issues of disputed authorship relating to several poems are dealt with under *UT and WT ('Us Two' and 'We Two'), thought to have referred to Charlotte and Branwell but more likely to refer to Charlotte's authorial characters the Marquis of Douro and Lord Charles *Wellesley.

The influence of *Blackwood's Edinburgh Magazine* on the young Brontës' writing practice and conception of authorship should not be underestimated. The title-pages with their clear lettering, elaborate colophons, and lists of booksellers; the editorial notes, lists of contents, advertisements, and variety of contents all reflect this authoritative model. Contents are signed and dated by different authors (Charlotte's pseudonyms) and range from articles, essays and reviews, to poems, serials, Gothic or supernatural tales, and conversations. The 'Military Conversations' (formerly 'Nights' under Branwell's editorship) amongst the Duke of Wellington and his cronies mimic the masculine tavern atmosphere of *Blackwood's* 'Noctes Ambrosianae'; but Charlotte gradually changes the tone and content, renames the serial simply 'Conversations', and introduces discussion on the sister arts.

By gaining control of what was the central literary feature of the *Glass Town and Angrian saga at this stage, Charlotte was able to develop it according to her own taste. Lord Charles's 'ghostly propensities' in 'Strange Events' and 'An Extraordinary Dream', for example, reflect her increasing interest in 'the truth of supernatural interference with the affairs of men' (Alexander *EEW*, 1. 269). 'Strange Events' suggests Charlotte has read *Swift's *Gulliver's Travels*, since Lord Charles imagines himself not only as the figment of 'another creature's brain' but also as a tiny figure in the hand of a huge creature in the likeness of himself (Alexander *EEW*, 1. 257–8). 'An Extraordinary Dream' is inspired by the many ghoulish tales in the pages of *Blackwood's*, such as John Galt's tale 'Buried Alive'.

Charlotte still worked closely with Branwell, who had relinquished the editorship voluntarily and who promised to contribute 'now and then', although his contribution seems to have been chiefly verbal criticism which Charlotte transposed into poetic contributions by 'WT' criticizing her own 'Foolish romances' (see 'Lines Spoken by a Lawyer', probably Branwell's character Sergeant *Bud, in Alexander *EEW*, 1. 94–5). Her com-

bative reply, heralding the end of 'Dullness' and her enthusiasm for more imaginative subjects, follows in the same magazine. Editorship gave her the opportunity to rapidly develop a variety of voices and styles, in particular those of the serious romantic Douro (later Duke of *Zamorna), the pompous Captain *Tree, and the critical Lord Charles who was to become her favourite narrator. She obviously had fun composing whimsical advertisements, such as 'The Art of Blowing One's Nose' taught by Monsieur Pretty-foot of No. 105 Blue Rose Street, or Richard (Young Man) *Naughty's offer to kill 'Rare lads' at Ned Laury's Inn (see BODYSNATCHING). One of the best-known articles is 'A Day at Parry's Palace' in which Lord Charles satirizes Emily Brontë's *Parry's Land with its realistic Yorkshire scenery of stone walls and factories 'breathing thick columns of almost tangible smoke', its northern dialect, uncouth table manners, and diet of roast beef, Yorkshire pudding, mashed potatoes, and apple pie (Alexander *EEW*, 1. 229–33). 'A Frenchman's Journal' traces the origins of the friendship between the Marquis of Douro and Young *Soult the Rhymer, Branwell's poetic persona; but most of the items referring to Soult reflect Charlotte's mockery of her brother's lack of humour, his pretentiousness, and deadly seriousness about becoming a great poet (see Alexander *EEW*, 1. 237). Despite her romantic effusions, Charlotte's grasp on reality is already keener than that of Branwell. Her insight into her brother's (and her own) posturing gradually develops into the brilliantly comic character Patrick Benjamin *Wiggins.

Alexander, Christine (ed.), assisted by Vanessa Benson, *Branwell's Blackwood's Magazine* (1995).
—— 'Readers and Writers: *Blackwood's* and the Brontës', *Gaskell Society Journal*, 8 (1994), 54–69.
Bock, Carol, *Charlotte Brontë and the Storyteller's Audience* (1992).

Young Men's Play, the first of the Brontë children's plays to be recorded (in *'History of the Year', by Charlotte). Begun in June 1826, after the arrival of a box of wooden toy soldiers, the 'Young Men's Play'—together with elements from *Our Fellows' Play and the *Islanders' Play—formed the basis of the *Glass Town and Angrian saga. 'A Romantic Tale' or 'The Twelve Adventurers' by Charlotte (in *'Two Romantic Tales') is the first story relating to this play about the *Twelves or 'Young Men'. Eighteen months later Branwell documented the play in greater detail, recording earlier sets of toy soldiers and listing the names of the Twelves: *Crashey, Cheeky, Wellesley (see ZAMORNA, DUKE OF), *Parry, Alexander *Sneaky, Captain John *Ross, *Bravey, *Gravey, Guelph, Stumps (killed en route to Africa), Monkey,

Tracky, and Cracky (Stumps is later 'made alive' and Tracky and Cracky disappear from the saga). Only Wellesley and Guelph (Duke of *York) feature in 'A Romantic Tale', but it is Branwell's Twelve who become the Young Men of the Glass Town and Angrian saga.

A distinctive feature of the Young Men's Play and Our Fellows Play is the 'old young men tongue', a bizarre language spoken holding one's nose. The transliteration of this suggests that it is an early attempt to reproduce Yorkshire dialect. It survives in the saga in the 'antediluvian' speech of the inhabitants of Stumps' and *Monkey's Islands, and is spoken by Dr Hume *Badey, who is also acknowledged as one of the Twelves. At some stage, a number of characters also had botanical names such as Tree, Bud, Flower, Arbor, Leaf, and Scrub; or they may be survivors of an earlier game. John Leaf, for example, the Glass Town Thucydides, is described as one of the first historians of the Glass Town, keeping records, speeches, and writing 'The Acts of the Twelves'. Associated with the botanical names is the father and son feature of the game: Captain Bud and Sergeant *Bud, Captain Tree and Sergeant *Tree, and the like, which extends to other characters such as Marshal Soult and Young *Soult the Rhymer, Naughten and Richard (Young Man) *Naughty.

Alexander *EW*, pp. 27–39.

Zamorna, Duke of (Arthur Augustus Adrian Wellesley, Marquis of Douro, King of Angria),

occasional early pseudonym of Charlotte Brontë and eldest son of the Duke of Wellington whom he replaces as Charlotte's favourite character. In the early juvenilia Zamorna (then Douro) is a young Apollo, noble and talented; a poet, soldier, and statesman, who is fatally attractive to women. At first he is the godlike antithesis to the Duke of *Northangerland, the fallen angel and sinister destroyer of thrones, but gradually his character degenerates and becomes more subtle. Drawing from Sir Walter *Scott's romantic heroes, *Milton's Satan, and the tortured *Byronic hero, Charlotte moulds Zamorna into a complex being who captures not only her imagination but her heart. When she is emotionally vulnerable his very image arouses and consoles her (see ROE HEAD JOURNAL, THE), yet she is also able to maintain an ironic distance through her cynical narrator Lord Charles *Wellesley, Zamorna's irritating and envious younger brother. To contend with Zamorna's increasingly complex personality and background of affairs and marriages spiralling out of control, Lord Charles—in mock desperation—employs the doppelgänger motif by creating a 'fictitious' twin for Zamorna in his malicious tale The *Spell. By 1839, Zamorna's sexual appeal has lost its allure (see CAROLINE VERNON), but elements of his character help inform the subsequent heroes of her novels, in particular *Rochester in Jane Eyre (see also WEST, ARTHUR RIPLEY).

The Marquis of Douro appears in both the *Young Men's Play and the *Islanders' Play, but he begins to emerge as a significant Glass Town character in Charlotte's manuscripts of 1830. He is tall and handsome with a 'slightly Roman nose', large brown eyes like his father, and dark curly auburn hair (see portraits drawn by Charlotte in Alexander & Sellars, pls. XXVIII and XXXVIII, pp. 215, 226). He is a captain in the Royal Regiment of the Horse Guards and member of various literary and cultural societies. An accomplished author, his preference is for writing poetry (chiefly for the *'Young Men's Magazine'), but he later publishes anonymous articles for political propaganda or to counteract the libellous accusations of Lord Charles. Whereas the Marquis is lofty, elegant, serious, and melancholy, Charles fraternizes with all, loves scandal, and is lively and deceitful. The increasing antipathy between these brothers leads to a variety of 'fictitious' slanders about the Marquis, his love affairs, and his supporters. Much of the interest in Douro's character is created by Charles's cynical narrative perspective.

Zamorna marries first Lady Helen Victorine *Gordon, who dies giving birth to his first son Ernest Edward Gordon *Wellesley (known as 'Fitzarthur'), and then the gentle Marian *Hume, Marchioness of Douro and mother of Lord *Almeida. As Zamorna's chivalrous and noble character becomes increasingly ruthless and ambitious, the need for a more robust mate leads to a third marriage with Mary Percy, beloved daughter of Northangerland. They have three sons and a daughter (see PERCY, MARY HENRIETTA). Nor is Zamorna ever without one or two mistresses. The most tragic is his cousin Rosamund *Wellesley; the oldest and most loyal is Mina *Laury. His illegitimate son by *Sofala, with whom he had an early affair, is the mute dwarf *Finic, who becomes his servant. Even in sedate middle age Zamorna manages to ensnare the young Caroline *Vernon, though Charlotte's attitude to his womanizing is no longer admiring but one of amused tolerance as he hovers over his prey 'like a large Tom-Cat' (Alexander EW, p. 196).

Zamorna's relationship with Northangerland is central to the *Glass Town and Angrian saga. After the *War of Encroachment Zamorna demands his own kingdom of *Angria as reward for his services and there builds his capital *Adrianopolis, making Northangerland his prime minister. When Zamorna is opposed by *Ardrah and his Reformist army from Verdopolis, Northangerland turns against Zamorna, defeats him, and sends him into exile. To punish Northangerland, Zamorna sends Mary to Alnwick where she languishes on the verge of death. Assisted by Warner and Mina Laury, Zamorna returns from exile and retakes his kingdom, while Northangerland retreats into retirement. Zamorna and Mary are reunited but their relationship has now degenerated from high romance into domestic comedy.

Throughout these political and military events, analysis of Zamorna's character remains the focus of Charlotte's writing. He is increasingly referred to as 'the young satrap of Angria', an image suggestive of his growing tyranny and ostentatious splendour. His ambition is encapsulated in his symbol of the rising sun. Charlotte planned that he should eventually become an imperial despot

Charlotte Brontë, 'Arthur Adrian, Marquis of Douro', pencil drawing, *c.*1833.

Zamorna, Duchess of

(see LEAF FROM AN UNOPENED VOLUME, A). To women he is 'viciously beautiful', and has 'the basilisk's fascination': 'There is a charm, a talisman about him which wins all hearts and rivets chains round them which can never be undone' (Alexander *EEW*, 2(2). 17, 26). But his deceitful smile and glancing eyes 'bode no good'. He becomes a fully-fledged Byronic hero: 'All here is passion & fire unquenchable. Impetuous sin, stormy pride, diving and soaring enthusiasm, war and poetry are kindling their fires in all his veins, and his wild blood boils from his heart and back again like a torrent of new-sprung lava. Young duke—young demon!' (Alexander *EEW*, 2(2). 93). We are told that to objects of his regard he is an angel but 'a very Lucifer' to those he hates (Alexander *EEW*, 2(1). 66). His childhood antagonism towards Quashia *Quamina is pursued relentlessly to the end. He patronizes Edward *Sydney until he finds that Sydney has a mind of his own. His ministers are his flatterers, reformed aristocratic rakes and military commanders, except for his brother-in-law Edward *Percy and the astute Warner Howard *Warner whose political relationship with Zamorna echoes that of Peel and *Wellington. As a patron of the arts, Zamorna gathers painters and poets around him, and as king (and eventually emperor), he builds marble mansions in Adrianopolis for his artistic favourites: Sir William *Etty, Sir Edward de Lisle, Sir John Martin *Dundee, Sir Henry *Chantry, Sir Edwin *Hamilton, and Alexander *Soult.

Zamorna, Duchess of. See PERCY, MARY HENRIETTA.

Zamorna, province and city of. Named after its defender in the *War of Encroachment, in the *Glass Town and Angrian saga, the Angrian province of Zamorna is 170 miles long and 112 miles broad, with a population of 1,986,000. Its governor is Viscount *Castlereagh and its capital, Zamorna, is a thriving industrial town like neighbouring *Edwardston. Both towns are situated on the Olympian River, and are involved in the woollen trade, with the 'Piece Hall' as the centre of activity. The Angrian name Zamorna is derived from the town and province of Zamora in Spain, situated on the Douro River.

Zamorna Palace, Zamorna's residence in *Adrianopolis, Angria, built on the River Calabar in the grand imperial style of the palaces in John *Martin's historical paintings of the ancient world. It is a vast edifice of marble pillars of 'the noblest Grecian moulding'. Comparison with the architecture of Wellesley House demonstrates the Duke of Zamorna's change in taste and ambition (Alexander *EEW*, 2(2). 266). Fort Adrian can be seen 5 miles across the water and the immense green plain of Saldanha Park lies behind the palace. Opposite stands Northangerland House. The building is occupied by Quashia Quamina when he captures the city during the Angrian wars.

Zenobia. See ELLRINGTON (ELRINGTON), LADY ZENOBIA, COUNTESS NORTHANGERLAND.

Zenobia, Alexandrina, speaker of four of Anne Brontë's poems and possibly the same character as 'Alexandria Zenobia Hybernia' in Anne's list of Gondal characters. She may also be 'Alexandria', the mother of an illegitimate child in Emily's poem 'I've seen this dell in July's sun'; and perhaps the girl Zenobia who, aged 13, promises to meet a boy Alexander in Exina, Gondal, in two years' time (see ALEXANDER, LORD OF ELBË).

Zillah, the housekeeper at *Wuthering Heights during Heathcliff's possession and informant of Ellen Dean when the latter is banned from the Heights. Although she dislikes much of what she sees, she keeps to herself and refuses to interfere.

Charlotte Brontë, 'Zenobia Marchioness Ellrington', pencil drawing 1833.

DIALECT AND OBSOLETE WORDS

In the Brontës' day most of the inhabitants of Haworth were Yorkshire dialect speakers; and since Charlotte Brontë complained that there was not a single 'educated' family in the place, it is likely that the 'maisters'—the mill owners, gentlemen farmers, and independent craftsmen— used at least some dialect forms as well as broad northern vowels, especially when speaking to their employees. The well-educated and well-travelled Mr Yorke in *Shirley*, like his prototype, the Gomersal mill owner Joshua Taylor, is portrayed as equally fluent and forcible in dialect, 'standard' English, and French, but he was probably unusual in keeping the two English forms distinct. Within Haworth Parsonage, the dialect of the faithful servant Tabitha Aykroyd, born and brought up in Yorkshire, was familiar to the Brontës from an early age, and it was faithfully recorded in the speech of Hannah in *Jane Eyre*, the servant Martha in *Shirley*, and perhaps also Nancy Brown in *Agnes Grey*. Branwell Brontë probably heard more freely spoken dialect than any of his sisters. He and Charlotte used vigorous, fluent, dialect speech to characterize the servants and cronies of their Angrian 'great men'. The 'strong twang' of General Thornton is used both for comic purposes and to indicate his honesty. The Brontës would be alert to the pronunciation and nuances of the local dialect partly because their own speech, influenced by their Irish father, Cornish mother and aunt, and the various teachers in their schools, was different: Mary Taylor recorded that when Charlotte first arrived at Roe Head school she 'spoke with a strong Irish accent'. Emily was intrigued by Tabby's Yorkshire version of 'Peel a potato', and sought to write it down phonetically, 'pillapatate'. She would later represent with a high degree of phonetic accuracy the dialect speakers in *Wuthering Heights*. Yorkshire people would consider that the Brontë sisters spoke 'less gruff than we talk here, and softer', as Ellen Dean remarked of Edgar Linton in *Wuthering Heights*, a novel in which speech differences have a strong influence on personal relationships. The surly, 'gruff' servant Joseph, a broad dialect speaker, resents the refined speech of the Lintons, and affects not to understand Isabella's request to accompany her into the house: 'Mim! mim! mim! Did iver Christian body hear owl like it? Minching un' munching! Hah can Aw tell whet ye say?' In *Jane Eyre* too, Jane and the 'coarsely-clad little peasants' who are her scholars at Morton at first 'have a difficulty in understanding each other's language'.

Thus in the Brontës' novels dialect reinforces character, helps to mark the class divide, and enhances the impression of real locality. It is never a mere ornament, a conventional device to provide local colour, or a stock source of comedy, as it often was in stage dramas. The Brontës used dialect in the way Sir Walter Scott, James Hogg, and Maria Edgeworth used it, as an integral part of their novels. For Scott, dialect speakers exemplified one aspect of the ancient traditions and 'manners belonging to an early period of society' hardly known to English readers. Dandy Dinmont in *Guy Mannering* brings to life the speech and habits of farmers in a 'wild country, at a time when it was totally inaccessible' except to a traveller on foot or horseback. The dialect-speaking farm-servants of *Wuthering Heights*, inhabiting a similar wild isolation, proved to be equally strange to English urban readers and reviewers.

The Brontës also knew and admired the writings of James Hogg. The vigorous dialect of the servants, the gaoler, and others in Hogg's *The Private Memoirs and Confessions of a Justified Sinner*, and its function as part of a choric commentary on the tense drama of the main events, would encourage the Brontës to follow suit. They would recognize the close kinship of Scottish and Yorkshire dialect, in for example the maid's testimony at Bell Calvert's trial: 'Na, na, I wadna swear to ony siller spoons that ever war made . . . lay them by, lay them by, an' gie the poor woman her spoons again.' Charlotte Brontë also loved and often quoted Scottish ballads, and songs by Burns.

Dialect and Obsolete Words

Some echoes of Irish speech may be detected. Mr Brontë had used an approximation to Irish pronunciation for some words spoken by Nanny in *The Maid of Killarney*, and the Brontës probably knew Maria Edgeworth's *Castle Rackrent* (1800) with its gossiping newsmonger and dialect-speaker Judy M'Quirk, and the narrator Thady, whose garrulous narrative is interspersed with dialect words which, as Edgeworth notes, were characteristic of 'many of Thady's rank'. Like Charlotte Brontë, and unlike Emily, Edgeworth glosses some of the dialect words and customs, noting that 'childer' was used for 'children' (as it was in Yorkshire), 'gossoon' for a little boy, 'fairy-mounts' for barrows, and 'Banshee' for 'a species of aristocratic fairy' whose singing warned of imminent death. Charlotte was to use the 'Banshee' hauntingly in *Villette*.

The following notes on Yorkshire dialect are intended as a brief guide to the list of dialect words used in the Brontës' works. They are based in part on K. M. Petyt's article 'The Dialect Speech in *Wuthering Heights*', in *Wuthering Heights* (Clarendon edn.), app. 7, pp. 500–13.

Pronunciation

The standard English pronunciation of the vowel in 'round' is a diphthong, but in Yorkshire dialect it is a monophthong, 'ah'. See 'ahr', 'bahn', 'daht', in the Table. The 'u' of 'come', 'up', 'sup' is broad, approximating to 'coom', 'oop', 'soop'. The Brontës note some diphthongal vowels where standard English has long single sounds: 'fooil' for 'fool', 'gooid' for 'good', 'Looard' for 'Lord'. Generally speaking, Yorkshire vowels tend to be fuller, more open, and made further back in the mouth than in standard English. Thus Emily writes 'fowk' for 'folk', 'owld' for 'old', 'noa' (approximating to 'naw') for 'no', 'yoak' ('yawk') for 'yoke'. Initial 'h' is often dropped by dialect speakers, but the Brontës do not usually indicate this.

Morphology

Dialect plural forms such as 'een' for 'eyes', 'shoon' for 'shoes', 'childer' for 'children' may be used. Personal pronouns are 'Aw' or 'Ee' for 'I'; 'thah', 'tuh', or 'thee' for the second-person singular (used in speaking to children, intimate friends, and by servants to their equals in rank, but not to the 'gentry'); 'shoo' for 'she', 'ye' or 'yah' for 'you', 'em' for 'them'. Possessive pronouns include 'maw', 'thy', 'ahr', or 'wer' (our). The reflexive 'himself' becomes 'hissen', 'ourselves' becomes 'werseln', pronounced '[h]issen', 'wersen', with a strong stress on the second syllable. 'Shall' and 'should' become 'sall', 'sud', or simply 's' alone: 'we's hear hah it's tuh be' = 'we shall hear how it is to be'. Other words may be shortened or run together: 'the' becomes 't', 'of the' becomes 'ut' or 'ot'; 'with' becomes 'wi'', 'and' becomes 'an' or 'un'; 'over' may be 'o'er', 'always' 'allus', and 'do not' 'dunnut'. 'Nobbut', meaning 'only', is probably an elided 'nothing but' or 'nowt but'. 'Have' may be omitted from perfect tenses, as in 'yah been' for 'you have been'.

Semantics

Some words which look familiar may have a different meaning in dialect from that in standard English: to starve can mean 'to be very cold', a hole or hoile may be a room, and gate or gait may mean either 'way' or 'road'. 'Road' can also mean 'way' in the abstract sense of 'manner', as in 'goa on i' that road'. 'Nor' or 'nur' may mean either 'than' or 'nor' as in standard English: 'Aw sud uh taen tent uh t'maister better nur him' means 'I should have taken care of the master better than he [did]'. The word 'like' has its standard meanings, but is also used quasi-adverbially before or after a word, adding to it the suggestion of 'as it were', 'so to speak', or giving a vague emphasis, as in 'St. John is like his kirstened [christened] name' in *Jane Eyre* (ch. 29). Words which survive only in dialect may have to be given a conjectural or approximate meaning from their context, since there may be no exact equivalents in standard English. As K. M. Petyt points out, other words in the Brontës' works may or may not be authentic dialect: 'Unfortunately, Joseph Wright's great *English Dialect Dictionary* is not reliable here: written evidence was insisted on as necessary and sufficient for a usage to be included, so if a form occurred in *Wuthering Heights* it was entered without query' (*Wuthering Heights* (Clarendon edn.), p. 512). One might add that the absence of holograph manuscripts for Emily's and Anne's novels and the notorious inaccuracy of Newby's printing add to the difficulty of authenticating and interpreting obscure expressions like 'pale t' guilp off' in *Wuthering Heights* (ch. 13).

The principal dialect speakers in the Brontës' novels are Nancy Brown in *Agnes Grey*, Hannah in *Jane Eyre*, Moses Barraclough, Joe Scott, and Mr Yorke in *Shirley*, and Hareton Earnshaw and Joseph in *Wuthering Heights*. In the juvenilia Sdeath always uses dialect; Thornton, Edward Percy, and others sometimes do so. The Table includes dialect words in the major novels, and some of those used in Emily's poems, in Charlotte's early writings and letters, and in Branwell's works. The chapter or volume and page-references are given to indicate typical usage and context, not to provide a complete list of examples.

Table: The Brontës' Use of Dialect

adj.	adjective
AG	*Agnes Grey*
BB Works	*The Works of Branwell Brontë*, ed. Victor A. Neufeldt, 3 vols. (1997, 1998, 1999)
EBP	*The Poems of Emily Brontë*, ed. Derek Roper, with Edward Chitham (1995)
EEW	*An Edition of the Early Writings of Charlotte Brontë*, ed. Christine Alexander, vol. 1 (1987), vol. 2(1–2) (1991)
JE	*Jane Eyre*
Letters	*The Letters of Charlotte Brontë*, ed. Margaret Smith, vol. 1 (1995), vol. 2 (2000)
P	*The Professor*
S	*Shirley*
sb.	substantive
Sc.	Scottish
T	*Tenant*
vb.	verb
WH	*Wuthering Heights*

References to the novels are to chapter and page of the Clarendon edition; references to other works are by volume and page. A semicolon separates references from different works; a comma separates references from the same work.

Dialect word	Meaning	Work	Reference ch./vol.	pp.
aat	out	*BB Works*	3	267
abaat	about	*BB Works*	3	146, 148
aboon	above	*BB Works*	3	441
agate/agait	on hand, afoot	*JE*; *WH*	28; 2	428; 21
ahint	behind	*BB Works*	2	121
ahr	our	*WH*	10	128
allas	= allus			
allus	always	*WH*	13	176
alow	ablaze	*S*	19	382
an	if	*BB Works*; *WH*	1; 2	4; 12
anent	opposite, against	*AG*	11	97, 100
another guess	a different	*AG*; *EEW*	11; 2(2)	101; 102
as what	whatever	*AG*	4	44
as where	wherever	*WH*	5	50
ask (Sc.)	lizard	*S*	7	118
atin	eating	*BB Works*	1	23

Dialect and Obsolete Words

Dialect word	Meaning	Work	Reference ch./vol.	pp.
at nothing	for anything	AG	4	45
at onst	at once	WH	13	174
aught	anything	AG	11	93
aw	I (1st person pronoun)	BB Works; WH	2; 9	117; 104, 107
awn	own	BB Works	3	420
aye	yes	BB Works	1	277, 373
ayont (Sc.)	beyond, after	S	13	290
bahn (to do)	bound to do, going to do	WH	24	307
baht	without	WH	13, 33	174, 388
bamming	playing a trick on	BB Works	3	172
ban	curse	WH	10	128
band	rope, string	S	3	49
barn	bairn, child	EEW; T; WH	2(1); 43; 11	46; 390; 134
beaten	exhausted	WH	4	44
beck	small brook, stream	JE; S; WH	9; 2; 10, 13	88; 38; 116, 164
ben	within, right inside	EEW	2(2)	310
bicker	flicker	BB Works	2	25
bide	live, dwell	WH	32	370
biggin'	building	S	30	613
bits of	small, of little value	S	3	49
boddle (Sc.)	=bodle			
bodle (Sc.)	Scottish coin of little value: see 'plack'	EEW	2(2)	106, 231
bogard	ghost	BB Works; S	2; 5	636; 68
bogle (Sc.)	goblin	EEW	2(2)	125
boit	boot	BB Works	2	527
bout	time, occasion	S	3	49
bow (vb.; Sc.)	bay, bark	S	7	118
brae (Sc.)	slope above a river-bank, hill-slope	EBP	—	148
		EEW; S	2(2); 24	330; 485
braid (Sc.)	broad	EEW	2(2)	322
braw (Sc.)	fine, brave, handsome	BB Works; V	2; 37	121; 629
brust (vb.)	burst, break	WH	33	388
bucking-basket	laundry-basket	S	36	714
bullister (Sc.)	sloe, wild plum	S	7	118
call	abuse, find fault	AG	11	93, 99
callant (Sc.)	lad, youth	V	26	431
cannie (Sc.)	lucky, safe to meddle with	V	25	402
cant	brisk, cheerful	S; WH	9; 7	160; 69
cantrip (Sc.)	witch's trick, or any mischievous conduct	EEW	2(1)	257
canty	brisk, cheerful	AG; WH	6; 22	54; 281
cheap (to be cheap of)	to get off lightly with	P	25	266
childer	children	JE; S	28; 8	426; 149
chitty-faced	having a small or babyish face	S	33	657
clatter (vb.)	to beat, strike	S	32	652
clatter (sb. & vb.)	chatter, gossip	Letters	i	194
clishma-claver (Sc.)	foolish talk	EEW	2(2)	231
clomp	walk heavily	AG	2	17
crack	brisk talk, gossip	EEW; S; T; V	2(1); 23; 4; 27	130; 463; 34; 450
crack	lively lad, a wag	EEW	2(2)	262

Dialect and Obsolete Words

Dialect word	Meaning	Work	Reference ch./vol.	pp.
cranky	shaky, crazy	WH	13	173
crock	smut, smudge	JE	18	240
croft	enclosed ground used for tillage or pasture	S	22	435
cushat	wood-pigeon or ring-dove	S	24	487
custen dahn	cast down	S	5	67
dahn	down	S	5	67
daht	doubt, be afraid	WH	13	172
dead-thraw	death-throe	S	37	725
dean	dingle, deep hollow	BB Works	3	187
deave aht	knock out	WH	13	172
den	dingle; deep hollow between hills	S	2	38
dip-tail	pied wagtail	EEW	1	197
doit	small coin; bit; jot	EEW	2(1)	53
donned, donning	dressed, dressing	WH	19, 7	247, 69
down-draughts	down-dragging or depressing influences	S	22	431
down of	distrustful of	T	43	389
dree (adj.)	cheerless, dreary	WH	14	188
dree one's weird	suffer one's destiny	EEW	2(2)	158
E/Ee	I (1st-person pronoun)	WH	33, 32	384, 371
eea, eees	yes	WH; BB Works	32; 2	371; 166
elf-bolt	fairy arrowhead	T	12	150
enah	presently, soon	WH	10	128
end, better	better kind or class	JE	14	166
erne	eagle	EEW	2(2)	340
ever (seldom or)	never (seldom or)	Letters	1	218, 408
ew-platter	plate made of yew-wood	EEW	2(1)	32
faal	= fahl			
fahl	foul, evil, ugly	JE; WH	38; 9	575; 103, 107
fain of	glad about	WH	30	356
fairish (sb.)	fairy	EEW; S; WH	2(1); 37; 18	46; 740; 239
faishion (vb.)	= fashion			
fand (vb., pret.)	found	JE; S	28; 3	426; 48
fashion (vb.)	bring oneself	AG; WH	11; 2	96; 18
feck (sb.)	part, portion	S	3	52
felly	fellow, admirer	WH	32	374
fettle off	kill	AG	5	48
fettle up	tidy up	AG	11	96
fey	fated to die	EEW	2(2)	105
flay/fley	frighten	S	5, 37	68, 740
flaysome	fearful, awful	WH	2	12
fley	= flay			
flighted	?frightened	WH	4	44
flit, flitting	move, removal	WH; P	4; 22	41; 19
fornent	opposite	BB Works	2	637
fra	from	BB Works	1	344
frame (vb.)	(1) go	WH	5, 13	53, 167
	(2) invent	WH	11, 24	142, 300
fresh	partly intoxicated	S	3	49
fry	state of worry or perplexity	S	1	10
gaberlunzie (Sc.)	beggar	EEW	2(2)	231

Dialect and Obsolete Words

Dialect word	Meaning	Work	Reference ch./vol.	pp.
gait, gate	way	BB Works; WH	2; 32	637; 379
gang (vb.)	go	WH	13	167
gaumless	stupid	WH	21	267
gawking	staring, gaping	BB Works	1	120
gein/gien	given	BB Works	3	177, 421
get agate	get started, begin	S	18	366
get owered	pass over, finish (intr.)	AG	12	106
getten (participle) to	got to, reached	BB Works	2; 3	223; 216, 422
gird (sb.)	fit, spasm of pain	S	3	51
girn	grin	S, WH	30; 10	603; 128
girn	grin, snarl, show the teeth	WH	17, 34	217, 411
girt (adj.)	great	WH	9	102
gleg	sharp, keen	S	18	364
gnarl	snarl	WH	1	8
gooid	good	BB Works	2	117
grat (Sc.)	wept	WH	9	95
grave (vb., Sc.)	bury	S	7	119
greasehorn	flatterer	P	5	42
guess, another	a different	AG; EEW	11; 2(2)	101; 102
hahs/hahse	house	WH	9, 13	108, 175
hahsiver	howsoever, anyway	WH	32	372
happed	stacked, heaped up	P	4	33
happen	perhaps	AG; BB Works; S; WH; JE	1; 2; 3, 30; 11, 29, 38	15; 122; 51; 358; 113, 436, 575
hard-handed	stingy, close-fisted	S	7	126
harry	carry	WH	34	411
haulf, by the	'by the half' = much	WH	32	372
hazing	a thrashing	BB Works	3	254
hisseln/hissen	himself	WH	30	354
hit (vb.)	reach	S	3	48
hoile/hoyle	hole/room/corner/ place/opening	BB Works; S	2; 3; 23	60, 108; 153; 464
		WH	13, 32	175, 383
holly-oaks	hollyhocks	S	23	461
holm	meadow, esp. near a river	JE	9	88
hoody	piebald grey & black crow	EEW	1	288
hor	her (poss. adj.)	WH	9	107
hotch	heave	EEW	2(1)	32
house	main communal room	WH	21	259
howe of night	middle of the night	S	32	639
howsiver/ howsomdever	however	BB Works	1, 2	285, 370
ing	meadow, esp. near a river	JE	9	88
intull	into	BB Works	2	167
jocks	?provisions	WH	32	374
just i' now/just e' now	by and by, ere long	S	18	372
kail (Sc.)	cabbage	Letters	1	214
keck, give a	to make a sound as if about to vomit	EEW	1	141
kedge	brisk, lively	EEW	1	84
ken (Sc.)	know	BB Works	1	326

Dialect word	Meaning	Work	Reference ch./vol.	pp.
kittle	fickle, unstable	S	18	370
lace (vb.)	beat, thrash	WH	3	26
lady-clock	ladybird	EEW; JE	1; 23	197; 314
laik	play a game	WH	3	26
laith	barn	WH	2	12
lake-lasses	playmates, companions	S	37	740
Lallans(Sc.)	Lowland Scottish dialect	EEW	2(2)	322
lameter	cripple	JE; S	37; 26	556; 523
larum	uproar, hubbub	EEW	2(2)	167
lift	rear up	EEW	2(2)	117
lig dahn	lie down	S; WH	3; 13	48; 175
lig hold of	lay hold of	S	5	68
light of (vb.)	chance upon	S	4	65
like, loike (adv.)	so to speak, as it were	BB Works; JE; WH	1; 29; 13	345; 436; 172
likely	desirable, fitting	JE; T	9, 28; 24	93, 427; 215
likker	more likely	WH	9	104
linn (Sc.)	waterfall	EEW	1	283
loike	= like			
loundering	severe, resounding	S	30	606
low (sb.)	flame	S	4	65
luddend	?	BB Works	1	400
lugs	ears	WH	3	26
madling	fool, flighty creature	WH	13	175
mak' (sb.)	make, sort, species	S	3	52
marred	spoilt	WH	8, 13	89, 175
mask	face, head, manifestation	JE	12	136
maun (Sc., vb.)	must (cf. mun)	S	7	119
mavis	song-thrush	EEW	2(2)	61
maw	my	WH	9	104
measter	master	BB Works	2	108
meeterly	tolerably	WH	13	173
mell	meddle, interfere	BB Works; WH	3; 13	421; 174
mensful	decent	WH	32	370, 383
messter	Mister	BB Works	2	109
mich	much	BB Works	1	345
middle-night(Sc.)	midnight	EBP	—	73
mim	prim, affected	S; T; WH	8; 32; 13	144; 290; 168
minching	mincing (speech)	WH	13	168
mools (Sc.)	mould, earth	WH	9	95
much made of	made much of, treated as a favourite	V	1	6
mud (vb., pret.)	might, must	BB Works; WH	2; 13	636; 172
muh (vb.)	may	WH	33	387
mun (vb.)	must	BB Works; WH	2; 33	117, 157; 387
nab	prominent hill	WH	21	262
nabbut/nobbut	only	BB Works; WH	2; 2	121, 167; 12
nave	fist	WH	13	172
nicher	snicker, cackle, neigh	EEW; JE	2(2); 19	123; 246
noan	(1)not	BB Works; JE; WH	2; 11; 9	121; 114; 106
	(2)none	BB Works; WH	2; 10	570; 128
nor	than	BB Works; JE	1; 38	443; 575
norther/nother	neither	BB Works; WH	2; 19	108, 109; 249
nothing, at	for anything	AG	4	45

Dialect and Obsolete Words

Dialect word	Meaning	Work	Reference ch./vol.	pp.
nowt	nothing, worthless thing	WH	2, 32	18, 370
o'ered/owered	over, finished	AG; WH	12; 3	106; 26
offald/offalld	worthless, wicked	WH	9; 18	104, 241
oftens	often	AG	11	95
on	of	BB Works; WH	1; 10, 34	345; 128, 412
onding on	heavy with (snow)	JE	4	41
'only	lonely	JE	37	553
onst	once	WH	13	174
orderations	arrangements, management	S	8	154
owered	= o'ered			
owt	anything	AG	11	101
pabble (vb.)	bubble	EEW	2(1)	32
pale t'guilp off	?knock the pan off	WH	13	172
pared	changed for the worse	S	9	160
pawky	shrewd, knowing	S	8	143
pawsed	?kicked or pushed	WH	3	26
penny-fee	wages, money	P	18	146
piecen	join broken threads in spinning	JE (MS)	13	145 n.
pike	turnpike gate	WH	10	128
pine	starve	S; WH	8; 13	153; 175
plack	small copper coin	EEW	2(2)	106
plack and bodle	to the last farthing	EEW	2(2)	231
play up	scold	S	23	464
plisky	rage, tantrum	WH	13	175
plisky (Sc.)	trick	BB Works	1	267
plotter (vb.)	blunder, flounder	WH	9	104
poortith	poverty	EEW	1	321
pooty	small, young	S	15	314
praise/prease	object of praise	EEW	2(1)	282
put about	vex, harass	S	24	496
quaigh (Sc.)	drinking-cup, sometimes made of wood	Letters	1	227
quean	saucy girl	WH	33	388
raised	highly excited	V	23	368
ranny	sharp, shrewish	EBP	—	35
raton/rotten/ratton	rat	EEW	1; 2(2)	25; 233, 263
ratton	rat	BB Works; S	2; 4	526; 58
re-piecen	rejoin threads	EEW	2(2)	249
reaming	foaming, brimful	Villette; WH	25; 32	402; 374
redd up	tidied up	JE	37	561
red-wud (Sc.)	completely mad	EEW	2(2)	233
reek (Sc.)	thick smoke	Letters	1	214
reeve (vb.)	to twist (?)	EEW	2(2)	117
rig (sb.)	?ridge	WH	9	104
rive (vb.)	pull with force, tear off	EEW	2(2)	132
road, that	in that way	WH	30	358
roup (vb.)	cry, shout, roar	EEW	2(2)	106
rum (adj.)	fine, good, valuable	EEW	2(1)	148
rusty	(of meat) rancid	JE	5	57
sackless	?dispirited	WH	22	280
sair (Sc.)	sore, sad	Letters	i	441

Dialect word	Meaning	Work	Reference	
			ch./vol.	pp.
scorney	scornful, contemptuous	EEW	2(1)	271
scrawk (sb.)	scratch or mark with a pen	EEW	2(2)	95
scroop	back, spine	WH	3	26
scrunty (Sc.)	stunted	S	7	119
sheepshanks, na (Sc.)	a person of no small importance	EEW	I	287
shoo	she	WH	33	388
shoon	shoes	EEW	2(1)	281
side (vb.)	move aside, tidy away	AG; WH	11; 32	96; 379, 383
sin	since	BB Works; JE	3; 28	267; 426
skelp (vb., Sc.)	bound along, move briskly	BB Works	1	93
skift (vb.)	shift, skip	WH	24	305
smoor	smother	S	7	119
snook	poke one's nose in	T	7	56
snoozled	nuzzled	WH	3	37
snow, wreath of	snowdrift	EBP	—	49
snow-wreath	snowdrift	AG; S; T	11; 24; 42	91; 476; 384
somut	something	BB Works	1	344
sort	deal effectively with	Letters	2	566
sough	ditch, boggy stream	WH	10	116
sough/sugh	soft murmur (of water)	JE	12	135
spang (vb.)	spring, leap	EEW	2(1)	24
stalled of	bored with, weary of	S; WH	18; 30, 31	364; 359, 363
stark	rigid, stiff in death	WH	34	411
starved	very cold, frozen	JE; WH	7, 34, 30	69, 504; 358
starving	freezing	WH	9	107
stoup	drinking vessel	BB Works; EEW	1; 2(2)	281; 106
sugh	= sough			
sumph	simpleton, blockhead	EEW	2(2)	372
sumphishness	stupidity	Letters	1	509
sup, a good	a fair amount	AG	1	15
syne (Sc.)	later	V	24	382
tached	taught	S	9	160
taed (Sc.)	toad	S	7	118
tak' tent/take tent	take care, beware	S; WH	23; 17	464; 230
taking (sb.)	(1) plight	WH	14	188
	(2) state of anger	WH	30	359
teed	tied	S	3	49
tent, take	see tak' tent			
tha/thaw	thou, you	BB Works	1, 2	401, 117
thereanent	about that matter	V	20	307
thible	wooden stirring stick or spoon	EEW; WH	2(2); 13	113; 172
thrang/throng	(1) busy	WH	30	353
	(2) dense, close, thick	EEW	2(2)	107
thrapple/trapple (Sc.)	windpipe, throat	EEW	2(2)	233
threap (vb.)	(1) quarrel	AG; JE	11; 29	100; 438
	(2) rebuke, assert vehemently	BB Works	2	167
tinkler	tinker, gipsy, outlaw	JE	18	241
tint (participle)	lost. Cf. 'tyne'.	BB Works	2	643
tit	small horse, nag	BB Works	3	189
to-nig'	last night (perhaps only said in the morning)	S	20	400

Dialect and Obsolete Words

Dialect word	Meaning	Work	Reference ch./vol.	pp.
toppin	head	*EEW*	2(1)	28
trade	course of action, conduct	*S*	8	150
trapple	= thrapple			
tuh	you (2nd person singular)	*WH*	13	167
tull	to	*BB Works*	2	504
twal' (Sc.)	twelve	*S*	13	290
tyne (Sc.)	lose	*JE*	24	341
unlikely	unsuitable, inconvenient	*JE; Letters; WH*	34; 1; 19	503; 432; 247
up uh	set on, determined on	*WH*	10	128
used coming	used to come	*AG*	11	94
uses burning	is in the habit of burning	*S*	19	379
usquebaugh (Sc.)	whisky	*Letters*	1	227
varmint/vermin	rascal (applied playfully to an animal or child)	*Letters*	1; 2	361, 598
war	worse	*S; WH*	20; 2, 9	399; 18, 104
wark (sb.)	work, trouble	*WH*	13	174
waur (Sc.)	worse	*S*	7	118
wearifu' (Sc.)	causing trouble or weariness	*S*	6	92
weird	destiny	*EEW*	2(2)	158
wer	our	*S; WH*	5; 32	68; 373
whamled	rolled	*BB Works*	2	170
while + time	until	*AG*	12	107
whudder (Sc.)	blow wildly, stormily (cf. wuther)	*S*	7	119
wick (adj.)	alive, lively	*BB Works; WH*	3; 5	421; 51
wick (sb.)	week, weeks	*WH*	32	369
wisht/whisht	hush	*BB Works; WH*	1; 9, 18	362; 92, 240
wollsome	wholesome	*WH*	13	173
wor, war	were, was	*BB Works*	2; 3	108; 148
work (sb.)	fuss, disturbance	*S*	1	15
worky-day	workaday	*AG; P*	22; 12	189; 101
wuther (vb. & sb.)	blow wildly, storm	*S; V; WH*	33; 16; 1	661; 240; 4
wynd	lane, alley	*EEW*	2(2)	265
yamp (Sc.)	hungry, peckish	*BB Works*	3	142
yate	gate	*WH*	9	104
yaw	you	*BB Works*	2	108, 109, 157
yellow-wymed (Sc.)	yellow-bellied	*S*	7	118
yourn	yours	*Letters*	1	317, 327

BIBLIOGRAPHY

The Brontës' Published Writings

Novels

Brontë, Anne, *Agnes Grey* (1847)

—— *The Tenant of Wildfell Hall* (1848)

Brontë, Charlotte, *Jane Eyre* (1847)

—— *Shirley* (1849)

—— *Villette* (1853)

—— *The Professor* (posthumously published, 1857)

Brontë, Emily, *Wuthering Heights* (1847)

The Clarendon editions of each novel (1969–92), under the general editorship of Ian Jack, have texts based on the first editions (except for *The Professor*, based on the holograph manuscript), full introductions, descriptive lists of early editions, textual and explanatory notes.

Poetry

Brontë, Anne, Charlotte, and Emily, *Poems* by Currer, Ellis, and Acton Bell (1846).

Brontë, Anne and Emily, *Wuthering Heights and Agnes Grey: with . . . a Selection from their Literary Remains*, [ed.] Currer Bell (1850).

Brontë, Branwell, poems published in the *Bradford Herald, Halifax Guardian*, and *Leeds Intelligencer* (1841–7).

Brontë, Revd Patrick, *Winter Evening Thoughts* (1810).

—— *Cottage Poems* (1811).

—— *The Rural Minstrel* (1813).

—— (poems within prose works) in *The Cottage in the Wood* and *The Maid of Killarney* are included in *Brontëana*, ed. Joseph Horsfall Turner (1898).

—— *The Phenomenon* (1824).

—— *On Halley's Comet* (1835).

Collected Poems

Brontë, Anne, *The Poems of Anne Brontë*, ed. Edward Chitham (1979).

Brontë, Branwell, *The Poems of Patrick Branwell Brontë*, ed. Victor A. Neufeldt (1990).

Brontë, Charlotte, *The Poems of Charlotte Brontë*, ed. Victor A. Neufeldt (1985).

Brontë, Emily, *The Poems of Emily Brontë*, ed. Derek Roper with Edward Chitham (1995).

—— *Emily Jane Brontë: The Complete Poems*, ed. Janet Gezari (1992).

—— and Anne, *The Poems of Emily Jane Brontë and Anne Brontë* (Shakespeare Head edn., 1934) (includes facsimiles of the Law Collection holograph manuscripts of 31 poems by Emily and 10 by Anne).

Other Writings

Brontë, Branwell, *The Works of Patrick Branwell Brontë: An Edition*, ed. Victor A. Neufeldt, vol. 1 (1997), vol. 2 and vol. 3 (1999) (includes prose and verse).

—— and Charlotte, *The Miscellaneous and Unpublished Writings of Charlotte and Patrick Branwell Brontë*, 2 vols. (Shakespeare Head edn., 1936, 1938) includes transcripts of some early writings 1829–39, 24 facsimiles of holograph manuscripts, and Branwell's translations of Horace's *Odes*, Book 1 (1840).

Bibliography

Brontë, Charlotte, *An Edition of the Early Writings of Charlotte Brontë*, ed. Christine Alexander;
    vol. 1. *1826–1832* (1987); vol. 2(1). *1833–1834*; 2(2). *1834–1835* (1991); vol. 3. *1836–1839* (forth-
    coming 2004).
—— *Five Novelettes*, ed. Winifred Gérin (1971)
—— *Ashworth*, ed. Melodie Monahan, *Studies in Philology: Texts and Studies* 80/4 (1983).
—— *Emma*, in *The Professor* (Clarendon edn.), app. 6.
—— 'John Henry' in *Shirley* (Clarendon edn.), app. D.
—— and Emily, *The Belgian Essays*, ed. Sue Lonoff (1996).
Brontë, Revd Patrick, *The Cottage in the Wood* (1815, 1818), *The Maid of Killarney* (1818), two
    sermons, and miscellaneous writings are included in *Brontëana*, ed. Joseph Horsfall Turner
    (1898).

Letters
The Brontës: Their Lives, Friendships and Correspondence (Shakespeare Head edn.), ed. T. J. Wise
    and J. A. Symington, 4 vols. (1932).
The Letters of Charlotte Brontë, with a selection of letters by family and friends, ed. Margaret
    Smith, vol. 1. *1829–1847* (1995), vol. 2. *1848–1851* (2000), vol. 3. *1852–1855* (forthcoming 2004).
The Letters of Mrs Gaskell, ed. J. A. V. Chapple and Arthur Pollard (1966).
Further Letters of Mrs Gaskell, ed. John Chapple and Alan Shelston (2000)

Art
Alexander, Christine, and Sellars, Jane, *The Art of the Brontës* (1995)

Bibliographies and Reference Works
Alexander, Christine, *A Bibliography of the Manuscripts of Charlotte Brontë* (1982).
—— and Rosengarten, Herbert J., 'The Brontës', in Joanne Shattock (ed.), *The Cambridge
    Bibliography of English Literature*, vol. 4 (3rd edn., 1999).
Allott, Miriam, *The Brontës: The Critical Heritage* (1974).
Christian, Mildred G., 'The Brontës', in Lionel Stevenson (ed.), *Victorian Fiction: A Guide to
    Research* (1964).
Evans, Gareth and Barbara Lloyd, *Everyman Companion to the Brontës* (1982).
Glen, Heather (ed.), *The Cambridge Companion to the Brontës* (2002).
Oxford Dictionary of National Biography (2004).
Pinion, F. B., *A Brontë Companion* (1975).
Rosengarten, Herbert J., 'The Brontës', in George H. Ford (ed.), *Victorian Fiction: A Second
    Guide to Research* (1978).
Smith, Walter E., *The Brontë Sisters: A Bibliographical Catalogue of First and Early Editions
    1846–1860* (1991).
Symington, J. A., *Bibliography of the Works of All Members of the Brontë Family and Of
    Brontëana* (incomplete, compiled c.1932–40) (published as vol. 20 of the Shakespeare Head
    Brontë edn., 2000).
Wise, T. J., *A Bibliography of the Writings in Prose and Verse of the Members of the Brontë Family*
    (1917).
Yablon, G. Anthony, and Turner, John R., *A Brontë Bibliography* (1978).

Biographies
Barker, Juliet, *The Brontës* (1994).
Barnard, Robert, *Emily Brontë* (2000)
Chitham, Edward, *A Life of Emily Brontë* (1987).
—— *A Life of Anne Brontë* (1991).
Davies, Stevie, *Emily Brontë: Heretic* (1994).
Du Maurier, Daphne, *The Infernal World of Branwell Brontë* (1960).